ENCYCLOPEDIA
OF
FRONTIER
BIOGRAPHY

ENCYCLOPEDIA
OF
FRONTIER
BIOGRAPHY

IN THREE VOLUMES
VOLUME II
G-O

by
DAN L. THRAPP

Published by the
University of Nebraska Press
Lincoln and London
in association with
The Arthur H. Clark Company
Spokane, Washington

First Bison Book printing: 1991
Most recent printing indicated by the last digit below:
10   9   8   7   6   5   4   3   2   1

Library of Congress Cataloging-in-Publication Data
Thrapp, Dan L.
Encyclopedia of frontier biography / by Dan L. Thrapp.
p. cm.
Reprint. Originally published: Glendale, Calif.: A. H. Clark Co., 1988.
Includes bibliographical references and index.
Contents: v. 1. A–F—v. 2. G–O—v. 3. P–Z.
ISBN 0-8032-9417-4 (set: paper).—ISBN 0-8032-9418-2 (v. 1: paper).—ISBN
0-8032-9419-0 (v. 2: paper).—ISBN 0-8032-9420-4 (v. 3: paper)
1. Pioneers—West (U.S.)—Biography—Dictionaries.   2. West (U.S.)—
Biography—Dictionaries.   3. Frontier and pioneer life—West (U.S.)—
Encyclopedias.   4. West (U.S.)—History—Encyclopedias.   I. Title.
[F596.T515   1991]
920.078—dc20
91-15482. CIP

Reprinted by arrangement with the Arthur H. Clark Company and Dan L. Thrapp

Abbreviations used in the bibliographical citations

AHS   Arizona Historical Society.

Amelia Williams   Amelia Williams, "A Critical Study of the Siege of the Alamo and of the Personnel of Its Defenders." *Southwestern Historical Quarterly,* Vol. XXXVI, No. 4 (Apr. 1933); XXXVII, Nos. 1-4 (July, Oct. 1933, Jan., Apr. 1934).

Appleton   *Appleton's Cyclopaedia of American Biography.* N.Y., D. Appleton & Co. 1887.

BAE   Bureau of American Ethnology.

Bancroft (plus title)   Hubert Howe Bancroft, *Works,* 39+1 vols. San Francisco, The History Co., 1874-1890.

Barry, *Beginning of West*   Louise Barry, *The Beginning of the West.* Topeka, Kansas State Historical Society, 1972.

BDAC   *Biographical Directory of the American Congress 1774-1971.* Washington, Government Printing Office, 1971.

BHB   Kenneth Hammer, *Little Big Horn Biographies.* Crow Agency, Montana, Custer Battlefield Historical and Museum Assn., 1965.

Black Hawk War   *The Black Hawk War 1831-1832,* 4 vols., comp. and ed. by Ellen M. Whitney. Springfield, Ill., Collections of the Illinois State Historical Library, Vols. XXXV-XXXVIII, 1970-78.

Bourke, *On Border*   John G. Bourke, *On the Border with Crook.* N.Y., Charles Scribner's Sons, 1891; (several other editions: with Index, Glorieta, New Mex., Rio Grande Press, 1969).

Bourne, *De Soto*   *Narratives of the Career of Hernando de Soto in the Conquest of Florida, as Told by a Knight of Elvas,* 2 vols., ed. by Edward Gaylord Bourne. N.Y., Allerton Book Co., 1922 (reprint, N.Y., AMS Press, 1973).

CE   *The Columbia Encyclopedia,* 3rd edn.

Chittenden   Hiram M. Chittenden, *The American Fur Trade of the Far West,* 2 vols. Stanford, Calif., Academic Reprints, 1954.

Chronological List   *Chronological List of Actions, &c., with Indians from January 1, 1866 to January 1891.* Washington, Adjutant General Office, 1891.

Clarke, *Lewis and Clark*   Charles G. Clarke, *The Men of the Lewis and Clark Expedition.* Glendale, Calif., Arthur H. Clark Co., 1970.

Coleman, *Captives*   Emma Lewis Coleman, *New England Captives Carried to Canada between 1677 and 1760,* 2 vols. Portland, Me., Southworth Press, 1925.

Cullum   George Washington Cullum, *Biographical Register of the Officers and Graduates of the U.S. Military Academy at West Point, N.Y.,* 8 vols. Boston, Houghton, Mifflin Co., 1891-1910.

DAB   *Dictionary of American Biography,* 22 vols. plus supplements. N.Y., Charles Scribner's Sons, 1958.

DCB   *Dictionary of Canadian Biography,* vols. I-IV. University of Toronto Press, 1966-1979.

Deeds of Valor   *Deeds of Valor…How American Heroes Won the Medal of Honor,* 2 vols., ed. by W.F. Beyer, O.F. Keydel. Detroit, Perrien-Keydel Co., 1907.

De Soto Expedition Commission   *Final Report of the U.S. de Soto Expedition Commission,* John R. Swanton, chairman. House Executive Document 71, 76th Cong., 1st Sess. (Serial 10328), Washington, Government Printing Office, 1939.

Dimsdale   Thomas J. Dimsdale, *The Vigilantes of Montana.* Norman, University of Oklahoma Press, 1953.

DNB   *Dictionary of National Biography,* 21 vols. London, Oxford University Press, 1973.

Dockstader   Frederick J. Dockstader, *Great American Indians.* N.Y., Van Nostrand Reinhold Co., 1977.

EA   *Encyclopedia Americana.*

EB   *Encyclopaedia Britannica.*

EHI   *Record of Engagements with Hostile Indians within the Military Division of the Missouri, from 1868 to 1882,* compiled from official records. Washington, Government Printing Office, 1882.

Farish   Thomas Edwin Farish, *History of Arizona,* 8 vols. San Francisco, Filmer Brothers Electrotype Co., 1915-1918.

fl.   Flourished (Birth/death date not known, but subject active at dates shown).

Griswold   Gillett M. Griswold, "The Fort Sill Apaches: Their Vital Statistics, Tribal Origins, Antecedents." Unpublished manuscript courtesy of Field Artillery Museum, Fort Sill, Oklahoma, 1970.

Handbook of Indians   *Handbook of North American Indians,* 20 vols., William C. Sturtevant, general editor. Washington, Smithsonian Institution, 1978.

Heitman   Francis Bernard Heitman, *Historical Register and Dictionary of the United States Army, from 1789 to 1903,* 2 vols. Washington, Government Printing Office, 1903 (and 1965 reprint).

Hodge, HAI   *Handbook of American Indians North of Mexico,* 2 vols., ed. by Frederick Webb Hodge. Washington, Smithsonian Institution (BAE Bulletin 30), Government Printing Office, 1907, 1910.

HT   *The Handbook of Texas,* 2 vols., ed. by Walter Prescott Webb, H. Bailey Carroll. Austin, Texas State Historical Assn., 1952.

Hunter TDT   *The Trail Drivers of Texas,* 2 vols., comp. and ed. by J. Marvin Hunter. Nashville, Cokesbury Press, 1925 (reprint N.Y., Argosy-Antiquarian, 1963).

Langford   Nathaniel Pitt Langford, *Vigilante Days and Ways.* Missoula, Montana State University, 1967.

Leach, *Flintlock*   Douglas Edward Leach, *Flintlock and Tomahawk: New England in King Philip's War.* N.Y., Macmillan Co., 1958.

McWhorter, *Hear Me*   Lucullus V. McWhorter, *Hear Me, My Chiefs! Nez Perce Legend & History,* ed. by Ruth Bordin. Caldwell, Ida., Caxton Printers, 1952.

MH   *Medal of Honor Recipients — 1863-1963,* 88th Cong., 2nd Sess., Senate Subcommittee on Veterans' Affairs. Washington, Government Printing Office, 1964.

MM   *The Mountain Men and the Fur Trade of the Far West: Biographical Sketches of the Participants,* 10 vols., ed. by LeRoy R. Hafen. Glendale, Calif. Arthur H. Clark Co., 1965-1972.

Montana, Contributions   *Contributions to the Historical Society of Montana,* 10 vols. Helena, 1876-1940.

Mormonism Unveiled   *Mormonism Unveiled; or the Life and Confessions of... John D. Lee... also... Mountain Meadows Massacre.* St. Louis, Bryan, Brand & Co., 1877 (and later printings).

NARS   National Archives and Records Service, Washington, D.C.

NCAB   *National Cyclopaedia of American Biography,* 60 vols. N.Y., Clifton, N.J., James T. White & Co., 1898-1981.

O'Neal, *Gunfighters*   Bill O'Neal, *Encyclopedia of Western Gunfighters.* Norman, University of Oklahoma Press, 1979.

Orton   Richard H. Orton, *Records of California Men in the War of the Rebellion, 1861-67.* Sacramento, State Office, 1890 (Index: J. Carlyle Parker, *A Personal Name Index to Orton,* Vol. 5, Gale Genealogy and Local History Series. Detroit, Gale Research Co., 1978).

Oscar Williams   *The Personal Narrative of O(scar) W(aldo) Williams 1877-1902: Pioneer Surveyor - Frontier Lawyer,* ed. by S.D. Myres. El Paso, Texas Western Press, Univ. of Tex. at El Paso, 1968.

Parkman   Francis Parkman, *Works — Frontenac Edition,* 16 vols. Boston, Little Brown and Co., 1899.

Password   published by the El Paso Historical Society.

PCA   Roscoe G. Willson, *Pioneer and Well Known Cattlemen of Arizona.* Phoenix, McGrew Commercial Printery (for Valley National Bank), 1951, 1956.

Porrua   *Diccionario Porrua de Historia, Biografía y Geografía de Mexico,* 2nd edn. Mexico, D.F., Editorial Porrua, S.A., 1965.

Powell   William H. Powell, *Powell's Records of Living Officers of the United States Army.* Philadelphia, L.R. Hamersley Co., 1890.

Price, *Fifth Cavalry*   George F. Price, *Across the Continent with the Fifth Cavalry, 1883.* N.Y., Antiquarian Press, 1959.

REAW   *Reader's Encyclopedia of the American West,* ed. by Howard R. Lamar. N.Y., Thomas Y. Crowell Co., 1977.

Register   *Society of Montana Pioneers, Volume I, Register,* ed. by James U. Sanders. Helena, the Society, 1899.

Sand Creek Massacre   *The Sand Creek Massacre: A Documentary History,* intro. by John M. Carroll. N.Y., Sol Lewis, 1973.

Swanton, *Tribes*   John R. Swanton, *The Indian Tribes of North America.* Washington, Smithsonian Institution (BAE Bulletin 145), Government Printing Office, 1953.

Sylvester   Herbert Milton Sylvester, *Indian Wars of New England,* 3 vols. Boston, W.B. Clarke Co., 1910.

Thwaites, EWT   *Early Western Travels, 1748-1846,* 32 vols., ed. by Reuben Gold Thwaites. Cleveland, O., Arthur H. Clark Co., 1904-1907 (reprint: N.Y., AMS Press, 1966).

Thwaites, JR   *The Jesuit Relations and Allied Documents: Travels and Explorations of the Jesuit Missionaries in New France, 1610-1791,* 73 vols., ed. by Reuben Gold Thwaites. Cleveland, Burrows Bros., 1896-1901 (reprint: N.Y., Pageant Book Co., 1959).

Twitchell, *Leading Facts*   Ralph Emerson Twitchell, *The Leading Facts of New Mexican History,* 2 vols. Cedar Rapids, Ia., Torch Press, 1911, 1912 (reprint: Albuquerque, N.M., Horn & Wallace Pubrs., 1963).

Williams, Amelia   *see* Amelia

Williams, Oscar   *see* Oscar

ENCYCLOPEDIA
OF
FRONTIER
BIOGRAPHY

G

Gaines, Edmund Pendleton, army officer (Mar. 20, 1777-June 6, 1849). B. in Culpeper County, Virginia, he was a brother of George Strother Gaines and was raised in North Carolina and Tennessee. In 1795 he was lieutenant of a militia rifle company for service against Indians and January 10, 1799, was commissioned an ensign in the 6th Infantry, becoming a second lieutenant of the 4th Infantry February 16, 1801, his career thereafter being mainly in the regular army. He transferred to the 2nd Infantry April 1, 1802, becoming first lieutenant April 27. Until 1804 he was assigned to survey and improve the Natchez Trace from Nashville, Tennessee to Natchez on the Mississippi, and in 1804 became commandant at Fort Stoddard at the confluence of the Alabama and Tombigbee rivers. February 19, 1807, acting on information from a citizen, Gaines arrested Aaron Burr who had been charged with treason, conveying him to Fort Stoddard, and then sending him east, later testifying at Burr's Richmond trial. Gaines became a captain ten days following the arrest. He determined at this point to quit the army, obtained a long leave, read law and commenced practice in Mississippi, but the War of 1812 saw him return to active duty; he became a major of the 8th Infantry March 24, 1812, and ended the war a Brigadier General and brevet Major General. In 1815 he was assigned to command the southern frontier with 1,000 men to control the Seminole and Creek countries. He ordered Fort Scott built at the confluence of the Flint and Chattahoochee rivers to control the nearby Negro Fort on the Apalachicola River, Florida, until the blowing up of the latter by Lieutenant Colonel Duncan Clinch's 4th Infantry which eliminated that threat to border peace. Gaines commanded during the First Seminole War of 1817-18 with Andrew Jackson and remained at his post after Jackson returned to Tennessee. Gaines commanded the Western Division of the army with headquarters at St. Louis from 1821 through the period of the 1831-32 Black Hawk troubles. He thus was superior to Atkinson

who commanded the right wing of the department and who was field commander during the Black Hawk War of 1832. Gaines was at New Orleans in January 1836 when he heard of the Seminole troubles in Florida and put to sea from New Orleans February 4, 1836, unaware that Winfield Scott had been named to the special command in Forida, although he was not yet arrived. Gaines reached Tampa February 9. With just under 1,000 men he commenced a march into the interior February 13. Enroute he buried the remains of Dade's command which had been wiped out by Seminoles December 28. Gaines's force was ambushed on the Withlacoochee River February 26; in an eight day siege he lost five men killed and 46, including himself, wounded, a bullet having knocked out two of his teeth. His campaign was made indecisive by the arrival in Florida of Scott, conflicting orders between the two ranking officers, paucity of rations and imperfect communications everywhere, these all fueled by the bitter hatred between Gaines and Scott. Gaines shortly left Florida over which as Western Army commander he should have been given oversight, and a court of inquiry in 1837 cleared him of military misconduct while censuring both him and Scott for failure to work more closely together. Gaines still commanded the Western Department at the outset of the Mexican War, was court-martialed for improper calling up of volunteers to support Zachary Taylor, but the case eventually was dismissed; later Gaines commanded the Eastern Department of the army. He died at New Orleans of cholera. He was of middle height with a gaunt face and athletic build. He was intelligent, remarkably candid, choleric in relations with Scott and other ranking officers, frequently in dispute with the War Department over trivialities as well as more important matters, able, conscientious and devoted to his country. He was married three times, his first two wives predeceasing and the third surviving him.

James W. Silver, *Edmund Pendleton Gaines, Frontier General.* Baton Rouge, La. State Univ.

Press, 1949; Heitman; Francis Paul Prucha, *The Sword of the Republic.* N.Y., Macmillan Co., 1969; *Black Hawk War,* I, II; John K. Mahon, *The History of the Second Seminole War.* Gainesville, Uni. of Fl. Press, 1967; CE.

Gaines, George Strother, pioneer (1784-Jan. 21, 1873). B. in Stokes County, North Carolina, he was raised in Tennessee; in 1805 was appointed assistant factor of the government trading house at St. Stephens, Alabama (then in Mississippi Territory), becoming factor within a year. Gaines immediately developed friendships among the Choctaws, was trusted by them and his influence led eventually to the dominance of American traders over the Spanish among that people. Gaines became one of the most important pioneers of the Tombigbee Valley of Alabama. He persuaded the Choctaws not to accede to Tecumseh's solicitations for support in 1811 or 1812 and was influential in enlisting hundreds of them to fight for the Americans in the Creek War of 1813-14. He resigned as factor in 1819 and in 1822 became a merchant at Demopolis, Alabama, also serving in the legislature. From 1830-56 he was a merchant at Mobile, Alabama and promoted many developments within that state and Mississippi. He was important in persuading most of the Choctaws to move to the present Oklahoma in 1830, they insisting that he select lands there for them to settle upon, which he did. Gaines moved to Mississippi following his retirement from business at Mobile, and served in the Mississippi legislature in 1861. He died at State Line, Mississippi; the town of Gainesville, Alabama was named for him. He was a brother of Edmund Pendleton Gaines.

Thomas McAdory Owen, *History of Alabama and Dictionary of Alabama Biography,* 4 vols. (1921). Spartanburg, So. Car., Reprint Co., 1978; *Mobile Daily Register,* June 19, 27, July 3, 10, 17, 1872, Jan. 25, 1873; information from the Ala. Dept. of Archs. and Hist.; Anna Lewis, *Chief Pushmataha: American Patriot.* N.Y., Exposition Press, 1959.

Galbraith, Isaac: *see* Gilbreth, Isaac

Galbraith, Robert M., cattleman, banker (Sept. 1, 1844-Sept. 11, 1942). B. at Sheffield, England, of Scot father and English mother, he reached Wyoming by the 1880's where he was arraigned with five others for alleged participation in the lynching July 20, 1889, of Ella Watson and James Averell. The charge followed testimony by eye-witnesses placing him at the scene. With the others Galbraith was released under $5,000 bond; the witnesses against them "disappeared" before the October grand jury considered the case, all the accused being released without indictment or trial. Galbraith afterward entered the banking business at Little Rock, Arkansas, "became wealthy and retired," and died at his home at Pine Bluff, Arkansas at the age of 98, the death due to senility and the results of a fall, according to his death certificate. His wife had predeceased him.

Galbraith death certificate; Alfred James Mokler, *History of Natrona County, Wyoming, 1888-1922.* N.Y., Argonaut Press, 1966 (first published in 1923).

Gale, Joseph Goff, pioneer (Apr. 29, 1807-Dec. 13, 1881). B. at Washington, D.C., he was well educated. Gale accompanied Ewing Young from Taos to California in 1831, and was trapping on the Snake River in 1832-33. He accompanied Joe Walker from the Rockies to California in 1834 and reached Oregon late that year, then for four years worked out of Fort Hall. He married a woman of the Umatilla tribe, perhaps being related through her to Chief Joseph of the Nez Perces. Gale settled in the Willamette Valley in 1838. He joined a group of pioneers in building a ship with which it was intended to hunt sea otter, but after sailing it to San Francisco Bay the ship was sold and the adventurers drove livestock back to the Willamette Valley in 1843. Gale was elected one of three "governors" of Oregon that summer. He returned to California in 1848, settling first near San Jose, then near Fort Tejon; he returned to Oregon c. 1862. He died in Eagle Valley, eastern Oregon.

Kenneth L. Holmes article, MM, Vol. VII.

Galeras, Juan, military figure (c. 1518-post 1552). B. at Almendralejo, Spain he reached Mexico and at 22 joined Coronado's expedition to explore the American southwest. He was with the advance element that captured Háwikuh, the initial pueblo of Cibola, New Mexico. Galeras then took part in García López de Cárdenas's exploration to the northwest and discovery of the Grand Canyon. With Pablos de Melgosa and another he made the first attempted descent into the chasm, although the trio could get only one-third of the way down. Galeras was with Coronado in the march to Quivira, in central Kansas, in the summer of 1541. In early 1548 he testified at Mexico City on behalf of Cárdenas, then in Spain, who had been charged with misconduct on the expedition, and in 1552 testified for Coronado at Mexico City.

George Parker Winship, *The Coronado Expedition, 1540-1542,* BAE, 14th Ann. Rep., Wash., Govt. Printing Office, 1896; Herbert Eugene Bolton, *Coronado: Knight of Pueblos and Plains.* Albuquerque, Univ. of New Mex. Press, 1964; George P. Hammond, Agapito Rey, *Narratives of the Coronado Expedition,* Albuquerque, 1940.

Galey, John Henry, oil, mining figure (Feb. 4, 1840-Apr. 12, 1918). B. at Barker, Pennsylvania, he became a school teacher at 16. Shortly after E.L. Drake in 1859 brought in the first oil well at Titusville, Pennsylvania, Galey became interested in the business; he was "one of the most energetic and enterprising of oil operators; many of the greatest fields developed in America . . . owe their existence to him." His first notable success was the "Maple Shade" gusher, brought in in 1860 in Venango County, Pennsylvania. Galey developed many innovations in the industry, drilled the first two wells at Coalinga California, expanded into gas field operation and into mining in Alaska, Idaho, Arizona and elsewhere. Galeyville, on the east slope of the Chiricahua Mountains of Arizona, was named for him, being laid out in 1880 (Galey had come to Arizona in 1879). In November 1881, Galey opened the Texas Mine, built a smelter at Galeyville and "mining activities zoomed and died like a skyrocket." He constructed a road 25 miles north to San Simon, a railroad point; since his ore was not self-fluxing, a suitable flux was brought from the Granite Gap region of New Mexico to the east. Galeyville periodically was menaced by hostile Apaches, but with minor results. But the Texas Mine ore never paid off well, Galey was said to have lost about $180,000 of his own and others' funds, and his exodus is controversial. According to one account, he attempted to salt the mine and unload it on some unsuspecting Boston financiers, but his scheme failed. Galey re-entered the oil

business in the east and prospered, it was reported. He was married three times, and died at Joplin, Missouri.

NCAB, Vol. XVIII, 18-19; James A. Long, "Turkey Creek Wildcat." *Frontier Times,* Vol. 48, No. 3 (Apr.-May 1974), 14-16, 42-43; Harold F. Williams et al, *The American Petroleum Industry,* Vol. II. Evanston, Ill., Northwestern Univ. Press, 1963, 78-80.

Galinée, Rene de Bréhant de: *see* Bréhant de Galinée, Rene de

Gall (Pizí), Hunkpapa Sioux chief (1840-Dec. 5, 1894). He was b. on the Moreau River of South Dakota and orphaned as a child; although he had other names, he was best known to his people as Pizí, "The Man Who Goes in the Middle." Gall became a noted warrior almost from his youth. It was said to have been Gall who killed First Lieutenant Eben Crosby October 3, 1872, when First Lieutenant Lewis D. Adair was wounded mortally near Heart River Crossing, Dakota, while hunting. Gall came to his greatest attention with the Battle of the Little Big Horn where he was said by McLaughlin to have "led the Sioux," which was not quite the case. Gall was one of 25 leading chiefs of warrior societies (and 225 minor warrior chiefs) in the engagement, and may even have been a foremost one, but he was not the leader of any but his own society's fighting men and his fame as "the commander of the Sioux" was manufactured long after the event by whites seeking to depose Sitting Bull and install the more malleable Gall in his place as leading chief. In 1890 Gall himself told magazine writer Francis Holley, as quoted by Marquis: "I can't say that I or anyone else was in command," and his description of the fight from his vantage point bears out his disclaimer. Marquis believed it unlikely that Gall ever told the agent or anyone else that he had commanded at the Little Big Horn and that Gall "really was a brave and honorable man," a rating the oldtime Indians who knew him unanimously conferred upon him. Gall was in the village first struck by Reno's detachment and was a leader in bringing his warriors into the attack against the major, driving him out of the river valley and to the hill where he was besieged. Gall then turned with his warriors to the principal Custer fight and was believed to have had an important impact on the outcome of that engagement. Gall went with Sitting Bull to Canada after the Custer fight, but in 1880 he and Crow Chief withdrew from the Sitting Bull people and surrendered to Major Guido Ilges at the Poplar River camp in Montana, January 1, 1881. He settled ostensibly as a farmer on the Standing Rock Reservation, Dakota. He was reported by McLaughlin to have denounced Sitting Bull as "a coward and a fraud," but this statement is suspect. Marquis wrote that the agent McLaughlin, "fostered a rift between Sitting Bull and Gall," McLaughlin's book revealing that "it took three years of besieging before he could get Gall to say anything against Sitting Bull. Then Gall merely agreed to the agent's arguing that Sitting Bull was in error as to the best course for the Indians to follow." Gall became a friend of the whites, endorsed the government plan for education of children and 1889 was appointed a judge of the Court of Indian Affairs; on March 2 that year he was instrumental in winning support for the last agreement with the Sioux by which a large reservation was divided into separate smaller reservations with some land ceded to the United States. McLaughlin said Gall was "a man of noble presence and much esteemed for his candor and sagacity by the whites with whom he came in contact." He died at Oak Creek, South Dakota.

Hodge, HAI (Gall article written by McLaughlin); Thomas B. Marquis, *Sitting Bull; Gall the Warrior*, p.p., n.p., 1934; Edgar I. Stewart, *Custer's Luck*. Norman, Univ. of Okla. Press, 1955.

Gallagher, Jack, desperado (d. Jan. 14, 1864). B. at Ogdensburg, New York, he was in Doniphan County, Kansas, in 1859, thereafter going on to Colorado. In early 1863 he killed a man at Denver and fled to Montana, making the trip with a Toponce-led party which left Denver February 2, and reached Bannack May 14; Gallagher drifted quickly toward outlawry. He was one of three noted gunmen deputized by the notorious Sheriff Henry Plummer and was stationed at Virginia City. Here he foiled prosecution of three desperado colleagues for the street murder June 26 of John W. Dillingham, all being freed although equally guilty. In August of 1863 Gallagher joined the Walter W. DeLacy expedition to explore previously inaccessible portions of the Snake River, returning to Virginia City September 23. Gallagher became involved in a saloon dispute with blacksmith Jack Temple over a dog fight and wounded him seriously, although not mortally. With Bill Hunter, another prominent desperado he robbed a Mormon enroute to Salt Lake City of a large amount of greenbacks, and presumably murdered him. The Vigilance Committee determined upon Gallagher's execution and on January 14, 1864, he was arrested, examined and with four others hanged in a building in Virginia City, praying, cursing, and drinking whiskey to the last. It is reported that after burial his head was somehow secured, the skull boiled clean, and that it is used today by a secret fraternal organization in the community for their rites.

Langford; Dimsdale, 168-69; *Montana Contributions*, 1 (1876), 117, 141; Dick Pace, *Golden Gulch*. Virginia City (Mont.) Trading Co., 1970.

Gallagher, Johnson (Corn Hole Johnny), gambler (c. 1847- post 1885). Also known at times as Three-card Johnny, Chuck-luck Johnny, Gallagher was a gambler from boyhood. He was at Newton, Kansas, in 1872-73, was fined for some offense at West Wichita, and was a familiar in other Kansas. cowtowns. He became acquainted with Wyatt Earp, Luke Short and others. Johnny had been known in Ft. Worth's "Hell's Half Acre," later was familiar with Las Vegas, New Mexico, and perhaps Tombstone, Arizona, always a well-known, if shadowy figure. He returned to Dodge City, Kansas, for Short's 1883 "war" with civic authorities, and was run out of town.

Ed Bartholomew, *Wyatt Earp: The Untold Story, Wyatt Earp: The Man & the Myth*, Toyahvale, Tex., Frontier Book Co., 1963, 1964; Nyle H. Miller, Joseph W. Snell, *Great Gunfighters of the Kansas Cowtowns, 1867-1886*. Lincoln, Univ. of Nebr. Press, 1967.

Gallego, Juan military officer (c. 1490-post 1541). B. in Coruña, Spain, he reached New Mexico and at about 50 joined the Coronado expedition in 1540 as a veteran and reliable military officer and frontiersman. He brought seven horses, a crossbow and other accoutrements of Spanish arms, along with a reputation for being "a terrific fighter." He went with Coronado in charge of the pack train, a task of great responsibility. He probably was not present at the capture of Háwikuh, the first pueblo of Cibola, but was sent with Melchior

Diaz and others, including the discredited Fray Marcos de Niza with reports and dispatches to Viceroy Antonio de Mendoza at Mexico City, a 3,000-mile round trip. He was directed to bring back a fresh supply train. Late in 1541 he reached Culiacán, Sinaloa on his way north. He had come through a country torn by the Mixton War and had now to force his way through a Sonora aflame with Indian revolt which had virtually depopulated the region of Spanish. Yet Gallego had a mission: he believed Coronado "in the land of the Turk," i.e., Quivira, and desperately in need of Gallego's supplies. Castañeda compared the subsequent deeds of Gallego favorably with those of the days of chivalry. From his 22 men Gallego chose seven and moved swiftly north, falling like a thunderbolt upon Indian settlements, one after another, slaughtering, dispersing, burning, destroying everything before him, day after day. He fought countless actions. His name became a terror to the hostiles as he progressed steadily north with his tiny band, the bulk of his force following after. For ten days his personal offensive continued. In the region of Suya, Sonora he executed many Indians as punishment for rebellion. In all his actions Gallego lost not a single man and but one was wounded, struck in the eyelid by a poisoned arrow, his life saved through prompt application of quince juice, the poison antidote, although he lost an eye. Gallego met Coronado on the San Pedro River in southern Arizona as the commander moved south, discouraged and defeated in his expedition's great ambition of discovering gold and rich kingdoms to plunder. Gallegos, bitterly disappointed, did not greet Coronado with the phrase, "I am glad you are coming back," according to Castañeda. Had he not encountered the general, the historian added, he would have taken his small command all the way to Quivira, "and they would have reached it without great risk, such was Gallego's discipline and leadership, and so well were his men trained and experienced in war." Day reports that in 1886 on the headwaters of Pawnee Creek in Finney County, Kansas, a sword blade was found, on its corroded surface the name, "Juan Gallego," and the inscription in Spanish: "Draw me not without reasons; sheathe me not without honor." Day concludes the name might be that of a sword maker in Mexico, for a duplicate weapon is at the National Museum of Mexico City, but added that "it is more stirring" to reflect on the possibility that this was truly the sword of Gallego, its work done and passed on as a symbol of Spanish arms from tribe to tribe to its final resting place. No further word of Juan Gallego of the 16th century has been found.

George Parker Winship, *The Coronado Expedition, 1540-1542*, BAE, 14th Ann. Rept., Wash., Gov. Printing Office, 1896; Herbert Eugene Bolton, *Coronado: Knight of Pueblos and Plains*. Albuquerque, Univ. of New Mex. Press, 1964; A. Grove Day, *Coronado's Quest*. Berkeley, Univ. of Calif. Press, 1964.

Gallegos, Baltasar de, military officer (fl. 1538-1543). A kinsman of Cabeza de Vaca, survivor of the Pánfilo de Narváez expedition to Florida, Gallegos joined the 1539 De Soto expedition into the southern United States and became one of its most prominent participants. He was appointed chief constable and captain of infantry and became *maestre de campo,* or field commander, after the disastrous March 8, 1541 battle with the Chickasaws in Alabama, retaining that post until De Soto died May 21, 1542. Gallegos took his wife with him, but whether only so far as Cuba or on the expedition itself is unknown (several wives did accompany expedition members throughout). From the town of Ucita on Tampa Bay Gallegos was sent with 100 men inland "to procure an Indian if possible," for an informant for De Soto. Instead he "captured" a Spaniard, Juan Ortíz, who had lived in the country for a dozen years being a survivor of the ill-fated Narváez expedition. Ortíz proved a most important addition to the De Soto operation being familiar with Indian languages and customs and providing beneficial services until his death in Arkansas two years later. Frequently Gallegos was assigned special missions, which he ever performed in the acomplished manner of a tough, ruthless, loyal officer, completely dependable. Sometimes he was directed to report his discoveries in writing with two separate letters, one secretly telling De Soto the truth about what he had found; the other to describe in glowing terms his alleged discoveries in order to boost morale among the men, morale being ever a vital consideration of the leader. Gallegos may have precipitated the disastrous battle at Mauvila, Alabama when he jerked the martin-skin cape from an arrogant chief and when Indians objected, Gallegos with his cutlass "laid open his back," and the battle was on. Whether he was among the 148 Spaniards wounded in the debacle was not reported. On a subsequent occasion when Francisco Osorio and others were caught depredating without permission in an Indian town, thus creating trouble for the expedition, De Soto insisted that two be beheaded; Gallegos and other leaders conspired with the interpreter to mis-translate what Indians of the village said in order to assure De Soto the natives held no ill-will. The ploy succeeded; the executions did not take place. When De Soto was on his deathbed he called his officers and "principal personages" to him, thanked them, "confessed his deep obligation to them all...for their great qualities, their love and loyalty...in the sufferance of hardship," and asked their forgiveness for any wrong he might have done them. Gallegos replied for the assemblage, consoling De Soto as best he might and urging him to appoint a successor to command the expedition. De Soto named Luis Moscoso de Alvarado for this positon. From this time Gallegos fades from view in written accounts of the expedition although no doubt he continued to fulfill his duty loyally. He had succeeded Moscoso as field commander after the sanguinary action at the Chickasaw town, and it may be that Moscoso bore resentment against Gallegos thereafter. No primary account dwells on the relationship between the two important men. Apparently Gallegos went on with survivors to Mexico and returned at length to Spain.

Bourne, *De Soto*, I, II; *De Soto Expedition Commission*.

Gallegos, Hernán, soldier (fl. 1581-1589). Gallegos was aide to Francisco Sanchez Chamuscado, commanding the tiny military escort for Friar Agustín Rodriquez on his missionary entrada of New Mexico in 1581-82. Rodriquez remained in New Mexico to receive martyrdom, while Chamuscado died enroute back to Santa Bárbara, Nueva Vizcaya. Gallegos' extended narration of the expedition's course and adventures is the best account of it, his statement presented at Mexico City upon his return in 1582. Little of biographical nature has been reported of him, but he was an intelligent and observant man with a fine memory and lucid style of expression. Gallegos became a contender for authorization to conquer and settle New Mexico, and went to Spain to further his ambition. He was unsuccessful although still in Spain in 1589.

George P. Hammond, Agapito Rey, *The Rediscovery of New Mexico, 1580-1594.* Albuquerque, Univ. of New Mex. Press, 1966; Twitchell, *Leading Facts.*

Gallegos, Juan, chaplain (fl. 1538-1543). Probably a brother of Baltasar de Gallegos, he was a Franciscan or Dominican priest or religious who accompanied the De Soto expedition to southern United States. Garcilaso reported that Juan Gallegos "died in Texas," toward the end of the long expedition, "but this is doubtful."

De Soto Expedition Commission.

Galpin (Gilpin, Kiplin), Charles E., frontiersman (d.c. 1870). Galpin arrived in the North Plains by 1834, married a "very intelligent" Yanktonais Sioux woman of fine character and for many years engaged in the upper Missouri fur trade. He was at Fort William (the later Fort John, then Fort Laramie), Wyoming probably at the time it was built, in 1834. When the first stockade was up, he and John Sabille, another trader, were sent to Bear Butte in the Black Hills where they induced Bull Bear with 100 lodges of Oglala Sioux to move to the Platte, "the first appearance of the Sioux in that region," it was said. Galpin still was trading in the Fort Laramie region in 1842, but later removed to the upper Missouri where he settled in to trade with his wife's people. In November of 1862 Galpin, descending the Missouri with some Idaho miners, ran into hostile Sioux moving into the Missouri country from the great Minnesota uprising. The Indians hailed the boat, urged that it tie up on their shore; Mrs. Galpin, although unaware of the Minnesota troubles as yet, sensed something wrong. She and the men of the party, after going ashore as requested, quickly pushed the boat back into the stream as an ambush was sprung. At this point a white woman ran down to the shore and called that white women and children were held captive by the hostiles. Galpin's party continued to Charles Primeau's trading house just above Fort Pierre where they told of the prisoners, who eventually were rescued. When the Jesuit, Jean-Pierre De Smet in May 1868 reached Fort Rice, North Dakota with authority of the Peace Commission to visit the hunting, or "hostile" Sioux under Sitting Bull on Powder River and urge them to accept a formal peace, he persuaded Galpin and his wife to accompany him. De Smet desired also at some point to extend his missions to the Sioux country; he had a reputation among that people for honesty and candor, as had Galpin. De Smet and the Galpins left with an escort of 80 Sioux including many famous chiefs on this mission, which was attended by considerable risk, The Sitting Bull camp was located on the Yellowstone, four miles above the Powder, and included 600 lodges. The non-treaties were prepared for the delegation; it was hoped they would accept it peacefully, which they did. June 19 the party arrived. There was dissension among the Sioux, some urging that the whites be killed, but Galpin and De Smet were taken into the lodge of Sitting Bull, where they were safe. Mrs. Galpin, a general favorite, visited other lodges, talking peace. A major council was held next day. Galpin recorded the speeches. Sitting Bull himself would not go to Fort Rice to sign the treaty, but he sent Gall and Bull Owl and they did so July 2, 1868. Galpin was sutler at various army posts and Indian agencies during his late life. He died on the Indian reservation at Grand River, South Dakota.

Montana, Contributions, Vol. X (1940), 305; George E. Hyde, *Red Cloud's Folk*. Norman, Univ. of Okla. Press, 1957; Doane Robinson, *A History of the Dakota or Sioux Indians*. Minneapolis, Ross & Haines, 1956; Stanley Vestal, *Sitting Bull: Champion of the Sioux*. Norman, 1969.

Galvez, Bernardo de, military officer (c. 1746-Nov. 30, 1786). B. at Málaga, Spain, he was the favorite nephew of the powerful José de Galvez which did no harm to his career. He served in a war with Portugal and another in North Africa and fought Apaches in Nueva Vizcaya (Chihuahua) from 1769 to 1772, being several times wounded. Galvez went to Louisiana in 1776 as colonel and commander of the Louisiana regiment, becoming governor in 1777. He married a beautiful Creole girl which helped make him popular among the people, and by assenting to supply American colonists with arms and other essentials for their war with Britain he reinforced his position among the colonials. He encouraged Canary Islanders to settle in Louisiana, and Acadians as well. When Spain declared war

on Britain in 1779, Galvez's operations were brilliant. He captured Baton Rouge and Natchez in 1779, Mobile in 1780 and Pensacola, Florida, in 1781, his campaign largely responsible for the acquisition by Spain of both East and West Florida at the treaty of Paris in 1783. He was rewarded with military promotions and the title of Count of Galvez. He was named in 1785 to succeed his father, Matías de Galvez (1717-1784) as Viceroy of Mexico, but died of fever at Mexico City shortly after taking office. A daughter was born eight days after his funeral.

Noel M. Loomis, Abraham P. Nasatir, *Pedro Vial and the Roads to Santa Fe.* Norman, Univ. of Okla. Press, 1967; Porrua; CE; Nasatir, *Before Lewis and Clark.* St. Louis, Hist. Docs. Found., 1952.

Gamez, Juan de, explorer (d. Oct. 18, 1540). A nephew of Hernando de Soto and b. in the province of Jaen, Andalusia, Spain, Gamez joined De Soto in the 1539 expedition into southern United States and was killed in the bloody battle with Indians at Mauvila, Alabama.

Bourne, *De Soto,* I, II.

Ganado Mucho, Navaho headman (c. 1809-1893). A prominent Navaho leader and stockman, his name meant "much cattle," illustrating his wealth and influence. He was accused by white ranchers near Navaho lands of stealing their stock, but there is no evidence that he did so, and he was ever ready to return any stolen or strayed animals he came across. When the Navahos attacked Fort Defiance, Arizona in 1859 Ganado Mucho sympathized with the war party, but remained aloof and counseled patience and peace. In 1861 Colonel Canby, commanding in New Mexico called a peace conference, but nothing came of it save expressions of good intentions on both sides. In 1865 Ganado Mucho led his people on the sad trek from their homeland to the Bosque Redondo Reserve on the Pecos River in the Fort Sumner area of eastern New Mexico. The experiment was disastrous for the Navaho, did little for peace in New Mexico and June 1, 1868, Ganado Mucho signed the treaty worked out with Sherman and Samuel Tappan returning them to their old lands in northeastern Arizona and northwestern New Mexico. Ganado Mucho struggled for fair dealing for the Navaho as long as he lived, though with varied success. He died at his home near Kagetoh, Arizona.

Frank McNitt, *Navajo Wars*. Albuquerque, Univ. of New Mex. Press, 1972; Dockstader.

Gannon, Thomas, lawman (d.c. Apr. 5, 1868). On December 5, 1867, Gannon was elected the first sheriff of Ellis County, Kansas, with headquarters at Hays City. Frequently he asked military assistance in chasing horse thieves and desperadoes; he took his job seriously, but his reign was short. In early April, 1868, he disappeared, "believed by many to have been murdered from ambush to prevent his giving evidence as a witness in a criminal case." His successors were J.V. Macintosh, a druggist, then Isaac Thayer, who took over in 1869; he was a veteran of the Beecher Island Indian fight.

Joseph G. Rosa, *They Called Him Wild Bill*. Norman, Univ. of Okla. Press, 1974.

Gannon, William, soldier (c. 1849-Dec. 30, 1941). B. at Manchester, England, he enlisted October 24, 1870, at Brooklyn, New York, in Company F, 8th Infantry, serving five years in the Indian country. His company was assigned to a Yellowstone River expedition; Gannon's outfit was sent to Fort D.A. Rice, Dakota Territory, thence through the Bad Lands to Montana. "During the march," he later wrote, "their were many hold ups the Sioux & other tribes rushing through Camp and fireing into the tents... Indians held up Command for some time in the Bad Lands... Several Skirmishes on the return March...," in one of which Gannon may have been wounded. He was detailed with bull wagons to bring supplies from various posts to the command and "I got through without loss." The company later was assigned to Fort D.A. Russell at Cheyenne, Wyoming, to the Red Cloud Agency, Dakota, and eventually to Fort Whipple, Arizona, where Gannon did mounted provost duty until his discharge as a sergeant. He went to Guaymas and Acapulco, Mexico, thence to San Francisco, Yerba Buena, Monterey and Los Angeles, California. He died at 91, his wife having predeceased him.

Information from H. William Gannon, grandson, Apr. 24, Dec, 2, 1976.

Gantt, John, fur trader (1790-Feb. 14, 1849). B. at Queen Anne, Maryland, and taken by his parents to Kentucky, he was commissioned in the army in 1817, remaining 12 years and rising to captain. He served at frontier posts, and was with Leavenworth on the Arickara campaign; Gantt was on Atkinson's Yellowstone expedition of 1825. On May 12, 1829, he was found guilty by court martial of falsification of pay accounts and was dismissed from the army. In 1830 he joined Jefferson Blackwell in a fur-gathering partnership, in 1831 began operations in the upper Rocky Mountains but shortly transferred to the upper Arkansas River, establishing a trading post, being the first to trade with the Arapahoes and Cheyennes in any volume. The Gantt-Blackwell firm went out of business in 1834, as Bent was establishing his fort. Gantt guided Henry Dodge's 1835 expedition to the Colorado Rockies. He was agent for the Potawatomis at Council Bluffs in 1838-39, guided emigrants to Fort Hall in 1843, went on to California where he became a worthy pioneer. He died of heart trouble at George Yount's ranch in the Napa valley.

Heitman; Harvey L. Carter article, MM, Vol. V.

Gantt, Richard, scout (fl. 1868). Gantt was mustered in August 19, 1868, as one of the "First Independent Company of the Kansas State Militia," an informal organization at Hays City, Kansas. He quickly left however to join George A. Forsyth and his 50 scouts and plainsmen seeing action at the battle of Beecher Island, beginning in mid-September on the Arickaree fork of the Republican River, eastern Colorado. Gantt was severely wounded early in the fight with hostile Cheyennes and other Indians.

Blaine Burkey, *Custer, Come at Once!* Hays, Kan., Thomas More Prep, 1976; George A. Forsyth, "A Frontier Fight." *Harper's New Monthly Mag.,* Vol. XCI, No. DXLI (June 1895), 56.

Garakont(h)ié, Daniel, Onondaga chief (d.c. Dec. 25, 1677). A chief although possibly not a hereditary one, of the Onondaga, he was a skilled orator, became very pro-French and after his formal baptism amid impressive rites at Quebec, he remained a staunch Christian until his death. Probably it was he who was called Sagochiendagehte, a name applied to the principal chief of the Onondagas and used for other purposes of distinction as well. He always seemed to have favored peace, several times returned French prisoners of the Iroquois to the St. Lawrence settlements and saved many who had fallen into Iroquois hands from torture and burning. In 1658, Garakontié was credited with warning the 60 or so Frenchmen connected with the mission established among the Onondagas of a secret plot to massacre them all in retaliation for supposed slights suffered by the Iroquois among French Canadian villages; they escaped in an adventurous episode, thanks to his foresight and friendship. The Jesuit Simon Le Moyne wrote on August 25, 1661 of a subsequent mission to the Onondagas that he had met Garakontié whom he found "a man of excellent intelligence, of a good disposition, and fond of the French, of whom he has gathered as many as twenty in his village— rescuing them, some from the fires of the Agnieronnons (Mohawks) and others from captivity; so that they regard him as their Father, their Protector, and their sole refuge in this barbarous land..." Garakontié was credited with a major role in bringing about a new, if short-lived peace, in 1661. He rescued the Jesuit Charles Le Moyne in 1665, taking him with other prisoners and Cayugas and Senecas as well as Onondagas, to Quebec on a fresh peace mission. Following the Tracy expedition against the Mohawks in 1666, which made a lasting impression on the Iroquois, Garakontié helped promote the work of the Jesuit missions, and after giving it deep thought over many years, decided he wished baptism, going to Quebec where the rite was performed by Francois de Laval de Montmorency, first bishop of New France, and with Governor Daniel de Remy de Courcelle as godfather whose first name Garakontié adopted. The chief for the rest of his life continued a model Christian, learning something of reading and writing, and staunchly defending his Catholic faith against jibes by New York Protestants. When Frontenac was feted on his arrival at Quebec in 1673, Garakontié was the first to speak on behalf of the Indian allies of the French. He died about Christmas Day in 1677 and was buried in the European fashion by the Jesuit Jean de Lamberville, who wrote to his superior: "One knows the obligations under which the whole Colony lies to garakontié. He has saved from the fires of the Iroquois more than 26 Frenchmen, whom he ransomed, fed, and sheltered in his own Cabin, until he could personally bring them back to us. He saved the lives of more than 60 other frenchmen by the secret warning that he gave of the designs which the Iroquois entertained... He was the first who induced his Countrymen to make peace with us; who, for that purpose, came many times on an embassy to Quebec; who concluded the peace; and who, since that time, has Preserved it to us by his authority and Counsels, always turning elsewhere the weapons of the Iroquois... He was highly regarded, not only by those of his own nation,...but even our frenchmen held him in...great esteem..." The Jesuit Pierre Millet wrote in the *Relation* of 1669-71 from the Iroquois country, that Garakontié "can be said to be entitled, alone, to more esteem and consideration than all the others... He is an incomparable man, and the soul of every good work accomplished here: he upholds the Faith by his personal repute; he maintains the Peace by his authority; he controls the spirits of these Barbarians with a skill and prudence which equals that of the wisest men of Europe... He can justly be called the Protector of (the French) Crown in this country; he has a zeal for the Faith comparable to that of the first Christians..."

HAI, I, p. 488; Thwaites, JR, XLI, 255n2; XLVII, 73-77, 97-101, 215; LI, 239-45; LIII, 55-57; LIV, 47-49; LV, 55-63; LVI, 41-47; LVII, 133-41; LXI, 21-33; DCB.

Garcés, Francisco Hermenegildo, Franciscan missionary (Apr. 12, 1738-July 19, 1781). B. at Morata del Conde, Aragon, Spain, he entered the Franciscan order at 15, was ordained at 25 and volunteered as a missionary to American Indians, entering the college of Santa Cruz de Querétaro, Mexico, in 1766. He entered the mission field in 1768, reaching San Xavier del Bac, near Tucson, Arizona, June 30. In August he made his first tour among Indians of the Gila River, traveling alone, and the next year probed the country of the Apaches. In 1771 he reached the Colorado River on an extensive journey, followed it to its mouth and returned to Tucson after a three month absence. In 1773 the problem arose of a land route from the Arizona to California missions. Anza, stationed at Tubac, was assigned to open such a road and January 2, 1774, left Tubac with an expedition including Garcés and Fray Juan Díaz; the party reached San Gabriel Mission, near Los Angeles March 22, 1774, Garcés returning to

San Xavier del Bac late in May. In 1775 Garcés joined a second Anza expedition; he reached the Yuma Indian rancheria of Chief Palma near the present Fort Yuma January 3, 1776, leaving there with two Indian companions February 14 upriver. Near the present Needles, California he turned westward, discovered the Mojave River, followed Cajon Pass into the Los Angeles basin and reached San Gabriel again. From there he traveled northwest into the San Fernando Valley and Antelope Valley, crossed the Tehachapi Range into the San Joaquin Valley, reaching the Kern and White rivers. He then went back to the Mojave River and from there east to the Moqui towns of northeastern Arizona, returned to the Colorado River, followed it to Fort Yuma and returned to San Xavier del Bac September 17, 1776. He had been away 11 months, traveled 700 leagues and had contacted an estimated 24,500 Indians. The Indian known to the Spaniards as Chief Palma, probably Salvador Palma who with his brother Ygnacio Palma headed important bands of the Yuma (Quechan) Indians on the Lower Colorado, had asked for missionaries and under orders of Carlos de Croix, Garcés returned to that tribe, though he found their attitude had cooled. Garcés warned against it, but authorities ordered missions established and in 1780 this was done by a cavalcade from Mexico which started two of them: Purisíma Concepción, at Fort Yuma, and San Pedro y San Pablo farther upstream. Garcés and Juan Antonio Barreneche were stationed at Fort Yuma. The natives came to resent the whites more deeply and July 17, 1781, an outbreak occurred while Garcés was saying Mass. Palma had ordered that Garcés and his companion be spared, but two days later they were found by a warrior and clubbed to death, as were two other missionaries at the upriver station. A probable total of 95 whites were killed including 31 soldiers, 20 male settlers, 20 women and 20 children, while 76 whites were captured by the Indians and held in bondage in this "disaster of almost unprecedented proportions in the history of Spain's conquest of (its California) frontier," and the Yumas were never again subdued by the Spanish. Remains of the missionaries were recovered in December 1781 and eventually buried at the college of Querétaro, July 19, 1794.

Maynard Geiger, O.F.M. *Franciscan Missionaries in Hispanic California.* San Marino Huntington Library, 1969; Jack D. Forbes, *Warriors of the Colorado.* Norman, Univ. of Okla. Press, 1965.

Garcia, Felipe, Yaqui soldier (Feb. 24, 1877-Mar. 30, 1977). B. in Sonora, Garcia, a Yaqui Indian, joined Pancho Villa during the Mexican Revolution but with the collapse of the Villistas, he fled Mexico for Arizona. He acted bit parts in several motion pictures. Garcia died at Tucson, Arizona.

Tucson, *Arizona Daily Star,* Apr. 4, 1977.

Garcilaso de la Vega (The Inca), historian (1537-1616). B. at Cuzco, Peru, of a Spanish father and a mother of royal Inca blood, he became known as among the earliest great Peruvian historians. He went to Spain in 1560 and about 1567 met a survivor of the De Soto expedition of 1538-43 into the southern United States (probably Gonzalo Silvestre, a Portuguese). From Silvestre as his principal informant, if it were he, and from Alonso de Carmona of Priego, Spain, and Juan Coles of Zafra, Spain, he compiled a narration, *La Florida del Inca,* one of the four primary narratives of the De Soto endeavor. His work was completed in 1591, published in 1605 in Portuguese and in 1723 at Madrid; a French version appeared in 1670 and a shortened English edition was published in 1881 at Philadelphia. A fine translation by John and Jeannette Varner, using the 1605 Lisbon collated with the 1723 Spanish editions, the best available, was published in 1951 by the University of Texas Press, and reissued in paperback in 1980. The text is without alterations except where necessary for translation clarification. Garcilaso is best known for his *Royal Commentaries of Peru* (1609-1617); none of his works are of significance in American frontier history however, save that of De Soto.

Bourne, *De Soto,* I, Intro.; Garcilaso de la Vega, *The Florida of the Inca.* trans. by John and Jeannette Varner. Austin, Univ. of Tex. Press, 1980.

Gard, (Sanford) Wayne, newsman, historical writer (June 21, 1899-Sept. 24, 1986). B. at Brocton, Ill., he was graduated from Illinois College at Jacksonville, had a master's degree from Northwestern University and studied at Columbia University. He was a wire editor for the Associated Press at Chicago in 1925-26 and an editorial writer for the *Chicago Daily*

News, Des Moines Register & Tribune and *Dallas Morning News.* His books included *Book Reviewing* (1927); *Sam Bass* (1936); *Frontier Justice* (1949); *The Chisholm Trail* (1954); *Fabulous Quarter Horse: Steel Dust* (1958); *The Great Buffalo Hunt* (1959), and *Rawhide Texas* (1965). Gard's principal literary interest was in the southwest, his subjects honestly researched and carefully written, his prose "revealing the courage, daring, and enterprise of Southwestern pioneers, and preserving their 'place in the heroic phase of western expansion'." He died at Dallas. Gard was married and fathered a son.

Who's Who in Texas Today, Austin, N.Y., Pemberton Press, 1968; *Western Hist. Quar.,* Vol. XVIII, No. 2 (Apr. 1987), 241; information from Beatrice Zeeck, Lubbock, Texas.

Gardner, Alexander, photographer (Oct. 17, 1821-Dec. 10, 1882). B. at Paisley, Scotland, he was interested in chemistry, became apprenticed to a jeweler, then turned to newspaper work becoming an editor of the *Glasgow Sentinel,* where his attention turned to photography. He came to the United States in 1849, bringing his family over in 1856, settling first at a utopian community he had co-founded, Clydesdale, Iowa on the Mississippi and eventually at New York City. He worked for Matthew Brady at New York from 1857 until 1862 when he became official photographer for the Army of the Potomac, later establishing a studio at Washington, D.C. with Timothy H. O'Sullivan. Between 1863-65 he and O'Sullivan compiled their monumental photographic history of the Civil War, Gardner during that period taking his well-known portraits of President Lincoln. In 1867 he photographed railroad construction from Kansas City to Hays City, Kansas, then joined a 35th Parallel railroad survey expedition, accompanying it across New Mexico and Arizona and into California. He assembled a valuable collection of around 127 views and pictures of people and other phases of the survey. Three collections of these exist: one at the Boston Public Library, another held by the Missouri Historical Society and a third by the George Eastman House. Gardner's photographs are sometimes technically imperfect but of considerable historic interest. He abandoned photography during the last decade of his life, devoting himself to social reform matters.

James E. Babbitt, "Surveyors Along the 35th Parallel: Alexander Gardner's Photographs of Northern Arizona, 1867-1868." *Jour. of Ariz. Hist.,* Vol. 22, No. 3 (Autumn 1981), 325-48.

Gardner, Charles (Mountain Phil, Big Phil the Cannibal), frontiersman (d. c.1874). B. at Philadelphia he was imprisoned in 1844 for some infraction during anti-Catholic riots that swept the city, escaped and fled west where he joined the Arapaho and lived with them occasionally thereafter. According to Wynkoop, who knew him well, Gardner was "one of the most singular characters" of his times, "of gigantic stature and repulsive aspect" whose fame extended everywhere in the trans-Missouri. Although Gardner was "supposed to have committed every crime known," yet he had some few good traits: he was of occasional generous impulses, was said to be loyal once he had given his friendship, and at times was considerate toward the traveler who came his way. Gardner seems to have been an occasional cannibal. Once he was sent with dispatches and an Indian companion in mid-winter on some errand of General William Harney, was caught in a prolonged snowstorm and ate his companion before returning from the mission. While trapping for Carson in the present Colorado he was reported to have killed and eaten his Indian woman during a hard winter. Wise frontiersmen learned never to "walk in front of him," or so the tales went. Gardner told W.N. Byers, a Colorado pioneer, in 1859 that he had "killed and eaten two Indians and one white man (a Frenchman)," although of course there were those who doubted that he had ever practiced cannibalism at all. That he was a "rough" there was no-question, however. April 14, 1860, while Indian men were absent from Left Hand's Arapaho village, Gardner and a group of drunken whites invaded the lodges and raped women and young girls, although veteran mountain man John Poisal defended his aged Indian wife at point of pistol and ran the intruders off. Left Hand's wife, sister and daughter were reportedly among the victims; Poisal caused a violent protest against the outrage to be published in the *Rocky Mountain News* on April 18, but since only Indian women were the victims nothing was done about it; had white women been involved a mass lynching no doubt would have followed. Wynkoop wrote in 1876 that Gardner was "killed a couple of years ago in an affray in Montana."

LeRoy R. Hafen, "Mountain Men—'Big Phil, the Cannibal'." *Colorado Mag.*, Vol. 13 (1936), 53-58; Margaret Coel, *Chief Left Hand: Southern Arapaho.* Norman, Univ. of Okla. Press, 1981.

Gardner, Johnson, mountain man (d. c. 1833). Gardner appeared on the Bear River in the upper Rockies in 1824 with free trappers, remaining in the region the rest of his life. He trapped an area since known as Gardner's Hole and the river flowing from it bears his name along the Upper Yellowstone. About 1831. Gardner and companions brutally executed two Arickara Indians in retaliation for the killing of Hugh Glass and two others, and Gardner was said to later have been similarly executed by Arickaras.

Aubrey L. Haines article, MM, Vol. II.

Gardner, Raymond Hatfield (Arizona Bill), scout (July 5, 1845-Jan. 29, 1940). B. at Loganport, Louisiana, he was said to have been kidnapped by Comanches at 2, no doubt in Texas, was traded to the Sioux and at 15 escaped and became a U.S. Army courier. Later on he was said to have been a pony express rider and perhaps an army scout at various times. He joined Buffalo Bill Cody's Wild West Show in 1892. Gardner died at San Antonio, Texas, and was buried in an unmarked grave. Through research of Master Sergeant George Miller, Gardner's army service was established, the body reinterred in the Fort Sam Houston National Cemetery on November 11, 1976.

Kansas City Times, Nov. 26, 1976; *Frontier Times,* Vol. 6, No. 8 (May 1929), 352.

Gardner, Rowland, pioneer (1815-Mar. 8, 1857). B. at New Haven, Connecticut, he moved as a young man to Seneca County, New York, married and fathered four children. He moved to Steuben County, New York, and in 1853 went west and settled eventually at Clear Lake, Iowa, moving in a year or two to Dickinson County. Here his homestead was attacked by Inkpaduta's hostiles and the family wiped out save for Abigail who was taken captive by the Indians (and later freed).

Abbie Gardner Sharp, *History of the Spirit Lake Massacre.* Des Moines, Iowa Printing Co. 1891.

Garemand, Charles, captive (1645-post 1659). The son of Pierre Garemand, a farmer at Cap Rouge, Quebec, Charles and his father were captured by Iroquois in June 1653, and carried off to the Oneida villages in the present New York State, where Pierre probably was burned to death, while Charles lived with his captors for at least 14 years. In mid-November 1655, Dablon and Chaumonot asked Oneida leaders for his deliverance, but this was not forthcoming. In April 1659 the Oneidas still refused to free "the little Frenchman," whereupon he passes from view. On June 1, 1660, eight Iroquois, or "yroquoised Hurons," captured Pierre Garemand's widow and four children near their farm, the woman "dangerously wounded." But a group of eight Frenchmen and some 20 Montagnais pursued the raiders, three of whom were drowned, five brought in alive of whom three were burned at Quebec, one given to Three Rivers (no doubt for burning), and the other spared.

Thwaites, JR, XXVII, 313n12; XXXVIII, 109. 169, 175; XLV, 91, 155-57.

Garistatsia (Le Fer), Mohawk chief (d. May 1663). A famous war leader "renowned by the many disasters that have often made us mingle our tears with our blood," Le Fer headed a mixed party of Mohawks and Onondagas that raided the French settlements along the St. Lawrence in the spring of 1663. The enemy was come upon by Algonquin warriors who surprised them at night. The Algonquin chief Gahronho, himself a noted warrior, sought out Garistatsia and in a hand-to-hand fight, slew him, the Iroquois were routed, and a French captive freed.

Thwaites, JR, XLVII, 303; XLVIII, 99-105.

Garland, Hamlin, writer (Sept. 14, 1860-Mar. 5, 1940). B. at West Salem, Wisconsin, his family moved in 1869 to an Iowa farm from where he attended the Cedar Valley Seminary at Osage, Iowa, graduating in 1881 and when his parents moved again to near Aberdeen, South Dakota, he staked a land claim in McPherson County although this interest quickly palled. He desired to become a writer and in 1884 moved to Boston for nine years. He wrote articles and stories for popular publications and several books and in 1893 moved to Chicago, traveled west to the Rockies, the Southwest and Mexico, visited Indian country, became a friend of Theodore

Roosevelt and in 1898 joined the Alaskan gold rush without notable profit. In 1915 he settled at New York, always continuing to write, his books numbering 30 including fiction, fact and autobiographical. Among his volumes of frontier interest were *Main-Travelled Roads* (1891); *Boy Life on the Prairie* (1899); *Moccasin Ranch: the Story of Dakota* (1909); *Other Main-Travelled Roads* (1910); *They of the High Trails* (1916); *A Son of the Middle Border* (1917); *A Daughter of the Middle Border* (1921); *Book of the American Indian* (1923); *Trail Makers of Middle Border* (1926), and *Back-Trailers of the Middle Border* (1928). He died at Los Angeles following a cerebral hemorrhage.

Neal B. Houston, "Hamlin Garland: 1860-1940." *Arizona and the West,* Vol. 11, No. 3 (Autumn 1969), 209-12.

Garland, John, army officer (1792-June 5, 1861). B. in Virginia he was commissioned a first lieutenant in the 35th Infantry March 31, 1813, thus seeing service in the War of 1812. He participated in the aftermath of the Black Hawk War of 1832, escorting Black Hawk and other noted prisoners from Fort Monroe, Virginia to Rock Island, Illinois. He was active in Florida's Second Seminole War (1835-42), virtually ending the conflict with treacherous capture of the last considerable band of hostiles by promising them a feast with plenty of liquor and when all had gathered having a trap sprung on them. Garland became major of the 1st Infantry October 30, 1836, lieutenant colonel of the 4th Infantry November 27, 1839, colonel of the 8th Infantry May 7, 1849, and won brevets to Brigadier General in the Mexican War in which he was cited for his conduct in four battles. He was appointed to command the Department of New Mexico from July 20, 1853, proving "capable and efficient as well as popular with the citizens." During his administration he took measures against the Utes and to counter Davidson's disastrous defeat by Jicarillas in 1854. In 1856 he ordered out Captain Daniel T. Chandler's expedition against Mogollon Apaches which reported light contact with the enemy and one unfortunate attack on a peaceful rancheria on the return. Garland also was much pre-occupied with Navaho affairs during his term, but led no major expeditions against them, nor undertook any decisive action. He was

succeeded September 15, 1858, as commander of the Department of New Mexico by Bonneville. Garland died in New York.

Heitman; *Black Hawk War,* II, Pt. II, p. 1189; John K. Mahon, *History of the Second Seminole War.* Gainesville, Uni. of Fl. Press, 1967; Robert M. Utley, *Frontiersmen in Blue.* N.Y., Macmillan Co., 1967; Frank McNitt, *Navaho Wars.* Albuquerque, Univ. of New Mex. Press, 1972; Constance Wynn Altshuler, *Chains of Command.* Tucson, Ariz. Hist. Soc., 1981.

Garlington, Ernest Albert, army officer (Feb. 20, 1853-Oct. 16, 1934). B. in South Carolina, he was graduated from West Point June 15, 1876, assigned to the 7th Cavalry, but did not join until August 1, 1876, after the Custer Big Horn fight. He was promoted to first lieutenant June 26 to fill a vacancy caused by that affair. Garlington remained with the Sioux expedition until September 1876. In a Nez Perce campaign the next summer he participated in the Battle of Canyon Creek, Montana. He continued to serve at northern Plains posts, much of the time on scout duty while also regimental adjutant. Garlington joined the Signal Office of Washington, D.C., early in 1883, and was selected to head a Greely Relief Expedition to Lady Franklin Bay, northeastern Ellesmere Island, being described as "the man (to be chosen) above all others in the Army — sober, persistent and able." The relief ship, the sealer, *Proteus,* was crushed in the ice off Cape Sabine, Ellesmere Land, July 23, although the complement was saved. Garlington then returned to St. John's, Newfoundland, aboard the *Yantic.* He was roundly scored by the public press for the debacle, but officially held virtually blameless and was not court-martialed, as some quarters suspected he might be. Garlington was returned to frontier duty at Fort Buford, Dakota Territory, doing some scouting. In the Wounded Knee affair December 29, 1890, he was shot in the elbow but won a Medal of Honor for "distinguished gallantry." He was promoted to captain December 3, 1891, was member of the board to revise Cavalry Drill Regulations, and was named inspector general with rank of major in 1895, continuing in that capacity through successive promotions for several years, becoming Inspector General of the Army from 1906 to 1917. He participated in engagements near Santiago, Cuba, in 1898, and was present at the surrender of the Spanish forces; later he served tours in the Philippines. He retired as a Brigadier General in 1917, but was recalled to active duty in 1918, serving in the office of the Chief of Staff. Garlington died at Coronado, California. He wrote a volume on Cavalry tactics, and a brief treatise on Troop L, 7th Cavalry, as well as a history of the 7th Cavalry that appeared in the *Journal of Military Service Institute.*

John M. Carroll, Byron Price, *Roll Call on the Little Big Horn, 28 June 1876.* Ft. Collins, Colo., Old Army Press, 1974; Edgar I. Stewart, *Custer's Luck.* Norman, Univ. of Okla. Press, 1955; A.L. Todd, *Abandoned.* N.Y., McGraw-Hill, 1961; Robert M. Utley, *Last Days of the Sioux Nation.* New Haven, Yale Univ. Press, 1963.

Garman, Charles: *see* Charles Garemand

Garnett, Richard Brooke, army officer (Nov. 21, 1817-July 3, 1863). B. in Essex County, Virginia, he went to West Point and was commissioned a second lieutenant of the 6th Infantry July 1, 1841, serving in the Florida war against the Seminoles in 1841-42. Garnett became a first lieutenant February 16, 1847, but saw no active service in the Mexican War. He was commandant at Fort Laramie, Wyoming from July 19, 1852, until May 18, 1854, and almost caused a Sioux uprising when he sent young Second Lieutenant Hugh Fleming with 23 men to arrest a Miniconjou Sioux who had taken a shot at a soldier. Firing broke out and six Indians were killed, the officer retiring without his prisoner. Only a great effort by Agent Fitzpatrick prevented an outbreak. Garnett became captain May 9, 1855. He resigned his commission to become a Confederate Brigadier General in the Civil War and died in Pickett's charge at Gettysburg, his body never identified; years later his sword was found in a Baltimore pawnshop.

Heitman; Cullum; Robert M. Utley, *Frontiersmen in Blue.* N.Y., Macmillan Co., 1967; Ezra J. Warner, *Generals in Gray: Lives of the Confederate Commanders.* Baton Rouge, La. State Univ. Press, 1959.

Garnett, Robert Selden, army officer (Dec. 16, 1819-July 13, 1861). B. in Essex County, Virginia, Garnett was graduated from West Point and commissioned in the 4th Artillery in 1841 and served at Buffalo and Fort Ontario, New York. He was breveted twice for several

actions in the Mexican War, transferred to the 7th Infantry in 1848, served two years against the Seminoles in Florida and two years at Texas frontier posts. He became a captain in 1851 and transferred to the 1st Cavalry March 3, 1855; he became a major in the 9th Infantry March 21, 1855, commanding an expedition against Puget Sound Indians. In 1858 Garnett commanded Fort Simcoe, Washington, on the present Yakima Reservation. He was directed to wage war on hostiles following the Steptoe defeat earlier in 1858 and according to Brown artfully managed to create great numbers of "hostiles" where none had existed before. His orders were cruel; a number of Indians were executed under flimsy pretexts or none at all, most of them being not hostile and some even friendly, by troops maneuvering under Garnett's orders. Garnett resigned his commission April 30, 1861, became a Brigadier General in the Confederate Army and was killed in action at Carricks Ford, Virginia.

Heitman; William Compton Brown, *The Indian Side of the Story.* Spokane, Wash., C.W. Hill Printing Co., 1961; *General George Crook: His Autobiography,* ed. by Martin F. Schmitt. Norman, Univ. of Okla. Press, 1960; NCAB.

Garnett, William, preacher (c. 1812-Mar.6, 1836). B. in Tennessee, he migrated to Texas where he lived at Robertson's Colony at the Falls of the Brazos where he was a Baptist preacher and known as a "man of unblemished character." He joined the Texas forces fighting for independence against Mexico, became an admirer of Travis, and died at the Alamo.

Amelia Williams, XXXVII, 260-61.

Garnier, Baptiste (Little Bat), scout, hunter (1854-Dec. 16, 1900). B. at Fort Laramie of a French father and Sioux mother. His father was killed by an Arapaho Indian in 1856 at Deer Crossing on the Platte (Glenrock, Wyo.), his mother died soon thereafter, and Little Bat was raised until 15 by rancher Elias W. Whitcomb (see entry) himself married to an Indian woman. He then lived with various families until the winter of 1871-72, when he settled in with John Hunton on a ranch on the Chugwater, 27 miles southwest of Fort Laramie. Bat married a woman, half Sioux, half French. He served as an army scout for Merritt in 1872, Crook in 1876, and at various times thereafter, "barely escaping" in the massacre at Wounded Knee in 1891, he having been interpreter in negotiations seeking to forestall the fight and having been caught unarmed in the melee. He was a famous and successful hunter; in one day he and Hunton killed 97 elk between present Douglas and Casper, Wyoming. Little Bat showed Hunton the oil seeps on Salt Creek, making Hunton probably the first white man to observe oil in Wyoming. James Cook said Little Bat was "well-known to army people" of that era as scout and hunter, was "good-natured, even-tempered" and a "fine specimen of physical manhood." Brininstool praised his "bump of location," and his great ability as a hunter. Crook had a high regard for Bat and arranged for federal employment at $100 a month for life. Garnier thought Crook's death in 1890, "the hardest thing that ever happened to me." Bat was shot and wounded mortally by a bar-keeper, Jim Haguewood, at Crawford, Nebraska, who was half-drunk at the time. He was buried at Fort Robinson.

Nebr. State Hist. Soc., Fort Robinson Museum files; James H. Cook, *Fifty Years on the Old Frontier*. New Haven, Yale Univ. Press, 1923; E.A. Brininstool, *Fighting Indian Warriors*, Harrisburg, Pa., Stackpole Co., 1953.

Garnier, Charles, Jesuit missionary (May 25, 1606-Dec. 7, 1649). B. at Paris, he became a Jesuit and in 1636 arrived in Canada to labor among the Hurons whose language he learned swiftly and so perfectly that he amazed his hosts by his eloquence in it. A man of remarkable sanctity, he worked with the Hurons until 1639 when he went to the Tobacco Nation with Isaac Jogues; they were forced to return to the Hurons. A second attempt at a mission failed, but a third in 1647 succeeded and Garnier with others established two stations in the Tobacco Nation. One of them, St. Jean, was overrun by attacking Iroquois December 7, 1649, and Garnier was slain. He was canonized by Pope Pius XI on June 29, 1930. A lengthy description of his death and his preceding life is found in the *Jesuit Relations* for 1650, pp. 111-15, and 119-45.

Thwaites, JR, VIII, 307-308n52; XXXV.

Garnier, Julien, Jesuit missionary (Jan. 6, 1643-Jan. 30, 1730). B. in Brittany, he reached Canada October 27, 1662, spending three years studying for the priesthood and learning Indian languages. He became a priest in 1668, the first Jesuit to be ordained in Canada. April of 1668 he went to the Oneida mission in present New York State where he was associated with Bruyas, then worked with the Onondagas; he remained in the Iroquois country until 1685. He moved then to Caughnawaga, Quebec, to work among Christianized Iroquois. From 1702 until 1709 he worked among the Senecas. From 1716-19 he was superior of all Jesuit missions in New France, then returned to Caughnawaga until 1728. He died at Quebec. He was said to have been able to converse in Algonquin, but was a complete master of Huron and five Iroquois dialects. With his more than 67 years of missionary work, he was the Jesuit with the longest record of labors and who lived longest in Canada.

Thwaites, JR L, 323-24n17; DCB.

Garrard, (Hector) Lewis, traveler, writer (June 15, 1829-July 7, 1887). B. at Cincinnati, his father died when Lewis was 7; the boy, never of robust health, journeyed to the Gulf coast at 16, roaming into Texas and hunting and fishing in the Louisiana bayou country. Fremont's report of his 1842-43 expedition stirred Garrard's imagination and he determined upon a western journey of his own. On September 1, 1846, he left Westport Landing with a freight caravan under Cerán St. Vrain bound for Bent's Fort, where he remained for some months. Early in 1847 he joined a William Bent band of volunteers to avenge the murder of Governor Charles Bent, a brother of William's, which occurred during an uprising at Taos, New Mexico. Garrard's is the only eye-witness account extant of the trial and hanging of the "revolutionaries." On his western tour, conducted interestingly at about the same time as those of Ruxton and Parkman, Garrard encountered a galaxy of notable mountain figures: St. Vrain and some of the Bents, Jim Beckwourth, Lucien B. Maxwell, Kit Carson and others, and his vivid descriptions of them, of his journey, and of the natural features of the country have combined to make his narrative report, *Wah-to-Yah and the Taos Trail* (1850) one of the enduring classics of the time and place, although written when Garrard was barely out of his teens. His only other published works were *Chambersburg in the Colony and the Revolution* (1856) and *Memoir of Charlotte*

Chambers (1856). Upon his return east, he studied law, then medicine at the University of Pennsylvania, graduating in 1853. In 1854 he and a brother, Israel, visited the Minnesota frontier; they acquired a tract on Lake Pepin and named it Frontenac, residing there and at nearby Lake City for many years. Garrard married in 1862, fathering two sons who died in infancy and two daughters who survived to maturity. Lewis's ill health prevented his continued practice of medicine or military service in the Civil War, although three brothers became Generals, two in the Volunteer service. Garrard lived the last years of his life at Cincinnati and died at Lakewood, New York. His book of the West is "not only one of the most interesting but...one of the most historically valuable of the many accounts of the Santa Fe traders, the Indians of the southwestern border, the 'mountain men' of the Rockies, and the American conquest and reconquest of New Mexico."

Carl I. Wheat introduction, *Wah-to-Yah & the Taos Trail.* Palo Alto, Calif., Amer. West Pub. Co., 1968; Roy W. Meyer, "New Light on Lewis Garrard." *West. Hist. Quart.,* Vol. VI, No. 3 (July 1975), 261-78.

Garretson, Martin S., bison conservationist (c. 1866-Dec. 21, 1955). Garretson, b. in the east, first went to the Plains in the 1880s where he "became experienced as a plainsman on cattle ranches from Texas to Montana." At that time there remained remnants of the great buffalo herds in Montana, but only bleached bones on other parts of their former range. Garretson met many of the buffalo hunters, the bone pickers and the cattlemen who replaced them, developed an abiding interest in the buffalo and became a charter member of the American Bison Society, founded at the New York Zoological Park December 8, 1905. He became secretary of the society in 1917 and one of its foremost spokesmen, and in 1923 also was named curator of the National Museum of Heads and Horns in the New York Zoological Park. His book, *The American Bison: The Story of Its Extermination as a Wild Species and Its Restoration under Federal Protection,* seemed definitive at its appearance and remains a standard work. Garretson also was active in the preservation of the pronghorn antelope which for a time appeared threatened with extinction although today, like the buffalo, seems

assured of continued existence. Garretson retired from both of his formal positions in 1945, and died at 89 at Plainfield, New Jersey.

New York Times, Dec. 22, 1955; Martin S. Garretson, *The American Bison.* N.Y. Zoological Soc., 1938.

Garrett, Buck, lawman (May 24, 1871-May 6, 1929). B. in Tennessee he was raised near Paris, Texas, and at an early age became a deputy U.S. marshal. He was recruited by Tom Smith as one of 22 gunmen to go to Wyoming to serve warrants on "dangerous outlaws," as part of what became the 1892 Johnson County War, Garrett one of Smith's lieutenants. He attended the attack on the KC Ranch house where Nick Ray and Nate Champion were killed and with the others was captured at the TA Ranch after a battle; eventually the Texans were released on their own recognizance and returned home, never having been tried. In 1905 Garrett was elected chief of police at Ardmore, Oklahoma, and in 1910 successfully ran for sheriff of Carter County of which Ardmore is county seat. Garrett and his deputy, Bud Ballew, attempted to arrest Arch Campbell and when Campbell went for a gun, Ballew killed him. Later they sought to arrest Steve Talkington, a gambler who also resisted and was killed by Ballew. According to Riotte, "One of the surprising things that I found out about Sheriff Buck Garrett was that he never killed a man... either as chief of police or sheriff. In fact, I was told that he very seldom wore a gun... Nevertheless, he never hesitated to enter into a fight or brawl to make an arrest." Garrett became one of the famous lawmen of his day in the west. He was 6 feet, 2 inches in height and weighed 200 pounds a fine horseman and good with his fists. He became a powerful figure in the county, one who sometimes hired attorneys to defend people he had arrested if they could not afford it themselves, and many tales are told of his kindnesses, although he was increasingly controversial. He came to cross-purposes eventually with the Ku Klux Klan, which he considered dangerous to a peaceable society. This led to his defeat for re-election in January 1922. He had made considerable money, in oil and other projects, and spent it as it came in. Eventually he suffered a stroke in Oklahoma City, was brought back to Ardmore by his wife from whom he had been separated, and she attended him until his death at almost 58. His widow died in 1958 and their only son, Raymond, died in 1965; all three are buried at Ardmore.

Helena Huntington Smith, *The War on Powder River*. N.Y., McGraw-Hill Book Co., 1966; Louise Riotte, "Buck Garrett, Man and Legend." *True West,* Vol. 17, No. 3 (Jan.-Feb. 1970), 22-25, 44-45; Garrett death certificate.

Garrett, Patrick Floyd Jarvis (Pat), lawman (June 5, 1850-Feb. 29, 1908). B. in Chambers County, Alabama, he grew up on a family farm in Claiborne Parish, Louisiana, and received some education. He was a trail driver, then became a buffalo hunter out of Fort Griffin, Texas. In November 1876, he killed Joe Briscoe, a youthful skinner whom he liked but with whom he fell into dispute. He quit hunting in 1878 with the buffalo about gone, and moved over to Fort Sumner, New Mexico, where he tried hog ranching for a time; he married Apolinaria Gutierrez at Anton Chico, New Mexico, in January 1880. The marriage was a success and she bore him eight children. In 1880 he was elected sheriff of Lincoln County, New Mexico, already wracked by civil strife. On December 19, Garrett laid a trap at Fort Sumner for Billy the Kid, and someone in his posse, perhaps Garrett, mortally wounded Tom O'Fol(l)iard, a Kid henchman. December 21 Garrett shot Charles Bowdre, another key follower of the Kid, at Stinking Springs, whereafter Billy and others of the band surrendered. They were taken to Santa Fe, then to Mesilla for trial. The Kid was convicted, and Garrett transported him to Lincoln with the execution set for May 13, 1881. Billy killed two guards and broke jail April 28 while Garrett was collecting taxes at White Oaks, New Mexico. July 14, Garrett killed the Kid at Pete Maxwell's place, Fort Sumner. With his boozing friend, Ash Upson (who did the actual writing), Garrett produced his famed *The Authentic Life of Billy the Kid...* Garrett did not stand for re-election. For six months he headed the LS Pat Garrett Rangers, so-called, organized to quell rustling by disgruntled cowboys in the Texas Panhandle; he resigned when he understood he was supposed to kill rather than arrest them. Garrett returned to Roswell, participating in a plan to irrigate considerable acreages in the Pecos Valley. The Pecos Valley Irrigation and Investment Company was organized in 1885, but after a flamboyant start the company sank into receivership, long after Garrett, whose vision had led to its founding, was forced out. After running unsuccessfully for sheriff of the newly-formed Chaves County, New Mexico, Garrett moved to Uvalde County, Texas, where he lived quietly. He paid special attention to a blind daughter, Elizabeth, "and all evidence indicates that she adored him." She became his most famous child, a popular public speaker, good writer, accomplished musician, a close associate of Helen Keller and wrote the official New Mexico state song and other melodies. He named one of his race horses after John Nance Garner, later vice president of the United States, who wrote a Garrett son, "I knew your father as an honorable, honest, patriotic American. When the movies slander him, they slander their betters." Garrett grew restless and when Albert J. Fountain and his son mysteriously disappeared in the White Sands, New Mexico area February 1,1896, Garrett returned to that Territory, where he was hired as a territorial private detective to work on the mystery. In 1898 warrants were issued for Oliver Lee, Jim Gililland and Bill McNew, all ranchers, for the slaying, although Garrett lacked court-acceptable evidence. In a shootout at Wildy Well east of Orogrande, New Mexico, Garrett was bested by Lee and Gililland, and one man was wounded mortally. Lee and Gililland later were tried at Hillsboro, New Mexico, and acquitted. Garrett was appointed by President Theodore Roosevelt collector of customs at El Paso. The appointment was not renewed after Garrett's two-year term. Pat left El Paso for a Dona Ana County ranch he owned where he passed the last two years of his life increasingly depressed; he became quarrelsome and insulting and came into financial distress. Garrett became involved in a maze of confusions embracing Wayne Brazel, W.W. Cox, James B. (Jim) Miller, Carl Adamson and others, and he was shot in the back of the head while journeying by wagon to Las Cruces with Adamson and Brazel. No one knows who killed him, although Brazel confessed, was tried and acquitted. Most specialists seem to think Miller did it from ambush; some believe the killer was Cox or Adamson or someone else. Metz virtually alone believes Brazel killed the old lawman and has marshaled evidence for a good case, although few others accept his conclusion. Garrett was buried at Las Cruces, his body today lying in the Masonic graveyard. Metz, considering Garrett a "complex man," wrote that "There never was a western sheriff quite like Garrett. He was an individualist, a dreamer, a man who never paid his bills but in most respects was as honest as anyone...a quiet, sarcastic, introspective family man, loyal to his friends...and an agnostic who actually understood the word."

Leon Claire Metz, *Pat Garrett: The Story of a Western Lawman.* Norman, Univ. of Okla. Press, 1974.

Garry, Spokan: *see* Spokan Garry

Garvey, Thomas, army officer (c. 1848-Apr. 30, 1892). B. in Galway, Ireland, he enlisted in the 2nd Artillery August 10, 1863, rising to sergeant by mid-1868. He was commissioned a second lieutenant in the 1st Cavalry October 7 of that year and became a first lieutenant June 20, 1872. He operated in Arizona against hostile Yavapais and Apaches, having several fights in the summer of 1872, none of consequence. In December he struck Delshay's band north of old Fort Reno, Arizona, killing 14 hostiles though the leader escaped. In November, 1881 Garvey with a small detachment of soldiers and Indian guides slipped into Sonora after hostiles, but were picked up by Mexican authorities and eventually returned north of the Line. Garvey became a captain December 19, 1884. He was dismissed from the service March 26, 1888, dying four years later. He was 5 feet, 10 inches in height, with grey eyes, brown hair and a fair complexion.

Heitman; Dan L. Thrapp, *The Conquest of Apacheria.* Norman, Univ. of Okla. Press, 1967; Thrapp, *General Crook and the Sierra Madre Adventure.* Norman, 1972.

Gass, Patrick, soldier, explorer (June 12, 1771-Apr. 3, 1870). B. at Falling Springs, Cumberland County, Pennsylvania, he was raised in Maryland and at Wellsburg, West Virginia. He enlisted in a ranger force in 1792, being stationed as a frontier soldier near the present Wheeling, West Virginia, but apparently saw no action. At Wheeling, however, he met Lewis Wetzel, the Indian killer. After peace was restored by the victory of Wayne at

Fallen Timbers, Gass turned to carpentry and worked on a house for James Buchanan, later President. When Washington called for volunteers to put down the 1794 Whiskey Insurrection, Gass found that he was "too much of a patriot to resist the government, and loved good old Monongahela too well to enlist against the Whiskey Boys; so he wisely remained neutral." In 1799 while tension with the French was rising, Gass enlisted in the army for five years under Jonathan Cass, rising to sergeant. In 1803 he volunteered as a private for the Lewis and Clark Expedition (he was promoted to sergeant August 26, 1804, to succeed Floyd who had died). A most reliable man, Gass accompanied the expedition to the Pacific and return, keeping a careful and valuable journal. On October 10, 1806, after the return to St. Louis, Lewis gave Gass a certificate stating that "the ample support which he gave me, under every difficulty; the manly firmness which he evinced on every necessary occasion; and the fortitude with which he bore the fatigues and painful sufferings incident to that long voyage, intitles (sic) him to my highest confidence and sincere thanks, while it eminently recommends him to the consideration and respect of his fellow citizens." Gass went to Vincennes, Indiana, and Louisville, Kentucky, where he and others rejoined Lewis and Clark, escorting a deputation of Indians to Washington. They met Jefferson and were discharged, Gass receiving his pay in gold and returning to Wellsburg. Here he arranged for publication his journal which appeared seven years before the official Lewis and Clark narrative was published: *A Journal of the Voyages and Travels of a Corps of Discovery ...*, edited by David McKeehan (1807). Gass re-enlisted and served at Kaskaskia, Illinois, for four years. At Nashville, Tennessee, he was drafted into the regiment raised by Jackson to fight the Creek Indians but with an option to enlist in the army for five years, which he elected, serving initially under Gaines. Gass took part in the assault on Fort Erie in the War of 1812, and was conspicuous in the Battle of Lundy's Lane, Canada, on July 25, 1814, where he lost an eye — which he considered a lucky accident since it assured him an $8 a month pension for life Discharged in June 1815, he returned to Wellsburg and, past 40, retired into obscurity. At 58 he married Maria Hamilton, 20, and fathered seven children before her death in 1846. On Christmas Day. 1854 while on a pension mission to Washington he met President Pierce. Gass was long the sole survivor of the Lewis and Clark Expedition. He had an alcohol problem late in life, but endured almost to the age of 99. He died and was buried at Wellsburg.

History of the Expedition Under the Command of Lewis and Clark, ed. by Elliott Coues. N.Y., Dover Pub., 1965.

Gates, Thomas, colonial administrator (c. 1560-1622). B. in Devonshire, he was reported by Willison to be "in his late forties" in 1609, and by that time had lived a full life of adventure. He had been knighted for his services on a 1596 expedition against Cádiz and before that, in 1585-86 had been a lieutenant on Drake's expedition which incidentally removed Raleigh's first colony from Roanoke Island, publishing an account of the expedition in 1589. Gates had commanded troops in Normandy, in the Azores, in Ireland and in the Low Countries. He was one of the grantees in the 1606 charter of the Virginia and Plymouth companies, investing heavily in the former. In 1609 he commanded the "third supply" to the colony at Jamestown, a fleet of nine ships and more than 500 colonists; his ship and another were wrecked in the Bermudas, remaining there some months before pinnaces were built with which the adventurers gained Virginia, their castaway experience forming the theme for Shakespeare's *The Tempest.* Most of the 500 Jamestown colonists having perished during the preceding winter, Gates determined to abandon the endeavor and had sailed down the bay when he met Lord de la Warr heading a new relief party, and turned back. Gates later returned to England and brought out still another contingent for the Virginia colony, remaining as governor from 1611 to 1614. His rule resulted in a firmer establishment for the struggling colony; he fought off Indian attacks, ruthlessly executed some captured tribesmen and strengthened the colony's defenses. Willison said he died in the Netherlands.

George F. Willison, *Behold Virginia: The Fifth Crown.*N.Y., Harcourt, Brace and Co., 1952; CE; DAB; Thwaites JR, IV, 253n5.

Gatewood, Charles Baehr, army officer (Apr. 6, 1853-May 20, 1896). B. near Woodstock, Virginia, of a Secessionist family, he attended West Point. Upon graduation he was assigned in 1877 to the 6th Cavalry and embarked upon a singular career in the Apache country as commander of Indian scouts. His experience in the numerous Apache outbreaks was perhaps more extensive and more indispensable than that of any other officer. Gatewood took part in many actions of the Victorio War of 1879-80, including the hard pursuit of the hostiles into Chihuahua in 1879; the heavy action in the San Andres Mountains of New Mexico in 1880, and several fights in the Black Range. He accompanied Crook's great expedition into the Sierra Madre in 1883 after the hostiles, afterward being assigned to manage some of the returned Indians on the Fort Apache Reservation. Gatewood had an important role in the Geronimo campaign of 1885-86; it was he who was selected by Miles to enter Mexico, locate the enemy and persuade him to surrender, and Gatewood performed this duty to the letter, although in poor physical health at the time. His intrepid entry into Geronimo's camp and arguing that Indian to finally give himself up is perhaps the highlight of the last southwestern Indian war, although Gatewood never received any particular recognition for his intrepidity and devotion to duty on the part of Miles or other officers of the Miles faction. This is not only to Miles' eternal discredit, but also to that of his country. Gatewood served as an aide to Miles in Southern California; in 1889 he rejoined his regiment at Fort Wingate, New Mexico. He went with the 6th Cavalry to the Dakotas for the 1890-91 Sioux trouble, was on leave for some months because of poor health, rejoined his regiment at Fort McKinney, Wyoming, where he was injured severely in a dynamite explosion coincident to the so-called Johnson County War. He was forced to retire permanently from active duty and died at Fort Monroe. "His reward for services that have often been described as unusual, was like that of many another soldier who has given his all that his country might grow and prosper: for himself a free plot of ground in Arlington Cemetery, and to his widow a tardy seventeen dollars a month." The Arizona Historical Society holds a monumental collection of primary material as the Gatewood Collection, assembled by the officer's son, Major Charles B. Gatewood; it covers many phases not only of Gatewood's career, but of related subjects.

Gatewood Collection; Britton Davis, *The Truth About Geronimo.* New Haven, Yale Univ. Press, 1929; Charles B. Gatewood, "The Surrender of Geronimo." *Proceed. of the Ann. Mtg. and Dinner of Order of Indian Wars of the U.S.* Wash., 1929; Dan L. Thrapp, *Al Sieber, Chief of Scouts.* 1964, *The Conquest of Apacheria.* 1967, both pub. by Norman, Univ. of Okla. Press.

Gaucher, Pierre (Iroquois Peter), resident among Flatheads (d. May 1856). An Iroquois, or part-Iroquois, he and others of his people went as beaver trappers to live among the Flatheads about 1816. A Catholic, he went in 1839 with Iroquois Aeneas to St. Louis to obtain priests for the Flatheads, De Smet being sent out in response. Gaucher was of strong support to the Jesuits. He also was a successful farmer and stockman by the 1850s. He was killed when thrown from his horse in the Big Hole Valley of Montana while chasing an elk; his neck was broken.

George F. Weisel, *Men and Trade on the Northwest Frontier.* Missoula, Mont. State Univ. Press, 1955.

Gaujot, Julien Edmond, army officer (Oct. 22, 1874-Apr. 7, 1938). B. at Keweenar, Michigan, he was appointed captain, 2nd West Virginia Infantry in 1898 and commissioned in 1901 a 1st lieutenant, 10th U.S. Cavalry. As captain of K Troop, 1st U.S. Cavalry, he earned a Medal of Honor at Agua Prieta, Sonora, for crossing a field of fire to obtain permission of a rebel commander to receive the surrender of beleaguered Mexican Federals and escort such forces, together with five Americans held prisoner, to the American line. He served in France in World War I with the 15th Cavalry, retired in 1934, and died at Radford, Virginia.

True West, Vol. 23, No. 4 (Mar.-Apr. 1976), 4-5.

Gaultier du Tremblay, Francois, explorer (Oct. 29, 1715-July 30, 1794). B. at Sorel, Quebec, he went west with his father, Verendrye at 15 and in 1732 helped build Fort St. Charles on the Lake of the Woods. In 1738 he journeyed to the Mandan country of present North Dakota, arriving December 3.

In 1742 he returned to the Mandans once again during an expedition organized by his brother, Louis-Joseph, the Chevalier de La Verendrye. In that year and the next they explored as far as the Pawnee villages, but made no important discoveries. After 19 years in the west he returned to the St. Lawrence Valley, but in 1752 became an interpreter at a trading post at the present Ashland, Wisconsin. By 1755 he had returned once more to Montreal where he remained the rest of his life. He was the last of the Verendryes, although less distinguished than most.

DCB, III, IV.

Gay, George, pioneer (1810-1882). B. in Gloucestershire, England, he became a seaman and in 1832 reached California aboard the whaler, *Kitty.* There he deserted his ship and joined Ewing Young's trapping party, working the northern California mountains. In 1835 with a company of eight men led by John Turner, coming overland to Oregon the company was attacked by Rogue River Indians, all of the whites being wounded and two killed. Gay thereafter made Oregon his home, marrying an Indian woman and settling in the later Yamhill County, on the upper Willamette River. In 1837 he was one of the company under Young that drove California cattle to the Willamette, enroute senselessly killing a native in supposed retaliation for the action two years earlier; it led to his being wounded a second time. Gay built the first brick house in Oregon which he opened to all visitors with "unbounded hospitality." At one time he had accumulated considerable wealth in horses and cattle, but he died poor.

Thwaites, EWT, XXX, 274n.; Bancroft, *Oregon,* 1; Stephen Dow Beckham, *Requim for a People.* Norman, Univ. of Okla. Press, 1971.

Gay, Mervin G., pioneer (1827-Feb. 22, 1883). B. in Louisiana, he reached Arizona about 1858, according to James Tevis, having been "run out of Texas for horse stealing" and with a $250 price on his head. Tevis installed him as manager of a merchandising operation on the San Pedro River, trading with emigrants. Tevis reported that Gay stole the livestock accumulated for sale, blaming their absence on Indian depredations. However, his version may not be the whole story. In 1861 Gay moved to Tucson. His son was killed by

Apaches September 28, 1870. Gay conducted business enterprises at Tucson until his death from pneumonia.

James H. Tevis, *Arizona in the '50's*. Albuquerque, Univ. of New Mex. Press, 1954; *Latest from Arizona! The Hesperian Letters, 1859-1861*, ed. by Constance Wynn Altshuler. Tucson, Ariz. Pioneers' Hist. Soc., 1969.

Gaytan, Juan, explorer (fl. 1538-1543). A nephew of a Roman Catholic cardinal of Siguenza, Guadalajara, Spain, he joined De Soto's expedition into southern United States and was made treasurer of it. In the fierce 1539 battle of Napetaca, probably on a headstream of the Suwannee River, Gaytan captured a youth who reported that he was from a distant territory (in western South Carolina), ruled by a woman and with plenty of gold; De Soto took him at his word and the expedition spent months in 1540 looking for the place, finding it at last but learning it had no precious metals although it was indeed ruled by a woman. Nothing further is reported of Gaytan who was a survivor of the expedition, reaching Mexico in 1543 and returning to Spain.

Bourne, *De Soto*, 1; *De Soto Expedition Commission*.

Geiger, Maynard J., Franciscan priest, historian (Aug. 24, 1901-May 13, 1977). B. at Lancaster, Pennsylvania, he moved at 12 with his family to Los Angeles where he was forced for economic reasons to drop out of high school after the second year. He was accepted by the Franciscan Order to study for the priesthood, however, and was ordained June 9, 1929, at Mission Santa Barbara, California. He earned a doctorate in history at the Catholic University of America at Washington, D.C. in 1937. June 3, 1937, he became archivist and historian for the Franciscan Province of Santa Barbara, a position he held for 40 years as "a model archivist," according to Nunis. During his tenure the documentary and library holdings trebled and in 1970 a new complex was dedicated to hold the collection. He produced 13 books and contributed regularly to scholarly journals, a bibliography of his works listing 200 titles. Among his major publications were *Book of Historical Dates of the Province of Santa Barbara* (1945); trans. and annot., *Palou's Life of Fray Junipero Serra* (1955); *The Life and Times of Fray Junipero Serra, O.F.M., or the Man Who*

Never Turned Back. 2 vols. (1959); *The Serra Trail in Picture and Story* (1960); *A Pictorial History of the Physical Development of Mission Santa Barbara from Brush Hut to Institutional Greatness* (1963); *Mission Santa Barbara, 1782-1965* (1965); *Franciscan Missionaries in Hispanic California, 1769-1848: A Biographical Dictionary* (1969), and with Clement W. Meighan, *As the Padres Saw Them: California Indian Life and Customs as Reported by the Franciscan Missionaries, 1813-1815* (1976).

Doyce B. Nunis Jr., "Maynard J. Geiger, O.F.M., 1901-1977." *Arizona and the West*. Vol. 20, No. 3 (Autumn 1978), 199-202.

Gentleman of Elvas, chronicler (fl. 1538-1557). Probably the most important of the four chroniclers of the De Soto expedition into southern United States was he who called himself the Fidalgo of Elvas, an important city of south Portugal. His identity has never been satisfactorily established. There were nine or more members of the expedition from Elvas, any survivor a possibility as a candidate. The manuscript sometimes had been attributed to Alvaro Fernandez "but his case is little better than the others." Alvaro Fernandez and his brother, Benito, joined the expedition; Benito drowned in Florida, but Alvaro weathered all its vicissitudes, reached Mexico and eventually Portugal again. He never came to special prominence in the endeavor and his name is mentioned in the various chronicles only once, as having joined it before it left for Cuba. That in itself might speak for his authorship of the narrative except that many, perhaps most members of the 611-man expedition are not mentioned at all in any primary document. (In this connection, see entry for another possible candidate: Gonzalo Silvestre). The chronicle first was printed at Elvora, Portugal, in 1557, just 14 years after the operation's conclusion. In 1609 it was translated and printed by Hakluyt in England and has been reprinted several times since. Its authenticity and accuracy were once questioned, on largely supercilious grounds, but both have been proven beyond any reasonable doubt by the subsequent appearance of the Biedma and Ranjel narratives, particularly the latter. The Elvas work is now generally accepted for what it is: a trustworthy, honest and quite objective record of a most remarkable adventure.

Unfortunately little biographical information on Fernandez has been uncovered.

Bourne, *De Soto,* I; *De Soto Expedition Commission.*

Gentles, William, soldier (c. 1830-May 20, 1878). The soldier who killed Crazy Horse, the great Sioux chief, was b. in County Tyrone, Ireland, and enlisted April 2, 1856, at New York City in the U.S. Army. He was described then as a laborer. On his first enlistment, in Company K, 10th Infantry, he saw duty in the Mormon War and was discharged at Fort Laramie in 1861. He then enlisted in the 1st Missouri Engineers and served during the Civil War. He enlisted in the 14th Infantry and was on sentry duty at Fort Robinson, Nebraska, September 5, 1877. When Crazy Horse was brought in and found he was to be held under confinement in the guard house, he resisted, and Gentles' bayonet pierced the Indian's abdomen, penetrating both kidneys and coming within one-half inch of going through his body; it is uncertain whether Gentles meant to stab him or whether the chief fell against the blade. Crazy Horse died about midnight from internal bleeding. Gentles was hidden from the excited Indians and spirited to Camp Sidney, Nebraska. He died at Fort Douglas, Utah, of asthma. Gentles was 5 feet, 8½ inches tall, with grey eyes, brown hair and a ruddy complexion; the Indians described him as a heavy-set man with a full beard, reddish in hue.

The Killing of Chief Crazy Horse, commentary by Carroll Friswold, ed., intr., by Robert A. Clark, Glendale, Calif., Arthur H. Clark Co., 1976.

Gerard (Girard), Frederick Francis, interpreter (Nov. 14, 1829-Jan. 13, 1913). B. at St. Louis, he attended Xavier College four years and went to Fort Pierre, South Dakota, in September, 1848, and to Fort Clark, North Dakota, the following year, becoming fluent in Arikara and Sioux. In 1855 he accompanied Basil Clement to the headwaters of the Platte, then became an Indian trader at Fort Berthold until 1869. On Christmas Day in 1863 Berthold was attacked by 600 Yankton Sioux of Two Bear's band, the fighting lasting from 9 a.m. until 4 p.m., the Indians trying to fire the block houses; the fort was defended by Gerard and 17 men and they killed about 40 of the Sioux, wounding some 100, Gerard said. The hostiles were driven off by Assiniboines, the whites deserted, and Gerard remained at the place alone for 10 days. He married an Arikara woman and fathered two daughters. Gerard became a government interpreter at Forts Buford and Stevenson, North Dakota and was employed as an interpreter at Fort Abraham Lincoln in 1872. He was hired May 12, 1876 as interpreter for Arikara and Sioux scouts on the Custer Sioux expedition and was assigned to the Reno command; he was missing after the valley fight June 25 but rejoined the command on Reno Hill the night of June 26. Gerard testified at the Reno Court of Inquiry at Chicago later, being congratulated by some for "telling the truth" about affairs on Reno Hill; he commented that some officer witnesses plainly were intimidated and he was "amused to see how bad their memories became" in the brief time since the fight had occurred. He opened a store at Mandan, North Dakota in 1883, moved to Minneapolis in 1890 and was hired by Pillsbury Mills as an advertising agent, perhaps among the people he knew well. He died at St. Cloud and was buried at St. Joseph, Minnesota.

BHB; *Custer in 76: Walter Camp's Notes on the Custer Fight,* ed. by Kenneth Hammer. Provo, Utah, Brigham Young Univ. Press, 1976; W.A. Graham, *The Custer Myth.* Harrisburg, Pa., Stackpole Co., 1957, 250-51.

German family, pioneers. This family, spelled Germaine by Nelson Miles (although he knew the correct spelling), consisted of the father, John (b. Sept. 3, 1830), the mother, Liddia or Lydia Cox German (b. Oct. 8, 1829), and seven children: Rebecca J. (Jane) (b. Jan. 16, 1854); Stephen W. (b. Sept. 17, 1855); Katherine (Catherine) E. (b. Mar. 21, 1857); Joanna C. (b. June 3, 1859); Soph(i)a L. (b. Aug. 11, 1862); Julia Arminda (b. Mar. 23, 1867), and Nancy Adelaide (Addie) (b. Apr. 26, 1869). The family lived near Morganton, Georgia, from where the father had served in the Confederate army. The Germans left Morganton April 10, 1870, and by September reached Howell County, Missouri, where they settled for a time. In 1873 they moved to Stone County, Missouri, for a few months, then on to Elgin, Kansas. August 15, 1874 they resumed their wagon trek westward for Colorado. September 11, 1874 their wagons were attacked by a Cheyenne war party ten miles south of Monument, Kansas, and about

30 miles east of Fort Wallace. Killed were John and Lydia, the parents; and Stephen, Rebecca (Jane) and Joanna, the latter because she had long hair an Indian thought would make an attractive scalp, and Rebecca (Jane) because she bravely assailed an Indian with an axe during the melee. Catherine and Sophia, Julia and Addie were borne off captives, their sagas comprising a celebrated legend of the West. The Cheyennes made for the Canadian River country and Texas Panhandle and when they split up the two older girls, Catherine and Sophia were kept together as were the younger pair, Julia and Addie. November 8 First Lieutenant Frank Baldwin attacked Gray Beard's camp of 100 lodges on McClellan Creek, Texas, routing the Cheyennes and recapturing Julia and Addie German, aged 7 and 5; they had been abandoned as the Indians fled and were found dirty, cold, hungry and terrified but were promptly clothed and kindly treated, being sent to Kansas. On March 6, 1875 about 820 Cheyennes including Gray Beard and Stone Calf, the chief whose band held Sophia and Catherine surrendered at Darlington, Indian Territory, bringing in and freeing the two girls aged 13 and 18, "alive though badly used." One of them was reported pregnant, although which is not stated. The four sisters eventually were reunited in Kansas where they remained with Mr. and Mrs. Patrie Corney, Fort Leavenworth, despite entreaties of relatives to return to Georgia. They were educated by the Corneys although Nelson Miles had been appointed their legal guardian; he secured a Congressional appropriation of $10,000 for their care, the principal to be set aside during their minority and the interest used for their support. When they grew up each received $2,500. All four married. Catherine wed Amos Swerdfeger and died at Atascadero, California August 6, 1932. (Nancy) Adelaide married Frank Andrews and settled at Bern, Kansas, where she became mother of 11 children, the grandmother of eight or more. About 1940 she moved to Santa Ana, California, where she lived three years with her sister, Julia; in 1943 she moved to Kansas City to live with a daughter, Mrs. Ada Stephens and died at Mrs. Stephens' home July 5, 1943, being buried at Bern. Sophia became Mrs. Feldman and spent most of her life on a farm near Humboldt, Nebraska; she died at Falls City, Nebraska March 4, 1949,

Julia became Mrs. Brooks and died at 92 on June 1, 1959 at Santa Ana, California.

Girl Captives of the Cheyennes: A True Story of the Capture and Rescue of Four Pioneer Girls 1874 (Catherine's narrative), rev. and ed. by Grace E. Meredith, niece of Catherine. Los Angeles, Gem Pub. Co., 1927; Nelson A. Miles, *Personal Recollections.* Chicago, Riverside Pub. Co., 1897; Lonnie J. White, "Indian Battles in the Texas Panhandle, 1874," White, *Hostiles & Horse Soldiers.* Boulder, Colo., Pruett Pub. Co., 1972; information from Larry Jochims, Kan. State Hist. Soc.; information from Nebr. Hist. Soc.

Geronimo (Goyahkla: He Who Yawns), Apache war leader (c. 1823-Feb. 17, 1909). B. into the Bedonkohe Apache people near the upper Gila River probably on the Arizona side of the boundary with New Mexico, Geronimo himself said his year of birth was 1829, but that is too late by five or six years. Most of what is known of Geronimo's early life is taken from his "autobiography" which was translated into English as he spoke by Ace Daklugie, son of Juh whose close companion he ever was; Daklugie's words were taken down by S.M. Barrett, an educator, and published in 1906 as *Geronimo's Story of His Life.* It must be carefully interpreted for while accurate enough presumably on details, its chronology is mixed and of course it is somewhat self-serving, in addition to which Barrett added flourishes which a careful reader must delete. The book for example quotes Geronimo as asserting his people hunted the buffalo, but this is most improbable, it being likely that this Apache never saw a buffalo until an old man. The Bedonkohe to some extent followed Mangas Coloradas and with that great chief Geronimo and his family and others journeyed in 1850 to Janos where in the absence of the men Mexicans killed the camp's women and children, Geronimo losing his mother, his wife and three children. This decided the course of his active life: from that day forward he hated Mexicans with a blind passion, and there is no doubt he killed many to avenge the deaths of his kindred. The first great battle of revenge occurred about a year after the loss of his family, the Apache reported. In that engagement he won his Mexican-given name of Geronimo. About 1851 he saw his first Anglo whites. Around 1858 Juh and Geronimo and their followers won a "great victory" near Namaquipa,

Chihuahua; there were many Apache raids on Mexico in those years, Geronimo often taking part, learning his trade as a warrior, developing his "power," becoming in time a war leader and attracting followers, although he never became a "chief," and always deferred to the true chiefs of his people. With discovery of gold at Pinos Altos, New Mexico, the increase in travel over the Butterfield Overland Mail route and growing white population, abrasion between the Apaches and Anglos increased and open hostilities occured by the start of the Civil War. Geronimo was not present at the "Bascom affair," but sided with Cochise afterward; he is reported by some to have been present at the Battle of Apache Pass, July 14, 1862, and no doubt took part in other affairs of the time as did many Apaches. Not much is known of his activities during the immediately subsequent years, because he was over-shadowed by abler, greater chiefs and warriors, but he operated during this time usually under or in association with Juh. In May 1871 he apparently was with Juh during the fight in which Lieutenant Howard B. Cushing was killed in the Whetstone Mountains, Arizona. January 9, 1877, Geronimo's band was struck by Lieutenant J.A. Rucker and a command which had trailed the hostiles for many days following stock thefts. In the action near the Leitendorf Mountains of southwestern New Mexico Geronimo lost 10 men — among the few defeats the Chiricahuas had suffered at the hands of U.S. troops save during the Civil War and immediately afterward. Geronimo then went to the Ojo Caliente Reservation in New Mexico where Victorio's people were, was incensed because he could not draw rations for the latest period during which he had been hostile, was arrested and ironed by Agent John Clum and moved in the spring to San Carlos. Four months later Clum's successor, Agent H.L. Hart had Geronimo freed. On April 4, 1878, he bolted once more for Mexico in company with Juh, Ponce and other wild spirits. During the Victorio War in 1879 Geronimo operated with Juh, at times their raids seeming to complement those of the Mimbres, if perhaps accidentally. In late 1879 Geronimo and Juh surrendered and settled for the time on the San Carlos Reservation. In late 1881 after the Cibecue incident, Juh and Geronimo took their people south once more into the Sierra

Madre, henceforth to center their activities in Mexico. From Mexico in the spring of 1882 was organized the most sensational raid in Apache annals. This was directed at San Carlos where Loco, with Victorio's death the leader of most of the Mimbres, and hundreds of his people resided. The raid no doubt was planned and executed by Juh, with Geronimo his subordinate and associate. A contrary point of view is expressed however by Debo who writes Juh entirely out of the adventure and places its conception and execution wholly upon Geronimo. If Geronimo did accomplish this miracle it was the most stupendous event of a life not noted for anything else remotely of that calibre. Debo bases her view largely on the absence of mention of Juh by Betzinez and what scant Apache records have come down. An Indian operation like this did not involve a tight body of raiders maneuvering like cavalry, but fluid groupings operating independently while more or less committed to some common goal. It is possible that Betzinez did not accompany Juh's band, or think to write of him, since he was concerned with his own relationship to Geronimo. Evidence placing Juh in a leadership role on the other hand is overwhelming. The American consul at Chihuahua reported Juh was at Casas Grandes as the raid was being organized and was determined to lead it. Mackenzie's reliable spy at Corralitos reported that "Ju, Apache Chief, here. Think it will go for San Carlos..." Pangburn, acting Indian agent at San Carlos reported "there is good reason to believe that Juh himself was here." Willcox reported that "Juh and Geronimo" were leading the raiders. Captain MacGowan, a conservative and reliable officer said Natiotish "met Hoo...near Eagle Creek... This information can be relied upon." Ace Daklugie said Juh led the raid. Crook wrote that "ju and Hieronymo" led the Loco breakout. And there is even more persuasive evidence: in all of Geronimo's long and spotted career there is no precedent or parallel for the Loco operation, nothing in his record to demonstrate that he had the imagination to conceive of such an enterprise, or the capacity to carry it out, or could rally followers enough to make it work. With Juh, however, the situation is reversed; there is an exact parallel. In 1879 when the hard-pressed Victorio was trying to escape into Mexico from the Black

Range against strong troop resistance, it was Juh — no particular friend of Victorio's — who came to his assistance. Juh-led warriors rushed up from Mexico, slammed into the ranches and communities along the Rio Grande and created such confusion and panic among the whites that Victorio could save himself and his people. Juh was the *one* strategist and supreme tactician among the latter-day Apaches, and he was the mastermind who conceived and led the great Loco breakout, the most stunning feat of Apache arms in recorded times. All this has significance because the reverse would distort the record and personality and capacity of Geronimo and make of him something he was not. As a guerilla leader he was outstanding; as a savior of his people he was nowhere; the role did not fit his personality, his life-style, his abilities. To make it appear so gives him qualities he did not possess. Geronimo afterward remained in the Sierra Madre until Crook's great 1883 expedition by which time Juh had died. Geronimo then agreed to come in to San Carlos, reaching the reservation early in 1884. In May 1885 he broke out again, taking many followers and associates with him back into the northern Mexico mountains where they remained for about 17 months during which Geronimo did little raiding, but his associates a great deal, each bit of hostility adding to the fearsome reputation of Geronimo himself, however unworthy he may have been of such notoriety. He agreed to surrender in late March 1886 to Crook, then was flushed back onto the warpath with a handful of followers by an American bootlegger who probably felt he could profit more from Apache hostility than tranquility. Miles replaced Crook and Gatewood persuaded Geronimo to surrender to Miles, which he did in early September 1886. He and his people, and the balance of the Chiricahuas were shipped to Florida, then to Alabama and finally settled near Fort Sill, Oklahoma, where Geronimo died of pneumonia. He had become a monumental attraction in his late years, his fame far outstripping the deeds of his years of hostility in which he had proven himself an able partisan leader and that is about all. But his name is firmly fixed in the American mythology and will never be supplanted nor is interest in it likely to diminish much in the foreseeable future. Geronimo himself however never was of the capacity of Mangas Coloradas, Delgadito, Cochise, Victorio or Juh, nor could his record in any way rival theirs in anything short of fiction. He married seven or nine times and may or may not have produced offspring who survived him. Geronimo was buried at Fort Sill, Oklahoma, where a modest monument marks his grave.

Literature abundant; Angie Debo, *Geronimo: The Man, His Time, His Place.* Norman Univ. of Okla. Press, 1976; review of the foregoing by Dan L. Thrapp, *Jour. of Ariz. Hist.,* Vol. 18, No. 1 (Spring 1977), 99-101.

Geronimo, Robert, Apache (1890-Oct. 25, 1966). B. at Mt. Vernon Barracks, Alabama, where Geronimo and other Apaches were held in exile, Robert was named for the doctor who delivered him, Army Assistant Surgeon Robert Bruce Benham. There is some doubt whether Geronimo was the child's father. The mother, Ih-tedda, later known as Katie Cross Eyes (see entry), was the seventh wife of Geronimo, who kidnapped her from the Fort Apache reservation while he was hostile in November, 1885. Ih-tedda gave birth to Lenna, and later to Robert but in 1890 or thereabouts secured permission to return to her people at the Mescalero Reservation in New Mexico. Geronimo is said to have next seen the boy in 1905 at Chilocco Indian School, Oklahoma. Ih-tedda married at Mescalero, Old Cross Eyes, a former army scout, and not until Robert was 13 did she claim him to be Geronimo's son. Many of the old Apaches refused to believe in the relationship. Nevertheless, Robert became the best known supposed offspring of Geronimo; he died at the Mescalero hospital, aged 77, of pnuemonia complicated by diabetes and perhaps a light stroke. Surviving him were sons Robert Jr. and Larry, and three daughters.

Correspondence, Eve Ball with author; correspondence Mrs. C.B. Beyer with author; Griswold; Alamogordo,N.M., *Daily News,* Oct. 26, 1966.

Gerry, Elbridge, frontiersman (July 18, 1818-Apr. 10, 1875). B. in Massachusetts, he entered the employment of Bent and St. Vrain about 1840, then joined the American Fur Company. He married a Sioux girl c. 1842, and when she died, another Sioux. Gerry became an Indian trader on the South Platte and upper Arkansas rivers, eventually owning a horse ranch near the present Greeley, Colorado. He was often a go-between for Indians and whites. He is buried on his ranch.

Ann W. Hafen article, MM, Vol. VI.

Gervais, Jean Baptiste, frontiersman (1790-Nov. 27, 1870). B. in Quebec, he joined the North West Company in 1807 and was stationed at Red River until 1819, when he joined the Hudson's Bay Company, being sent to the Columbia River in 1822. He was with Ogden's brigade on the Snake River in 1824, and continued trapping for the HBC for several seasons. By 1829 he was working for Smith, Jackson and Sublette in the upper Rockies and became one of five partners who bought out that firm in 1830 as the Rocky Mountain Fur Company. It was sold in 1834, and Gervais continued as a free trapper, quitting the Flathead country for Oregon about 1850. His half Indian wife died leaving five children, in 1851. Gervais volunteered for service in the Yakima Indian war of 1855. He died near Oregon City.

Harriet D. Munnick article, MM, Vol. VII.

Gervais, Joseph, pioneer (1777-July 14, 1861). B. in Quebec, he had become a buffalo hunter on the Arkansas River by c. 1796. His later movements are indistinct but in 1810 he was one of the overland Astorians, reaching Oregon in February 1812. He was a member of expeditions exploring the Willamette Valley and in 1813 joined the North West Company after it purchased Astoria, later shifting to the Hudson's Bay Company. Gervais became a free trapper and in the late 1820s settled in the Willamette country, trapping occasionally, and taking part in other pioneer activities. He was one of those exacting vengeance on the Clallam Indians of the Olympic Peninsula for their slaughter of five HBC men in 1828. He also was of the party recovering Jedediah Smith's goods after the Umpqua River disaster. He married three times

Kenneth L. Holmes article, MM, Vol. VII.

Ghent, William James, writer (Apr. 29, 1866-July 10, 1942). B. at Frankfort, Indiana, he became a compositor, eventually editing trade publications in New York and edited the *American Fabian* in 1897-98. He was interested strongly in social causes all of his life and most of his book publications reflect

that concern. Ghent joined the staff of the *Dictionary of American Biography* in 1927 and contributed numerous articles to it, most dealing with frontier figures and characters. He also wrote the *Road to Oregon* (1929) and *The Early Far West* (1931). LeRoy R. Hafen recalled that when writing his draft of a biography of Thomas Fitzpatrick he learned that Ghent, "a good popular writer, was working on the same subject." The two agreed to pool resources upon Ghent's assurance he could produce a popular account and sell it to a leading magazine for publication. The Depression made such a sale impossible however, and Ghent agreed to accept $100 in advance on his share of the royalties while Hafen arranged for the book to be published in a small edition in Colorado. *Broken Hand: The Life of Thomas Fitzpatrick...* appeared in 1931. Within two years it went out of print and became increasingly sought after. Hafen alone later produced a revised edition. Ghent moved to Washington, D.C., where he spent the late years of his life.

Who Was Who; LeRoy R. Hafen, *Broken Hand: The Life of Thomas Fitzpatrick.* Denver, Old West Pub. Co., 1973.

Gholson, Benjamin Franklin, frontiersman (Nov. 17, 1842-Apr. 3, 1932). B. in the present Falls County, Texas, he was the grandson of a veteran of the Battle of New Orleans and the son of Albert G. Gholson (1818-1860), who came from Kentucky to Texas in 1832 and fought in the war of independence. Eventually Ben Gholson settled at what became the communty of Gholson in Lampasas County. From 1858 to 1860 he served several hitches in the Texas Rangers, taking part in pursuits of Indian raiders and occasional skirmishes with them or in other wilderness adventures. The *Handbook of Texas* says that Gholson "assisted in the recapture of Cynthia Ann Parker" in the so-called battle of Pease River, but Gholson, in the lengthy interview printed in *Frontier Times* did not mention that incident, although he described his Indian fighting activities in some detail. He had enlisted in the Ranger company of J.M. Smith in March 1860, took part in a rather unsuccessful operation against the Comanches in the Wichita Mountains, and resigned August 11, 1860. Richardson said that Captain Lawrence S. Ross effected the capture of Cynthia Parker December 19, 1860, and makes no mention of

Smith or Gholson. Ross's Irish lieutenant, Thomas Kelliher, was the ranger who actually captured Cynthia Ann, according to Richardson. Gholson served the Confederacy in the 2nd Texas Cavalry, then became a stockman in Lampasas County, his cattle grazing into neighboring counties. He was married, and lived in Evant, a short distance from Gholson.

Frontier Times, Vol. 4, No. 11 (Aug. 1927), 46-51; HT; Rupert Norval Richardson, *The Frontier of Northwest Texas 1846 to 1876.* Glendale, Calif., Arthur H. Clark Co., 1963.

Gibbon, John, army officer (Apr. 20, 1827-Feb. 6, 1896). B. near Holmesburg, Pennsylvania, later part of Philadelphia, he went to West Point from North Carolina, was commissioned a second lieutenant in the 4th Artillery September 13, 1847 and sent to Mexico duty after hostilities ceased. In Florida he took part in operations against the Seminoles from 1849-50, becoming a first lieutanant in the latter year. Gibbon assisted in removal of the bulk of the Seminoles from Florida to Indian Territory from May, 1853 until August 1854. He taught at West Point, then was on frontier duty in Utah from 1860-61 when he returned to Fort Leavenworth. Gibbon's Civil War service was outstanding. He emerged a Major General of Volunteers and brevet Major General in the army, commanding a corps in the final phases of the conflict. He had been wounded at Fredericksburg and again at Gettysburg and thereafter walked with a decided limp which caused Plains Indians to refer to him as "No Hip Bone," or "One Who Limps." Gibbon became colonel of the 36th Infantry July 28, 1866, and colonel of the 7th Infantry March 15, 1869. He commanded Fort Kearny, Nebraska, from December 1866 to the following May, Fort Sanders, Dakota, to December 1868, Camp Douglas, Utah, in 1869-70, then went to Fort Shaw, Montana, and commanded also the District of Montana until late 1872. He returned to Fort Shaw in mid-1874. March 21, 1876 he assumed command of the Yellowstone Expedition, or the so-called Montana Column which was to move from Fort Shaw on the Sun River, 83 miles north of Helena to the Yellowstone and down that stream to make contact with Custer and Terry when joint operations against hostile Indians suspected to be south of the Yellowstone were contemplated. By this time Gibbon was regarded as "a typical officer of the old school, not much given to 'fuss and feathers' but one of the sturdy, substantial sort who could be depended upon to carry out his orders." Gibbon's command reached Fort Ellis, near Bozeman, Montana, March 28. The Infantry left on the 30th for the Yellowstone, Gibbon himself following with four troops of the 2nd Cavalry April 1. He had heard by now of Crook's battle with hostiles on Powder River March 17 and supposed the enemy therefore would move north; so instead of crossing the river as had been planned, Gibbon moved down its north bank. April 9 he had a conference with the Crows from whom he obtained 23 scouts and two squawmen: Thomas Leforge and one, Bravo. April 13 the march was resumed, the Big Horn reached April 19 but on the 21st Gibbon was advised that Crook would not move before May 15 at the earliest, the Dakota column under Terry and Custer no sooner and Gibbon with his modest command (24 officers and about 400 men) was directed to remain at Fort Pease, below the mouth of the Big Horn on the Yellowstone. For the next two months Gibbon's forces patrolled and scouted in the valley of the Yellowstone with no major incident. In June Gibbon was directed to meet Terry aboard the *Far West* near the mouth of the Rosebud, conferences taking place from June 9 to 21. The 22nd Custer moved out, up the Rosebud, his final word from Gibbon being to leave some Indians for the others to fight. Custer had his battle and met his death June 25; the Gibbon-Terry column reached the scene two days later, Gibbon spending two days burying the dead; the wounded were moved 15 miles to the mouth of the Little Big Horn where the steamer *Far West* awaited them. Gibbon resumed command of Fort Shaw and the District of Montana, exercising it until 1878. Meanwhile, in the summer of 1877 he took a battalion against the Nez Perce Indians, leading his reduced command into the Battle of Big Hole, Montana where again he was severely wounded, this time in the thigh, on August 9; the action was the most savage of the Nez Perce campaign with two officers, 21 enlisted men and six civilians being killed, five officers, 31 enlisted men and four civilians being wounded, some mortally; between 60 and 90 Indians were slain, more than half of them women and children. While the fight itself was at best a standoff and more realistically a white reverse, the Nez Perce could ill afford their losses. Gibbon was in command of the Department of Dakota briefy in 1878-79, commanded Fort Snelling, Minnesota in 1879 and the Department of the Platte in 1884. He became a Brigadier General July 10, 1885. He commanded the Department of the Columbia from 1885-91, and the Division of the Pacific from late 1890 until his retirement, April 30, 1891. He died at Baltimore. Gibbon wrote a number of magazine articles of continued interest; his account of the Custer campaign appeared in the *American Catholic Quarterly Review* for April and October 1877 and has been reprinted.

Cullum; Heitman; Edgar I. Stewart, *Custer's Luck*. Norman, Univ. of Okla. Press, 1955; Robert M. Utley, *Custer and the Great Controversy*. Los Angeles, Westernlore Press, 1962; *Gibbon on the Sioux Campaign of 1876*. Bellevue, Nebr., Old Army Press, 1970 (reprint of the *Amer. Catholic* articles).

Gibbons, Edward, merchant, soldier (d. Dec. 9, 1654). B. in England, his adventures are unrecorded until he appears in America as a member of Thomas Morton's convivial company at Merry Mount (Ma-re Mount) in Massachusetts. He seems to have avoided seizure when Morton was taken and next turns up at the Piscataqua colony at the site of today's Portsmouth, New Hampshire, where his probable brother, Ambrose Gibbons, was a settler. He was fined for drunkeness and related offenses at one time, and may have been a partisan of Anne Hutchinson. Gibbons withal was "Undoubtedly a man of abilities and activity," and rose steadily in colonial positions, accumulating considerable resources in his capacity as businessman and sometimes fur trader. Palfrey wrote that "in his private capacity, Gibbons was a merchant, and, it is to be feared, not a prudent, perhaps not a scrupulous one." Gibbons in June of 1637 took a pinnace of 30 tons to Bermuda, but foul weather drove him to the West Indies. He arrived at Hispaniola, he said, "but not daring to go into any inhabited place there, but to go ashore in obscure places, (he and his crew) lived of turtles and hogs, etc." Cotton Mather, sometimes careless in choosing his sermon sources, preached that the starving crew drew lots to see whose body should feed the rest, and then they prayed, when a large fish "leaped into the boat"; after this fortuitous

event, hunger again descended when the same process was gone through, and as they prayed a "large bird" landed on the boat to supply their needs a little while. Once more starvation loomed and once more they went through the ritual, according to Mather, when a French "man-of-war" with his prize bore down upon them. The French captain who, Palfrey assumed could be none other than a free-booter common enough in the area, recognized Gibbons as an old friend, loaded the Massachusetts ship with hides, tallow and other things, gave Gibbons the prize to take back to New England to sell for him, and sent them happily off for home. This tale struck Palfrey as concocted "to cover up a transaction between a Massachusetts official and a West-Indian Buccaneer," but nothing further was reported done about it. Gibbons was representative of the Massachusetts general court from 1638-47. In 1644 when a militia was organized, he was chosen to command the Suffolk Regiment with the title of sergeant-major; he was Major General of militia from 1649-51, and captain of the ancient and honorable artillery company, described as "a man of resolute spirit, bold as a lion, very generous and forward to promote all military matters; his forts are well contrived and batteries strong and in good repair." Gibbons advanced more than 2,500 pounds to Charles La Tour, secured by a mortgage of La Tour's fort and lands in Acadia, and lost it all on the capture of that place by d'Aulnay de Charnisay in 1647. In 1643 Gibbons was one of the commissioners who formed the confederation among the colonies of Massachusetts, Plymouth, Connecticut and New Haven. His military capability was called into service during periods when Indian unrest threatened the settlers. Gibbons died at Boston.

Thwaites, JR, XXXVI, 239n10; Appleton, II, p. 635; John Gorham Palfey, *History of New England During the Stuart Dynasty*. 3 vols. Boston, Little, Brown and Co., 1865, II, pp. 225-27n.

Gibbs, Alfred, army officer (Apr. 22, 1823-Dec. 26, 1868). B. on Long Island he was graduated from West Point and commissioned a brevet second lieutenant in the Mounted Rifles July 1, 1846, becoming a second lieutenant December 31, 1847. He was breveted to captain during the Mexican War, then was assigned to California where his concern was more with deserters to the gold fields than with military operations as such. He became a first lieutenant May 31, 1853. On March 8, 1857, in New Mexico he pursued eight Mimbres Apaches who had stolen mules near Robledo, New Mexico, caught up with them near Cooke's Springs and killed six, receiving in the process a lance wound which had a permanent effect upon his health. Gibbs became a captain May 13, 1861, was captured by Texas troops at San Augustine Springs, New Mexico, in July but was exchanged, and ended the Civil War a Brigadier General of Volunteers and a brevet Major General of the army and Volunteers. He became major of the 7th U.S. Cavalry July 28, 1866, placing his mark upon the regiment "more than any officer save Custer." Ill health kept him at Fort Leavenworth during Custer's winter campaign of 1868-69 and he died of "congestion of the brain." He was buried at Portsmouth, Rhode Island.

Heitman; Cullum; Robert M. Utley, *Life in Custer's Cavalry*. New Haven, Yale Univ. Press, 1977.

Gibson, George, frontiersman (d. 1809). B. in Mercer County, Pennsylvania, he probably was raised in Kentucky, joined the Lewis and Clark Expedition and was considered for the position of sergeant after the death of Sergeant Floyd although Gass won out. He must have had some Missouri River experience before the expedition, since he served occasionally as interpreter. He was a hunter, horseman and played the violin and he married following the expedition. Clarke says he may have been one of the men under Pryor who attempted to return the Mandan chief Shahaka to his home in 1807 after a trip to Washington, but were rebuffed by the Arikara and sent back down the river. Gibson died at St. Louis.

Raymond W. Settle, Nathaniel Pryor article, MM, Vol. II: *History of the Expedition Under the Command of Lewis and Clark*, ed. by Elliott Coues. N.Y., Dover Pub., 1965; Clarke, *Lewis and Clark.*

Gibson, Hoot (Edmund Richard Gibson), actor (Aug. 6, 1892-Aug. 23, 1962). A motion picture performer, he was born in Tekamah, Nebraska, and is said to have been nicknamed because he once hunted owls in a cave. He claimed he was a wild horse hunter when he went to work for the Selig Polascope Co., movie producers, first as a stunt man, then as a cowboy star, beginning with a bit part in "The Squaw Man" in 1913. He earned up to

$14,500 a week and made — and spent — about $6 million, he estimated. He ended his motion picture career c. 1946, except for a bit part in "The Horse Soldiers" for John Ford in 1959, his 310th film. During his last years Gibson was a greeter in a Las Vegas gambling casino. He died in southern California and was buried at Los Angeles.

New York Times, Sept. 20, 1959; *Los Angeles Times,* Aug. 24, 1962.

Gibson, John, army officer, Indian trader, adventurer (May 23, 1740-Apr. 16, 1822). B. at Lancaster, Pennsylvania, he was a classical scholar, well educated for the time. In 1758 he was a member of Brigadier General John Forbes' expedition against the French-Indians which, after one reversal, resulted in the occupation of the burned and abandoned Fort Duquesne (Pitt). After the peace of 1763 he settled at the post as Indian trader; shortly afterward, as he and two others were descending the Ohio by canoe, they were seized off Beaver Creek, his two companions burned but Gibson saved through adoption by an Indian woman who had lost a son to war, a common practice. He remained several years with the Indians, became fluent in their tongue, and developed an affinity for their culture and customs. He was released in 1764 through efforts of Col. Henry Bouquet and settled again at Fort Pitt, resuming his occupation. In 1774 he took a conspicuous part in Lord Dunmore's War against the Shawnees and others, particularly in negotiating the peace in the course of which he received from the great Logan the speech, delivered to Gibson alone and by him translated and made public, although much of the rhetoric appears to stem from Gibson's classical studies rather than the Indian mind; still there is no reason to doubt its basic authenticity. He may have been related to Logan by marriage. After several civilian assignments, Gibson in the Revolution was named to command a Virginia regiment and after service in the east, was sent about 1778 to Pitt, assuming temporary command of the post. In one affray on Cross Creek, Gibson with a few men surprised a small band of hostile Mingos under Little Eagle, a noted war chief who fired at the white commander, his ball narrowly missing, when Gibson, with his sword, swiftly cut off the Indian's head. This was said to be the the origin of the Indians' nickname, "Long-knives" for Virginians and ultimately other whites, and Gibson ever afterward was known as the "Longknife warrior." Gibson was left by McIntosh in command of Fort Laurens, on the west bank of the Muskingum R., Ohio. Invested for six weeks from January, 1779, by British Indians, the garrison was reduced virtually to starvation. He was to have been second in command of George Rogers Clark's westward expedition, but was prevnted from so serving by Brodhead whom he succeeded as temporary commandant at Fort Pitt, being relieved in turn by Irvine. Gibson became Major General of militia following the Revolution, served in civilian capacities in western Pennsylvania, helped Butler negotiate the 1789 treaty with the Iroquois, sided with the government during the "whiskey rebellion," earning thereby the enmity of many, in 1800 was appointed secretary of the Territory of Indiana, and assisted Harrison at the council of Vincennes with Tecumseh. He died at Braddock's Field, Philadelphia. He was, said Butterfield, "a friend to the Indians," and, in sum "a brave soldier and an honest man."

C.W. Butterfield, *An Historical Account of the Expedition Against Sandusky under Col. William Crawford in 1782.* Cincinnati, Robert Clarke Co., 1873; DAB.

Giddings, George H., stage line operator (1823-Dec. 12, 1902). B. in Susquehanna County, Penna. he reached Texas in 1846, a decade after his brother, Giles A. Giddings had been killed in the Battle of San Jacinto. Giddings studied law at Brenham, Washington County, Texas, and opened his practice, but within months joined a Ranger force, took part in an Indian campaign under Thomas Smith, burying the bodies of victims of a raid by hostiles, suffering an assault by a large party of them, then trailing the band to the Wichita Mountains where in a battle the whites were victorious and prisoners taken. After some months of patrolling the frontier, Giddings served in the Mexican War with Texas outfits, but saw no major action. He briefly was a surveyor, a clerk in a San Antonio, Texas, concern, traded into Mexico and achieved some financial independence. In 1853 Giddings secured a contract to carry mails between San Antonio and Santa Fe; when Congress on March 3, 1857, called for bids for a mail line from San Antonio to San Diego, California, James Birch won out, and

Giddings was named agent for the eastern division, and sold or leased his own stock and equipment to the larger concern for the expanded service. On March 3, 1858, Birch was lost at sea. Giddings won his contract, the service henceforth called the Giddings Line. The description of the fate of his line after the Butterfield line commenced operating is most unclear, but it appears that Giddings continued his project until 1861 despite the competition, financial problems and other difficulties. After the Apache Pass incident in early 1861 which sent Cochise on the warpath, the Giddings line suffered heavy losses due to hostile actions; his brother, James was among the whites killed by Apaches. George Giddings immediately went to Arizona to investigate conditions, reporting upon the evidence of depredations he found. With the Civil War his contracts expired and the line ceased to function, Giddings reporting his losses to Indian actions at $231,720. As a supposed Union sympathizer, he was sent to Austin to try to prevent Texas secession, but instead joined the Confederacy and "rendered valuable service to the south in both civil and military capacities." Giddings remained active in Texas affairs after the Civil War. He died at Mexico City.

Emmie Giddings W. Mahon, Chester V. Kielman, "George H. Giddings and the San Antonio-San Diego Mail Line." *Southwestern Hist. Quar.* Vol. LXI, No. 2 (Oct. 1957), 220-39.

Gilbert, Charles Champion, army officer (c. 1822-Jan. 17, 1903). B. in Ohio, he was graduated from West Point and commissioned a second lieutenant in the 1st Infantry September 27, 1846, serving in the Mexican War and on frontier duty, 1848-50 and 1855-61, being stationed at West Point between the periods in the field; he became a first lieutenant in 1850 and a captain in 1855. He emerged from the Civil War a major with three brevets, joined the 28th Infantry in 1866 and the 7th Infantry as a lieutenant colonel in 1868. Sherman suggested in 1877 that Gilbert succeed Howard in the wearying pursuit of the Nez Perce, making from Idaho for Canada, but Howard rejected the suggestion. Gilbert then failed to contact Howard in Montana through refusal to accept sound advice as to where Howard might be located. Gilbert retired March 1, 1886, and died at 81.

Heitman; Powell; McWhorter, *Hear Me.*

Gilbreth, Isaac, trapper (c. 1796-pre 1860). B. at Boston he was by trade a blacksmith and became a Rocky Mountain trapper in 1825. He reached California with Jedediah Strong Smith in 1827 having survived the Mohave Indian attack which killed most of the party on the Colorado River. He decided to remain in California to which Smith gave his assent and Governor José Maria de Echeandía his licence. Gilbreth, whose name often is spelled Galbraith went to Monterey, California, then to Los Angeles but returned to Monterey. A crack shot, he once amused himself by shooting the heads off blackbirds at 20 paces. Gilbreth was employed variously as a blacksmith at the missions of Santa Barbara, San Gabriel and San Luis Rey. He left California probably in 1832 with David E. Jackson and was at St. Louis in late 1834, apparently settling in Saline County, Missouri. Gilbreth reportedly died at Independence, Missouri, before the Civil War. A huge and powerful man, he willed his giant skeleton to a physician friend.

Bancroft, *Pioneer Register;* Dale L. Morgan, *The West of William H. Ashley.* Denver Old West Pub. Co., 1964.

Gildea, Augustus M. (Gus), frontiersman (Apr. 23, 1854-Aug. 10, 1935). B. in Dewitt County, Texas, he was a cowboy by 1866, and is said to have fought Indians in Texas. Gildea was a Texas Ranger and became a law officer at Del Rio, Texas, moving to New Mexico by 1878, where he became a partisan, or at least a friend, of John Selman, reportedly coining the term, "Selman's Scouts," for John's band; Gildea was listed with Selman by Lew Wallace as wanted for investigation of at least four murders. He worked as a cowboy and range guard for John Chisum. In Arizona he worked as a cowboy in the San Simon area. He died at Douglas, Arizona

Ed Bartholomew, *The Biographical Album of Western Gunfighters.* Houston, Frontier Press of Tex., 1958; Leon Claire Metz, *John Selman, Texas Gunfighter.* N.Y., Hastings House, 1966.

Gililland (Gilliland) James Robert, cattleman (Mar. 22, 1874-Aug. 8, 1946). B. in Brown County, Texas, he came with his family to the Mimbres River country of southern New Mexico in 1886, the next year moving to the Sacramento Mountains east of the Rio Grande. He worked as a cowboy, sometimes associated with Oliver Lee, and with Lee was implicated in the disappearance in February 1896, of Albert J. Fountain and his young son, but in a trial he was cleared. Among other killings in which Gililland was suspected of having some part, although never convicted of any of them, were those of Matt Coffelt and Charley Rhodius in 1893, Deputy Sheriff Kent Kearney in 1898, and Alec Lee, about 1933. Married, Gililland raised cattle in the San Andres Mountains, New Mexico, for 37 years, then retired to Truth or Consequences, then called Hot Springs, New Mexico. Gililland never talked in depth about the Fountain case and "his secret knowledge passed away with him," according to Keleher. Metz, however, reports Gililland's alleged confession.

William A. Keleher, *The Fabulous Frontier.* Albuquerque, Univ. of New Mex. Press, 1962; Leon Claire Metz, *Pat Garrett: The Story of a Western Lawman.* Norman, Univ. of Okla. Press, 1974.

Gillem, Alvan Cullem, army officer (July 29, 1830-Dec. 2, 1875). B. at Gainesboro, Tennessee, he was graduated from West Point in 1851 and joined the 1st Artillery, becoming a captain by 1861 after service against the Florida Seminoles and on the Texas frontier. He served to Major General of Volunteers with Tennessee units during the Civil War (in which forces under his command killed the noted Confederate cavalry raider John M. Morgan in September 1864). In 1866 he became a colonel in the 24th Infantry, transferred to the 11th Infantry in 1869 and to the 1st Cavalry in 1870. Gillem was a personal friend of President Andrew Johnson, was given reconstruction duty and after Johnson's term ended was sent to the Texas frontier once more. In early 1873 he was assigned to command army forces engaged with the Modoc Indians in California's lava beds, and although his health began to fail shortly after taking over the duty, he "arose from his sick bed" to carry on the frustrating conflict; he was relieved in the spring with the exasperating campaign not yet decided. On his return to Benecia Barracks his condition worsened and he went on sick leave in January 1875; he died near Nashville, Tennessee.

Heitman; Ezra J. Warner, *Generals in Blue: Lives of the Union Commanders.* Baton Rouge, La. State Univ. Press, 1964; Keith A. Murray, *The Modocs and Their War.* Norman, Univ. of Okla. Press, 1965.

Gillett, James Buchanan, Texas Ranger, frontiersman (Nov. 4, 1856-June 11, 1937). B. at Austin, the son of James S. Gillett, the family moved to Lampasas in 1872. Gillett began cowboy work the next year in Coleman County. He worked for several outfits, had a brush or two with Indians, saw a colleague murdered, and joined Company D, Texas Rangers, under Captain Dan W. Roberts June 1, 1875. In late August he had his first pursuit and skirmish with hostiles — Apaches — and that fall participated in the policing of Mason County, torn by a feud. In September 1876, he joined Company A, Frontier Battalion, under Major John B. Jones, taking part in scouting, police work, pursuit of rustlers and breaking up Mexican filibuster organizations. He was selected for Company E, a picked body of men, by its lieutenant, N.O. Reynolds. He was with a ranger detachment that escorted John Wesley Hardin from Austin to Comanche, and thence to the penitentiary at Huntsville. Helped clean up Kimble County, in the course of it killing Dick Dublin, noted outlaw. About 1879 the Reynolds company moved to San Saba, to scout Lampasas and several other counties, operating principally against outlaws. In July 1878 he went with a ranger detachment to Round Rock where the notorious Sam Bass was mortally wounded, although Gillett was not in that fight. As a sergeant Gillett was ordered with Lieutenant George W. Baylor's company to El Paso following the El Paso "Salt War." For about a year he operated against Apaches, including Victorio. He, with Baylor, first visited the site of Victorio's Candelaria massacre, and was prevented only by Mexican objections from being in at the death of that war chief of the Mimbres Apaches. Many adventures with an assortment of outlaws, renegade Apaches and other lawless elements followed. He captured Abran and Enofre Baca, wanted as murderers, the latter in Old Mexico, and delivered them to Socorro, New Mexico. Gillett resigned as a ranger in the fall of 1881. He served as city marshal of El Paso for several years, resigning April 1, 1885. He managed a large ranch for six years, then his own in the Marfa area, and near Roswell, New Mexico. He died at Temple, Texas, and was buried at Marfa. Although never commissioned, he was a good ranger. His book is one of the better first person accounts of the Texas Rangers when they operated upon the frontier.

James B. Gillett, *Six Years with the Texas Rangers.* New Haven, Yale Univ. Press, 1925; HT.

Gillette, Warren Caleb, frontiersman (Mar. 10, 1832-Sept. 8, 1912). B. at Orleans, New York, he worked at various occupations until 1862 when he went up the Missouri aboard the *Shreveport,* making his way to Deer Lodge, then became a pioneer merchant at Bannack and at Virginia City after the 1863 gold discovery there. He moved about 1867 to Helena, Montana. He joined the 1870 Washburn expedition for the Yellowstone country, remaining behind to look for the lost Truman Everts who was rescued by another party. Gillette established a 12,000 acre sheep ranch near Deer Lodge, and died at Helena.

Aubrey L. Haines, *Yellowstone National Park: Its Exploration and Establishment.* Wash., Nat. Park Service, 1974.

Gilliam, Cornelius, frontiersman (d. Mar. 28, 1848). Gilliam, whose antecedents are unknown although he probably was a Missourian, claimed to have fought in the Black Hawk War of 1832 in the Midwest, and in the Seminole War probably as a captain with Missouri Volunteers. In the battle of Okeechobee December 25, 1837, a white reverse, Zachary Taylor charged that the Missourians had broken in disorder after a volley or two and could not be reformed, and this Gilliam took as a personal insult, which it may have been; he blamed poor tactical direction for the defeat in which 26 whites were killed outright and 112 wounded to 11 dead and 14 wounded for the Indians. In 1844 Gilliam headed a company of 307 emigrants from Missouri for Oregon. By that time he had been a preacher, a county sheriff and had served in the Missouri Legislature, and "he was, indeed, just the robust, impulsive, sympathetic, willful, and courageous leader the men of the border would choose." The trip was a harsh one, ending in near winter weather as they reached Oregon late in the year. Gilliam became a prominent settler in Oregon; he also engaged in exploring remote areas of the territory. In 1847 he was named colonel of a regiment of volunteers raised to avenge the November 29 massacre of Marcus

Whitman and others at the Whitman Protestant mission at Walla Walla, Washington. He was killed accidentally while drawing a rope from a wagon, one end of the cord becoming entangled with a rifle and the weapon firing the fatal bullet.

Thwaites, EWT, XXX, 174n.; Bancroft, *Oregon,* I; Clifford M. Drury, *Marcus and Narcissa Whitman and the Opening of Old Oregon.* Glendale, Calif., Arthur H. Clark Co., 1973

Gilmer, John Thornton (Jack), stagecoach man (Feb. 22, 1841-1892). B. at Quincy, Illinois, he left home at about 15, crossed the plains to California, accumulated about $3,000 but lost it and turned stage driver. He claimed to have "turned the first wheel" of the Wells, Fargo Overland stage line across the plains and worked for that company for 10 years, also freighting for Russell, Majors and Waddell. He drove on the Central Overland, California and Pike's Peak Express Company's lines for Ben Holladay. He married in 1866 and settled for a time at Fort Bridger, Wyoming, but in 1869 when the railroad was completed, moved to Salt Lake City. He then bought into Montana stage lines, and expanded his operations due to his great administrative and organizing ability. He developed mining and staging interests all over the west. He fathered 11 children, six of whom survived him.

Agnes Wright Spring, *The Cheyenne and Black Hills Stage and Express Routes.* Lincoln, Univ. of Nebr. Press, 1965.

Gilpin, William, pioneer (Oct. 4, 1815-Jan. 20, 1894). B. on "the battlefield of Brandywine," Pennsylvania, the *Dictionary of American Biography* gives his year of birth as 1813 and Bancroft as 1822. He went to West Point from July 1834 to February 1835, but did not graduate. Gilpin was commissioned a second lieutenant in the 2nd Dragoons June 8, 1836, becoming a first lieutenant October 19, fought briefly under Jesup in the Seminole War in Florida and resigned April 30, 1838. In 1843 he went to Oregon with Fremont but left the expedition at The Dalles and spent the winter of 1843-44 in the Willamette Valley, returning to the States in 1844. Gilpin later served in the Mexican War as major of the 1st Missouri Cavalry. After service in Mexico Gilpin, by now a lieutenant colonel led a force of 1,200 cavalry, infantry and artillery onto the Plains

to assure communications to the Rocky Mountains. The troops wintered in the vicinity of the later Colorado Springs and in the summer of 1848 operated to some extent against Indians, although no engagements of consequence were reported. In 1861 Gilpin became first territorial governor of Colorado in recognition of "his services as an explorer of the Great West," these services not further defined. Disgruntled Coloradans forced his removal in 1862, after territorial troops had scored their great Civil War successes in New Mexico and before their record was tarnished at Sand Creek. Gilpin lived at Denver the rest of his life, and died there. A railroad enthusiast he was a promoter of a railroad to the Pacific and once urged a worldwide rail network uniting the Old World and the New by way of Bering Strait.

REAW; Bancroft, *Nevada, Colorado & Wyoming;* Thwaites, EWT, XXX, 39n.; DAB.

Girard, Joseph Basil, army surgeon (Dec. 26, 1846-Aug. 25, 1918). B. at Courniere, Puy-de-Donne, France, he graduated in medicine from the University of Michigan in 1867, and entered the army as an assistant surgeon, serving in the Department of the Platte 1867-71 at Forts Morgan, Colorado; D.A. Russell, Laramie, Fetterman and Fred Steele, Wyoming; and Sidney Barracks, Nebraska. Girard was in the Department of Arizona from 1872 until 1876 during Crook's operations against the Apaches; he was in the field on Indian operations from 1872-73 and at various Arizona posts thereafter. From 1876-79 he was assigned to the Department of the East based at Fort Wayne, Michigan, then he was stationed at Fort Davis, Texas, from 1879 until 1881 when he returned to the Department of Arizona. Girard was attending surgeon at the hanging March 3, 1882, of three Apache scouts who allegedly had mutinied against the army at Cibecue, Arizona, August 30, 1881. Girard was assigned to eastern posts from 1884 until 1887 when he returned to Fort Lowell, Arizona. He later served in Hawaii and the Philippines and retired December 26, 1910, as a colonel. He lived in retirement at San Antonio, Texas.

Heitman; Powell; *Who Was Who;* Sidney B. Brinckerhoff, "Aftermath of Cibecue" (with portrait of Girard). *Smoke Signal,* Tucson Ariz. Corral of Westerners, 36, 1978.

Gird, A.K., scout (d. 1877). Gird was described by Stanton G. Fisher as "a brave and good scout," who joined Fisher's scout company in Idaho for the 1877 Nez Perce campaign. Gird, said Fisher, "was killed last fall in the Judith Basin (of Montana) by one, Major Read," or perhaps, Reed. Fisher himself was a brave and reliable scout.

"Journal of S.G. Fisher." *Montana Contributions,* II, 1896, 274.

Gird, Richard, pioneer, developer, miner (Mar. 29, 1836-May 30, 1910). B. at Litchfield, New York, and well educated for the day, he left home at 16 for California where he learned mining and assaying. In 1858 he went to Valparaiso, Chile, as a civil engineer and in the early 1860s to Arizona, purportedly bringing the first assaying outfit to the Territory. With William D. Bradshaw he ran a ferry across the Colorado to Ehrenberg and opened a wagon road to Prescott, fighting off Indians from time to time threatening their freight wagons. In 1868 he completed the first "official" map of Arizona Territory, moved to San Francisco but returned to Arizona in 1874. As a prospector he joined Al and Ed Schiefflin to establish the silver strike that launched Tombstone, and was a primary mill and construction developer and businessman of the area. His later life is incidental to his frontier experience. He sold out and although with absolutely no written obligation to do so, hunted up the Schiefflin brothers, giving them enough of his larger profits so they all ended up with equal benefits from the Tombstone strike. Gird retired from Arizona a fairly wealthy man, established a 23,000 acre ranch and eventually founded on it Chino, California; he was a progressive, inventive rancher and farmer whose impact was enduring. He also ranched by proxy from 1885 in Sonora, eventually selling the land to William Greene, who established on it the Cananea Consolidated Copper Co. Gird died in California.

Odie B. Faulk, *Tombstone: Myth and Reality.* N.Y., Oxford Univ. Press, 1972.

Girty, George, partisan (1751-c.1811). B. near present Harrisburg, Pennsylvania he was captured at the fall of Fort Granville, Pennsylvania, in the summer of 1756, and taken to Kittanning, Pennsylvania, where with his brothers he was forced to witness the torture-slaying of his stepfather. The Armstrong expedition in September 1756, failed to rescue him and his brothers, James and Simon, and George Girty was taken across the Allegheny River, later returned to Kittanning, then given to the Delawares by whom he was adopted and with whom he lived until 1759 when the Indians were persuaded to surrender their captives at Pittsburgh. George, having learned the Delaware tongue, became an occasional interpreter. He was a sometimes trader to the Indians and remained at Pittsburgh during Lord Dunsmore's War, a fairly respected citizen. In 1778 he joined Capt. James Willing's company of U.S. marines as a second lieutenant, the unit proceeding to the Mississippi and down it to New Orleans, in operations against British "planters." Girty deserted May 4, 1779, fleeing through many adventures to Detroit, where he arrived August 8. He was employed as interpreter and sent to the Shawnees with headquarters at Wapatomica, becoming as much an English agent among those Indians as interpreter, and was looked upon by the British as faithful and loyal. George was a member of Capt. Henry Bird's expedition against Kentucky in 1780 and was of considerable assistance bringing many prisoners back as far as the Shawnee villages, whence they were dispatched to Detroit. George and James Girty fought bravely in defense of the Indian village at Piqua, Ohio, against George Rogers Clark. With Joseph Brant George Girty attacked and destroyed Colonel Archibald Lochry's 100-man company of Pennsylvania Rangers on August 24, 1781, on the Ohio River below the mouth of the Great Miami in present-day Indiana, and successfully skirmished with the Americans afterward. He was not a member of the expedition against Wheeling in September, despite contrary rumors. George was with the Delawares at Sandusky, Ohio, when Crawford drove toward the Indian towns, and fought bravely in the action, afterward withdrawing to remain with the Delawares. His action toward the captured American scout, John Slover, was heartless and cruel; Slover escaped though under sentence of death by torture. Later in 1782 George was a member of Capt. William Caldwell's large expedition against Kentucky, taking part in several actions including the battle of Blue Licks. He did not take part in the later expedition against Wheeling. January 7, 1791, he accompanied Simon Girty and about 300 Indians in an attack on Dunlap's Station, eight miles from the present Hamilton, Ohio, but the attack failed. Girty "so gave himself up to savage life that his identity is with difficulty traced" thereafter. George married among the Delawares and had several children. During his latter years he became a drunkard. He died at the trading post of his brother, James, about two miles below Fort Wayne, Indiana. Of his appearance nothing is known; he was brave and faithful to the British and to his Indian allies.

Consul W. Butterfield, *History of the Girtys.* Cincinnati, Robert Clarke & Co., 1890.

Girty, James, partisan, Indian trader (1743-Apr. 15, 1817). B. near present Harrisburg, Pennsylvania, he was captured at Fort Granville in the summer of 1756, was forced to witness the torture-slaying of his stepfather at Kittanning, and eventually was adopted by the Shawnees. He mastered their tongue quickly and after he and other white prisoners were turned in at Pittsburgh in 1759 he became a part-time interpreter, with his brothers frequenting Indian camps in the vicinity periodically. By 1772 he lived by choice among the Shawnees much of the time and in that year he assisted the Rev. David Jones in compiling a dictionary of Shawnee. He and his brothers had many white friends at Pittsburgh, where James remained during Lord Dunmore's War. British agents, Alexander McKee among them, persuaded him in Ohio to join the British cause in 1777 and Girty "helped, in no small degree," to turn the Shawnee from the American to the British standard. James reached Detroit in August, but returned immediately to the Shawnee, engaged at $2 a day to interpret or make war with them as occasion required. On June 15, 1778, he and Simon, his brother, McKee and others were adjudged guilty of treason by the Pennsylvania government. Commissioned by Hamilton to continue his work, James left his headquarters at Wapatomica, below present Zanesville, Ohio, on a raid into Kentucky, which apparently had some success. Simon Kenton, captured on an Ohio adventure, after considerable abuse reached Wapatomica where his life was saved by Simon Girty. The Girtys were called to Detroit in 1780, then joined the Bird expedition into Kentucky. On

August 6 James and George Girty were prominent in the defense of Piqua, an Ohio Indian village, against George Rogers Clark. James helped the Sandusky Indians against Crawford in 1782, and took part in Caldwell's foray into Kentucky later that year and Captain Andrew Bradt's excursion against Fort Henry and Wheeling in September. James Girty established a trading station at St. Mary's, Ohio, near the present community of that name, and married an English-speaking Shawnee woman known as Betsey. For seven years he enjoyed a monopoly of the Indian trade in his vicinity. Under threat of American encroachments he removed to Gosfield, Essex County, Ontario, alternating his trading activities between Ohio and Ontario, ultimately settling down in the latter region, having been given grants of land by the Crown. He was too infirm to take part in the War of 1812, suffering much from rhuematism. He fathered a son and daughter; his Indian wife died about 1800. James Girty was more temperate in habit than his notorious brothers, was tall and lithe, and may have been "painted worse than he was."

Consul W. Butterfield, *History of the Girtys.* Cincinnati, Robert Clarke & Co., 1890.

Girty, Simon Sr., frontiersman (c. 1700-1751). B. in Ireland he emigrated to Pennsylvania, settling about five miles north of present Harrisburg where August 10, 1747, he was licensed as an Indian trader. Two years later he removed to Sherman's Creek, Perry County. Girty, his wife, the former Mary Newton of English birth, and their four sons, Thomas, Simon Jr., James and George, were forcibly ejected upon Indian demand by white authorities on May 22, 1750, and returned to their former home. Here Girty was killed while drunk by an Indian hang-about known as The Fish; the Indian later was killed by John Turner; who subsequently married Mrs. Girty.

Consul W. Butterfield, *History of the Girtys.* Cincinnati, Robert Clarke & Co., 1890.

Girty, Simon Jr., partisan or renegade (1741-Feb. 18, 1818). B. near present Harrisburg, Pennsylvania, he was captured by French/Indians at Fort Granville in the summer of 1756, taken to Kittanning where he and his brothers were forced to witness the torture-murder of their stepfather, and ultimately was

carried away by Senecas, adopted and soon
learned their language. He was freed at
Pittsburgh in 1759, picked up the Delaware
tongue and learned passable Wyandot
(Huron). Employed as interpreter at Fort Pitt
he became a man of some influence among
whites and reds. Girty was active in Lord
Dunmore's War of 1774 as interpreter and
scout, his antipathy toward Indians at this
time pronounced. He was responsible for
"interpreting" Logan's celebrated speech for
John Gibson, who recorded it for history.
Simon was commissioned a militia second
lieutenant, although he could neither read nor
write. He took his oath of allegiance February
22, 1775; the militia soon was disbanded,
however. Dunmore listed him among the
whites he considered loyal to the Crown.
Affections of the borderers were by no means
clear nonetheless, since Girty accompanied
James Wood on a wilderness sweep to
encourage tribes to rally to the colonies' cause.
When George Morgan became agent for
Indian affairs at Fort Pitt in mid-1776, he
hired Girty and others as interpreters, and for
their influence among the wild Indians; Girty
was discharged August 1 for "ill behavior."
Lieutenant-Governor Henry Hamilton meanwhile had reached Detroit November 9, 1775,
and began attempts to rally the tribes to the
Crown. Girty received a new commission as
second lieutenant in Captain John Stephenson's company of Patriot forces, but resigned
in August 1777. Hamilton that year had
commenced sending Indian allies against
frontier settlements as far distant as Wheeling,
Virginia. Suspected with Alexander McKee of
disloyalty to the Patriot cause, Girty was
examined and acquitted; he made a useful
reconnaissance of the Seneca County for the
Patriots, and participated in Brigadier-
General Edward Hand's abortive expedition
against hostiles on the Cuyahoga River, his
only military action in the Patriot cause.
When McKee fled to the British he took along
Girty, Matthew Elliott and others, leaving
Fort Pitt March 28, 1778, spending some time
with the Shawnees and reaching Detroit by
June 15 when Girty was hired as interpreter at
$2 (16 York shillings) a day, his field of
operations to be the Ohio wilderness and
border settlements. From this time forward
Girty was loyal to British interests. The
Pennsylvania government declared him and
other defectors traitors. Simon Girty,

assigned to the Mingos, found them settled in
the valley of the Scioto as far as present
Columbus, Ohio, and on tributaries of the
Great Miami River. He and his brother,
James, joined in a raid on Kentucky; it had
small success. Simon was instrumental in
saving the life of Simon Kenton, an acquaintance from Lord Dunmore's War days,
captured while operating with George Rogers
Clark's Illinois expedition, in October 1778.
Under Hamilton's directive Girty in January
1779 led a scout to reconnoiter Fort Pitt and
western Pennsylvania and, if possible, obtain
John Gibson's scalp. They attacked a small
party of soldiers near Fort Laurens (Bolivar,
Ohio), defeating them; Girty's identity
becoming known, his reputation as a
"renegade" mounted, although he never truly
was such. Girty regained Detroit February 4,
bearing captured letters from Gibson revealing that Girty was to receive little mercy if
taken, and arousing on Girty's part implacable
hatred against his old acquaintance, Gibson.
Girty accompanied Captain Henry Bird to
rally Ohio Indians against Laurens and other
American posts. On February 22 the war
party, mostly Wyandots and Mingos, reached
Laurens; a small party of whites was trapped
and annihilated, but a siege, though prolonged, was ineffective and the Indians
returned to their villages. A bounty of $800
was offered for Girty's scalp by the Americans
at this time, it was said. Girty took part in
frequent forays against the Pennsylvania
frontier and his reputation grew. Despite
legends to the contrary, Girty was neutral as
regards the Moravian missionaries working
with Ohio Indians, although sourly so. April
1, 1780, Indians took prisoners from an Ohio
River boat, among them Catherine Malott,
19, of Maryland, whom Girty subsequently
married, although he was not present at the
action. The Girtys were at Detroit in March
and accompanied Bird against Kentucky
again, taking Ruddle's Station, or Fort
Liberty, on the Licking River, after Simon
Girty's negotiations for its surrender, then
reduced Martin's Station similarly, Simon
returning to the Ohio Mingos. In early 1781 he
was ordered from the Mingos to the
Wyandots, with whom he raided and lived
subsequently. He next led a small foray on
Kentucky. Girty saved from torture death
Henry Baker, 18, captured near Wheeling.
Simon joined a massive movement of Indians,

Butler's Rangers and others into southern Ohio to counter an expected thrust of George Rogers Clark against Detroit. On the banks of the Ohio River, Simon Girty had an altercation with Joseph Brant, the Mohawk leader then an officer in the British forces, who struck him on the head with a sword, seriously wounding Girty and leaving him with a permanent scar and perhaps some mental impairment. Girty had recovered by January 1782. He came into abrasive contact then with the Moravians, receiving from De Peyster at Detroit instructions to remove them thence, though not to plunder or harm them; he turned the commission over to a Frenchman, Francois Le Villier, while Girty joined a plundering expedition with Wyandots to the Ohio, having some small success. Although described from personal experience by some missionaries as a "white savage," and a "madman," Girty could be kind, as he was to Christian Fast, 17, captured by the Indians but ultimately freed. On March 8, 1782, more than 90 Christian Indians at the Moravian settlement at Gnadenhutten, Ohio, were massacred by David Williamson and lawless Pennsylvania militia. A large force under Colonel William Crawford left Pennsylvania for an attack on the Sandusky villages May 25. In an action June 4 Crawford was defeated and captured; Simon and George Girty took part in the battle, the former not prominently, however. Crawford subsequently perished by torture; Girty's role in this celebrated incident is well known and, if cruel, yet was ambiguous. In his position he perhaps was forced to act as he did. He accompanied Captain William Caldwell into Kentucky, attacking Bryant's Station, and taking part in the battle of Blue Licks, August 19, 1782. Girty led a small raid to within five miles of Pittsburgh, taking scalps, in May 1783, his last foray into the American settlements; on this raid he captured an American youth, but treated him kindly. He worked thereafter as interpreter for the British at Detroit, and was maintained for the remainder of his life at half-pay. He married Miss Malott in August 1784, settling at Amherstburg, Essex County, Ontario. Yet for the next decade he was an influence through British instigation in Ohio Indian hostility toward the Americans and in the series of campaigns and wars that ensued. After the treaty of Fort McIntosh he apparently made visits to Sandusky and other Indian villages, seeking to stir the natives against the Americans. He led a party of Indians that attacked Dunlap's Station on the Ohio River early in January 1791; one captive was savagely tortured with Girty's apparent permission. On November 5, he bravely took part in Little Turtle's stunning victory over St. Clair, and may have directed the Indian who killed Major General Richard Butler, highest ranking American officer to die in the Indian wars. On June 25, 1792, he led an attack on Fort Jefferson, near present Greenville, Ohio. He was prominent in an attack June 30-July 1, 1794, on Fort Recovery, in present Mercer County, Ohio, a defeat for the Americans. Girty was present at the battle of Fallen Timbers, August 20, 1794, although he took little active part and escaped after the Indians were defeated by Anthony Wayne, returning to Detroit. Girty made one more visit to the Maumee Indian country of Ohio, then retired to Canada. Occasionally an interpreter, he lived on his farm with his family, some of his children rising to local prominence. His wife left him for a time because of his drunkeness and brutality when intoxicated. In 1800 Girty broke his right ankle and thereafter was lame; his eye-sight began to fail by 1811. He was driven from his home by events of the War of 1812, but returned in 1816, blind and crippled, was reconciled with his wife who was religiously inclined. He was given a military funeral by British troops from nearby Fort Malden. Girty was 5 feet, 9 inches, tall, had black hair and eyes, his face was round and full, his neck short, his build robust. "In his prime he was very agile." His hair turned grey in his last years. He had good qualities, was not so base or evil as Americans borderers — many of the same stripe as he — often made out, but was loyal to the British cause, to his Indian friends and although occasionally brutal, he also possessed more elevated characteristics.

Consul W. Butterfield, *History of the Girtys.* Cincinnati, Robert Clarke & Co., 1890.

Girty, Thomas, frontiersman (1739-Nov. 3, 1820). B. near present Harrisburg, Philadelphia, he was captured as an infant at Fort Granville, near present Lewistown, Philadelphia, in 1756, and taken by Indians to Kittanning, Philadelphia, where with his brothers and mother he was forced to witness the torturing of his stepfather. He was rescued by Lieutenant Colonel John Armstrong's expedition against Kittanning September 8, 1756, and taken to Pittsburgh. He apparently sought a home "in the west," after Pontiac's War, was married before 1768 and settled at Pittsburg, at one time packing for Indian traders. He figures in minor legal matters in 1776 and 1777, and still was living in Pittsburgh, in 1781. The next year he joined in an inconsequential petition to Irvine and in 1783 with his half-brother, John Turner, visited his brother, Simon Girty at Detroit, but with what result is not known. Although his loyalty to the American cause was suspect late in the Revolution, he was sent as an emissary to the Sandusky, Ohio, Indians in 1788, with a mission to divide and weaken them if possible. He performed valuable services as a scout against the Ohio Indians from 1792 to 1794. He died at Girty's Run, across the Allegheny and a few miles from Pittsburgh, having raised a respectable family and himself earning a reputation for worthiness.

Consul Butterfield, *History of the Girtys.* Cincinnati, Robert Clarke & Co., 1890.

Gist, Christopher, soldier, frontiersman (c. 1706-July 25, 1759). B. in Maryland, he received a good education and became a surveyor by profession and an explorer and frontiersman by inclination. By 1750 he was living in the Yadkin, North Carolina, country near Daniel Boone. October 31, 1750 he was appointed by the Ohio Company to explore the trans-Allegheny as far as later Louisville at the falls of the Ohio River. He visited Shannopin's Town, later Pittsburgh, crossed the Ohio and reached several Indian towns, including Pickawillany, Ohio, near present Piqua where the Picks, part of the Shawnees, lived. After exploring Kentucky to some extent he returned to the Yadkin. The next year he discovered the Blue Stone River, in Mercer County, West Virginia, and Gist's River, in the Cumberland Mountains of present Russell County, Virginia. In 1753 settled briefly at Brownsville, Philadelphia, returned to Maryland in November, joined George Washington on a mission from Governor Dinwiddie to Fort Duquesne and the two journeyed westward, Gist twice saving Washington's life. Gist was with Washington in the defeat of Coulon de Jumonville, May 28, 1754, and the surrender of Fort Necessity, July 4, 1754. Gist served as scout in the

Braddock campaign and took part in the unfortunate battle July 9, 1755, later being made captain of a company of scouts. In 1756 he went south to the Cherokee country, attempting to enlist Indians for the British cause; he was an Indian agent briefly. Gist died of smallpox, in Virginia, on the road from Williamsburg to Winchester. He was an able, intelligent explorer of great courage and persistence and did much to advance the frontier in the trans-Allegheny; his journals have extraordinary value.

DAB; *Documentary History of Dunmore's War 1774,* ed. by Reuben Gold Thwaites, Louise Phelps Kellogg. Madison, Wisc. Hist. Soc., 1905; *Christopher Gist's Journals,* ed. by William M. Darlington. Pittsburg, J.R. Weldin & Co., 1893 (1966, xii).

Gist, Nathaniel, frontiersman (Oct. 15, 1733-c. Jan. 1, 1815). The son of Christopher Gist (1706-1759), he was b. in Maryland and by 1753 had traded with the Overhill Cherokee, those of the Carolina-Tennessee-Georgia region. Much later he formed a liaison with a Cherokee girl and probably fathered the great Cherokee Sequoyah (see entry). In 1754 Gist was again among the Cherokee at Echota town in the present Monroe County, Tennessee. He returned to Virginia in time to take part in the Braddock campaign, serving as lieutenant in his father's 17th Company of Rangers of Washington's regiment; he was in the disastrous defeat of Braddock. In 1756 Gist served in his father's company scouting and ranging the Virginia frontier against French Indians, in 1757 became a captain and in 1758 took 200 Cherokee in the John Forbes campaign that reoccupied Fort Duchesne (see Forbes entry). In 1760 Gist and Daniel Boone hunted in the mountainous wilderness near the Holston River, a tributary to the Little Tennessee, Gist later exploring Cumberland Gap. His union with the Cherokees could not have come in 1760-61 as has been stated since he then was an officer with the Byrd-Stephen regiment of Virginians operating against the Cherokees. Afterward he settled for a time in the Cherokee towns on the Little Tennessee and there entered his relationship with the Cherokee woman. Gist was in the Overhill Cherokee towns in 1775 when Richard Henderson and his associates purchased from the Indians large portions of Kentucky and Tennessee. From the Cherokees that year he visited West Florida and returned to central Tennessee, becoming deeply involved in the complicated intrigues coincident with the start of the American Revolution and its repercussions on the frontier. He seemed on the one hand to intrigue with the British and Tories, and on the other to be loyal to Virginia, warning the Cherokees not to go to war against the border settlers. When Colonel William Christian began his retaliatory campaign against them, Gist under a truce flag joined him. Initially he was "thought to be a spy, but the prejudice against him soon wore off and he became very popular" with the Revolutionists. He went on to Virginia, explained his actions to the governor and Council of State, and was cleared. January 1, 1777 Gist was appointed colonel of the Continental forces and sent south by Washington to bring the Cherokee to sign a treaty of friendship at Fort Patrick Henry, Long Island, on the Holston River near the present Kingsport, Tennessee. Gist advocated fuller use of Indian auxiliaries in the American cause. He later commanded Red Stone Fort in Pennsylvania, campaigned in South Carolina and was captured at Charleston; he retired January 1, 1781. In 1793 he moved from Virginia to Kentucky, receiving a grant of 7,000 acres of bluegrass land for his services as a Revolutionary War soldier. His home became a center noted for hospitality. He named it Canewood, and there he died "about the close of the War of 1812." He was described in his maturity as "stout-framed and about six feet high and of a dark complexion," cordial to all and although in 1783 he had married a white woman, Judith Cary Bell, remained perfectly open about his earlier relationship with the Indian girl by whom Sequoyah had been born.

Samuel C. Williams, "Nathaniel Gist, Father of Sequoyah." *East Tenn. Hist. Soc. Pub.* No. 5 (Jan. 1933), 39-54.

Gladwin (Gladwyn), Henry, military officer (Nov. 19, 1729-June 22, 1791). B. in England, probably in Derbyshire, Gladwin became a lieutenant in the 48th Infantry Regiment August 28, 1753 and sailed for America in 1754-55. His outfit and the 44th Foot which accompanied it, "two of the most worthless regiments in the army," were under overall command of Major General Edward Braddock. Gladwin attended the July 9, 1755 Monongahela battle in which he was wounded and Braddock killed. He took part in an attack on Louisbourg in 1757 and in December became a captain. In 1758 Gladwin transferred to the 80th Light Armed Foot, a regiment raised by Thomas Gage for wilderness fighting, was wounded at Fort Carillon (Ticonderoga) in 1758 and in 1759 was promoted by Amherst to acting major (he was confirmed in that rank in December, 1760). As acting commander of the 80th he participated in the successful actions against French Forts Carillon and St. Frédéric on Lake Champlain in the summer of 1759, accompanied Amherst's operation against Montreal that year and became commander of the captured Fort de Levis (Fort William Augustus) near present Ogdensburg, New York. In 1761 he was directed by Amherst to lead an expedition to Niagara, and by William Johnson to continue from there to Detroit where he arrived September 1, so ill he was forced to return to England in October. He came back to Detroit in 1762 with instructions to found posts on Lake Superior and exercise general supervision over northwestern establishments. Gladwin tended to be abrupt and had little patience with Indians, whom he termed dogs and barely tolerated. His personality may have exacerbated the ruffled feelings of Pontiac and others, though they seemed already to be plotting a revolt against the British. May 1, 1763 about 40 Ottawas (Pontiac's people) reconnoitred Fort Detroit. Gladwin on May 7 received private information (the source of the intelligence is in dispute) that Pontiac planned mischief and would by ruse assail Fort Detroit the following day. He alerted the garrison and intrepidly nipped the Indian endeavor, but on Monday, May 10, Pontiac openly attacked the post and its environs and a long siege began, continuing until October 30. Gladwin, whose garrison numbered 122 soldiers with eight officers and about 40 fur trade figures of uncertain loyalty, remained firmly in control, knowing that "promotion was certain to be the reward of success; and almost as surely the torture-stake would be the penalty of failure." The post was well supplied with provisions and water, communications could be opened at times with Niagara, and at critical junctures Detroit was resupplied and reinforced. Although the Indians occasionally mustered as many as 1,000 warriors, a siege was not to their liking, French pledges of assistance were unfulfilled, and as the season wore on their numbers dwindled. In October Pontiac learned that the English and French had made a peace. He suggested a truce, and Gladwin accepted. Detroit and Fort Pitt had been the only British posts in the northwest to hold out, the former largely through Gladwin's ability and courage. Gladwin wrote to Amherst that the Indians "have lost between eighty and ninety of their best warriors, but if your excellency still intends to punish them for their barbarities, it may be easier done, without any expense to the crown, by permitting a free sale of rum, which will destroy them more effectually than fire and sword," adding in the same passage that if Amherst desired to smooth over the difficulties, "which I hope you will," it might be done through intervention by William Johnson who was liked, trusted and influential among the tribesmen. Upon Amherst's recommendation Gladwin was promoted to lieutenant colonel and became deputy adjutant general in America. He had wearied of wilderness operations however, and returned to England in 1764. He declined to serve in America during the Revolutionary War but became a colonel on the retired list in 1777 and a Major General November 20, 1782. He died near Chesterfield, Derbyshire. Gladwin was married and fathered 10 children.

Charles Moore, "Henry Gladwin and the Siege of Pontiac." *Harper's New Monthly Mag.,* Vol. XCV, No. DLXV (June 1897), 77-93 (including portraits of Gladwin and his wife); Howard H. Peckham, *Pontiac and the Indian Uprising.* Univ. of Chicago Press, 1961; *Journal of Pontiac's Conspiracy 1763.* Detroit, Mich. Soc. of Colonial Wars, 1910; Parkman, *The Conspiracy of Pontiac,* 2 vols.; Lee McCardell, *Ill-Starred General: Braddock of the Coldstream Guards.* Univ. of Pittsburgh Press, 1958; DAB.

Glanton, John Joel, scalp hunter (1821-c. 1850). B. in South Carolina, he was at San Antonio, Texas, by 1836. Glanton married into a Mexican family, but his wife reportedly was killed by Indians, generating his lifelong hatred of them. At 15 Glanton was said to have been a scout with Fannin's command, but escaped the Goliad massacre. He was said to have been back in San Antonio March 18, 1840, for the celebrated "Council House

Fight," in which a Comanche peace delegation was betrayed, 35 of them killed along with eight whites. Glanton was outlawed by Sam Houston for unspecified offenses, but served in the Mexican War under Jack Hays and others, and reportedly was mustered out April 30, 1848, in Mexico. Later that year he became a scalp hunter, heading a band for that purpose, some asserting that they turned in Mexican as well as Indian scalps for bounty; ultimately Glanton and some others were "chased out of Mexico," for these or kindred activities. They settled on the lower Colorado River near present Yuma, killed the owner of a ferry and took it over and set themselves up in business, charging exhorbitant fees and otherwise abusing their neighbors until the Yuma Indians revolted, drove them into the desert and killed Glanton and about a dozen others. Glanton was described as a "thickset, rough-looking man."

Ed Bartholomew, *Biographical Album of Western Gunfighters.* Houston, Frontier Press of Tex., 1958; Bancroft, *History of Arizona and New Mexico.*

Glass, Hugh, mountain man (d.c. 1833). Nothing is known of his birth or early years save that he probably was of Irish descent, and was educated. He may have been a seaman and a Gulf of Mexico pirate, probably with the Lafittes (Laffites). Escaping the buccaneer ship to the Texas coast, he and another wandered inland, the legend goes, and were captured by Indians identified improbably as Pawnees. Escaping once again to St. Louis, he joined Ashley for the 1823 expedition up the Missouri River. Glass was wounded at the Arickara battle; recovered, he was one of 13 men who moved overland to the relief of a fur-gathering crew left at Fort Henry, at the mouth of the Yellowstone River. Late in August 1823, Glass was severely mauled by a grizzly and left with two volunteer companions, young Jim Bridger and John S. Fitzgerald, it is said. These became convinced he could not live, and abandoned him; Glass recovered sufficiently to crawl 300 miles down the Grand River to the Missouri, was befriended by Indians, and eventually reached Fort Kiowa, above the confluence of the White and Missouri rivers. Recovered, Glass reportedly pursued the two who had abandoned him, back up the Missouri and the Yellowstone to the Big Horn where he found

Bridger and spared him because of his youth; Glass continued by way of the Platte down to Fort Atkinson on the Missouri seeking Fitzgerald, having one narrow escape after another, only to discover finally that the man he sought had joined the army and was beyond reach. Glass traded to Santa Fe, trapped the Ute country, was dangerously wounded by an arrow. Recovered he continued as a free trapper, then became a meat hunter out of Fort Union. He was killed with Edward Rose and another on the Yellowstone River ice below the Big Horn by Arikaras.

Literature abundant; John Myers Myers, *Pirate, Pawnee and Mountain Man*. Boston, Little Brown and Co., 1963; Aubrey L. Haines article, MM; Vol. VI; Dale L. Morgan, ed., *The West of William H. Ashley, 1822-1838*. Denver, Old West Pub. Co., 1964.

Glass, John Nelson, army officer (Nov. 2, 1853-Aug. 15, 1892). B. at Ripley, Tennessee, he was graduated from West Point, became a second lieutenant in the 6th Cavalry August 9, 1878, and was promoted to first lieutenant March 20, 1885. Glass was stationed most of his career in the Indian country, serving at Forts Grant, Lowell, Huachuca and the San Carlos Indian Reservation in Arizona; Forts Bayard and Wingate, New Mexico and Fort Washakie, Wyoming. As commander of Indian scouts, and with his troop he saw much scouting and campaigning after hostile Indians, taking part in Morrow's extended pursuit of Victorio into Chihuahua in the autumn of 1879, scouts along the Gila and other actions. An intelligent and highly literate man, Glass wrote hundreds of letters (most of them preserved) to his wife and relatives; many are vivid, detailed descriptions of his life as a frontier soldier and of his campaigns, gifted with touches of humor and occasionally poignancy. Some are at the Arizona Historical Society at Tucson; others are held by Glass's descendants. At Fort Washakie Glass "started out to take a long ride in the cool of the evening," being ill, when his horse shied, the officer was thrown and his neck broken; he "lived only a few minutes." Glass was fluent in French and German, and understood some Apache. At one point he was court-martialed and convicted after accusing his superior officer of cowardice; President Cleveland remitted the sentence.

AHS Archives; Heitman; Cullum; *Annual Association of Graduates* (West Point), 1893.

Glenn, Edwin Forbes, army officer (Jan. 10, 1857-Aug. 5, 1926). B. near Greensboro, North Carolina, he was graduated from West Point in 1877. In 1888 he instituted military training and taught mathematics at the University of Minnesota; he earned a law degree from that school in 1890 (and received honorary degrees from five colleges). He was admitted to the Minnesota bar and became judge advocate of the military Department of Dakota and of the Department of the Columbia from 1896-98. Glenn commanded exploring and relief expeditions to Alaska in 1898-99. He retired in 1919 as a Brigadier General. He died at Glendon, North Carolina. He was author of *Glenn's International Law* (1895) and *Rules of Land Warfare* (1914).

Who Was Who; Cullum.

Glenn, Hugh, fur trader, businessman (Jan. 7, 1788-May 28, 1833). B. in Berkeley County, present West Virginia, he moved to Cincinnati by 1811, supplied provisions to forces during the War of 1812, becoming acquainted with Jacob Fowler in doing so. A banker and businessman, he contracted to supply frontier army posts and Indians involved in removal programs into the trans-Mississippi country. By 1819, due to the nation's financial difficulties, irregularities in fulfilling his contracts, and other factors, Glenn had come into difficulties. He secured a license to trade with Indians "westward to the mountains," joining Fowler and others and in late 1821 they started up the Arkansas River. Captured by Kiowas, Glenn was rescued by Arapahoes. He learned of the Mexican revolution and visited Taos, charting a new route in doing so. His party trapped nearby mountains. Glenn commenced his return trip June 1, reaching St. Louis July 15. He visited the west once or twice again, but his business empire had crumbled; he died at Cincinnati.

Harry R. Stevens article, including details of Glenn's many-faceted financial and business dealings, MM, Vol. II.

Glidden, Frederick Dilley (Luke Short), writer (1908-Aug. 18, 1975). B. at Kewanee, Illinois, he became a newspaperman, then perhaps the most popular writer of western stories of his time. Commenting on the report that "all newspapermen are disappointed writers," Glidden once said, "in me you behold a writer who is a disappointed newspaperman. I've been fired from more newspapers than I like to remember, even if I could." He reportedly spent two years as a trapper in sub-Arctic Canada before turning to writing, which he did about 1936. He wrote more than 50 novels (his brother, Jonathan Glidden, also was a popular writer under the name of Peter Dawson). Glidden assumed the name Luke Short as suggested by his agent after a publisher objected that his own "was too phoney," and only later learned "that the name had once belonged to a no-good western gunman." He was married and fathered three children, two of whom survived him. Glidden died at Aspen, Colorado, where he had lived for many years.

Western Writers of Amer., *The Roundup*, Vol. XXIII, No. 10 (Oct. 1975), 10; *Contemporary Authors*, Vol. 21-22, Detroit, Gale Research Co., 1969.

God(e)froy, Jacques, fur trader, interpreter (1722-1795). B. either at Three Rivers or Detroit, he became a fur trader, proficient in several Indian languages and served as interpreter for many years at Detroit "acquiring great influence over the savages" who resorted there. In 1760 he took an oath of allegiance to Britain. Godfroy was sent by Major Gladwin to seek an interview with Pontiac on behalf of the English cause, but returned unsuccessful, was arrested on suspicion of treason but soon released. Later he was sent to the Illinois with four other Canadians. They not only pillaged an English trader, but aided Indians to capture Fort Miami and for this Godfroy was sentenced to be hanged for treason. But because of his talents as interpreter he was saved from the gallows and in August, 1764 sent with Morris for whom he performed faithfully. On one occasion, in Pontiac's camp, a young Indian sought to stab Morris to death, but was wrestled back by Godfroy who thus saved the captain's life. From that camp Morris and Godfroy resumed their mission to the Illinois. They had another close call at Fort Miami, Morris being captured by Indians and almost put to the torture; during his ordeal Godfroy staunchly stood by him and eventually caused him to be freed. Repeatedly threatened with death if he persevered in his journey to the Illinois, Morris with Godfroy returned to Detroit, reaching there September 17, lucky to be still alive. After this adventure, Godfroy

settled anew at Detroit, became much respected and esteemed and one of the wealthiest of the French colony. His death occurred probably at Detroit.

Thwaites, JR, LXX, 303nl; Thwaites, EWT, I, p. 302n.; Parkman, *The Conspiracy of Pontiac*, II.

Godefroy, Jean Paul, fur trader (c. 1602-c. Oct. 20, 1668). B. at Paris, the son of a court official, he reached Canada about 1626 and became an interpreter and trading clerk probably at Three Rivers. He made at least two trips to France, became commander of a ship and from 1648-50 admiral of a trading fleet. He entered a seal hunting company at Tadoussac, and traded for furs with the Indians. In June 1851, he and Gabriel Druillettes, a Jesuit, were sent to New England in an attempt to reach an accord for a combined war against the Iroquois; the proposal was refused by authorities of Plymouth and Massachusetts colonies and the emissaries returned to Canada. Godefroy, who was related to Jean Godefroy de Lintot, became a prominent colonist in New France, but returned to the mother country about 1657 with his wife and one of his two daughters; he died in France.

Thwaites, JR, IX, 305-306n4; DCB.

Godefroy de Normanville, Thomas, interpreter (c. 1610-Summer 1652). B. in Normandy, he was a younger brother of Jean Godefroy de Lintot and a relative of Jean Paul Godefroy. He reached New France about 1626 and quickly absorbed enough of Indian languages to serve as interpreter under Champlain. When the English occupied Quebec from 1629 to 1632, Godefroy lived among the Indians, settling upon French return in the Three Rivers region. He spoke Algonquin, Iroquois, and probably Huron, an Iroquoian tongue. He was captured by the Iroquois three times, the first with Marguerie in February 1641; then in the spring of 1648 and again in August 1652. He escaped the first two times, but was killed in the Iroquois villages in present New York State on the last occasion.

Thwaites, JR, XXI, 23ff; 311nl; DCB.

Godey, Alexis (Alexander, Antoine), frontiersman (1818-Jan. 19, 1889). B. of French parents at St. Louis, Godey entered the Rocky Mountain fur trade in his teens, for in 1835 he was trapping with Bridger and Carson in the upper Rocky Mountains and as far as the Humboldt River. He may have made the Green River rendezvous in 1836 after wintering at Fort Hall. Godey was probably at Pueblo, Colorado, in 1842 when the first fort on the site was constructed. Carson was for years his close associate, and with him he joined Fremont on the second, third and fourth expeditions. Godey won high praise from Fremont for his coolness, the officer asserting that Carson, Godey and Dick Owens, if in Napoleon's army, would all be field marshals. Godey's best known exploit while with Fremont was a pursuit he and Carson undertook in 1844 in southern California to retrieve horses stolen by Indians from a Mexican party; they recovered the horses, a captive boy, and killed two Indians, Godey reportedly doing in both. He was a lieutenant with the California Battalion in 1846 and fought in the action at San Pasqual, being sent afterward by Kearny to San Diego with others seeking assistance. On their return, the party was captured by the Mexicans, but Godey soon was released. He was one of the strong figures of the fourth Fremont expedition; it was he who led rescuers to the snowbound survivors among the high southern Rockies. Godey joined a California-bound party in 1849, reaching Sutter's Fort September 15, visiting Monterey and opening a hotel at San Juan Bautista. He married Maria Antonia Coronel, a sister of Antonio Francisco Coronel, California pioneer, although he previously had had a succession of Indian wives. Coronel fought the Americans in 1846-47, later became state treasurer. Godey became a sheep rancher near Bakersfield, California, and for twenty years worked for Edward Fitzgerald Beale on his ranch system. Attending a Los Angeles circus, according to Favour, Godey "got too close to a lion and was scratched severely, dying from blood poisoning." He left an estate of about $10,000 and was buried at Bakersfield.

Harvey Lewis Carter, "Dear Old Kit": The Historical Christopher Carson. Norman, Univ. of Okla. Press, 1968; Alpheus H. Favour, Old Bill Williams: Mountain Man. Norman, Univ. of Okla. Press, 1962; Bancroft, Pioneer Register; Los Angeles Times, Jan. 21, 1889, a one-paragraph item confirming his death and place of burial; Walt Wheelock, "Alexis Godey." Los Angeles Westerners' Branding Iron, No. 73, June 1965.

Godfrey, Edward Settle, army officer (Oct. 9, 1843-Apr. 1, 1932). B. at Kalida, Putnam County, Ohio, he enlisted in 1861 in the 21st Ohio Infantry, then went to West Point and after graduation was commissioned a second lieutenant in the newly activated 7th Cavalry in 1867 at Fort Harker, Kansas, and made a first lieutenant within a year. He performed scouting and frontier service in Kansas and Indian Territory, participated in the battle of the Washita, and led the pursuit downstream until he became aware of extended further Indian villages in that direction; on his withdrawal he heard what must have been the firing marking destruction of Elliott and his detachment. Godfrey served in the southeast from 1871-73, then returned to the upper Plains to take part in Stanley's Yellowstone expedition, two brushes with hostiles being reported. He was on the 1874 Black Hills expedition. Godfrey commanded K Company and was with Benteen at the Little Big Horn, gained Reno Hill and took a prominent part in events there during the remainder of the fight and afterward. His writings of the engagement have been a prime source for historical writers ever since. Best known is his "Custer's Last Battle," which appeared in Century magazine in January, 1892 and was republished with additions, in Contributions to the Historical Society of Montana, IX, pp. 141-225. His diary covering the period of the Big Horn campaign was published posthumously. After the death of Weir late in 1876 Godfrey came to command Company D of the 7th. In 1877 he participated in the campaign against the Nez Percé, was severely wounded at Snake Creek in the Bear Paw Mountains, brevetted major for "most distinguished gallantry," and was given a Medal of Honor. In 1879 he testified before a Court of Inquiry investigating the conduct of Reno at the Custer fight. In 1890 Godfrey took part in the battles of Wounded Knee and Drexel Mission, South Dakota. He was injured in a train wreck while returning from this campaign and never fully recovered, his later assignments reflecting his condition. In 1897 he was in Arizona and New Mexico, served in Cuba and later in the Philippines, first with the 12th Cavalry, then with the 9th of which he was colonel, was promoted to Brigadier General and retired in October 1907. When he died at Cookstown, New Jersey, he was believed to be the last survivor save Colonel Charles Varnum of the Little Big Horn fight. His diary and papers are preserved at the Library of Congress. Godfrey was married twice, his first wife having predeceased him, and fathered children.

The Field Diary of Lt. Edward Settle Godfrey, ed. by Edgar I. and Jane R. Stewart. Portland, Ore., Champoeg Press, 1957; Edgar I. Stewart, *Custer's Luck*. Norman, Univ. of Okla. Press, 1955; John M. Carroll, Byron Price, *Roll Call on the Little Big Horn, 28 June 1876*. Ft. Collins, Colo., Old Army Press, 1974.

Godfroy, Frederick C., Indian agent (1828-June 15, 1885). B. at Monroe, Michigan, he commenced study for the Roman Catholic priesthood, then transferred to the University of Michigan but left before graduation. He worked in mercantile establishments in Michigan until 1876, on July 1 of that year becoming agent for the Mescalero Apache Agency of New Mexico; Godfroy was partial to the Murphy-Dolan faction of the developing Lincoln County troubles, but had his hands full managing his Apaches. It was a time when the restless Ojo Calientes were sidling onto the Mescalero reservation and they had to be cared for; when white desperadoes were raiding Mescalero horse herds; when military cooperation with the agent was wholly or usually lacking. An investigation of the agency uncovered various flaws in its management and March 15, 1879, S.A. Russell succeeded Godfroy. He died at Plattsburgh, New York, and was buried at Buffalo, New York.

Robert N. Mullin notes; William A. Keleher, *Violence in Lincoln County, 1869-1881*. Albuquerque, Univ. of New Mex. Press, 1957.

Godin, Antoine, Iroquois mountain man (pre-1810-c. May 22, 1836). Hired by the North West Company for service in the Oregon country, he roved the mountains for many years. In July 1832, it was Godin and another who murdered a Blackfoot for his blanket, thus precipitating the celebrated battle of Pierre's Hole. Godin was shot treacherously by Blackfeet near Fort Hall.

Aubrey L. Haines article, MM, Vol. II.

Golden, Johnny, gambler (c. 1854-1876). B. in Illinois, he was a gambler at Kansas City, and reached Fort Griffin, Texas, about 1876. Here

he became enamored of beauteous Lottie Deno, and she of him, switching her affections from a married saloon keeper to Golden. Golden was arrested on a trumped-up charge and assassinated, reportedly at the instigation of the unnamed saloon keeper who is said to have paid officers $250 for the killing. "No investigation of the affair was ever made."

Carl Coke Rister, *Fort Griffin on the Texas Frontier*. Norman, Univ. of Okla. Press, 1956; *Frontier Times,* Vol. IV, No. 4 (Jan. 1927), 1-3; Vol. IV, No.5 (Feb. 1927), 56; Ed Bartholomew, *Wyatt Earp: The Untold Story*. Toyahvale, Tex., Frontier Book Co., 1963, 308.

Goldsby, Crawford: *see* Cherokee Bill.

Golling, Elling W. (Bill), artist (1878-c. Apr. 16, 1932). B. at Pierce City, Idaho, he was raised after the death of his mother by relatives at St. Johns, Michigan, at Chicago and briefly in New York State, before going west again, reaching Lewiston, Idaho, where he settled on his father's ranch. Here he commenced drawing. After several years he returned to Chicago to complete his grade school education and worked at a variety of jobs; in 1896 he went west once more, roamed and worked at odd jobs on the upper Great Plains, eventually reaching Montana where he continued cowboying and once again, early in 1903, took up art. He sold his first pictures at Sheridan, Wyoming, others at Chicago where he had returned to study briefly at the Academy of Fine Arts. In the west again he devoted himself to a career in art, pursuing it until his death of a heart attack. His work, particularly his pen-and-ink drawings, are vivid fragments of his life as a "working cowboy, and a good one," who had a talent for recording what he knew and saw and at that, too, was very good. He also did numerous oil paintings of quality, although he has only in recent years come into his own as an important art figure of the northern Plains cattle country

R.H. Scherger, "Paint Bill." *Mont. Mag.,* Vol. XV, No. 2 (Spring 1965), 68-85.

Gomes, Estevao, explorer, adventurer (c. 1483-spring 1538). B. probably in Oporto, Portugal, Gomes sailed with Magellan's fleet, but deserted the flotilla and brought his ship back to Spain in 1521. In 1524 he coasted the

North American continent from Cuba to Cape Race, seeking a passage to the Pacific and to the Orient; Gomes seized 58 or more Indians from Maine or Nova Scotia and took them to Spain, where they were freed by Charles V. In 1535 Gomes accompanied Mendoza to the Rio de la Plata and in 1537 he was with Ayolas on his traverse of the Gran Chaco, being killed by Indians on the return. The best brief account of Gomes' life is by L.A. Vigneras in the *Dictionary of Canadian Biography, I.*

Gonnor, Nicolas de, Jesuit missionary (Nov. 19, 1691-Dec. 16, 1759). B. in Lucon diocese, France, he became a Jesuit, reached Canada in 1725 and in 1727 accompanied Guigas to the Sioux mission. He then was stationed for a time at Caughnawauga, Quebec, but found difficulty in learning the Iroquois tongue, although he spent another five years there at a later period. The rest of his career was spent in eastern Canada; he died at Quebec.

Thwaites, JR, LXVIII, 331n36.

Goodale, Greenleaf Austin, army officer (July 4, 1839-Feb. 17, 1915). B. at Orrington, Maine, he enlisted in the 6th Maine Infantry May 7, 1861, and was commissioned a first lieutenant in the 77th U.S. Colored Infantry January 2, 1864, emerging from the Civil War a captain with two brevets, one earned at Gettysburg. He became a first lieutenant in the 23rd Infantry July 28, 1866, and served at various posts throughout the west. He commanded Fort Klamath, Oregon during the period that led to the Modoc War of 1872-73, but was relieved after a year in June 1871 before the conflict broke out. Goodale became a captain in 1878, commanded Fort Mackinac, Michigan and was superintendent of Mackinac National Park from March 4, 1886, until 1890. He became a Brigadier General at his retirement in 1903.

Heitman; Powell; Keith A. Murray, *The Modocs and Their Wars.* Norman, Univ. of Okla. Press, 1965; *Who Was Who.*

Goodale, Tim, frontiersman (c. 1800-post 1864). B. in Illinois, he reached the Rocky Mountains about 1839 and about 1843 was living in the Greenhorn settlement, eastern Colorado, spending years in the vicinity of that or neighboring communities, and trapping as well. He went to California about

1850, and from 1854-56 he operated a Green River ferry. He guided periodically. He was guide for Major E.L. Berthoud who discovered Berthoud Pass in the Colorado Rockies in 1861. Goodale lived near the later Bellevue, Colorado, until 1864 when he moved to the Bitterroot Valley of Montana where he died some years later.

Harvey L. Carter article, MM, Vol. VII.

Goodfellow, George E., frontier physician (Dec. 23, 1855-Dec.7, 1910). B. at Downieville, California, he was appointed to Annapolis at 16, beat up a bully, was suspended and turned to medicine, graduating with honors in 1876 from Cleveland Medical College. He practiced briefly at Oakland, then went to Prescott where his father was a mining engineer and built up a sizable practice, becoming an army contract surgeon, serving at Whipple Barracks and Fort Lowell, near Tucson. Goodfellow secured permission to serve with Custer's 7th Cavalry, but his papers from Washington were delayed and he missed the Little Big Horn affair. He left the army in 1880, removing to Tombstone where for 12 years he was leading physician, surgeon, coroner and self-taught expert on bullet punctures, becoming, it is said, one of the foremost gunshot wound experts in the nation. He said he once "performed assessment work" on a corpse, finding it "rich in lead, but too badly punctured to hold whiskey." He got a lynch mob off the hook as coroner by officially noting that the deceased "came to his death from emphysema of the lungs — a disease common to high altitudes — which might have been caused by strangulation, self-inflicted or otherwise." Dr. Goodfellow cited one instance where a bullet, after passing through Morgan Earp, lodged in the thigh of a presumably innocent bystander who died. "His injury was inconsequential and hardly more than an abrasion," adjudged Goodfellow. "Technically he died from shock. The simple fact is the man was scared to death." He was called upon to perform many types of surgery, a skill to which he gave full attention, being proud of his dexterity, "thought deeply and performed valuable researches," and made frequent journeys east to advance his professional knowledge. He was a linguist, and avid student of geology (rushing to Bavispe, Sonora, May 31, 1887, to investigate results of a severe earthquake), yet warm-hearted enough to speed into Sonora on another occasion to treat a village suffering from smallpox ravages, for which President Porfirio Diaz presented him with a fine horse. Goodfellow could be contentious, engaged in law suits over civil matters, but also supported community betterment projects. He made major contributions toward surgery of the prostate gland, first successfully performing the operation of prostatectomy. He was among the first to use spinal anaesthesia and to advocate open air treatment for tuberculosis. He became a prominent surgeon in San Francisco but after the 1906 earthquake returned to Mexico as surgeon in chief for the Southern Pacific railroad of that country. He died at Los Angeles.

Thomas E. Gibson, "George E. Goodfellow." *Surgery, Gynecology, and Obstetrics,* Vol. LIV, (April 1932), 716-18.

Goodnight, Charles, cattleman (Mar. 5, 1836-Dec. 12, 1929). B. in Macoupin County, Illinois, he reached Milam County, Texas, ten years later in company with his step-father and mother and in 1857 settled in Palo Pinto County where he became a ranger and Indian scout. He was with Jack J. Cureton in the December 18, 1860, Pease River fight in which Comanche Chief Peta Nocona was wounded mortally. During the Civil War he also served as scout and guide for a frontier regiment. By 1865 he had assembled some stock and was in search of markets. He and Oliver Loving decided to trail cattle west to New Mexico; the route they blazed from Fort Belknap on the Red Fork of the Brazos River, Texas, to Fort Sumner, New Mexico, became known as the Goodnight-Loving Trail, being afterward heavily used. After Loving was killed by Indians Goodnight continued driving cattle to New Mexico for several years; in 1871 he worked with John Chisum in a profitable relationship. In 1875 Goodnight developed a trail known for him from Alamogordo Creek, New Mexico to Granada, Colorado, but a Colorado ranching endeavor did not succeed. In 1876 Goodnight settled in Palo Duro Canyon in the Texas Panhandle, being the first major stockman to select that region although he was followed by many others. In 1877 he blazed a trail from his ranch to Dodge City, a roadway also followed by later drovers. That year he entered a partnership with John G. Adair, the firm known as the JA

Ranch, and in time, it was said, they ran 100,000 cattle on a million acres of land. Goodnight was a progressive with regard to stock, raising Durham, Hereford and Angus cattle at various times. One of his great contributions to the nation was his preservation on the JA Ranch of a small herd of buffalo, all that was left of the great southern herd virtually wiped out by hide hunters. With some of this wild stock he attempted unsuccessfully to raise "cattalo," or a cross of buffalo and Angus; the product was largely infertile. From his buffalo stock however, came animals that contributed their gene pools to those of a few northern buffalo and are represented today in the Yellowstone herd and most other extant herds; without this influx of genes from the southern animals the nation's surviving buffalo specimens would be much less robust and representative. In 1879 when stock thieves made heavy inroads into his herds, Goodnight warned Texas Ranger Captain George W. Arrington that if he didn't control the rustlers, Goodnight himself would raise 75 men and end stock thievery forever. The depredations were curtailed. In 1880 Goodnight was a founder of the Panhandle Stockmen's Association to improve cattle breeds and rid the region of outlawry. His JA Ranch was divided in 1887 between Goodnight and his partner's widow, Cornelia Adair, and three years later Goodnight sold out his share. In his last years he invested in a Mexican mining operation, worked a small ranch at the Panhandle town named for him, and spent his winters at Tucson, Arizona, where he died. He was, according to Haley, "the most representative cowman that the West has known."

J. Evetts Haley, *Charles Goodnight: Cowman & Plainsman.* Norman, Univ. of Okla. Press, 1949; DAB; HT; Walter Prescott Webb, *The Texas Rangers.* Boston, Houghton Mifflin Co., 1935; *Frontier Times,* Vol. 5, No. 1 (Oct. 1927) 28-30; Vol. 10, No. 3 (Dec. 1932), 131-44.

Goodrich, John Calvin, adventurer (c. 1809-Mar. 6, 1836). He was a resident of Tennessee in 1826 when Congressman Sam Houston recommended him for purser in the Navy; apparently he was not appointed. In 1834 he reached Texas with a brother, Benjamin Briggs Goodrich and settled in the later Grimes County. He fought as a private in the Texas war of independence and died at the

Alamo. Benjamin Goodrich in a rousing letter to another brother written from Washington (or New Washington), Texas, described on March 15, 1836, John's death and the fall of the Alamo, "one of the very best documents that we have from the Texas side, immediately after the event of the Alamo Massacre." Washington, Texas, was not distant from where the decisive battle of San Jacinto would be fought.

Amelia Williams, XXXVII, 261-63; HT.

Goodrich, Silas, frontiersman (fl. 1804-1825). B. in Massachusetts he joined the Lewis and Clark Expedition January 1, 1804. He was fond of fishing and perhaps the best man of the party at it, sometimes catching examples of novel species. He re-enlisted in the army following the exploration, Clark noting that he was dead by 1825.

History of the Exploration Under the Command of Lewis and Clark, ed. by Elliott Coues. N.Y., Dover Pubns., 1965; Clarke, *Lewis and Clark.*

Goodwin, Grenville, ethnologist (July 20, 1907-June 30, 1940). B. at Southampton, Long Island, he was sent for college preparation to the Mesa Ranch School in Arizona where he met Dean Byron Cummings who suggested he come to the University of Arizona to study anthropology. Goodwin did so briefly, but was uninterested in an academic degree and went to live at Bylas, Arizona, among the western Apaches. He studied carefully the communities around Bylas, Fort Apache, Canyon Day and Cibecue, traveled to other parts of the western Apache country and visited places in Sonora and Chihuahua which figured in Apache history. Although he never received a college degree he carried out some graduate work for the University of Chicago shortly before his death. In his field work he became acquainted with such professional anthropologists as Morris Opler, then concentrating on the Chiricahuas, and Harry Hoijer, a linguist and Athapascan specialist then of the University of Chicago, later of the University of California at Los Angeles, learning from him methods of transcription of unwritten languages. Goodwin commenced with no special training nor techniques. He came to know many Apache families and they to know him. He visited and chatted and listened, seeking older people who wanted to talk

about old times. He was invited to every kind of gathering and social event and from these took voluminous notes, added to by correspondence with many specialists who came to accept him as one of them. Beginning in 1935 he published in various journals and in 1937 was a consultant for John Collier's Indian Bureau work in establishing a tribal government apparatus among the San Carlos Apaches. His report was a pioneer effort in applied anthropology. In 1939 he went to the University of Chicago for graduate study in anthropology and to complete a monograph, *The Social Organization of the Western Apache* (1942), a volume that made him a major figure in North American ethnology. The book was published posthumously, for as he completed it he died of a brain tumor. He had planned a series of monographs and two additional volumes based upon his work or correspondence have appeared: *Western Apache Raiding and Warfare,* ed. by Keith H. Basso (1971), and *Grenville Goodwin: Among the Western Apache, Letters from the Field,* ed. by Morris E. Opler (1973). Spicer wrote that "anthropology and the Apaches lost much by Grenville Goodwin's early death. His promising work was cut short, but even so he succeeded in laying the foundations for a sound ethnology of a people whom he had learned during ten; years to understand and respect." Goodwin died at Los Angeles and was buried at Tucson; he was survived by his widow, Janice T. Goodwin and son, Neil Goodwin.

Edward H. Spicer, "Grenville Goodwin." *Arizona and the West,* Vol. 3, No. 3 (Autumn 1961), 201-204; Goodwin death certificate.

Goodyear, Miles Morris, mountain man, trader (Feb. 24, 1817-Nov. 12, 1849). B. at Hamden, Connecticut, he gained some education. In 1836 he encountered Oregon-bound Marcus Whitman and other missionaries beyond Fort Leavenworth and accompanied them to Fort Hall. He hunted and trapped, perhaps in company with Indians of various tribes, until late 1842. He moved to Fort Bridger and accompanied Stewart to the Green River valley in 1843. Goodyear helped establish Fort Buenaventura, September 1846, on the Weber River above its junction with the Ogden (the site of the future city of Ogden), and left for Los Angeles in late 1846, arriving in January 1847. Returning with horses he guided the Mormons toward the Salt Lake Valley in 1847, and sold them his fort and land for just under $2,000 in gold. Goodyear drove 230 horses from California to St. Joseph, Missouri, where he wintered in 1848-49. Learning of the California gold strike, he returned there, made a rich find in the Yuba River bed, but caught a chill and died.

Eugene E. Campbell article, MM, Vol. II.

Gookin, Daniel, Indian defender (1612-Mar. 19, 1686). B. in either Ireland or England, Gookin had reached Virginia by 1630 and within a few years was granted 2,500 acres later added to, on the James River. He subsequently lived in Maryland, then moved to Massachusetts since he was a Puritan; Gookin visited England and other colonies often, held minor political offices, and some military positions as well. He was interested in Indian welfare, "his efforts on their behalf were second only to those of (John) Eliot." Gookin's defense of the "praying Indians," i.e., Christian Indians, during the bloody King Philip's War, made him very unpopular in New England, although he led a party of Christian Indians as scouts against the hostiles during that conflict. He wrote "An Historical Account of the Doings and Sufferings of the Christian Indians of New England," published in the *Transactions of the American Antiquarian Society* (1836); "Historical Collections of the Indians in New England," *Massachusetts Historical Society Collections* (1792), and a history of New England which was not published. Gookin married twice, his first wife having died.

Leach, *Flintock;* DAB; Francis Russell, "Apostle to the Indians." *Amer. Heritage,* Vol. IX, No. 1 (Dec. 1957), 4-9, 117-19.

Gordon, Charles Garnett, army officer (September 28, 1837-Oct. 26, 1898). B. near Chapel Hill, North Carolina, Gordon enlisted in Company B, 2nd California Cavalry September 14, 1861, went to New Mexico with the California Column and was discharged at Fort Sumner, New Mexico April 25, 1864, for disability. He was commissioned a second lieutenant in the 6th Cavalry September 26, 1867, becoming a first lieutenant February 21, 1870. He was wounded in the leg in the Apache attack on Fort Apache, Arizona, September 1, 1881.

Gordon took part in the pursuit of Loco following the April 1882 emeute from the San Carlos Reservation, Arizona, toward Mexico and his company was incorporated in the Forsyth column which followed Loco into Sonora, but was too late to engage the hostiles. Gordon had become a captain August 30, 1881, and retired October 5, 1887.

Heitman; Orton; Dan L. Thrapp, *General Crook and the Sierra Madre Adventure.* Norman, Univ. of Okla. Press, 1972; information from David Perry Perrine, historian of the 6th Cavalry.

Gordon, Jack (Peter Worthington), renegade, adventurer (c. 1822-c. Dec. 14, 1864). B. to a prominent Virginia family, Worthington at 17 killed a man and fled west under the pseudonym Jack Gordon; he concocted a false tale of his origins: that he was of English birth and as a seaman jumped ship in this country. Gordon said he served with Colonel Alexander Doniphan's command during the Mexican War, but killed another man north of El Paso in January 1847 and was imprisoned. He broke jail and fled northwest arriving as he later reported at an Apache rancheria where he was welcomed, the band fortunately at peace. His principal occupation with the Apaches was "trading or an agent for trading." Eventually he "married" an Indian girl, learned a bit of the language, and joined Apache raiding parties harassing Mexican settlements, coming ever more securely into the Indians' confidence. After one depredation his band was trailed by Captain Enoch Steen (see entry) and a detachment of the 1st Dragoons 80 miles westward from the Rio Grande. In a sharp fight near the Santa Rita copper mines on August 16, 1849, Gordon (as he later conceded to John Nugent) shot and seriously wounded Steen. When Jack Hays (see entry) reached El Paso in September 1849 he sought as guide someone who could help him establish contact with the Gila Apaches for whom Hays had been named agent. Steen recommended Gordon, if he could be contacted, adding that "he would steal, lie and kill, but he (would be) true to you." Gordon, still sought for the earlier slaying, visited El Paso surreptitiously and Hays arranged for his assistance. Nugent described Gordon at this time as "about five feet eight or nine inches in height, robust in frame, and wonderfully modeled for strength and muscular activity, while in endurance he excelled any white man or Indian I ever met."

Light haired and blue eyed, his face was colorless as to blood, but embrowned by years of exposure." Gordon agreed to bring some Apaches for a talk with Hays near Picacho Peak, six miles westerly of Las Cruces, New Mexico. Gordon and Hays met there, the former reporting the Indians agreed to talk, but in the Santa Rita country. However just before the scheduled meeting a Mexican punitive force under José María Elías González engaged the Apaches in a sharp battle in which Gordon assisted his Indian friends. This affair so nettled the Apaches that it precluded any meeting with Hays. Gordon accompanied the white party to Tucson, from where the Hays group went on to California. Gordon's Apaches, according to Calhoun, in early November fell upon 25 German emigrants northwest of El Paso, killed seven or eight and captured the rest, seeking to exchange them for Apache prisoners of the Mexicans. Shortly thereafter Gordon found his way to California where he was arrested at San Jose for horse theft, sentenced to two years, broke jail and spent an evening with Jack Hays (then sheriff of San Francisco County) before going on his way. Jack mined near Coarse Gold Gulch in Madera County for awhile and in 1853 joined Harry Love (see entry) and his rangers searching out the notorious bandit Joaquin (Murrieta). Shortly afterward he left California for west Texas once more. In late 1854 he became a stage driver for the Henry Skillman-George Giddings mail line between El Paso and San Antonio. His earlier friendship with the Apaches and reputation as a hardened frontiersman may have led to his employment; these factors may also have been the root cause of his firing late in 1855. Shortly the El Paso customs house safe was robbed of $2,300, the thieves later identified as Gordon with William Miller, Edward Russell and William McElroy (also known as William Blair). By mid-1856 McElroy was feuding with Ben Dowell, later to become El Paso's first mayor. With Gordon, McElroy plotted to kill Dowell, but the latter learned of the plan and was prepared when the pair appeared at his place of business August 7, McElroy was killed; Gordon fled, all the way back to California. Prospector Joshua Henshaw recalled that Gordon operated in the Kern River country with a band of "highway robbers," although his faulty memory placed the date a year or two early. He yarned about Gordon's near-losing engagement with a

wounded grizzly. Later Gordon lived near Tulare Lake with an Indian woman and may have fathered a daughter by her. He was reported involved in the disappearance of several men near Tailholt, Tulare county, and was believed the killer of a Dutch or German prospector from whom $4,000 was missing when the body was found. Gordon entered into a hog-raising enterprise with Samuel Groupie but hard feelings arose and in a shootout at Tailholt, Gordon was wounded mortally, Groupie seriously but not fatally; an autopsy December 15, 1864 cleared Groupie. In the hours before his death Gordon did what he could to provide for an Indian girl living with him, perhaps his daughter.

James Kimmins Greer, *Colonel Jack Hays: Texas Frontier Leader and California Builder,* N.Y., E.P. Dutton, 1952; John Nugent, "Scraps of Early History," III, IV, *The Argonaut.* Vol. II, No. 10, 11 (1878); George P. Hammond, Edward H. Howes, eds., *Overland to California on the Southwestern Trail 1849: Dairy of Robert Eccleston,* Berkeley, Univ. of Calif. Press, 1950; Nancy Hamilton, *Ben Dowell: El Paso's First Mayor,* El Paso, Univ. of Texas, Southwestern Studies Monograph 49, 1976; Annie Heloise Abel, *The Official Correspondence of James S. Calhoun,* Washington, Govt. Printing Office, 1915, pp. 45-46, 73; Wayne R. Austerman, *Sharps Rifles and Spanish Mules: The San Antonio-El Paso Mail,* College Station, Tex. A&M Univ. Press, 1985; Austerman, "The English Apache," *Real West,* Vol. 29, No. 207 (Feb. 1986), 42-48; Austerman, Correspondence with author; William B. Secrest, "Jack Gordon," *Lawmen & Desperadoes: A Compendium of Noted Early California Peace Officers, Badmen and Outlaws, 1850-1900,* manuscript in preparation; Secrest, correspondence with author.

Gordon, Mike, frontiersman (1850-July 19, 1879). B. in Canada, he had served in the 5th Cavalry and later was an army scout on the Plains. He had reached Wichita and Dodge City, Kansas, by 1875. He may have had trouble of some sort over a woman at Wichita; in 1878 he was reported in Fort Worth, Texas, where he had a difficulty again concerning a woman. At Las Vegas, New Mexico. he "began to bluff by drawing a pair of sixes and firing promiscuously," and Doc Holliday killed him. Again the trouble apparently was over a woman.

Ed Bartholomew, *Wyatt Earp: The Man & the Myth.* Toyahvale, Tex., Frontier Book Co., 1964.

Gordon, William, adventurer (c. 1800-c.1850). His birth and death dates are conjectory; b. probably in Tennessee, he fought with Jackson at the Battle of New Orleans January 8, 1815, and was wounded and captured in the first Seminole War. Gordon was at St. Louis in 1818, accompanied John C. Sullivan surveying Indian country in Illinois and by 1822 had entered the fur trade with the Missouri Fur Company. He escaped a Blackfoot massacre on the Yellowstone River (1823), and twice went "beyond the mountains" — i.e., to the Oregon country. When Leavenworth indecisively broke off his attack on the Arickara villages, Gordon and Angus McDonald surreptitiously fired the dwellings of the Indians. With Jedediah Smith and others, Gordon wintered among the Crows, was robbed by that people, and in 1825 associated with the Atkinson-O'Fallon Yellowstone Expedition. Gordon reached St. Louis in 1826, may have worked for Smith, Jackson and Sublette in the Rockies, and in 1829 was with the American Fur Company. He had taken a Yankton Sioux wife and continued upper Rockies trapping until 1831 when he became a Missouri River trader in the Nebraska country. In 1832 he was engaged in a campaign against the Sauks and Foxes of Illinois. He occasionally served as a special Indian sub agent and often attended treaty councils. He is mentioned in Chouteau accounts as late as 1846 and in 1847 guided emigrants to Oregon. He is said to have been struck by lightning while swimming his horse across the Yellowstone during a violent storm; the date is unknown.

Charles, E. Hanson Jr. article, MM, Vol. IX.

Gore, Sir St. George, shooter (1811-Dec. 3, 1878). B. at Sligo, Ireland, he was the eighth baronet of that title. He fancied himself a "sportsman," a term which in his mind was perverted into a license to slaughter any creature that moved; his two-year expedition to the American West proved an example so stark and so savage of his obsession that even the Indians protested his wasteful driving away of the game upon which they depended, and frontiersmen of principle were dismayed by his single-minded pursuit of ruthless killing. His leisurely course through the wild land was marked by a trail of reeking carcasses. With an annual income of $200,000, money was no obstacle to his pleasure. Gore

outfitted at St. Louis, used Fort Laramie as a base and hunted in Colorado and Wyoming, then hired Bridger to guide him into the Yellowstone country. His procession included four six-mule teams and wagons, two three-yoke ox conveyances and 21 French carts, 40 employees, 112 horses including some of the finest, three milk cows, 14 dogs. One wagon was required for Gore's weapons: 75 rifles, 12 or more shotguns, a large number of pistols; two vehicles were required to move his fishing gear and an expert fly-maker was in his retinue. One wagon could be converted into a bedroom. A brass bedstead could be dismantled for transfer, and there were an iron table and washstand and a huge linen tent with a striped lining. An observor wrote that the individual was "of medium height but rather stout, bald head, short side-whiskers, a good walker but indifferent horseman, a good shot from a rest but rather indifferent offhand... He rarely, if ever, went (hunting) unattended, his party usually comprising seven men. He never loaded his own gun, but after firing passed it to an attendant, who gave him another already charged." In the evenings he sometimes read books to Bridger who found Shakespeare too high-flown for his taste, but appreciated Baron Munchausen. Blackfeet ran off 21 of the party's horses; Gore traded with the Crows for more. Agent Alfred J. Vaughan protested Gore's actions in the Indian country, but there was no official action against him and he reached St. Louis in the late spring of 1856, supremely proud of his butchery of 2,500 buffaloes by his own count, 40 grizzly bears, countless elk, deer, antelope and small game. He had become incensed at what he believed an attempt to take advantage of him when he offered his outfit for sale, so he gathered his wagons, harness, saddles and supplies on the bank of the Missouri, set it afire, waited until the embers cooled and had all scrap iron picked up and tossed into the water. Then he went on downstream, quitting at last the frontier he had disgraced.

Montana, Contributions, Vol. X, 1940, 296; Mark H. Brown, *Plainsmen of the Yellowstone.* N.Y., G.P. Putnam's Sons, 1961.

Gorges, Ferdinando, promoter (c. 1566-1647). B. at Ashton, Somersetshire, England, and related to Sir Walter Raleigh, he early had an outstanding military career and was knighted for his services at Rouen in 1591. He was military governor of Plymouth, England, from 1596 until 1602 and again from 1604 to 1629. Gorges seems to have participated in the conspiracy of the Earl of Essex, although he recovered in time to testify against the Earl "and save his own neck." He then became interested in Waymouth's voyages to the New England coast and determined to colonize the area, hopefully to be awarded the region as a baronial fiefdom. Gorges thus became a leading figure in formation of the Plymouth Company, and may have been somehow responsible for the Pilgrims' eventual settlement in Massachusetts, rather than Virginia. He and John Mason also became backers of the Sagadahoc colony established in 1607 at the mouth of the Kennebec River in Maine, though it failed the following year. Gorges directed many fishing and trading endeavors his company developed along the New England coast. Under his auspices Captain John Smith tried three times to establish a Maine settlement, but all failed. Gorges helped obtain for his company a new charter in 1620 in which New England was for the first time defined as that territory between 40 degrees and 48 degrees North Latitude, but little financial support was forthcoming. After the Pilgrim band settled within the territory granted to Gorges and his colleagues, it secured his "fatherly interest" as the first permanent establishment in New England, but he struggled against the Massachusetts Bay and Salem colonies, which he regarded as irregular interlopers into his domain. In 1623 David Thompson established a settlement at the mouth of the Piscataqua River (the community subsequently known as Portsmouth, New Hampshire), but after 1641 it gradually came under Massachusetts jurisdiction. In 1634 Gorges and Mason divided their grant, Gorges taking the lands east of the Piscataqua and thus assuming the sole proprietorship for what later became Maine. In 1629 Edward Godfrey had founded a settlement at the mouth of the York River; in 1641 Gorges conferred a charter upon it and named it Gorgeana, but when Massachusetts in 1652 assumed authority over the region following Gorges' death, it was renamed York. Gorges had received full title to the province of Maine in 1639, but could not colonize his realm, and his grant passed to his heirs, who had no effective control over the region which quietly slipped at length under

Massachusetts auspices. Gorges' grandson in 1677 formally sold all rights in Maine to Massachusetts for £1,250. Gorges was a man not without faults but "in spite of his always devious schemes and greedy ambitions, (he) deserves to be well remembered for doing more than any other individual to promote the early colonization of New England."

CE; EA; Thwaites, JR XXXVI, 242-43n20, 21; George F. Willison, *Saints and Strangers.* New York, Reynal & Hitchcock, 1945; James Phinney Baxter, ed., *Sir Ferdinando Gorges and His Province of Maine.* 3 vols., Boston, The Prince Society, 1890; Henry Sweetser Burrage, *Gorges and the Grant of the Province of Maine, 1622.* Portland, Printed for the State, 1923.

Goupil, Rene, Jesuit surgeon, martyr (May 13, 1608-Sept. 29, 1642). B. at Saint-Martin, Angers, France, he was the first Jesuit martyr in North America, perishing at the hands of the Iroquois. Jogues wrote that Goupil did not become a priest because of "bodily indispositions," but went to New France to serve the Society of Jesus there and in hopes that his health would improve. For two years he fulfilled "the meanest offices" about the mission headquarters, and being a surgeon, assisted in caring for the ill as well. Because the Hurons badly needed a surgeon's services, he prepared to work in that country. He left Three Rivers August 1, 1642, with Isaac Jogues and about 40 others, mostly Hurons, in a flotilla of canoes, bound for the Huron country, but within a few days the party was captured by a war band of Iroquois and Goupil and Jogues with some others taken south into present New York State. "Upon the road," wrote Jogues later, Goupil "was always occupied with God (and he) showed a willing acceptance of the death which God was sending him. He gave himself to him as a sacrifice..." Goupil suffered the most barbarous torture stoically. On September 29 he was dispatched by a tomahawk near the present Auriesville, New York. Jogues eventually returned to Canada, though later was taken again by the Iroquois and killed. Goupil and Jogues were among those Jesuit martyrs canonized June 29, 1930, by Pope Pius XI.

Thwaites, JR, XXVIII; DCB.

Graffenried, Christopher, Baron de: *see* De Graffenried

Graham, Isaac, trapper, partisan (Sept. 1, 1800-Nov. 8, 1863). B. at Fincastle, Virginia, trained as a jockey, he reached Missouri in 1818 and by 1830 was at Fort Smith, Arkansas, heading west in a party of would-be trappers under Robert Bean. After some adventures they reached the Taos area. In the spring Graham and others trapped north to the North Platte River, returning to Taos with a fair catch. In 1832 with others Graham trapped to the Green, joined the rendezvous, took part in the battle of Pierre's Hole, trapped as far west as the Humboldt river, then returned to the upper Rockies in fur-gathering activities. By 1836 Graham had arrived at Los Angeles and took part in political turmoil, becoming the principal in the so-called "Graham affair," commenced April 7, 1840. He and other Americans were arrested for treason and exiled to Mexico where, in June 1841, at a second trial they were cleared and returned to Monterey. He became a lumberman, but sided with Michel-torena in strife that terminated with the February 20, 1845, "Battle of Cahuenga" near Los Angeles. Graham was a very controversial figure in California, burdened with both worthy and unworthy character-istics, and his was a significant life.

Doyce B. Nunis, Jr., article, MM, Vol. III; Nunis, *The Trials of Isaac Graham.* Los Angeles, Dawson's Book Shop, 1967: this has a bibliography and analysis of sources on Graham's career.

Graham, James Duncan, army officer (Apr. 4, 1799-Dec. 29, 1865). B. in Prince William County, Virginia, he went to West Point and was commissioned a third lieutenant in the Corps of Artillery July 17, 1817, becoming a second lieutenant October 14 and a first lieutenant September 8, 1819. He was assigned to the Stephen Long expedition of 1819-20 to the Rocky Mountains, accom-panying Long to Council Bluffs on the Missouri from where he went with O'Fallon overland to the Pawnee villages, then was ordered to take the expedition steamship, *Western Engineer* back to the Mississippi. He met the returning party in the fall of 1820 at Cape Girardeau, Missouri. Graham thence-forth was connected with the Topographical Engineers in most of his assignments. From 1822-29 he was on topographical duty in Vermont and elsewhere and he later took part in nearly all federal boundary surveys of the period, including those in the northeast and along the Canadian and Texas-Mexican boundaries. He became a major in the Topographical Engineers July 7, 1838. In 1850-51 as astronomer and scientist with the Mexican Boundary Survey it is written, Mount Graham in Arizona (10,516 feet) was named for him but this cannot be, since the peak bore its name years before James Graham arrived in the present Arizona. For a decade from 1854 he worked at developing harbor facilities on the Great Lakes, during that time discovering the existence of a lunar tide on those bodies of water. Graham became a lieutenant colonel August 6, 1861, and a colonel of Engineers June 1, 1863. He was married.

Cullum; Heitman; Thwaites, EWT, XIV-XVII; Will C. Barnes, *Arizona Place Names.* Tucson, Univ. of Ariz. Bull. 2, 1935.

Graham, John, partisan (d. Sept. 21, 1887). B. on a farm near Boone, Iowa, he went to California in the 1870s with his older brother, Tom, and in 1882 the pair moved to Globe, Arizona, where they determined to start a cattle ranch in Pleasant Valley to the north. They soon launched their operation, which prospered until they began branding maver-icks and hiring gunmen and desperadoes to ride and rustle for them. This led inevitably to a feuding relationship with the Tewksbury family although originally the two groupings had been friendly. John Graham was not involved in the opening gun battle of the Pleasant Valley War August 9, 1887 when two Graham people were killed, three injured for no Tewksbury losses. For some unspecified reason a warrant was issued for John Graham. Apache County Deputy Sheriff James D. Houck (incidentally a Tewksbury partisan), trying to serve it, mistook 18-year-old William (Billy) Graham for John on August 17 and mortally wounded him. September 2 John and Tom Graham and some of their faction attacked the Tewksbury home, killing John Tewksbury and William Jacobs and laying siege to the place (see Tom Graham entry). John Graham had no part in the famed September 4, 1887, shootout at Holbrook in which four of the Graham partisans were eliminated by Sheriff Commo-dore Perry Owens. John Graham and Charley Blevins were killed at Perkins store in the valley by a posse headed by Sheriff William

Mulvenon of Yavapai County who sought to arrest them; instead they went for their guns, and lost. Graham was mortally wounded by a rifle shot and Mulvenon demanded, "Johnny, why didn't you put up your hands when I told you to; didn't you know me?" Graham shook his head. Mulvenon turned away, saying, "He knows he is a damn liar. He knew me."

Clara T. Woody, Milton L. Schwartz, *Globe, Arizona*. Tucson, Ariz. Hist. Soc., 1977; Earle R. Forrest, *Arizona's Dark and Bloody Ground*. Caldwell, Ida., Caxton Printers, 1964.

Graham, Thomas H., partisan (c. 1854-Aug. 2, 1892). B. on a farm near Boone, Iowa, he and his brother John left home in the 1870s and went to California, after about a decade moving to Arizona. At Globe Tom Graham met Ed Tewksbury who described the fine stock range in Pleasant Valley to the north; Tom Graham accompanied Tewksbury to the region, liked it, remained with the Tewksburys for some days and eventually drove cattle into the valley. The Grahams and Tewksburys remained friends for some time until the Grahams began to indulge in rustling, which turned the Tewksburys against them and laid the seed for the sanguinary Pleasant Valley War of 1887 and afterward. Graham was formally charged with stealing cattle and was brought to trial, but no witnesses appeared against him and he and his brother were cleared; later the Tewksburys were charged with stealing stock from Tom Graham, but that case also was dismissed. Graham was charged with the ambush-murder of a Basque sheepherder in February 1887, but nothing came of it. September 2, 1887, after fights and incidents had left four Graham partisans dead or missing and five wounded for no Tewksbury casualties, Tom Graham, oldest among his brothers and hence leader of the faction, led an attack on the Tewksbury ranch in which John Tewksbury and William Jacobs were shot from ambush and siege laid to the house in which four of their enemies held out. The investment was maintained for 11 days, according to report (although Forrest denies this), during which half-wild hogs devoured portions of the two corpses within view of the house, the Grahams denying impassioned pleas for a burial truce. Whether Tom Graham was in on the September 17 battle in which his side lost one man (Harry Middleton) mortally wounded and another shot for no

Tewksbury losses is unknown. Tom Graham was not present at Perkins Store when his brother John was killed September 21 by a sheriff's posse, nor was he at his home nearby. In fact, Tom Graham had had enough of the war and withdrew from Pleasant Valley for the Salt River Valley, although he retained his holdings. Now 33 he married a 17-year-old Baptist minister's daughter, Anne Melton October 8, 1887 (she died at Phoenix at 94 on May 31, 1961). Graham surrendered to Prescott Sheriff William Mulvenon at Phoenix October 16, was taken to Prescott and released on $3,000 bail pending a Grand Jury hearing in December. The Tewksburys also were required to face the jury at that time. Graham meanwhile made a swift two-day visit to Pleasant Valley, hired a few cowboys and directed his foreman to manage the ranch on shares, quickly leaving again under wary Tewksbury scrutiny. In December the Prescott Grand Jury indicted Graham as well as the Tewksburys, but after postponements the cases were dropped. The courts thus failed to end the feud, and bushwhacking, lynching and vigilante action continued for some time. When George Newton, a Tewksbury partisan, disappeared at a Salt River crossing April 10, 1892, Ed Tewksbury suspected Tom Graham of having something to do with it. Graham was shot, the last of the vendetta to be murdered, while enroute to Tempe with a wagonload of grain, by two men, identified by witnesses as Ed Tewksbury and John Rhodes. Before he died Graham himself named the pair as his assailants. Both were taken into custody, but neither was finally convicted nor sentenced for the assassination. Clara Woody did the best research on the Pleasant Valley War, and in her considered view "they weren't man-killers, either family (the Grahams or the Tewksburys). It was the outlaws and the officers (who were swept in as the feud developed) who shot," although her judgment might be overly generous.

Clara T. Woody, Milton L. Schwartz, *Globe, Arizona*. Tucson, Ariz. Hist. Soc., 1977; Earle R. Forrest, *Arizona's Dark and Bloody Ground*. Caldwell, Id., Caxton Printers, 1964; Woody to author, May 20, 1968.

Graham, William, partisan (c. 1869-Aug. 18, 1887). B. on a farm near Boone, Iowa, he was said by Forrest to be a half-brother to Tom and John Graham although Woody says merely he was their brother. He reached Pleasant Valley, Arizona, in 1883 and joined the older two in their ranching and, some suspected, rustling operation. Billy took no recorded part in the earliest phases of the feud with the Tewksburys but he was young and high spirited and there was no doubt where his sympathies lay. Late on August 17, 1887, eight days after the first gun battle of the vendetta which became known as the Pleasant Valley War, Graham was returning from a Phoenix dance and was crossing a creek north of the Graham ranch headquarters when he met James D. Houck, a Tewksbury partisan and deputy sheriff of Apache County who claimed he held a warrant for John Graham and mistook Billy for the older man. In a gunfight Houck mortally wounded Graham who died the next day at the Graham ranch.

Clara T. Woody, Milton L. Schwartz, *Globe, Arizona.* Tucson, Ariz. Hist. Soc., 1977; Earle R. Forrest, *Arizona's Dark and Bloody Ground.* Caldwell, Id., Caxton Printers, 1964.

Graham, William Hicks, gunman, lawyer (July 21, 1829-Oct. 16, 1866). B. at Philadelphia and of diminutive stature, Graham read law and migrated to San Francisco where he clerked for Probate Judge R.N. Morrison. A newspaper criticized Morrison, and Graham challenged the editor to a duel, the editor being William Walker, later a celebrated filibuster. In the duel January 12, 1851, at the old Mission Dolores Graham wounded Walker before two Supreme Court justices, the sheriff, various police officers and a collection of lawyers and other witnesses. In July 1851 Graham and a former friend, George Frank Lemon engaged in a shootout in Portsmouth Square, Graham being shot in the mouth and left arm; in a second duel a month later at Benicia Graham seriously wounded Lemon. Discovering that his antagonist would live, he challenged him to a third duel, which was not held. In the mid-1850s Graham had passed the California Bar but still managed to get in a shooting scrape now and again. He joined the gold rush to Nevada and eastern California in 1862. In Nevada he killed Jack McBride. In Montgomery, California, he came into dispute with Yank McGuire over a court case. In a saloon they shot it out, Graham killing McGuire while being slightly wounded himself. Eventually Graham came to regret his violent career and the transitory fame from

it: "Such a reputation is a curse to anyone," he said. "Every reckless fool who wants to get his name up as a desperado thinks he is duty-bound to have a difficulty with you, while you are expected to resent every grievance, real or imaginary, with the knife or pistol." Graham died quietly at Los Angeles, almost in obscurity.

Information from William B. Secrest; Secrest, "Gunfighters of Old California." *Calif. Highway Patrolman,* Vol. 43, No. 4 (June 1979), 8-9, 38-52.

Graham, William Y., frontiersman (1817-Feb. 16, 1878). B. in New York State of Scots parentage he was appointed by President Jackson to West Point from which a brother was graduated (another went to Annapolis). William Graham, however had a "personal difficulty" with the commandant, and did not graduate. He was some time in Florida and went to St. Louis in 1845. He spent the winter of 1845-46 on the Upper Mississippi and in 1846 with others accompanied the Santa Fe trading expedition of Eugene and Thomas Leitensdorfer; because of the Mexican War their endeavor, while unsuccessful, was less profitable than they had hoped. Graham late in 1846 became a government courier between Santa Fe and Leavenworth, continuing in that capacity until the end of the war. Probably in 1849 he joined the rush to California, remaining there as trader and miner until 1861 when he went up the Missouri River aboard the ill-fated *Chippewa* which blew up before reaching Fort Benton. Graham came to Goldcreek with Perry McAdow and Abraham Sterne Blake. He and others prospected a dry gulch where Pioneer, Montana, later was located, made some good finds and wintered with the two Stuarts and probably McAdow and Blake. In 1864 Graham was a discoverer of Deer Lodge Lode. He went on to become a well-known pioneer of Montana and served on the Council in the 9th Territorial Legislature. He died at Philipsburg, Montana.

Bancroft, *Washington, Idaho & Montana.* 617, 683; *Montana, Contributions,* II (1896), 64, 122; Deer Lodge, Mont., *New North West,* Mar. 1, 1878; U.S. Census, 1870, Bozeman City, Gallatin County; information from the Mont. Hist. Soc.

Grandmaison, Louis, pioneer (c. 1834-July 27, 1867). B. in Canada Grandmaison went to work as an adobe brickmaker at Fort Owen in the Bitterroot Valley of Montana May 20, 1860, and afterward was reported at Hell Gate (the later Missoula) and Deer Lodge, Montana. He was stabbed to death at Stevensville, Montana by a Frenchman, the cause probably whiskey; the prisoner whose name was unknown, was to be sent to Missoula the next day, but whether that was done, and with what result, is unknown.

George F. Weisel, *Men and Trade on the Northwest Frontier*. Missoula, Mont. State Univ. Press, 1955.

Granger, Gordon, army officer (Nov. 6, 1822-Jan. 10, 1876). B. at Joy, New York, he was graduated from West Point and commissioned a brevet second lieutenant in the 2nd Infantry July 1, 1845, transferring to the Mounted Rifles (3rd Cavalry) July 17, 1846, and becoming a second lieutenant May 29, 1847. After the Mexican War his service was on the frontier, Granger becoming a first lieutenant May 24, 1852, and a captain May 5, 1861. He served in Oregon and Washington before 1851 when, on a leave of absence, he studied military tactics in Europe, upon his return in 1852 being assigned to Forts Merrill, McIntosh and Ringgold Barracks, Texas. He was in a skirmish with Indians at Golindrina Pass, Texas, June 18, 1853, and engaged Lipan Apaches on the Nueces River April 13, 1856. Granger was stationed at Fort Craig, New Mexico in 1859-60. He had a superior Civil War record highlighted by a brilliant role at Chickamauga, September 19-20, 1863. Granger emerged from the war a brevet Major General of the army and July 28, 1866, became colonel of the 25th Infantry and of the 15th Infantry December 20, 1870. He became commander of the District of New Mexico where Apache difficulties were his principal problem. He conferred in 1871 with Cochise whom authorities were endeavoring to settle on a New Mexico reservation. The effort met with no success, Cochise refusing even to consider a trip to Washington, D.C., where the matter might be pressed. One of Granger's greatest problems was resettlement of the Mimbres Apaches from their homeland near Ojo Caliente on a detested new reservation near Tularosa in western New Mexico, but this effort ultimately failed, too. Granger died in his office at Santa Fe. He was described as outspoken and rough in manner but "kindly and sympathetic at heart." One of his junior

officers, conceding that Granger was "a fine officer in some respects," added that he was "a foul mouthed brute...and a hard drinker," and some officers' wives avoided him, a fact which nettled Granger. He was married.

Cullum; DAB; Dan L. Thrapp, *Victorio and the Mimbres Apaches*. Norman, Univ. of Okla. Press, 1974; Frank D. Reeve, ed., "Frederick E. Phelps: A Soldier's Memoirs." *New Mex. Hist. Rev.*, Vol. XXV, No. 3 (July 1950), 196-97.

Grant (Skene), Alexander, army officer (1838-Mar. 28, 1875). B. in Canada, his correct name according to Heitman was Alexander Grant Skene. He enlisted in the 1st Artillery April 11, 1861, and by September 4, 1865, was a sergeant major. He was commissioned a second lieutenant of the 1st Cavalry September 10, 1866, becoming a first lieutenant May 1, 1868. He joined E Troop of the 1st at Camp McDowell, Arizona, in April 1867, and I Troop in Oregon in July 1868, returning with it to Arizona in 1871. Grant took part in Crook's 1872-73 offensive against Apaches and other hostile Indians, having engagements twice at the Red Rocks in central Arizona. In May 1873 he left with his company for Nevada and died at Camp Halleck.

Heitman; Constance Wynn Altshuler, *Chains of Command*. Tucson, Ariz. Hist. So., 1981.

Grant, Blanche Chloe, writer, artist (Sept. 23, 1874-June 19, 1948). B. at Leavenworth, Kansas, she was educated at Indianapolis, at Vassar Collge, and at various art institutions, becoming an illustrator and landscape painter. Miss Grant was best known in a frontier sense for the first editing of *Kit Carson's Own Story of his Life* (1926); she did it from one of two typewritten copies taken from the original manuscript of Carson's dictated memoirs, the manuscript now at the Newberry Library. Miss Grant obtained her copy from Charles L. Camp, and "performed a valuable service to historical scholars by making it available in print." She also did important research on Lewis Garrard, author of the frontier classic, *Wah-to-Yah and the Taos Trail*, as pointed out by Wheat in his introduction to the Grabhorn Press edition. Her biographical sketches of artists of Taos are held by the Bancroft Library. After studying and working as an artist in the East, Miss Grant moved to Taos in 1920 from Lincoln, Nebraska, living in New Mexico the remainder of her life. She published: *Taos Today* (1925); *One Hundred Years Ago in Old Taos* (1925); *Taos Indians* (1926); *When Old Trails Were New: The Story of Taos* (1934), in addition to editing the Carson narrative.

Woman's Who's Who of America, 1914-15. N.Y., Amer. Commonwealth Co., 1914; *Who's Who in New Mexico,.* Albuquerque, Abousleman Co., 1937.

Grant, Frederick Dent, army officer (May 30, 1850-Apr. 11, 1912). B. at St. Louis and the son of Ulysses S. Grant, he was graduated from West Point in 1871 when he joined the 4th Cavalry. As a lieutenant colonel and aide de camp to Sheridan he accompanied Custer's 1874 Black Hills expedition. On it he kept a daily journal which he filed with his report September 7 to the Adjutant General; his reaction to the findings of the expedition were mixed: he reported immediately following it that gold had been discovered, said in his report that it had not been found in any quantity, later confirmed that it was importantly present; he may have tailored his official summary for policy reasons. Reactions of colleagues of the Custer party to Grant's personal behavior also were mixed. Grant reported that he remained largely on the frontier until 1881, when he resigned from the Army, becoming minister to Austria, then police commissioner of New York City. He rejoined the Army in time for the Spanish American War, becoming a Major General by 1906 and holding important commands until his death.

Who Was Who; Herbert Krause, Gary D. Olson, *Prelude to Glory.* Sioux Falls, S.D., Brevet Press, 1974.

Grant, James, army officer (1720-Apr. 13, 1806). B. at Ballindalloch, Banffshire, Scotland, he studied law, received an army commission in 1741 and became captain of the 1st Royal Scots in 1744, fought in Flanders and served many years in Ireland. Grant became major of the 77th Foot, or Montgomerie Highlanders regiment in February 1757 and came with it to America. In September 1758 with 800 men he was sent to reconnoitre Fort Duquesne, Pennsylvania. He divided his force to draw the enemy into an ambuscade but September 14 was himself surprised and routed with a loss of a third of his men in killed, wounded and missing, Grant and 19 of his officers being captured in what Parkman called "this mismanaged affair." Nevertheless Grant became a lieutenant colonel of the 40th Foot in 1760 and was named governor of East Florida. In 1760 he was sent by Amherst to serve with Montgomerie and 1,300 regulars against the "mountaineers" (probably Indians) of Carolina and take part in May in an expedition against the Cherokees. In a fight at Estatoe, a Cherokee village, 60 to 80 hostiles were killed June 1-2, while at Etchoe on June 27 the British fought their way out of an ambush losing 17 killed and 66 wounded among the regulars, other losses among the provincials. Montgomerie and Grant withdrew having failed their objective of burning out the enemy, leaving them convinced the withdrawal indicated weakness. Grant succeeded to the family estate and in 1772 became brevet colonel and in 1775 colonel of the 55th Foot. In 1776 as a Brigadier he returned to America, fighting in several battles of the Revolution and in the West Indies. He became a Major General in 1777, Lieutenant General in 1782, and General in 1796, serving at times in Parliament. Fond of good living he became in his later years "immensely corpulent." He died at 85 at Ballindalloch.

DNB; Parkman, *Montcalm and Wolfe,* II; David H. Corkran, *The Cherokee Frontier.* Norman, Univ. of Okla. Press, 1966.

Grant, Richard, frontiersman (Jan. 20,, 1794-June 21, 1862). B. in Canada, he entered the fur trade about 1815 with the North West Company, joining the Hudson's Bay Company after the 1821 merger. Following service at a number of Canadian wilderness posts, he was assigned to Fort Vancouver in 1841, taking over direction of the Snake River operations from Ermatinger, remaining in charge for about 10 years out of Fort Hall. Grant was important to emigrants traveling toward the Pacific, advising many to head for California instead of Oregon, some following his advice. The Mormon trade also was important to him. The fur trade dwindled away by 1850 and the next year Grant retired, settling near Fort Hall. He moved eventually to near Missoula, Montana, then back to The Dalles, Oregon, and died at Walla Walla. He was more than 6 feet tall, English in appearance, and was "very popular" with the pioneers.

Merle Wells article, MM, Vol. IX; George F. Weisel, *Men and Trade on the Northwest Frontier.* Missoula, Mont. State Univ. Press, 1955; *Montana Contributions,* II (1896); John S Galbraith, *The Hudson's Bay Company as an Imperial Factor, 1821-1869.* Berkeley, Univ. of Calif. Press, 1957.

Grattan, John Lawrence, army officer (c. 1830-Aug. 19, 1854). B. in Vermont he went to West Point from New Hampshire and became a brevet second lieutenant of the 6th Infantry July 1, 1853, being stationed at Fort Laramie, Wyoming. An emigrant's abandoned cow was shot by a Miniconjou Sioux, High Forehead; A Brulé head man, Conquering Bear (Brave Bear), offered at Fort Laramie to pay for the cow with a more valuable horse, but nothing was done. An attempt by Man Afraid of His Horse to settle the matter was rejected. Grattan, apparently eager for Indian fighting laurels, had convinced the post commander, Second Lieutenant Hugh Brady Fleming, that he deserved to lead the next expedition to meet with Indians and was given this authority with instructions "to receive the offender (the man who had killed the cow)..., to act upon his own discretion, and to be careful not to hazard an engagement without certainty of success." Grattan, with Sergeant William Faver, Corporal Charles McNulty, 25 privates, two musicians and an interpreter, Lucien Auguste set out for the Sioux camp with two cannons on August 19, 1854, the interpreter, sure he was to be killed, getting pretty drunk enroute. Grattan, boasting of his intent to settle the matter and welcoming a fight if it came to that, penetrated the Brulé village where in a conference High Forehead refused to surrender, nor Grattan to accept any compromise. A fight erupted, Grattan and all his command save one were killed outright as was Conquering Bear; the lone survivor, Private John Cuddy, was wounded mortally and brought to the fort where he succumbed August 21, making no statement. The Grattan incident, the most celebrated white defeat on the Plains until the Fetterman affair in 1866, opened the way to decades of warfare and bitterness in Indian-white relations.

Lloyd E. McCann, "The Grattan Massacre."

Nebraska History, Vol. XXXVII, No. 1 (Mar. 1956), 1-26; George E. Hyde, *Spotted Tail's Folk.* Norman, Univ. of Okla. Press, 1961.

Graves, Franklin Ward, pioneer (c. 1789-Dec. 25, 1846). B. in Vermont, he and his wife, Elizabeth (c. 1799-Mar. 7, 1847) and their nine children joined the Donner party from Marshall County, Illinois, for California, leaving Independence, Missouri in May (see George Donner entry). Graves was an intelligent, courageous man and on several occasions saved members of the company embarrassment from Indians or other exigencies met. At the snowbound camp east of the Sierra Nevada he alone knew how to make snowshoes which ultimately were necessary to get survivors out of their deadly valley; he left with the "Forlorn Hope" party, but the trek was too much for him. On his deathbed he urged his daughters to make use of his body to avoid starvation, although they rejected the suggestion. He died on Christmas Day. Elizabeth Graves and their son, Franklin Ward Jr., 5, died March 7. They with other members of the family had started from their cabin with the Second Relief Party of James Reed; at the north end of Donner Lake Elizabeth Graves cached what money the family had (it was never located). Mrs. Graves and her son met their end at the snowbound Summit camp where a storm had trapped those seeking to flee to California. The other Graves children survived.

C.F. McGlashan, *History of the Donner Party.* Stanford Univ. Press, 1947; Bancroft, *Pioneer Register.*

Graves, William (Whiskey Bill), desperado (d. Jan. 26, 1864). Listed by Red Yager as a roadster, or primarily a holdup man of the notorious Henry Plummer band of southwestern Montana desperados, Graves was said by Langford to possess probably the only silk hat in Montana. He was involved to some extent in much of the outlawry perpetrated by the organized desperados in and near Bannack and Virginia City. When vigilante activity commenced and numerous band members were executed, Graves withdrew to the Bitterroot Valley of western Montana, being captured at Fort Owen near the present Stevensville. He was the only victim of the popular tribunal to be executed in the supposed favorite fashion of the times: from horseback. He was mounted behind a vigilante, rope around his neck secured to an overhead tree limb. The accuser cried, "So long, Bill!" and raked the horse with his spurs; the animal lunged forward and Graves was no more. He had "made no resistance, but refused all confession."

Dimsdale; Langford; Birney.

Gravier, Jacques, Jesuit missionary (May 17, 1651-c. Apr. 23, 1708). B. at Moulins, France, he became a Jesuit and in 1685 reached Canada, the next year being sent Michilimackinac. In 1688 he went to the Illinois country to succeed Allouez. Gravier was a "missionary of great ability and efficiency, and an excellent linguist," and a dictionary of the Illinois language, supposedly compiled by him, is extant. Gravier was superior from 1695 to 1698 at St. Ignace on Mackinac Strait, but aside from that interval remained in his Illinois mission stations until late in 1705 when a Peoria Indian, imbued with the boasting of northern nations that the way to assert themselves was to dominate the isolated missionaries, took revenge for a fancied slight and fired five arrows at the priest. Two shafts glanced off his breast, a third tore his ear, the fourth was stopped by the collar of his cassock and a fifth dangerously wounded him in the arm, the stone head remaining imbedded after the shaft was withdrawn and the deep wound becoming dangerously infected. Amateur treatment was applied generously, but did little good. Gravier was sent to Mobile for medical attention and in 1706 to Paris for a continuation of it. His wound never healed however. In early 1708 he returned to America and resumed as best he could his missionary labors but died in April from the effects of the injury. The dates of April 17, 23 and 26 are variously given for his demise.

Thwaites, JR, LXV, 264nll, LXVI, 51-65, LXXI, 156.

Gray, Andrew Belcher, surveyor (July 6, 1820-Apr. 16, 1862). B. at Norfolk, Virginia, the son of a British consul, he early studied engineering and surveying under Andrew Talcott, onetime Army engineer. With Talcott he participated in a survey of the Mississippi Delta, but left at 18 to serve as midshipman in the infant Texas Navy, in which his brother, Alfred Gilliat Gray (1818-1876) was an officer before going on to a Union command in the

Civil War. Andrew Gray was appointed by Texas a surveyor and member of a commission under Memucan Hunt to define the boundary between Texas and the United States, winning praise for his work. He was employed by the War Department on a survey of the Keweenaw Peninsula of Michigan's Lake Superior country. Gray returned to Texas with the opening of the Mexican War, serving against Plains Indians during that conflict. In 1849, on a brief trip to California he surveyed the site of San Diego. Gray was named by President Polk principal surveyor of a joint Mexican-U.S. Boundary Commission; his service was brief but significant, he and others opposing Bartlett's placing of the border line from the Rio Grande to the Colorado which ultimately resulted in the Gadsden Purchase being necessary. Gray was replaced on the survey after his dispute with Bartlett by William Emory, and went to New York where, early in 1852, the Texas Western Railroad Company was organized; Gray was selected to make its survey for a southern route to the Pacific coast, and reached San Antonio in late 1853 to organize his expedition of only 19 men, all of whom however were hardened frontiersmen. From Fort Chadbourne the party crossed the Staked Plains to El Paso, explored the Laguna de Guzman, south of the Border, then surveyed a route westward through the Chiricahua Mountains, across the San Pedro River, into the Santa Cruz Valley and eventually along the Gila River to the Colorado, with a subsidiary exploration into Sonora. Eventually the party reached San Diego; Gray's report of a *Survey of a Route for the Southern Pacific R.R. on the 32nd Parallel* was published in 1856. Gray was married that year. He settled for a time in Arizona, residing at Tucson and surveyed mining property and carried out government projects, among other undertakings charting the Pima-Papago Reservation along the Gila River in 1859. In 1861 he joined the Confederate Army, becoming an engineer on Mississippi River fortifications, and while carrying out a survey for Beauregard he was killed by a boiler explosion on a riverboat.

The A.B. Gray Report, ed. by L.R. Bailey. Los Angeles, Westernlore Press, 1963.

Gray, Dixie, Lee, cowboy (d. Aug. 13, 1881). A son of the onetime Tombstone, Arizona, justice of the peace, Mike Gray, young Gray accompanied Newman Haynes Clanton and others driving cattle from New Mexico to Arizona. In Guadalupe Canyon, Arizona, the group was fired on while asleep by a party of Mexicans and largely massacred.

Ed Bartholomew, *Wyatt Earp: The Man & the Myth.* Toyahvale, Tex., Frontier Book Co., 1964.

Gray, Robert, sea captain (May 10, 1755-Summer 1809). B. at Tiverton, Rhode Island, he commanded a privateer during the Revolutionary War and became a competent navigator. Boston merchant Joseph Barrell and five others, desiring to open the China trade in September 1787, at a cost of $50,000 sent out the *Columbia Rediviva* under Captain John Kendrick with the sloop, *Lady Washington* under Gray to make for the northwest coast. They rounded Cape Horn and reached Nootka Sound, Vancouver Island a year later, although it is possible they were not the first American vessels on that coast: the ill-fated Captain Simon Metcalfe with the brig, *Eleanora* may have preceded them in 1787 or 1788. In July 1789 Kendrick and Gray switched vessels, Gray now commanding the *Columbia.* Kendrick, commander of the expedition sent Gray to Canton with sea otter furs thusfar collected. Gray arrived in China in November, exchanged his furs for oriental products of value in the United States, rounded the Cape of Good Hope and returned to Boston August 10, 1790 — the first American captain known to have circumnavigated the globe. The *Columbia* was refitted and left Boston under Gray as commander and part owner in September 1790, arriving at Vancouver Island in June 1791. After wintering there his chief mate and several seamen were slain by Haida Indians among the Queen Charlotte Islands. Gray traded up and down the coast, seeking to avoid the Spanish while filling his holds. Because of his sometimes imperious ways, Gray's shore post was attacked by his estimate of 3,000 Indians January 18, 1792, but the assault was beaten back easily because the rather complex Indian plot was uncovered and thwarted before the action began. In March, by way of retaliation Gray ordered men of his command to sack the Indian town from which the assault had been launched; the place had been deserted and the whites burned

upwards of 200 buildings, destroying the fine handiwork which embellished the place. Gray cruised southward as spring arrived and in April sighted the great river discovered by Bruno de Hezeta August 17, 1775, naming it for his ship, the *Columbia.* Hezeta had been unable to enter the estuary because of the current, but guessed it was the mouth of a great river and Spanish maps since had labeled it "Hezeta's Entryway." Because the Spanish had endeavored to keep its existence secret "there was some justice to its being renamed by Gray." In his first attempt, Gray too failed to penetrate the mouth of the river. A few days later he discovered Gray's Harbor to the north, then returned and May 11, 1792, succeeded in entering the mouth of the Columbia, went upstream about 25 miles and traded with Indians for ten days. In May, off Vancouver Island the *Columbia* beat back an Indian effort to avenge the burning of the native town or, as some accounts have it, in revenge for Gray's subsequent assault upon a village where Indians refused to trade with him. Gray again left the northwest coast with his furs, exchanged them at Canton for China goods and sailed for home, once more completing a circling of the world, arrriving at Boston July 20, 1793. As Samuel Eliot Morison wrote, "On her first voyage, the *Columbia* solved the riddle of the China trade. On her second, empire followed in her wake." By giving the United States a claim to discovery of the Columbia River Gray also gave a claim to Old Oregon which ultimately secured the northwestern states for the nation. Gray married a Boston woman by whom he had five children including one son who died at 6, and settled down as a master of coasting vessels. Gray developed yellow fever on a voyage to Charleston, South Carolina, died and was buried at sea. Gray was the complete materialist. In Cook's view he was "practical, consistent, and ruthless," again "cruel and vengeful," and not an attractive character, although his ability and efficiency were undeniable.

Warren L. Cook, *Flood Tide of Empire.* New Haven, Yale Univ. Press, 1973; Francis E. Smith, *Achievements and Experiences of Captain Robert Gray.* Tacoma, Wash., Barrett-Redfield Press, 1923; Bancroft, *Northwest Coast,* I.

Gray, William H., mission worker, pioneer (Sept. 8, 1810-Nov. 4, 1889). B. at Fairfield,

New York, his father died and he was raised by a Presbyterian clergyman brother, learning the cabinet trade and studying medicine. Converted, he was interested in mission work and may have been influenced to go to Oregon by Samuel Parker's lectures in 1834-36. He was asked to go to Oregon during ;the winter of 1835-36 by the American Board of Commissioners for Foreign Missions, a Congregationalist-founded organization in which Presbyterian and other denominations soon cooperated. Gray agreed and joined Whitman for the trek west. Gray was of help in getting the missionaries installed, housed and attending to their material needs. He went to Fort Vancouver, then returned to the States on the northern route by way of Lake Coeur d' Alene, Clarks Fork of the Columbia and Fort Laramie. At Ash Hollow, Nebraska, his party was attacked by 300 Sioux; his five Indian companions were killed, Gray had two horses shot under him and received two bullets through his hat, clipping off hair locks. He had contacted many tribes on his transits of the west, and stressed the need for more missionaries. Three additional missionaries and one lay worker were sent in 1838 because of his appeals. Gray married in February, 1838 and conducted the missionary party westward with fur caravans, arriving at Whitman's station near the present Walla Walla, Washington in August. In 1842 Gray resigned and settled in the Willamette Valley of Oregon where he became a prominent pioneer, engaging in steam boating. In 1864 he wrote a *History of Oregon* of 684 pages. He also wrote on Whitman and moral and religous aspects of Indian problems, and collected funds for a Whitman monument. Mrs. Gray died at Clatsop, Oregon December 8, 1881, and Gray at Portland. They left seven children.

Myron Eells, *Marcus Whitman; Pathfinder and Patriot.* Seattle, Alice Harriman Co., 1909, Appendix C.

Graydon, James (Paddy), frontiersman (c. 1842- Nov. 9, 1862). B. in Ireland, he was a onetime soldier and curiously successful "farmer" in the Sonoita Valley of the later Arizona, the census of 1860 showing his property valued at $13,000, an oddly-sizable sum for the place and time. Although he gave his occupation as farmer, he also ran an inn of sorts, the United States Boundary Hotel,

three miles from Fort Buchanan and within easy reach of its payroll. He accompanied Dr. B.J.D. Irwin from Buchanan to Apache Pass in February 1861, being instrumental in capturing three Coyotero Apache adult men, no doubt taken by a ruse of some kind. Irwin took them with his detachment to the Pass and to Lieutenant George Bascom's camp. The hostages later were hanged in supposed retaliation for Apache killing of white captives, thus climaxing the Bascom-Cochise affair, a celebrated incident in Apache-white relations. Graydon, captain of the Independent Spy Company at the Battle of Valverde, New Mexico, suggested on the eve of the engagement, February 20, 1862, the driving of two elderly mules loaded with explosives, the fuses lighted, into the Confederate camp to set off panic; the mules refused to go, however, calling for a hasty retreat by the Union side from the vicinity. On October 18, 1862, Graydon and some of his men approached the Gallinas Springs, New Mexico, camp of the Mescalero chiefs Manuelito and José Largo, then because of Kit Carson's offensive against the tribe, enroute to Santa Fe to ask for peace. Graydon entered the camp with his men, ostensibly peaceably inclined, but firing soon broke out, Graydon himself killing Manuelito with a shotgun, José Largo and nine others were also killed and about 20 wounded. The scandal had repercussions; Graydon was accused of murder by Dr. John Marmaduke Whitlock, a Kentuckian, and challenged the physician to a duel at Fort Stanton, New Mexico. Whitlock suffered a minor wound in the wrist; Graydon was shot through the lung, dying four days later. In reprisal the physician was killed and his body then riddled by "one hundred and thirty gunshot wounds" by Graydon's men, one report said.

Benjamin H. Sacks, "New Evidence of the Bascom Affair." *Arizona and the West,* Vol. 4, No. 3 (Autumn 1962), 265; Arizona Census, 1860; Lawrence Kelly, *Navajo Roundup.* Boulder, Colo., Pruett Pub. Co., 1970; "A Pioneer Story: The Tragical Death of J.M. Whitlock in 1868." *New Mex. Hist. Rev.,* Vol. XVI, No. 1 (Jan. 1941), 104-106; Jerry Thompson, "The Vulture over the Carrion: Captain James 'Paddy' Graydon and the Civil War in the Territory of New Mexico." *Jour. of Ariz. Hist.,* Vol. 24, No. 4 (Winter 1983) 381-404.

Great Mohawk (Togouiroui), Mohawk chief (d. June 5, 1690). A man "of unusual ability and character, who possessed great influence with his tribesmen," he was known as Kryn, a Dutch name, at Albany, New York. He was credited with leading the Mohawks to triumph over the Mohicans. In 1672 he became attracted to Christianity and settled with his wife and the regular bands of recruits he brought from the Mohawk villages of the present New York State to the Christian Iroquois settlements of New France. The Great Mohawk came to be as much admired by the French as by his own people. He led the Iroquois Christians in the Denonville force which attacked the Senecas in 1687; in February of 1690 he was leader in the French-Indian assault on Schenectady during King William's War. In June of 1890 he and his warriors joined in a campaign against the Salmon River settlements; when their allies, the Algonquins and Abenakis during the night mistook them for the enemy and attacked, the Great Mohawk was the first to fall.

Thwaites, JR, LXII, 255, LXIII, 177-81, 231, 302n13; DCB, I.

Greek George, camel driver: *see* Caralambo, George.

Green, John army officer (Nov. 20, 1825-Nov,22, 1908). B. in Germany he served as enlisted man to first sergeant in the Mounted Rifles July 1, 1846, to July 5, 1855, when he was commissioned a second lieutenant of the 2nd Dragoons (2nd Cavalry), becoming a first lieutenant March 3, 1861. Green became a captain August 13 of that year and emerged from the Civil War in the same rank, becoming major of the 1st Cavalry June 9, 1868. He was stationed at Camp Grant, Arizona, in 1869 and from there made an extended reconnaissance of the White Mountain country to the north, returning in November to select a site for Camp Ord which ultimately became Fort Apache, established in 1870 and destined to become one of the more famous posts during the Indian wars. On his first reconnaissance Green had learned of the presence of three white men among the White Mountain Apaches, Corydon Cooley, Albert Banta and Henry Dodd, instantly leaped to the conclusion they were selling guns to the Indians (they were not, being only prospectors) and reportedly threatened them with execution; he also was willing to massacre Indians suspected of being hostile, but junior officers prevented such atrocity, and Green came to be appreciated and liked by peaceful Apaches. Green was very active in the Modoc War of 1872-73 in northeastern California and southern Oregon, and it was at his probably unwise direction that the Battle of Lost River occurred and the conflict launched. Green took part in most of the important engagements in the war including the first Battle of the Stronghold January 17, 1873 when he showed such notable intrepidity in leading his troops against well-placed, able and sharpshooting Modoc warriors that he won a Medal of Honor and a brevet to Brigadier General. Green became a lieutenant colonel of the 2nd Cavalry July 3, 1885, and retired by reason of age November 20, 1889. He was married to Mary Yeager in 1878 and lived in retirement at Hoboken, New Jersey although he is reported to have died at Boise, Idaho.

Heitman; Powell; Lori Davisson, *Fort Apache Arizona Territory: 1870-1922.* Tucson, Westerners, Smoke Signal 33, Spring 1977; Keith A. Murray, *The Modocs and Their War.* Norman, Univ. of Okla. Press, 1965.

Green, W.M., Texas Ranger (1854-Dec. 23, 1930). B. in Hill County, Texas, he served with the Texas Rangers in 1871-72 and was a leader in organizing The Texas Ranger Association at Weatherford, Texas in 1920. He was elected major commandant, holding the office until death at Colorado, Texas. He was survived by his widow, two sons and three daughters.

Frontier Times, Vol. 8, No. 5 (Feb. 1931), 207.

Green(e), George, scout (May 14, 1840-Oct. 2, 1913). B. in Massachusetts, Greene and his 16-year-old wife moved to Lincoln, Kansas, where he became a merchant about 1866. Greene was one of Forsyth's scouts in the battle of Beecher Island in September, 1868. Eventually Greene sold out his Lincoln business and moved to Washington State, where he is ;said to have become a business leader remaining so until his death, when he was listed as a "retired merchant." He died at Sedro Woolley, where he was buried.

Simon E. Matson, ed., *The Battle of Beecher Island,* Wray, Colo., Beecher Island Battle Mem. Assn., 1960, 80 (Greene's picture is on page 5); death certificate.

Green Horn, Comanche chief: *see* Cuerno Verde

Greenwood, Caleb, frontiersman (c. 1763-1850). B. in Virginia or Tennessee, he may have gone west to escape punishment for a slaying and probably arrived at St. Louis about 1808. He joined the overland Astorians, but did not accompany them all the way to the Pacific. By 1812 he was with Manuel Lisa, then became a free trapper, and in 1815 had reached the Arkansas River in present eastern Colorado; the next year he returned to St. Louis. Greenwood then trapped the upper Missouri country, perhaps lived among the Crows for a time, and c. 1827 married a Crow-French woman, fathering children; his wife died at St Louis in 1843. In 1844 Greenwood guided emigrants bound for Oregon but at Fort Hall took part of them to California instead, reaching Sutter's Fort in December. He returned to Fort Hall, remaining there until 1846 diverting as many wagon parties as he could from Oregon to California. In 1847 he took part in the Donner relief expedition, and settled in El Dorado County, California.

Harvey L. Carter article, MM, Vol. IX.

Gregg, John Irvin, army officer (July 19, 1826-Jan. 6, 1892). B. at Bellefonte, Pennsylvania, he enlisted in the Mexican War, emerging a captain and spent the years between that conflict and the Civil War in the iron business in Pennsylvania. He was commissioned a captain of the 3rd Cavalry May 14, 1861, transferred to the 6th Cavalry August 3, 1861, and became colonel of the 16th Pennsylvania Cavalry November 14, 1862. Gregg emerged from the Civil War a brevet Major General of Volunteers. On July 28, 1866 he became colonel of the 8th U.S. Cavalry, assigned to Arizona. The 8th was "a rough sort of regiment," plagued by numerous desertions as was not uncommon in postwar outfits. Gregg was sometimes in the field, taking part in a hard little fight July 9, 1867, on Music Mountain, in northwestern Arizona in which Captain James Williams received an arrow wound that ultimately proved mortal. Gregg directed the Hualapais (Walapais) War of 1867-68 in northwestern Arizona. He was retired for disability incurred in line of duty April 2, 1879. He died of a heart condition at Washington, D.C., and was buried at Arlington Cemetery.

Heitman; Dan L. Thrapp, *The Conquest of Apacheria.* Norman, Univ. of Okla. Press, 1967; NCAB, X, 497.

Gregg, Josiah, trader, explorer, writer (July 19, 1806-Feb. 25, 1850). B. in Overton County, Tennessee, he was taken to Illinois at 3 and Missouri at 6, growing up in Howard County. Intellectually inclined, he tutored in mathematics as a child, whittled his own quadrant at 12, studied surveying at 16, made notes of his observations and read good books. He never married. He tried teaching at 18, then medicine, finally the law, giving up each in part because of his chronic ill-health and in May 1831, joined a caravan for Santa Fe, following the course of two older brothers. By the time he reached New Mexico he was conversant in Spanish, was a bookkeeper for merchant Jesse Sutton and had become a good businessman himself. For nine years, until 1840, he crossed the Plains four times, extending his trading to the cities of interior Mexico. On his last trip he blazed a new trail, from Van Buren, Arkansas, to Santa Fe, a route favored by many later California Gold Rushers. From his observations and geographical studies and notes he published, in 1845, "the most complete and reliable map of the prairies then in existence." In 1841 he made a brief tour of Indian territories in Oklahoma. He drove mules to Texas, then settled for a time at Van Buren, writing his famous *Commerce of the Prairies* from his notes and years of observation and experience. In 1845 he again studied medicine, at length taking a degree and ultimately establishing a brief practice in Mexico. He took part in the Mexican War, probably in part as a correspondent (he wrote an eye-witness account of the Battle of Buena Vista), but served also as guide, interpreter, and supplied cartographical information, at first with Brigadier General John Wool, then with Colonel Alexander Doniphan, whence he returned to New York and then to Missouri. From there he revisited Saltillo, Mexico, went to Mexico City in pursuit of botanical interests, and from Mazatlan to San Francisco. In October 1849, he was at a mining camp on the Trinity River. From there he led a very difficult exploring expedition over the coast ranges to discover Humboldt Bay. He died following a fall from his horse. His gravesite is lost, but his monuments are his noteworthy book, his journals and his geographical discoveries.

Josiah Gregg, *Commerce of the Prairies,* ed. by Max L. Moorhead. Norman, Univ. of Okla. Press, 1954; *Diary and Letters of Josiah Gregg,* ed. by Maurice Garland Fulton, intr. by Paul Horgan, 2 vols. Norman, 1941, 1944.

Gregory, Herbert E., geologist (Oct. 15, 1869- Jan. 23, 1952). B. at Middleville, Michigan, he was graduated from Yale in 1869 and took his doctorate there in 1899. He taught geology at Yale from 1896 to 1936, when he became professor emeritus; he also served with the United States Geological Survey. Gregory's interests were far-ranging: Juanita Brooks said he was "an avid student of the history of southern Utah," coming incidentally to believe that John D. Lee, aside from his religion and participation in the Mountain Meadows Massacre, should, "hold a prominent place in the history of the area for his explorations." Gregory also was interested in the Pacific: he was chairman of the Committee on Pacific Investigations of the National Research Council, a regent of the University of Hawaii, and was director of the Bernice P. Bishop Museum at Honolulu from 1919 to 1936. He died and was buried at Honolulu.

Who Was Who; Juanita Brooks, *The Mountain Meadows Massacre.* Norman, Univ. of Okla. Press, 1966.

Greiner, John, Indian superintendent (Sept. 14, 1810-May 13, 1871). B. at Philadelphia, he was state librarian of Ohio when appointed Indian agent of New Mexico in 1849 and became territorial secretary while at Santa Fe. He became embroiled with Edwin Vose Sumner over who was actually superintendent of Indian affairs in New Mexico. Greiner concluded one of the first treaties between the United States and the Mimbres Apaches, finalized July 11, 1852. He returned to Ohio, became editor of the Zanesville, Ohio, *Times* in 1865 and wrote popular jingles of the day.

Dan L. Thrapp, *Victorio and the Mimbres Apaches,* Norman, Univ. of Okla. Press, 1974; Calvin Horn, *New Mexico's Troubled Years,* Albuquerque, Horn & Wallace, Pub., 1963.

Grey, John (Ignace Hatchiorauquasha), Iroquois mountain man, pioneer (c. 1800-c. 1844). Although only half-Iroquois, he had an "Iroquois outlook on life." He probably was

b. on the St. Lawrence River in eastern Canada, receiving some education. Grey may have been a member of a North West Company Snake River brigade in 1818 and later explored enough of the upper Rocky Mountains to have natural features named for him, including Gray's Hole, and Gray's Lake. A free trapper, he sometimes seemed contentious and to Alexander Ross, at least, was "a damned rascal," largely because of his independence and insistence upon his rights. Grey joined Ashley about 1825 as a free trapper. He survived an ambush by Indians March 9, 1832, later engaging in a knife fight with Milton Sublette on Bear River after Sublette had "insulted" Grey's daughter, and several times survived savage fights with grizzly bears. After two decades of adventurous and frequently prosperous trappping, he and other Iroquois and French-Canadians settled in 1836 near Independence-Westport, Missouri, at the site of the later Kansas City. In 1841 he was guide and hunter as far as Green River for the Bidwell-Bartleson California party, returning to Kansas City in September. His property was washed out in an 1844 flood; his widow and family moved after 1850 to Fort Scott, Kansas. Grey was an influential "bridge (across) the cultural gap between Indians and whites during the years of the fur trade."

The Rocky Mountain Journals of William Marshall Anderson, ed. by Dale L. Morgan, Eleanor Towles Harris. San Marino, Calif., Huntington Library, 1967; Merle Wells article, MM, Vol. VII.

Grey (Pearl) Zane, writer (Jan. 31, 1875-Oct. 23, 1939). B. at Zanesville, Ohio, named for an ancestor, Grey was graduated from the University of Pennsylvania in 1896 as a dentist. He worked at that profession in New York City until 1905 and played some semiprofessional baseball. His first writing appeared in 1902, his first novel, *Betty Zane,* in 1903, and his first great success, *Riders of the Purple Sage,* in 1912. He wrote scores of novels, mainly of western slant, traveled to odd corners of the west in company with such genuine frontier types as Charles Jesse (Buffalo) Jones, with whom he roped mountain lions in the Grand Canyon country. Grey was an accurate observer, and although his novels fall into cliche patterns, they possess elements of value, including fine descriptions of country the writer usually had seen firsthand, and occasional vignettes of good characterization. He shared his love for the West with a taste for history and passion for fishing; his pursuit of big game fish on distant oceans he chronicled in some very readable books. Although a type, Grey was a fluent writer and left an enduring legacy of work of considerable variety. He died at Altadena, California.

Literature abundant; Maggie Wilson, "The Wonderful World of Zane Grey." *Arizona Highways*, Vol. 60, No. 8 (Aug. 1984), 30-37.

Grey Chief (Grey Head), Crow chief (fl. 1852). A chief and band leader of the river Crows, Grey Chief came into Fort Union January 8, 1852, with his people. He was given his name, Kurz wrote, "on account of his grey hair, which, however, is a perfect yellow in spots," and he was not grey headed from age which added to the singularity of his appearance. He always wore a fur cap with a red feather

Journal of Rudolph Friederich Kurz. Lincoln, Univ. of Nebr. Press, 1970.

Grierson, Benjamin Henry, army officer (July 8, 1826-Sept. 1, 1911). B. at Pittsburgh, Pennsylvania, he was a merchant for five years at Meredosia, Illinois, before the Civil War. Commissioned major of the 6th Illinois Cavalry October 24, 1861, and colonel April 12, 1862, he ended the war a Major General of Volunteers and with a distinguished record as a cavalry officer. His 600-mile raid in April and May of 1863 as far south as Baton Rouge, Louisiana, materially assisted Grant in the Vicksburg campaign and was a daring operation of merit and consequence. He became colonel of the black 10th Cavalry July 28, 1866, organizing and training the regiment which became an outstanding frontier outfit. Grierson was described by Utley as a mild-mannered, big hearted man who did not fare well in the postwar army. His lack of West Point credentials, his warm identification with black troops and "the active personal enmity of General Sheridan helped make his frontier career frustrating and undistin-guished," although not without its highlights. In 1868 he examined the site of the future Fort Sill, Oklahoma, in December was one of three officers reconnoitering the area, commenced its construction January 8, 1869, and was in charge of initial work on it. The post became

the center of efforts to control the southern Plains Indians and after 1876 to protect them. Grierson was an advocate of Grant's Peace Policy toward the Indians. He carried out the arrest of Kiowa chiefs Satanta, Big Tree and Setangya following the Warren wagon train raid in 1871. Grierson was active against Comanche and Kickapoo Indians in West Texas and in the spring of 1880 cooperated with Colonel Hatch of New Mexico against the Mescalero Apaches suspected of aiding and abetting Victorio in his guerilla war against New Mexico troops. During the summer of 1880 Grierson directed heavy scouting in West Texas to ward against Victorio's coming north out of Mexico. The Apache did so twice however, each time being turned back by Grierson's forces. July 30 Grierson himself with a small escort was trapped on "Devil's Ridge," northward of Fort Quitman, Texas, by Victorio's hostiles, having "a very bad time until rescue arrived." In August he fought Victorio again, this time in the celebrated action at Rattlesnake Springs in West Texas; the Indians were rebuffed and returned to Mexico for the last time. Grierson in December 1888 left the 10th Cavalry to become commander of the Department of Arizona in succession to Miles. He was promoted to Brigadier General April 5, 1890, and retired July 8 of that year. His first wife died in 1888, and he married again in 1897, his second wife surviving him. Grierson died at his summer home at Omena, Michigan.

Heitman; Robert M. Utley, *Frontier Regulars.* N.Y., MacMillan Co., 1973; Dan L. Thrapp, *Victorio and the Mimbres Apaches.* Norman, Univ. of Okla. Press, 1974; E.L.N. Glass, *History of the Tenth Calvary 1866-1921.* Tucson, Ariz., Acme Printing Co., 1921; William H. and Shirley A. Leckie, *Unlikely Warriors: General Benjamin Grierson and His Family.* Norman, 1984.

Griffin, John Smith, missionary (1807-Feb. 1899). B. at Castleton, Vermont, he took his theological education at Oberlin, Ohio, graduating in 1838. He conceived the idea of starting an independent and self-supporting mission to the northwest Indians, obtained funds from the Litchfield, Connecticut, Congregational Church, secured the services of Asahel Munger, a skilled craftsman, for his material assistance, married in St. Louis and reached Fort Hall, Idaho, in 1839. There he left Munger and went on to Lapwai, a Nez Perce mission operated by the Reverend Henry H. Spalding where he wintered. March 16, 1840 the Griffins left to start a mission among the Shoshone, suffering incredible hardships in the mountains as they tried to force their way through winter snows, and reached the Fort Boise area where they intended to commence work. Griffin's Indians abandoned the effort and eventually the Griffins did, too, recognizing that it was hopeless. They finally arrived at the Whitman's Walla Walla missions where they rested and at length went on to Fort Vancouver. In 1841 Griffin established a settlement at the Tualatin Plains, Oregon, and became a prominent Oregon pioneer.

Thwaites, EWT, XXVIII, 275n.; Clifford M. Drury, *Marcus and Narcissa Whitman and the Opening of Old Oregon,* 2 vols. Glendale, Calif., Arthur H. Clark Co., 1973.

Griffith, A(lonzo) Kinney, novelist (Aug. 25, 1897-May 21, 1981). B. in Pennsylvania of a white father and an Ireland-born mother, his primary occupation was listed as mechanic, employed by the federal government. He lived in Arizona for many years before his retirement to Mariposa, California, some years before his death at Merced, California. Griffith wrote three books: *The Big Scalphunter: A Saga of the Great Southwest* (1961); *Mickey Free: Manhunter* (1969), and *First Hundred Years of Niño Cochise: The Untold Story of an Apache Indian Chief* (1971). Griffith also wrote shorter pieces for magazines. Although his writings were represented as factual, this author has never succeeded in locating any recognized authority on the subjects concerned who was impressed with the factuality or authenticity of much he produced. His autobiographical sketches seem similarly fanciful in important respects.

Griffith death certificate; "In Memoriam." *True West,* Vol. 28, No. 10 (Nov. 1981), 8; Griffith, *Mickey Free: Manhunter.* Caldwell, Id., Caxton Printers, 1969, author's blurb.

Griffith (Cameron), Goldie, rough rider (Sept. 30, 1893-Jan. 6, 1976). B. at Kinmundy, Illinois, she was the daughter of show people. In 1912 she joined the 101 Ranch as a performer both in the arena and in early motion pictures. In 1913 she joined the Buffalo Bill Wild West show, appearing with it also in 1916-17 as trick rider and bronco buster. She took part in rodeos until 1922. Goldie married first Harry Sterling, a bronc and trick rider, and second, Tim Cameron, also a rodeo rider; both marriages ended in divorce. She died at Boulder, Colorado.

Frontier Times, Vol. 50, No. 3 (May 1976), 54.

Griggs, Robert Fiske, explorer, botanist (Aug. 22, 1881-June 8, 1962). B. at Brooklyn, Connecticut, he earned a doctorate at Harvard in 1911. He served as a botanist in U.S. and Texas government posts, taught at Fargo (North Dakota) College, Ohio State and George Washington universities and served with the National Research Council. He was a member of expeditions to Puerto Rico, 1901; Guatemala, 1902; Alaska, 1913, 1915-19, 1930. In 1916 he discovered the "Valley of 10,000 Smokes," which had developed following the stupendous Mt. Katmai, Alaska eruption of 1912. Griggs had studied a small field of seething fumaroles, then found the great valley by accident when noting, enroute to camp, a towering cloud of steam. "We climbed up the little eminence that hid the source," he recalled. "The sight that flashed into view was one of the most amazing visions ever beheld by mortal eye." The valley ceased its major fuming after about 30 years, but remains a national park. Griggs named dozens of mountains, lakes, harbors, passes, and in 1959 the U.S. government named the highest mountain in the area Mt. Griggs, in a cairn atop which his ashes lie today.

New York Times, Travel Sec., Mar. 18, 1973; *Who's Who in America.*

Grijalva, Merejildo, interpreter, scout (c. 1842-1916). B. of Opata parentage or perhaps of Mexican lineage, he also was called Chivero (Goat herder) and was captured at 10 by Chiricahua Apaches under Cochise by whom he was adopted and, being intelligent, whose language he quickly learned. He became Cochise's primary interpreter and even raided with his warriors. Michael Steck, New Mexico Indian agent noticed the boy and became attracted to him, believing him valuable for interpreter purposes. Steck arranged for James Tevis, Overland stage company agent to Apache Pass to slip the boy onto a coach for the Rio Grande which was done, Merejildo thenceforth working for Steck; Sweeney believes that this kidnapping

— for that is what it was — incensed Cochise and was a factor in the Chiricahua chief's ultimately turning hostile. Merejildo, as he was almost universally known, went on to become "one of the outstanding guides and scouts of the Southwest" during critical years. He worked out of a number of posts in Arizona and New Mexico; he and his brother, Francisco, worked as scouts under Crook in 1872-74. Merejildo accompanied John Clum who took Apaches to the East on one occasion. He married, lived at Tucson, then near Fort Thomas, worked at San Carlos as a "farmer" at $1,000 a year for some time and occasionally became involved in minor troubles caused by drinking or gunplay. Merejildo at last established a ranch near Solomonville, Arizona, where he died.

Rita Rush, "'El Chivero' — Merejildo Grijalva." *Arizoniana*, Vol. I, No. 3 (Fall 1960), 8-10; Charles D. Poston biographical article in Tucson *Arizona Star*, Oct. 3, 1880; James H. Tevis, *Arizona in the '50's*. Albuquerque, Univ. of New Mex. Press, 1954, 169; Edwin R. Sweeney to author, June 18, 1982.

Grimes, Ahijah W. (High, Caige), lawman (July 5, 1850-July 19, 1878). B. at Bastrop, Texas, his nickname, "High," apparently derived from his mother's maiden name, and he was almost exactly one year older than desperado Sam Bass through whose agency he would die. Grimes was trained as a printer, served three months with the Texas Rangers until December 1877, and became a deputy with Deputy Sheriff Milt Tucker at Georgetown, Texas; Grimes was located at Round Rock, also in Williamson County. When Bass and two of his men entered Round Rock at 4 p.m., preliminary to an attempt on the bank, Grimes and Moore, although previously alerted and warned not to attempt to arrest the dangerous men, suspected they were armed and accosted them in Henry Koppel's store. The three bandits commenced firing simultaneously, putting six bullets into Grimes who fell dead near the door without having drawn his gun. After being mortally wounded himself later, Bass stated, "If I killed Grimes, it was the first man I ever killed." Grimes was married, had fathered three children, and was in strict performance of his duty when shot down; yet it was the desperado, Bass, who became immortalized in legend and myth, and Grimes who was

forgotten save for his role in Bass's career. "It is only natural," wrote Tipton, "especially in frontier areas, to make legendary heroes of the 'bad' men and ignore the good; Texans are no exception." Vandals are reported to have defaced Grimes' headstone so that it was removed from the cemetery where he had been buried with Masonic honors.

Robert W. Stephens, *Texas Ranger Sketches*. Dallas, p.p., 1972 (with photograph of Grimes); Wayne Gard, *Sam Bass*. Lincoln, Univ. of Nebr. Press, 1969; correspondence with Van C. Tipton, Georgetown, Tex.; *Frontier Times*, Vol. 5, No. 1 (Oct. 1927), 22-23.

Grinnell, George Bird, naturalist, ethnologist (Sept. 20, 1849-Apr. 11, 1938). B. at Brooklyn, New York, Grinnell was graduated from Yale in 1870 and joined a paleontology expedition under O.C. Marsh, collecting mammal fossils from the central Plains, Wyoming and Utah. He served as naturalist and paleontologist for Custer's 1874 expedition to the Black Hills, reporting however that "the rapidity of our travel" precluded exhaustive observations. He found game abundant in the area and fossils widely present although only a cursory investigation was possible. Grinnell accompanied William Ludlow to the Yellowstone country in 1875. He earned his doctorate from Yale in 1880. Grinnell became editor, and eventually owner, of *Forest and Stream* magazine, managing it from 1876 to 1911. He helped draft plans for the New York Zoological Park, and in 1899 was a naturalist for the Alaskan expedition of Edward H. Harriman. Grinnell had met Frank North and his Pawnee scouts on his earliest western expedition, and developed a deep interest in the Plains Indians, visiting them for many summers, accompanying the Pawnees and others on buffalo hunts and taking part in their various activities. His books, in addition to a juvenile series of frontier-oriented works, included: *Pawnee Hero Stories and Folk Tales* (1889); *Blackfoot Lodge Tales* (1892); *The Story of the Indian* (1895); *Trails of the Pathfinders* (1911); *The Indians of Today* (1911); *Beyond the Old Frontier* (1913); *Blackfeet Indian Stories* (1913); *The Fighting Cheyennes* (1915); *When Buffalo Ran* (1920); *The Cheyenne Indians*, 2 vols. (1923); *Bent's Old Fort and Its Builders* (1923); *By Cheyenne Campfires* (1926); *Two Great Scouts* (1929). , He also co-edited a number of hunting and conservation books. As he observed the wholesale destruction of western game animals, Grinnell became an ardent conservationist. In 1886 he was a founder of the Audubon Society. In 1887 he joined Theodore Roosevelt and others in organizing the Boone and Crockett Club, was co-editor of its publications for some time, and its president from 1918-37. In 1911 he helped found the American Game Association, a protective group. A strong supporter of the National Parks system, he fought to prevent hunting within the reserves and was largely responsible for creation of Glacier National Park in 1910; in 1925 he became president of the National Parks Association. He died at New York City. Grinnell's influence in many fields: paleontology, natural history, ethnology, conservation, wildlife preservation, was very great at a critical time, and proved of lasting benefit for the nation and the preservation of its resources.

Literature abundant; DAB; *Who Was Who;* John F. Reiger, "George Bird Grinnell." *Ariz. and the West,* Vol. 21, No. 1 (Spring 1979), 1-4.

Grollet, Jacques (Santiago), seaman, adventurer (c. 1664-post 1705). B. at La Rochelle, France, he was a member of the La Salle expedition which left France in 1684 for the New World, basing itself at Matagorda Bay, Texas. Grollet may have been one of the conspirators who did away with La Salle on the Trinity River of Texas March 19, 1687; at any rate, he survived. Two years later, May 1, 1689, he and L'Archévèque were picked up at Fort St. Louis on the Lavaca River near Matagorda Bay by a Spanish expedition out of Mexico under Alonzo de Leon. Grollet was taken to Mexico, eventually reached New Mexico and in 1699 was residing at Santa Fe. Here he was friendly with L'Archévèque and Meusnier, another survivor of the La Salle expedition. When last heard from, in 1705, Grollet lived at Bernalillo on the Rio Grande south of Santa Fe.

Aldolphe F.A. Bandelier, "The Betrayer of La Salle." *Nation,* vol. XLVII, No. 1209 (Aug. 30, 1888), 166-67; Parkman, *La Salle and the Discovery of the Great West.*

Groner, Con, lawman (1845-post 1887). Groner was a railroad engineer who quit that profession in 1876 and became widely known as sheriff of Lincoln County, Nebraska. Billed as "the cowboy sheriff of the Platte," Groner toured with Buffalo Bill Cody's Wild West show for several seasons, one of them along with Doc Middleton, a horse thief whose nemesis he had sought to be. During the winter of 1877-78 then Second Lieutenant Homer W. Wheeler in pursuit of Indian marauders out of Fort McPherson, Nebraska, had been joined by 20 cowmen under Groner who frightened off the Indians before Wheeler could strike them. As sheriff Groner seriously sought Middleton for the reward money, but he never caught up with him although he did arrest Charles Fugit, Doc's particular buddy; Groner was wounded slightly by Fugit when apprehending him. Groner was billed in Cody's shows as having arrested six members of Middleton's gang, balking a train holdup, and arresting a fabulous number of murderers, horse and cattle thieves and assorted desperadoes. He was described as "a large, beefy man" and his law office headquarters were at North Platte, Nebraska.

Don Russell, *The Lives and Legends of Buffalo Bill.* Norman, Univ. of Okla. Press, 1960; *Man of the Plains: Recollections of Luther North 1856-1882,* ed. by Donald F. Danker. Lincoln, Univ. of Nebr. Press, 1961; John Carson, *Doc Middleton, the Unwickedest Outlaw.* Santa Fe, Press of the Territorian, 1966, 16.

Groseilliers, Médard Chouart, Sieur des, explorer (c. July 1618-c.1696). B. in the French province of Chie, he reached Three Rivers, Quebec, by 1641 and spent some time in the Huron country, later perhaps being sent to Lake Superior by the Jesuits. By 1646 he was back on the St. Lawrence where he served as a soldier at Quebec and later as a river pilot. His first wife, by whom one son survived to maturity, died in 1651 and Groseilliers married Marguerite, half-sister of Pierre Radisson, his close friend, and with whom he achieved lasting fame as an explorer and fur trader. By his second wife he fathered four children. In 1654 Groseilliers and probably Radisson (see Radisson entry for discussion of his participation), traveled into the Indian country of the Great Lakes, traversing Lake Huron, perhaps reaching Lake St. Clair, crossing overland to Lake Michigan and probably visiting Lake Superior, returning to the St. Lawrence by way of the Straits of Michilimackinac and the Ottawa River, bringing with them a valuable cargo of furs.

He remained in the settlements until he and Radisson in mid-1659 again set out for the wilderness. They reached Chequamegon Bay on the southern shore of Lake Superior and went overland to winter at Lac Court Oreilles in the present Sawyer County, Wisconsin. With spring they spent six weeks among the Sioux, returned to Lake Superior and crossed to its northern shore; their further explorations are uncertain, but Radisson said they had touched Hudson Bay or, more likely, James Bay which in the time allotted is conceivable, if barely. By August 19 they were back in Montreal, accompanied by 300 Ottawas in 60 canoes and bringing 200,000 livres worth of beaver. Although this wealth perhaps saved the colony from economic disaster, the furs were seized, the pair fined and Groseilliers thrown in jail probably because he had undertaken the expedition without sanction. The incensed explorers determined to sell their talents to the English and "a train of events, therefore, was started by them which would come to an end only with the British conquest of Canada in 1763." Groseilliers visited France, returned and in 1662 was foiled in an attempt to go by sea from Percé, on the tip of the Gaspé Peninsula, to Hudson Bay by ship and instead went to Boston with Radisson. Here support was won for several attempts to reach the Bay by sea, but the essays failed. The pair were persuaded to go to England in an attempt to win the support of Charles II; they were taken at sea by a Dutch privateer, landed in Spain and made their way across Europe to England where they observed the effects of the Plague and Fire of 1665 and 1666. After several further attempts, Groseilliers and Radisson set out in two small ships in 1668, and while Radisson's vessel failed to reach Hudson Bay, Groseilliers' achieved the goal; Charles Fort was established at the mouth of the Rupert River, near the head of James Bay; the next year Radisson took possession of Port Nelson at the mouth of the Nelson River. From the work of the explorers the Hudson's Bay Company was formed May 2, 1670. For the succeeding five years Groseilliers and his brother-in-law were engaged by the company in explorations and enterprises related to the fur trade, the burgeoning enterprise thoroughly alarming the French of the St. Lawrence settlements and in the homeland. About 1675 the pair spent a year in France,

and in 1676 Groseilliers returned to Canada, spending some time with his family at Three Rivers, but by the 1680's they again were in the Hudson Bay country working with Canadian organizations. After two years of confusing difficulties with Canadian bureaucracy rather than wilderness exigencies, they returned to France, from where Radisson was persuaded to reenter the employ of the Hudson's Bay Company, and Groseilliers returned to New France. The date and place of his death is not certainly known (although he may have died at Sorel, Quebec, on the date given), nor are the events of his final years. But his career had been important: to him is largely due the insight which led to establishment of the Hudson's Bay Company and the reestablishment of that great body of water as a key to control of the fur trade of the continent; his intelligence was marked and his influence with both Indians and whites was considerable.

Thwaites, JR, XXVIII, 319-20n32; XLII, 219-21, 296n11; DCB; DAB.

Groston, de St.-Ange et de Bellerive, Louis, army officer (1698-Dec. 27, 1774). B. at Montreal he was taken with his father's family to Fort St. Joseph, near Niles, Michigan, in 1720. The next year Louis escorted Charlevoix through the western country, and two years later with Etienne de Veniard de Bourgmond went to Fort d'Orleans, about 280 miles up the Missouri, remaining on the river until 1736. Groston became commander of a French post at Vincennes, Indiana, upon the death at the hands of Chickasaws of Bissot de Vinsenne, remaining there until 1764, then taking command of Fort de Chartres, which he delivered to the English October 10, 1765. Bellerive went to St. Louis, joined the Spanish service and was in command there until 1770. Until his death at St. Louis he was a captain of Spanish Infantry. He never married.

Thwaites, JR, LXX, 316-17n40; DCB, IV.

Grouard, Frank, scout (Sept. 20, 1850-Aug. 15, 1905). Grouard was b. in the Society Islands of the South Pacific, the son of Benjamin Franklin Grouard, a Mormon missionary, and a native woman. Grouard Sr. had been sent to the islands as a missionary by Joseph Smith in 1843 and brought his three sons back to Utah in 1852, then made his home at San Bernardino, California, until he withdrew from the church "to become a member of a spiritualist group." Frank Grouard was adopted into the family of Addison Pratt which moved to Beaver, Utah, from where Frank ran away at 15, reaching Helena Montana. Four years later, about 1869, while a mail carrier he was captured by Sioux near the mouth of Milk River, Montana, and for six years he lived among that people, learning their language and, he said, becoming acquainted with Crazy Horse and Sitting Bull. Grouard said that before he left the Sioux he was instrumental in 1874 in opening the way for negotiations for the Indians to cede the Black Hills; later he removed to the Red Cloud Agency, then went to live with an agency trader, J.W. Deere. Grouard heard that Crook, then at Fort Laramie, desired to see him. He was hired by Crook as scout for the 1876 campaigns along with about 35 others, some of them famous frontier names. Grouard had a major part in Crook's operations that year. He was in the attack on an Indian village (erroneously believed to have been Crazy Horse's village) on March 17, in the battle of the Rosebud on June 17, on the famous Sibley Scout of early July in which he and Big Bat Pourier seem to have been responsible for salvaging the command which had a nearly miraculous escape, on the Big Horn and Yellowstone expedition and in the skirmish at Slim Buttes, Dakota, on September 9-10. Grouard had a role in events leading to the slaying of Crazy Horse at Fort Robinson on September 5, 1877, and his interpretation, or misinterpretation, may have been a factor in the great Indian's death; Grouard said he believed Crazy Horse was planning a white massacre, a belief arising from his faulty understanding of what the Indian had said. Grouard continued serving as a scout in Wyoming and Nebraska, was attached to the Pine Ridge Reservation in 1890-91 during the Messiah ferment that led to the affair at Wounded Knee, and rendered valuable services to the whites at this time. During his later years Grouard operated against desperadoes who were active in the region and "there can be little doubt that he played a major role in the suppression of these gentlemen of the road." About 1894 Joe DeBarthe, a newspaperman, wrote down Grouard's story which is a standard source for the events it covers, even if it contains flaws largely resulting from its nature as a recollection, plus DeBarthe's interpolations.

Despite these imperfections, "the Grouard account possesses real intrinsic merit, and its good points far outnumber the bad." Grouard was highly praised and valued by Crook who according to Finerty once said "he would rather lose one-third of his command" than be deprived of his services; Bourke and others praised him highly. Grouard was strongly built, muscular, about 6 feet in height and weighed about 200 pounds; he was a dead shot and skilled in all plainsman's arts, was of undoubted courage, reliability and had a "shrewd, native intelligence" to match his physique.

Joe DeBarthe, *Life and Adventures of Frank Grouard.* Norman, Univ. of Okla. Press, 1958; John F. Finerty, *War-Path and Bivouac.* Lincoln, Univ. of Nebr. Press, n.d.; J.W. Vaughn, *The Reynolds Campaign on Powder River.* Norman, Univ. of Okla. Press, 1961; Vaughn, *With Crook at the Rosebud.* Harrisburg, Pa., Stackpole Co., 1956.

Grounds, Billy, desperado (Nov. 26, 1862-Mar. 29, 1882). His real name was said to have been Boucher. B. in Texas, Billy left home on his 19th birthday, 1881, and went to New Mexico and Arizona. Suspected of rustling and murder, he and Zwing (Zweig) Hunt were surprised at a ranch near Tombstone, Arizona, by Deputy Sheriff Breakenridge and a posse. Grounds was killed as was Deputy John C. Gillespie; Hunt was wounded seriously.

Allen Erwin, *True West,* Vol. XIII, No. 3 (Jan. -Feb. 1965), 71; Ed Bartholomew, *Wyatt Earp: The Man & the Myth.* Toyahvale, Tex., Frontier Book Co., 1964.

Grover, Abner S. (Sharp), scout (c. 1825-July 16, 1869). Forsyth said Grover was "a plainsman of somewhere between forty and fifty years of age" in 1868, "who had passed his life hunting and trapping along the northwestern border" adding that "I judged from his manner and his swarthy complexion that he had in his blood a dash of the French voyageur, probably from among his mother's people. He ... spoke the dialect of the Sioux, and knew many of their tribe personally." Grover told Forsyth in 1868 that he had been on the Plains 30 years. Brady quotes Louis H. Carpenter that Grover had "married a Sioux woman and had lived for years with the Indians," graphically describing his trailing skill. By the middle of 1860s Grover was in

Kansas, working as scout out of various army posts. In August 1868, he and Will Comstock were directed by Lieutenant Fred H. Beecher to enter the Cheyenne chief Turkey Leg's camp west of Fort Hays to secure information about hostiles. Comstock was killed and Grover seriously wounded. Not fully recovered, he was enlisted as chief scout for Forsyth's company of plainsmen. The party was besieged on Beecher's Island September 17-25, holding off many Cheyennes and others in a memorable siege-battle although casualties were not inconsiderable. On October 18, 1868, Grover, as scout for Carr and Carpenter, took part in an action against Cheyennes on Beaver Creek, Kansas, Carr paying tribute to Grover's interpreting ability and his bravery. Grover was killed at Pond City, Kansas, by John Morrissey, "in a row," as Carpenter put it. Reuben Waller claimed special knowledge that Grover had killed Comstock and that Grover had been killed "by one of the boys who was in the Beecher fight with him," but his version is at variance with the record on both counts. Forsyth said Grover was of "keen eye, a good shot, and a cool head," and that he was about 5 feet, 10 inches tall, "rather sparsely built, little given to conversation, and apt to be somewhat moody..."

Blaine Burkey, *Custer, Come At Once!* Hays, Kan., Thomas More Prep, 1976; Cyrus Townsend Brady, *Indian Fights and Fighters.* Lincoln, Univ. of Nebr. Press, 1971; George A. Forsyth, *Thrilling Days in Army Life.* N.Y., London, Harper & Bros., 1900.

Grover, Cuvier, army officer (July 24, 1829-June 6, 1885). B. at Bethel, Maine, he was graduated from West Point in 1850, and assigned to the 1st Artillery. He served at Fort Leavenworth from 1850-53, then was assigned to engineering duty with the exploration through the region now traversed by the Northern Pacific Railroad. In January and February 1854, with only four men, he accomplished a crossing of the Rocky Mountains on snowshoes "in the midst of hostile Indians." His report on climatic conditions removed many objections to building a northern rail line. Grover was assigned to Fort Crawford, Wisconsin, in 1855-56, Fort Snelling, Minnesota, 1856-57, took part in the Mormon "War," and was named provost marshal for the Territory of Utah. At the outbreak of the Civil War he was in command of Fort Union, New Mexico. Called upon by Confederates to surrender, he burned his supplies and by a "brilliant forced march" reached the Missouri River with his command, although at permanent cost to his health. His Civil War record was good; he served in the eastern armies and was breveted Major General. Mustered out, he became lieutenant colonel of the 3rd Cavalry, then colonel of the 1st Cavalry, serving at a succession of western posts, although he "had no use for frontier service": Fort Larned, Kansas; Fort Craig, Fort Selden, New Mexico; Camp Verde, Arizona; Fort D.A. Russell, Fort Fetterman, Wyoming; Fort Vancouver and Fort Walla Walla, Washington. Since his Red River campaign he had suffered "frequently" from nervous prostration and facial neuralgia, and died at Atlantic City where he went seeking relief. Grover married twice.

NCAB, Vol. V, 49-50; DAB; Cullum; F. Stanley, *Fort Craig.* Pampa, Tex., Pampa Print Shop, 1963.

Grover, Sylvester, soldier (c. 1865-post 1925). His year of birth is conjecture. On October 10, 1885, Grover, of Troop C, 4th Cavalry, and a soldier named Hickman, Troop F, 4th Cavalry, were taking from Lang's ranch, New Mexico, dispatches from Crawford in Mexico to Crook at Fort Bowie, Arizona. At "Cowboy Pass," they were ambushed by Apaches, Hickman killed, Grover wounded and his horse hit. Grover saved the dispatches, found shelter among the rocks, held off the Indians and was rescued by passing discharged scouts and soldiers; he received a certificate of merit for his action.

Winners of the West, Dec. 30, 1925.

Grummond, George Washington, army officer (d. Dec. 21, 1866). From Michigan, Grummond enlisted as first sergeant of Company A, 1st Michigan Infantry May 1, 1861, was commissioned a captain September 12 and resigned July 14, 1862. He became a major of the 14th Michigan Infantry March 9, 1863, a lieutenant colonel April 20 and was mustered out July 18, 1865. He was commissioned a second lieutenant of the 18th U.S. Infantry May 7, 1866, and assigned to Wyoming, reaching Fort Phil Kearny on the Bozeman Trail east of the Big Horn Mountains September 17 with his pregnant wife, Frances, having met her in Tennessee and married her after conclusion of the Civil War. Fort Phil Kearny was harassed by incessant Indian attacks all about, its details subject to assault whenever they ventured beyond the guns of the post. Grummond sided with Captain William J. Fetterman in a rift which developed between that officer and the post commander, Colonel Henry B. Carrington. November 25, 1866, Grummond was of a pursuit force that recovered steers the Indians had run off. December 6 in a confused melee north of the post in which Carrington had sought to punish hostiles, Lieutenant Horatio Bingham was killed and Grummond all but cut off, slashing his way free with his saber; he said he "shut his eyes and literally slashed his way out... Grummond said he could hear his saber 'click' every time he cleaved an Indian's skull." December 21 Grummond was given command of a detachment of about 20 men of the late Lieutenant Bingham's C Company, 2nd Cavalry and directed to join Fetterman in an operation north of the post. No man of the Fetterman command returned. Grummond was killed after he apparently had cut off an Indian's head with his saber. His body was mutilated after death. Frances Grummond transferred the remains to Tennessee for ultimate interment. She married Carrington April 3, 1871, following the death of Carrington's first wife and wrote an autobiography, *My Army Life* (1911), published a year before her second husband's death.

Dee Brown, *Fort Phil Kearny: An American Saga.* N.Y., G.P.Putman's Sons, 1962; J.W. Vaugn, *Indian Fights: New Facts on Seven Encounters.* Norman, Univ. of Okla. Press, 1966.

Guadalajara, Diego de, explorer (fl. 1654). Assigned by the Mexico City viceroy, the Count of Alba to explore the Concho River country of Texas for reported pearls, Guadalajara left Santa Fe with 30 soldiers and 200 Indian auxiliaries and followed the route of Hernán Martín and Diego del Castillo to the Concho. There the expedition contacted the Jumanos Indians, became involved in intertribal warfare and not equipped to deal with such, returned to Santa Fe.

Herbert Eugene Bolton, *Spanish Exploration in the Southwest, 1542-1706.* N.Y., Charles Scribner's Sons, 1916; HT; Bancroft, *North Mexican States and Texas,* I, 384-85.

Gudrid, wife of Karlsefni, Norse woman (fl. c. 1000-1005). Daughter of a wealthy farmer, Thorbjorn Vifilsson, Gudrid was b. in Iceland and was termed by Eirik's Saga "very beautiful and a most exceptional woman in every respect." She was raised as a foster daughter by a man named Orm and his wife Halldis, close friends of Gudrid's parents. Her parents and Orm and Halldis determined to migrate to Greenland where Gudrid, a devout Christian, married Thorstein Eiriksson (one Saga reports she was married once previously), and according to the Greenlanders' Saga took part with her husband in an unsuccessful voyage to Vinland the ensuing summer. Thorstein died in some sort of plague in Greenland the following winter. Thorfinnr Karlsefni, a wealthy Iceland merchant came to Greenland on a trading expedition, and with the blessing of Eirik the Red, Gudrid's guardian, married the widow. She accompanied Karlsefni to Vinland, or some site on the American mainland on a colonizing voyage involving 160 people, and remained in North America more than three years although native hostility and other factors eventually caused them to withdraw. While in America, Gudrid gave birth to Snorri Karlsefnisson, the first white child known to have been born on this continent. Upon dissolution of the settlement attempt Gudrid, her husband and Snorri returned to Greenland and ultimately to Iceland where they settled permanently. Snorri developed a distinguished lineage, which included several bishops and other noteworthy Icelanders. When Karlsefni died, Gudrid made a pilgrimage to Rome; upon her return she became a nun and a recluse, living out her life in Iceland.

Magnus Magnusson, Hermann Palsson, *The Vinland Sagas: The Norse Discovery of America.* Baltimore, Penguin Books, 1965; Gwyn Jones, *The Norse Atlantic Saga.* N.Y., Oxford Univ. Press, 1964.

Guerin, Jean, Jesuit donne (d. Sept. 1662). Guerin, whose place of birth is not recorded, was a *donne,* or lay assistant to the Jesuits of New France, working with and for them more than 20 years with "devotion and fidelity." He labored with missionaries among the Iroquois, Hurons, Abenakis and Algonquins. In 1660 he accompanied the ill-fated Menard from Three Rivers into present Michigan to winter among the Ottawas. Menard went on into Wisconsin in search of remnants of the Hurons and disappeared in the forest, but he was not accompanied at the time by Guerin who had been left in charge of a fledgling church at Keweenaw Bay, west of Marquette in Upper Michigan. Guerin was killed by the accidental discharge of a firearm.

Thwaites, JR, XXI, 319n24.

Guerrier, Edmund Gasseau Choteau (Hawk, Ed Geary), frontiersman (Jan. 26, 1840-Feb. 22, 1921). The son of William Guerrier and Tah-tah-tois-neh, a full-blood Southern Cheyenne, Ed Guerrier was b. in an Indian village along the Smoky Hill River in Kansas, according to Dixon and Ruth. His mother died in the 1849 cholera epidemic and the boy returned to live with his father, a Fort Laramie trader who sent him in 1851 to St. Mary's Mission, Kansas, to be educated. From there he went to St. Louis University but when his father was killed in 1858 he withdrew and came under the guardianship of Henry F. Mayer, sutler at Fort Lyon, Colorado who once said of his charge, "I know him to be an upright, intelligent, correct young man. He is entirely reliable. I trust every word he says." For several years he occupied himself with a variety of Plains jobs from horse herding to bullwhacking but by 1864 was back with his mother's people, settling with George Bent in Black Kettle's camp. Guerrier and Bent each wrote a letter from the chief to Fort Lyon authorities seeking peace, Guerrier's addressed to Major Wynkoop, commanding. The letters led to a conference with Governor Evans and Chivington near Denver and eventual encampment at Sand Creek, 40 miles northeast of Lyon. Here the band was attacked by Chivington and his Colorado Volunteers November 29, 1864, in what became notorious as the Sand Creek Massacre. Guerrier was not hit, but fled with Bent who was wounded. They rode back toward Lyon, Bent to receive treatment for his wound at his father's home and Guerrier determined to give up, saying he did not care what the soldiers did to him. He surrendered at the fort and was not treated badly. Major Anthony, then commander of the post, questioned him and he gave some information but nothing of importance about the location of the Plains tribes. Unlike George and Charles Bent, Guerrier seems never to have

ridden with the hostiles, but his sympathies were with them. He was hired by Indian Agent Jesse Leavenworth as courier and interpreter and was present at negotiations leading to the Treaty of the Little Arkansas in October 1865. He then worked as trader for various firms but in April 1867 Wynkoop, now agent for the Cheyennes persuaded him to scout and interpret for Hancock; Guerrier with John S. Smith and Dick Curtis interpreted for the General in spring council with the Cheyennes and other Indians, but none of the interpreters could comprehend what Hancock was trying to say and the Indians they translated for understood even less. Hancock ordered Guerrier to remain in the Indian camp all night and report any unusual events; Guerrier saw that the tribesmen, fearing another Sand Creek, were silently stealing away but "he did not hurry to report." Hancock ordered Custer to pursue the withdrawing Indians and Guerrier and Will Comstock served as scouts, although how effectively is uncertain since Bent said that Guerrier habitually rode ahead of the column warning stray hostiles to keep away, the troops were coming. On this campaign Guerrier first came upon the bodies of Kidder and his men, killed by hostiles. He left Custer in July. Guerrier was an interpreter (although not named as such) at the Medicine Lodge Council in October 1867 along with John Smith, George Bent and others; Julia Bent, whom Guerrier later would marry, also was present but not as an interpreter. In the winter of 1868-69 Guerrier scouted for Carr and the 5th Cavalry in operations against the southern Plains Indians, his services extending into the summer of 1869. He "barely missed" the important Battle of Summit Springs, Colorado, in July. Guerrier accompanied the Cheyennes as they gradually withdrew into the present Oklahoma and a restricted reservation and for a time was trader out of Camp Supply. With Comanche interpreter Philip McCusker he accompanied a delegation of chiefs to Washington, D.C., in 1871, his portrait apparently taken at that time by a Bureau of Ethnology photographer (Hyde, facing p. 103). Another Guerrier portait is in Nye (255) and another accompanies the Dixon article. He was granted 440 acres of land along the North Canadian River near Darlington and settled there. In 1875 he married Julia Bent, daughter of William Bent and either Owl Woman or Yellow Woman (the matter is not clear), who survived him, by his marriage becoming brother-in-law of George Bent. Guerrier was interpreter at the important conference between Little Wolf, a Northern Cheyenne and Agent John D. Miles in 1877. He was an important informant for Grinnell on Cheyenne customs, beliefs and history (his summary of Cheyenne history is included in Lubers). To many Oklahoma whites Guerrier became Geary, then Ed or Ned Geary, and Geary, Oklahoma, was named for him in 1898. He died at Geary, near his flourishing ranch , and is buried there. He left his widow and a son, William.

David Dixon, "Edmund Guerrier: A Scout with Custer." Little Big Horn Associates *Research Review,* Vol. XIV, No. 2 (Dec. 1980), 3-8; George E. Hyde, *Life of George Bent.* Norman, Univ. of Okla. Press, 1968; H.L. Lubers, "William Bent's Family and the Indians of the Plains." *Colorado Mag.,* Vol. XIII, No. 1 (Jan. 1936), 19-22; *Sand Creek Massacre; George Bird Grinnell, The Fighting Cheyennes.* Norman, 1956; Blaine Burkey, *Custer, Come At Once!* Hays, Kan., Thomas More Prep, 1976; Stan Hoig, *The Sand Creek Massacre,* Norman, 1974; Wilbur Sturtevant Nye, *Plains Indian Raiders,* Norman, 1968; information from David Dixon; information from Kent Ruth, Geary, Okla.

Guerrier, William, trader (d. Feb. 16, 1858). A Frenchman, his name is spelled variously. As "Bill Garey" he was an interpreter in 1845 at Bent's Fort when Delawares and Cheyennes met in council; he then became a trader at Hardscrabble (Pueblo), Colorado. In partnership with Joseph B. Doyle he took six wagons with goods for the upper Arkansas Indian trade out from Westport in 1846. Two years later at Westport he formed a partnership with Seth Ward for the Indian trade, each supplying about $1,500 in cash for trade goods; they took five large wagons to the upper Arkansas where they secured 6,000 buffalo robes bringing them back to Westport in 1849. By 1851 Guerrier and Ward were in the Platte Valley, operating a trading post at the "Narrows," about 20 miles east of Fort Laramie, Wyoming. Guerrier and Ward apparently attended the assembly of northern Plains tribes in September 1851 at Horse Creek near Scott's Bluff. In 1852 the partners moved their establishment to Sand Point, near the present Guernsey, Wyoming, nine

miles west of Fort Laramie. In addition to the trading, in which Guerrier handled most of the Indian business, Ward that with whites and emigrants, they built a toll bridge across the North Platte River and entered the cattle business to some extent, trading for worn-out oxen from emigrants. Guerrier married a Cheyenne woman and his son, Edmund G. Guerrier became a noted scout and interpreter and barely escaped the Sand Creek Massacre of 1864. William Guerrier was blown up when sparks from his pipe ignited a powder keg at a trading camp on the Niobrara River near the present Lusk, Wyoming.

Barry, *Beginning of West; Sand Creek Massacre,* 156; MM, III.

Guigas, Michel, Jesuit missionary (Jan. 22, 1681-Feb. 6, 1752). B. at Condom, France, he became a Jesuit and reached Canada in 1716. After a year at Quebec he was sent to the Ottawa mission at St. Ignace, on the Strait of Mackinac. In 1727 he commenced a new mission among the Minnesota Sioux, accompanying an expedition to build a fort at Lake Pepin, but the next year the French were forced to leave by hostile Fox Indians (although they returned in 1735). Guigas, descending the Mississippi from Fort Beauharnois was captured October 15, 1728 by Mascouten and Kickapoo Indians. He narrowly escaped being burned at the stake and was held prisoner for five months, but in that time won so great an influence over his captors as to persuade them to conclude a peace with the French and conduct him to the country of the Illinois. He returned when it was possible to Fort Beauharnois and remained in the west, working among the Sioux or at Mackinac until 1739. He went then to Saguenay in eastern Canada for a year, and returned to Quebec where he lived until his death.

Thwaites, JR, LXVIII, 329-30n27; Edward Duffield Neill, *History of Minnesota,* 4th ed. Minneapolis, Minn. Hist. Co., 1882, 183-86, 851-55; DCB, III.

Guilfoyle, John Francis, army officer (Oct. 1, 1853-Oct. 27, 1921). B. in Maryland, he went to West Point becoming a second lieutenant in the 9th Cavalry in 1877, and being assigned to frontier duty at Socorro, Texas. In 1878 he took part in a Ute expedition and escorted a boundary commission party, then served at

Colorado posts in 1878-79. He was scouting and acting engineer officer for the District of New Mexico in 1879-80, and was stationed at Fort Stanton and then Fort Craig in 1880-81. On May 16, 1881, Guilfoyle was sent from Fort Cummings "to hunt down some small bands of hostile Indians who are annoying the settlements" in the Sacramento Mountains east of the Rio Grande. Presumably he was so engaged in early July when Nana, veteran Apache war leader, launched his devastating 1,200-mile raid through southern New Mexico, and Guilfoyle proved his near-nemesis, dogging the trail for long distances, and fighting several sharp skirmishes with the Apaches. It was an epic endeavor. Guilfoyle was breveted first lieutenant for three of his fights with Nana: at White Sands, New Mexico, July 19; in the San Andres Mountains, July 25, and at Monica Springs, west of Socorro, August 3, 1881. He was promoted to first lieutenant November 1. Guilfoyle undertook scouting missions in Kansas and Colorado to 1883, then served at Fort McKinney, Wyoming, and Fort Robinson, Nebraska. He was at Pine Ridge, South Dakota, in 1890, at the start of the Wounded Knee affair and was cited posthumously "for gallantry in action against hostile Sioux Indians near Catholic Mission at White Clay Creek, South Dakota, December 30, 1890." Afterward he served at Fort Robinson from 1891-95, assisted in quelling an Idaho miners' strike in 1895; served at Fort Washakie, Wyoming, and Fort Duchesne, Utah, and was in the Philippines ;in 1900-1901. He retired a colonel in 1917, and died at New Haven, Connecticut.

Heitman; Cullum; Harold Miller, "Nana's Raid of 1881." *Password,* Vol. XIX, No.2, (Summer 1974), 51-70.

Gunnison, John Williams, army officer (Nov. 11, 1812-Oct. 26, 1853). B. at Goshen, New Hampshire, he was graduated from West Point in 1837, appointed a second lieutenant of the 2nd Artillery, the next year joining the topographical engineers with which he served as captain until his death. Gunnison took part in the Seminole War of 1837-38, participated in the removal of Cherokees to Indian Territory in 1838, and returned to the Seminole Wars. He undertook surveys in the southeast and in the Great Lakes region until 1849 when he joined Howard Stansbury's expedition studying the Great Salt Lake country and a central railroad route to the Pacific coast. At Salt Lake City he became interested in the Mormons and their religio-political state, publishing *The Mormons, or Latter-Day Saints, in the Valley of the Great Salt Lake* (1852), which was not unfavorable to the sect and generally well received. From 1851-53 Gunnison took part again in surveys in the Great Lakes region. Early in 1853 he was assigned to conduct a survey across central Colorado and Utah. By October the 37-man party had threaded Cochetopa Pass, followed the Grand River and crossed the Green and had reached Sevier River, northeast of Sevier Lake, Utah. Here Gunnison and seven others were killed in an ambush purportedly laid by Paiutes, although some aspects of the affair are curious, and controversy about it exists to this day, some sources believing that a combined force of Indians and Mormons attacked the Gunnison party. Ghent, writing in the *Dictionary of American Biography,* said "these charges were...discredited by further investigation, and it is generally conceded that the act was committed solely by the Indians in revenge for certain aggressions by parties of emigrants." These "aggressions," if any, were never clearly identified and supported; it is true, however, that the Mormons at the time were engaged in an Indian "war," which commenced by their records July 18, 1853, and would continue until May 23, 1854, with "many Indians" and about 19 whites being killed (including the members of the Gunnison party), but these summaries do not include any aggressions by "gentiles" upon the Indians as a cause of hostilities. Heitman says that Gunnison was "killed by a band of Mormons and Indians." Bancroft, while himself placing no credence in it, reports that "by many the Gunnison massacre has been and is still ascribed to the agency of the Mormons." Wise writes that Gunnison, far from rashly inviting the attack, had operated with experienced caution, knowing he was in the country of potentially hostile Indians, pointed out the singularity of the attack in which rifle fire was an important element while, he said, the Indians "were said to have few if any rifles of their own," and most significantly, that the only things looted from the camp were "notebooks and scientific instruments...,when in ordinary circumstances no Indians would have recognized their value..." Brigham Young, according to Wise, sent out his best Indian man, Dimick Huntington, who "succeeded in recovering" from friendly Indians the instruments and records of the party, although how this was done during an Indian war while the natives, by Mormon accounts, were openly hostile was not explained. It is true that the Mormon guide, William Potter, was among the casualties. Three Indians turned over as perpetrators of the affair, were tried in a federal court at Nephi City, found by a Mormon jury to be guilty of manslaughter, contrary to instructions of the non-Mormon judge who had directed that they either be found guilty of murder or acquitted. They soon escaped from custody.

Literature abundant: DAB; Heitman; Nolie Mumey, *John Williams Gunnison.* Denver, Artcraft Press, 1955; James H. Simpson, *Navaho Expedition...*, ed. by Frank McNitt. Norman, Univ. of Okla. Press, 1964; Bancroft, *Utah;* William Wise, *Massacre at Mountain Meadows.* N.Y., Thomas Y. Crowell Co., 1976; Frank Esshom, *Pioneers and Prominent Men of Utah.* Salt Lake City, Western Epics, 1966.

Gutierrez, Pablo, prospector (fl. 1844). A laborer for John Sutter, Gutierrez reported to Bidwell in March 1844, that he had discovered gold on Bear River, in the Sierra Nevada, but nothing came of it because the Micheltorena revolt intervened. Gutierrez was captured and hanged by José Castro, one of the partisans, probably in late 1844 or 1845.

John Bidwell, *Echoes of the Past.* N.Y., Citadel Press, 1962.

Gutiérrez de Lara, José Bernardo Maximiliano, revolutionist (Aug. 20, 1774-May 13, 1841). B. at Guerrero, Tamaulipas, Mexico, he was a property owner and blacksmith until about 1810 when he joined insurrectionists fighting against Spain. Sent to the Rio Grande area he was dispatched by the rebels to request aid of the United States; he reached Washington late in 1811 with a letter of introduction to James Monroe, then secretary of state, who assured Gutiérrez that if the United States extended aid, it would do so to expand its own territories, not to assist struggling independence movements for their own sake. After some time in the east, Gutiérrez returned to Natchitoches where he associated with U.S. Lieutenant Augustus

William Magee, and together they planned a revolutionary expedition into Spanish Texas. Magee was made colonel and "real commander of the proposed expedition," while Gutiérrez was given the title of General, thus to Mexican settlers "intimating that he was the head" of it. Efforts were made to enlist Texas Indians as auxiliaries. The expedition was composed of "some men of respectable character," but also some freebooters, several of whom had cause to detest Magee for his cruelty to their kind on previous occasions. Probably about 60 men in all were enlisted. Henderson believed that "Major General James Wilkinson, commander of the United States Army in the Southwest, seems to have known and approved of the recruiting of the force," and enlistments were made openly. The expedition crossed the Sabine River and invaded Texas probably on August 12, 1812. Nacogdoches was easily occupied. A month later the march inland was resumed. La Bahía (Matagorda Bay) was occupied, but within three days a strong Royalist army laid siege to the place, the siege lasting four months. Repeated engagements ended with victory for the Republicans, but in early February Magee died "under mysterious circumstances," the Republicans were strongly reinforced, and the Spanish fell back to Bexar (San Antonio) by mid February 1813. The Republicans captured that place, killing a considerable number of Spanish and butchering officers captured, a provisional state government was formed, independence declared, Gutiérrez elected governor and commander-in-chief of the army, holding other positions also. Although the revolutionary force grew in numbers, its discipline declined as did its morale. Yet another victory was won over a large Spanish force under Elizondo June 17, 1813. Gutiérrez was court-martialed, presumably for his role, if any, in the murder of Spanish officers upon the initial capture of Bexar, and he resigned August 4. A fresh Mexican force of about 2,000 men under Arredondo attacked August 18 and destroyed the Republican forces; more than 112 prisoners were shot and the total dead numbered 1,000, while the Spanish loss was 55 killed, 178 wounded and two missing. Gutiérrez was not present at this battle, having left Bexar after his resignation for Natchitoches. He went to New Orleans, declined an offer to operate against Spanish

Pensacola, cooperated in several expeditions into Texas including the James Long operations; his independence role was recognized by Iturbide after Mexican independence, and Gutiérrez returned to Guerrero, served as governor of Tamaulipas and fulfilled military offices. He died at Santiago, Nuevo Leon.

Harry McCorry Henderson, "The Magee-Gutiérrez Expedition." *Southwestern Hist. Quar.*, Vol. LV, No.1 (July 1951), 43-61; Porrua; HT; Bancroft, *North Mexican States and Texas, II,* 17-32.

Guyenne, Alexis F. Xavier de, Jesuit missionary (Dec. 29, 1696-1762). B. at Orleans, France, he became a Jesuit and reached Louisiana with Beaubois in 1726, being sent to the Alabamas Indians where the French had built a post known as Fort Toulouse. He was, in the words of Le Petit, "much exposed to the cruelty of the Savages," and he might be forced "to seek a more abundant harvest on the banks of the Mississippi," the priest warned in 1730. Later Guyenne indeed went to minister to the Arkansas Indians. He was superior of the Illinois mission from 1749-56, and died in that mission area.

Thwaites, JR, LXVII, 342n44, LXVIII, 219-21, LXXI, 169.

Guymonneau, Jean Charles, Jesuit missionary (Mar. 14, 1684-Feb. 6, 1736). B. in France he became a Jesuit and reached Canada in 1715, serving 20 years in the Illinois mission where he died of pleurisy.

Thwaites, JR, LXVIII, 309, 335n50, LXXI, 164.

Guyot, Arnold, explorer (Sept. 28, 1807-Feb. 8, 1884). B. in Switzerland he became one of the first scientific explorers of the Great Smoky Mountains of Tennessee-North Carolina. Earlier visitors had penetrated portions of the range and described something of its flora and fauna, but Guyot studied them with a scientist's care, spent months among them, measured their heights for the first time and had drawn the first map showing the range in detail. A geographer by profession, Guyot taught physical geography and history at the University of Neuchatel until political conditions forced him to emigrate to America. He taught geology and physical geography at Princeton for the rest of his life. Guyot became interested in the physical structure of the Appalachians, during the 1850s exploring them and becoming particularly attached to the Smokies which he considered "the master chain of the Appalachian System."He ascertained as thoroughly as he could with the means at hand the precise elevations of the tallest peaks and the high points of the one "mule path" penetrating the uplift itself, his calculations turning out to be quite accurate by today's standards. He named many of the points he located and a map drawn under direction of his nephew, E. Sandoz, now held by the U.S. Coast and Geodetic Survey makes possible their identification. The Civil War brought a halt to his work in the region which became the Great Smoky Mountains National Park dedicated in 1940 from an area of about 460,000 acres evenly divided between North Carolina and Tennessee; the region had been set aside for a park in 1926 and the reserve itself was established in 1930.

Paul M. Fink, "Early Explorers in the Great Smokies." *East Tenn. Hist. Soc. Pubns.* No.5 (Jan. 1933), 55-68.

Guzman, Francisco de, adventurer (fl. 1538-1543). B. at Seville the illegitimate son of a "gentleman," he joined the De Soto expedition into southern United States and served with it until in 1542 it reached Arkansas. At Chaguate, a southern Caddoan town near the Washita River, Guzman deserted the expedition because, wrote the Gentleman of Elvas, he was fearful of having to pay gambling debts to some other member in the form of an Indian girl, "his concubine," to whom he obviously was deeply attached. De Soto learned of the defection two days later and sent a message back to the chief directing him to find and forward the young man "but the Chief never did." Upon his return to Chaguate De Soto learned that the Spaniard was in another village. He wrote him a letter, "sending ink and paper that he might answer," said that the expedition was about to leave the region for good, reminded the wayward youth "of his being a Christian," added that he was unwilling to leave him among heathen, that his error would be pardoned, and if he was being held against his will to let De Soto know by writing. The messenger brought back the paper with only the man's name and rubric on it, signifying that he was still alive; De Soto sent a dozen mounted men after him, but Guzman hid until they had given up and departed. Preferring his Indian girl and the Indians to civilization he was never heard of again.

Bourne, *De Soto, I.*

Guzman, Juan de, military officer (d. July 5, 1543). B. at Talavera de la Reyna, Spain, he joined the 1539 De Soto expedition into the southern United States and was made a captain of infantry succeeding Maldonado who had been sent on a separate mission. Guzman served capably, as is supposed, throughout the endeavor and had a major role in the sacking of Anilco, a Quapaw village on the south side of the Arkansas River in Arkansas. Guzman was named a joint commander of one of the brigantines with which the expedition survivors sought to descend the Mississippi River. When the flotilla was attacked by hostile Indians in scores of canoes, Guzman was sent with 25 armored men in canoes to repel the enemy. The Indians encircled the Spaniards and "with great fury closed hand to hand with them...," the Christians falling into the water, and, by the weight of their armor, going to the bottom." Eleven whites were killed, among them Guzman; survivors said "they saw the Indians get into the stern of one of their canoes with Juan de Guzman, but whether he was carried away dead or alive, no one could state."

Bourne, *De Soto,* I; *De Soto Expedition Commission.*

Gwin, William McKendree, pioneer (Oct. 9, 1805-Sept. 3, 1885). B. in Sumner County, Tennessee, he was named for a Methodist bishop, William McKendree, his father being a frontier preacher, Indian fighter and friend of Andrew Jackson. Gwin studied medicine at Translyvania University, Lexington, Kentucky, and practiced at Clinton on the Mississippi frontier in order to be with his brother, who shortly was killed in a duel. President Jackson then appointed William Gwin a U.S. marshal for Mississippi and on one occasion sent him to Texas for a secret talk with Sam Houston about possible annexation of Texas. In 1840 he was elected to Congress, serving a single term. Gwin was unfortunate in land speculations and in mid-1849 reached California, instantly becoming involved in politics and the move toward statehood. He was elected senator. His pro-slavery views

were well known and in 1861 he was arrested but paroled in December. In 1863 he went to Paris where he interested Napoleon III in a project to settle southern Sonora and Chihuahua and was named the French mining governor of the territories. He went to Mexico in 1864 but could not persuade Maximilian to take up the plan. Gwin was regarded by the United States as a Confederate agent in Mexico. Grant called him a "rebel of the most virulent order," and Seward wrote to army officers to caution them about "the duke of Sonora." Gwin made a second trip to France, then returned to Mexico where he could foresee the coming downfall of Maximilian; eventually Gwin slipped out of Mexico and reached San Antonio, Texas. The Confederacy had fallen. Gwin was arrested October 2, 1865, at New Orleans. Seven months later he refused parole on condition he leave the United States, but was released anyway, still under parole, May 7, 1866. Among Gwin's contributions to the United States: he served as go-between of Jackson and Houston regarding Texas annexation; he helped bring statehood to California; he was of great importance in founding the Pony Express and advocated transcontinental railways; he was the first man known to have negotiated for sale of Alaska to the United States; he was instrumental in establishing the Atlantic cable, and urged the acquisition of Hawaii by the United States. By 1866, however, his public career was finished and he died in obscurity at New York City. He had been married twice and fathered six children. Gwin appears to have been more loyal to the United States than his wartime actions suggested, proud of his high positions and ambitious for his country, but he was not above "subtle intrigue" at times and certain deviousness beclouded his major achievements.

Rex R. Magee, "The Duke of Sonora." Potomac Corral of Westerners *Corral Dust,* Vol. III, No. 3 (Sept. 1958), 17-19; DAB; BDAC; standard reference works.

Gylam, Lewis J. (Jack), lawman (d. Dec. 1, 1873). A Texan, Gylam had settled in Lincoln County, New Mexico, before the Horrell clan arrived in 1873. In 1872-73 he was the second sheriff of the county, succeeding William Brady after Brady's first term in office. Lawrence G. Murphy had backed him for sheriff but the two fell out and after Gylam was ousted the Texan became bitter and had threatened to kill both Murphy and Murphy's partner, James J. Dolan. Following Gylam's death Murphy accused him of malfeasance in office. When the Horrell brothers arrived Gylam resided at their ranch, perhaps having known them previously. He, Dave Warner and Ben Horrell resisted arrest by Lincoln constable Juan Martinez and when a gunfight erupted Gylam and the others were killed, as was Martinez. A report said that Gylam and Horrell were shot down by aroused townspeople after having surrendered.

Robert N. Mullin notes; Mullin, ed., *Maurice G. Fulton's History of the Lincoln County War.* Tucsonon, Univ. of Ariz. Press, 1968.

H

Hacker, John, borderer (Jan. 1, 1743-April 20, 1821). B. near Winchester, Virginia, three weeks after the arrival of his parents from England, he was a brother of William Hacker Sr., and the first settler on Hacker's Creek, near Buckhannon, present West Virginia. He moved there in 1769; his first crop was destroyed by roaming buffalo. He brought his family to his cabin by 1770, and almost immediately set out to hunt buffalo, perhaps in retaliation. He picked up the trail of a small herd, followed it for days, exploring the land about the Little Kanawha River as he did so, eventually determining that the area was rich in game. On a later occasion, caught in a fierce snow and cold spell in the remote mountains, unable to kindle a fire, he lashed two of his horses together, wrapped himself in his thin blankets and slept in the warm crevice between their bodies. Hacker married and fathered the children who perpetuated the name in the border country; his brother, William may not have married, or if he did so, his family was massacred by Indians. John Hacker died on Hacker's Creek, present West Virginia.

Lucullus V. McWhorter, *Border Settlers of Northwestern Virginia.* Hamilton, O., Republican Pub. Co., 1915.

Hacker, Mary, pioneer (b. 1776). On Dec. 5, 1787, she barely survived a massacre of whites on Hacker's Creek, western Virginia, being struck, stabbed seven times, scalped and left for dead while others were in fact killed by a war party led or accompanied by Leonard Schoolcraft, a renegade. Mary grew to maturity, married a man named Wolf, settled on Wolf's Run, Lewis County, present West Virginia, but never fully recovered; she died of a nasal hemorrhage.

Lucullus V. McWhorter, *Border Settlers of Northwestern Virginia.* Hamilton, O., Republican Pub. Co., 1915.

Hacker, William Sr., borderer (1740-before 1840). B. in England, he was two years older than his brother, John; he was brought by his parents to near Winchester, Virginia, where he was raised. He followed John to the vicinity of Buckhannon, present Lewis County, West Virginia, and became a border rover and Indian fighter, associating with such men as Jesse Hughes and John Cutright. His marital status is uncertain; there are reports that he was married and that his family was massacred by Indians, accounting for his subsequent hatred of them; it is also said that he married a second time, but confirmation is lacking for either marriage. He was a party with Hughes and Cutright in the murderous attack in 1772 on the peaceful Delaware Captain Bull's village, in which about 15 were butchered in retaliation for depredations by quite another band. With Jacob Scott and Elijah Runner he took part in the murder of Bald Eagle, another peacefully-inclined Delaware chief, about the same time; these outrages did much to bring a 20-year Indian war down upon the settlements. On one occasion when Cutright was severely wounded, Hacker tipped a ramrod with a handkerchief, rammed it into the bullet-hole and withdrew the rod, the cloth staunching the flow of blood and saving Cutright's life, whereafter William was known locally as "Surgeon Hacker." It is said he was "the foremost in danger, the bravest in peril & the first to assist in need." Shortly after the slayings of Bald Eagle and Bull, he is said to have moved to the vicinity of Red Banks (Hendersonville), Kentucky, and either died near there or went subsequently to Canada where, one report said, he "became wealthy." He had died before 1840, according to one informant, perhaps many years before.

Lucullus V. McWhorter, *Border Settlers of Northwestern Virginia.* Hamilton, O., Republican Co., 1915.

Hackett, Fred B., wild west show figure (c. 1880-Feb. 16, 1975). B. at Boston, he ran away at 16 to become a Wyoming cowboy. Married in 1905, he and his wife, Lila, joined the Buffalo Bill Wild West Show in 1914, she as trick rider and fancy shot, he as rough rider and in charge of properties. He was a good friend of the Sioux, well acquainted with the Pine Ridge Reservation, often visiting there, was adopted into the Oglala tribe, and for a time was ration clerk at the agency. Hackett became an elevator safety engineer, as his profession. He was internationally known for his collections of Indian artifacts, documentary material on wild west shows, and photographs of performers. He was one of 15 organizers of the Chicago Corral of The Westerners, and died in that city.

Westerners Brand Book, Chicago Corral, Vol. XXXI, No. 11-12 (Jan. -Feb. 1975), p. 84.

Hafen, LeRoy R., historian (Dec. 8, 1893-Mar. 8, 1985). B. at Bunkerville, Nevada, he was graduated in 1916 from Brigham Young University at Provo, Utah, earned a master's degree in history at the University of Utah, his dissertation published as *Handcarts to Zion: The Story of a Unique Western Migration, 1856-1860* (1960), a volume of the *Far West and Rockies* series. Hafen secured his doctorate under Herbert Eugene Bolton at the University of California at Berkeley in 1924. By then he had married Ann Woodbury (May 31, 1893-Dec. 13, 1970) and started a family. He became State historian of Colorado, curator of history at the Colorado Historical Society and editor of *Colorado Magazine,* positions he held until 1954, when he retired from them to join the BYU faculty and devote maximum time to historical research and writing. His output was prodigious, and thoroughly professional, Hafen winning wide esteem for his published works. He wrote about 50 articles appearing in *Colorado,* and among his many books were: *The Overland Mail* (1926), based upon his doctoral thesis: ed., *History of Colorado,* 3 vols. (1927); with W.J. Ghent, *Broken Hand: Chief of the Mountain Men* (1931); ed., *Villard's Past and Present of the Pike's Peak Region* (1932); *Colorado, the Story of a Western Commonwealth* (1933); with F.M. Young, *Fort Laramie and the Pageant of the West* (1938); with C.C. Rister, *Western America* (1941); ed., *The Pike's Peak Gold Rush Guidebooks of 1859* (1941); ed., *Overland Routes to the Gold Fields 1859* (1942); ed. *Colorado Gold Rush: Contemporary Letters and Reports* (1941); with Ann Hafen, *Colorado: a Story of the State* (1943, 1953, 1967); *Colorado and Its People,* 2 vols. (1948); ed. *Ruston of the Rockies* (1950); ed.

Ruxton's Life in the Far West (1951); with Ann Hafen, *the Far West and Rockies Historical Series,* 15 vols. (1954-61); ed., *Mountain Men and The Fur Trade of the Far West,* 10 vols. (1965-72); *Broken Hand: The Life of Thomas Fitzpatrick: Mountain Man, Guide and Indian Agent* (1973), and *Joyous Journey of LeRoy R. and Ann W. Hafen: An Autobiography* (1973). He was visiting professor at the University of Glasgow, Scotland in 1947-48, and spent 1950-51 in research on a Rockefeller fellowship at the Henry E. Huntington Library of San Marino, California. After Ann died, Hafen, as his wife had wished, married her sister, Mary Woodbury. He died at 91 at his winter home, Palm Desert, California.

Westerners, Los Angeles Corral *Branding Iron,* No. III, Sept. 1973, 14-15; *Colorado Heritage News,* July 1985, 2; *LeRoy R. and Ann W. Hafen: Their Writings and Their Notable Collection of Americana Given to Brigham Young University Library,* Provo, Utah, including an extended bibliography.

Haguewood, Jim, killer (fl. 1900). Bartender at Dietrick's saloon, Crawford, Nebraska, where, on December 16, 1900, he shot and mortally wounded Baptiste (Little Bat) Garnier, army scout and hunter. Haguewood "had been having family troubles," and drinking heavily; the dispute was over a matter of little consequence, and Bat had considered Haguewood his friend. Haguewood was tried and acquitted.

James H. Cook, *Fifty Years on the Old Frontier.* New Haven, Yale Univ. Press, 1923; E.A. Brininstool, *Fighting Indian Warriors.* Harrisburg, Pa., Stackpole Co., 1953.

Hahtalekin, Nez Perce chief (c. 1843-Aug. 9, 1877). Josephy gives Hahtalekin's age as 34 on the eve of the 1877 hostilities between the non-treaty Nez Perce and troops in Idaho and Montana. Hahtalekin headed the Paloos (Palouse) band of Nez Perce which counted 16 warriors with buffalo hunting and combat experience, all "reputedly heroic fighters." The band, or tribe had had an extensive homeland until the treaty of 1855 at Walla Walla when they were restricted to a much smaller area near the confluence of Snake and Palouse rivers. The treaty was signed by Hahtal-ee-kin who, if the age given by Josephy for the 1877 chief is correct, may have been his father. Nez Perce chiefs, as a rule, were succeeded by their sons. Hahtalekin joined the other four non-treaty Nez Perce chiefs after the battle of Clearwater. According to Josephy he was killed at the Battle of Big Hole, Montana; McWhorter seems to suggest the possibility that he was killed September 30 in the Battle of Bear Paw Mountains.

Alvin M. Josephy Jr., *Nez Perce Indians and the Opening of the Northwest.* New Haven, Yale Univ. Press, 1965; McWhorter, *Hear Me;* Charles J. Kappler, ed., *Indian Treaties, 1778-1883.* N.Y., Interland Pub. Co., 1972, p. 706.

Haight, Isaac Chauncey, Mormon pioneer (May 27, 1813-Sept. 8, 1886). B. in Windham, Greene County, New York, he early became a convert to the Church of Jesus Christ of Latter-day Saints, and was at Nauvoo, Illinois at the death of Joseph Smith, prophet and founder of the sect. In 1853 Haight was director of church emigration to Utah, among other duties purchasing supplies, and in 1854 was sent to Cedar City, Utah, to take charge of an iron works. He had an important role in the Mountain Meadows Massacre of September 11, 1857, and thereafter went into hiding. Under public pressure, he was excommunicated in 1870 by leaders of the church, but was reinstated by Brigham Young four years later "having evidently been able to shift full responsibility (for the affair) to (John D.) Lee" and others. Haight lived for a time in Manassa, Colorado, and at Thatcher, Arizona, where he took his mother's maiden name of Horton. He died at Thatcher of "affection of the lungs."

Juanita Brooks, *Mountain Meadow Massacre.* Norman, Univ. of Okla. Press, 1966; William Wise, *Massacre at Mountain Meadows.* N.Y., Thomas Y. Crowell Co., 1976.

Haiglar, Catawba chief (d. Aug. 30, 1763). Known to the English colonists as King Haiglar he probably became head chief of the Catawba around 1750. Generally disposed toward peace, he offered his services to the governor of South Carolina when a Cherokee war broke out in 1759, joined Colonel Grant's forces and was active at the hard battle of Etchoe. Haiglar was temperate and May 26, 1756, in a letter requested authorities to cease the sale of alcohol to members of his tribe for which it had ruinous effects. In 1763 the Shawnee waylaid, killed and scalped him when he was returning to South Carolina from the Waxhaw region of North Carolina.

Haiglar was described as of sterling character, just in his dealings, true to his word and greatly beloved by his people.

Hodge, HAI; Swanton, *Indians of the Southeastern United States,* 104.

Hale, bronco Apache (d. Mar. 11, 1890). B. probably on the San Carlos Reservation in Arizona, Hale became an army scout and associate of the Apache Kid, who held the rank of sergeant or first sergeant. He broke out with the Kid following the melee in which Al Sieber was wounded, was retaken (see Pas-lau-tau biography for details), tried twice and was involved in the famed stagecoach bolt near the present Kelvin, Arizona, November 2, 1889, when two whites were killed and one left wounded. Hale was in the fight on the Gila with Lieutenant James Waterman Watson and a detachment, including scouts, and was killed while Pas-lau-tau was wounded mortally.

Jess G. Hayes, *Apache Vengeance.* Albuquerque, Univ. of New Mex. Press, 1954; Dan L. Thrapp, *Al Sieber, Chief of Scouts.* Norman, Univ. of Okla. Press, 1964.

Hale, John, rancher (d. Apr. 14, 1881). Hale is said by Gillett to have been foreman on a Manning brothers' ranch near El Paso, and by Metz to have been apparently running his own ranch, but a friend of the Mannings and their group. When George Campbell was on the dodge briefly following his shooting up of El Paso, he stayed with Hale. In the famous El Paso shootout which ensued, Dallas Stoudenmire killed Hale after Hale had killed former Texas Ranger Gus Krempkau. Hale's body was taken to his ranch for burial, the remains later transferred to the present Concordia Cemetery site. Hale was married.

James B. Gillett, *Six Years with the Texas Rangers.* New Haven, Yale Univ. Press, 1963; Leon CLaire Metz, *The Shooters.* El Paso, Mangan Books, 1976.

Hale, Owen, army officer (July 23, 1843-Sept. 30, 1877). B. in New York, he enlisted in the 7th New York Cavalry October 23, 1861, and was commissioned a second lieutenant May 9, 1863, emerging from the Civil War a first lieutenant and brevet captain. He was commissioned a first lieutenant in the 7th U.S. Cavalry July 28, 1866, becoming a captain March 1, 1869. Hale served in the 7th under the overall command of Miles in 1877 as they sought to trap Chief Joseph and his Nez Perce in the Bear Paw Mountains of Montana, short of their Canadian goal. The morning of September 30 was "extremely stormy and inclement." Brady quotes Hale: "My God! Have I got to go out and be killed in such cold weather!" He was killed instantly within twenty yards of the Indians as the Nez Perce decimated the attacking units of the 7th Cavalry advancing upon their positions.

Heitman; Cyrus Townsend Brady, *Northwestern Fights and Fighters.*   Garden City, N.Y., Doubleday, Page & Co., 1923.

Haley, John, scout (fl. 1868). Haley was one of about 50 frontiersmen under George A. Forsyth at the battle of Beecher Island, being wounded slightly on its first day, September 17, 1868. Haley had died by 1905, according to the *Beecher Island Annual* for that year.

George A. Forsyth, "A Frontier Fight." *Harpier's New Monthly Mag.,* Vol. XCI, No. DXLI (June 1895), 56.

Half King (Scrunihatha, Tanacharison), Seneca chief (c. 1700-Oct. 1, 1754). He first came to prominence about 1748 when he lived near Logstown, Pennsylvania. It was to Half King that most highranking visitors to Indians of the Ohio region came for advice and assistance. Half King was a noted figure on the Indian side of a treaty with Virginia commissioners in 1752; the pact acknowledged the tacit right of Virginia to move into the area. Half King accompanied Washington on his 1753 journey to the Ohio country and his 1754 military expedition to Fort Necessity, the chief asserting he had killed Jumonville, the French officer, during skirmishing at Great Meadows, Pennsylvania, May 28, 1754 in revenge for the French slaying of his father, as he believed. The chief has sometimes been confused with a Huron chief, Half King of Sandusky, Ohio. The Seneca Half King died of pneumonia at the home of John Harris on the site of today's Harrisburg, Pennsylvania.

Hodge, HAI.

Hall, Charles Scott, army officer (July 6, 1851-May 2, 1929). B. in Indiana he went to West Point and was commissioned a second lieutenant in the 13th Infantry June 15, 1876, and after service in the south and east was assigned to Fort Cummings, New Mexico, in 1878. In 1882 during the Loco emeute from

San Carlos, Arizona, he commanded Indian scouts, operating for a time with Forsyth in Mexico and locating the camp of Mexican Lieutenant Colonel Lorenzo Garcia who had fought the Apaches and now directed Forsyth to leave Mexican soil forthwith, which Forsyth did. Hall also commanded Indian scouts during the Geronimo campaign out of Ford Bayard, New Mexico. He became a first lieutenant March 1, 1887, and resigned February 15, 1897. He followed civilian pursuits for the remainder of his life except that he was captain of two Illinois Volunteer regiments during the Spanish American War, neither called to active duty. He died at New Orleans, Louisiana.

Cullum; Dan L. Thrapp, *Al Sieber, Chief of Scouts.*   Norman, Univ. of Okla. Press, 1964.

Hall, Hugh, frontiersman (1772-post 1828). B. at Carlisle, Pennsylvania, he joined the Lewis and Clark Expedition, then settled at St. Louis and was still living in 1828, according to Clark.

History of the Expedition Under the Command of Lewis and Clark, ed. by Elliott Coues.   New York, Dover Pubns, Inc., 1965; Clarke, *Lewis and Clark.*

Hall, (Jesse) Leigh, lawman (Oct. 9, 1849-Mar. 17, 1911. B. at Lexington, North Carolina, he reached Texas in 1869 where he changed the spelling of his middle name to Lee and dropped the first name, becoming famous in Texas history simply as Lee Hall. He was city marshal of Sherman, Texas, a deputy sheriff of Denison and was named a second lieutenant of the Special Force, a division of the Texas Rangers, under Captain L.H. McNelly. In this organization Hall served from August 10, 1876 to February 29, 1880 and with it he achieved a reputation as one of the greatest of Texas Rangers. Hall soon became a captain. He helped break up the Sutton-Taylor feud, one of the most noted in Texas annals, and arrested King Fisher, no mean feat, and other criminals only slightly less notorious. Shortly after leaving the Rangers Hall married; he fathered five daughters. He managed a ranch for five years, served as agent for the Anadarko Indians and was indicted for embezzlement and making false claims but the suits were dismissed for lack of evidence. In the Spanish American War he raised two companies of volunteers and served in the Philippines as leader of the Macabebe Scouts, receiving a brevet for gallantry and being mustered out October 6, 1900. He was buried at the National Cemetery at San Antonio, Texas.

Dora Neill Raymond, *Captain Lee Hall of Texas.* Norman, Univ. of Okla. Press, 1940; Walter Prescott Webb, *The Texas Rangers.* Boston, Houghton Mifflin Co., 1935, 288-94; Robert W. Stephens, *Texas Ranger Indian War Pensions.* Quanah, Tex., Nortex Press, 1975.

Hall, Martin Hardwick, historian (Aug. 30, 1925-Jan. 18, 1981). B. at Calexico, California, he was graduated from the University of New Mexico in 1950, earned a master's degree from the University of Alabama in 1951 and a doctorate from Louisiana State University in 1957. He taught at several southern universities and colleges before 1964 when he joined the history department of the University of Texas at Arlington, becoming a full professor of history. He wrote four books on Texas and Texans during the Civil War including *Sibley's New Mexico Campaign* (1960) and his masterwork, *The Confederate Army of New Mexico* (1978), compiled with Sam Long. Among his many published papers two were of particular frontier interest: "Captain George M. Frazer's Arizona Rangers, C.S.A.," *Password,* Volume XIX, No. 2 (Summer 1974), 71-77, and "Captain Thomas J. Mastin's Arizona Guards, C.S.A.," *New Mexico Historical Review,* Volume XLIX, No. 2 (April 1974), 143-51.

Council on Abandoned Military Posts' *Headquarters Heliogram,* Nov. 1981; information from Sandra L. Myres.

Hall, Sharlot Mabraith, writer, historian (Oct. 27, 1870-Apr. 9, 1943). B. in Lincoln County, Kansas, she was brought by her parents to the Prescott, Arizona, region in 1881. She commenced writing poetry at an early age, and became interested in the history and lore of central Arizona. She never married. Miss Hall was associate editor of *Out West* magazine in 1906-1907, but devoted her life to preserving the history of her chosen area, and for many years was curator of what became the Sharlot M. Hall Museum at Prescott. One of her poems was important in the admission of Arizona as a state in its own right in 1912. Miss Hall became a revered and beloved figure in her adopted land. She published a volume of poetry, *Cactus and Pine,* in 1911, and another appeared after her death, *Poems of a Ranch Woman.* She died at Prescott.

Ariz. Hist. Soc. archives; Sharlot M. Hall Museum archives.

Hall, William Preble, army officer (June 11, 1848-Dec. 4, 1927). B. in Randolph County, Missouri, he was graduated from West Point, assigned to the 19th Infantry in 1868 and a year later transferred to the 5th Cavalry, joined at Fort McPherson, Nebraska, took part in the Republican River expedition and an engagement with hostile Indians at Prairie Dog Creek. He reached Arizona with the regiment in 1872. Out of Fort Crittenden he engaged in three Apache skirmishes. In 1876 he participated in the Big Horn and Yellowstone expedition and engaged in the War Bonnet (Hat) Creek action against the Cheyennes and Slim Buttes affair with the Sioux. Hall was quartermaster for the Wind River expedition of 1877 and for field operations in Wyoming in 1878, and was chief quartermaster for an operation against Colorado Utes in 1879, participating in raising the siege at Milk River. At Rifle Creek October 20, 1879, he successfully led a small command out of a perilous situation through a screening of superior hostile forces, winning a Medal of Honor for the feat. Hall was made captain in 1876, major in 1893, lieutenant colonel in 1897 and colonel in 1901. He was assistant adjutant general for the Department of Puerto Rico in 1899-1900, promoted to Brigadier General and was adjutant general of the army from March 5, 1907. He retired June 11, 1912.

George F. Price, *Fifth Cavalry.*

Haller, Granville Owen, army officer (Jan. 31, 1819-May 2, 1897). B. at York, Pennsylvania, he was commissioned a second lieutenant of the 4th Infantry November 17, 1839, served at Fort Leavenworth and Fort Gibson, Indian Territory, and was attached briefly to Old Fort Holmes at the mouth of Little River, Indian Territory. In October 1841 he was sent to Florida, accompanying Belknap's expedition into the Big Cypress Swamp after hostile Seminoles in December. He served in Texas in the army of occupation, became a first lieutenant July 12, 1846, and won two brevets in the Mexican War. He became a captain

January 1, 1848. From New York he embarked on the U.S. Store Ship Fredonia around Cape Horn to Vancouver Barracks, Washington Territory, where he arrived in June 1853 and was assigned to Fort Dalles, Oregon. Following the Ward wagon train massacre of 1854 just east of Boise in which Shoshones killed 19 of 21 whites, Haller with 26 enlisted men and as many volunteers left The Dalles and "chastised in a measure" the Indians believed responsible, Burns describing it as an "Indian hanging expedition." The next year Haller scouted to the headwaters of the Missouri River, then returned to The Dalles where he found the Indians "greatly excited," the Yakimas under arms and their agent, A.J. Bolan, or Bolon, murdered by them. Haller led an expedition of 102 men and four officers into the Yakima country, engaged the hostiles in the Simcoe Valley, but after three days was forced to withdraw with 21 casualities to the Indians 40. Haller made further expeditions into the Yakima country under Major Rains and Colonel George Wright in 1855 and 1856. He then took part in western Washington operations until ordered to Fort Mojave, Arizona, in 1860 and to Washington D.C., serving as a major in the Civil War in the East until he was dismissed July 25, 1863 by Secretary Stanton for alleged "disloyal conduct and the utterance of disloyal sentiments," a charge later refuted. He was commissioned a colonel in the infantry July 1, 1879 (to rank from 1873), assigned to the 23rd Infantry and retired February 6, 1882, living thereafter at Seattle. He was married and fathered children.

Heitman; Powell; Bancroft, *Washington, Idaho and Montana;* Robert Ignatius Burns, S.J., *The Jesuits and the Indian Wars of the Northwest.* New Haven, Yale Univ. Press, 1966.

Ham, Zachariahs, frontiersman (fl. 1825-1836). An able trapper and mountain man, nothing is known of his birth and little of his death. As leader of a party of trappers he discovered Ham's Fork, a tributary of Black's Fork of the Green River about 1825. He reached Los Angeles in 1831 with the William Wolfskill party. He was reported to have drowned in the Colorado River, perhaps about 1836.

Bancroft, *Pioneer Register;* John E. Baur article, MM, Vol. IX.

Hamblin, Albert, Snake Indian (c. 1842-post 1859). Albert was adopted by Jacob Hamblin, Mormon Indian specialist, about 1850, lived with the Hamblin family three years in northern Utah and six years in southern Utah. On May 20, 1859, he was sent by Hamblin to Carleton, investigating the Mountain Meadows Massacre of September 11, 1857, to be interviewed; Albert spoke "very good English." He described the massacre which he said he and another English-speaking Indian boy, John, had witnessed; Albert blamed Indians entirely for the butchery, no doubt being coached carefully before testifying. Carleton said that two of the recovered children from the emigrants' train had pointed Albert out "as an Indian whom they saw kill their two sisters," and added that "Albert had evidently been trained in his statement..., keeping always the Mormons in the background and the Indians conspicuously the prominent figures and actors," but under close questioning admitted that Prime Coleman, Amos Thornton, Richard Robinson and a man named Dickinson were present.

James Henry Carleton, "Mountain Meadows Massacre." Hse. Exec. Doc. 605, 57th Cong., 1st Sess., (Serial 4377).

Hamblin, Jacob, missionary to Indians (Apr. 12, 1819-Aug. 31, 1886). B. at Salem, Ohio, he settled near Spring Prairie, Wisconsin, when he was converted to Mormonism. His wife, although baptized in the new faith, soon deserted him, and Hamblin migrated to Utah, reaching Salt Lake City September 1, 1850. He was appointed in 1857 head of the Santa Clara Indian Mission, five miles from St. George, in southern Utah. His connection with the Mountain Meadow Massacre in September 1857, was oblique. He did not attend the slaughter, although his half brother, Oscar, did so, but Jacob collected and helped place the surviving children and received $2,961.76 from the federal government for his part in caring for them. Hamblin may have been instrumental in averting a repetition of the debacle on another train, the Duke party. Originally a friend of John D. Lee, there was a falling out, and Hamblin's testimony was pivotal in the trial which led to Lee's execution for the Mountain Meadow affair, Lee referring to Hamblin as "the fiend of hell" as a result. Leading a party into northern Arizona in 1858, he became the first since Escalante to cross the Colorado River, in those regions. He visited the seven villages of the Hopis, and left four missionaries, including his younger brother, among them. Hamblin made almost annual trips into northern Arizona, coming to know the country thoroughly, his work largely instrumental in the establishment of several Mormon settlements along the Little Colorado River and elsewhere. He was the first white man to thoroughly explore the area, the first to go down the Colorado River through Black and Boulder Canyons in a boat, his account assisting the later voyages of J.W. Powell for whom Hamblin served occasionally as guide. In 1874 he went alone into the Navaho country to avert a war; captured by hostiles, he later was released. "Jacob Hamblin, with his ideal of friendliness, of fair-dealing and peace... did more single-handed to bring about a mutual understanding than all the soldiers that ever marched into Arizona." So faithful was he that Brigham Young, December 15, 1876, gave him the title, "Apostle to the Lamanites," the Lamanites, in Mormon teachings, being the Indian peoples. Hamblin moved in 1879 to Springerville, Arizona, where poverty gradually overtook him and he wandered, to Alpine, to Pleasanton, New Mexico, to Old Mexico, and back again to Pleasanton where he died. First buried there, his body subsequently was moved to Alpine. A tall, lean, quiet man, Hamblin was deeply religious and considered thoroughly honest by all who knew him. He never killed an Indian, although narrowly avoiding it once when his weapon missed fire.

Literature abundant; Juanita Brooks, "Jacob Hamblin, Apostle to the Indians." *Ariz. Highways,* Vol. XIV, No. 4 (Apr. 1943), 31-35; Juanita Brooks, *The Mountain Meadows Massacre.* Norman, Univ. of Okla. Press, 1962; Juanita Brooks, *John D. Lee.* Glendale Calif., Arthur H. Clark Co., 1962; Paul Bailey, *Jacob Hamblin, Buckskin Apostle.* Los Angeles, Westernlore Press, 1948; Charles S. Peterson, *Take Up Your Mission: Mormon Colonizing Along the Little Colorado River 1870-1900.* Tucson, Univ. of Ariz. Press, 1973.

Hamblin, Oscar, Mormon pioneer (Apr. 4, 1833-pre-1892). B. in the east (his parents reached Utah in 1850), he was a half-brother of the Mormon Indian specialist Jacob

Hamblin, and was with John D, Lee at the Mountain Meadows Massacre of September 11, 1857, as Jacob was not, according to *Mormonism Unveiled,* p. 379. This says he died before publication of the book in 1892.

Frank Esshom, *Pioneers and Prominent Men of Utah.* Salt Lake City, Western Epics, 1966; *Mormonism Unveiled;* Juanita Brooks, *Mountain Meadows Massacre.* Norman, Univ. of Okla. Press, 1962.

Hamell, Augustin, frontiersman (1800-c. 1860). Perhaps b. in Canada, Hamell may have come to the upper Missouri country after consolidation of the North West Company and Hudson's Bay Company in 1821. He was at Fort McKenzie in 1835 and also lived at various times at Fort Clark, Fort Union and Fort Benton. He built several trade houses known as Hamell's Houses. He was fluent in Blackfoot and married a Blackfoot woman, the union solemnized several years afterward by Father Point in 1846. Hamell had had one daughter by a previous marriage, and had ten children by the second, one daughter, Mrs. Susan Arnoux, still living in 1940 at Browning, Montana. Hamell was an interpreter for Isaac Stevens at Fort Benton September 21, 1853, called by Stevens "an intelligent voyageur who had been in the country many years." Sometime later Hamell moved his family downriver in a mackinaw boat to Sioux City and settled on a farm near Yankton, South Dakota. He died at 59. Armells Creek, a Fergus County, Montana, branch of the Missouri River, was named for him in one of his name-variants.

Montana Contributions, Vol. X, 1940, 261-62.

Hamilton, pioneers (d. Sept. 11, 1857). A family of this name, composition unknown, perished with the Fancher emigrant wagon train, wiped out by Mormons and Mormon-led Indians at Mountain Meadows, southwestern Utah.

William Wise, *Massacre at Mountain Meadows.* N.Y., Thomas Y. Crowell Co., 1976.

Hamilton, James A: *see* Archibald Palmer

Hamilton, John Morrison, army officer (June 1, 1839-July 1, 1898). B. in Ontario, Canada, he enlisted in the 33rd New York Infantry May 1, 1861, being commissioned a second lieutenant in the 9th U.S. colored Infantry regiment December 24, 1863, and ending the Civil War a first lieutenant. He served in Texas, helped organize the 9th U.S. Cavalry, June 6, 1867, became a captain in the 39th Infantry and December 30, 1870, transferred to the 5th Cavalry, joining the regiment at Fort McPherson, Nebraska in July. In January 1872 he reached Camp McDowell, Arizona. Hamilton took part in the Apache campaign of 1873, was engaged in the fight at Pinto Creek and in the spring of 1874 participated in operations against Apaches, having a role in five fights; he was breveted to major for his part in tnem. In June 1875 he was stationed at Fort Riley, Kansas and served against hostile Indians in Kansas, in Nebraska and on the Powder River campaign of 1876. Hamilton performed field service in northern Wyoming in 1877, in Idaho in 1878 and with the Ute Expedition of 1880, then was stationed at Fort Robinson, Nebraska. Hamilton was killed at the battle of San Juan in Cuba.

Heitman; Price, *Fifth Cavalry*.

Hamilton, Joseph Varnum, fur trader (1811-Aug. 23, 1867). B. at Fort Madison, Iowa, the son of army officer Thomas Hamilton, he joined the American Fur Company "at an early date." At one time he was an acting Indian agent. He lived in South Dakota late in life and died at Fort Randall.

Montana Contributions, Vol. X, 1940, 280.

Hamilton, Louis McLane, army officer (July 21, 1844-Nov. 27, 1868). B. in New York City and raised at Williamsburg on Long Island and Poughkeepsie, New York, Hamilton was a grandson of Alexander Hamilton of Washington's Cabinet, while his maternal grandfather was Louis McLane, U.S. Senator and Secretary of the Treasury and of State in Jackson's Cabinet. Louis Hamilton enlisted July 21, 1862, and was commissioned a second lieutenant of the 3rd Infantry September 27. He commanded a company at the battle of Fredericksburg, won a brevet at Chancellorsville and another at Gettysburg. He was commanding at Fort Lyon, Colorado, when commmissioned July 28, 1866, a captain in the newly organized 7th Cavalry. June 24, 1867, Hamilton with a small detachment turned back an estimated 45 attacking Sioux near the forks of the Republican River. Later in the summer of 1867, Hamilton commanded a

detachment which followed Custer east from the Plains Indian warfront in the celebrated incident which led to Custer's court-martial although Hamilton, of course, was not implicated in any wrong-doing. In the November 1868 campaign toward the Washita, Hamilton had been assigned officer of the day duties with the rear guard, but pleaded to move toward the expected fight with his command, and secured a substitute officer for his official duty, thus freeing himself to advance with Custer. Hamilton charged into the village of Black Kettle's Cheyennes at Custer's side and was killed instantly by a single bullet through the region of the heart. Suggestions that his death may have been from a misdirected, or even intended, soldier's bullet, seem unwarranted. He was buried at Camp Supply, Indian Territory, with Sheridan, Custer and other officers as pall-bearers. In January 1869, Hamilton was reburied at Poughkeepsie, New York, where his parents lived.

Hamilton's personnel file, Nat. Archives; George A. Custer, *My Life on the Plains*. Lincoln, Univ. of Nebr. Press, 1966; Stan Hoig, *Battle of the Washita*. Garden City, N.Y., Doubleday & Co., 1976.

Hamilton, William T., frontiersman (Dec. 6, 1822-May 24, 1908). B. in upper England, he reached New Orleans in 1825 and eventually St. Louis. In 1842 he joined Bill Williams and George Perkins in a trading-trapping expedition to the Rocky Mountains, the party disbanding in 1845 at Fort Laramie. Hamilton continued to roam and trap the upper Rockies, visited St. Louis briefly in 1848, returned to the mountains and by July 4, 1849, had reached California where Hamilton and others engaged in Indian fighting and killing for some years, continuing this occupation as far north as Washington Territory. In about 1859 he established a trading post at the present Missoula, Montana, was elected sheriff; in 1864 he sold the post and moved to Fort Benton, Montana, trading and being elected sheriff of Chouteau County, later becoming a deputy U.S. marshal. In 1869 he moved to southern Montana, in 1876 joined Crook for the Rosebud campaign, then returned to the present Columbus, Montana, where he lived the last 29 years of his life. In 1905 he published his book. He died at Billings.

Hamilton, *My Sixty Years on the Plains*. ed. by Donald J. Berthong, Norman, Univ. of Okla. Press, 1960; L. Custer Keim article, MM, Vol. IX.

Hamner, George, Rough Rider (May 23, 1873-Feb. 6, 1973). B. at Faber's Mill near Charlottesville, Virginia, he became a telegrapher and worked for Western Union from Kenova, West Virginia, to Wagon Mound, New Mexico. He reported by telegraph all 21 rounds of the John L. Sullivan-James J. Corbett championship fight at New Orleans September 7, 1892. May 6, 1898, he enlisted at Santa Fe in Troop F, of the New Mexico squadron of what became known as the Rough Riders. Hamner after service in Cuba was mustered out in August 1898, went to Virginia Medical School, became a physician in 1903, served as a medical officer in World War I and died at veterans hospital near Tampa, Florida. Only two other Rough Riders survived him, Frank Brito and Jesse Langdon.

Dale L. Walker, "The Last of the Rough Riders." *Montana: Mag. of Western Hist.*, Vol. XXIII, No. 3 (July 1973), 40-50.

Hancock, James C., pioneer (July 27, 1860-Dec. 29, 1937). B. at Clermont, near Indianapolis, he was a direct descendant of the John Hancock who signed the Declaration of Independence. He reached Arizona and on January 19, 1881, arived at Galeyville on the eastern slopes of the Chiricahua Mountains. He became the "law" at Galeyville and nearby Paradise, and occasionally entered the cattle business, but with no marked success. Hancock knew most of the gunmen, outlaws, rustlers and characters of southeastern Arizona; his recollections were pungent and generally accurate. He was at Tombstone, Arizona, when Johnny-Behind-the-Deuce was saved from a lynch mob, and denied that Wyatt Earp had anything to do with preserving the man's life. Hancock was convinced Virgil Earp, not Brocius, killed city marshal Fred White in order to get his job; in this he was mistaken. Hancock was a justice of the peace, postmaster and storekeeper at Paradise and though he died at Douglas, Arizona, his body was returned to Paradise for burial.

AHS Archives; Ed Bartholomew, *Wyatt Earp: The Man & The Myth.* Toyahvale, Texas, Frontier Book Co., 1964.

Hancock, Winfield Scott, army officer (Feb. 14, 1824-Feb. 9, 1886). B. at Montgomery Square, near Norristown, Pennsylvania. Graduated from West Point in 1844. Participated in Mexican War, winning brevets at Contreras and Churubusco. Served in Third Seminole War in 1850's, the Utah Expedition of 1857, and was made Brigadier General of Volunteers in 1861, serving with distinction in the Civil War, particularly at Gettysburg, where he was badly wounded. He became a Major General in the regular army in 1866. In the summer of 1867 he led the costly and ineffective expedition against hostile Cheyennes and others on the central plains, as a side issue of which indirectly pressed for the court-martial of George Armstrong Custer on charges of being absent without proper leave from his command, causing deserters to be shot without trial, and other alleged offenses. Subseqently Hancock was in command of the Department of Louisiana and Texas, 1867; Department of Dakota, 1870-72; Division of the Atlantic, 1872-86, and Department of the East. He was nominated for President by the Democratic Party, 1880. Hancock was an able officer, better in formal battle than in Indian campaigning. He earned high praise from Grant and others under whom he served. He was buried at Norristown, Pennsylvania.

DAB; Lawrence A. Frost, *Court-Martial of General George Armstrong Custer.* Norman, Univ. of Okla. Press, 1968.

Hand, Dora (Fannie Keenan), actress (c. 1844-Oct. 4, 1878). A variety actress of considerable experience, she was married to Theodore Hand, a musician, but divorced him in Indiana. She reached St. Louis from Memphis in 1876 and two years later moved on to Dodge City, Kansas, where she appeared as a vocalist in several variety shows. She lived with a friend, Fannie Garrettson, on the south side of the tracks and was shot and killed accidentally by an assassin who apparently had hoped to slay a male companion of Miss Garrettson (some said this man was Mayor James H. Kelley), who was absent the night of the incident. James W. Kenedy was charged with the slaying, but was acquitted.

Nyle H. Miller, Joseph W. Snell, *Great Gunfighters of the Kansas Cowtowns, 1867-1886.* Lincoln, Univ. of Neb. Press, 1967.

Handsome Lake, Seneca prophet (1735-Aug. 10, 1815). B. at Conawagus on the Genesee River, the half-brother of Cornplanter, he became chief of the Turtle Clan of the Senecas. As a young man he was frequently drunk, and finally suffered an extended illness. About 1800 he collapsed, apparently dead, his body was dressed in ceremonial clothing and prepared for burial. When all had gathered for the death ceremony he returned to consciousness and from that day became a teacher and prophet. His religion bore obvious Christian influences, but was opposed by missionaries, although it has endured side by side with Christianity. For 15 years Handsome Lake said he was instructed from time to time by three messengers from the Creator. He formed a code of 130 sections his people were to follow. They included admonitions to shun liquor, respect the poor, that a rich man could not enter heaven, to obey Indian customs and the government, that greatness came from service, not possessions, to further education. He received support from President Jefferson and others, and was of great influence for good among his people. He died at Onandaga.

CE; "Handsome Lake," by Aren Akweks, in *Sa-Ko-Ri-On-Nie-Ni: Our Great Teacher,* Hogansburg, N.Y., Akwesasne Counselor Org., St. Regis Mohawk Reservation, n.d.; *Handbook of Indians,* 15.

Handy, John Christopher, surgeon (Oct. 20, 1844-Sept. 25,1891). B. at Newark, New Jersey, he went with his parents to California in 1853 and at 19, ten years later, earned a degree from San Francisco's Cooper Medical School. He became a contract surgeon with the army and in 1867 was assigned to Fort Apache, Arizona, where he served two years, then to Camp Thomas, Arizona. He learned to speak Apache "fluently." In 1868 Cochise, the militant Chiricahua Apache, sent word to Department of Arizona Commander Thomas C. Devin that he was willing to talk peace. Devin directed Captain Frank W. Perry with Dr. Handy and, oddly enough, Mrs. Handy, who may have been Apache, with a Coyotero guide to meet the hostile chieftain. The talk reportedly was cordial but little came of it. Nothing more is heard of this Mrs. Handy. On October 28, 1870, Handy killed the post trader named Huey at Fort Thomas, fled to Tucson, was tried and acquitted with the defense that the affair was one of "honor." In July 1878 Handy married for a second time, on this occasion to Mary Page Scott (d. Jan. 28, 1893), daughter of Larcena Pennington Page Scott, and by her fathered four boys and one girl. He earned many friends and as many enemies as a Southern Pacific railroad company physician and chancellor of the University of Arizona; Handy was a man of "wild and terrible temper," and in the words of Arizona Historical Society secretary Edith Stratton Kitt "a veritable Dr. Jekyll and Mr. Hyde." Handy was mortally shot by attorney Francis J. Heney whom he had accosted at Tucson for conducting Handy's wife's divorce proceedings. Heney (c. 1859-Oct. 13, 1937), later became a California Superior Court Judge in the San Francisco area. Handy's son, John C., who had sworn to kill Heney, changed his mind upon meeting him and they became fast friends, remaining so for the rest of Heney's life.

Ariz. Hist. Soc. archives, Hayden file.

Hanks, O.C. (Camilla, Comelio, Charley Jones, Deaf Charley), desperado (c. 1863-Apr. 16, 1902). Described as "somewhat deaf" in a Pinkerton wanted circular, Hanks was born at Cuero, DeWitt County, Texas, of worthy ancestry; by legitimate profession he was a cowboy. He was charged with rape, wanted in New Mexico for murder, and in 1881 went to Montana with a herd of longhorns and "worked on cattle ranges for several years as a peaceable, well-liked cowboy." He was arrested in Teton County, Montana, in 1892 and given ten years for holding up a Northern Pacific train near Big Timber; he was released April 30, 1901. He joined Butch Cassidy, Longabaugh and Harvey Logan for the holdup July 3, 1901, of a Great Northern train near Wagner, Montana. In this affair $65,000 in unsigned bank notes was taken, difficult to pass. The gang went to San Antonio, Texas, where Hanks was killed in his boarding house while resisting arrest. He was described by the Pinkerton agency as 5 feet, 10 inches, in height, 156 pounds, of good build with a sandy complexion, auburn hair and blue eyes.

Thomas M. Stell, "The Killing of Camilla Hanks." *Frontier Times,* Vol. 53, No. 2 (Feb.-Mar. 1979), 9, 61; Charles Hall, *Documents of Wyoming Heritage.* Cheyenne, Wyo. Bicentennial Commiss., 1976;

Charles Kelly, *Outlaw Trail: The Story of Butch Cassidy.* N.Y., Bonanza Books, 1959.

Hanna, Robert, army officer (January 17, 1848-Dec. 4, 1908). B. in Attica, Indiana, he was graduated from West Point and commissioned a second lieutenant in the 6th Cavalry in 1872. In Arizona Hanna became a scout commander and in May 1877 went south from the Hualapais country in northwestern Arizona to Fort Huachuca near the Sonora border with 35 Hualapais scouts and Dan O'Leary, chief of scouts. When the Mimbres Apaches broke out of San Carlos, Hanna was on a scout in the vicinity and with Rucker's 6th Cavalry command engaged in an arduous and lengthy pursuit of part of the fleeing hostiles to the east and northeast, catching up and causing them casualties and taking captives. He also was engaged from time to time in scouting along the border, sometimes after Mexican smugglers and again after Apache hostiles. In 1878 he was assigned to West Point and promoted to first lieutenant; by 1882 he again was in Arizona where on one occasion he overtook Mexican smugglers pretending to be Apaches to avoid customs difficulties. Hanna became a captain in 1888 and for a time commanded Fort Wingate, New Mexico, and Fort Lewis, Colorado. He was in the field during the Pine Ridge campaign in Dakota in 1890-91. Hanna retired for disability in line of duty February 24, 1891. He engaged in the railroad business in California in 1891-92 and was interested in a company making Navy torpedoes thereafter. He died, probably at Sag Harbor, Long Island.

Heitman; Cullum; Dan L. Thrapp, *Victorio and the Mimbres Apaches.* Norman, Univ. of Okla. Press, 1974; information from David Perry Perrine.

Haozous, Sam, Mimbres Apache (1868-Dec. 5, 1957). A great grandson of Chief Mahko of the Bedonkohes and descended on his mother's side from Mangas Coloradas, he and his people were taken from the Warm Springs Reservation in New Mexico to San Carlos, Arizona, in 1877. Sam was with Victorio in the breakout from San Carlos in September 1877, and was returned there from New Mexico with Loco. Haozous was with the Loco band seized at San Carlos by Juh and driven in 1882 to the Sierra Madre. He returned to Arizona after the Crook 1883 expedition into Mexico. In May of 1885 he went out with Geronimo and remained out until the surrender of that band in early September 1886 when with the rest of his people he was exiled to Florida. In Alabama he married a San Carlos woman and fathered one son, Cecil Haozous; his wife returned to Arizona and Sam married again, fathering two children, his wife and infant children dying at Fort Sill. Sam then married Blossom White, half-white daughter of interpreter George Wratten, fathering five more children. Sam Haozous died at Apache, Oklahoma. His tape-recorded life story, which requires some explanation and interpretation, was printed verbatim in the April 1978, *Tel-Ectric Topics,* Kingfisher, Oklahoma.

Griswold; Angie Debo to author, June 7, June 19, 1978.

Harby, Levi Myers, naval officer, soldier (1793-1870). B. at Charleston, South Carolina, he enlisted in the Navy in 1807, fought in the War of 1812, was captured by the British and escaped from Dartmoor after 18 months. He may have commanded a ship under Decatur in the so-called Algerine War of 1815 against the Barbary pirates. He resigned his commission December 4, 1827, fought in the Seminole War, and joined American volunteers in the 1835-36 Texas struggle for independence. Recommissioned a captain, he later fought with the Confederacy in the Civil War, commanding the ship *Neptune* at the Battle of Galveston.

Honoring 1776 and Famous Jews in American History. Phila., Joseph Jacobs Pubn., 1975; *New Standard Jewish Encyclopedia.* Garden City, N.Y., Doubleday & Co., 1970.

Hardenbergh, James Richmond, army officer (1841-1912). B. at New Brunswick, New Jersey, he received military training at Peekskill (New York) Military Academy and went west with his father before the Civil War. Hardenbergh inherited considerable money and used part of it to raise a company of the 1st Washington (Territory) Volunteer Infantry which he commanded for a time, was second lieutenant from August 31, 1862, until March 23, 1865, serving at Fort Steilacoom and Fort Vancouver, Washington, and at Fort Boise, Idaho, participating in campaigns against the Snake Indians. Subsequently he served as second lieutenant in 1865 in Company E, 2nd California Cavalry but saw no action before his muster out on June 8, 1865 (Heitman says he was mustered out June 2, 1866). Hardenbergh became a second lieutenant of the 9th U.S. Infantry April 5, 1866, and a first lieutenant July 28, He was assigned initially to Camp Cady, California, and in the summer of 1866 had a sharp skirmish with Paiute Indians, three soldiers being killed with no hostile losses. By January 1867 he was assigned to Camp El Dorado on the west bank of the Colorado River in the present Nevada. After El Dorado had been demoted to outpost status Hardenbergh remained briefly but reported to Camp Mojave, Arizona, in the fall of 1867, spent two months supervising construction of an outpost at Paiute Spring, California, and in January 1868 was transferred to Camp Independence, California where he served until his discharge at his own request September 7, 1870. He spent the rest of his life at San Francisco and Oakland, California and was buried in the National City Cemetery at the San Francisco Presidio.

Dennis G. Casebier, *Battle at Camp Cady*. Norco Calif., p.p., 1972; Casebier, *Camp El Dorado, Arizona Territory*. Tempe, Ariz. Hist. Found. 1970; Casebier, *Fort Pah-Ute, California*. Norco, Calif., Tales of the Mojave Road Pub. Co., 1974

Hardin, John, Indian fighter, officer (Oct. 1, 1753-May 1792). B. in Fauquier County, Virginia, he was moved as a child with his family to southwestern Pennsylvania, then a wilderness where he learned woodcraft skills and Indian ways to stand him in good stead later. In 1774 he took part as an ensign in Lord Dunmore's War and was wounded. He served in the Revolution with Daniel Morgan's riflemen, and took part in such engagements as Saratoga. In 1786 after he moved with his family to Nelson (Washington) County, Kentucky, he volunteered for George Rogers Clark's Wabash expedition, being appointed quartermaster. He participated in several forays into Indian territory. In 1788 and 1789 he led punitive scouts against the Shawnees. As a colonel of Kentucky militia he participated in the Harmar expedition of 1790 against the Miami towns of Ohio, carelessly leading his men into an ambush on October 19; his force, excluding most of the militia which fled at first fire or before, was cut to pieces. Hardin and Harmar were investigated

by a court of inquiry, but exonerated because of the undependability of the militia. A subsequent court-martial termed Hardin's conduct "that of a brave and skillful officer." The following June he rendered good service with Charles Scott's expedition against Indian towns on the upper Wabash River. On June 1 Scott sent Hardin with 60 mounted infantry and a troop of horse to attack the villages separately. Hardin smashed into the towns, took numerous prisoners and then discerned a stronger village unknown to Scott, and attacked it not awaiting orders, swiftly carrying it. General Wilkinson sent him under flag of truce in 1792 to negotiate a peace with the Miami tribes, but at what is now Hardin, Ohio, he was murdered by ostensibly friendly Indians under somewhat controversial circumstances. A few days before his death he had been commissioned a Brigadier General. "Despite his experience, eminent military talents, and unquestioned courage, Hardin was better qualified to command a company than a regiment."

DAB; Scott's report to Secretary of War, printed in *Indianapolis Gazette*, Sept. 5, 1826; Francis Paul Prucha, *The Sword of the Republic*. N.Y., Macmillan Co., 1969.

Hardin, John Wesley, gunman (May 26, 1853-Aug. 19, 1895). B. at Bonham, Fannin County, Texas, he was the son of a frontier Methodist preacher and was named for the founder of Methodism. He received some education, which he furthered during his later life, and had an average home environment with little advance indication that he was to become the most effective gunman in Texas' history. The basis for any account of his life is his own autobiography which Robert G. McCubbin, a student of it, considered "an accurate and amazing account," which lists approximately 27 of Hardin's reputed 30 or 40 killings. Hardin lived in Polk and Trinity counties while maturing. He killed a Negro in November 1868, and before the year was out had killed three more men, including two white soldiers. There may have been two more slayings before 1871 when he went with a trail herd up the Chisholm route to Abilene, according to his own account killing five men enroute and three at the destination. Back in Texas he married Jane Bowen, but could not stay out of trouble and killed four men at various times, then surrendered to the sheriff of Cherokee County. The next month, in October 1872, he broke jail, tried stock raising, but was "drawn into" the Sutton-Taylor feud in 1873 and 1874 through reported relationship with one of the principal families involved. The latter year he started up the Chisholm Trail once more, but killed Charles Webb, deputy sheriff of Brown County, enroute. This increased the search for him by law authorities and others, and he dodged around Texas, then went to Florida and the southeast, adding six more dead men to his list for certain, and several possible slayings as well. Texas Rangers captured him peacefully at Pensacola, Florida, July 23, 1877. Hardin was tried at Comanche, Texas, for the murder of Webb. On September 28, 1878, he was sentenced to 25 years in prison. In jail at Austin awaiting the outcome of his routine appeal, Hardin claimed to have met, among other inmates, such frontier notables as John Ringo, Manning Clements (a relative), Sam Pipes and Albert Herndon of the Sam Bass gang, Bill Taylor and other stellar figures of the outlaw galaxy of the day. Hardin was taken to Huntsville, Texas, for his imprisonment. He engineered and took part in many escape attempts, by his own account, all of which failed, but time in prison also was spent constructively, for he read widely and deeply, studied mathematics and pursued his intellectual interests, becoming, it would appear, a quite literate man judging from his autobiography. McCubbin believed this work basically "as Hardin wrote it," and not that of a ghost, although an editor may have smoothed it out to some extent. Hardin studied theology in prison, became superintendent of the Sunday school, a member of the debating society, and read law on the basis of a list of books recommended by a prominent outside educator and attorney, Andrew Todd McKinney. Upon his release (in 1894 he was granted a full pardon) Hardin joined his children in Gonzales County (his wife had died the year before), entered an 1894 political campaign which became quite heated, and when his candidate lost, moved to Karnes County. Early in 1895 he married Callie Lewis, a young woman of London, Texas, but the marriage failed. Hardin went to El Paso, Texas, to handle a case for Jim Miller, a noted assassin whose wife was Hardin's cousin. Miller, who had killed many men as a hired slayer, requested Hardin's help as an attorney to prosecute a man who had attempted to slay Miller, the case being handled at El Paso. The jury failed to reach a verdict and pending a retrial, Hardin commenced the practice of law, soon drifting into old habits. He was accused of holding up a faro game April 16, 1895, at the Gem Saloon, and paid a light fine. He began living with a woman, Mrs. Helen Bulah McRose. Standing at the Acme Saloon bar, he was shot in the back of the head by John Selman, a 58-year-old gunman of vast experience and dark misdeeds, who was cleared but himself killed a short time later. Hardin was an intelligent man of violent prejudices, flash temper, considerable ego and an odd mixture of good and bad qualities. To a large extent he was a product of his time, but he also was the type of man who made his times what they were. Under different circumstances he might have become a productive citizen, risen to high places, but in the post-Civil War Texas environment it was almost inevitable that he should become what he was, the most notorious of all those who defied the law.

John Wesley Hardin, *Life of John Wesley Hardin As Written by Himself,* intr. by Robert G. McCubbin. Norman, Univ. of Okla. Press, 1961; Lewis Nordyke, *John Wesley Hardin, Texas Gunman.* N.Y., William Morrow & Co., 1957; Jack DeMattos, "Gunfighters of the Real West: John Wesley Hardin." *Real West,* Vol. 27, No. 196 (Apr. 1984), 44-54.

Hardy, William Harrison, pioneer (Apr. 25, 1823-June 23, 1906). B. in Allegheny County, New York. He never was in military service, but in 1849 was elected captain of a wagon train of 100 bound for California, and was called "captain" thereafter. A merchant in Placer County Hardy amassed some wealth, removed to Arizona and in 1864 established a ferry and founded Hardyville on the Colorado River near the head of steam navigation, nine miles above Camp Mojave. Hardy established a toll road from his town to Prescott, had skirmishes with the Indians at various times, opened a mine and mill. In 1866 he was elected a member of the Territorial Council from Mohave County. After the railroad crossed the river at Needles, farther south, Hardyville waned and so did Hardy's fortunes, although the community retained some importance until the first decade of the 20th century. Only a cemetery now remains of the place. Hardy, virtually penniless, died from cancer at Whittier, California, and is buried there. Although he had a robust hatred of Indians, Hardy was a worthy pioneer.

Dan L. Thrapp, *Al Sieber, Chief of Scouts.* Norman, Univ. of Okla. Press, 1964.

Hargous, Charles Emelio, army officer (Apr. 13, 1844-Mar. 10, 1891). B. in New York he became a first lieutenant in the 15th New York Engineers December 1, 1862, and was mustered out in 1863. The next year he was re-commissioned in the 15th and became captain in 1865. In 1866 Hargous was commissioned a second lieutenant in the 40th Infantry and transferred to the 5th Infantry in 1869. He was stationed at Fort Keogh, Montana for a time under Miles. Although the year of his retirement was to have been 1908, he was retired March 9, 1891, and died the following day.

Powell; Heitman; Thomas H, Leforge, *Memoirs of a White Crow Indian.* Lincoln, Univ. of Nebra. Press, 1974, 265-66.

Harlan, John Jefferson (Off Wheeler), confidence man (c. 1853-post 1889). B. in Ohio he reached Kansas by 1872. a year later raping a 16-year-old girl on a freight train between Newton and Emporia, was convicted of the crime May 1 and given seven years but was pardoned April 26, 1877. He was described by prison records as 5 feet, 9 inches tall with a light complexion, brown hair, blue eyes and by profession a painter. He had become known as Off Wheeler because of his powerful physique. A later description said he was of medium height "but extraordinary breadth, having shoulders like those of a buffalo bull. He has a pleasant, good humored countenance..." After release from the penitentiary Harlan was reported at Dodge City, Kansas; Las Vegas and Lamy, New Mexico; Benson and Tombstone, Arizona; the Colorado mining camps; Texas, California and Oklahoma. He may have been a lawman of sorts at Benson where he was directed by Sheriff John Behan (see entry) of Tombstone to arrest a murderer and bring him to Tombstone, which was done. August 9, 1881, Harlan while drunk shot at an Indian, missed him, and was fined $50 and costs for assault with intent to kill. December 24, 1881, Harlan killed bartender Harry Kistner at Lamy following a quarrel. Harlan and his friends drifted about the southwest, plying variations of their bunco trade as opportunity arose, in and out of court on charges as light as vagrancy and occasionally more serious, almost invariably evading or mitigating punishment by nimble wits, and at times being run out of some community by threats of lynching. In 1889 he was settled in Oklahoma Territory, reportedly near Guthrie.

Ed Bartholomew, *Wyatt Earp: The Man & the Myth.* Toyahvale, Texas, Frontier Book Co., 1964; Philip J. Rasch, "John Jefferson Harlan: Bunco Steerer." London, English Westerners Soc., *Brand Book,* Vol. 21, No. 1 (Winter 1982), 1-8.

Harmar, Josiah, army officer (Nov. 10, 1753-Aug. 20, 1813). B. at Philadelphia he was educated in a Quaker school and commissioned captain of the 1st Pennsylvania Battalion October 27, 1775, becoming major of the 3rd Pennsylvania October 1, 1776. He ended the Revolutionary War a lieutenant colonel and brevet colonel. He commanded the army from August 12, 1784, becoming a brevet Brigadier General July 31, 1787. Harmar as commander of the army stationed in Ohio was a witness to the Treaty of January 21, 1785 with the chiefs of the Wyandots, Delawares, Chippewas and Ottawas but was not a formal signatory to the pact, concluded at Fort McIntosh, 30 miles downriver from Pittsburgh. In 1785 Harmar tried without success to expel whites settling in Indian country north of the Ohio. He was engaged in Indian fighting in 1785-86 and the next year occupied Vincennes and several Illinois towns. In 1789 Harmar moved his head-quarters to Fort Washington (today's Cincinnati, Ohio), and September 1790 in response to directives from the Secretary of War attacked the Miami towns. His force of 1,453 men, only 320 of them regulars, found the towns deserted, burned them and headed back toward Fort Washington. October 18 about 300 militia and regulars were sent to seek hostiles, but returned having accomplished little. The following day Colonel John Hardin of the Kentucky militia set out himself with 180 militia and 30 regulars, ran into an ambush and suffered severe losses. October 21 came a second white defeat when Harmar sent 300 militia and 60 regulars back to the villages to surprise any Indians who had returned. They found Indians, but the militia abandoned the regulars to pursue them and the hostiles killed Major John P. Wyllys, the commander, and again caused considerable losses. Harmar sped back to Fort Washington, his militia "completely demoralized and out of control." It had been an outright defeat: Harmar had lost 75 killed and 3 wounded of his regulars, 108 dead and 28 wounded of the militia for a total of 183 killed and 31 wounded to an estimated Indian loss of 120, which was really a guess. Harmar attempted to report a success in that "our loss was heavy, but the headquarters of iniquity were broken up," and a court of inquiry cleared him. But his adventure caused the enemy to grow in arrogance and boldness and made necessary the expedition a year later of Arthur St. Clair which terminated in a far worse catastrophe, and the 1794 operation of Anthony Wayne which finally cleared things up. Harmar possessed courage but not the capacity to wage war against Indians, and white frontiersmen did not like him. He resigned his commission as commander of the army January 1, 1792. During his last years Harmar was adjutant general of Pennsylvania.

Heitman; DAB; Francis Paul Prucha, *The Sword of the Republic.* N.Y., Macmillan Co., 1969.

Harmer, Alexander F., soldier, illustrator (Aug. 21, 1856-Jan. 8, 1925). B. at Newark, New Jersey, he enlisted in the army in 1872 and again in 1881, serving on the frontier; between enlistments he studied at the Philadelphia Academy of Fine Arts, and became an illustrator whose work appeared in *Harper's Weekly,* with John G. Bourke's *An Apache Campaign in the Sierra Madre* (1886) and *The Snake-dance of the Moquis of Arizona* (1883), and elsewhere. Harmer accompanied Crook's great Sierra Madre Expedition in 1883 and made most of the sketches that appeared in Bourke's book on the spot. He did oils and watercolors in addition to pen and ink works. After 1890 he became interested in the Mission Indians of California and the missions themselves and ranchero life in that state, most of his later work being concerned with those subjects. He died at Santa Barbara, California.

Robert Taft, *Artists and Illustrators of the Old West 1850-1900.* N.Y., Bonanza Books, 1953.

Harney, William Selby, army officer (Aug. 22, 1800-May 9, 1889). B. near Nashville, Tennessee (Heitman says he was born and entered the army in Louisiana), he studied at a local academy and took private instruction in navigation in order to enter the Navy, but on February 13 1818, he was commissioned a second lieutenant in the 1st Infantry. He became a first lieutenant in 1819, transferred briefly to the 1st Artillery in 1821 and back again to the 1st Infantry in which he was promoted to captain May 14, 1825. He served in the Black Hawk War in Illinois and Wisconsin in 1832 and participated in the decisive Battle of Bad Axe, Wisconsin, August 2. Harney became major and paymaster May 1, 1833, and was made a lieutenant colonel of the 2nd Dragoons August 15, 1836. He came to some prominence in the Second Seminole War in Florida (December 28, 1835-August 14, 1842). April 24, 1838 he led an attack on the camp of Arpeika (Sam Jones), a Mikasuki chief, but the results were inconclusive. Described as then 6 feet, 3 inches in height and magnificently proportioned, Harney could command by his mere presence but unfortunately "displayed some qualities of a bully, especially where 'inferior' races were concerned." He commanded a force of 26 men assigned to protect a trading post on the Caloosahatchee River and the night of July 23, 1839 the detachment was attacked by Indians, Harney escaping down a forest path clad only in shirt and underdrawers; 18 men were killed or captured by the hostiles. In December, 1840 Harney led an expedition in search of a Seminole, Chakaika who had launched the surprise attack earlier. When Seminole canoemen became lost the officer ordered Indian women to show him the way, threatening to hang their children if they refused. They declined to do it, and he did not carry out his threat. Approaching Chakaika's camp in the dark, Harney against orders dressed and painted his men like Indians and surprised the enemy, Chakaika was shot, some Indians were captured whom Harney ordered hanged and the officer returned to Fort Dalles (present site of Miami) after 12 days. Harney was breveted colonel and June 30, 1846, was promoted to colonel, making him the army's ranking Cavalry officer under Scott; the two never got along. Scott had Harney court martialed for disobedience of orders in Mexico, Harney appealed to superiors at Washington, and Scott was reprimanded lightly. Despite these contretemps however, Harney performed brilliantly in the Mexican War and was breveted Brigadier General. In the aftermath of the Grattan defeat by the Sioux, Harney was summoned home from Paris where he was on leave to lead a punitive expedition against that powerful tribe. He left Fort Kearny, Nebraska August 24, 1855, at the head of 600 Dragoons and with the announcement, "By God, I'm for battle — no peace." September 3 he attacked the Brulé Sioux camp of Little Thunder, killing 85, wounding five and capturing 70 women and children at Ash Hollow on Blue Water Creek, Nebraska; it was one of the celebrated victories over Indians presumed hostile during the Plains wars. Harney proceeded to Fort Laramie and from there made a wide sweep to the north and east, skirting the Black Hills and Dakota badlands and reaching Fort Pierre October 20. His operations, then and subsequently, thoroughly cowed the Sioux for the time being. However he ran afoul of the Indian Bureau in trying to arrange a treaty with them, and it was not approved. Harney returned to Florida briefly for the third, and final, Seminole War which lasted from 1855 to 1858. In 1857 he was given command of the Utah Expedition, but shortly was succeeded by Albert Sidney Johnston. Harney was promoted to Brigadier General June 14, 1858, and given command of the Department of Oregon. The next year he ordered seized the disputed island of San Juan in Puget Sound, thus bringing a controversy with Britain to a head and for this action he was recalled. He was given command of the Department of the West with headquarters at St. Louis, but was deprived of his command in May 1861 as a result of suspicions — unwarranted — of Southern sympathies. Harney was retired in 1863 and given a brevet Major Generalcy in 1865. He married twice, fathered three children, and died at Orlando, Florida.

Heitman; CE; DAB; John K. Mahon, *History of the Second Seminole War*. Gainesville, Univ. of Fa. Press, 1967; Robert M. Utley, *Frontiersmen in Blue*. N.Y., Macmillan Co., 1967.

Haro, López de: *see* López de Haro, Gonsalez

Harper, James, soldier (1786-c. 1813). B. in Berkeley County, Virginia, he was raised near Cincinnati, Ohio, and enlisted in the War of 1812, serving under Harrison on the Northwestern frontier. He was caught in an Indian

ambuscade bearing scalps at his belt, was taken to "some point on the Lakes and burned at the stake."

Lucullus V. McWhorter, *Border Settlers of Northwestern Virginia*. Hamilton, O., Republican Pub. Co., 1915.

Harrell: *see* Horrell

Harrington, Frank, scout (Jan. 9, 1827-Jan. 12, 1907). B. in New York State, he enlisted in an Illinois regiment in 1862 and was discharged the following year for disability, moving to Kansas and settling in the Saline Valley. In August 1868, he joined the Forsyth scouts. He with Louis Farley and George B. Clark were sent to the north bank of the riverbed opposite Beecher Island to act as sharpshooters in the September fight; all were wounded, Harrington by an arrow over the left eye, then a glancing blow by a bullet in the same region, but which did not penetrate the skull. Harrington died at Konawa, Oklahoma.

Simon E. Matson, ed., *The Battle of Beecher Island*. Wray, Colo., Beecher Island Battle Meml. Assn., 1960, 59.

Harrington, Henry Moore, army officer (Apr. 30, 1849-June 25, 1876). B. at Albion, New York, he went to West Point from Michigan and was commissioned a second lieutenant in the 7th Cavalry June 14, 1872. After service in the southeast he went to Dakota in 1873, accompanied David Stanley's Yellowstone expedition that year and Custer's Black Hills Expedition in 1874. Harrington was with Custer's Sioux expedition and was lost at the Battle of the Little Big Horn, although his remains were not identified. The Sioux Chief Gall told Walter Camp that he had heard from four eye-witnesses that one soldier "rode through the Indians on a very swift horse which they could not catch. They told that after chasing him for about a mile or two the soldier drew his pistol and killed himself. This they could not understand, because the man's horse was swifter than theirs and was continually getting farther away from the pursuers." Editor Kenneth Hammer speculated that this man "may have been" Harrington.

Cullum; BHB; *Custer in 76: Walter Camp's Notes on the Custer Fight*. Provo, Utah, Brigham Young Univ. Press, 1976.

Harrington, James (Jimmie), stage driver (fl. 1881). Harrington was driver of the Concord stage on which John P. Clum left Tombstone for Benson, Arizona, December 14, 1881. The stage purportedly was attacked by desperadoes intent upon assassinating Clum, in his belief, but they were foiled. Clum left the vehicle five miles out of Tombstone and reached Benson, 20 miles distant, the next day.

John P. Clum, *It All Happened in Tombstone.* Flagstaff, Ariz., Northland Press, 1965.

Harrington, John, soldier (c. 1848-post 1899). B. at Detroit, he was a sailor by profession but whether on the Great Lakes or at sea was not stated. He enlisted for five years in Company H, 6th Cavalry December 19, 1870. Harrington was one of six men in the famous buffalo wallow fight September 12, 1874, near the Washita River, Texas, and was seriously wounded in the hip during the engagement with about 125 Kiowa Indians, his account of the action as vivid as any. One man was killed and four of the defenders wounded. For this action Harrington on November 4 was given the Medal of Honor, as were his companions. Harrington ended his enlistment at Fort Bowie, Arizona a corporal, re-enlisted in January and was discharged a sergeant with "excellent" character five years later at Fort Niobrara, Nebraska, and continued to re-enlist through 1899. He was described in his early enlistments as of light complexion with blue eyes, dark hair, and 5 feet, 5 3/4 inches in height.

Harrington service records, NARS; MH; *Deeds of Valor,* II; *Indian Campaign on the Staked Plains, 1874-1875,* ed. by Joe F. Taylor. Canyon, Tex., Panhandle-Plains Hist. Soc., 1962.

Harrington, Mark Raymond, anthropologist (July 6, 1882-June 30, 1971). B. at Ann Arbor, Michigan, he was graduated from Columbia University in 1907, and worked successively for the American Museum of Natural History, Peabody Museum, Harvard, Heye Museum, University of Pennsylvania Museum, Museum of the American Indian, and the Southwest Museum. He wrote many books, from *Sacred Bundles of the Sac and Fox Indians,* (1914), to *Dickon Among the Lenape Indians,* (1938). He also wrote some fiction. Harrington was discoverer of the Ozark Bluff Dweller culture in Arkansas and

Missouri, explored many sites in Nevada and California and did research in Cuba. He lived with and was familiar with many Indian tribes across the continent. A conservationist, he would permit no bird, mammal or reptile to be killed on any of his expeditions. He was friendly, fond of jokes, a good mimic and had a wide spectrum of friends.

Who's Who in America; Branding Iron, Los Angeles Corral, Westerners, June 1959, No. 49, which includes a bibliography; *Branding Iron,* Dec. 1971, No. 103.

Harriot, Thomas, explorer, scientist (1560-July 2, 1621). B. at Oxford, England, he became a mathematician and astronomer of note. He graduated from Oxford February 12, 1580, then was engaged as mathematical tutor to Sir Walter Raleigh. Raleigh sent Harriot as surveyor and scientific observor to Roanoke Island, North Carolina with a 1585 colonial endeavor, Harriot working closely with John White, artist of the party. The two wintered among Indians on the southern shores of Chesapeake Bay. Harriot's activities extended beyond the scientific, for he and Edward Nugent June 1, 1586, killed and beheaded Wingina, a locally-prominent chief of the Secotan tribe of Algonquins, the chief suspected of plotting destruction of the white colony although since detailed verbal communication was impossible no one positively knew his intent; the slaying had calamitous effect upon the colony's future. Harriot returned to England with those colonists brought back by Sir Francis Drake in 1586 and made no further visits to America. He wrote the widely-circulated *True Report of... Virginia,* first published at Frankfurt-am-Main by Theodor de Bry in 1590. A near contemporary of Galileo, Harriot made significant astronomical and mathematical discoveries, but ill health plagued him much of his life, preventing publication of some of his most important findings. He succumbed to cancer of the nose, possibly induced by the long-continued taking of snuff. He died near Isleworth, west London.

Thomas Harriot, *A Briefe and True Report of the New Found Land of Virginia,* intro. by Paul Hulton, N.Y., Dover Publns., Inc., 1972; Paul Hulton, *America 1585: The Complete Drawings of John White.* Chapel Hill, Univ. of No. Car. Pr. and British Mus. Pubns., 1984; DNB; Samuel Eliot Morison, *European Discovery of America: The Northern Voyages.* N.Y., Oxford Univ. Pr., 1971.

Harriott, Isaac H., pioneer (Sept. 24, 1833-Mar. 8, 1857). B. at Boundbrook, Somerset County, New Jersey, he was taken to Illinois at 5, to St. Louis in 1848 and to Pekin, Illinois the next year where he commenced to read medicine. He later moved to Atlanta, Illinois, St. Paul, Minnesota, and in 1856 to Lake Okoboji, Iowa where he commenced to practice medicine. He was killed in the Spirit Lake Massacre perpetrated by Inkpaduta, a Sioux Indian and his followers.

Abbie Gardner Sharp, *History of the Spirit Lake Massacre.* Des Moines, Iowa Printing Co., 1891.

Harris, Alexander (Shorty), frontiersman (Dec. 28, 1845-Oct. 7, 1932). B. in Indiana, Harris was a rancher, trapper, scout and cowboy in western Nebraska, Wyoming and elsewhere, traded oxen along the trails westward, and engaged in trail drives to Montana, Wyoming, Kansas, Colorado, Indian Territory, New Mexico, Arizona and California. He engaged in the raising of purebred stock in Nebraska and Wyoming. Harris reported he had confronted and faced down Wyatt Earp at Socorro, New Mexico, but whether in 1882 or 1884 is not known. Harris died at Minden, Nebraska, and was buried at Hyannis, Nebraska.

Ed Bartholomew, *Wyatt Earp: The Man & the Myth.* Toyahvale, Tex., Frontier Book Co., 1964.

Harris, Edward, lay scientist and traveler (Sept. 7, 1799-June 8, 1863). B. at Moorestown, New Jersey, he was a gentleman-farmer of some means who met John James Audubon in 1824, gave him financial aid and friendship, the two remaining close for the rest of their lives. Harris was a "well-informed bird specialist, a scientific agriculturist, a careful businessman, (who) led an ordered and intelligent life." In 1837 the two made an ornithological excursion to the Louisiana and Texas coasts. In 1843 they made an extended journey up the Missouri River, on which Harris kept a minute and useful journal and made geological and other scientific observations. He died at Moorestown.

Up the Missouri With Audubon: The Journal of Edward Harris, ed. by John Francis McDermott. Norman, Univ. of Okla. Press, 1951.

Harris, George Montgomery, army officer (c. 1846-May 12, 1873). B. in Pennsylvania he went to West Point from Georgia, was commissioned a second lieutenant in the 10th Infantry June 15, 1868, and joined the 4th Artillery July 14, 1869. With his battery he took part in the Modoc War of 1872-73 in northeastern California and was severely wounded in the disastrous Thomas-Wright attack on the Indians April 26, 1873. When he was thought killed outright "even old soldiers wept. He was idolized by his men because of his bravery." Lieutenant Boutelle assisted in carrying him from the field. His mother, in Philadelphia, was notified of her son's wounding, boarded a train for San Francisco, took a local to Redding, California, found a stage to Yreka, California, hired a supply wagon to the top of a nearby bluff and rode a mule into the hospital station. Her son died 24 hours later.

Heitman; Keith A. Murray, *The Modocs and Their War.* Norman, Univ. of Okla. Press, 1965; Richard Dillon, *Burnt-Out Fires.* Englewood Cliffs, N.J., Prentice-Hall, 1973.

Harris, Jack, adventurer (d. July 11-12, 1882). B. in New England, he was said to be descended from Major General Israel Putnam. He fought with William Walker's filibustering expedition in Nicaragua about 1855, was wounded and his left hand crippled. Despite this he became a professional gambler. He accompanied Colonel Albert Sidney Johnston's 1857-58 Mormon expedition as hunter and scout, and saw Civil War service as a Confederate. He settled in San Antonio becoming a minor political boss. Harris became involved in a dispute with Ben Thompson, a city marshal of Austin and noted gunman, and was killed by Thompson from darkness in a vaudeville house-saloon Harris owned with others. Harris was a large, dark man, and although some modern writers call him "Peg-leg," there was nothing wrong with his legs.

Taylor Thompson, "Thrilling Tales of Frontier Days." *Frontier Times,* Vol. I, No. 6 (Mar. 1924), 8-9; Floyd Benjamin Streeter, *Ben Thompson, Man With a Gun..* N.Y., Frederick Fell, 1957.

Harris, John, frontiersman (fl. 1829-1834). Probably b. in Missouri, he reached Santa Fe with his son, Robert, in 1829, and in 1831 led a trapping party into Colorado, but had returned to Taos by January 25, 1832. He then led a group eastward, working the southern Plains rivers; all his trapping ventures were unsuccessful. He may have returned to Missouri.

David J. Weber article, MM, Vol. VII.

Harris, Moses, army officer (Sept. 6, 1839-June 27, 1927). B. at Andover, New Hampshire, he enlisted in the 4th Cavalry March 19, 1857, and was sent to Fort Leavenworth. He was on an expedition against the Cheyennes from May to October under Colonel Edwin V. Sumner and in an action at Solomon's Fork, Kansas, July 29. In the summer of 1858 he marched with the troop to the Sweetwater River and returned to Fort Riley, Kansas. Under Major John Sedgwick he was on an expedition from May to August 1860 against the Kiowa Indians and in an action at Blackwater Springs, Kansas July 11. Harris had risen to sergeant by May 18, 1864, when he was commissioned a second lieutenant of the 1st Cavalry, becoming a first lieutenant August 15 and winning a Medal of Honor two weeks later at Smithfield, West Virginia. From 1866-69 Harris took part in "various scouts and skirmishes" from Fort Lyon, Indian Territory, and during the summer of 1869 marched with his troop to Camp Grant, Arizona, where he scouted for Apache hostiles, "taking part in several small engagements" until March 1870. From March to May he was engaged in constructing a wagon road to the new Camp Apache from Camp Thomas, Arizona; he became a captain June 20, 1872 and in the summer of 1873 was at Sitka, Alaska. Harris spent the following summer in the Wallowa Valley of Oregon "watching restless Nez Perce Indians under Chief Joseph." In 1878 he participated in the campaign against Snake and Bannock Indians and in October 1881 was sent to Arizona and engaged in the pursuit of Apache Juh and Geronimo in their dash from San Carlos to Mexico; he also scouted for hostile Apaches during the Loco emeute from San Carlos in the spring of 1882. From 1884-86 he was engaged in scouting from Fort Custer, Montana. Harris was sent to Yellowstone National Park August 15, 1886, taking over August 17 as first military superintendent and remaining there until May 31, 1889. He became major of the 8th Cavalry in 1892 and retired March 7, 1893. He died at Rochester, New York aged 88, "a most remarkable soldier and man" in the words of Aubrey L. Haines.

Heitman; Powell; Hiram Martin Chittenden,

Yellowstone National Park. Cincinnati, Robert Clarke Co., 1905; information from Aubrey L. Haines; *Superintendent's Ann. Rep. (Yellowstone) for 1928,* p.28.

Harris, Moses (Black), mountain man (d. c. May 13, 1849). B. in Union County South Carolina, he may have been with Ashley in his first ascent of the Missouri River in 1822; he certainly was a member of the 1823 party, taking part in the disastrous battle against the Arickaras, June 1. He brought news of the upper country to St. Louis by January 22, 1824. Back in the Rocky Mountains with Jedediah Smith and others in 1825, Harris was one of four who first circumnavigated Great Salt Lake; later he visited the Yellowstone region. His yarns about petrified trees and Yellowstone wonders became mountain classics. Harris was back and forth between the mountains and St. Louis several times, becoming one of the half dozen most famous mountain men. He was present at the founding of Fort William (Laramie) in 1834, and three years later was depicted by artist Alfred Jacob Miller who accompanied a Stewart party to the rendezvous. In 1840 he engaged in a bloodless shooting bout with Robert Newell over a minor difference. He guided one of the largest emigrant companies to Oregon in 1844; in 1845 he rescued a party of stranded emigrants in central Oregon. He was back at St. Joseph in 1847, returned to the mountains in 1848 and to Missouri again, contracting cholera at Independence in 1849 where he died, an "enigma," but a "man of real significance in the early history of the West."

Literature abundant but scattered; the best summary is an article by Harvey L. Carter, MM, Vol. IV.

Harris, Thomas W., pioneer (Aug. 20, 1827-post 1899). B. in Woodford County, Kentucky, he reached Fort Hall in 1851, entered the employ of John Owen of Fort Owen in the Bitterroot Valley of western Montana, and was a trusted and loyal associate of Owen for many years. He made expeditions for Owen, including some to the Overland Trail where he bartered for emigrants' used-up stock. He married an Indian woman or possibly a halfbreed, in 1862 worked for the Indian Department as a farmer and in 1863 became a Missoula County commissioner. Eventually he developed his own farm on Three Mile Creek near Fort Owen. He and John Owen had a falling out resulting in an 1866 lawsuit which Harris lost. He remained on his Three Mile Creek farm thereafter.

George F. Weisel, *Men and Trade on the Northwest Frontier.* Missoula, Mont. State Univ. Press, 1955; *Montana Contributions,* II (1896); *Montana Genesis: Stevensville,* (Mont. Hist. Soc., 1971).

Harrison, Montgomery Pike, army officer (c. 1826- Oct. 7, 1849). B. in Indiana he was the grandson of the ninth President, William Henry Harrison, and the older brother of Benjamin Harrison, the 23rd President. Montgomery Harrison graduated from West Point and became a brevet second lieutenant of the 7th Infantry July 1, 1847, a second lieutenant of the 5th Infantry September 11 and served in the Mexican War. From 1848-49 he did frontier duty at Fort Smith, Arkansas and joined the Marcy Expedition to Santa Fe in 1849, Marcy ordered to follow the main Canadian River and give what advice and assistance he could to gold seekers heading for California. Harrison was killed by Indians near the Colorado River of Texas. Black Beaver, the famed Delaware scout followed up his trail and deduced that Harrison, who had frequently said he was not intimidated by tales of wild Indians, believed most of them friendly, and had vowed he would treat them so, on the day of his death was riding alone. He sighted two Indians, probably renegade Kiowas and met up with them. The three dismounted to have a smoke in a grassy spot when the Indians seized the officer's rifle and shot him, then stripped the body and mutilated it. They were not apprehended. A coffin was made of a wagon bed and the body, packed in charcoal, was taken back to Fort Smith for burial. Harrison was 23 at his death.

Heitman; Cullum; Rupert Norval Richardson, *The Frontier of Northwest Texas 1846 to 1876,* Glendale, Calif., Arthur H. Clark Co., 1963; Grant Foreman, *Marcy and the Gold Seekers.* Norman, Univ. of Okla. Press, 1939.

Harrison, Richard, Mormon pioneer (fl. 1857). Richard Harrison was a Mormon of high standing in Iron County, Utah at the time of the Mountain Meadows Massacre, September 11, 1857, and is placed there at the scene by John D. Lee and by *Mormonism Unveiled,* either participating in or consenting to the tragedy. Afterward he and his wife retained one of the orphaned children of the slain emigrants.

Juanita Brooks, *John D. Lee.* Glendale, Calif., Arthur H. Clark Co., 1962; *Mormonism Unveiled,* 379.

Harrison, William B., adventurer (c. 1811- Mar. 6, 1836). B. in Ohio, he reached Texas in January 1836, from Tennessee and was captain of the Tennessee Volunteers, Crockett's men. As such he perished at the Alamo.

Amelia Williams, XXXVII, 264.

Harrison, William Henry, military officer, politician (Feb. 9, 1773-Apr. 4, 1841). B. at Berkeley, Charles City County, Virginia, he attended Hampden-Sidney College, Virginia, studied medicine and was commissioned an ensign in the 1st Infantry August 16, 1791. He became a lieutenant June 2, 1792, and was assigned to command the 1st Sublegion September 4. He was an aide to Wayne in his Ohio campaign after Harmar's defeat and the St. Clair debacle, helped build Fort Washington at the present site of Cincinnati and took part in the August 20, 1794, Battle of Fallen Timbers in which Wayne broke the power of the Shawnees and their allies; white casualties were 107 killed and wounded, the Indian loss unknown. Harrison became a captain May 15, 1797. He commanded Fort Washington until June 1, 1798, when he resigned from the army to enter politics. He became secretary of the Northwest Territory in 1798 and the next year defeated (by one vote) Arthur St. Clair Jr. to become delegate to Congress, resigning May 14, 1800. Harrison strongly reflected the frontiersmen's point of view in Northwest territorial matters. He was active in creation of Indiana as a separate Territory, being named governor and Indian commissioner in 1801 and retaining those positions until 1813. During his administration he was instrumental in concluding a series of treaties with Indians including that of Fort Wayne September 30, 1809, in all opening 33 million acres to white settlement while compressing into tighter and more remote regions the several Indian tribes, thereby generating their restlessness and discontent. This led inevitably to the Battle of Tippecanoe. Tecumseh, under pressure from white encroachments, developed plans for a confederacy of Indian tribes to oppose further pressure, which he had every right to do, while Harrison quickly perceived that he must destroy this Indian "threat" to further land-opening ambitions. When Tecumseh went south in the summer of 1811 to solicit support from the Creeks and other tribes, Harrison seized the opportunity to clean out the Indian center, presided over by Tecumseh's brother, Tenskwatawa (The Prophet), in the chief's absence. Harrison had no authority to move on the town. To do this he must penetrate the territory of a power with which the United States was at peace. Nevertheless he led his command of 1,000 regulars and militia, knowing that the Prophet would be unable to keep his warriors from attacking the invading force, even if he wished to do so. President Madison, who alone possessed authority to order such an operation was inperfectly informed about what was underway. When Harrison's forces reached the Prophet's town he encamped on Tippecanoe River (in the Wabash country of Indiana) and, as he anticipated, the Indians launched a dawn attack November 7, 1811. The troops were nearly overrun at the outset, but rallied and fought off repeated assaults. Indians had been assigned to kill the "rider on (Harrison's) grey horse," but the commander's mount was ridden by Colonel Abraham Owen who was shot to death, while Harrison himself, astride a dark bay, escaped unscathed. The engagement was not a decisive victory. Rather it was a stand-off, although the whites held the ground and eventually burned the Prophet's town. White losses were 62 killed or wounded mortally and 126 less seriously wounded; the Indian loss was estimated at 25 or 35 killed with an unknown number wounded. Yet, Tecumseh's allies scattered, his ambitions now lay in ruins, and he would join the British side in the War of 1812. Harrison and his supporters, to justify his operation and its results, mounted a publicity campaign "which elevated the battle to the status of legend and carried Harrison eventually to the White House." It was not the first, nor would it be the last such effort to achieve comparable goals. Harrison was named Brigadier General August 22, 1812, and March 2 Major General and commander in the Northwest. He was defeated in January 1813, by British General Henry A. Proctor but recovered and moved

against Detroit where the British on October 5 were beaten in the Battle of the Thames in which Tecumseh was killed, shot reportedly by Colonel Richard M. Johnson (see entry), of Kentucky. Harrison resigned from the army May 31, 1814. His subsequent political history is beyond the scope of this work. He died of pneumonia exactly one month after being sworn in as the ninth President of the United States.

Literature abundant; BDAC: Heitman; Glenn Tucker, *Tecumseh: Vision of Glory,* Indianapolis, Bobbs-Merrill Co., 1956; Reed Beard, *The Battle of Tippecanoe...,* Chicago, Hammond Press, 1911.

Hart, Caleb Lawson (Loss), lawman (1862-Jan 31, 1934). B. in Park County, Texas, he removed with his parents to Indian Territory in 1879, engaged in blacksmithing and cattle ranching and served as a deputy United States marshal under J.J. Dickerson, T.B. Needles and J.J. McAlester, for 11 years in all. On June 8, 1894, he killed Bill Dalton near Elk (Poolville), Indian Territory, northwest of Ardmore. Hart two years later settled at McGee, Indian Territory, survived a smallpox attack and engaged in merchandising. He is buried at McGee.

Charles J. Mooney, "The Man Who Killed Bill Dalton." *Golden West,* Vol. X, No. 2 (Jan. 1974), 14-15, 49.

Hart, Edward (Little), gunman (d. Sept. 1878). Little Hart was a gunman associated with the Horrells during their New Mexico stay and "war," but whether he came with them from Lampasas, Texas, is uncertain. At any rate he was akin in temperament and bellicosity. On their withdrawal from New Mexico in early 1874 Hart killed Joe Haskins, a settler of good repute, simply because he had a Mexican wife and Hart didn't like Mexicans. Hart, Billy Applegate, Zachariah Crumpton and a cowboy named Still broke off from the main exodus and stole four mules and two race horses from Aaron Willburn of Roswell, New Mexico; the rancher secured a posse and trailed the rustlers to Hueco Tanks, arriving early one morning while the thieves were asleep, the posse killing Crumpton and Still. Hart returned to Lampasas with the Horrells, remaining about four years. He went back then to New Mexico and joined the Seven Rivers Warriors, or outlaws where he sought to head up this Dolan-leaning faction. John Selman, who aspired to the leadership himself, killed Hart by shooting him unawares through a tabletop.

Robert N. Mullin notes; Leon Claire Metz, *John Selman: Texas Gunfighter.* N.Y., Hastings House, 1966; Philip J. Rasch, "The Horrell War." *New Mex. Hist. Rev.,* Vol. XXXI, No. 3 (July 1956), 223-31.

Hart, William Surrey (Bill), actor (Dec. 6, 1870-June 23, 1946). B. at Newburgh, New York, he was taken west as a child, growing up, he reported, in contact with Sioux and cowboys on the northern plains. He became a stage actor at about 17 and during 20 years in the theatre appeared in Shakespearean and classical roles; he also became a competition walker, that being a recognized and popular sport at the time. His motion picture career began in 1914 with two-reel films; from 1915 to 1925 he was perhaps the most popular western star, his final major picture being "Tumbleweeds," 1925. He wrote several young people's books and an autobiography, and died at Newhall, California, on his small ranch, now a park.

EA; William S. Hart, *My Life East & West.* Boston and N.Y., Houghton Mifflin Co., 1929.

Harte, Francis Brett (Bret Harte), writer (Aug. 25, 1836-May 5, 1902). B. at Albany, New York, his first poem was published at 11. He journeyed to California in 1854, spending 17 years there, working on the Union (now Arcata) *Northern Californian,* wrote an editorial assailing a massacre of local Indians and being forced to remove to San Francisco, he obtained government positions and wrote short stories, satires and articles on the side. With Anton Roman, a bookseller-publisher, he founded the *Overland Monthly* and edited it, writing for it his famous "The Luck of Roaring Camp" (August 1868) and other pieces, including "The Outcasts of Poker Flat" and "The Heathen Chinee." His first collection of short stories, including his Mother Lode tales, appeared in 1870. He never again approached that writing peak, removing shortly from California to live and work the rest of his life in the East and abroad. He died at Camberley, Surrey, southwest of London and is buried in Frimley churchyard.

Literature abundant.

Harvey, Alexander, fur trader (c. 1808-July 20, 1854). B. at St. Louis, he joined the American Fur Company in 1831 and was on the upper Missouri River by the next year. He was with Maximilian's party up the river in 1833 and, being "an energetic and active man without fear and of great physical strength," was sent ahead from Fort Union to build Fort McKenzie. Larpenteur wrote that he was "the boldest man that was ever on the Missouri... six feet tall, weighing 160 or 170 pounds and inclined to do right when sober." His feats of endurance, strength and courage were legendary, although he was hated and despised for cruelty and callousness. On complaints of employees in the winter of 1839-40, he was summoned to St. Louis and made the trip alone and afoot. Chouteau, in admiration, sent him back to Fort McKenzie where, when he returned, he summoned the men who had testified against him and beat them up, one by one. He killed Isadore Sandoval at Fort Union in 1841. In February, 1844, Harvey, a vindictive and violent man, determined to take revenge against Blackfeet for a dispute with a war party the year before. Francois Chardon, nominally in charge of the post, was an habitual drunkard and Harvey lured a number of Blackfeet (of a party different from the offending one) to within range of a cannon he had loaded with a variety of missiles. He ordered an Irishman to fire the gun, and when told it would be murder and the order refused, he knocked the Irishman down and fired it himself, felling at least four Indians either killed outright or wounded mortally, and wounding 17 others. Harvey then rushed upon the fallen, splitting their skulls with an axe, scalping them and, Weippert was told by an eye-witness, "licked the blood from his axe, saying 'I will serve all the dogs so!'" This massacre became celebrated in fur trade legend. Harvey with Chardon built Fort F.A. Chardon (Fort F.A.C.) at the mouth of the Judith River later in 1844 and remained in charge when Chardon went down the river. Harvey may have intimidated Chardon; at any rate there probably was bad blood between them, and followers of Chardon planned to kill Harvey, but the attempt failed. Harvey went down the river and against all fur company efforts to dissuade him, reported the illegal sale of liquor by traders on the upper Missouri.

Nothing came of the charges, but Harvey then joined Robert Campbell and others in organizing the St. Louis Fur Company in opposition to Chouteau. Harvey was chief organizer of the company, making his headquarters at its Blackfoot post, Fort Campbell. "No one ever accused him of dishonesty, laziness or cowardice." He must have married, for in his last note to Campbell, written July 17, 1854, he begged him to care for his daughters, Edeline and Susan. Harvey was buried at Fort Pierre.

Montana, Contributions, Vol. X, 1940, 302-304.

Harvey, Jack, frontiersman (1836-Mar. 13, 1868). B. probably at Dunkirk, New York, he had reached Kansas by 1862, taking part in the border scrimmaging as one of Captain William S. Tough's Buckskin Scouts, and becoming a friend of James Butler (Wild Bill) Hickok. He participated in the capture of Fort Smith, Arkansas, and was badly wounded at Cane Hill, Arkansas. Harvey was captured by the Confederates in 1864, but they did not know who he was and released him. After the war he became distinguished as a scout for various army commands on the plains, including the Hancock expedition of 1867. Harvey died of tuberculosis at Ellsworth, Kansas.

Joseph G. Rosa, *They Called Him Wild Bill,* 2nd ed.   Norman, Univ. of Okla. Press, 1974.

Harwood, William A., pioneer (1847-Mar. 5, 1913). B. in Delaware, he reached Arizona about 1876 and became a prospector, and lumber merchant. He was affiliated in some way with the Schieffelin brothers in the vicinity of Tombstone, where he probably was the first mayor. He was a member of the Legislature from Cochise County in 1885. He died at Tombstone.

Ed Bartholomew, *Wyatt Earp: The Man & The Myth,*   Toyahvale, Tex., Frontier Book Co., 1964.

Hasbrouck, Henry Cornelius, army officer (Oct. 26, 1839-Dec. 17, 1910). B. at Newburgh, New York, he was graduated from West Point May 6, 1861 and became an officer in the 4th Artillery, taking part in the battle of Bull Run, the defense of Washington and, after two years instruction in philosophy at the Point, the final battles around Richmond, refusing a brevet as major for gallant, meritorious services at the siege of Petersburg.

Still an artillery captain, he took part in the 1873 Modoc War in northeastern California and was the key officer in ending the series of army defeats and turning the war against the Indians. During the action of Sorass Lake, Hasbrouck's light battery, mounted as cavalry, and two troops of the 4th Cavalry were camped at the lake May 10. Captain Jack, garbed in the uniform of the assassinated General Canby, led his 33 Indians in an attack on the force. One detachment was absent from the camp; the Indians stampeded the horses and mules and "for a time things looked serious." Hasbrouck rallied his men, checked the advance and "by a series of brilliant charges," put the Modocs to flight and sent them down the long road to dispersion and ultimate defeat. Hasbrouck won his brevet as major for this action. He was on a minor expedition against Nevada Indians in 1875, remaining in the field until 1878. In the summer of 1887 he witnessed maneuvers of the French army. During the Spanish-American War he served in Cuba, becoming commander of the Department of Pinar del Rio. He became a Brigadier General in 1902 and retired. He died at Newburgh and was buried at West Point.

42nd Annual Reunion of Assn. of Graduates of USMA, 12 June 1911.

Has-cal-te, bronco Apache (d. April 1, 1894). B. probably on the San Carlos Reservation, Arizona, Has-cal-te was tried for second degree murder of a freighter, convicted in October, 1889 at Globe, Arizona and sentenced to 12 years at Yuma Territorial Prison. Being transported in a stagecoach in which were the Apache Kid and several other convicted men, the prisoners on November 2, 1889, overcame their guards near the present Kelvin, Arizona and escaped, leaving two dead whites and one wounded. Has-cal-te, Say-es and El-cahn hid out along Mescal Creek, a tributary to the Gila River until Say-es killed a relative of Has-cal-te, whereupon the latter turned himself in and revealed the hiding place of the others; troops captured Say-es and killed El-cahn in September 1890. Has-cal-te and Say-es were sent again to Yuma prison where they were lodged together in Cell 13. Say-es died March 29 and Has-cal-te followed him in death, both succumbing to consumption.

Jess G. Hayes, *Apache Vengeance.*   Albuquerque, Univ. of New Mex. Press, 1954; Dan L. Thrapp, *Al Sieber, Chief of Scouts.* Norman, Univ. of Okla. Press, 1964; William Sparks, *The Apache Kid, a Bear Fight...* Los Angeles, Skelton Pub. Co., 1926.

Haskell, Charles M., adventurer (c. 1813-Mar. 6, 1836). Charles M. Haskell was a cousin of Charles Ready Haskell (b. Sept. 12, 1817, near Nashville) and also probably b. in Tennessee, reaching Texas from Louisiana. Houston, on January 30, 1860, wrote that "I sent him with Bowie and Bonham from Goliad to the Alamo, with an express to blow up the Alamo, on the 17th of Jany. 1836." Charles M. Haskell was killed at the Alamo; Charles Ready Haskell fell at Goliad, March 27, 1836. Haskell County, Texas, was named in honor of Charles Ready Haskell.

Amelia Williams, XXXVI, 278; XXXVII, 234; HT.

Haskell, Harry L., army officer (Sept. 24, 1840-Oct. 25, 1908). B. at Clinton, Maine, he enlisted at 21 in the 125th New York Infantry and became sergeant major, August 26, 1862. He was commissioned a second lieutenant in that regiment March 16, 1863, and ended the war a captain with a creditable record, including scouting operations in the Shenandoah Valley, being captured and exchanged, and participation in the Battle of Gettysburg and the Wilderness Campaign. He was wounded at Spottsylvania, May 12, 1864. After duty in Georgia he became acting adjutant of Major John Green's infantry battalion, seeing service against the Nez Perce in Idaho and Wyoming. He was aide de camp to Colonel Orlando Bolivar Willcox in Arizona from March 1878 to September 1882. During this time, as chief of scouting operations on the southern border of Arizona and New Mexico, he effected in December 1879, the surrender of Juh and Geronimo and 108 hostile Chiricahuas after a daring interview without escort with them in their camp in the Guadalupe Mountains. Chronically ill most of his life from a series of ailments and injuries, Haskell nevertheless received regular promotions. He was named to the 12th Infantry in 1867 and was made major in 1899, lieutenant colonel of the 30th Infantry in 1901, colonel of the 12th, 1903, Brigadier General, 1904, when he was retired for disability. He had contracted malaria in Cuba and on Luzon during the Spanish American War, and died at San Diego from amoebic dysentery, also acquired during that conflict. Haskell, of medium height and fair appearance, was an able officer of considerable bravery and useful service. He was married but had no children.

Harry L. Haskell, Military and Pension Records, NARS.

Haskell, Thales Hasting, Mormon pioneer (Feb. 21, 1834-June 13, 1909). B. at North New Salem, Massachusetts, he early joined the Mormon sect, reached Nauvoo, Illinois, shortly before its evacuation, and became "a good frontiersman, always being included in every dangerous mission." He was a member of the Southern Indian Mission of 1854 and succeeding years, charged with establishing a working relationship with the Paiutes of southern Utah to facilitate settlement of the area. Haskell accompanied Jacob Hamblin to Salt Lake City in the late summer of 1857, and was not present at the Mountain Meadows Massacre of September 11. He was long associated with Hamblin. In the spring of 1858 the Mormons were excited about the true significance, if any, of the Joseph C. Ives exploration by steamboat of the Colorado River; Hamblin sent Haskell to board one of the boats as a "Mormon renegade," to learn what he could of the designs of the exploration party. He reported back a very distorted concept of the expedition's purposes; Ives in his *Report Upon the Colorado River of the West in 1857 and 1858,* wrote an amused version of this spying activity by Haskell whom "we perceived (to be) a Mormon.... For some reason he chose to make a mystery of his personality and told a clumsily contrived and impossible story... (several) discrepancies (in his tale) did not argue well for (his) sanctity... (He) departed with early dawn to join his companions, first extracting all the information he could..." Haskell and his wife settled at Pinto, Utah, then went to Bluff in southeastern Utah where they lived seven years, moving to Manassa, Colorado, in 1886. Haskell "was always on the frontier, always on the exploring expeditions. He wrote verse and songs." He died at Manassa.

Juanita Brooks, ed., *Journal of the Southern Indian Mission.* Logan, Utah State Univ. Press, 1972; Ives, *Report upon the Colorado River of the West.* 36th Cong., 1st Sess., Hse. Exec. Doc. 90, Wash., 1861.

Haskin, Peter V., army officer (fl. 1864-1870). B. in New York he was a first lieutenant in the 6th New York Cavalry in 1864-65, commissioned a second lieutenant in the 5th U.S. Cavalry in 1867, in late 1868 was transferred to the frontier in Kansas as a first lieutenant, took part in several expeditions and skirmishes including the decisive victory over the Cheyennes July 11, 1869, at Summit Springs. He resigned and returned to civil pursuits.

Price, *Fifth Cavalry.*

Haslam, Robert H. (Pony Bob), Pony Express rider (1840-Feb. 29, 1912). B. at London, England, he became "one of the most daring, resourceful, and best-known riders" of the Pony Express in 1860-61. Haslam helped build stations along the route, then was assigned the 75-mile run between Friday's Station near Lake Tahoe on the California-Nevada border and Buckland's Station (Fort Churchill), to the east. In May 1860, the Paiute Indians became hostile. On one occasion Haslam rode his route eastward, at Buckland's Station found that his relief rider refused to proceed; Bob was offered $50 if he would take the mail on. He accepted, continuing to Smith Creek, 190 miles from his point of origin, his elapsed time 18 hours. The westbound mail arrived after he had but a brief rest and he started westward. After a ride of 30 miles he found the station keeper at Cold Springs killed and all horses swept off by Indians. At Sand Springs, 37 miles farther west he persuaded the station keeper to accompany him to the Sink of the Carson — fortunately since after their departure the station was attacked by hostiles. At Buckland's Station Haslam's bonus doubled to $100 and he continued to Friday's Station, an overall ride of 380 miles in 36 hours, the feat "surrounded with perils on every hand," and his record never bested in the history of the organization. During his days with the Express Haslam twice was wounded by Indians, once, it was reported, struck in the jaw by an arrow while carrying Lincoln's Inaugural Address. Eventually Haslam took over a ride between Reno and Virginia City, Nevada, after the telegraph had made the Pony Express proper obsolete. Later he rode the 100-mile route between Queen's River and Owyhee, Idaho. In the 1870s Haslam was deputy U.S. marshal at Salt Lake City and later was messenger on a stage line between Salt Lake City and Denver. For many years he was associated with Buffalo Bill Cody's Wild West Show. At one time he was its advance agent, "a task to which he brought no experience and little capacity." In 1890 he accompanied Cody on an abortive attempt to locate Sitting Bull and head off a feared Sioux uprising, but nothing came of the endeavor. Haslam eventually became a clerk or steward at the Congress or Auditorium Hotel in Chicago. He died at Chicago, his small headstone paid for in part by Cody. Haslam was married.

Raymond V., Mary Lund Settle, *Saddles and Spurs.* Lincoln, Univ. of Neb. Press, 1972; Don Russell, *The Lives and Legends of Buffalo Bill.* Norman, Univ. of Okla. Press, 1960; Kate B. Carter, *Riders of the Pony Express.* Salt Lake City, Pony Express Mid-Century Memorial Commission of Utah, 1974; Fred R. Egloff, "Trails Paved Under," Chicago, *Westerners Brand Book,* Vol. XXXIX, No. 2 (May-June 1982), 11; Haslam death certificate.

Hasson, Patrick, army officer (Dec. 23, 1834-Sept. 20, 1927). B. in Ireland he enlisted January 12, 1856, from Philadelphia in the 4th Infantry and rose to sergeant by 1861. Two months after enlistment he joined Company E, 4th Infantry in southern Oregon, then in the field in Buchanan's expedition against the Rogue River Indians, Hasson taking part in the actions of Ma-ka-nootney village and the Big Bend of the Rogue River. Hasson served under Crook and Judah on various scouts and expeditions during 1857-58 in northern California, Oregon and Washington, including the Garnett expedition against the Yakima and Coeur d'Alene Indians during the fall of 1858. In 1859 Hasson was of the command of Colonel Silas Casey in the occupation of San Juan Island at the mouth of Puget Sound during the dispute with England over sovereignty. In 1860 he was transferred to Fort Yuma, California, where he was discharged in January 1860, his enlistment having expired. Hasson was unsuccessful in obtaining a commission in the Regular Army during the Civil War, working instead as a civilian in the War Department. January 22, 1867, he was commissioned a second lieutenant in the 14th Infantry, becoming a first lieutenant in 1872 and a captain April 8, 1889. He was sent to Arizona in 1867, taking part in Price's expedition against the

Hualapais Indians with elements of the 8th Cavalry (although an infantry officer). On November 3, 1867, he had a fight near the Oaks and Willows, northwestern Arizona with a large force of hostiles, reporting 32 Indians killed. On November 7 or 8 he and his men killed 20 Indians and captured 16 in a fight near Fort Rock, between Prescott and Hardyville. Hasson himself and seven of his men were wounded, the officer winning a brevet for his action. He served on the Powder River campaign with Crook from August 1876 until January 1877, and operated under Mackenzie in 1881, forcing the Utes from Colorado to Utah. Hasson retired March 28, 1892, living in retirement at Vancouver, Washington, where he died. He fathered two sons one of whom, John Patrick Hasson, born at Fort Douglas, Utah, April 10, 1878, became a commissioned officer, being first lieutenant of the 5th Cavalry by 1902. The other son, Charles J. Hasson, was born June 25, 1875, at Fort Cameron, Utah.

Order of Indian War Collection, U.S. Army Milit. Inst., Carlisle Barracks, Pa; Heitman; *Chronological List;* Dan L. Thrapp, *Conquest of Apacheria.* Norman, Univ. of Okla. Press, 1967.

Hastings, David H., army officer (c. 1815-Sept. 22, 1882). B. in Ireland, he enlisted July 19, 1837, in the 2nd Infantry rising to first sergeant by November 17, 1845. He then enlisted in the 3rd Artillery and Army Engineers, serving to first sergeant by July 14, 1848. He was wounded at Contreras, Mexico, and severely wounded in the capture of Mexico City during the Mexican War. Hastings was commissioned a brevet second lieutenant of the 1st Dragoons June 28, 1848, becoming a second lieutenant December 27, 1848, and a first lieutenant October 22, 1854. In New Mexico with his regiment he participated in several Indian campaigns and commanded the military escort for Major William H. Emory during the Mexican border survey following the Gadsden Purchase south of the Gila River. Stationed at Fort Buchanan, Arizona, Hastings was injured severely October 7, 1857 when his horse fell with him during an Indian chase. Hastings' remaining service was in the east. He became a captain January 9, 1860, joined the 1st Cavalry August 3, 1861, and became a major with the 5th Cavalry September 23, 1863, retiring

December 7 of that year. He died at Baltimore.

Heitman; Price, *Fifth Cavalry;* Constance Wynn Altshuler, *Chains of Command.* Tucson, Ariz. Hist. Soc., 1981.

Hastings, Lansford Warren, expansionist (c. 1818-c. 1868). B. probably in Knox County, Ohio, in 1842 he led the first planned overland wagon migration of any size to Oregon although only 24 years of age. Surveyed the townsite of Oregon City. In 1845 he published *The Emigrants' Guide to Oregon and California,* one of the early guidebooks of the region. He left California in the autumn of 1843 and by way of Mexico City reached New Orleans in February and Missouri in March, apparently not going by way of Texas or conferring with Sam Houston as popular myth has it. Nor is there any real evidence that he sought to become "president" of an independent California. In 1846 he went with a party east from California as far as Fort Bridger and Black Fork on the Green River, seeking to divert Oregon-bound emigrants to California by way of the cut-off named for him, down Weber Canyon, past the present Salt Lake City, the Utah-Nevada desert and the Sierra Nevada; great difficulties caused by thirst and other natural obstacles attended those who took this ill-conceived route. He served as captain, Company F, California Battalion in 1846. After marriage and several years law practice he moved his family to Arizona City, the later Yuma. A Secessionist he devised an elaborate though unfeasible plan to capture southern California, Arizona and New Mexico for the South during the Civil War. Defeat of the Confederacy sent him to Mexico and Brazil, seeking some site for colonization by unreconciled southerners. He published a guidebook to the Amazon region at Mobile in 1867, and died on his return from Brazil. A controversial person he also was an enigma on several counts; even his birth year is unknown since he gave his age variously on two censuses. He is held responsible by some for the fate of the Donner party, trapped in the Sierra Nevada while trying to follow his recommended cut-off. He was, said one historian, "a figure of more than secondary importance during the years 1843-46," although the exact extent of his contributions is not fully assessed.

Thomas F. Andrews, "The Ambitions of Lansford W. Hastings: A Study in Western Myth-Making." *Pacific Hist. Rev.,* Vol. XXXIX, No. 4 (Nov. 1970), 473-91; Lansford W. Hastings, *Emigrant's Guide to Oregon and California,* hist. note and biblio. by Charles Henry Carey. Princeton University Press, 1932.

Hatch, Edward, army officer (Dec. 23, 1832-Apr. 11, 1889). B. at Bangor, Maine, he studied two years at Norwich University, Northfield, Vermont, and in 1848 made a voyage as a seaman, but didn't take to that profession and moved to Iowa, determined to become a lumberman. On August 12, 1861 he was commissioned captain of the 2nd Iowa Cavalry, becoming major September 5, lieutenant colonel December 11, and colonel June 13, 1862. He ended the Civil War (after hard service under Sherman) a brevet Major General of Volunteers and became colonel of the 9th U.S. Cavalry July 28, 1866, the next year receiving a belated brevet of Major General in the army for Civil War service. Hatch was stationed in Texas after the Civil War, having his hands full with turbulence along the Mexican border, and clashing head on with Lieutenant Colonel Nathan Augustus Monroe Dudley, also of the 9th Cavalry, the difficulty arising from a race riot at Jefferson, Texas, October 4, 1868 with several lynchings. In 1876 Hatch became commander of the Military District of New Mexico while Dudley commanded Fort Union; during much of the Lincoln County War in New Mexico the antagonism between the two surfaced from time to time. Most of Hatch's problems in New Mexico came however from Apache difficulties. He cooperated fully with John P. Clum, Arizona agent who removed the Mimbres Apaches from Ojo Caliente, New Mexico, to San Carlos Reservation in 1877, but many of those removed broke out under the able Victorio and regained their southern New Mexico homeland. Settled at last on the Mescalero Reservation, Victorio was flushed out of that reserve and onto the warpath by error, and from then on was Hatch's principal headache. For more than a year he depredated and battled through the southern part of the Territory, seemingly immune to capture and Hatch was roundly battered by the local press for not more promptly taking the hostiles into custody or killing them; neither was easy to do. Victorio

finally was defeated by a civilian chief of scouts and his Indians and driven from the Territory, ultimately to be slain in Mexico. Hatch's judgment was not always of the best. In April 1880 he became convinced that Victorio's principal source of munitions and recruits was the Mescalero Reservation in New Mexico, and after troop elements had been defeated by the hostiles in the San Andres Mountains, Hatch with an immense force swooped down on the Mescalero Reservation in an attempt to dismount and disarm the Apaches there. A few were killed and others bolted, about 50 of them joining Victorio, thus adding to the strength of that chief and the length of his war and negating Hatch's primary purpose. In 1879 Hatch had been diverted by the necessity to send troops to contain Colorado Utes in case the Milk River troubles should spread southward (they did not), and was one of a commission of three investigating the difficulties and attempting to identify who among the Utes was responsible for the killings that accompanied them. Twelve Indians were so identified and listed for trial if they could be apprehended. Meanwhile Hatch's New Mexico problems had not lessened; his wife died of smallpox at Washington, D.C., and October 30, 1881, Hatch was succeeded in command of the district by Ranald Mackenzie of the 4th Cavalry. In March 1889 he was thrown from his buggy at Fort Robinson, Nebraska, fracturing a hip. Seemingly recovering, he died suddenly. During his career Hatch had taken part in 40 battles and skirmishes.

Heitman; Philip J. Rasch, "The Men at Fort Stanton." *English Westerners' Brand Book,* Vol. 3 (Apr. 1961), 2-8; Robert M. Utley, *Frontier Regulars.* N.Y., Macmillan Co., 1973; Dan L. Thrapp, *Victorio and the Mimbres Apaches.* Norman, Univ. of Okla. Press, 1974.

Hatch, Edwin A.C., Indian official (Mar. 23, 1825-Sept. 13, 1882). B. at New York, he may have seen service with a volunteer organization in the Mexican War, since he was referred to as "major," though not listed by Heitman. He reached Minnesota in 1843, settling at St. Paul. Hatch was appointed first agent for the Blackfoot Indians in 1855, holding the position for less than two years when he was succeeded by Alfred J. Vaughan. Hatch was presented to the Indians at a treaty council in October 1855, then established the agency at

Fort Benton, Montana. His "two most noteworthy achievements" included a rousing ball for fur traders at the post December 31, 1855, which lasted for two days and two nights, and overseeing distribution of annuities. During eight months in 1856 he was not at Fort Benton, but at Fort Union, awaiting arrival upriver of the annuities which were distributed September 22-23. His only annual report was written in July 1856, but since he had spent so little time with his charges, it was short on detail. Hatch returned to Minnesota and died at St. Paul.

Montana Contributions, Vol. X, 1940, 270; John C. Ewers, *The Blackfeet: Raiders on the North- western Plains.* Norman, Univ. of Okla. Press, 1958.

Hatch, Ira, Mormon Indian specialist (Aug. 5, 1835-Nov. 25, 1927). The son of Ira Stearns Hatch, he was b. perhaps in New York or Ohio. He was of the Southern Indian Mission from 1854, sent to south Utah to work with the Indians, and in this he found his life's calling. It is said he learned to speak fluently 13 Indian tongues, including the difficult Navaho. "Always he lived on the frontier, moving as he was called to places where tact in Indian relations was needed." Hatch led a band of Indians who tracked down and slaughtered three men who sought to escape to California from the beleaguered Fancher emigrant train at the Mountain Meadows site of the September 11, 1857, massacre. Hatch's party killed two of the men as they slept in the Santa Cruz Mountains, wounded a third, and Hatch himself was said to have slain him later. A paper or notebook the victim was carrying was taken either by Hatch or by an Indian and ultimately was destroyed by John D. Lee, or turned over to higher church authority. Hatch was sent in 1860 to northern Arizona with Jacob Hamblin to become a missionary to the Moqui (Hopi) Indians. Hatch's only wife was Sarah Spanesbank, daughter of a Navaho chief and a Paiute woman; he fathered three sons and a daughter. Hatch died at Fruitland, New Mexico.

Frank Esshom, *Pioneer and Prominent Men of Utah,* Salt Lake City, Western Epics, 1966; Juanita Brooks, *Mountain Meadows Massacre.* Norman, Univ. of Okla. Press, 1966; Brooks, *John D. Lee.* Glendale, Calif., Arthur H. Clark Co., 1962; Brooks, ed., *Journal of the Southern Indian Mission.* Logan, Utah State Univ. Press, 1972;

William Wise, *Massacre at Mountain Meadows.* N.Y., Thomas Y. Crowell Co., 1976.

Hatch, Ira Stearns, Mormon pioneer (Feb. 9, 1800-Sept. 30, 1869). B. at Winchester, New York, he joined the Mormon sect in 1832, was ordained elder in 1852, having reached Utah in 1849 after service with the Mormon Battalion and before that with the Nauvoo Legion. Ira Stearns Hatch was made a member of the Seventy shortly before his death. He was the father of Ira Hatch, a noted Indian specialist and interpreter.

Frank Esshom, *Pioneers and Prominent Men of Utah.* Salt Lake City, Western Epics, 1966.

Hatch, John Porter, army officer (Jan. 9, 1822-Apr. 12, 1901). B. at Oswego, New York, he was graduated from West Point and commissioned a brevet second lieutenant in the 3rd Infantry July 1, 1845. He transferred to the Mounted Rifles (3rd Cavalry) July 17, 1846, and became a second lieutenant April 18, 1847. Hatch participated in the military occupation of Texas and in the Mexican War, winning two brevets. In February 1849 he was at Camp Sumner, near Fort Leavenworth, departing in May on an overland march with the regiment to Oregon, reaching Fort Vancouver October 1. He returned east in late 1850 and was stationed in Texas in 1852 and in 1856 in New Mexico. Hatch in 1857 took part in Bonneville's expedition against the Gila Apaches, participating in the fight at the Canyon de los Muerto Carneros on May 24. Later he was stationed at Fort Defiance, in 1858 taking part in an operation against the Navahos and commanding troops in a skirmish near the Laguna Negra September 25, 1858. Hatch became a captain October 13, 1860, and a Brigadier General of Volunteers September 28, 1861, going through the Civil War in that rank while becoming a major in the 4th Cavalry October 27, 1863. Most of his postwar positions were administrative, his service in Texas, Indian Territory, Montana and Washington. Hatch became lieutenant colonel of the 5th Cavalry January 15, 1873, transferred to the 4th Cavalry and became colonel of the 2nd Cavalry in 1881. He retired January 9, 1886, living in New York City until his death. He was married and his widow, a son and daughter survived him.

Cullum; Heitman; Powell; Price, *Fifth Cavalry.*

Hatcher, John L., frontiersman (c. 1812-c. 1897). B. in Botetourt County, Virginia, he reached St. Louis about 1835, going west with a Bent and St. Vrain party and being employed at Bent's Fort for several years. He lived for a time with the Kiowas. He was guide for Lieutenant J.W. Abert, exploring the Texas Panhandle. In 1846 he traded for mules in Old Mexico, met Lewis Garrard in New Mexico (who wrote about Hatcher), became an Army scout during the Mexican War and after, and was in an out of Bent's Fort frequently. In 1853 he drove sheep to California, returning to Santa Fe December 25. He became a noted southwestern scout and freighter. Hatcher returned to Missouri in 1858 and drove sheep to California again, settling in the Sonoma Valley in 1859; in 1867 he moved to Oregon. He died on his farm in Linn County, Oregon

Harvey L. Carter article, MM, Vol. IV; Lewis H. Garrard, *Wah-to-yah and the Taos Trail.* Norman, Univ. of Okla. Press, 1955.

Hatchiorauquasha, Ignace: *see* John Grey

Hatfield, Charles Albert Phelps, army officer (Dec. 9, 1850-June 19, 1931). B. in Alabama he was a West Point graduate who joined the 4th Cavalry in 1872. According to Patch he was of the West Virginia Hatfield clan that feuded so sanguinarily with the McCoys. He "must have inherited at least one of the habits of his ancestors for on one occasion, when he had trouble with another officer, he invited him to 'shoot it out' before breakfast." The duel was averted. Hatfield performed frontier duty in Texas from 1872-75, served at Fort Sill, Oklahoma, from 1875-77, then returned to Texas where he resumed scouting activities. Hatfield took part with Mackenzie in the raid across the Rio Grande in May 1873, attacking the Lipan and Kickapoo villages in Mexico, and he probably participated in the Palo Duro Canyon, Texas, fight against Comanches September 28, 1874. He won a brevet for a fight May 16, 1886, against hostile Apaches in the Santa Cruz Mountains of Sonora. Hatfield served at Washington State posts and in Idaho from 1890. He went to Cuba in 1899, serving there until 1901; was in the Philippines intermittently from 1901 to 1911, and served on the Mexican border from 1912 to 1914 when he retired, a colonel. He returned briefly to active duty in 1917. Hatfield died at Baltimore, Maryland. He had

some artistic talent, was a particular friend of John Bigelow who wrote *On the Bloody Trail of Geronimo,* and wrote several magazine articles on frontier matters late in life.

Heitman; Cullum; Joseph Dorst Patch, *Reminiscences of Fort Huachuca, Arizona.* Wash., p.p., 1962; "Ranald S. Mackenzie's Official Correspondence Relating to Texas, 1871-1873," ed. by Ernest Wallace. *Museum Journal,* Lubbock, Tex. Tech. College, Vol. IX (1965).

Hauser, Samuel Thomas, frontiersman (Jan. 10, 1832-Nov. 10, 1914). B. at Falmouth, Kentucky, he went to Missouri as a railroad surveyor in 1854. About 1860 he attempted to halt the legal lynching of a man, was nearly shot himself, protested the incident in a local newspaper and was forced to leave the community. He boarded a Missouri River steamer, reaching Fort Benton in 1862 and continued overland to the Salmon River placers, then returned to Bannack and Grasshopper Creek, Montana. In 1863 he joined James Stuart's Yellowstone expedition. He narrowly escaped a night attack by Indians on the party, a thick notebook over his heart stopping a bullet. In 1865 Hauser and William F. Sanders established a bank at Virginia City, Montana. In 1870 Hauser was a member of the Washburn Yellowstone expedition, using his engineering skill to measure the height of waterfalls, of geysers and to map Yellowstone Lake. His business interests continued to expand. He died at Helena, Montana.

Aubrey L. Haines, *Yellowstone National Park: Its Exploration and Establishment.* Wash., Nat. Park Service, 1974.

Hawkins, Benjamin, Indian agent (Aug. 15, 1754-June 6, 1816). B. in Granville (later Warren) County, North Carolina, he was studying at Princeton College at the outbreak of the Revolutionary War when he was appointed to George Washington's staff as French interpreter. He returned to North Carolina in 1778, became a member of the legislature and served in the Continental Congress from 1781-84, 1786 and 1787. In 1785 he was named a commissioner to deal with Cherokees, Choctaws, and Chickasaws; he concluded the Hopewell Treaty of November 28, 1785, with the Cherokee; the Hopewell Treaty with the Choctaws January 3, 1786, and the Hopewell Treaty with the

Chickasaw January 10. Hawkins was senator from 1789-95 when he was appointed by Washington to negotiate with the Creek Confederacy, arriving at the important Colerain Treaty June 29, 1796. He had now dealt with the most important Indian bodies of the southeast and Washington appointed him agent to the Creeks and general superintendent of all Indian tribes south of the Ohio; he accepted at once and spent the rest of his life in this capacity. He established his headquarters initially at Fort Hawkins in the Creek nation, on the Ocmulgee River opposite the present Macon, Georgia. Hawkins of course paid many visits to the Upper Creeks at Tuckabatchie and the Lower Creeks at Coweta and became one of the best-known Indian agents in American history; since he was already quite wealthy there never was any significant hint at his agency of the corruption that seemed endemic in many others, and although Hawkins was criticized from time to time there seemed little doubt of his devotion to public service. He eventually moved his headquarters to the Old Agency on the Flint River in Crawford County, Georgia. Hawkins devoted much attention to teaching his Creek charges husbandry and agriculture. He created a large model farm, a plantation that served as an agricultural college for the Indians. Until the War of 1812 he held the Creeks and other Indians at peace. When Tecumseh visited the Creeks, Hawkins attended at least one of his councils with the southern Indians, although the troubles the great Shawnee stirred up culminated in the Creek War of 1813-14 which Hawkins, because of ill health, was unable to prevent. During it however he raised a regiment of friendly Creeks, financing it from his own pocket and turned over command to William McIntosh (see entry). Hawkins was bitterly opposed not only to the Creek War but its consequences: the loss to the Creeks of much of their ancestral lands through the Fort Jackson Treaty. He died at the Old Agency and was buried on his plantation near Roberta, overlooking the Flint River, Crawford County, Georgia. Hawkins was highly literate. He wrote *Sketch of the Creek Country in 1798 and 1799* (Part I, Vol. 3, *Collections,* Georgia Historical Society, 1848) and *Letters of Benjamin Hawkins, 1796-1806* (Georgia Historical Society, 1916). He left a great deal of manuscript material upon his death, but much of it was destroyed by fire shortly afterward.

Merritt B. Pound, *Benjamin Hawkins, Indian Agent.* Athens, Univ. of Ga. Press, 1951.

Hawkins, John (Jacob Hawken), mountain man (fl. 1828-c. 1849). Perhaps b. in St. Louis, he went up the Missouri and became a beaver trapper, working with Bridger and other notables. He probably was a son of the famous gunsmith, Jacob Hawken, but there is much confusion about his true name and place within the family. He took part in an 1835 skirmish with the Blackfeet, and had other adventures. About 1840 he was employed by Bent, St. Vrain & Company, visiting St. Louis occasionally, but spending most of his time in the southwest, trapping and trading. He may have returned to St. Louis thereafter.

Janet Lecompte article, MM, Vol. IV.

Hawkins, Joseph H., legislator, expansionist (d. fall 1823). B. at Lexington, Kentucky, the date of his birth is uncertain, but he served in the Kentucky legislature from 1810-13 and as United States Representative from 1814-15. He moved in 1819 to New Orleans where he befriended Stephen F. Austin and became interested in Texas colonization projects, although he apparently never visited Texas himself. Hawkins purchased and outfitted vessels to transport colonists, paid seamen and made personal loans to colonists, spending about $30,000 supporting colonization undertakings in Texas. The circumstances of his death are not reported.

BDAC; HT.

Hawkins, Joseph M(ark?), adventurer (c. 1799-Mar. 6, 1836). B. in Ireland, he reached Texas from Louisiana, "a man of intelligence and influence." From his signature to his letters he seems to have been known by his middle name, perhaps to avoid confusion with some other Joseph Hawkins. He died at the Alamo.

Amelia Williams, XXXVII, 264-65.

Hawley, John, Mormon pioneer (fl. 1857). A man of this name was placed by *Mormonism Unveiled* at the Mountain Meadows Massacre of September 11, 1857, either participating in or consenting to the tragedy. He was said to have died in the Indian Nation before 1892.

Mormonism Unveiled, 379.

Hawley, William, Mormon pioneer (fl. 1857-1892). A man of this name was placed by *Mormonism Unveiled* at the Mountain Meadows Massacre of September 11, 1857, either participating in or consenting to the tragedy. He was reported in 1892 as living at Fillmore, Utah.

Mormonism Unveiled, 379.

Hayden, Ferdinand Vandiveer, geologist, public figure (Sept. 7, 1829-Dec. 22, 1887). B. at Westfield, Massachusetts, he was raised on a farm near Rochester, New York, studied at Oberlin College, Ohio, and graduated in medicine in 1853 from Albany Medical College, New York. He accompanied paleontologist Fielding Bradford Meek to the Dakota Badlands on an 1853 expedition. The following year he went farther north along the Missouri, and in 1856 reconnoitred the Fort Benton, Montana, area. With a military expedition he explored the Yellowstone River and Black Hills of South Dakota. In 1858 he undertook the geological exploration of Kansas, and in 1859 returned to the upper Missouri and Gallatin basin of Montana. During the Civil War Hayden served the Union Army as surgeon. In 1865 he was named professor of geology and mineralogy at the University of Pennsylvania, holding the position in absentia while continuing field work. In 1867 he conducted a geological survey of Nebraska and in 1869 was put in charge of the forerunner of the United States Geological Survey, continuing for several years in that position. He completed a highly successful expedition in 1869 from Denver through the mountains to Santa Fe. In 1871 Hayden led an expedition into the Yellowstone country, spurred by reports of its wonders. The 34-man group joined with a military party in the Yellowstone Valley and explored the area for more than a month. In his 500-page report and by every means Hayden urged creation of a national park covering the region and on March 1, 1872, President Grant signed the bill establishing Yellowstone as the nation's first such reserve. When the United States Geological Survey was launched in 1879, Hayden continued with it, retiring in 1886 because of poor health. He died at Philadelphia.

Ferdinand Vandiveer Hayden and the Founding of the Yellowstone National Park. Wash., U.S. Dept. of Inter., Geol. Survey, 1973; DAB; EB; EA.

Haydon (Hayden), pioneers (d. Sept 11, 1857). A family of this name, composition unknown, perished with destruction of the Fancher emigrant wagon train at Mountain Meadows, southwestern Utah, at the hands of Mormons and Mormon-led Indians.

William Wise, *Massacre at Mountain Meadows.* N.Y., Thomas Y. Crowell Co., 1976.

Hayes, Bob (Sam Hassell, John West), outlaw (c. 1874-Nov. 18, 1896). B. in Iowa, he went into outlawry in Texas where he was sentenced to five years for horse rustling, broke jail and reached New Mexico early in 1895, becoming one of the High Fives outlaw gang of the Christians (see William Christian biography for their record). He took part in the Nogales, Arizona, bank holdup August 6, 1896, at Rio Puerco, New Mexico, and train holdup October 2, 1896; was with George Musgrave October 19 at the shooting of George T. Parker southwest of Roswell. Hayes took part in minor outlawry, savagely beating an aged postmaster at Separ, New Mexico, who resisted his demand for money, and was killed in a gunfight at a Diamond A horse camp in the Animas Mountains, southwest New Mexico.

Jeff Burton, *Black Jack Christian: Outlaw.* Santa Fe, Press of the Territorian, 1967.

Hayes, Edward Mortimer, army officer (Dec. 23, 1842-Aug. 15, 1912). B. in New York, he enlisted as a musician in the mounted service in 1856, was assigned to the 5th Cavalry and sent to Camp Cooper, Texas, participating in a series of actions against hostile Indians: Brazos River, Wichita Village, Small Creek; he was on the Wichita expedition of 1858-59 and in the affair at Pecan Bayou. His enlistment expiring he returned to Ohio and in the Civil War entered the military telegraph service, later serving in the 10th Ohio Cavalry as a commissioned officer, was mustered out a brevet major and became a second lieutenant in the 5th Cavalry. In 1868 he was assigned to frontier service, participating in Indian campaigns in Kansas, Colorado and Indian Territory. On July 11, 1869, he was prominent in the decisive victory at Summit Springs over the Cheyennes. When Colonel Carr ordered the bugler to sound the charge on the hostile villages, the man was paralyzed by fear, and Hayes, who had been a musician, snatched the instrument from him and blew a perfect call.

Although much of the time quartermaster, Hayes sought and accepted participation in whatever combat was at hand, and invariably acquitted himself well. He was on the Big Horn and Yellowstone expedition of 1876 and at the battle of Slim Buttes, Dakota, September 9 of that year. He became captain in 1874, major of the 7th Cavalry in 1893, lieutenant colonel of the 4th Cavalry in 1899, colonel of the 13th Cavalry in 1901, and a Brigadier General in 1903, retiring that year.

Heitman; Price, *Fifth Cavalry.*

Hays, John Coffee (Jack), ranger, frontiersman (Jan. 28, 1817-Apr. 25, 1883). B. at Little Cedar Lick, Wilson County, Tennessee, he reached Texas from Mississippi where he had worked as a surveyor, pursuing that profession intermittently in Texas. He reached Texas shortly after the battle of San Jacinto, and was employed surveying land titles but because of his fighting qualities, soon led Texas Ranger units against Indians and Mexican guerillas. According to some accounts, he served under Henry W. Karnes and Erastus (Deaf) Smith against frontier marauders. In 1840 the Ranger forces were enlarged and Hays became a captain, taking part in memorable fights against the Comanche at Plum Creek in 1840, Enchanted Rock in 1841, at Bandera Pass in 1842, and the battle of the Salado against Mexican forces under Adrian Woll six miles east of San Antonio in 1842. In the Mexican War, Hays was colonel of the 1st regiment, Texas Mounted Volunteers, taking part in the battles at Monterrey and Mexico City; he was mustered out in 1848 upon his return to Texas. He was a member of a commission to settle a boundary dispute between Texas and the United States with regard to the territory of New Mexico. On April 11, 1849, Hays was named first agent for the Gila Apaches, but found it impossible to establish contact with that hostile people, although "some of my own companions were killed by them at the very time they were intimating an intention to treat with us," and he resigned his office from San Diego, California, January 3, 1850. Hays had been accompanied to California by a sizable party attracted by Gold Rush reports, he proceeding to the San Francisco Bay region. He was elected sheriff of San Francisco County in 1850, re-elected in 1851, and served until 1853 when he was appointed by President Pierce surveyor-general of the state. In this capacity Hays is said to have laid out the city of Oakland, and became one of its greatest promoters. When the Pyramid Lake War erupted in Nevada in 1860 with the ambush and nearly complete destruction of a group of 105 volunteers, Hays was placed in command of a force of 549 more determined volunteers, bolstered by 207 regulars under Captain Joseph Stewart, 3rd Artillery. At the mouth of the Truckee River, a resounding victory over the Indians was gained; this was Hays' last Indian fight. He entered the real estate business, and became a major financial and development figure of Oakland, but was an invalid late in life. He died near Piedmont, Alameda County, California. Married, he fathered six children, two surviving to maturity.

DAB; HT; Dan L. Thrapp, *Victorio and the Mimbres Apaches.* Norman, Univ. of Okla. Press, 1974; Russell R. Elliott, *History of Nevada.* Lincoln, Univ. of Nebr. Press, 1973.

Hays, William Jacob, artist (Aug. 8, 1830-Mar. 13, 1875). B. at New York City, he studied art under John Rubens Smith, and in 1860 visited the upper Missouri River country, his trip resulting in work of current and lasting value. He went up the river aboard the *Spread Eagle,* a steamboat, leaving St. Louis May 3 and reaching Fort Union June 15. He continued upstream, sketching as he progressed, his field works "important because they portray a number of the trading posts of the upper Missouri, for some of which there are no other pictorial records," and for his animal pictures. He commenced his descent July 9 and by July 27 had reached St. Louis. Some of the results of his western trip have enduring value: "The Herd on the Move," now at the Gilcrease Institute, Tulsa, Oklahoma; "The Stampede," called for some modern reason the "Buffalo Hunt," and "The Wounded Bison," perhaps Hays' most famous painting, both held by the American Museum of Natural History of New York. Besides his western trip, Hays made a journey to Nova Scotia and did much work in the Adirondacks, producing pictures of fauna and flora for the most part. He spent his last years in ill health and died at New York.

Robert Taft, *Artists and Illustrators of the Old West: 1850-1900.* N.Y., Bonanza Books, (post 1953); DAB.

Hazen, Eli Warnock, soldier (Apr. 29, 1839-Jan. 1, 1908). B. at New Castle, Pennsylvania, Hazen went to California with the Gold Rush or afterward. In August 1861, as a "carriage trimmer" he enlisted in Company E, 1st California Volunteer Infantry, with Captain Thomas L. Roberts his commanding officer. Hazen with his company was part of the California Column, which marched eastward to the Rio Grande; he was mustered out at Los Pinos (Pinos Altos?), New Mexico, on August 31, 1864. He kept a diary of his marches and mileages, and extended notes on the incidents of his service and some of the places visited. These include fresh details of the Battle of Apache Pass, where Roberts' company was heavily engaged, a narrative that is of prime historical value, interesting comments on Tucson and other places. Hazen continued east after the war, spending the rest of his life as a New Castle farmer. He died of pneumonia and was buried at New Castle. Hazen was married and fathered two children.

"The California Column in the Civil War: Hazen's Civil War Diary," ed. by Konrad F. Schreier, Jr. *Jour. of San Diego Hist.,* Vol. XXII, No. 2 (Spring 1976), 41-48.

Hazen, William Babcock, army officer (Sept. 27, 1830-Jan. 16, 1887). B. at Hartford, Vermont, he was raised in Ohio, graduated from West Point in 1855, was assigned to the 4th Infantry at Fort Reading, California, but shortly moved to Fort Lane, Oregon. He was occupied for some time with Rogue River and Klamath Indian hostilities and with assembling the former enemy on new reservations in the face of native reluctance and white suspicion and threats. After 19 months Hazen was ordered to Texas, reaching Fort Davis February 13, 1858, from where he scouted against hostile Mescalero Apaches and other peoples; he was transferred to Fort Inge, near Uvalde, where again he operated against disruptive elements, earning a brevet for two actions. Hazen was severely wounded in a skirmish with Comanches, terminating his Texas frontier career. His Civil War record was good, Hazen emerging as a Major General of Volunteers, and being brevetted up to Major General for gallantry in important battles. He was named colonel of the 38th Infantry in 1866, first serving as acting assistant inspector general of the Department

of the Platte. He made his initial inspection with a small soldier detachment and Ambrose Bierce as civilian topographer; Bierce had been a topographical officer in Hazen's Civil War brigade, agreed to join the expedition after authorities rejected Hazen's request for an army topographical engineer, and his maps were included in the final inspection report. In addition to Forts Reno and C.F. Smith, Wyoming, the Hazen party visited Forts Cooke and Benton, Montana, and finally Fort Douglas, Utah. August 10, 1868, Sherman named Hazen agent of the southern of two large Indian districts formed as a result of Grant's Peace Policy, the district generally in the present state of Oklahoma. Hazen's management of it was complicated by such military operations as Custer's Washita expedition and the work of Indian Bureau agents. He helped select the site for the future Fort Sill, first called Camp Wichita, but it was difficult to make farmers out of erstwhile warriors, and his work was not very successful; his services as special agent concluded June 30, 1869. He was named to the Southern Superintendency of Indian affairs, implementing formation of an intertribal government for the so-called Five Civilized Tribes in Oklahoma. He left the Indian service in 1870, traveled to Europe where he was an observer of the Franco-Prussian War, then served his regiment at Fort Gibson, Indian Territory, Fort Hays, Kansas, and was instrumental in the expose of Belknap's corruption. His career was often controversial; Hazen took issue with railroad promoters' rose-colored descriptions of High Plains regions by which they hoped to persuade uninformed immigrants to settle their lands. In December 1880, he was promoted to Brigadier General and placed in charge of the Army Signal Corps; he became the center of a controversy over the Greely Arctic Expedition, and a court-martial found him guilty of unduly criticizing the Secretary of War, although "the finding did not hurt his career." He died of kidney poisoning. Hazen was married.

Marvin E. Kroeker, *Great Plains Command: William B. Hazen in the Frontier West.* Norman, Univ. of Okla. Press, 1976.

Hazlett, Bill, gunman (d. June 22, 1881). B. perhaps in Shawnee County, Kansas, he and his brother established a ranch in the Animas Valley, New Mexico. For some reason they developed enmity toward desperadoes Billy the Kid Leonard and Harry the Kid Head and in a gunbattle at Owl City, New Mexico, June 6, 1881, the Hazletts killed both, perhaps to avert depredation of their ranch or mining property. Ike reportedly shot Leonard in the heart; Bill shot Head in the stomach; he was wounded six more times as he stumbled off to die. Jim Crane may have accompanied Leonard and Head; he reportedly led the band of up to 20 cowboys who returned and killed the Hazletts, who are said to have killed two more and wounded three of the Crane party before being slain at Eureka (Hachita), New Mexico.

Ed Bartholomew, *Wyatt Earp: The Man & the Myth.* Toyahvale, Tex., Frontier Book Co., 1964; Peter Hertzog, *A Directory of New Mexico Desperadoes.* Santa Fe, Press of the Territorian, 1965.

Head, Mark, mountain man (c. 1812-1847). B. in Virginia, he matured in Missouri, and became a Rocky Mountain trapper about 1832, being present at the famed battle of Pierre's Hole between trappers and Blackfeet in July 1832. Head was a member of Joe Walker's California expedition of 1833-34. In 1834 he took Sir William Drummond Stewart at his word, chased an Indian who had stolen Stewart's best horse, and scalped him for the $500 the Scotsman had off-handedly promised, the incident being "a little more than I looked for," as Stewart conceded. In May 1835, Head was mauled by a grizzly. He had a number of engagements with the Blackfeet and Sioux. On a bet he tried to tomahawk a bear to death, and again was mauled, losing most of his scalp. Head, having become the generally acknowledged epitome of the mountain man, remained in the Rockies, one adventure following another, until January 1847, when he met George Ruxton at the old Pueblo on the Arkansas. He and another were captured at the Red River settlement following the Taos uprising, and were murdered. Head, according to George Simpson, "possessed the most remarkable aptitude for getting into scrapes and out of them in a damaged condition of any man I ever knew."

Harvey L. Carter article, MM, Vol. I.

Heald, Weldon F., conservationist, writer (May 1, 1901-July 28, 1967). B. at Milford,

New Hampshire, he received a degree in architecture from Massachusetts Institute of Technology about 1923, then moved to Altadena, California, where he married Phyllis Warde in 1930. Heald had spent much of his youth in Switzerland, becoming enamored of mountains and wilderness, his tastes reflected in his slogan: "God bless America — and let's save some of it!" During World War II Heald served in the Army as a climatologist and at various times was consultant to the Secretary of the Interior on conservation matters. After the war the Healds settled on a ranch in Cochise County, Arizona, until they moved to Tucson in 1955 where he died following a heart attack. A longtime member of the Sierra Club, American Alpine Club and other organizations of that type, he became a strong voice for conservation and wilderness preservation, authoring some 650 magazine articles, largely in support of those causes. He co-authored *The Inverted Mountains* (1948); wrote several *Scenic Guides to the West,* devoted to a state apiece; contributed to several travel guides of the U.S., and with his wife wrote *Sky Island* (1968), related to the Healds' experience at their Chiricahua Mountains ranch; it was published posthumously. In 1973 Heald Peak, a 6,934 foot elevation of the Paiute Mountains, Kern County, California, was named for him and a plaque installed on its summit April 27, 1974.

Information from Phyllis W. Heald, June 24, July 10, 1974.

Healy, John, army officer (Sept. 12, 1891-Nov. 2, 1970). B. in Middlesex County, Virginia, he was graduated from the Virginia Military Institute and William and Mary College. He worked for United Fruit Company in Central America, then was commissioned in the army, serving with the 3rd, 4th, 10th, 26th and 305th U.S. Cavalry units. Healy spent much time at Fort Huachuca, Arizona, owned a cattle ranch near Hereford, Arizona, and finally retired with rank of lieutenant colonel after World War II. He was deeply interested in army history and was largely responsible for development of the Fort Huachuca Historical Museum, one of the better institutions of its kind. It was largely through his efforts that the museum's archives were created and built up.

The Huachuca Scout, Section E, Mar. 3, 1977.

Healy, John J., frontiersman (c. 1835-Sept. 15, 1908). B. in County Cork, Ireland, some calculations suggest his year of birth was around 1841, but his obituary indicates it was earlier. At 15 he joined Walker's first filibuster expedition to Nicaragua. At 17 he signed up in the 2nd U.S. Dragoons and was sent to Utah with the Albert Sidney Johnston expedition being mustered out at Camp Floyd in August 1860. He reached Portland, learned of gold strikes in Idaho and took the first boat of the 1861 season up the Columbia, at The Dalles outfitting with pack animals. He reached the Clearwater country and prospected, taking claims in the Oro Fino region of Idaho, south of Pierce City. Healy, George Grigsby and others prospected toward the Salmon River and in August 1861, made a strike that resulted in establishment of Florence, Idaho and which launched the great Salmon River gold rush, though Healy earned only $1,500 from his find. He spent the winter of 1861-62 at Elk City, early the next spring with three companions working up the merciless Salmon River gorge and by one miracle after another at last gaining the open country of Lemhi Valley, the first whites on record to make the frightful journey — and they were not followed by many others. In the ultimate straits from starvation they were rescued by the first Pike's Peakers coming up from Colorado. With some of them they threaded Lemhi Pass and gained the valleys of southwestern Montana. Healy prospected western Montana and as far north as Edmonton, Alberta, but made no other important discoveries, turned to townsite promotion though the town he selected, Boulder, Montana, wouldn't grow much. He tried working an Indian reservation farm at Sun River, took up Indian trading, like many another using whiskey to boost profits. With A.B. Hamilton in 1869 he built Fort Hamilton (which shortly became Fort Whoop-Up) at the confluence of the St. Mary and Oldman rivers, Alberta. It was the "most famous of the whiskey forts" and here Johnny Healy "ruled with an iron hand," but again he made little profit, his partners at Fort Benton, Montana, raking in most of it. When the Mounted Police ended the whiskey trade in 1874 Healy returned to Fort Benton. In June 1877 he became sheriff of Chouteau County, Montana, quickly establishing himself as a legendary lawman of utter fearlessness and few scruples. "He enforced the law with a brutality that sometimes left the line between crime control and lawlessness vague, though always with a dash and verve that excited attention," his threat to hang horse thieves whenever caught, for example, proving not an idle one. He became part owner of the Fort Benton *Record,* ran a sawmill, joined a brief — and fruitless — gold rush to the Bear Paw Mountains and weathered countless adventures with Indians and white desperadoes. He lost the election of 1882 and left Montana for Alaska, establishing a trading post at Dyea, in the southeastern part of the Territory, outfitting prospectors long before the Klondike Gold Rush commenced. In 1895 he chartered a small steam schooner and went from Seattle to St. Michael at the mouth of the Yukon, establishing posts for the North American Transportation & Trading Company, which he incorporated. When the Klondike strike was made in August 1896, Healy's ship the *Portland* brought to Seattle the first large number of successful miners with their more than $1 million in gold dust. Healy expanded his operations, stores and warehouses, contracted for a number of river steamers and induced Michael Cudahy, wealthy Chicago meat packer, to back him financially. Healy's ultimate attention was turned toward construction of a trans-Siberian railroad to be reached by a tunnel under the Bering Sea, the work hopefully to be financed by Russian and French funds. In 1906, already an elderly man, he headed a party which in the dead of winter traveled afoot from Dawson to Fairbanks and thence to Valdez on the Alaskan coast. He died at Los Angeles, California. In his early manhood Healy was five feet, five inches tall, swarthy, blue-eyed and had some education.

Fort Benton (Montana) *River-Press,* Sept. 23, 1908; John Linton Struble, "Johnny Healy Strikes It Rich." *Idaho Yesterdays,* Vol. 1, No. 3 (Fall 1957), 22-28; Paul F. Sharp, *Whoop-Up Country: The Canadian-American West.* Norman, Univ. of Okla. Press, 1973; David Lavender, *The Rockies,* N.Y., Harper & Row, 1968.

Heap, David Porter, army officer (Mar. 1843-Oct. 25, 1910). B. at San Stefano, Turkey, the son of a U.S. minister to that country, Heap was graduated from West Point in 1864 and won a brevet for his services during the siege of Petersburg, Virginia. In February 1870, he became chief engineer of the military Department of Dakota, accompanying his

superior, Major John W. Barlow on a
reconnaissance of the Upper Yellowstone in
1871. The 1871 Chicago Fire consumed
Barlow's notes and photographs, and Heap,
who had returned to St. Paul, was able from
his own records to "produce the first map of
the Yellowstone region based on adequate
instrumental observations." The remainder of
his military service was not on the frontier,
Heap retiring a Brigadier General in 1905. He
died at Pasadena, California.

Aubrey L. Haines, *Yellowstone National Park:
Its Exploration and Establishment.* Wash., Nat.
Park Service, 1974.

Heard, Isaac V.D., attorney, pioneer (Aug. 31,
1834-June 17, 1913). B. at Goshen, New York,
Heard reached St. Paul, Minnesota, April 21,
1851, became a clerk in the offices of
prominent lawyers and was elected city
attorney in 1856. The next year he was
appointed county attorney and for several
years thereafter was alternately city or county
attorney. Heard was a member of Sibley's
staff at the time of the Sioux uprising of 1862
and was with the relief party that hastened to
New Ulm to raise the Indian siege. He was
acting judge advocate at the trial of the Sioux
who were hanged at Mankato following the
devastating hostilities. A classical student, his
*History of the Sioux War and Massacres of
1862 and 1863* (1863, 1975) became the
standard work on that bloody affair and has
remained an important source of information
until this day. Heard participated in numerous famous law cases of his time, founded the
first reform school for juveniles in the state
and was a popular and generally respected
lawyer who always had a positive outlook on
public affairs. Because of illness he returned to
Goshen in 1883, remaining there until his
death. He was buried at St. Paul.

St. Paul Dispatch, June 20, 1913; Minn. Hist.
Soc. *Scrapbook,* Vol. 72, p. 81.

Heath, Henry, soldier (c. 1845-c. 1920). A
particular friend of Franklin J. Niles (later
marrying Niles' sister), Heath and Niles
enlisted in January 1863, in the 6th Iowa
Cavalry for campaigning and fighting with
Sully on the North Plains frontier for two and
one-half years. Heath is often mentioned in
Niles' voluminous letters home, particularly
those to Niles' sister, and his service paralleled
that of Niles in most particulars. As acting

sergeant, Heath carried a truce flag when
Sully went out to confer with leaders of the
hostile Sioux July 28, 1864, before the battle
of Killdeer Mountain. With Niles, Heath
suffered from typhoid fever at Fort Randall in
1865, but recovered, was mustered out
October 17, married Louisa Niles, and
presumably lived the rest of his life in Iowa.

Lee E. Echols, "We're A-Goin' to Fight the
Indians." *Frontier Times,* Vol. 50, No. 3, (Apr.-May
1976), 6-11, 45-51.

Heavy Runner (Tail That Goes Up the Hill),
Blackfoot chief (d. Jan. 23, 1870). A
determined friend of the whites (recognized as
such by Alfred Sully and other responsible
frontier figures), he was shot as the first victim
of the Baker massacre of Piegans on the
Marias River, Montana. Baker's attack had
followed depredations by Blackfeet under
Mountain Chief and others against the whites,
and on Sheridan's irritable order to "strike
them hard." General de Trobriand's orders to
Baker told him not to molest Heavy Runner's
people, but unfortunately the Indian camps
were mixed and although upon detection of
the approach of soldiers Heavy Runner raced
up the hill with a "paper," no doubt to show it
was a friendly village, firing began and he was
first to fall. The attack remains highly
controversial despite efforts by its apologists,
contemporary with the action and contemporary today, to explain it away. It had far-
reaching effects on the management of
Indians by officialdom, and on depredations
against whites by the Blackfeet.

Montana, Contributions, Vol. X, 1940, 276;
Robert J. Ege, *Strike Them Hard!* Bellevue,
Nebr., Old Army Press, 1970; John C. Ewers, *The
Blackfeet: Raiders on the Northwestern Plains.*
Norman, Univ. of Okla. Press, 1958.

Hebard, Grace Raymond, historian, writer
(July 2, 1861-Oct. 11, 1936). B. at Clinton,
Iowa, she was a graduate of Iowa State
University with an earned doctorate from
Illinois Wesleyan University, and was
admitted to the Wyoming bar in 1898. Never
married, Miss Hebard was a draftsman for the
U.S. Surveyor General's office and the U.S.
Land Office at Cheyenne, Wyoming, from
1882-91, and became a professor of political
economy at the University of Wyoming in
1906. Among her appointments was as a
member of the committee to mark the Oregon

Trail through Wyoming; she was state historian for the Colonial Dames. She wrote: *The History and Government of Wyoming* (1904); *The Pathbreakers from River to Ocean* (1911); *Sacajawea, Pilot for Lewis and Clark* (1907); *The Bozeman Trail*, with E.A. Brininstool (1921); *Chief Washakie* (1929); *Sacajawea, a Guide and Interpreter of the Lewis and Clark Expedition* (1933); *The Pony Express and Telegraph Line in Wyoming* (1935). Her home was at Laramie, Wyoming.

Who Was Who.

Heckewelder, John Gottlieb Ernestus, Moravian missionary (Mar. 12, 1743-Jan. 31, 1823). B. of a prominent Moravian family at Bedford, England, Heckewelder was educated initially in English Moravian schools. He reached Pennsylvania in 1754, received further education at Bethlehem, Pennsylvania. Indicating a strong desire for missionary work, he was first assigned to assist Christian Frederick Post in removing Delaware villages from the Susquehanna to the Muskingum, in Ohio; this effort was aborted by the Pontiac War, but Heckewelder entered Indian work in 1763, quickly absorbing the language and customs of the natives, and in 1771 began full time missionary work, remaining in it for 15 years. With David Zeisberger he assisted in the removal of bands of Delaware Indians from Pennsylvania to Ohio, helping establish the famed communities of Schoenbrunn and Gnadenhutten on the Muskingum River. In 1781 he and others were captured by English-allied Indians, held on the upper Sandusky River, and twice called to Detroit, but eventually he was permitted to return to his Ohio missionary endeavors. He was not present at the massacre by border ruffians of 96 Christian Indians at Gnadenhutten. Heckewelder was married in 1780, his wedding said to have been the first of a white couple in Ohio. He retired from missionary work in 1786, but continued to engage in Indians affairs, sometimes for the government. He was present at the Vincennes negotiations in 1792 and the following year served a western country peace mission, each resulting in an informal agreement which in neither case seems to have been ratified. In 1801 Heckewelder returned to Gnadenhutten, remaining in charge there for nine years, although most of the Indians had been transferred to Fairfield, Ontario. From 1810

until his death Heckewelder wrote of Indian life and customs as he had come to know them. Among his important writings in English were: *History, Manners, and Customs of the Indian Nations Who Once Inhabited Pennsylvania and the Neighboring States* (1819); *A Narrative of the Mission of the United Brethren among the Delaware and the Mohegan Indians from its Commencement in the Year 1740 to the Close of the Year 1808* (1820); *Names Which the Lenni Lenape or Delaware Indians Gave to the Rivers, Streams, and Localities within the States of Pennsylvania, Maryland and Virginia, with their Significations* (1822). Heckewelder was a rigidly honest man of high intelligence and great industry. He had something of a scientific turn of mind, was attracted to botany and natural history as well as to the aborigines, and his extensive writings and other papers are of permanent value, as were his personal labors within his own lifetime. He was survived by three daughters when he died at Bethlehem, Pennsylvania.

Paul A.W. Wallace, *Thirty Thousand Miles with John Heckewelder.* University of Pittsburgh Press, 1958; John Heckewelder, *History, Manners, and Customs of the Indian Nations Who Once Inhabited Pennsylvania and the Neighboring States,* intr. by William C. Reichel. Phila., Hist. Soc. of Pa., 1876; DAB.

Hedding, Elijah, Indian convert (c. 1825-July 1844). The son of the Walla Walla chief Peupeu-mox-mox (Yellow Serpent), Hedding was raised at the Methodist mission in the Willamette Valley of Oregon and named for a Methodist bishop; he spoke English well and was educated in the six years he spent at the mission. In 1844 about a dozen Cayuse, Nez Perce and Walla Walla Indians including Elijah's father decided to visit Sutter's Fort in California to exchange horses, mules and furs for cattle, driving them back to Oregon to form the nucleus for tribal herds. From Sutter's post the Oregon Indians made a small raid, picking up 22 horses and mules stolen by California Indians; when they returned the animals of course were claimed by American and Spanish settlers, the Indians maintaining they had become their own property. In the course of the dispute Elijah Hedding was murdered by a Kentuckian, Grove C. Cook, "already notorious as a man who hated Indians and shot them without provocation."

The incident greatly incensed the Oregon Indians and the affair was a factor in the subsequent massacre of the Whitmans November 29, 1847. There are varying reports of the Hedding killing, but in Bancroft's words it is "reasonable to suppose...that Elijah was deliberately murdered by Cook."

Thwaites, EWT, XXX, 229n; Bancroft, *California,* V; Alvin M. Josephy Jr., *The Nez Perce Indians and the Opening of the Northwest.* New Haven, Yale Univ. Press, 1965; Clifford M. Drury, *Marcus and Narcissa Whitman and the Opening of Old Oregon.* Glendale, Calif., Arthur H. Clark Co., 1973.

Hedges, Cornelius, pioneer (Oct. 28, 1831-April 29, 1907). B. at Westfield, Massachusetts, he was graduated from Yale and Harvard Law School, engaged in law practice and newspapering in Iowa and in 1864 headed for the Montana gold fields. He walked from Independence, Iowa, to Virginia City, Montana, worked several claims without much fortune, and settled at Helena, Montana. He was a member of the 1870 Washburn Yellowstone expedition as special correspondent for the *Helena Herald,* and became a proponent of reserving the Yellowstone area for the public good; although he is credited with broaching the idea at a campfire meeting at Madison Junction September 19, 1870, he was the third person known to have advanced the suggestion. His contribution lay rather "in that series of fine articles, so descriptive of the Yellowstone region, which he contributed to the *Helena Herald* on his return." He became prominent in several fields in Montana's development and died at Helena.

Aubrey L. Haines, *Yellowstone National Park: Its Exploration and Establishment.* Wash., Nat. Park Service, 1974.

Heffington, Bill, pioneer (c. 1846-post 1927). In 1850 he reached Parker County, Texas, near South Bear Creek, where his father, Stephen, took up 320 acres and commenced farming; this was about 18 miles southeast of Weatherford. At 17 Bill Heffington joined a company formed to protect Parker County from Indian raids while the Civil War was underway to the east. He engaged in "several Indian fights," including a tardy and slight role in the disastrous action at Dove Creek in January 1865, when the Texans suffered their worst defeat from Indians, on this occasion at the hands of peacefully-inclined Kickapoos enroute for Mexico. Bill's brother Tom had 18 bullet holes in his clothing, one slight wound, and had his horse killed in the action. Bill Heffington continued fighting frontier raiders until well into the 1870's. He lived late in life at Marble Falls, Texas.

Frontier times, Vol. 5, No. 1 (Oct. 1927), 17-19.

Heinmot Hihhih, White Thunder: *see* Yellow Wolf

Heintzelman, Samuel Peter, army officer, pioneer (Sept. 30, 1805-May 1, 1880). B. at Manheim, Pennsylvania, he graduated from West Point and was commissioned a second lieutenant in the 2nd Infantry July 1, 1826. He served at Belle Fontaine and Jefferson Barracks, Missouri, and at Forts Mackinac and Gratiot in Michigan for six years. In 1831, assigned to the Corps of Topographical Engineers he assisted surveying Lakes St. Clair, Huron and Michigan. From 1835-42 he was in Florida working with the Quartermaster Corps, on the periphery of the Second Seminole War, but not actively engaged in it. He had become a first lieutenant March 4, 1833, and a captain November 4, 1838. Heintzelman served in the Mexican War, winning a brevet. He was sent to California, operating against Indians for a time and while commander at San Diego, he founded November 27, 1850, Camp Independence, its name changed in 1852 to Fort Yuma; its intent was to guard the southern route to California, but later it became a primary supply base for Arizona posts. Heintzelman took up any business opportunity that came his way, owning real estate in San Diego while in Arizona he heavily engaged in mining. He became president of the $2 million Sonora Exploring and Mining Company, a corporation made up of eastern investors brought together by Charles Poston and others. It operated several mines near Tubac and in southern Arizona until the Civil War and the subsequent evacuation of troops forced it to shut down. Some of the mines showed promise, but none was the big strike and profits were sporadic and never lavish. Nor were his other enterprises particularly lucrative, although he made some money on them. Heintzelman was a good officer and did not let his moonlighting interfere with his duties. After four years he returned east July 15, 1854. He became major of the 1st Infantry March 3, 1855. He thereafter engaged in Texas Indian campaigns and in Rio Grande border scuffles with the Mexican bandit, Juan Cortina. His Civil War service was good but he was said to have lacked initiative and to have "magnified difficulties." He ended the war a Major General of Volunteers and was retired February 22, 1869, as a Major General in the army. He died at his Washington, D.C., home. He was married and fathered children.

Cullum; Diane M.T. North, *Samuel Peter Heintzelman and the Sonora Exploring & Mining Company.* Tucson, Univ. of Ariz. Press, 1980; Jay J. Wagoner, *Early Arizona: Prehistory to Civil War.* Tucson, 1975.

Heitman, Francis Bernard, military editor, historian (Apr. 10, 1838-Mar. 6, 1926). B. at Cincinnati, Ohio, he was employed by the War Dept. in 1856. He compiled and edited: *Historical Register of the Officers of the Continental Army During the War of the Revolution, April 1775 to December 1783* (1893); and *Historical Register and Dictionary of the United States Army, From Its Organization September 29, 1789 to March 2, 1903* (1903). He died at Washington, D.C.

Herringshaw's Library of American Biography; Nat. Archives and Records Service.

Heizer, Robert Fleming, archeologist, anthropologist (July 13, 1915-July 18, 1979). B. at Denver he early became interested in archeology and was graduated from the University of California at Berkeley in 1936, earning his doctorate there in 1941. By then he already had 28 scientific studies and other writings in print. He taught at the University of Oregon, University of California at Los Angeles, and at Berkeley during his professional life, "becoming the key figure in California and Nevada archeology," at the same time deeply involved in anthropology and ethnohistory of southwestern Indians. He expanded his interests into Mexico and Central America. Heizer founded the University of California Archeological Survey, his teams cataloguing more than 13,000 sites of Indian habitation in California and three of his many works generated further southwestern studies: *An Introduction to the Archaeology of Central California* (1939), with J.B. Lilard and Franklin Fenenga;

Archaeology of Humboldt Cave, Churchill County, Nevada (1956) with A.D. Krieger; and *Prehistoric Rock Art of Nevada and Eastern California* (1962), with Martin A. Baumhoff. In 1970 he was invited to edit Volume 8 of the massive *Handbook of North American Indians,* the California volume and "typically, Heizer's was the first to be organized, finished, and herded into print" of the 20-volume series. Others of his major works included, (ed.) with M.A. Whipple, *The California Indians: A Source Book* (1951, 1971), and (ed.) *The Destruction of California Indians* (1974). His *The Natural World of the California Indians* (1980), appeared posthumously. Heizer was married and the father of four children. The most complete bibliography of his many works was in the *Journal of California and Great Basin Anthropology,* Volume 1 (Winter 1979), 246-67.

Clifton B. Kroeber, "Robert F. Heizer: 1915-1979." *Ariz. and the West,* Vol. 23, No. 3 (Autumn 1981), 209-12.

Helgi, merchant (d. c. 1006). An Icelandic merchant, he and his brother, Finnbogi sailed from Norway to Greenland and there joined Eirik's natural daughter Freydis on a commercial expedition to the New World. There Freydis by treachery caused to be murdered Helgi, Finnbogi and all their party in order to steal their ship and its cargo of lumber and other New World products. Where this occurred is uncertain, but it may have been in northern Newfoundland.

Magnus Magnusson, Hermann Palsson, *The Vinland Sagas: The Norse Discovery of America.* Baltimore, Penguin Books, 1965.

Helm, Chat(ham E.), frontiersman (Apr. 12, 1824-Oct. 18, 1905). B. in either Kentucky or Missouri he was raised in Fairfax County, Missouri, and about 1850 went overland to California where he joined his brothers, Daunt (John), Weid (William Johnson), James (Tex?) and perhaps Turner in a gold camp near Georgetown, El Dorado County. Chat may have joined in the general turbulence the clan seemed to attract, but came to no lasting prominence in northern California during his years there. He with Weid and Daunt (and possibly Turner) were reported to have visited the Montana mining camps around 1863. Although not hanged as was their more notorious cousin, Boone

Helm, they were run out of the region, it is said, by vigilante warnings. Although a miner at times, and farmer in his later life, Chat and his brothers were believed by descendants to have been primarily gamblers and opportunists. Chat seemed to have some knowledge of Sioux country and either he or Weid (depending upon who told the story) once held up a Yuma, Arizona, card game and escaped across the Colorado River with the sizable pot. Weid, Turner and Chat in the 1870s established homesteads east of Warner Springs, California, Chat specializing in the raising of apples but also running a little stock and becoming involved in a series of shooting affrays, on one occasion killing an Indian who had protested Helm's cutting off the water supply for a native village. There were unsubstantiated rumors of other killings since Chat, like the other Helms, was a frontiersman with the bark on who defended his rights and ambitions with guns when he deemed it necessary. Chat like Weid married a white woman. He fathered three boys and perhaps some daughters, his sons becoming prominent and respected later on in the Warner Springs area. Around 1900 he moved to Los Angeles, died there and was buried locally.

Colin Rickards, history of the Helm clan, manuscript in preparation; Dan L. Thrapp, "Poor Tom Cover." Westerners Los Angeles Corral *Brand Book XV*, 1978; information from John T. Helm Jr.; *San Diego Union*, Aug. 26, 1974; Helen Hunt Jackson, *A Century of Dishonor*. Boston, Roberts Bros., 1891, 489.

Helm, Daunt (John), frontiersman (c. 1820-c. 1888). The date of birth is conjecture and that of his death speculation based upon a variety of sources. Daunt Helm, who like most of his brothers was illiterate, was born either in Kentucky or Missouri and raised in Fairfax County of the latter state. With his brothers, Davenport, James, and Weid (and perhaps Turner) he went to California in 1849 settling in a gold camp near Georgetown in El Dorado County. Daunt is a shadowy figure during his entire life. Whether he accompanied another brother, Chat and Weid to Montana around 1863 is not established, but if they went he probably did also; report has it that the three were run out by vigilantes early in 1864. A decade later Daunt was living east of Warner Springs, San Diego County, California, where Chat, Weid and Turner had homesteads although Daunt himself never married and refused to settle down. He helped herd his brothers' livestock which sometimes ranged down onto the desert during the cold months, or in the highlands at other times of the year. There are scattered reports from various sources that a Helm was lynched in the 1870s either in San Bernardino or San Diego counties; the only possible candidate would have been Daunt, but he was never lynched as investigation demonstrates. Judy Van der Veer wrote that "on the knoll (east of the Warner's Ranch stage station) is the lonely grave of a man who was hanged from a cottonwood tree beside the stage station," and John Helm's marker is the only stone found on the rise; Van der Veer could not recall where she had picked up the report of the lynching nor could other possible sources she mentioned confirm it, so the legend remains a mystery. In September 1884 the wealthy and respected Thomas Wells Cover of Riverside, California disappeared on the Anza Borrego desert east of Warner Springs while hunting the Peg Leg Smith lost gold deposit; Cover had been one of the six discoverers of the fabulous Alder Gulch, Montana gold placers in 1863 and reportedly was prominent among the vigilantes who had hanged Boone Helm and others. For a variety of reasons foul play came to be suspected in the Cover disappearance. If that were indeed the case logical suspicion would point toward the Helm brothers, with Daunt the most likely suspect, but he was never charged nor was murder in fact ever proven nor Cover's remains ever certainly found. Daunt's gravestone gives his date of death as 1873 which seems obviously in error; John T. Helm, historian of the clan, said that "the date is definitely incorrect." He recalled that his own father, Turner's son, once remarked that Daunt's year of death might have been his own year of birth, or 1888. Turner's daughter, Mary Jane, born in 1870 vividly recalled Daunt as living with Turner and the others and "from time to time was chased off for abusing the brothers' children." She compared him to a "brute," and strongly remembered his "distaste for work." The reason why Daunt alone among the brothers has a stone marker on his grave, and for the misleading date chiseled upon it are unknown, but speculation has been assembled in *Poor Tom Cover.*

Information from John T. Helm Jr.; Dan L.

Thrapp, *Poor Tom Cover,* manuscript in preparation; Judy Van der Veer, "On History's Trail to San Felipe." *Westways,* Vol. 53, No. 1 (Jan. 1961).

Helm, Davenport, frontier rowdy (fl. 1849-1855). A cousin of Boone Helm, Davenport was raised in Fairfax County, Missouri. With his brothers, James, Daunt (John), Weid (William Johnson) Helm and possibly (Harmon) Turner Helm he left in 1849 for the California gold fields. The clan settled near Georgetown, El Dorado County. Here about 1854 Davenport was on the dodge after a killing; subsequently he was shot to death in Sonoma County, California.

Colin Rickards, a history of the Helm family, manuscript in preparation; Dan L. Thrapp, "Poor Tom Cover." The Westerners Los Angeles Corral, *Brand Book XV,* 1978.

Helm, (Levi) Boone, desperado (Jan. 28, 1827-Jan. 14, 1864). B. in Lincoln County, Kentucky, he was taken with his family in 1831 to Log Branch, Monroe County, Missouri, where he matured as a wild and unruly young man, inclined toward bowie knives, horseplay, alcohol and rough companions. He did not serve in the Mexican War, although three of his brothers did. In 1849 Boone and his brothers, David, Fleming and perhaps Alonzo went overland to California, settling at Murderers Bar on the Middle Fork of the American River, spending more time gambling than mining. Here Fleming was killed in a card game dispute, David killed Fleming's slayer and the remaining Helm boys were back in Missouri by mid-1850. In early 1851 Boone Helm married Lucinda Browning, 17 who gave birth to a daughter and sued for divorce, cheerfully assented to by her errant husband. September 14, 1851, Boone Helm murdered Littlebury Shoot, a neighbor and friend because Shoot refused to accompany Helm to Texas. Captured within two days, Helm was jailed but escaped and fled south. He was pursued by Littlebury's loyal brother, William Shoot who employed agents to hunt Helm down in Indian Territory and return him for trial. Legal delays and changes of venue resulted in his being held in custody beyond the limit allowed by law and Helm was freed and made once more for California where he probably lodged for a time with his hard-bitten cousins: Daunt (John), Chat (ham), Weid (William

Johnson), Davenport and perhaps (Harmon) Turner Helm. Whether Boone took part in the turbulence his kinfolk persistently generated can only be surmised, but if he abstained it was the only time in his life he would do so. Dimsdale wrote that Helm "either killed or assisted in the killing of nearly a dozen men in the brawls so common at that time," a figure which might not be too far off the mark if Helm's whole Pacific Coast experience were summarized. In the spring of 1858 having committed a "murder" as distinct from a "killing," Boone fled to The Dalles, Oregon. Later that year he planned to follow the Overland Trail eastward with six companions. One man, frightened by Helm's incessant boasting of his criminal past, fled back to The Dalles, but the other six pushed on into the wilderness as winter descended. They had a fight with Digger Indians on the Raft River, Idaho and near the Bannack River one of the whites was slain by Indians. Winter closed in savagely and when spring came only Boone Helm was alive, found by John W. Powell and party of Montana's Bitterroot Valley to be subsisting upon the remains of one of his late companions. Whether he had done in the others, for food or otherwise, can never be learned. Powell gave Helm a new suit of buckskin and a horse and took him to Salt Lake City. There Helm was credited with killing two citizens, joined a band of horse thieves stealing from the army and a mail company and in California killed an army man who had indentified him with criminal activities. He fled then to Los Angeles, quickly got into fresh trouble, went north and reached Oregon again where he perfected himself at road agentry and, it was whispered, committed several murders. He reached British Columbia where on one occasion he boasted to authorities that he had killed and eaten a companion during a cold snap, whether idle braggadocio or otherwise was never explained. In June 1862 Boone killed an unarmed miner in a crowded saloon at Florence, Idaho, and fled. Arrested in British Columbia he escaped jail at Cariboo, was arrested again at Olympia, Washington but escaped once more, was recaptured and returned to Florence to be tried for the saloon murder, was acquitted and found his way into southern Idaho where a relative outfitted him with a horse and cash in the belief Boone would go to Texas and join the Confederate army, though in fact he had no such intention. Instead he went to southwestern Montana where gold had been discovered and camps were booming. Here Helm joined the Henry Plummer band of desperadoes, his notoriety assuring him a prominent place in the organization. He was listed by Red Yager as a "roadster," or general purpose desperado with the band. Birney reports that Helm, Alex Carter and Bob Zachary murdered the Cavalier (Chevalier) brothers for their gold in mid-October 1863 and no doubt he was in on other bits of deviltry from time to time. He was arrested at Virginia City, Montana, on January 14, 1864, by vigilantes and hanged with four others in an unfinished building on the town's principal street. Helm was game to the last, showed no fear of dying and shouted his support for Jefferson Davis as the trap was pulled from under him. There is a curious possibility that William Shoot, brother of Helm's initial victim, may have presented evidence that was largely responsible for Helm's execution; Shoot's presence at Virginia City was established not long afterward and much of the testimony and evidence against Helm would seem to have no other possible origin, but the actual date of Shoot's arrival at the camp is unestablished at this writing.

Colins Rickards, history of the Helm clan, manuscript in preparation; Dan L. Thrapp, *Poor Tom Cover*, manuscript in preparation; Dimsdale; Hoffman Birney, *Vigilantes*. Phila., Penn Pub. Co., 1929; Langford; Colin Rickards, "Boone Helm —Man Eater!" *True West*, Vol. XX, No. 4 (Mar.-Apr. 1973), 6-9, 18-21, 30-32, 46-54.

Helm, Teofulio, pioneer (Feb. 24, 1874-Apr. 19, 1967). One of several sons of (Harmon) Turner Helm by his first Mission Indian wife, Teofulio was b. in the Warner Springs area of southern California and lived in the San Felipe Valley, becoming one of the most prominent citizens of eastern San Diego County. He served as deputy sheriff for more than 40 years, and in other public capacities. He denied that he was related to the wild Chat(ham) and Weid (William Johnston) Helm individuals, although they were older brothers of his father. Teofulio had personal knowledge of lynchings, Indian removals and other aspects of life on a modified frontier, but was respected and widely liked. For him was named Teofulio Summit, a 3,636-foot

promontory near Warner Springs. He died at Escondido, California.
San Diego Union, July 26, 1975.

Helm, Tex (James?), frontiersman (fl. 1849-1865). This man was either a brother or a cousin of Boone Helm. He went to California with others of the clan in 1849, later moving to Idaho. Here he provided the funds to clear Boone Helm of a murder charge at Florence, Idaho, then supported him until he found work as a miner, which he quickly abandoned. Tex supplied him with more money and a horse in the belief Boone would head for Texas to join the Confederacy. Tex Helm was never accused of any outlawry so far as the record shows. He was killed by a horse in 1865 at Walla Walla, Washington.

Colin Rickards, history of the Helm family in preparation; Langford.

Helm, Thomas Jefferson, frontiersman (c. 1824-1904). B. in Tennessee, he moved with his family several times and left for the West after his widowed mother had settled in Indiana. He may have been married before leaving and reportedly fathered a son. By 1860 he was a miner at Pinos Altos, New Mexico, gold camp, and about that time became a partner of Thomas J. Mastin in a ranching venture. He was a second lieutenant in the Arizona Guards formed by Mastin in 1861, the organization thereafter enrolled in Confederate service. Upon Mastin's death October 7 from an Apache arrow wound, Helm was elected captain, October 31, 1861, and re-elected July 1, 1862. It was to Helm that John Robert Baylor, Confederate officer and "governor" of Arizona, issued his famous instructions of March 20, 1862, directing that he gather in Apaches by treachery, kill the adults, enslave the children, taking precautions "to allow no Indian to escape." The Confederates abandoned New Mexico before the directive was acted upon. Helm was at New Orleans in 1873, and was married to Bettie Grooms in 1884 at Austin, Texas, where he lived the remainder of his life, Helm St. being named for him. He died at Austin.

Martin Hardwick Hall, "Captain Thomas J. Mastin's Arizona Guards, C.S.A.." *New Mex. Hist. Rev.,* XLIX, No. 2 (Apr. 1974), 153-51; Hall's correspondence with author, Sept. 23, 1974.

Helm, (Harmon) Turner, frontiersman (1832-

c. 1898). B. in Missouri he was raised in Fairfax County, the youngest in a family of 21 boys and 1 girl. At the age of 14 he signed on, as a "waterboy" he later recalled, in Napoleon B. Giddings' company of Sterling Price's 2nd Regiment of Missouri Mounted Volunteers for Mexican War service. The company reached New Mexico, participated in quelling the Taos rebellion and was mustered out within a year of its enlistment. In 1849 Turner headed for the California gold fields, either with his brothers, Davenport, James, Daunt (John) and Weid (William Johnson Helm) or apart from them. While they settled in El Dorado County, Turner resided, at least for a time, near Red Bluff in Tehama County. Whether he accompanied his brothers if they went to Montana around 1863 is uncertain; one report places him there. It was said they all were run out by vigilantes. Turner, the only one of the California Helm clan who could read and write, became something of a leader of them, although younger than the others. He bought a house at Los Angeles around 1864 (shortly after the Montana vigilante episode), where the boys made their headquarters when in the area. Later Turner settled on a homestead east of Warner Springs in San Diego County, as did Chat and Weid; Daunt lived with them, never marrying nor settling down. In January 1873 a mule was stolen from Turner Helm who tracked the thief beyond San Berdardino coming upon an Indian named José dining on the animal's roasted flesh. Helm brought the culprit back to Julian, California, where he became the beneficiary of primitive plea bargaining; during the night he was taken from the jail and murdered, apparently by the disgruntled Turner. In 1884-85, even before suspicion centered on Daunt for being involved with the desert disappearance of Thomas Wells Cover, a wealthy Riverside, California, planter and earlier a discoverer of the Alder Creek gold placers in Montana, Turner sent notes to Riverside parties alleging that another had killed Cover, seeking to shunt investigation from the Helm boys; his letters were dramatically mistimed however, and merely added fuel to popular opinion which largely focused on the Helms, although none was ever charged nor in fact was murder ever proven to have been done. Turner married his first wife in the Napa Valley country of upper California; she died before he moved south. Later he married two

Indian women is succession. By the first he fathered three children and by the next, four children. He died near Santa Ysabel, California, of a prostate infection and was buried on a knoll not far from his ranch, east of Warner Springs; the headboard has disappeared and the grave since been rifled, as is supposed.

Colin Rickards, a history of the clan, manuscript in preparation; Dan L. Thrapp, "Poor Tom Cover," Westerners Los Angeles Corral *Brand Book XV*, 1978; information from John T. Helm; San Diego *Evening Tribune*, June 11, 1937.

Helm, William Johnson (Weid), frontiersman (Oct. 18, 1828-Jan. 21, 1909). B. in Missouri he was raised in Fairfax County, and in 1849 set out for the California gold fields with his brothers: Davenport, James (Tex?), John (Daunt), and possibly (Harmon) Turner Helm, all of them first cousins of the more notorious Boone Helm. They settled near Georgetown, El Dorado County, in the gold country, to mine and as often to gamble, drink whiskey and generate disturbances. In 1850 they joined a lynch mob that hanged a murderer. They still were in El Dorado County when Boone Helm arrived on his second visit to California in 1854, cleared though not acquitted of a murder count. He may have associated with his cousins for a time although details are lacking. Weid killed a man at Georgetown sometime in the mid-1850s and fled to Los Angeles; a decade later he was arrested in southern California and returned to Georgetown for trial, but was freed, either by acquittal or dismissal. There were allegations that Weid, with his brothers, Chat, Daunt and possibly Turner were in the Montana mining camps around 1863 but rather than being hanged as was their cousin Boone, were run out by vigilante warning. There is no confirmation for this, nor denial of it. Weid appears to have had some experience with Sioux country however. Either Weid or Chat once held up a Yuma, Arizona, card game it was reported and fled across the Colorado River and back to their base with the pot, supposedly sizable. Weid, Chat and Turner established homesteads east of Warner Springs, California, farmed a little, raised cattle and claimed grazing rights "clear to the Colorado River," enforcing their pretensions in a number of shooting scrapes whose consequences have never been clearly defined (some of Weid's cattle turned feral below the Warner highlands and ran loose until around 1915, being killed off by hunters about that time). Weid married and fathered ten legitimate children including three sets of twins (plus three sets of still-born twins) and assorted illegitimate children "mostly from midwives attending his wife in childbirth...his attitude was any squaw he could catch was fair play," according to John T. Helm Jr., grandson of Turner and a historian of the family. A niece recalled Weid: "He had one good (blue) eye, smoked a pipe and was over 6 foot tall with a flowing beard that reached his chest," although none of the Helm boys actually were much over 5 foot, 9 inches tall; photographs show them wearing high-heeled boots which may have added to the impression of height. Weid died in Los Angeles County, the death certificate asserting the body was returned to Temecula for burial; in fact it was taken on to a family plot in Cañada Verde, east of Warner Springs and buried beside Turner, who died around 1898. The grave is unmarked today.

Dan L. Thrapp, "Poor Tom Cover," Westerners Los Angeles Corral *Brand Book XV*, 1978; information from John T. Helm; Colin Rickards, a history of the Helm clan, manuscript in preparation.

Henderson, Bill rustler (d. June 3, 1876). He is reported to have been leader of a gang of desperadoes, mainly rustlers, operating in the Fort Griffin area of Texas; ultimately the gang stole 26 horses from a ranch, were dispersed by a posse, Henderson and others making for Dodge City, Kansas. Here Henderson and Hank Floyd were arrested by Sheriff Bassett, returned to Albany, seat of Shackelford County, Texas, and lynched.

Carl Coke Rister, *Fort Griffin on the Texas Frontier.* Norman, Univ. of Okla. Press, 1956.

Henderson, George B. (John Powers), cattleman (d. summer 1890). Probably b. in Pennsylvania, he was a policeman in the coal and iron camps there, became "mixed up in the killing of a man" and went to Wyoming where he became range manager for the 71 cattle company in the Sweetwater country. He was said to have been a participant in the notorious lynching of Ella Watson and James Averell in July 1889, but was not formally charged as were six others. He is reported to have followed Ralph Cole, a witness against

the alleged lynchers shortly after the incident, shot him and burned his body. Henderson was "shot at several times and had had numerous quarrels" after the lynching. On July 31, 1889, he was narrowly missed by an assassin's bullet which wounded one of his team horses. Not long afterward he came into dispute with John Tregoning, a night herder for the 71 ranch and was shot and killed by him. Sentenced to life, Tregoning within two years escaped the penitentiary, supposedly with assistance from the warden's daughter; he was not retaken.

Alfred James Mokler, *History of Natrona County Wyoming 1888-1922.* N.Y., Argonaut Press, 1966.

Henderson, Richard, army officer (c. 1815-Dec. 28, 1835). B. at Jackson, Tennessee, he was graduated from West Point in 1835, in July being appointed brevet second lieutenant of the 2nd Artillery and sent to Fort Brooke, Florida, to take part in the Seminole War. He already had decided he did not want to remain in the Army and had petitioned the President for release, which had reached him two days before he joined the doomed Dade command. He kept the information to himself and although now technically a civilian, kept to his assignment. When the command was ambushed, Henderson was wounded, his left arm broken, early in the affair; he was slain as were all but three of the 108-man command.

Cullum; Frank Laumer, *Massacre!.* Gainesville, Univ. of Fla. Press, 1968.

Hendrick (Theyanoguin), Mohawk chief (c. 1680-Sept. 8, 1755). B. near the present Westfield, Massachusetts, as a Mahican (Mohegan), he was son of a Mohawk mother and a Mahican father and at a young age moved to the Mohawks and was admitted into the Wolf Clan. He was converted to Christianity by the Dutch pastor Godfrey Dellius of Fort Orange (Albany, New York) around 1690 and became a preacher to his adopted people. He resisted Jesuit persuasion and although he visited the St. Lawrence settlements late in the century, remained with his people in New York. In Queen Anne's War (1701-13) Hendrick sided with the British although in no important way and in 1710 went to London with Peter Schuyler and Colonel Francis Nicholson; he and his three chiefs colleagues pleaded for English missionaries and Hendrick became a lay preacher in the Church in England. He again visited England in 1740. In King George's War (1645-48) Hendrick was active against the French of Canada but his expedition was blunted by the enemy and he and a few followers barely made it back to Mohawk country. He worked closely with William Johnson trying to keep the Iroquois aligned with the British, while protecting his people as best he could from loss of lands and debauchery by traders. He frequently represented the Iroquois at councils with the British, these meetings culminating in the 1754 Albany Congress where Hendrick stingingly criticized his white allies for neglecting frontier defenses and leaving their Indian allies open to French attack. Late in the summer of 1755 he helped enlist Indians to accompany Johnson's expedition against Crown Point on Lake Champlain. As Hendrick surveyed the battle-field-to-be, he remarked to Johnson, "If my warriors are to fight (here) they are too few; if they are to die, they are too many," and here, on Lake George, Hendrick was killed although the French under Dieskau were defeated. The chief's loss was mourned sincerely on both sides of the Atlantic for he was famed as a staunch friend of the English and "perhaps the outstanding Indian of this period in North America" in the British view. During his later life he was often referred to, not sarcastically, as King Hendrick. He was as noted as an orator as he was as a statesman and warrior.

Hodge, HAI; DAB; DCB; Dockstader.

Henely, Austin, army officer (c. 1848-July 11, 1878). B. in Ireland, he enlisted in the 11th Infantry September 14, 1864, and rose to quartermaster sergeant by September 14, 1867, entering West Point July 1, 1868. He was commissioned a second lieutenant in the 6th Cavalry June 14, 1872. April 23, 1875 Henely with a detachment from H Company of the 6th Cavalry and K of the 19th Infantry attacked Cheyennes on Sappa Creek, Kansas, killing between 19 and 27 (the reports differ) of the Indians for the loss of two soldiers. It was a clean victory, aided by Homer Wheeler, then a civilian, as guide and eight Medals of Honor were awarded to white participants. In August Henely was transferred to Camp Bowie, Arizona from where he engaged in scouting after Apachès. He became a first

lieutenant November 15, 1876. In March 1877 he reported to Kautz the presence of the noted hostile, Geronimo at the Warm Springs Agency of New Mexico. This set in motion a series of events that were to lead to hostilities for a decade, beginning with the removal of the Warm Springs or Mimbres Apaches to San Carlos Reservation in Arizona. Henely was very active as a scout commander and was a close friend of Tony Rucker, equally enthusiastic at this pursuit. Henely and Rucker were drowned together in a flash flood near the later Camp Rucker on the west side of the Chiricahua Mountains of Arizona; one report said that Rucker plunged into the torrent to rescue Henely who had been washed away, while another said that both young officers had been drinking at the sutler's store before the tragedy.

Cullum; G. Derek West, "The Battle of Sappa Creek (1875)." *Kan. Hist. Quar.,* Vol. XXXIV, No. 2 (Summer 1968), 150-78; Barry C. Johnson, "Austin Henely: Centre of the Sappa Creek Controversy." *English Westerners' Brand Book,* Vol. 7, No. 3 (Apr. 1965), 11-12; Dan L. Thrapp, *Victorio and the Mimbres Apaches.* Norman, Univ. of Okla. Press, 1974; E.R. Martin, "Old Camp Rucker: Its Place in History." *Periodical* 39, Vol. XI, No. 1 (Spring 1979), 42-49.

Hennepin, Louis, Recollet priest, explorer (May 12, 1626-c. 1705). B. at Ath, Belgium, he became a Recollet priest and after varied experiences in Europe was sent with four others of his society to New France with La Salle in 1675. Early in 1676 he went to Fort Frontenac (the present Kingston, Ontario), but in 1678 returned to Quebec. Here he again met La Salle who brought instructions for the priest to join his exploration party, which Hennepin did. The expedition reached Niagara Falls December 8, built a fort during the winter, and by 1680 Hennepin was at Fort Crevecoeur in Illinois. Here he was directed by La Salle to accompany Accault and Auguel exploring the upper Mississippi River, with Accault apparently the leader of the group although one could not discern this fact from Hennepin's writings. Hennepin claimed in all seriousness that the trio first went south to the mouth of the Mississippi, then back up to fulfill the original instructions, but of course this part of his narrative is fictitious. On the 11th of April on the upper river the three were captured by a war party of Sioux who

intended to strike the Miamis; the Frenchmen's lives were spared and they do not
appear to have been mistreated. With their
escort they moved north along the river to St.
Anthony's Falls, which Hennepin named,
then continued northward overland to the
Thousand Lakes (Mille Lacs) region east of
the present Brainerd, Minnesota, reaching
there April 21, 1680. Hennepin spent his time
studying the habits, language and culture of
the tribe. During the summer he went with a
band of Sioux to the Wisconsin River, where
he was met up with by Duluth, who persuaded
the Sioux to let the trio come into his custody;
by fall they had passed Green Bay and were at
Michilimackinac where they wintered,
reached Quebec the next summer and
Hennepin arrived at Le Havre, France the
same year, retiring to a convent to write his
book, *Description de la Louisiane*. It was
quite popular, going through many editions.
His subsequent works, *Nouveau Voyage*
(1696) and *Nouvelle Decouverie* (1697) each
magnified his experiences and findings a bit
more until very little reliability can be placed
in any save the earliest account and there far
from completely. His exaggerations and
misstatements of fact are sufficiently reported
by Parkman and Neill. Hennepin spent the
remainder of his career in Europe, the details
having no frontier interest and his troubles
and problems generally of his own manufacture. He was, wrote Jean Roch Rioux in the
Dictionary of Canadian Biography, "a
fearless disseminator of the faith, but also an
independent person, disagreeable into the
bargain, (and) he more than once antagon-
ized his associates, provoked dissension, and
made enemies for himself."

Literature abundant: Parkman, *La Salle and the
Discovery of the Great West;* Edward Duffield
Neill, *The History of Minnesota,* 4th ed. Minne-
apolis, Minnesota Historical Co., 1882, 822-31.

Henri, Jean, explorer (d. c. 1690). A member
of the La Salle expedition that founded Fort
St. Louis on Matagorda Bay, Texas, he
survived the breakup of that endeavor and
became a chief of a Nebadache tribe, a Caddo
people. Hearing of him, Alonso de Leon in
1683 went to the Indian village and interro-
gated Henri, whom he called Juan Jarri or
something similar; the Frenchman's replies
were not satisfactory and De Leon sent him to

Mexico City for further examination; from
there he was returned to the Presidio of
Monclova, Nueva Leon, where De Leon was
commandant. Henri became guide for De
Leon's 1689 expedition which discovered the
ruins of Fort St. Louis and three more
Frenchmen were picked up. Henri died before
De Leon's 1690 expedition.

HT; Herbert Eugene Bolton, *Spanish Exploration in the Southwest, 1542-1706.* N.Y., Charles
Scribner's Sons, 1916.

Henry, Andrew, fur trader (c. 1775- Jan. 10,
1832). B. in Fayette County, Pennsylvania, he
was well educated but wrote almost nothing
that has survived. In 1806 he became a partner
in a Missouri lead mine. Henry joined Lisa
and others in forming the St. Louis Missouri
Fur Company and in 1809 became field
captain, leading an expedition to the Three
Forks, in the Montana mountains, where in
April 1810, he commenced building a fort.
Blackfeet difficulties prevented very successful fur gathering and in 1811 Henry and his
party appeared among the Mandans after
exploring the Montana-Idaho wilderness,
discovering Lake Henry, building a post near
present St. Anthony, Idaho, and splitting his
party into three important segments, each
with a role in exploration of the northwest.
Henry returned to St. Louis, enrolled in the
War of 1812, becoming a major. In 1822 he
became associated with Ashley in a renewal of
the northwestern fur hunt and left in April for
the upper Missouri. Henry intended to winter
at the mouth of the Yellowstone River, but
pushed on up to near the mouth of the
Musselshell River. In exploring toward Three
Forks, he lost four men to Blackfeet and
withdrew in April 1823, to the mouth of the
Yellowstone River. Learning of Ashley's fight
with the Arikaras, Henry pushed downstream by boat, joined Ashley for the
inconclusive Leavenworth campaign against
the Arikaras, and Henry and a party of
trappers then began the overland return to the
Yellowstone. They were attacked by Mandans
but continued, Henry wintering in 1823-24 at
his Yellowstone post, and in the fall of 1824
bringing a good fur catch to St. Louis. He
retired to his home in Washington County,
Missouri, where he died.

Literature abundant; Louis J. Clements article,
MM, Vol. VI.

Henry, Guy Vernor, army officer (Mar. 9, 1839-Oct. 27, 1899). B. at Fort Smith, Indian Territory, he was graduated from West Point in 1861 and assigned to the 1st Artillery, becoming colonel of the 40th Massachusetts Infantry in 1863, earning three brevets in action and ending the Civil War with that organization, having received a Medal of Honor for gallantry at Cold Harbor, Virginia. He became captain of the 3rd Cavalry late in 1870. In 1871, in Arizona, he commanded the first company of Apache scouts organized by George Crook, and led them on a successful scout, demonstrating the solution to the Apache problem. In December 1874, he was ordered from the Red Cloud Agency into the Black Hills to remove miners illegally in that Sioux country; his detachment was caught in a violent blizzard and - 40 degree temperatures, and all were nearly frozen to death, Henry applying for sick leave in February to recover. On June 16, 1876, he had an important role in the Rosebud action under Crook, being knocked off his horse by a .44 caliber slug through the face that destroyed one eye and closed the other temporarily. Hostiles rode over his body, but were driven back by friendly Crow and Shoshone scouts in hand-to-hand fighting, the scouts recovering the officer. Henry also saw service against Indians in Utah, Wyoming, Nebraska and Dakota. He took part in the White River Ute expedition in 1879 following his return from a European tour. He became major of the 9th Cavalry in 1881, seeing service at Wounded Knee and in related operations; lieutenant colonel, 7th Cavalry, in 1892, served in the 5th Cavalry, transferred to the 3rd Cavalry again, and became colonel of the 10th Cavalry in 1897. He became a Brigadier General, then Major General of Volunteers in the Spanish American War, and Brigadier General in the Army. Henry was military governor of Puerto Rico from December 1898 to May 1899. His home was at Washington, D.C.

Heitman; *Who Was Who;* J.W. Vaughn, *With Crook at the Rosebud.* Harrisburg, Pa., Stackpole Co., 1956.

Henson, Matt(hew Alexander), polar explorer (Aug. 8, 1866-Mar. 9, 1955). B. probably in Philadelphia, he was taken by Robert Edwin Peary to Nicaragua as his "valet" on an 1887 expedition to survey a possible route for a trans-isthmus canal, and remained with Peary on all his subsequent exploration trips over a 22-year period, including that to the North Pole. On this famous expedition, Matt Henson kept a diary recording on April 6, 1909, his pride that "I . . . had the honor of representing my race in the historic achievement." According to Henson, the black got to the vicinity of the Pole first, then waited for Peary and the four Eskimos to come up. "It looked just like any other place on the ice," he once remarked. By executive order of President Taft, Henson was appointed clerk in the New York Customs Office, retiring in 1936 and living on a meagre pension from then until his death in Harlem. His wife, Lucy, died in 1968. Henson's story was told in a book, *Dark Companion,* by Bradley Robinson (1947).

New York Times, Mar. 10, 1955.

Hentig, Edmund Clarence, army officer (Aug. 24, 1842-Aug. 30, 1881). B. at Marshall, Michigan, his mother, Sarah Macomb Rucker, was niece of Major General Alexander Macomb, commander in chief of the Army from 1828-41, and sister of Brigadier General Daniel H. Rucker. Hentig enlisted in 1863. After the Civil War he became a sailor on the Great Lakes, but was commissioned June 12, 1867, a second lieutenant in the 6th Cavalry, serving in Texas for three years. He then was transferred to Kansas where he served until 1876, when he was assigned to Arizona, becoming captain and commanding a company at Fort Apache. In late August 1881, Hentig and his cousin, First Lieutenant William Stanton were ordered out on a scout under Colonel Eugene A. Carr, directed to go to Cibecue Creek and arrest a medicine man, Noch-ay-del-klinne, who was suspected of inciting the Apaches to war against the whites. The command arrested the Indian, then camped for the night on Cibecue Creek despite the general excitement the operation had aroused among Apache followers of the medicine man. Suddenly gunfire erupted, some of the Apache scouts mutinied, and Hentig and his orderly were shot down at first fire. They and other casualties were buried at night on the scene before the battered command withdrew to Fort Apache. Later the bodies were transferred to the National Cemetery at Santa Fe; the marker from that cemetery commemorating the incident now stands at Fort Apache. A short-lived camp was named for Hentig, located on Ash Creek on the present San Carlos Reservation in Arizona. Hentig was married and had a foster daughter.

David Perry Perrine, "Camp Hentig—Nobody Remembers It!" *Periodical* 32, Vol. IX, No. 2 (Summer 1977), 3-15; Dan L. Thrapp, *General Crook and the Sierra Madre Adventure.* Norman, Univ. of Okla. Press, 1972.

Hereford, Benjamin H., pioneer, attorney (c. 1829-July 2, 1890). B. in Virginia, he studied law, crossed the Plains with ox teams via the Santa Fe Trail, spent two years in Chihuahua City, and reached Sacramento, California, in 1855. He practiced law there for two years, later at Virginia City, Hamilton and elsewhere in Nevada and again at San Francisco. He reached Tucson, Arizona, in 1875. Bartholomew said that he was a deputy sheriff for a time in Nevada. In Arizona he established a San Pedro Valley ranch at what became known as Hereford, where a smelter was erected; when it closed down the community faded. Revived in 1892 it again was named Hereford, this time for Ben's son, Frank H. Hereford (1861-1928), also an attorney. For a time Frank was assistant editor of the Tombstone *Epitaph,* and it is said witnessed the OK Corral fight in October 1881. Ben died at Kansas City.

Portrait and Biographical Record of Arizona: Commemorating the Achievements of Citizens Who Have Contributed to the Progress of Arizona and the Developement of Its Resources. Chicago, Chapman Pub. Co., 1901; AHS Archives; Ed Bartholomew, *Wyatt Earp: The Man & The Myth.* Toyahvale, Tex., Frontier Book Co., 1964.

Herendeen, George B., scout (Nov. 28, 1846-June 17, 1919). B. at Parkman, Geauga County, Ohio, he was orphaned at 13, served in the Civil War, lived for a time in Indiana and then went to Denver, to New Mexico and later to Montana. In 1874 he accompanied the Yellowstone Wagon Road and Prospecting expedition, and in June 1875 was one of 43 men headed by "Major" F.D. Pease, agent to the Crows, who established a trading post called "Fort Pease" on the north bank of the Yellowstone River, below the mouth of the Big Horn. Eighteen of the party returned to Bozeman early in February 1876, asserting that the fort was under continuous siege from the Sioux. James Brisbin with a detachment

of the 2nd Cavalry on a relief mission found six men killed and 19 survivors still holding out. It is not known which group Herendeen was with. He was with Gibbon's column as a scout and courier in 1876, but reached and became a part of the Custer command about June 22 and on June 25 was attached to Reno's battalion. He was in Reno's fight in the valley with the Sioux, was missing for a time, but rejoined the battered command on Reno Hill remaining for the rest of the fight. Herendeen was scout during the Nez Perce campaign. He testified January 27-28, 1879, at the Reno Court of Inquiry. Following his Indian scouting activities he lived in the Montana communities of Bozeman, Lewistown and Great Falls until 1889 when he moved to Harlem, Montana. He died there of pneumonia. He was described as 5 feet, 8 inches in height, was of fair complexion with brown hair and blue eyes.

Barry C. Johnson, "George Herendeen: Montana Scout." *English Westerner's Brand Book,* Vol. 2, Nos. 3, 4 (Apr., July 1960); BHB; *Montana Contributions,* II (1896), 1966; Edgar I. Stewart, "Major Brisbin's Relief of Fort Pease." *Montana,* Vol. 6, No. 3 (Summer 1956), 23-27.

Hernandarías de Saavedra, explorer (d. Oct. 21, 1541). The grandson of the marshal of Seville, Hernandarías joined the De Soto expedition into the southern United States and became prominent as a fighting man. He was wounded mortally October 9, 1541, at Tula, probably a Caddoan village, on the Arkansas River in western Arkansas. Hernandarías lingered until October 21 when "he died like a Catholic knight, commending his soul to God."

Bourne, *De Soto,* II.

Hernandez, Joseph Marion, militia officer, politician (Aug. 4, 1793-June 8, 1857). B. at St. Augustine, Florida, when it was under Spanish control, he transferred his allegiance to the United States when it took over Florida, served as delegate to Congress from 1822-23 and was a member and presiding officer of the territorial House of Representatives. Hernandez was appointed a Brigadier General of Volunteers during the Second Seminole War, serving from 1835 until 1838. His militia were involved in some hard skirmishes early in the war, the most severe being that on January 17, 1836, at Anderson's

Plantation when the St. Augustine Guards under Benjamin A. Putnam were routed with 50 percent casualties. Hernandez had difficulties with militia who would not leave their homes unguarded while on military service, and with regulars who would not follow the orders of a volunteer officer. In September 1837 he captured King Philip. Under Jesup's direction, Hernandez captured by treachery Osceola, Coa-hadjo, about 71 warriors and others October 21, 1837, an infamous act which brought lasting calumny upon Jesup. Hernandez ran unsuccessfully for the U.S. Senate in 1845, then moved to Cuba where he became a planter in Coliseo district, near Matanzas where he died and was buried.

BDAC; John K. Mahon, *History of the Second Seminole War.* Gainesville, Univ. of Fla. Press, 1967.

Hernandez, Pablo (Juan C. ?), adventurer (c. 1833-post 1857). B. in either New Mexico or California, Hernandez at 11, Andreas Fuentes, and others were traveling from New Mexico to California when they were attacked by Indians near the Mohave River in the southern California desert. Several were killed but Fuentes and Hernandez escaped afoot, being rescued about April 15, 1844, by Fremont, homeward bound on his second expedition. Kit Carson and Alexis Godey recovered their stolen horses. Hernandez accompanied the Fremont party eastward, was adopted into the household of Senator Thomas Hart Benton, and educated. Subsequently he returned to southern California where, according to report, he became a stock thief or bandit, eventually making his way into Sonora. When the Crabb filibuster expedition penetrated Sonora, Hernandez, who reportedly had acted as go-between for Pesqueira and Crabb when the expedition was conceived, now was said to have been instrumental in securing Crabb's surrender for eventual execution (April 7, 1857) of the adventurer and all his band save one. One of his letters while involved in this affair is extant, in which he boasted that he personally had severed the head of Crabb and preserved it in spirits.

Robert H. Forbes, *Crabb's Filibustering Expedition into Sonora, 1857.* Tuscon, Arizona Silhouettes, 1952; Harvey Lewis Carter, '*Dear Old Kit': the Historical Christopher Carson.* Norman, Univ. of Okla. Press, 1968; *Frontier Times,* vol. 4, No. 5 (Feb. 1927), 44-48.

Herndon, Albert, train robber (fl. 1878-84). Probably b. in Dallas County, Texas, he may have been about the age of his friend, Sam Pipes, with whom he joined the Sam Bass outlaw gang in the spring of 1878, assisted in the Mesquite Springs, Texas, train robbery, was captured by Texas Ranger June Peak, sentenced to life imprisonment July 17, 1878. He was pardoned by President Cleveland for volunteering for nursing service aboard a quarantined ship in New York harbor. He was of medium build, weighed 150 pounds, had brown hair and mustache.

Wayne Gard, *Sam Bass.* Lincoln, Univ. of Nebr. Press, 1969.

Herring, Valentine Johnson (Rube), frontiersman (1812-c. 1883). B. in Illinois, he received a fair education and in 1831 was hired at St. Louis by John Gantt for a trapping expedition to the Rockies. He joined William Sublette in the upper country by 1833. He returned to St. Louis, was hired by Wyeth and reached Fort Hall, eventually becoming a free trapper. He was in charge of Fort Lancaster, eastern Colorado, in 1841-42, though he spent considerable time at Taos. He shot and killed Henry Beer in a duel over a Mexican woman with whom Herring permanently took up, although they did not formally marry. Rube converted to Mormonism in late 1846, but defected when Mormons refused his services as a guide next spring, although he was considered to be still of that faith for some years. In 1849 he and his woman journeyed to California, settling at length in San Bernardino County. He became superintendent of schools in 1853, was a justice of the peace and county assessor, sheriff in 1859 and held other offices. The English writer, George Ruxton, was entranced by Herring and left a memorable, though overly fictitious, portrait of him.

George Frederick Ruxton, *Life in the Far West.* Norman, Univ. of Okla. Press, 1951; Janet Lecompte article, MM, Vol. IX.

Hersey, Timothy Fletcher, pioneer (Aug. 17, 1827-May 11, 1905). B. at Sumner, Oxford County, Maine, his father took the family in 1834 to the Rock River country of Illinois. Tim was educated at Beloit, Wisconsin, becoming proficient in surveying while through his father, a miller, he learned that trade as well. He had many contacts with Wisconsin

Indians and lived in that state until 20, working at logging and freighting. He then located in Joe Daviess County, Illinois, where he was married. In 1857 he arrived in Kansas, the first settler in Dickinson County and the founder of Abilene. In 1858 he became a government contractor, furnishing hay, grain and fuel for installations as far as the Rocky Mountains. He had many skirmishes with Indians. In 1857 a party of Missourians was besieged by Cheyennes near the present Clay Center, Kansas; Hersey and thirteen other citizens, along with thirty soldiers came to the relief, finding two men killed and a woman injured. In the resulting action with the hostiles three of the Hersey party were wounded, one mortally. During the Civil War Hersey was an Indian trader. Afterward he contracted with Joseph G. McCoy to survey a cattle trail from Abilene to Wichita, Kansas, an extension of the Chisholm Trail, the route known as the Hersey, McCoy or Abilene Trail. In 1860 he was a guide for the Smoky Hill River Expedition to locate a road between the Platte trail on the north and the Arkansas Trail on the south, to connect Leavenworth and Denver. Indian skirmishes cost them one man killed and another wounded. Hersey once claimed he had been in 25 Indian engagements in his career; he was wounded by arrows on several occasions. November 15, 1869, he emigrated to the Solomon Valley and located the community of Beloit, Kansas, erecting a mill, operating a hotel and strongly boosting the town among prospective settlers. Hersey held various public offices from time to time. In 1881 "when Kansas was settled up," he headed for the Tongue River country of Wyoming where he erected a sawmill and later a flour mill, selling out in 1883. He went to Denver in 1893 and prospected in Colorado until 1901 when he moved to Castle Rock, Washington, where he died.

United States Biographical Dictionary: Kansas Volume. Kansas City, S. Lewis & Co., 1879; Timothy Fletcher Hersey file, Kan. State Hist. Soc.; *Frontier Times,* Vol. 8, No. 5 (Feb. 1931), 197-98.

Hertel, (Joseph) Francois, partisan (c. July 1, 1642-c. May 20, 1722). B. at Three Rivers where his father, Jacques Hertel of Normandy was the first settler (having reached Canada in 1615), Francois became a militia-man at 15 since Three Rivers was exposed to seemingly incessant Iroquois attacks. In July 1661 he was captured by Mohawks who took him to their villages in the present New York State, subjected him to some torture (he reported his left thumb torn off and a finger on his right hand burned), was adopted by an Indian family and held for two years. During this time he well learned the Iroquois tongue, as he later came to understand Algonquin and various dialects, it being stated at one time that "he understands almost all the Indian languages." During his captivity he managed to smuggle letters to the Jesuit, Simon Le Moyne at the Onondaga villages, the priest describing him as "of comely appearance, and delicate," though he became tough enough to win a lasting reputation as a guerrilla fighter and become "le Héros" (the Hero) to the French and in Canadian folklore. He escaped his Iroquois family and reached Three Rivers by late 1663, being employed as an interpreter and serving as a militia-man. He was married in 1664 at Montreal, fathering 10 sons, all of whom fought valiantly for Canada in the wilderness reaches of the frontier, often leading or accompanying Indian war parties. Hertel senior was in numerous brushes and affrays with the constant enemy; he was a member of Remy de Courcelle's futile expedition against the Iroquois in February 1666 and of Tracy's more effective campaign later in the year. In 1673 he assisted in the building of Fort Frontenac at the present Kingston, Ontario, and five years later was sent on a mission to Hudson Bay, returning with furs for which he had not been authorized to trade, so he was imprisoned, his pelts confiscated and he heavily fined; he was released shortly, and the fine remitted. With the troubles leading up to King William's War (1688-97) Hertel came into his own. He was charged with command of all the tribes allied to the French, and in this capacity he developed woods-ranging war tactics that proved highly effective. Early in 1690 Frontenac authorized three war parties to attack New England targets, Hertel's directed to Dunstable, Massachusetts but diverted during two months cautious scouting of the wild country to Salmon Falls, New Hampshire. Hertel had left Three Rivers January 28 with 25 Canadians, 20 Sokokis and 5 Algonquins, numbering in his command three of his sons and a nephew. They reached their goal the night of March 27. The attackers "made their onset between break of day & Sunrise when most were a bed & no watch kept neither in fort nor house." According to French accounts 43 English were killed, including women and children, 54 taken prisoner, 27 houses burned and 2,000 cattle destroyed; English sources assert about 30 English were slain along with two attacking Frenchmen and two Indians, one Frenchman taken prisoner, and that the enemy claim of 2,000 cattle killed was wildly exaggerated. Hurrying his prisoners northward Hertel learned he was being pursued by a sizable body and ambushed it at the Wooster River crossing where an additional 20 English were killed; Hertel's nephew, Louis Crevier was slain and a son, Zacharie Hertel, wounded in the knee and crippled for life. With the English repulsed, Hertel and 36 followers left the prisoners in the care of his remaining personnel to be hustled off to Canada, and hastened to join René Robinau de Portneuf in an assault on Caso Bay, or Falmouth, at the site of Portland, Maine. More than 400 were gathered to make this attack, while the defenders numbered fewer than 100 fighting men and as many non-combatants. After several days of siege, the English survivors surrendered on a pledge by Portneuf of quarter, but as quickly as they had quitted their fortifications and laid down their arms the Indians fell upon them, slaughtering many more; the survivors were taken to Canada. "The Hertels, father and sons, rapidly became the terror of the English and the enemy Indians. Their feats were without number," wrote one authority but with a lack of detail although the Hertels seem in fact to have been foremost and very active in the forest war that raged for many bloody years along the fringes of the two empires. Hertel was commandant of Fort Frontenac from 1709 to 1712; he reported that no party or expedition had gone against the enemy "that has not included the father and some of his sons," and his adventures must have been numerous; he became perhaps the most famed frontier soldier of New France. Parkman wrote that "To the New England of old he was the abhorred chief of Popish malignants and murdering savages. The New England of to-day will be more just to the brave defender of his country and his faith." Frontenac tried from 1689 to obtain for him letters of nobility, but for many years the French court resisted since it had never heard of Hertel and for other reasons. When Frontenac asked that "the fees be omitted because of the Hero's poor financial condition," Jean Baptiste Colbert, chief minister to King Louis XIV, retorted that "if he were too poor to pay for the seals he was to poor to support the position and so denied him." Finally in 1716 Louis granted the request, and the parchment was delivered to Hertel. He died at Boucher-ville, across the river from Montreal. "A complete study of the martial exploits of Francois Hertel and his sons has not yet been made," but it would be a narrative of supreme adventure were it thoroughly done.

Literature abundant, but scattered; the best narrative is DCB, II; see also Parkman, *A Half Century of Conflict, Count Frontenac and New France Under Louis XIV;* Coleman, *Captives,* I; Thwaites, JR, XLVII, 83-87, 315n3.

Hertel de la Fresnière, Zacharie Francois, army officer (c. 1665-c. June 18, 1752). B. probably in Three Rivers, Quebec, he was the first of 10 sons of Francois Hertel, the noted partisan commander and like him took part in raids against the New England frontier. He was wounded in the attack on Salmon Falls, New Hampshire, March 28, 1690, and crippled for life, but not incapacitated. He was captured by Iroquois in 1691 and held for three years, then returned to Three Rivers. As a captain in 1731 he was assigned to supervise construction of Fort St. Frederic at Crown Point on Lake Champlain. He was made a knight of the order of St Louis in 1745, and died at Montreal. Hertel de la Fresnière was married.

DCB, III.

Hertel de Moncours, Pierre, Canadian officer (Mar. 19, 1687-Feb. 28, 1739). The 10th son of Francois Hertel, Moncours was a fighting man like his father and six brothers. In 1731 he was commandant of the garrison at Fort St. Frederic near Crown Point on Lake Champlain; three years later he was in command at Green Bay, Wisconsin, but after disputes with fur traders there he was recalled in 1736.

DCB, II.

Hertel de Rouville, Jean Baptiste, partisan (Oct. 26, 1668-c. June 28, 1722). B. at Three Rivers, Quebec, he early served his country in

Indian skirmishes on the frontier against the Iroquois and accompanied his father, Francois Hertel and two brothers on the 1687 expedition of Governor Brisay (Marquis de Denonville) against the New York Senecas. He also accompanied his father on the raid against Salmon Falls, Hew Hampshire, although whether he took part in the subsequent raid against Falmouth (Portland), Maine is not reported. In 1704 he carried out his most famous raid from the American frontier point of view, that against Deerfield, Massachusetts. "The object of the attack was an unoffending hamlet, that from its position could never be a menace to the French, and the destruction of which could profit them nothing," wrote Parkman. "The aim of the enterprise was not military, but political," because it was targeted so as not to offend the dreaded Iroquois while preventing the Abenakis from swerving their alliance from the French to the English. Rouville left the Mission St. Louis at Caughnawaga, near Montreal, in the dead of winter, his snowshoe command including four of his brothers among the 50 Canadians along with 200 Abenaki and Iroquois Indians from Caugnawaga, a settlement for Mohawks who had been converted and moved to Canada. The attack force reached the vicinity of Deerfield February 28, 1704. Snow had drifted to nearly the top of the 8-ft. palisade while it lay three feet deep on the level. At 2 a.m. the attackers crept over the solid crust, slipped over the palisade and launched the assault against the sleeping little community of fewer than 300 people, including 20 soldiers sent to help out in event of a French and Indian attack, but the sentinels, if any, were drowsing. Seventeen of the 43 houses of the place were burned; the exact number of casualties is not known with certainty, but the best authorities say 54 were killed and 111 taken captive of whom 18 or 20 were slaughtered enroute to Canada. Rouville and 22 of his followers including one of his brothers, the adjutant, were wounded and three killed. Rouville, however, recovered and led an expedition in the autumn against the English at Plaisance (Placentia), Newfoundland. In 1708 he was co-commander of an expedition of Indians and French which struck Haverhill on the Merrimack River in Massachusetts just before dawn on August 29. The attackers "were not very successful," in firing the under 30 structures in the place, and

few were burned though 48 men, women and children were slain; in their withdrawal the French command was ambushed and nine killed including René Hertel de Chambly, Rouville's brother. The next year Rouville led a minor raid once more against the Deerfield environs; there were few casualties on either side. Rouville had acquired a dread reputation among the English colonials for "to preserve the goodwill of his Indian allies he had been constrained to permit the carrying out of acts of barbarity that were unworthy of civilized beings," nor was he viewed objectively by the enemy; under the circumstances it was difficult to do so. He was sent by the French to Boston in 1710 on a diplomatic mission, but the rest of his career was spent in eastern Canada. He was made a knight of the order of St. Louis a few months before his death. He was twice married and left descendants. Parkman publishes a portrait of him, facing p. 56 of *A Half Century of Conflict, I.*

Parkman, *A Half Century of Conflict,* I; Coleman, *Captives;* DCB, II.

Hertel de Saint Francois, Etienne, army officer (Nov. 8, 1734-July 18, 1760). B. at St. Francois du Lac, Quebec, and a member of the famous Hertel family of French-Canadian warriors, Etienne at 14 was a cadet with colonial troops at Fort St. Frederic on Lake Champlain. He then served eight years at the fortress of Louisbourg, and later was posted to Michilimackinac on the Strait of Mackinac. He was killed in operations against the English near Lotbiniere, above Quebec.

DCB, III.

Hervey, James Madison, attorney (July 4, 1874-Jan. 31, 1953). B. at Stephenville, Texas, his father, Austin Flint Hervey was a supplier for buffalo hunters at Fort Griffin, Texas, and a brother, Virgil was killed there. Hervey lived at Lincoln, New Mexico, in 1886 and Roswell in 1887. He was graduated from the University of Michigan law school in 1899. While Attorney General of New Mexico (1907-1909) he became deeply interested in the case of the murder of Pat Garrett (February 29, 1908) who had been a friend of his father; he believed those guilty should be discovered. Among the many uncertain elements of his inquiry is whether he caused to be destroyed the Fornoff report. Hervey's summation of what he had learned was printed in *True West* by his arrangement eight years after his death by which time he presumed all of the principals would be dead; he wrote it probably around 1952. Hervey had interviewed Carl Adamson, the only witness to the shooting of Garrett, supposedly by Wayne Brazel. Inconsistencies in the reports of the killing bothered Hervey and he persuaded Fornoff to undertake an intensive investigation, Fornoff at the time "a noted peace officer and captain of the State Mounted Police." Fornoff and Hervey became convinced that Garrett was killed by Jim Miller in the pay of "a wealthy ranchman near El Paso" and perhaps others because of Garrett's delving into the Fountain murders. Robert N. Mullin, a serious student of Lincoln County affairs, over a period of 60 years attempted to locate the Fornoff Report or a copy of it, but was unsuccessful and believed the original had been destroyed. No true copy has been located.

Colin Rickards, *How Pat Garrett Died.* Santa Fe, Palomino Press, 1970; James Madison Hervey, "The Assassination of Pat Garrett." *True West,* Vol. 8, No. 4 (Mar.-Apr. 1961), 16-17, 40-42; Robert N. Mullin, "The Key to the Mystery of Pat Garrett." Los Angeles Westerners *Branding Iron* 92 (June 1969) 1, 4-5.

Hess, Hezekiah, Virginia borderer (Oct. 9, 1756-Oct. 4, 1848). B. in Dutchess County, New York, he was brought to Hampshire County, Virginia, when under 1 year old, where he resided until 1822 when he moved to Lewis County, Virginia. In June 1776, he volunteered as Indian scout, ranging the border stream valleys, protecting the settlements from marauders. He volunteered again during the 1777 season, engaging in one action with a large enemy band. Hess continued such service in 1778 and 1779, and there is an unconfirmed report that he fought in the War of 1812. He was denied a pension however, and died in penury.

Lucullus V. McWhorter, *The Border Settlers of Northwestern Virginia.* Hamilton, O., Republican Pub. Co., 1915.

Hesse, Fred George S., cattleman (Apr. 3, 1853-Mar. 3, 1929). B. in Essex, England, he came to the United States in 1863, completed his education at Washington D.C., and went to San Antonio, Texas, where he became a cowboy and eventually ranch foreman. In 1876 he drove a trail herd to Wyoming for the English brothers, Moreton and Dick Frewen who located their 76 Ranch on the middle fork of the Powder River. Hesse remained with them until they sold out around 1888 and about 1890 started his own 28 Ranch on Crazy Woman Creek not far from Buffalo, Wyoming. Here he inevitably became embroiled in growing tensions between big cattlemen and small ranchers that would lead in 1892 to the Johnson County War, with Hesse of course on the side of the major stockmen. Smith believed Hesse was a leader in concentrating opposition to the small ranchers and their supposed rustling activities; it is hinted that Hesse, a hard and fearless man, about November 20, 1891, may have killed Orley E. (Ranger) Jones with whom he had had differences. The murder never was solved. Feelings against Hesse rose in Buffalo, the center for the small ranchers, and December 17, 1891, he and Frank M. Canton, suspected of another murder were forced to flee the town "not to return until they came with the invading army." Hesse was one of the pillars of the cattlemen invaders of Johnson County where it was intended to assassinate a number of suspected stock thieves. Hesse was picked up with the other invaders by United States Cavalry elements, but he was never convicted of misdeeds. He returned to his 28 Ranch in 1894, the old animosities still around but dormant. His ranching activities prospered, his holdings growing from the 160 acres he homesteaded to about 4,000 acres supporting at one time four bands of sheep and 2,500 head of cattle. Hesse also became involved in financial affairs in Buffalo and was a leaseholder in the Billy Creek oil field. He was married and the father of two sons and a daughter. He died at Buffalo.

Sheridan (Wyoming) *Journal,* Mar. 5, 1929; Helena Huntington Smith, *The War on Powder River.* N.Y., McGraw-Hill Book Co., 1966; information from the Western History Research Center, Univ. of Wyo.

Heth, Henry, army officer (c. 1821-Sept. 27, 1899). B. in Virginia, he was graduated from West Point, commissioned a brevet second lieutenant of the 1st Infantry July 1, 1847, and a second lieutenant of the 6th Infantry September 22. He was made first lieutenant June 9, 1853, and captain of the 10th Infantry March 3, 1855. Heth was on frontier duty at

Fort Atkinson, Kansas, from 1848-53, and at Fort Riley, Kansas, from 1854-55. He was sent on the Sioux campaign of 1855 and in the action at Blue Water, Nebraska, in 1856. He was responsible for a Cheyenne outbreak in 1856 when, in April a small band of Indians came to the Upper Platte Bridge, Nebraska, to trade; in a dispute over ownership of a horse Heth tried to arrest three Cheyennes. One Indian was killed, another imprisoned and the third escaped to the Black Hills, his tribesmen commencing heavy depredations upon the emigrant road. Heth was on the Utah Expedition of 1858-60. He left Union service for the Confederacy April 25, 1861, becoming a Southern Major General.

Heitman; Cullum; Robert M. Utley, *Frontiersmen in Blue.* N.Y., MacMillan Co., 1967.

Hewit, Henry Stuart, physician (Dec. 26, 1825-Aug. 19, 1873). B. at Bridgeport, Connecticut, he graduated from Yale and studied medicine privately, receiving his degree from the University of New York in 1847. He joined the army as contract surgeon and left New York for Vera Cruz, Mexico, March 19, 1848. He contracted yellow fever but recovered and eventually returned to New York. He left with the 3rd U.S. Artillery for California via Cape Horn, arriving April 23, 1849, and accepting a commission as army assistant surgeon. He accompanied Captain William H. Warner on an exploring expedition to the headwaters of the Sacramento and Humboldt rivers; Warner was killed by Indians and remnants of the expedition reached San Francisco again. After a short visit to Hawaii, he was ordered to Fort Yuma as its first physician, reaching there December 1, 1850, with part of the 2nd Infantry under brevet Major Samuel P. Heintzelman. Differences quickly arose between Hewit and Heintzelman, compounded by the distant Oatman massacre and Hewit's belief Heintzelman, did not do enough to rescue two kidnapped girls. Hewit resigned from the army June 10, 1851, returned to San Francisco and left for Panama enroute to New York aboard the steamship *Union,* which was wrecked off the Lower California coast, Hewit riding muleback north for 100 miles in four days to San Diego to report the disaster. He finally reached Bridgeport again by mid-September 1851, taking his family back to San Francisco where he established a private

practice as a surgeon, until they returned east about 1855. He served the Union Army from 1861-65 as surgeon, being breveted lietenant-colonel, earning praise from Sherman and others for his dedicated work. He fathered 11 children, six of whom survived with distinguished careers. Hewit died at New York City and was buried at Bridgeport.

Arizona Medicine, (Jan. 1969), 62-70.

Hewitt, Christian Cyrus, army officer (c. 1848-Oct. 3, 1905). B. probably at Wheeling, (West) Virginia, he was graduated from West Point and commissioned a second lieutenant in the 19th Infantry June 17, 1874, assigned to Fort Wallace, Kansas. In early October he was engaged in pursuit of hostile Cheyennes who had attacked a German family of emigrants, killing five and capturing four girls. April 23, 1875, he was with Henely in the Battle of Sappa Creek, Kansas, the last major action of the 1874-75 hostilities on the central Plains. He helped capture four Cheyennes believed guilty of killing a buffalo hunter near Fort Wallace in the spring of 1875. Hewitt remained on the Plains and in New Mexico during most of the rest of his army service, becoming a first lieutenant June 15, 1882, and a captain June 4, 1892. He retired for disability in line of duty February 2, 1901, with rank of major and died at Wheeling.

Cullum; Powell; Heitman.

Hewitt, John Napoleon Brinton, ethnologist, linguist (Dec. 16, 1859-Oct. 14, 1937). B. at Niagara Falls, New York, he became a student of American Indian linguistics, mythology and sociology, and for many years was employed by the Bureau of American Ethnology at the Smithsonian Institution. His publications were numerous. He spoke and made extensive studies of Chippewayan, Creek, Delaware, Maya, Seri, Waicura and Polynesian; for a number of years before his death he was a member of th executive committee of the U.S. Board of Geographic Names. Among his publications were: *Polysynthesis in the Languages of the American Indian* (1893); *Era of the Formation of the Historic League of the Iroquois* (1894); *The Cosmogonic Gods of the Iroquois* (1895); with W.J. McGee *The Seri Indians* (1898); *The Name Cherokee and Its Derivation* (1900); *Orenda and a Definition of Religion* (1902); *Iroquoian Cosmology* (1904); (ed.)

Introduction to Seneca Fiction, Legends and Myths (1919); *A Constitutional League of Peace in the Stone Age of America: The League of the Iroquois and Its Constitution* (1920); (ed.) Edwin Thompson Denig, *Indian Tribes of the Upper Missouri* (1930); *Status of Women in Iroquois Polity Before 1784* (1932); with Percy James Robinson *Toronto During the French Regime* (1933); (ed.) *Journal of Rudolf Friedrich Kurz* (1937); *Treaties with the Six Nations of Iroquois of New York* (1939).

Who's Who; New York Times, Oct. 20, 1937.

Hezeta, Bruno de, navigator (c. 1751-1807). A Basque from Bilbao, he was commissioned in the Spanish navy and was one of six officers sent from Spain to Mexico to take part in explorations of the Northwest Coast of America and to assure and extend Spanish footholds there in the face of a perceived threat from Russian and British expansionists. He reached Mexico City in October 1774 and was assigned to captain the *Santiago* with Juan Perez (see entry) as second in command, already an experienced explorer in the intended part of the globe. The *Santiago* would be accompanied by the schooner *Sonora* with Juan de Ayala in command and Juan Francisco de la Bodega y Quadra, second officer. The ships left San Blas March 18, 1775, Hezeta's instructions to reach Latitude 65 degrees if he could, and then work southward along the coast. He spent nine days in a northern California anchorage he called Santíssima Trinidad, near today's Trinidad, California. July 13 the expedition reached the Washington coast near Point Grenville. Here the *Sonora* found itself in an entanglement of shoals. While attempting to secure fresh water ashore it lost the six-man landing group to an Indian ambush, the vessel itself barely escaping to rejoin the *Santiago,* and then continuing northward. Hezeta reached no more than 49 degrees north latitude, although the *Sonora,* separated from the parent ship had gone on to 58 degrees 30 minutes, on the upper reaches of the Alaskan panhandle before turning back. August 11 Hezeta brought about and headed southward, cruising as near the coast as he dared. August 17 he discovered what he called the Bay of the Assumption of Our Lady, but the current was so strong that he could not effect an entrance, so judged it formed the mouth of some great river; it was the earliest reported sighting by a European of the Columbia River, 17 years before its official discovery by Robert Gray. The 29th of August Hezeta reached Monterey Bay on the California coast. The *Sonora* at length joined him there and November 7 the two vessels returned to San Blas. Although remaining active in the Pacific waters for some time, Hezeta made no more voyages of exploration. He was transferred to the Philippines, then to Cuba, commanded naval bases from 1787 at Rosas and Algeciras and died at Málaga.

Warren L. Cook, *Flood Tide of Empire.* New Haven, Yale Univ. Press, 1973; Bancroft, *Northwest Coast, I.*

Hiawatha, Mohawk statesman (c. 1545-c. 1580). The name is the title of a chieftainship hereditary in the Tortoise (Turtle) clan of the Mohawks, the most famous holder of it being the first known to bear the name. A founder of the League of the Iroquois he was a reformer, statesman, medicine man and prophet, a disciple of Dekanawida (see entry) and, being a noted orator, and since his mentor had a serious speech impediment, spokesman for him. The two engineered reforms to end intertribal strife and the promotion of universal peace, at least between and among the five tribes of the Iroquois Confederation. They advanced for example a regulation to set the price of a human life at ten strings of wampum, a cubit in length: a murderer, instead of sparking a savage blood feud, must pay the bereaved family ten strings of wampum for the death he had caused and an additional ten strings for his own life made forfeit by his crime. Though by birth a Mohawk, Hiawatha began his work among the Onondaga but, meeting vicious opposition he transferred his labor to the more receptive Oneida. They agreed to accept his program for a law-based association of states providing the Mohawks would do the same, the confederation commencing with these two tribes plus the Cayuga. The Onondaga then were approached again and finally agreed to join if the Seneca would also do so. Hiawatha with Dekanawida developed in time into half-mythical figures, accomplishing deeds hitherto reserved for the Iroquois gods and becoming the central figures in cycles of interrelated legends. Longfellow, in his epic poem, *Hiawatha,* has confused the Mohawk law-giver with a Chippewa legend, so that his figure is not at all representative of the true Hiawatha, who remains a great innovator of political thought among the American Indians and particularly the Iroquois, even though he worked somewhat in the shadow of his great mentor, Dekanawida.

Hodge, HAI; Thomas R. Henry, *Wilderness Messiah*. N.Y., William Sloane Associates, 1955.

Hickman, Sotha, borderer (June 10, 1748- post July 17, 1832). B. in eastern Maryland, he removed to Monongalia County, Virginia (present West Virginia) and served as a scout out of Nutter Fort, the present Clarksburg, West Virginia, in 1780-82 under William Lowther and others. He once was captured while trapping on Little Kanawha River, Virginia, and taken to the Indian towns on the Scioto River, Ohio, from whence he escaped.

Lucullus McWhorter, *The Border Settlers of Northwestern Virginia*. Hamilton, O., Republican Pub. Co., 1915.

Hickok, James Butler (Wild Bill), gunfighter, frontiersman (May 27, 1837-Aug. 2, 1876). B. at Homer (later Troy Grove), Illinois, he received some schooling. He assisted his father in running an Underground Railroad station in their home until his parent's death in 1852; at an early age he demonstrated a sense of rudimentary justice and fair play. He drove a canal team briefly and in 1856 with his brother, Lorenzo, left for the west, landing from a Missouri River steamboat at Fort Leavenworth. With John M. Owen he joined James H. Lane's Free State Army in Kansas, remaining with it more than a year. In March 1858, he was elected constable of Monticello, Kansas, farming on the side. He left Monticello late that year, an infatuation with a local girl being broken up, and hired out to Russell, Majors, and Waddell for two years of driving coaches and wagons. He may have reached Santa Fe, during this period, possibly meeting Kit Carson, may have returned to Illinois briefly in 1859, went back to Kansas and met William F. Cody (Buffalo Bill) that year, and the next met Joseph A. Slade. He, Slade and others, tracked down Indians who had run horses off from a western Nebraska Pony Express station, recapturing the animals plus a herd of Indian ponies. Hickok then was assigned to Rock Spring Station, near Fairbury, Nebraska, where on July 12, 1861, he had his celebrated fight with David McCanles, and wounded, possibly mortally, Woods and Gordon who were despatched by others, the account of the fight being magnified almost beyond description by George Ward Nichols in a *Harper's* article that made "Wild Bill" nationally famous. Hickok was cleared by court action. He enlisted as a civilian scout in the Union Army at Leavenworth in 1861, took part in the Battle of Wilson's Creek August 10, and by October 30 was hired as a wagonmaster for the army in Missouri, serving on and off about a year; during this time he somehow earned his nickname, which could have originated in any of several wild adventures. Presumably as a scout, courier or sharpshooter, he took part in the savage Battle of Pea Ridge, Benton County, Arkansas, March 6-8, 1862. Hickok did not kill Brigadier General Benjamin McCulloch during that action, as has been alleged. He may subsequently have been attached to the 8th Missouri State Militia as scout or a "spy," as reconnaissance personnel were sometimes called. In the wild border country Hickok could well have experienced many remarkable adventures during the war, but the accounts which have surfaced in numerous printed collections are contradictory, confusing, rarely subject to authentication, and seem generally unreliable; Rosa has done the best job of sifting them. Following hostilities, Hickok settled briefly at Springfield, Missouri, here shooting Davis (Dave) Tutt July 21, 1865; he was acquitted. In 1866 he was appointed a deputy U.S. marshal at Fort Riley, Kansas, where his brother, Lorenzo, was wagon master. Bill concurrently performed other tasks for his friend, Richard Bentley Owen, post quartermaster, and sometimes was described as a scout or "guide." In this capacity he may have guided Sherman from Riley to Fort Kearny, Nebraska, a mission for which Cody subsequently — and erroneously — received credit. From Kearny he guided a tourist party on an excursion into western Nebraska, then returned to Riley, where Lt. Col. George A. Custer now commanded the 7th Cavalry. The two became acquainted. Hickok continued his employment as deputy marshal under U.S. Marshal Charles Whiting. He worked against thieves, army deserters and other lawbreakers, some of his adventures being recorded. During the summer of 1868 enroute to Atchison, Kansas, he met the future lawman, Bill Tilghman, then a boy of 12, and Tilghman's sisters, making a strong impression on them. The last date on which Hickok is known to have operated as a deputy marshal is May 2, 1870, when he was at Junction City, Kansas. Hickok was a scout for the expedition of Winfield Scott Hancock to the southern Plains Indians in 1867, continuing to scout for the army on occasion until February 28, 1869. The first dime novel of Wild Bill's "adventures" appeared in July 1867, to be followed by many more in subsequent years. Hickok was chosen sheriff of Ellis County, Kansas (in which Hays City was the largest community) at a special election August 23, 1869. In August he killed Bill Mulvey, and in September Samuel Strawhun, both shootings considered justifiable. Hickok was defeated in the general election and Peter Lanihan succeeded him as sheriff. July 17, 1870, he killed a soldier and wounded another in a saloon fight at Hays and hastily departed that community, surfacing later at Topeka, Kansas. On April 15, 1871, he was named city marshal of Abilene, Kansas, where he encountered John Wesley Hardin, Ben Thompson and other noted frontier figures. On October 5, 1871, he fatally wounded Phil Coe and killed by mistake Mike Williams. On December 13, he was dismissed as marshal because the trail drives were over and the town no longer needed his services. In 1872 he went to Georgetown, Colorado, staying with Charley Utter; later he moved to Kansas City. Bill took part in a "grand buffalo chase" at Niagara Falls, New York, in August 1872, and late in September he appeared in a fair at Kansas City. In 1873 he joined Buffalo Bill in a New York show, but was not happy in it; he left the troupe at Rochester, New York. In 1874 he participated briefly in another stage production at New York City, then returned to the plains, where he guided sporting parties and settled for a time at Cheyenne, Wyoming. Here his eyes commenced to trouble him. March 5, 1876, he married Agnes Lake, with whom he had corresponded for several years (Hickok never was married, nor even particularly friendly with Calamity Jane Cannary, and "documentation" alleging that the two were wed is spurious). Hickok and his wife honeymooned at Cincinnati; he went to St. Louis to organize a miners' expedition for the Black Hills, abandoned that project

and proceeded to Cheyenne where with Utter and others he went to Deadwood, South Dakota, enroute being joined by Calamity Jane, according to report. At Deadwood, August 2, 1876, Hickok was assassinated by Jack McCall who later was executed for the shooting. Hickok was buried first at Ingleside, near Deadwood, then in 1879 the body was moved to the Mt. Moriah Cemetery where it remained. For some reason Calamity Jane's body was buried 20 feet from Hickok at Mt. Moriah, the two in death thus being more closely associated than they were in life. Rosa, a careful student, reported that he could confirm only seven killings by Hickok, with several "probables," but concedes that four years of wild experiences during the Civil War, part of the time as sharpshooter or scout, "might have produced at least half" of the high total of "considerably over a hundred" victims alleged by sensationalists, although himself believing this figure "grossly magnified." Rosa added that "when he died his alleged personal claim was only thirty-six." Aside from his war service, Hickok engaged in showdowns "only when provoked," and normally, when sober at any rate, he was "mild-mannered, courteous, and peaceful," although self-assured, courageous and deadly when aroused. In spite of the high level of publicity attending his movements, commencing with the Nichols article, it seems odd that he would have developed his fearsome reputation on such a low man-count as research provides, and there are many gaps in his life which, as Rosa admits, might account for unrecorded activities. Be it said that Hickok was a legend in his own time and appears to have fully deserved his reputation.

Literature abundant; the best treatment of his life and sifting of the almost countless legends and yarns about him and his activities, is Joseph G. Rosa, *They Called Him Wild Bill*, 2nd ed. Norman, Univ. of Okla. Press, 1974.

Hicks, John (Tuckose Emathla), Seminole head chief (c. 1774-1833). John Hicks' Town was a Mikasuki settlement west of Payne's savannah in northern Florida in 1822 and its chief was Tuckose Emathla, or John Hicks. He was a large man, 6 feet, 2 inches in height, his proportions classical and "one can assume that he was descended from chiefs through the female line." Hicks signed the Camp Moultrie Treaty of September 18, 1832, which sought to limit the lands occupied by Florida Indians, but did not sign the Additional Article which specified reservations for certain principal chiefs, among them Neamathla, most prominent chief of the time in northern Florida. The next year when Neamathla, dissatisfied with the proposal to limit his people to a small reserve, allegedly sought to generate an uprising, Governor Duval abruptly removed him as head chief and installed Hicks in his place, presumably considering Hicks more amenable. The Office of Indian Affairs rejected Duval's request to name Hicks "governor of the red men in Florida," but said Hicks would be "distinguished by a great medal, and acknowledged as the chief of his people." Duval was cautioned against interfering in such internal Indian affairs as "the making and unmaking of chiefs." In 1824 Hicks turned down an invitation to visit Washington to talk with white leaders, but two years later, in May 1826 he and five other Seminoles visited Washington, D.C., with Abraham their interpreter. Hicks and the others expressed themselves as opposed to removal of the Seminoles to the west; they were unhappy on the reservations assigned to them; they wanted the white men to return their black slaves the whites had seized under one pretext or another; they wanted no more talk about book learning for their children. The whites had obtained the book, they said, by deceit and it had been denied to the red men in their view forever. Hicks signed the Payne's Landing Treaty May 9, 1832, which was to prepare the way for removal of the Seminoles across the Mississippi. He went with a delegation to the future Indian Territory in early 1833 to approve lands set aside for the Seminoles, Hicks representing the aged chief Sam Jones, considered too feeble to make the trip. Hicks signed the resulting Fort Gibson Treaty of March 28, 1833, in Jones's name. Hicks died, probably in Florida, in the late summer or early autumn of 1833. He was succeeded by Micanopy as head chief.

John K. Mahon, *The History of the Second Seminole War.* Gainesville, Univ. of Fla. Press, 1967; Edwin C. McReynolds, *The Seminoles.* Norman, Univ. of Okla. Press, 1967.

Higbee, John M., Mormon official (c. 1828-post Feb. 1894). Higbee was major of the Iron County, Utah, militia and as such had a key role in the Mountain Meadows Massacre of September 11, 1857. He was courier between the assassins and Isaac C. Haight, Mormon stake president at Cedar City, Utah, purportedly relaying instructions for the murders from William H. Dame, commander of militia. Higbee also was a leader among the 54 whites who assisted an indeterminate number of Indians in the butchery. It was reported that it was Higbee who touched off the slaughter by calling to the armed Mormons to "Do your duty!" as they guided the emigrants from their arms and the safety of their wagon corral, and the slaughter thereupon commenced. Some authorities are unclear on the point. At any rate, following the sordid affair, Higbee went into hiding, part of the time in Arizona. He was released from his church position July 31, 1859, indicted in 1874 but not brought to trial, and when he returned at length to Utah "it was the opinion of many Mormons that he should be absolved of all responsibility (for the crime) and restored to full fellowship in the church." He had returned to Utah permanently after the execution of John D. Lee. Higbee gave an account in 1894 of the massacre, signed it as by "Bull Valley Snort," but unquestionably it was made by Higbee, according to Brooks, who reproduces it.

Juanita Brooks, *Mountain Meadow Massacre.* Norman, Univ. of Okla. Press, 1966; William Wise, *Massacre at Mountain Meadows.* N.Y., Thomas Crowell Co., 1976; Bancroft, *Utah.*

Higgins, Christopher Power, pioneer (Mar. 1830-Oct. 14, 1889). B. in Ireland he received a business education in the United States and in 1848 joined the Dragoons with whom he served five years. He was a member of the Isaac Stevens expedition from St. Paul to Puget Sound in 1853 when a route for a railway was charted. Higgins visited Fort Benton, Montana, in 1855. In September 1858 he took part (perhaps as a packer) in George Wright's campaign against the Coeur d'Alene, Shoshone and associated tribes. In 1860 Higgins formed a partnership with Francis L. Worden; they packed merchandise into Montana, establishing a post at Hell Gate Ronde, about four miles below the present Missoula, Montana, which they founded. In 1862 the partners established a store at Gold Creek and in 1863 another at LaBarge City (Deer Lodge). In 1864 they moved their Hell Gate Ronde operation to the present site of Missoula, also erecting a grist mill and lumber mill, both of which prospered. The new site was known for a time as Wordensville, but at Worden's urging was changed to Missoula. In 1870 the partners opened a bank of which Higgins became president. He also was interested in horse raising and owned several ranches and mining properties. He married, fathered nine children and died at Missoula.

Bancroft, *Washington, Idaho & Montana,* 784; *Montana Contributions,* Vol. II (1896), 247.

Higgins, Francis Edmund (Frank), lumberjack evangelist (Aug. 19, 1865-Jan. 4, 1915). B. at Toronto, he eventually became a fulltime logging missionary for the Evangelistic Committee of the Presbyterian Church and later, for its Board of Home Missions, originating with work among Minnesota woodsmen. He spent much of his life supervising and promoting this field. In other states he established logging missionaries patterned upon those he had developed in Minnesota. Higgins grew up in the frontier environment of Shelburne, Ontario, felt the urge to preach and began as a Methodist minister in Minnesota in 1890 but two years later he was dropped by the denomination, and became a Presbyterian at Barnum, Minnesota. Once, while watching a log drive, a "pig" invited him to preach a sermon, and there his career was launched. "I went out as a lumberjack and did the things the men did," he once wrote. Of a powerful physique, he became a competent woodsman himself and "he gained their confidence by becoming one of them." Higgins still, however, was not ordained to the ministry, partly because he lacked the necessary education and, probably polish. Once he visited a dying logger who related how listening to Higgins had converted him, and urged Higgins to continue; this determined him upon his life's work. He became a North Woods legend even in his own time. Formally he became pastor of a Bemidji church in the heart of the logging country, a rough-and-tumble camp, where among its saloons and dives he did the work of a Christian minister. He took charge also of a Presbyterian congregation in the logging town of Farley, 10 miles from Bemidji. Finally he was ordained in 1902 by the Duluth Presbytery and resigned his formal charges that November for a "parish in the pines," as he called it, hiking with a pack on his back to the logging camps or, in winter, making his

visitations with dogteam, becoming more and more popular among the lumberjacks, some of whom walked miles to hear him. His services were simple and informal, not lacking in dignity, and Higgins, a man of vivid personality, spoke conversationally, trying to reform the morals and conduct of his listeners, while well aware of the almost insuperable obstacles they faced in living Christian lives amid the temptations all around them. His favorite subject was the Prodigal Son and, one logger remarked, he "preached the gospel of the Right Hook," though he was a compassionate man, with a genuine liking for the rough lumbermen. He used some of his own converts as missionaries eventually until he had five of them working in areas Higgins could not reach himself; his public speaking and his writings spread his fame to the nation and focused much interest on logging camp work. Higgins died at Shelburne, Ontario, his boyhood home, of cancer, survived by his wife and daughter.

Harold T. Hagg, "The Lumberjacks' Sky Pilot." *Minnesota Hist.,* Vol. 31, No. 2 (June 1950), 65-78.

Higgins, John Calhoun Pinckney (Pink), cattleman, gunman (1848-Dec. 18, 1914). B. in Georgia, his name was said to really have been O'Higgins, but his Irish immigrant father dropped the "O". The family took him to Austin, Texas, then to a ranch they established in 1857 in Lampasas County, Texas. Pink was a leader in the Ku Klux Klan for a time, owned a meat market and saloon until they burned, and engaged in skirmishes with hostile Indians, being twice wounded. As a cattleman he delivered several herds to Kansas railroad points, on at least one occasion combining his stock with a herd of the Horrell brothers. The Horrells became involved in a saloon shootout with Texas State Police March 19, 1873, at Lampasas. O'Neal said that of the four police killed in that engagement, one was Higgins' son-in-law, and this may have generated the feud between the families. In 1874 Higgins found Zeke Terrell, a Horrell rider with a Higgins' cow he had shot; Higgins killed Terrell, stuffed him into the body of the dead animal and told law officers where they could find a miracle taking place: a cow giving birth to a man. The next year Higgins killed Ike Lantier, purportedly a onetime Quantrill guerilla and former buffalo hunter, also an employee of the Horrells. January 22, 1877

Higgins shot down the unarmed Merritt Horrell in the Lampasas saloon on the grounds he suspected him of rustling, much later being acquitted of Horrell's murder. March 22 Higgins and some of his men sought to ambush Tom and Mart Horrell near Lampasas and wounded both but were driven off by the Horrells. June 14, 1877, the Horrells and Higgins factions fought a gunbattle at the town square of Lampasas. Frank Mitchell, Higgins' brother-in-law and an innocent bystander, was killed; Bill Wren, Higgins' lieutenant was badly wounded and the fight eventually was called off. In July 1877 Higgins and 14 of his followers engaged in a two-day siege of the Horrell ranch, but without important result. Texas Ranger John B. Jones in late July and early August persuaded the factions to sign a truce which held, if barely. About 1884 Higgins came into disagreement with a citizen of Ciudad Acuña, Mexico, over the sale of some horses, and killed him. About 1900 Higgins moved his ranch to 13 miles south of Spur, in Kent County, West Texas. Here he came into dispute with Bill Standifer and in an October 4, 1903, fight killed him. Higgins was reported in all to have killed from 14 to 18 men and once said there might have been more. He died of a heart attack at his ranch. Higgins was 6 feet, 2 inches, tall and weighed 190 pounds.

Jerry Sinise, *Pink Higgins, The Reluctant Gunfighter and Other Tales of the Panhandle.* Wichita Falls, Tex., Nortex Press, 1973; HT; O'Neal, *Gunfighters;* Bill O'Neal, "The Horrell Brothers of Lampasas." *Frontier Times,* Vol. 54, No. 3 (Apr.-May 1980), 6-7, 42-45.

High Head Jim: *see* Jim Boy

High Horn (Spemicalawba), Shawnee chief (c. 1775-Nov. 24, 1812). Known to the whites as Captain James Logan, he was captured in 1786 as a boy by James Logan of Kentucky and raised and educated by him, adopting Logan's name as his own; Logan sent him back to his tribe, by now a firm friend of the whites. His mother was Tecumseh's sister. High Horn attempted unsuccessfully to deter Tecumseh from hostilities against the whites. In the War of 1812 High Horn enlisted with the Americans, serving as scout and spy in the Ohio country. Charged with lacking good faith because he withdrew before a superior force, High Horn set out with two com-

panions down the Maumee River to prove his loyalty. The three encountered British Captain Matthew Elliott with five Indians, killed the officer and two Indians although High Horn was wounded mortally in the affair, dying two days later in the American camp. He was buried with honors (the town of Logansport, Indiana is named for him). High Horn was described as of fine physique, good features, intelligent, sincere and of good humor. His usual residence was at the Shawnee town of Wapakoneta, Ohio.

Hodge, HAI.

Hi Jolly: *see* Philip Tedro

Hill, Howard, archer, photographer (Nov. 13, 1900-Feb. 4, 1975). B. in Shelby County, Alabama, he was educated at Auburn University and came to wide attention as a superlative archer and competent wildlife photographer. Given his first bow at 6, he swiftly developed skill. He won 196 consecutive archery tournaments and for seven straight years was national archery flight champion. A man of great strength and coordination, he could pull a 175-pound bow back 26 inches. Because of his skill he was a stand-in for actor Errol Flynn in such motion pictures as "Robin Hood," where archery was a feature. Hill came to notice as a big game hunter with the bow, claiming to have killed every species of game on the North American continent as well as most species in Africa. He was believed the first white hunter to kill a fullgrown bull elephant with a bow and arrow, and took other types of dangerous game at will. He was featured in a number of film documentaries. In one of these, "The Last Wilderness," he was shown using his skills in Wyoming. Hill died at Birmingham, Alabama.

Howard Hill, *Hunting the Hard Way.* Chicago, Wilcox & Follett Co., 1953; *New York Times,* Feb. 6, 1975.

Hill, Joe, desperado: *see* Joe Olney

Hill, Robert Thomas, geologist (Aug. 11, 1858-July 28, 1941). B. at Nashville, Tennessee, he moved to Comanche, Texas, in 1874, becoming an amateur geologist and paleontologist. He studied later at Cornell University and worked for John Wesley Powell of the U.S. Geological Survey for a time, returning to Texas in 1887. He already had published a paper or two with responsible scientific organizations, and intensive field work in Texas and the Southwest spurred a steady stream of scientific reports and popular articles. He expanded his interests to include the West Indies and Central America. "The total of Hill's writing (much of it still unpublished) represents one of the most distinguished series of studies of North American geology ever struck off from the brain of one man." His popular writings included articles on history, Indian life and personal reminiscences. He died at Dallas, his body cremated, and his ashes spread over Round Mountain, near Comanche, the first geological feature that had caught his youthful eye.

HT; Oscar Williams.

Hill, Thomas, frontiersman (d. 1756). A white friend of the Delaware Indians, Hill was carrying a message to them from the governor of Pennsylvania when he was murdered by a war party of Iroquois on the trail between Minisink and Wyoming Valley, Pennsylvania. Since the Delawares frequently adopted the name of a deceased white friend, his name may have come into use at that time by an Indian family; at any rate there is a family of Hills in the tribe from about that time, descendants including the famous mountain man, Tom Hill, and his son of the same name, a Nez Perce interpreter and leader; Haines found no indication that the Delaware Hills had any white blood.

Francis Haines, "Tom Hill — Delaware Scout." *Calif. Hist. Soc. Quar.,* Vol. XXV, No. 2 (June 1946), 139.

Hill, Thomas, painter (Sept. 11, 1829-June 30, 1908). B. in Birmingham, England, he migrated to the U.S. as a child, studied art at the Pennsylvania Academy, and settled in California about 1870, becoming a foremost landscape artist specializing in Sierra Nevada scenes. His "Driving the Last Spike" is the "best-known picture of the ceremony of joining the rails" of the transcontinental railroad. It now hangs in the state capitol, Sacramento, California. Hill died at Raymond, California.

DAB; Robert Taft, "The Pictorial Record of the Old West." *Kan. Hist. Quar.,* Vol. XVIII, No. 2 (May 1950), 115.

Hill, Tom, mountain man (c. 1811-c. 1860). B. probably in the Sandusky, Ohio, settlement of the Delaware Indians, he may have been half Delaware, half white (although Haines finds no evidence Hill was part white), his father perhaps Isaac or John Hill, both of whom Haines considers full-blood Indians. The Delawares were forced to leave the Sandusky reserve for one in Kansas from where Tom Hill became a mountain man. In the spring of 1834 he, Kit Carson, Joe Meek and two other whites fought off a large band of Comanches between the Cimarron and Arkansas rivers. In 1837 Tom Hill was with Carson on the Yellowstone; when Manhead, leader of the Indian hunters was killed by Blackfeet, Carson named Hill to take his place. Two years later Hill joined Nez Perce who had come to the buffalo ranges to hunt. Hill married a Nez Perce woman from Kooskia, and from this union came a son, also named Tom Hill, who figured in later Nez Perce history. Tom the elder came to a position of influence among the Montana Nez Perce, according to Haines, "being credited with a following of 8 or 9 chiefs and 1,000 Indians, which included almost all of the Nez Perces in the Montana country at that time." Drury, writing of the Oregon country missionaries, found that Hill "was an agnostic and a bitter critic of the way the white men had treated the Indians in the East," of which he had personal experience. The missionary Henry Spalding of Lapwai mission of Idaho called Hill a "blasphemous and debased infidel," but Spalding was rigid in his moral beliefs and Hill doubtless made things as difficult as possible for Protestant missionaries, although he got on well with Catholics, according to Whitman. The missionary considered Hill a man of "considerable talent who exercised a strong influence against all whites — but most especially against us missionaries." That influence spread among the Cayuses as well as the Nez Perce. He told the tribesmen what had happened to Indian lands in eastern United States and warned of their coming fate if white men continued to arrive in Oregon. This was the simple truth, events bearing out his predictions. November 24, 1845, Hill visited Whitman for the first time at Waiilatpu Mission near the present Walla Walla, Washington. The two were impressed with each other, though not sharing common views. In explaining his opposition to mission work Hill said that "religion was too sacred a thing for fallible beings to practice," and since they could not uphold its tenets fully "it was better to have nothing to do with it." Hill said after talking with Whitman, inspecting his establishment and studying his works that "he had been deceived by false reports" about the missionary and now had a better opinion of him. Yet his negative impact upon the unconverted Indians had had much to do with stalling the missionary enterprise and ultimately perhaps bringing about the Whitman massacre, in which however Hill had no direct role. Hill was described at this time by one who had met him as "a finely formed man... nearly six feet tall," who spoke both English and Nez Perce well, and was "richly and gorgeously dressed... in full Indian costume. His hunting shirt was deerskin dyed red and cut full of holes and fringed. This was worn over a striped shirt. His pants were of the same material as his hunting shirt and fringed down the side... He wore moccasins decorated with porcupine quills, and his long hair hung about his shoulders." In 1846 with the Walla Walla chief Peu-peu-mox-mox, Hill led a mixed band of 40 Indians into California on a retaliatory raid to punish whites who had murdered the chief's son a year previously, but the Mexican War broke out and Tom joined Fremont's forces with which his old friend, Carson was serving, and distinguished himself by bravery in subsequent affairs. November 16, 1846, Hill was wounded in a skirmish at Natividad Rancho near Monterey, recovering quickly. He became a trusted despatch bearer and a member of Fremont's bodyguard. Tom Hill did not return to the northwest. Eventually he settled on the Delaware Reservation in Kansas where he was given land in compensation for his military service (he had enlisted, rather than serving solely as a scout). He died in Kansas around 1860. Tom's son, who told McWhorter he was half Delaware and half Nez Perce, was raised among the Nez Perce. In the campaign of 1877 he and his people who had been hunting buffalo joined the Joseph bands as they traversed Lolo Pass and came down into Montana. Hill accompanied them to the Bear Paw Mountains where he was the most prominent Nez Perce interpreter at the two conferences between Joseph and Miles. This Tom Hill indicated he was born about

1841 and was still living at 70 on July 17, 1911. It is possible he was the Tom Hill who died about 1923.

Francis Haines, "Tom Hill: Delaware Scout." *Calif. Hist. Soc. Quar.,* Vol. XXV, No. 2 (June 1946), 139-47; Francis Haines, *The Nez Perces.* Norman, Univ. of Okla. Press, 1955; Clifford M. Drury, *Marcus and Narcissa Whitman and the Opening of Old Oregon,* 2 vols. Glendale, Calif., Arthur H. Clark Co., 1973; Drury, *Diaries and Letters of Henry H. Spalding,* Glendale, 1958.

Himollemico (Hornotlimed), Mikasuki Seminole chief (d. Apr. 1818). During the First Seminole War of 1817-18 Himollemico dwelt at Fowl Town in northwestern Florida, but was forced to flee farther south. November 30, 1817, three ships reached the mouth of the Apalachicola River, but because of contrary winds were unable to ascend the stream. First Lieutenant Richard W. Scott (see entry) with a boat and 40 men was sent to their assistance. On the return the boat was ambushed by Himollemico and his warriors, all the whites being killed except six men who swam to safety. Twenty soldiers left to aid the vessels and as many sick and injured women and men also fell into Himollemico's hands and were slain and scalped. The hostiles then withdrew to the town of Mikasuki which later was stormed by American troops; most of the Indians escaped, but Himollemico was taken and with Chief Francis (see entry) was executed by Jackson's directive.

Hodge, HAI; Edwin C. McReynolds, *The Seminoles.* Norman, Univ. of Okla. Press, 1967.

Hinkle, Milton David, rodeo man (Oct. 15, 1881-Feb. 29, 1972). B. on the XIT ranch near Bovina, Texas, he was the son of George Hinkle, onetime sheriff of Ford County, Kansas. Milt won his first bronc riding contest in 1896 at Silver City, New Mexico, and may have mounted as many broncs as any man. He broke horses for the government during the Spanish-American and First World wars, and traveled with many of the top wild west shows of the period, including those of Buffalo Bill, Pawnee Bill and Charles Thompson. He was said to have been the first white cowboy to bulldog for exhibition, and twice won steer wrestling championships. He bulldogged for variety from autos, motorcycles, and was seriously injured in 1931 performing the feat from an airplane. Hinkle, while a member of the U.S. Border Patrol, was chosen a bodyguard for Theodore Roosevelt's expedition to the River of Doubt, Brazil. He traveled with numerous circuses and became a rodeo promoter. He died at Kissimmee, Florida, where he had made his home for many years.

Homer C. Walton, "Milt Hinkle: A Great Old Cowboy Has Finished His Circle." *True West,* Vol. 20, No. 1 (Sept.-Oct. 1972), 36ff.

Hinojos, Blas de, army officer (d. Feb. 28, 1835). Hinojos left Santa Fe, New Mexico, February 8, 1835, with a force of around 1,000 men, mostly citizen volunteers but including also Pueblo warriors, among them some from Jemez and their war captain, Salvador. Second in command was Juan Antonio Cabeza de Baca, wealthy rancher and alcalde of Peña Blanca. At Washington Pass in northwestern New Mexico the disorganized mob fell into a well-laid Navaho ambush. How many Mexican and Pueblo casualties there were was never reported, but Hinojos and Cabeza de Baca were killed and Salvador was forced to leap off a precipice to his death, so casualties must have been many. One report said that 35 Navahos were killed, a suspect estimate.

Frank McNitt, *Navajo Wars.* Albuquerque, Univ. of New Mex. Press, 1972; Josiah Gregg, *Commerce of the Prairies.* Norman, Univ. of Okla. Press, 1954.

Hite, Cass, frontiersman, prospector (c. 1858-1912). B. in Missouri, the year given for his birth is conjecture based upon his known activities. His father was a '49er, visiting California briefly. Cass left home at 16 and prospected in Montana and other promising areas, and was in Telluride, Colorado, in the mid-1870's. It was rumored that he killed a man there, killed another at Green River, Utah, for which he did two years in the penitentiary and was released, seriously ill. He was nursed to health by Hanksville, Utah, Mormons and in 1883 settled at what became known as Hite's Crossing of the Colorado, where he remained until 1898. He is said to have discovered the arches of Natural Bridges National Monument. Always panning for gold, with no sensational success, Hite moved downstream a dozen miles to Tickapoo Creek, a Colorado tributary from the west, where he died, the precise date being unknown.

Charles Kelly, "Lost Silver of Pish-la-ki." *Desert Mag.,* Vol. IV, No. 2 (Dec. 1940), 5-8; John V. Young, "Cass Hite's Dandy Crossing." *Westways,* Vol. 56, No. 10 (Oct. 1964), 43-45.

Hoback, John, mountain man (d. Jan. 1814). A Kentuckian, he became a trapper for the Missouri Fur Company in 1809, was guided with others to the Three Forks by Colter, trapped the upper Rockies with the Astorians and was killed by Indians with John Reed and his trappers. The Hoback River and Hoback Mountains in western Wyoming were named for him.

Harvey L. Carter article, MM, Vol. IX.

Hobart, Charles, army officer (Aug. 6, 1836-Aug. 21, 1926). B. at Hingham, Massachusetts, he crossed the Plains and January 16, 1862, was commissioned a second lieutenant of the 1st Oregon Cavalry. In July 1865 near the confluence of the forks of the Malheur River, Oregon a command under Hobart had a fight with about 70 Indians, taking some casualties. Hobart reported that "I think white men must have been among them, for they told us in good English to 'come on, you sons of bitches, we can whip you anywhere.' They had considerable soldiers' clothing among them and appeared to have plenty of arms and ammunition." He became a first lieutenant October 12, 1865, and was mustered out July 25, 1866. Hobart became a first lieutenant in the 8th U.S. Cavalry July 28, 1866, and was sent with his regiment to Arizona. On April 16, 1867, he was a company officer under Captain James Monroe Williams when the expedition struck an Apache rancheria in the Black Mountains east of Prescott, reporting 54 Apaches killed for the loss of one soldier killed, another wounded; there was no indication how many of the slain Indians were men. Hobart and other officers were commended by McDowell for their work. As regimental adjutant Hobart left Arizona for the District of Nevada with Colonel John Irvin Gregg, but following promotion to captain March 26, 1868, and graduation from the adjutant's assignment, he returned to Arizona. Hobart transferred to the 3rd Infantry December 29, 1873, became major of the 15th Infantry April 25, 1895, lieutenant colonel of the 8th Infantry August 8, 1898, and retired September 17 of that year. He died at Washington, D.C.

Heitman; W.M. Hilleary, *A Webfoot Volunteer,*

Oreg. State Univ. Press, 1965; *Arizona Miner,* Apr. 20, July 13, 1867; Constance Wynn Altshuler, *Chains of Command.* Tucson, Ariz. Hist. Soc., 1981.

Hodge, Frederick Webb, Indian man (Oct. 28, 1864-Sept. 28, 1956). B. at Plymouth, England, he was brought at 7 to the United States and was raised at Washington, D.C., and was attending the forerunner of George Washington University when he was offered the position as stenographer in the office of John Wesley Powell, then chief of both the U.S. Geological Survey and the Bureau of American Ethnology. When Cushing was organizing the Hemenway Southwestern Archaeological Expedition, Powell suggested Hodge as field secretary. Hodge worked for the next three years with Cushing and Bandelier at excavations in the Salt River Valley of Arizona and the Zuni valley of New Mexico. Hodge returned to Washington and in 1894 became editor for the BAE *Reports and Bulletins.* At the same time he was assigned to prepare an ethnological encyclopedia to be called the "North American Indian Synonymy" which eventually became the monumental, two-volume, 2,202-page *Handbook of American Indians North of Mexico* (1910). In 1895 Hodge visited every pueblo in New Mexico and Arizona in his studies. For 15 years after 1899 he served with distinction as editor of the *American Anthropologist* and of various volumes sponsored by the American Anthropological Association. In 1907 he commenced to edit Edward S. Curtis' *North American Indian,* which eventually ran to 20 volumes. In addition, Hodge had been executive officer of the Smithsonian Institution from 1901-1905, became ethnologist-in-charge of the BAE, holding that position until his resignation from Federal service in 1918 when he joined the Museum of the American Indian at New York City. From this position he continued his field studies in the Southwest while never letting up on his editorial tasks. At 67 in 1932 he became director of the Southwest Museum at Los Angeles and during 22 years of leadership brought that institution "to the unique prestige it enjoys today in the field of American Indian studies." His writings included about 435 items; he served on many scientific and public service organizations and was widely honored as "a patriarch of American Indian studies." He

wrote *History of Hawikuh, New Mexico, One of the So-called Cities of Cibola* (1937), and edited or was one of the editors of: *Spanish Explorers in the Southern United States* (1907); *The Memorial of Fray Alonso de Benavides, 1630* (1916); *Letters and Notes on the Texan Santa Fe Expedition 1841-1842* (1930); *The Indian Tribes of North America, with Biographical Sketches and Anecdotes of the Principal Chiefs,* by Thomas L. McKenney and James Hall (1933); *History of New Mexico by Gaspar Perez de Villagra* (1933), and *Fray Alonso de Benavides' Revised Memorial of 1634 with Numerous Supplementary Documents . . .* (1945). He died at Santa Fe, a month short of his 92nd birthday.

John Alexander Carroll, "Frederick Webb Hodge." *Arizona and the West,* Vol. 1, No. 3 (Autumn 1959), 202-05.

Hodges, George, frontiersman (fl. 1850-1852). Hodges apparently reached the Bitterroot Valley of western Montana with John Owen who founded the famed Fort Owen in 1850. A brief diary in possession of the Montana Historical Society records his travels and adventures for about six months and additional notes indicate he was active in the area for a year beyond that. He was a packer with general frontier experience, capable and occasionally he lost stock to the Indians, as did most of his contemporaries. Notes in the back of his diary attest to wide and intelligent interests, but nothing further is known of him.

George F. Weisel, *Men and Trade on the Northwest Frontier.* Missoula, Mont. State Univ. Press, 1955.

Hodges, Thomas J. (Tom Bell), outlaw (c. 1824-Oct. 4, 1856). From Rome, Tennessee, he became a physician and reached California during the gold rush after service in the Mexican War. He tried his profession, then mining, gambling, grand larceny for which he was imprisoned briefly, and finally outlawry. Escaping jail with him were Bill White, Jim Smith, Ned Connor, all aliases, and others. Hodges took the name of Tom Bell and with his gang commenced preying upon travelers in the Mother Lode country, although there is no record that he ever killed anyone. He soon arranged connections with various stations used by the California Stage Company, including the California House, 28 miles from

Marysville on the Camptonville Road. Near here Bell, with six companions, on August 12, 1856, attempted the first stagecoach robbery in California history. A woman passenger was killed, several citizens wounded. Two of the gang were killed in the affair, others, including Hodges were wounded and White, captured, confessed, implicating all. Hodges was seized along the upper Merced River and lynched forthwith.

William Banning, George Hugh Banning, *Six Horses*. N.Y., Century Co., 1930.

Hodges, Tom, frontiersman (c. 1826-c. 1870). B. in Alabama, he reached Arizona by early 1864 when he stated that he was a miner. He later operated "the first well-regulated saloon" in Prescott but had other specialties, McClintock describing him as "a noted gunman of that period" and "a quarrelsome individual" who also achieved fame as an Indian fighter and guide for military and volunteer organizations in their pursuit of hostiles. He was sergeant-at-arms for the Third Territorial Assembly of 1866 when a proposal to organize a band of rangers was discussed but not formally approved. Nonetheless on November 23, 1866, Prescott citizens requested Hodges to raise 30 men for 90 days and "a liberal sum was subscribed for the outfit, and also for Indian scalps." The rangers were quite successful. In late December they attacked a rancheria south of The Willows, a station on the Hardyville-Prescott road, killing 23 Indians with the loss of J. Hartman killed and several wounded. An Indian woman was allowed to escape but in general the Prescott *Miner* noted that "we are glad to know our Yavapai Rangers do not think it worth their trouble to make prisoners..." On subsequent expeditions, according to Conner, the Rangers under Hodges "made some pretty good 'killings'." Conner added that Hodges proved "an effective operator against the Apaches (sic)... and his men fought without money or price." Hodges was guide for Captain James Monroe Williams who in April 1867 led his 8th Cavalrymen in several attacks on hostiles northeast of Prescott in which 54 Indians were reported slain, Hodges said to have rendered "excellent service." In 1868 Hodges apparently was living in the vicinity of the later Phoenix when he was visited by Captain Samuel B.M. Young of the 8th Cavalry who

hired him as guide for operations against the Apache Mohaves east of Hardyville, Arizona. Hodges was said to be the only white man of the period to know that hostile country well. On April 21, 1869, at Wickenburg, Arizona, he killed J. Burton Sparks, a 35-year-old Kentuckian whom McClintock said also had served as scout and guide, and fled into Sonora. There he shortly died or was slain, wrote McClintock, the circumstances unreported.

Prescott, *Arizona Miner*, Nov. 30, 1866, Jan. 12, Apr. 20, July 13, Aug. 17, 1867; James H. McClintock, *Arizona*. Chicago, S.J. Clarke Pub. Co., 1916, I, pp. 192-93; Farish, III, IV; Daniel Ellis Conner, *Joseph Reddeford Walker and the Arizona Adventure*. Norman, Univ. of Okla. Press, 1956; U.S. Census for Ariz., 1864.

Hodgkiss, W.D., frontiersman (d. 1864). B. in New York State, he entered the fur trade in 1832 with Bonneville and as a sub-leader in 1833 he headed a trapping party up the Salmon River. Hodgkiss was still in the fur trade a decade later, for in 1843 from the Platte River he wrote to Andrew Drips about rivals in the business. Hodgkiss was employed at Fort Pierre, and in 1863 was in charge of Fort Union, where he died. He had married an Indian woman and fathered children; some decendants live still in South Dakota.

Montana, Contributions, Vol. X, 1940, p. 305; Dale L. Morgan, Eleanor Towles Harris, eds., *The Rocky Mountain Journals of William Marshall Anderson*. San Marino, Calif., Huntington Library, 1967.

Hodgson, Benjamin Hubert, army officer June 30, 1848-June 25, 1876). B. at Philadelphia he went to West Point and was commissioned a second lieutenant of the 7th Cavalry June 15, 1870, and performed scouting and frontier duty in Colorado and at Fort Leavenworth until March 1871 when he was assigned to southeastern posts until April 1873 when he went to Yankton, Dakota Territory. He was on David Stanley's Yellowstone Expedition of 1873 and Custer's Black Hills Expedition the following year. After a leave of absence he rejoined his regiment at Fort Abraham Lincoln, Dakota, in April 1876 and served on the Sioux expedition as adjutant (of Companies A, G, and M) to Reno. Hodgson was in the valley fight with Reno, and was killed at the river crossing. He was buried first on Reno Hill, the body exhumed in July 1877 and reinterred in Laurel Hill Cemetery, Philadelphia.

Cullum; BHB; Charles Kuhlman, *Legend into History*. Harrisburg, Pa., Stackpole Co., 1952.

Hoentubbee, Choctaw warrior (d. 1860). A prominent Choctaw warrior, he attended many councils Tecumseh had with the southern Indians in 1811 or 1812 and was a principal source for reconstruction of those visits of the great Shawnee appearing in Halbert and Ball, *The Creek War*. Hoentubbee died in Kemper County, Mississippi, and his son, Charley Hoentubbee related to the historians everything his father had told him about Tecumseh.

H.S. Halbert, T.H. Ball, *The Creek War of 1813 and 1814*. University of Ala. Press, 1969.

Hogue, Edward O., lawman (c. 1847-May 1877). B. in France, he became a policeman at Ellsworth, Kansas, in 1872, later city marshal, then a deputy sheriff, winning respect for bravery. When the police force was fired over the Whitney-Thompson affair, Hogue was given Ben Thompson's arms and alone was left to "make arrests." He may have served briefly later as city marshal, but was defeated in a race for sheriff in November 1873. In 1875 he was reported a deputy sheriff at Dodge City, Kansas. He died in Wyoming.

Nyle H. Miller, Joseph W. Snell, *Great Gunfighters of the Kansas Cowtowns, 1867-1886*. Lincoln, Univ. of Nebr. Press, 1967.

Holatah Emathla, Seminole chief (d. June 3, 1836). A brother of Charley Emathla, Holatah Emathla was chief of several hundred Seminoles, was never hostile to the whites, and usually acceded to white demands regarding his people. He signed the Camp Moultrie Treaty of September 18, 1823, limiting the Florida Indians to reservations. He signed the Payne's Landing Treaty of May 9, 1832, paving the way for removal of the Seminoles from Florida across the Mississippi, and he was a member of the delegation to the future Indian Territory to inspect lands to which the Seminoles would be transported, his name on the Fort Gibson Treaty of March 28, 1833, although later he and two others claimed they did not sign it, that someone else had done so in their names. Holatah Emathla however always favored emigration, and this brought him into jeopardy with Seminoles who opposed removal. Following the assassination of his brother, Charley, Holatah Emathla and others favoring emigration hastily took their people to Tampa Bay for white protection. They became the first important band of Seminoles to leave for Indian Territory. He with more than 400 of his people left for New Orleans in early April, reached Little Rock, Arkansas, in May and started their trek overland to their new homes, but Holatah Emathla died before reaching there. He was buried, according to an army officer of the escort "on a handsome eminence overlooking the stream, one and a half miles from the Canadian (River)... He was of pleasing manners, and good person, cool, crafty, and politic," but added that "he was wanting in decision, and could not be depended upon."

John K. Mahon, *History of the Second Seminole War*. Gainesville, Univ. of Fla. Press, 1967; Grant Foreman, *Indian Removal*. Norman, Univ. of Okla. Press, 1969.

Holbrook, Stewart H., writer (Aug. 22, 1893-Sept. 3, 1964). B. in Vermont, he went to Winnipeg at 18 to work for a newspaper, played semiprofessional baseball and was a traveling actor. He returned to New England in 1911 and became a logger. He enlisted in World War I, seeing service in France. Afterward he worked as a logger in British Columbia, commenced to write and from 1923 devoted full time to it. His first book, *Holy Old Mackinaw*, in 1938, was about logging. He specialized in books of the Pacific Northwest, railroads, and subjects related to forests and wilderness. He died at Portland, Oregon.

New York Times, Sept. 5, 1964

Hole-in-the-Day (Bagwunagijik), Chippewa chief (c. 1790-1846). The date of b. is conjecture. Hole-in-the-Day was a member of the warlike Noka, or Bear clan and was recognized as a chief by the government for bravery and fidelity to the Americans in the War of 1812. He succeeded Curly Head as war chief in 1825 and his subsequent life was devoted to fighting the powerful Sioux. It was Hole-in-the-Day who triumphantly ended the long struggle between Sioux and Chippewa over fishing and hunting grounds in the Lake Superior region. Only government action prevented Hole-in-the-Day from planting a village on the Minnesota River and driving the Sioux out onto the western plains. At a Prairie du Chien council he acknowledged that the Sioux for long had possessed the territory from the Mississippi to Green Bay and north to Superior, but said his people had won it by right of conquest. The Chippewa had an early advantage in the struggle for they initially had access to French firearms while the Sioux did not, "but in the later feuds which Hole-in-the-Day carried on the two peoples were equally armed." Hole-in-the-Day almost was converted to Christianity, promising to become a believer "after one more battle" with the Sioux, but didn't get around to it. When he died he was succeeded as chief by his son of his own name (b. c. 1825) who carried on the war with the Sioux. At the time of the Sioux uprising of 1862 the younger Hole-in-the-Day was accused of plotting a complementary revolt but he did not join the Sioux. Young Hole-in-the-Day visited Washington, D.C., several times, married a white woman reporter he met on one of his trips and became very wealthy, no doubt through agreements he had reached with the whites over Chippewa lands and in other ways. It was during his chieftainship that the Chippewa were gradually restricted to the White Earth Reservation, although Hole-in-the-Day resisted white pressure attempting to force him to relocate there. He was murdered by men of his own tribe at Crow Wing, Minnesota June 27, 1868.

Hodge, HAI.

Holladay, Ben, transportation figure (Oct. 14, 1819-July 8, 1887). B. in Nicholas County, Kentucky, he removed to western Missouri, operating a store and hotel at Weston, and trading with Kansas Indians. In the Mexican War he helped supply Kearny's Army, and afterwards purchased wagons, oxen and transportation equipment at surplus prices. In partnership with T.F. Warner he freighted goods to Salt Lake City, winning the friendship and support of Brigham Young. He drove cattle to California, selling them profitably, and eventually purchased the Central Overland California and Pike's Peak Express Company from Russell, Majors and Waddell; under Holladay "the overland stagecoach service . . . reached its greatest extent." He suffered sizeable losses, however,

in the Cheyenne uprising on the Plains in the mid-1860s, and Holladay sold his stagecoach empire to Wells, Fargo and Company in 1866, partly because he saw that the railroad would doom overland traffic by coach. He had begun steamship operations on the west coast and expanded them, his vessels serving an area from Alaska to Mexico, Holladay also becoming a major figure in Oregon railroad affairs, but eventually he lost out; by 1876 he was broken financially. He died at Portland, Oregon. With little schooling, Holladay became and retains his place as one of the greatest trasportation figures America has produced, and his impact on the frontier was immense and enduring. A major collection of his papers and correspondence was donated in 1959 by his son, Ben Campbell Holladay, to the Oregon Historical Society.

Ellis Lucia, *The Saga of Ben Holladay.* N.Y., Hastings House, 1959; *Los Angeles Times,* Nov. 26, 1959; DAB.

Holland, Tapley, adventurer (c. 1812-Mar. 6, 1836). A resident of Grimes County, Texas, Holland was at the Alamo. When, according to legend, Travis with his sword drew a line in the dust and asked those defenders who were willing to stay to the death to come across it, Tapley Holland was the first man to leap to the the side of Travis. Rufus Grimes vouched for the story, and said he had known Tapley Holland well. Holland died at the Alamo.

Amelia Williams, XXXVII, 265.

Holland, William Jacob, entomologist, paleontologist (Aug. 16, 1848-Dec. 13, 1932). b. of Moravian missionary parents at Bethany, Jamaica, he reached Bethlehem, Pensylvannia, in 1863 and was graduated from the Moravian Seminary, 1867; Amherst College, 1869; and Princeton Theological Seminary, 1874, being ordained in both the Moravian and Presbyterian denominations. After pastoring several churches, in 1891 he became chancellor of Western University at Pittsburgh continuing his natural history investigations. A close friend of Andrew Carnegie, he inspired creation of the Carnegie Museum at Pittsburgh and became its director from 1898 until 1922, when he became director emeritus. His many writings included the encyclopaedic and still definitive, *The Butterfly Book* (1898) and *The Moth Book* (1903), but his paleontological interests also were strong, and he conducted field work and studies in Utah and elsewhere. Holland participated in the discovery and was first to scientifically describe *diplodocus carnegiei*, the largest dinosaur until then uncovered, being longer than the famed brontosaurus, although not so heavy. He was principal organizer of the American Association of Museums and its first president; he traveled widely. Holland died at Pittsburgh.

Family recollections; DAB.

Holliday, John Henry (Doc), dentist, gunman (Aug. 14, 1851-Nov. 8, 1887). B. at Griffin, Georgia, his family moved during the Civil War to Valdosta, Georgia, where he reportedly became closely attached to a cousin, Martha Ann (Mattie), who eventually became Sister Mary Melanie after entering St. Vincent's Convent at Savannah, October 1, 1883, a Sister of Mercy. Holliday, who may have contracted tuberculosis from his mother who died of that ailment, took part in a plot to blow up the courthouse at Valdosta, and may consequently have fled to a dental school at Baltimore, although none of the three such schools then extant had a record of his attendance. Upon his return he reportedly took part in a bloodless shooting incident in 1872 near Valdosta, practiced dentistry briefly at Atlanta, then moved to Dallas, where he developed his taste for whiskey and gambling, and reportedly shot an irate patient. At Jacksboro, Texas, Holliday was said to have shot three soldiers, one mortally, and left Fort Griffin for shooting someone else. He hastened to Denver, which he reached in 1876, being known there as Tom McKee. He became involved in a knife fight and went to Cheyenne and Deadwood, returning to Fort Griffin in 1878, where he became associated with Wyatt Earp, if the two had not met in Kansas earlier, and with Kate Elder. Holliday, it is said, had shot still another man, and Kate helped him escape from jail; he later married her. The two returned to Dodge City, where Doc practiced dentistry until he migrated to Las Vegas, New Mexico, in late 1878 or 1879. He shot and wounded one, Charlie White, and killed Mike Gordon, but, being a friend of Hoodoo Brown who dispensed "justice" in Las Vegas, he was not troubled for his actions. Holliday took part in the bloodless railroad "war" in Colorado: He was suspected of robbing the Santa Fe-Las Vegas stage August 18, 1879, and again on August 30, along with a

train robbery October 14, and possibly another later. He is said to have accompanied Wyatt Earp to Tombstone, for by early 1880 he was in that community, working at three of his four "professions," dentistry, gambling and pandering, and reportedly at the fourth, stage robbery. He was strongly suspected of instigating the March 15, 1881, stage robbery in which Bud Philpot and Peter Roerig were killed. On a signed statement by Kate Holliday, he was arrested and Behan's investigation led to a charge of murder against him, but Kate was persuaded to abandon Tombstone and Doc was released, though still under bond, at the time of the October 26, 1881, OK Corral fight. Holliday was suspected in some quarters of having something more than a casual interest in the killling of Jim Crane, Old Man Clanton and others who purportedly perished at the hand of "Mexicans," Crane supposedly possessing information about the March stage robbery. Before the Tombstone gunfight Holliday, probably believing Ike Clanton possessed information against him, sought to goad Clanton into a fight so he could kill him, but Ike would have none of it. Holliday, armed with a shotgun and a pistol (whose holster was shot away), took a prominent part in the "battle," in which the two McLaurys and Billy Clanton were killed and Ike Clanton wounded, as were Virgil and Morgan Earp; Holliday had no official police position. Holliday and Wyatt Earp were arrested by Behan, but released December 1, on Judge Spicer's finding "no sufficient cause" against him. Behan saved Doc's life that month when he was threatened by saloonman Milt Joyce, and Holliday refused to fight Ringo, who wanted to kill him. Jailed again February 11, 1882, for the murder of Billy Clanton, Doc once more was released, as was Wyatt Earp. Holliday helped the Earps murder Frank Stilwell at Tucson March 18, and Indian Charley (Florentino Cruz) two days later. He accompanied the Earps and others to Colorado, being casually suspected of a killing or two along the way, going to Pueblo and Denver, where he was jailed. Colorado, on May 29, 1882, refused to extradite him to Arizona on the murder charge. The Denver *Republican,* May 22, 1882, published a lengthy interview with Doc, giving his side of recent events. Said to have been baptized a Roman Catholic, Doc died of tuberculosis at Glenwood Springs, Colorado, where an ornate tombstone marks his grave. Holliday was about 5 feet, 10 inches, or less in height, weighed about 150 pounds, was blond and had pale blue eyes. His hair grayed before his death.

Ed Bartholomew, *Wyatt Earp: The Untold Story, Wyatt Earp: the Man & the Myth*, Toyahvale, Tex., Frontier Book Co., 1963, 1964; G.G. Boyer, *Illustrated Life of Doc Holliday*. Glenwood Springs, Colo., Reminder Pub. Co., 1966; Albert S. Pendleton Jr., Susan McKey Thomas, "Doc Holliday's Georgia Background." *Jour. of Ariz. Hist.*, Vol. XIV, No. 3 (Autumn 1973), 185-204.

Hollister, Cassius M. (Cash), lawman (Dec. 7, 1845-Oct. 18, 1884). B. near Cleveland, Ohio, he went to Kansas in 1877, visiting Wichita and Caldwell where he was a hotel clerk, being elected mayor October 28, 1879. He was embroiled in several weaponless fights, was superceded April 6, 1880, as mayor, and appointed deputy U.S. marshal early in 1883. On April 8, 1883, with Henry Brown and others he had a gunfight south of Hunnewell, Kansas, with rustlers in which one rustler was killed, another dangerously wounded. Once he journeyed to Indian Territory to investigate a murder and brought back suspects. November 21, 1883, he and Ben Wheeler killed Chet Van Meter who had resisted arrest. Hollister resigned as deputy marshal September 9, 1884, but continued as deputy sheriff of Sumner County. He was killed by Robert Cross, a Texas desperado, in an attempted arrest. Cross later was taken.

Nyle H. Miller, Joseph W. Snell, *Great Gunfighters of the Kansas Cowtowns 1867-1886.* Lincoln, Univ. of Nebr. Press, 1967; Wayne T. Walker, "Cash Hollister — Border Lawman." *Real West*, Vol. 25, No. 183 (Mar. 1982). 14-17.

Hollister, William Welles, sheepman, pioneer (Jan. 12, 1818-Aug. 8, 1886). B. near Hanover, Licking County, Ohio, Hollister in 1852 joined a wagon train called the Buckeye Boys' Caravan and headed for California. Reaching Hangtown (Placerville), the outfit was sold, and Hollister went on to San Francisco. Unable to book passage by ship homeward immediately, he went to San Jose, where he observed large herds of sheep, grazing apparently on clover burrs, which he examined and found "full of nutritious seed." He decided to "go back to Ohio...and drive a band of graded Merino sheep back to

California to raise choice breeds, better animals than the scrubby Mexican variety." He interested a brother and sister, collected 6,000 Merino sheep, 50 herdsmen, 15 wagons, and started for California again March 9, 1853. The drive went out over the central route, passed Salt Lake City, had a fight with Paiutes on the Virgin River and reached Cajon Pass, California, with barely 1,000 sheep remaining. About 1,000 lambs were born before the flock reached Monterey County, California, 15 months after leaving Ohio. Hollister established a ranch in Tecolotito Canyon, east of Santa Barbara, where he and others acquired a 35,000 acre Mexican land grant called San Justo and his sheep ranching thrived. When a community arose there developed also a dispute over what to name it, some holding out for San Justo until one objector blurted: "Theys too damned many towns (here) named after saints. I move we name our town after a sinner — let's call it Hollister," and Hollister it was called and remains. William Welles Hollister died at Santa Barbara, California.

Graham Hollister, "Colonel Hollister's Westward Trek." Potomac Corral of Westerners, *Corral Dust*, Vol. VI, No. 3 (June 1961), 20-21, 24; Walter A. Tompkins, "The Upstart from Ohio." *Kenyon Alumni Bulletin,*Gambier, Ohio, Vol. XVIII, No. 4 (Oct.-Dec. 1960).

Hollow-horn Bear, Brulé Sioux chief (Mar. 1850-March 15, 1913). B. in Sheridan County, Nebraska, at 16 he accompanied his father, Iron Shell in an operation against the Pawnees, the battle at the site of the present Genoa, Nebraska. He was too young to have taken part in the Fetterman action of 1866 in Wyoming but two years later participated with other Brulé in operations against troops, once in Wyoming and again near the present Crow Agency, Montana. In 1869 he participated in actions against workman constructing the Union Pacific railroad. Hollow-horn Bear became a captain of police at the Rosebud Agency, South Dakota; as such he arrested his predecessor, Crow Dog for the August 5, 1881, murder of Spotted Tail. Five years later Hollow-horn Bear resigned. In 1889 Crook conferred with the Rosebud Sioux on attempts by the government to break up the large reservations; Hollow-horn Bear, a noted orator, represented the Sioux but Crook succeeded in his mission largely by playing upon disaffections among the Indians and rifts between their leaders. Hollow-horn Bear continued to uphold the rights of the Sioux, sometimes with success. March 4, 1905, he was one of the native Americans to ride in President Theodore Roosevelt's inaugural parade and in 1922, almost a decade after his death, his portrait was used on a 14-cent stamp. Hollow-horn Bear died of pneumonia and was buried at Washington, D.C.

Hodge, HAI; George E. Hyde, *Spotted Tail's Folk.* Norman Univ. of Okla. Press, 1961; Dockstader.

Holmdahl, Emil L., soldier of fortune (1883-Apr. 8, 1963). B. at Fort Dodge, Iowa, he ran away at 15, joined the 61st Iowa Infantry and served in the Philippines. He transferred to the 20th U.S. Infantry and when his enlistment expired, joined a soldier of fortune group during the Boxer Rebellion in China. He served under Lee Christmas in Honduras, and under Emilio Kosterlitzky in the Mexican rurales. He soldiered under Madero, then Carranza, Villa and Obregon. Accused of violating the neutrality laws of this country, he was sentenced to 18 months, but before he entered the penitentiary the Pershing expeditions was organized and Holmdahl, useful as a scout and guide, was pardoned. He served in France in the 16th Engineers in World War I, rising to Captain. After the war he prospected in Mexico. Villa's grave was desecrated February 5, 1926. Holmdahl was in the vicinity but denied having committed the deed although suspicion pointed to him. He entered the oil business subsequently. Holmdahl died at Van Nuys, California.

Los Angeles Times, Feb. 19, 26, 1967.

Holmes, William H., prospector, lawman (c. 1833-Nov. 2, 1889). If the W.B. Holmes listed in the 1864 census as living at Tuscon is the Hunkydory Holmes of later fame, he was b. in New York but must early have moved to Texas for Hayes (who gives his middle initial as A.) asserts that he reached Arizona as "a native of Texas." The census states that he had come to Arizona in 1863. He must have been familiar with some of the wild spots of the Territory by 1872, for in that year according to Spring he was a guide for Thomas Miner in one phase of the noted Miner gold searching expedition. Hayes said he came to Arizona as a hawker of Methodist tracts "but gave up the

Christian work for the more adventurous life of a prospector," being in Globe at the start of its boom about 1876. He staked out a rich silver claim "which netted him a small fortune," but spent it defending himself after he had killed Banjeck Marco, another prospector who allegedly attempted to jump his claim. After his acquittal he tried politics, did odd jobs, wrote poetry and entertained in saloons. His best known poem was "Hunkydory," from which derived his nickname (Hayes prints its text). Holmes had a record of a heart condition when Glenn Reynolds, the sheriff deputized Holmes to assist him in moving the Apache Kid and several other prisoners from Globe to the railroad at Casa Grande enroute to the Territorial Prison. Near the present Kelvin, Arizona, four of the prisoners (although not the Apache Kid) overpowered Reynolds and Holmes; Reynolds was shot dead and Holmes died, presumably of a heart attack since his body bore no wound. Holmes' lever-action Winchester and pistol were taken off by his assailants.

Jess G. Hayes, *Apache Vengeance.* Albuquerque, Univ. of New Mex. Press, 1954; *John Spring's Arizona,* ed. by A.M. Gustafson. Tucson, Univ. of Ariz. Press, 1966; Dan L. Thrapp, *Al Sieber, Chief of Scouts.* Norman, Univ. of Okla. Press, 1964.

Holston (Holstein), Stephen, frontiersman (fl. 1748-1777). By 1748 Holston, who "was of an adventurous turn," while on a hunt had discovered the Holston River which flows from southwestern Virginia into eastern Tennessee to join the Little Tennessee River near today's Knoxville. It carved a route for early settlement extending into Tennessee and was famed in border annals. Sometime after 1748 Holston settled on the Little Saluda, South Carolina, but after Cherokees severely frightened his wife during his absence, he moved his family back to the Holston River in present Botetourt County, Virginia. Building canoes, he and others explored their way down the Holston to the Tennessee, down it to the Ohio, thence to the Mississippi and down it to Natchez when he returned to Holston upon which he had made the earliest settlement. This was located at the head spring of the Middle Fork, but he quitted the place sometime before 1774 for Culpeper County. He returned to the Holston River country later, however, served in the battle of Point Pleasant in Lord Dunmore's War in 1774, and was reported still in the militia in 1776 or 1777. "As we hear no more of him, he probably did not long survive this period," according to Draper.

Alexander Scott Withers, *Chronicles of Border Warfare,* ed. by Reuben Gold Thwaites. Parsons, W. Va., McClain Printing Co., 1970, information included from Lyman C. Draper, 59n.

Holt, Jack (Charles John Holt), actor (May 11, 1888-Jan. 18, 1951). B. at Winchester, Virginia, the son of an Episcopal priest, he was said to be a descendant of John Holt, Lord Chief Justice of England, and John Marshall, Chief Justice of the United States. He studied engineering at the Virginia Military Institute and went to Alaska with an exploration and mining company, becoming a prospector and packer. He returned to Oregon, worked briefly on a ranch, then entered motion pictures at San Francisco about 1913, becoming in time a major western star. He appeared in one of the finest silent westerns, Emerson Hough's "North of 36," a picture of a cattle drive to Kansas in which genuine longhorns were used and stampedes filmed. Holt broke a leg early in the process, and most riding sequences in which he figured were shot from the other side of his horse, in order not to reveal his cast. Holt appeared in a great variety of adventure pictures. During World War II he was commissioned a captain in the Quartermaster Corps, being stationed at the El Reno, Oklahoma, Remount depot readying mules and other animals for far-flung battle theatres. He received his discharge in 1944 as a major. His final film was "Across the Wide Missouri," a picture of the early mountain men. He died at Los Angeles, California.

Los Angeles Times, Jan. 19, 1951; personal acquaintanceship with author.

Hooker, Henry Clay, cattleman (Jan. 10, 1828-Dec. 5, 1907). B. at Hinsdale, New Hampshire, he is said to have served in the Union Army during the Civil War, whence came his title of "colonel," but if so this is unconfirmed by Heitman or Powell. Hooker went west in 1865, lost his business in an 1869 San Francisco fire, but secured a contract to supply army posts and Indian agencies in Arizona with beef and removed to that territory, operating out of Tucson. In 1872 he established the famous Sierra Bonita Ranch at a cienega between Willcox and old Fort Grant. It became one of the best known ranches in the west, visited by such celebrities as Crook, Miles, Owen Wister, Whitlaw Reid, Augustus Thomas, Wyatt Earp and many others. Hooker bred fine trotters, believed guests should "dress" for dinner, and after his 1877 marriage the ranch became the scene of social gatherings. At the height of his operations Hooker had some 20,000 cattle ranging 250,000 acres, and the "Crooked H" brand he established is used to this day, believed the oldest continuously-used brand in Arizona, as the ranch house is among the oldest in the state. Hooker died at Los Angeles, where he was buried. A major pioneer figure, he was controversial in some respects, but generally was respected.

Roscoe G. Willson, *Pioneer Cattlemen of Arizona,* Vol. I. Phoenix, Valley Nat. Bank, 1951; Lee E, Echols, "I Shall Be a Borrower of Money." *True West,* Vol. 26, No. 4 (Mar.-Apr 1979), 12-15, 43-48; Gertrude Hill, "Henry Clay Hooker: King of the Sierra Bonita." *Arizoniana,* Vol. II, No. 4 (Winter 1961), 12-15; Earle R. Forrest, "The Fabulous Sierra Bonita," *Jour. of Ariz. Hist.,* Vol. 6, No. 3 (Autumn 1965), 132-46.

Hooker Jim (Hooka, Ha-kar-jim), Modoc war leader (c. 1825-1879). The leader of one band of Modoc Indians, he was in the forefront of hostility during the Modoc War of 1872-73 in northeastern California, caused when whites tried to force the Modocs to move to the Klamath Reserve, Oregon. His early career is obscure although like other Modoc warriors he no doubt took part in sporadic hostility against emigrant wagon trains during and following the California gold rush. He was prominent in events leading to the Modoc War, leading the foray which resulted in the slaying of about 14 settlers following the Lost River Battle of November 29, 1872, which opened the conflict. For this he later was indicted in Oregon, although never tried. Hooker Jim with Captain Jack and the rest of the militant Modocs faded into the Lava Beds south of Tule Lake to begin their long resistance against white troops. He took part in the first Battle of the Stronghold in which nine soldiers were killed and a great many more might have been, had Hooker Jim been in command of the Indian side. Jim and

Curley Headed Doctor, increasingly militant and at odds with Captain Jack, came to head up their own faction, and this proved fatal to the Indian cause. Hooker Jim was a member of the assassination party that murdered Canby, Thomas and badly wounded Meacham April 11, 1873, taking no part in those killings but trying to shoot L.S. Dyar, Klamath Indian agent and in other ways encouraging the slaughter. He had a role in the second Battle of the Stronghold April 26 when four officers and 18 enlisted men were killed and about 18 others wounded. But the Indians were forced to retreat southward of the best defensive positions. Hooker Jim and his faction came to cross-purposes with Captain Jack in May and split off, leading to disintegration of the fighting force. With others of his faction, Jim surrendered about May 22. From that time forward, to save his life, he worked with the army to bring in those hostiles still out, including Captain Jack. He became one of the the "Modoc bloodhounds," who ferreted out the erstwhile hostiles, and was a prime government witness at the court martial of Captain Jack and five other alleged ringleaders, leading to death verdicts for all and the execution of four. Hooker Jim and his band were among the 153 Modocs sent to Indian Territory, where he died at the Quapaw Agency six years later.

Keith A. Murray, *The Modocs and Their War.* Norman, Univ. of Okla. Press, 1965; Jeff C. Riddle, *Indian History of the Modoc War.* Medford, Oreg., Pine Cone Pubrs., 1973; Bancroft, *Oregon,* II, 555-636, *California Inter Pocula,* 446-560; Dockstader.

Hoover, Jake, hunter-prospector (c. 1850-Apr. 14, 1925). A Montana frontiersman who befriended Charlie Russell in 1880, Hoover had come to Fort Benton at 16 on the steamboat, *St. John,* and made for the gold diggings at Last Chance Gulch (Helena). He discovered Tenderfoot Bar, a rich placer, though he profited little. Turned cowboy, he became foreman of the O.H. Churchill outfit along the Sun River, at various times afterward was a trapper, meat hunter, roamer, and associate of every type of frontier character, throughout Montana country. He discovered "more rich mines than any other prospector—without reaping a rich reward." He started a stampede on the Yogo in 1871, when the first sapphires in the region

accidently were discovered. When Russell came to Montana as a youth, Hoover took him in and housed him for two years, giving him the basic knowledge of frontier life that often was reflected in Russell's art. Hoover remained in Montana until the 1920s, but died at Seattle.

Mont. Hist. Soc. archives; Harold McCracken, *The Charles M. Russell Book.* Garden City, N.Y., Doubleday & Co., 1957.

Hopkins, Charles, Mormon pioneer (fl. 1857-1876). Hopkins was a president of Cedar City, Utah, and holding a responsible public position at the time of the Mountain Meadows Massacre, September 11, 1857. *Mormonism Unveiled* places him at the scene, either participating in or consenting to the tragedy. In October he visited Salt Lake City, conferring with Brigham Young about the affair, in company with Philip Klingonsmith and John D. Lee. He was dead by the time of the September 1876 trial of Lee.

Juanita Brooks, *John D. Lee.* Glendale, Calif., Arthur H. Clark Co., 1962; Brooks, *Mountain Meadows Massacre.* Norman, Univ. of Okla. Press, 1966; *Mormonism Unveiled,* 379.

Hopocan (Captain Pipe, Konieschguanokee), Delaware chief (c. 1725-1794). An hereditary sachem of the Wolf clan of the Delawares, he was tribal war chief with a reputation for wisdom and oratory. In the French and Indian War of 1756-63 he fought against the British with courage and skill and in 1763 or 1764 tried to seize Fort Pitt by strategem, but was foiled and himself captured. After the peace he settled with his people on the upper Muskingum River, Ohio, until the Revolutionary War when he sided generally with the British against the Americans (though not consistently) while informing the British commander at Detroit that he would commit no barbarities during the conflict, having little interest in it save to win subsistence for his people. In May 1782 however, Colonel William Crawford fell into his hands after the rout of his regiment of volunteers near the upper Sandusky and Crawford was put to the torture and burned at the stake in a celebrated horror incident of the 18th century frontier. After the Revolution Hopocan was signatory to the January 21, 1785, Fort McIntosh Treaty and one at Fort Harmar, Ohio January 9, 1787 (never ratified by Congress). In 1780 he moved to what became known as Captain Pipe's village about ten miles southeast of Upper Sandusky, Ohio.

Hodge, HAI.

Horn, Thomas, scout, assassin (Nov. 21, 1860-Nov. 20, 1903). B. near Memphis, Scotland County, Missouri, he became an ardent hunter and fine shot in his youth. At 14 he ran away to Santa Fe, where he said he worked as a stage driver, learned to speak Spanish and about 1876 reached Prescott where he met Al Sieber. His career for the next few years is virtually unknown, and his autobiography sheds scant light since it is largely fictitious, and rarely dependable. The trouble with most biographies of this interesting character is that their research concentrates on his later career and accepts with little question his own account of his years in Arizona; no dependable biography covering his early years exists. Horn was fluent in Spanish but he apparently spoke little if any Apache although he claims to have been adept in that language as well. According to Sieber, Horn became an Army packer in 1882 (Barnes said a "scrub packer," meaning without other responsibility), and no doubt was at the significant Tupper-Rafferty Enmedio fight in northern Sonora in April 1882; his version of it is surprisingly dependable. Horn was among the 76 packers who accompanied Crook on his great 1883 Sierra Madre expedition, but was less prominent than most of the others, being unmentioned by any of the diarists or in any official account of that adventure. Nevertheless, Horn was a diligent and at that time honest, hard-working packer as he must have been to serve Crook. He had no recorded role in the Crook-hostile negotiations in the Sierra (although his "autobiography" makes him the star) and came back from Sonora as little known as when he went south. Sieber wrote (unless someone else added to his letter) that he gradually placed Horn in charge of Apache scouts during Al's absence, and came to depend upon him for such assistance. Thus in late 1885 when Sieber was recalled to San Carlos, Horn was named by Crawford (not by Sieber) chief of scouts for a pursuit of Geronimo into the Sierra Madre. On January 11 occurred the conflict between U.S.-led scouts and Mexican irregulars in which Crawford was wounded mortally and Horn wounded in the left arm; an example of the manner in which Horn embroiders the truth may be seen by comparing his official description of the incident (HED 1, 49th Cong., 2nd Sess., Ser. 2460) with what he wrote for his autobiography, pp. 218-29, some 16 years later. Tom is equally fictional in narrating his part in the surrender of Geronimo. Gatewood, in his recital of the surrender of that Apache says that in leaving Fronteras to meet with the hostile he took an escort of six or eight enlisted men "and Tom Horn and Jose Maria as additional interpreters," and that is all he says of Horn, indicating he was there solely as a Spanish-English interpreter. This is not in any way to deprecate the very real courage Horn displayed by going with Gatewood and his few companions into the camp of the enemy, but he was not the pivotal character of the meeting and by the record had no more to do with Geronimo's surrender than to interpret from Spanish to English and back again when occasion required. Horn was discharged with the surrender of Geronimo, since white chiefs of scouts were no longer in great demand. He mined for a time near Aravaipa, Arizona. His role in the Pleasant Valley War is as obscure as he has made his role in the Indian campaign. He said he was sent into the feuding district by Sheriff Buckey O'Neill of Yavapai County, Arizona, as a mediator and that he also served as deputy for sheriffs Commodore Perry Owens of Apache County and Glenn Reynolds of Gila County. But O'Neill was not sheriff at the time, there is no confirmation of Horn's use by Owens and Reynolds; he may not have been a deputy for any of them. Horn possibly killed Mart (Old Man) Blevins whose slayer has been a mystery. Horn told Joe LeFors that he killed his first man when he was 26, adding "he was a coarse S.O.B." Horn became involved in the feud on the Tewksbury side in the spring of 1887; he was then 26, to become 27 on November 21. Blevins, killed in July 1887 is the only victim of the feud at that early date whose killer both is unknown and who might reasonably fill Horn's description. Horn was a superlative roper; he won a steer-roping contest at Globe, Arizona on July 4, 1888, and beat out the redoubtable Charley Meadows in a Phoenix contest in November 1890 or 1891 with the record time of 49.5 seconds, excellent for the conditions, the stock and the timing devices then in use. In 1890 he joined the Pinkerton Detective Agency at Denver, and four years later became a stock detective for the Swan Land and Cattle Company of Wyoming. About this time he seems to have developed his interest in murder-for-pay, although he may have engaged in that pursuit as far back as the Pleasant Valley War days. He admitted to LeFors that for $600 apiece he had shot William Lewis in August and Fred Powell in September of 1895, both small ranchers in the Laramie Mountains area. He dropped down to Arizona then to avoid the heat, running a cow ranch for E.A. Jones of Aravaipa. On November 7, 1896, he wrote U.S. Marshal William K. Meade at Tucson offering to shoot up the William (Black Jack) Christian band then harassing the Territory "if there is anything in it for me." He wrote that "I can stand a better show to get them by going alone and will go and get some of them at least and drive the rest out of the country... *No cure no pay* is my mottoe. So if I don't get them it costs no one a cent." This surely is not the offer of an amateur assassin. However, Black Jack Christian was killed April 28, 1897, while Robert Christian disappeared under mysterious circumstances from Fronteras, Sonora, December 9, 1897, and was never certainly seen again. During the Spanish American War Horn hired on at Tampa, Florida April 23, 1898, as a packer and August 1 was promoted to chief packer at $133 a month; he was discharged September 6, 1898. He was hired for his special type of work to stop rustling in Brown's Hole, northwestern Colorado in 1900. Horn, or James Hicks as he then called himself on July 8, 1900, killed Madison M. Rash at his Cold Spring Mountain ranch; on October 3, 1900, he killed Isom Dart, a black rancher at his Summit Spring cabin. Horn later boasted in a letter to Joe LeFors that "I stopped cow stealing (by the Brown's Hole 'gang') in one summer," apparently by the two killings and frightening other men out of the area. Horn lost one fight, to knife-wielding Newt Kelly in a Baggs, Wyoming saloon, receiving a severe side wound. He again became a stock detective in Wyoming. On July 19, 1901 a 13-year old boy, William Nickell was killed from ambush in the Iron Mountain region, apparently having been mistaken in dim light for his father. A week or so later his father, Kels P. Nickell was shot in the arm and hip by another ambush fusillade. Deputy U.S. Marshal LeFors — and others — suspected Horn was guilty of both shootings. In a famous interview with Horn, purportedly to interest him in taking a rustler cleanup job in Montana (which Horn was eager to accept), LeFors got Horn to admit the Nickell shootings, the conversation taken down by a concealed court reporter. Horn later complained that he was drunk at the time, a defense belied by his subsequent letters attempting to explain what he had really said and how his words were "twisted" by those determined to prove his guilt. His conviction was affirmed by the State Supreme Court, and he was hanged. His execution for the William Nickell shooting is still controversial in some quarters but the fairness of the verdict and sentence in view of Horn's career can hardly be disputed. Horn was six feet, two inches in height, deep-chested, erect and of considerable strength. He was described in his early manhood by an army officer who knew him well as very light complexioned with sandy hair and blue eyes. Much of the controversy around Horn is based upon statements in his book and its authorship. Dobie noted that Coble conceded to having "edited" it, and found a copy at Denver in which was penciled a statement by Hattie Horner Louthan that she had ghost-written the book. Someone else wrote that "whether Horn was guilty or not, a good case could be made for hanging anyone who wrote that book!"

Literature abundant: Tom Horn, *Life of Tom Horn Written by Himself: A Vindication.* Denver, Louthan Book Co., 1904; Dan L. Thrapp, *Dateline Fort Bowie.* Norman, Univ of Okla. Press, 1979; Charles B. Gatewood, "The Surrender of Geronimo." *Proceed of Annual Meeting...of Order of Indian Wars,* 1929; "'No Cure, No Pay,' a Tom Horn Letter," ed. by Larry D. Ball. *Jour. of Ariz Hist,* Vol. 8, No. 3 (Autumn 1967), 200-02; John Rolfe Burroughs, *Where the Old West Stayed Young.* N.Y., William Morrow and Co., 1962; Joe LeFors, *Wyoming Peace Officer: The Autobiography of Joe LeFors.* Laramie Wyo. Printers, Inc., 1953.

Hornaday, William Temple, zoologist (Dec. 1, 1854-Mar. 6, 1937). B. at Plainfield, Indiana, he was educated at Iowa State College, received his doctorate of science at the University of Pittsburgh in 1906 and also studied in Europe and at Yale. From 1875-79 as a collecting zoologist he visited Latin America, India, Ceylon, the Malay Peninsula and Borneo. He was chief taxidermist at the U.S. National Museum from 1882-90. During this time he wrote *The Extermination of the American Bison,* which was included in the Report of the National Museum, 1886-87, and also was published separately by the Government Printing Office in 1889; it is not error-free, but remains a basic work on its subject. Hornaday spent the years from 1890-96 in the real estate business at Buffalo, New York, then in 1896 became the first director of the New York Zoological Park, retaining the post until his retirement in 1926. Here he came to national and international attention as a conservationist of dedication and zeal, active in promoting game sanctuaries and laws for protection of wildlife generally. He was decorated by several foreign governments and many organizations for his work in these directions. Hornaday took the initiative in creation of the Naional Bison Range, Moise, Montana; the Wichita National Bison Range of Oklahoma and the Elk River Game Preserve, Montana, while supporting the Bayne Law to prohibit the sale of native game and tariff laws to prohibit importations of wild bird plumage into this country for millinery purposes. He also organized the Permanent Wild Life Protection Fund in 1913. In addition to his work on bison, Hornaday wrote *Two Years in the Jungle* (1885); *Taxidermy and Zoological Collecting* (1892); *The American Natural History* (1904); *Camp-Fires in the Canadian Rockies* (1906); *Camp-Fires on Desert and Lava* (1908); *Our Vanishing Wild Life: Its Extermination and Preservation* (1913); *Wild Life Conservation in Theory and Practice* (1914); *Minds and Manners of Wild Animals* (1922); *Tales from Nature's Wonderlands* (1924); *A Wild Animal Round-up* (1925); *Wild Animal Interviews* (1928), and *Thirty Years War for Wild Life* (1931). He lived in retirement at Stamford, Connecticut.

Who Was Who; CE.

Horner, Jacob, soldier (Oct. 6, 1854-Sept. 21, 1951). B. at New York City, he was taken by his parents to Alsace when less than 4 and at 15 returned to New York, worked in meat markets and on coastal ships, returned to Europe in 1874. In January 1875 he arrived at New Orleans where he worked some months

as a meat cutter, narrowly escaped a lynching for a minor offense, reached St. Louis aboard a riverboat and April 7, 1876, enlisted for five years in Company K, 7th Cavalry. He arrived at Fort Abraham Lincoln, Dakota Territory in time to march out on the Sioux expedition May 17, 1876. He was on detached duty at Yellowstone Depot from June 11 to July 4, and thus missed the Little Big Horn battle. Subsequently he was assigned to join Terry and Gibbon near the Little Big Horn site. He served under Sturgis in an effort to strip Standing Rock Agency Indians of their horses and recover loot taken in the Custer fight. In the summer of 1877 Horner took part in the Nez Perce campaign and fought in the battle of Canyon Creek, September 13, against Chief Joseph's hostiles. Horner was married April 18, 1880, at Fort Totten, North Dakota, and fathered five children. He left the army a sergeant in 1881 and became a butcher, retiring from that occupation in 1930. He divided his later years between Bismarck, North Dakota, and Los Angeles where he was sometimes consulted by motion picture people on a late 19th century cavalryman's life. The last survivor of the 7th Cavalry of the 1876 campaign, he died at Bismarck. He was five feet, six inches, in height, with black eyes and hair and a dark complexion.

Roy P. Johnson, "Jacob Horner of the 7th Cavalry." *No. Dak. Hist.,* Vol. 16, No. 2 (Apr. 1949), 75-100.

Horner, Joe: *see* Frank M. Canton

Horrell, Ben(jamin), cattleman, gunman (d. Dec. 1, 1873). One of the Arkansas clan which moved before the Civil War to Lampasas County, Texas, he was too young to serve in that conflict. In March 1873 he may have taken part in the Horrell clan's storming of a jail at Georgetown, Williamson County, Texas, to free their wounded brother, Mart, and Jerry Scott, a Lampasas saloon-keeper. That year the five Horrell brothers and their followers migrated to Lincoln County, New Mexico. On December 1 several Horrells went to Lincoln on a spree. A Mexican constable, Juan Martinez tried to arrest three of the party: Ben, Dave Warner, and Jack Gylam (Gilliam?); they declined to give up their arms. Returning with assistance Martinez and his opponents engaged in a gunbattle in which Ben Horrell, Dave Warner and Gylam were killed, the incident precipitating the so-called Horrell War in Lincoln County. It was rumored that Horrell and Gylam were shot down after surrendering, and that Ben's gold ring was stolen by someone who chopped off his finger to get it.

Robert N. Mullin notes; Maurice Garland Fulton, "The Horrell War of 1973." written for English Westerners *Brand Book*, (Jan 1957); Philip J. Rasch, "The Horrell War." *New Mex. Hist. Rev.*, Vol. XXXI, No. 3 (July 1956), 223-31; Bill O'Neal, "The Horrell Brothers of Lampasas." *Frontier Times*, Vol. 54, No. 3 (Apr.-May 1980), 42.

Horrell, C.O.M. (Mart), cattleman, gunman (d. Dec. 15, 1878). One of the Arkansas-born clan that settled in Lampasas County, Texas, before the Civil War, Mart with his brothers Sam and Tom served in Terry's Texas Rangers (8th Texas Cavalry) during the conflict, then returned to Lampasas. March 19, 1873 Mart, Tom and Merritt Horrell with their brother-in-law Bill Bowen (Clint Barkley) who was evading a murder charge, and others were confronted in Jerry Scott's Matador Saloon at Lampasas by Captain Thomas Williams and seven men of the State Police, attempting to arrest Bowen. In a resulting gunfight Mart was wounded, Williams and three of his police killed and others routed. Mart, Scott and two others were lodged in a jail at Georgetown in neighboring Williamson County, Texas. When Mart was sufficiently recovered to travel his four brothers and others broke him out. The five Horrell boys migrated to Lincoln County, New Mexico, where December 1, 1873, Ben Horrell was killed resisting arrest at Lincoln. December 20, 1873, the surviving Horrells shot up a Mexican wedding dance party in retaliation, killing four and wounding two. A month later Sheriff Alex H. (Ham) Mills with a posse of 60 Mexicans surrounded the Horrell people at Casey's Mill, near Picacho on the Rio Hondo. No casualties were reported from the all-day battle. The Horrells pulled out for Texas again, on the way killing five Mexican freighters they met 15 miles from Roswell, New Mexico and doing a bit of rustling enroute. They settled again near Lampasas. March 26, 1877, Mart and Tom Horrell were ambushed by Pink Higgins and some of his gunmen four miles east of Lampasas where they were headed for a court appearance. Tom was wounded and Mart nicked, but routed the attackers. In early June the Horrells attacked

a Higgins line camp and shot two men. June 14, 1877, a gun battle erupted between the Horrell and Higgins factions at the Lampasas town square; Higgins had a man wounded, a bystander was killed but the Horrells suffered no casualties. A two-day battle at the Horrell Ranch in July when the Higgins men attacked resulted in two Horrell men being wounded. July 25 the Horrell men killed a Higgins rider north of Lampasas. The Texas Rangers under Sergeant N.O. Reynolds captured the Horrells and Ranger John B. Jones negotiated a truce between the factions. September 8, 1878, Mart and Tom Horrell were arrested on suspicion of killing a Bosque County merchant in a robbery. December 15 a mob of 100 stormed the jail at Meridian, Texas, where they were held and shot them to death in their cells. Mart's son, J.S. Horrell inherited something from his father's combativeness, killing four men who wounded him at his Lampasas county farmhouse some years later.

Robert N. Mullin notes; Philip J. Rasch, "The Horrell War," *New Mex. Hist. Rev.*, Vol. XXXI, No. 3 (July 1956), 223-31; Robert N. Mullen ed., *Maurice G. Fulton's History of the Lincoln County War.* Tucson, Univ. of Ariz. Press, 1968; Bill O'Neal, "The Horrell Brothers of Lampasas." *Frontier Times*, Vol. 54, No. 3 (Apr.-May 1980), 6-7, 42-45.

Horrell, John, cowman, gunman (fl. c. 1860-c.1870). The oldest of the six sons of Samuel Horrell from Arkansas, John with the others settled in Lampasas County, Texas, before the Civil War in which he is not recorded as having participated. Sometime afterward he migrated to Las Cruces, New Mexico where he was killed in an obscure gunfight, the first of the brothers to die.

Bill O'Neal, "The Horrell Brothers of Lampasas." *Frontier Times*, Vol. 54, No. 3 (Apr.-May 1980), 6.

Horrell, Merritt, cattleman, gunman (d. Jan. 22, 1877). One of the Arkansas-born Horrell family, Merritt settled with his five brothers on cattle land in Lampasas County, Texas before the Civil War, too young to take part in that conflict. He married, his brother-in-law being Bill Bowen (Clint Barkley) who soon was indicted for murder. March 19, 1873, Merritt with his brothers, Mart and Tom were at Jerry Scott's Matador Saloon in Lampasas when Captain Thomas Williams and men of the State Police sought to arrest Bowen. A gunfight erupted in which Williams and three of his men were killed and Tom and Mart were wounded. Merritt was with his brothers who stormed the Georgetown, Williamson County jail to free the recovering Mart and Scott. Merritt joined his brothers in their brief exodus to New Mexico in 1873-74, taking part in their gunbattles there and returning with them to Lampasas County where in February 1874 he was wounded slightly in a fight with a group of "Minute Men" regulators. In September 1874 Merritt and Bill Bowen surrendered on charges arising from the Matador Saloon shootout, but in 1876 were acquitted. The Horrells had come into a feuding relationship with cattleman-gunman Pink Higgins, who accused them of rustling his stock. Higgins shot the unarmed Merritt Horrell to death in the Matador Saloon without apparent cause.

O'Neal, *Gunfighters;* Bill O'Neal, "The Horrell Brothers of Lampasas." *Frontier Times,* Vol. 54, No. 3 (Apr.-May 1980), 6-7, 42-45; Philip J. Rasch, "The Horrell War." *New Mex. Hist. Rev.,* Vol. XXXI, No. 3 (July 1956), 223-31; Robert N. Mullen, ed., *Maurice G. Fulton's History of the Lincoln County War.* Tucson, Univ. of Ariz Press, 1968.

Horrell, Samuel Sr., cattleman (d. c. 1864). Of the Arkansas Ozarks, Horrell and his six sons, John, Ben, Mart, Tom, Sam and Merritt moved sometime before the Civil War to Lampasas County, Texas, establishing what became a cattle ranch on Lucy Creek a few miles northeast of the community of Lampasas. They were a gun family, clannish, brave and feud-inclined. Although three of the boys, Mart, Tom and Sam fought with Terry's Texas Rangers (the 8th Texas Cavalry) throughout the Civil War, old Sam apparently did not, and he had died before the end of the conflict.

HT; Bill O'Neal, "The Horrell Brothers of Lampasas." *Frontier Times,* Vol. 54, No. 3 (Apr.-May 1980), 6; Charles Leland Sonnichsen, *I'll Die Before I'll Run, The Story of the Great Feuds of Texas.* N.Y., Devin-Adair Co., 1962.

Horrell, Samuel W., farmer, gunman (fl. 1861-78). The oldest member of the combative Horrell family of Arkansas origin, he settled with the rest in Lampasas County, Texas, where he married and sought to raise his "large family of children." He was a farmer and generally more quietly disposed than his brothers, though as belligerent when aroused. He served during the Civil War in Terry's Texas Rangers (the 8th Texas Cavalry) which operated east of the Mississippi. Sam was not known to have taken part in the Matador Saloon shootout March 19 1873, when four State Police were killed and Mart and Tom Horrell wounded. However he was with his brothers and a number of others who stormed the Georgetown, Williamson County jail to extract Mart and Jerry Scott, the saloon keeper. He accompanied the clan then to New Mexico, settling in Lincoln County. When Ben, the youngest brother was killed resisting arrest, Sam, Mart and Tom with others on December 20, 1873, raided a Mexican wedding dance in retaliation, killed four and wounded two of the revelers. Sam took part in other gunfights as the Horrells eased back into Texas, settling again in the Lampasas area. In June 1877 Sam may have participated in an attack on a line camp belonging to Pink Higgins, with whom the Horrells had come into a feuding relationship; two Higgins men were wounded, one fatally. On June 14, 1877, Sam, Mart, Tom and four followers engaged in a gunbattle with Higgins and his two principal partisans in the Lampasas town square; Frank Mitchell, Higgins' brother-in-law was wounded mortally while William R. Wren, his chief aide was seriously wounded. A July gunfight between Higgins and Horrell factions at the latter's ranchhouse ended inconclusively. Sam, with Tom and Mart Horrell were arrested later that month by Texas Rangers, and signed a truce July 30; a like paper signed August 2, 1877, by Higgins, Wren and R.A. Mitchell ended the shooting, although the feud tapered slowly. Sam settled quietly on his ranch in Lampasas County until 1880 when, according to O'Neal, he removed to New Mexico where he lived quietly until his death at a date unreported.

O'Neal, *Gunfighters;* Bill O'Neal, "The Horrell Brothers of Lampasas." *Frontier Times,* Vol. 54, No. 3 (Apr.-May 1980), 6-7, 42-45; Philip J. Rasch, "The Horrell War." *New Mex. Hist. Rev.,* Vol. XXXI, No. 3 (July 1956), 223-31; James G. Gillett, *Six Years With the Texas Rangers.* New Haven, Yale Univ. Press, 1925.

Horrell, Thomas L., cattleman-gunman (d. Dec. 15, 1878). One of the combative Horrell brothers of Arkansas origin, Tom figured prominently in most of their troubles with authorities and feud-rivals. He settled with the others in Lampasas County, Texas, before the Civil War in which he served, with brothers Sam and Mart in Terry's Texas Rangers (the 8th Texas Cavalry) east of the Mississippi. He and Pink Higgins, also a Lampasas cattleman, engaged in a joint drive to Abilene in 1872. Arriving there they had a dispute in a saloon which nearly ended in a shootout and which may have originated the violent feud between them which broke out two years later. March 19, 1873, one-eyed Tom, with three of his brothers and others were involved in a gunfight when Captain Thomas Williams of the State Police attempted to arrest Bill Bowen, a Horrell relative by marriage. Four police were killed and Tom and Mart Horrell wounded, though not too seriously to take part in a storming a month later of the Georgetown, Williamson County jail to free the recovering Mart, whereupon the clan moved to New Mexico, settling in Lincoln County. When the youngest brother, Ben, was killed resisting arrest by a Mexican constable, Tom, Sam, Mart and two others December 20, 1873 assailed a Mexican wedding dance in retaliation, killing four and wounding two. After considerable additional gunplay in New Mexico the clan moved back to Lampasas County. March 26, 1877 Tom and Mart Horrell were ambushed near Lampasas where they were headed for a court hearing, and Tom was wounded seriously. Higgins partici-pants were released by authorities and Tom led a party to a Higgins line camp where they killed one and wounded another of the enemy. On June 14, 1877, in a shootout at the Lampasas town square, Frank Mitchell, a noncombatant was killed and Bill Wren, a Higgins leader, wounded. Carson Graham, a Higgins man, was killed by Horrells July 25 outside of Lampasas. July 28 Texas Rangers arrested Tom and his brothers who were persuaded by Major John B. Jones to sign a truce, Higgins, Wren and Bob Mitchell signing for the other faction three days later, thus ending the feud, if not the hostility. May 28, 1878, a Bosque County merchant was shot to death in a robbery and Tom and Mart Horrell were implicated by a former follower. They were arrested and held in the Meridian, Bosque County, jail. The jail was stormed by more than a hundred masked men and the two shot to death in their cell.

O'Neal, *Gunfighters;* Bill O'Neal, "The Horrell

Brothers of Lampasas." *Frontier Times,* Vol. 54, No. 3 (Apr.-May 1980), 6-7, 42-45; Philip J. Rasch, "The Horrell War." *New Mex. Hist. Rev.,* Vol. XXXI, No. 3 (July 1956), 223-31; Robert N. Mullin, ed., *Maurice G. Fulton's History of the Lincoln County War.* Tucson, Univ. of Ariz. Press, 1968; Walter Prescott Webb, *The Texas Rangers.* Boston, Houghton Mifflin Co., 1935.

Horse Guard, Crow chief (b.c. 1822). A halfbreed, he won great renown for his warrior prowess and became chief of a band of up to·70 lodges. By 30 he had taken part in about 30 wars or raiding expeditions, "always returning with scalps or horses and getting his party back in safety." He had the features of a white man. Horse Guard signed the River Crow Treaty at Fort Hawley July 15, 1868, and was in the Judith Basin in 1874-75.

Montana Contributions, Vol. X, 1940, 287.

Horton, Azariah, Presbyterian missionary (c. 1715-Mar. 2, 1777). B. possibly in New York, he was the first Presbyterian to be officially commissioned as a missionary in colonial days. He was graduated from Yale in 1735, ordained by New York Presbytery in 1740, and appointed two years later to work among Indians of eastern Long Island. Two of the churches he founded there still exist, one at Poosepatrick on the Great South Bay in south Brookhaven, and one at Shinnecock, two miles west of Southampton. In 1748 he became pastor of a white congregation at South Hanover, New Jersey. Horton was dismissed in 1776 and died the following year.

Alfred Nevin, *Encyclopaedia of the Presbyterian Church in the United States of America,* Phila., Presby. Encyclopaedia Pub. Co., 1884

Houck, James D., pioneer (c. 1847-Mar. 21, 1921). B. in Ohio he fought in the Civil War with a Wisconsin regiment, went to Wyoming shortly after the war and gradually drifted to Arizona where he arrived in 1870. In 1874 he became a mail rider and courier between Fort Whipple (Prescott), Arizona and Fort Wingate, New Mexico, and in 1877 estab-lished a trading post between Wingate and Holbrook, Arizona, trading with the Navahos until 1885. He represented Apache County for a term in the 13th Territorial Legislative Assembly. As a deputy under Sheriff Commodore Perry Owens of Apache County, Houck had some involvement in the Pleasant

Valley War that broke out in 1887 north of Globe, Arizona. August 17, 1887, he mortally wounded William Graham, aged 18, Graham dying two days later. Houck related several versions of the event though without significant variations in the climax. In September 1887 he was somewhat involved in the killing of John Graham and Charles Blevins at Perkins Store in Pleasant Valley. Forrest asserted Houck was principal instigator of the August 11, 1888, lynching of Jim Stott, Jim Scott and Billy Wilson which he termed "the most dastardly act" of the vendetta. Others disagree. Woody believed that the trio were indeed rustlers and that the hanging occurred about as Houck told it, with or without his help. He with five others had arrested the three, then quietly turned them over to a company of largely Tewksbury partisans who hanged them. She adds, "from this point on, Pleasant Valley was free of cattle stealing. Tattered remnants of the rustling ring had fled and the vigilante group disbanded, its mission fulfilled." Houck had begun his JDH sheep ranch near Heber, Arizona before the feud erupted and continued building and expanding it afterward. In 1900 he bought Cave Creek Station, 35 miles north of Phoenix, Arizona, and developed it as a shearing camp for sheepmen wintering their animals in that warm region. He became a Maricopa County deputy sheriff and also operated a stage and mail service. Although he prospered for some years, hard times came with reduced sheep grazing, drought, a dwindling of interest in the Cave Creek property, the maturing and departure of his seven children, a divorce from his first wife and remarriage, and Houck eventually took a lethal dose of poison. He was buried at Phoenix.

Frances C. Carlson, "James D. Houck: The Sheep King of Cave Creek." *Jour. of Ariz. Hist.,* Vol. 21, No. 1 (Spring 1980), 43-62; Earle R. Forrest, *Arizona's Dark and Bloody Ground.* Caldwell, Ida., Caxton Printers, 1964; Clara T, Woody & Milton L. Schwartz, *Globe, Arizona.* Tucson, Ariz. Hist. Soc., 1977.

Hough, Emerson, writer (June 28, 1857-Apr. 30, 1923). B. at Newton, Indiana, he studied for the law, but turned to journalism, then became branch manager for *Field and Stream* magazine at Chicago. Hough was interested in the frontier west, and was a dedicated

conservationist and strong proponent of the national park system and preservation of wildlife. He died at Evanston, Illinois. He wrote, among his many titles: *The Cowboy,* 2 vols. (1897); *the Story of the Cowboy* (1897); *The Girl at the Halfway House: A Story of the Plains* (1900); *The Settlement of the West: A Study in Transportation (Century* Magazine, Nov., Dec., 1901; Jan., 1902); *The Mississippi Bubble* (1902); *The Way to the West* (Boone-Crockett-Carson) (1903); *The Story of the Outlaw* (1907); *The Young Alaskans* (1908); *54-40 or Fight* (1909); *Out of Doors* (1915); *Getting a Wrong Start: A Truthful Autobiography* (1915); *The Magnificent Adventure* (a novel based on Meriwether Lewis) (1918); *The Passing of the Frontier* (1918); *The Sage-Brusher* (1919); *Maw's Adventure: The Story of A Human Being in the Yellowstone* (1921); *The Covered Wagon* (1922); *North of 36* (1923); *The Frontier Omnibus* (1936).

EA: DAB: Library of Congress Index.

House, Thomas, blacksmith, adventurer (fl. 1800-1807). B. in Jefferson County, Tennessee, he was a blacksmith by trade and joined Philip Nolan on his 1800-1801 wild horse hunting expedition to the Trinity River of Spanish Texas. Nolan was killed by Spanish soldiers and House, his brother, John, and others of the company were taken prisoner. John escaped but Thomas House was removed to Chihuahua City. Here he engaged in lengthy escape plots with his scattered campanions, but nothing came of them. When last reported by Pike, himself briefly in what amounted to custody, House was confined to his quarters "in a very bad state of health."

Bennett Lay, *The Lives of Ellis P. Bean.* Austin, Univ. of Texas Press, 1960.

Houston, Sam(uel), statesman (Mar. 2, 1793-July 26, 1863). B. in Rockbridge County, Virginia, he moved with his widowed mother and the family in 1807 to Maryville, Tennessee, where he was scantily educated. Houston spent three years with the Cherokees, learned their language and customs and "developed a deep sympathy for the Indian character," as well as an independence of spirit that would guide him all his remarkable life. He enlisted March 28, 1814, in the army, becoming sergeant, ensign and third lieutenant before the climactic engagement with the Creeks at Horseshoe Bend, Alabama, where he was wounded March 28, 1814. His gallantry came to the attention of Andrew Jackson, however, and he was promoted to second lieutenant and ultimately first lieutenant. He resigned from the army March 1, 1818, and commenced the study of law. He opened practice at Lebanon, Tennessee, was elected district attorney at Nashville in October 1818, was appointed adjutant general of Tennessee and in 1821 was named Major General of militia. He served in Congress as representative from 1823-27 and was elected governor of Tennessee in 1827. A brief marriage ended unhappily; Houston resigned his office, journeyed to western Arkansas and for six years worked among the Cherokees and other Indians, smoothing over intertribal frictions, negotiating for his Indian friends at Washington, D.C., established a trading post on the Verdigris River near Fort Gibson, was admitted to Cherokee citizenship, took an Indian wife and was a loyal friend and counselor to the tribe. In late 1832 Houston made his first trip to Texas, going as far as San Antonio, partly to report on Indian affairs and perhaps other matters to Andrew Jackson, his longtime friend, negotiate a pact of some kind between his adopted peoples, and for other reasons. He returned to Texas to attend the 1833 convention as a delegate from Nacogdoches. During succeeding months and years Houston rose to prominence with the upswelling of sentiment against Mexico and in favor of independence. November 12, 1835, he was elected Major General of the Texas army. He signed the declaration of independence March 2, 1836, and two days later was elected commander in chief of the army. News of the fall of the Alamo and the Goliad massacre came in swift succession; Houston withdrew before the advance of the triumphant Santa Anna troops, but on April 21, 1836, turned about, pounced upon the deceived enemy and wiped out Mexican power in Texas forever at the Battle of San Jacinto, himself wounded in the action. The ankle injury never completely healed. September 5, 1836, Houston was elected president of Texas, securing United States recognition, the release of Santa Anna from embittered Texans and his dispatch to Washington, D.C., as a "hostage for peace," and otherwise fulfilled an uneventful term of office. Since he could not legally succeed himself, he served in the Texas congress. He

married for a third time May 9, 1840, to Margaret Moffette Lea of Alabama, and this, like his second, was a happy marriage. In 1841 Houston again was elected president of Texas, tried to repair the damages wrought by his predecessor, Mirabeau B. Lamar, although he himself authorized against his better judgment the disastrous Somervell Expedition and the equally unfortunate Snively Expedition. His term expired in 1844. Houston probably favored annexation of Texas by the United States, and worked assiduously, if by circumlocution, to bring it about. He attended the deathbed of Jackson in the States, preventing his casting his vote for annexation. From 1846 for nearly 14 years he served as U.S. Senator from Texas, not speaking frequently "but when supporting the Union or defending the rights of the Indians, he rose more than once to real heights of impassioned and well-controlled eloquence." He was offered and declined a generalship during the war with Mexico, and was bitter that the United States did not establish at least a protectorate over all of Mexico upon its conclusion. Houston's voting record in the Senate supports further the picture of him as a man of complete integrity and great vision, in both qualities far above most of his colleagues and contemporaries. He was always strongly for Union, for expansion, for order, for justice and civil rights, for common sense and honor. His position was classically southern only on the question of a railroad to the Pacific by the southern route. In 1859, despite the opposition he had aroused by his pro-Union stand, Houston once more was elected the chief administrator of Texas. The state was vociferously pro-southern, but Houston continued to voice his opposition to secession, denounced those who favored it as "reckless and mischievous agitators," and pointed out what he clearly saw: the disaster for Texas that would result from acceptance of their position; the less clear-sighted and less mentally acute citizenry, however, could not perceive what he saw so vividly. Believing that the Union might still be preserved, Houston tried to initiate a movement for a southern convention to work out a compromise. He followed the directive of the Texas legislature and put the question of secession to a referendum but when the populace backed that disastrous course Houston denied that their vote carried with it any necessary adherence to the Confederacy, but instead had reinstated the state's former independence; upon that grounds, as he insisted, he declined to take the oath of allegiance to the Confederate government, the office of governor was declared vacant, and Houston withdrew. He declined an offer of Union military forces to re-establish his position and retired to his farm near Huntsville, where he died, survived by his wife and eight children. It is difficult to assess Houston as other but the noblest and greatest figure Texas has thus far produced, and it seems fitting that the largest city of the state should bear his name.

Literature abundant.

Hovey, Eugene, victim (c. 1852-Apr. 18, 1873). B. in Yreka, California, according to Riddle (Dillon says in Wisconsin), Hovey (whom Murray says was 19) was a well-liked, quiet civilian packer during the Modoc War of 1872-73 and was murdered and mutilated in a savage way while unarmed and leading a pack mule with supplies for the troops. Hooker Jim and Bogus Charley shot him while two accompanying newspaper writers, Edward Fox and H, Wallace Atwell ran for their lives.

Jeff C. Riddle, *Indian History of the Modoc War.* Medford, Ore., Pine Cone Pubs., 1973; Richard Dillon, *Burnt-Out Fires.* Englewood Cliffs, N.J., Prentice-Hall, 1973; Keith A. Murray, *The Modocs and Their Wars.* Norman, Univ. of Okla. Press, 1965.

Howard, Guy, army officer (Dec. 16, 1855-Oct. 22, 1899). The oldest child of Oliver Otis Howard, he was b. at Augusta, Maine, and in Oregon was commissioned a second lieutenant of the 12th Infantry August 31, 1876. He was aide to his father during the Nez Perce campaign of 1877 winning a brevet at Camas Meadows, Idaho, August 20, and was present at the Bear Paw Mountains, Montana surrender of Chief Joseph and most of his people. Howard became a first lieutenant July 19, 1882, a captain January 7, 1893, transferring to the Quartermaster Department that month. He became a major of volunteers in 1898 and briefly a lieutenant colonel of volunteers. He was killed in action near Arayat, Philippine Islands.

Heitman; information from Library, Bowdoin College, Brunswick, Me.

Howard, Joseph, frontiersman (fl. 1827-1849), the son of Thomas Proctor Howard, Joseph went up the Missouri River with Ashley in 1827, and was in the American Fur Company records from 1830. He married an Indian woman named Margaret and a son, Joseph, was baptized at St. Louis in 1839 when the elder Joseph was on a trip downriver. He remained generally on the upper Missouri until 1849.

Montana Contributions, Vol. X, 1940, 280.

Howard, Joseph, frontiersman (c. 1839-Dec. 28, 1894). The son of Joseph Howard, a fur man, Joseph junior was b. of a Piegan mother at Fort Benton, Montana, taken to St. Louis where he was baptized August 22, 1839, and returned to Fort Benton in 1851. He was described by John Owen as a "stout, hard, young half-breed, inured to all hardships of the mountain life." Howard settled in 1873 on a ranch near Chouteau, Montana, where he died.

Montana Contributions, Vol. X, 1940, 280.

Howard, Oliver Otis, army officer (Nov. 8, 1830-Oct. 26, 1909). B. at Leeds, Maine, he went to West Point and was commissioned a brevet second lieutenant of Ordnance July 1, 1854, and a second lieutenant February 15, 1855, serving at various arsenals until 1857 when he operated against Seminole Indians in Florida, becoming a first lieutenant July 1 that year. His Civil War service was distinguished. He lost an arm at Fair Oaks, won a Medal of Honor and the thanks of Congress for his services at Gettysburg, ending the war a Major General of Volunteers, a Brigadier General of the army and a brevet Major General. President Andrew Johnson named him commissioner of the Bureau of Refugees, Freedman and Abandoned Lands in May 1865, Howard holding the position until June 1872. He became highly controversial in connection with that work, largely because of his support for the newly-freed blacks which was underpinned by his strong religious convictions and sense of fair play. He was a Christian of Congregational affiliation, and a founder of Howard University, serving as its first president. In 1872 President Grant named him a special Indian commissioner and directed him to go to the Southwest and attempt to settle the knotty problems caused by white excesses and consequent Apache unrest and hostility. He left Wahsington March 7, returned briefly in June and went back to New Mexico in July to complete his work. In its course he conferred at length with Victorio, trying to settle difference between that great chief and the agents, and through his acquaintance with that leader was enabled to go with Jeffords, his aide, Joseph Alton Sladen, and others to Cochise in the Dragoon Mountains of southeastern Arizona. After an 11-day visit with Cochise that chief agreed to come to peaceful terms which included establishment of a reservation for him and a general settlement of differences betweeen the Chiricahuas and the whites. It was a notable feat on Howard's part. He also visited other troubled spots in the southwest, investigated the Camp Grant Massacre and interviewed Indian survivors of it and assiduously tried to fulfill his mission of bringing peace with justice to the region. Frontier officers and westerners found what they perceived to be Howard's sanctimoniousness hard to swallow at first, but his "peace theories (were) strongly tinged with common sense," he consulted whites as well as Indians, and developed some valuable areas of agreement, arranged agreements with tribes and bands, rearranged reservation boundaries and on the whole left a positive image. Howard commanded the Department of the Columbia from July 1874 until 1880, and was the field commander during most of the sanguinary Nez Perce campaign of 1877, being in some part responsible for its outbreak because of the imperiousness with which he dealt with the much-abused non-treaty Nez Perce leaders and the impossible demands he placed upon them. Elements working under his overall command engaged in the bloody battles, or defeats suffered at the hands of the Nez Perce, and he pursued them in their withdrawal from Idaho into Montana, northwestern Wyoming and across Montana again to the Bear Paw Mountains of the latter where the climactic battle was fought, although by Miles rather than Howard who had not yet come up; he arrived only in time for the surrender. Howard's conduct of the military phases of the Nez Perce campaign were on the whole commendable, even extraordinary for one of his age and somewhat dwindling vigor. He also was overall commander in operations against the Bannocks and Paiutes in 1878. Howard was superintendent of the U.S. Military

Academy from June 21, 1881, to September 1, 1882, when he became commander of the Department of the Platte until 1886. He became a Major General March 19, 1886, and commanded the Military Division of the Pacific for two years, thus was overall supervisor of the operations against Geronimo in their final phases, although never in the field. He commanded the Division of the East from 1888 until his retirement November 8, 1894. Howard wrote much, his books including *Chief Joseph: His Pursuit and Capture* (1881); *My Life and Experiences Among Our Hostile Indians* (1907), and *Famous Indian Chiefs I Have Known* (1908). His two volume *Autobiography* also appeared in 1907. Oliver Knight, in the *Reader's Encyclopedia of the American West* wrote that "The quality of Howard's dealings with the Indians is open to dispute," with some believing he treated them with understanding in the interest of equal justice for both white and native. On the contrary, Knight concluded, "The record indicates, however that the self-righteous Howard lacked the temperament, empathy, and knowledge to deal with the Indians effectively, in council or in the field." Howard was honest, compassionate and of undoubted personal courage and on the whole his career on the frontier was distinctly positive. He died at Burlington, Vermont.

Heitman: Powell; Cullum; Dan L. Thrapp, *Victorio and the Mimbres Apaches.* Norman, Univ. of Okla. Press, 1974; Thrapp, *The Conquest of Apacheria.* Norman, 1967; McWhorter, *Hear Me;* Howard's own books.

Howard, Thomas Proctor, explorer (b. 1779). Raised at Brimfield, Massachusetts, he enlisted with the Lewis and Clark expedition January 1, 1804, although Clark said of him that "he never drank water." He married at St Louis and had a son, Joseph. A Montana creek in 1805 was named briefly for him.

Clarke, *Lewis and Clark.*

Howard, William J., frontiersman (c. 1829-Jan. 1924). At 24 Howard, who owned a ranch 20 miles west of Mariposa, California, joined Harry Love in the California Rangers in an attempt to extirpate banditry in central California, his ranch to be headquarters. Howard helped Love recruit the 20 men considered necessary and accompanied the posse on its long circuitous search for the bandit Joaquin, also known as Murrieta, and his principal lieutenant, Three Fingered Jack. The pair were run down and killed July 25, 1853, on Cantua Creek, near present Coalinga, California. Howard became the last surviving member of the California Rangers and kept in touch with those he could contact as long as they lived. He died at Portland, Oregon, aged 97.

William B. Secrest, "Hell for Leather Rangers." *True West,* Vol. 15, No. 4 (Mar.-Apr. 1968), 20-23, 48-49.

Howie, Neil, lawman (c. 1834-Mar. 1874). B. in Scotland he came to the United States in boyhood and was raised in Wisconsin. He went to Colorado and in 1863 reached the Beaverhead River country of southwestern Montana. Notorious Henry Plummer tried unsuccessfully to recruit him for his outlaw band, called The Innocents; Howie was brave enough for them, but too principled to accept. In the fall he went to Salt Lake City, returning with a freight cargo. Howie at great personal risk captured Dutch John Wagner, delivering him to the vigilantes who dispatched him January 11, 1864, at Bannack. Howie apparently continued active in the affairs of the vigilantes, although details are unreported. In the spring of 1864 Governor Sidney Edgerton appointed him sheriff of Madison County; he served bravely and well during the flour riots of April 1865 although there was no bloodshed and Howie gracefully gave in to popular demands for food, when these became overly insistent. When succeeded as sheriff he was appointed first deputy U.S. marshal for Montana, holding the position as long as he remained in the Territory. July 25, 1867, Howie was commissioned colonel of the 1st Montana Volunteer Cavalry, a militia outfit. He and his men completed building Fort T.F. Meagher and Fort Howie on the North Fork of the Musselshell River. In late August he and his men had a fight with Crows who were attacking whites, about the only action against hostiles the militia recorded. Howie had troubles with mutinous volunteers and in other ways, but was among the best of the officers serving the Territory in militia organizations. He went to Wyoming to help out a brother arrested for murder; when the brother was pardoned Howie went on to Colorado and in 1872 to Utah. He became assistant superintendent of the Remington Company's Quartz Works on

the island of Trinidad off the mouth of Venezuela's Orinoco River, Trinidad then being a British Crown Colony. Either on Trinidad or the nearby mainland Howie accompanied a pack train one day when he was accosted by a revolutionary force and killed a lieutenant and sergeant; later he shot a captain to death in a saloon, but was not held for these affrays. Within months however he died on Trinidad of fever, purportedly malaria. Howie was intrepid, left a host of friends, and was an interesting man, being attracted to violence as well as such aesthetic things as a lovely landscape, a rare flower or unusual animal.

Nathaniel Pitt Langford, *Vigilante Days and Ways.* Missoula, Mont. State Univ. Press, 1957; *Benton Weekly Record,* Fort Benton, Mont., Oct. 6, 1881; *Helena* (Montana) *Weekly Herald,* June 18, 1874.

Howland, John Dare, artist (May 7,1843-Sept. 10, 1914). B. at Zanesville, Ohio, he was the son of a river boat captain and at 14 went up the Missouri River for fur trader Robert Campbell. He worked at various posts, lived with the Indians, hunted buffalo (reportedly with a bow and arrow), and learned a great deal about wilderness life, which he enjoyed. He served as scout during the 1862-64 troubles with the Sioux and other northern Plains tribes, and eventually settled at Denver. Howland studied art in France and became an accomplished painter of vigorous Plains scenes and aspects of the life he had known. He painted Black Kettle, the Cheyenne chief and prominent Indians of several tribes. Howland was secretary of the Indian Peace Commission in 1867-69, and witnessed nine treaties. He died at Denver.

Kate Howland Charles, "Jack Howland, Pioneer Painter of the Old West." *Colo. Mag.,* Vol. XXIX, No. 3 (July 1952). 170-75.

Howling Wolf, Cheyenne war chief (c. 1840-June 2, 1927). The son of Minimic, or War Shield, principal chief of the tribe, Howling Wolf early took a prominent role in Cheyenne wars with other tribes and the whites. If there was no previous Howling Wolf he must have been born around 1840 for he was a mature warrior by the mid-1860s. He was active in collaboration with the Sioux and others opposing the 1865 Connor expedition on the northern Plains; he also was prominent in the central Plains hostilities of the late 1860s and was one of the leaders in the attack on the Kidder party in July 1867. Howling Wolf was active against Miles on the south Plains in 1874-75 when he finally surrendered, only to be sent to Fort Marion, Florida, with other late hostiles. While there he completed a series of a dozen drawings of Cheyenne life as he had known it, from the first coming of the whites until the death of Roman Nose. In 1878 he returned from Fort Marion to the Darlington Agency, Oklahoma, where for a time he became a Christian and ardent pro-white, quickly becoming disillusioned however and returning to the traditional anti-white focus of his earlier years. In 1884 he was elected chief of the Dog Soldiers. Howling Wolf struggled against implementation of the Dawes Act of 1887 with its attempt to break up Indian tribal life and eventually strip them of what little land had been left to them. He died in an automobile accident at Waurika, Oklahoma. He was married three times and fathered eight or ten children.

George E. Hyde, *Life of George Bent,* Norman, Univ. of Okla. Press, 1968; Dockstader.

Hoyt, Edward Jonathan (Buckskin Joe), frontiersman (Oct. 4, 1880-Apr. 20, 1918). B. at Magog, Quebec, he is said to have won his nickname in the 1850's hunting and trapping among Canadian Indians. He also showed some talent for music, learning to play 16 instruments, acquiring local fame, before he became attracted to steamboat and wagon circuses in the eastern and central United States, at times performing as aerialist and acrobat. He enlisted in the Union Army in the Civil War, serving with the Army of the Potomac, and when the war ended went to Kansas, settling on the site of the present Arkansas City. For 20 years he made personal expeditions into the Rockies and Indian Territory. In 1879 he was at Leadville, Colorado, where he became acquainted with Haw Tabor, sank a number of mining shafts, did not prosper much and adventured. He came to know the western slope of the Rockies and Ute country, and was there during the Ute uprising and the Meeker massacre; a tiny Colorado community of Hoyt was said to have been named for him. Hoyt prospected in Nova Scotia in 1884. In 1888 he entered show business with Pawnee Bill and in 1889 joined the land rush into Oklahoma. From 1890 to 1891 he said he had served as deputy U.S.

marshal for Kansas and Oklahoma, then organized his own Buckskin Joe Wild West show, a venture never too successful. In 1897 he prospected and worked mines in Honduras for four years before a revolution forced him out. He disposed of his Kansas and Oklahoma interests in 1909 and moved to Los Angeles, California, where he died.

Buckskin Joe: The Memoirs of Edward Jonathan Hoyt, ed. by Glenn Shirley. Lincoln, Univ. of Nebr. Press, 1966.

Hoyt, Henry Franklin, physician (1854-post 1929). B. on a farm near St. Paul, Minnesota, he accompanied the David Stanley Yellowstone Expedition in 1873 as one of an astronomical party assisting surveyors for a northern railroad. In 1874 he commenced the study of medicine at St. Paul and in 1876 at the time of the James-Younger bank robbery attempt at Northfield obtained the cadaver of Charlie Pitts (Sam Wells), one of the desperadoes killed September 21. He had the skeleton mounted and kept it with him at Chicago when he entered Rush Medical School that fall. Before graduation he practiced medicine in 1877 at Deadwood, South Dakota, and in the fall of that year went to the Texas Panhandle where he said he was one of the first formally trained (although not yet graduated) physicians to practice there. He became friends with Billy the Kid who sold him a horse when he left the region in 1878. After completing his education, Hoyt practiced at St. Paul, held minor public offices and in 1899 went with the army as a surgeon of Volunteers to the Philippines where he said he took part in 25 engagements. Eventually he retired to Long Beach, California, where in 1925 he was awarded the Silver Star for his Philippine service.

Henry F. Hoyt, *A Frontier Doctor.* Boston and N.Y., Houghton Mifflin Co., 1929; Colin Rickards, "Bones of the Northfield Robbers." *Real West,* Vol. 22, No. 161 (Jan. 1979), 28-31, 60.

Hrdlicka, Ales, anthropologist (Mar. 29, 1869-Sept. 5, 1943). B. in Humpolec, Bohemia, he emigrated to the U.S. with his father in 1882, and earned medical degrees. In 1898 he went to Mexico with the Norwegian, Carl Lumholtz, to do anthropometric work among the Indians. He made expeditions into the southwest for the American Museum of Natural History, but in 1903 joined the

National Museum of the Smithsonian
Institution where he built up one of the world's
largest human skeletal collections. He traveled
worldwide in his investigations and in pursuit
of his specialty: bodily measurement variations
between different peoples. He was interested in
early migration and man's origins and did
much work in the Aleutian Islands. He
believed man's arrival in the New World was
not much more than 15,000 years ago, but that
was before recent evidence suggesting that his
appearance was considerably earlier. Hrdlicka
wrote widely. He died at Washington, D.C.

EA; CE

Hubbell, John Lorenzo, Indian trader (Nov.
21, 1853-Nov.11, 1930). B. at Pajarito, New
Mexico, south of Albuquerque, he had
numerous adventures in Utah among the
Paiutes and among the Hopis in Arizona, in
1871 settling first at Fort Defiance on the
Navaho Reservation, then establishing a
trading post at Ganada. There and around St.
John's he engaged for some time in disputes
with lawless elements, asserted that "I didn't do
any of the killing myself, but I supplied the guns
and ammunition for the fighting, was, in fact,
the man behind the guns." He was elected
sheriff of Apache County in 1882 and served
two adventurous terms. He was elected senator
from his county to the first state legislature of
Arizona, convening in 1912. Hubbell had a
reputation for honest dealing with the Indians,
spoke Navaho fluently (and, being half
Spanish, that language as well), claimed to be a
friend of several important Indians, including
Victorio and Geronimo among the Apaches,
Ganado Mucho, Manuelito and others among
the Navahos. He died following a stroke and is
buried near Ganado.

Farish VI; Dorothy Challis Mott, "Don Lorenzo
Hubbell of Ganado." *Ariz. Hist. Rev.,* Vol. IV, No.
1 (Apr. 1931), 45-51; Robert M. Utley, "Portrait for a
Western Album." *Amer. West,* Vol. XV, No.5
(Sept./Oct. 1978), 10.

Hudson, pioneers (d. Sept. 11, 1857). A family
of this name, composition unknown, perished
as part of the Fancher emigrant wagon train at
Mountain Meadows, southwestern Utah,
destroyed by Mormons and Mormon-led
Indians.

William Wise, *Massacre at Mountain Meadows.*
N.Y., Thomas Y. Crowell Co., 1976.

Hudson, Henry, discoverer (d. c. summer
1611). Since Hudson was already in middle age
when he definitely appears in history in 1607,
he must have been born about 1575, although
the date is lacking. An English navigator and
explorer, he had a wide reputation upon his
initial appearance, being then employed by the
English Muscovy Co. to seek a route to the Far
East via the Arctic. He set a "farthest north"
record, attaining 81 degrees North Latitude,
and assembled information which led to
founding of the Spitzbergen whaling industry.
A second expedition in 1608 seeking a
northeast passage likewise failed to accomplish
its purpose. The Dutch East India Co. then
contracted for his services in a similar pursuit,
but this 1609 expedition was headed off by ice
above North Cape and Hudson contravened
his instructions by putting about in his ship, the
Halve Maen (Half Moon) to seek a northwest
passage by way of America instead. He entered
Chesapeake Bay, Delaware Bay and New York
Bay, and was believed first to ascend the
Hudson River (named for him) as far as the site
of the later Albany, laying the basis for the
Dutch claim to the area. In an English harbor
on his homeward journey he was forbidden by
the Privy Council to return to the Netherlands,
and re-entered English service. He sailed from
London April 17, 1610, with a mixed crew
aboard the *Discovery,* and with orders from his
private backers to explore Davis Strait and
beyond. By way of Husdon Strait, which may
have been discovered by Sebastian Cabot, he
entered Hudson Bay after a quickly put-down
mutiny, and explored widely, wintering near
the mouth of Rupert River. Dissension,
disease (principally scurvy) and an ill-
managed company enhanced unrest. The
homeward voyage was commenced June 12,
1611; on June 24 off Charlton Island, Hudson,
his son, John, 19, and six others were put into
a ship's boat and cast adrift. The triumphant
ship's crew subsequently lost three men in a
fight with Eskimos, a mutiny ringleader died
and the remainder barely managed to reach
south Ireland and thence London. Inquiries
continued for several years; finally four of the
mutineers were arraigned before an Admiralty
court on a charge not of mutiny, but of murder;
they were acquitted for "it was not murder to
turn experienced seamen adrift near a shore
that was neither totally barren nor unin-
habited." Hudson's fate was never finally

determined. His achievements give him "a very high rank in the band of navigators from the British Isles" laying the geographical groundwork for immense commercial and development enterprises, some enduring to this day. Hudson was a man with both excellent and deplorable qualities; his undoing was largely because of his own leadership failings.

Literature abundant: DCB; CE; C.A. Weslager and A.R. Dunlap, *Dutch Explorers, Traders and Settlers in the Delaware Valley 1609-1664.* Phila., Univ. of Pa. Press, 1961.

Hudson, Richard, pioneer (Feb. 22, 1839-Apr. 16, 1912). B in England he was orphaned and brought by relatives to America, educated at Brooklyn and San Francisco, having reached California in 1852. He went to the Oroville, California, mines in 1856 and in 1861 helped raise the short-lived 1st California, then joined Company I, 5th California Infantry, becoming first sergeant. In January, 1863, he was commissioned second lieutenant and transferred to Company G and June 22, 1865, to Company D, then E, 1st California Veteran Infantry; he was mustered out at Fort Union, New Mexico, October 17, 1866. During his service he was said to have participated in some Indian skirmishes, but details are lacking. In 1868 he was appointed captain of militia by New Mexico Governor Robert Mitchell, promoted to major by Governor Lew Wallace, and to colonel of the 1st New Mexico Regiment by Governor Lionel A. Sheldon. In 1866 Hudson went to the gold camp of Pinos Altos, New Mexico, becoming a prominent settler, engaging in freighting, staging, mining and related activities. In 1868 upon organization of Grant County he became its first sheriff, serving two years. He then served as judge of the Probate Court for four years. In 1871, a year after founding of Silver City, New Mexico, he settled there; Hudson Street is named for him. For a time he operated what he called Hudson Hot Springs (Faywood Hot Springs), engaged in the cattle business and was named agent for the Mescalero Apaches by President Harrison. He married (his wife and Harvey Whitehill's wife were sisters) and fathered a daughter. He died and was buried at Deming, New Mexico, where he had lived for some years.

Information from Silver City Museum, N. M.; Orton; correspondence with Mrs. Myrtle W. Carlisle, Deming.

Huff, Peter, pioneer (d. Sept. 11, 1857). Huff, from Benton County, Arkansas, his wife whose name is not known, and at least three children were of the Fancher emigrant wagon train which left Fort Smith, Arkansas, in late March 1857, for California. At Mountain Meadows, Utah, the 140 members of the train were wiped out by Mormons and Mormon-led Indians. The youngest child, Sophronia Huff, may have been spared and returned to Arkansas.

William Wise, *Massacre at Mountain Meadows.* N.Y., Thomas Y. Crowell Co., 1976.

Huffman, Laton Alton, photographer (Oct. 31, 1854-Dec. 28, 1931). B. near Castalia, Iowa, among his ancestors were frontiersmen who had scouted with Brady and fought with the Wetzels and others. Raised on a farm, he became enamored of outdoor life, early studied photography in his father's studio at Waukon, Iowa, opening a studio of his own at 21 at nearby Postville, Iowa. In 1878 he moved to Moorhead, North Dakota, and by 1880 had reached Fort Keogh, Montana, apparently by way of western Kansas. He took over a studio at the post; out of it he became a noted frontier photographer, recording views of most of the major activities of his times: buffalo and hide-hunting, cattle roundups, sheep and sheepmen, the coming of the railroads, ranch life, frontier communities, and Indians, including both portrait and group shots. With Eugene Lamphere he established a ranch on Lame Deer Creek, operating it for a short time. The Northern Pacific Railroad reached Miles City in 1881, bringing sight-seers and hence a market for Huffman's pictures, enabling him to expand his widespread operations. He began also to sell photographs to eastern publications, traveled to Yellowstone and other scenic or historically interesting places, and by 1883 had more than 300 negatives "of the staying kind." Huffman occasionally guided hunting parties as his fame grew. He worked briefly in Chicago, then opened a studio temporarily at Billings, Montana, occasionally held political office, became something of an institution in Montana, counseled scientists from his fund of specialized knowledge of zoology, ethnology and geography. "If there is one quality which sets the Huffman collection apart from the work of others... it is the intimate nature of the subject matter. Huffman was part of the society which he photographed and many of his pictures portray not only certain individuals but... various details about their daily life. Herein probably lies their unique appeal." Huffman had a sense of humor, was resourceful and diligent and no effort was too great to capture a desired subject. He had some shortcomings, however. He bought negatives from others and sometimes identified these as his own work; he relied upon his memory for data on certain pictures, and his recollection on occasion was faulty. Sometimes he wrote an identifying line on a print and later a different identification on a duplicate print. He may sometimes have back-dated pictures to increase their sale potential. "Even with these small blemishes, the Huffman pictures constitute one of the finest pictorial records of life on a western frontier." Huffman, who was married, died of heart attack at Billings, Montana, never having completed an autobiography which he had roughly mapped out.

Mark H. Brown, "L.A. Huffman — Frontier Photographer." Yellowstone Corral of Westerners, *Hoofprints*, Vol. 5, No. 2 (Autumn-Winter 1975), 3-21; Mark H. Brown, W.R. Felton, *The Frontier Years: L.A. Huffman, Photographer of the Plains.* N.Y., Bramhall House, 1955; Brown, Felton, *Before Barbed Wire: L.A. Huffman, Photographer on Horseback.* N.Y., Bramhall House, 1956.

Hughes, Barney, prospector (1817-Oct. 16, 1909). B. in Ireland, he reached New York in 1829 and California in 1854, by trade a "moulder." In 1858 he arrived in British Columbia, remaining two years. Henry Edgar, with him a later discoverer of Alder Gulch, first met Hughes at Orofino, Idaho, in 1861. In January 1862, they went together to Florence, Idaho, then moved into Montana. They left Bannack together February 4, 1863, for Deer Lodge. On May 26 they were of a party of six who located the important Alder Gulch placers in southwestern Montana. In 1864 Barney sold his Alder Gulch interest for about $40,000 in dust. In the fall he started for British Columbia, and at Missoula gave all but $3,000 of his wealth to a brother to take to San Francisco to be coined. The brother invested in San Francisco real estate and lost it all; this took the heart out of Barney. He died at Wisdom, Montana.

Muriel Sibell Wolle, *Montana Pay Dirt.* Denver, Alan Swallow Pubr., 1963; Henry Edgar, "Barney Hughes: An Appreciation." *Montana Contributions,* Vol. VII, 1910, 197-98.

Hughes, Elias (Ellis), scout (1757-Dec. 22, 1844). B. in present Hardy County, Virginia, he was a younger brother of Jesse Hughes and also famous as a trans-Allegheny scout. He removed to Harrison County while young and took part in the Battle of Pt. Pleasant in the 1774 Lord Dunmore's War. With the Revolution, Hughes volunteered in the Virginia militia, serving as ranger under Capt. James Booth until the spring of 1778 when his father was killed by Indians (according to report along with Hughes' fiancee). He was named captain of rangers or scouts under Lowther and served thus until 1781, when he served again as private until 1783, and continued his scouting activities until 1795 when Wayne brought peace to the Ohio country. Hughes was a marvelous hunter and "the recognized champion rifle shot on the western waters." He assisted in the building of Nutter Fort, West Virginia, and was regarded by his superiors and others as brave and efficient. In 1797 he moved to the Muskingum River, Ohio, and the next year to Licking County, Ohio, being hunter for the surveying party that platted the first landholdings there. He continued his work with scout militia organizations and in the War of 1812 was captain of militia and commissioned second lieutenant, Colonel Rennick's Regiment, Mounted Ohio Volunteers. He died near Utica, Ohio, Hughes "on all subjects except Indian warfare was ... taciturn, but was fond of relating his exploits and successes as a scout; sitting up whole nights, sometimes, to relate... his hair-breadth escapes and adventures, and the thrilling stories, heroic acts and deeds of renown in which he had borne a part. He was unassuming, temperate, honest, mild-mannered, unpretending, unambitious, but firm, determined, unyielding, and some thought him vindictive." He was blind the last 16 years of his life, took up "religious subjects"; he was buried with full military honors. Like his more famous brother, he hated Indians, particularly hostile ones or thieves, with an abiding passion, although he may not have been so cruel or merciless as Jesse.

Lucullus V. McWhorter, *The Border Settlers of Northwestern Virginia.* Hamilton, O., Republican Pub. Co., 1915.

Hughes, James, cattleman (c. 1865-Nov.22, 1899). B. in New Mexico, the son of Nick

Hughes, he was a cattleman in eastern Arizona and western New Mexico during the turbulent years of the Earps and Clantons, was a friend of Curly Bill Brocius and other enigmatic figures. He died at Shakespeare, New Mexico, and is buried there.

Ed Batholomew, *Wyatt Earp: The Man & the Myth.* Toyahvale, Tex., Frontier Book Co., 1964; Emma Marble Muir, "A Pioneer Ranch." *Around Here: The Southwest in Picture and Story,* Vol. X, No.1 (1952), 66, 74-75, 80-83.

Hughes, James Bryan, army officer (May 17, 1863-Jan. 21, 1933). B. in North Carolina, he was a West Pointer who joined the 10th Cavalry as a second lieutenant in 1884, becoming a first lieutenant in 1891. He was posted to Arizona in time to see arduous field service chasing the elusive Apache Kid and others following the Kid's 1887 breakout after the wounding of Al Sieber. He was a member of the court-martial in late June 1887 to try the Kid and his colleagues (who had surrendered voluntarily) for charges connected with the affair. Hughes left Arizona in the spring of 1892, being assigned to Fort Custer, Montana, and remaining at this and other Montana posts until 1898. His service in the Spanish American War and subsequent operations was credit-able; he won the Silver Star for gallantry in an action at Santiago, Cuba, July 1, 1898, became captain in the 1st, then the 4th Cavalry regiments in 1899 and served actively in military efforts connected with the Philippine Insurrection. He suffered in 1913 a "disability not incident to the service," was "in arrest" from September 27 to December 21 of that year, on sick leave from January 3 to March 7, 1914 when he retired as major. He died at Washington, D.C.

Cullum; Heitman; Dan L. Thrapp, *Al Sieber, Chief of Scouts.* Norman, Univ. of Okla. Press, 1964.

Hughes, Jesse, scout, Indian fighter (c. 1750-c. Oct. 1, 1829). Of Welsh extraction, he was b. perhaps in Allegheny County, Virginia, in the winter when snow was deep and starving wolves howled around the cabins; he grew up to be as cruel and merciless as a wolf and one of the greatest scouts of the Allegheny frontier. Hughes was "the best trailer among the whites and could trail with any Indian on the border." He was a fine hunter, not so good a shot as his brother, Elias, though he could approach game more closely and thus killed about as much.

He, Elias and William Lowther carried out the first actual exploration of the Little Kanawha River, and its main tributary, Hughes River, about 1772, the latter named for Jesse Hughes. Hughes was of inestimable value to the tiny border settlements with his unceasing scouting, knowledge of Indian ways, warding off of war parties and warning of those too strong to be distracted. His roving expeditions extended beyond the Virginia border and into western Pennsylvania, and he killed many Indians. Although it is probable that he scouted at times for militia and military groups, there is no proof that he enlisted; this however, is not conclusive, since such records are missing for many who so served. In 1772 he was prominent in the murder of Bald Eagle, a Delaware chief living at peace in northwestern Virginia, and a short time later, in the massacre of Captain Bull, another Delaware chief and his village of 15 persons, also living at presumed peace with the whites. Captain Bull, in his death agonies, was seized by Hughes and dragged through the fire "while he was yet kicking." Hughes then skinned the Indian's thigh and used the material to patch his moccasins. Hughes was a man of many adventures; once a rattlesnake awakened him trying to get under his covers. The snake was dispatched and in the morning Jesse found in a hollow log of the cabin wall another live rattlesnake and five copperheads. "Jesse Hughes was the recognized chief of the Virginia scouts." He served with Lowther and was on the expedition when John Bonnett was killed. One of his daughters, Mary, was captured in 1787 by Indians, taken to Ohio, and peacefully freed by her father in 1790. Jesse may have been a subaltern in Lowther's ranger company in the early 1790s, for occasionally he was directed to take men and scout the frontier. In 1791 he survived the fight in which Nicholas Carpenter and others were killed while trying to supply Ft. Harmar, Ohio. Lithe and swift of foot, even as an old man he won a match race with one far younger. His last Indian adventure is recorded for the year 1793. He moved to the Wabash country of Indiana in 1797 or 1798, the following year to eastern Kentucky, in the spring of 1800 to western Virginia and settled on Turkey Run, in present Jackson County, West Virginia. He died near Ravenwood; his gravesite is unknown. Hughes was about 5 feet, 9 inches in height, weighed 145 pounds; he had thin lips, a narrow chin, sharp, slightly Roman nose, little beard, light hair, his eyes were grayish-blue ("Hughes had eyes like a rattlesnake," said one who knew him). He was irritable, vindictive, suspicious and "his hatred, when aroused knew no bounds. Yet...he was true to those who gained his friendship." One woman who had known Hughes in her girlhood, said his "countenance was hard, stern and unfeeling; his eyes were the most cruel and vicious I ever saw. He was profane and desperately wicked. He was very superstitious, and a firm believer in witchcraft .... His temper was fierce and uncontrollable, often finding vent in the abuse of his family.... He never worked but spent his time in hunting and scouting.... When scouting his dress consisted only of the long hunting shirt, belted at the waist, open leggings, moccasins, and a brimless cap, or a handkerchief bound about his head."

Lucullus V. McWhorter, *The Border Settlers of Northwestern Virginia.* Hamilton, O., Republican Pub. Co., 1915.

Hughes, John Reynolds, Texas Ranger (Feb. 11, 1855-June 3, 1947). B. at Cambridge, Illinois, he lived six years in Indian Territory with various tribes (becoming a warm friend of Quanah Parker), then engaged in the cattle business along the Travis and Williamson counties line in Texas. He entered the Texas Rangers as a private August 10, 1887, at Georgetown, Williamson County, and retired January 15, 1915, his being the longest service in the organization in point of years, and one of the most notable. Hughes served in every Texas county along the Rio Grande River, being promoted up to captain "by my superior officers being killed (successively) by bandits," his appointment as captain dated July 4, 1893. "For several years I did not expect to live to the age that I have. I expected to be killed by criminals. An officer who hunts desperate criminals has no business having a wife and family, and I have remained single." In August 1888 he arrested Catarina Garza, who started the so-called "Garza War," later arrested Charles F. Dodge, wanted at New York, and numerous other desperate men. "Unfortunately, I have been in several engagements where desperate criminals were killed. I have never lost a battle...and never let a prisoner escape. The longer I hold a prisoner the closer I watch him." Hughes never revealed how many men he had killed in line of duty but he "never

took human life except it was a case of kill or be killed." He was particularly known for his detective skills. Webb quotes an assessment by a border citizen: "Hughes had a mixed reputation. With many of those who knew him, he took a place next to McNelly amongst border captains and peace officers. Others... rated him...below Brooks and Rogers. Their charge against him was that he was susceptible of being influenced by clever stories and lacked the ability of McNelly, Brooks, and Rogers to distinguish...between the true and the false." Hughes was deeply religious, never drank or smoked or gambled. In ill health he shot himself at 92 at Austin, with his old frontier model Colt .45.

Robert N. Mullin notes; *Frontier Times,* Vol. 5, No. 1 (Oct. 1927), 4-8; Walter Prescott Webb, *The Texas Rangers.* Boston, Houghton Mifflin Co., 1935; Virgil E. Baugh, "A Pair of Texas Rangers: Bill McDonald and John Hughes." Washington, D.C., Potomac Corral of Westerners, Great Western Series, No. 9, Dec. 1970.

Hughes, Nicholas (Nick, Old Man), cattleman (c. 1843-June 16, 1920). B. in Ireland he emigrated to the United States at 15 and joined the 5th Infantry (misrepresenting his age) in 1858, re-enlisting and served through the Civil War, much of it in New Mexico. He was mustered out a corporal, November 7, 1866, at Fort Union, New Mexico. He tried ranching briefly in Old Mexico, then settled for a time in Bernalillo County, New Mexico, tried Old Mexico for a few years again, then removed to the San Simon Valley, Arizona, where he established a ranch in 1878, building a headquarters like an adobe fort, impervious to Indian or white bullets and sometimes tested by one or the other. Many desperadoes, John Ringo, Curly Bill and the like, were welcome there, as was everyone else, Hughes and his family remaining neutral in all disputes. In 1883 Hughes started a ranch at Shakespeare, New Mexico; late in the decade he sold out and began another southeast of Lordsburg, which he ultimately sold to John T. Muir. He died at a veterans' home at Los Angeles and is buried there.

Emma Marble Muir, "A Pioneer Ranch." *Around Here: the Southwest in Picture and Story,* Vol. X, No. 1 (1952), 66, 74-75, 80-83.

Hughes, Thomas Sr., borderer (d. Apr. 1778). His birthplace is unknown as is its date, but he apparently resided on the Wappatomaka, the south branch of the Potomac River in Virginia, from 1757. He removed to the Upper Monongahela River, in the trans-Allegheny region, about 1769 or 1770, and was killed on Hacker's Creek by Indians. Among the children of Thomas were Jesse, Elias and Thomas Jr., all noted scouts and Indian fighters.

Lucullus V. McWhorter, *The Border Settlers of Northwestern Virginia.* Hamilton, O., Republican Pub. Co., 1915.

Hughes, Thomas Jr., scout (c. 1754-Oct. 1837). B. possibly in present Hardy County, Virginia, he, like his famous brothers, Jesse and Elias, had an "inordinate passion for sport and adventure" and became "one of the most capable and persistent scouts on the Virginia frontier." He lived on the West Fork of the Monongahela River (Harrison County), Virginia, by 1774 and from then until 1779 he was active as a ranger under Lowther. "His consummate skill in woodcraft, his bravery and caution, soon won for him a subaltern leadership. He was subsequently commissioned a Lieutenant of Indian Spies," a position he held until 1784. He continued informal scouting activities until 1795; "as a scout Lieutenant Thomas Hughes was surpassed only by his two renowned brothers." Hughes moved to Jackson County, West Virginia, about 1795, living there until his death. Late in life his mind became "entirely gone," and although examiners agreed that "he did good service," as a scout, he was denied a pension because his work "was rendered in the Indian Wars, and not in the War of the Revolution." He was illiterate as was his brother Jesse, but that did not interfere with his functions as an officer of rangers.

Lucullus V. McWhorter, *The Border Settlers of Northwestern Virginia.* Hamilton, O., Republican Pub. Co., 1915.

Hui-shen, explorer (fl. AD 499). A Buddhist priest reached Ching-chou in southern China, reporting he had visited a land he called Fusang, 7,000 miles eastward, and provided a description of it; he also said that five mendicant priests had preceded him, reaching Fusang in AD 458, teaching the people something of their faith. The story, as related in Vol. 54 of Liang Shu (the history of the Liang Dynasty), written in the 7th century, AD, has been widely reprinted though nothing new has been added. A French specialist on China in 1761 deduced that Hui-shen had reached the west coast of America in the region of Mexico; historians are divided, although there is no reason to doubt that some voyage of the sort was possible and may well have been accomplished.

A History of the Chinese in California: A Syllabus, ed. by Thomas W. Chinn. San Francisco, Chinese Hist. Soc., 1969.

Humaña, Antonio Gutiérrez de, explorer (fl. 1593-1594). From Santa Bárbara, Nueva Vizcaya (Chihuahua), Humaña and some of his people joined Captain Francisco Leyva de Bonilla in a campaign to punish depredating Indians in the present Chihuahua. They determined thereafter to make an entrada into New Mexico although forbidden to do so by Governor Diego Fernándo de Velasco of Nueva Vizcaya. Humaña and Leyva nonetheless went up the Rio Grande to San Ildefonso, one of the Tewa towns about 25 miles north of the present Santa Fe. After about a year they went eastward through the towns of the Pecos and Vaquero Indians to the buffalo plains, then worked northeastward toward Quivira. They crossed two large rivers and passed through sizable rancherias (Bolton thinks near today's Wichita, Kansas) where the houses were made of poles and straw. A disagreement arose between Humaña and Leyva over some unreported matter and one afternoon Humaña killed Leyva with a knife, then took command of the expedition whose size is unreported. Not long afterward the Indians reportedly destroyed Humaña and his men, the only survivors being five Indians who escaped, three becoming lost on the plains, two reaching the New Mexico pueblos where one was slain and the only survivor, Jusepe being interviewed in 1601 by Oñate.

George P. Hammond, Agapito Rey, *The Rediscovery of New Mexico, 1580-1594.* Albuquerque, Univ. of New Mex. Press, 1966; Herbert Eugene Bolton, *Spanish Exploration in the Southwest, 1552-1706.* N. Y., Charles Scribner's Sons, 1916.

Hump (Etokeah), Miniconjou Sioux chief (c. 1848-Dec. 1908). One of the most hostile of the non-treaty Sioux, Hump was chief of the Miniconjous and as such had a leading role in the December 1866 fight against Fetterman in

Wyoming when 81 whites were killed above Fort Phil Kearny. In 1876 he again was prominent in the Custer fight on the Little Bighorn although his horse was killed and he was wounded early in the battle and so, he said, "I did not get in the final fight." Graham reprints Hump's narrative of the engagement as he saw it. Afterward Hump and his people numbering about 550, accompanied Sitting Bull to Canada and "were among the last who surrendered to (American) authorities." A historian remarked that "Hump and his sub-chiefs were most jealous of their rights as headmen and strictly adhered to all of the old-time customs... Long after all of the other Indians had adopted citizens' dress they adhered to the breech cloth and the blanket, kept up the heathen dances, wore long hair and lived in the old fashioned, clustered villages." In company with many Sioux, Hump and his band were enthused by the Ghost Dance movement of the late 1880s. However when army Captain Ezra P. Ewers, an old friend, pointed out that armed resistance would be futile, Hump carefully separated his band from the dancers and retired to Pine Ridge Agency, a safe distance away. He refused to join those who wished to retaliate for the slaying of Sitting Bull. After the Wounded Knee debacle of December 29, 1890, Hump and some other chiefs went to Washington, D.C., where they sought relaxation of restrictive policies, but were not completely successful. Hump died on Cherry Creek, a tributary to the Cheyenne River of South Dakota and was buried in the Episcopal Cemetery near there.

Dockstader; W.A Graham, *The Custer Myth: A Source Book of Custeriana.* Harrisburg Pa., Stackpole Co., 1957; Doane Robinson, *A History of the Sioux Indians.* Minneapolis, Ross & Haines, 1956.

Humphries, John, Mormon pioneer (fl. 1855-1892). Humphries appears to have worked at an iron foundry in southern Utah where on January 1, 1855, he was "almost suffocated" by coke fumes, and was "semi-buried" to clear his lungs by breathing "in the fresh turned up earth." *Mormonism Unveiled* places him at the scene of the Mountain Meadows Massacre of September 11, 1857, either participating in or consenting to the tragedy. The book, published in 1892, reported him then living at Cedar City, Utah.   .

Journal of the Southern Indian Mission, ed. by Juanita Brooks. Logan, Utah State Univ. Press, 1972; *Mormonism Unveiled,* 379.

Hunt, Alexander Cameron, lawman, politician (Dec. 25, 1825-May 24, 1894). B. in New York State he reached Denver in 1859 and in June 1862 was appointed United States Marshal for the District of Colorado. He testified March 15, 1865, at Washington, D.C., on the Sand Creek Massacre although he had not been present and spoke only of what he had learned at Denver from participants. He said many of the 100-day men of the 3rd Colorado Cavalry did not know what Indians they were fighting, or why they were attacking them until after the action when white civilians informed them. They "killed everything alive in the camp that they could get at. I believe that was part of the understanding, that none should be spared." Hunt said he and others "always regarded Black Kettle and White Antelope as the special friends of the white man" and knew of no hostile acts by them. He thought Chivington's motive in leading the attack was "hope of promotion" as had happened to Carson, Harney and others. Hunt was appointed governor of Colorado by President Johnson in May 1867, serving until June 1869. He became interested in railroads and proprietor of one line, sometimes riding "100 miles a day on horseback, superintending railroad work." He became interested in coal mines near Laredo, Texas, and Mexican railroads but retained his principal residence at Denver. He died at Chicago.

Sand Creek Massacre; Bancroft, *Nevada, Colorado & Wyoming.*

Hunt, Richard (Zwing, Zweig), desperado (1858-May 31, 1882?). B. in Washington County, or perhaps Bosque County, Texas, he reached Arizona with Billy Boucher (Grounds) by about 1880 and became associated with Brocius and other free spirits in eastern Arizona and western New Mexico. He was suspected of rustling and believed implicated in the killing in a robbery at Charleston, Arizona, of a son of Judge B. L. Peel of Tombstone; Hunt and Grounds on March 29, 1882, were surprised at the Chandler ranch near Tombstone. In a resulting shootout, an officer and Grounds were killed and Hunt, wounded through a lung, was taken to a Tombstone hospital, from which he escaped April 27 with the aid of a relative, Hugh Hunt.

Hugh said that after fleeing they had had a battle with Indians, Zwing was killed and Hugh had buried him in the Dragoon Mountains; this was possible for the Loco campaign was then underway. It was also reported, however, that Zwing returned to San Antonio, Texas, and thereafter led a law-abiding life. On June 10, 1882, the Tombstone *Epitaph* reported that Zwing Hunt "was a child of circumstances and a creature of excitement. Generous to a fault, rash to the extremity of foolishness, and as brave as an Arabian fire-worshipper...Zwing would do to go tiger hunting with...."

Ed Bartholomew, *Wyatt Earp: the Man & The Myth.* Toyahvale, Tex., Frontier Book Co., 1964; Bartholomew, *Western Hard-Cases,* pp. 82-84. Ruidoso, N.M., Frontier Book Co.,1960; Bartholomew, *Biographical Album of Western Gunfighters.* Houston, Tex., Frontier Press of Tex., 1958.

Hunt, Theodore, naval officer, fur trader (1782-Jan. 21, 1832). B. at Trenton, New Jersey, he was a cousin of Wilson Price Hunt. He became a Navy midshipman at 16 and as a lieutenant took part in the war with the Barbary Pirates. He resigned from the Navy, perhaps because of illness, in 1811 and at St. Louis in 1814 became a partner of Manuel Lisa, making one brief trip up the Missouri for trade. Thereafter he resided at St. Louis where he is buried.

E. Lee Dorsett article, MM, Vol. IV.

Hunt, Thomas, sea captain (fl. 1614). Hunt commanded a ship under Captain John Smith which visited the New England coast in 1614; here he was left behind by Smith with instructions to make up a cargo of fish and beaver pelts and return it to Europe. Hunt believed there would be more profit in slaves, and ruthlessly seized seven from the Nauset tribe of Cape Cod and 20 from Patuxet on the site of Plymouth, Massachusetts. He took these hapless people to Málaga, Spain, selling them for 20 pounds sterling apiece, most disappearing from view. Friars brought a few to Christianize, among them Tisquantum, the later Squanto, who managed to escape to England before returning as an interpreter to New England. Hunt's vicious deed had far-reaching repercussions; for years Indians along the Massachusetts coast were inveterately hostile to traders and fishermen and many casualties were caused although later they became friendly with Plymouth colonists and cooperated faithfully with them.

Almon Wheeler Lauber, *Indian Slavery in Colonial Times.* Williamstown, Mass., Corner House Pubrs., 1979; Hodge, HAI; Sylvester; George F. Willison, *Saints and Strangers.* N. Y. , Reynal & Hitchcock, 1945.

Hunt, Wilson Price, fur trader (Mar. 20, 1783-Apr. 13, 1842). B. at Asbury, New Jersey, he became a St. Louis merchant at 21 and in 1809 met with John Jacob Astor concerning the latter's scheme for a northwestern fur empire. Hunt became leader of the overland Astorians and was to take charge of the Columbia River post where the project would center. The land party left St. Louis late in 1810, wintering a few miles below the junction of Missouri, Kansas and Nebraska. The group left up the river April 21, 1811, engaging in a "race" of sorts with Manuel Lisa of a competing company for the last few hundred miles to the Arikara villages. The overland party, leaving the Mandan villages, reached the Big Horn in late August, the Green River and then the Snake. An attempt to negotiate the river in dugouts proved impracticable. After great hardships, and the splintering of his party with the loss of some personnel by mishap and otherwise, Hunt reached the Columbia January 21, 1812, and Astoria February 15. Hunt now learned of the loss of the *Tonquin,* the ship which brought the other half of the enterprise to the Oregon coast, but concentrated trapping was underway, nonetheless. Aboard a second supply ship, the *Beaver,* Hunt visited the Russian governor, Count Baranoff, at Sitka, picked up 75,000 seal skins at the Pribilof Islands and sent them to Canton, himself remaining on the Hawaiian Islands where he chartered another ship, the *Albatross,* to return to Astoria. His British-Canadian colleagues, aware of the War of 1812 now underway, sold Astoria to the North West Company in Hunt's absence; duplicity seems obvious. Hunt, indignant, finalized the sale and left by sea for China, reaching New York at last in 1816 and St. Louis in 1817. He settled there for the rest of his life, and died at that city.

Literature abundant; Washington Irving, *Astoria,* many editions; DAB; William Brandon article, MM, Vol. VI.

Hunter, Bill, desperado (d. Feb. 3, 1864). Hunter was an unusual sort of desperado, alternating outlawry with honest labor in the mines or anywhere else to pick up a dollar; he had many friends among honest men, and a number continued to respect him far beyond his demise. He was a member of the Montana Plummer gang, had robbed and assisted in murdering at least one traveler, was a "roadster," and had become a desperado so long previously that Red Yager even accused him of drawing Yager into outlawry, thus earning a special enmity from Red. When the five Plummer desperadoes had been picked up and hanged at Virginia City, Montana, January 14, 1864, Hunter slipped through the encircling net with help from some vigilantes who refused to believe him guilty of anything, according to report. He escaped to the Gallatin valley of Montana. Here he was finally accosted by vigilantes and taken to a tree for execution. There being no drop immediately available, several of the accusers grabbed the loose end of the rope that had been swung over a limb and together ran with it to jerk Hunter upward into eternity. It was reported that in his final contortions, although clearly unconscious, he had freed one arm, symbolized the drawing of a revolver and the cocking and shooting of it six times.

Dimsdale; Langford.

Hunter, George, Mormon pioneer (Mar. 20, 1828-post 1892). A resident of Cedar City, southern Utah, he and other militiamen were charged with mutinous conduct in 1853 when they threatened with arms those who sought to take their "surplus" cattle to Salt Lake City on Brigham Young's orders; this charge apparently was dismissed. *Mormonism Unveiled* places Hunter at the scene of the Mountain Meadows Massacre of September 11, 1857, either aiding in or consenting to the tragedy. The book listed him as of Cedar City in 1892.

Journal of the Southern Indian Mission, ed. by Juanita Brooks. Logan, Utah State Univ. Press, 1972, 70-71, Appendix VI, 155-59; *Mormonism Unveiled,* 379.

Hunter, John Dunn, captive, frontiersman (c. 1797-c. Feb. 1, 1828). By Hunter's narrative, he was seized probably by Kickapoo Indians from some frontier situation at an age too early to permit recollection of his parents or the circumstances, then was acquired successively by Pawnees, Kansas and Osage Indians, maturing among the latter and becoming more Indian than white. During his extended life among the latter tribe he became a full-fledged warrior, taking at least one scalp, journeying with other men of the band on hunting and war trips and making two extended journeys that somewhat tax credulity: one of about a year and one-half to the Pacific in the region of the mouth of the Columbia; the second from the Mandan country to near the source of the Mississippi during which winter hardships almost did in the party, but at last it regained the Osage villages. There is evidence both for and against accepting these accounts as basically genuine. Hunter eventually returned to the white settlements in 1816 initially to warn a trader, George P. Watkins of an attempt to be made upon him by drunken Osages; gradually he came to absorb and develop his white inheritance, became something of a fur and produce trader on the lower Mississippi and, having gained a rudimentary education, journeyed east to perfect it at Philadelphia and other cities where he wrote his *Memoirs of a Captivity Among the Indians of North America* (1823, with subsequent editions). Something of a success on both sides of the Atlantic, Hunter traveled to London where he spent the winter of 1823-24, "the *Lion* of the fashionable world." He was presented at court and won the attention of many prominent men and societies. He returned with the notion of somehow preserving and ameliorating the fate of his Indian friends threatened as he believed by debauchery and extermination at the hands of the spreading white societies. He visited Thomas Jefferson, who was convinced of his integrity and the reality of his adventures, and proceeded down the Ohio to the Mississippi, settling among a colony of Cherokees in desperate straits 50 miles above Nacogdoches. He went to Mexico City to gain for them recognition of their land titles. Here, early in 1826, he broached the proposition to encourage colonization of the northern Spanish frontier by some 30,000 Indians. He argued they would prove a bulwark against the expected influx of American settlers who could only strike for independence from Spain or Mexico when strong enough to do so. His proposed establishment of the Republic of Fredonia, caused something of a diplomatic furore, with the British generally favorable, the Americans opposed, and the Mexicans uncertain. Stephen Austin, as was to be expected, stoutly opposed the notion and wrote Hunter to that effect, being largely instrumental in crushing the short-lived "state." Hunter's associate, Richard Fields, a halfbreed Cherokee chief, was murdered, as was Hunter mainly, it is suspected, through the machinations of a soldier of fortune, Peter Ellis Bean, and others at the instigation of Austin. Hunter's book had proven controversial, perhaps because it presented in a most favorable light the culture and mores of the wild Indians in an age when to most Americans they were vermin, and presented the white border culture by contrast in an unfavorable light when most Americans considered it the vanguard of an enlightened society. His book was attacked by such informed individuals as William Clark and Pierre Chouteau, the less knowledgeable Lewis Cass, and others; it was defended by Catlin and Jefferson and has been freely used by such Indians specialists as Clark Wissler, Frederick Hodge and various students. In the introduction to a 1973 edition, Richard Drinnon, its editor, sums up the evidence and concludes, "I believe Hunter to have been an honest man." Drinnon rather overstates his case at times, but on balance his is a judicious and informed view. Hunter was short, swarthy, strongly-built, of amiable and grave disposition.

John Dunn Hunter, *Memoirs of a Captivity Among the Indians of North America*, ed. by Richard Drinnon. N. Y., Schocken Books, 1973.

Huntington, Dimmick B., Mormon pioneer (May 26, 1808-Feb. 1, 1879). B. at Watertown, New York, he became a convert to Mormonism and reached Utah July 28, 1847, with the Mormon Battalion veterans. He became a high priest of the church and served as an Indian missionary for 40 years, being also an Indian interpreter and farmer. According to Carleton's *Report* on the Mountain Meadows Massacre, a Paiute chief named Touche, in the 1870's living on the Virgin River, reported receiving a letter in the summer of 1857 from Brigham Young to the effect that "the emigrants were to be killed," the letter brought to him by Huntington. Huntington, an early settler of Provo, Utah, was living at Salt Lake City at the time Carleton compiled his report. According to Wise, "the shadowy, elusive Huntington was a member of the inner circle" around Young, and Young's key Indian man when conducting business with the "Laman-

ites." His role and participation, if any, in the massacre itself is unclear.

Frank Esshom, *Pioneers and Prominent Men of Utah*. Salt Lake City, Western Epics, 1966; William Wise, *Massacre of Mountain Meadows*. N. Y., Thomas Y. Crowell Co., 1976.

Hurley, John, cowboy (1848-Jan. 25, 1885). John Hurley was a cowboy who was often mixed up in Lincoln County War events in New Mexico, sometimes being employed by the House—i.e., the Murphy-Dolan faction. He lived on the Ruidoso before the troubles and had a small farm. Hurley was a member of the posse which murdered Tunstall, one of the Mathews force which ambushed Frank McNab on April 29, 1878, attended the Five Days' Battle at Lincoln in July 1878 and was present at Stinking Springs when Billy the Kid was captured December 21, 1880. Hurley, who operated a saloon just off post limits at Fort Stanton in 1880, also was a deputy to Pat Garrett, Lincoln County sheriff, that year. In 1885 he was deputy to Sheriff John Poe. He was killed with Jasper Corn by Nicolas Aragon when Aragon was attempting to escape jail through a hole in the roof.

Robert N. Mullin notes; "Frank Warner Angel's Notes on New Mexico Territory 1878," ed. by Lee Scott Theisen. *Arizona and the West*, Vol. 18, No. 4 (Winter 1976), 354.

Hurricane Bill: *see* William A. Martin

Hurst, John scout (c. 1847-Apr. 19, 1920). B. probably at Ogdensburg, New York, he reached California, enlisting at La Porte, August 16, 1861, in Company F, 1st California Infantry, which arrived at Yuma January 1, 1862, and marched by way of Tucson and Apache Pass to the Rio Grande, being stationed principally at Fort Craig and scouting for hostile Apaches in Socorro County and elsewhere in New Mexico. Hurst was mustered out August 31, 1864, at Los Pinos, New Mexico, and with other veterans accompanied a wagon train returning empty to Fort Leavenworth from Fort Union. He hired out as a teamster and hauled freight to frontier posts "with more or less scrimmages with the Indians." Hurst was one of Forsyth's scouts at Beecher Island, his story appearing in *The Battle of Beecher Island*, pp. 39-44. After the engagement, Hurst went to Fort Harker (Ellsworth), Kansas, and worked as wagonmaster hauling goods and supplies for two years. In 1870 he joined the Hays City, Kansas, police force, but was shot and crippled by one George Clinton, who was hanged by vigilantes for the incident. Hurst, when well enough to travel, journeyed to his home at Ogdensburg; in 1873 he went to Renville County, Minnesota, returned to Ogdensburg, went back to Minnesota in 1881, but in 1900 returned to Ogdensburg for good. He was notably religious. Hurst died at Ogdensburg.

Battle of Beecher Island..., Wray, Colorado, Beecher Island Battle Memorial Assn., 1961; information from Mary H. Smallman, Canton, N.Y., St. Lawrence County (N.Y.) Historian.

Huse, Guy Evans, army officer (c. 1855-Apr. 30, 1893). B. in New York, Huse was graduated from West Point and joined the 4th Cavalry in 1879. He saw service with Wirt Davis in the Geronimo war of 1885-86, but resigned for reasons of health September 1, 1886. He became major of engineers in the Army of Chile and later a railroad engineer, working on the Tehuantepec Railroad of Mexico and other Latin rail routes. He died in Guatemala.

Heitman; Cullum.

Hutton, Oscar, scout, Indian man (c. 1833-c. 1873). B. in Virginia, he reached California in 1850, spending the rest of his life "on the frontier and in Indian country." Hutton was literate and examples of his writing are extant. Bourke wrote of him that "Hutton had had a wonderful experience in the meanest parts of our great country... All over the great interior basin west of the Rockies Hutton had wandered in the employ of the United States with some of the Government surveying parties...(He) had seen so much of hardship that it was natural to expect him to be meek and modest in his ideas and demeanor, but he was, on the contrary, decidedly vain and conceited," as about the fact that he had six toes on each foot, more than any other man of his acquaintance. Hutton, whom Bourke termed "a good and brave man," had reached Arizona during the Civil War and November 3, 1865, was commissioned second lieutenant and commanding officer of Company F, Arizona Volunteers, a largely Mexican outfit stationed at Camp Date Creek and in Skull Valley, near Prescott from where he scouted and fought hostile Indians for about a year. His command originally numbered 85 men, but soon dwindled to 35. February 24, 1866, two of his rangers were lost to Indian action. In August with 14 of his men and 12 citizens Hutton attacked about 70 Indians who had raided a wagon train, killing 23 with a loss of one man killed and another wounded. His men always were short of basic supplies and operated often under extreme hardships. The rangers were mustered out in the fall of 1866. Hutton became post guide at Fort Grant, Arizona, about 1868; from this time he ably guided and scouted for Cushing and other officers, taking part in long expeditions and several significant engagements, reporting that he had "perhaps seen as much active service against the Indians as any man living in Arizona." He was with Whitman when Aravaipa Apaches began to come into Fort Grant where they were rationed and settled a few miles from the post in Whitman's attempt to bring peace to the region. "I acted as Spanish interpreter at nearly every talk with them," he stated. "I have never seen Indians on a reservation, or at peace about a military post under so good subjection, so well satisfied and happy, or more teachable and obedient than were these.... I was repeatedly requested to watch every indication of anything like treachery on their part, and I will give it as my deliberate judgment, that no raiding party was ever made up from the Indians fed at this post." His statement was taken following the Camp Grant massacre of more than 100 of these Indians by a Tucson raiding party of Anglos, Mexicans and Papago Indians in April 1871. A mule kick crushed Hutton's jaw and he never recovered from the shock, dying, as Bourke supposed, "quite as much from chagrin at being outwitted as from the injury inflicted." He left his widow of Mexican birth and a son. His year of death is conjecture.

Bourke, *On Border;* Farish, IV: U.S. Census for Ariz., 1870; *U.S. Board of Indian Commissioners. Peace with the Apaches of New Mexico and Arizona. Report of Vincent Colyer, Member of Board— 1871.* Wash., Govt. Printing Office, 1872.

Huvé, Alexandre, priest (fl. 1704-1727). A French secular priest, he was named assistant to the Mobile, Alabama, parish in 1704 and in addition did missionary work among the Apalachee refugees who had fled from the English colonies to the Gulf coast. The Jesuit Gravier, perhaps with prejudice, described him in 1708 as one "who Knows not a single word in the Savage tongue, although he has been here 4 years," adding that although a missionary to the Apalachees "he Knows not a word of their language, and he hears confessions, baptizes, marries, and administers Communion and extreme unction, Without understanding the savages...The Apalaches have driven him away twice, — both because he does not learn their language, and because he is very particular about his food, for they...feed him." He was in charge of the Mobile parish from 1710 until 1721 and it was reported that "he struggled on for some years, till having become almost blind, he returned to France in 1727."

Thwaites, JR, LXVI, 131, 342-43 n28.

Hyde, George, E., Plains Indian historian (June 10, 1882-Feb. 2, 1968). B. at Omaha where he lived all his life, Hyde early became interested in Plains history, although partially blind and totally deaf by 20, taking up writing "as about the only thing I could do." He became acquainted with Indians initially in 1898 when Omaha was host to the Trans-Mississippi Exposition; he went to their camps, earned their trust and deepened his interest. In 1912 he was hired as assistant to George Bird Grinnell, then working on the Cheyenne tribe, and played a major role in the assembly and writing of Grinnell's *The Fighting Cheyennes* (1915) and later Indian books. Because of his handicaps, Hyde did much of his research by correspondence and through the assistance of friends, and established lifelong relationships with such people as George Bent. He depended upon the staff at the Omaha Public Library to obtain published material on loan and in his later years friends and associates transcribed manuscript materials at the National Archives and other repositories for him. His first book, written with George F. Will of Fargo, North Dakota, a correspondent of half a century whom Hyde never met, was *Corn Among the Indians of the Upper Missouri* (1917). He wrote *Rangers and Regulars* (1933); *The Early Blackfeet and Their Neighbors* (1933); *The Pawnee Indians* (1934, 1951, 1973); *Red Cloud's Folk: A History of the Oglala Sioux Indians* (1937-1957); *A Sioux Chronicle* (1956); *Indians of the High Plains* (1959); *Spotted Tail's Folk: A History of the Brulé Sioux* (1961): *Indians of the Woodlands* (1962), and *Life of George Bent: Written from His Letters,* ed. by Savoie Lottinville (1968). He died of cancer at 84.

John Dishon McDermott, "George E. Hyde: 1882-1968." *Arizona and the West,* Vol. 17, No.2 (Summer 1975), 103-06.

Hyde, Richard W., stockman (Nov. 22, 1840-Apr. 18, 1914). His place of birth is not reported but by the 1850s he was a freighter, hauling goods from Nebraska City to Denver late that decade. Thereafter he was a stockman in Montana, buying cattle at Salt Lake City and driving it north to his range. In this occupation he was associated at times with William F. Drannan, a frontiersman known principally for his yarn-spinning and embellishments upon his career. Hyde settled finally at Mineral Wells, Texas, where he died, to be buried next to Drannan.

W.N. Bate, "Frontier Legend." *Old West,* Vol. 8, No. 3 (Spring 1972), 6-15, 32-42, 52.

I

Iberville: *see* Le Moyne, sieur d'Iberville, Pierre

Ietan, Oto chief (d. Apr. 1837). Said to have been the son of Big Horse (Shonga-tonga) his name may come from some exploit against the Ietan tribe, the name for the Comanches or some other Plains people. Ietan's Indian name was Shamonekusse or Shongmunecuthe, meaning prairie wolf, or coyote. In 1821-22 he accompanied a deputation of chiefs to the East; they reportedly tried to count the people of New York by means of notched sticks, but quickly gave that up as hopeless. He died from a wound inflicted while pursuing some young braves who had seduced two of his wives. Ietan was known among his people for wit, sagacity and warlike prowess.

Thwaites, EWT, XIV, 232n.

Ieuch, Henry (Dutch Henry, Henry Stewart), rustler (d. Jan. 9, 1910). Not much is known of the birth or early life of Dutch Henry Ieuch, who sometimes is confused with Dutch Henry Born (see entry), but who rustled horses and roamed the upper Great Plains and southern Canada in the early 1900s whereas Born had operated farther south. "To his friends, Dutch Henry Ieuch was a good-natured, amiable man, who was generous to a fault. To others he was a tough, virtueless renegade," as Walker reported. Ieuch operated with a gang of horsethieves who freed him from a Culbertson, Montana jail and fled aboard the sheriff's horse which he ultimately sold to a Canadian Mounted policeman from whom the sheriff had to buy him back. A member of the gang, Alex McKenzie was alleged to have killed Dutch Henry in Roseau County, Minnesota in April 1906 on the basis of flimsy identification of a disfigured corpse; McKenzie was sentenced to life. Mounted Police however reported that they killed Dutch Henry in 1910 about 60 miles south of Moose Jaw, Saskatchewan, and this report generally was credited. McKenzie was pardoned October 25, 1913.

Wayne T. Walker, "Born and Ieuch: The Two Dutch Henrys." *Real West,* Vol. 26, No. 193 (Oct. 1983), 46-47, 52-54.

Ignace la Mousse (Old Ignace), Iroquois Christian leader (d. 1837). Educated at Caughnawaga, a Christian station for Iroquois and Canadian Indians he went to the Rocky Mountains between 1812 and 1820 to work for either the North West Company or the Hudson's Bay Company as a trapper. Ignace married into the Flatheads among whom he settled, teaching the people what he knew or remembered of his religious training under Canadian Catholics. In 1835 he undertook a mission to secure a Black Robe (Jesuit) from Canada to instruct his Flathead people, but hearing that the Jesuits also were at St. Louis he went there, taking along two sons to be baptized, but no Jesuit was able to accompany him home again. In 1837 he headed a second delegation, but on the South Platte his party was overrun by Sioux who initially dismissed Ignace because he was dressed like a white man. He was unwilling to forsake his companions however, declared himself an Indian whereupon, after a brave defense, all of his party including himself were slain. In 1840 his son, Young Ingatius who had remained at Westport after the initial trek, accompanied De Smet back to the Flatheads.

Thwaites, EWT, XXVI, 230n.

Ignacio, Wiminuche Ute chief (1828-Dec. 9, 1913). B. in the southwestern Colorado San Juan country he became a chief of the Wiminuche band of Utes of that region, but whether a hereditary chief or he earned the title by merit is unreported. His father was a noted medicine man. Gradually he assumed more authority and by the death of Ouray in 1880 became chief of all the southern Utes. He refused to be drawn into the so-called Ute War of 1879, remaining aloof and keeping his people quiet, for he ever was a peace-loving leader. He died at Ignacio (population about

600) named for him and the site of tribal headquarters for the Southern Ute Reservation. Located southeast of Durango, Colorado, it is the home for people of the Wiminuche, Mouache and Capote Ute bands and was established in 1873.

Dockstaker; *Federal and State Indian Reservations.* Wash., U.S. Dept. of Commerce, 1974.

Ih-tedda (Katie Cross Eyes), Apache (1851-probably pre-1940). Her name is said to mean "Young Girl," and Ih-tedda met Geronimo at San Carlos in 1877-78, though not then as his wife. She did not join the exudos of the Geronimo hostiles in May of 1885, but remained on the Fort Apache Reservation, Arizona. In November 1885, Geronimo and Perico stole her and another to replace wives captured by troops. Ih-tedda, as his seventh wife, surrendered with Geronimo September 3, 1886, was shipped to Florida, thence to Alabama, and gave birth to a daughter, Lenna, and a son, Robert, who became Robert Geromimo although there is some doubt who was the father. About 1890 Ih-tedda returned to the Mescalero Reservation in New Mexico, where she married Old Cross Eyes, a former army scout, and became known as Katie Cross Eyes.

Griswold; correspondence, Eve Ball with author.

Ilges, Guido Joseph Julius, army officer (Nov. 10, 1835-Jan. 13, 1918). B. in Ahrweiler, Coblenz, Prussia, he became an attorney at Vincennes, Indiana, and served in General Jim Lanes's "Frontier Guards" in the defense of Washington, D.C., in March and April 1861 until Lincoln disbanded the organization which never had been part of the formal military establishment. Ilges then was commissioned a captain of the 14th Infantry and came out of the Civil War with brevets to lieutenant colonel for gallantry with the Army of the Potomac. He was sent to Arizona where he was active in scouting and operations against hostile Indians. In 1865 he was at Camp Grant. In 1867 he effected the release of a captive boy from the Apaches and adopted Ernest Amelung, sending him to San Francisco to live with Ilges's aunt until the child's relatives could be located; Amelung was found to have an uncle in Germany and went to live with him. Ilges on April 3, 1867 led a scout against Apaches in the Tonto Basin; March 25, 1868, he had a fight with hostiles at

Cottonwood Springs. He became a major of the 7th Infantry December 10, 1873. September 25, 1877, with a company of infantrymen and citizen volunteers Ilges fought the Nez Perce of Chief Joseph at Cow Creek Canyon, Montana, taking light casualties. He might have held the Nez Perce until Howard came up with his forces had they been stronger; rather he retired to Cow Island and let the Indians go on to Bear Paw Mountain. October 22, 1878, with troops from Fort Benton, Montana, which he then commanded, Ilges captured a camp of 35 metís, or half-breeds from the Red River of Canada, and sent them home. Ilges transferred to the 5th Infantry in December 1879. December 5, 1880 with five companies of his regiment he moved through bitter weather from Fort Keogh to Camp Poplar River, Montana. January 2, 1881 with a command of about 300 officers and men he attacked a strong camp of Sioux on the other side of the Missouri, killing eight and forcing about 300 to surrender; January 9 about 20 additional were captured and January 29 some 64 others taken, all without casualities to the troops save severe frostbite because of the savage weather. Among the captured was the great Sioux chief, Gall, who had participated in the Custer fight on the Little Big Horn River, Montana five years earlier; Iron Dog, another noted war leader, also was taken. February 12, 1881, Ilges reported arresting 185 hostile Sioux in a Yankton camp at Redwater, Montana. February 6, 1882, Ilges became lieutenant colonel of the 18th Infantry. He was dismissed from the service after a court martial October 31, 1883 (for financial irregularities, although no dishonesty was involved), and moved to Cincinnati, Ohio, where he was a journalist with local German-language newspapers for 18 years and weightmaster at a hay market for 15 years. In 1912 he received a visitor: Ernest Amelung whom he had rescued from the Apaches 45 years earlier. Amelung had returned to the United States at 22 and was then interpreter for the War Department. Ilges came on very hard times in his advanced age. He applied for a pension in 1917, stressing that he was crippled from injuries, nearly blind and with no resources and must go to a poorhouse unless a pension were granted. At length he was given $30 a month; the check for $90 for the last three months of his life was returned uncashed — it had arrived a few days after his death. When he joined the army in 1861 he was listed as 6 feet, 2 1/2 inches in height, with a dark complexion, brown eyes and black hair.

Heitman; *Chronological List; Record of Engagements;* W.A. Graham, *The Custer Myth.* Harrisburg, Pa., Stackpole Co., 1957, 89; *Winners of the West,* Nov. 30, 1935; Ilges pension record, Nat. Archives.

Illingworth, William H., photographer (1884-c. Mar.17, 1893). B. in England, he was brought to Philadelphia as a child and in 1850 to St. Paul, Minnesota. At 20 William Illingworth studied photography at Chicago. In 1866 he accompanied the Fisk emigrant expedition to Montana, the 30 stereoscopic pictures he produced forming the basis for a studio-gallery he opened at St.Paul in 1867. He recorded many views of early times in Minnesota, the collection now largely at the Minnesota Historical Society. Illingworth accompanied and photographed the 1874 Custer expedition to the Black Hills, securing about 70 dramatic and valuable pictures of its progress and its work. Most of them are held by the South Dakota State Historical Society. Married three times, his first two wives died, he divorced the third and shortly afterward shot himself, by one account because of ill health.

Herbert Krause, Gary D. Olson, *Prelude to Glory.* Sioux Falls, S.D., Brevet Press, 1974; Henry Wall, "Restless, Troubled Opportunist: Portrait of a Pioneer Photographer." *Ramsey County History,* Vol. IV, No. 1 (Jan. 1968), 9-11.

Imoda, John Baptist Camillus, Jesuit priest, missionary (Nov. 29, 1829-June 17, 1886). B. at Turin, Italy, he was assigned to Montana Indian missions in 1859 at the age of 30, reaching Montana by way of California after rounding Cape Horn in a sailing vessel from Italy. He learned the Blackfoot language and preached in it. Following the fight January 23, 1870, of brevet Colonel E.M. Baker and the Piegans on the Marias River, Montana, Imoda went to the Piegan camp on the Belly River in Canada, persuaded them to make a "lasting peace" with the Americans, and April 11, 1870, reported on the success of his talks to brevet Major General Alfred Sully. In 1873 he came under supervision of the newly-formed Bureau of Catholic Indian Missions, Washington, D.C. Imoda was paid tribute for bravely going among Indians during a smallpox epidemic "when no other dared to do so." Under administrative decision of the Grant administration, Imoda and other Catholic missionaries were barred from working with the Blackfeet, although he wrote a strong protest against the decision to J.B.A. Brouillet, director of the Bureau of Catholic Indian Missions. He died at Helena at the residence of Bishop John B. Brondel.

Francis J. Weber, "Grant's Peace Policy: A Catholic Dissenter," *Montana,* Vol. XIX, No. 1 (Winter 1969), 56-63; Robert J. Ege, *Strike Them Hard!* Bellevue, Neb., Old Army Press, 1970.

Indian Annie, character (d. 1883). Annie lived in a shack behind the Grand Central Hotel, Ellsworth, Kansas, in 1867, becoming associated with James Butler (Wild Bill) Hickok and considered by some his wife; if so she was a common law wife. She later married Ben Wilson and they had a daughter, Birdie; after Wilson died Annie supported herself and daughter with odd jobs and fortune telling. Annie died in a home for the indigent, presumably at Ellsworth.

Joseph G. Rosa, *They Called Him Wild Bill,* 2nd ed. Norman, Univ. of Okla. Press, 1974.

Indian Charley: *see* Florentino Cruz

Indian George (Bah-Vanda-Sava-Nu-Kee), Panamint chief (c. 1843-1943). B. in Death Valley, California, he could recall the Jayhawker wagon train laboring through in 1849 although he was "just a boy" at the time. He matured to earn fame as a guide for surveyors, prospectors and bighorn sheep hunters in the Panamint and nearby ranges. He early took the name of a Dr. S.G. George, a lost-mine seeker who came through the Indian country and perhaps was guided by the chief, who became known thereafter as Indian George; later he assumed the last name of Hanson. He always was for peace with the whites. He is supposed to have guided two prospectors who made the noted silver discovery in the Panamints, although George did not share their wealth. When he died aged about 100 he was buried in a secret unmarked site in the Panamint Range of his people.

Roberta M. Starry, "Indian George — Most Famous Guide and Scout of the Panamint Tribe." *True West,* Vol. 27, No.3 (Jan.-Feb. 1980), 34-36, 60-61.

Ingalls, Rufus, army officer (c. 1820-Jan. 15, 1893). B. in Maine, he went to West Point and was commissioned a brevet second lieutenant in the Rifles July 1, 1843, and a second lieutenant of the 1st Dragoons March 17, 1845. He did frontier duty at Fort Jesup southwest of Natchitoches, Louisiana in 1843-45 and was at Fort Leavenworth in 1845-46 and in the Mexican War in 1846-47, winning a brevet for the fights at Embudo and Taos, New Mexico. Ingalls became a first lieutenant February 16, 1847. He served in California in 1848-49, at Fort Vancouver, Washington, 1849-52 and at Fort Yuma, California, in 1853. He was on brevet Lieutenant Colonel Edward Steptoe's expedition across the continent by way of Great Salt Lake to Washington Territory from 1854-56, remaining in the northwest until 1861. Ingalls emerged from the Civil War a Brigadier General of Volunteers and army lieutenant colonel and most of his subsequent service was in the Quartermaster Department. He became Brigadier General and the Quartermaster General February 23, 1882, and retired July 1, 1883. He died at New York City.

Cullum; Heitman; Powell.

Ingraham, Prentiss, soldier of fortune, writer (Dec. 22, 1843-Aug. 16, 1904). B. in Adams County, Mississippi, he was well educated, served in the Civil War, in Withers' Mississippi Regiment of light artillery as a lieutenant, and was commander of scouts in Ross's Brigade, Texas Cavalry, being once captured and twice wounded. After the war he fought with Juarez in Mexico, for Austria in a war with Prussia, in Crete, in Africa and in a Cuban unsuccessful 10-year struggle for independence. His adventures and extensive travels gave him material for approximately 1,000 dime novels and other writings including numerous plays, short stories and even poems. He was one of the most prolific of Beadle and Adams stable of dime novelists. He did far more to promote the career of Buffalo Bill than Buntline. His first play to be enacted by Cody was in 1879, something called "The Knight of the Plains; or, Buffalo Bill's Best Trail," a production in which Cody appeared from coast to coast. Ingraham was still writing Buffalo Bill stories at his death, in 1904, and it is said produced more than 200 of them. He also wrote of Texas Jack Omohundro and others, and books signed by such notables as their own work. In his spare time he acted as press agent for Cody's Wild West show, but he won greatest notice by his unending stream of novels which, while "without distinction, are written in a surprisingly correct and easy fashion and are wholesome in their general teachings." One of his plays ran for several years. Ingraham was married, fathered three children and died at the Beauvoir Confederate Home.

Don Russell, *The Lives and Legends of Buffalo Bill.* Norman, Univ. of Okla. Press, 1960; DAB.

Ingram, David, adventurer (fl.1568). Probably born at Barking, Essex, England, Ingram told Sir Francis Walsingham, Queen Elizabeth's secretary of state, that as a sailor, with 100 others, he went ashore in 1568 near present Tampico, Mexico, from Sir John Hawkins' plundering expedition, rather than starve afloat. About 75 went southward, were defeated by the Spanish, and only two, Miles Philips, and Job Hortop eventually reached England again. Ingram, Richard Browne and Richard Twide, with others, set out northward. Most were killed by Indians, but the three, 11 months later, reached a river mouth 60 leagues west of Cape Breton Island, Nova Scotia. They found the French ship Cargarine, M. Champaigne (not Champlain), master, and by 1569 were back in England. Walsingham's examiners secured Ingram's tale in 1582; it was published in 1589 in the first edition of Richard Hakluyt's "Principal Navigations," then dropped as overly fictitious. Ingram's dictated and carefully recorded narrative tells of elephants "twise as big as a horse," Indian kings enriched by precious stones, etc. Yet underneath the embroideries there is an undoubted bedrock of truth, and Ingram may well have walked from Mexico to somewhere on the east coast. His descriptions of buffalo, of "great playnes and greate and huge woodes" are reasonable, and he probably saw the flamingoes, the now extinct great awk, and various other species which he describes. Ingram thought he had walked 2,000 miles but on the course he probably followed, by way of Florida, it was closer to 3,000. Nothing is known of his later life.

Los Angeles Times, Nov. 21, 1955; Richard Hakluyt, "The Relation of David Ingram," from *The Principal Navigations.* Ann Arbor, Readex Microprint Corp., 1966.

Inkpaduta (Scarlet Point), Sioux leader (c. 1815-c.1879). The son of Wamdesapa, a Wakpekute chief, he was b. on the Watonwan River, South Dakota, his mother a Sisseton. His father was said to have been a man of violent temper who killed Tasagi, principal chief of the Wakpekutes and thus was outlawed by the band. When Wamdesapa died about 1848, Inkpaduta succeeded him as chief of the renegade faction and his first subsequent exploit was in 1848 to imitate his father by the slaying of the new chief of the Wakpekutes, Wamundeyakapi, together with 17 of his warriors as they slept in their hunting camp in the present Murray County, Minnesota. Although not a party to the Traverse des Souix 1851 council, he collected from those who had been there much of their annuities, doing so by intimidation. Inkpaduta became incensed with the whites after Henry Lott, a bootlegger and horse thief in 1854 killed his brother and family. The winter of 1856-57 was severe, the Indians reduced to near starvation and on one begging trip among the whites an Indian killed a settler's dog which had bitten him; a posse thereupon disarmed the Indians, leaving them with no means to hunt. Somehow they recovered their weapons, or obtained others, and on March 8 and 9, 1857, killed 34 settlers near Spirit Lake and took three women prisoner; later they killed another settler and captured another woman. Two weeks later they struck Springfield, near the present Jackson, Minnesota, and killed more whites. Inkpaduta's force consisted of only a dozen or so men and military pursuit proved ineffectual. He was not captured but two of the women were ransomed and the other two slain in captivity. Through the efforts of Little Crow, a Sioux to become famous in Minnesota's later annals, some men of Inkpaduta's band were tracked down and killed, but he and a core of supporters escaped to the west. He thereafter largely made his home with the Yanktonais but retained sporadic contact with the Santees for some years. It was reported, although never confirmed, that he conferred with Little Crow before the bloody 1862 outbreak and may have taken a minor role in it although again he escaped punishment. "From that time forward," wrote Robinson, "his ubiquity was amazing," It· also borders on the unbelievable. Robinson reports him "everywhere from the Canadian line and the Bad

Lands down to Nebraska and central Minnesota and wherever he appeared, murder and theft marked his trail, yet while carrying on this guerilla work he was the leader in every battle fought with the white troops after Wood Lake.... He was at the affair at Fort Abercrombie (September 3-6, 1862) and was present in the battles of Big Mound (North Dakota, July 24, 1863), Dead Buffalo (July 26, 1863) and Stony Lake (July 28, 1863). He was with the Yanktonais at the time and by common consent the leadership fell to him. This was probably the first time that the management of a large number of Indians in battle with the soldiers had been entrusted to him and the superb manner in which he covered that retreat... marked him at once as a soldier of high executive ability, and won for him the admiration of the Indians who thereafter were glad to fight under his leadership." He was at Whitestone Hill, north of the present Ellendale, North Dakota, September 3, 1863, but fortune was not with him and the Indians, according to white reports, suffered disastrous losses. Inkpaduta who now according to some historians had soared from a wandering outlaw with a negligible following to a military master in command of more than 1,000 warriors roamed freely thereafter on the buffalo plains, murdering and depredating when occasion arose. July 28, 1864, he fought Sully in the Battle of Killdeer Mountain, north of the Black Hills and in the running fights in the Bad Lands, although by now practically without weapons. He migrated to Canada but made forays below the border from time to time. When the Red Cloud operations were conducted along the Bozeman Trail he was with that chief and later joined Crazy Horse; in the Custer Battle of the Little Big Horn Inkpaduta was with the Indians facing Reno. He survived that action and again migrated to Canada where he died around 1879, still free. Robinson concedes that in seeking a scapegoat for the savage depredations along the frontier, whites were apt to blame them upon any Indian they knew about or could name, adding that "it is not impossible that he is unjustly charged with some of (the depredations), but such men as Joseph LaFrambois and John B. Renville...were firm in the belief, for which they gave good reasons, that either Inkpaduta personally or his young men, acting under his initiative, were responsible" for the offenses listed. Inkpaduta was a tall, well-built Indian whose face was deeply pitted by smallpox. He was married and fathered four sons and a daughter.

Doane Robinson, *History of the Dakota or Sioux Indians.* Pub. by State of So. Dak., repr. by Ross & Haines, Minneapolis, 1956; Abbie Gardner Sharp, *History of the Spirit Lake Massacre.* Des Moines, Iowa Printing Co., 1891; Robert M. Utley, *Frontiersmen in Blue.* N.Y., Macmillan Co., 1967; Roy W. Meyer, *History of the Santee Sioux.* Lincoln, Univ. of Nebr. Press, 1967.

Inman, Henry, army officer, writer (July 30, 1837-Nov. 13, 1899). B. at New York City, he enlisted in the army at 20 on March 9, 1857, and served four years in the 9th Infantry in Oregon and California, taking part in quelling Indian troubles. He was transferred east and joined the 17th Infantry in 1861 being commissioned a second lieutenant May 14 and a first lieutenant October 24. He came out of the Civil War a captain and brevet major, later being breveted lieutenant colonel for service against Kansas Indians. As quarter-master at Fort Harker, Kansas, he signed on and was authorized to pay the 50 scouts who accompanied Forsyth to the battle of Beecher Island. Although an "energetic and popular quartermaster officer," Inman had persistent trouble with his paper work and accounts, due probably more to carelessness than design. He was tried for a third time in 1870-72 on charges ranging from embezzlement to giving false receipts and as a result was dismissed from the service; although he spent the rest of his life trying to clear his record, he was unsuccessful. In 1878 he entered journalism with the *Larned* (Kansas) *Enterprise,* being associated with various news-papers and news organizations thereafter. He published *Stories of the Old Santa Fe Trail* (1881); *In the Van of Empire* (1889); *The Old Santa Fe Trail, the Story of a Great Highway* (1897); in 1898, *Tales of the Trail, The Ranche on the Oxhide, A Pioneer from Kentucky,* and *The Great Salt Lake Trail,* the latter in collaboration with William F. Cody. Inman also published *Buffalo Jones' Forty Years of Adventure* in 1899. He was married and died at Topeka, Kansas.

Heitman; *Who's Who;* Appleton; DAB.

Iretaba, Mohave chief (c. 1808-May 3, 1874). B. probably in the vicinity of the present-day Needles, California, of the Neolge or Sun Fire clan, he became a subchief under Cairook (Kairook) and in time the leader of the Huttoh-pah band of the powerful Mohave tribe. He was a guide for Ives in the 1849-50 exploration by boat of the Colorado River, in 1851 guided Sitgreaves and later guided Whipple on their surveys. In the course of these he became a good friend of the whites, although his knowledge of their ways was ever limited. In 1856 he purchased the captive Oatman girls from the Yavapais and turned them over to the whites. Whether he had any role in the 1858-59 hostilities against whites is not known, but when Cairook and other leaders were taken hostage and imprisoned at Fort Yuma, Iretaba probably was not with them. Cairook was killed trying to escape, and Iretaba assumed his role as head of the tribe. In January 1861 he arrived in Los Angeles, "a large man, with good Indian features, giving evidence of intelligence," and "not only the head chief of (his) tribe, but really possessed of more influence in the Colorado country than any other chief." Discovery of gold at La Paz and elsewhere on the lower Colorado the following year brought a rush of whites, causing new difficulties. John Moss, a noted frontier figure for whom Iretaba had served as guide on a successful prospecting trip, took Iretaba in November 1863 with Antonio Azul, a Pima chief to Washington, D.C., by way of San Francisco, Panama and New York. Iretaba met President Lincoln, and reached his homeland again late in June 1864. The Colorado River Reservation set aside for his Mohaves in 1865 was the first Indian reservation in Arizona, and still exists. His persistent friendship for the whites may have been difficult on occasion. In June 1867 a La Paz saloon keeper lured Iretaba's favorite wife into his establishment, got her drunk and raped her; the chief sought him out, lost a fist fight to him and then caused the white to be arrested. Quickly freed the saloonkeeper accosted Iretaba again, hitting him over the head with a revolver; had the chief reacted like a white and killed the other, it would have gone down as another Indian outrage, no doubt. In 1872 Iretaba informed Crook of the identity of Indians who had perpetrated the Wickenburg stagecoach massacre November 5, 1871, in which the well-known Frederick Loring was killed along with several others. Iretaba's role in bringing to task the ringleaders incensed many Mohaves. While remaining a friend of the whites, the chief lost some influence with his people who thought he had sold them out, and disbelieved the "lies" he told of the wonders he had seen in the East. His death near the Colorado River was ascribed variously to old age or smallpox, the exact cause remaining uncertain. Dockstader gives the date of his death as June 17, 1878.

William B. Secrest, "Iretaba's Outrageous Lie," *Frontier Times*, Vol. 48, No. 6 (Oct.-Nov. 1974), 22-23, 43-44; Dan L. Thrapp, *Al Sieber, Chief of Scouts*. Norman, Univ. of Okla. Press, 1964; Dockstader.

Iron Jacket (Pohebits Quasho), Kotsoteka Comanche chief (d. May 12, 1858). A chief and medicine man of a major division of the Comanches, he was believed by his fellows able to blow aside with his breath leaden missiles and arrows and so be immune to injury or death. His name probably came from his wearing a Spanish armor of mail. He was killed near the Antelope Hills on the South Canadian River in battle with Texas Rangers under John S. (Rip) Ford and Shapley Prince Ross. The Rangers broke up his armor to salvage pieces of it for souvenirs.

W.J. Hughes, *Rebellious Ranger: Rip Ford and the Old Southwest*. Norman, Univ. of Okla. Press, 1964; HT; Noel M. Loomis, Abraham P. Nasatir, *Pedro Vial and the Roads to Santa Fe*. Norman, 1967.

Iron Shirt, Tanima Comanche leader (fl. 1865). Iron Shirt, whose name probably came from his wearing a Spanish mail armor cuirass, was reported living in 1865, but few biographical details of his life are preserved. However there were other Indians named Iron Shirt on the Plains in the 19th century among the Cheyennes, Kiowas, Kiowa Apaches and perhaps other tribes. George Bent wrote that "The Mexicans had a number of these old coats of mail and traded several of them to the plains Indians," citing various instances of the use of such armor (92-93), Grinnell also speaks of the use of such armor by Indians (74-75).

Noel M. Loomis, Abraham P. Nasatir, *Pedro Vial and the Roads to Santa Fe*. Norman, Univ. of Okla. Press, 1967; George E. Hyde, *Life of George Bent*. Norman, 1968; George Bird Grinnell, *The Fighting Cheyennes*. Norman, 1956.

Iron Tail, Sioux show performer (c. 1850-May 29, 1916). Described as a "war chief and head of all the Indians in the show," Iron Tail toured for years with Buffalo Bill's Wild West organization beginning in 1901. He claimed to have been the model for the Indian relief on the buffalo nickle, but the designer, James Fraser said that he used at least two Indians for the representation: Iron Tail and Two Moon. In the performance, Iron Tail led the attack on the Deadwood Mail stagecoach as a regular feature. He later appeared in the Miller Brothers 101 shows.

Don Russell, *The Wild West: A History of the Wild West Shows*. Fort Worth, Tex., Amon Carter Museum of Western Art, 1970.

Iroquet, chieftain (fl. 1609-1624). Chief of an Algonquin people called Iroquet, the Indian named Iroquet met Champlain at Quebec in 1609 with a Huron war leader seeking French assistance against the Iroquois of present New York State. Champlain, accompanied their expedition, taking part in a fight near Lake Champlain, scoring an immediate victory but the action proving a long-range disaster for the French. In 1610 Iroquet conferred with Champlain, initiating the long-lasting alliance between French, Algonquin and Huron peoples; at this meeting Champlain persuaded Iroquet to take to his camp with him a French lad who may have been Etienne Brulé; the boy was to be given the rudiments of the Iroquet language. Iroquet and Champlain also met in 1611 and in 1615 Iroquet headed the Algonquins who joined the Hurons in a Champlain-led expedition against the Iroquois south of Lake Ontario. Following this raid, Iroquet and the Hurons had a falling out over Iroquet's leniency to a captive the Hurons wanted to torture to death and in a resulting fight Iroquet suffered two arrow wounds. He was last heard of in 1624, when he returned from a successful beaver-trapping endeavor in the Neutrals country.

Thwaites, JR, V, 288-89n52; DCB.

Iroquois Aeneas (Young Ignace), migrant to the Flatheads (d. c. 1880). One of the original band of Iroquois to migrate as beaver trappers to the Flatheads, Aeneas' portrait was painted by Point (p. 48). In 1839 he and another went to St Louis seeking priests and conducted De Smet back to the Flatheads; Aeneas also served De Smet in 1841 and accompanied him to the Crows in 1842. He may have farmed near Fort Owen in the Bitterroot Valley of Montana in 1851-53. In 1854 he guided some parties for John Mullan of the Stevens expedition. About 1857 he settled near St. Ignatius Mission, Montana. He was buried near Arlee, Montana.

Wilderness Kingdom: Indian Life in the Rocky Mountains: 1840-1847. The Journals & Paintings of Nicolas Point, S.J. N.Y., Holt, Rinehart and Winston, 1967; George F. Weisel, *Men and Trade on the Northwest Frontier.* Missoula, Mont. State Univ. Press, 1955.

Iroquois Peter: *see* Pierre Gaucher

Irvine, Caleb, army officer, frontiersman (Sept. 1825-Feb. 6, 1891). B. in Robinson County, Tennessee, he enlisted July 14, 1846 for Mexican War service reaching Mexico City and becoming first sergeant of Mounted Rifles by 1848 when he became a brevet second lieutenant of Mounted Rifles and a second lieutenant in 1850. He resigned June 30, 1851, in Oregon. He served under Loring in an 1849 expedition from Fort Leavenworth to Oregon. He was at The Dalles, Oregon, when he accepted an invitation from his acquaintance John Owen in September 1851 to join him as a civilian at Fort Owen in the Bitterroot Valley of western Montana. Irvine made regular trips for Owen to the Overland Trail each summer to trade with emigrants for worn out stock to be recouped on Montana grass. He had brushes with Blackfeet and other Indians. Irvine farmed for a time, worked for the Indian Department, mined on Gold Creek, Montana, and in 1863 joined the rush to Alder Creek, Montana. He became probate judge of Deer Lodge County, serving until 1890 as probate judge or justice of the peace at Deer Lodge, Butte and Anaconda. His first wife was an Indian woman who died in 1859; his second was an English woman he married in 1866.

Heitman; George F. Weisel, *Men and Trade on the Northwest Frontier.* Missoula, Mont. State Univ. Press, 1955.

Irvine, William, army officer (Nov. 3, 1741-July 29, 1804). B. in Ireland, he was educated at Dublin, studied medicine and was named a surgeon on a British ship, serving in the Seven Years' War. He reached Carlisle, Pennsylvania, in 1764, supported American independence, raised a Pennsylvania regiment, and

was appointed a colonel. His command took part in the expedition against Canada, where he was captured and later exchanged. He saw hard service in the eastern campaigns, was made a Brigadier General in 1779 and two years later was assigned to the north-western frontier, stationed at Fort Pitt. He remained there until after the Revolution, harassed by mutinies and Indian raids. He died at Philadelphia.
DAB

Irvine, William C. (Billy), cattleman (Mar. 3, 1852-July 27, 1924). B. at Carlisle, Pennsylvania, he became a foreman in 1873 for George Bosler and his brother, also from Carlisle, who ran 30,000 head of cattle in the sandhills country of Nebraska. After three years Irvine bought 4,000 head of cattle in Texas and drove them to a ranch on the North Platte River in Wyoming. He remained in the cattle business until 1884 when he returned to Pennsylvania, in 1886 going back to Wyoming and again becoming a stock raiser. He was organizer and manager of the Converse Cattle Company and the Ogalalla Land and Cattle Company, a businessman and a power in the Wyoming Stock Growers Association of which he was president from 1896-1911. With Wolcott he was credited with being a most active leader of the "invasion" of Johnson County in the 1892 operation of big cattlemen against small stockmen they suspected of rustling, and avoided any serious prosecution of his role through the influence of powerful friends. Irvine held many political and business positions of importance in his later life. He was married. He died at Santa Monica, California.

Helena Huntington Smith, *The War on Powder River.* N.Y., McGraw-Hill Book Co., 1966; information from Western Research Center, Univ. of Wyo.; *Man of the Plains: Recollections of Luther North 1856-1882.* Lincoln, Univ. of Nebr. Press, 1961.

Irving, John Treat Jr., writer (Dec. 2, 1812-Feb. 27, 1906). B. at New York City he became an attorney and in 1833 accompanied U.S. Commissioner Henry L. Ellsworth who sought to arrange with the Plains Pawnees for the well-being of the Delawares, removed to the west of the Mississippi. From this excursion Irving wrote *Indian Sketches Taken During an Expedition to the Pawnee*

Tribes, published at Philadelphia in 1835. The remainder of his life has little frontier interest. Irving was a nephew of Washington Irving.

Thwaites, EWT, XXIII, 390n.; George E. Hyde, *The Pawnee Indians.* Norman, Univ. of Okla. Press, 1974.

Irving, Washington, writer (Apr. 3, 1783-Nov. 28, 1859). B. at New York City, his apprenticeship to a lawyer was ended by ill health and he traveled abroad from 1804-1806; he later passed his bar examination, but was little inclined toward legal work and his fame stems from his writings. It was assured by appearance of *A History of New York* (1809), sometimes known as Diedrich Knickerbocker's History of New York, and *The Sketch Book of Geoffrey Crayon, Gent.* (1820), which includes his Hudson River fables, "The Legend of Sleepy Hollow," and "Rip Van Winkle." After many years abroad, his reputation as a writer assured, Irving returned to this country. In 1832 he visited present-day Oklahoma, leaving Fort Gibson, Arkansas, in October and traveling by way of the present communities of Tulsa, Keystone, Ingalls, Guthrie, Norman, Shawnee, Okmulgee and returning to Fort Gibson by early November. From this came his small book, *A Tour of the Prairies* (1835). In 1834 John Jacob Astor made available to him documents relative to his fur-trading enterprises in the Northwest, enabling him to write *Astoria* (1836). From the interest thus aroused came also *Adventures of Captain Bonneville, U.S.A.* (1837). Irving was the first great American writer to be fully appreciated abroad, and his best work lives today almost as freshly as when penned. His *Astoria, Bonneville* and *Tour* have enduring value. Irving died at Tarrytown, New York.

Literature abundant.

Irwin, Bernard John Dowling, army surgeon (June 24, 1830-Dec. 15, 1917). B. at Roscommon, Ireland, he was graduated from New York Medical College and became an army assistant surgeon August 26, 1856, serving at Fort Defiance and then at Fort Buchanan, Arizona. In January 1861 Apaches stole cattle and a boy, the future Mickey Free, from the John Ward place near Buchanan on Sonoita Creek and Second Lieutenant George Nicholas Bascom was sent to Apache Pass to contact the Chiricahua chief, Cochise and

rescue the boy, if possible (see Bascom biography for details). Possibly because the Bascom party required medical assistance, Dr. Irwin and a small escort left Buchanan for Apache Pass February 9. The next day in the Sulphur Springs Valley Irwin reported he had struck an Apache raiding party including a Coyotero chief and two warriors driving stolen stock; after a hard chase of six or seven miles his soldiers, Irwin said, although mounted on mules had overtaken and captured the three adult Apaches, who were bound and with the cattle delivered to Bascom at Apache Pass. Irwin's account is suspect, however: mules would be unable to overtake horsemen in a long chase, and adult warriors could never be taken alive in such a manner as the doctor described; since the Coyoteros had no direct relationship with Cochise's Chiricahuas it seems obvious they were seized by a ruse of some sort, probably having voluntarily come into Irwin's camp as no doubt they had stolen the stock in Mexico and would not suspect U.S. soldiers of seeking to avenge such a raid. At Apache Pass the famous confrontation between Cochise and Bascom meanwhile had come about. In a long and involved sequence of events Cochise executed four white prisoners he had taken, and although Bascom demurred, Irwin insisted that the whites execute the six Apache men held prisoners: Irwin's three and three taken by Bascom. To overcome the lieutenant's reluctance, Irwin insisted upon his "right" to hang his three prisoners and that he would do so in any event, so Bascom was persuaded to do the same with his own captives. Thus was initiated what turned out to be a quarter century of Apache hostility, precipitated by Irwin's intransigence. Nevertheless, in 1894 he was awarded the first Medal of Honor "earned" for operations against Indians, not as has been written because he had "captured" the three Coyoteros, but because he "voluntarily took command of troops and attacked and defeated hostile Indians he met on the way" to Apache Pass. Irwin served in the east during the Civil War. April 7, 1862, at the Battle of Shiloh he improvised one of the first field hospitals in military history, commandeered unused tents, blankets and medical supplies until he had a 300-bed makeshift hospital serving both Union and Confederate wounded; his work developed into extended use of field hospitals, now a standard Army medical practice. Irwin became a major (surgeon) September 16, 1862. From 1882 until 1885 he was medical director of the Department of Arizona and became a lieutenant colonel September 16, 1885, a colonel August 28, 1890, and retired June 28, 1894; he became a Brigadier General on the retired list in 1904. He was married and fathered three children. Irwin is said to have known something of five languages.

Heitman; B.J.D. Irwin, "The Apache Pass Fight." *Infantry Journal*, Vol. XXXII, No.4 (April 1928), 368-75; Benjamin H. Sacks, "New Evidence on the Bascom Affair." *Arizona and the West*, Vol. 4, No. 3 (Autumn 1962), 261-78; field plaque, Shiloh Nat. Milit. Park, Tenn.; Constance Wynn Altshuler, ed., *Latest From Arizona!* Tucson, Ariz. Pioneer' Hist. Soc., 1969; Altshuler, *Chains of Command.* Tucson, Ariz. Hist. Soc., 1981.

Isa-tai (Eschiti, Coyote Shit, Rear End of a Coyote), Kotsoteka (Qhahada, Kwahadi) Comanche medicine man (c. 1842-Nov. 10, 1914). B. a Kotsoteka or Quahada Comanche, Isa-tai while young became a medicine man and according to Nye, a minor war chief who pretended to supernatural powers: he predicted the outcome of heavenly phenomena, it was reported he could belch up wagonloads of cartridges, then swallow them again, and that his medicine could protect his followers from white bullets. Naturally he attracted a devoted following. When an uncle on December 10, 1873, was slain by white troops while enroute home from a successful Mexico raid, Isa-tai brooded. At length he announced he had conversed personally with the Great Spirit, being told that the Caddoes, Wichitas and other Indians were degenerating swiftly because they adopted the ways of the whites. To become a powerful nation again the Comanches must go to war and kill off all the whites they could. At a tribal medicine dance in May 1874 on Red River he and Quanah Parker (see entry) emerged with a sizable war party including principally Quahada Comanches, Cheyennes and a few Kiowas. June 27 they attacked an aggregation of 28 buffalo hunters and others at Adobe Walls in the Texas Panhandle, but Isa-tai's medicine swiftly failed. Three hunters were killed outright and another by accident for a loss of about nine Indians killed and others wounded. Isa-tai took no part in the fighting, observing

the action from a distant hilltop; his horse was wounded and a Comanche rider near him struck by a spent bullet fired by buffalo hunter Billy Dixon (see entry) at a measured distance of 1,538 yards, nearly seven-eighths of a mile. The shot stunned but did not kill the Indian. Nevertheless, the prophet's medicine had proven false. Angry Cheyennes sought to flog him, but were dissuaded. Isa-tai later explained that his power had been nullified by a Cheyenne who had broken a taboo, killing and skinning a skunk enroute to the battle; thus Isa-tai was not at fault. The Comanches forgave him and forgot the incident. The medicine man came in with the bulk of his people in 1875 and settled near Lawton/Fort Sill, Oklahoma, where Isa-tai, regarded as "that comical fellow," raised a family and lived the remainder of his life. Several photographs of him are held by the Museum of the Great Plains at Lawton, and the Panhandle-Plains Historical Museum, Canyon, Texas. At the age of 72 Isa-tai died at his home near Lawton.

Information from Paula M. Williams, Museum of the Great Plains, Lawton; T. Lindsay Baker, Panhandle-Plains Hist. Mus.; William D. Welge, Okla. Hist. Soc.; Rupert Norval Richardson, *The Comanche Barrier to South Plains Settlement.* Glendale, Calif., Arthur H. Clark Co., 1933; W.S. Nye, *Carbine and Lance.* Norman, Univ. of Okla. Press, 1951; Ernest Wallace, E. Adamson Hoebel, *The Comanches: Lords of the South Plains.* Norman, 1952; George Bird Grinnell, *The Fighting Cheyennes.* Norman, 1956; G. Derek West, "The Battle of Adobe Walls (1874)." *Panhandle-Plains Hist. Rev.,* Vol. XXXVI (1963), 1-36.

I-see-o (Tahbone-man, Plenty Fires), Kiowa scout (c. 1851-March 11, 1927). B near Fort Larned, Kansas, in his mid-teens in late 1867 he went on a first raid, against the Navahos of New Mexico, returning in time to attend the Medicine Lodge Treaty council in Kansas, the Kiowas signing October 21. For about five years they were at peace, aside from occasional raids on tribal enemies, but the establishment of Fort Sill and depredations of the buffalo hunters drove the southern Plains tribes to war against the exposed Texas frontier. July 12, 1874, he was with Lone Wolf's band in the Lost Valley fight near Jacksboro, Texas, where the rangers under John B. Jones were defeated. In the fall of

1874 Lone Wolf and his band in turn were defeated at Palo Duro Canyon in the Staked Plains by Mackenzie's 4th Cavalry. Lone Wolf took his party to Fort Sill where on February 25, 1875, they surrendered and Tahbone-mah changed his name to I-see-o (Plenty Fires). Eventually he became a scout for the Fort Sill command. In 1889 Hugh Lennox Scott, an army officer accomplished in Indian sign language, arrived at the post and during nine years I-see-o worked closely with him, at first communicating by signs. The two with others were instrumental in quelling a movement toward a ghost dance hysteria such as had gripped the northern Plains tribes. The Kiowa helped temper other irritating influences. In the 1890s when the all-Indian Company L of the 7th Cavalry was enlisted, I-see-o became first sergeant under Scott (although over-age by normal standards for enrollment). In 1897 when the company was disbanded, I-see-o enlisted again for five years as a scout, serving as a courier for Miles. With the Spanish American War he enlisted once more, but remained at Fort Sill during the conflict. After the war he lived with his family at Big Bend on the Washita. In 1915 he accompanied a delegation to Washington where he once more encountered Scott, by now army Chief of Staff. Scott took him to Newton Baker, Secretary of War and persuaded Baker to give him permission to enlist I-see-o as a sergeant in the army for life. February 1, 1915, Scott wrote Colonel Granger Adams, commander at Sill to "let him live on the reservation or out among his people, as he elects, and see that he gets pay, clothing and rations. . . until he dies. He is old and medieval, his mind is back in the middle ages, and he has simply been stunned by civilization. I do not see how he has survived this long. When the government needed him, he was supremely loyal, against the wishes of his own people." The army erected a cottage for him, but I-see-o preferred to live in the old ways, generously distributing his pay regularly to hangers-on, but being cared for nonetheless. In January 1927 he contracted pneumonia which led to his death, the passing of the last Kiowa scout, the last Indian scout, at Fort Sill.

Fred Frank Blalock, "Last of the Fort Sill Indian Scouts — Plenty Fires." *Frontier Times,* Vol. 54, No. 4 (June-July 1980), 6-11.

Ishi, Yahi Indian (c. 1860-March 25, 1916). Ishi, described as the last stone-age Indian in the contiguous United States, was discovered lost, starving and emotionally exhausted in a corral next to a slaughterhouse operation at Oroville, California August 29, 1911. Law authorities were called and placed Ishi in jail for his own protection from curious throngs. His case was widely-reported, coming to the attention of Alfred L. Kroeber of the University of California at Berkeley's Museum of Anthropology and an anthropologist went to Oroville to interview him, taking along a partial vocabulary of the Yana Indian language, since it was felt that this or a dialect of it would most probably be his tongue. In the course of an extended interview some words indeed seemed intelligible to him and it was determined finally that he was a Yahi Indian, southernmost portion of the Yana tribe. Soon Ishi was taken to the museum where he lived in happiness and without want for the remaining near-five years of his life. It was learned that he apparently was the last of his people; his only male companion had been slain by a white, other survivors had drowned, his mother died of illness and ultimately only Ishi had been left to wander in loneliness and despair until he reached Oroville. During his life at the museum Ishi became very close to the museum staff, spending his days describing his tribal customs, religious beliefs, traditions and language and demonstrating his wilderness skills in archery, survival techniques, woodcraft and craftmanship; once he took a trip back to the land that had been his people's but the effect was traumatic, and he did not remain. He enjoyed learning to take care of himself, to market, to wander about the Bay area communities, ride on trolley cars, and investigate the ways of the strange white world. At length he developed tuberculosis and from this he died, his body cremated as was the custom of his people.

Saxton Pope, *Hunting With the Bow & Arrow.* N.Y., G.P. Putnam's Sons, 1925; Theodora Kroeber, *Ishi in Two Worlds.* Berkeley, Univ. of Calif. Press, 1961.

Ish-ish-kais-kais (Frank Escaloom), Cayuse leader (d. June 3, 1850). A brother of the chief, Tomahas of the Cayuse, Ish-ish-kais-kais took a major part in the Whitman Massacre of

November 29, 1847 in Washington Territory, shooting Judge L.W. Saunders, Narcissa Whitman and Nathan Kimball and later took Kimball's 16-year-old daughter as a wife against her will. He was baptized and confirmed into the Roman Catholic Church, named John and was hanged at Oregon City for his part in the uprising with four other Cayuse leaders.

Clifford M. Drury, *Marcus and Narcissa Whitman and the Opening of Old Oregon,* 2 vols. Glendale, Calif., Arthur H. Clark Co., 1973.

Ives, George, desperado (1836-Dec. 21, 1863). B. at Ive's Grove, Racine County, Wisconsin, he was attractive in appearance, nearly 6 feet tall, of light complexion, smooth shaven and with "lively blue eyes." He left a widowed mother and several sisters to go west in the mid-1850s, mining in California, serving as packer for Wright or Steptoe in Washington Territory, and Henry Edgar met him in 1858 in British Columbia. As a herder of government mules at Walla Walla, Washington, he developed a taste for rustling, making off with animals while leaving the impression they had perished in severe winter weather. Ives became "a gambler and a rowdy in all the mining settlements of the Salmon River," showing up at Lewiston, Pierce City, Elk City, Florence and Warren's Diggings and by that time a close friend of Alex Carter, another burgeoning desperado. Ives reached the Beaverhead country of Montana by 1862 and was a resident of Bannack that winter where he met or renewed his acquaintance with Henry Plummer, a noted desperado leader who shortly would be elected sheriff of Bannack and Virginia City, Montana. Ives readily joined his band. He was a member of James Stuart's Yellowstone expedition of 1863 and in one of several brushes with hostile Indians was wounded slightly. Ives became among the best known, or most notorious of the "roughs" working with Plummer, and some of his holdups, his murderous threats to others and similar indiscretions are well documented. Ives became a clerk for a grazer of public horses at Virginia City, a position which made it possible for him to learn where travelers intended to go and often how much gold dust they were taking, information invaluable to the Plummer band. Ives and another desperado, Stephen Marshland in November 1863 held up a stage between

Virginia City and Bannack and in another holdup tried to murder Anton M. Holter, a noted businessman and cattleman. In early December 1863 he murdered Nicholas Tbalt, an inoffensive and popular young German and for this he was arrested by James Williams in the initial stirringa of the vigilante movement that was to sweep Montana clean. Ives was brought to Nevada City, near Virginia City, Montana, tried by an impromptu court and jury of 24 men and hanged, the first of the Plummer band to be so disposed of. Literature on Ives is more extensive than any other of the Montana desperadoes save Henry Plummer.

Dimsdale; Langford; Birney; Helen Fitzgerald Sanders, *A History of Montana,* 3 vols. Chicago & N.Y., Lewis Pub. Co., 1913, I, pp. 198-216.

Ives, Joseph Christmas, military officer (1828-Nov. 12, 1868). B. at New York City he was appointed from Connecticut to West Point and July 1, 1852, became a brevet second lieutenant of ordnance. He transferred to the topographical engineers March 18, 1853, becoming a second lieutenant April 30, 1855, and a first lieutenant July 1, 1857. Ives served with Amiel Whipple (see entry) on the 35th Parallel Pacific Railroad Survey in 1853-54 and in 1857-58 conducted an important exploring expedition up the Colorado River from the Gulf of California toward Black Canyon. A special steamer, the *Explorer* was built on the Atlantic coast for the expedition, tested on the Delaware River, dissembled and shipped in sections to the West coast and re-assembled at the mouth of the Colorado River, "its like never seen before that time or since." Ives used it as far as the head of navigation at Black Canyon, then continued his upstream work by skiff. He subsequently explored by land the route eastward to Fort Defiance over the high plateau region north of the San Francisco peaks and past the Hopi Indian mesas. His description of his journey, published as "Report on the Colorado River of the West" (HED 90, 36th Cong., 1st sess.) was interesting, lively and of historical importance. Ives was an engineer and architect for the Washington national monument and served as astronomer and surveyor for a commission determining California's boundaries. He became a captain of engineers for the Confederacy rising to colonel and aide-de-camp to President Jefferson Davis. He resided at New York City

after the Civil War and died at 40 in that
community.

Heitman; Cullum; Frank C. Lockwood, *Thumbnail Sketches of Famous Arizona Desert Riders
1538-1946,* Tucson, Univ. of Ariz. Bulletin 11,
1946; standard reference works.

J

Jaastad, Benjamin Olsen, pioneer, writer (Jan. 14, 1886-June 24, 1965). B. in Norway he was brought by his parents as an infant to Wisconsin where he remained until 17, moving then to his father's homestead in North Dakota from where he bought a roundtrip ticket to Tucson, Arizona, arriving November 15, 1906 — and never using the return part of his passage. He learned the sash and door trade, but also became interested in southwestern history, and worked closely with Edith Stratton Kitt and others similarly inclined. Jaastad was intelligent, curious, perceptive, tireless and had an amused tolerance for the foibles of the pioneers, many of whom he came to know personally. His most remembered work was *Man of the West* (1956), published by the Arizona Pioneers' Historical Society, a biography of George Washington Oaks from Jaastad's friendship and many interviews with him. He also contributed notes on Judge Charles Meyer, Samuel Hughes, Jeff Kidder and other prominent Arizonans of his era, as well as of the Dragoon Springs Stage Station, Juan Bautista de Anza, Pedro Font and similar historical figures. Jaastad died at Tucson.

Ariz. Hist. Soc. archives.

Jackson, Paiute chief (fl. 1857). A leader of the southern Paiute band known as the Santa Clara Indians of extreme southwest Utah, Jackson and some of his people were instrumental in tracking down and slaying three men who had escaped the besieged Fancher train emigrants at Mountain Meadows before the massacre of September 11, 1857. They sought apparently to reach California. Jackson recovered a paper or document dropped by one of the three; this he turned over to his friend and president of the Mormon Indian mission, Jacob Hamblin, from whom John D. Lee subsequently took and purportedly destroyed it; the paper supposedly contained a list of those with the train and other revealing information.

Juanita Brooks, *The Mountain Meadows Massacre.* Norman, Univ. of Okla. Press, 1966.

Jackson, Andrew, military officer, politician (March 15, 1767-June 8, 1845). B. in the Waxhaw settlement (present Lancaster County), South Carolina as he believed (although North Carolina also claims his birthplace), Jackson's father died before the boy was born; an older brother died in 1779 in a Revolutionary War incident. Andrew and another brother were captured by the British August 1, 1780, in the engagement of Hanging Rock and contracted smallpox while under confinement; the brother died. Jackson's mother died while doing volunteer work aboard a prison ship in Charleston Harbor so that by 14 Andrew was left alone, having almost no education but a lively intelligence and boundless energy. No attempt will be made in this essay to trace Jackson's career in detail, except as it impacted upon the frontier. It was a full, episodic and nationally significant life, featuring a living legend whose every movement seemed to generate endless controversy; his however was often a positive influence. At Salisbury, North Carolina, Jackson read law and was admitted to practice at McLeanville, November 12, 1787, the next year migrating to the Nashville district of Tennessee. He was delegate to a Tennessee constitutional convention, served a term in Congress and a year as U.S. senator, was a popular judge of the state Supreme Court from 1798 until 1804 when he settled on his estate, "The Hermitage," engaging in land speculation and mercantile and planting pursuits for several years. Charles Dickinson of Nashville insulted Jackson's wife, Rachel, but apologized. Jackson heard later that he had repeated his remarks and difficulties between the two intensified over this and other matters. May 30, 1806, Jackson killed Dickinson in a duel beyond the state line in Kentucky. Late in 1812 Jackson was commissioned by Governor William Blount a Major General of Tennessee Volunteers. By 1813 he had already raised and equipped 2,500 men. He sent one element under John Coffee (see entry) as far south as Natchez on the Mississippi, but they saw no action and returned to Nashville in early 1813. August 30 occurred the appalling defeat at Fort Mims in southern Alabama to the Creeks under William Weatherford (see entry), several hundred defenders being slain. Jackson moved south in October. Coffee commanded in a fight at Tallasehatche, Alabama, November 3 in which 183 Creeks were slain for a loss of 46 whites, five of them killed. At Talladega November 9 Jackson attacked the Red Stick, or war-party Creeks, reporting 300 killed for a loss of 100 whites, 17 of whom died. Jackson unfortunately now was held at Fort Strother on the Coosa River by lack of supplies and "mutinous" troops who had fulfilled their enlistments. By January 1814 however he was reinforced and resupplied and readied a new offensive. He was successful in a fight at Emuckfau Creek, but bested by the Hillabee Creeks who had turned hostile through white error. More volunteers reached him and by late February he had a command of 2,000 infantry, 700 cavalry and 600 Indians (500 Cherokees and 100 friendly Creeks). Jackson moved toward Horseshoe Bend on the Tallapoosa River where the main body of Creeks was barricaded under direction of Menewa. Here on March 27 was fought the Battle of Horseshoe Bend, a white victory that effectively ended the Creek War. Jackson's men counted 557 Creek dead (there were no wounded), and estimated that around 300 had drowned seeking escape. The Jackson forces lost 203, including 49 killed. Menewa escaped. Weatherford was not at the Horseshoe Bend battle but, fully anticipating execution, rode into Jackson's camp some time later and surrendered, surprised to find himself treated with courtesy and dignity. Jackson considered Weatherford possessed of elements of "true greatness," and a man of "reckless personal courage" whom he could admire. He hurried Weatherford off to The Hermitage to reside as guest for months until the intense white feeling against him eroded and he could safely return to southern Alabama. Already a national hero by his Horseshoe Bend victory, Jackson found himself elevated to new heights by his stunning defeat of British regulars January 8, 1815, at New Orleans; he had become the towering hero of the War of 1812. He had been made a Brigadier General of the U.S. Army April 19, a Major General May 1, 1814, and won the formal thanks of Congress and a special gold medal for his New Orleans

triumph. In late 1817 Jackson was ordered to the Georgia-Florida frontier under conditions that were not minutely spelled out and not clear to him. By March, still uncertain of the nature of his mission, he moved into Spanish Florida, initiating what became the First Seminole War. Two British subjects, Alexander Arbuthnot and Robert C. Ambrister (see entries), were taken suspected of influencing Indians against the Anglos, tried by drumhead courts and executed, Ambrister shot and Arbuthnot hanged. These legal assassinations of British subjects generated prolonged international difficulties. Jackson's Florida campaign proved indecisive and although the territory was purchased from Spain in 1819 and Jackson served briefly as governor, he soon returned to Tennessee, being discharged from the army June 1, 1821. Jackson became President March 4, 1829, serving eight full years. He was widely regarded as the frontiersman-President, but the major impact of his term upon the frontier was his support and implementation of the Indian Removal Act of 1830, thus presiding over much of a sordid chapter of American history. Although Jackson's role in this remains controversial among historians, it did nothing to enhance the luster of his name or historical image. Prucha, in a "reassessment" of Jackson's Indian policy believed him not anti-Indian, however pro-frontiersman. Jackson believed that a dense white population in the deep south would add more to the security of the United States than would a loose aggregation of Indian tribes, and he was committed to the view that only a "civilizing" process, whatever that meant, would safeguard Indians from eventual extermination. This, Jackson thought, could best take place if the Indians were remote from corrupting white influences and pressures, and that removal offered the best opportunity for Indian and white tranquility and progress; he never of course considered white removal from contact with the Indians, for the whites had votes and the Indians none. Prucha believed Jackson's attitude was basically one of "justice and fairness," though with scant sympathy for what he considered barbarism. He had castigated Weatherford, for example, for "taking sides with an ignorant set of savages" since he was "a man of good sense and almost a white man," Weatherford being only one-half to one-quarter Creek. On another occasion

Jackson said he could not see "why the Red man more than the white, may claim exemption from the municipal laws of the state within which they reside," although he said nothing about their being due the protection of the laws of the same state, a state which had been somewhat arbitrarily superimposed upon the Indian culture by invaders who had no inherent rights except by force over those of the natives. The removal policy had its roots as far back as Jefferson's administration. It was endorsed enthusiastically by Jackson as a way to "protect" the Indian civilizing process, provide land for white settlers, bolster security against foreign invaders, and quiet "the clamor of Georgia against the federal government," especially since Jackson would make no move to enforce the Supreme Court ruling against that state in Indian matters. This was not because of Jackson's "immorality," but "because the political situation of America would not permit it," which seems lame enough. Prucha stressed Jackson's concern that the removals take place in a kindly spirit, by persuasion rather than compulsion, and with the assent of the tribesmen. But in 1830 the Choctaws were forced to accept the notorious Treaty of Dancing Rabbit Creek and their removal in 1833 was "characterized by great suffering." The Chickasaws were obliged arbitrarily to move, the Creeks, in some respects more civilized than the white intruders, "suffered heavy loss of life" during their forced migration in 1834-35, while the Cherokees in 1838 were ruthlessly shunted from their homeland over the "Trail of Tears" with a loss of 25 percent of their number. Surely none of these migrations was initiated with the cheerful assent of the people concerned, and most of them occurred while Jackson was Chief Executive. Jackson might fairly be judged not on what he said from time to time, even taking into account his propensity for inconsistency, but by his deeds. He died at The Hermitage. Among the best of the short summaries of his life, career and impact is the essay by Thomas D. Clark in *The Reader's Encyclopedia of the American West*.

Literature abundant; REAW; Francis Paul Prucha, "Andrew Jackson's Indian Policy: A Reassessment," *Journal of American History*, Vol. LVI, No. 3 (Dec. 1969), 527-39; Prucha, "Indian Removal and the Great American Desert," *Indiana Mag. of Hist.*, Vol. LIX, No. 4 (Dec. 1963), 229-332; BDAC.

Jackson, David E. fur trader (c. 1790-Dec.24, 1837). It has been said that Jackson participated in the Battle of New Orleans in 1815. In 1822 he joined Ashley to trap the upper Rockies. He took part in the Arikara fight June 2, 1823, and probably in the Leavenworth action in August. He participated in fur trade operations in the Rockies until 1826 when he joined Smith and William Sublette in acquiring Ashley's interests. Thereafter he managed part of the firm's trapping undertakings and made a trip or two to Missouri. In 1828-29 he wintered among the Flatheads; Jackson's Hole was named for him, as were Jackson Lake and Jackson, Wyoming. The firm sold out in 1830 to the Rocky Mountain Fur Company, the partners reaching Missouri by October. Jackson, with Smith and Sublette, entered the Santa Fe trade, reaching the New Mexico city with a wagon caravan July 4, 1831, after Smith had been killed by Comanches. Jackson went on to California, reaching San Diego in November, and journeying north almost to San Francisco. He bought California mules and some horses, returned with them to New Mexico, and went on to Missouri. His health poor, Jackson remained in the Mississippi valley until he died of fever at Paris, Tennessee. Although never to achieve great personal fame, he was a more positive influence on the opening of the West than history records.

Literature abundant, but incomplete; see Carl D.W. Hays article, MM, Vol. IX.

Jackson, Frank, desperado (c. June 10, 1856-c. 1930?). B. in Llano County, Texas, Jackson was a tinner at Denton, Texas, when in 1874 he became acquainted with Sam Bass. An orphan, Jackson killed Henry Goodall, a black desperado and horse thief, in 1876. The next year he reluctantly joined Bass. The outlaws held up a stage near Fort Worth, Texas, December 22, 1877, and another January 26, 1878. Turning to train robbery, they held up a Houston and Texas Central express at Allen, Texas, February 22, 1978, and March 18 they held up another at Hutchins, Texas. On April 4, the band, reinforced by two former associates who broke jail in Nebraska, held up a Texas and Pacific train at Eagle Ford, Texas. At Mesquite, Texas, they held up another, against stronger resistance and with little profit, men being wounded on both sides. The brigands were considerably hounded by posses and the tumult they had generated. One member was killed June 13, 1878, at Salt Creek, Texas. Once Jackson saved the life of the traitor, Jim Murphy, whom Bass and another had decided to kill, and who was to betray the band. After casing several banks, Bass settled on one at Round Rock, Williamson County, Texas. Murphy tipped off the Texas Rangers who reached the town and on July 19, 1878, in the legendary gunbattle a law officer and a bandit were killed outright, Bass mortally wounded and a second lawman wounded seriously. Jackson accompanied Bass out of town and, directed to save himself, escaped unhurt. It is reported that he returned to Denton County briefly, then vanished. Siringo said he saw him in Montana. Other reports put him in California, elsewhere in Texas, in New Mexico; as late as 1927 efforts were made to get Williamson County to drop the charge against him for murder of the Round Rock deputy sheriff.

Wayne Gard, *Sam Bass.* Lincoln, Univ. of Neb. Press, 1969; *Frontier Times,* Vol. 3, No. 5 (Feb. 1926), 23; *Frontier Times,* Vol. 4, No. 12 (Sept. 1927), 15.

Jackson, George, frontiersman (Jan. 9, 1757-May 17, 1831). B. in Cecil County, Maryland, he moved with his parents to Moorefield, Virginia (now West Virginia), and in 1769 to Jackson's Fort (now Buckhannon, West Virginia). He was captain of scouts in the first military company organized in the Buckhannon settlement, in 1779, and joined Clark at Pittsburgh for the planned expedition against Detroit. He had general command of various bands of scouts, being succeeded by Lowther. Jackson later became colonel in the militia "and is inseparably connected with the early history of the Upper Monongahela" in the trans-Allegheny country, revealing "energy and daring courage." Jackson studied law, was a member of the First Virginia Assembly in 1788, and held other political offices, was a member of Congress and moved to Zanesville, Ohio, about 1806, where he farmed and also held political offices. He died at Zanesville and was buried in Falls Township, nearby.

BDAC; Lucullus V. McWhorter, *The Border Settlers of Northwestern Virginia.* Hamilton O., Republican Pub. Co., 1915.

Jackson, Helen Maria Fiske Hunt, writer (Oct. 15, 1830-Aug. 12, 1885). B. at Amherst, Massachusetts, her first husband, Edward Bissell Hunt, an army engineer, died in an 1863 accident and in 1875 she married a wealthy Quaker railroad man, William Sharpless Jackson, living thereafter mainly at Colorado Springs, Colorado. She had commenced placing poetry in 1866, her first novel was published in 1876, and she began to take an interest in Indians after hearing Poncas lecture at Boston in about 1880. She wrote *A Century of Dishonor* in 1881, sending a copy to each member of Congress at her own expense. She was sent by the government as a special commissioner to investigate conditions of the Mission Indians, and in 1883 filed a *Report on the Condition and Needs of the Mission Indians,* which she thought ineffective. A collection of her articles, *Glimpses of California and the Missions,* appeared in 1903. She turned to fiction to dramatize her convictions about Indian abuses, writing *Ramona,* an indictment of cruelty and treachery in treatment of native Americans. It appeared in 1884, and for many years the drama was played annually on the slopes of Mt. San Jacinto, California, proving as popular and enduring as the novel. Mrs. Jackson died at San Francisco.

DAB; Lawrence Clark Powell, "Ramona". *Westways,* Vol. 60, No. 7 (July 1968), 13-15, 55; Michael T. Marsden, "Helen Hunt Jackson." *Arizona and the West,* Vol. 21, No. 2 (Summer 1979), 109-12.

Jackson, James, army officer (Nov. 21, 1833-post 1903). B in New Jersey he enlisted in the 12th Infantry in 1861, was commissioned in 1863 and ended the Civil War a first lieutenant, transferring in 1866 to the 30th Infantry and becoming a captain in 1868. He joined the 1st Cavalry on the last day of 1870. Jackson commanded the garrison troop at Fort Klamath (the post commanded by Major Green) late in 1872 when orders were issued to arrest Captain Jack, an attempt which would ignite the Modoc War of 1872-73 in southern Oregon and northeastern California. Jackson led out the mission that resulted in the Battle of Lost River, November 29 and the slaying by Modocs of more than a dozen settlers thereafter. Jackson was ordered to support Bernard in the December 2 action at Land's Ranch southeast of Tule Lake, but his command arrived after the affair had terminated. Jackson's Company B was in the Battle of the Stronghold in the Lava Beds south of Tule Lake January 17, the Indians holding off the white soldiers easily causing them about nine killed and 30 wounded, including three officers. Jackson's troop was with Mason in the second Stronghold Battle in mid-April, but their effect was slight since Mason took pains to see that no one under him was exposed to Modoc fire. On April 26 however the Thomas-Wright force was decimated in an attack south of the Stronghold, and Jackson's company was part of the relief, assisting in extracting the wounded and dead from this worst defeat of the war. Jackson and his company were attacked in the engagement at Sorass Lake May 10, losing several enlisted men killed or wounded mortally, but this was the last action of any significance in the war, the Modocs commencing to surrender soon after. Jackson was in the engagements at Clearwater and Camas Meadows, Idaho in the 1877 Nez Perce campaign, winning a Medal of Honor for gallantry in the latter engagement August 20 for recovering under heavy fire with the aid of a couple of troopers the body of one of his soldiers who had been killed. He also won a brevet for the Lost River affair of 1872 and the Clearwater action of July 12, 1877. He became a major of the 2nd Cavalry January 23, 1889, a lieutenant colonel of the 4th Cavalry in 1897, transferred to the 1st Cavalry on August 11 of that year and retired November 21, 1897.

Keith A. Murray, *The Modocs and Their War.* Norman, Univ. of Okla. Press, 1965; Cyrus Townsend Brady, *Northwestern Fights and Fighters.* Garden City, N.Y., Doubleday, Page & Co., 1923; Powell: Heitman.

Jackson, Sheldon, Alaska churchman, reindeer promoter (May 18, 1834-May 2, 1909). B. at Mineville, New York, he was graduated from Princeton Theological School and ordained to the Presbyterian ministry in 1858, conducting school for Choctaws at Spencer, Indian Territory, and eventually directing mission work for his denomination in the Rocky Mountain west. He visited Alaska in 1877 and in 1884 became superintendent of mission work in that territory, the next year being appointed the first superintendent of public instruction for Alaska, retaining that federal post until his

death. He traveled and explored widely, setting up schools as quickly as funds and resources became available. In order to relieve hunger among the Eskimos, he urged the importation of reindeer to replace food supplies destroyed by the natives or white hunting. Against vigorous opposition and in the face of many discouragements, his plan was put into operation: the first 16 reindeer, purchased in Siberia, reached Unalaska in 1891 and within a few years 1,280 of the animals were imported and desirable ranges stocked; by 1930 these had multiplied to approximately 700,000 head in various herds. He described this endeavor in his *Introduction of Reindeer into Alaska...*(1890) and other writings. Jackson also wrote *Alaska, and Missions on the North Pacific Coast* (1880), and *The Presbyterian Church in Alaska... (1877-84)* (1886). He died at Asheville, North Carolina. Short of stature his health was never robust, although his energy was immense. He was married.

Jackson's writings; *Who Was Who; DAB.*

Jackson, "Teton," desperado (d. 1893). Possibly b. in Missouri he said he became an outlaw "for an affair that happened in the early days in Joplin, Missouri," the nature of it not specified. In 1876 he was said to have been a scout briefly for Crook on the Yellowstone and Big Horn Expedition. Afterward he headed a band of Jackson Hole horse thieves which according to Campbell numbered around 300, each, "wanted for a major crime in some part of the United States." In 1887 he was captured in the Big Horn Basin by Frank Canton, then sheriff of Johnson County, Wyoming, and sentenced in Idaho (from where he had stolen horses) to 14 years. Canton befriended him by mail, sending him money and tobacco, yet was high on Jackson's list of those he most wanted to kill when he got out. Around 1890 he knifed a guard and escaped. In 1892 he gave an "interview" to a Casper, Wyoming, newspaperman, reciting his version of his career and practices. He was captured and returned to Boise, attempted once more to escape jail and was killed in the effort. He was described by Campbell as 6 feet, 2 inches, in height, weighing around 300 pounds, with black eyes, red hair and a red beard.

Robert B. David, *Malcolm Campbell, Sheriff.* Casper, Wyo., S.E. Boyer & Co., 1932, 84-89.

Jackson, William Henry, photographer, artist (Apr. 4, 1843-June 30, 1942). B. at Keeseville, New York, he became a photographer at Troy, New York, in 1858. He ran a photography studio at Rutland and Burlington, Vermont, from 1860 until 1866, except for a year as an enlisted man in a Vermont regiment during the Civil War. Jackson went overland to California where he remained from 1866-67, then returned to Omaha, Nebraska, where he established a studio from 1868-70, photographing construction of the Union Pacific railroad. As official photographer of the Hayden Survey from 1870-78 he was first to photograph the Yellowstone region, his pictures being instrumental in the decision to create the National Park. He took many thousands of glass-plate negatives of western scenes, mining camps and such places as Mesa Verde and the Pueblos. In 1879 he established a studio at Denver where he remained for 20 years, while periodically taking trips as far as Canada, Mexico, England and Siberia. In 1898 he moved to Detroit, establishing the Detroit Publishing Company with partners and in 1924 transferred to Washington, D.C., where he took up painting; at the age of 93 he executed Old West murals for the new Department of the Interior Building. About 7,000 of his glass negatives, ranging in size from 5 by 7 inches to 18 by 22 inches are held by the Colorado Historical Society, and 10,000 are in the collections of the Ford Museum at Dearborn, Michigan. Jackson was author of *The Pioneer Photographer — Rocky Mountain Adventures with a Camera* (with H.R. Driggs) (1929) and *Time Exposure* (1940), an autobiography. His photographs are very widely used even today for their historical interest, clarity and beauty. He married twice, fathered four children, and died at New York at 99, deservedly famous as one of the most important picture makers of the Old West.

Who Was Who; EA; CE; Mountain and Plain History Notes (Colo. Hist. Soc.), Vol. 16, No. 3 (Mar. 1979).

Jacobs, John, Mormon pioneer (Dec. 7, 1825-post 1892). B. at Byglandsfjord, Norway, he became a Mormon and reached Utah in 1849 with the Ezra T. Benson company. He settled at Lehi, Utah, in 1851, and moved to Cedar City, Utah, in 1853. A man of his name was placed by *Mormonism Unveiled* at the Mountain Meadows massacre, September 11, 1857, either participating in or consenting to the tragedy. In 1858 he moved back to Lehi. Jacobs was an Indian wars veteran and for 32 years was counsellor in the deacons quorum of his church. He married twice.

Mormonism Unveiled, 380; Frank Esshom, *Pioneers and Prominent Men of Utah.* Salt Lake City, Western Epics, 1966.

Jacobs, John M., pathfinder (fl. 1842-1864). Jacobs was described in 1863 by diarist Samuel Word whose wagon train he had guided to Montana as "a mountaineer who has spent 21 years of his life in this country," which would make his arrival in the Rocky Mountains about 1842. If he then was a mature man it would make his year of birth about 1820 or 1825, though this is conjecture. Johnson reported he once was described as "a red-bearded Italian," but this soubriquet is not repeated elsewhere. In 1856 with Robert Dempsey, Jacob Meek and Robert Hereford, Jacobs in trading along the Oregon Trail accumulated 600 cattle and horses and drove them to Montana where he settled along the Beaverhead River with his Indian wife and family. Here he met the Stuarts in 1858. Stuart tells various incidents of frontier life in which Jacobs figured, including his purchase from a Hudson's Bay Co. trader of an English-made tiger-shooting rifle which he found unsatisfactory being unable to "kill any game with it." The reason, Stuart discovered after trading Jacobs out of the weapon was that he only half-loaded it because he feared the recoil, which Stuart conceded "was tremendous." Jacobs served as a wagon train pilot from Montana to Walla Walla, Washington, and then returned. In the late winter of 1862-63 Jacobs and his 8-year-old daughter and John M. Bozeman, a Georgian with four years experience in the mountains, left Bannack to trace what Jacobs already knew was a feasible wagon route to the Montana goldfields. It led from the North Platte along the eastern face of the Big Horn mountains, and became known as the Bozeman Trail, although it was more Jacob's than Bozeman's. Crows intercepted them south of the Yellowstone and stole their weapons, ammunition and food and left them three wornout horses to ride. The trio continued their exploratory journey, sometimes subsisting upon grasshoppers since game was scarce. May 11 the Stuart exploration party discerned them in the distance and, realizing they were whites, sent men to meet them but the trio feared they were Indians and took flight; no contact was made. Jacobs and his companions reached the Trail at the present Glenrock, Wyoming, and persuaded 45 wagons of emigrants to try their shorter route to the goldfields. Near the Big Horn Mountains Sioux forced the wagons to turn back; only a party of eight horsemen evaded the natives and continued on the route into Montana. In 1864 Jacobs piloted a wagon train from the North Platte to Montana, arriving in July, but this time took the so-called Bridger Trail west of the Big Horns rather than east of them on his own route. The eastern road became known to old-timers as the Jacobs and Bozeman Cut-off, and later to emigrants as the Bozeman Trail; a penciled map showing it notes that it is "Jacobs' Map of His and Bridger's Routes to Virginia City," and indicates it was drawn by Jacobs or under his direction very early in the route's history. The daughter who had accompanied Jacobs and Bozeman in charting the route died on Prickly Pear Creek, about two and one-half miles from Clancy which is ten miles south of Helena, Montana. The death occurred in the winter of 1865-66.

Great Falls (Mont.) *Tribune,* Jan. 13, 1963; Granville Stuart, *Forty Years on the Frontier.* Glendale, Calif., Arthur H. Clark Co., 1925; Dorothy M. Johnson, *The Bloody Bozeman.* N.Y., McGraw-Hill Book Co., 1971; Grace Raymond Hebard, E.A. Brininstool, *The Bozeman Trail,* 2 vols. Arthur H. Clark Co., 1922, 1960; Note by N. Merriman, Feb. 23, 1878, held by Mont. Hist. Soc.

Jacobs, Swen, Mormon pioneer (fl. 1857-1892). A man of this name was alleged by *Mormonism Unveiled* to have been at the scene of the Mountain Meadows massacre of September 11, 1857, either participating in or consenting to the tragedy. The book, published in 1892, said he was "of Cedar City," Utah.

Mormonism Unveiled, 380.

James, Alexander Franklin (Frank), desperado (Jan. 10, 1843-Feb. 18, 1915). B. in Clay County, Missouri, he was an older brother of Jesse. Frank probably fought in the 1861 Battle of Wison's Creek under the Confederate Sterling Price, but returned home, either on parole or for some other reason, in 1862.

He joined the guerilla, William Clarke Quantrill perhaps in the fall of 1862. He probably was one of Quantrill's men under Shelby in November and December, and participated in the Lawrence, Kansas, raid August 21, 1863. He was in Texas during the winter of 1863-64, and accompanied Quantrill into Kentucky where the guerilla leader was wounded fatally, Frank James and others surrendering at Samuel's Depot on July 26, 1865. Thereafter he gradually moved into outlawry with his brother (see Jesse James' biography for summary). Following Jesse's assassination, Frank James moved about variously, according to report, but on October 5, 1882, surrendered to Gov. Thomas Crittenden at Jefferson City. Cases against him, by February of 1885, had collapsed or been dismissed, or were no longer pressed. His life was fairly exemplary thereafter. Frank held a number of jobs, and for a time tried stage and circus life, but without much success. He died at the old James farm in Clay County; his wife, Annie, lived until July 6, 1944.

See Jesse James biography for references.

James, Edwin, explorer, linguist, naturalist (Aug. 27, 1797-Oct. 28, 1861). B. at Weybridge, Vermont, he was graduated from Middlebury College, then privately studied medicine, geology and botany and in 1820 became scientist with Stephen H. Long's expedition to the central Rocky Mountains. The party followed the Platte and South Platte rivers, reaching the front range in July. On July 14 James, with Second Lieutenant William Henry Swift and an old mountain man, Joe Bissonette, made the first recorded ascent of what became known as Pike's Peak, west of present Colorado Springs. Long named the spectacular mountain James Peak in his honor, but custom and Fremont decreed otherwise. The expedition explored toward the headwaters of the Arkansas, Red and Canadian rivers, then moved back to the settlements and dissolved in Missouri. James wrote the only extensive official report: *Account of an Expedition from Pittsburgh to the Rocky Mountains performed in the Years 1819 and '20,* but it was too scientific and too realistic to achieve much popular favor. As an Army surgeon James was stationed at Fort Crawford, Wisconsin, and Mackinac, became interested in Indian languages, compiled spelling books in those tongues, translated the New Testament into Ojibway, with the invaluable assistance of John Tanner who had worked for 30 years with that people in various capacities and from whose experiences James also wrote: *A Narrative of the Captivity and Adventures of John Tanner* (1830, 1956). In 1837-38 James was agent for the Potawatomi Indians at Old Council Bluffs, Nebraska, then settled at Rock Spring, Iowa, where he died. He was described by acquaintances as "a fine scholar," and "a man of undoubted integrity and intelligence." He also was an ardent abolitionist and held strong temperance views.

DAB; David Lavender, *The Rockies.* N.Y., Harper & Row, Pubrs., 1968; *The Book of a Thousand Tongues.* N.Y., United Bible Societies, 1972; Walter O'Meara, *The Last Portage.* Boston, Houghton, Mifflin Co., 1962.

James, George Wharton, writer (Sept. 27, 1858-Nov. 8, 1923). B. in Lincolnshire, England, he came to this country in 1881, migrating to the southwest in search of health. A Methodist minister until a messy divorce, he traveled and wrote widely about his adopted land, some of his books of fine quality, including *The Wonders of the Colorado Desert,* which appeared in 1906. Others of his more than 40 volumes include a *Tourist's Guide Book to Southern California* (1894); *In and Around Grand Canyon* (1900); *In and Out of California Missions* (1905); *Through Ramona's Country* (1908), and *The Lake of the Sky, Lake Tahoe* (1916). He died at St. Helena, in northern California.

Lawrence Clark Powell, "George Wharton James: The Wonders of the Colorado Desert." *Westways,* Vol. 62, No. 2 (Feb. 1970), 4-7, 52.

James, Jesse Woodson, desperado (Sept. 5, 1847-Apr. 3, 1882). B. in Clay County, Missouri, he was son of a Baptist preacher, who left when Jesse was 2 to hunt gold in California and shortly died there. Jesse and his brother, Frank, were raised by their strong-willed mother, Zeralda, who subsequently married twice. A southern woman, she owned slaves. The Missouri-Kansas border was the scene of much guerilla activity, turbulence and lawlessness as the boys grew up. Early in the Civil War William Clarke Quantrill emerged as an outstanding guerilla leader, ruthless and active. Although Frank James joined Quan-

trill about 1862, Jesse did not become a guerila until 1863 or 1864, appearing then with Bloody Bill Anderson's fragment of Quantrill's partisans. Jesse killed Union Major A.V.E. Johnson in a savage fight near Centralia, Missouri. He was wounded in the finger in 1864. He may have been with the George Shepherd guerillas who drifted into Texas in late 1864, remaining there for the winter, returning to Missouri in the spring of 1865. There is no solid record that the James boys sought clemency after the war. Jesse received a severe chest wound in partisan fighting in 1865. When recovered he and Frank lived apparently peacefully for about four years, farming in Missouri, but robberies became increasingly common from the first daylight robbery of a bank, at Liberty, Missouri, February 13, 1866, through 1868 and Jesse and Frank emerged as leaders of a gang of desperadoes, even though proof of their participation in the early crimes is not clear. At any rate the James boys' move into lawlessness became complete. In this career, from 1866 until 1882, Jesse and Frank probably took part in at least 12 bank robberies, seven train robberies, four stagecoach robberies, and assorted other deviltry such as the robbery of the Kansas City Fair September 26, 1872. Their activities ranged as widely as West Virginia, Alabama, Arkansas, Iowa, Kansas and Minnesota, although most of it occurred in Missouri. Their first train robbery was on the Rock Island at Adair, Iowa, in which a train was derailed, the engineer scalded to death, his fireman badly burned and several passengers injured. In all of the recorded James' escapades, at least 11 citizens were killed and about 10 injured, although the actual no doubt was above that, and this does not count the outlaws slain or wounded. The James' most disastrous escapade was at Northfield, Minnesota, September 7, 1876, when two civilians were killed, one wounded, outlaws Clell Miller and Bill Chadwell were killed in town while Charlie Pitts was killed later by a posse, all the other outlaws — three Youngers and the two Jameses — were wounded, either in town or in fights as they strove to get away. The Jameses made it back to Missouri, but the Youngers were captured. Eventually a price of $10,000 apiece was placed on the James brothers through efforts of a new Missouri governor, Thomas T. Crittenden. Robert Ford shot

Jesse in the back of the head in a St. Joseph bungalow to collect the reward. James was an unusual outlaw, but he was aided in his extraordinarily long career by the circumstances of the place and the time. Yet he is of the stuff of myths, and his perpetual place in American folklore is assured.

Literature abundant; William A. Settle Jr., *Jesse James Was His Name ... or ... Fact and Fiction Concerning the Careers of the Notorious James Brothers of Missouri.* Columbia, Univ. of Mo. Press, 1966; Paul I. Wellman, *A Dynasty of Western Outlaws.* Garden City, N.Y., Doubleday & Co., 1961.

James, Marquis, writer (Aug. 29, 1891-Nov. 19, 1955). B. at Springfield, Missouri, he worked on midwestern and New York newspapers and edited the *American Legion Monthly* from 1923-32. James wrote a number of books, those of frontier interest including *The Raven: A Biography of Sam Houston* (1929), and *Andrew Jackson, the Border Captain* (1933). He also wrote an autobiography, *The Cherokee Strip: A Tale of an Oklahoma Boyhood* (1945). James died at Rye, New York.

Who Was Who.

James, Theodore, outlaw (fl. 1897). Linked in late times to the Black Jack Christian band of outlaws (see William Christian biography for details), he took part in the highly successful train robbery November 6, 1897, at Grants Station, New Mexico, was captured and held briefly at Fronteras, Sonora, was freed and disappeared "without stirring a ripple."

Jeff Burton, *Black Jack Christian: Outlaw.* Santa Fe, Press of the Territorian, 1967.

James, Thomas, frontiersman (Nov. 1, 1782-Dec. 17, 1847). B. in Maryland, he joined the St. Louis Missouri Fur Company in 1809, reaching the Mandan villages in September and because of a dispute, became a free trapper. His two companions were killed by Indians while James trapped the upper Missouri country; he rejoined the company and returned to the Three Forks area. James went back to St. Louis in 1810, spent three years in Pennsylvania, several years thereafter at various pioneering enterprises. In 1821 with others and a keelboat load of supplies, he ascended the Arkansas River and reached Santa Fe December 1, after an adventurous

crossing of the plains. He returned to St. Louis in 1822. The next year he again entered the South Plains; after harsh adventures with the Comanches, he returned to St. Louis in 1824. He undertook various frontier activities, commanded a scout company during the Black Hawk War. About 1846 he dictated to Nathaniel Niles, an attorney, his autobiography: *Three Years Among the Indians and Mexicans,* published in that year at Waterloo, Illinois, and in various editions since. It is a "substantially accurate," engaging and occasionally very revealing narrative, and portrays its subject as a good observor, honest and intelligent.

Thomas James, *Three Years Among the Indians and Mexicans.* N.Y., *Citadel Press,* 1966.

James, Will, artist-author (June 6, 1892-Sept. 3, 1942). B. Joseph-Ernest-Nephtali Default at St. Nazaire de Acton, Quebec, of French parentage, he grew up at Montreal. He swallowed some lye at 10, and nearly died. In 1907, at 15, he went west to be a cowboy, working in Saskatchewan and Alberta for three years, becoming involved in a barroom shooting incident, in which no one was killed. After a short visit east he returned to western Canada, then moved into Montana, adopting the name of Will James. He was in Idaho in 1911, chasing wild horses and beginning to sketch the scenes around him. He wandered widely in the northwest for several years. He centered on Nevada, was arrested in November 1914, for cattle rustling and sentenced to Nevada State Prison at Carson, being paroled April 11, 1916. He already had a wide local fame as a "drawer" of horses, cattle and cowboys. He drifted to Los Angeles where he rode broncs and stunt rode for motion pictures. He returned to Nevada and Montana and ranch jobs. James served less than a year in the 21st Infantry, being mustered out in 1919. A bucking horse accident laid him up for a time and in August 1919, he entered the California School of Fine Arts at San Francisco. At Maynard Dixon's suggestion, he quit art school, making his first sale of cowboy pictures to *Sunset* magazine, where they appeared in the January 1920, issue. He was married July 7, 1920, to Alice Conradt, sister of his good friend, Fred. He studied briefly at Yale Art School and finally, after several disappointments, sold an article with pictures, "Bucking Horses and Bucking

Horse Riders," to *Scribner's Magazine,* for $300. From that time on his success was assured. His first book, *Cowboys North and South,* appeared in 1924. *Smoky,* his first great success, appeared in 1926. James bought a ranch out of Pryor, Montana, which he named the Rocking R. In 1930 his other great success, *Lone Cowboy,* a heavily fictionalized "autobiography," was published. In all, James wrote and illustrated 24 books, some of them collections of portions of others. He always had an alcohol problem, compounded by tension over attempts to conceal his true origins, fearing these would detract from his cowboy image. In the mid-thirties Alice divorced him and James rapidly slid down hill. His art work, best when done with pencil, satisfactory in ink, had begun to suffer. He died at Hollywood "from alcoholic complications."

Anthony Amaral, *Will James: the Gilt-Edged Cowboy.* Los Angeles, Westernlore Press, 1967.

Jameson, Green B., engineer (c. 1807-Mar. 6, 1836). B. in Kentucky, he was a resident of Brazoria, having reached Texas in 1830, initially practicing law. He was the chief engineer at the Alamo and at least five of his letters, or reports, to Houston and others are extant. Jameson supervised the remounting of the guns of the improvised fortress, and was killed in the Mexican assault upon it.

Amelia Williams, XXXVII, 266; HT.

Jameson, J(ohn) Franklin, historian (Sept. 19, 1859-Sept. 28, 1937). B. at Somerville, Massachusetts, he earned his doctorate at Johns Hopkins University in 1882 and taught at Brown University from 1888-1901, then at the University of Chicago (1901-1905), which he left to become director of the historical research department of the Carnegie Institution; he remained there until 1928. In this capacity he directed an in-depth study of the federal archives which led to creation of the National Archives as they exist today and the National Historical Publications Commission. Jameson organized a study of American-related documents abroad and out of this and other research came the 19-volume *Original Narratives of Early American History,* for which he was general editor. He was a founder of the *American Historical Review* and its managing editor for many years and was a leader in the creation of the *Dictionary of*

American Biography, a standard reference work. He became chief of the manuscripts division of the Library of Congress in 1928, remaining in that position until his death. Jameson died at Washington, D.C. In addition to the above, his works of frontier interest included *Willem Usselinx: Founder of the Dutch and Swedish West India Companies* (1887); *The History of Historical Writing in America* (1891); *Dictionary of United States History* (1894, 1931), and *Privateering and Piracy in the Colonial Period* (1923).

Literature abundant: DAB; EA; CE.

Janis, Antoine St. Charles, frontiersman (c. 1800-c. 1840). B. near St. Louis, he went to the Rockies with Ashley in 1824 and became a mountain man. He worked for William Sublette and the Rocky Mountain Fur Company in 1832, attended the rendezvous at Pierre's Hole, and "had an account" with the American Fur Company from 1837 to 1839. Reportedly he was killed by Blackfeet on the Yellowstone River.

Janet Lecompte article, MM, Vol. VIII.

Janis, (Joseph) Antoine, frontiersman (March 26, 1824-Apr. 10, 1890). B. near St Louis he became a fur man, reaching the mountains about 1841 after receiving a good education. He became a trader at Fort Laramie, married an Oglala Sioux woman and fathered 10 or more children by her. He became a Sioux interpreter in 1855, guided Johnston during the Mormon War, and went to Colorado following the gold strike, in early 1859 building a cabin on Cache la Poudre and assisted in locating the town of Colona, Colorado. He moved to the Pine Ridge Reservation in 1878 and died on White Clay Creek, Nebraska, being buried at Pine Ridge.

Janet Lecompte article, MM, Vol. VIII.

Janis, Nicholas, frontiersman (Oct. 12, 1827-Sept. 13, 1902). B. near St. Louis, he reached Fort Laramie in 1845, married an Oglala Sioux woman, and fathered nine children. He became a trader, visited Colorado following the Cherry Creek gold strike, guided prospectors, was an interpreter at the upper Cheyenne agency until 1862, ranched on the North Platte River, 30 miles east of Fort Laramie, selling out in 1880 when he moved to Pine Ridge, South Dakota, where he died.

Janet Lecompte article, MM, Vol. VIII.

Jaramillo, Juan, military officer (fl. 1540-1547). Juan Jaramillo, from Villanueva de Balcarrota in Castile was possibly a nephew of the Juan Jaramillo who fought valiantly with Cortez in the conquest of Mexico and who married Marina, Cortez's former mistress; the elder Jaramillo remained in Mexico during the Coronado campaign of 1540-42 on which Juan Jaramillo the younger served creditably. He wrote a brief but valuable narrative of the operation, useful because of the clarity of the descriptions, distances and other military matters with which it is concerned and so of supreme benefit to today's historians. He accompanied Coronado to Quivira in 1541 on which journey he is the best authority. Jaramillo testified for Coronado in 1547 at the inquiry into the leader's management of his expedition. He wrote his narrative, it was said, "many years" after conclusion of the adventure, but no date is given.

George Parker Winship, *The Coronado Expedition, 1540-1542.* BAE, 14th Ann. Rep., Wash. Government Printing Office, 1896; Herbert Eugene Bolton, *Coronado: Knight of Pueblos and Plains.* Albuquerque, Univ. of New. Mex. Press, 1964; A. Grove Day, *Coronado's Quest.* Berkeley, Univ. of Calif. Press, 1964; George P. Hammond, Agapito Rey, *Narratives of the Coronado Expedition.* Albuquerque, 1940.

Jaycox, Henry H., frontiersman (c. 1834-Jan. 20, 1901). B. in Montgomery County, New York, he migrated to Wisconsin where he married and fathered a son, Henry Lafayette Jaycox (B. at Eagle, Wisconsin, May 13, 1859, died at Prescott, Arizona, March 16, 1947). Henry Sr. left for California in 1858 and his wife divorced him for desertion. He reached Arizona in 1864, being a member of the second King Woolsey expedition into Indian country, March 29-April 17, 1864, and the third Woolsey expedition of 92 men which left Woolsey's Agua Fria ranch June 1, 1864, and returned 87 days later after exploring eastern Arizona as far as Fort Goodwin. By 1870 Jaycox was on the Verde River, Arizona, where he farmed, mined and served as guide for the army against Indians, being considered qualified at that pursuit. After the sale of mining properties he moved to Oregon in July 1875, married again and fathered three daughters, but his second wife also divorced him and he returned to Arizona by 1882. He died at Hooker's Ranch on the Salt River, Gila County. Jaycox Mountain and Jaycox Tank in Coconino County were named for him.

Ariz. Hist. Soc., Hayden File.

Jeffords, Thomas Jonathan, frontiersman (Jan. 1, 1832-Feb. 19, 1914). B. in Chautauqua County, New York, Jefford's middle name is sometimes erroneously given as Jefferson; his uncle was named Thomas Jefferson Jeffords (b. April 2, 1811), but the frontiersman's birth records show his middle name to be Jonathan. Jeffords was educated and may have read law; one unconfirmed report said that he practiced briefly at Denver in his young manhood. He became a Great Lakes sailor and rose to skipper lake boats, retaining the title of "captain" for the rest of his life. The report that he also operated river boats on the Mississippi and/or Missouri is probably mistaken. Jeffords said he laid out the road from Fort Leavenworth to Denver in 1858 although by then the route was well known, and that he reached Taos, New Mexico, in 1859. In that year he drove stage on the Butterfield route and had an arrow scar to show for it. He prospected in the San Juan Mountains of southwestern Colorado in 1860. By 1862 he was in central New Mexico where he said he participated (as a civilian) in the Battle of Valverde February 21 between Union and Confederate forces, and in some manner came to the attention of Edward R.S. Canby, commanding Union forces in the region. Jeffords said that Canby sent him with dispatches for Carleton from Mesilla to Tucson, the mission effecting a contact and future cooperation between the California Column and Union forces in New Mexico. Jeffords said he remained with Carleton for the remainder of the Civil War. Around 1866 Jeffords became conductor along the stage route from Tucson to Mesilla and said he later became mail superintendent, in 16 months losing 14 men killed by Indians. Desiring to assure the safety of his personnel from Apache attack, Jeffords in 1867 dared to ride alone into Cochise's Dragoon Mountains rancheria and confer with the chief who was sufficiently impressed by Jefford's boldness and bravery to spare his life and come to an agreement with him to the effect that Jefford's drivers would be immune from Apache attack thereafter. Jeffords came to be called by Cochise *shik-isn,* or "brother," which he transliterated as "Chickasaw." The pact held and Jeffords and Cochise remained on friendly terms as long as the Chiricahua lived although Jeffords confessed late in life that he never turned his back to Cochise and ever kept his arms ready when in his company. In 1870 he and Elias Brevoort (see entry) formed a trading partnership to deal with the Mimbres Apaches; in order to get rid of an overly-observant agent, Charles Drew (see entry), they trumped up charges that he was an alcoholic and supplied whiskey to the Indians. Their allegations were disproven and the traders lost their license. On several occasions Jeffords upon request contacted Cochise or other Apache leaders for army officers or important civilians who wished to discuss or settle some matter. In June 1871 he was sent by New Mexico Indian superintendent Nathaniel Pope to find Cochise and if possible persuade him to come in to Cañada Alamosa, New Mexico for talks. Jeffords located Cochise in the Dragoon Mountains, but was unable to persuade him to visit New Mexico; he was paid $500 by Pope for this singular endeavor. Jeffords' most famous such undertaking was to escort Oliver Otis Howard in 1872 to Cochise's camp; the meeting was successful to all concerned. Howard granted Cochise a reservation in southeastern Arizona and persuaded Jeffords to become the first — and only — agent for the Chiricahuas, a condition Cochise had insisted upon. Jeffords was an effective agent in that his friendship for Cochise determined his success in keeping the Chiricahuas off of the warpath north of the Border, if not into Mexico, but he was somewhat controversial, charges occasionally leveled that he furnished arms and ammunition to the Apaches, that his rationing methods were inexact and that he was applying for and securing about 30 percent more rations than he had Indians. Howard always defended his character, however, pointing out that defamation from certain sources was not necessarily derogatory to the man, that Jeffords had the courage the post called for, while Dudley, who also knew both Jeffords and Cochise, said that the former was "the best Indian man" he had ever met. As to the ration problem, Jeffords himself pointed out that the Chiricahua reservation was on the path to Mexico, that he must ration numerous Apaches transiting on raids or war or to visit, for otherwise he could not hold Cochise's people, while the only count that was made

which occurred after the reservation was closed, failed to consider the numerous Apaches who by then had fled into the Sierra Madre. When after the death of Cochise the Chiricahuas were moved out of their reserve to that of San Carlos, Arizona, Jeffords was left without that kind of employment, a relief to him. In 1879 Jeffords, with Archie McIntosh and Captain Harry L. Haskell contacted Juh and about 100 of his hostile fellows in the Guadalupe Mountains, daringly visited them and persuaded them to surrender, one more example of Jeffords' intrepidity. Virtually through with his Indian activities, Jeffords thereafter moved about considerably and tried a number of occupations, few profiting him very much although many were associated with mining in some form. He was deputy sheriff at Tombstone in November 1882 and scouted a bit during Miles's Geronimo campaign of 1886. In 1892 he settled at Owls Heads about 35 miles north of Tucson where he continued to mine sporadically. While not a gregarious man, he had warm friends and could be congenial — within limits — upon occasion. He died at Owls Head and was buried at Tucson. In 1964 his grave was marked by a headstone arranged for by the Daughters of the American Colonists. Forbes described him in 1913 as "a straight, tall, somewhat slender man of about 165 pounds, with a sparse, reddish beard." Ben Jaastad (see entry) said he knew Jeffords about that time and "his hair and whiskers were white as snow and he was bent with age." He wore steel-rimmed spectacles for reading purposes by that time. Jeffords never married and was not known to have fathered children.

Farish, II, 228-40; C.L. Sonnichsen, "Who Was Tom Jeffords?" *Jour. of Ariz. Hist.,* Vol. 23, No. 4 (Winter 1982). 381-406: this article includes an excellent portrait of Jeffords; Dan L. Thrapp, *Victorio and the Mimbres Apaches.* Norman, Univ. of Okla. Press, 1974; Ben Jaastad, "George (Washington) Oakes, 1840-1917," manuscript at the Ariz. Hist. Soc. (note: the published version of this paper, *Man of the West: Reminiscences of George Washington Oaks.* Tucson, Ariz. Pioneers' Hist. Soc., 1956, omits most of the Jeffords references); R.H. Forbes, letter on Jeffords to the *Jour. of Ariz. Hist.,* Vol. 7, No. 2 (Summer 1966), 87-88; Thrapp, unpublished manuscript on Cochise; information from Elsie B. Jacques.

Jenkins, John, army officer (Nov. 27, 1751-

Mar. 19, 1827). B. at New London, Connecticut, he held various occupations, including that of constable before moving to the Wyoming Valley, Pennsylvania, in 1769 and taking part in the so-called Pennamite War. He enlisted in the army August 26, 1776, was captured by Indians November 1777 and taken to Niagara, the next spring to Montreal and then to Albany, New York but while being transferred to a grand Indian council at Kanadaseago, New York, he escaped. He reached home after much privation June 2, 1778, bringing intelligence of the advent upon the Wyoming Valley of Joseph Brant and Butler, and was in command of Forty Fort when the settlers marched out to meet them and turn back the invaders. Jenkins became a lieutenant in Captain Spalding's company and served until April 1779 when he was requested to meet with General Washington to whom he brought valuable information relating to the Indian country into which Sullivan was preparing his expedition; Jenkins served as scout for it, keeping an interesting journal and receiving Sullivan's formal thanks for his services. Jenkins served variously thereafter and was at Yorktown where he served under Steuben. He resigned his commission March 1, 1782. He settled at Exeter, Pennsylvania, where he lived the remainder of his life. He was married and fathered eight children.

Journals of the Military Expedition of Major General John Sullivan. Glendale, N.Y., Benchmark Pub. Co., Inc., 1970.

Jenkins, John, victim (July 28, 1815-Sept. 15, 1848). B. at Walnut Hills, Warren County, Mississippi, he became editor of the Vicksburg *Sentinel* December 13, 1844, and came into a feuding relationship over political matters with Henry A. Crabb and some other who ran a rival paper. In a street fight, Jenkins stabbed one of the pair and was shot by one or both of them, being mortally wounded. Henry Crabb removed to California and went on to become a noted and ill-fated filibuster.

Miss. Dept. of Arch. and Hist.; Jenkins' tombstone in the Vicksburg city cemetery; Vicksburg *Evening Post,* Apr. 12, 1932.

Jenness, John C., army officer (d. Aug. 2, 1867). B. in Vermont, he enlisted in the 17th New Hampshire Infantry November 25, 1862, and was commissioned a first lieutenant in the 1st New Hampshire Artillery September 19, 1864, being mustered out June 15, 1865. He was commissioned a second lieutenant of the 27th U.S. Infantry July 28, 1866, becoming a first lieutenant March 5, 1867, and was shot by Sioux Indians in the celebrated Wagon Box Fight near Fort Phil Kearny, Wyoming.

Grace Raymond Hebard, E.W. Brininstool, *The Bozeman Trail.* Glendale, Calif., Arthur H. Clark Co., 1960.

Jerome, Lovell Hall, army officer (Aug. 6, 1849-Jan. 17, 1935). B. in New York he was graduated from West Point, commissioned a second lieutenant in the 2nd Cavalry June 15, 1870 and assigned to Fort Ellis, Montana. He escorted a surveying party for the Northern Pacific Railroad from July to September 1872 and occasionally was engaged in scouting. He was under arrest at Fort Ellis in 1876. In 1877 he was on the Nez Perce expedition of Miles. Jerome was present October 1, 1877, when Miles lured Chief Joseph out for a parley during the affair at Bear Paw Mountains; Jerome then wandered into the Indian camp, perhaps as he later reported, at Miles' direction to see that the Nez Perce did not cache their weapons before surrender. At any rate, Miles seized Joseph and the Indians, when they heard of it, seized Jerome. While Joseph, by Indian accounts, was mistreated after being seized under a flag of truce, the Nez Perce treated Jerome with consideration and respect, although some wanted to kill him. He was allowed to keep his sidearms and supplied with food and sleeping equipment. His seizure nullified any plans Miles may have had to retain Joseph and the chief ultimately was permitted to return to the Indian camp, Jerome thereupon being freed. It is worth noting that Jerome received neither a Medal of Honor nor a brevet for his role in the Bear Paw battle, as did other officers who placed themselves in less jeopardy, perhaps indicating Miles' dissatisfaction with his reconnoiter. Jerome again was arrested and held at Fort Snelling, Minnesota, from December 1878 until April 1879, when he resigned his commission. He enlisted in Company H, 8th Cavalry March 16, 1880, and served to corporal until January 31, 1882, when he was mustered out. He became general manager of the John Weir Mining Company of Mosby Creek, Tennessee, a zinc mining operation. During the Spanish American War he tendered his services to the War Department, but they were not accepted. He died at New York City.

Heitman; Cullum; McWhorter, *Hear Me;* Alvin M. Josephy, *The Nez Perce Indians and the Opening of the Northwest.* New Haven, Yale Univ. Press, 1965.

Jesup, Thomas Sidney, army officer (Dec. 16, 1788-June 10, 1860). B. in Berkeley County, Virginia (now West Virginia), he was commissioned from Ohio a second lieutenant in the 7th Infantry May 3, 1808, becoming a first lieutenant December 1, 1809 and a major by the end of the War of 1812 when he was in the 1st Infantry. He became a lieutenant colonel of the 3rd Infantry April 30, 1817, colonel adjutant general in 1818, Brigadier General and Quartermaster General May 8, 1818 and was breveted Major General May 3, 1828, for 10 years in one grade. Although a Quartermaster General, and a good one, Jesup was given a field command in Alabama May 19, 1836, when a Creek outbreak sparked grave fears at Washington that these noted fighters might join the Florida Seminoles in a massive Indian war. Jesup acted vigorously in Alabama until Winfield Scott, his military superior ordered him to desist until Scott had troops in Georgia ready to concert an offensive. Jesup carried his case to Washington and Scott was ordered out of the theater, Jesup to assume command. December 8, 1836, he succeeded Richard Keith Call, a Brigadier General in the territorial militia, in command of the army in Florida where Seminole hostility had proven deeper and more difficult to eradicate than had been expected. Jesup was given a free hand. His idea was to push depots ever deeper into Florida and from them to pressure the Seminoles without letup until they surrendered when all could be shipped to Indian Territory. Difficulties arose immediately over the fact that many blacks operated with the Seminoles and white Floridians assumed such were runaway slaves, this though the Indians themselves owned some slaves. Also white Floridians and their publications twisted everything Jesup said to their advantage and his disadvantage. Added to these, many of his men were ill-trained militia, proper communications between elements of his command were lacking, and terrain posed almost

insuperable problems. Yet he persevered. He established a detention camp near Tampa, adding to it gradually such Seminoles as would surrender, including the important chiefs Micanopy, Jumper, Cloud and Alligator. June 2, 1837 however Osceola with a force of 200 quietly reached the camp and cleaned it out with up to 700 Seminoles liberated. Jesup initially offered to resign as a result, then thought better and determined to remain to justify himself. Around July 1 the name of his command was changed to Army of the South. By offering blacks freedom and protection if they would quit the hostiles and come in (even if for a variety of reasons the pledge was not often kept) the problem of black support for Seminole hostility was virtually solved. The weary Jesup also decided that the government was wrong in trying to ship west the Seminoles before Seminole lands were needed for white settlement. Jesup decided that he must ignore flags of truce if he were to break up the enemy leadership: he took Coacoochee (Wildcat) and Blue Snake captive after they had come in for talks and in October 1837 ordered Osceola and others, including 71 warriors arrested under similar circumstances; these deeds made Jesup infamous in many circles, although he believed it necessary to fulfill his mission. "General Jesup may ... have convinced himself of the honorableness of his conduct, but was still writing justifications of it twenty-one years later," observed Mahon. Jesup launched a major offensive in late October 1837 with the largest army to assemble in Florida during the Seminole wars, nearly 9,000 men in all. A column led by Jesup himself engaged the Indians January 24, 1838, in the Battle of Loche-Hachee; while the hostile loss was unknown the Anglos and their allies had 7 killed and 31 wounded, including Jesup himself: a bullet shattered his glasses and laid open his cheek. In May 1838 Jesup was relieved of command by Zachary Taylor and resumed his duties as Quartermaster General at Washington. He continued in that capacity in all for 42 years until his death; no other officer ever held a staff position so long, and the organization he created in that department persisted long after him. Mahon wrote that "Jesup was the most important white individual in the Seminole War (although) reactions to his policies were violent then, and they still are." He died at Washington, D.C., and was buried in Arlington National Cemetery.

Heitman; John K. Mahon, *History of the Second Seminole War.* Gainesville, Univ. of Fla. Press, 1967.

Jett, William Bladen, frontier soldier (Nov. 27, 1858-Dec. 7, 1941). Born on the Northern Neck of Virginia, Jett enlisted April 9, 1881, and was assigned to the 4th Cavalry, joining in Colorado and sent shortly to Arizona. Posted to Fort Huachuca, he was of the detachment ambushed by Chihuahua's Apaches June 8, 1885, in Guadalupe Canyon, near the New Mexico-Arizona-Old Mexico lines, when three men were killed. He was discharged April 9, 1886, spent some time as a cowboy and rancher in southern Arizona. He joined the Methodist Episcopal Church at Phoenix the next year and returned to Virginia, training for the ministry; he was a preacher for about 30 years. Jett's principal significance is for his autobiography covering his army and frontier years, including the only eye-witness account of the Guadalupe Canyon fight. He was a good soldier, but contentious, opinionated and stubborn, and must have been a trial to his officers. He died at Petersburg, Virginia.

"The Reluctant Corporal: The Autobiography of William Bladen Jett," ed. by Henry P. Walker. *Jour. of Ariz. Hist.,* Vol. XII, Nos. 1, 2 (Spring, Summer 1971), 1-50, 112-44.

Jim Boy (High Head Jim, Tustenaggee Emathla), Creek prophet, chief (c. 1790-1851). From Auttose, Alabama, he commanded the hostiles in the battle of Burnt Corn July 27, 1813, which opened the Creek War of 1813-14. By report he had given away Creek plans for hostilities to Sam Moniac (McNac) earlier; in any event the whites precipitated and lost the encounter. Jim Boy may have been in on the Fort Mims massacre of August 30, 1813, but it is not known what other actions he participated in during the war. After the conflict he settled near Polecat Spring where he built a town called Thlopthlocco. In 1818 he served with the Creeks under William McIntosh against the Seminoles. During the Creek troubles of 1836 he attached himself to those friendly to the whites. At the close of difficulties he was asked to raise a force of Creeks to fight in the Second

Seminole War in Florida; he raised 950 men, forming a regiment commanded ultimately by David Moniac (see entry). Jim Boy was in the second Battle of Wahoo Swamp November 17-21, 1836, and the Battle of Lake Monroe, February 8, 1837, in addition to a number of skirmishes. When he returned home he found his family had been transported in his absence to Indian Territory and all his property destroyed despite the promise of General Jesup that his people would be cared for and any damage to his property in his absence compensated for; neither promise was kept. Four of his nine children had been among 236 Creeks drowned in the sinking of the emigration steamship *Monmouth.* Jim Boy's home in the Creek Nation in Indian Territory was at Wetumpka, where he died. He was described as a fine looking man, six feet tall and with a commanding air.

H.S. Halbert, T.H. Ball, *The Creek War of 1813 and 1814.* Univ. of Ala. Press, 1969; Albert James Pickett, *History of Alabama.* Birmingham Book and Mag. Co., 1962 (as High Head Jim); Thomas McAdory Owen, *History of Alabama and Dictionary of Alabama Biography,* 4 vols. (1921), II, Spartenburg, So. Car., Reprint Co., 1978; Jim Boy's portrait is opposite p. 188, Grant Foreman, *Indian Removal.* Norman, Univ. of Okla. Press, 1969.

Jim Dickie, Delaware hunter (d. post 1849). A member of Jim Swanock's band, he reached the Rockies in the middle 1830s, becoming a trapper and hunter, being last reported at Fort Barclay, New Mexico, June 18, 1849.

Harvey L. Carter article, MM, Vol. VII.

Jim Mike, Rainbow Bridge guide: *see* Mike, Jim.

Joaquin, California outlaws (fl. 1850s). Best known of the several desperadoes named Joaquin was Joaquin Murrieta, but the California Legislature named five as wanted in 1853: "Joaquin Muriati, Joaquin Valenzuela, Joaquin Carillo, Joaquin Botellier and Joaquin Ocomorenia." Many believe that Murrieta, most famous of all, was largely fictitious, a creation of novelist John Rollin Ridge (Yellow Bird), "because he needed the money," and adopted without question by numerous fact writers and even serious historians. Secrest differs, and presents evidence to support his case. The legend centered around the shootout of Murrieta and "Three-Fingered Jack" Garcia with California Rangers Captain Harry Love (see entry) and his 20 men in 1853; it is widely believed that the true Murrieta had escaped into Old Mexico and the head Love brought in — for which the rangers received a $6,000 reward — was of an innocent man. Murrieta, this version goes, went south from Maricopa County to Monterey County, San Luis Obispo County, Los Angeles and had reached San Diego by July 4, before fading into Mexico where he was reported living much later. Secrest's research, on the other hand found that Joaquin Murrieta, who had been depredating in Calaveras County, central California, for two months beginning in January 1853, had ceased his activities four months before Love took up his trail. Love's rangers had been organized by Assemblyman P.T. Herbert of Mariposa County, who became one of them. Love captured Jesus Felíz, brother-in-law of the wanted man and forced him to guide the rangers to Murrieta's camp on Cantua Creek. Early on July 25, 1853, Love caught up with the gang, eight of whom were slain. One known as Murrieta was shot by rangers Bill Henderson and John White. *Tres Dedos*, or Three-Fingered Jack, was also killed. Bill Byrnes (see entry) cut off Murrieta's head and someone severed the head and hand of Three-Fingered Jack, the trophies preserved in whiskey until the rangers reached Stockton when they were transferred to alcohol-filled glass jars for exhibition purposes. Almost immediately tales were generated that the one head was not that of Murrieta but of an Indian horse handler named Chappo, but the ranger claims were supported by much evidence, including identification of the Murrieta head by one of his own associates. From Millerton and Mariposa, Love gathered 17 affidavits from people who had known Murrieta and were convinced that the head was his. Added to these were detailed descriptions of the head by the *Stockton Journal*, August 12, 1853, the San Francisco *Herald*, the Columbia *Gazette*, and Love's letter to the editor of the California *Alta* in March 1855. Whereas a biography of Joaquin Murrieta by Frank Latta (1980) reported that the supposed Murrieta head was clearly that of an Indian, Secrest presents persuasive evidence from contemporary sources that it was not. Murrieta himself had

been described in life as tall, handsome, with a light beard and mustache, light brown wavy hair, light complexioned and with blue eyes, his features distinctly Spanish. Witnesses reported the preserved head depicted those characteristics, being also identified by a facial scar Joaquin was known to have possessed. Love exhibited Joaquin's head for $1 a view in the central California mining camps (where Murrieta was well known) for several months; eventually the trophy was acquired by Dr. Jordon's San Francisco Museum where it spent 40 years before being destroyed in the 1906 San Francisco earthquake and fire.

William B. Secrest, "Who Died at Cantua Creek?" *Real West*, Vol. 27, No. 196 (Apr. 1984), 36-41; Joseph Henry Jackson, "The Creation of Joaquin Murieta." *Pacific Spectator*, Vol. II, No. 2 (Spring 1948), 176-81; Ramon F. Adams, *Six-Guns and Saddle Leather*. Norman, Univ. of Okla. Press, 1969, 536-38; Remi and Margaret Nadeau, "Joaquin: Dead or Alive?" *Westways*, Vol. 62, No. 8 (Aug. 1970), 45-46, 51; Remi Nadeau, *The Real Joaquin Murieta: Robin Hood Hero or Gold Rush Gangster?* Glendale, Calif., Zeta Pubs Co., 1975; Raymond F. Wood, "New Light on Joaquin Murrieta." *Pacific Historian*, Vol. 14, No. 1 (Winter 1970), 54-65.

Jogues, Isaac, Jesuit missionary (Jan. 10, 1607-Oct. 18, 1646). B. at Orleans, France, he was ordained a Jesuit priest in 1636, leaving in April for Canada and going immediately to the Huron mission, where he learned the language and labored for six years. He attempted unsuccessfully with Garnier, another Jesuit, to found a mission among the Tobacco nation and in September 1641, with Charles Raymbault, met Chippewas near Sault Ste. Marie. In 1642, after visiting Quebec, he and his companions, including some Hurons, were ambushed by Iroquois and taken to the Mohawk villages where they were tortured, some burned alive and another Frenchman murdered. Jogues and another were given to Indian families as slaves, still recovering from their savage wounds suffered under torture. In August 1643, Jogues escaped with the help of the Dutch commandant at Rensselaerswyck (Albany) and a Protestant, and November 5 left New Amsterdam (New York) aboard a Dutch vessel, reaching Rennes, France, January 5, 1644. The following spring he returned to

Montreal. In July Mohawk envoys reached Three Rivers to conclude a peace treaty; this eventually was finalized and ratified in Canada in May 1646. Jogues (who had learned the Iroquois tongue), and Jean Bourdon were sent to the Mohawks for Indian ratification, then returning to Quebec. In September 1646, Jogues was sent again to the Mohawk country to spend the winter, but the Indians had recommenced hostilities against the French. They captured Jogues, taking him and a companion, Jean de la Lande, to the Mohawk town of Ossernenon (now Auriesville, New York, just west of Amsterdam on the Mohawk River). Enroute Jogues became perhaps the first white man to see Lake George. A tribal council decided to free the prisoners, but the two were assassinated by "fanatical members of the Bear clan," felled by tomahawk and not by torture. "Thus," wrote Parkman, "died Isaac Jogues, one of the purest examples of Roman Catholic virtue which this Western continent has seen... When acting under orders he knew neither hesitation nor fear." Information of the murders was sent to Canada by Willem Kieft, governor of New Netherlands. With seven others of his faith killed by the Indians, Jogues was canonized June 29, 1930 by Pope Pius IX.

Thwaites, JR IX, 313-14n41, XXV, 43-73; DCB; Parkman, *The Jesuits in North America, II.*

Johnny-Behind-the-Deuce: *see* Michael O'Rourke.

Johnson, scout (fl. 1870's). Whether this man was a half-breed Lipan-Tonkawa, or a half-breed Mexican-Lipan, is uncertain; they may have been the same, or different, men, but in either event "Johnson" was a major scout for Mackenzie during the 1874 Staked Plains operation that in September featured the last army-Comanche engagement in Texas. Johnson was hired at Fort Concho (San Angelo), Texas. By Carter he was called Tonkawa Johnson, and said his mother was a Lipan, although he could speak little of the tongue. Johnson is generally credited with guiding Mackenzie into Palo Duro Canyon, east of present Canyon, Texas, for the climatic engagement.

R.G. Carter, *On the Border with Mackenzie.* N.Y., Antiquarian Press, 1961.

Johnson, Arkansas, desperado (d. June 13,

1878). B. probably in Missouri, he was a petty thief whose real name was said to be either Huckston or McKeen; he was married and with the help of his wife broke jail with Henry Underwood at Kearney, Nebraska; the two went to Texas and joined the Sam Bass gang. Johnson took part in a Bass train robbery at Eagle Ford, Texas, April 4, 1878, and another at Mesquite Station April 10; both were relatively unproductive. He was slightly wounded in a brush with a posse June 9, eight miles south of Denton, Texas, and was killed in a fight with June Peak's Rangers on Salt Creek, west of Cottondale. Peak credited Sergeant Thomas Floyd with killing Johnson, but there are other claimants. Johnson was of heavy build, 5 feet, 8 inches, in height, ruddy complexion, with blue eyes and light hair; he was bearded and his face bore smallpox scars.

Wayne Gard, *Sam Bass.* Lincoln, Univ. of Nebr. Press, 1969; *Frontier Times,* Vol. 3, No. 5 (Feb. 1926), 24-25.

Johnson, Bill, lawman (d. Apr. 17, 1881). Johnson was hired as assistant marshal of El Paso about mid-September 1880, being described by Metz as "the town drunk." Nevertheless, he survived the brief reigns as marshal of A.I. Stevens, George Campbell and Ed Copeland, but was fired by a fourth, Dallas Stoudenmire. This ignited a feud between the two. Johnson missed the April 14, 1881, fight in which Stoudenmire and others felled four victims, but three days later attempted to ambush Dallas and Doc Cummings, missed with a double-barreled shotgun and himself was slain.

Leon Claire Metz, *The Shooters.* El Paso, Mangan Books, 1976.

Johnson, Dorothy Marie, writer (Dec. 19, 1905-Nov. 11, 1984). B. at McGregor, Iowa, she was graduated from Montana State University in 1928, worked as a magazine editor in New York before returning in 1950 to teach journalism at the University of Montana (the new name for her alma mater) at Missoula, and commenced writing novels and non-fiction western books. Among her writings were *Indian Country* (1953); *Famous Lawmen of the Old West* (1963); *Some Went West* (1965); *Warrior for a Lost Nation: A Biography of Sitting Bull* (1969); *Montana* (1970); *Western Badmen* (1970); *The Bloody Bozeman* (1971); with R.T. Turner, *The Bedside Book* of *Bastards* (1973), and *All the Buffalo Returning* (1979). Johnson's writings were popular, interesting and moved at a good clip, but they were rarely researched thoroughly and according to Ramon F. Adams sometimes contained "errors too many to list." She died at Missoula of Parkinson's disease, having ordered her tombstone engraved: "PAID," commenting that "God and I know what it means, and nobody else needs to know." She never married.

Adams, *Six-Guns and Saddle Leather,* Norman, Univ. of Okla. Press, 1969; *Contemporary Authors,* New Revision Series 6.

Johnson, Edwin W., lawman (Dec. 13, 1853-Dec. 5. 1931). B. in Clark County, Arkansas, Johnson's first name was given as Edward in a biographical article by his son, but as Edwin on his death certificate. At 23 he was a deputy sheriff at Arkadelphia, Arkansas. In 1880 he went to Texas and became a deputy under Cooper Wright of Clay County. Johnson was active in suppressing fence cutting in the 1880s. For two years, either before or after the Marlow affair he was a deputy under Ol Brown of Young County, Texas. In March 1885 he was appointed deputy U.S. marshal, sent to Graham, Texas, and served four years, generally in the western part of Indian Territory, the later Oklahoma. February 29, 1888 Johnson lost his right arm in a gun battle with Bob James at Wichita Falls, Texas, but by practice learned to shoot well with his left hand. In the summer of 1888 the five Marlow brothers were indicted for horse theft and Johnson with the assistance of others arrested four of them, Charlie, George, Alf, and Llwellyn (Lep), the fifth, Boone Marlow being absent from home at the time. The four were jailed at Graham, in the early fall escaping but shortly being retaken. Later they made bond. Boone was arrested by Fort Sill authorities and jailed at Graham December 12, 1888, but was mistakenly released on bond. When it was learned that he was wanted for murder, officers went to the Marlow place five days later. One officer was killed from ambush; four Marlow brothers were taken, Boone again evading arrest. Local feeling being high it was decided to move the Marlows from the Graham jail to Weatherford, a railhead 60 miles distant, for shipment to Dallas. Johnson organized an eight-man protective force and with the prisoners left the Graham jail at 9:30

p.m. January 19, 1889. The convoy was attacked by a mob at a creek crossing; a major battle erupted, Johnson killing one mobster but being wounded in his one good hand, a shot "literally tearing it to pieces." He weathered repeated hails of bullets although incapacitated by his wound. There were ten battle casualties: five dead and five wounded. Among the dead were Johnson's chief deputy, Sam Criswell and two Marlow brothers, Lep and Alf, the other two Marlows being wounded. Two members of the mob, Bruce Wheeler and Frank Harmonson also died. Politically-inspired legal entanglements and suits by the Marlows cast a shadow over Johnson who was even indicted for allegedly being one of the mob although Charlie Marlow gave him credit for doing all he could for the boys, and it was generally conceded that he was a very brave man and in no way to blame for the affair; eventually he was fully exonerated, his case never having reached the trial stage. In about 1916 Johnson moved to Los Angeles, California and was deputy sheriff there until his death. He was described by his son as a man who "seldom ever joked, but was high-tempered and quick to resent an insult." Johnson's wife pre-deceased him.

Edward W. (Ted) Johnson, "Deputy Marshal Johson Breaks a Long Silence." *True West,* Vol. 27, No. 3 (Jan.-Feb. 1980), 6-11, 48-54; Johnson's death certificate.

Johnson, Guy, Indian official (c. 1740-Mar. 5, 1788). B. in Ireland, he was probably a nephew of William Johnson whose youngest daughter by Catherine Weisenburg he married in 1763. He reached America about 1755 and commanded a ranger company under Amherst in 1759-60 against the French. In 1762 his uncle, who was superintendent of Indian affairs made Guy deputy superintendent; he had been acting as secretary of the Indian department and also had some skill as a mapmaker. Upon William Johnson's death in 1774, Guy Johnson became superintendent of Indian affairs and worked assiduously to retain the loyalty of the Iroquois of New York State as the Revolution loomed. In 1775 he went to Oswego, New York, where his wife died, leaving him with two daughters whom he took to Montreal. Here he lost control over Canadian Indians but was reconfirmed as agent of the Six Nations. He made his headquarters at Niagara in 1776 with his deputy, John Butler, then joined Howe's army at New York in 1777 but after Burgoyne's defeat tried to get back to Montreal, not reaching that city until 1779. He went to Niagara again that autumn and directed Indian and Loyalist raids against the New York frontier and took credit — or responsibility — for the raid which perpetrated the Wyoming Valley Massacre of 1778 in Pennsylvania. Guy Johnson turned over the Indian superintendency in 1783 to John Johnson, William's son, and returned to England. He died at London.

CE; DAB; DNB; Barbara Graymont, *The Iroquois in the American Revolution.* Syracuse (N.Y.) Univ. Press, 1972; Arthur Pound, *Johnson of the Mohawks.* N.Y., Macmillan Co., 1930.

Johnson, James, pioneer (d, 1847). B. in England, he apparently reached Guaymas, Sonora, about 1825; James Johnson is often confused with John J. Johnson, the scalphunter, but they were distinct individuals. James Johnson engaged in pearl fishing in the waters of the Gulf of California; from 1833-34 he made several trips between Sonora and California aboard the ship *Facio,* representing "some kind of Sonora company." Eventually he bought into the San Pedro rancho of Manuel Gutiérrez in California, but financial hard times came upon him, he was accused of taking part in the Apalátegui Revolt of 1835, and his ranching interests eventually were removed to San Diego County, presumably where he died. His widow lived on for more than 30 years, as did two sons and three daughters. Johnson was described as a large stout man "of variable temperament."

Bancroft, *Pioneer Register;* Rex Strickland, "The Birth and Death of a Legend: The Johnson 'Massacre' of 1837."*Arizona and the West,* Vol. 18, No. 3 (Autumn 1976), 257-86.

Johnson, John Indian official (Nov. 5, 1742-Jan. 4, 1830). The son of William Johnson and Catherine Weisenburg, he fought with his father in a campaign during the Pontiac Conspiracy (1763-66) and was knighted in 1765 at London where he had gone to further his education. As the oldest son of his father he succeeded to the baronetcy and vast estates when William Johnson died in 1774 and also became Major General of militia as his father had been. As a Loyalist he fled New York in

1777 and went to Montreal where he was commissioned a lieutenant colonel and placed in command of a ranger force, the Royal Greens. He was with St. Leger at Fort Stanwix in 1777, was at Oriskany later that year and in 1778 led a raid into the Mohawk Valley, continuing his guerilla operations in 1779 out of Niagara and Oswego. He raided into the Mohawk Valley and the Schoharie Valley in 1780, causing much devastation. Johnson went to England in 1781 returning the next year, succeeding his cousin, Guy Johnson as superintendent general and inspector general of the Six Nations and Indians in Quebec and with a commission as British army colonel. He died in Canada where he had been given money and land to compensate for the loss of his legacy in New York State. He was married.

DCB; DAB; CE; Barbara Graymont, *The Iroquois in the American Revolution.* Syracuse (N.Y.) Univ. Press, 1972; Arthur Pound, *Johnson of the Mohawks.* N.Y., Macmillan Co., 1930.

Johnson, John (Turkey Creek Jack), lawman, desperado (fl. 1872-1882). This may have been the Jack Johnson who in November 1872 as marshal of Newton, Nebraska, killed desperado Mike Fitzgerald who had slain Justice of the Peace George Halliday. Later he went to the Black Hills where he reportedly killed two men and shortly left for Arizona. He was one of Wyatt Earp's followers operating around Tombstone in 1880-82, and was suspected from time to time of participating in lawless events. Johnson had a role in the murder of Frank Stilwell at Tucson March 20, 1882, and Florentino Cruz two days later. He then quitted Arizona with the Earp people and disappears from the record.

Ed Bartholomew, *Wyatt Earp: The Untold Story.* Toyahvale, Tex., Frontier Book Co., 1963; Bartholomew, *Wyatt Earp: The Man & the Myth.* Toyahville, 1964.

Johnson, John J., scalphunter (c. 1805-Autumn 1852). B. in Kentucky, he was a hatter by trade, his year of birth conjecture (he was said to have come to Mexico as "a very young man" although the given date of his migration is incorrect). Johnson arrived at Santa Fe from Missouri in July 1827 as a member of the James Glenn party. August 6 Johnson received a trade permit allowing him to visit Sonora, and went southward with

Glenn and James Ohio Pattie, returning to Santa Fe in 1828. Johnson received permission to go to Sonora again in 1828, 1829 and 1831, no doubt engaging in trade. He probably by 1830 had settled at Oposura, Sonora, making that community the center of his widespread operations until his death. From trade, his interests expanded into mining and land ownings, mainly centered near San Marcial. In 1835 he married Delfina Gutierrez who had been educated at Oposura, and fathered four sons, Ricardo, Julian, Ismael and Manuel. Late in March 1837, Apaches raided Noria, 30 miles north of Oposura, causing casualties and taking captives. About this time a group of Missouri mule buyers led by Charles Ames and Bill Knight, reached Johnson's ranch headquarters; since few mules had been left by Apaches in the country, Ames and his party agreed to accompany Johnson and men he would gather, in a raid on Apache camps to the northeast, hopefully to recover booty taken from Noria and acquire Indian-held mules for sale in the States. The expedition left Oposura April 3, 1837, with 17 Anglos and five Mexican mule packers. At Fronteras Johnson persuaded Antonio Narbona Jr., presidio commandant, to loan him a small swivel gun; Johnson and his crowd left Fronteras April 12 and rode north, hunting Apaches, probably passed through Guadalupe Canyon and on April 20 sighted an Indian camp perhaps at Juniper Springs in the present Hidalgo County, New Mexico. Johnson found the camp headed by Juan José Compá, a Mimbreno Apache chief. Johnson lied about the reasons for being in the country, his explanations were accepted, and he was permitted to remain; two days later, April 22, having mounted and loaded the swivel gun, Johnson at 10 a.m. treacherously attempted to assassinate as many of the Apaches as he could, loot being his objective. Although Juan José, his brother, Juan Diego and Marcelo, a third chief, were among the initial victims, no doubt made sure of at the outset by the Anglos, the Apaches seem to have rallied quickly and in a two-hour fight chased the whites off but not until about 20 Apaches had been killed and others wounded, no doubt in the initial surprise of the assault. Pursued by the angered Indians, Johnson managed to regain Janos Presidio, where on April 24 he penned a report of the affair to José Joaquin Calvo, interim governor of Chihuahua, then

withdrew to Oposura. He and his men ultimately received 100 pesos for their fight, many details of which remain perplexing while Strickland, who appears to have done the best research on the incident, is unpersuasive at several controversial points. The attack, and particularly the slaughter of the chiefs, had far-reaching repercussions, particularly on Mexican-Apache relations, but also with regard to Anglo-Apache affairs and can scarcely be justified in any direction. When gold was discovered in California, Johnson and some of his sons made trips there; on one of them John Johnson died in the vicinity of an Arizona community that is unidentified. His descendants have in some cases reached positions of some prominence in Sonora.

Rex W. Strickland, "The Birth and Death of a Legend: The Johnson 'Massacre' of 1837." *Arizona and the West*, Vol. 18, No. 3 (Autumn 1976), 257-86.

Johnson, Julian, pioneer (fl. 1860). The second son of John J. Johnson, assassin of Juan José Compá and other Mimbres Apaches, Julian settled ultimately at Gilroy, California, where he was a telegrapher in 1860; he was confused by Wilson and others with his father, who never resided in California, although he traveled there on business occasionally. Later Julian moved to Piedmont, near San Francisco. He married an Anglo woman and fathered five children, including four sons. His son, John, left descendants and was a man of some means.

Rex W. Strickland, "The Birth and Death of a Legend: The Johnson 'Massacre' of 1837." *Arizona and the West*, Vol. 18, No. 3 (Autumn 1976, 285.

Johnson, Lewis, military officer (Mar. 20, 1841- Sept. 23, 1900). B. in Germany, he enlisted in the 10th Indiana Infantry April 18, 1861, was commissioned a first lieutenant September 18 and became colonel of the 44th Colored Infantry September 16, 1864, ending the Civil War a brevet Brigadier General of Volunteers. He became first lieutenant of the 41st U.S. Infantry July 28, 1866, a captain December 12, 1867, and transferred to the 24th Infantry, a black regiment November 11, 1869, commanding G Company. In the spring of 1888 the regiment was ordered to Arizona and New Mexico, Johnson and John L. Bullis being assigned to San Carlos where Bullis became acting Apache agent June 1 and Johnson commander of the post. On November 24, 1891, Bullis was succeeded as agent by Johnson, his longtime friend. Both men had been involved in the firing of Al Sieber, a chief of scouts of 20 years experience, and in a prolonged scandal concerning alleged irregularities at San Carlos. Johnson also was concerned with bronco Apaches and the wearying attempts to chase down the Apache Kid (see entry), then charged with various misdeeds in the southwest and in Old Mexico; he was never caught. Archie McIntosh, famed scout for Crook, offered to get the Kid, but dropped his offer after Johnson treated him "in a very Impolite & Harch way. I got disgusted..." Johnson was responsible for the arrest of Eskiminzin (see entry) and the shipment east of that chief and about 40 of his people on the unwarranted charge of secretly giving support to the Kid. Johnson retired with rank of major April 25, 1895, and died five years later.

Heitman; Powell; Dan L. Thrapp, *Al Sieber, Chief of Scouts.* Norman, Univ. of Okla. Press, 1964; information from Angie Debo; McIntosh to John G. Bourke, July 31, 1895, Bourke Collection, Box 2, folio 22, Nebr. Hist. Soc; William G. Muller, *The Twenty Fourth Infantry.* Fort Collins, Colo., Old Army Press, 1972

Johnson, Nephi, Mormon Indian interpreter (Dec. 12, 1833-June 6, 1919). B. at Kirtland, Ohio, he early joined the Mormon faith, reached Utah in 1848 and became a missionary to the Indians from 1853 until 1865, serving as scout and guide and learning the Paiute language and having much influence over them. "Few men in the vicinity could speak their language as well. The Paiutes in turn had great confidence in him." At the time of the Mountain Meadows massacre, Johnson was living at Enoch, Iron County; upon the summons of Isaac C. Haight, he went to Mountain Meadows with John M. Higbee and was interpreter when Lee made arrangements for the final butchery with the Indians and Mormons on one side, the Fancher company of California-bound emigrants on the other. In his 1906 affidavit, Johnson said that some of the 54 white men present "did not approve of the killing" and declined to shoot the gentiles they were assigned to slay, so that the Indians had to complete the work.

Johnson lived the latter part of his life at Mesquite, Nevada, where before his death he seemed heavily moved by remorse at recollection of the Mountain Meadows tragedy, as recounted by Brooks, who prints Johnson's graphic affidavit of the affair. He died at Mesquite and was buried there.

Juanita Brooks, *The Mountain Meadows Massacre.* Norman, Univ. of Okla. Press, 1966; Brooks, *John D. Lee.* Glendale, Calif., Arthur H. Clark Co., 1962; William Wise, *Massacre at Mountain Meadows.* N.Y., Thomas Y. Crowell Co., 1976; information from Myrtle Jensen Beber.

Johnson, Richard Mentor, soldier, politician (Oct. 17, 1781-Nov. 19, 1850). The man whom legend insists killed Tecumseh was b. at Bryants Station, Kentucky. He studied law, was admitted to the Bar in 1802, entered politics in 1804 and was elected to Congress in 1807. He served in the War of 1812 as colonel of Kentucky Volunteers and commanded a regiment under Harrison at the Battle of the Thames October 5, 1813. Johnson was generally considered the individual who shot and killed the great Indian, Tecumseh, in that engagement. He served in Congress, in the Senate and House of Representatives for most of the rest of his life, and was Vice President of the United States under Van Buren from 1837-41. He died at Frankfort, Kentucky.

BDAC; Heitman; Tecumseh: *Fact and Fiction in Early Records,* ed. by Carl F. Klinck, Englewood Cliffs, N.J., Prentice-Hall, Inc., 1961, 201-19.

Johnson, William, Indian superintendent (1715-July 11, 1774). B. at Smithtown, County Meath, Ireland, he reached America in 1738 to oversee an estate belonging to an uncle near Fort Hunter at the confluence of the Mohawk River and Schoharie Creek, New York. Johnson shortly became a substantial businessman, successful farmer, land speculator and Indian trader and soon was involved in public affairs and of increasing influence with the Six Nations of the Iroquois. During King George's War (1745-48) he attempted to organize Indian scouting and raiding parties, in February 1748 became colonel of the 14 militia companies on the New York frontier and three months later colonel of the militia regiment for Albany, positions which "opened great opportunities for patronage" and which he held the rest of his life. He won contracts to supply various frontier forts, sometimes padding his accounts and profiting considerably. Johnson lived in feudal magnificence in his fortified stone mansion, Johnson Hall. He formed a liaison in 1739 with Catherine Weisenburg, a German or Dutch indentured servant who had escaped from her owner, and married her upon her deathbed in 1759 legitimizing their three children; he then (or earlier) formed a liaison with Molly Brant, sister of the important Mohawk Joseph Brant, and probably married her in Indian fashion. At any rate Johnson argued early for development of relations with the powerful Iroquois and in April 1755, Braddock, then commander in chief of North America named him superintendent of Indian affairs in the northern parts of the continent, principally New York. Johnson was appointed commander of an expedition to take Fort St. Frederick at Crown Point on Lake Champlain, while Braddock would attack Fort Duchesne and Shirley strike Fort Niagara; all three expeditions failed of their objective, but Johnson's force founded Fort William Henry and defeated a Dieskau command at Lake George, Johnson himself being wounded. It was no great victory, according to Gwyn but in 1757 Parliament made Johnson a gift of 5,000 pounds sterling for it and he was awarded a baronetcy. Johnson resigned the commission from Braddock late in 1755 and concentrated on matters concerned with his Indian superintendency. He recruited nearly 1,000 Indians for John Prideaux's expedition against Niagara in July 1759 and when Prideaux was killed, Johnson assumed command, his first action destroying a French relief force approaching from the Ohio Valley; the fort surrendered July 25, cutting "the main artery of the French fur trade." With his Indians, Johnson accompanied Amherst to Montreal in 1760, soon returning to his Mohawk Valley home. With the fall of French America, Johnson's duties as Indian superintendent expanded and his success and influence with the Iroquois grew, largely because they considered him honest and dependable. One of his principles was that "the purchase of Indian lands should be controlled at a pace determined by the tribe's willingness to sell." Yet he had difficulties, largely because of lack of centralized purpose by the British who left Indian affairs too much to the individual colonies, and Johnson's need for police powers to enforce intelligent and

forward-looking regulations which therefore were largely ignored on all sides. He differed with Amherst in his desire to supply Indians with arms, and in favoring negotiations with them rather than confrontations. After 1760 Johnson met often with Indians, with Pontiac at Oswego in 1766 and with others in his manse. He presided over and was influential in the establishment of the Fort Stanwix Treaty of 1768 which ostensibly was meant to separate the races by establishing boundaries for each, but which often also gave an opening for Johnson's persistent land speculation and profiteering. The treaty was designed in part however to protect the Indians, and may have done so to some extent. Johnson was overcome by "a fainting and suffocation" during an Indian council at his home and died without lingering. The rumor was quickly started that he had died a suicide, having received unsettling dispatches shortly beforehand, but this was not generally credited. Johnson had eight children by Molly Brant surviving him. In his will he referred to them as his natural children by his "housekeeper," provided for and permitted them to take his name. His Indian liaisons, and there were others, greatly extended his influence among the Mohawks and other Iroquois as well as adding fluency in their language to his tongue. He has generally been esteemed as a worthy and respectable man, but Gwyn shows that he lost no opportunity to profit at the expense of the Crown or Indians, amassed a huge personal fortune and through the advantages of his office and long intimacy with the Indians "he was indeed one of their principal exploiters; his actions speak louder than any words of his." However, in Parkman's view, "compared with the Indian traders who infested the border, he was a model of uprightness" and when he came to a position of power in Indian agreement in New York "there was joy through all the Iroquois confederacy." He remains a towering figure of the northeastern frontier and a man of significance upon 18th century American history.

Literature abundant: Julian Gwyn, DCB, IV, 394-98; Arthur Pound, *Johnson of the Mohawks.* N.Y., Macmillan Co., 1930; Barbara Graymont, *The Iroquois in the American Revolution.* Syracuse (N.Y.) Univ. Press, 1972; William L. Stone, *Life of Joseph Brant.* N.Y., George Dearborn and Co., 1838; Parkman, *Montcalm and Wolfe,* I;

Robert B. Roberts, *New York's Forts in the Revolution*. Rutherford, N.J., Fairleigh Dickinson Univ. Press, 1980.

Johnson, William, adventurer (fl. 1812-1840). Johnson was an English seaman who deserted to the Americans and served aboard the *Constitution* in the War of 1812, notably at the defeat of the British ship *Guerrière* August 19, 1812. He afterward became a trapper for the Hudson's Bay Company and reached Oregon in 1839 with his Indian wife and family. Johnson was sheriff in the first provisional government, and settled on a claim near the present South Portland, in the Willamette Valley. McLoughlin said that eventually Johnson "left by sea and never returned to Oregon."

Thwaites, EWT, XXIX, 17n.

Johnson, William Harrison, frontiersman (d. Aug. 16, 1878). B. in Marion County, Ohio, he was a captain in the Quartermaster department during the Civil War, being commissioned November 18, 1862, and resigning March 6, 1865. He was mustered out in Texas and drove a small cattle herd to New Mexico, being wounded in both legs by hostile Indians on the eastern New Mexico Plains and was nursed to health on the Beckwith ranch near Seven Rivers, Lincoln County. Over the strenuous objections of Hugh Beckwith, an ardent Secessionist, Johnson married one of Hugh's daughters, Camelia (March 30, 1857-August 18, 1939). Johnson acquired a ranch nearby in partnership with John Wallace Olinger. The ranch prospered amazingly even to the point where John Chisum, the principal cattleman in the area, called Johnson "the worst cattle thief in the Pecos." Johnson held a deputy's commission from Sheriff Brady and became embroiled in the Lincoln County War on the Dolan-Murphy side; in fact Hugh Beckwith accused Johnson of luring his son, Robert Beckwith, into the affair. Johnson was killed by Hugh Beckwith in a dispute over ranch management. Johnson left his widow and two infant children.

Robert N. Mullin notes; Philip J. Rasch, Lee Myers, "The Tragedy of the Beckwiths." *English Westerners Brand Book 90*, Vol. 5, No. 4 (July 1963).

Johnston, Albert Sidney, army officer (Feb. 2, 1803-Apr. 6, 1862). B. at Washington, Kentucky, he was graduated from West Point in 1822, serving in the 2nd and 6th Infantry regiments until 1834 including duty as a regimental adjutant during the Black Hawk War. He resigned in 1834 because of his wife's illness, farmed in Missouri until 1836 when after his wife's death he went to Texas, serving in the Texas army, on August 5 being appointed adjutant general, and in 1837 becoming senior Brigadier General in command of the army, succeeding Felix Huston. A duel with Huston resulted in Johnston's being seriously wounded. He was appointed secretary of war for Texas in 1838 and the next year led an expedition against the Cherokees in East Texas. Married a second time in Kentucky he and his wife settled in Brazoria County, Texas. In the Mexican War he was colonel of the 1st Texas Rifles. In 1849 he was commissioned paymaster, United States Army, serving on the Texas frontier until named colonel of the 2nd Cavalry and appointed to command the Department of Texas from 1856. He commanded the Utah Expedition of 1858-60, and managed to assist the settlement of the Mormon question without open warfare. For three months Johnston commanded the Department of the Pacific at San Francisco; he resigned his commission April 10, 1861, rejected a Federal offer of a command second only to Winfield Scott, reached Texas overland, went on to meet with Jefferson Davis. Johnston was appointed a general officer and assigned to command the Western Department. He was mortally wounded at Shiloh, April 6, 1862, and "with him went one of the greatest hopes of the Confederacy." His body was entombed at New Orleans until 1867 when it was moved to Austin, Texas. He was described as over 6 feet tall, with broad shoulders, massive chest, square jaw and piercing eyes that "suited the frontier."

Literature abundant: Heitman; Cullum; DAB; HT.

Johnston (Johnson), John, frontiersman (c. 1823-Jan. 21, 1900). Of Scot descent and b. in New Jersey, he reportedly became a partner of John L. Hatcher (1812-1897) around 1843, going with him to the Rocky Mountains. They reached the Uintahs and once in a skirmish each killed two Arapahoes and Johnston, it is said, learned the art of scalping. After the usual mountain adventures with grizzlies,

Indians and other wild life, in 1846 he reportedly married a Flathead woman. In the spring of 1847 in Johnston's absence, the saga goes, Crows killed her and their unborn child. This set Johnston off on a Crow-killing spree that lasted for many years, according to legend. The tales relate that he not only killed and scalped Crow warriors, but extracted and ate their livers; some historians doubt the validity of the entire legend. Johnston became known as the Crow killer (Dapiek Absaroka) which like all myths or legends includes incidents no doubt overblown. For example it has been said that he killed in all 300 Crows, which seems unlikely in view of the estimated total of around 450 Crow warriors in those times, with no record of any disaster of such proportions. February 24, 1864, Johnston at St. Louis enlisted in Company H, 2nd Colorado Cavalry, remaining in the army 19 months, most of the time a sharpshooter in west-of-the-Mississippi actions. He was mustered out September 23, 1865. Johnston returned to the northern Plains and Rockies where his movements are indistinct but reportedly led to garish adventures, without much supporting documentation. In the late 1870s he visited Leadville, Colorado, briefly. Sheriff Tom Irvine of Custer County, Montana, named Johnston deputy stationed at Coulson, Montana. He held the job for a year, then returned to wilderness roaming. Until the late 1880s he trapped in the mountains, refusing purported offers to join Buffalo Bill or other wild west shows, and around 1895 his health failing, he left the mountains. He entered the Veterans Administration hospital at Los Angeles in December 1899 and died a month later, being buried in the hospital's cemetery.

Raymond W. Thorp, Robert Bunker, *Crow Killer: The Saga of Liver-Eating Johnson.* Bloomington, Ind. Univ. Press, 1958; Mark H. Brown, *The Plainsmen of the Yellowstone.* N.Y., G.P. Putman's Sons, 1961.

Johnston, Phillip, soldier (Sept. 15, 1892-Sept. 14, 1978). B. in Kansas, Johnston served with the Army in France in World War I; in World War II he suggested using Navahos to transmit war zone messages to avoid coding and confuse the Japanese; the Marine Corps accepted his suggestion, made him a technical sergeant in charge of recruiting Navaho speakers in Arizona, New Mexico and Utah.

In 1969 Johnston was given a special congressional medal for his work. He was a graduate of Northern Arizona University, Flagstaff, and Occidental College, Los Angeles, employed for 28 years as a city civil engineer in the latter community. He died at San Diego and was buried at Glendale, California.

Arizona Daily Star, Sept. 15, 1978.

Johnston, Velma Brown (Wild Horse Annie), conservationist (Mar. 5, 1912-June 27, 1977). B. in Nevada, around 1950 Velma Johnston and her husband, Charley, a Reno hay grower, saw a motor van crowded beyond capacity with wild horses being taken to the slaughterhouse in Nevada and Velma thereupon set out upon her great and lasting crusade to provide relief from persecution for wild horses and burros of the western arid lands. Her work commenced slowly but gathered momentum. In 1959 she led the drive which caused Congress to pass a bill prohibiting planes and trucks from being used to round up the animals. In 1971 she helped in passage of the wild Free Roaming Horse Act to further protect feral horses and burros. She became president of the International Society for the Protection of Mustangs and Burros and also of the Wild Horse Organized Assistance Society. Late in life she wrote an autobiography, *Mustang — Wild Spirit of the West.* In November 1980 the Little Book Cliffs Wild Horse Range northeast of Grand Junction, Colorado, was dedicated to her memory; the area of 27,000 acres had a herd in that year of 80 wild horses and was the third such refuge in the nation, created in 1974. Other refuges include the Pryor Mountain Wild Horse Range near the Wyoming-Montana border and the Nellis Bombing range, formerly part of the Nellis Air Force Base in Nevada. Velma Johnston died of cancer at 65 at Reno, Nevada; her husband had preceded her in death.

New York Times, June 28, 1977; Tucson, *Arizona Daily Star,* Nov. 8, 1980; Velma Johnston death certificate.

Jolliet, Adrien, fur trader, explorer (c. 1641-c. 1669?). An elder brother of Louis Jolliet, he was b. probably at Quebec and early became a fur trader, perhaps initially a voyageur. June 13, 1658, he and another were captured by Iroquois on the St. Lawrence River and taken to the Onondaga villages of New York State.

The pro-French chief Garakontié returned them to Quebec late in September. In 1660 Jolliet and others traded into the Ottawa country, accompanying the Jesuit Menard to Lake Superior. In the spring of 1666 he again contracted to obtain furs from the Ottawa. Late in 1668 Talon, intendant for New France, directed Jolliet and Jean Peré to visit Lake Superior, seek out a reported copper lode, and then search for an easier water route than via the Ottawa River for bringing ore to Montreal. On the return by way of Lakes St. Claire and Erie, Jolliet on September 24 met the La Salle exploration party near the present Hamilton, Ontario, and described for them the route he had charted via the lakes rather than the tortuous river. The *Dictionary of Canadian Biography* says Jolliet died during his return; there is no other confirmation, but he is not mentioned again in the literature. In 1664 he had married Jeanne Dodier, by whom he had a son.

Thwaites, JR, XLIV, 101,322n9; XLVI, 302n6; DCB, I 626.

Jolliet Louis, explorer (c. Sept. 21, 1645-summer 1700). B. at Quebec, he studied at the college of the Jesuits at Quebec, and took minor orders in 1662. Musically inclined, he was organist for some time at the college, but left the seminary in 1667, went to Paris briefly, and upon his return entered the fur trade. By 1671 he was at Sault Ste. Marie, where he no doubt heard rumors of the great river of the West. He was selected to locate it and learn into what sea it flowed; by 1672 he was at Michilimackinac, where he met Father Marquette who had been commissioned to accompany, and perhaps to nominally lead the expedition. It left in May 1673, with seven men in two canoes, going probably by way of Green Bay and the Fox and Wisconsin rivers to the upper Mississippi of which they were the nominal white discoverers, and continuing down it past the Missouri and Ohio to the mouth of the Arkansas River. About mid-July they started back, going up the Illinois River to a portage near present Chicago, and thence to familiar Lake Michigan once more. It was an epic journey of exploration. The party regained the French mission at Green Bay called St. Francis Xavier late in September 1673. Jolliet remained at Sault Ste. Marie during the winter, transcribing his journal and map and leaving duplicates with

the Jesuits, leaving in May 1674, for Quebec. His canoe capsized enroute, three men were drowned and his documents lost, while the copies he had left at Sault Ste. Marie were destroyed by fire. He reconstructed the events of the journey as best he could from memory. He was married in 1675, sought to settle in the Illinois country in 1677, but permission was denied, and he continued in the fur trade, in 1679 being commissioned to travel as far as Hudson Bay in its interests. He reached James Bay, contacted amicably a party of Englishmen, and returned to Quebec. His fur enterprises were extensive; Jolliet visited Labrador in 1694 and engaged to some extent in fisheries. He was named hydrographer and was known as something of a cartographer as well as a pioneer and frontiersman. The last three years of his life are only dimly known. For his feats of exploration, Jolliet was rewarded with the gift of Anticosti Island in the Gulf of St. Lawrence (seized briefly by the British), and later was given a seigniory near Quebec. "His broad education, his culture, the diversity of his talents as much as his courage and ambition, made of him one of the greatest and most illustrious sons of his country."

Literature extensive: DCB; DAB; CE; Raphael N. Hamilton, *Marquette's Explorations: The Narratives Reexamined.* Madison, Univ. of Wisc. Press, 1970.

Jolliet, Zacharie, fur trader (c. 1650-pre 1692). B. probably in Canada, he studied at the Jesuit college at Quebec as had his older brother, Louis, and like him he entered the fur trade at an early age. On October 1, 1672, the brothers joined with five others in forming a fur trading company to operate among the Ottawa and reached Michilimackinac in early December. Zacharie remained at Sault Ste. Marie to take care of business matters while his brother, with Marquette and four of the trading partners the next spring engaged in the great journey of discovery to the upper Misssssippi. April 13, 1679, Louis and Zacharie Jolliet and seven other Frenchmen reached Hudson or James Bay by way of the Saguenay, returning to Quebec by late October. Most of the later mention of Zacharie was in connection with the Hudson Bay fur trade and strife with the English traders active there. Thwaites says that since the woman Zacharie Jolliet had married in 1678 had married again by November 1692,

Zacharie must by that date have been deceased.

Thwaites, JR, LXIV, 273n1; DCB, I, 394, 396.

Joncaire, Louis Thomas, Chabert de, interpreter, Indian man (c. 1670-June 29, 1739). B. in Provence, France, he reached Canada as a cavalry sergeant in the late 1680s and soon was captured by the Senecas who sentenced him to be executed. Joncaire reported that he broke the nose of a Seneca chief who tried to burn his fingers, and so impressed the Indians that they adopted him; his son said that as he was about to be execu.ed, he was adopted by one of the Iroquois women. In any event, he quickly learned their language, their mannerisms, and became something of a Seneca himself, retaining their friendship and trust as long as he lived. He was an important instrument in a peace arranged in 1701 ending a French-Iroquois war. In Queen Anne's War he was charged with keeping the Iroquois neutral; his great rival was the half-breed, Louis Couc Montour, interpreter for the English who sought to nullify Joncaire's efforts. In the summer of 1709 Joncaire caused the assassination of Montour by deception, an incident which displeased Vaudreuil who said he would have preferred Montour to be captured so he could be properly hanged. August 7, 1711, Joncaire again was instrumental in swinging Indians collected for a Montreal council to declare for war on the side of the French. In 1720 Vaudreuil sent Joncaire to the Senecas to quietly win permission for the French to establish a post at Niagara, after it had been learned that the English planned to build such a fort. Joncaire commanded at Niagara until 1726. In 1731 he was named by Beauharnois to command a group of Shawnees who had migrated from the Susquehanna to the Allegheny River, prevent them from trading with the English and hopefully to move them still farther along to Detroit, but Joncaire died at Niagara before he completed this mission.

Thwaites, JR, LXIX, 293n30; DCB, II.

Jones, Ben, frontiersman (c. 1840-c. 1894). Jones, a man who had grown old on the frontier and young William W. Walker, his partner, were spending the night at Wyoming's KC Ranch April 8-9, 1892, when cattlemen invaders attacked and killed Nate Champion and Nick Ray. Jones and Walker were let go through efforts of friends among the invaders although they were vital witnesses. Because of their knowledge their careers turned hectic. Warned not to enter Casper, Wyoming, they lived on starvation diets for days, afraid to go into town. The cattleman's lawyer, Fred H. Harvey advised them to leave the country, adding that the stockmen would pay them for staying away until everything was settled. At last they were spirited off, barely escaping one legal thicket after another in Wyoming and Nebraska until they reached Kansas City and were safely shipped by rail to Westerly, Rhode Island, where they stayed at the Windsor Hotel for nearly two years, the Wyoming Stock Growers' Association paying their bills so long as they were away from Wyoming and could not testify against the cattlemen. Jones and Walker each were paid at last with $2,500 checks for their inconvenience — but the checks bounced: "no funds." Jones had married a 45-year-old Westerly woman expecting to settle there on the cattlemen funds. After the check debacle he wrote the association at Cheyenne and got a "scorching" reply demanding that he not again contact the organization (the danger of punishment for the guilty now being past). "Ben thought there was some mistake" and determined to go to Cheyenne and try to straighten matters out. He left Rhode Island and neither his wife nor Walker ever heard from him again, the latter assuming that he might have been "knocked off by the cattle barons," although no proof ever surfaced.

Daisy F. Baber, as told by Bill Walker, *The Longest Rope: The Truth About the Johnson County Cattle War.* Caldwell, Id., Caxton Printers, 1940; Robert B. David, *Malcolm Campbell: Sheriff.* Casper, Wyomingana, 1932.

Jones, Banjamin, mountain man (c. 1785-June 1835). B. in Virginia of English parentage, Jones left home at 16 and went to Kentucky, reaching St. Louis by 1802 or earlier; his year of birth given above is conjecture. He probably met Alexander Carson. There is no proof that he was associated with the Lewis and Clark Expedition, nor that Carson was, but in both cases it was possible they were engages as far as the Mandan Villages. With Carson, Jones became one of a party of 20 under Ezekiel Williams leaving St. Louis for the upper

Missouri and the mountains on January 25, 1807. Jones and Carson, returning downstream after a two-year hunt in the upper country met the Astorians in May 1811 and joined the Wilson P. Hunt party as guide and hunters, being "acquainted with the whole of the country between the Mandans and the Aricaras." In 1813 when he finally returned to St. Louis, Jones bought land on the Mississippi River, but became restless and went to Santa Fe in 1825 with the Sibley survey expedition, remaining in the southwest four years. He moved his family to Carondelet, Missouri, and later to a tract on Gravois Creek near Wilson Hunt. When he died of cholera he left his wife and five children, 14 slaves, 54 books and considerable real estate, making provision for his children's education and providing that the slaves bequeathed them "should never be sold by them or their heirs, 'under any pretence whatever'."

Stella M. Drumm, "More About the Astorians." *Ore. Hist. Quar.,* Vol. XXIV, No. 4 (Dec. 1923), 357-59; Louise Barry, *The Beginning of the West.* Topeka, Kan. State Hist. Soc., 1972; Clarke, *Lewis and Clark.*

Jones, Buck (Charles B. Gebhard), actor (Dec. 12, 1889-Dec. 1, 1942). B. in Vincennes, Indiana, he reportedly was raised near Red Rock, Oklahoma, where he is said to have learned ranch work. He is reported to have enlisted in the army, seen service on the Mexican border and in the Philippines where he was wounded by a bandit, and became an army pilot with the First Aviation Squadron before World War I. He is said to have become an auto race driver, in 1913 joined the Miller Brothers 101 Ranch show, worked with various circuses, and was employed first by Universal, then Fox and Columbia motion picture studios, becoming a western star. He is said to have appeared in about 200 films. He was caught in the Boston night club fire that took 500 lives, dying two days later.

Los Angeles Times, Dec. 1, 1942.

Jones, Calvin, frontiersman (Mar. 6, 1822-Oct. 15, 1888). B. in Kentucky, he was raised in Missouri and at 17 went west with a wagon train. He took part in the huge 1840 mountain men raid on southern California horse ranches, when 5,000 head were driven off. Jones became a beaver trapper, returned to California for a year in 1845, pursued various

activities east of the Rockies, was a freighter and herded sheep for Lucien Maxwell. He died at Pueblo, Colorado.

Harvey L. Carter article, MM, Vol. VI.

Jones, Charles G., soldier (Jan. 3, 1873-Jan. 2, 1967). B. at Iron Hill, Iowa, he served in the army in Arizona and New Mexico from 1894 to 1896, taking part in several scouts after the Apache Kid and other broncos. He was considered a veteran of the Indian wars. He worked as a railroad brakeman in Iowa, and as a businessman, and died at Cedar Rapids, Iowa.

Cedar Rapids Gazette, Jan 3, 1967.

Jones, Charles Jesse (Buffalo Jones), adventurer, conservationist (Jan. 1844-Oct. 1, 1919). B. in Tazewell County, Illinois, he grew up in McLean County. He early was attracted to natural history, studied two years at Wesleyan University at Bloomington and at 21 went west. He settled in Doniphan County, Kansas, started a nursery and married a woman descended from Izaac Walton, went broke and moved his wife and son to the future Osborne County, Kansas, where he built a sod house and commenced hunting buffalo, at first for their own needs, then for the market. He was on the plains in the core of the buffalo-hunting period, from 1869 onward and never calculated how many buffalo he killed, but guessed it was "thousands." He was in occasional Indian skirmishes, including a fight March 18, 1877, near the present Amarillo, Texas with Comanches who had quit their reservation for a hunt. Even by that time Jones occasionally had captured buffalo calves, gentled and sold them for $7.50 or exhibited them at county fairs. He was a founder in 1878 of Garden City, Kansas, along with the Fulton brothers and others and was elected mayor. He got into real estate and occasionally drove a team of buffalo calves through the streets of the town for the novelty of it. Gradually Jones came to appreciate the danger that buffalo were facing extinction and what their loss would mean. In April 1886 he set out from Kendall, Kansas, toward western Texas to see if any buffalo were left; he found a few and commenced roping calves, catching four the first day, more later on until a total of 18 were roped and taken alive. For this and similar feats he came to be nationally known as Buffalo Jones. Emerson Hough, a writer, and others concerned about preserving some remnant of the buffalo became interested. Jones established a buffalo ranch across the Arkansas River from Garden City, and experimented crossing buffalo and cattle; the result, called cattalo, were sturdy and possessed good qualities, but too often were sterile. With his calves and buffalo purchased from other Plains stockmen and buffalo partisans, Jones between 1886 and 1889 accumulated about 50 head. He bought the Sam I. Bedson herd of 86 buffalo, including some cattalo from Winnepeg, Alberta, for $50,000 in 1888 (in an aside roping a moose calf, and shipping it back to Kansas) and sent them by railroad, with considerable difficulty to Garden City. He commenced selling a few animals to zoos, parks and to individuals who wished to raise the animals, on one occasion taking ten buffalo to Liverpool, England, for a customer willing to pay $10,000 for them, delivered. His attempt to start a buffalo ranch in Nebraska failed however and because of financial difficulties Jones was forced to sell his buffalo in 1895, some to Michel Pablo in Montana, others to a California rancher. In 1897 he went to the Canadian arctic to rope musk-ox, an animal until then rarely if ever exhibited in the United States. He had numerous difficulties with Indians opposed to his project, but wintered near Great Slave Lake and in February, when he figured the cold weather had driven the musk-oxen south, commenced his hunt. He and John R. Rea eventually roped five calves, but they were killed by superstitious Indians, wolves ate the remains and Jones returned to Kansas by way of the Yukon and the Aleutians. His feat in capturing the animals had aroused wide interest, his fame had extended, but his profits had not. With Henry Inman he wrote an autobiography, *Buffalo Jones' Forty Years of Adventure* (1899). He captured a bighorn for the National Zoological Park. By 1900 Jones again had become interested in establishing wildlife refuges and when he learned that a buffalo herd was to be started at Yellowstone Park he asked Theodore Roosevelt for the job of building it; in 1902 he was made Yellowstone Park game warden. He built a compound for his embryonic herd, developed from animals from Montana and Texas. Jones did "a fine job" in getting the herd

established, but he came into difficulty in managing his men, being outraged by their use of alcohol, tobacco, and playing poker. They refused to work for him any longer, and he was fired. Jones decided to establish a buffalo and cattalo experimental ranch and preserve on the Kaibab Plateau north of the Colorado in Arizona. He obtained animals from Montana and California, they arriving at Lund, Utah, in June 1906. From there they were trailed to the selected site. These animals were the nucleus of the herd maintained today in the House Rock Valley to the east of the Kaibab. In Arizona Jones captured mountain lions and hunted wild horses with Zane Grey and others. Jones persuaded Charles S. Bird, a wealthy industrialist of Willapah, Massachusetts, to finance a trip to Africa on which he promised to rope any kind of game. Two southwestern cowboys, Marshall Loveless and Ambrose Means, a dozen cow ponies and several hounds were taken along, reaching Nairobi March 3, 1910. In adventurous escapades they managed to rope warthogs, elands, zebras (and ride one bareback), a rhino, a lioness (which was presented to the New York zoo and lived until 1921); in 1913 Jones went to the Congo after gorilla, but that effort was not as successful, the expedition breaking up in disarray and bad feelings between Jones and the sponsors. Jones also had contracted an African fever and he died five years after at Topeka, Kansas. Buffalo Jones was one of a kind. His supporters, and they were many, believed he had become a true conservationist after his earlier days as a butcher of buffalo and other wild animals; his detractors considered him at best a mountebank (albeit an adventurous one) at worst something of a confidence man. But many of his experiences were real, and his influence in preserving the buffalo and other fauna was considerable. His place in frontier history is assured.

Robert Easton, Mackenzie Brown, *Lord of Beasts: The Saga of Buffalo Jones.* Tucson, Univ. of Ariz. Press, 1961; Zane Grey, *The Last of the Plainsmen.* N.Y., Grosset & Dunlap, 1911; Martin S. Garretson, *The American Bison.* N.Y., Zoological Soc., 1938; David A. Dary, *The Buffalo Book.* Chicago, Swallow Press, 1974.

Jones, Horace P., scout, interpreter (Mar. 29, 1829-Nov. 16, 1901). B. at Jefferson City,

Missouri, he received a fair education before he was 17 when his family migrated to Texas, settling at Jefferson, Marion County. Jones wandered across Texas as a young man, visiting the buffalo country and contacting various Indian tribes. He learned Comanche and became proficient in sign language. In 1855 he was employed as a farmer at the "Upper Reservation" on the Clear Fork of the Brazos in Throckmorton County where the Penateka Comanches settled. He was attracted to these Indians and they to him, adopting him into the tribe and depending upon his counsel in matters of Indian-white affairs. These Indians were moved in late 1858 or 1859 to the Washita, Indian Territory, Jones accompanying them and becoming interpreter at the Washita Agency near Fort Cobb. He personally witnessed the recapture of Cynthia Ann Parker in 1860 while interpreter with L.S. (Sul) Ross's Ranger company. On the night of destruction at the Wichita Agency, October 23, 1862, and massacre of the Tonkawa Indians, Jones narrowly escaped death from the attacking Delawares and Shawnees. A year or two after the Civil War Jones was post scout and interpreter at Fort Arbuckle and later at Fort Sill in the present Oklahoma. He was a man of intellect and complete honesty with whites and Indians, who trusted him implicitly. In 1883 because he was unable to save any money he was persuaded to start a ranch on an allotment southwest of Signal Mountain near Fort Sill, each of his friends giving a cow to get him started (Quanah Parker gave two). Around 1884 the army cut his pay from $100 to $50 a month, but Sheridan when he heard of it, restored the original amount, with the lost back pay made up. Jones died at Fort Sill, thoroughly respected and with a wide friendship.

Joseph P. Thoburn, "Horace P. Jones, Scout and Interpreter." *Chronicles of Okla*, Vol. II, No. 4 (Dec. 1924), 380-91.

Jones, J. Milum, pioneer (c. 1825-Sept. 11, 1857). Jones, his wife whose name is not known and a child, possibly Felix Jones whose age is unknown, were from Johnson County, Arkansas. They joined the Fancher emigrant wagon train leaving Fort Smith, Arkansas, late in March 1857, bound for California. The elder Joneses were slain with

others of the company at Mountain Meadows, Utah, by Mormons and Mormon-led Indians.
William Wise, *Massacre at Mountain Meadows.* N.Y., Thomas Y. Crowell Co., 1976.

Jones, Jack: *see* William W. McGaa

Jones, John A., frontiersman (Jan. 6, 1855-Aug. 29, 1879). B. in Braxton County, Virginia (today's West Virginia), he was the oldest son of William Heiskell Jones (1830-1908), and with his father reached the site of the present Roswell, New Mexico, July 4, 1866, his father becoming the first white resident of the Pecos River valley. In either 1872 or 1875 he killed a purported claim jumper named Reilly or Riley near the site of the present Picacho, New Mexico; he and other members of the family went to Tucson to avoid retaliation, but left under obscure circumstances and returned to New Mexico where John killed another man in a dispute over a calf; the Joneses fled to the Pecos where they settled at what became Old Seven Rivers. They prospered until a Felix outfit, consisting of two brothers and their families killed a boy named Hart whom John Jones had rescued from Apaches and adopted formally. John pursued the Felix clan down the Pecos and killed seven men and older boys (Angel referred to the Felix clan as the Phallis family). John, Jim and Bill Jones participated in the Five Days' Battle at Lincoln in July 1878, but for unclear reasons. Later John Jones killed John Beckwith, his associate it was rumored in collecting "stray" cattle from largescale ranchers, and after having differed with Beckwith over a division of the spoils. Jones was killed three days later in Pierce Canyon by Robert Olinger, a friend and perhaps a relative by marriage of Beckwith's.

Robert N. Mullin notes; Philip J. Rasch, Lee Myers, "The Tragedy of the Beckwiths." *English Westerners' Brand Book 90,* Vol. 5, No. 4 (July 1963).

Jones, John B., Texas Ranger (Dec. 22, 1834-July 19, 1881). B. in Fairfield District. South Carolina, he was brought by his father to Texas in 1838. Jones was a graduate of Mt. Zion College, Winnsboro, South Carolina, returned to Texas and enlisted as a private in Terry's Rangers during the Civil War, rising to adjutant of the 15th Texas Infantry and by

1863 to adjutant general of a brigade. After the war he visited Mexico and Brazil, seeking sites for colonies for disgruntled Confederates, but recommended against both countries. On May 2, 1874, he was named major of the Frontier Battalion, and by July 10 six companies of Texas Rangers, 75 men in each, were enlisted to comprise it. The companies were stationed along the frontier from the Red River to the Rio Grande, charged with keeping Indians out and controlling outlawry within. The first important Indian fight was at Lost Valley, near Jacksboro, July 12, 1874, when Jones with 28 men attacked 100 or more Indians thought to be Kiowas, Comanches and Apaches. Jones lost two men killed, two wounded, and killed three enemy and wounded several, being lucky to get away without more serious losses. He effected a truce in the Horrel-Higgins feud of Lampasas County, settled the Mason County feud, cleaned up lawless Kimble County. He was instrumental in the destruction of the Sam Bass gang of train robbers at Round Rock in July 1878. Jones was sent in 1877 to El Paso in connection with the so-called Salt War, temporarily settling the affair, which however flared again after he left. Jones was made a member of the commission named by U.S. and Texas authorities to investigate the affair, as a result of which he took the side of the Americans as against the Mexicans involved. In January 1879, he was named adjutant general of Texas, continuing to direct the activities of the Frontier Battlion until his death. Jones was 5 feet, 8 inches, tall, black hair and black eyes, mustached, with an alert face. He was a quiet, tactful man, but with the aura of command, rode fine horses, was of high intelligence and great courage. He was temperate in habits, neither smoked nor drank and led "the finest force of Rangers that Texas has had." Little known, save by the specialist, he was among the greatest of Ranger officers.

DAB; HT; Walter Prescott Webb, *The Texas Rangers.* Boston, Houghton Mifflin Co., 1935; James B. Gillett, *Six Years With the Texas Rangers.* New Haven, Yale Univ. Press, 1925.

Jones, John M. (Jonesy), soldier-trumpeter (c. 1847-June 17, 1877). B. at Wheeling, (West) Virginia, he enlisted in Company F, 1st Cavalry and became a trumpeter. He was generally liked, though he had a fondness for whiskey which led him occasionally into

trouble. Once he deserted, but rejoined his troop under a general amnesty. In 1877 in Idaho he was in the guardhouse when Howard, impatient with reluctance of Nez Perce Chief Tuhulhulzote to accede to demands to give up his country and go on the reservation had the Indian jailed. In prison Tuhulhulzote and Jones became friends. Later Jones told a friend that if it came to war he knew he would not be harmed; Tuhulhulzote had promised him that. Jones was with an advance element of Captain Perry's command on the first day of hostilities. As they approached the hostiles, Jones commenced to blow a call to advance when he was shot from his horse by Fire Body (Otstotpoo), the first white soldier to fall in the Nez Perce war. Jones was 5 feet, 4 inches, in height and had hazel eyes, sandy hair and a ruddy complexion.

McWhorter, *Hear Me;* John D. McDermott, *Forlorn Hope: The Battle of White Bird Canyon and the Beginning of the Nez Perce War.* Boise, Ida. State Hist. Soc., 1978.

Jones, John Percival, pioneer, legislator (Jan. 27, 1829-Nov. 27, 1912). B. in England he was brought as a child to Ohio and reached San Francisco in 1850 around the Horn in the bark *Eureka.* He prospected the Feather, Stanislaus and Yuba Rivers, then entered business at Weaverville, California. In 1861 he became sheriff of Trinity County and by report established some reputation for Indian fighting. He was elected a state senator in 1863, became a financial figure in San Francisco, made a fortune in Comstock, Nevada, silver mines, was elected to the U.S. Senate, and from thence forward was a considerable financial, business and promoting figure in the Far West. Later he developed the Treadwell Mine in Alaska, settled on a ranch at Santa Monica, California, and there he died.

BDAC; Charled W. Dillon, "J.P. Jones — Fortune's Favorite." *True West,* Vol. 23, No. 3 (Feb 1976), 26-30.

Jones, John Stycks, freighter, businessman (May 20, 1811-July 11, 1876). B. at Lexington, Kentucky, he moved while young to Natchez, Mississippi where he managed a plantation for Jefferson Davis, a cousin of his wife. Jones then located in Pettis County, Missouri with his brother, Charles O. Jones (b. March 9,

1814, in Henry County, Kentucky — died post 1880), and became a noted Great Plains freighter before the Civil War; Charles Jones also engaged in this occupation to some extent. By 1848 there were indications Jones already was interested in Plains transportation. On March 5, 1850, with James Brown he contracted to freight government stores from Leavenworth to Fort Hall and ten days later advertised to take 80 men through to California if they would drive teams to Fort Hall, planning to go on to California with empty wagons from that point. His wagons left May 21, but Jones apparently altered his plans and returned to Independence, Missouri, from Laramie August 1, having made "one of the quickest trips" ever made from that post. In September he, Brown and William H. Russell contracted to deliver government freight from Leavenworth to Santa Fe and thereafter he was a major figure in the South Plains trade, although on this trip winter conditions caused the partners a "heavy loss of animals" just short of Santa Fe. Congress eventually reimbursed the company for these losses. In February 1851, Jones and Russell (Brown having died) signed a two-year contract to deliver army stores from Leavenworth to Santa Fe and Albuquerque. Their trains set out about March 1, but the 22nd many of the wagons were destroyed by a prairie fire supposedly set by Pawnees, the teamsters fleeing to safety across the Arkansas River. In May three more wagon trains were dispatched westward by Jones and Russell and later that month the partners secured a contract to freight government grain from Leavenworth to Fort Kearny, Nebraska, for two years. In 1858 Jones formed a partnership with Joseph L. Cartwright, also of Pettis County, Missouri, to freight supplies across the Plains. Their first train was of 156 wagons, the freight delivered to Camp Floyd, Utah, 40 miles from Salt Lake City; their oxen and other stock were driven on to California, where it was sold. When gold was discovered in Colorado they commenced about 1859 hauling to that region. At the Cherry Creek camp they were offered 75 town lots and five acres of land if they would establish a trading business. This was done, the partners constructing the first brick commercial house in Denver. During 1859-60 business was so brisk that 500 wagons were employed. Jones, Russell and Cartwright were among the

organizers of the first stage line to operate from Leavenworth to Denver and perhaps to Salt Lake City, the Leavenworth & Pike's Peak Express Company, but Jones shortly withdrew. His freighting business continued until after the Civil War when because of overextension, the structure collapsed. He later rebuilt his fortune. Jones figured in many Colorado enterprises and died after a short illness at Boulder.

Barry, *Beginning of West;* information from Helen Darrah of the Pettis County Hist. Soc., Missouri; James Baker, LeRoy R. Hafen, *History of Colorado,* Vol. 5. Denver, Linderman Co., 1927; *Rocky Mountain News,* July 12, 1876, p. 4.

Jones, Orley E. (Ranger), victim (c. 1868-Nov. 28, 1891). B. probably in Nebraska he became a cowboy and a locally-famed bronc buster, and migrated to Johnson County, Wyoming, in 1887. The next year he rode for the EK Ranch and later homesteaded a tract on Red Fork near the present community of Mayoworth. He came into a feuding relationship with the English rancher, Fred G.S. Hesse as an element of the Johnson County troubles that were pointing toward armed conflict. He was ambushed and shot in the back by one of two men who were suspected in some quarters as being Frank M. Canton and Fred Hesse; both shortly fled the country and did not return until they came in with the invading "army" the following April. Neither ever stood trial for the slaying of Ranger Jones, which remained officially unsolved.

Helena Huntington Smith, *The War on Powder River.* N.Y., McGraw-Hill Book Co., 1966; Baber, Daisy F., *The Longest Rope.* Caldwell, Id., Caxton Printers, 1940.

Jones, Sam: *see* Arpeika

Jones, Thaddeus Winfield, army officer (July 30, 1848-Mar. 27, 1939). B. in North Carolina, he was graduated from West Point, named to the 10th Cavalry in 1872, and stationed in West Texas. Jones saw considerable active service against Comanches and on the frontier generally. May 7, 1875, he had a brush with hostiles on the North Concho River, recovering 33 head of stolen stock. From May 10 to December 24, 1875, he was of the great expedition under Shafter leaving Fort Concho (San Angelo, Texas) to explore the Staked Plains; after many hardships the command reached Three Rivers, New Mexico, then returned. Jones made notes for a sketch-map of the route and region that "was one of the finest and most important that ever went to the Engineer Officer, and other maps of that part of Texas today are almost copies of it." In April 1877, Jones was of a command from Fort Griffin, Texas, that surprised a Comanche village at Lake Quemado, Texas, with good results. He was named a first lieutenant in 1879, and in August 1880, it was he and his two companies that launched the decisive and interesting battle with Victorio at Rattlesnake Springs, West Texas, one of the better known actions of the Victorio War. Jones became a captain in 1891, and was stationed at Fort Apache, Arizona, later being stationed at Fort Bedford, North Dakota, and Fort Assiniboine, Montana. He became a colonel of Volunteers in 1898, was in the campaign against Santiago, Cuba, winning a Silver Star for gallantry against Spanish forces July 1, 1898; he was stationed in the Philippines at various times from 1899 to 1906, and served from 1901 in the 13th, 7th, 8th and 3rd Cavalry regiments. He retired about 1907 and died at 90 at Long Beach, California.

Heitman; Cullum; William G. Muller, *The Twenty Fourth Infantry.* Fort Collins, Colo., 1972; E.L.N. Glass, *The History of the Tenth Calvary 1866-1921.* Tucson, Ariz., p.p., 1921; Dan L. Thrapp, *Victorio and the Mimbres Apaches.* Norman, Univ. of Okla. Press, 1974.

Jones, Thomas, lynching victim (c. 1854-Mar. 15, 1885). A twin brother of Elizabeth Taylor, he was lynched with her. Both were born in Wales and buried in the Spring Ranche Cemetery, Nebraska (see Elizabeth Taylor biography for details and reference).

Jones, William, ethnologist (Mar. 28, 1871-Mar. 29, 1909). A Fox Indian, he was b. on the Sauk and Fox Reservation in Indian Territory, his father an Indian and his mother an Englishwoman. He was educated at Harvard and obtained a masters degree and doctorate at Columbia where he studied under Franz Boas, specializing in American Indian ethnology and linguistics. In 1907 he brought out *Fox Texts,* Algonquian lore presented in the native language with translations and considered "among the best American texts that have ever been pub-

lished." In 1906 he went to the Philippines for the Field Museum of Natural History of Chicago and was killed by headhunters along the Cagayan River, Luzon.

Dockstader.

Jones, William B., pioneer (d. Sept. 12, 1857?). It is possible that a man of this name from Caldwell County, Missouri, was a member of the Fancher train of emigrants, besieged at Mountain Meadows, Utah, and destroyed September 11, 1857; if so he may have slipped away from the train September 10 with John H. Baker and another, seeking to gain California. The three were killed by Mormon-led Paiutes near Santa Clara, in extreme southwestern Utah. Subsequently a journal or document, bearing the name of William B. Jones, was recovered by an Indian and purportedly destroyed by John D. Lee, one of the leading figures in the massacre.

Juanita Brooks, *The Mountain Meadows Massacre.* Norman, Univ. of Okla. Press, 1966; William Wise, *Massacre at Mountain Meadows.* N.Y., Thomas Y. Crowell Co., 1976.

Jones, William T., frontiersman (c. 1848-Oct. 13, 1879). Jones moved to Dona Ana County, New Mexico, with his father, Samuel, at least by 1850; in 1878 Bill was an officer of the third district court, county clerk and ex officio clerk to the commissioners at Mesilla. In 1879 the stirring of Victorio's Apaches led to the organization of the local militia. Finerty, who called him "a fine looking man," said Jones was elected captain. In October 1879, Jones and 16 other militiamen hurried north to a point on the west side of Las Uvas Mountains, about 30 miles northwest of Las Cruces, where they clashed with Juh and his fighting men. Killed were Jones, Cleto Sanchez, Nepumuseno Barragan, Pancho Brehan and Nepumuseno Lara. Jones' body alone was removed to Mesilla where it was buried in the family plot; the other victims were buried where they fell.

Information from Keith Humphries, Las Cruces, New Mex.; *Las Cruces Bulletin,* Nov. 13, 1975; Dan L. Thrapp, *Victorio and the Mimbres Apaches.* Norman, Univ. of Okla. Press, 1974; manuscript by Daniel Aranda, "An Episode from Victorio's War"; "Frank Warner Angel's Notes on New Mexico Territory 1878," ed. by Lee Scott Theisen. *Arizona and the West,* Vol. 18, No.4 (Winter 1976).

Jordan, George, soldier (1848-post 1900). B. in Williamson County, Tennessee, Jordan enlisted in the all-black 9th Cavalry in 1866 when it was organized, ultimately becoming a sergeant. On May 13-14, 1880, Jordan with detachments of K, E and I companies, defended old Fort Tularosa, New Mexico, against part of Victorio's Mimbres Apaches. On August 12, 1881, he was prominent in Captain Charles Parker's fight with Nana in Carrizo Canyon, west of Sabinal, New Mexico. For these two actions Jordan was awarded the Medal of Honor. Jordan retired in 1897 and died at the U.S. Soldier's Home, Washington, D.C.

William H. Leckie, *The Buffalo Soldiers.* Norman, Univ. of Okla. Press, 1967.

Josanie (Ulzan(n)a), Apache warrior (1821-Dec. 21, 1909). A full brother of Chihuahua, Josanie was a noted raider whose feat often was described under the name, Ulzana. He was a Chiricahua, a warrior with Chihuahua and Geronimo. Josanie served as scout in the 1881 campaign against Nana, and may have absorbed something of the older man's indomitable spirit as the Army units futilely chased him. On his great raid of November-December 1885, Josanie usually is credited with killing 38 people, but Aranda counts — and lists by name — 45 killed by him and wrote that there may have been still others. In any event, it was an epic adventure, and incidentally the subject for one of the few honest and worthy motion pictures about the Apache wars, "Ulzana's Raid," of 1972. Josanie surrendered with his brother, Chihuahua, to Crook in March 1886, the prisoners shipped to Florida exile in April. Josanie had two known wives and fathered at least seven sons, two of whom survived him and were taken to Mescalero, New Mexico, by foster parents after Josanie's death. The others of the family are buried at Fort Sill, Oklahoma.

Griswold; Daniel D. Aranda, "Josanie — Apache Warrior." *True West,* Vol. 23, No. 5 (May-June 1976), 38-39, 62-64.

Joseph, Chief (Hin-mah-too Yah-lat-kekt: Thunder Rolling in the Mountains), Nez Perce leader (c. 1840-Sept. 21, 1904). Dockstader gives his year of birth as between January and April 1832, but in any event it occurred in the Wallowa Valley, Oregon. He was the son of Old Joseph, a half-Cayuga, half-Nez Perce married to a Nez Perce woman and became a chief upon the death of his father which occurred in 1871, as young Joseph believed. Joseph had two brothers, Olikut, five years younger, and Sousouquee, or Cecushcecue (Dark, or Brown), older than the other two and who was killed before the 1877 Nez Perce War. While Olikut became a buffalo hunter through periodic trips to the eastern plains and through this activity also learned in war, for there were many Nez Perce enemies to fight in that country, Joseph made but a single trip as a young man to the buffalo country and knew nothing of war. He was however courageous, wise and one with a pronounced taste for diplomacy and much skill in that calling. Joseph with his people belonged to the non-treaty Nez Perce. For six years he rejected white pressure to give up their beloved Wallowa Valley and settle with the treaty Nez Perce in Idaho; his band was wealthy in stock and Joseph thereby became the most noted spokesman for the non-treaty Indians and was considered by Howard and others the dominant chief, although he was but one of five non-treaty chiefs, the others: Looking Glass, White Bird, Tuhulhulzote and Hahtalekin with his Paloos band. Joseph's group numbered between 55 and 60 fighting men; Looking Glass, 40; White Bird, 50; Tuhulhulzote, 30 and Hahtalekin, 16 men "counting himself." Joseph ever inclined toward peace. It is said he attended a Sioux council in 1874 where war against the whites along the Yellowstone was discussed, but refused to go along with it. In 1877 General Howard, acting upon instructions, directed Joseph to bring his people and stock upon the Idaho reservation or be driven in by cavalry. Jeseph then quitted the Wallowa Valley with his followers, some 350 in all and camped with other non-treaty bands along Whitebird Creek and the Salmon River, in Idaho. About a score of young men from other bands led a raid that caused casualties among white settlers, and precipitated the Nez Perce War of 1877 which was less a "war" than a brilliant hegira executed amid pools of battle in which the Nez Perce, counting only 191 fighting men of whom about 50 were considered "warriors," i.e., trained, experienced combatants, conducted themselves with great skill and success. From Whitebird Creek in western Idaho for 1,200 miles across Idaho, Yellowstone Park and the width of Montana toward Canada, through four major battles and 14 other skirmishes, the Nez Perce developed one of the most highly sung sagas of American history — but it was not led by Joseph, at least militarily although he is often credited with its genius."Joseph, the war chief, is a creature of legend," wrote McWhorter who did the most extended research among Indian survivors of that exodus. "Joseph, the Indian Napoleon, does not emerge from the Nez Perce chronicles of their great fight for freedom." His fame arose mainly from army officers who pursued and sometimes fought the Indians, and their inference was natural: Joseph was prominent in the negotiations preceding outbreak of the war, and he was the sole chief at the surrender. Thus it became, and has remained, Joseph's exploit, Joseph's war. Despite the fact that he was no warrior chief, he was a brave fighter as an individual. He fought with other Nez Perce in the battles of White Bird Canyon, June 17; Clearwater, July 11-12; Big Hole Basin where he was in charge of the horse herds during part of the action, and at the Bear Paw Mountains, September 30-October 5 when surrender of 431 Nez Perce took place. On October 1 Joseph was lured into conference by Miles under a flag of truce; when Miles urged him to surrender Joseph demurred. Thereupon Joseph was seized and, according to Indian accounts which appear reliable, treat most harshly, being bound, rolled into a blanket and left near the mule picket line overnight. Meanwhile Lieutenant Jerome probably at Miles' direction, reconnoitered the Indian camp when, upon learning of Joseph's seizure, the Nez Perce captured the lieutenant. Although some wished to kill him, others objected, and he was retained with humanity and consideration until an exchange for Joseph could be arranged. Joseph rejoined his people. Whites who knew Joseph, including army officers were invariably impressed by his superior qualities, ability and personality. His character gradually acquired so much respect from the American people that they insisted upon release of his people from their hated Oklahoma exile and return to the northwest. Although Miles and Joseph agreed at the surrender that the Nez Perce would be returned at once to their homeland, the understanding was reversed by Washington and they were sent to Oklahoma where many

died or became ill. In 1833, 33 women and children were allowed to return to their old home; the next year 118 others were permitted to do so. Joseph and about 150 of his band were not allowed to go to Idaho but were sent to the Colville Reservation, Washington. In 1897 and in 1903 Joseph visited Washington, D.C., meeting with President McKinley on his first trip and Theodore Roosevelt on the second; he also talked with Miles and Howard. He died at Nespelim on the Colville Reservation; the Indian agent said he had become reconciled to his lot in his final years, urging education of the children of the tribe and discouraging gambling and drunkeness. Joseph was more than 6 feet tall, handsome, an able orator; he was married three times, his two wives surviving him.

Literature abundant; Hodge, HAI; McWhorter, *Hear Me;* Lucullus V. McWhorter, *Yellow Wolf: His Own Story.* Caldwell, Id., Caxton Printers, 1940; O.O. Howard, *Nez Perce Joseph.* Boston, Lee and Shepard, 1881; Nelson A. Miles, *Personal Recollections of Nelson A. Miles.* Chicago, Riverside Pub. Co., 1897.

Joseph, Old Chief: *see* Wellammootkin

Joset, Joseph, Jesuit missionary (Aug. 27, 1810-June 19, 1900). B. in Courfaivre, the French district of Berne, Switzerland, he entered the Society of Jesus in 1830 and after 13 years training in Europe was ordained and served a year in France. He was accepted for the Rocky Mountain missions in 1843 and reached St. Mary's Mission in the Bitterroot Valley of Montana late in 1844. De Smet named him superior of St. Joseph's Mission to the Coeur d'Alene Indians and he served largely among that people for half a century, although stationed briefly on occasion at St. Paul's and St. Michael's missions. He established the Coeur d'Alene mission "so solidly" that it became one of two principal centers of Jesuit work in the region. Joset died at 90 having been 70 years a Jesuit and 56 a missionary. Burns said Joset had an "appealing countenance, with steady eyes and a happy smile." He was distinctly spiritual, "an excellent missionary, a good religious, but odd and highly imaginative," and he was steady in devotion and daily life. Although a leader he lacked administrative talent. Joset was kind to his co-workers, humble in recognition of his own faults, adept in Indian languages and composed some ethnological writings. He was pivotal in settlement of the 1858 Indian war and was ever a man of peace.

Robert Ignatius Burns, S.J., *The Jesuits and the Indian War of the Northwest.* New Haven, Yale Univ. Press, 1966.

Joutel, Henri, explorer (c. 1645-post 1722). B. at Rouen, France, his father was a gardner for the La Salle family. Henri after about 16 years in the French army met Rène Robert Cavalier, sieur de La Salle in 1684 and agreed to join his expedition to establish a settlement somewhere near the mouth of the Mississsippi River. He became a confidante of La Salle, and his detailed journal is perhaps the best account of the fatal enterprise, the death of his superior and the escape of six survivors of the expedition to French Canada and eventually the homeland. The expedition sailed from La Rochelle about July 23, 1684, three of the four ships (one having been captured by the Spanish) reaching the Gulf of Mexico and coasting westward, missing the mouth of the Mississippi, La Salle's goal, and after several tentative landings, put in at Matagorda Bay, near the present Houston. A settlement called Fort St. Louis was constructed at Lavaca Bay, northwestern arm of Matagorda Bay, where two of the ships were wrecked, the fourth returning to France. La Salle made several exploratory journeys, one to the Rio Grande, others in search of the Mississippi, while Joutel, often left in command at the base, struggled to control dissatisfaction and unrest, and at least once thwarting a plot to kill him. January 12, 1687, Joutel accompanied La Salle on a renewed attempt to locate the Mississippi and reach Canada, from which a ship might be procured or succor found; on March 19 La Salle was assassinated on a southern branch of the Trinity River, while Joutel was away from camp; he and others were spared the leader's fate. With six companions (one of whom drowned enroute), Joutel set out to reach Canada overland in May 1687. He reached Fort Lewis (at Starved Rock, Illinois), September 14, concealing from the French there as they had from the Indians earlier, the fact of La Salle's demise; Joutel said the truth was held back from the Indians " to keep them still in Awe and under Submission," while it was intended to reveal the facts of the tragedy first to the Court, should they ever regain France. The reasons for concealing La Salle's death from the Frenchmen they met, including the faithful Tonty who joined them at Fort Lewis October 27, are less clear, but Joutel and his party apparently felt they could travel through the French possessions with more authority if it was believed they had been sent by La Salle instead of barely surviving the debacle of his great scheme. The Joulet party left Fort Lewis March 21, 1688, arriving May 10 at Michilimackinac, at Montreal July 17, Quebec the 29th and returned to La Rochelle October 9 and Rouen the 17th. Joutel apparently retired to Rouen where the Jesuit Charlevoix had a long interview with him late in December 1722, the last certain notice we have of his career. Charlevoix praised Joutel as a "very upright man," and aside from the strange failure to report to the New World French the details of his commander's death "everything that appears concerning him is highly favorable." Certainly his journal, which first appeared in English in 1713, is more reliable and a superior document to that of Douay who was not above embroidering or falsifying the facts for his own purposes, failures never charged against Joutel. His narrative is also important for its ethnological content.

Henri Joutel: A Journal of La Salle's Last Voyage. N.Y., Corinth Books, 1962; Parkman, *La Salle and the Discovery of the Great West,* 462.

Joy, Christopher (Kit), cowboy, desperado (c. 1860-post 1884). B. probably in Texas, he was called by Bartholomew a "Tombstone character," but he was best known around Silver City, New Mexico. He worked as a cowboy for Harvey Whitehill, noted lawman, and others. On November 24, 1883, he and three others robbed a Southern Pacific train at Gage, 15 miles west of Deming, New Mexico. Through good detective work by Wells Fargo's James B. Hume and others, they were identified; Joy and Mitch Lee, who had killed engineer Theophilus C. Webster in the holdup, were captured at Horse Springs, New Mexico, in January 1884, and returned to the county jail at Silver City. On March 10 they broke out, four train robbers and two others. Caught up with about three miles north of town they fought a running gunbattle for about five miles. George Washington Cleveland, black, a train robber and Carlos Chavez, under death sentence for murder, were killed; Lee supposedly mortally wounded, was captured; Joy killed Joseph N. Lafferr, a posseman, and escaped, and Frank Taggart, another train robber, surrendered as did Spencer, a horse thief. Taggart and the wounded Lee were lynched, Spencer was returned to jail. Joy lurked in the Gila River rough country where he had numerous friends until he was wounded severly in the left leg and captured about March 22, 1884. The leg was amputated. He was tried at Hillsboro, New Mexico, November 15-19, found guilty of second degree murder, and given life.

This is Silver City, New Mexico, 1882 1883 1884. Silver City, The Enterprise, 1963.

Joyce, Milton E., saloonman (c. 1847-c. 1890). He was b. in Virginia. There was a Justice of the Peace M.E. Joyce at Hays City, Kansas, in 1869, who held an inquest over a Will Comstock victim. An M.E. Joyce was assistant marshal at Hays City in 1870, and took the census. This Joyce however was probably Marcellus E., b. in Ireland and who died at Leavenworth, Kansas in 1884. Milt Joyce was at Tombstone by 1880, and was operator of the Oriental Saloon in 1881, losing heavily during the disastrous fire June 22 that year. Joyce believed that the Earp people were responsible for killing Newman Haynes Clanton and others in Guadalupe Canyon in August 1881, to "make sure of killing Jim Crane," who had purported evidence of Holliday's complicity in a stage holdup. About the end of that year Joyce muttered to Wyatt Earp and Holliday that perhaps another stage would be robbed soon. One of them slapped Joyce. The next day Joyce armed with two guns sought a fight with Holliday, but Sheriff Behan disarmed him, asserting there had been enough killing in Tombstone; Joyce was fined $15 for disturbing the peace. Later Holliday is said to have shot Joyce in the hand. Joyce remained in the area for years. He and a partner owned a ranch and mine across the New Mexico line in the early 1880s and in 1885 he and Frank Leslie owned a ranch about twenty miles from Tombstone. In 1884 Joyce and others, including Nellie Cashman, went on a lost mine hunt in Baja California without result. By 1893 he was referred to in the newspapers as "the late Mr. Joyce."

Ed Bartholomew, *Wyatt Earp: The Man & The Myth.* Toyahvale, Tex., Frontier Book Co., 1964; Blaine Burkey, *Custer, Come At Once!* Hays,

Kan., Thomas More Prep, 1976; 1880 U.S. Census for Ariz.

Juan de Fuca (Apostolos Valerianos), navigator (c. 1536-c. 1602). A Greek b. on the island of Cephalonia, largest of the Ionian Islands, he became a seaman and "pilot," or navigator for ships. He went to the West Indies and entered the service of Spain, remaining thus employed for 40 years and "sailed to and from many places," in both Atlantic and Pacific waters. Juan de Fuca reported he was in a Spanish ship returning from the Philippines and China which was taken off Lower California by "Captain Candish Englishman," thus losing 60,000 ducats ($135,000) of his own goods. This incident may have been the seizure of the galleon, *Santa Ana* by the English seaman Thomas Cavendish in 1587. Juan de Fuca said that he was pilot for three small Spanish ships which the Viceroy of Mexico sent northward along the American coast seeking the Straits of Anian, the mythical Northwest Passage. But a mutiny, he said against a sodomical captain, aborted that voyage "without any effect of thing done" and the captain was held for trial in Mexico. The account was not supported until recent scholarship. Cook points out that this no doubt was the revolt against Captain Sebastian Pérez de Castillo, captain of the *San Jose* who was charged with an "unnatural offense," and was to have been tried by the Mexico Audiencia but succumbed in prison before the case reached court. Juan de Fuca said that shortly afterward, in 1592 the Viceroy sent him with a small caravel and a pinnace to seek the Straits of Anian. He coasted north reaching Latitude 47 degrees where he found a broad inlet that opened up inland with numerous islands, that he went ashore in various places, contacted the skin-clad natives, believed that the strait emptied into the "North Sea," and returned to Acapulco, hoping for a generous reward from the Viceroy; as this did not materialize he went to Spain, to Italy, and then returned to Greece, hoping until the last that he would receive some reward, if not from Spain then perhaps from England for his discovery. The only contemporary account of his alleged adventures came through an English collector of historical documents, Michael Lok who interviewed Juan de Fuca at Venice in 1596 and remained in touch with him through correspondence until 1602 when he learned the old seaman had died on Cephalonia. At the outset Lok believed him to be about 60 years of age. Lok was an associate of Richard Hakluyt, famed geographer and editor of narratives of exploration, who was left Lok's record of his information from Juan de Fuca; Hakluyt bequeathed it to Samuel Purchas, by whom it was published in 1625 (Warren Cook carries the latest reprinting of it). The Greek's account was accepted as valid until the 1790s when failure to discover a transcontinental strait where the pilot said he had located it brought the story into discredit. Juan de Fuca's latitude however is reasonably accurate for his times, the actual location of the Juan de Fuca Strait is between 48 degrees 25 minutes and 48 degrees 38 minutes, and the Greek's description of it closely fits reality. The most persuasive reason for doubting the voyage, as Cook points out, is lack of Spanish or Mexican supporting documentation, but this can easily be explained by the destruction through fire of much Mexican archival material of the times and the fact that the voluminous archives of Mexico City and Seville have never been examined in thorough detail. On the whole, Cook makes a case for caution in condemning as spurious the narrative and Juan de Fuca's great voyage is seen as not inherently impossible but rather bordering on the probable.

Warren L. Cook, *Flood Tide of Empire.* New Haven, Yale Univ. Press, 1973, incl. Appendix A; Thwaites, EWT XXVIII, 31n.; Bancroft, *Northwest Coast,* I

Juan Diego, Mimbres Apache chief (d. Apr. 22, 1837). A brother of Juan José Compá, Juan Diego, a mighty raider on Mexican resources, was killed with Compá by John Johnson in a famous massacre at the south end of the Animas Mountains of present New Mexico.

Rex W. Strickland, "The Birth and Death of a Legend: The Johnson 'Massacre' of 1837." *Arizona and the West,* Vol. 18, No. 3 (Autumn 1976), 257-86.

Juan José Compá, Mimbres Apache chief (d. Apr. 22, 1837). B. probably in present southwestern New Mexico, Juan José appears to have been head chief of the Mimbres. He apparently was raised by the Rafael Elías Gonzalez family in Sonora, his surname,

Compá, according to Strickland possibly a variant of Compay, the patronym of the Elías family. Wilson reports that Juan José was educated for the priesthood, could read and write, keep accounts, and "was really quite an educated man. The Mexicans murdered his father, which prompted him to leave the whites, and place himself at the head of his people, and wage war against the Mexicans," though he remained friendly with the Anglos. Wilson said that he had been a good friend of Juan José over a period of about two years and his "friendship was in every way valuable to us." In 1831 Colonel José Joaquin Calvo signed a treaty with 29 Apache chieftains at Santa Rita, in southern New Mexico; their country was divided into three zones and Juan José Compá was made "general" over one of them, with headquarters at Janos, but the treaty was unsuccessful in establishing and maintaining peace. From 1833-35 there were frequent Apache raids on Mexican establishments. Apaches of unknown identification made a raid on Noría, 30 miles north of Oposura (Moctezuma), Sonora, late in March 1837. An American domiciled at Oposura, John J. Johnson, collected 17 followers and five Mexican packers and set out on a punitive or raiding expedition April 3. By his account to Governor Calvo, written April 24, Johnson initially followed the trail of the Noría raiders, but quickly lost it; he went then to Fronteras, Sonora, where the commandant at the presidio, Antonio Narbona Jr., loaned him a small field piece suitable for packing on a little Sonora mule. Johnson left Fronteras April 12, heading north, passed perhaps through Guadalupe Canyon and at the southern extremity of the Animas Mountains found Juan José's rancheria near a dry lake bed. The Mimbres leader was suspicious of anyone coming out of Mexico, but his misgivings were allayed by Johnson. April 20 Johnson ransomed a 12-year-old girl, Autora, or Aurora (1825-1879) who, by his report (which is not above suspicion) suggested that the Indians planned treachery against him. On April 22 his field piece was loaded with what scrap was available, the Apaches lured in some number around the target, a bag of pinole or something similar, when the gun was touched off by Johnson himself. One account said that Juan José, lured some distance away on the pretext of examining a mule, was dispatched gorily by Benjamin Leaton and

Johnson, but it is difficult to see how that incident and the massacre could be carried out upon unalarmed Indians in any synchronized fashion. At any rate the whites followed up the gun blast with rifle fire and a score of Apaches were said to have been killed, others wounded. Among the fallen, Johnson said, were Juan José, his brother, Juan Diego, and Marcelo, the latter two also chiefs; three of the 20 casualties were women. The Johnson party was quickly driven off by the aroused Apache survivors, but without reported losses, although some of his group which included members of a mule-buying expedition, returned directly to Santa Fe, and may have suffered casualties. Wilson reported that the incident generated intense Indian hostilities against Anglos. Of the several versions of the affair, Cremony's is thoroughly unbelievable and can be discounted; Wilson's is inaccurate on dates and some details, but contains valuable information; Gregg's version is generally as accurate as Strickland's, with less diversionary verbiage; McGaw's is drawn from Strickland's sources in large part, and is substantially accurate; Strickland's has important information about Johnson's family and descendants, and the best re-construction of the incident, but it might be well to weigh it against studies which offer a somewhat different point of view. When this has been done his version is seen to support the generally-held view that the affair was a callous, cruel and treacherous massacre, provoked with little cause and no reward in view, given the absence of important loot in the Apache camp.

Josiah Gregg, *Commerce of the Prairies,* ed. by Max L. Moorhead. Norman, Univ. of Okla. Press, 1954; *Benjamin David Wilson's Observations on Early Days in California and New Mexico,* ed. by Arthur Woodward. Hist. Soc. of Southern Calif. Ann. Pubn., 1934, 74-150; William Cochran McGaw, *Savage Scene: The Life and Times of James Kirker.* N.Y., Hastings House, 1972; Rex W. Strickland, "The Birth and Death of a Legend: The Johnson 'Massacre' of 1837." *Arizona and the West,* Vol. 18, No. 3 (Autumn 1976), 257-86; Ralph A. Smith, "Apache Plunder Trails Southward, 1831-1840." *New Mex. Hist. Rev.,* Vol. XXXVII, No. 1 (Jan. 1962), pp. 20-42.

Juana Maria, castaway (c. 1803-Oct. 19, 1853). Last of the San Nicolas Island Indians living off the coast of southern California, she

was abandoned about 1836 when the rest of her people were transported to the mainland. Juana Maria lived for 18 years alone on San Nicolas, supposedly without contact with any other human being. She was rescued by George Nidever, erstwhile mountain man, later engaged in otter hunting, and others. Brought to Santa Barbara, California, September 8, 1853, she was treated kindly but falling ill, died shortly afterward. She was baptized with the name of Juana Maria moments before her death, and was buried at Santa Barbara Mission. Her language, of which only traces were recorded, apparently had a Shoshonean affiliation.

Original Accounts of the Lone Woman of San Nicolas Island, ed. by Robert F. Heizer and Albert B. Elsasser. Ramona, Calif., Ballena Press, 1973.

Juanico, Navaho headman (fl. 1823-1853). Usually identified with the Cienega Grande area on the eastern approach to the Canyon de Chelly, Juanico was one of the more important headmen of the Navahos during the first half of the 19th Century. He was a foremost spokesman at the Paguete council of February 12, 1823, with Colonel José Antonio Vizcarra, then governor of New Mexico. The council, if anything, "widened the gulf separating the two sides," the Navahos returning to raiding and the Spanish to sending expeditions after them. Vizcarra himself led an immense (1,500-man) punitive sweep into Navaho country that same summer. He picked up the trail of Juanico's band and followed it; a skirmish occurred August 9 amid very difficult mountain terrain with mixed results, although some livestock was taken. The expedition was not very successful, killing some Navahos and a few Utes, mistaken for Navahos. Juanico attended Doniphan's treaty council of 1846 and signed the resulting pact. August 31, 1853, he and other headmen arrived at Santa Fe as a delegation to meet the new governor, David Meriwether. Thereafter he fades from view.

Frank McNitt, *Navajo Wars.* Albuquerque, Univ. of New Mex. Press, 1972; David M. Brugge, "Vizcarra's Navajo Campaign of 1823." *Arizona and the West,* Vol. 6, No. 3 (Autumn 1964), 223-44.

Juchereau de la Ferté, Denis Joseph, army officer (c. June 19, 1661-c. Aug. 8, 1709). B. at Quebec he reached Lake Superior with fur traders in 1683 and in 1684 took part in La

Barre's ineffectual campaign against the Iroquois. He was back in the Ottawa country in 1685 and at Michilimackinac in 1686, the next year taking part in Denonville's campaign against the New York Senecas. His other activities seem confined to Canada, part of which time he served aboard warships. He died at Quebec.

DCB, II.

Juchereau de St. Denis, Louis, explorer, army officer (Sept. 17, 1676-June 11, 1744). B. at Quebec, he accompanied Iberville in 1699 on the latter's second voyage to Louisiana and accompanied Bienville in exploring between the Red and Ouachita rivers in 1700-1701. Shortly afterward he was named commandant of the Fort du Mississippi, 18 miles up from the river's mouth, holding the position until 1707; he went up the river to the Ohio about 1704 to briefly take charge of a tannery his late brother, Charles had established for the preservation of buffalo hides and other skins. Louis also explored westward into Texas and in 1713 Cadillac directed him to seek a new trade route to New Spain. In the course of fulfilling this mission he founded the important frontier community of Natchitoches, Louisiana, traded his way across Texas and reached Piedras Negras, Mexico, in July 1714. Here Juchereau was imprisoned, taken to Mexico City, then accepted as a guide for Spanish forces into Texas where it was determined to found Spanish missions, among those one at Nacogdoches, Texas, another important frontier post. Juchereau, being released by the Spanish, reached Mobile by mid-1716. He promptly engaged in smuggling between the French and Spanish colonies; his goods were impounded and Juchereau again went to Mexico City, this time to try and regain possession of his property. He was imprisoned for a few months, then released, permitted to sell his goods and go back to Louisiana but never to re-enter Texas. By 1719 he was back at Natchitoches. He served the French forces in the war against Spain in 1719-20 and was given command of the Natchitoches region where in 1721 he resumed his subrosa trade with Texas. In 1731 his men massacred members of the Natchez tribe who had moved to the vicinity of Natchitoches after the Natchez uprising and massacre of French along the Mississippi. He died at Natchitoches and was buried in its church.

Ross Phares, *Cavalier in the Wilderness: The Story of the Explorer and Trader Louis Juchereau de St. Denis.* Baton Rouge, La. State Univ. Press, 1972; John Francis Bannon, *Spanish Borderlands Frontier, 1513-1821.* N.Y., Holt, Rinehart and Winston, 1970; DCB, III.

Juchereau de St. Denis, Nicolas, colonist (c. 1627-Oct. 4, 1692). B. near Chartres, France, he reached Canada with his father in 1634 and eventually became a major landholder and active in various colonial enterprises. As head of a militia company he took part in the Courcelle and Tracy expeditions against the New York Iroquois in 1666, but his other activities were confined to Canada.

DCB, I.

Juchereau de St. Denys, Charles, entrepreneur (Dec. 6, 1655-Aug. 27, 1703). B. in Canada, he early became an army officer and interested in the fur trade, initially by making sizable loans to traders in the Indian country. In 1700 he was a founder of the Compagnie du Canada for the export of fur and that year, at Paris, he secured a concession for the tanneries on the lower Ohio River, which may have been planned with a view to exploiting the possibilities in buffalo hides, among the first such schemes for commercial use of the product on record. He was granted the concession in part with a view to curtailing illicit contacts between French coureurs de bois and the English traders already penetrating that region. He left Montreal May 18, 1702, and reached Illinois late in the year. His party built a fort near the mouth of the Ohio and established various other posts, one perhaps at the site of the later Fort Massac (1757-1814), 11 miles below the present Paducah, Kentucky, and on the north side of the Ohio. "The legend of a massacre at this place may have had its origins in some misfortune dating from Juchereau's time." Juchereau's death, possibly from an epidemic, cut short the enterprise and only part of several thousand skins of buffalo, deer, bear and wolf were ever salvaged and Juchereau's men were scattered.

Thwaites, JR, LXV, 268n28; Roger E. Henn, "First Great Buffalo Slaughter." Chicago, *Westerners Brand Book,* Vol. XXXIII, No. 8 (Dec. 1976), 59, an article inaccurate but descriptive; DCB, II.

Judah, Henry Moses, army officer (c. 1821-

Jan. 14, 1866). B. in Maryland he went to West Point from New York and was commissioned a brevet second lieutenant of the 8th Infantry in 1843. He was sent to Forts Marion and Brooke, Florida from 1843 until 1845 and then was with the military occupation of Texas in 1845-46. Judah became a second lieutenant of the 4th Infantry April 19, 1846, and a first lieutenant in 1847 during his service in the Mexican War, when he earned two brevets. He served in eastern posts from 1848-53 and was sent to Fort Vancouver, Washington in 1853, becoming captain September 29, 1853. He was stationed at northern California posts, principally in Humboldt County, from 1853-58, part of the time on scouting missions. Judah was on the march to Oregon in 1858 with the 4th Infantry and served at Forts Vancouver and Steilacoom until 1860. He was at Fort Yuma, California in 1860-61. He became colonel of the 4th California Infantry September 6, 1861 and a Brigadier General of Volunteers March 21, 1862. Judah then went east for Civil War duty, emerging a brevet colonel. He died at Plattsburg, New York. Crook served under Judah in California and Oregon, writing "I had such contempt for him that his sight was obnoxious to me," and alleged that he was drunk on duty almost as often as he was sober, and very little effective in Indian operations.

Heitman; Cullum; *General George Crook: His Autobiography,* ed. by Martin F. Schmitt. Norman, Univ. of Okla. Press, 1960.

Judson, Edward Zane Carroll (Ned Buntline), writer (Mar. 20, 1823-July 16, 1886). B. at Stamford, New York, his date of birth is uncertain since he gave three different ones during his lifetime and his tombstone bears a fourth, which is used here. Judson ran away to sea as a youth, a cabin boy; on August 7, 1837, he enlisted at the Philadelphia Navy Yard as Second Class Boy. After some service at sea he was appointed acting midshipman February 10, 1838, served on the frigate *Constellation* and other vessels, including some cooperating with the army during the Seminole War. He resigned from the Navy May 14, 1842. Much of what he wrote of himself is as unreliable as the myriad dime novels he subsequently published, but it appears that his Navy career was eventful, if not particularly rewarding. He had married his first wife while in the navy and said he had spent the next two years in the

Yellowstone country with the North West Fur Company, but there is no evidence except his wayward word for it. By May 1844, he was at Pittsburgh, Pennsylvania, launching *Ned Buntline's Magazine,* which lasted for two issues. Buntline, as Judson came to be known, began to write pieces for established magazines. He edited six numbers of the *Western Literary Journal and Monthly Magazine,* then left without paying its bills; in Tennessee he captured two of three men wanted for murder, and was paid $600 bounty, started another publication in Nashville, became involved with the wife of Robert Porterfield and killed her husband. A mob tried to lynch him, but someone cut the rope and Buntline, his neck intact, was unindicted by a grand jury and freed. He went to New York, resurrected the publication he had commenced at Nashville, claimed he served in the Mexican War, became involved in numerous escapades, did a year for fomenting a riot, was indicted at St. Louis for inciting another riot in which some men were killed, jumped bail, and during all this time wrote more and more titles of the endless stream of dime novels which made him the best known and, at about $20,000 a year, the best paid writer in America. He served briefly in the Civil War, "his record being thoroughly discreditable," and in 1869, hunting new material, he became acquainted with Buffalo Bill at Fort McPherson, Nebraska. Legend asserts that Buntline picked Cody as a likely subject and made of him the national figure he became through the lurid novels he produced about him; Russell shows this not to be the case, that Cody did more for Buntline than Buntline did for Buffalo Bill, and that in any event Buntline wrote only about four books on the Buffalo Bill theme. However Buntline did write the atrocious play, "The Scouts of the Plains," which launched Cody and Texas Jack Omohundro in show business, Buntline himself appearing in it initially. Buntline married at least five times; on occasion his soul-mates were multiple at a given time. He established various estates, but in his elder years suffered increasingly, it is said, from old wounds which he had received in a variety of ways, some legitimately, although he wrote and wrote until his death. Personally Buntline was not an unattractive character, usually cheerful and according to most, genial, with as many friends as detractors, although to many the appellation, "the great rascal" fitted him. He was buried at Stamford, New York.

Jay Monaghan, *The Great Rascal.* N.Y., Bantam Books, 1953; Don Russell, *The Lives and Legends of Buffalo Bill.* Norman, Univ. of Okla. Press, 1960.

Juh, Apache chief, war leader (c. 1825-Nov. 1883). B. on the upper Gila River, probably in southern New Mexico or eastern Arizona, Juh was a leading man of the Nednai Apaches, married first Ish-keh, grand-daughter of the noted Bedonkohe chief, Mahko, and the first cousin of Geronimo. Juh established himself as a superb combat leader in 1855 in a battle with Mexicans near Namiquipa, Chih.; reportedly was at the Battle of Apache Pass, July 15, 1862, and probably led the warriors who slew Cavalry Lieutenant Howard B. Cushing and two others May 5, 1871. He and Geronimo escaped into Sonora upon the breakup of the Chiricahua Reservation in southeastern Arizona in 1876, but Juh reappears in 1879 when he cooperated with or had a hand in some of the bloodiest work attributed to Victorio in southern New Mexico. He and Geronimo surrendered in 1880 and were moved to the San Carlos Reservation of Arizona. He may have had some role in the Cibecue affair in the summer of 1881, then led a bolt southward to his "stronghold" in the Sierra Madre of Sonora. From there he, probably Geronimo and others, in the spring of 1882 filtered north to San Carlos again and herded Loco and hundreds of followers south into Mexico to be with their wild clansmen. When Crook penetrated the Sierra Madre in 1883, Juh avoided him and declined to come in. He died following a fall from his horse into the Casas Grandes River, Chihuahua, but whether he was drunk or suffered a heart attack is not known. Juh was among the greatest of Apache war leaders, exhibiting marked qualities of command and an understanding of strategy; he was notably cruel. He was described as 6 feet or more tall, dark-skinned, weighed about 225 pounds, had a speech impediment. The meaning of his name is uncertain. He left one surviving son, Ace Daklugie, in this country.

Dan L. Thrapp, *Juh: An Incredible Indian.* El Paso, Tex. Western Press, 1973; Eve Ball, *Indeh: An Apache Odyssey.* Provo, Utah, Brigham Young Univ. Press, 1980.

Jukes, Samuel, Mormon pioneer (fl. 1857-1876). Jukes, a resident of Cedar City, Utah, was placed by *Mormonism Unveiled* at the Mountain Meadows Massacre of September 11, 1857, either participating in or consenting to the tragedy. He was indicted in the 1870's for participation in the murders, but was not tried. *Mormonism Unveiled,* published in 1892, said he was then of Cedar City.

Juanita Brooks, *John D. Lee.* Glendale, Calif., Arthur H. Clark Co., 1962; *Mormonism Unveiled,* 379.

Jules: *see* Bene (Beni) Jules

Julien, Denis, frontiersman (c. 1775-c. 1836). B. possibly near St. Louis, he was the father of at least three children by his Indian wife, and became trader to the Iowa Indians on the Des Moines River, at least by 1805. He may have been related to Etienne Julien, also a trader, and may later have worked the upper Mississippi country. By about 1825 he was engaged in the fur business on the Missouri, was involved in a shooting incident at Fort Atkinson December 26, 1825, and by 1827 was reported at Taos. He left there for the Uintah Basin of later Utah. He inscribed his name on "Inscription Rock" near the confluence of the Whiterocks and Uintah rivers in 1831, and in 1836 chiseled his name or initials in several places on Green River canyon walls; one, on May 3, at Hell Roarin Canyon, another at Cataract Canyon of the Colorado, and others elsewhere. He apparently was the first to navigate the canyons of the lower Green and upper Colorado, and probably lost his life to rapids in the latter river, its first supposed white victim.

Otis Dock Marston article, MM, Vol. VII.

Jumonville, Joseph Coulon de Villiers de, army officer (Sept. 8, 1718-May 28, 1754). B. at Verchères, Quebec, he entered the French colonial regulars as an officer, and was killed in what "proved to be the opening shot in the Seven Years' War," or French and Indian War as it often is known. Jumonville had been at Green Bay in 1733 where, in a battle with the Fox Indians, his father, a brother and a brother-in-law were killed and another brother, Louis Coulon, who would avenge Jumonville's death, was wounded. In 1739 Jumonville took part in Bienville's operation against the Chickasaws. He is said to have seen action against frontier New York outposts thereafter. Jumonville was assigned to Fort Duquesne in 1754. On May 23 he was sent with 30 men to scout George Washington's position at the soon-to-be-called Fort Necessity. Regardless of the intent of Jumonville, Washington logically decided that his secretive movements about the English position were of hostile nature and on May 28 with 40 men stole upon the hidden camp and opened fire in the best frontier tradition. Ten Canadians, including Jumonville, were killed and all but one of the others taken prisoner. Eccles, in the *Dictionary of Canadian Biography,* sees the incident as an unprovoked attack not upon hostile soldiers, but upon "an embassy" of peaceful intent. But Washington reported, "Instead of coming as an Embassador, publicly, and in an open manner, they came secretly, and sought after the most hidden retreats... encamped there and remained hidden for whole days together, at a distance of not more than five miles from us; they sent spies to reconnoiter our camp..." With three-quarters of a century of experience in bloody raids by French and Indians upon unsuspecting hamlets and border positions (and English-supported Indian attacks upon French outposts as well), the frontiersman's reaction could only have been to do what was done.

Thwaites, JR, LXX, 312-13n32; Frederick Tilberg, *Fort Necessity National Battlefield Site, Pennsylvania.* Wash., Natl. Park Service Hist. Handbook, Series 19, 1954; DCB, III.

Jumper (Otee Emathla, Onselmatche), Seminole chief (c. 1796-Apr. 18, 1838). A Red Stick Creek who had fought against Jackson in the First Seminole War of 1817-18, he said he was of Yamasee descent. Jumper rose in his band to become chief Micanopy's sense-bearer, that is, his lawyer, or advocate. Whites characterized him variously as cunning, intelligent, deceitful, active, brave, eloquent and described him as with small, deadly eyes, contracted forehead and protruding nose. He was a foremost leader in the Second Seminole War which broke out in 1835. Sprague wrote that Jumper was "naturally endowed with great fluency of speech, and with a voice peculiarly musical and attractive. He attained an ascendancy over all classes, and became the most important man in councils and consultations." Jumper signed the Payne's Landing Treaty of May 9, 1832, which laid the groundwork for removal of the Seminoles from Florida, and his name was attached to the Fort Gibson Treaty of March 28, 1833, but he later denied he had signed it and in 1835 adamantly refused to emigrate, as did four other chiefs. These five were "removed" as chiefs by Indian Agent Wiley Thompson, which did nothing to damage their standing with their people but signed Thompson's death warrant. Jumper was a leader, perhaps the leader, in the Dade massacre of December 28, 1835, which opened the Second Seminole War. In late February Jumper, Alligator and others led the so-called Fort Izard siege of Gaines and his command, in several days costing the whites five men killed and 46 wounded. Jumper was in the Battle of Hatcheelustee, January 27, 1837, and with Micanopy and Abraham came in for a talk February 3. On March 6 he and others agreed to surrender, according to Jesup and by the end of May Jumper was in a detention camp at Tampa Bay. But June 2 Osceola and Sam Jones stealthily cleaned the camp out and there went hopes for immediate peace. Jumper missed Hernandez's capture-by-treachery of Osceola and Coa Hadjo because, it was reported, he was ill with measles, a disease then rampant among Florida Indians. On December 19, 1837, Jumper surrendered again with 63 of his followers and this time it was for good. He and hundreds of other Seminoles were sent to New Orleans where they were confined at Fort Pike to await transport to their new homes in the trans-Mississippi. At Fort Pike Jumper died, "a distinguished chief... who for a long time had been dying of consumption," said a newspaper. He was "buried in the afternoon. In his coffin were placed his tobacco, his pipe, his rifle, and other equipment according to his people's custom. The military and a number of citizens attended his funeral, which was conducted with all the honors of war."

John K. Mahon, *The History of the Second Seminole War.* Gainesville, Univ. of Fla. Press, 1967; Edwin C. McReynolds, *The Seminoles.* Norman, Univ. of Okla. Press, 1967; Grant Foreman, *Indian Removal,* Norman, 1969; John T. Sprague, *The Origins... of the Florida War.* N.Y., D. Appleton & Co., 1847.

Jusepe, Gutiérrez, Mexican Indian (c. 1572-post 1599). A native of Culhuacan, about 50 miles north of Mexico City, he was taken by Antonio Gutiérrez de Humaña, probably as a servant northward to Nueva Vizcaya where in 1593 Humaña joined Captain Francisco Leyva de Bonilla in punitive operations against Indians depredating against the northern frontier. The expedition, without royal sanction later penetrated New Mexico, spending about a year near San Ildefonso, 25 miles north of Santa Fe. Then it went eastward to the buffalo plains and northeastward across two large rivers, probably into Kansas near either the present Great Bend or Wichita. Here they came upon a sizable settlement, the houses of poles and grass thatching and agricultural produce raised; the people perhaps were Wichitas. Jusepe said that a dispute arose between Humaña and Leyva as a result of which Humaña stabbed Leyva mortally with a butcher knife, then took command of the expedition. Five of the Indian followers at this point fled southward (Humaña and his party subsequently were wiped out to a man by Indians), but three became lost on the plains, Jusepe and another regaining the New Mexico pueblos where Jusepe's companion was killed. When he heard of Spanish being at the Pueblo of San Juan Bautista he made contact with them and was interviewed at length February 16, 1599, by Oñate, his testimony taken down and constituting the only narrative of a survivor of the Humaña-Leyva expedition.

George P. Hammond, Agapito Rey, *The Rediscovery of New Mexico, 1580-1594.* Albuquerque, Univ. of New Mex. Press, 1966; Herbert Eugene Bolton, *Spanish Exploration in the Southwest, 1542-1706.* N.Y., Charles Scribner's Sons, 1916.

Juzan, Pierre, trader (d. c. 1840). Pierre and William Juzan who may have been brothers, or cousins, probably were descended from a de Juzan, aide to Pierre-Benoit Payen de Noyan (1700-1765), a military officer under Bienville who took part in several expeditions against the Chickasaws and Natchez. De Juzan was killed May 26, 1736, in the disastrous French attack on the Chickasaw town of Akia (Ackia) west of the Tombigbee River in northern Mississippi; in the affair won by the Chickasaws the French lost 24 regulars killed and 52 including Payen de Noyan wounded, along with 22 killed and wounded among their Choctaw auxiliaries. Pierre Juzan was a noted 18th century French-Indian trader among the Choctaws, centered at Chunk(e)y Town, at the present Union, Mississippi. Juzan had married a niece of Pushmataha and raised a family; he spoke English, French and Choctaw with equal fluency. Gradually he developed trading houses at several points among the numerous Choctaw and a second residence at Coosha, in the present Lauderdale County, Mississippi. Juzan died at Tuscahoma, on the Tombigbee River in Alabama. Some time after his death his family emigrated to Indian Territory where most of the Choctaws had resettled.

H.S. Halbert, T.H. Ball, *The Creek War of 1813 and 1814.* Univ. of Ala. Press, 1969; Albert James Pickett, *History of Alabama.* Birmingham Book and Mag. Co., 1962.

K

Kamaiakan, Yakima chief (c. 1800-c. 1877). The principal chief of the Yakimas and confederate tribes of eastern Washington under the treaty of 1855 he also was a leader in the war which shortly began and continued for three years. He was born at Ahtanum Creek near Tampico, Washington and in 1839 went to Waiilatpu to ask for a missionary but his request was rejected because of jealousy between the Protestant missionaries so he turned to the Roman Catholics. The discovery of gold in the mid-1850s led to an influx of whites and the danger of major clashes with the Indians, and Governor Stevens of Washington Territory in 1855 negotiated a number of treaties to obviate that possibility, Kamaiakan acceding under protest. In September 1855 a war began and Kamaiakan declared it his intention to keep all whites out of the territories he considered his own. October 4-5, 1855, an engagement occurred in the Simcoe Valley, the 84 soldiers under Major Granville Haller withdrawing in the face of superior forces. The uprising became general. May 17, 1858, a force under Colonel Steptoe was defeated near the present Colfax, Washington, but Colonel George Wright defeated the Kamaiakan Indians in September in two engagements, the chief being wounded. Kamaiakan refused to sue for peace and crossed into British Columbia. He and his family lived in the Kutenai country for some time but eventually returned to his homeland where he lived in obscurity until his death. He died at his camp at Rock Lake, his grave later desecrated by whites. He was described as 6 feet, 1 inch in height, of proud bearing, an eloquent speaker and intelligent. He was married several times.

Hodge, HAI; Dockstader; Bancroft, *Washington, Idaho and Montana;* Bill Gulick, "Kamiakin — War Chief of the Yakimas." *True West,* Vol. 31, No. 5 (May 1984), 12-18.

Kane, John Henricks, army officer (fl. 1855-1870). B. in Ireland, he early emigrated to the United States and on June 6, 1855, enlisted in the 2nd (which became the 5th) U.S. Cavalry, serving in Texas until the state seceded. As a sergeant he was commissioned a second lieutenant in 1863, earned a brevet and ended the war as a first lieutenant. By October 1868 he was on the frontier engaging in Indian affairs, served with the Canadian River expedition, was promoted to captain late in 1868, served with the Republican River expedition and at the decisive victory of Summit Springs, July 11, 1869, over the Cheyennes. Kane was discharged July 15, 1870, because of a reduction in the size of the army, and became a stock raiser in Texas.

Price, *Fifth Cavalry;* Heitman.

Kane, Paul, artist (Sept. 3, 1810-Feb. 20, 1871). B. at Mallow, Cork County, Ireland, he emigrated to Canada as a child, and studied art in the U.S., France and Italy, returning to Canada in 1845 where he became a painter of note; his frontier work is particularly worthy. In 1847 he visited Waiilatpu Mission and Dr. Marcus Whitman near present Walla Walla, Washington, sketched a number of Cayuse Indians, some of whom were principals shortly afterward in the massacre in which Whitman and more than a dozen others lost their lives. Kane subsequently painted portraits from his field sketches, adding touches of ferocity in keeping with the later deeds of violence he had heard about. Kane is believed also to have done the only life sketches of Marcus and Narcissa Whitman (reproduced by Drury). Kane's travels to the Northwest, 1845-48, resulted in works today highly prized (many are in the Royal Ontario Museum, Toronto, and the Parliament Buildings, Ottawa). He also wrote: *Wanderings of an Artist among the Indian Tribes of North America* (1859; 1924).

EA; J. Russell Harper, ed., *Paul Kane's Frontier.* Ft. Worth, Tex., Amon Carter Mus., 1971; Clifford M. Drury, *Marcus and Narcissa Whitman and the Opening of Old Oregon,* 2 vols. Glendale, Calif., Arthur H. Clark Co., 1973.

Kane, Thomas Leiper, army officer (Jan. 27, 1822-Dec. 26, 1883). B. at Philadelphia, he was a brother of arctic explorer Elisha Kent Kane, became a lawyer and was an abolitionist, becoming an agent of the Underground Railroad. Although he never became a Mormon, he was a friend of Brigham Young for 30 years and is something of a hero to the Mormon faith, having been an intermediary for the Saints on several pivotal occasions. Kane and Young met when the former became ill of "swamp fever" along the Mississippi and was nursed to health by Mary Ann Angel Young, Brigham's wife. Kane was said to have been the first Pennsylvanian to enlist in the Civil War, being commissioned by President Lincoln and Gov. Andrew Curtin to enlist a regiment of frontier sharpshooters, his "Bucktail Regiment" becoming one of the most decorated units of the Union Army. As a Brigadier General of Volunteers he defended Culp's Hill at Gettysburg, being wounded three times, as a result of which he was forced to resign although named a brevet Major General in 1865 for his work. Kane was instrumental in formation of the so-called Mormon Battalion in the Mexican War, in the Mormon move from Nauvoo, Illinois, to the Salt Lake valley, and for successful mediation of the 1857 "Mormon War." Arising from a sickbed at Philadelphia when he heard of the supposed insurgency, Kane traveled by steamboat to Panama, thence to San Francisco, south to Los Angeles and by horseback to Salt Lake City where he conferred with Young, taking the Mormon leader's views to Ft. Bridger where he met with Albert Sydney Johnston, bringing the two factions into accord and accompanying the federal forces peacefully into Utah the following spring. A statue to his memory as "The Immortal Friend of Utah and Its People," was erected in the rotunda of the Utah State Capitol, a duplicate placed at Kane, Pennsylvania, a community named for him.

California Intermountain News, July 19, 1973; DAB.

Kane, William Henry (Jim), soldier, scout, rancher (c. 1863-July 1945). B. in Hamilton County, Ohio, he enlisted May 8, 1880, in Troop D, 4th Cavalry, becoming a sergeant by 1884. He was discharged May 7, 1885, and became a scout for the army in Apache operations and eventually a freighter. He was a ranch partner of William Bladen Jett (see

entry) for a brief period. For 53 years Kane was a cattle raiser near Clarkdale, Arizona. He died at Long Beach, California.

"The Reluctant Corporal: The Autobiography of William Bladen Jett," ed. by Henry P. Walker. *Jour. of Ariz. Hist.,* Vol. XII, No. 1 (Spring 1971), 24, photo p. 25, 47n32.

Ka-ni-ache (Coniachi, Quix(n)iachi, Moache Ute chief (c. 1818-summer 1880). His first appearance on the historical record was in 1849 when he was an important band leader of the Moache Utes (a segment of the Southern Utes), their homeland focused on the Cimarron River of northeast New Mexico; sometimes he was considered head chief of the Moaches. Ka-ni-ache that year attempted to bring in Ute leaders suspected of complicity in the slaying of Bill Williams and Benjamin Kern in the southern Colorado mountains. He failed and was confined briefly; he escaped, although wounded slightly in doing so. Under the name of Quixiachigate he signed the December 30, 1849, treaty with the United States, being described on the document as "principal chief" of the Utes. While generally for peace and amenable to talks with the whites, Ka-ni-ache was not averse to arms and occasionally harassed travelers and others, although his forays rarely were sanguinary in intent. In 1855 he was wounded in an attack on a wagon party. He was a steadfast friend of Kit Carson's and the two often conferred (Carson then was the Ute agent) when Ka-ni-ache visited Taos. Once the chief saved Carson's life when another Indian sought to shoot him. Carson appears to have had respect for the Indian's control over Moache bands. The Moaches were enemies of the Navahos, Cheyennes, Arapahoes and Kiowas at various times, and Ka-ni-ache was a "prized scout" in certain of Carson's operations against these tribes, including that which led to the first Battle of Adobe Walls. In the autumn of 1866 Ka-ni-ache and his fighters had an engagement with troops under Lieutenant Colonel Andrew J. Alexander on the Purgatoire River near present Trinidad, Colorado. The affair, which followed alleged depredations, had mixed results: the whites claimed 13 Indians killed while the chief said he lost no men; the whites conceded losing one man killed and two wounded. White sentiment for removal of the Moache Utes to southwestern Colorado where a reservation had been established grew. Ka-ni-ache and other Indians visited Washington, D.C. and on March 2, 1868, a treaty was "signed," although Ka-ni-ache later denied he understood or had himself signed the document. He did sign a subsidiary agreement implementing the first later in 1868, but again its terms were misinterpreted to him and he signed under misapprehensions. Eventually Ka-ni-ache signed another treaty, September 13, 1873, providing for removal of his people to the western reservation where he became subsidiary to the famed Ouray. Ka-ni-ache was killed by lightning in the late summer of 1880 shortly following the death of Ouray.

Morris F. Taylor, "Ka-ni-ache." *Colo. Mag.,* Vol. 43, No. 4 (Fall 1966), 273-302; Vol. 44, No. 2 (Spring 1967), 139-61.

Kanipe, Daniel Alexander, soldier (Apr. 15, 1853-July 18, 1926). B. near Marion, McDowell County, North Carolina, he enlisted as Knipe August 7, 1872, in Company C, 7th Cavalry, With his organization he accompanied the Yellowstone Expedition of 1873 commanded by Colonel David Stanley, and in 1874 was on Custer's Black Hills expedition. May 17, 1876, he left with the regiment from Fort Abraham Lincoln, Dakota Territory on Custer's operation against the Sioux. Kanipe was with Reno in a scout with six troops up Powder River, then to the Tongue and the Rosebud where an Indian trail was struck though lack of rations forced the command back to the Yellowstone. June 22 the regiment under Custer commenced the movement up the Rosebud and over to the Little Big Horn where a large Sioux encampment was struck June 25 and Custer and much of his command wiped out. When within sight of the Indian camp, Kanipe was sent back with a message to Captain Thomas M. McDougall urging him to bring the packs up quickly, then joined Reno's command on the bluffs and thus was spared the fate of the rest of Company C. After the arrival of Terry, Kanipe with others toured the site of the battle; he said George Custer's body was stripped but not mutilated. Kanipe always believed that had Reno and Benteen carried out Custer's plan of attack the massacre of the 7th Cavalry troopers would not have occurred. He was discharged a sergeant August 7, 1877. In World War I he became a captain in the 19th North Carolina

militia. He died at Marion. Kanipe was married; he was described as 5 feet, 11 inches in height, with light hair, fair complexion and hazel eyes.

Montana, Contributions, Vol. IV (1903); *Custer in '76: Walter Camp's Notes on the Custer Fight.* Provo, Utah, Brigham Young Univ. Press, 1976; BHB.

Kanosh, Paiute chief (Feb. 1821-1884). B. as the eldest of four sons of a widow who left the mountains of eastern California and migrated to Utah, the family settled near the present Kanosh, Utah. His wisdom won for Kanosh the leadership of about 500 Pah Vant (Paiute) Indians of the valley. Kanosh was friendly toward the whites. Several times he journeyed to Salt Lake City to confer with Brigham Young and settle differences; he ruled his people with a "firm but kindly hand; his word was law and nearly always he was able to stop any uprising." Kanosh also was intelligent. He had, according to Mormon belief, a "rather clear concept of the Gospel as taught by the Latter-day Saints and taught the Gospel to his tribe." He had four wives, three of whom died tragically: the first lost her mind and Indians put her to death; the second was very jealous and killed the third, a Cherokee, then, berated for doing so, starved herself to death. His last wife lived with him until his death. Mourned by whites and reds alike, he was buried at Kanosh.

Information from Edward L. Black (b. June 6, 1868), a Utah pioneer, with the original at the museum at Fillmore, Utah, reprinted in Nolie Mumey, *John Williams Gunnison.* Denver, Artcraft Press, 1955, p. 174n.

Karlsefni, Thorfinnr, colonist (fl. c. 1005). The first European known to have attempted a settlement on North America, Karlsefni was an intelligent and able Icelander who had become wealthy through numerous trading voyages. In Greenland he married Gudrid, widow of Thorstein, a son of Eirik the Red and in some undetermined year shortly after the turn of the millenium he and Snorri Thordransson led a colonization effort involving about 160 people including five women, to Vinland, or some place on the lands to the west, perhaps Newfoundland. They established a base camp at Straumfjord, a place where the tides or currents were very strong, and eventually moved on south to establish the first real colony where they remained a year or more. Native hostility and other factors drove them out at last, but not before Gudrid had given birth to Karlsefni's son, the first white child known to have been born in America. On the return of Karlsefni's ship the party stopped off in Labrador and incidentally kidnapped two native children, taking them to Greenland where they matured. Karlsefni eventually went to Norway, then settled permanently in Iceland, where he died having founded a distinguished lineage, which included several bishops of the Catholic church. The location of Karlsefni's main base may have been at L'Anse aux Meadows on the northern peninsula of Newfoundland; the site of his colonization attempt is uncertain and the subject of much controversy. Geographical clues given in the Sagas add more confusion than light to the subject.

Magnus Magnusson, Hermann Palsson, *The Vinland Sagas: The Norse Discovery of America.* Baltimore, Penguin Books, 1965; Gwyn Jones, *The Norse Atlantic Saga.* N.Y., Oxford Univ. Press, 1964; DCB.

Katumse, Penateka Comanche chief (fl. 1849-1859). When the Penateka Comanche head chief, Old Owl, died in 1849 Katumse and other chiefs assumed leadership, although never over the whole band, it would appear. It was a time of hardship due to the influx of whites and by 1852 Katumse's people, numbering more than 700, were reported "suffering extreme hunger bordering on starvation," and the chiefs complained that debauchery was destroying their followers. Katumse settled with his people on the Brazos Reservation in Texas until that was phased out when he moved northward toward the present Oklahoma.

Rupert Norval Richardson, *The Comanche Barrier to South Plains Settlement.* Glendale, Calif., Arthur H. Clark Co., 1933.

Kautz, August Valentine, army officer (Jan. 5, 1828-Sept. 4, 1895). B. at Ispringen, Baden, Germany, he was taken as an infant by his parents to Brown County, Ohio. He enlisted in 1846 in the 1st Ohio Infantry and served through the Mexican War under Taylor, going to West Point in 1848 and being commissioned a brevet second lieutenant in the 4th Infantry in 1852 and a second lieutenant the

following March. He was assigned to Oregon and Washington territories until the Civil War, scouting in the Rogue River valley from 1853 to 1855, was wounded in a skirmish with hostile Indians October 25, 1855, and again wounded March 1, 1856, near Puget Sound. Stationed at Fort Steilacoom, on the eastern shore of Puget Sound, Kautz in 1857 made the first recorded ascent of Mt. Rainier (14,408 feet) and one of its 26 glaciers is named for him. Kautz was acting quartermaster to the 1858-59 Northwest Boundary Commission, and in 1859-60 was on leave in Europe. He had made first lieutenant December 4, 1855, and captain of the 6th Cavalry May 14, 1861. His service in the Civil War was distinguished, Kautz emerging as a brevet Major General of the army; he had taken part in the capture of Morgan and his raiders, was chief of cavalry for the XXIII Army Corps and for the Department of Virginia and became a division commander. In May and June of 1865 Kautz was a member of the military commission which tried the conspirators for the assassination of President Lincoln. He became a lieutenant colonel of the 34th Infantry and transferred to the 15th Infantry March 15, 1869. While stationed at Fort Stanton, New Mexico he organized several successful expeditions commanded by Howard Cushing against the Mescalero Apaches before they were established permanently on their present reservation. Kautz became colonel of the 8th Infantry July 8, 1874, joining his regiment in Arizona and in March was named commander of the Department of Arizona, succeeding Crook who had been his classmate at West Point. Kautz's Arizona assignment was troubled by Indian unrest and abrasive contacts with John Clum, contentious agent for the San Carlos Apaches who had an ingrained contempt for all army officers. Yet Kautz maintained order fairly well and resisted the temptation to publicly chastise the agent. During his Arizona tour his interest in mining developed and he also explored the Canyon de Chelly and other little known regions of the Navaho country in northeastern Arizona. March 5, 1878, he was relieved by Willcox. Kautz served in California and elsewhere, becoming a Brigadier General April 20, 1891, and commanded the Department of the Columbia until his retirement January 5, 1892. He lived at Seattle until his death. Kautz was studious, hard-working and energetic. He wrote *The Company Clerk* (1863); *Customs of Service for Non-Commissioned Officers* (1864); *Customs of Service for Officers of the Army* (1866) and a report on operations south of the James River during the Civil War. He kept a voluminous diary, 27 volumes of which for the years 1857-95 are at the Library of Congress. In 1865 he married the daughter of Governor David Tod of Ohio; she died in 1868 and in 1872 he married a Cincinnati woman by whom he had a son and two daughters.

Cullum; Powell; Heitman: Weldon Heald to author, Jan. 19, 1958; Dan L. Thrapp, *The Conquest of Apacheria.* Norman, Univ. of Okla. Press, 1967; Andrew Wallace, "Duty in New Mexico: A Military Memoir." *New Mex. Hist. Rev.,* Vol. L, No. 3 (July 1975), 231-62; DAB.

Ka-ya-ten-nae, Jacob (Kaahteney, etc.), Apache war leader (1858-Jan. 1918). B. a Mimbres Apache in southern New Mexico and a close follower of Victorio and Nana, Ka-ya-ten-nae was a resourceful and valiant fighter during the Victorio War of 1879-80. When Victorio was trapped at Tres Castillos, Chihuahua, in October 1880, Ka-ya-ten-nae was with Nana on a scout for ammunition and thus missed the massacre. He was considered by some to have become a sub-chief. Ka-ya-ten-nae accompanied Juh and Geronimo in the April 1882 raid on San Carlos to free Loco and several hundred Mimbres Apaches who then were herded to Mexico. Betzinez reported that Ka-ya-ten-nae was among the able fighters who sat out the Garcia massacre of many of the Loco band, and Al Sieber largely supported this belief. Following Crook's great expedition into the Sierra Madre in 1883 Ka-ya-ten-nae and other recalcitrants came in to San Carlos for his first reported stay on a reservation. Britton Davis found him restless, moody and a potential trouble-maker, suspected of organizing a break-out. Ka-ya-ten-nae attempted to ambush Davis, but was thwarted. The Apache was arrested, tried by an Indian court and sentenced to three years in Alcatraz prison in California. Crook however urged holding him for one month under heavy guard, then allowing him to "go about the Island [of Alcatraz] and the city of San Francisco so that he may observe and become acquainted with the manner of living of the whites and thus learn something which may be of benefit to his people when he is returned to

the reservation, which I recommend be done at such time as the experience given him be for their interests and his own." This procedure was followed. When Geronimo sought to surrender to Crook in March 1886 at Canyon de los Embudos, Sonora, Crook directed Ka-ya-ten-nae to mingle with the hostiles, assess their sentiments for war or peace, and persuade any who might listen to surrender; the Apache performed this mission satisfactorily. When the Geronimo band surrendered later in the year Ka-ya-ten-nae was sent with the Chiricahuas, hostile and friendly alike, into Florida exile. He had become stepfather to James Kaywaykla, last survivor of the Victorio massacre. Ka-ya-ten-nae was Kinzhuna's brother and was related to Chihuahua; he married twice and took the first name of Jacob while a prisoner. He went with the other Apache captives from Florida to Alabama and thence to Fort Sill, Oklahoma. In 1913 he was allowed to settle on the Mescalero Reservation in New Mexico where he died of pneumonia. Richard H. Harper, a missionary on the reservation, reported that the Apache, however wild and turbulent before Crook's disciplinary action, in New Mexico became "not at all militant in appearance; was, indeed, so mild and respectful... it seemed difficult to realize that what history records about him could be true." He was of medium size, but robust and very strong.

Griswold; Dan L. Thrapp, *Conquest of Apacheria,* Norman, Univ. of Okla. Press, 1967; Frank C. Lockwood, *The Apache Indians,* N.Y., Macmillan Co., 1938; Jason Betzinez, *I Fought With Geronimo,* Harrisburg, PA, Stackpole Co., 1959.

Keais, John Low, army officer (c. 1812-Dec. 28, 1835). B. in North Carolina, he was an orphan of considerable intellectual ability, his particular interest mathematics. He was graduated from West Point in 1835 and in July commissioned a second lieutenant, 3rd Artillery and sent to Fort Brooke, Florida, to take part in the Seminole War. He was with Dade whose 108-man command was virtually destroyed. Keais was disabled by having both arms broken at the first fire. He "got one of the men to tie both arms with a handkerchief, and was placed against a tree, where he was tomahawked by the negroes" who accompanied the Seminole Indians. Keais's injuries prevented his use of a small pistol he carried in his pocket and the attackers overlooked it when they overran the battleground, the weapon being recovered by a subsequent search party.

Cullum; Heitman; Frank Laumer, *Massacre!* Gainesville, Univ. of Fla. Press, 1968.

Kearny, Stephen Watts, army officer (Aug. 30, 1794- Oct. 31, 1848). B. at Newark, New Jersey, he was commissioned a first lieutenant in the 13th Infantry March 12, 1813, was lightly wounded at the battle of Queenston Heights above the Niagara River, Canada, on October 13 and captured, but soon exchanged. He became a captain April 1, 1813, transferred to the 2nd Infantry May 17, 1815 and by 1819 was on the frontier. He accompanied Atkinson in founding Camp Missouri (the later Fort Atkinson) near Council Bluffs (on the present site of Fort Calhoun), Nebraska in 1819 and the next year accompanied Captain Matthew J. Magee overland to the later Fort Snelling, Minnesota, seeking the best military route to the mouth of the St. Peters River. In September 1820 he was sent to Fort Smith, Arkansas, briefly, arriving coincidentally with the returning Long's expedition from the Rockies. Kearny transferred to the 1st Infantry June 4, 1821, was breveted major for ten years in grade in 1823 and promoted to major of the 3rd Infantry May 1, 1829. In 1825 he had accompanied Atkinson to the Yellowstone, leaving Council Bluffs May 16 by keelboats, meeting the Ponca Indians June 9, reaching the Mandan villages July 26 and the mouth of the Yellowstone August 17. Here they met Ashley coming in from the mountains with 100 packs of beaver and adventures to tell. The Atkinson party went on 120 miles above the Yellowstone to the Porcupine, then swung about downstream, reaching Council Bluffs September 19 after an almost eventless journey. In August, 1828 Kearny took command of Fort Crawford at Prairie du Chien, Wisconsin, remaining there a year before being transferred to Missouri's Jefferson Barracks, which he helped construct. He participated briefly in quelling Winnebago troubles in Wisconsin, but soon was back in Missouri. Once more he had to return to Wisconsin in 1830 however, to cool a brief inter-tribal flareup. He was transferred to Fort Leavenworth and from there in 1831 went to Fort Towson in present Oklahoma, to rebuild and reoccupy the post in anticipation

of its use to control Indians removed to the vicinity from east of the Mississippi. Kearny became lieutenant colonel of the newly organized 1st Dragoons March 4, 1833, and in September led a detachment into Iowa, commencing construction of Fort Des Moines. He became colonel of the regiment July 4, 1836, while stationed at Leavenworth, many considering him in effect the father of the United States Cavalry into which the dragoons eventually evolved. In 1842 Kearny became commander of the Third Military Department, stationed first at Leavenworth, then at St. Louis, his mission to protect 1,000 miles of frontier with about 600 soldiers, besides keeping war-inclined tribes at peace with one another and policing a number of reservations. For a decade he led or oversaw a succession of escorts, patrols and expeditions into troubled areas. In 1845 he took five companies of the 1st Dragoons along the Overland Trail to South Pass, Wyoming on a 99-day expedition. June 16 he held a council with the Sioux near Fort Laramie; he reached South Pass, 850 miles from Leavenworth and started the return July 1, having brought the first United States troops ever seen this far to the west. From Laramie the column dropped down to Bent's Fort and returned by way of the Arkansas River, counciling with the Cheyennes enroute and regaining Leavenworth August 1. Kearny became a Brigadier General June 30, 1846, assigned to command the Army of the West in the Mexican War, leading his 1,660 men to Santa Fe, which was entered without opposition and serving as military governor of New Mexico for a month. A civil government organized, he set out for the Pacific coast September 25, 1846, with 300 dragoons, 200 of whom were sent back from Socorro, New Mexico when Kearny was informed California already had surrendered to Fremont and Stockton — a premature announcement. With his thinned column he proceeded westward through Apache country to Tucson, the Gila River and down it to the Colorado which was forded November 25. December 2 the column reached Warner's Ranch on the highlands beyond the Imperial Valley desert. At San Pasqual on December 7-8, 1846, Kearny fought his only real engagement, if a minor one, with the Mexicans, and suffered a reverse. Twenty-two Americans were killed (only two by gunfire, the rest by lance wounds) and about 16 were wounded of 45 to 50 men engaged, while the enemy of 70 men under Andres Pico suffered indeterminate losses, but around 10 per cent. From San Diego the combined forces of Kearny and Commodore Robert Field Stockton left December 29 for Los Angeles, engaging in two minor skirmishes enroute and occupying the community January 10. Almost immediately an acrimonious dispute arose between Kearny and Fremont, who had come down from the north, as to who was in overall command; the squabble does not belong in this sketch, but it was resolved in Kearny's favor. After brief service in Mexico Kearny was breveted Major General and returned in 1847 to Leavenworth. A disease contracted at Vera Cruz, Mexico, had seriously impaired his health and he died at St. Louis at the home of Meriwether Lewis Clark, an army major. He was married and fathered children.

Dwight L. Clarke, *Stephen Watts Kearny: Soldier of the West*. Norman, Univ. of Okla. Press, 1961.

Keemle, Charles, frontiersman (Oct. 1800-Sept. 28, 1865). B. at Philadelphia he became a journalist and worked at Vincennes, Indiana, in 1817 but soon removed to St. Louis. He joined the Missouri Fur Company in 1820, being stationed on the Yellowstone River, trapping as far as the Three Forks. On May 31, 1823, he survived a Blackfoot attack that killed seven and wounded four trappers, taking command of the others and bringing them safely out. Keemle took part in Leavenworth's indecisive attack on the Arickaras, wintered in 1823-24 with the Crows, then returned to civilization for good. He died at St. Louis.

Charles E. Hanson Jr., article, MM, Vol. VIII.

K(e)iser, Benjamin, interpreter (d. Apr. 23, 1856). Ben K(e)iser's mother was stolen in Kentucky when a small child by Shawnees and when she grew up became the wife of a Shawnee chief, so Ben was half Shawnee though his date of birth is not reported. He was a Rocky Mountain trapper and hunter who by 1851 was working for John Owen of Fort Owen in the Bitterroot Valley of Montana; he served as interpreter for John Mullan in October 1854 and for Isaac I. Stevens at the working out of Flathead and Blackfoot treaties in 1855 although the Rev.

Adrian Hoecken believed he was not sufficiently fluent in Flathead. Stevens spoke highly of him, believed him well versed in English, very reliable as interpreter and a remarkable frontiersman. K(e)iser was married to an Indian woman and fathered children. He died in the Bitterroot Valley.

John Fahey, *The Flathead Indians.* Norman, Univ. of Okla. Press, 1974; George F. Weisel, *Men and Trade on the Northwest Frontier.* Missoula, Mont. State Univ. Press, 1955.

Keiser, William, frontiersman (d. Sept. 27, 1867). Known as "Buffalo Bill," he died on the Little Prickly Pear Creek, east of Helena, Montana.

Montana, Contributions, Vol. X, 1940, 282.

Keith, Gordon W., soldier (fl. 1876). A trooper of Company C, 5th Cavalry, he and Harry Anderson were riding as couriers when they attracted the attentions of hostile Cheyennes near Warbonnet (Hat) Creek, near present Montrose, Nebraska. This opened the way for Cody's celebrated "duel" with Yellow Hand, or Yellow Hair, on July 14, 1876.

Don Russell, *The Lives and Legends of Buffalo Bill.* Norman, Univ. of Okla. Press, 1960.

Keleher, William Aloysius, lawyer, writer (Nov. 7, 1886-Dec. 18, 1972). B. at Lawrence, Kansas, he was graduated from Washington and Lee University in 1915. Already established at Albuquerque, and with newspaper and other experience behind him, Keleher began the practice of law in 1915. His first book, the *Maxwell Land Grant,* published in 1943, dealt with the history of land grants in New Mexico. The second, *The Fabulous Frontier,* came in 1945 (rev., 1962); *Turmoil in New Mexico 1846-1868,* (1952); *Violence in Lincoln County, 1869-1881,* (1957); *Memoirs: 1893-1969,* (1970). He was a reliable historian.

Who's Who in America; Western Writers of Amer., *Roundup,* Vol. XXI, No. 2 (Feb. 1973).

Keliher, Michael, victim (d. Mar. 2, 1880). New to Las Vegas, New Mexico, and suspected to be carrying much money, Keliher was murdered by John Joshua Webb and William (Dutchy) Goodlet in the Goodlet and Robinson Saloon. Webb, who lifted the wallet, was sentenced to hang, but escaped jail.

William A. Keleher, *Violence in Lincoln County 1869-1881.* Albuquerque, Univ. of New Mex.

Press, 1957; Colin Rickards, *Mysterious Dave Mather.* Santa Fe, Press of Territorian, 1968.

Kell, William Hudson, army officer (Apr. 19, 1841-Feb. 9, 1916). B. at Steubenville, Ohio, he enlisted in the 1st Ohio Infantry in 1861, later serving in the 2nd and 18th Ohio Infantry regiments through the Civil War, being with Sherman on the Atlanta operation. In 1872 he was commissioned a second lieutenant in the 22nd Infantry, joining at Fort Rice, North Dakota. He was with the Yellowstone Expedition from June to September 1873, served in Louisiana briefly and returned to Montana in 1876. Under Lieutenant Colonel Elwell Stephen Otis he was in a skirmish with the Sioux July 29, 1876, at the mouth of the Powder River, and another the night of October 10, 1876, under Captain Charles Wright Miner at Deadwood Creek (Spring Creek), Montana. Miner had attempted to take a train of 94 wagons from Glendive Creek to a cantonment on the Tongue, but several hundred Indians under Sitting Bull wounded some of his animals, captured 47 mules and forced the train back to Glendive Creek. Colonel Otis then reformed the train, substituted soldiers for demoralized civilian drivers and with reinforcements started out again. In a daylong fight October 15 both Kell and Miner won brevets for gallantry, repeatedly charging the enemy. At one point the hostiles fired the prairie, the wagons in four side-by-side columns advancing through the flames and eventually won out; Sitting Bull sent in a note telling the whites to get off his buffalo range, Otis replying by note that if the Indian desired more fighting, he would accomodate him. Kell was with the advance of Major Henry M. Lazelle's command July 9, 1877, when it surprised an Indian camp at Sentinel Buttes, Montana and routed the enemy. After service in the east Kell was stationed at San Antonio, Texas in 1879, in the field along the San Juan River of Utah late in 1883 and in the spring of 1884, then was stationed at Fort Keogh, Montana. He became a first lieutenant in 1879, captain in 1891 and retired as a major December 15, 1899. He was promoted to lieutenant colonel on the retired list April 23, 1904. Kell died at New York City.

Powell, Heitman; EHI; *Chronological List;* 1916 *Army Register.*

Kelley, Andrew, soldier, Indian man (c. 1844-c. 1918). B. in Queens County (present Laois (Laoighis, Leix) County), Ireland, he emigrated to the United States and in 1867 enlisted in Company B, 15th Infantry, assigned to Fort McRae, New Mexico where he remained three years, a time of importance for bringing in of the hostile Mimbres Apaches under Victorio and others; Kelley learned something of their language or perhaps could communicate with them in the Spanish they understood. After his enlistment he worked at times for the Indian Bureau from 1870 until 1882; he became well acquainted with Victorio and others of his band, and was trusted by them. February 7, 1879, Victorio, then out, came near the post of Ojo Caliente, New Mexico, and Kelley was sent to confer with him, leading to a meeting betweeen that hostile and Second Lieutenant Charles W. Merritt, but only a temporary surrender was effected. January 20, 1880, the hostiles again sent word to Kelley that they would surrender but not to the military, whom they did not trust. Little came of this, either. Even while working for the Indian department Kelley also pursued ranching and mining. The ghost town of Kelley, New Mexico, two miles southeast of Magdalena and about 27 west of Socorro was probably named for him since he was reported to have operated a lead-zinc mine and sawmill in its vicinity. Stanley attributes the name of the town to a "John" Kelly who, he said, died in the 1880s after falling into an abandoned mine shaft, but this must have been a different man. Andy Kelley established a ranch along Cañada Creek, then took up a homestead below Elephant Butte Dam. In 1896 he became assessor of Sierra County, retaining the position for a decade when he moved to Paraje, Socorro County, entering business. A deed was recorded in his name at Hot Springs (the later Truth or Consequences), Sierra County, May 21, 1914. A patent from the United States to his heirs was dated in Sierra County records September 29, 1920; thus Kelley must have died between the two dates, although there is no death certificate on file for him in New Mexico.

Dan L. Thrapp, *Victorio and the Mimbres Apaches.* Norman, Univ. of Okla. Press, 1974; George B. Anderson, *History of New Mexico: Its Resources and People,* Vol. I. Chicago, Pacific

States Pub. Co., 1907; F. Stanley, *Fort Tularosa* (New Mexico) *Story.* Pep, Texas, p.p., 1968, 12; Nat. Archives enlistment records.

Kelley, Hall Jackson, expansionist (Feb. 24, 1790-Jan. 20, 1874). B. at Northwood, New Hampshire, he received a college education and by 1818 was a teacher at Boston, within five years publishing some educational materials before his teaching career ended in 1823. Professionally a mathematician and surveyor as well, he also became interested in Oregon and its colonization, founding the American Society for Encouraging the Settlement of the Oregon Territory. Among his recruits was Nathaniel J. Wyeth, who almost alone among his influential converts eventually reached Oregon — although by that time he had severed relations with Kelley. Kelley's various aggregations of prospective settlers fell apart. He raised enough money however to take himself to New Orleans, across New Mexico and up the coast to California and eventually, with Ewing Young's assistance, reached Oregon (deathly ill of malaria) where he was succored by John McLoughlin of the Hudson's Bay Co. He returned to Boston in 1836 and never went back to Oregon, although his writing of it was published in a House of Representatives Report (101, 25th Cong., 3rd Sess., appendix). Kelley "was an impressive fanatic, possessed some real ability, and exerted an appreciable influence on ...American colonization of Oregon."

DAB; Bernard DeVoto, *Across the Wide Missouri.* Boston, Houghton Mifflin Co., 1947.

Kelley, Harrison, attorney, army officer (Nov. 2, 1838-Sept. 15, 1905). B. in St. Joseph County, Michigan, he was graduated from the University of Michigan law school in 1864, opening a practice at Sturgis, Michigan. Kelley enlisted in the 11th Michigan Infantry early in 1865 and reached Tennessee as a second lieutenant by the end of the war. In 1867, married, he emigrated to Oregon by way of Panama, settling at Jacksonville where he became editor of the *Oregon Sentinel,* practiced law and engaged to some extent in mining. When the Modoc Indian outbreak occurred in 1872 he organized and became captain of Company A of the Oregon militia. With it he saw considerable action in the California Lava Beds; in one action a man was killed beside him and the losses included about a fourth of his command. "The captain was shot at many times, but was not seriously hurt. He manifested great bravery, courage and coolness...." After the Modoc affair he returned to the practice of law at Jacksonville and moved to Burns, Oregon in 1890 where he became the first mayor; in 1889 he was appointed receiver of the federal land office at Burns and in 1896 became county clerk. He was the father of one daughter. Harrison Kelley is often confused with Captain William Kelly by historians writing of the Modoc war, although William Kelly died in 1871 before the Modoc affair began.

An Illustrated History of Baker, Grant, Malheur and Harney Counties. Spokane, Western Hist. Pub. Co., 1902; information from Woodbridge K. Geary, grandson of Kelley, Sept. 2, 1978.

Kellogg, (Eva) Louise Phelps, historian (May 12, 1862- July 11, 1942). B. at Milwaukee, she was graduated and earned a doctorate under Turner at the University of Wisconsin (1901) and studied at the University of Paris and the London School of History and Economics. After a brief period of teaching at the University of Wisconsin, she joined the State Historical Society of Wisconsin where she remained during her professional life. For some time she was editorial assistant to Reuben G. Thwaites, with him producing several historical studies: *Frontier History of Dunmore's War* (1905); *Revolution on the Upper Ohio* (1908), and *Frontier Defense on the Upper Ohio* (1912). She also edited, or wrote: *Frontier Advance on the Upper Ohio* (1916); *Frontier Retreat on the Upper Ohio* (1917); *Early Narratives of the Northwest 1634-1699* (1917); *Charlevoix's Journal of a Voyage to North America,* 2 vols. (1923); *The French Regime in Wisconsin and the Northwest* (1923); *Juliette A. Kinzie Wau-Bun* (1932); *The British Regime in Wisconsin and the Northwest* (1935), and *Historic Wisconsin* (1939). She became the first woman president of the Mississippi Valley History Association (1926) and received many honors. She never married and lived at Madison, Wisconsin, until her death.

Notable American Women 1607-1950. A Biographical Directory, Edmund T. James, ed. Cambridge, Belknap Press of Harvard Univ. Press, 1971; *Who Was Who.*

Kellogg, Marcus Henry (Mark), newspaperman (Mar. 31, 1833-June 25, 1876). B. at Brighton, Ontario, of New England parentage he was the third of ten children of the family which moved in 1835 to Toronto and before 1839 to Watertown, New York. The Kelloggs then moved to Bowmainville, Canada, thence to Marengo and Waukegan, Illinois while Mark learned the telegrapher's trade at nearby Kenosha, Wisconsin; in 1851 they settled at LaCrosse, Wisconsin. Here Mark worked for the old Atlantic and Pacific Telegraph Company and at 28 married Martha (Mattie) L. Robinson, their daughters being Cora Sue, born in 1862 and Martha (Mattie) Grace in 1863. Kellogg did not serve with Union forces in the Civil War, but became a newspaperman on the LaCrosse *Democrat.* His wife died in 1867, the daughters were turned over to an aunt and in 1868 Mark became assistant editor of the Council Bluffs, Iowa *Daily Democrat,* but shortly left that employment. His movements until 1873 are uncertain although he may have been in New York part of this time, or perhaps Minnesota or even Dakota. He became assistant editor of the Bismarck *Tribune* probably with its appearance in July 1873. November 11, 1873, he was foreman of a coroner's jury investigating the shooting of David Mullen by soldiers from the nearby Fort Abraham Lincoln. In the summer of 1874 he was foreman of a hay camp north of Bismarck. Returning to town he studied law and did some work for the *Tribune.* He went east in early 1876 and returned on the same train with Custer and his wife; the train became snowbound and Kellogg improvised a telegraph key and brought Tom Custer with a sleigh to the rescue. Thus Kellogg went with the Custer column when it left the fort May 17, replacing his employer, Clement A. Lounsberry who, having known Custer since Civil War days originally had planned to accompany the expedition. During the march Kellogg had three articles published in the *Tribune,* the dispatches dated May 31, June 12 and June 21, the latter from the mouth of the Rosebud. Kellogg was killed with Custer at the battle on the Little Big Horn, his body discovered on June 29. The New York *Herald* which had printed one of his dispatches, had a monument erected at the site of its discovery and burial, 200 yards southeast of the Custer Monument. Vaughn has compiled the definitive account of the Kelloggs and particularly of Mark.

J.W. Vaughn, "The Mark H. Kellogg Story." *Westerners New York Posse Brand Book,* Vol. Seven, No. 4 (1961), 73-75, 84-91; John C. Hixon, "Custer's 'Mysterious' Mr. Kellogg," and "Mark Kellogg's Diary." *No. Dak. Hist.,* vol. 17, No. 3 (July 1950), 145-76; *Custer in '76: Walter Camp's Notes on the Custer Fight,* ed. by Kenneth Hammer. Provo, Utah, Brigham Young Univ. Press, 1976.

Kellogg, Sanford Cobb, army officer (May 10, 1842-Feb. 7, 1904). B. at Troy, New York, he enlisted May 29, 1862, in the 37th New York Militia and was commissioned a captain of Volunteers March 11, 1863, emerging from the Civil War in the same rank, and with three brevets. He was commissioned a second lieutenant in the 18th Infantry February 23, 1866, and a first lieutenant May 15, being assigned to the 5th Cavalry December 15, 1870, and joining the regiment at Fort McPherson, Nebraska. He was promoted to captain January 11, 1871, assigned to Arizona. While enroute however he was called to Chicago to serve on the staff of Lieutenant General Sheridan, taking part in a reconnaissance of the Yellowstone River as far as the Powder and engaging in several skirmishes with Sioux. He rejoined his company in Arizona in April 1873, remaining until July 1875, serving at several posts. Moved back to the Plains he took part in the Big Horn and Yellowstone expedition being engaged at War Bonnet Creek, Wyoming, and Slim Buttes, Dakota. Kellogg was stationed at Fort D.A. Russell, Wyoming, with a period of field service in Idaho and took part in the Ute campaign in Colorado in 1879. He escorted Sheridan to Yellowstone National Park in 1881. Kellogg became a major of the 4th Cavalry January 14, 1892. He retired September 23, 1898, and died at Washington, D.C.

Heitman; Powell; Price, *Fifth Cavalry.*

Kelly, Charles, desperado (fl. 1864). Rescued from starvation when snowbound in Montana by John White and Rudolph Dorsett, Kelly repaid the kindness by stock thefts; tracked down by the pair, he was captured, but worked loose and killed White and Dorsett in April 1864. Kelly was traced to Deer Lodge, Montana, Lewiston, Idaho, Walla Walla, Washington, Portland, Oregon, and San Francisco, where he disappeared.

Dorothy M. Johnson, *The Bloody Bozeman.* N.Y., McGraw-Hill Book Co., 1971.

Kelly, Charles, historical writer (Feb. 3, 1889-April 19, 1971). B. at Cedar Springs, Michigan, his father was a Baptist minister "until he was starved out," attempted to run a Chicago mission for the poor which also proved unsuccessful and decided to found a religious colony in Tennessee. The family of six boys had a hard time with the autocratic preacher who "beat us once a week for the good of our souls." Charles left home in 1910 and studied briefly at Valparaiso (Indiana) University, then knocked about the country for a few years. At Great Falls, Montana, he became friendly with cowboy artist Charles M. Russell; painting and music were Kelly's twin hobbies, although he could make a living at neither. In 1918 he joined the Army but did not see service abroad. He settled at Salt Lake City in 1919, married and became partner in a printing company. In Utah he found historical research more fascinating than either of his other interests. Out of field work came his first book, *Salt Desert Trails* (1930), which he published himself. He also wrote: with Hoffman Birney, *Holy Murder: The Story of Porter Rockwell* (1934); with Dale L. Morgan, his lifelong friend, *Old Greenwood* (1936, 1965), a biography of Caleb Greenwood, mountain man, and with Maurice L. Howe, *Miles Goodyear* (1937). Kelly wrote *The Outlaw Trail: The Story of Butch Cassidy and the "Wild Bunch"* (1938, rev. ed. 1959) the work considered by Adams "an excellent history"; it is among the finest books published on outlaws of the Great Basin country. In 1938 Kelly also edited *The Journals of John D. Lee,* and, for recreation, descended much of the Colorado River with two others. He wrote more than 100 articles on western history, some published in the *Utah Historical Quarterly* of the Utah State Historical Society of which Kelly eventually became an honorary life member. He moved in 1940 to Wayne County, Utah. In 1943 he became custodian of Capitol Reef National Monument; in 1950 was appointed park ranger and two years later became superintendent of the monument, retiring in 1959 when he and his wife returned to Salt Lake City. There he died. There were no children. Kelly was something of an iconoclast and was cynical almost to the point of misanthropy. In 1937 he wrote "I belong to no organizations of any kind whatever, never go out socially, not interested in politics, and hate radios..." He was never known to belong to any church and while earlier he had joined an

extremist fringe organization or two he found no more satisfaction in them than in people in large quantities. He was regarded by most as "a difficult man," and his eulogist conceded he had a "barbwire personality." But with it he had "a generosity of spirit, an underlining of kindness and loyalty to those who earned his respect and admiration." He was thoroughly honest, his research solid, his judgments usually valid and his writing clear, concise and highly readable. Each of his works was a contribution of merit.

Information from the Utah State Historical Society.

Kelly, Edward O. (Red), killer (1842-Jan. 13, 1904). B. in Missouri, Kelly was a onetime town marshal of Bachelor City, Colorado, a deputy sheriff of Hinsdale County, Colorado, and a policeman and streetcar driver at Pueblo. A man of violent temper, in 1891 he killed Ed Riley at Pueblo, a black, because Riley had accidentally stepped on his toes. In Missouri he had been "well acquainted" with the James family, though in what connection in uncertain. On June 8, 1892, at Creed, Colorado, he shot Bob Ford, who had killed Jesse James, in a clear-cut assassination. Among the various reasons given is that Ford mistreated Kelly's mother long before in Missouri, but this is scarcely credible; more reasonable is the supposition that Kelly was at one time a member of the James' gang. Arrested immediately, he was sentenced July 12, 1892, to life imprisonment in the Canon City penitentiary. Missouri friends won his pardon October 4, 1902. On July 16 of that year Ford's widow, Dol, had committed suicide after corresponding with Kelly. Kelly was arrested January 30, 1903, at Pueblo, charged with drunkeness and vagrancy. He was killed at Oklahoma City during an altercation with Joe Burnett, a policeman. He was unmarried, and well educated.

Denver *Republican,* Jan 15, 1904; Nolie Mumey, *Creede: History of a Colorado Silver Mining Town.* Denver, Artcraft Press, 1949; Paul I. Wellman, *A Dynasty of Western Outlaws.* Garden City, N.Y., Doubleday & Co., 1961; Ramon F. Adams, *Burs Under the Saddle: A Second Look at Books and Histories of the West.* Norman, Univ. of Okla. Press, 1964.

Kelly, Hiram B., pioneer (Oct. 14, 1834-June 2, 1924). B. in Sheridan County, Missouri, he and his father joined the Gold Rush in 1849, mining for three years in California, then returned to Missouri. Hi Kelly became a freighter from Independence in 1853, going to Santa Fe that year and the next. In 1855 he began working for a mail contractor between Independence and Santa Fe, making a number of trips and occasionally having difficulties with Indians. He quit the mail service after badly freezing both legs in December 1857, the next year freighting to Utah where he arrived in 1859. He joined the Colorado gold rush in 1860, prospecting near Leadville, then went to Fort Laramie, Wyoming, where he obtained a hay contract. He worked for Ben Holladay on the overland stage line, his immediate boss being Joseph A. Slade, but quit in 1863. The next year he married the half-Sioux daughter of Peter Richard (a cousin of John Richard Jr.), the marriage producing eight children. Hi Kelly traded with emigrants on the overland trail, sometimes in Wyoming, again in Colorado. Occasionally he obtained small herds of cattle, selling them when opportunity arose, contracted to supply poles for the transcontinental telegraph line, ran a store for a time and freighted, often harassed by hostile Indians. In 1870 he established a ranch on Chugwater Creek, southeastern Wyoming, and many years was a cattleman, becoming a pillar of the Wyoming Stock Growers Association; he sold his 3,200-acre ranch to Scottish interests for $250,000 in 1884 and moved to Cheyenne, but continued to buy and sell ranch properties although his principal interests became mining and unfortunate real estate transactions. By 1900 he was about broke and in 1902 moved to the Denver area, settling at suburban Edgewater. His wife died in 1922 and Hi Kelly died just short of his 90th birthday, being buried next to his wife in the Fort Collins, Colorado, cemetery.

Brian Jones, "Hi Kelly: Pioneer." English Westerners *Brand Book,* Vol. II, No. 3 (Apr. 1969), Pub. 148, pp. 6-10. ·

Kelly, James (Nigger Jim), cowboy (c. 1839-Feb. 1912). B. in present Williamson County, Texas, he was named for James Olive, father of Isom Prentice (Print) Olive, and became a long time friend and employee of Print's. Jim, born a free man, was a "peerless" horse trainer and all-round cowboy and eventually became Olive's trail boss. He usually was armed and

had no fear of any man, white or black, being known to some as a "bad nigger," but to Print as a loyal friend. On July 27, 1872, his boss was being shot up by James W. Kenedy, a white Texan, in an Ellsworth, Kansas, card parlor; Kelly from the window shot the aggressor, seriously wounding him and probably saving Olive's life. Kelly returned with the recuperating Olive to Texas by train. Jim later accompanied Bob Olive with a trail herd to central Nebraska, where the Olive outfit located. Kelly apparently had no role in the famous Nebraska lynching of Ketchum and Mitchell, for which Olive and eight others were indicted February 19, 1879 and briefly imprisoned. With Olive in the penitentiary, Jim went back to Texas in 1880, but returned to Nebraska with another trail herd, remaining there for the rest of his life. He "spent his declining years" at Ansley, Nebraska, where he died and is buried.

Harry E. Chrisman, *The Ladder of Rivers.* Denver, Sage Books, 1962.

Kelly, Luther Sage (Yellowstone Kelly), scout (July 27, 1849-Dec. 17, 1928). B. at Geneva, New York, he enlisted in March 1865 in the 10th Infantry at Rochester, New York. He thought he had joined the Volunteers, but was retained after Civil War hostilities and was ordered west, being stationed at Fort Wadsworth, South Dakota, where he worked out his enlistment. Thereafter he traveled the Yellowstone country as hunter and trapper and for a time as dispatch bearer made monthly round trips between Fort Union and Devil's Lake. He also learned something of the Sioux language. In 1873 he was guide and scout for George A. Forsyth on a reconnaissance up the Yellowstone River, discharged on the return at Fort Buford, North Dakota. Kelly was chief scout for Miles from 1876 to 1878, serving on a number of campaigns including one against Sitting Bull and another on the Tongue River against Sioux and Cheyennes. He was in the 1877 action at Cow Island with the Nez Perce and asserted it was he who first located the Chief Joseph band of Nez Perce at the Bear Paw Mountains of Montana, where many of them were captured by Miles. Kelly was in Colorado for the 1880 Ute conflict. Subsequently he was a War Department clerk at Chicago, Governors Island and at Washington, D.C. In 1898 he was a guide for Captain Edwin Forbes Glenn on an Alaska exploring trip and in 1899 guided the Harriman expedition in Alaska. As a captain of Volunteers he went to the Philippines and saw much active service. Kelly in 1904 became agent for four years at the San Carlos Apache Reservation of Arizona, then tried to work a gold mine in Nevada with little profit, and in 1915 settled on a fruit ranch at Paradise, California, where he died. He was buried at Kelly Mountain, Billings Montana. He was married.

Luther S. Kelly, *"Yellowstone Kelly": The Memoirs of Luther S. Kelly.* Lincoln, Univ. of Neb. Press, 1973; DAB.

Kelly, William, army officer (June 23, 1818-Dec. 28, 1871). B. at Hillsey, England, he migrated to Canada where he married Mary Ana Louisa Wright at Halifax, Nova Scotia May 15, 1837, in Anglican rites. Kelly enlisted in the 3rd Infantry in 1843 at Fort Gratiot, Michigan, transferred to the 4th Infantry in 1847, serving with it to sergeant by 1853 when he left the service. He had reached Oregon in 1849 and become the father of five children. He became postmaster of Vancouver, Washington Territory, in 1854 and in 1855-56 was county treasurer and clerk of the U.S. district court; he raised a company to fight Indians, and was made captain of it. In late 1861 he raised a company for the 1st Oregon Cavalry, the organization becoming Company C of that regiment and Kelly its captain; he served with it until 1866. In 1863 Kelly assisted in construction of Fort Klamath in southern Oregon and in building a road to it. When Kelly saw that the Klamath Indians were destitute during the fort's first winter, he advanced them beef and flour on his own initiative and responsibility, the action having "a most salutary effect in conciliating the Indians and rendering future control of them easy and economical." In 1865 he headed an escort party for Byron J. Pengra's survey of the road from Fort Klamath over the Cascade Mountains to the Owyhee mining country. Kelly became captain in the 8th U.S. Cavalry upon leaving the 1st Oregon in July 1866, serving with that regiment until his death. He was breveted major for an action April 5, 1868, against hostile Indians on the Malheur River, Oregon. Shortly thereafter Kelly moved with his Company C to Arizona, serving briefly in Nevada and California enroute . In November 1869 he accompanied

John Green to select a site for the future Fort Apache. The location chosen, Kelly was left in charge while Green and other officers explored the vicinity, during their absence conferring with Es-kel-dah-silah, a noted White Mountain Apache leader and other principal figures living in the vicinity of the future post. In early 1871 he was at Fort Bayard when Apaches ran off horses and mules from Silver City, New Mexico. Kelly and his company quickly took up pursuit, overtaking the Indians February 12 in the Chiricahua Mountains some 30 miles south of Camp Bowie where a sharp fight ensued; among the 14 Indians killed was Salvadore, the son of Mangas Coloradas. From Fort Selden, New Mexico, Kelly in the autumn received an extended sick leave because of "chronic dysenterry" from which he died at Denver enroute to Oregon. His widow survived him less than a year, dying on Christmas Day, 1872, in Oregon. This Captain Kelly was not the same as Captain Harrison Kelley of the Oregon Volunteers who fought in the Modoc War and with whom he has been confused by some historians.

Nat. Archives military and pension file for William Kelly; Oreg. Hist. Soc. Archives; Ariz. Hist. Soc. Archives; Las Cruces, New Mex., *The Borderer,* Apr. 13, 27, 1871; Bancroft, *Oregon* II; *Morning Daily Oregonian,* Portland, Jan. 1, 1872.

Kemble, Edward Cleveland, newspaperman (1828-Apr. 10, 1886). B. in New York State, he left the east coast February 4, 1846, aboard the *Brooklyn* bound around Cape Horn for San Francisco, chartered at $1,200 a month by Mormons under Samuel Brannan and carrying 238 passengers, almost but not all of them members of the Church of Jesus Christ of Latter-day Saints. She reached San Francisco on July 31, by way of Honolulu after a rough passage. Kemble, who may not have been a Mormon, became the first printer, perhaps the first reporter, at San Francisco. He enlisted in Company G, California Battalion, and his reports were considered worthy and reliable by Bancroft. From April 1847, he was editor of the *San Francisco Star,* founded the Sacramento *Placer Times,* and edited the *Star and Californian* and *Alta California* until 1855. He is known, among other things, for initially labeling the discovery of gold at Sutter's Mill in 1848 "humbug," which it assuredly was not. Kemble returned to the east in 1855, during the Civil War became paymaster of Volunteers and emerged a brevet lieutenant colonel of Volunteers. In 1867 he returned to the Pacific coast as inspector of Indian affairs, remaining some years. He went east again, joined the Associated Press at New York, where he remained until his death. In 1974 he was elected to the California Newspaper Hall of Fame.

Bancroft, *Pioneer Register;* Heitman; Los Angeles *Herald-Examiner,* Dec. 7, 1974.

Kemper, Samuel, adventurer (c. 1777-1815). B. in Fauquier County, Virginia, Kemper was "a man of good stock." With his father and probably his brothers, Reuben and Nathan, he migrated to Ohio in 1800 and in 1801 to southern Mississippi. His brothers figured in the West Florida uprising in 1804, but Samuel apparently refrained. However he joined the Magee-Gutiérrez Expedition to free Spanish Texas, being named major, in 1812. He figured prominently in its adventures as far as Bexar (San Antonio). He made possible the occupation of Nacogodoches August 12, 1812. With Magee's death Kemper took command of the Anglo contingent of the operation at La Bahía (Matagorda Bay) in February 1813. Under Kemper's guidance the expedition broke up a siege and advanced on Bexar. Kemper and Ross led a slashing attack that routed the Spanish at Rosalis, and Kemper insisted upon an unconditional surrender of Bexar. Kemper was host for a dinner April 1 for the defeated Spanish officers, Salcedo and Herrera. Salcedo disarmed his men on April 2, and on April 3, the Spanish officers were murdered by the insurgents. This so incensed Kemper that he withdrew, reaching Natchitoches May 7; he resisted all urgings to bestow his undoubted talents upon the filibuster cause again. Kemper died of measles at St. Francisville, Louisiana.

Harry McCorry Henderson, "The Magee-Gutiérrez Expedition." *Southwestern Hist. Quar.,* Vol. LV, No. 1 (July 1951), 43-61; Harris Gaylord Warren, *The Sword Was Their Passport: A History of American Filibustering in the Mexican Revolution.* Baton Rouge, La. State Univ. Press, 1943; Julia Kathryn Garrett, *Green Flag Over Texas.* N.Y. and Dallas, Cordova Press, 1939.

Kendall, George Wilkins, writer, adventurer (Aug.22, 1809-Oct. 21, 1867). B. at Mount Vernon, New Hampshire, he learned the printing trade and worked for Horace Greeley in New York, and also at Washington, Raleigh, North Carolina, and Boston. He worked for a time with Francis Asbury Lumsden, founding January 25, 1837, with him the New Orleans *Picayune.* In 1814 he joined the Texan Santa Fe Expedition and became its primary chronicler. With others of the ill-fated adventure, he was captured in New Mexico, spent two years in a Mexican prison, and from his experience wrote *Narrative of an Expedition Across the Great South-western Prairies from Texas to Santa Fe: Narrative of the Texan Sante Fe Expedition,* which went through various editions, the latest in 1966. During the Mexican War in 1846 Kendall accompanied Zachary Taylor, Ben McCulloch's Texas Rangers, and General William J, Worth, becoming one of the first war correspondents of record and establishing a primitive kind of pony express to get his dispatches from the field to his newspaper. Kendall was mentioned in dispatches and himself captured a battle flag and was wounded. He spent several subsequent years at Paris, covering events for his newspaper. Upon his return he moved to a sheep ranch in the later Kendall County (named for him) in Texas, maintaining his association with and interest in his New Orleans publication. He took an oath of allegiance to the Confederacy in July 1862, although not active militarily, and organized and armed bands to guard the frontier against Indian attack. He died at his ranch.

Kendall's writings; DAB; HT.

Kendrick, John, navigator (c. 1740-c. Dec. 12, 1794). B. at Harwich, Massachusetts, he became a ship's captain, was a Revolutionary War privateer and a trader. He commanded the *Lady Washington-Columbia* expedition of 1787-89, on which Robert Gray also shipped, to Nootka Sound on the western coast of Vancouver Island, British Columbia. Kendrick in 1789 sent Gray from the Northwest Coast to China with a cargo of otter skins and other trade goods while Kendrick remained on the American coast. Later in 1789 Kendrick in the *Lady Washington* went to Hawaii, where he envisioned developing a trade in pearls and sandalwood, although the attempt proved abortive. He continued to China where he remained 14 months, returning in March 1791 to the Northwest Coast, enroute visiting Japan, his the first American flag vessel to drop anchor at that country. Indians sought to capture the ship off the Queen Charlotte Islands, but Kendrick forestalled them. He continued trading between China and the Northwest Coast until 1794 when on a visit to Hawaii the *Washington* lay off Honolulu, adjacent to the British trader *Jackal*. Her captain, William Brown fired off a salute to a native king's war victory. Unfortunately one of the cannon had not previously been relieved of its shot, which tore through the side of Kendrick's ship, killing the captain and others. Kendrick, wrote Cook, was "the most popular trader with the (American) natives." He was the antithesis of his colleague. "In contrast to the cruel and vengeful (Gray), Kendrick sought and earned the affection and respect of Indians and Spanish alike." Kendrick was filled with wildly improvident schemes for magnificent undertakings: such things as reversing the prevailing westerlies of the Atlantic and turning the Gulf Stream into the Pacific by means of a canal across Mexico, "but with all his fooleries he was a wonderful man," acknowledged a contemporary.

Warren L. Cook, *Flood Tide of Empire.* New Haven, Yale Univ. Press, 1973; DAB; Bancroft *Northwest Coast,* I.

Kenedy, James W., cowboy, gunman (fl. 1872-1880). The son of noted Texas pioneer Mifflin Kenedy who had married Mrs. Petra Vela de Vidal of Mier, Mexico, Kenedy went up the trail to Kansas. At Ellsworth he engaged in gambling and July 27, 1872, in a dispute over cards, seriously wounded I.P. (Print) Olive, being wounded seriously himself by Nigger Jim Kelly, Olive's trail boss. On April 4, 1878, he is alleged to have fired two shots at night into a house south of the Dodge City tracks, trying to hit Mayor James (Dog) Kelley, who had thrown him out of a saloon in another gambling dispute. The following afternoon in a heavy snowstorm, he was followed up by a posse seeking him for the killing of actress Dora Hand by his nocturnal shooting. The pursuers included Bat Masterson, Charles Bassett, Bill Tilghman and perhaps Wyatt Earp. Near Meade City, Kansas, Kenedy was wounded through the shoulder, his horse killed, and he was returned to Dodge where in October 1878, he was

aquitted at a "private" trial. December 9 his father reached Dodge to return James to Texas. In November 1880, Kenedy was reported mistakenly to have shot and killed Earp on Sand Creek, Colorado. Kenedy was said to have died in Texas "some years later."

Nyle H. Miller, Joseph W. Snell, *Great Gunfighters of The Kansas Cowtowns, 1867-1886.* Lincoln, Univ. of Nebr. Press, 1967; Harry E. Chrisman, *the Ladder of Rivers.* Denver, Sage Books, 1962; Joseph G. Rosa, *The Gunfighter: Man or Myth?* Norman, Univ. of Okla. Press, 1969.

Kenedy, Mifflin, cattleman (June 8, 1818-Mar. 14, 1895). B. at Downington, Pennsylvania, in 1834 he sailed as a cabin boy to Calcutta, returning the following year; from 1836 to 1846 he served aboard riverboats on the Mississippi and tributaries and as a lightboat skipper in the Mexican War, later engaging in overland trade with Mexico. He also raised sheep in Hidalgo County, Texas, but sold out. In 1860 he joined Richard King for a short time in cattle ranching, with sheep, goats and mules as sidelines. He maintained his interest in river boats and trading along the Rio Grande. Kenedy was one of the first Texas ranchers to fence his lands, beginning in 1869, but he sold out in 1882 having turned his attention to railroad construction. He married Mrs. Petra Vela de Vidal of Mier, Mexico, in 1852, and among his children was James W. Kenedy, who twice got into shooting scrapes in Kansas, the second time extracted by his father who returned him to Texas. Mifflin Kenedy died at Corpus Christi and is buried at Brownsville, Texas.

HT; Ed Bartholomew, *Wyatt Earp: The Untold Story.* Toyahvale, Tex., Frontier Book Co., 1963; Harry E. Chrisman, *The Ladder of Rivers.* Denver, Sage Books, 1962.

Kennedy, Richard M., lawman (1848-1921). B. at Syracuse, New York, he became a deputy under Sheriff Red Angus of Johnson County, Wyoming, and served as such during the Johnson County War. Kennedy was sheriff of the county from 1901 to 1907. He died at Buffalo, Wyoming.

Archives and photograph, Gatchell Museum, Buffalo, Wyo.

Kennerly, Henry Atkinson, pioneer (Dec. 2, 1835-July 9, 1913). The son of a onetime army officer and a daughter of Pierre Menard who had trapped the Three Forks of Montana in 1810, Kennerly accompanied Alfred Cumming to attend the 1855 council with Blackfeet on the Judith River. He returned to Montana in 1863 and became a prominent pioneer, dying at Cut Bank.

Montana Contributions, Vol. X, 1940, 273.

Kensler, Toussaint, frontiersman (d. Nov. 19, 1874). A Sioux half-breed, he was accused of killing Adolph Pirreo April 9, 1872, at John Phillip's ranch near Fort Laramie, Wyoming. He escaped and sent back the horse he stole during his brief freedom, saying, "he had no right to keep it." He lived for some months with Sioux and Arapahoes in the Black Hills, while a petition signed by the Sioux chiefs Red Cloud and Spotted Tail in his behalf and sent to President Grant had no effect. He was taken and hanged at Cheyenne, Wyoming.

Charles Hall, *Documents of Wyoming Heritage.* Cheyenne, Wyo. Bicentennial Commis., 1976.

Kent, Andrew, adventurer (c. 1794-Mar. 6, 1836). B. perhaps in Pennsylvania, he went to Texas by way of St. Charles County, Missouri, in 1828. He resided at Gonzales, east of San Antonio in 1836, entering the Alamo with the 32-man relief force March 1, and dying with its defenders. Kent County, Texas, is named for him.

Amelia Williams, XXXVII, 268; HT

Kenton, Simon, frontiersman (Apr. 3, 1755-Apr. 29, 1836). B. in Culpeper County, Virginia, believing at 16 he had killed a love rival he adopted the name of Simon Butler and fled to Fort Pitt, becoming acquainted with Simon Girty. In 1771 he descended the Ohio River to the Great Kanawha River and thence to present West Virginia, engaging in trapping until spring of 1773 when Indians drove his party away. He returned to Fort Pitt in 1774, was employed as a scout in Lord Dunmore's War against Shawnees, reportedly saving the life of Daniel Boone, among other deeds of daring. Thereafter he went to Kentucky, trapping and farming in a minor way in present Mason County. George Rogers Clark used Kenton as a scout in his 1777-78 Illinois expedition, where he proved important in operations against Kaskaskia and Vincennes. Kenton returned to Harrodsburg, Kentucky, and was associated with Boone on several expeditions. In 1778 he was captured

in Ohio with two others on a horse-hunting trip and was condemned by Indians to torture and death. He was rescued by Simon Girty but was again captured. Girty succeeded in having him conveyed to Sandusky, Ohio, where the Mingo chief, Logan, persuaded a French trader to ransom and take Kenton to Detroit as a prisoner of war. Kenton escaped in June 1779, returning to Kentucky where he aided in driving British and Indians out of the region. He continued his border service until 1782 when, learning that the victim of his youth still lived, he resumed his proper name. In 1793 he served in the army of Anthony Wayne which defeated the Miamis at Fallen Timbers. Kenton removed to Ohio in 1800, settling on Mad River near present Urbana. In 1805 he was made Brigadier General of militia. In 1813 he served with Kentucky troops aiding William H. Harrison in his invasion of Canada and fought with courage at the battle of the Thames. Kenton was converted in a Methodist Episcopal Service in 1819 and died at Bellefontaine, Ohio. He was around 6 feet tall, blonde, blue or gray eyes, figure broad-shouldered and trim, his voice pleasing. He was true in friendship, honest, fearless and resourceful. He was one of the most noteworthy and able of trans-Allegheny frontiersmen and deserves a high place in the annals of the border.

NCAB, III, 527-28; Patricia Jahns, *The Violent Years.* N.Y., Hastings House, 1962, a biography slightly fictionalized.

Keogh Myles Walter, army officer (Mar. 25, 1840-June 25, 1876). B. at Orchard, County Carlow, Ireland, he left that country in 1860. In Italy he was commissioned in the Papal armies and before leaving Rome in 1862 he was presented with the Pro Petri Sede medal and the Cross of the Order of St. Gregory the Great; he probably wore one of them at his death. Keogh joined the Union Army as a cavalry captain in 1862, serving with Shields, Stoneman and others with distinction, revealing outstanding bravery. He is said to have taken part in more than 100 battles, winning a brevet as lieutenant colonel. He became a second lieutenant of the 4th Cavalry in 1866. Later that year he was made a captain in the 7th Cavalry, probably having met Custer during the Civil War. With this organization he perished in the fight against Sioux and Cheyennes on the Little Big Horn.

According to the chief, Red Horse, his astonishing courage in that action revealed him to have been "the bravest man they (the Sioux) had ever fought." His badly wounded mount, Comanche, was the only living creature recovered from the field by the whites after the engagement. Keogh had close family connections in Ireland (a sister was the grandmother of Francis Cardinal Spellman), but he was a victim of melancholy and depression which apparently led to gambling and rather heavy drinking. He enjoyed sports. His body was stripped but not mutilated, and a Catholic medal was not removed by the Indians.

Carroll Friswold, *Frontier Fighters and Their Autograph Signatures.* Keepsake No. 87, Westerners, Los Angeles Corral, 1968; Edgar I. Stewart, *Custer's Luck.* Norman, Univ. of Okla. Press, 1955; Francis B. Taunton, "The Man Who Rode Comanche." *Sidelights of the Sioux Wars,* London, English Westerners' Soc., 1967.

Keokuk, Sauk leader (c. 1780-Apr. 1848). B. on the Rock River, Illinois, he was not an hereditary chief, but rose to lead his people through merit and oratory. His mother was reported to have been half French. Keokuk was a devious, ambitious and at times unscrupulous man, eventually becoming the leading councilor of the Sauk assembly and for a time greatly popular among the people he had chosen to assiduously cultivate. At the time of the Black Hawk difficulties however, Keokuk seemed so passive that he lost influence among both wings of the tribe and Black Hawk emerged to the fore. About this time the league with the Foxes came into effect, brought about largely by Keokuk who had turned to them after losing favor with his own people. Black Hawk, because of tribal divisions, had not the strength to counter the whites and swiftly lost his 1832 war, at which time Keokuk once more emerged as the principal power of the nation. By the government he was made chief of the Sauks, an advancement which aroused ridicule from both Sauks and Foxes since he was not of the ruling clan, and also stirred the ire of Black Hawk who openly challenged the new chief. The one point at which Keokuk became honored by the tribesmen was in his demand at Washington, D.C., by right of conquest to the Iowa lands claimed by the Sauk and Fox peoples. He died in Kansas, but in 1883 his remains were reinterred in the city park at Keokuk, Iowa and a monument raised over his grave. A bronze bust of Keokuk also stands in the capitol at Washington.

Hodge, HAI.

Kern, Benjamin Jordan, physician (Aug. 3, 1818-Mar. 14, 1849). B. at Philadelphia, Kern was the oldest of three talented brothers who became prominent in the exploration of the West. Benjamin was persuaded by Edward, a brother who had accompanied Fremont on a previous expedition, to join as physician the fourth expedition of that explorer; this attempted to cross the southern Rocky Mountains in winter and ended disastrously, 11 men perishing in the deep snows of the impassable San Juan Mountains of southern Colorado, the others barely escaping with their lives southward to Taos. Benjamin accompanied the veteran guide of the expedition, Old Bill Williams, back into the San Juans in late winter to salvage abandoned records and equipment. The two were killed, supposedly by Utes, although McNitt and others believe that Mexican packers had a role in their demise.

Robert Taft, *Artists and Illustrators of the Old West: 1850-1900.* N.Y. Bonanza Books, 1953; James H. Simpson, *Navaho Expedition...,* ed. and annot. by Frank McNitt. Norman, Univ. of Okla. Press, 1964; Robert V. Hine, *Edward Kern and American Expansion.* New Haven, Yale Univ. Press, 1962; Alpheus H. Favour, *Old Bill Williams: Mountain Man.* Norman, Univ. of Okla. Press, 1962.

Kern, Edward Meyer, artist (Oct. 26, 1823-Nov. 23, 1863). B. at Philadelphia, he was one of several talented brothers, three of whom were active in exploration of the West. Kern was hired as artist on Fremont's third expedition leaving St. Louis in mid-1845, crossing the Rockies to Salt Lake City and then continuing to California where Fremont became involved in the war against Mexico and the takeover of the southwest. Kern served as a lieutenant under Fremont from July 1846 until April 1847, spending much of his time at Fort Sutter or the vicinity, participating in minor Indian skirmishing. He sailed for home in November. Edward persuaded his brothers, Benjamin and Richard, to join him on Fremont's disastrous fourth expedition in 1848. This was designed to effect a winter crossing of the southern Rocky Mountains to demonstrate the feasibility of a railroad route on that latitude; severe weather hampered and at last stalled the expedition in the San Juan Mountains of southern Colorado, 11 men perished and the others barely reached Taos, New Mexico, where Edward and Richard were stranded without resources. Benjamin had returned in late winter to the mountains with Bill Williams to recover items abandoned by the explorers and was killed by Utes or others. Richard and Edward joined Lieutenant James Simpson for the expedition under John M. Washington into the Navaho country, penetrating the Canyon de Chelly and other secluded sites, the Kerns serving as artists and topographers. Edward returned east via Leavenworth in the summer of 1851 with an expedition under John Pope seeking an improved route across tha Plains; he continued to Philadelphia. Kern applied for a position as artist-topographer on Matthew Perry's expedition to Japan, but settled for a berth on the North Pacific Expedition of Commander Cadwalader Ringgold, sailing June 11, 1853, aboard the USS *Vincennes* in company with four sister ships. The expedition rounded Cape of Good Hope and reached Hong Kong, where Ringgold was invalided home as insane, although he later recovered and assumed other commands. The *Vincennes* and other ships, now under John Rodgers, eventually explored northward along Japan to the Bering Straits, Kern spending some weeks on the Siberian mainland with a landing party; taken off, he and his group with the expedition reached San Francisco October 13, 1855, leaving February 2 for the South Pacific, Cape Horn and home, visiting Tahiti enroute. Kern was back at Philadelphia in July 1856. In 1858 he joined another North Pacific expedition, this time under John Brooke, visiting California, Hawaii and Japan, and returning home by summer 1860. He was commissioned a captain of topographical engineers, according to his biographer (although there is no listing for him in Heitman) and served under Fremont briefly in Missouri; in November his commission was "revoked" because it was irregular, his biographer asserted. Kern returned to Philadelphia where he died. He had been an epileptic. He was described as tall and thin, with hair, mustache and spade beard dark red, and with

grey eyes; he was good humored, gregarious and energetic. Kern County and the Kern River of California are named for him. His watercolors and oils are owned by the National Collection of Fine Arts and other ranking museums but "his image of the West was to be seen in large part through the dark glass of a lithographer." The most extensive collection of Kern letters and journals is at the Huntington Library of San Marino, California.

Robert V. Hine, *Edward Kern and American Expansion.* New Haven, Yale Univ. Press, 1962; Robert Taft, *Artists and Illustrators of the Old West: 1850-1900.* N.Y., Bonanza Books, 1953; James H. Simpson, *Navaho Expedition...*, ed. and annot, by Frank McNitt. Norman, Univ. of Okla. Press, 1964.

Kern, Richard Hovendon, artist, topographer (1821-Oct. 26, 1853). B. at Philadelphia, he and two brothers became artists and participated in important explorations of the Rocky Mountain west. Kern was a member of the disastrous fourth Fremont expedition of 1848 which crossed the Sangre de Cristo Range amid heavy winter weather, was halted in the San Juan Mountains by snow and cold; 11 men died and the Kerns were rescued barely in time and taken to Taos, completely soured on Fremont. Destitute, Richard and his brother Edward removed to Santa Fe. A third brother, Benjamin, had been killed by Utes or others with Bill Williams in the San Juans (Richard is said to have named Bill Williams Mountain, a prominent peak in northern Arizona, for his friend who had perished with his brother). In the summer Richard and Edward Kern were employed by Lieutenant James Hervey Simpson of the Topographical Corps to do illustrations and maps for his report on an overland journey from Fort Smith. The Kerns joined Simpson and Colonel John M. Washington for an extended 1849 reconnaissance into the Navaho country, penetrating for the first time Canyon de Chelly, making charts and pictures and crowding their journals with facts uncovered, engaging in a skirmish or two with Indians, circling south to Morro Rock where they copied inscriptions of explorers and travelers for centuries past and where Richard chiseled another: "Lt. J.H. Simpson, U.S.A., and R.H. Kern, artist, visited and copied these inscriptions, September 17, 1849." The Kerns may have participated in a miner survey or two by Simpson during the next year, padding meagre returns from their art work with civilian employment by the army. In 1851, Richard Kern joined the Sitgreaves exploring and survey expeditions from Zuñi, New Mexico, which it left September 24, 1851, arriving at Fort Yuma on the lower Colorado River November 30. Kern's illustrations accompany Sitgreave's official report. Kern went on to California, where he was guest of John Sutter. He supplied Senator Gwin of California with a written description of a possible southern railroad route, and became something of a national authority on the subject, it is said. In 1853, back in the east, Richard Kern was hired as artist and topographer for John W. Gunnison's 38th Parallel railroad survey. The expedition crossed the plains, the Sangre de Cristo and San Juan ranges (in summer this time), threaded Cochetopa Pass, and eventually reached the Sevier river and valley in western Utah. Here Gunnison, Richard Kern, and five others were killed, allegedly by Paiutes, northeast of Sevier Lake. Kern was described as stocky, a bit paunchy, musically inclined and of a light-hearted nature; his photograph shows him to have been handsome and pleasant of visage.

Robert Taft, *Artists and Illustrations of the Old West: 1850-1900.* N.Y., Bonanza Books, 1953; James H. Simpson, *Navaho Expeditions...,* ed. and annot. by Frank McNitt. Norman, Univ. of Okla. Press, 1964; Robert V. Hine, *Edward Kern and American Expansion.* New Haven, Yale Univ. Press, 1962; Bancroft, *Utah;* Nolie Mumey, *John Williams Gunnison.* Denver, Artcraft Press, 1955.

Keseberg, Lewis, pioneer (May 22, 1814-1895). B. at Berleburg, Westphalia, Prussia, he was married June 22, 1842, reached America with his wife May 22, 1844, and emigrated from the States to California in 1846 with the Donner company (see George Donner entry). In his party were Phillipine Keseberg, his wife (d. January 30, 1877), his one-year-old son, Lewis Keseberg Jr. (d. December 24, 1846), and his daughter, Ada, 3 (d. February 24, 1847). Keseberg was not popular with many of the emigrants; he was suspected of beating his wife, for one thing. October 14, 1846, he and a man named Wolfinger, a fellow German reputedly wealthy, lagged behind the train. The company

camped and at length Keseberg came up, reporting Wolfinger would be along shortly. Three men went back to search, found Wolfinger's wagon, its oxen unhitched and grazing nearby but no trace of the man nor of Indians who might have killed him. It was conjectured Keseberg killed Wolfinger for his money but the case never proven; Joseph Rhinehart who died December 16, 1846, reportedly confessed he had had something to do with the murder. At the snowbound camp near Donner Lake Keseberg emerged as the greatest suspected villain. He was said to have been the first to resort to cannibalism. There were dark suspicions of his having murdered or hastened the deaths of six of the weakening travelers including little George Foster and Tamsen Donner, wife of George Donner, train captain who already had perished. The Second Relief Party under Reed arrived in late February with provisions for Keseberg and others still alive, but Keseberg himself remained at the site until the Fourth Relief Party's coming in April when he went out with it to Sutter's Fort. At the suggestion of Sutter Keseberg filed suit for slander against some who verbally assailed him; he was granted $1 — and forced to pay court costs. There was no law east of the Sierra and west of Salt Lake and no proper legal inquiry ever was made to ascertain the facts. If there was no proof of his guilt, there also was none of his innocence. His accusers were many and their primary testimony is not to be dismissed lightly. Soon after his arrival at Sutter's Fort Keseberg took charge of the schooner *Sacramento,* freighting wheat to San Francisco and working seven months for Sutter; he went to Sonoma and worked as long for Vallejo. After an illness he returned to Sutter's Fort and operated a boarding house, made good money and built a $10,000 home. In 1851 he bought the Lady Adams hotel at Sacramento, later sold it for a good profit, but a fire destroyed hotel and resources of the purchaser, so he cleared nothing. Returning to Sutter's Fort he started a brewery, finally selling out for $50,000, but a massive flood of 1860-61 washed out all his resources, leaving him broke again. At another time he was partner of Sam Brannan in a distillery at Calistoga. His wife died and of the four of his 11 children still living two were "hopelessly idiotic." Keseberg descended into extreme poverty, able to obtain work for only about three months each year. Because of the excesses of his idiot children he could not live near other people. McGlashan interviewed him twice, became convinced he had not murdered Tamsen Donner "and of his comparative blamelessness in many other matters." Others were not so generous. Keseberg died at 81 at the Sacramento County Hospital. He was described as 6 feet tall, weighing around 175 pounds, well proportioned with clear blue eyes, regular features, light hair and beard and a rapid, loud and "somewhat excited" manner of speech. He spoke German, English, Spanish and French.

C.F. McGlashan, *History of the Donner Party.* Stanford Univ. Press, 1947; George R. Stewart, *Ordeal by Hunger.* N.Y., Ace Books, 1960; Bancroft, *Pioneer Register.*

Ketchum, Ami (Whit), blacksmith (d. Dec. 11, 1878). Trained as a blacksmith but something of a rancher, Ketchum and Luther Mitchell were considered by the Print Olive people of Custer County, Nebraska, rustlers against whom they developed a grievance. Robert A. Olive, as a deputy sheriff attempting to arrest the two was shot fatally late in November 1878. Subsequently Ketchum and Mitchell were picked up by Sheriff Barney Gillan, turned over to Print Olive and lynched, their bodies then burned; the incident was celebrated on the Nebraska frontier. Olive and another were convicted, sentenced to life imprisonment, but eventually went free.

Solomon D. Butcher, *Pioneer History of Custer County, Nebraska.* Denver, Sage Books, c. 1965, 43-62.

Ketchum, Samuel W., desperado (c. 1854-July 24, 1899). B. on Richland Creek, San Saba County, he and his younger brother, Tom (Black Jack), left Texas about 1890, worked as cowboys in the Pecos Valley of New Mexico for a time, then turned desperado. They killed a Carrizozo, New Mexico, merchant, robbed stages, trains, post offices and other establishments, and in 1897 robbed two trains in Arizona spending intervals in Old Mexico. On September 3 that year the Ketchum gang held up a train near Folsom, New Mexico; Sam and others held up a train at virtually the same site July 11, 1899. A posse caught up with them in Turkey Canyon, Colfax County; a fight ensued in which Sheriff Edward J. Farr of Walsenberg,

Huerfano County, Colorado, was killed. Two of the three bandits, Sam Ketchum and William H. (Bill) McGinnis (William Ellsworth (Elza) Lay), were wounded, as were five of the eight members of the posse, in addition to Farr. Henry M. Love, a posse-member, succumbed to his wounds four days later. Sam was taken to the penitentiary at Santa Fe where he died of blood poisoning from his wound. "The Ketchum gang was blamed for a good many crimes which they may not have committed. Apparently they had connections with a larger organization of outlaws," i.e., the Wild Bunch.

HT; Ed Bartholomew, *Black Jack Ketchum: Last of the Hold-up Kings.* Houston, Frontier Press of Tex., 1955; Jeff Burton, "Suddenly in a Secluded and Rugged Place," *Brand Book,* Vol. XIV, Nos. 3, 4 (April, July 1972), London, English Westerners' Soc.; Peter Hertzog, *Legal Hangings.* Santa Fe, Press of Territorian, 1966.

Ketchum, Thomas E. (Black Jack), desperado (c. Oct. 31, 1863-Apr. 29, 1901). B. on Richland Creek, western San Saba County, the youngest of three boys, he left Texas about 1890, possibly because of a crime, and worked as a cowboy in the Pecos Valley, New Mexico. By 1894 his older brother, Sam, had joined him and they commenced criminal careers, killing a merchant near Carrizozo, robbing various establishments, holding up stages and trains. In 1897 they robbed two trains in Arizona, spending intervals largely in Old Mexico. They robbed a train near Folsom, New Mexico, September 3, 1897. On August 16, 1899, Tom tried to hold up a train at virtually the same site by himself, was seriously wounded by the conductor, Frank E. Harrington, and was picked up beside the tracks the next day. His arm was amputated September 9, while he was awaiting trial; he was sentenced to hang October 5, 1900 at Clayton, under a New Mexico law making "molesting a train" a capital crime. He had gained weight in jail and the drop was too great, the rope severing the head from the body. Sheriff Salome Garcia was not blamed for a bungled job, however.

HT; Peter Hertzog, *Legal Hangings.* Santa Fe, Press of Territorian, 1966; Ed Bartholomew, *Black Jack Ketchum: Last of the Hold-up Kings.* Houston, Frontier Press of Tex., 1955; Ramon F. Adams, *Burs Under the Saddle.* Norman, Univ. of Okla. Press, 1964; Jack DeMattos, "Black Jack

Ketchum." *Real West,* Vol. 27, No. 197 (June 1984), 18-20, 52.

Keyes, Edward Livingston, army officer (Aug. 28, 1843-post 1899). B. in Massachusetts, he was commissioned a second lieutenant in the 5th Cavalry July 27, 1872, reaching Camp McDowell, Arizona, November 30. He took part in the Apache campaigns of 1872-74, engaged in actions at Red Rock Springs and on Pinto Creek, and was twice nominated for a brevet. Keyes reached Camp Supply, Indian territory, in July 1875 and participated in the Sioux campaign of 1876, having a role in the Battle of Slim Buttes, Dakota, September 9-10. He published a book of poetry in 1882 and wrote articles for popular magazines as late as 1899.

Price, *Fifth Cavalry,* 569-70; Heitman; Jerome A. Greene, *Slim Buttes, 1876: An Episode of the Great Sioux War.* Norman, Univ. of Okla. Press, 1982.

Kia-ma-sump-kin, Cayuse leader (d. June 3, 1850). He was a leader in the Cayuse tribe of the Walla Walla region of Washington Territory and accused of joining in the conspiracy that led to the Whitman Massacre November 29, 1847, although he protested his innocence and Drury believed that he was not guilty. Nevertheless he, with four other Cayuse leaders, was sentenced to hang. He was baptized and confirmed into the Roman Catholic Church, given the name of James, and executed with the others at Oregon City.

Clifford M. Drury, *Marcus and Narcissa Whitman and the Opening of Old Oregon,* 2 vols. Glendale. Calif., Arthur H. Clark Co., 1973.

Kicking Bird (Tene-angpote), Kiowa chief (c. 1835-May 5, 1875). His grandfather was a Crow captive taken into the Kiowa tribe, but little is known of Kicking Bird's early life although he became a chief of marked ability. Hodge wrote that "in tribal traditions and cermonial rites he was a thorough adept, and as a warrior he won a name, but had the sagacity to see the hopelessness of the struggle with the whites and used all his influence to induce the tribe to submit to inevitable conditions." He signed at Wichita the first agreement to accept a reservation on August 15, 1865, and the Medicine Lodge Treaty of October 21, 1867, which placed the Kiowa-Comanche-Plains Apache reservation in the present Oklahoma. He took no part in most subsequent hostilities. When white authorities failed to fulfill their agreement to release Kiowa chiefs imprisoned in Texas he lost faith in the government and almost joined 1874 hostilities against Tonkawa and white buffalo hunters, but eventually induced the bulk of his tribesmen to return to the agency at Fort Sill, Oklahoma, and henceforth was recognized by the whites as head chief of the Kiowas; he assisted in establishment of the first school for his people. When charges accumulated that he was a "woman," and a coward he gathered a band for a Texas raid and fought a troop detachment victoriously, regaining repute for courage and success in war. He died suddenly, by poison his friends were convinced, and at the request of his family was buried with Christian rites.

Hodge, HAI; Mildred P. Mayhall, *The Kiowas.* Norman, Univ. of Okla. Press, 1962; Wilbur Sturtevant Nye, *Plains Indian Raiders.* Norman, 1968, 216-17.

Kid Curry: *see* Harvey Logan

Kidder, Alfred Vincent, archeologist (Oct. 29, 1885-June 11, 1963). B. at Marquette, Michigan, he was graduated from Harvard in 1908 and earned a doctorate there in 1914. From 1915 until 1929 he directed excavations at Pecos, New Mexico, for Phillips Academy, Andover, Massachusetts; before that he had conducted archeological reconnaissances in Colorado and Utah and in 1909 had traveled in Egypt and Greece. Out of his New Mexico work came two of his many publications: *Pottery of Pecos* (1931, 1936), and *Artifacts of Pecos* (1932). In 1917-18 Kidder was an Infantry officer serving to captain with the 91st Division of the AEF, participating in the St. Mihiel, Argonne-Meuse and Ypres-Lys offensives and becoming chevalier of the Legion of Honor. He wrote with S.J. Guernsey, *Archeological Exploration in Northeastern Arizona* (1917) and *Basket-maker Caves in Northeastern Arizona* (1921). Kidder accompanied the Charles A. Lindberghs on a highly publicized air trip in October 1929, over Yucatan Mayan ruins, observing that the trip accomplished as much in 25 hours as ground expeditions could do in five years. By that time he had become a specialist on the Mayas. From his studies of early civilizations came his firm conviction that ours will crash as quickly as it was born, a prediction he often voiced.

Kidder was honored by many universities and societies and received numerous honorary degrees. He was president of the Society for American Archeology in 1937 and of the American Anthropological Association in 1942. He was married and fathered five children; he died at Cambridge, Massachusetts.

New York Times, June 14, 1963; *Who Was Who;* Robert Wauchope obituary of Kidder in *Amer. Antiquity*, Vol. 31, No. 2, Pt. I (Oct. 1965), 149-71, including Kidder bibliography.

Kidder, Jeff P., lawman (c. 1875-Apr. 5, 1908). B. in South Dakota, Kidder was a cowboy when he joined the Arizona Rangers in 1903, swiftly moving up to sergeant. He was a good shot, a brave man, but had a violent temper, in 1905 coming into trouble for pistol-whipping men in Bisbee, Arizona, paying a fine of $50 for one offense, the disposition of another being unreported. He joined Captain Thomas H. Rynning on at least one unofficial mission into Mexico to search for three missing Americans. They were not found. On December 31, 1906, Kidder killed Tom T. Woods at Douglas in a gun battle. Kidder accompanied Harry Wheeler and other Rangers on a difficult and supposedly dangerous mission to the Papago country to arrest a murderer in 1907; the man was taken and the Rangers returned without loss. April 4, 1908, Kidder engaged in a hard gun battle with Mexican police at Naco, Sonora, about 300 yards below the line. He was wounded in the stomach by a 45 caliber bullet; three Mexicans were wounded, one of whom died. Kidder tried to reach the American side of the line, but gave out, his ammunition was exhausted, he was captured and was dragged to a Mexican jail, suffering "brutal" treatment. The facts of the affair are controversial. Kidder died from his wound. Wheeler said Kidder "was one of the best officers who ever stepped foot in this section of the country. He did not know what fear was..., had rendered excellent service" frequently under circumstances of extreme danger.

Joseph Miller, *The Arizona Rangers.* N.Y., Hastings House, 1972.

Kidder, Lyman Stockwell, army officer (Aug. 31, 1842-c. July 12, 1867). B. at Braintree, Vermont, he was the son of Jefferson Parish Kidder (1815-1883), a noted jurist and legislator. Lyman Kidder moved to St. Paul, Minnesota, in 1858. He enlisted in the Curtis Horse Regiment November 1, 1861, serving from fourth corporal to fifth sergeant by May 27, 1863; the regiment became the 5th Iowa Cavalry on June 25, 1862. Kidder wrote that he was "stationed at Camp Benton, Missouri, Fort Sherman, Kentucky, Forts Donelson and Henry, Tennessee, and between these points — where I participated in several skirmishes with guerillas." He was discharged from the 5th Iowa to accept an appointment as first lieutenant in the 1st Minnesota Mounted Rangers, being mustered in June 6, 1863. He was "with it during the entire Indian Campaigns, being in the battles of Big Mound (July 24), (Dead) Buffalo Lake (July 26) and Stony Mound (July 28, 1863)." He was mustered out November 28 because of expiration of his term of service, enrolled in Company E of the Independent Battalion of Minnesota Cavalry on August 26, 1864, and served two years, being stationed at Fort Ripley, Sauk Center and "on the frontier stockade line, all in Minnesota, until the 1st day of May 1866 when I was discharged at Fort Snelling." Kidder described himself as a "printer" in civilian life, refused to follow his father's career into law, and was commissioned a second lieutenant of the 2nd U.S. Cavalry January 22, 1867, being assigned to the Kansas-Colorado frontier. Kidder, with an Indian guide, Red Bead, a Sioux chief, and ten enlisted men, was ordered June 29 to take dispatches from Fort Sedgwick on the south fork of the Platte River in Colorado, to Custer from Sherman, Custer being camped on the Republican River in Nebraska; if he didn't find Custer he was to follow his supposed route to Fort Wallace, Kansas. Kidder never reached Custer, who learned that the lieutenant was bringing important communications to him, and he and scout Will Comstock closely searched for Kidder on their way to Wallace. On July 12 (Heitman erroneously gives the date as July 21), the mutilated bodies of the Kidder party were found, gathered into a small compass, near Beaver Creek, close to the headwaters of the Solomon River. Since there were no white survivors, for many years the details of the fight could not be learned. George Bent ultimately revealed, however, that Kidder had run into a hunting camp of Sioux with a few Cheyennes, was run to earth in a small hollow where his party was surrounded and all killed. No Cheyennes were wounded but two Sioux were slain: Yellow Horse, a brother-in-law of John Smith, and another. The Cheyennes included Good Bear, Two Crows, Tobacco and others; the Sioux were under Pawnee Killer, a noted chief. Brininstool's thesis that Kidder was wholly inexperienced, "had as yet seen no Indian warfare, nor had he any experience in dealing with the red man," while his detail "with a single exception... was composed of mere boys" and that the mission was "plain suicide," has been followed by Frost and others, but is plainly in error. Kidder was an experienced soldier, had fought guerrillas in Kentucky and Tennessee and Sioux in Minnesota and had served many months on the frontier in the aftermath of the great Minnesota Sioux war; his men were of an average age for soldiers of that or virtually any later period, not "mere boys," and his Indian guide was a warrior of much experience and acclaim; Kidder just ran out of luck. His father contacted Custer to ascertain details and learn if there were any way to identify the body of his son, all the victims having been buried in a common grave. Kidder learned that one body had an odd fragment of shirt still in place when found; he identified this as a garment made for young Kidder by his mother as he left for army duty, and thus the body was identified and returned to St. Paul, Minnesota, for burial; the other bodies were reburied in a military cemetery at Fort Wallace.

Kidder manuscript of his early career, So. Dak. State Hist. Research Center; Heitman; *Roster and Record of Iowa Soldiers in the War of the Rebellion,* IV. Des Moines, Ia., State Printer, 1910, 845-52, 936; *Minnesota in the Civil and Indian Wars 1861-1865,* II. St. Paul, Minn., Pioneer Press Co., 1899; E.A. Brininstool, *Troopers with Custer.* Harrisburg, Pa., Stackpole Co., 1952; Lawrence A. Frost, *The Court-Martial of General George Armstrong Custer.* Norman, Univ. of Okla. Press, 1968; George E. Hyde, *Life of George Bent,* ed. by Savoie Lottinville. Norman, 1968.

Kieft, Willem, governor (c. Sept. 10, 1597-Sept. 27, 1647). B. at Amsterdam and trained as a merchant, he failed in business in France and perhaps elsewhere and September 2, 1637, was named by the Dutch West India Company to succeed Wouter van Twiller as director-general (governor) of New Nether-

land, based at the mouth of the Hudson River in present New York. He wintered in Bermuda and arrived at his post March 28, 1638, never having been to the New World before and knowing nothing of Indians, according to De Vries. He proved to be "an active, but injudicious and quarrelsome governor," of immense ineptitude in handling natives, a man in De Vries's view thoroughly unfit for the position. Over the years minor depredations led to murders of Indians and Dutch, the tension exacerbated by Kieft's attempt to tax the natives in pelts, corn and wampum, they little understanding such a requirement and thinking it punishment for wrongs they had not committed. Dutch trading practices which cheated the Indians also were a factor, although they were no worse and may have been somewhat more honest in mercantile affairs than other Europeans. Kieft authorized soldiers to attack a friendly village of Wiechquaeskeck (Raritan) Indians, a division of the Delawares at midnight, February 25, 1643, near Pavonia (Jersey City). From 80 to 120 were hacked to death by Dutch soldiery, who considered it "a deed of Roman valor, in murdering so many in their sleep." The Indians naturally sought revenge and soon the warfare became general, involving nearly a dozen bands of northern New Jersey, the lower Hudson valley and Long Island, clearing out the isolated Dutch settlements and virtually besieging New Amsterdam (New York City), capital of New Netherland. Among the 40 white victims was the brilliant Anne Hutchinson and virtually all her family; she had been ousted from Massachusetts for liberal religious views and settled near the present Pelham Bay, New York, where the massacre took place. In March 1644 a strong white force, nominally under Dr. Johannes la Montagne, a Huguenot physician and councilor to Kieft but effectively led by John Underhill (see entry), attacked a populous town near Pound Ridge in eastern Westchester County, New York. The village was surrounded and after an estimated 180 Indians had been shot down, the many huts were fired, trapping the occupants. The Delaware loss, according to the Indians, was around 500, though some said 700. The overall Indian dead in two years of war, wrote Trelease, was about 1,000 (in a 1646 letter the Jesuit, Isaac Jogues, in a position to learn the facts first hand, put it at 1600 "including women and children").

Kieft was held accountable by Dutch colonial officials for the disastrous war and was replaced as director-general by Petrus Stuyvesant. Kieft left New Amsterdam August 16, 1647, aboard the *Princes* which was wrecked on the British coast and 59 persons, among them Willem Kieft, were lost, as were the records and documents he was carrying back to Holland. His death was little regretted in New Netherland for he had "come close to destroying the colony."

*Narratives of New Netherland 1609-1661,*ed. by J. Franklin Jameson.   N.Y., Barnes & Noble, 1967; C.A. Weslager, A.R. Dunlap, *Dutch Explorers, Traders and Settlers in the Delaware Valley 1609-1664.*   Phila., Univ. of Pa. Press, 1965; Weslager, *The Delaware Indians: A History.*   New Brunswick, New Jer., Rutgers Univ. Press, 1972; Allen W. Trelease, "Dutch Treatment of the American Indian, with Particular Reference to New Netherland," *Attitudes of Colonial Powers toward the American Indian,* Howard Peckham, Charles Gibson, editors.   Salt Lake City, Univ. of Utah Press, 1969, 47-59; *Handbook of Indians,* 15; DAB; REAW.

Kildare, Maurice, *see* Richardson, Gladwell

Kile, John, soldier (c. 1846-July 18, 1870). B. at Troy, New York, he enlisted in Company G, 37th Infantry, in 1867, and was discharged the next year. He enlisted at Chicago in May 1870, in Company I, 7th Cavalry, and was posted to Fort Hays, Kansas. Here he was mortally wounded and a trooper companion, Jerry Lonergan, wounded less seriously by James Butler (Wild Bill) Hickok, in a saloon at Hays City on July 17, in "a drunken row," and "not in the line of duty."

Joseph G. Rosa, *They Called Him Wild Bill,* 2nd ed.   Norman, Univ. of Okla. Press, 1974.

Kilmartin, John (Jack), soldier, scout (c. 1847-July 1876). B. in Canada, he enlisted at Philadelphia April 9, 1868, in Company F, 3rd Cavalry, commanded by Howard B, Cushing (see entry), and served with it in the southwest. Under Cushing's energetic leadership the company participated in operations against Mescalero Apaches in New Mexico and West Texas, and against other Apaches in Arizona to where the organization was transferred March 2, 1870. May 5, 1871, Kilmartin, as acting corporal won a Medal of Honor for his prominent role in the fight with

Juh's Chiricahuas in which Cushing and two others were killed. After discharge in 1873 Kilmartin moved to Fort Sill, Oklahoma, where he became a civilian scout, meanwhile acquiring part interest in Whaley's Ranch, in Texas south of the Red River. With former Sergeant John B. Charlton (see entry) and the noted scout Jack Stilwell, Kilmartin took up the trail of stock thieves near Fort Sill and followed them south, stopping for the night at the ranch where his wife, "a hard-faced woman," was employed as cook. Early next morning she blew out his brains with a pistol as he lay asleep, apparently desiring to rid herself of an encumbrance to her liaison with Whaley, who is not further identified; nothing was done to her for the murder. Nye wrote that "Kilmartin was one of the best scouts who ever served at Fort Sill. He was quiet, unassuming, and possessed of absolute courage. Had he survived it is likely that his fame would have equaled that of Stilwell and Ben Clark" (see entry). Charlton, via Carter places the time of Kilmartin's death as late May 1875.

Dan L. Thrapp, *The Conquest of Apacheria.* Norman, Univ. of Okla. Press, 1967; Robert G. Carter, *The Old Sergeant's Story.*   N.Y., Frederick H. Hitchcock, 1926, 123-26; Wilbur Sturtevant Nye, *Carbine & Lance.*   Norman, 1969.

Kilpatrick, Ben (The Tall Texan, John Arnold), desperado (c. 1877-Mar. 13, 1912). B. in Concho County, Texas, he was one of a family of six boys and grew up as a cowboy, becoming 6 feet, 2 inches, tall, light complected with eyes pale yellow and a violet spot in each. He was considered "absolutely fearless," a good shot and became a noted member of the Ketchum gang and later of Butch Cassidy's Wild Bunch; he was an accomplished train robber, and reportedly had several killings linked to him, though details are lacking. Kilpatrick is among Wild Bunch members in the celebrated photograph taken at Fort Worth. He probably took part in the Wagner, Montana Great Northern train robbery of July 3, 1901, and was arrested at St. Louis November 8, being sentenced December 12 to 15 years while his girl friend, Laura Bullion, got a lesser term. He was released June 11, 1911. In March he and a former cellmate, Ole Beck, attempted to rob a Southern Pacific express near Sanderson, Texas. Messenger David A. Trousdale, 32, a new guard, killed Kilpatrick with an ice mallet, then killed Beck with Kilpatrick's rifle.

Charles Kelly, *The Outlaw Trail: The Story of Butch Cassidy and the "Wild Bunch."* N.Y., Bonanza Books, 1959; James D. Horan, *The Wild Bunch.* N.Y., Signet Books, 1958.

Kilpatrick, George, desperado (c. 1875-post 1901). A brother of Ben Kilpatrick, he was born probably in Concho County, Texas, and lived with the family near Eden, Texas. He was suspected of participating in the killing of Oliver Thornton about March 27, 1901, but there is no record of his indictment. On April 2, 1901, he and Will Carver engaged in a shootout with Sheriff Elijah S. Briant and deputies at Sonora, Texas, Carver being killed and Kilpatrick wounded five or more times. He recovered and was questioned about the Thornton slaying, but was not held. Reportedly, "careless with branding stock," he was said to have been killed for that or some other reason, and is supposed to be buried at Paint Rock, Texas.

John Eaton, *Will Carver, Outlaw.* San Angelo, Tex., Anchor Pub. Co., 1972; James D. Horan, *The Wild Bunch.* N.Y., Signet Books, 1958.

Kimbell, George C., adventurer (c. 1810-Mar. 6, 1836). Kimbell, a lieutenant in the Texas armed forces, lived at Gonzales in 1836, and was one of the 32-man relief force that reached the Alamo, San Antonio, March 1, where they perished with the other defenders. Kimble County, Texas, although spelled differently, was named for George Kimbell.

Amelia Williams, XXXVII, 268; HT.

Kimbell, Rush G., Texas Ranger (Feb. 15, 1855-Jan. 18, 1954). B. at Memphis, Tennessee, he was said to be related to Dr. Benjamin Rush of Pennsylvania, a signer of the Declaration of Independence for whom he was named. He moved to Texas where at about 20 or 25 he joined the Texas Rangers (as did two of his brothers), serving in Company D, Frontier Battalion in West Texas. He may have been with Sergeant Edward A. Sieker in his fight July 1, 1880, with outlaws in which a Ranger and a desperado were killed. Corporal Kimbell on September 25, 1880, took a small squad in pursuit of horse thieves who had stolen animals from Fort Terrett. Four Rangers dropped out when their horses broke down, but Kimbell and Bill Dunham

continued the pursuit toward New Mexico, accosting the rustlers October 8. In a resulting gun battle, one desperado was wounded mortally and the other, also wounded, was brought in to Fort Davis, Texas. About 1889 Kimbell moved to Altus, Oklahoma where he operated a retail grocery for the rest of his life. He died less than a month before his 99th birthday. He was married.

Walter Prescott Webb, *The Texas Rangers.* Boston, Houghton Mifflin Co., 1935; Kimbell death certificate; information from Mrs. Oletha Hinton, Altus, Okla.

Kind, Ezra, frontiersman (d. c. July 1834). B. probably in Pennsylvania, he reportedly crossed the Missouri River about 1832, and may have gone to Santa Fe as a teamster. In 1833, he with T. Brown, De Lacompt, G.W. Wood, R. Kent, William King and Indian Crow, somehow reached the Black Hills, it is said, and discovered gold, the party being massacred by Indians, presumably Sioux. Kind, the last to die, purportedly carved their story on a stone discovered in 1887 by Louis Thoen, a stonemason and reportedly an honest, upright man, near Spearfish, South Dakota, on the west side of Lookout Mountain. The stone is in the Adams Memorial Museum, Deadwood, South Dakota. John Cashner, amateur historian, investigated and received letters (since lost), from T. Brown's nephew who said his uncle left Missouri in 1832-33 with a man named Kent and disappeared. J.C. Adams of Ash Hollow, Pennsylvania, wrote that an uncle, Bela Kent, had disappeared with an adventurer named Kind in the 1830's. The carving's authenticity is not fully established, but has never been disproven.

Chicago Daily News, Aug. 21, 1939; Watson Parker, *Gold in the Black Hills.* Norman, Univ. of Okla. Press, 1966.

King, Charles, adventurer (fl. 1800-1821). Said to be from Natchez, Mississippi, he joined Philip Nolan for the latter's 1800-1801 wild horse hunting expedition to the Trinity River of Spanish Texas and after Nolan was killed, King and the others were captured and taken to Chihuahua. A carpenter and illiterate, he was permitted to practice his trade. When all foreigners in Mexico were freed by Royal edict in 1820, King and some others made their way to Fort Smith on the

Arkansas river, arriving early in 1821. Nothing more is known of him.

Bennett Lay, *The Lives of Ellis P. Bean.* Austin, Univ. of Tex. Press, 1960; MM, Vol. III, p. 29.

King, Charles, army officer, novelist (Oct. 12, 1844-Mar. 17, 1933). B. at Albany, New York, of a distinguished family, he was raised at Milwaukee, Wisconsin, where his father was editor and part owner of the *Milwaukee Sentinel.* Charles King was graduated from West Point in 1866, joined the 1st Artillery, transferred to the 5th Cavalry as a first lieutenant in 1870, and by 1874 was in Arizona, stationed at Camp Verde. He had fights with hostile Apaches at Diamond Butte, Black Mesa and Sunset Pass, where he was seriously wounded and lost much of the use of his right arm for life. From Fort Hays, Kansas, in 1876 he participated in the Sioux campaign in the North Plains, was regimental adjutant on the Big Horn and Yellowstone expedition, and was engaged in actions on the south branch of the Cheyenne River, War Bonnet (Hat) Creek and on September 9 at Slim Buttes, Dakota. He was acting assistant adjutant general of the Wind River expedition against the Nez Percé in Wyoming in 1877, was promoted to captain in 1879, and was forced to leave active service for disability from his wound. In 1880 he became professor of military science and tactics at the University of Wisconsin becoming colonel and adjutant general of the state with rank of Brigadier General. In the Spanish-American War he was commissioned Brigadier General of Volunteers, took part in actions during the Philippine Insurrection, was commissioned Brigadier General of the Wisconsin National Guard in 1904 and Major General in 1929. By June 30, 1932, he was credited with 70 years of active service. His most famous non-fiction book of frontier interest is *Campaigning with Crook,* which appeared initially as a series of feature stories in the *Sentinel;* its first book appearance was as a 500-copy paperback in 1880; it was reissued, somewhat modified, in 1890 by Harpers, and has since come out in various editions. His first novel, *The Colonel's Daughter,* appeared under a different title in 1882, launching an apparently inexhaustible stream: King wrote 61 books in all, the overwhelming majority fiction, not read too much today but giving a vivid picture of 19th century military life and experiences in three

areas of conflict: the Civil War, the Indian Wars, and the Spanish-American War; King was one of the few men entitled to wear campaign badges from five major campaigns including World War I when he helped train Wisconsin and Michigan men for the 32nd Division. When it was suggested that he be retired at 75 years of age, the orders came down that King's status was not to be changed without "direct authority of the Chief of Staff." King died at 89 from injuries received when he tripped over a rug and fell. He died at Milwaukee. He was married.

C.E. Dornbusch, *Charles King: American Army Novelist,* foreward by Don Russell. Cornwallville, N.Y., Hope Farm Press, 1963; Charles King, *Campaigning with Crook,* intr. by Don Russell. Norman, Univ. of Okla. Press, 1964; Curtis E. Green, "Captain Charles King: Popular Military Novelist." *Arizoniana,* Vol. II, No.2 (Summer 1961), 23-26; Oliver Knight, *Life and Manners in the Frontier Army.* Norman, 1978.

King, Clarence, geologist, writer (Jan. 6, 1842-Dec. 24, 1901). B. at Newport, Rhode Island, he was graduated from Yale in 1862, having been an outstanding athlete. He heard of the ascent of Mt. Shasta by William H. Brewer, went overland to California, met Brewer by chance on a riverboat to San Francisco and was appointed assistant geologist of the Whitney survey directed by Brewer and James T. Gardiner. Between 1867 and 1877 he surveyed a 100-mile-wide area from Colorado to the California boundary, his seven-volume *Report of the Geological Exploration of the Fortieth Parallel* "reached perhaps the highest standard yet attained by government publications." He introduced the system of denoting topography by contour lines, stressed laboratory work, and in 1878 became first head of the new western survey department of the U.S. Geological Survey. His greatest non-scientific work was *Mountaineering in the Sierra Nevada* (1872), a classic. He entered private mining engineering work in 1881. King's friends included Henry Adams, Willliam Dean Howells and others. For the last 14 years of his life he was secretly married to a black woman, a onetime housemaid, by whom he had five children. King suffered a financial disaster in the crash of 1893, committed himself for a year to an asylum in New York City. Howells believed King "always vaguely meant to write a great work of fiction," although it is not proven that he ever set about it, though he revealed in conversations with delighted friends his talent in that direction. He sent his wife to racially less-prejudiced Canada, providing funds for her care, when he felt himself to be mortally ill of tuberculosis, and died at Phoenix. Mt. Clarence King, a spectacular 12,909-foot peak in the Sierra Nevada, was named for him.

DAB; Lawrence Clark Powell, "Clarence King's Mountaineering in the Sierra Nevada." *Westways,* Vol. 62, No. 5 (May 1970), 14-17, 48-49.

King, Francis, M., lawman (d. July 6, 1865). A southern California sheep rancher and deputy to Sheriff Tomas Sanchez, King and his brother, Sam Houston King, became involved in a feud with Robert S. Carlisle, a Chino California, rancher. In a gun battle at the Bella Union Hotel, Los Angeles, King and Carlisle were killed, Sam Houston King wounded. He recovered, was tried for murder and acquitted.

Los Angeles Times, Oct. 14, 1956.

King, Frank E., pioneer (d. Sept. 11, 1857). King, probably b. about 1827, joined the Fancher emigrant wagon train somewhere on the Great Plains and accompanied it to Mountain Meadows, Utah, where it was destroyed by Mormons and Mormon-led Indians, King being murdered with the rest.

William Wise, *Massacre at Mountain Meadows.* N.Y., Thomas Y. Crowell Co., 1976.

King, Sandy (Red Curly, Ferguson), desperado (d. Nov. 9, 1881). Reportedly born at Allegheny City, Pennsylvania, he might have been the individual known as Luther King, a Tombstone character who walked out of jail there March 28, 1881, and disappeared. Sandy may have taken part in the ambush of a Mexican pack train in Jeff Davis County, Texas, in 1879, or another in southern Arizona or Sonora somewhere. He and Russian Bill may have been in a "hard-fought battle" in early November 1881, with ranchers who had lost stock, near "Downing's Ranch," Arizona; at any rate he became active in the Deming-Shakespeare area of New Mexico. At least once he was charged with murder. He was jailed at Shakespeare, New Mexico, by Deputy Sheriff Dan Tucker of Deming; Russian Bill joined him in the jail. At 2 a.m. the pair were hanged from the rafters in the

bar room of the Shakespeare Hotel, King for outlawry, Bill for being "a damned nuisance." It is sometimes said that King was the man hanged as a nuisance, but this is in error. King was a hard, dangerous man of courage and a record, and he was hanged for cause. Bill was the nuisance. King died game.

Philip J. Rasch, "AKA 'Russian Bill'." Westerners, Los Angeles Corral, *Branding Iron,* No. 86, Mar. 1968, pp. 12-13;Ed Bartholomew, *Wyatt Earp: The Man & the Myth.* Toyahvale, Tex., Frontier Book Co., 1964; *Service Record Book of Men and Women of Hidalgo County.* Lordsburg, N.M., VFW Post 3099, 1949.

King, William, P., adventurer (c. 1812-Mar. 6, 1836). He and his brother, John G. King (b. c. 1810), lived a dozen miles above Gonzales and responded to Travis's appeal for help for the Alamo, reaching the beleaguered redoubt March 1 with 30 other Gonzales men. All died with its defenders.

Amelia Williams, XXXVII, 269; HT.

King Hendrick: *see* Hendrick

King Philip: *see* Metacom

Kingsbury, Ezra Wolcott, army officer, frontiersman (June 11, 1830-Feb. 9, 1900). B. in Connecticut, in 1859 he married and joined the Colorado gold rush, becoming a "trader" in Park or Lake county, Colorado. Kingsbury did not remain in Colorado exclusively, however. On July 12, 1861, he was on a westbound stage that reached Rock Creek Station, Nebraska, an hour after the celebrated affair in which Wild Bill Hickok killed Dave McCanles while two other men also lost their lives. Later Kingsbury embellished the story and regaled writer George Ward Nichols with it, Nichols subsequently interviewing Hickok who went along with the joke and recited a wild and fictitious account of the "battle" to which Nichols and later J.W. Buel and others gave nationwide and lasting publicity. On August 26, 1862, Kingsbury was commissioned captain commanding a company of the 3rd Colorado Infantry which became the 2nd Colorado Cavalry, serving in this regiment during the Civil War, principally in eastern Kansas and western Missouri. It's major operations were against Sterling Price and for his role Kingsbury was cited on Major General Samuel Curtis's roll of honor. Kingsbury was active in operations against guerilla and bushwacker outfits. His report of August 18, 1864, detailing a frustrating pursuit of such bands, told that he extracted information from a local settler by means of "a little hanging" which loosened his tongue. Kingsbury was mustered out at Fort Leavenworth September 23, 1865. In a special election August 10, 1867, he was chosen sheriff of Ellsworth County, Kansas, and was reaffirmed in a regular election November 5, beating out Hickok, M.R. Lane and three others. At one time it was reported Hickok came to Kingsbury's rescue when the sheriff was threatened by Samuel Strawhun, a combative individual whom Wild Bill killed September 27, 1869. Although still sheriff, Kingsbury according to Rosa "disappeared" from Ellsworth early in 1869, his deputy, Chauncey Whitney taking his place until E.A. Kesler formally was named sheriff March 1. Kingsbury probably had rushed to Kansas City where his infant son, John Light Kingsbury died on March 21; later that year a daughter was baptized into the Episcopal Church, so the confinement of Mrs. Kingsbury may have kept him in the city. In November 1869 Kingsbury won a suit against a construction firm for injuries in an accident, being awarded $16,041.66; the defendants demanded a new trial but the result of their request is not reported. Late in 1869 Kingsbury was appointed revenue agent for St. Louis and Kansas City; in 1870 he was appointed general store keeper for western Missouri in the Revenue Department. He was discharged in 1873 because of opposition by members of the so-called Whiskey Ring, but was reinstated in 1875, holding the position at least until the early 1880s. By 1890 he was licensed as a storekeeper on the extensive San Carlos Apache Reservation in Arizona. Here, probably for political and other reasons, he ran afoul of army officers managing the reserve, John L. Bullis and later, Lewis Johnson. The extended dispute resulted in two formal investigations at the reservation, the leveling of vicious charges and incidentally the firing of chief of scouts Al Sieber after 20 years of faithful and unrivaled service, Sieber being a fairly innocent bystander who however had sided with Kingsbury. After leaving Arizona some time subsequently, Kingsbury went to Chicago where he resided until his death when he was listed as an insurance agent. He was

survived by his widow (d. April 24, 1925), two sons and a daughter. Kingsbury was described as 6 feet, 1 1/2 inches tall, with gray eyes and hair that had turned gray by age 55. He was buried at Chicago.

History of Jackson County, Missouri. Cape Girardeau, Mo., Ramfre Press, 1881, pp. 800-01; information from Colo. Div. of State Archives and Public records; Blanche V. Adams, "The Second Colorado Cavalry in the Civil War." *Colo. Mag.,* Vol. 8, No. 3 (May 1931); John H. Nankivell, *History of the Military Organizations of the State of Colorado.* Denver, W.H. Kistler Staty. Co., c. 1935; information from Jackson County (Mo.) Hist. Soc. and Westport Hist. Soc., Kansas City; *War of the Rebellion,* Ser. I, Col, XLI, Pt.I; Kingbury's pension file, Nat. Archives; Joseph G. Rosa, *They Called Him Wild Bill,* 2nd ed. Norman, Univ. of Okla. Press, 1974; Dan L. Thrapp, *Al Sieber, Chief of Scouts,* Norman, Univ. of Okla. Press, 1964.

Kingsbury, Henry Peoble, army officer (Apr. 25, 1850-Feb. 1, 1923). B. in North Carolina, he was graduated from West Point and commissioned a second lieutenant of the 6th Cavalry June 12, 1871. Kingsbury was on frontier duty at Fort Riley, Kansas until January 1872, then at Fort Harker, Kansas, Camp Supply, Indian Territory, and in Texas and Kansas again until 1875 when he became a first lieutenant. He was sent to Arizona that year, being engaged in scouting and operations against the Apaches, through 1881. Kingsbury became a captain October 5, 1887, major of the 3rd Cavalry January 23, 1900, lieutenant colonel of the 8th Cavalry February 25, 1903, and its colonel August 31, 1906. He retired April 25, 1914, and died at Washington, D.C.

Cullum; Heitman; Powell.

Kinkhead, Mathew, pioneer (1795-c. 1860). B. in Madison County, Kentucky, he may have fought briefly against Indians during the War of 1812 in the Missouri country. He went to Santa Fe in 1825 and perhaps to Taos where he joined William Workman in a distillery operation and in 1826-27 was host to runaway Kit Carson. By 1830 he had become a citizen of Mexico and within five years received a land grant in the Mora River valley east of the mountains; later he moved to the site of the present Pueblo, Colorado. He opened a cattle ranch operation 30 miles west of Pueblo in

1834. Kinkhead moved to Sacramento, California, about 1849, where he reportedly became quite wealthy from ranching and shipping.
Janet Lecompte article, MM, Vol. II.

Kinman, Seth, frontiersman (Sept. 29, 1815-Feb. 24. 1888). B. near Uniontown, Pennsylvania, he moved to Illinois at 15 and in 1849 went to California but returned to Illinois for two years in 1850. He then took his family to northern California where he became a market hunter; he claimed to have killed 800 grizzlies in Humboldt County. Kinman made several trips to Washington, D.C., presenting elkhorn chairs to Presidents from Buchanan to Hayes. Kinman accidentally shot himself in the leg, the wound leading to amputation and ultimately his death. He was buried in Humboldt County, California.
Chad L. Hoopes article, MM, Vol. V.

Kinney, Charles, frontiersman (c. 1803-pre-1867). He reached Taos by 1829, received a land grant at Mora, New Mexico, in 1835, worked out of various plains trading posts, including Lupton's, trapped as far west as the Humboldt River, was an occasional guide and associate of Kit Carson and others. He was generally respected.
Janet Lecompte article, MM, Vol. IV.

Kinney, Henry Lawrence, promoter, empire builder (June 3, 1814-Mar. 3, 1862). B. in Pennsylvania, he went to Illinois in 1830, becoming a merchant and acquiring the title of colonel; he removed to Texas in 1838, settling at Brownsville. The next year he is said to have commenced construction of landing facilities and buildings at what became Corpus Christi, conducting a smuggling operation because of high Mexican tariffs, and acquiring vast lands by one ruse or another. On July 16, 1842, he bought 10 leagues between the Nueces River and Oso Creek from Capt. Enrique Villereal, of the Mexican state of Tamaulipas, including the site of Kinney's ranch and trading post. Comanches occasionally raided that far south; in one skirmish Kinney was wounded twice, three of his men were killed along with seven Indians. Once he was imprisoned briefly at Matamoros, Mexico, for allegedly supporting an insurgency, but nothing came of the charge. Indians, and Mexican and Texas

outlaws ravaged the countryside, a constant threat. He prospered during the Mexican War when land he claimed south of the Nueces River was secured for the United States. Kinney was cited for bravery in the battle of Monterrey, having acted as scout, guide and translator for the American troops. With war's end Corpus Christi, which had enjoyed a boom from troops and hangers-on during hostilities, declined as did Kinney's fortunes. He then sought to organize a real estate boom, advertising the glories of Corpus Christi in northern, eastern and European papers, including such lures as the statement that "pears grow wild" in the area, not explaining that they were prickly pear cactus. In 1849 Kinney was elected to the state senate for four terms. His first partner at Corpus Christi had been William Aubrey; he now took another, William Leslie Cazneau, an adventurer like himself, and they charted a road inland to northern Mexico (Cazneau was founder of Eagle Pass, on the Rio Grande), Corpus Christi becoming thus the port for upper Mexico. Meanwhile Kinney had married; he had left Pennsylvania, it is said, because of a jealous husband, had failed to win the hand of Daniel Webster's daughter, Julia, in Illinois, lived for a time with Geneviva Hinajosa Perez, and in 1850 married Mary Webb Herbert, a widow and daughter of a judge. The marriage was unhappy and Mrs. Kinney soon removed to Galveston with her children. Kinney embarked upon a projected conquest of Nicaragua in 1854, contracting for 30 million acres on the Mosquito Coast, but his financial backing failed, his men wandered off to join William Walker, and Kinney, broke, returned to Texas. He was elected to the legislature, but resigned in 1861 on a plea of ill health but actually because he had little sympathy with the secession, although he offered his services as agent in Mexico to both Lincoln and Jefferson Davis and later did some purchasing there for the Confederacy. He was shot at Matamoros under controversial circumstances; the site of his grave is unknown.
HT; Dee Woods, "King of the Wild Horse Desert." *Best of the West,* no Vol., no No., 1973, 22-23, 49-50.

Kinney, John, desperado (1847-Aug. 28, 1919). b. in Hampshire, Massachusetts, he migrated westward with his family, and enlisted in Company E, 3rd Cavalry, in 1867 at Chicago, being discharged at Fort McPherson, Kansas, in 1873. By 1875 he had reached the Rio Grande valley below Mesilla, New Mexico; on January 1, 1876, he and others shot through windows at revelers from the 8th Cavalry of Fort Seldon, killing three, including two soldiers. November 2 he killed Ysabel Barela under controversial circumstances. December 17 he entered the El Paso Salt War and killed or was responsible for the killing of four Mexicans. He operated a saloon briefly at El Paso, with occasional explosive results, his place being called "a hangout for the most parasitical." He and others he enlisted joined the James J. Dolan faction in the Lincoln County War and had a role in the siege of the McSween home and the killing of McSween. For four days he was a deputy sheriff of Doña Ana County, New Mexico, guarding Billy the Kid in his transfer from Mesilla to Lincoln. Despite recurrent legal difficulties, he opened a butcher shop at Mesilla, but also headed a gang of rustlers operating widely through the Territory. His gang was broken up and Kinney taken prisoner by New Mexico state militia. Kinney was convicted and sentenced to five years, being sent to a penitentiary at Lansing, Kansas, but legal maneuvers got him out, the case quietly dismissed. Kinney went to Omaha, to Iowa, returned to El Paso, operated a feed lot and corral at Kingman, Arizona, dealt in mining claims and finally settled at Prescott where he died. He claimed to have entered Cuba on a dangerous mission with a few companions, survived, and was rescued by Leonard Wood, which might be true. He died respected by people who did not know his background. Kinney was 5 feet, 5 inches tall, weighed 180 pounds, had brown hair, hazel eyes, was married once and fathered a daughter.

Robert N. Mullin, "Here Lies John Kinney." *Jour. of Ariz. Hist.*, Vol. XIV, No. 3 (Autumn 1973), 223-42.

Kino, Eusebio Francisco, priest-missionary (Aug. 10, 1645-Mar. 15, 1711). B. of Austrian lineage at Segno, Tyrol (now Italy), he was educated in mathematics and astronomy in Germany, entered the Society of Jesus in 1665, and was ordained a priest. Kino volunteered repeatedly for missionary service hoping to go to the Orient, but was sent to the western hemisphere instead. After some mishaps, he reached Mexico May 9, 1681; his first assignment, establishment of a mission in Baja California, was a failure. In 1687 he was sent north and that year he began his 24 years on the frontier, establishing his first mission among the Indians: Nuestra Señora de los Dolores, in Sonora. In 1691 he made the first of about 40 expeditions into what is now Arizona. He labored mostly among the Pimas. At the time of his arrival, the mission of Cucurpe on the Rio San Miguel, 75 miles south of the present Nogales, was northernmost of the Jesuit missions; at his death Kino had extended the missionary and cultural frontier of New Spain northward to the Gila River, and westward to the Rio Magdalena and the Altar Valley. He often rode 30 to 35 miles a day, "carried Christianity into areas ... where it had never been before: catechism was taught, baptism administered, and Mass celebrated." Kino explored Arizona as far as the Casa Grande ruins, which he was probably the first white to see, and the Gila River as far west as present Yuma and the Colorado River, proving that California was not an island. "His revised maps of the west coast of North America showed that California was accessible overland from the expanding frontier of New Spain." They were so well drawn that they were not improved upon for a century. Kino also was something of a rancher and cattleman, and taught the Pimas to diversify their agriculture and expand it. His missionized Indians numbered some 30,000 of a variety of tribes and he baptized 4,000, the number being limited, as he said, by lack of priest coworkers to give catechetical instruction. "In his 65th year Padre Kino rode a familiar trail to Magdalena to dedicate a small new chapel...During the Mass of Dedication, he became ill," near midnight he died and was buried on the gospel side of the chapel by his friend, Padre Augustín de Campo. A bust of Father Kino (no likeness from life is known), has been placed in Statuary Hall of the Capitol at Washington, D.C. On May 24, 1966, his remains were located and identified at Magdalena where the chapel in which he had been buried had disintegrated by reason of time and neglect; a larger church had replaced it. A monument was to be built over the grave.

Literature abundant: EB; DAB; Charles Polzer, *A Kino Guide: His Missions— His Monuments.* Tucson, Ariz., Southwestern Mission Research

Center, 1968; Fay Jackson Smith, John L. Kessell, Francis J. Fox, *Father Kino in Arizona.* Phoenix, Ariz. Hist. Found., 1966; *Los Angeles Times,* July 9, 1966.

Kintpuash: *see* Captain Jack

Kiotseaeton, Mohawk chief (fl. 1645-46). A famous Mohawk orator and envoy to the French in 1645 seeking peace between the two peoples, he with Couture and others attended a grand council at Three Rivers in July 1645, at which were represented also the Hurons and several other Canadian tribes. The council was followed by a second in 1646 and a controversial treaty emerged, in which the Algonquins were somewhat short-changed, and the Mohawks awarded a share of the fur trade, their principal objective. Despite the treaty, hostilities soon resumed, resulting in 1649 in virtual destruction of the Huron nation.

Thwaites, JR, XXVII; DCB; George T. Hunt, *The Wars of The Iroquois.* Madison, Univ. of Wisc. Press, 1940.

Kipp, James, fur trader (1788-June 2, 1880). B. near Montreal, he became a Red River hunter and trapper at 20, and by 1818 was on the upper Missouri River, joining the Columbia Fur Company about 1822. He built the first post for the Blackfeet in 1831. Kipp had some education. He married Earth Woman, daughter of Four Bears, a Mandan chief, and was said to have been the only white man who mastered the Mandan language. He is reported to have had several other Indian families as well, and a white wife and children who lived on his farm home near Independence, Missouri. Joe Kipp, born November 29, 1849, on the Heart River, North Dakota, was his son by his Mandan wife. James Kipp retired about 1860 or 1865 to his farm and died at the age of 93 at Parkville, Missouri, where he is buried.

Montana Contributions, Vol. X, 1940, 270; Ray H. Mattison article, MM, Vol. II; Annie Heloise Abel, *Chardon's Journal at Fort Clark, 1834-39.* Pierre, Dept. of Hist. of So. Dak., 1932, 225-26 n.80.

Kipp, Joseph (Joe), scout, frontiersman (Nov. 29, 1849-Dec. 12, 1913). B. on Heart River near the present Bismarck, North Dakota, he was the son of James Kipp and Earth Woman,

daughter of Four Bears, famed Mandan chief. At 6 he was taken by his Indian trader father to Fort Berthold on the Missouri, and two years later to Fort Union near the mouth of the Yellowstone River. Fur trader Andrew Dawson took the boy to western Montana among the Blackfeet where he received some education at Jesuit missions. Late in 1861 Joe went to St. Louis, returning to Montana the following year when he clerked for the American Fur Company at Fort Benton. Later he received nine months schooling at Bryant & Stratton College, Peoria, Illinois. Kipp went back to Montana in 1867, worked for traders, prospected, and became guide and interpreter at Fort Shaw on the Sun River above its junction with the Missouri. He was chief scout for Major Eugene M. Baker (see entry) for the January 1870 campaign against Piegans believed hostile. The Indians were in two camps on the Marias River. One, under Heavy Runner, was known to be peaceful; the other, that of Mountain Chief, was considered hostile. Baker could not tell them apart, but Kipp assured him he would know which was the enemy. Baker, who had been drinking heavily, attacked the wrong village despite Kipp's insistence that it was Heavy Runner's camp. The resulting massacre of more than 170 Indians (none of whom fired a shot) became one of the most controversial frontier incidents in the Northwest. Although Kipp was in no way to blame, the event so unsettled the Indians he moved to Canada to avoid their hostility. In the winter of 1873-74 at Fort Whoop-Up, Alberta, Kipp killed the turbulent Calf's Shirt, noted Blood chief (who at an earlier time while drunk had sought to murder John Imoda, Jesuit missionary). Later in 1874 Kipp returned to Montana. He remained among the Blackfeet, trading, became a rancher, engaged in other pioneer activities and, fluent in eight languages including the difficult Mandan, frequently interpreted during negotiations with various native peoples. He died of pneumonia at Browning, Montana, leaving his widow, three sons and two daughters, and "mourned by the whole population" of the Blackfeet Reservation.

Information from the Mont. Hist. Soc.; *Great Falls Tribune,* Dec. 19, 1913; *Cut Bank* (Montana) *Tribune,* Dec. 18, 1913; M.A. Leeson, ed., *History of Montana 1739-1885.* Chicago, Warner, Beers and Co., 1885; *Montana Contributions,* X (1940), 207n75, 275n108; Robert J. Ege, *Tell Baker to*

Strike Them Hard! Bellevue, Nebr., Old Army Press, 1970.

Kirchner, Carl, Texas Ranger (Nov. 19, 1867-Jan. 28, 1911). B. in Bee County, Texas, he served as Ranger from 1889 to 1895, becoming first sergeant through hard and effective service. "A participant in a number of gunfights, it is said he killed several men . . . experiencing great danger over an extended period." It was Kirchner who saved the Ranger contingent in an 1893 battle near Tres Jacales, Mexico, not far from San Elizario, Texas, an action in which Captain Frank Jones was killed. Kirchner considered this his narrowest escape. He wired Ysleta for reinforcements which arrived in time to secure the body of Jones from Mexican authorities. After his Ranger service, Kirchner settled at El Paso, entering business. In 1904 he was hired with two others by the Mexico government to guard a money shipment to Vera Cruz. He died in El Paso of typhus contracted while inspecting casualties of a Mexican civil disturbance in the vicinity of Juarez. Webb lists Kirchner's first name as Karl.

Robert W. Stephens, *Texas Ranger Sketches.* Dallas, p.p., 1972; Walter Prescott Webb, *The Texas Rangers.* Boston, Houghton Mifflin Co., 1935; Oscar Williams.

Kirker, James, scalp hunter (Dec. 2, 1793-1853). B. near Belfast, Ireland, he reached New York City in 1810. He served on a privateer in the War of 1812, was captured off Brazil but his prison ship in turn was taken by the U.S. frigate, *Constitution,* and Kirker returned to New York where he was mustered out with enough prize money to start in the grocery business. In 1817 he went to St. Louis, entered business, but went up the Missouri in 1822 with Ashley and later, reportedly, joined Leavenworth for the indecisive campaign against the Arikaras. By 1824 he was at Santa Fe, returned to St. Louis the following year, and went back to New Mexico almost immediately. He visited the Santa Rita copper mines with the Patties and in 1827 joined them for a trapping expedition, but shortly became a guard for ore trains from Santa Rita to Chihuahua. In 1835 Kirker acquired a license to trade with the Apaches, initiating his relationship with that people, although his activities with them during the middle 1830s

are uncertain. Kirker was reportedly proclaimed an outlaw for his affiliation with these Indians and fled to Bent's Fort until the confusion settled. In 1837 the notorious Johnson affair precipitated general hostilities between Apaches and Mexicans and Kirker, with more than a score of recruits, entered the Indian hunting business which generated turmoil rather than quelling it. His precise activities during this period are not satisfactorily defined; he apparently took part in several skirmishes with the Apaches. He "retired" for a time on a ranch near Corralitos, Chihuahua, then resumed hunting Indians for their scalps, but the accounts of his subsequent operations seem undependable. Kirker attended Doniphan's capture of Chihuahua City, but again, the extent of his assistance to the officer is uncertain. He helped fight the Utes in 1848, according to report, returned to Ireland briefly, and in 1849 went from St. Louis to California by way of Santa Fe. In California he lived by market hunting. He died at Oak Springs, near Mt. Diablo, and was buried at Pleasanton.

William Cochran McGaw, *Savage Scene: The Life and Times of James Kirker, Frontier King.* N.Y., Hastings House, 1972; Ralph A. Smith, "The Scalp Hunter in the Borderlands 1835-1850." *Arizona and the West,* Vol. VI, No. 1 (Spring 1964), 5-22; Review of McGaw by David J. Weber in *New Mex. Hist. Rev.,* Vol. XLIX, No. 2 (Apr. 1974), 175-77.

Kirkland, Samuel, Presbyterian missionary (Nov. 20, 1741-Feb. 28, 1808). B. at Norwich, Connecticut, the son of Daniel Kirtland, he modified the spelling of his name and was one of the Connecticut Congregationalists who called themselves Presbyterians although the denominational purity of that classification is not quite clear. Upon graduation from the College of New Jersey (Dartmouth College), he desired to become a missionary among the Iroquois, his wish "enthusiastically endorsed" by William Johnson, British superintendent for the New York Indians. He commenced work among the Senecas in 1764 and in 1766 moved to the Oneidas among whom he labored most of the rest of his life. At the outset he effectively taught temperance and took positive steps to enforce it, his views sometimes modified when rum seemed necessary as a political lure. In 1769 he married Jerusha Bingham and she proved popular with Indian women and of great importance to her husband's ministry. They became central to the lives of their Indians and very influential among not only Oneidas but Tuscaroras as well, shortly extending their mission to them. In late 1770 Kirkland placed himself under a Boston missionary organization which, with Harvard, managed to contribute to his support, the first regular income he had enjoyed and expanding his capacity to materially assist the people. This in turn inclined them toward Boston, soon to become a revolutionary center, as the font of their good, which had significant implications during the Revolutionary War. As this event loomed, Johnson and his successors became cool toward Kirkland as partial to the freedom cause. Kirkland was influential in preventing Lord Dunmore's War in 1774-75 from spreading to the Iroquois and becoming a general Indian uprising, a conflict which might have cooled the rising revolutionary fervor. On July 10, 1775, Kirkland traveled to Philadephia to confer with members of the Second Continental Congress of Indian affairs, sensing the imminence of a break in American-British relations and the need to keep as many of the Iroquois neutral as possible, if not to ally them with the colonial cause. This was made difficult by the persistent encroachment of frontier whites on Indian lands and the resistance to these factions only by the British, or so it seemed to the Indians. Nevertheless, Kirkland was of critical importance in keeping the Oneidas and Tuscaroras neutral throughout the Revolution, although for much of the time he was a chaplain with the American army at Fort Stanwix, with Sullivan's 1779 expedition into the Mohawk Valley, and elsewhere. At the close of hostilities, however, he returned to his station at Canowaroghare, New York. He helped in formulating the Treaty of Fort Stanwix, October 22, 1784, signing the pact as a witness. In 1788 he toured Seneca country and conferred with his lifelong friend Joseph Brant (who however had sided with the British during the War) on Indian welfare. Kirkland received a 4,000 acre grant from New York for his Indian services. In 1789 he completed a census of Iroquois by families. When the Miamis and other Indians resoundingly defeated St. Clair November 4, 1791, Kirkland, at the request of War Secretary Henry Knox visited the western part of

Iroquois country and persuaded the excited Senecas and others that only disaster would accompany their joining in any general war against the whites. He persuaded them to send a large delegation of chiefs to Philadelphia and the Six Nations remained friendly with the United States. In January 1793 with the approval of George Washington and Alexander Hamilton, Kirkland obtained a charter from New York State for the Hamilton Oneida Academy, designed to provide higher education for both Indian and white young men; the Indian interest was limited and eventually that emphasis was dropped. The school, Hamilton College at Clinton, New York, continues to this day. Kirkland carried on his Indian missionary work until death, retaining Iroquois respect and affection throughout. All of his known papers, either in manuscript form or by reproduction are held by the Hamilton College Library; they contain much ethnological data.
    Barbara Graymont, *The Iroquois in the American Revolution.* Syracuse, (N.Y.) Univ. Press, 1972; DAB; CE.

Kirkland, William Hudson, pioneer, cattleman (July 12, 1832-Jan. 20, 1910). B. at Petersburg, Virginia, he reached Tucson, Arizona, from California January 17, 1856 and was there when Mexican soldiers left (following the Gadsden Purchase of 1853-54); he and two companions lashed mesquite poles together for a flagstaff and raised the first American flag over the community. For $20 Kirkland purchased twenty acres of land from the departing Mexican soldiery and established the intitial Anglo cattle "ranch" in the area, soon expanding its size; in 1857 he drove 200 head from Sonora to stock it but they were stolen by 1860. He was married May 26, 1860, in the first wedding of an Anglo couple in Tucson, it was reported. Kirkland moved to Wilmington, California in 1861, selling his "Terreon Ranch" on which he claimed to have lost $21,000 in so doing. He drove a Butterfield stage for a time and returned to Arizona in 1863. Kirkland settled in Kirkland Valley (named for him) in Yavapais County, farmed and mined and in 1868 moved south again, operating a sawmill in the Santa Rita Mountains and taking up other pioneer activities. On one occasion he said his mountain camp was jumped by Apaches he believed led by Cochise who jabbed his rear with a lance and ordered him to rustle up a meal. "I didn't know I could cook, but I found by God I could cook pretty well!" he later confessed. At any rate the food was satisfactory enough that Cochise let him go. Kirkland held various minor public offices and was a freighter in his latter years. He died at Winkelman, Arizona, and was buried near Tempe, Arizona. He fathered seven children.

Hayden file, Ariz. Hist. Soc.; Jay J. Wagoner, *Early Arizona.* Tucson, Univ. of Ariz. Press, 1975; Will C. Barnes, *Arizona Place Names,* 1st ed. Tucson, 1935.

Kitchen, Pete(r), frontiersman (1819-Aug. 5, 1895). B. near Covington, Kentucky, he was taken by his parents to Tennessee as a child and in 1846 became a teamster with Zachary Taylor's army in south Texas, ending the Mexican War a wagonmaster. In 1849 as a teamster he accompanied the Mounted Rifles from Fort Leavenworth to Fort Vancouver, Oregon Territory. Pete then went south to California and in 1854 arrived in Arizona, acquiring a small herd of cattle which he located on the Santa Cruz River about 25 miles south of Tucson, becoming a supplier of beef to army garrisons at Calabasas and Fort Buchanan. In 1861 hostile Indians, perhaps Apaches, burned him out. When the Civil War erupted, Kitchen moved to Tucson, and later resided at Magdalena, Sonora with his common-law wife. He returned to Arizona probably in 1868, settling midway between Calabasas and the Mexican border where he built a fortress-ranch headquarters and where he farmed irrigated land and grazed his growing herds of cattle. Hostile Indians drove out most of the settlers, but not Kitchen. They ran off his horses in January 1869, his sheep in February, his oxen in June, killing scattered whites in the course of their raids. Kitchen endured. His place became a haven of security in the ravaged Santa Cruz valley, visited by travelers, army officers and adventurers alike, all guaranteed Pete's famous hospitality. By 1870 Kitchen began hauling produce to Tucson, a growing trade he maintained for years despite the hazards of incessant Indian attacks. In 1871 he was host to Howard Cushing on that officer's last, fatal scout after Apaches. Raids on the Kitchen place continued in 1872, some of his employees were killed but Kitchen himself was unscathed. From 1873-76 he was a local mail carrier while

his farm continued to prosper and sales of his produce to army and Tucson merchants expanded steadily. In 1873 he bought a house at Tucson, although he could not live there for any length of time, spending most of his working hours at his Potrero Ranch. A convivial and gregarious man, Kitchen always enjoyed his sip of whiskey and a gambling game (which he usually lost) and he traveled as far away as Prescott and San Carlos to sign contracts for sales of produce. The last Indian raid on the Potrero was in March 1877. Beginning about 1875 Kitchen occasionally held mining properties, selling them to investors when he could. With arrival of a railroad at Nogales on the border south of him in 1882 Kitchen's role as a frontier patriarch faded. He sold out for $5,000 in February 1883 and moved to Tucson where he lived the rest of his life. Through the years he has become a folk hero of the Arizona frontier, a status merited on several counts; he was the type of which sagas are woven and legends created; he was a positive influence.

Elizabeth R. Snoke, "Pete Kitchen: Arizona Pioneer." *Arizona and the West,* Vol. 21, No. 3 (Autumn 1979), 235-56; Gil Proctor, *The Trails of Pete Kitchen.* Tucson, Dale Stuart King, 1964.

Kitt, Edith Stratton, historian (Dec. 15, 1878-Jan. 19, 1968). B. at Florence, Arizona, she became the savior and builder of what is now the Arizona Historical Society, and the recorder of much primary information from the region's pioneers. She married George Farewell Kitt, a Tucson, Arizona, merchant, mothered two children, then completed her education at the University of Arizona and became secretary for the floundering historical society in 1925. She rebuilt and shored it up by her almost unaided efforts until it became one of the strongest and most influential such organizations in western United States, She also pioneered the *Arizona Historical Review,* and contributed many valuable articles to it. After her retirement in 1947 she continued collecting pioneer information for then Senator Carl Hayden; she retired again in 1953 after seeing that collection assume significant proportions, but continued as a volunteer worker for the AHS. Mrs. Kitt died at Sacramento, California, and was buried at Tucson.

Jour. of Ariz. Hist., Vol. VII, No. 1 (Spring 1966), pp.v-viii; Vol. IX, No. 2 (Summer 1968), 113-17.

Kittson, William, fur trader (c. 1795-Dec. 25, 1841). B. in Canada, he was adopted by one whose name was Kittson and served with the British during the War of 1812. In 1817 he became a clerk to the North West Company and by 1819 was working at Fort Nez Perces (Walla Walla). When the NWC merged with the Hudson's Bay Company, Kittson continued with the new firm, being stationed at Spokane House. He joined Ogden with the Snake River brigade in 1824, keeping a diary which gives valuable insights; after the first Snake River expedition, Kittson was assigned to Kootenai, Flathead, and other posts. He died at Fort Vancouver.

Gloria Griffen Cline article, MM, Vol. IX.

Klingonsmith, Philip, Mormon adventurer (Apr. 3, 1815-July 1881). B. at Brush Creek, Westmoreland County, Pennsylvania, he was trained as a blacksmith, joined the Mormon faith in 1846 and by 1850 was in Utah. He became a bishop at Cedar City, Utah, in 1852. In 1857 he took part in the Mountain Meadows massacre in southern Utah, and was the first to confess complicity, on April 10, 1871. He testified at the first trial of John D. Lee. He had been sent to Nevada to mine lead near Pioche. He moved to Arizona and the *Salt Lake Tribune* for August 4, 1881, said he had been found dead in a prospector's hole in Sonora, presumably murdered, perhaps as a "traitor" or possibly to prevent damaging revelations. He was dark-complected, of good build, with black hair and grey eyes.

Journal of the Southern Indian Mission: Diary of Thomas D. Brown, ed. by Juanita Brooks. Logan, Utah State Univ. Press, 1972; Brooks, *Mountain Meadows Massacre.* Norman, Univ. of Okla. Press, 1966 (this includes as Appendix IV, the text of Klingonsmith's affidavit about the massacre and circumstances surrounding it).

Kluckhohn, Clyde Kay Maben, anthropologist (Jan. 11, 1905-July 29, 1960). B. at Le Mars, Iowa, he studied at Princeton, was graduated from the University of Wisconsin in 1928, studied at the University of Vienna in 1931-32, was a Rhodes Scholar and earned a master's degree at Oxford and doctorate from Harvard in 1936. He was associated with Harvard from 1934. Kluckhohn's major specialty was the Navaho Indian people until World War II when he became director of the Far Eastern unit of the U.S. Office of War

Information, advisor to MacArthur and was professor at the University of Tokyo during the occupation of Japan. He was director of the Russian Research Center at Harvard for seven years, when he resigned to return to anthropological work; he was president of the American Anthropological Association, a member of the Academy of Sciences, and won various awards for his work. Among his voluminous publication output, that referring to the wilderness and American Indians were: *To the Foot of the Rainbow* (1927); *Beyond the Rainbow* (1933); *A Bibliography of the Navajo Indians* (1940); *An Introduction to Navajo Chant Practice* (1940); *The Navajos in the Machine Age* (1942); *Mirror for Man ... Human Behavior and Social Attitudes (1944); Navajo Witchcraft* (1944); with Dorothea Leighton, *The Navajo* (1946); with Leighton, *Children of the People: the Navajo ...*(1947); with Albert L. Kroeber, *Culture ... Concepts and Definitions* (1952). Kluckhohn died of a heart attack while fishing the Pecos River of New Mexico.

Los Angeles Times, July 31, 1960; *Who Was Who.*

Knapp, Orson Claudius, army officer (d. Apr. 16, 1877). B. in Ohio he enlisted in the 13th Ohio Infantry in 1861 and transferred to the 15th U.S. Infantry, being commissioned in 1863 and ending the Civil War a first lieutenant; he became captain in 1867 and was appointed agent to the Modoc and Klamath Indians, Oregon in 1869 but his lack of experience and knowledge of the natives was a causative factor in the outbreak led by Captain Jack which initiated the Modoc War of 1872-73 in northeastern California. Knapp shortly was relieved by John Meacham, brother of the Indian Superintendent for Oregon, Alfred B. Meacham. Knapp was discharged from the army at his own request October 25, 1870 and returned to his home at Bellefontaine, Ohio, where he died.

Heitman; Jeff C. Riddle, *Indian History of the Modoc War.* Medford, Ore., Pine Cone Pubs., 1973; Keith A. Murray, *The Modocs and Their War.* Norman, Univ. of Okla. Press, 1965.

Knappen, Nathan H., newspaperman (Aug. 20, 1855-Dec. 26, 1877). B. in Wisconsin, he became editor of the *Bismarck* (North Dakota) *Tribune* in 1873 briefly, and in 1874 served as special correspondent for that journal with the Custer Black Hills expedition. He was the most insistent of the several journalists accompanying the movement that gold in substantial quantities had been discovered. Two weeks after his return to Bismarck Knappen left to join the *Perham* (Minnesota) *News,* and abandoned it for other publications. He died at Albert Lea, Minnesota.

Herbert Krause, Gary D. Olson, *Prelude to Glory.* Sioux Falls, S.D., Brevet Press, 1974.

Knight, Mormon pioneer (fl. 1857). A man of this surname, not Samuel Knight, was placed by *Mormonism Unveiled* at the scene of the Mountain Meadows massacre of Utah, September 11, 1857, either participating in or consenting to the tragedy. Nothing further is reported of him.

Mormonism Unveiled, 380.

Knight, John, physician, frontiersman (d. Mar. 11, 1838). A resident of Westmoreland County, Pennsylvania (the portion that later became Fayette County), he enlisted in 1776 in the 13th (afterward known as the 9th, then the 7th) Virginia Regiment, which Colonel William Crawford (see entry) commanded. Knight on August 9, 1778 was named surgeon's mate and later became assistant surgeon at Fort Pitt. He was invited by Crawford to join as surgeon the 1782 expedition against the Shawnees of Sandusky, Ohio and accepted. He left Pittsburgh for Ohio May 21 and arrived the following day at Mingo Bottoms, where the expedition was mustered. Knight was with Crawford when he was captured by Delawares allied with the Shawnees; while under sentence of execution himself, Knight was forced to watch the frightful torture and death of Crawford. He then was taken to a Shawnee town for his own execution, but escaped June 13 in the present Hardin County, Ohio, and reached Fort Pitt July 4 "in the most deplorable condition man could be in and be alive." He wrote a narrative of his experiences, published by Hugh H. Brackenridge, later a Pennsylvania Supreme Court judge. Knight remained a surgeon in the 7th Virginia at Fort Pitt until the close of the Revolutionary War. October 14, 1784 he married Polly Stephenson, a relative by marriage of Crawford's. Subsequently Knight moved to Shelbyville, Kentucky, where he died, leaving his widow who survived him by about a year, and ten children.

Consul Butterfield, *An Historical Account of the Expedition Against Sandusky under Col. William Crawford in 1782.* Cincinnati, Robert Clarke & Co., 1873; Butterfield, *History of the Girtys,* Cincinnati, Clarke, 1890 (repr. 1950).

Knight, Samuel, Mormon pioneer (Oct. 14, 1832-post 1892). B. at Conesville, Broome County, New York, his father was a convert to Mormonism who died on the plains enroute to Utah. Knight lived at Santa Clara but had taken his wife to Jacob Hamblin's higher ranch near Mountain Meadows for the birth of their first child, and Knight took part in the Mountain Meadows massacre, September 11, 1857, according to Brooks and *Mormonism Unveiled.* An affidavit of Knight's, giving his version of the massacre, is held in Latter-day Saints church files, but was not made available to Brooks for her study. On October 7, 1857, when the Duke company of emigrants was attacked by Indians on the crossing of the lower Virgin River, Knight and Leavitt were sent by Hamblin to persuade the Indians to limit their ravages to the taking of stock, or so it was reported; if the account is true, Knight and his partner had a role in saving the lives of those emigrants. Knight's testimony at Lee's trial is unreliable.

Juanita Brooks, *The Mountain Meadows Massacre.* Norman, Univ. of Okla. Press, 1962; Frank Esshom, *Pioneers and Prominent Men of Utah.* Salt Lake City, Western Epics, 1966; *Mormonism Unveiled.*

Knight, William, physician, scalp hunter (d. Nov. 8, 1849). B. at Baltimore, Maryland, he was educated as a physician and reached Santa Fe by way of Indiana "in early life" before 1837, suggesting that he was born about 1815. He married a New Mexico woman and was naturalized a citizen of Mexico. Through his restless, adventurous nature he became well acquainted with the Gila region, and served as guide for the Charles Ames mule-purchasing party from Santa Fe to Moctezuma, Sonora, in 1837. The Ames group of rugged frontiersmen eagerly joined the John Johnson expedition seeking retribution and plunder from the Mimbres Apaches, and on April 22, 1837, treacherously attacked and wantonly slaughtered Juan José Compá, two other chiefs, and about 17 additional Indians who had hospitably received them, touching off a prolonged period of Apache-white warfare, all for a pittance of compensation. Knight returned to Santa Fe, in 1841 traveled to California with the Workman-Rowland party, returned to Santa Fe and in 1842 took his family to California, where he settled first at Los Angeles, then in Yolo County, enduring normal pioneer hardships. He was a violent man, "quick to resent an offense, and disposed to settle all (such) in frontier style." Visiting Sutter's Fort on one occasion, he came into dispute with Sutter, "promptly drew a brace of pistols from his belt, and, laying them on a table before (Sutter), invited him to choose one and... settle the affair... The invitation was, of course, declined." Knight's Landing on the Sacramento River was named for him. Knight served Micheltorena in a California insurrection, was a signer of the San Jose call to foreigners, and took an active part in the Bear Flag revolt, probably serving in the California Battalion. After the discovery of gold he established Knight's Ferry on the Stanislaus River. Knight was widely famed as a hunter. On one occasion after California had been won, Knight took swift offense over an imagined slight arising from his piano playing and challenged a distinguished Californian, General Mariano Guadalupe Vallejo, to instantly "step out on the plaza to settle the matter with either knife, pistol or rifle, which ever that gentleman liked best," and was persuaded only with difficulty of innocence of any attempt by Vallejo to insult him. Knight died at his Stanislaus ferry site, reputedly a wealthy man, though his children received nothing and "the whole affair (is) hidden in the shadow of an unfathomable mystery." Three of his daughters were married and still living in 1885.

Illustrated Atlas and History of Yolo County, Calif. San Francisco, DePue & Co., 1879, p. 31; Bancroft, *Pioneer Register;* Rex W. Strickland, "The Birth and Death of a Legend: The Johnson 'Massacre' of 1837." *Arizona and the West,* vol. 18, No. 3 (Autumn 1976), 257-86.

Knipe, Daniel A: *see* Daniel Alexander Kanipe

Knox, Felix, gambler (d. c. Apr. 20, 1882). A man of small stature, he had served as a drummer boy in the 8th Cavalry "for many years," although he reportedly took part in actions against the Apaches, and became an accomplished gambler, even a "short card man." He was lame, one leg permanently injured in a fight over cards at old Fort Grant, Arizona. One source said he "was not a particularly pleasant sort of an individual, in a social way," while another said "his manners were very nice." Knox was a partner of William T, McNelly, a former 8th Cavalry comrade, in a saloon at Globe, Arizona, with Knox running the gambling part of the enterprise. He had a cow ranch on the upper Gila River. Returning to Globe from the ranch with his wife and child and a Mexican workman, the party was accosted two miles from York's Ranch by Apaches fleeing from San Carlos toward Mexico. According to the generally accepted legend, Knox turned the wagon around, kissed his wife and baby goodbye, dropped to the ground with his rifle and held the Apaches at bay while the others escaped, being ultimately killed himself. There is a minor controversy over details of the affair, but Knox was killed and his body was not mutilated, possibly, as has been suggested, because the Indians respected his courage.

Correspondence, Clara T. Woody with author, Jan. 14, 1969, and earlier; James H. McClintock, *Arizona.* Chicago, S.J. Clarke Pub. Co., 1916, Vol. I, 236; *This Is Silver City, 1891, Silver City Enterprise.* Silver City, N.M., 1967, 29-30.

Kohrs, Conrad, cattleman (Aug. 5, 1835-July 23, 1920). B. at Wewelsfleth, Holstein, Denmark, he went to sea at 15, shipping on a schooner to Brazil, the Cape Verde Islands, Argentina and the United States. He returned to Europe to have an injured leg doctored, then went once more to New York and thence to the Mississippi valley where he worked rafting logs and lumber from Minnesota to St. Louis. He became a citizen of the United States October 5, 1857, in Scott County, Iowa. In 1858 he went by way of Panama to California, mined for a time and in 1858 went to the Fraser River, British Columbia, where the gold was in better supply, but when winter came Kohrs returned to California, then to Iowa and sold saugages at New Orleans until 1861. He returned to Iowa, went briefly to New York, then crossed the Plains reaching Montana in 1862. He prospected at Gold-creek, then accompanied the strike at Grasshopper Creek, establishing a butcher shop at Bannack, Montana, for Henry

Crawford. When Plummer shot Cleveland, Kohrs carried the mortally wounded man into Crawford's shop to die and Plummer thereby engendered deep suspicions of Crawford and threatened to kill him. Crawford shot Plummer in the arm with a rifle from ambush, then fled to the states, leaving Kohrs the butcher business which Kohrs soon expanded into a cattle raising and marketing operation. With the discovery of gold in Alder Gulch he moved his butcher business to Virginia City, operating in partnership with Ben Peel, the arrangement continuing until Peel left Montana in 1866, Kohrs buying him out for $17,500. In traveling about picking up cattle for his business, Kohrs had several brushes with highwaymen and some narrow escapes. He served with the vigilantes who cleaned up Montana in 1863-64. He was at Virginia City for the hanging of Helm, Gallagher, Parish, Lane and Lyons; he also attended the hanging of Marshland, Bunton, Shears, Graves, Skinner, Cooper and Zachary. The cleanup simplified business operations for Kohrs as thereafter "there was no danger in riding the road carrying money." Kohrs furnished cattle to various butchers in the territory, and also bought hogs and sheep for his own butcher business at Summit, above Virginia City. In 1864 he founded a ranch near Deer Lodge, Montana, on which he fattened and conditioned cattle and horses. Kohrs' business expanded steadily as Montana gold rushes continued and population grew and he came to have a virtual monopoly of the beef industry in the Territory. In late 1867 he returned to the middle west, married and went back up the Missouri River to Fort Benton, Montana, then overland to Deer Lodge once more, which thereafter remained his permanent headquarters. Kohrs continued active in mining enterprises as well as stock raising and marketing, but Texas cattle commenced coming in and for that and other reasons his pleasant monopoly was broken. He, his wife and children visited Europe in 1871, returning to Montana in the spring of 1872. Kohrs bought shorthorn cattle in Iowa and sought to upgrade his herds, while prices continued to lower and profits tended to disappear. Nevertheless, Kohrs' expansion was steady, he becoming the largest and best known cattleman in Montana. In 1878 he bought his first thoroughbred horses, a start toward breeding up his horse herds as well as the cattle. Kohrs was always interested in civic affairs and politics. He was county commissioner for Deer Lodge County, was elected to the Territorial Legislature in 1885 and the Montana Constitutional Convention in 1889. In 1902 he was a state senator and in 1904 as a Montana delegate voted to nominate his friend Theodore Roosevelt for President. Kohrs died at Helena. His widow reached the age of 96 when she died, also at Helena, October 29, 1945.

Conrad Kohrs: An Autobiography. Deer Lodge, Mont., Platen Press, 1977.

Kolb, Emery, photographer (Feb. 15, 1882-Dec. 11, 1976). B. at Wilkinsburg, Pennsylvania, he was educated at Pittsburgh, and reached Grand Canyon in 1902 to join a brother Ellsworth L. Kolb (Jan. 4, 1877-Jan. 9, 1960), for a three month job as porter at the Bright Angel Camp. The Kolbs bought a photography studio at Williams, Arizona, for $425, but "I got tired of taking pictures of saloon girls," and with the help of Ralph Cameron (Oct. 21, 1863-Feb. 12, 1953), later a senator from Arizona who had built Bright Angel Trail down into the canyon and made it a toll-route, Kolb and his brother moved their studio to the South Rim of the Canyon. Later Kolb built a studio at Indian Gardens, four miles down the Bright Angel Trail into the Canyon; the National Park Service, after determining to tear down the structure about 1965, purchased and preserved it instead, because of its historic interest. Kolb and his brother had made pioneering trips on the river. In December 1911, in two rowboats, they traversed much of the Colorado's course through Grand Canyon and took the first motion pictures of it. In 1919 Emery Kolb accompanied an expedition to the Valley of Ten Thousand Smokes, Alaska, as photographer; from 1921 until 1923 the Kolbs worked with the United States Geological Survey on a study of the Colorado River canyons. Kolb made his living largely by taking pictures of tourists on mules, commenting "I guess I've taken more pictures of faces and mules than any other living man," but his own fame as explorer and pioneer of the Grand Canyon region made him the target of tourist cameras as well. He died at Flagstaff, survived by a daughter. Ellsworth died at Los Angeles.

Lon Garrison, "A Camera and a Dream." *Ariz.*

Highways, vol. XXIX, No. 1 (Jan. 1953), 30-35; Ellsworth and Emery Kolb, "Experiences in Grand Canyon." *Nat. Geog. Mag.,* Vol. XXVI, No. 2 (Aug 1914),99-184; Tucson, *Arizona Daily Star,* Dec. 12, 1976.

Kone, Edward Reeves, trail driver (Mar. 15, 1848 - Jan. 30, 1933). B. in Montgomery County, Texas, his family moved to Hays County in 1855. He learned ranch work, attending roundups in Hays, Conmal, Guadalupe and Caldwell counties and in 1866 accompanied a Longhorn herd to Louisiana, starting at San Marcos and progressing through Bastrop, Navasota, Nacogdoches to New Iberia. It was an eventful trip, but not much profit in it. Kone studied law, became county attorney at 20 and served briefly as sheriff of Hays County. He held a number of public positions, being corporation judge for Austin when he died.

Frontier Times, Vol. 8, No. 6 (Mar. 1931), 249-56, 273-77; HT.

Konkapot, Mahican sachem (c. 1700-c. 1775). In 1724, already as a sachem, he joined in a treaty ceding the upper and lower Housatonic townships of western Massachusetts to the whites. He was commissioned a "captain" in 1734 by Governor of Massachusetts/New Hampshire Jonathan Belcher and succeeded to the chieftaincy about 1744. Konkapot early embraced Christianity and invited the Moravians to work among his people, who became known as the Stockbridge Indians after they were Christianized; some went to join Christianized Pennsylvania Indians. Konkapot took the Christian name of John and thenceforward was often known as Captain John. He was recognized by colonial authorities as head of the Mahicans and long was the patriarch of the Stockbridge settlement. He died around 1775, on the eve of the American Revolution.

Hodge, HAI.

Kosterlitzky, Emil(io), adventurer (Nov. 16, 1853-Mar. 2, 1928). B. at Moscow of a Russian father and German mother, Kosterlitzky at 10 was taken by his parents to Charlottenburg, near Berlin, Germany. Four years later he entered a military school at St. Petersburg, Russia. Subsequently he transferred to the Royal Naval College, Moscow, and in 1872 was assigned to a training ship for a world cruise. December 3, 1872, for reasons unknown, Kosterlitzky jumped ship at Puerto Cabello, Venezuela. His movements from then until he reached Guaymas, Sonora April 29, 1873 are not defined. Persistent rumors have it that Kosterlitzky reached the United States at one time, enlisted in E or D Troop, 3rd Cavalry, or in the 6th Cavalry or in the 8th Cavalry, rose to non-commissioned rank, deserted and made his way to Mexico. Lieutenant General Philip Sheridan, then commanding the Military Division of the Missouri, wrote January 30, 1877, to Kosterlitzky's sister in answer to an inquiry that her brother "deserted from the United States Military Service on the 25th of July last (1876), as reported herein by his company commander." Yet Smith, who has done the most extended research on Kosterlitzky, cites documents showing that he was promoted to first sergeant in the Mexican Army July 2, 1876, and five months later was commissioned alférez, meaning ensign or second lieutenant. Smith concludes that rumors of Kosterlitzky's having served in and deserted from some United States regiment, and Sheridan's statement, resulted from confusion of identities, that a Polish soldier whose name is not given but which resembled Kosterlitzky's did desert, but that Kosterlitzky himself never served in any United States Army unit, as he himself steadfastly maintained. To the contrary, on May 1, 1873, Kosterlitzky enlisted in the Mexican Army (his first name ever thereafter converted to Emilio), became a corporal June 3, 1874, and his entire Mexican military career thereafter documented fully. Following his commissioning, he rose by regular promotions to colonel of the National Guard by December 28, 1906; meanwhile he performed parallel service in the Gendarmeria Fiscal, the famed Rurales or mounted police of Sonora which he joined April 21, 1885, by July 10, 1910, becoming commander of the 3rd Zone, Sonora, always under the favor of Porfirio Diaz to whom he was ever loyal. Although Kosterlitzky's career in the National Guard element of the Mexican Army was long and full, spanning the region from the sanguinary Yaqui-Mayo Wars of southern Sonora to the rugged Apache campaigns of the Sierra Madre in the 1880s, his greatest fame derived from his leadership of the dread Rurales, maintaining iron-fisted order over a tumultuous citizenry for many years. A strict disciplinarian, he could be harsh and ruthless as he was tireless and incorruptible, while at the same time generally fair-minded, courteous, soldierly and willing to listen to testimony in favor of some supposed criminal he had taken. "In his time he freed many men, and he shot many men," concluded Smith. Kosterlitzky was not above a tall tale, now and then, as for example his yarn of having captured Geronimo and turning him over to Lawton upon request; no such incident ever occurred. But many other events just as flamboyant did take place and Kosterlitzky, in his meticulous way, recorded most of them. He and his Rurales were of service in quelling a strike-riot at the Cananea, Sonora copper mine June 1, 1906, and various other disturbances at different times. His acquaintanceship among United States army officers and officials north of the Border was extended, Kosterlitzky being generally respected among them as he was by Mexican counterparts. After Diaz was forced into exile May 25, 1911, Kosterlitzky on February 12, 1912, retired from the Mexican Army, but upon request by President Francisco Madero resumed active service September 11. Turmoil generated by the disintegrating Mexican political situation however led him on March 13, 1913, following a futile battle of his force, outnumbered seven to one by insurgents, to surrender at Nogales, Arizona to Captain Cornelius C. Smith Sr., of the U.S. 5th Cavalry. On August 12 he and his men were interned at Fort Rosecrans, near San Diego, California. Kosterlitzky's unrivaled experience and knowledge of the Mexican borderlands, his familiarity with foreign languages (he was fluent in Russian, German, Spanish, English, French and Italian), his intelligence and reliability led to his appointment as Special Employee of the U.S. Department of Justice March 26, 1917; he became a special agent of the department at Los Angeles May 1, 1922, rendering, in the words of J. Edgar Hoover, services "of great value in investigations along the Mexican border and on the West Coast." Kosterlitzky resigned this position because of failing health September 4, 1926. He died at Los Angeles, leaving his widow, three daughters and three sons; he was buried at Calvary Cemetery.

Cornelius C. Smith Jr., *Emilio Kosterlitzky: Eagle of Sonora and the Southwest Border.* Glendale, Calif., Arthur H. Clark Co., 1970; author's file on Kosterlitzky.

Kress, Mortimer N. (Nebraska Wild Bill), frontiersman (Aug. 31, 1841-July 4, 1914). B. near Williamsport, Pennsylvania, he served in the 1st Pennsylvania Cavalry in the Civil War, then migrated to Nebraska where in 1870 he was settled on the Blue River, and had come to be known as "Wild Bill," "Wild Bill of the Blue," or, as Burger has it, "Nebraska Wild Bill," though how he acquired his soubriquet is unknown. "He went around with two revolvers and a very fierce look," but by some "was considered a thorough coward," and not a genuine tough. He hunted buffalo and trapped for a time. Camped on the Republican River with John (Jack) Ralston, the pair late in March or early April 1873, killed three prominent Sioux: Whistler, Badger and Handsmeller (or Stinking Hand), who had peacefully approached the camp and were slain by treachery. This so aroused the Sioux that Bill "never dared come up on the Republican after that." An army investigation revealed the facts of the matter in general, but Ralston had disappeared and Kress was not formally accused of the crimes. He was described as handsome, well set-up, graceful, about 6 feet in height with blue eyes and black hair which late in life turned white. He died on the Blue River, Nebraska.

Joseph G. Rosa, *They Called Him Wild Bill.* Norman, Univ. of Okla. Press, 1974; Solomon D. Butcher, *Pioneer History of Custer County, Nebraska.* Denver, Sage Books, 1965, 89-90.

Kroeber, Alfred Louis, anthropologist (June 11, 1876-Oct. 5, 1960). B. at Hoboken, New Jersey, he was raised in New York City, from childhood learning German, English, Latin and Greek. He entered Columbia University at 16, in his senior year coming under the influence of Franz Boas who had been appointed to the faculty in 1896. Until then anthropology did not exist as a distinct, unified academic discipline although Kroeber accepted the date of 1860 as the beginning of "organized anthropology." He majored in literature and took Boas's course in Indian languages as an intellectual exercise, but in 1897 Peary brought six Eskimo from the Central Arctic and Kroeber studied their language and culture, this leading to his first publications, on Eskimo folklore, appearing in 1898 and 1899 and a paper on Eskimo ethnology in 1900. He undertook a trip west in

1899, visiting the Arapaho, Ute, Shoshone and Bannock Indians, took other courses in anthropology, accepted a fellowship in the subject and earned his doctorate in 1901 with a dissertation on Arapaho art. While little interested in social reform aspects of anthropology as such he came to seek a perspective and destroy ethnocentric thinking about primitives by the more advanced peoples. Kroeber commenced his professional career at the University of California at Berkeley in 1901, spending the rest of his life with that institution and coming at length to be generally recognized as "the dean of anthropology." His work coincided with development of the field as a recognized and valued science, its study a profession which later students might choose "without excessive confusion or risk." During six decades his influences in the developing discipline was immense even if it remains premature to attempt to assess fully his impact. Steward discusses his theoretical views in some depth. In his career Kroeber published more than 500 papers, books and studies, 70 discussing the ethnology of California; about 25 concerning American Indian cultures; 20 devoted to folklore and as many to archeology. One of his outstanding works was the 1,000-page *Handbook of the Indians of California* (1925, several printings since) and *Cultural and Natural Areas in Native North America* (1939) was another, it too having gone through several printings. His *Anthropology* (1948) was considered "probably the most important single work ever written in anthropology" and was based upon a preliminary book of the same name published in 1923. The 850-page second edition presents a basic resume of virtually all recent fields of anthropology, appraisals of new trends, and Kroeber's views with the exception of social science and the structual components of the discipline. Kroeber's vast array of publications "will be for many decades an almost inexhaustible mine not only of information but of problems, concepts, and hypotheses." Among his monuments are one of the world's great research museums and one of the most vigorous departments of anthropology, both essentially his creations. He was widely honored in his lifetime. In 1926 he married "to the delight of everyone," Mrs. Theodora Krakow Brown, a widow who had been his seminar student; it was a very happy union.

After Kroeber's death she became author of the best-selling *Ishi in Two Worlds* (1961), the biography of the last stone-age Indian in the contiguous United States whom her husband, after his discovery had caused to become a resident at the university museum for nearly five years before Ishi's death from pnuemonia. During this time the Indian and the scientist became warm friends and Ishi a fount of information about his people, their culture, language and folk beliefs. Kroeber died at Paris in his 85th year.

Julian H. Steward, "Alfred Louis Kroeber: 1876-1960." *American Anthropologist*, Vol. 63, No. 5, Pt. I (Oct. 1961), 1038-1087, incl. bibliography compiled by Ann J. Gibson and John H. Rowe of 538 items published by Kroeber.

Kruling, Charles (Dutch Charley), partisan (fl. 1878). Charley lived on the Pecos River in the vicinity of Seven Rivers, New Mexico, and became embroiled in the Lincoln County War. He was a member of the posse that killed Tunstall, and was badly wounded in the ankle by George Coe during the Five Days' Battle at Lincoln in July 1878; he spent months in the Fort Stanton hospital recuperating. In 1878 he accepted Wallace's amnesty for the war's participants.

"Frank Warner Angel's Notes on New Mexico Territory 1878," ed. by Lee Scott Theisen. *Ariz. and the West,* Vol. 18, No. 4 (Winter 1976).

Kuhlman, Charles, Custer historian (Jan. 15, 1872-Sept. 18, 1959). B. at Davenport, Iowa, he was graduated in 1897 from the University of Nebraska, earned a master's degre in 1900 and a doctorate from the University of Zurich in 1901, returning to teach European history at Nebraska before a loss of hearing forced him to turn to farming near Billings, Montana. In the 1930s he became interested in the nearby Custer battle ground and for the remainder of his life studied and wrote about the action there. Kuhlman, "who brought a superior mind to the study of the Custer fight," came to stand, according to Utley, "in a class by himself." He approached the battle situation "with no preconceived notions, no preformed prejudices, no party to champion ... no man ever studied the terrain longer or understood what it said better." His works represent to many minds a cornerstone in the study of the Custer event, their worthiness generally acknowledged even by those who disagree with Kuhlman's conclusions. He died at Columbus, Montana, having been "stone deaf for most of his later life." His definitive work was *Legend into History* (1951, 1952); he also wrote *Did Custer Disobey Orders at the Battle of the Little Big Horn?* (1957), based upon a paper read August 26, 1946, before the Billings Rotary Club; a lengthy Custer article, "informative and of much value," printed in the *Bismarck, North Dakota, Tribune,* August 13, 1939; *Custer and the Gall Saga,* p.p. (1940, 1969); and *The Frank Finkel Story: Possible Custer Survivor?* (n.d., c. 1970).

Cover flap on *Legend into History;* Robert M. Utley, *Custer and the Great Controversy.* Los Angeles, Westernlore Press, 1962; foreword to the *Frank Finkel Story;* information from Fay Kuhlman, Charles Kuhlman's daughter-in-law.

Kurz, Rudolph Friederich, artist, fur trader (Jan. 8, 1818-Oct. 16, 1871). B. at Bern, Switzerland, Kurz said that "from my earliest youth primeval forest and Indians had an indescribable charm for me," and after he became an accomplished artist he set sail for America, arriving at New Orleans December 24, 1846. He reached St. Louis by river steamer January 17 and spent the years until 1852 in the Upper Missouri country. He witnessed a number of historically important events, was employed as a fur company clerk at Forts Berthold and Union, felt a deep sympathy for the Indians, and could be critical of important personages who visited that country while he was there. He kept a detailed, unfailingly interesting journal of his years on the upper frontier, today available in an economic edition. Kurz was a perceptive, if occasionally a caustic, observor (Taft calls him, "the philosophical Kurz"), and his witness to the activities of Edwin Denig, Audubon, Catlin, Culbertson and many others, as well as his observations of Indians, their customs and manner of life, have historical and ethnological value. His art also is useful. After his years in the upper country, Kurz reached St. Louis May 25, 1852, ill and not sure what to do with himself or his collection of skins, artifacts and sketches. "As I now dare assume that my studies are sufficiently thorough and comprehensive to justify my executing paintings true to life," he wrote in his journal, "and as I am offered no

better outlook for earning my bread as artist in St. Louis than in any of the other new States, owing to the prevailing lack of interest in painting, I must, though with heavy heart, dispose of a large part of my Indian collection in order to get money enough to travel to New York or to Paris, where I hope to find more encouraging prospects." He returned to France by steerage and reached his Bern home September 24 quite "unexpected by my family." The rest of his life was spent in Europe and Kurz was almost unknown in this country until the 1937 publication of his remarkable journal in the *Bureau of American Ethnology Bulletin 115,* from which it has been textually reprinted. Kurz died at Bern; he deserves to be much better known and appreciated than is the case.

Journal of Rudolph Friederich Kurz, trans. by Myrtis Jarrell, ed. by J.N.B. Hewitt. Lincoln, Univ. of Nebr. Press, 1970.

Kusz, Charles L., Jr., frontier editor (c. 1849-Mar. 27, 1884). B. at Albany, New York, he went to Colorado in 1875, struck it rich at Leadville in 1879, but lost his fortune reportedly by way of an absconding wife. In 1880 or 1881 he established himself at Manzano, Valencia County, New Mexico, eventually becoming publisher of *The Gringo & Greaser,* a semi-monthly newspaper. It was a fearless, open sheet of originality and humor. He made enemies through his writings, and was assassinated by two men who were never captured.

Peter Hertzog, *The Gringo & Greaser.* Santa Fe, N.M., Press of Territorian, 1964.

Kyle, John Gowdy, army officer (c. 1849-Mar. 30, 1877). B. in Ohio he went to West Point and was commissioned a second lieutenant in the 1st Cavalry June 15, 1870, being posted to the northwest. He was engaged in scouting and other duties during the preliminaries to the Modoc War of 1872-73 in southern Oregon and northeastern California. He saved an ammunition wagon from being looted by Indians in the December 2, 1872, fight at Land's Ranch, southeast of Tule Lake. In the first Battle of the Stronghold, January 17, 1873, Kyle was wounded, he having assumed command when Perry was hit and knocked out of the fight. Kyle's severe shoulder wound caused his evacuation to Fort Klamath where he recovered sufficiently to return to duty, taking part in rescuing the remnants of the Wright-Thomas command and in the action at Sorass Lake, May 10. In 1874 he accidentally was shot again at Fort Bidwell, California, and spent 1875 at Fort Klamath, Oregon, but from January to November 1876 was confined to a government insane asylum in Washington where he died; he had been promoted to first lieutenant while officially insane.

Heitman; Richard Dillon, *Burnt-Out Fires,* Englewood Cliffs, N.J., Prentice-Hall, 1973.

L

LaBarge, John B., steamboat captain (c. 1820-May 1, 1885). B. at St. Louis and a brother of Joseph and Charles LaBarge, he became with them captain of Missouri River steamboats, spending some 45 years in this field and captaining a number of different craft. "About the year 1842," he once recalled, "I went up to the mouth of the Yellowstone. Then there were but one or two steamboats going every year, and we made but one trip in a season, known as the mountain trip, but the balance of the season was occupied in making trips between St. Louis and Council Bluffs, and intermediate points. I took the first steamer, the *Chippewa* (later blown up), to Fort Benton, in 1859.... About 1865 I went up to Benton, carrying the first government troops that went across to Oregon from Benton by the same route followed by Lewis and Clark.... Commencing in 1868 the traffic began to fall away.... Then began the decline in the mountain trade...." LaBarge was one of the more famous river captains, and was universally esteemed. He died on his boat at St. Louis and was buried at Calvary Cemetery in that community.

Information from the Mo. Hist. Soc.; *Missouri Republican,* Dec. 10, 1879; May 2, 6, 1885.

LaBarge, Joseph, steamboat captain (1815-Apr. 2, 1899). B. at St. Louis, his father a Canadian, his mother Spanish, and his two brothers river captains like himself; Charles was killed in a boat explosion in 1852, John died in 1885. Joseph was the oldest. His father, Joseph Marie LaBarge, had gone up the Missouri with Ashley and taken part in the fight at the Arikara villages. Young Joseph at 16 with a party of traders, took part in the battle of Bad Axe, with Blackhawk, August 2, 1832, on the Wisconsin border. He became apprentice clerk on the steamboat *Yellowstone* of the American Fur Co., plying the Missouri River. In 1833, on his second trip, one man was killed and three wounded by Sioux fire, the captain and pilots died from cholera, and LaBarge brought the boat safely in to Fort Atkinson. He was not allowed to land, however, because of the threat of disease, and continued downstream to the Illinois shore opposite St. Louis, to avoid the ship's being impounded and burned. The boat, owned by Pierre Chouteau Jr., was sent back upriver to Fort Union with its cargo. He made four trips for the company, designed a stern-wheeler named the *Assiniboin,* but she burned in 1835. LaBarge received his pilot's license at 19, designed and built a second boat having left the Chouteau company, and went into freighting and trading on his own. By 1864 there were 47 steamers on the Missouri and by 1880 about 75. LaBarge, having become a captain, built 15 boats in his career; running the river was always hazardous by reason of weather, Indian ambushes and floating debris. LaBarge won contracts for the delivery of Indian annuities and government supplies to Fort Benton, but the 1863 drought wiped him out and Chouteau, better financed, regained the lush contracts. Railroads finally killed steamboating on the rivers and after about 40 years on the Missouri LaBarge retired to his home at St. Louis. He had known many of the frontier greats: Jim Bridger, DeSmet, Kit Carson, Joseph Smith, Custer, Fremont among them, and his career spanned the active life of steamboating on the Missouri. He died at St. Louis.

Joe Koller, "Pilot on the River of Hazards." *Best of the West,* no vol., no no. (1973), 16-17, 47-49; William E. Lass, *A History of Steamboating on the Upper Missouri.* Lincoln, Univ. of Nebr. Press, 1962.

Labatie, J(e)an, interpreter (fl. 1646-1649). French by birth according to his remark to emissaries to the Iroquois, Labatie served as interpreter at Fort Orange (Albany), New York, and his letter of October 30, 1646, is "the best authority" on the death of the Jesuit Jogues, martyred by the Mohawks. The French interpreter who in 1653 assisted the Jesuit Poncet, another captive of the Iroquois, probably was Pierre Radisson, rather than Labatie.

Thwaites, JR, XXXI, 289-90n6; XXXIII, 137; XXXIX, 266n15; Parkman, *Jesuits in North America*, II.

LaBiche (La Buche, Milhomme), Francois, interpreter (fl. 1804-1828). Recruited for the Lewis and Clark Expedition at Kaskaskia, he was an expert riverman who managed one of the pirogues and also was a useful interpreter and hunter. He accompanied Lewis and some Indians to Washington, D.C., after return of the expedition and a man of that name, perhaps he, was active around St. Louis as late as 1828. Lewis spoke highly of him. There are two rivers in the northwest named for LaBiche.

History of the Expedition Under the Command of Lewis and Clark, ed. by Elliott Coues, N.Y., Dover Pubns., 1965; Clarke, *Lewis and Clark.*

Labonte, Louis, frontiersman (c. 1785-Sept. 12, 1860). B. near Montreal, he was employed by the American Fur Company at St. Louis in 1808, and joined Wilson Price Hunt of the overland Astorians in 1811. He was employed at Astoria and later at Fort Vancouver, becoming associated with the Hudson's Bay Company and assigned at times to establishments in the interior. He was discharged at Montreal in 1830, and returned to Oregon becoming a pioneer settler along the Willamette.

Harriet D. Munnick article, MM, Vol. VII.

La Bretonniere, Jacques Quintin de, Jesuit missionary (May 5, 1689-Aug. 1, 1754). B. at Meaux, France he became a Jesuit and reached Quebec in 1721, being assigned to the mission at Caughnawauga, Quebec, where he spent most of his career. He accompanied Iroquois warriors of that mission on expeditions against hostile tribes, including the Foxes in 1728 and the Chickasaws in 1739.

Thwaites, JR, LXVIII, 331n35.

La Chasse, Pierre de, Jesuit missionary (May 7, 1670-Sept. 27, 1749). B. at Auxerre, France, he became a Jesuit and arrived in Canada in 1700, soon to be placed in the Abenaki mission on the Penobscot River of the present Maine where he remained for 18 years. In 1708 he caused a census to be made of the Abenakis of the Kennebec region; he also played a positive role in the events of Queen Anne's War (1701-13), stimulating the

"patriotism" of the Indians. After 1713 he was prominent in French attempts to hold the alliance with the Abenakis. In 1719 he became superior of the Jesuit missions in New France, holding the office until 1726. He continued actively supporting the Indians' allegiance to the French; in 1724 he wrote a letter memorializing the "martyrdom" of Rale who had been killed by the English in August of that year. He spent the last years of his life at Quebec, where he died.

Thwaites, JR, LXVI, 346n42; DCB, III.

Laclède Liguest, Pierre de, founder of St. Louis (c. 1724-Spring 1778). B. at Bedous in the French Pyrenees, he reached New Orleans from La Rochelle in 1775, and remained eight years before entering a business association with a wealthy merchant, Gilbert Antoine Maxent for an eight-year monopoly to develop trading opportunities in the middle Mississippi Valley. In August 1763 Laclède went upriver with 13-year-old René Auguste Chouteau; they arrived November 5 at Ste. Genevieve, Missouri, the only settlement then on the west bank of the Mississippi in that latitude. To winter he crossed to Kaskaskia on the Illinois side, settling in at Fort Chartres. In December Laclède and Chouteau crossed the river and inspected the west bank from the Missouri River southward, selecting as the site for a trading post on the shelving bank a point high enough to be safe from spring inundation; it is where downtown St. Louis is today. Building commenced in February 1764. Laclède persuaded many of the French settlers of Kaskaskia to move to his new location once word of the end of the French and Indian War had been received and it was known that otherwise they would come under the British flag. Within a year more than 40 families had settled at the new site — when word arrived that Spain had acquired Louisiana and they would now come under Spanish rule, although the town remained firmly French as was its culture. For 18 months Laclède had been *de facto* ruler of Upper Louisiana but was "a benevolent dictator." He never held any official position of authority in the Missouri country or elsewhere. With his trading empire established firmly, Laclède in 1769 bought out Maxent. His business affairs became badly snarled and he spent two years at New Orleans attempting to straighten them out. In the spring of 1778, seriously ill, he left for St. Louis by river craft and died enroute, being buried on the west bank near the mouth of the Arkansas River. In 1757 he had formed a liaison with a respected married woman, Marie Thérèse Chouteau who with her son, René Auguste Chouteau left her husband for him, never having been divorced. Thus his children, through whom he founded an enduring family, did not by French law bear his name but that of his consort, Chouteau.

John Francis McDermott, "Myths and Realities Concerning the Founding of St. Louis," in *The French in the Mississippi Valley.* Urbana, Univ. of Ill. Press, 1965; Noel M. Loomis, Abraham P. Nasatir, *Pedro Vial and the Roads to Santa Fe,* Norman, Univ. of Okla. Press, 1967.

La Demoiselle (Old Briton) Piankashaw, (Miami) chief (d. June 21, 1752). An important chief of the Piankashaw band of the Miamis, he led a revolt in 1747 against the French practice of monopoly trading which he felt held the Indians in thrall at best. He moved his chief village from the Kekionga area, on the Maumee River at the site of the present Fort Wayne, Indiana, to just below the junction of Loramie Creek and the Great Miami River; the new village was called Pickawillany, more available to the British and within easy support range of Delawares and Shawnees. This threatened a complete break with the French and caused a schism among the Miamis. The French were alarmed on several counts. Céleron's Ohio River expedition did little to overawe La Demoiselle and Pickawillany grew into a major trading center. A military/Indian effort to wipe out the village came to nothing, and the French turned to Charles Langlade, a mixed-blood trader who gathered some Indians and destroyed the town June 21, 1752. La Demoiselle was boiled and eaten, a feature of "the kind of practical diplomacy which was most effective on the frontier." Anson wrote of La Demoiselle that "His influence on the French-English imperial struggle in the Ohio Valley continued after his death. If he had been able to maintain his village, the English might have driven a wedge between Louisiana and New France," adding that "La Demoiselle deserves, but has not gained the recognition from the Miamis which he has already received from historians."

Thwaites, JR, LXIX, 187, 299n46; Bert Anson,

The Miami Indians. Norman, Univ. of Okla. Press, 1970; R. David Edmunds, "Old Briton," *Studies in Diversity: American Indian Leaders,* ed. by Edmunds. Lincoln, Univ. of Nebr. Press, 1980.

La Farge, Oliver Hazard Perry, writer (Dec. 19, 1901-Aug. 2, 1963). B. at New York City, La Farge was the great great grandson of the hero of the Battle of Lake Erie. He entered an anthropology class at Harvard and accompanied a field party to the Four Corners area, joining further expeditions there in subsequent years, meeting such noted southwest figures as the Rev. Berard Haile, Lorenzo Hubbell and Laura Adams Armer. His first book was also his greatest, *Laughing Boy,* a Navaho novel which appeared in November 1929, and was an instant success. He wrote other books none achieving the success of his first, although all are worthy, and became deeply involved in work for the Indians, probably his greatest service to his country and its aboriginal peoples. La Farge died at Albuquerque and is buried at Santa Fe.

Lawrence Clark Powell, "Oliver La Farge's Laughing Boy." *Westways,* Vol. 63, No. 12 (Dec. 1971), 22-24, 50-52.

Lafferty, John, army officer (Aug. 23, 1835-Oct. 15, 1899). B. at Utica, New York, he reached California May 16, 1859, settling at Stockton. He was appointed a first lieutenant in the 1st battalion of the Native California Cavalry, July 21, 1864. With a detachment Lafferty scouted through the Coast Range and the San Joaquin Valley of California for a band of highwaymen called the Mason and Henry gang, all secessionists. Through his efforts the band was broken up and "never afterward heard from." Lafferty joined the 8th Cavalry as a second lieutenant in 1866 and became a captain in 1876. He won a brevet for gallantry against the Paiute Indians in the Black Slate Mountains of Nevada February 15, 1867, when six of the hostiles were killed, and at Chiricahua Pass, Arizona, October 20, 1869, when Lafferty was wounded severely. In the latter very hard fight, probably against Cochise's band of Chiricahua Apaches, Captain Reuben F. Bernard praised Lafferty's conduct as "most gallant and daring," and with his incapacitation, "the cavalry arm has lost for a time a good and brave officer." Lafferty's lower jaw was partially shot away, and he lost all his front teeth. As a result of the

wound he retired June 28, 1878. He married in
1891, died at San Francisco, and was buried at
the San Francisco Presidio.

AHS Archives; Heitman; Bernard to Devin, Oct.
22, 1869, Letters Sent, Fort Bowie, Ariz., *Records
of United States Army Commands,* Record Group
98, Nat. Archives.

Lafitte (Laffite), Jean, pirate (either c. 1780-c.
1826, or April 22, 1782-May 5, 1854). By the
first reckoning, he was born at Bayonne or
Bordeaux, France, perhaps reached the lower
Mississippi aboard a French privateer in 1804
and by 1809 was established at New Orleans
with piracy interests at Barataria Bay, from
where he directed operations of 10 or 12 ships
commissioned by the Republic of Cartagena,
to prey on Spanish shipping in the Gulf of
Mexico. His Barataria Bay establishment was
broken up by U.S. forces September 16, 1814,
but the effective participation of many of his
men in the Battle of New Orleans won him a
pardon February 6, 1815, from President
Madison. Lafitte and his colleagues then
established a settlement at Galveston Bay.
This was broken up in 1821 by an American
naval expedition and after a few years the
Lafittes disappeared from view. According to
later scholarship, which has been challenged
but which seems persuasive, Lafitte was born
at Port-au-Prince, Santo Domingo, was
married to his second wife, Emma Hortense
Mortimore, of a prominent shipping family,
at Charleston, South Carolina, June 7, 1832,
settled at St. Louis where he manufactured
gunpowder, corresponded with Abraham
Lincoln, met Karl Marx and Friedrich Engels
and became interested in European commun-
ism, wrote his memoirs and died at Alton,
Illinois.

DAB; Stanley C. Arthur, *Jean Lafitte, Gentleman Rover.* New Orleans, Harmanson Pubr.,
1952.

Lafitte (Laffite), Pierre, buccaneer (Oct. 21,
1779?-Mar. 9, 1844?). Older brother of Jean
Lafitte and his colleague in piracy in the Gulf
of Mexico out of Barataria Bay and later
Galveston. (See his brother's entry for birth
and sources).

La Flesche, Francis, Omaha anthropologist
(Dec. 25, 1857-Sept. 5, 1932). B. at Omaha,
Nebraska, the brother of Susette La Flesche,
he went to white schools but also absorbed
Indian culture, taking part in tribal dances
and in final buffalo hunts on the Plains,
describing his mixed upbringing in *The
Middle Five: Indian Boys at School* (1900).
When Alice Fletcher in 1881 commenced her
study of the Omaha Indians, Francis became
her collaborator and interpreter, the two
working together for 25 years to produce *The
Omaha Tribe* (1911), an extended and in
depth study of that people and culture. While
working on this project La Flesche joined the
staff of the Senate Committee on Indian
Affairs at Washington, attended the National
University School of Law, and graduated with
two degrees. In 1910 he joined the Bureau of
Ethnology, remaining with it until his
retirement in 1930. Among his publications
were two important studies of the Osage tribe
(1928 and 1930) in *Bureau of American
Ethnology Reports,* and a *Dictionary of the
Osage Language* (1932). La Flesche died at
Macy, Nebraska. He was twice married.

Dockstader.

La Flesche, Susette (Bright Eyes), Indian
rights advocate (1854-May 26, 1903). B. on
the Omaha Reservation, Nebraska, she was
an Omaha woman of mixed Osage-French-
Omaha descent and was educated in Presbyterian schools. She taught at a reservation
school but soon became involved in Indian
affairs. She and her father, Joseph La Flesche
took up the cause of the Poncas who had been
removed by force to the Indian Territory and
desired to return to their homeland, the case
receiving national publicity and ultimately
being resolved in favor of the Poncas. She
married Thomas H. Tibbles, a writer for the
Omaha Herald who first had publicized the
Ponca story, and with her husband made
several lecture trips to the east "on Indian
rights and white wrongs." She was an effective
speaker and she and her husband appeared
before Congressional committees, Susette not
averse to Indians joining the American
mainstream, but desiring that their traditional
cultural values not be lost meantime. The
couple lived for a time at Washington, D.C.,
but returned to Lincoln, Nebraska where she
died, shortly before Tibbles ran for Vice
President on the Populist ticket. She was
buried at Bancroft, Nebraska.

Literature abundant; Dockstader.

Laforet, Francisco, trapper (c. 1793-post

1860). B. at Montreal, he reached New Mexico by 1826, and became a trapper, being at North Park, Colorado, when Thomas Smith lost his leg to a Ute wound. In 1830 as a free trapper he accompanied Yount and Wolfskill to California. Laforet returned to New Mexico, continued to trap, settling in 1842 at the present Questa, New Mexico, where he was host briefly to the English writer, Ruxton.

David J. Weber article, MM, Vol. VI.

Laframboise, Michel, fur trader (May 5, 1793-Jan. 25, 1861). B. near Montreal as Jean Baptiste Eugene Laframboise, he took his father's name, Michel. In 1810 he sailed aboard the *Tonquin* out of New York on John Jacob Astor's fur venture to the Oregon coast. When Astor's operation failed, he joined the North West Company and when it merged with the Hudson's Bay Company in 1821, Laframboise easily transferred his loyalty to HBC. He became an interpreter and active trader and trapper, generating controversy however over his dubious honesty, his womanizing, and other peccadillos. George Simpson considered him "a lying worthless blackguard." Nevertheless, he was a utility man for the company, completing missions requiring courage and tenacity. In 1832 he led an expedition as far south as the Sacramento Valley, returning to Fort Vancouver in 1833. His second California expedition in 1834 was followed by a third in 1835, a fourth in 1836-37, a fifth in 1837-38, and a sixth. They were fairly successful in fur gathering,·but ran into political complications. Laframboise settled on a farm on the Willamette River in 1841, but made one more California hunt in 1842-43 for the HBC. He retired from the company in 1845 and became a U.S. citizen in 1851. In some important ways very capable, Laframboise's personal weaknesses and inadequacies prevented his rise within the company and kept him from achieving the place in history his accomplishments warranted.

Doyce B. Nunis Jr. article, MM, Vol. V.

La Harpe, Benard de, trader (fl. 1718-1723). A onetime governor in Brittany, he secured a land concession northwest of Natchitoches, Louisiana, and arrived in the present Red River County, Texas, with 50 settlers in 1718, establishing a post among the Kadodahacho (Cadodacho) Indians. He traded along the

lower Canadian River. He returned to France in 1720 and was directed to occupy Matagorda Bay on the Texas coast, but did not locate it properly and, faced with considerable Indian hostility abandoned the coast for Louisiana again. December 24, 1721, he left New Orleans on a four month expedition up the Arkansas River, traveling 140 leagues by water and marching overland to some mountains, but his recommendation that the region be occupied by France was not carried out. He was at Pensacola in December 1722 when that city was returned to Spain as a result of the settlement of the Franco-Spanish War and February 12, 1723, sailed for the last time to France.

Noel M. Loomis, Abraham P. Nasatir, *Pedro Vial and the Roads to Santa Fe.* Norman, Univ. of Okla. Press, 1967; HT; Herbert Eugene Bolton, *Texas in the Middle Eighteenth Century.* Austin, Univ. of Tex. Press, 1916, 1970.

Laidlaw, William, fur trader (c. 1798-Oct. 1851). B. in Scotland, he became among "the ablest of the fur traders" of the upper Missouri River country. He reached St. Louis from Canada in 1822, joined the Columbia Fur Company and was in charge of its operations below the later Pierre, South Dakota. Laidlaw remained with the firm after it merged with the American Fur Company in 1827, and after 1834 became a partner in the Upper Missouri Outfit, at times in charge of Fort Union. He died insolvent at St. Louis, a man of mixed qualities; he married and remained faithful to a Sioux woman, fathering five daughters.

Ray H. Mattison article, MM, Vol. III.

La Jemerais, Christophe Dufrost de, army officer (Dec. 6, 1708-May 10, 1736). B. at Varennes, France, he was brought early to Canada and entered the army, serving among the Miamis and then at Fort Beauharnois on Lake Pepin, Minnesota. In 1729 he went to Montreal and in 1731 joined his uncle, Verendrye in constructing a post on Rainy Lake, the next year another at Lake of the Woods, then explored toward Lake Winnipeg. He was stationed in 1734-35 at the post on the Lake of the Woods, then moved to Fort Maurepas on the Red River, where he died.

Thwaites, JR, LXVIII, 335n49; DCB, II.

Lake, Stuart N., writer (Sept. 23, 1889-Jan.

27, 1964). B. at Rome, New York, he became a newspaperman at New York City, working for the *Herald* from 1911 until World War I when he served in France. Badly wounded by shrapnel he spent three years in a military hospital, and in 1921 moved to California, becoming a screen writer and technical adviser for western films. He gathered material for about four years on Wyatt S. Earp, much of it from Earp himself, and wrote the most controversial widely-sold book about a western character, *Wyatt Earp, Frontier Marshal* (1931); it has been devastatingly assailed by students and others acquainted with the times and personalities of whom Lake wrote, and much of it appears to be erroneous at best. Lake savagely defended his work, threatening law-suits for challenges to it, but facts are facts and it does not stand up well in the face of them. Lake died at San Diego, California, and was buried at Rosecrans National Cemetery on nearby Point Loma.

Los Angeles Times, Jan. 28, 1964; Ramon F. Adams, *Burs Under the Saddle.* Norman, Univ. of Okla. Press, 1964; superintendent, Rosecrans National Cemetery.

La Lande, Jean de, martyr (d. Oct. 18 or 19, 1646). A donne, or lay assistant to the Jesuit missionaries, bound by contract instead of religious vows, he was b. at Dieppe, France, and reached Canada by December 14, 1642. From then on until 1646 he was attached to the Three Rivers residence. In September 1646 he accompanied Jogues to the Iroquois country of the present New York State. The two were captured however and taken to the Mohawk town near today's Auriesville, New York, where a tribal council decided to set them free, but they were assassinated by fanatical members of the Bear clan of the Mohawks. News of the murders was sent to Canada by Willem Kieft, then governor of New Netherlands. La Lande was cannonized by Pope Pius XI, June 29, 1930.

Thwaites, JR IX, 314n41, XXXI, 123; DCB.

LaLande, Jean Baptiste, frontiersman (d. c. Feb. 7, 1821). Probably b. in Illinois, his name appears among the St. Clair County militia in 1790; he may have been the son of Alexander LaLande. In 1804 LaLande was sent with Jeannot Metoyer and José Gervais by the Kaskaskia, Illinois merchant, William

Morrison (d. 1837) to open trade with Santa Fe, but LaLande dropped contact, avoided reimbursing Morrison for goods and resources advanced for commercial purposes, and remained in New Mexico. One of Zebulon Pike's ostensible errands at Santa Fe was to recover some part of these resources from LaLande. The frontiersman and Pike met, the former said to have been hired as a spy for the Mexican government. When confronted by Pike he said he was too poor to pay Morrison's claim. LaLande died at Santa Fe, and it was reported that he left much property and many descendants.

Thwaites, EWT, XIX, 174-75n.; Noel M. Loomis, Abraham P. Nasatir, *Pedro Vial and the Roads to Santa Fe.* Norman, Univ. of Okla. Press, 1967; Richard E. Oglesby article, MM, Vol. VI; *Journals of Zebulon Montgomery Pike,* ed. by Donald Jackson. Norman, 1966.

Lalemant, Gabriel, Jesuit missionary (Oct. 3 or 10, 1610-Mar. 17, 1649). B. at Paris, he was a nephew of Jerome Lalemant (Apr. 27, 1593-Jan. 26, 1673), also a Jesuit and at times superior of the Jesuits in Canada, and a nephew of Jerome's brother, Charles Lalemant (Nov. 17, 1587-Nov. 18, 1674), a Jesuit as well, first superior of the Quebec Jesuits and important in establishing their work in Canada. Gabriel reached New France in the summer of 1646, spent two years working among French settlements and in August 1648, was sent to the Huron country. He worked with Brebeuf at the St. Louis Mission and with the descent upon it of an estimated 1,200 ferocious Iroquois warriors March 16, 1649, they were urged to flee, but refused; both were seized and perished under the cruelest torture. Lalemant's ordeal commenced at 6 p.m. on March 16 and continued until morning when he succumbed. The account of the deaths of the martyrs was secured by the donne, Christophe Regnaut, who obtained his information from Christian Hurons captured by the Iroquois, eyewitnesses to the tortures, who later escaped the enemy. Lalemant was canonized June 29, 1930.

Thwaites, JR, XXXIV, 25-37, 151-57, 245-46n1, 2; DCB.

La Liberte (Joseph Barter), frontiersman (c. 1775-1837). Andrew Henry listed a La Liberte at Fort Gabe, Canada, in 1799; Clarke believed he may have drifted down to the Oto along the lower Missouri; in 1804 he joined the Lewis and Clark Expedition, but deserted about August 1, 1804 and "we never saw him again," although he was picked up promptly among the Indians. He again escaped. A Canadian named Joseph La Liberte married a Julie Village at St. Louis January 11, 1835; he was then 60, and was buried May 31, 1837, according to Clarke.

History of the Expedition Under the Command of Lewis and Clark, ed. by Elliott Coues. N.Y., Dover Pubns., 1965; Clarke, *Lewis and Clark.*

Lamanse (Lamanzee, Lamazu), Chehalis Indian interpreter (fl. 1811). B. probably in the Gray's Harbor area of Washington, he picked up some English and served vessels as interpreter to tribes along the Northwest coast. He joined the *Tonquin* about June 5, 1811, and accompanied it to Newettee Inlet, Vancouver Island, where the ship was overrun by Indians and ultimately blown up and destroyed with all her complement save Lamanse who provided the only eye-witness account of the event. It is printed textually in Garbiel Franchere, *Adventure at Astoria 1810-1814,* and was discussed by Alexander Ross. Afterward Lamanse returned to Gray's Harbor and was interviewed on the tragedy by officials at Astoria.

Gabriel Franchere, *Adventure at Astoria 1810-1814.* Norman, Univ. of Okla. Press, 1967; Alexander Ross, *Adventures of the First Settlers on the Oregon or Columbia River.* London, Smith, Elder & Co., 1849; Chittenden.

Lamb, George A., frontiersman (Oct. 3, 1814-Apr. 21, 1836). B. in the Laurens District of South Carolina, he reached Walker County, Texas, by 1834, and took part in several expeditions against hostile Indians. As a second lieutenant in the Texas war of independence he was killed at San Jacinto. Lamb County was named for him.

HT.

Lamberville, Jacques de, Jesuit missionary (Mar. 24, 1644-Apr. 18, 1711). A younger brother of Jean de Lamberville, he too became a Jesuit, reached Canada in 1674 and was assigned to the Mohawk mission in present New York State. Here his most famous convert was Kateri Tekakwitha (1656-1680), the so-called Lily of the Mohawks.

Work among the Iroquois was perilous and on one occasion Lamberville narrowly escaped assassination by a drunken Indian. Jacques de Lamberville joined La Barre's futile Seneca expedition and then joined his brother, Jean de Lamberville at the Onondaga mission, remaining there as the only missionary among the Iroquois after his brother was summoned to Quebec in 1686. He served as chaplain at Fort Frontenac (Kingston, Ontario) during Denonville's 1687 expedition against the Seneca. Lamberville was stationed in St. Lawrence settlements until 1701 when he returned to the Onondagas, working among them until 1709 when he went back to Montreal, where he died. The *Dictionary of Canadian Biography* gives his year of death as 1710.

Thwaites, JR, LX 320-21n26; DCB, II.

Lamberville, Jean de, Jesuit missionary (Dec. 27, 1633-Feb. 6, 1714). B. at Rouen, France, he became a Jesuit and reached Canada in 1669, immediately assigned to the Onondaga mission in present New York State where he served, soon as superior, until 1687 when all missionaries were forced to leave. Lamberville was famed as a diplomat with a strong influence among the Iroquois and a good relationship among British and Dutch interests of New York State, and as well was appreciated and depended upon by the French. Intricacies of French colonial government and practices often tested the missionary's skills to the utmost. Lamberville was used by La Barre as an unwitting instrument in preparing for his "war" of 1684 and was instrumental in extricating the governor's hapless expedition from its debacle; again he was used by the French Governor Brisay de Denonville in the official's treachery (unsuspected initially by Lamberville) against the Iroquois and the priest to some extent mitigated the damage the governor had wrought. After leaving his mission among the Onondagas, Lamberville was chaplain to French garrisons at Forts Frontenac (Kingston, Ontario) and Niagara, during this period proving himself a man of prayer and a sometimes-fighter as well. Ill health, brought about by scurvy, forced his return to Montreal in February 1688, and he remained thereafter in New France until his return to Paris in 1692; he died at Paris (the *Dictionary of Canadian Biography* gives the date of his death as February 10, 1714). Lamberville was among the most trusted and adept of French diplomats working with the feared Iroquois, but his best efforts were nullified by official duplicity and obtuseness though his skills were universally conceded.

Thwaites, JR, LVI, 301n1; LXIV, 239-59; DCB, II.

Lambourne, Alfred, artist (Feb. 20, 1850-June 6, 1926). B. in England of Mormon parents who migrated to St. Louis in 1860, he left in an ox train for Utah in July 1866, reaching Salt Lake September 25. Lambourne became a scenic artist for the Salt Lake Theatre. He painted about 610 works and wrote 14 books. His art is amateurish but adds something to understanding of emigrant travel and presents early views of a wide scope of the West.

A.J. Simmonds, "Alfred Lambourne, Artist of the Salt Lake Trail." *Real West,* Vol. XIV, No. 20 (Feb. 1971) 28-29, 51-56.

Lame Bull (Lone Chief), Piegan chief (c. 1797-1857). A noted Piegan leader, war chief and later friend of the whites, Lame Bull was head of the Hard Top Knots band of about 100 lodges in 1853. He had led a small Piegan trading party attacked near Fort McKenzie, Montana, by Assiniboines and Crees in 1833. In March 1854, he led a large war party against the Crows. Mellowed somewhat by age and experience, he was first signer of the October 17, 1855, treaty arranged by Stevens at the mouth of the Judith River and Stevens found him sincere in a desire to live at peace with neighboring tribes. The next year he agreed to permit a Presbyterian mission among his people and spoke eloquently in explanation of his decision. In 1857, while hunting buffalo near the Sweetgrass Hills, Lame Bull's horse was tossed by an enraged bull, the chief's ribs crushed and his neck broken. One account said he was buried in his lodge and 20 horses were killed for his use in the next world; another legend has it that he was buried by whites at Fort Benton. He was physically small, but courageous, wise, and a famous man among his people. When President Franklin Roosevelt was inducted ceremonially into the Blackfoot tribe at Glacier Park in 1934, he was given the honorary name of Lone Chief in commemoration of the great Blackfoot.

Montana, Contributions, Vol. X, 1940, 271-72; John C. Ewers, *The Blackfeet, Raiders on the Northwestern Plains.* Norman, Univ. of Okla. Press, 1958.

Lame Johnny: *see* Cornelius Donahue

Lamme, Samuel Craig, trader (d. July 11, 1829). B. probably in Kentucky, he became a trader with headquarters at Franklin, Missouri, and stores at Liberty and Independence. He early went to Santa Fe, no doubt on a trading expedition for in June 1827 he, Louis Robidoux, Thomas Boggs and 14 others associated with the trade left Taos and reached Franklin in mid-July, concluding a "very profitable" trip and bringing back about $30,000 and several hundred mules from their venture. Lamme was one of those petitioning President Jackson for military protection on the Trail. In 1829 he set out with Charles Bent and with the first military escort for the merchants under brevet Major Bennet Riley. The military stopped at the Arkansas River while the civilian caravan crossed into Mexico territory. About nine miles westward Indians ambushed three men riding in advance, chasing down and killing Lamme who was mounted on a mule, "his body being completely riddled with arrows. His head was cut off, and all his clothes stripped from his body." The incident occurred in the present Kearny County, Kansas.

Barry, *Winning of West,* 144, 161; Josiah Gregg, *Commerce of the Prairies.* Norman, Univ. of Okla. Press, 1954; Henry Inman, *The Old Santa Fe Trail.* N.Y., Macmillan Co., 1897, 75.

Lamoose, Charles, Iroquois with Flatheads (c. 1824-pre 1891). A son of Old Ignace Lamoose, Charles went with his father to St. Louis in 1835 to obtain priests for his adopted people. He was said by artist Gustavus Sohon to be half Iroquois and half Pend d'Oreille, speaking English and French as well as native tongues. He died in the Bitterroot Valley of Montana.

George F. Weisel, *Men and Trade on the Northern frontier.* Missoula, Mont. State Univ. Press, 1955; John Fahey, *The Flathead Indians.* Norman, Univ. of Okla. Press, 1974, 69.

La Morinie, Jean Baptiste de, Jesuit missionary (Dec. 24, 1705-post 1764). B. at Perigueux, France, he became a Jesuit and reached

Canada in 1736, serving at Detroit until 1739 and at Michilimackinac from 1741 until 1752. He was later in charge of the Miami mission in the present Indiana until because of disturbances among Indians, French and English he sought refuge about 1760 in Illinois. He worked at Ste. Genevieve, Missouri, until the Jesuit expulsion, embarking in 1764 from New Orleans for France.

Thwaites, JR, LXX, 310n22, LXXI, 172.

La Mothe-Cadillac, *see* Laumet, Antoine.

La Motte, Nicholas de, French colonist (fl. 1613-18). La Motte as a lieutenant joined in France the company of La Saussaye, assigned by the Marquise de Guercheville to found a French colony which was begun at Saint Sauveur, near the present Bar Harbor, Maine. In July of 1613, the place was raided by Samuel Argall, a Virginia adventurer, and the colonists killed or captured. La Motte, who had bravely defended his ship, "showed fight to the last, and won the esteem of his captors." He was among the prisoners taken to Virginia and arrived finally back in France. In 1618 he returned to Canada with Champlain, remaining during the winter of 1618-19.

Thwaites, JR, II, 309n83; Parkman, *Pioneers of France in the New World.*

LaMotte de Saint Paul, Pierre, army officer (fl. 1665-1670). Often confused with others of the same surname, he reached Canada as a captain in the Carignan-Salieres regiment in 1665. The next spring he was assigned to build Fort Ste. Anne at the northern end of Lake Champlain on an island still called Isle La Motte for him (the post, too, sometimes was called Fort La Motte). It was from Ste. Anne that the Courcelle and Tracy expeditions started out on their Mohawk campaigns in 1666, but it is not known if LaMotte accompanied them. LaMotte became commandant of Montreal in about late 1668, and left for France in 1670.

Thwaites, JR L, 319-20n9; DCB.

Lane, Clubfoot George, desperado (d. Jan. 14, 1864). By 1862 Lane had become known as a horsethief and robber who escaped execution at the hands of Idaho vigilantes by turning himself in to the United States post at Fort Lapwai for incarceration. Freed, Lane migrated to southwestern Montana where in

1863 he was given a shoemaker's bench in the crowded store of Stuart and Dance at Virginia City; by this time he had come under Henry Plummer's malignant wing and served that notorious desperado as spy and "roadster," or road agent. He also was a messenger, taking news of the execution of George Ives to Plummer at Bannack. He was arrested quietly at Virginia City and learning that his sentence was death, asked for a minister with whom he spent the remaining hours of his life "in attending to the affairs of the soul." Lane was the first of five men executed that day to die, leaping from his support before it could be pulled from under him, and dying without a struggle. His club foot, in the sock he had worn on his execution day, subsequently was dug up to prove the location of the graves, and is on view in a Virginia City museum.

Dimsdale; Langford; Birney.

Lane, Joe, frontiersman (fl. 1868). Joe Lane was one of George Forsyth's party of plainsmen engaged in the Beecher Island fight south of the present Wray, Colorado, in September 1868. Forsyth wrote (*Thrilling Days,* 39-41) that one man proved an errant coward during the battle of the 17th-18th, but does not name him; Reuben Waller, in *The Battle of Beecher Island,* 89, said his name was Lane. But two Lanes were in the action, Joe and an M.R. Lane (see entry). Forsyth, in the Beecher Island publication, 10, said Joe Lane with others was either a Union or Confederate veteran (he does not mention M.R. Lane), and Schlesinger, Chalmers and others describe Joe Lane scouting in advance of the column for Indians, and on the island searching for dead Indians (and scalping at least one), so he seems innocent of the charge. Joe Lane was said to be living in 1908 at Red Bluff, Montana, but it is not known where or when he died. It is tempting to reflect on the possibility he might have been Joseph Samuel Lane, son of the redoubtable Joe Lane of Oregon. Young Joseph was b. October 14, 1827, at Evansville, Indiana, and died August 6, 1910, at Myrtle Creek, Oregon. He served as volunteer in the Oregon Indian wars of 1855-56; his brother, John (c. 1836-1914) went to West Point, resigned to join the Confederacy where he became an officer. It is possible that Joseph Samuel Lane also served in the Confederate army, given the strong Southern leanings of his father; in any event Joe Lane was an experienced fighting man. The enigma of his actual identity remains unresolved.

George A. Forsyth, *Thrilling Days in Army Life.* N.Y., Harper & Bros., 1900; *Battle of Beecher Island,* Wray, Colo., Beecher Island Battle Meml. Assn., 1960; *Man of the West: Reminiscences of George Washington Oaks,* rec. by Ben Jaastad, ed., Arthur Woodward. Tucson, Ariz. Pioneers Hist. Soc., 1956, 35-36; information from the Oreg. Hist. Soc.

Lane, Joseph, political leader, soldier (Dec. 14, 1801-Apr. 19, 1881). B. in Buncombe County, North Carolina, he was taken with his parents to Henderson County, Kentucky, where he was raised. In 1821 he moved to Vanderburg County, Indiana, farming, trading with New Orleans and often serving in the state legislature. He was commissioned colonel of the 2nd Indiana Volunteers July 1, 1846, promoted to Brigadier General July 1, and breveted Major General October 9, 1847, for his conduct at the battle of Huamantla, Mexico, becoming "one of the outstanding heroes of the (Mexican) War." He was appointed governor of Oregon, serving in public offices until 1861. As superintendent of Indian affairs, he forced the Cayuse Indians to give up the murderers of the missionary Whitman, and worked out a peace with the Rogue River Indians after a most risky encounter with them in which he came close to losing his life. He commanded an expedition against the Rogue River Indians in 1853, being wounded August 23 in a hard fight after which peace was concluded. As an avowed secessionist, Lane lost much of his popularity in Oregon; at least two of his sons served in the Confederate army. Lane was accused, probably falsely, of conspiring to create a Confederate republic in southern Oregon and northern California. If he had any such design, nothing came of it. He retired to a farm near Roseburg, Oregon and lived in near seclusion for the rest of his life. "His character for honest and fair dealing, his charm of manner and highmindedness, won for him the personal good will and even the friendship of many Oregonians who had become his relentless political enemies." In addition "he was one of the ablest and most vivid personalities of his time in western history."

Literature abundant: BDAC; DAB; Bancroft, *Oregon,* II; Stephen Dow Beckham, *Requiem for a People.* Norman, Univ. of Okla. Press, 1971.

Lane, M.R., frontiersman (fl. 1867-1868). In 1867 Lane was a resident of Ellsworth County, Kansas, and ran November 5 for sheriff against James Butler (Wild Bill) Hickok, Chauncey Whitney, Ezra Kingsbury and another; Lane lost, Kingsbury being elected. During the heated campaign however, Hickok accused Lane of slandering him, a charge Lane denied. A gunfight seemed imminent, since neither man would back down, but cooler heads prevailed and the battle was narrowly averted. In the summer of 1868 Lane enlisted in the 50-scout organization George A. Forsyth collected to fight Plains Indians. Forsyth, in an obvious reference to Lane (see Joe Lane entry) wrote "I was much impressed with his appearance... Tall, well built, brown hair and black eyes, a flowing beard midway to his waist, well mounted on his own horse, a good rider, and with a pleasing address, he... impressed... others also... He spoke of several Indian engagements in the far north in which he had taken part, and... I thought him... invaluable... Imagine my surprise and astonishment, therefore, when we had been attacked at dawn, to discover that my fine-looking scout was an absolute failure and a coward. He seemed paralyzed with fear, and had been among the first to finish and occupy his rifle-pit... and after firing a single shot he had lain sheltered in his pit, face downward, claiming that one of the Indians 'kept a bead drawn on him,'" while taunts from his comrades had made no effect. Oaks confirmed Forsyth's observations. Sackett reports, giving no authority, that Lane was discharged for cowardice once the command returned to Fort Wallace. Nothing further is reported of him. The question remains, how could a man eager to face Wild Bill Hickok in a stand-up gunfight, prove so weak in the face of an Indian attack? Charles F. Lummis perhaps had the answer in a general comment on cowboy-and-Indian fighting published much later, and not referring to this particular incident.

Joseph G. Rosa, *The Gunfighter: Man or Myth?* Norman, Univ. of Okla. Press, 1969; George A. Forsyth, *Thrilling Days in Army Life.* N.Y., Harper & Bros., 1900, 39-41; *Battle of Beecher Island.* Wray, Colo., Beecher Island Battle Mem. Assn., 1960, 89; *Man of the West: Reminiscences of George Washington Oaks,* rec. by Ben Jaastad, ed., Arthur Woodward. Tucson, Arizona, Ariz. Pioneers Hist. Soc., 1956, 35-36; S.J. Sackett, "Arickaree!" *Frontier Times,* Vol. 36, No. 3,

(Summer 1962), 6-11, 48-52; Dan L. Thrapp, *Dateline Fort Bowie: Charles Fletcher Lummis Reports on an Apache War.* Norman, 1979, 129-30.

Laney, Isaac, Mormon pioneer (Dec. 19, 1815-Oct. 31, 1873) B. in Simpson County, Kentucky, he was a convert to Mormonism who was severely wounded by a shotgun by a Missouri mob and reached Utah September 29, 1847, with the Captain Hunter company. He married once, and settled at Parowan, Utah. Here he went counter to church instructions and sold a small quantity of onions to the Fancher emigrants with whom Mormon authorities forbade any dealings whatever; several Mormons with clubs later set upon Laney for his indiscretion and "nearly beat him to death." He took no reported part in the Mountain Meadows Massacre of the Fancher wagoners on September 11, 1857. Laney remained loyal to the church and became one of the presidents of the Seventies quorum. He died at Salt Lake City.

Frank Esshom, *Pioneers and Prominent Men of Utah.* Salt Lake City, Western Epics, 1966; William Wise, *Massacre at Mountain Meadows.* N.Y., Thomas Y. Crowell Co., 1976.

Lang, Billy, cattleman (d. Aug. 13, 1881). An Animas Valley rancher, he had a place in the Cloverdale Springs area of southwestern New Mexico. He and a neighbor, Dixie Lee Gray, rounded up some of their stock to drive to the Tombstone market. Accompanying the drive was Newman H. Clanton, three cowboys: Charles Snow, Harry Ernshaw, Billy Byers, and Slim Jim Crane, a desperado. In the morning they were attacked by upwards of 20 Mexicans, according to report, and all killed but Byers and Ernshaw. Lang ran into a canyon, but fell, shot through the legs, fired his pistol until it was empty, killing one Mexican and wounding another. "He was the only one that did much fighting," Ernshaw reported. Reasons for the attack are obscure.

Ed Bartholomew, *Wyatt Earp: The Man & the Myth.* Toyahvale, Tex., Frontier Books Co., 1964.

Langdon, Jesse D., Rough Rider (1881-June 28, 1975). Probably b, in North Dakota he was raised near Fargo and at 17 enlisted in what became known as Teddy Roosevelt's Rough Riders for service in the Spanish American War. Langdon had gone to Washington to ask Roosevelt to be enlisted, was referred to San Antonio, Texas, where the entered service. In Cuba he participated in the two notable land actions of the Santiago campaign: at Las Guasimas and San Juan Hill. He observed the shooting of Captain William O. (Buckey) O'Neill of Prescott, Arizona, in the latter affair. Because Langdon was on furlough when the regiment was mustered out in August 1898, he was discharged December 7, the last of the outfit to be released. He and 13 other Rough Riders toured with Buffalo Bill Cody's Wild West Show in 1899. He practiced veterinary medicine in Washington State and was an unlicensed physician in a small town 70 miles from the nearest doctor. Langdon moved later to Lafayetteville, New York, the last of the Rough Riders. He died at Stanfordville, New York.

Dale L. Walker, "Last of the Rough Riders." *Montana: Mag. of Western Hist.,* Vol. XXIII, No. 3 (July 1973), 40-50; additional information from Dale L. Walker.

Langford, John, desperado (c. 1847-Aug. 25, 1869). A half-Indian, he "led a desperate life all over the border," before being lynched at Pond City, in Wallace County, Kansas. He confessed to killing six men, put the lynch rope around his neck and freely jumped to his death.

Nyle H. Miller, Joseph W. Snell, *Great Gunfighters of the Kansas Cowtowns, 1867-1886.* Lincoln, Univ. of Nebr. Press, 1967.

Langford, Nathaniel Pitt, explorer, writer (Aug. 9, 1832-Oct. 18, 1911). B. in Oneida County, New York, he entered banking at St. Paul, Minnesota in 1853, and in 1862 joined an expedition under James L. Fisk for the Idaho gold fields, but went to Bannack, Montana, instead, and the next year to Virginia City, Montana. He was a member of the executive committee of the Montana Vigilantes who wiped out the Plummer desperadoes, and most of the vigilantes were his friends; he refused to name most of them even when he wrote his book about their decisive activities 30 years later, In 1864 he was named collector of internal revenue for Montana, holding the position until 1868. He was a member of the 1870 Washburn Yellowstone expedition, wrote a book about it, and worked for establishment of Yellowstone National Park. After it was created he became its first superintendent, holding the position from 1872 until 1877. With James Stevenson on July 29, 1872, he made the first recorded ascent of the Grand Teton mountain. About 1885 he returned to St. Paul entering business, and died in that city. He wrote *Vigilante Days and Ways* (1890), and *The Discovery of Yellowstone National Park* (1905). Haines reports Lanford's date of death as 1909, which is in error.

Aubrey L. Haines, *Yellowstone National Park: Its Exploration and Establishment.* Wash., Nat. Park Service, 1974; Langford, *Vigilante Days and Ways,* intr. by Dorothy M. Johnson. Missoula, Mont. State Univ. Press, 1957; St. Paul *Pioneer-Press,* Oct. 19, 1911; information from the Minn. Hist. Soc.

Langlade, Charles-Michel Mouet de, partisan, trader (c. May 7, 1729-winter 1800-1801). B. at Michilimackinac of a French father and Ottawa mother he early came into a position of great influence among the Ottawa, the important chief, Nissowaquet being his uncle. Occasionally he accompanied their war parties. He became an officer in the colonial regulars. On June 21, 1752, he led a force of 240 Canadians and pro-French Ottawas, destroying the Miami village of Pickawillany (Piqua, Ohio), killed their chief Memeskia (La Demoiselle, Old Briton); the Indians ate him and one white and captured five other English traders who were escorted to Detroit or Quebec. Langlade was active in the French and Indian War and claimed to have planned the ambush of Braddock's force. He helped ambush Robert Rogers near Fort Carillon (Ticonderoga, New York) January 21, 1757. On Lake George in the summer of 1757 he was instrumental in capturing a British flotilla. Langlade was at the siege of Quebec and believed he could have thwarted it had reinforcements reached him in time. In addition to his war exploits he became a fur trader and engaged in winter trading among the Ottawas and Potawatomis. After the peace of 1763 he easily shifted his career to British interests. When Fort Michilimackinac was captured in 1763 as part of the Pontiac uprising, he saved from torture and death the British officers George Etherington and William Leslye and the life of Alexander Henry. During the American Revolution he effectively served the British cause with his Indian allies, was on Burgoyne's campaign and other operations of note. In 1780 he took Indians into the Illinois country to assist in an attack on Spanish St. Louis, but his force was routed. In all Langlade said he had taken part in 99 battles and was known for his intrepidity and intelligence. He was of medium height, square build and broad shouldered. He was somewhat bald, his surviving hair turning white in his advanced age. With thick eyebrows, he had black eyes, and a round face "full of expression." He died at Green Bay, Wisconsin. He fathered a son by an Ottawa woman and married a French woman by whom he had two daughters.

Parkman, *The Conspiracy of Pontiac;* Thwaites, JR, LXIX, 299n46; DCB, IV; Bert Anson, *The Miami Indians.* Norman, Univ. of Okla. Press, 1970; Patricia K. Ouradam, *The Menominee Indians: A History.* Norman, 1979; Joseph Tasse, "Memoir of Charles Langlade." *Wis. Hist. Collections,* Vol. VII, (1873-76), Madison, 1876, 123-87.

Lanihan (Lanahan), Peter (Rattlesnake Pete), lawman (d. July 18, 1871). In 1868, Lanihan was appointed a law enforcement officer of newly-incorporated Hays City, Kansas, continuing in that profession until his death. He may have been a deputy or under-sheriff for Hickok in 1869, though perhaps still a constable who worked with Bill. In November of that year he defeated Hickok in a two-man race for sheriff, taking over January 1, 1870. Lanihan was wounded mortally July 16, 1871, in a saloon brawl he was trying to break up.

Joseph G. Rosa, *They Called Him Wild Bill.* Norman, Univ. of Okla. Press, 1974.

Lansdale, Richard Hyatt, physician, Indian agent (Dec. 23, 1811-Apr. 19, 1898). B. in Montgomery County, Maryland, he was orphaned at 10, studied medicine at Troy, Ohio, moved to Indiana in 1834, to Illinois and eventually to Missouri in 1846. He served with the Missouri Volunteers in the Mexican War, migrated to California in 1849 and in 1850 went by sea to Oregon where he platted the town of Vancouver and then took up land on Whidbey Island, practiced and undertook various explorations. In 1852 Lansdale explored a route for a wagon road from Puget Sound up the Snohomish River by way of the great falls near present Snoqualmie, Washington, then southeastward probably by Snoqualmie Pass to the Yakima River and thence to the Columbia, said to be the first survey of the Yakima Pass by whites. In December 1854 he was made the first permanent agent of the Flatheads and also agent to the Upper Pend d'Oreilles and Kalispels. Asked to examine the Bitterroot (where the Flatheads traditionally had lived) and Flathead valleys to select a site for the reservation, Lansdale (a devout Methodist) recommended the latter because he believed the influence of the Jesuits who had established mission work there was beneficial for the Indians. His recommendation was partly responsible for the Flathead Treaty's assigning the tribe to what was first called the Jocko reservation (now the Flathead Reservation) which in 1891 led to the "tragic removal" of Chief Charlot and his people from the Bitterroot. Lansdale established his agency at the junction of the Jocko and Flathead rivers although it was moved by his successor in 1860 to near the present town of Arlee. Lansdale returned to the Pacific coast in 1856 although he came back in 1857 briefly before becoming agent in 1857 of the tribes north of the Columbia River and east of the Cascade Mountains. In 1873 he was named physician for the Snohomish Indians, serving them for three years, then removed to Olympia, Washington where he lived the remainder of his life except in 1879 when he was physician to the Quinault Indians. He was married twice, his first wife dying in 1841, and three of his children survived him. He was buried at Olympia.

George F. Weisel, *Men and Trade on the Northwest Frontier*. Missoula, Mont. State Univ. Press, 1955; *Montana Contributions*, X (1940); Bancroft, *Washington, Idaho & Montana*, 18, 29-30, 382; Robert Ignatius Burns, *The Jesuits and the Indian Wars of the Northwest*. New Haven, Yale Univ. Press, 1966; Olympia *Washington Standard*, Apr. 22, 1898.

LaRamee, J., frontiersman (June 8, 1784?-Nov. 1821). Possibly b. in Montreal, LaRamee's life is wrapped in mystery, but important place names in the West preserve his memory, including Fort Laramie, Wyoming. He may have come to this country in North West Company employ; he may later have become a free trapper. Supposedly he was killed by Arapahoes on the Laramie River, named for him.

John Dishon McDermott article, MM, Vol. VI.

L'Archévèque, Juan de (Jean), adventurer (c. 1671-Aug. 13, 1720). B. as Jean l'Archévèque at Bayonne, France he came to America in 1684 with La Salle at 12 or 13 years of age and was a member of La Salle's party based at Matagorda Bay, Texas. He joined the plot to murder La Salle and his most loyal retainers on March 19, 1687, on the Trinity River in Texas. The surgeon, Liotot did the actual slaying of the retainers, while L'Archévèque and others stood guard. L'Archévèque was the decoy who engaged La Salle in conversation when Duhaut (whose servant and myrmidon L'Archévèque was) murdered the French leader. L'Archévèque at this time was 16 which in Bandelier's words "indicated precocious depravity, or, perhaps, to be charitable, boyish ignorance." L'Archévèque had a special liking for Joutel and may have had something to do with the plotters' decision not to slay that man after they first had determined he must die, too. When the conspirators fell out, Duhaut and Liotot were slain and Hiens urged the killing of L'Archévèque as well, but the boy was absent at the time and before his return Joutel and two priests successfully argued that his life be spared. Hiens apparently was killed later by Indians. Two years after, on April 22, 1689, Spanish under Alonso de Leon from Mexico at last discovered La Salle's old Fort St. Louis, on the Lavaca River at the head of Matagorda Bay. It seemed quite abandoned but May 1 two men dressed and painted like Indians approached, L'Archévèque and Grollet, resolved to trust to Spanish clemency, surrendering to the southerners to whom they related a tale of hardship, of the disastrous end of the St. Louis colony and the fact that they personally had buried 14 of its dead. Although Parkman writes that L'Archévèque was sent to Spain for imprisonment, this did not occur, as he later conceded. For eight years the Frenchman drops out of sight, but in 1696 L'Archévèque had reached New Mexico (as did Pierre (Pedro) Meusnier and Jacques (Santiago) Grollet, both also of the La Salle expedition). L'Archévèque emerges as a soldier of the presidio at Santa Fe, claiming the hand of a widow of Thomas de Ytta, who had been murdered by a mulatto in Zacatecas. The Frenchman married her in 1697. In 1701 L'Archévèque became a property owner at Santa Fe, then a successful trader and finally a respected and experienced captain in forays against troublesome Indians. He was a member of the Juan de Ulibarri expedition of 1706 from Santa Fe to El Cuartelejo in eastern Colorado to bring back natives who had fled from the Picurís pueblo during the 1690s turmoil in New Mexico. His trading ventures extended as far south as Sonora, and he occasionally bought directly at the City of Mexico. At some date, his first wife apparently having died, he married again. L'Archévèque was prominent in Santa Fe war councils of 1715 and 1720; at the latter the question of a reconnaissance to the Arkansas river was discussed, L'Archévèque strongly endorsing it, his reasons including the probability that it would procure definite information regarding "his countrymen the French." Thus he became a member of the ill-fated Pedro de Villasur expedition of 1720 which progressed farther into the interior than any other Spanish endeavor of record. At dawn on August 13, on the Platte, either at the junction of its two forks or at its confluence with the Loup River, the expedition was surprised by Pawnees and perhaps other Indians, and 35 whites and 11 Indian allies were slain, among the fallen L'Archévèque. He left two legitimate and two illegitimate children and an estate of 6,118 pesos, respectable for the day. His son, Miguel de Archibeque, founded a family which flourished into recent times.

Adolphe F.A. Bandelier, "The Betrayer of La Salle." *Nation,* Vol. XLVII (47), No. 1209 (Aug. 30, 1888), 166-67; Parkman, *La Salle and the Discovery of the Great West;* Alfred B. Thomas, *After Coronado.* Norman, Univ. of Okla. Press, 1969; Oakah L. Jones Jr., *Pueblo Warriors & Spanish Conquest.* Norman, 1966; Alfred B. Thomas, "The Massacre of the Villasur Expedition." *Nebr. Hist.,* Vol. VII, No. 3 (1924), 68-81.

La Richardie, Armand de, Jesuit missionary (Jan. 4, 1686-Mar. 17, 1758). B. at Périgueux, France, he became a Jesuit and reached Canada in 1725, spent two years at the Lorette mission of Quebec and in 1728 was sent to work among the Hurons of Detroit. This work was most frustrating, virtually fruitless for years, but his efforts gradually were rewarded and by 1735 he could report that his charges were all converted. He remained among them until about 1753. He died at Quebec.

Thwaites, JR, LXVIII, 333n44.

Larios, Juan, Franciscan missionary (1633-c. 1675). B. at Sayula, Jalisco, Mexico, he

entered the Franciscan order in 1651, was a preacher at Guadalajara and a superior of convents at Armacueca and Atoyac. During a visit to Parral, Nueva Vizcaya, he was invited to become a missionary by Chichimeca Indians in Coahuila Province where he went in 1673, accompanied by a priest, Dionysio de Peñasco and lay brother, Manuel de la Cruz of the Franciscans, commencing important religious work that prospered under Antonio de Balcarcél Rivandeneira, alcalde mayor of Coahuila. April 30, 1675 Larios with Fernando del Bosque, Friar Dionísio de San Buenaventura, ten Spanish soldiers and Indian auxiliaries left Monclova (Guadalupe) on a missionary tour, shortly being joined by 100 other Indians. They reached the Rio Grande May 11, crossed near the present Eagle Pass and moved into Texas, making for the Sierra Dacate (Anacacho Mountain), the military to take royal possession, confer with Indians, aid the missionaries and report the expedition's discoveries. It crossed a branch of the Nueces River and reached a place they called San Pablo in the present Edwards County, Texas, enroute meeting a dozen tribes of Indians and recovering a Spanish boy captive who had forgotten his native tongue. By June the expedition had returned to Monclova. Although neither grand in scope nor in line of march, the effort was the earliest well-authenticated missionary journey across the Rio Grande south of the Pecos. Larios died in the mission fields after which his work fell into disorder until Alonso de Leon recontructed the city of Monclova and revived the settlements of Coahuila in 1689.

Herbert Eugene Bolton, *Spanish Exploration in the Southwest, 1542-1706.* N.Y., Charles Scribner's Sons, 1916; Porrua; HT.

Larn, John, lawman-gunman (March 1, 1849-June 24, 1878. B. probably at Mobile, Alabama, he moved to Colorado in his teens, killed a ranchman, and a month later a New Mexico sheriff, then migrated to the Fort Griffin area of Texas. By 1871 he became trail foreman for Bill Hays, noted Griffin stockman and in the fall drove 1,700 cattle to Colorado, "an event punctuated by killings, cattle rustling and a near shootout" with U.S. Cavalrymen. Back at Griffin differences arose between Hays and Larn over alleged rustling. Larn, with law and military men on his side, attacked a Hays drive, killing five men and capturing four who were assassinated "trying to escape." Larn "a most unusual man," whose enemies admired his virtues and friends conceded his faults, became foreman for Joseph Matthews and wed his daughter, Mary, a happy marriage. Larn became associated with John Selman, a noted gunman, both being members of the Shackelford County, Texas, vigilante committee, Larn for a time its head. February 15, 1876, Larn was elected sheriff, his vigilante and lawman impulses being hopelessly intertwined, and he had some 13 counties to police. William R. Cruger was his chief deputy; Selman may have been unofficial deputy at times. Larn broke up the Bill Henderson gang, shooting, lynching or otherwise disposing of its members. Lynchings from his jail were a common, sometimes multiple occurrence, and public sentiment against Larn and his crony, Selman, mounted. They were suspected also of rustling to build up their private herds. Following a savage shootout in which Larn did not participate though his friends did, January 17, 1877, Larn resigned (March 7) as sheriff, and Cruger appointed to succeed him. Larn and Selman withdrew from the vigilantes, were appointed deputy inspectors of hides and animals for Shackelford County, and continued their lawless ways with cattle and cattlemen. They gradually assembled a gang of about 16 men, and their operations became confused with enmity to "grangers," and took on some elements of a feud. Murders were committed, there were assassination attempts against Larn and Selman, and it became a "case now of open war against everybody." They defied the Texas Rangers who sought to arrest them. Selman escaped vigilante action, but Larn was taken the night of June 22, 1878, removed to Albany, Texas, and a masked group of nine or more executed him in jail, their leader reportedly a relative. He was buried at his Camp Cooper ranch, a stone marking the grave.

Leon Claire Metz, *John Selman, Texas Gunfighter.* N.Y., Hastings House, 1966; Ed Bartholomew, *Wyatt Earp: The Untold Story.* Toyahvale, Tex., Frontier Book Co., 1963.

Larpenteur, Charles, fur trader (1807-Nov. 15, 1872). B. in France, he reached America in 1818, remaining in Maryland until he was 21, going then to St. Louis where, in 1833, he hired out to William Sublette and Robert Campbell for a Rocky Mountain expedition.

They reached the trappers' rendezvous on the Green River in July; the company then built Fort William, at the mouth of the Yellowstone, intending it as competition with the American Fur Company's Fort Union nearby, but Sublette sold out to his rival during the winter. Larpenteur then joined the American Fur Company. His pen gives graphic insights into upper Missouri trading operations, describes the 1837 smallpox plague and other events. He left the AFC and in the spring of 1848 became a free trader to the Flatheads near Fort Benton, returned to the states in 1849, and after another year in the upper river country, tried to settle down to farming on the Little Sioux River, Iowa. However, the fur business continued to call him, and he spent several years more on a variety of trading ventures, his active career continuing until 1871, when he finally settled once more in Iowa. He died near Little Sioux. His journals and memoirs form "a remarkable document on the American fur trade."

Louis Pfaller article, MM, Vol. I.

Larrabee, Charles F., Indian agent (d. Nov. 1, 1912). B. in Maine, he enlisted in the 30th Maine Infantry as sergeant major January 11, 1864, and was commissioned a first lieutenant September 1. He ended the Civil War with brevets to major for work in several Louisiana engagements and was mustered out August 12, 1865. He was commissioned a second lieutenant in the 7th Infantry February 23, 1866, becoming a first lieutenant July 28. He was mustered out January 1, 1871. Larrabee was named to succeed George Stevens as agent at the San Carlos Apache Reservation in Arizona, arriving in March 1873. Dr. Reuben A. Wilbur was interim agent; he seems to have resented Larrabee's arrival to take over Wilbur's function. Larrabee found the Indians divided into two factions, each seeking the favor of the agent and warning against the other party. Larrabee became the focal point of a tangle of intrigue, conspiracy and turbulence too great for his inexperience to manage. Conditions steadily worsened and erupted May 27 with assassination of Jacob M. Almy, commander of troops stationed to preserve order at San Carlos and to protect the agency. With this, Larrabee had had enough and resigned June 18. His further activities are not reported.

Heitman; Dan L. Thrapp, *The Conquest of Apacheria.* Norman, Univ. of Okla. Press, 1967.

La Salle, René Robert Cavelier, sieur de, explorer (Nov. 21, 1643-Mar. 19, 1687). B. at Rouen, France, of a wealthy family, he entered the Jesuit order and showed intellectual promise, becoming interested particularly in mathematics. He remained with the Jesuits from 1658 until 1667 when he asked to be released from his vows because of "moral frailties," but more particularly because of his restlessness and unwillingness to consent to strict religious discipline. He reached Canada after mid-1667, establishing a trading post on a seigniory granted him by the Sulpitians near Lachine Rapids on the St. Lawrence above Montreal. La Salle became interested in western explorations and a possible route to China. In July 1669, he accompanied the Sulpitians Casson and Galinée in an abortive expedition to rediscover the Mississippi, but the party never got farther than Lake Ontario, although La Salle encountered there Louis Jolliet, enroute back to the settlements from Lake Superior. Little is known and much is speculated about La Salle's succeeding four years, Thwaites believing that "he seems to have spent much of that time in exploration and trade in the lower lake region, and that of the upper Ohio, of which he was probably the first white discoverer." Others disagree, including Céline Dupré in the *Dictionary of Canadian Biography* who doubts La Salle accomplished any notable explorations in this period or discovered the Ohio. Becoming friendly with Frontenac, La Salle went to France in 1674 and returned with a royal grant for the present Kingston, Ontario region, establishing a prosperous colony where commerce and agriculture were carried on by French and friendly Iroquois. But his imagination conceived designs far more grandiose than pioneering settlements. In 1678 La Salle obtained from Louis XIV permission to make explorations to the west in the name of the king, build forts and open communications with Mexico. "This enabled him to begin the execution of his own colossal schemes, which included far more — to build vessels above Niagara, and later on some branch of the Mississippi, (opening) a great route for commerce via that river and the Gulf of Mexico; to explore the region between Lake Erie and the Mississippi, and plant therein French colonies; and to secure for himself the commercial and perhaps viceregal control of this new empire." In 1679 above Niagara Falls, La Salle had constructed the

Griffon, a 45-ton vessel aboard which he sailed to Mackinac and Green Bay; she set out to return laden with fur, but never again was heard from (though her remains may have been found in 1955 in a cove on Russell Island in Georgian Bay); loss of the ship and cargo seriously embarrassed La Salle, who was engaged in further adventures. With a small party in canoes he entered the Illinois River, building Fort Crevecoeur near the present Peoria, Illinois, and wintered there. On February 29, 1680, La Salle sent Hennepin and two others to explore the upper Mississippi River. Hennepin had joined the explorer in 1678 at Quebec at the direction of his superior. On his small exploratory journey he reached the Falls of St. Anthony at the present Minneapolis-St. Paul before being distracted by Sioux. Leaving his faithful lieutenant Henri de Tonty in command at Fort Crevecoeur, La Salle returned to Montreal in the spring for supplies, but the men he left mutinied and partially destroyed the fort in Tonty's absence and deserted. La Salle had a facility for making enemies and suspecting of inimical design even his friends; he aroused the hostility of rival fur traders, Canadian merchants and the powerful Jesuits, yet persisted with his plans despite all obstacles, which involved one disaster after another and ever-deepening debts which each debacle made more weighty. In late 1681 with his most famous expedition he and Tonty entered the Mississippi and followed the river to its mouth, taking possession April 9, 1682, of the entire basin for his king and naming the country Louisiana in his honor; all this was a necessary preliminary step to implementing his vision of founding a French empire in the interior of the continent. In December of 1682 La Salle had constructed Fort St. Louis on Starved Rock above the Illinois River near the present Utica, and placed Tonty in charge. His friend and supporter, Frontenac was recalled to France and a successor, La Barre "proved bitterly hostile" to La Salle, who once more returned to the homeland. Granted by the king a squadron of four vessels and some 300 soldiers, artisans and colonists, La Salle's greatest expedition left La Rochelle August 1, 1684, bound for the Gulf of Mexico and the mouth of the Mississippi. One of the vessels was lost to Spanish corsairs before the expedition reached the Gulf; the others purportedly were unable to locate the mouth of the river and continued (by inadvertence or intent) westward. On January 1 a landing was made in the present Jefferson County, Texas, but this proved an unsatisfactory place for a colony; other unsuccessful essays included one from January 20 to February 4 in Matagorda County before, late in February, La Salle put in at Matagorda Bay which he found satisfactory for his purpose and erected a new "Fort St. Louis." One ship was lost with its cargo at the entrance to the bay; another was wrecked shortly afterward, leaving the explorer with no sea support since the fourth vessel had put back for France at the direction of its naval officer commanding. . La Salle made several exploratory journeys to the westward; on one of these he probably reached the Rio Grande, discovering several tribes of Indians inimical to the Spanish interest and willing to listen to the French. Some authorities believe his intent was to determine the strengths of Spanish posts and influence in this quarter. Realizing that to save his colony he must establish contact with the French in the Mississippi valley, La Salle then headed another expedition, this time to the northeast, searching for the great river. He set out in April 1686 with 20 men, reaching the town of the Cenis of the Hasinai confederacy, a Caddo people where he spent some time recovering from fever. Eight of the party survived to regain Fort St. Louis. A fresh expedition left January 12, 1687, and probably reached the Navasota River northwest of present Houston where La Salle was murdered by a disgruntled member of the expedition, the surgeon Liotot, a brutal man who himself was subsequently slain by others of the party. The colony La Salle founded at Matagorda Bay was a debacle from the start; only six survivors of his expedition were said ultimately to have reached France; several were taken by the Spanish subsequently, some of whom reached New Mexico (see L'Archévèque entry). A few others may have been adopted by Indian tribes to which they had deserted and a few children were salvaged from the ruins of Fort St. Louis after natives massacred remaining adults. Yet, despite the series of disasters, some of which were his own fault, La Salle possessed the elements of greatness. Parkman wrote that he was "without question one of the most remarkable explorers whose names live in history," and quotes La Salle's other lieutenant, Henri Joutel: "His firmness, his courage, his great knowledge of the arts and sciences, . . . and his untiring energy... would have won at last a glorious success for his great enterprise, had not all his fine qualities been counterbalanced by a haughtiness of manner which often made him insupportable, and by a harshness toward those under his command which drew upon him an implacable hatred, and was at last the cause of his death." Parkman adds, however, that "it is easy to reckon up his defects, but it is not easy to hide from sight the Roman virtues that redeemed them. Beset by a throng of enemies, he stands... above them all.... America owes him an enduring memory; for in this masculine figure she sees the pioneer who guided her to the possession of her richest heritage."

Parkman, *La Salle and the Discovery of the Great West;* Thwaites, JR, LVII, 315-17n2, LX, 319-20n21, LXV, 270n33; Harrison John MacLean, *The Fate of the Griffon.* Chicago, Swallow Press, 1975.

La Saussaye, Rene le Coq de, colonial commander (fl. 1612-13). La Saussaye became the agent for the Marquise de Guercheville to found a French colony south of Port Royal, Nova Scotia. He left France March 12, 1613, and reached Acadia May 16, recruited the Jesuits Pierre Biard and Enemond Massé at Port Royal, and traced the coastline southward to Frenchman Bay, Maine, where a settlement named Saint Sauveur was begun near the present site of Bar Harbor. The place was surprised July 2 by Samuel Argall of Virginia, the French ship taken and the colony occupied while La Saussaye took to the woods with a few others. He eventually came in for a conference with Argall, and was given permission to take a longboat with Massé and 13 other colonists. He reached France in October 1613, and fades from the historical record.

Thwaites, JR I-IV; Parkman, *Pioneers of France in the New World,* II, 128n; DCB.

Lassen, Peter, pioneer (Aug. 7, 1800-Apr. 26, 1859). B. at Copenhagen, he learned the blacksmithing trade and emigrated to the United States in 1828, landing at Boston, moving later to Keyesville, Chariton County, Missouri. Here he became a farmer and blacksmith, remaining until 1839 when in company with 10 men and two women (missionaries' wives) he accompanied an American Fur Company party to Fort Hall,

Idaho, where the women were left. Lassen went on to The Dalles, Oregon, thence by river to Fort Vancouver. He and others wintered on the Willamette River, then embarked on the *Lausanne* for Bodega Bay and went overland to Sutter's Fort, then to San Francisco and San Jose where Lassen resumed blacksmithing. In the spring of 1841 he built a sawmill at Santa Cruz, said to have been the first built in that part of California, selling out two years later. In 1844 he was naturalized a Mexican citizen and received the 26,000 acre Rancho Bosquejo land grant on Deer Creek in Tehama County. Here, surrounded by hundreds of Indians some of whom he hired to build and work his ranch structures, Lassen did not see a white man for seven months; his herds increased to 200 or 300 head and not one was ever molested by Indians. Lassen's gradually became a headquarters for Anglo travelers; in 1846 he became associated with Fremont and others and was "probably one of the Bears" in the Bear Flag revolt. In 1847 he started East but probably went no farther than Fort Hall, his mission having been to divert emigration to the Lassen route and into the upper Sacramento Valley; he returned to California the next year. In 1850 he sold half of his ranch and stock and engaged in unfortunate steamboat speculation at Sacramento, becoming financially ruined in the process; he lost what was left of his holdings to a partner who had turned out to be "a great rascal." Lassen settled in 1851 in Indian Valley, Plumas County. In 1854 he and others made the strike that resulted in the founding of Susanville, now the seat of Lassen County, which was named for him. Lassen became a farmer and miner in Honey Lake Valley, near Susanville. Named for him also was Lassen Peak, one of the contiguous states' most recent active volcanoes, erupting continuously from May 30, 1914, until June 1917, the peak itself having been discovered about 1821 by Luis Arguello; Lassen Volcanic National Park was established in 1916. While on a prospecting trip north of Pyramid Lake Lassen was killed by Indians "or possibly white men disguised as Indians." Two monuments mark his grave about six miles from Susanville.

Bancroft, *Pioneer Register;* "Peter Lassen." *Hutchings' Calif. Mag.,* Vol. III, No. 10 (Apr. 1859), reprinted in *Scenes of Wonder and Curiosity: Selected by Roger R. Olmsted from Hutchings'*

Magazine. Berkeley, Calif. Howell-North, 1962, 385-87, incl. portrait.

Lasuén, Fermín Francisco de, Franciscan missionary (June 7, 1736-June 26, 1803). B. at Victoria, Spain, he received his habit March 19, 1751, at 14, and came to Mexico in 1759. He was sent to the missions of Lower California in 1768, remaining there until the missions were turned over to the Dominicans in 1773 when he moved to San Diego, arriving August 30. He succeeded Junipero Serra in 1785 as president of the Alta California missions, and founded nine: Santa Barbara, December 4, 1786; Purísima, December 2, 1787; Santa Cruz, August 28, 1791; Soledad, October 9, 1791; San José, June 11, 1797; San Juan Bautista, June 24, 1797; San Miguel, July 25, 1797; San Fernando, September 8, 1797, and San Luis Rey, June 13, 1798. Late in life he wrote a defense of the mission system in answer to charges of cruelty and dishonesty. It is cited by Bancroft. During his 18 years as president, Lasuén saw 15,000 confirmed, 34,000 baptized; more than 15,000 Indians lived at the missions, 7,614 marriages had been blessed and the establishments all were flourishing. "A very able administrator, a character beloved by all, he ushered in the golden age of the missions." He died at San Carlos Borromeo.

Palou's Life of Fray Junipero Serra, trans. & annot. by Maynard J. Geiger, O.F.M. Wash., D.C., Acad. of Amer. Franciscan Hist., 1955.

La Tesserie, Jacques Descailhaut, sieur de, interpreter (1629-1673). B. in Nantes, France, he accompanied the Jesuit Beschefer to Fort Orange (Albany, New York) from Quebec in the summer of 1666. A fur trader, he was at one time member of the Sovereign Council of Quebec.

Thwaites, JR, L, 191, 325n20.

Laudonniere, Rene Goulaine de, French colonist (d. 1582). B. in the Poitou region of France, he could not have been much junior to Ribaut (b. c. 1520), and was a Huguenot by faith. He was named a lieutenant to Ribaut for the establishment, under auspices of Admiral Gaspard de Coligny, of the Huguenot colony in "Florida," the 1562 expedition investigating the St. John's River, Florida, and eventually beginning a settlement on Parris Island, South Carolina, naming their post

Port Royal. Laudonniere with Ribaut returned to France, reaching Dieppe July 20, 1562, the former with three ships and 300 colonists sailing in April 1564, to found a new colony, the hapless settlers of the first having killed their commander, barely escaped starvation, and returned to France. The fresh colonial attempt was made on the St. John's River, Florida, called by the French the River of May; here they built what Laudonniere called Fort Caroline, named for Charles IX. Initially the colonists got on well with the Indians, although the relationship later chilled and casualties were suffered in at least one French raid on Indian cornfields. Unrest seized the settlers, some of whom sailed to Spanish ports; when a few returned Laudonniere caused to be shot four judged ringleaders of the mutiny. He was prepared to give up his second Huguenot colony when Ribaut arrived with strong reinforcements August 29, 1565. A Spanish fleet under Pedro Menéndez de Aviles discovered the French settlement, surprised it with an overland expedition while the French fleet was seeking to attack the Spaniards at St. Augustine, and massacred cruelly most of those found. Laudonniere, wounded and desperately ill, escaped and regained France in January 1566. Laudonniere, buffeted by the Protestant-Catholic rivalry in his native land, retired to his estate where he wrote his account of the Florida adventure, published in 1586 at Paris and in an English translation by Hakluyt. Parkman describes Laudonniere as "pious... and an excellent marine officer" and obviously he was intelligent, of great courage and seems to have been a man of integrity.

Parkman, *Pioneers of France in the New World;* DAB; CE.

Laumet, Antoine (Antoine de la Mothe Cadillac), founder of Detroit (Mar. 5, 1658-Oct. 15, 1730). B. at Les Laumets, near Caumont, department of Tarn-et-Garonne, France, he became a controversial figure in French America, but a pioneer of true genius. He invented for himself a noble pedigree he was not born with, but received a good education before coming to America in 1683 as an immigrant with grand ambitions. Settled in Nova Scotia, he became familiar with the New England coast through service aboard a privateer, married his captain's daughter, Marie-Therese Guion in 1687, and

his fortunes improved; he was granted a seigniory on the Douaguek River in present-day Maine, including the island of Mt. Desert. He entered a trading partnership and reached Quebec in 1691. He made a worthy reconnaissance of the New England coast for the government and in 1694 was made commandant at Michilimackinac, between Lakes Huron and Michigan, a real responsibility. A failure as an administrator but adroit as a somewhat shady fur merchant, he returned to Quebec in 1697, going on to France the next year to propose the settlement on the Detroit River to serve as a French center at the edge of the wilderness. After a second hurried trip to France to defend his scheme, Cadillac reached the site of Detroit with 100 men in 1701 and set about making himself "master of the northwest." He soon commenced to feud with other French officials, his Indian administration suffered, his greediness mounted. In 1704 he was arrested but acquitted at Quebec. Finally in 1710, to get him out of Detroit, Cadillac was named governor of Louisiana, "without a doubt the most dismal colony in the French empire." He reached there in 1713, and attempted unsuccessfully to open communications with Mexico overland, discovered a supposed lead mine in the Illinois country, and resumed battling with other French officials. He was recalled, and in 1717 returned to France, his 34 years in the colonies "come to an inglorious end." He was jailed briefly, though the French government ultimately paid his salary arrears, honored him, gave him rights at Detroit which he never assumed since he did not return there. In 1723 he purchased the governership of a small town, Castelsarrasin, where he died. The *Dictionary of Canadian Biography,* which has the best account of his life, although distinctly anti-Cadillac, concludes that rather than being one of the "great early heroes" of France in the New World, he approached the status of one of the "worst scoundrels ever to set foot in New France," although enduring myth holds otherwise.

Literature abundant, though scattered; DCB; DAB.

Lauverjat, Etienne, Jesuit missionary (Jan. 25, 1679-Nov. 16, 1761). B. at Bourges, France, he became a Jesuit and reached Quebec c. 1710. After acquiring the Abenaki language he was assigned to the Pentagoet mission near the present Bangor, Maine, on the Penobscot River. Lauverjat won a reputation for militancy in urging his charges to resist English settlements on the Maine coast; in 1723 Thomas Westbrook of Massachusetts burned the Abenaki village and Lauverjat's chapel to avenge a previous attack against an English post. The missionary thought the Abenakis had to resist English encroachments or lose their missionaries and probably their faith. He left Maine in 1732 for Canada and returned in 1740 for two more years along the Penobscot. In 1742 he moved to a mission for the Abenakis at the mouth of the Missisquoi River in Vermont, leaving this post for Quebec in 1747. In 1749 he went to the ancient mission at Norridgewock in Maine, working there until 1754 when he retired to Quebec, where he died.

Thwaites, JR, LXVI, 345n41, LXXI, 163; DCB, III.

Law, John, financier (Apr. 21, 1671-Mar. 21, 1729). B. in Scotland, he killed a man in a duel and fled to Amsterdam where he studied banking and finance. He returned to Scotland and proposed a National Bank, also publishing a volume on his monetary theories; his ideas for a bank were rejected and he went to France where national finances following the death in 1715 of Louis XIV were in a perilous condition. Law won the support of the regent, the Duke of Orleans, for quick profit schemes, to benefit the Duke among others, and his national bank was chartered, authorized to issue paper money. By 1717 Law had acquired a trading monopoly for Louisiana and organized a Company of the West, which consolidated with the French East India company and other firms as the Company of the Indies, but popularly known as the Mississippi Company. His bank was made the Royal Bank, its money issues guaranteed by the state and Law progressed to become the leading financial figure of France, responsible even for much of the public debt. His Mississippi Scheme for the development of supposed (and illusory) resources in Louisiana won wild public support in a frenzy of speculation. Warned by earlier disappointments, the Company did not attempt to exploit the rumored but virtually non-existent mineral resources of the territory, but concentrated on agriculture, Law being given a grant on the Arkansas River, to which he

sent 200 German colonists; they quickly heard of the financial collapse of Law's scheme, abandoned their settlement and returned down the Mississippi, but were persuaded to settle about 30 miles above New Orleans at a place called subsequently the German Shore. With the inevitable collapse, Law was ruined, spending the last years of his life in Venice where he supported himself by gambling, which he had done most of his life anyway. His Mississippi Scheme, as it was popularly called, had led to the largest influx of colonists into Louisiana to that date, but it produced no other lasting benefits. In 1723 the seat of the government of Louisiana was transferred from Mobile to New Orleans and Louisiana became a royal province.

Literature abundant: Thwaites, JR, LXVII, 339-40n37; CE.

Lawson, John, frontiersman (d. Sept. 1711). B. probably in Yorkshire, England, he reached Charleston (Charles Town), South Carolina, by August 1700, and December 28 set out on a 1,000-mile journey or small expedition inland from the port through the piedmont country northward, then east again to the coast of North Carolina. He was interested in Indians and their ethnology and is among the best of early writers on the primitive people he encountered. He carefully noted the tribes and recorded what he could of their customs and linguistic affinities. Most of the peoples met with had already been decimated by smallpox and trader's rum. This was a time of rapid change among Carolina tribes, most dwindling so rapidly as to merge with such larger tribes as the Catawba and thus become ethnologically extinguished, this within a very few years. Thus Lawson's observations have much value. At Hillsboro, North Carolina, Lawson left the north-south Great Trading Path and reached the settlements in eastern North Carolina where he resided for some years. In 1705 he was an incorporator of Bath. Otherwise he took little part in local politics, but busied himself writing his book, published under an unwieldy title in 1709 at London; it bore in second and third editions (1714, 1718) its better known legend, *The History of Carolina.* Lawson had gone to England to secure its publication and while there in 1708 was named surveyor-general of North Carolina. Also at London he met Christopher de

Graffenried, a Swiss adventurer, joining him in a plan to establish a colony of Swiss and German Palatines in Carolina, centered on New Bern at the confluence of the Neuse and Trent rivers. The colony aroused suspicions and the antagonism of the Indians, including the Tuscaroras. In September 1711, Lawson invited De Graffenried to join in a scout up the Neuse River. The two were captured by Tuscaroras and taken to Catechna, a native village near the mouth of the river. Several councils were held, the first deciding upon the prisoners' release, but after a dispute between a chief and the contentious Lawson a later meeting decided both whites should be executed. De Graffenried talked his way out of the dilemma, but Lawson was unable to do so. De Graffenried said "I had heard before from several savages that the threat had been made that he was to have his throat cut with a razor... but some say he was hanged; others that he was burned. The savages kept it very secret how he was killed." Major Christopher Gale however in a letter of November 2, 1711, said he had heard the executioners stuck Lawson "full of fine small splinters of torchwood, like hogs' bristles, and set them gradually on fire." This is virtually identical with Lawson's own description of how some tribes burned their captives, which neither confirms nor invalidates the report. Since Lawson was famous, his death stirred deep emotions throughout the Carolinas. He was married and fathered children. His execution was the first hostility of the Tuscarora War which broke out September 22 and resulted ultimately in the Tuscaroras, or what was left of them, migrating northward to join their Iroquois kinsmen, the league thus becoming the Six Nations rather than the Five as it previously was known.

Douglas L. Rights, *The American Indian in North Carolina.* Winston-Salem, John F. Blair, Pubr., 1957; DAB; CE.

Lawson, Joseph, army officer (c. 1822-Jan. 30, 1881). B. in Ireland, he operated a grocery store until the Civil War when, although married and with four or five children, he entered service as a second lieutenant in the 11th Kentucky Cavalry. After the war he was commissioned a second lieutenant in the 3rd Cavalry, was promoted to first lieutenant, and served with Crook in the Powder River campaign of March 1876. He displayed great

courage at the Rosebud fight and in September 1879, distinguished himself in the action with the Ute Indians on the Milk River, Colorado. He died of paralysis at Fort Fred Steele, Wyoming. Considered quite a character, he was 5 feet tall, thin and wiry, with a straggly red beard generally stained with tobacco juice, was "known in every way a good fellow, a trusted and honest soldier," of great endurance.

J.W. Vaughn, *Indian Fights: New Facts on Seven Encounters.* Norman, Univ. of Okla. Press, 1966.

Lawton, Henry Ware, army officer (Mar. 17, 1843-Dec. 19, 1899). B. near Toledo, Ohio, he enlisted in the 9th Indiana Infantry in 1861, became a first lieutenant of the 30th Indiana, serving with Sherman's forces throughout the Civil War, rising to rank of lieutenant colonel, winning a Medal of Honor at Atlanta. He briefly studied law at Harvard, then accepted a commission in the 41st, later the 24th, black regiment of Infantry. In 1871 he was transferred to the 4th Cavalry, serving under Ranald S. Mackenzie in West Texas, mainly as a resourceful, dependable quartermaster, "habitually as energetic as it is possible for a man to be," in the words of his commanding officer. Obtaining supplies and keeping mule wagons flowing to swift-moving Cavalry units through all weather and terrain tested his abilities to the utmost, his successes justifying Mackenzie's unbounded confidence in him. It was Lawton's unpleasant duty to direct the slaughter of more than 1,000 Comanche ponies captured at Palo Duro Canyon in 1874. Lawton was present at Mackenzie's fight with the Dull Knife band of Northern Cheyennes on the north fork of the Powder River, Montana, November 25-26, 1876. One student gives Lawton much of the credit for Mackenzie's success in West Texas and Montana, characterizing him as "an administrative and logistical genius," who owed part of his ability to cope with any emergency "to his supreme contempt for army manuals and red tape." In 1886 under General Nelson Miles, Lawton headed a fruitless search of the Sierra Madre in Sonora for Geronimo and received his surrender after it had been arranged by Lieutenant Charles B. Gatewood. During the Spanish-American War he commanded the 2nd Division, V Army Corps, in actions before Santiago. He reached Manila in March 1899, and in helping put down the insurrection, as Major General of Volunteers, he was killed instantly directing troops opposite San Mateo, east of Manila. Lawton was 6 feet, 4 inches in height, of great vigor, intelligence, determination and soldierly ability, and was widely respected professionally.

DAB; Ernest Wallace, *Ranald S. Mackenzie on the Texas Frontier.* Lubbock, Tex., West Tex. Mus. Assn., 1964; *Ranald S. Mackenzie's Official Correspondence Relating to Texas, 1873-1879,* ed. by Ernest T. Wallace. Lubbock, 1968; Robert G. Carter, *On the Border With Mackenzie.* N.Y., Antiquarian Press, 1961.

Lawyer (Hol-lol-sote-tote), Nez Perce chief (c. 1794-Jan. 3, 1876). Described as "by far the most influential Indian of the Pacific Northwest during the 19th Century," Lawyer was born in Kamiah, northern Idaho, his father being Chief Twisted Hair who met Lewis and Clark in 1805 and his mother supposedly a Flathead woman. He won his soubriquet, it is said, because of his fluency in languages and his ability as a public speaker. Lawyer fought on the side of the whites in the celebrated Battle of Pierre's Hole in 1832, being wounded in the hip, an injury that never properly healed. He became friendly with many noted whites and Indians. Lawyer met Whitman and Parker in 1835, knowing enough English by that time to serve as interpreter. When the Treaty of 1855 was signed at Walla Walla, Lawyer's name, which he wrote out, headed the list of chiefs, the others signing with an "X." Lawyer worked closely with Protestant missionaries in the Northwest, teaching them Indian languages, and in other ways, although for years adamantly declining to become a confessing Christian. He defended the Protestant missionaries however against the criticism of the Roman Catholic Pierre Jean De Smet. When the priest said "it was bad for us to have wives," Lawyer retorted by asking "how the priest came into the world?" Lawyer assisted missionary Henry Spalding in translating Matthew, the first Gospel to be rendered into the Nez Perce tongue. At the age of 54 Lawyer became head chief of the Nez Perces following Ellis, appointed by Agent Elijah White in 1842 and who had died in 1848, and Richard, who was ineffective and dropped after one year; Lawyer remained head chief until 1871 when for reasons of age he resigned. He headed

2,500 Nez Perce taking part in the Walla Walla council of 1855 between 5,000 Northwest Indians on the one hand, and Governor Isaac I. Stevens on the other. When a conspiracy to slay the governor and other whites was generated by the Cayuses, Lawyer moved his lodge next to the governor's tent, thus shielding him from harm. In May 1858, when Colonel Steptoe was repulsed near present Rosalia, Washington, by hostile non-Nez Perce Indians, Lawyer brought 200 men to his rescue. The government failed to fulfill its obligations under the 1855 treaty, including payment to Lawyer of a $500 annual salary, and this caused unrest. The Nez Perces were summoned to another council at Lapwai May 15, 1863, at a time when gold miners were overrunning their lands. This council resulted in eliminating old Chief Joseph's Wallowa Valley from the Nez Perce country; several chiefs, including Joseph, refused to accede to this usurpation, the incident resulting in the fatal split of the Nez Perce into Treaty and Non-Treaty groups; Lawyer signed the treaty as did 49 other chiefs. Again the government failed to fulfill its pledges and the Nez Perce who had signed suffered from white corruption and unwillingness to abide by written promises. Lawyer wrote to President Lincoln, who was assassinated before the letter arrived, and was invited in 1868 with three other Nez Perce chiefs by President Johnson to visit Washington. On August 13 the Nez Perces signed a supplemental treaty. In 1871, by then a professing Christian, Lawyer was baptized by Spalding and on Christmas day Lawyer led his Christian followers in organizing the First Presbyterian Church of Kamiah. In his old age Lawyer became very religious. He died at his Kamiah home, described as "the noblest man in the Nez Perce tribe." Lawyer's life "stretched from before the time of Lewis and Clark . . . to the eve of the Chief Joseph uprising. Wiser than most of the other chiefs of the Oregon country, Lawyer saw that the white men with their superior skills and overwhelming numbers were bound to extend their rule over the natives. Any resistance was folly — and yet, his inherent sense of right called upon him to exert all of his powers of persuasion to obtain justice for his people. In him was a merging of the red and the white, the transition from the nomad to the farmer, and of the pagan to the Christian."

Clifford M. Drury, "I, the Lawyer: Head Chief of

the Nez Perce." N.Y. Corral, *Westerners Brand Book,* vol. 7, No. 1 (May 1960); Drury, *Chief Lawyer of the Nez Perce Indians.* Glendale, Calif., Arthur H. Clark Co., 1979.

Lay, William Ellsworth (Elza Lay, William H. McGinnis), desperado (Nov. 25, 1868 - Nov. 10, 1934). B. in Ohio, raised in Ohio and Iowa, he became one of the most noted Boston), he became one of the most noted members of the so-called Wild Bunch, and the gentleman brains of some of their most daring escapades. His family moved to Wray, Colorado, when he was small, Elza becoming a cowboy and minor rustler. His first holdup was of a peddler in Brown's Hole, Colorado, about 1884. He ran a saloon briefly near Fort Du Chesne, Uintah County, Utah, and reportedly tried counterfeiting, married and fathered two daughters. With George LeRoy Parker (Butch Cassidy) and others, "Robbers' Roost" was established southwest of Green River, Utah. On August 13, 1896, Lay, Cassidy and Bob Meeks held up the bank at Montpelier, Wyoming. Lay became Cassidy's chief lieutenant and was with him April 21, 1897, at Castle Gate, Utah, for a coal mine payroll holdup. Lay participated in the June 2, 1899, train robbery near Wilcox, Wyoming. In a resulting pursuit Sheriff Josiah Hazen of Converse County, Wyoming, was wounded mortally. With Cassidy and Harvey Logan Lay fled south through Brown's Hole, Robbers' Roost, into Arizona and thence to Alma, New Mexico, where they went to work for the WS Ranch, remaining some time, Lay under the name William H. McGinnis. Here he met Sam Ketchum, an outlaw also from Utah, and on July 11, 1899, they held up a Colorado and Southern Railway train near Folsom, New Mexico, with William Carver and Bruce Weaver. A posse located the bandits in a Turkey Canyon cave near Cimarron, New Mexico, and on July 16 a gunbattle erupted, resulting in death or mortal wounds for two possemen, lesser wounds for others, and, among the desperadoes, Ketchum was mortally wounded and Lay (or McGinnis) shot through chest and shoulder. He escaped but was arrested in Eddy County, New Mexico, August 16, tried and on October 10, 1899, sentenced to life imprisonment. He was released January 10, 1906, officially, although actually earlier, went south of the border and dug up his share

of the 1899 train loot, supposed to be $58,000. Afterwards, known sometimes as McGinnis instead of Lay, he married again and had a varied, but prosperous and lawful career. He died at Los Angeles and is buried in Forest Lawn Memorial Park cemetery.

Jeff Burton, "Suddenly in a Secluded and Rugged Place." *Brand Book,* English Westerners' Soc., Vol. XIV, Nos. 178, 180 (Apr., July 1972); Pearl Baker, *The Wild Bunch at Robbers Roost.* Los Angeles, Westernlore Press, 1965; Charles Kelly, *The Outlaw Trail: The Story of Butch Cassidy and the "Wild Bunch."* N.Y., Bonanza Books, 1959.

Lazelle, Henry Martyn, army officer (Sept. 8, 1832-July 21, 1917). B. at Enfield, Massachusetts, he was graduated from West Point in 1855 and commissioned a second lieutenant in the 8th Infantry. He performed frontier service against Indians from 1857-59, and was wounded through the lungs by a hostile in 1859. At the outset of the Civil War he was a first lieutenant, becoming captain June 11, 1861; he became colonel of the 16th New York Cavalry in 1863, resigning from the Volunteers the following year. Lazelle was commissioned major of the 1st U.S. Infantry in 1874 and saw service under Miles in Montana, sweeping up scattered hostiles after the Custer defeat. Commanding a mixed organization of ten companies he pursued the Sioux, Lame Deer's band in the summer of 1877, his advance striking the hostiles at Sentinel Buttes July 9, dispersing the enemy. Lazelle became lieutenant colonel of the 23rd Infantry in 1882 and colonel of the 18th Infantry in 1889, retiring November 26, 1894. He was promoted to Brigadier General in retirement. Lazelle was author of *One Law in Nature* (1872), and *Matter, Force and Spirit* (1895).

Powell; Heitman; EHI.

Lean Bear (Starving Bear, Awon-i-nahku), Cheyenne chief (1813-May 16, 1864). A prominent warrior and chief, Lean Bear first comes into view in 1851 at Fort Atkinson, Ford County, Kansas, when he sought to examine a ring on the hand of an officer's wife and was attacked by her husband and whipped out of camp; Lean Bear harangued his men and urged them to attack the post, but was quieted. In 1858 he captured Yellow Nose and his mother, a Ute woman; she escaped but Yellow Nose became "one of the most famous of Cheyenne warriors." In 1861 Lean Bear,

Black Kettle and others signed the Fort Wise (Fort Lyon) Treaty, later repudiated by some of the signatories as a "swindle." In March 1863 he and other chiefs visited Washington, D.C., met with Lincoln and, wishing to speak was "so nervous (at meeting Lincoln, the Great White Father) that he said he would like to have a chair to sit on while he talked," his remarks summarized in Hoig (1874). May 16, 1864, Lean Bear and another leading Cheyenne, Star, rode out from their camp on the Smoky Hill River, Kansas, to greet Lieutenant George S. Eayre of the Colorado Volunteers, unaware that Eayre was on a single-minded, Indian-killing expedition. Lean Bear wore on his chest the peace medal Lincoln had given him and bore the papers indicating he was no enemy of the whites. But while at a distance of 20 to 30 yards, Eayre gave the order to fire and both Indians were murdered; other Cheyennes chased Eayre and his command back to Fort Larned, killing four and wounding others although Black Kettle tried to stop the pursuit. The incident led to much central Plains hostility on the part of the aroused Indians.

George E. Hyde, *Life of George Bent,* Norman, Univ. of Okla. Press, 1968; George Bird Grinnell, *The Fighting Cheyennes.* Norman, 1956; Stan Hoig, *The Sand Creek Massacre.* Norman, 1961; Hoig, *The Western Odyssey of John Simpson Smith,* Glendale, Calif., Arthur H. Clark Co., 1974.

Lean Elk: *see* Poker Joe

Leas, J(ulius) Edwin, army officer (fl. 1867-1869). B. in Ohio, he was commissioned from Indiana a second lieutenant in the 5th Cavalry August 17, 1867, in April 1869 was assigned to frontier duty, took part in the Republican River expedition, the fights at Rock Creek and Summit Springs, resigned August 13, 1869, "and returned to civilian pursuits."

Price, *Fifth Cavalry.*

Leatherlips, Huron (Wyandot) chief (c. 1732-summer 1810). Leatherlips, whose Indian name was Shateyyaronyah was a chief by August 3, 1795, when he signed the Treaty of Greenville, Ohio, regarded as of honorable character and a firm friend of the whites. This latter attitude so inflamed Tecumseh that the great chief ordered Leatherlips executed on the grounds that he was a "wizard," and thus

prone to invoking evil upon his fellows. Tecumseh assigned Roundhead, another Huron chief to carry out the execution and to Leatherlips' brother the task of informing the fated man of his impending execution, the announcement consisting of a piece of birchbark with a tomahawk sketched upon it. The sentence was carried out on the Scioto River, about 14 miles north of the present Columbus, witnesses including a number of white men including a justice of the peace who sought to have the sentence set aside but without success. Leatherlips was tomahawked while kneeling beside his grave, after chanting his death song. The Wyandot Club of Columbus in 1888 erected a granite monument to Leatherlips in a park surrounded by a stone wall at the site of his execution.

Hodge, HAI.

Leaton, Ben(jamin), frontiersman (d. pre-Aug. 15, 1851). He was b. in either Amelia County, Virginia, or Nelson County, Kentucky, in all probability; family tradition suggests either and there were Leaton families in both, though the name is not common. Ben is not mentioned in the 1790 Census, and probably was born between 1800-1810. He was in the southwest at least as early as 1837, for he was a principal with John James (Juan) Johnson in the treacherous April 22 massacre that year in southern New Mexico of the Mimbres leader, Juan José Compá, two other chiefs and 18 additional Apaches for scalp money; according to McGaw, Leaton and Johnson were the instigators, and together did away with Juan José, although Wilson calls the colleague of Johnson "Gleason," and Ralph Smith thinks that Wilson's Gleason might have been James Glenn. McGaw, however, is most positive and has published Johnson's official report listing Leaton, who therefore must be accepted as the individual concerned. Leaton was believed by McGaw to have been associated with Kirker in further scalp-hunting in 1839, since his later colleague, John W. Spencer, was involved. Leaton has been called a Mexican War veteran; if true, he may have served with Doniphan's column from New Mexico as far as Chihuahua City, as did Kirker. Muster rolls of the Doniphan expedition do not list Leaton — nor Larkin Landrum, Spencer or John W. Burgess, his associates who also were said to have served; they may have accompanied Doniphan in the so-called Traders' Battalion, for which no muster roll exists. In 1848 Leaton bought an adobe mission-presidio 4.1 miles below the present site of Presidio, Texas, on the Rio Grande. The structure probably was built in 1684 as El Apostol Santiago, and re-established in 1773 as El Fortin de San José. Leaton's bill of sale from Juan Bustillos for the place was dated August 19, 1848, but he had been there earlier, perhaps as early as 1846. This layout became known as Fort Leaton and under Ben's initiative became the largest adobe structure in Texas, it is said, with some 40 rooms, as large as 30 by 40 feet and with ceilings 20 feet high; Leaton acquired in all 3,840 acres. Spencer and perhaps Burgess, may have been associated with him at one time or another in its ownership/ management. The place soon became a favorite stopping point for travelers, includ-ing an occasional army surveying or other expedition. In 1850, brevet Major Jefferson Van Horne, 3rd Infantry, stationed at El Paso, Chihuahua Governor Angel Trías Álvarez and a Mexican official, Emilio Laughberg, of the present Juarez, exchanged correspondence, the Mexicans accusing Leaton of purchasing from raiding Indians loot stolen from Mexican ranches, and supplying the hostiles with arms, powder and lead. Brevet Major General George Mercer Brooke, charged with defense of the Rio Grande frontier, alleged in his turn that the U.S. had grave cause for complaint with Chihuahua for hiring Americans to war on the Indians not only in Mexico, but in the Big Bend area; thus the case was not too clear from any viewpoint. Trías then replied that Leaton had proven lawless and "vicious," Leaton charged that the troubles had commenced with the Mexicans hiring scalp hunter Joel Glanton and his activities (and was considerably furthered by the activities of Leaton, Kirker and Johnson, but he did not mention that); Leaton claimed that rather than incite trouble, he had kept the peace and prevented important depredations on occa-sion, as perhaps he had. The legend persists in the Presidio country that Leaton once persuaded a number of Apaches to visit him at Fort Leaton and assassinated them with a concealed cannon; this event was no doubt a recital of the Johnson massacre in southern New Mexico, transmuted in the course of numerous retellings to Texas, and there is no good evidence that it or anything similar ever took place at Fort Leaton. Leaton died "mysteriously," perhaps at San Antonio, Texas, leaving his widow $8,000 in debt, it is said. His will, filed August 15, 1851, listed as beneficiary Juana Pedraza (b. 1812), his widow, and three children: Joe, Elizabeth and Bill Shepard Leaton. Juana later married Edward Hall, a Scotsman (b. c. 1821), an interpreter and customs house official. A feud reportedly developed between Hall and Burgess; the latter had Hall killed. Burgess, on Christmas Day 1875, was killed at Fort Davis by Bill Leaton, and Bill was killed in 1878 in a fight with the police chief at Ojinaga, Mexico, across the Rio Grande from Presidio. Joe Leaton reportedly died in the California gold fields. Leaton descendants of Texas today are from Elizabeth.

Carlysle Graham Raht, *The Romance of Davis Mountains and Big Bend Country*. El Paso, Rahtbooks Co., 1919; William Cochrane McGaw, *Savage Scene: Life and Times of James Kirker*. N.Y., Hastings House, 1972; Leavitt Corning Jr., *Baronial Forts of the Big Bend: Ben Leaton, Milton Faver and Their Private Forts in Presidio County*. San Antonio, Tex., Trinity Univ. Press, 1967; Joe A. Gibson, *Forts and Treasure Trails of West Texas*. San Angelo, Tex., Educator Books, 1969; Oscar Williams.

Leavenworth, Henry, army officer (Dec. 10, 1783-July 21, 1834). B. at New Haven, Connecticut, son of a Revolutionary War colonel, young Leavenworth became captain of the 25th Infantry April 25, 1812, major in the 9th Infantry, August 15, 1813, and won brevets for distinguished services at Chippewa and Fort Niagara. As a lieutenant colonel of the 5th Infantry in 1819 he established Fort Snelling at the junction of the Minnesota and Mississippi rivers. October 1, 1821, he was transferred to the 6th Infantry and became commandant at Fort Atkinson, Nebraska, near Council Bluffs. He left Atkinson June 22, 1823, for the Arikara villages on the upper Missouri, where Ashley's trappers had been defeated. Leavenworth called his five infantry companies the "Missouri Legion," being supported by various frontiersmen and Sioux irregulars. Although what artillery was available was used against the rudely barricaded village the results were inconclu-sive, with from 30 to 50 Indians killed, including noncombatants, and Leavenworth accepting the Arikara offer of a truce, after which they escaped unpursued. He was soundly criticized for his lack of drive and the bad impression made upon warlike Indians by his apparent indecision and failure to push the affair, but he may have been justified. One critic calls him a "brave and energetic officer," which his record would seem to bear out. With a brevet of Brigadier General, he was assigned to Green Bay, Wisconsin, then Jefferson Barracks, St. Louis, and in 1827 built Cantonment (subsequently Fort) Leavenworth. Early in 1834 he was in command of the entire southwestern frontier, instructed to negotiate peace among warring tribes. He set out from Fort Gibson on June 15, but in July was struck by a "bilious fever," and died at Camp Smith on the Washita. His body eventually was reburied at Fort Leavenworth. He was "a man of broad and varied culture," influential in improving standards in the young army, and was noted for his "clearness of judgment and energy in action."

DAB; Dale Morgan, *Jedediah Smith and the Opening of the West.* N.Y., Bobbs-Merrill Co., 1953.

Leavenworth, Jesse Henry, Indian agent (Mar. 29, 1807-Mar. 12, 1885). The son of Brigadier General Henry Leavenworth for whom Fort Leavenworth is named, Jesse was b. at Danville, Vermont, and said that in company with his father he had early become "well acquainted with Indian life and character on the border." He went to West Point and was commissioned a second lieutenant of the 4th Infantry July 1, 1830. He transferred to the 2nd Infantry in 1831 but resigned his commission October 31, 1836, and for two decades practiced civil engineering at Chicago. Leavenworth went to Colorado in 1860. In February 1862 he was authorized to raise six companies of volunteer infantry which largely constituted the 2nd Colorado Infantry of which he became colonel. In August the regiment was ordered to Fort Lyon, Colorado, and in April 1863 six companies were marched to Fort Leavenworth, Kansas. In June Leavenworth was placed in command of all troops on the Santa Fe Trail, with headquarters at Fort Larned, Kansas and "the Indians and the Confederates together gave him plenty of employment." In October 1863 Leavenworth was dishonorably discharged for enlisting a unit without proper

authority, but the dismissal later was changed to honorable. In 1864 he was named agent for the Kiowas, Comanches and Plains Apaches, taking over the agency at Fort Larned in October. The Chivington massacre at Sand Creek, Colorado, on November 29, 1864 provoked hostilities throughout the Plains, making it very difficult for Leavenworth even to contact his Indians, although eventually he did so through intermediaries. He was fortunate during much of his time as agent in having as guide and interpreter Jesse Chisholm who had been with Henry Leavenworth on the 1834 Comanche expedition on which the elder Leavenworth had died. Chisholm, reported Jesse Leavenworth "has been with these Indians almost all the time since. He has been upon that frontier; he has traded with them; he speaks their language perfectly... and has helped me more since (1864) than anyone else in keeping them quiet and protecting them. His information in regard to them is perfect and complete, and I get most of my information from him." Leavenworth testified at the Sand Creek investigative inquiry, although he had no direct connection with the Indians involved nor with the Chivington military effort, nor was he at the scene. He was asked merely for background information on the tribes involved in related or subsequent activities and under his purview as agent. Leavenworth's testimony shows him to be well-informed and intelligent in his understanding of wild Indians and their problems. Unfortunately his views were not implemented by others. He resigned in May 1868 and returned to his family at Milwaukee, where he lived until his death.

Robert M. Utley, *Life in Custer's Cavalry.* New Haven, Yale Univ. Press, 1977; Bancroft, *Nevada, Colorado & Wyoming; The Sand Creek Massacre;* Carolyn Thomas Foreman, "Col. Jesse Henry Leavenworth." *Chronicles of Okla.,* Vol. XIII, No. 1, Sec. II (Mar. 1935), 14-29.

Leavitt, Dudley, Mormon pioneer (Aug. 31, 1830-Aug. 15, 1908). B. at Hatley, Canada, across the border from Vermont, his parents became Mormon converts and moved the family in 1835 to Kirtland, Ohio, and in 1841 to Nauvoo, Illinois. In 1846 Dudley Leavitt left for Council Bluffs, Iowa, and in 1850 reached Utah. He remained in the Salt Lake Valley until 1855 when he went to southern

Utah with Jacob Hamblin, becoming a pioneer in the Santa Clara, Utah, country and in developing southern Utah communities. "We can only wonder as to Dudley's relation" to the Mountain Meadows massacre, wrote his granddaughter, Juanita Brooks. Lee's confessions put Leavitt at the scene of the tragedy; Leavitt never discussed the affair, Brooks reported, except once when he said, perhaps referring to the massacre, "I thank God that these old hands (of mine) have never been stained by human blood." He and Samuel Knight were sent by Hamblin, president of the Indian mission, to somehow maneuver Paiute Indians out of attacking a subsequent wagon train bound for California, the Duke party. The Indians had swept off 300 of the emigrants' cattle at the crossing of the Muddy, or lower Virgin River; the two missionaries recovered 100 head at the risk of their lives and turned them back to the travelers. Leavitt became first counselor to Hamblin in his Indian work. Leavitt married a number of wives and, with other polygamists, spent about ten years hiding from federal officers charged with putting down the practice, but the inference is that he never abandoned the several families. He died near Mesquite, Nevada.

Juanita Brooks, *Dudley Leavitt, Pioneer to Southern Utah*. St. George, Utah, p.p., 1942; Brooks, *The Mountain Meadows Massacre*. Norman, Univ. of Okla. Press, 1966.

Le Bailleur, sea pilot (fl. 1613). Le Bailleur was pilot for La Saussaye's expedition to found a French colony at Saint Sauveur, Mt. Desert Island, Maine; he escaped the capture of the place by the English under Samuel Argall, and later attempted to aid the Jesuit priest Pierre Biard although himself a Huguenot. Le Bailleur apparently succeeded in making his way back to France with La Saussaye or in some other way.

Thwaites, JR, I-IV.

Lebec, Peter, presumed trapper (d. Oct. 17, 1837). Nothing is known of his origin, birth or life except for his death which, according to one of the "briefest biographies on record," was caused by a grizzly bear. This occurred at the site of the later Fort Tejon, California. Lebec was buried beneath an oak on which was carved: "IHS Peter Lebeck killed by a X bear October 17, 1837." The bones were

disinterred in 1890, appearing to be those of a man about 6 feet tall, then reburied on the same site which now is marked by a stone; the carving from the tree is at the Kern County Museum, Bakersfield, California. Various stories are circulated of Lebec's origins, but all are fanciful and unsupported; research has turned up nothing.

Raymund F. Wood, *The Life and Death of Peter Lebec*. Fresno, Calif., Acad. Library Guild, 1954.

LeBlanc, William, frontiersman (1804-Jan. 1, 1872). B, in Canada, he reached New Mexico in the 1820s, becoming a trapper, then a trader at Buzzards' Roost, near Wetmore, Colorado. LeBlanc worked for Bent and St. Vrain, participated in the Santa Fe trade, escaped the Turley's Mill massacre in 1847 and was on the jury that condemned the insurrectionists. He died near Del Norte, Colorado.

Janet Lecompte article, MM, Vol. V.

Lebo, Thomas Coverly, army officer (Nov. 17, 1842-Feb. 23, 1910). B. at Potters Mills, Pennsylvania, he was commissioned in the 11th Pennsylvania Infantry in 1861, but transferred to the 1st Pennsylvania Cavalry, becoming a captain by 1865 and having twice been wounded. Lebo joined the 10th Cavalry in 1867 as a first lieutenant and served until 1894 on the frontier, being three times mentioned in General Orders "for good judgment, energy and conspicuous gallantry in action with Indians." He operated against Victorio in 1880 under Grierson in West Texas, and against Geronimo in Old Mexico in 1886. As major of the 6th Cavalry from 1893, he commanded that regiment at San Juan Hill, Cuba. Lebo became lieutenant colonel of the 1st Cavalry in 1899 and colonel of the 14th Cavalry in 1901. He was made a Brigadier General in 1905. After retirement he lived at Albuquerque, New Mexico, and died at Chicago.

Heitman; *Who Was Who;* information from David Perry Perrine; Jack C. Gale, "Lebo in Pursuit." *Jour. of Ariz. Hist.,* Vol. 21, No. 1 (Spring 1980), 11-24.

Le Boesme, Louis, Jesuit brother (Aug. 25, 1632-1709). B. at Saintes, Toulouse province, France, he was brought to Canada as a child and in 1648 went to the Huron mission where he remained two years. He then returned to France, entered the Society of Jesus and after his first vows went back to Canada in 1656, where it was reported he was wounded by Iroquois. He volunteered for duty in the Ottawa country upon his recovery. He went to the Onondaga Mission in 1657 and presumably was among the 60 Frenchmen who escaped an Iroquois plot to murder them, and regained the French settlements in March 1658. He apparently returned to France at some time, for he came back to Canada in September of 1663. After service in the Saguenay county, he was sent to the mission among the Illinois, where he was in 1683.

Thwaites, JR, XLII, 225,263; XLIV, 71; LXII, 215; LXXI, 149, 399n38.

Le Boullenger, Jean Antoine (Baptiste), Jesuit missionary (July 22, 1685-Nov. 4, 1740). B. at Rouen, France, he became a Jesuit and reached Canada in 1716. He did most of his missionary work, it is believed, in the Illinois country, being stationed usually at Kaskaskia, where he died.

Thwaites, JR, LXVIII, 330n28, LXXI, 165.

LeClaire, Antoine, interpreter, pioneer (Dec. 15, 1797-Sept. 25, 1861). B. at St Joseph, Michigan, of a French-Canadian father and a Potawatomi mother, he was sponsored by William Clark, learning English and a dozen or more Indian tongues; in 1818 he was employed at Fort Armstrong, Illinois, as an interpreter. On November 20, 1820, he married Margaret LePage at Portage des Sioux. LeClaire served as interpreter through the Black Hawk War and for many years, becoming "well known to every Indian in the area," and signed as interpreter 11 treaties. In the important September 1832 pact at the close of the Black Hawk War, the Indians insisted that he be given two sections of land for his devoted service. General Winfield Scott agreed because "we believe that he has been faithful to both sides, to the Americans as well as to the Sac and Fox nation." LeClaire prospered in land and trading enterprises, in later life was worth $500,000, and was a founder of Davenport, Iowa. In frontier history he is best known for Black Hawk's autobiography, a narrative purportedly dictated by the Indian, translated by LeClaire, and put into book form by its editor, John P. Patterson; there have been differences of opinion regarding the validity of the work, but Jackson concluded that it "is basically a tale told by an Indian from an Indian point of view." LeClaire reportedly weighed 385 pounds in 1844 but this "did not seem to hinder his movement about the country on horseback or in carriages." He died at Davenport.

Donald Jackson, ed., *Ma-ka-tai-me-she-kia-kiak: Black Hawk: An Autobiography.* Urbana, Univ. of Ill. Press, 1955; Charles Snyder, "Antoine LeClaire, First Proprietor of Davenport." *Annals of Iowa,* Third Ser., Vol. 23 (1941-1942), 79-117.

Le Clercq, Maximus, Recollet missionary (d. 1689). B. probably in France, he became a Recollet priest and arrived in Canada before 1684; he was a brother or cousin of Chrestien Le Clercq, also a Recollet missionary in New France. Maximus and a cousin, Zénobe Membré, another Recollet, accompanied La Salle on his 1684 expedition to the Gulf coast and were massacred at Fort St. Louis in the Illinois country in 1689.

Thwaites, JR, LXII, 272n9;DCB, I, 438.

Ledbetter, James F. (Bud), lawman (Dec. 15, 1852-July 8, 1937). B. at Madison, Arkansas, he became one of the great lawmen of the Southwest. He served as deputy sheriff of Johnson County, Arkansas, for 10 years, removed to Indian Territory July 27, 1894, and after a year as officer for an express company, was appointed a deputy U.S. marshal. He was elected chief of police of Muskogee, Oklahoma, in 1908-10, and lived at Muskogee for the remainder of his life. The nemesis of numerous desperadoes and outlaws, Ledbetter singlehandedly captured four members of the Jennings gang and once joked that it took him "about half an hour to make a preacher out of Al Jennings." Ledbetter was generally taciturn regarding his own countless exploits. "I was only a green country boy," he recalled, however, when he was 80. "But they always wanted me in on every case. I wasn't afraid, for one thing. Maybe I should have been. But I never got hurt much. As I look back on it now, I don't see how I could have kept from being killed if just by accident. But I wasn't. I always got through to come back on the next case. Some of those 'cases' were pretty bad." His death occurred at Muskogee it is believed.

Tulsa Daily World, May 21, 1933; Okla. Hist. Soc. Archives.

Lederer, John, explorer (c. 1644-post 1675). From Hamburg, Lederer reached Virginia at

26 and became the first European to explore the Piedmont and Blue Ridge Mountains and leave a record of his discoveries. "He helped open the great Indian trading Path toward the southwest for the fur traders...and he gave a valuable commentary on the Indian tribes (he) encountered." Lederer was studious, interested in medicine, the Indians and natural resources and he sought a pass or way through the Appalachians to the virtually unexplored country beyond. On his initial expedition he left March 9, 1670 and went northwest along the Pamunkey River, reaching the Blue Ridge northwest of present Charlottesville, Virginia, but was unsuccessful in finding a pass. His second and more extended expedition left May 20, 1670 and took him southwest into the Carolinas, perhaps across the border into South Carolina near the Catawba River. He learned that the mountains diminished to the southwest, and he might have rounded them except that he feared the Spaniards and withdrew. On a third expedition commenced August 20, 1670, he sought a pass to the northwest called Zynodoa by the Indians, which Cumming believed "the first mention of Shenandoah" and might have referred to the gap at Harper's Ferry. Again he failed to discover a route through the mountains. Lederer shortly left Virginia "under conditions obscure and clouded," but which may have to do with circumstances and personalities with which he had come to cross-purposes. He went to Maryland, was made a citizen, given a license to trade with Indians, but political circumstances altered in Maryland and again Lederer was left without an effective patron. He went in 1674 to Connecticut where he was befriended by John Winthrop Jr., the governor, but within a year had returned to Hamburg, promising to come back to America shortly. No further record of him has been found.

The Discoveries of John Lederer with Unpublished Letters...to Governor John Winthrop, Jr...., ed. by William P. Cumming. Charlottesville, Univ. of Va. Press, 1958; DAB.

Ledesma, Pedro de, military officer (c. 1518-c. 1580). B. at Zamora in Spain he reached Mexico in 1537. He joined the Coronado expedition in 1540 and went with it to Arizona and New Mexico. He had a role in quelling the Tiguex War on the Rio Grande River in New Mexico and went with Coronado to Quivira, in central Kansas. After the expedition he testified at Mexico City on behalf of Coronado during the lengthy investigation that resulted in clearing the leader of charges of mismanagement. Ledesma became an encomendero, settled on lands never before conquered and became alcalde mayor for various communities. In 1561 and 1563 he sent communications to the Crown in Spain suggesting means by which Mexico's economic situation might be bettered. He introduced new crops to cultivation, including the olive and worked toward the production of grapes for manufacture of wine. Ledesma promoted improvements in the production and marketing of livestock and animal products. He was a man of much vision and a positive influence in the ecomomy of Mexico.

Herbert Eugene Bolton, *Coronado: Knight of Pueblos and Plains.* Albuquerque, Univ. of New Mex. Press, 1964; *Porrua;* George P. Hammond, Agapito Rey, *Narratives of the Coronado Expedition.* Albuquerque, 1940.

Ledford, John E. (Jack), frontiersman (1843-Feb. 28, 1871). b. in North Carolina, he was said to have been a Quantrill guerilla, and served subsequently as a U.S. army scout with Jack Bridges, but resigned in April 1869, at Fort Dodge, Kansas. He was sometimes arrested on minor charges, but never convicted. He was accused of associating with rustlers involved in the theft of army mules April 5, 1870, at Bluff Creek, Indian Territory. In November 1870, he ran for sheriff at Wichita, Kansas, but did not win the office. December 22 he married. February 28, 1871, his hotel was surrounded by 5th Infantrymen under Second Lieutenant C.E. Hargous, led by Jack Bridges and Lee Stuart, a scout, apparently in pursuance of the mule-theft charge. Bridges was wounded, Ledford killed, but there are controversial aspects to the affair.

Joseph G. Rosa, *The Gunfighter: Man or Myth?* Norman, Univ. of Okla. Press, 1969.

Ledoux, Abraham, frontiersman (1786-c. 1842). B. in Canada, he reached St. Louis with his brother, Antoine, in 1812, joining fur trader Manuel Lisa for a season, then settling among the Pawnees. He joined the Long expedition as hunter and farrier. He married temporarily a Pawnee woman, but left the tribe about 1825, reaching Taos where in 1826 he married the daughter of a wealthy family by whom he had a son, José Julian

Ledoux, for whom the town of Ledoux, New Mexico, is named. Abraham died at Taos.

Janet Lecompte article, MM, Vol. III.

Ledoux, Antoine, frontiersman (1779-Nov. 1859). B. in Canada, he reached Missouri by 1812, joining Manuel Lisa for the Missouri River trade, spending then about 10 years in the western Plains, roaming as far as Taos. He lived frequently with the Pawnees and married a Pawnee woman; being wounded by a Pawnee in 1824, he quitted the tribe, reaching Taos in 1825 and spending the reminder of his life in the New Mexico area. He was buried at Mora, New Mexico.

Janet Lecompte article, MM, Vol. III.

LeDuc, Maurice, trapper (1808-1880). B. in Canada, he may have reached St. Louis with his father in 1820, and New Mexico a few years later, or perhaps that was LeDuc senior, and LeDuc junior joined Ashley; the two are not clearly differentiated until both were listed by the American Fur Company about 1832. The elder LeDuc reportedly was killed by a Paiute in the Great Basin. LeDuc junior continued as a "small, bad-tempered, shiftless ex-trapper who never learned to settle down" the rest of his life. He appears in Ruxton's *Life in the Far West,* and spent his time largely in eastern Colorado and New Mexico. He died at Lucien Maxwell's place on the Cimarron in New Mexico perhaps, or elsewhere in the region.

Janet Lecompte article, MM, Vol. VI.

Ledyard, John, explorer (1751-Jan. 10, 1789). B. at Groton, Connecticut, he was well-educated, studied law and intended to become a missionary to the Indians but instead went to sea; he joined a British regiment at Gibraltar, but was returned to his ship and eventually reached London where he met Captain James Cook, then preparing his third voyage of exploration. Ledyard shipped with Cook as a corporal of marines, leaving London July 12, 1766. Cook was killed in the Hawaiian Islands in 1779 and Ledyard with the other members of the expedition returned to London late in 1780. Ledyard refused to serve against his countrymen in the American Revolution and afterward returned to Connecticut. He was interested by his visit to Nootka Sound in a voyage of exploration to the northwest coast of America, and in Paris

met Jefferson, then U.S. minister, who was intrigued by Ledyard's career and pretensions. He found Ledyard "panting for some new enterprise. His immediate object at Paris was to engage a mercantile company in the fur trade..., in which, however, he failed. I then proposed to him to go by land to Kamtschatka, cross in some of the Russian vessels to Nootka Sound, fall down into the latitude of the Missouri, and penetrate to and through that to the United States. He eagerly seized the idea, and only asked to be assured of the permission of the Russian Government." Jefferson believed he had secured the permission of the Empress Catherine II for the crossing of Siberia. Ledyard reached St. Petersburg and arrived within 200 miles of Kamchatka where he wintered at Irkutsk, but the Tsarina had changed her mind, Ledyard was arrested, taken by carriage night and day without stopping to Poland, where he was put out, and returned to Paris. He then cast about for some new endeavor and after meeting with Sir Joseph Banks of London, determined to explore the sources of the Niger, an Africa river. En route to Cairo he visited Jefferson again at Paris, telling of his eventual plans to journey from Kentucky to the Pacific, but first must come Africa. At Cairo he made arrangements for his travels into the interior, but an illness caused by a violent rage brought his death and, wrote Jefferson, "thus failed the first attempt to explore the western part of our northern continent." Ledyard was tall, rangy and powerful in build; he was attractive, a visionary, and Jefferson considered him a genius. His dream of opening the Pacific Northwest which "brought him only discouragement and disaster came true for other men in less than a generation after his death."

CE; DAB; *History of the Expedition Under the Command of Lewis and Clark,* ed. by Elliott Coues. N.Y., Dover Pubns., 1965.

Lee, A. Mitchell, desperado (c. 1860-Mar. 11, 1884). A southwestern New Mexico cowboy, supposedly with a checkered past but good natured when not lawless and a cool customer, Lee killed engineer Theophilus Webster in a Southern Pacific train holdup at Gage, New Mexico, November 24, 1883, and was captured in January 1884, at Horse Springs, New Mexico. On March 10, he, Kit Joy who had participated in the robbery, and others broke jail at Silver City, New Mexico.

Lee, supposedly mortally wounded, and Frank Taggart, another train robber, were captured and lynched.

This is Silver City, New Mexico, 1882 1883 1884. Silver City, N.M., Enterprise, 1963.

Lee, Clell Forest, lion hunter (Apr. 15, 1905-Aug. 7, 1981). Lee was raised at Paradise, Arizona, on the north side of the Chiricahua Mountains and after graduation from high school became a government hunter with the U.S. Biological Service in New Mexico. During the early 1920s Lee visited the Blue River country in east central Arizona and eventually established a stock ranch there, working it the remainder of his life—when he was not off lion hunting. From 1938 until 1960 he and his brothers, Ernest and Dale guided hunters and hunted on their own in Mexico, Central and South America. During World War II Clell Lee was a deputy sheriff at Fry (now Sierra Vista), Arizona. The Lees attained wide renown as hunters of mountain lion, jaguar and bear, using a strain of hound called blue tick, developed by their father. Clell died at Blue and was buried there, being survived by his brother, Dale. Most knowledgeable people rated Clell Lee second only to Ben Lilly as a big game hunter of the southwest.

Arizona Daily Star, Aug. 21, 1981; information from Connie Shepperd, Alamagordo, New Mex., cousin of Lee.

Lee, James, pioneer (Mar. 17, 1833-Mar. 11, 1884). B. at Londonderry, Ulster, Ireland, he migrated to Canada as a youth and went to Missouri. In 1857 he went to Arizona with the Overland Mail Company as a hostler. When the stage line was discontinued in 1861, Lee turned to wagon freighting and mining; he went to Sonora early in the Civil War but returned to Tucson in 1864; the next year he declined an appointment from Governor Goodwin to recruit within Pima County Company D of the 1st Arizona Infantry to serve against Indians. He was naturalized February 14, 1870. Lee was involved at various times in Indian skirmishing, in mining activities and operated a flour mill at Tucson. In April 1871 with five other Anglos, around 50 Mexicans and nearly 100 Papagoes he took part in the Camp Grant Massacre in which around 100 Apaches, mostly women and children, were slain. With the others he was acquitted by a Tucson jury in December. Lee in 1874 ran as independent candidate for sheriff of Pima County and was beaten by one vote. He died of pnuemonia.

Hayden file, Ariz. Hist. Soc.; Don Schellie, *Vast Domain of Blood.* Los Angeles, Westernlore Press, 1968.

Lee, Jason, missionary, pioneer (June 28, 1803-Mar. 12, 1845). B. at Stanstead, Quebec, he was converted at 22 and studied for the ministry. He served eastern Methodist parishes before his ordination which occurred in 1832. The next year Lee was chosen head of a mission to the Flathead Indians of the far northwest, and accompanied by a nephew and three lay assistants he joined Nathaniel J. Wyeth's second expedition, arriving at Fort Vancouver, Washington, September 15, 1834. The Flathead mission project was abandoned and the missionaries settled in the Willamette Valley, ten miles northwest of present Salem, Oregon. In 1839 Lee took to Oregon a reinforcement party of about 75, arriving in 1840. However he gradually abandoned missionary work for development of the fledgling colony, was replaced as head of the mission, returned to the east where he died. His remains were reinterred at Salem in 1906. Jason Lee was a controversial character, "a good man, but he made mistakes of judgment," in the view of Clifford M. Drury, leading historian of Protestant missionaries and missions of the Northwest. Lee married twice, both mates predeceasing him. He left a daughter.

DAB; information from Clifford M. Drury.

Lee, Jefferson Harrison, frontiersman (c. 1836-Apr. 7, 1915). B. in Ohio, he came to Arizona with his Indiana wife from Colorado in 1864 and settled at what he named the American Ranch in the Williamson Valley northwest of Prescott, engaging in cattle raising and farming. The locality was infested with Yavapais Indians, driven to hostility by white ingressions and Lee spent much time fighting Indians and protecting his property. He was credited by contemporaries with "making more 'good Injuns' than any other man who lived in the County." For five years he never journeyed from his home to Prescott except by night when Indians were loath to move about; in his fields he was ambushed several times, but "in each case he was the victor in a sharp fight." At age 70 he went to Alaska seeking gold, remained away for two years until fire destroyed his Alaskan property when he returned to Arizona, where he died. He fathered five sons and two daughters.

Ariz. Hist. Soc., Hayden collection.

Lee, Jesse Matlock, army officer (Jan. 2, 1843-Mar. 26, 1926). B. in Indiana he enlisted November 13, 1861, in the 59th Indiana Infantry, was commissioned a second lieutenant October 3, 1862, and mustered out a captain in 1865, becoming captain of the 38th U.S. Infantry August 23 of that year. After again mustering out he became a second lieutenant in the 39th Infantry July 28, 1866, and a first lieutenant January 7, 1867, transferring to the 25th Infantry April 20, 1869, and to the 9th Infantry January 1, 1871. He was an Indian agent in Nevada from 1869-70 and by the middle 1870s was at Camp Sheridan and Camp Robinson on the northern Plains. He reported he took part in the "Powder River expedition," but did not provide a date and this could not have been Crook's March expedition and fight at Powder River which involved only cavalry units and personnel. In 1876 Lee was stationed at the Spotted Tail Agency for Brulé Sioux in South Dakota and from 1877-78 was agent there (Hyde says in one place he became agent in 1876, and in another, 1877; Lee reported it was in March 1877). Lee and Spotted Tail became good friends, each admiring the other. In September 1877, Lee contacted Chief Crazy Horse, who had come to the Spotted Tail Agency from the Red Cloud Agency, his proper station, and persuaded him to return with Lee to Camp Robinson, close to Red Cloud Agency. Conditions included that Crazy Horse could tell his side of the story of the past few days supporting his belief that his views had been misinterpreted, and that he would not be harmed. When the party reached Camp Robinson, Colonel Luther P. Bradley, in command, refused to talk with the Indian and ordered that he be turned over to the officer of the day, which meant he would go to the guardhouse. Lee's protestations to Bradley had no effect and in a succeeding melee Crazy Horse was killed, which Lee considered a great wrong. Hyde believed Lee "a strong agent" for Spotted Tail who should have been retained longer than he was, but he was

replaced as acting agent. He became a captain May 1, 1879, and that year was recorder for the Reno Court of Inquiry at Chicago. Lee was stationed at many frontier posts thereafter: Fort Omaha, Nebraska; Fort McKinney, Wyoming; Fort Douglas, Utah; Fort Russell, Wyoming; Forts Thomas and McDowell, Arizona. He was Indian agent for Cheyennes and Arapahoes in Indian Territory in 1885-86. Lee became a major in 1898, lieutenant colonel of the 6th Infantry in 1900, colonel of the 8th Infantry in 1901, Brigadier General in 1902 and Major General upon his retirement, January 2, 1907. He died at Washington, D.C. He was generally regarded as a superior officer, thoroughly honest and liked by enlisted men as well as officers.

Heitman; Powell; E.A. Brininstool, *Crazy Horse.* Los Angeles, Wetzel Pub. Co., 1949 (which has a portrait of Lee); Robert A. Clark, Carroll Friswold, *The Killing of Chief Crazy Horse.* Glendale, Calif., Arthur H. Clark Co., 1976; George E. Hyde, *Spotted Tail's Folk: A History of the Brulé Sioux.* Norman, Univ. of Okla. Press, 1961.

Lee, John Doyle, Mormon pioneer (Sept. 12, 1812-Mar. 23, 1877). B. at Kaskaskia, Illinois, he was descended from a soldier under George Rogers Clark on his mother's side and reportedly was a distant relative of Robert E. Lee on his father's. Lee became attracted to Mormonism and was baptized into the faith June 17, 1838, at Ambrosia, Missouri, south of Far West, Caldwell County; he became a member of the Danite band of Mormon militants, serving as bodyguard for Joseph Smith and Brigham Young. Lee took an active part in the guerilla-type turmoil that developed between Mormons and non-Mormons and in the exodus to Illinois that resolved that crisis; he and his family reached Illinois in February 1839. Lee went on a six month mission to Tennessee that year, and other missions subsequently, he being in Kentucky on such an endeavor when Joseph Smith was killed at Carthage, Illinois. Lee was adopted by Young. He commenced taking plural wives as early as 1845, marrying at least 19 women during his lifetime. He took part in the exodus from Nauvoo, Illinois, toward the West in 1846, but on August 28 Young assigned him to go to Santa Fe where he collected about $1,200 in pay received by the Mormon Battalion, and took it back to help finance the Saints' move to Utah. Lee left Winter Quarters June 3, 1858, for Utah, arriving before autumn. He farmed in the Salt Lake Valley until 1850, helped found Provo, Utah, then was directed to remove to Iron County, in south Utah, to help develop an agricultural support for iron mining and works the Mormons planned to develop there. Parowan, Utah, was created under his direction on a site he selected. He spent some time exploring the little known land to the south,though his principal efforts were pioneering. As southern Utah settled, Lee was among the most prominent pioneers, if not always the most popular; he was utterly faithful to his church and its leadership. January 1, 1856, he was placed in charge of the Iron County agency, one of five Indian agencies in the territory; he became probate judge, clerk and assessor of Washington County, when it was formed. Lee's role in the Mountain Meadows Massacre, September 11, 1857, is frequently discussed but remains unclear, although he was the scapegoat who alone was executed to expiate the crime, probably in some arrangement between authorities and the church to cleanse the record by this single action, although from 40 to 60 Mormons took part in the butchery of the 140 or so emigrants of the Fancher train. Lee was an undoubted foreman of the event, but responsibility for it extended through Haight to Dame who formally ordered it, receiving his directions to do so in all likelihood from some undefined higher authority. It was Lee, according to court testimony (admittedly taken after the church had decided upon his sacrifice), who persuaded the emigrants to leave the security of their impromptu fortress and walk out to be slaughtered and who designed the plan for the killings and directed it on the ground. Lee reported on the matter to Brigham Young and Wilford Woodruff at Salt Lake City. He returned south and continued his pioneering life. After a conference with Indian Superintendent Jacob Forney in April 1859, Lee and Philip Klingonsmith went into hiding while Cradlebaugh, bringing warrants for the arrest of suspected participants in the massacre, investigated the matter in southern Utah. On May 28 Lee returned home. In March 1859 Lee was dismissed as probate judge, although he continued to prosper economically. Disquiet in Utah over the massacre would not

still, in fact slowly continued to mount; many people, not all of them non-Mormons, were uneasy over the crime, still unsolved officially. In February 1870, Brigham Young suggested to Lee that he "move" away from his prosperous farming layout; in September Young repeated the advice. Lee moved to Kanab, Utah; October 8 he received word of his excommunication, a sure sign he was to be sacrificed. In 1871 with the anti-polygamy drive rising, Lee was directed to take "one or two" of his wives and retire to the Colorado River crossing at Lonely Dell, where he would establish what became known as Lee's Ferry, important for many years in the movement of colonists from Utah to Arizona. In 1872 he was host for the Powell Expedition, the leaders of which praised his hospitality highly. Lee was arrested by Sheriff William Stokes at Panguitch, Utah, November 7, 1874, where he had gone to visit a wife and family. He was tried in the summer of 1875, but only Klingonsmith, by then an apostate, testified against him, and a hung jury resulted, eight Mormons for acquittal, four gentiles for conviction. Lee was transferred in August 1875, from Fort Cameron, Beaver, to the Utah State Penitentiary. May 11, 1876, he was released on bail pending a second trial at Beaver. It began in December before an all-Mormon jury, but it was evident that this time the church had decided to give him up as a sacrifice, and he was convicted after abundant Mormon testimony; he was sentenced to be executed, selected shooting as the method to be employed, and was shot at the site of the massacre, affirming that for him "death has no terror." On April 20, 1961, the First Presidency and Quorum of the Twelve of the Mormon Church announced, "It was the action of the Council...that authorization be given for the re-instatement to membership and former blessings to John D. Lee."
    Juanita Brooks, *John Doyle Lee.* Glendale, Calif. Arthur H. Clark Co., 1961.

Lee, Oliver Milton, cattleman (Nov. 8, 1865-Dec. 15, 1941). B. at Buffalo Gap, 15 miles south of Abilene, Texas, Lee and his half-brother, Perry Altman, migrated to New Mexico in 1884, Lee already a fine horseman and expert shot. He had use for both skills in turbulent southern New Mexico where the Lincoln County War was a vivid, living memory. Eugene Manlove Rhodes, Lee's

good friend and a man who could be believed
in such things, said Lee had killed eight men
and many otherwise courageous individuals
feared and were wary of him. Lee and Altman
selected Dog Canyon on the west side of the
Sacramento Mountains as a place to settle,
then the eastern part of Dona Ana County.
Altman took up a place and as soon as he was
21 Lee also homesteaded. Lee and Altman
came into a feuding relationship with a faction
headed by John H. Good of the Tularosa
country; Good's son, Walter, was killed, and
after other incidents of shooting and burning,
John Good drifted out of the country, giving
Lee room to expand his holdings a bit. He
obtained more cattle, developed water,
erected windmills and built tanks, and his
circle cross brand became more influential
and Lee more controversial. On February 12,
1893, for example, Lee and probably Bill
McNew killed Charles Rhodius and Matt
Coffelt, near El Paso under pretense that these
cowboys were rustlers; they were not. Dark
motives were suspected, the killings adjudged
near-murders by some with knowledge of the
affair. Albert J. Fountain and his son, Henry,
8, turned up missing in February 1896, and
Lee was suspected of doing away with them.
One of Lee's men, McNew was arrested; Lee
and Gililland, other suspects, were caught up
with at Lee's Wildy Well Ranch, an extension
of his Dog Canyon layout, and in a resulting
shootout with a Pat Garrett posse, Deputy
Sheriff Kent Kearney was mortally wounded,
Garrett and his posse captured and shooed
back to Las Cruces. Lee and his men, now on
the dodge, hid out at the HG Ranch near the
Rio Grande, where Rhodes was horse
wrangler for Lee's half-sister and brother-in-
law, Mr. and Mrs. H.G. Graham; the
situation was compounded by the fact that
Lee was wary of surrendering to Garrett,
sheriff of Dona Ana County, cognizant of his
probable fate if he did. His friends at Santa Fe
succeeded in carving a new county, Otero, out
of Dona Ana County, and installing his
friend, George Curry, as sheriff; Otero
County would have jurisdiction in the
Fountain murder cases. Lee now offered to
surrender if he would not be turned over to
Garrett, and would not be placed in the Dona
Ana County jail, under Garrett's control.
Gene Rhodes helped with the surrender,
which occurred at Las Cruces, Lee and

Gililland being taken to Socorro to be jailed,
later moved to Alamorgordo, New Mexico.
The 18-day trial began May 25, 1899, at
Hillsboro, Sierra County, with powerful
political forces involved and all but overwhelming the simple trial for murder. Lee was
acquitted, the judgment in the opinion of
many having little to do with his guilt or
innocence. Metz wrote: "The vast majority of
Fountain's friends do not doubt that Lee,
Gililland, and McNew were all guilty as
charged.... They still regard the jury's verdict
of innocent as an appalling miscarriage of
justice.... One would expect to find an
opposite consensus among friends of the
accused, but that is not the case. No solid
agreement exists. Naturally some of Lee's
defenders deny that he or the others did
anything wrong, but *most* will admit that
there was a lot of truth in the accusations...."
Lee's role in the murder of Garrett, if any, is
also a source of intense controversy; there is
nothing concrete to tie him to it, but persistent
rumors abound that he was involved in some
sort of conspiracy to effect the slaying. Lee's
involuntary connection with the 1919 killing
of John T. Hutchings by F.M. Scanland and
in the 1920 killing near Washington, D.C., of
Scanland, also has never been quite clarified
nor all suspicions allayed. After 1900 Lee
participated prominently in public affairs. He
was representative and state senator almost
continually from 1918 to 1930, a director of
the Federal Land Bank of Wichita, Kansas,
and held other posts, contributing "valuable
services to New Mexico." But "the old ways of
the range clung to Oliver Lee and during the
time of his service in the State Legislature it
was an open secret...that at every session he
carried a forty-five in a leather holster...
nicely concealed beneath the folds of the
Prince Albert coat which he wore on all
occasions of state." He was active in efforts to
improve highways and in game conservation
legislation. Lee died at Alamogordo. He had
married Winnie Rhode, sister of A.P. (Print)
Rhode, and sister too of the wife of W.W.
Cox, and fathered nine children.

Literature abundant: William A. Keleher, *The Fabulous Frontier.* Albuquerque, Univ. of New Mex. Press, 1962; W.H. Hutchinson, *Another Verdict for Oliver Lee.* Clarendon, Tex., Clarendon Press, 1965; Leon Claire Metz, *Pat Garrett: The Story of a Western Lawman.* Norman, Univ. of

Okla. Press, 1974; C.L. Sonnichsen, *Tularosa: Last of the Frontier West.* Old Greenwich, Conn., Devin-Adair Co., 1972.

Lee, Stephen Louis, frontiersman (c. 1808-Jan. 19, 1847). B. probably in Kentucky, he reached New Mexico in 1824 and became a trapper based on Taos and a trader-merchant as well, with dealings in Chihuahua and with the states at times, making an occasional trip to the eastern settlements. He was killed in the insurrection at Taos.

David J. Weber article, MM, Vol. III.

Leeper, Matthew M., Sr., Indian superintendent (Apr. 27, 1804-July 22, 1894). B. in "the Carolinas" of Huguenot descent he became a lawyer and in Arkansas was "collector of public moneys under the Federal Government." He there married Lucy E. Washington (July 12, 1818-Mar. 8, 1899), whose grandfather was first cousin to George Washington. Recommended by Sam Houston, among others, Leeper was made agent from March 1857 to September 1859 at the Penateka Comanche Reservation on Clear Fork of the Brazos River, Texas. In view of the rising hostility of Anglo Texans, the Indians were moved in 1859 north of the Red River to the Wichita Agency (near Fort Cobb) in the present Oklahoma, Leeper then returning to Texas briefly, enroute being wounded seriously by hostile Indians. Later he became agent at the Wichita Agency, although a controversial individual or, in Nye's words, "a contrary soul." He differed with his superiors and subordinates and once was placed in arrest, but soon released. When the Confederacy took over the region, Leeper was appointed by Jefferson Davis superintendent of Indian affairs for the Southern government, with jurisdiction as before. On the night of October 23, 1862, the Wichita Agency was attacked by a strong force of Delawares and Shawnees (one report said Osages, and another laid it to the Caddoes), partial to the Union cause, who "literally cleaned out the reservation. Several hundred Tonkawas were killed and the remnant... scattered." It was reported that the four whites present, including Leeper, were also killed, but he escaped through an upstairs window of his beleaguered house and survived, making his way afoot to Sherman, Texas which he reached in the last straits two weeks later. With the end of the Civil War his years as agent were over, and he settled at Sherman, where for many years he was notary public. Leeper fathered four children, three daughters and a son, Matthew Jr., who was raised on the Comanche Reservation and thus learned that tongue from childhood, becoming an interpreter and eventually an army surgeon; two of Leeper's daughters also married army officers. Matthew Sr. and Lucy Leeper were buried at the West Hill Cemetery of Sherman.

Sherman (Tex.) *Daily Register,* July 23, 1894, Mar. 8, 1899; Matthew Leeper file, Office of Sec. of Interior Appointments Div., Tex.; Rupert Norval Richardson, *The Comanche Barrier to South Plains Settlement.* Glendale, Calif., Arthur H. Clark Co., 1933; W.S. Nye, *Carbine & Lance.* Norman, Univ. of Okla. Press, 1951; Mildred P. Mayhall, *Indian Wars of Texas.* Waco, Texian Press, 1965.

Leeper, (Leepere) Matthew M., Jr., army officer, surgeon (c.1854-June 4, 1904). B. in Arkansas, his father, Matthew M. Leeper Sr., was a somewhat controversial agent for the Penateka Comanches at their reservation on the Clear Fork of the Brazos River, Texas, and later at the Wichita Agency near Fort Cobb, Oklahoma. Thus Matthew grew up speaking Comanche as well as English and later picked up Kiowa. He was named agency interpreter while Lawrie Tatum was in charge and occasionally interpreted for talks with Satanta, Lone Wolf and other Kiowa leading men. When Tatum moved to the Kiowa agency near Fort Sill, Oklahoma, Leeper went along; he interpreted for the talk in which Satanta admitted he was responsible for the celebrated Warren wagon train raid in Texas, a confession which led to capture of the hostile leaders. Leeper was commissioned a second lieutenant in the 4th Cavalry July 27, 1872, probably by or at the instigation of Mackenzie who was well acquainted with his work, sometimes taking Leeper into the field with him for his knowledge of Comanche and Kiowas. Leeper commanded the detachment which arrested Aaron Wilson for the murder of an emigrant and his son in 1875, buried the remains and turned Wilson over to civil authorities for trial and execution. Leeper became a first lieutenant March 20, 1879, and resigned his commission May 5, 1880 after operations against Kiowas and Comanches had ceased. Of marked intelligence, he then became a surgeon/physician. On December 28, 1886, he was married at Holland, Erie County, New York, to Mary E. Norton of Delmar, Iowa, 12 years his junior. February 7, 1901, at Milan, Missouri, he was commissioned a captain surgeon of Volunteers under the name of Leepere and was sent to the Philippines where he was promoted to major surgeon November 5, 1901. Leeper(e) suffered an attack of Dengue fever at San Pablo, Laguna Province, and because of failing health he resigned September 27, 1902. Never fully recovering, he died at Glen Cove (Oyster Bay), Nassau County, New York. There were no children from the marriage; his widow returned to make her home at Calapan, Mindoro Province in the Philippines and subsequently remarried.

Leeper pension file, NARS; W.S. Nye, *Carbine & Lance*. Norman, Univ. of Okla. Press, 1951; R.G. Carter, *On the Border with Mackenzie*. N.Y., Antiquarian Press, 1961.

Lees, Isaiah W., detective (Dec. 25, 1830-Dec. 21, 1902). B. at Lancaster, England, he became a mechanical engineer and expert iron worker at Patterson, New Jersey, and reached California in the 1849 gold rush. He tried mining and then worked for the Union Iron Works at San Francisco where he became foreman of a crew repairing steamships. A chance conversation with a policeman turned him into an amateur detective; he solved the murder of José Rodriguez, his evidence resulting in the hanging December 10, 1852, of José Forni, first person legally executed at San Francisco under the American government. October 28, 1853, Lees joined the San Francisco police department and within three weeks became assistant captain and detective, embarking upon a distinguished 47-year career. Lees was a voracious reader of crime and detective material. He pored over newspapers and began clipping crime stories, pasting them in scrapbooks. When he arrested criminals he made careful notes and descriptions and kept a file for future reference. About 1854 or 1855 he started a rogues' gallery. He had daguerreotypes made of all criminals arrested, paying for the likenesses from his own pocket at first. His successes began to accumulate and in October 1859 he was appointed a captain of police. In the spring of 1863 he was instrumental in halting the schooner *J.M. Chapman,* surreptitiously

clearing San Francisco to commence a Confederate privateering career; Lees' detective work assured successful prosecution of her master and crew. The celebrated cases in which Lees participated were many: the Frank Deen confidence-man case; the purloined painting, *Elaine;* the celebrated Duncan case; the capture of Theodore Durant for the "crime of the century"; the Frank Miller affair; the Cordelia Botkin poisoning case, and many others. In 1897 Lees became chief of police at San Francisco, retiring in 1900. His rogues' gallery had grown to more than 10,000 pictures and names of criminals, his scrapbooks to several score and his crime library to around 1,000 volumes, only four of them fiction. Lees once remarked of his profession: "It's really not a pleasant business. It means work all the time — the hardest kind of work, both mental and physical. (A man) must come to his task gifted with a natural aptitude for logic, for reasoning from cause to effect — in a word, with a genius for shedding the noonday sun on the midnight of dark and tangled threads of crime." His funeral was among the most impressive in San Francisco's history. "The country never knew another like him," wrote his friend, William Pinkerton.

Information from William B. Secrest; Secrest, "Isaiah W. Lees." *American West,* Vol. XVII, No. 5 (Sept. -Oct. 1980), 28-29, 64-67.

Leese, Jacob Primer, pioneer (Aug. 19, 1809-Feb. 1, 1892). B. at Newelstown (St. Clairsville), Ohio, he joined the Rogers-Coffee Rocky Mountain trapping expedition in 1829 at Fort Smith, Arkansas, leaving in 1830 and wintering in New Mexico. He worked for Ceran St. Vrain at Taos and Abiquiu. Leese went to California in 1833, engaged in an unsuccessful mule-driving venture eastward and returned empty handed to Los Angeles. He resumed a commercial career, became a central California pioneer. In 1849 he visited China for trading reasons, in 1863 unsuccessfully engaged in a colonizing venture in Lower California, lived in Texas for some time and returned to California. He died at San Francisco following an accident.

Gloria Griffen Cline article, MM, Vol. III.

Le Fer: *see* Garistatsia

Leforge, Thomas H., "white Crow Indian" (July 9, 1850-Mar. 28, 1931). B. at Portsmouth, Ohio, he moved in infancy with his family to St. Joseph, Missouri, and in 1853 to Doniphan County, Kansas, where his playmates were Potawatomi children and where he absorbed something of their language. In 1864 his father became interested in Montana gold discoveries and took his family there by way of the Bridger Trail, west of the Bighorn Mountains. Two members of the party were lost to lightning. The family settled at Virginia City, Montana, for a year or more, then moved to Bozeman in the Gallatin Valley. In 1867 Leforge joined the Montana Militia, "composed largely of ex-ruffians of the Missouri-Kansas border," he said, and a short-lived outfit. Leforge continued a typical frontier existence, some hunting and trapping, a little logging, brushes with Piegan raiders. In the summer of 1868 he joined some Crow Indians in Livingston Canyon along Yellowstone River. He acquired the name Horse Rider among them by able handling of a fractious mount, retaining that appellation for 60 years. Leforge was adopted by Yellow Leggings and thus became a brother of Three Irons of the Mountain Crows. He became a close friend of Minton (Mitch) Bouyer, half-Souix but also affiliated with the Crows; they accompanied military scouts out of Fort Ellis occasionally. He also knew Jim Beckworth briefly before the latter's death. In 1870 a Crow Agency was established on Mission Creek, ten miles downstream from Livingston, Montana. Leforge, who now could speak Crow, was put on the agency payroll as blacksmith and general purpose man about 1870. He married a Crow girl named Cherry; it was a love match and endured until his wife died. Leforge and his adopted people had occasional skirmishes with Piegans, Sioux or Cheyennes, and a major action between Sioux and Crows, aided by Nez Perce, in 1873 near Pryor Creek. The Leforges moved to the new Crow Agency on Stillwater River about 1874, near the present town of Absarokee, Montana. There Tom continued as before to work at odd jobs about the agency and for the agent, participated in numerous scouts and forays with his adopted people and engaged in skirmishes with their enemies. Although he had scouted for Miles and Gibbon, he refused to scout against the Nez Perce in 1877 because of his respect and friendship for them. He did scout against the Bannacks in 1878, however. He counted

coups a few times. In 1876 he became associated with Crow scouts under Gibbon, James H. Bradley in command. In this operation his adventures were many; on one occasion he and others scouted terrain where Custer would fall, but it was a month before that event and they found no sign of interest. Although quite active during the campaign, Leforge never saw Custer, continuing to operate with Gibbon until he broke a collar bone in an accident and went to the field hospital, thus avoiding being assigned to Custer, as was Bouyer. After the Custer debacle Terry authorized Leforge to enlist Crow scouts for further operations and he signed up 50 who were taken by steamer from Pryor Creek down the Yellowstone to the mouth of the Bighorn. Eventually he and the Crows were assigned to Crook and still later Leforge joined Miles. He enlisted Crow scouts to serve out of new Fort Keogh, Montana and made one ineffectual scout with Brisbin; he engaged in other skirmishes, other adventures. His wife, Cherry, sickened and died. Leforge then married the widow of Mitch Bouyer. In 1877 he again served with Crow scouts under Lieutenant Gustavus Doane, and was stationed sometimes at the new Fort Custer, engaging in affrays with Sioux, Piegan or white horse thieves, He attempted ranching and mining in a minor way. In 1887 because he was drifting from Indian into white ways, he and his wife separated, she marrying again successfully. Leforge married a white woman at Columbus, Montana, joined a circus for a time, lived on a legacy, settled at Livingston, Montana, but then became bored and engaged in prospecting in Oregon and Washington, divorcing his wife who did not wish to leave Livingston. He married another white woman in Yakima, Washington. Leforge bought an Alaskan mine, sight unseen; it didn't pay out. He mined at Teller, near Nome on a second northern trip; it was financially unsuccessful, too, so he returned to Washington and went into the brick-making business; then tie-cutting. But the Crow country and Crow society memories proved strong. He returned to Montana in 1912 without his latest wife and two daughters. Back to the Crows. He was warmly greeted by his people and his six children, some adopted. Born an Ohioan, he died as he wished a Crow Indian at the Crow Agency, Montana. Leforge was an honest man, of accurate memory and had many friends among whites as well as among Indians — and some enemies. His recollections, revealed in many visits, were gathered, edited and published by Marquis.

Thomas H. Leforge, *Memoirs of a White Crow Indian,* as told by Thomas B. Marquis. Lincoln, Univ. of Nebr. Press, 1974.

LeFors, Joe, lawman (1865-Oct. 1, 1940). B. at Paris, Lamar County, Texas, his parents took him as an infant to a farm near Fort Smith in the Indian Territory; he was raised there and near Vinita in the Cherokee Nation. In 1878 James J. LeFors took his six boys by ox wagon toward the Texas Panhandle, near the Wichita Mountains having a brush with Comanches but being rescued, motion picture style, by soldiers of the 10th U.S. Cavalry. The family settled about a dozen miles south of Mobeetie, Texas, on East Cantonment Creek. In 1879 Joe accompanied a cattle drive of his brother Perry's from below Fort Concho to the Kansas line; then worked as a freighter from Dodge City to Mobeetie and Fort Elliott, Texas. In October he hired out as a mail rider between Fort Elliott and Fort Sill, Oklahoma; on one occasion he was chased by a party of Indians who were marauding off the reservation. The Indians became so troublesome that his father took him off the mail route and sent him to school at Caddo Grove, Texas, until 1881, the father meanwhile dying. Joe then returned to Mobeetie and hired out as a teamster once more, later working for cow outfits and doing general ranch work, running wild horses and once being innocently involved in a gunfight in which one man was killed, another wounded badly. In 1884 he accompanied a trail drive to Dodge City; the next year he was with a trail herd from Mobeetie to Buffalo, Wyoming. LeFors went to work for the Murphy Cattle Company of Wyoming, occasionally driving herds to Chadron, Nebraska, as the nearest rail point and remaining with the outfit until 1887 when he hired out to the Wyoming Land and Cattle Company. Rustling was everywhere according to LeFors, and he soon began having trouble with thieves, but gives few details. In 1890 the Murphy Cattle Company hired him to run an outfit in Montana on the Yellowstone River and he took the job "to get away from the rustlers." The concern had a contract to supply beef to the Sioux of Standing Rock

Agency and for five years he delivered stock there, learning the Sioux tongue and sign language. He heard of the 1892 Johnson County War "and could see two sides to it." In 1895 he became a livestock inspector in Wyoming for Montana cattlemen, identifying and returning stolen animals. Initially "I made some arrests but could get no convictions" in his work near Newcastle, Wyoming. LeFors then heard that rustled stock was being held in the Hole-in-the-Wall country along Buffalo Creek, southwest of Kaycee. He rode alone into that country at night, reconnoitered it for several days, locating stolen cattle, many with brands altered and a number of them Montana animals; parts of the country had not been rounded up since the Johnson County War, while lawmen kept their distance. He gradually developed a plan for a clearing out of the Hole-in-the-Wall, but it was dangerous work. In a fight with rustlers on South Beaver Creek, 50 miles south of Newcastle, LeFors' clothes were bullet-punctured, two of the rustlers were killed; he left the recovered stock with his men and took out after the third thief whom he arrested. In 1897 after numerous adventures with rustlers, LeFors again penetrated Hole-in-the-Wall and had a fight in which some men were shot on both sides, the LeFors party being bested and run out. He organized a fresh force of 54 men from Montana and Wyoming stock associations and law organizations, using them as cover for a large company of cowboys to do the range work. Although his force was threatened with ambush and attack by 60 or more whom he defined as "mainly outlaws," he succeeded in rounding up the Hole-in-the-Wall country at last, bringing out 1,163 head of stolen cattle, and, he concluded, leaving the area "a safer place for both an officer and property ever since." LeFors became increasingly effective as a livestock inspector, having had as many as 17 men in the Newcastle jail at once charged with cattle stealing, and attending court livestock theft cases in South Dakota as well as Wyoming. He was involved in a long chase after the June 2, 1899 Wilcox, Wyoming, train robbery, failing to catch up with some of those participating through no fault of his own. LeFors became a deputy U.S. marshal out of Cheyenne, being equally as effective in this role. Following the August 29, 1900 Tipton, Wyoming train robbery LeFors led a long hunt down into Brown's Hole and elsewhere, but failed to catch up with the robbers, again not his fault. When Willie Nickell was killed and Kels P. Nickell wounded LeFors was put on the case, operating under cover. He met Tom Horn for the first time and linked him with the case. In the most celebrated aspect of his career, LeFors interviewed Horn while a court reporter and another deputy U.S. marshal listened in an adjoining room, taking down the conversation verbatim; it was this information that was pivotal in the conviction of Horn for murder and his ultimate execution. LeFors in his autobiography said that Horn "was not drunk," although some believed he "might have been drinking" before the interview. Neither Horn nor LeFors bore the other any open ill-will after the trial. Later LeFors made an adventurous arrest of an important wanted and hostile Shoshone from the Wind River Reservation. In April 1908, he quit his position and went to work for the Wool Growers Association, with his duties to take up grievances between cattle and sheep men, and to put down depredations. Again he was successful in a series of interesting cases. Although he does not go into detail in his autobiography, LeFors mentioned that he had lived for some time in Argentina around 1912, that some of his "most hazardous and thrilling experiences were encountered on a trip up a river in Central America," and that the closest call he ever had "was when I was ship-wrecked on a little native schooner on the Caribbean Sea." He also made many trips into Mexico as an officer and as a private citizen. From 1921 he lived several years in southern California but then returned to Buffalo, Wyoming, where he died at his home, leaving his widow and a son.

Joe LeFors, *Wyoming Peace Officer.* Laramie, Wyo., Laramie Printing Co., 1953.

Left Hand (Niwot), Southern Arapaho chief (c. 1823-c. Dec. 1864). B. on the central Plains as was his brother, Neva, he learned English, Sioux and Cheyenne as a boy, the former at such fur trading posts as Forts Lupton, Vasquez, Jackson and Bent. He was tutored further in English by his sister's husband, John Poisal, a Kentuckian trader. Although an accomplished warrior, Left Hand remained generally aloof from hostilities against the whites. Around 1850 he married, his initial wife's name being unremembered; he prob-

ably married other wives thereafter. By the mid-1850s he was a chief. Conditions for the Plains tribes worsened and in the summer of 1858 Left Hand journeyed by wagon with his family eastward to Nebraska and Iowa, seeking information as to whether farming would enable his people to survive the dwindling of buffalo herds. He may have worked briefly for several farmers and at length, possessed of some agricultural knowledge, returned west with a wagon train of travelers, convinced his people would never settle down to farming since it was opposed to their whole way of life and history. Left Hand believed that his people might become cattle raisers, more in keeping with their life-style. The Colorado gold boom commenced late in 1858 and burgeoned quickly, Left Hand with some difficulty keeping Arapaho young men at peace although the whites quickly usurped their wintering lands at the base of the Rockies, Left Hand's centering about where Boulder, Colorado, now stands. The proximity of the whites meant that Left Hand's people suffered more depredations but he continued his staunch passivity despite white provocations. Left Hand, being absent, did not sign the unfortunate Fort Wise (Fort Lyon) Treaty of February 18, 1861 and strongly repudiated it, the Arapahoes generally coming to believe it was presented dishonestly and swindled them of lands they considered theirs. In the spring of 1861 Left Hand twice visited the Denver *Rocky Mountain News* office to explain that the Arapaho were peaceful, would continue so, and to explain the Indian position; on the second visit he was accompanied by Little Raven, head chief of the Southern Arapaho. Left Hand then visited a popular theater, strode out upon the stage and reiterated his sentiments. He missed going to Washington with a delegation of chiefs, the omission of this English-speaking Indian in his view contrived by Agent Colley and John Smith, noted Plains translator, "because he could speak English and (had he gone) Smith could not tell his lies." Little Raven would not go because Left Hand had been left out, and he trusted no other interpreter. Left Hand's brother, Neva, who understood some English did go however, and confirmed Left Hand's suspicion. In May Left Hand joined other chiefs in a conference with Governor John Evans at Denver at which the matter of Plains peace was discussed. Despite continued provocations and deliberate misunderstanding on the part of the whites of Indian intentions (which were principally to obtain food in a region largely swept clear of game by white excesses), Left Hand, Black Kettle and other chiefs adamantly declined to engage in hostilities, while Evans, Chivington and other white leaders as persistently edged toward war with the hapless Indians. Because of a purposeless attack upon a Left Hand peace delegation by Captain James W. Parmeter at Fort Larned, Kansas, some Southern Arapaho young men drifted off to join Cheyennes in hostilities, and this brought disfavor upon all, though Left Hand remained peaceful. In September 1864 Left Hand, Black Kettle and other chiefs invited the commander of Fort Lyon to their Smoky Hill River camps to settle differences; Wynkoop daringly made the trip with 140 men and two artillery pieces. White prisoners were turned over and most of the peaceful camp followed Wynkoop back to Fort Lyon, although Left Hand remained on the Smoky Hill River. He did not attend the September meeting at Camp Weld, near Denver of Black Kettle and other peaceful chiefs with Evans and Chivington, although Neva did. After the council, which ended with no firm white decision for peace, the Indians retired to near Fort Lyon where Left Hand and others joined them. Wynkoop was succeeded in command by Major Scott Anthony, a hard-liner. He instructed the Indians under Left Hand (with about 50 followers) and Black Kettle to camp on Sand Creek, some 40 miles northeast of the post and there on November 29, 1864, they were surprised by Chivington and his Colorado troops, about 148, mostly women and children, being killed. Although reported slain at Sand Creek, Left Hand rather was wounded mortally and died perhaps in the Smoky Hill camps if he succeeded in traveling that far. In his early manhood he was described as more than 6 feet tall, "strikingly handsome" and "much more intelligent than the average Indian." It was reported that he did not braid his hair, but wore it loosely over his shoulders.

Margaret Coel, *Chief Left Hand: Southern Arapaho*. Norman, Univ. of Okla. Press, 1981.

Left Hand, Southern Arapaho chief (1840-post 1889). B. on the central Plains he was no relation to the celebrated Chief Left Hand,

mortally wounded at Sand Creek, Colorado, in the Chivington Massacre of November 29, 1864. The younger man could not speak English. He probably received his name before 1867, and succeeded Little Raven as head chief of the Southern Arapaho upon the older man's death in the winter of 1889.

Margaret Coel, *Chief Left Hand: Southern Arapaho*. Norman, Univ. of Okla. Press, 1981.

Le Grand, Alexander, adventurer (c. 1800-post 1839). B. in Maryland, he was educated in law but turned to the frontier, reaching Santa Fe by 1823 and the next year leading a party of traders there from Missouri. He may have trapped the Rockies for a time, visited Chihuahua and Sonora; he reached Mexico City by November 1826. He became an agent to define and assist in settling a 48 million acre land grant in present Texas, New Mexico, Oklahoma and Colorado. He reached New Orleans where he assembled an expedition for carrying out his mission or, as some suspected, to carve an empire for himself, made a somewhat mysterious crossing of the plains, reaching Santa Fe November 15, 1827. He spent some nine years in obscurity, probably traveling widely through Mexico and the southern plains and mountains and becoming something of an authority on the South Plains Indian tribes. July 12, 1836, he became aide to Thomas J. Rusk, commanding the Texas army, attempted unsuccessfully to negotiate a treaty with Comanches and Kiowas, and returned to Texas to come into distinct disfavor with Houston. His last reported appearance was February 6, 1839, when he was quoted in an article in the *Telegraph and Texas Register*. He left Houston early in 1839.

HT; Raymond Estep article, MM, Vol. VII.

Leib, Edward Henry, army officer (c. 1840-May 17, 1892). B. in Pennsylvania, he enlisted in a state regiment in 1861, shortly being commissioned a second lieutenant in the 5th (then the 2nd) Cavalry April 26. He participated in eastern theatre operations during the Civil War, being breveted up to lieutenant colonel, rising to captain in regular command, and being severely wounded while commanding the regiment near Dinwiddie Court House March 31, 1865. He successfully fought guerillas in Tennessee in 1866. On the frontier he commanded Fort Harker, Kansas, in 1868-

69, and served at other posts, reached Arizona in 1872, moved north with the regiment in 1875, was in the engagement at War Bonnet Creek, Wyoming, was on the Big Horn and Yellowstone expedition and in the fight at Slim Buttes, Dakota, September 9, 1876. He was dismissed May 9, 1877, and became a special agent in the office of the Commissioner of Pensions at Washington, D.C. The House of Representatives Committee on Pensions in January 1880, strongly recommended increasing Leib's own pension from $30 to $50 a month, noting that he was wholly disabled from manual labor by wounds incurred while "the services he performed while in good standing as an officer have borne their fruits, and they are entitled to recognition." Leib died at Millersburg, Pennsylvania.

Heitman; Price, *Fifth Cavalry; Army and Navy Jour.,* Jan. 31, 1880, June 4, 1892.

Leifr Eiriksson (Leif the Lucky), discoverer (c. 971-c. 1020). B. in Iceland he was the son of Eirik the Red, the brother of Thorstein and Thorwald, famed in Vinland annals, and a half-brother of Freydis whose atrocities darken her memory. The legend of his discovery of America is no doubt apocryphal; it was Bjarni Herjolfsson in about 986 who was blown off course and became the first known European to raise the American coast. Leifr, a sea-going merchant, heard of Bjarni's landfalls while at the Norwegian court of King Olaf around 1000. He had been converted to Christianity and returned with a priest to Greenland, rescuing stranded seamen enroute and thus earning his nickname of "the Lucky." He bought Bjarni's ship (no report on what happened to his own), and in general retraced Bjarni's route, although in reverse and it is uncertain whether the landfalls he made were those Bjarni had raised initially. He discovered a place finally where salmon abounded in the streams, there was no frost in winter, the latitude was more southerly than Greenland, and grapes and grapevines were plentiful. He returned to Greenland about 1002, it is calculated. Leif's Vinland has been variously located by scholars as far south as Florida and as far north as Hudson Bay, although somewhere on the New England or New-foundland coasts seems to have most support. The archeological discoveries at L'Anse aux Meadows probably reflect the later colonization attempt of Karlsefni rather than Leif's

Vinland for the climate is far too harsh and other clues do not fit that location; in fact no Norse expedition after Leifr is known to have relocated his Vinland. Leifr himself did not visit Vinland again, but he lent his ship to his brother, Thorvald, who was killed by Skraelings on the continent, and to his other brother Thorstein whose abortive trip proved unsuccessful. Leifr succeeded his father, who died around 1002 as the chief patriarch of the Greenland settlements, married and produced progeny. Little is known of his later life.

Magnus Magnusson, Hermann Palsson, *The Vinland Sagas: The Norse Discovery of America.* Baltimore, Penguin Books, 1965; Gwyn Jones, *The Norse Atlantic Saga.* N.Y., Oxford Univ. Press, 1964; Farley Mowat, *Westviking.* Toronto, McClelland and Stewart, 1965; DCB.

Leigh, William Robinson, artist (Sept. 23, 1866-Mar. 11, 1955). B. at Falling Waters, West Virginia, he was said to be descended from Pocahontas. He studied art from childhood, continued his education in Europe and settled in 1896 at New York. After difficulty in persuading the artistic world that the American West was worth depicting for itself and in its own terms, he sold the Santa Fe railway on a plan for it to pay his passage west in exchange for paintings from the Grand Canyon country of Arizona. He worked at the Laguna and Zuni pueblos in 1907 and extended his theatre in succeeding years. In 1910 he accompanied a hunting party to Wyoming and thenceforward spent much time in various parts of the West of which he became a careful, colorful, graphic portrayer, his work eventually bringing him acclaim from critics and public alike. Leigh was one of the great depicters of the Southwest, although his talents were employed by the American Museum of Natural History to portray scenes as distant as Africa; Leigh also was a writer and lecturer and continued his art work until the last day of his 88-year life span. He died at New York City and was buried at Nyack, New York.

Who Was Who; June DuBois, "W.R. Leigh: Painter of Frontiers." *Amer. West,* Vol. XV, No. 2 (May-June 1978), 32-47.

Leipler, William, soldier (1845-post 1893). B. in Baden, he enlisted in Company B, 20th New York Cavalry, November 23, 1863; he later enlisted in Company F, 2nd Cavalry, late in

1866, and fought with it in the Piegan campaign, a Sioux campaign, at Lame Deer, Muddy Creek and Baker's operation on the Yellowstone, and in the Nez Perce campaign. In 1870 he was of the military escort that accompanied the Washburn Yellowstone expedition; he was of the party of volunteers that brought the lost Truman Everts back to civilization following his rescue. Leipler retired in 1893, when he removed to Buffalo, New York.

Aubrey L. Haines, *Yellowstone National Park: Its Exploration and Establishment.*   Wash., Nat. Park Service, 1974.

Le Maire, F., priest (fl. 1708). A secular priest of the Seminary of Foreign Missions, he was stationed for several years at Fort St. Louis (Mobile Bay, Alabama) where, in the perhaps prejudiced view of the Jesuit Gravier, he was "the chaplain of the fort, who neither chants, nor preaches, nor visits a single Soldier, — who thinks of nothing but eating, and for whom naught but contempt is felt." He had come to Louisiana at the instance of a wealthy friend to do missionary work among the Indians and remained several years.

Thwaites, JR, LXVI, 131, 342n28.

Le Mercier, Francois Joseph, Jesuit missionary (Oct. 3, 1604-June 12, 1690). B. at Paris, he became a Jesuit and in 1635 arrived in Canada where he labored among the Hurons and quickly absorbed their language. In June 1856, after the Iroquois had virtually destroyed the Huron nation, Le Mercier went with other Jesuits on a mission to the Onondagas in present New York State, remaining a year. Much of his life was spent in the St. Lawrence valley, twice being superior of missions and for a time vicar of Quebec. He returned to France in 1673, was named superior of the mission on Martinique, and remained there until his death.

Thwaites, JR, VIII, 290-91n11; DCB; Parkman, *The Jesuits in North America,* I.

Le Moyne, David, missionary worker (c. 1637- c. 1657). B. at Dieppe, he reached Canada and accompanied the Jesuits as a lay worker in their 1656-58 mission to the Onondagas in the present New York State. He died on the shore of Lake Cayuga (Tiohero) of the "bloody flux," or dysentery.

Thwaites, JR, LXIV, 27.

Le Moyne, Jacques de Morgues, artist (d. 1588). The first artist known to have worked in what is now the United States, Le Moyne accompanied the Huguenot, Rene Goulaine de Laudonniere's ill-fated expedition to Florida and the Carolinas in 1564; Le Moyne was one of the few survivors. His water colors of Indians, scenes, etc., were published by Theodore de Bry, along with the artist's narrative. He died at London.

George C. Groce, David H. Wallace, *New-York Historical Society's Dictionary of Artists in America 1564-1860.*   New Haven, Yale Univ. Press, 1957.

Le Moyne, sieur d'Iberville, Pierre, adventurer, colonizer (July 1661-July 9, 1706). The third son of Charles Le Moyne de Longueuil, he was a brother of Jean Baptiste le Moyne, sieur de Bienville and was b. at Montreal c. July 20. According to the *Columbia Encyclopedia,* he entered the expanding navy of Louis XIV and after a decade at sea returned to Canada. He took part in expeditions against British outposts in Hudson Bay in 1686, 1689, 1691, 1694 and 1697; in 1689 he was commissioned to command throughout the northern sea. Despite his courageous and sometimes brilliant successes, "Iberville received no support from France," or at any rate not much, and his work was without visible result. In 1690 during King William's War he took part in an attack on Schenectady, New York, led by his older brother, Jacques, sieur de Sainte Hélène, enhancing his growing reputation for Indian-like ruthlessness. He unsuccessfully attacked Fort Pemaquid (William Henry), Maine, in 1692, and four years later returned to destroy the post, as well as capturing St. John's Newfoundland in a campaign called "the cruelest and most destructive of Iberville's career." His greatest fame, however, came with his work in Louisiana, as the French claims in the lower Mississippi valley were called. In 1698 Iberville was commissioned in France to locate the mouth of the Mississippi River, "select a good site which can be defended with few men, and... block entry to the river by other nations." Leaving Brest with four ships late in the year, Iberville, accompanied by his brother, Bienville, built a temporary post at Biloxi Bay (the present Ocean Springs, Mississippi) and returned to France leaving Bienville in charge of a garrison of 80 men. He returned to Biloxi in January 1700, built another fort on the great river, 40 miles above its mouth, sought to counter machinations of British traders from Carolina and returned to France by way of New York where it is reported he sold 9,000 skins brought to his posts by Canadian coureurs de bois who did not wish to risk their illegal catch with Montreal traders. He believed, and there was support in France for his ideas, that coureurs de bois should be encouraged in their subrosa trade with the natives, since they would then be more active in opposing British traders slipping into the Mississippi valley. He argued for a strong French commitment to Louisiana and perhaps an alliance with Spain to permit France to use the Pensacola base in Florida. Failing this he urged construction of a strong French post in Mobile Bay; the crown authorized establishment of a colony there and approved Iberville's plans for development of the basin's strengths against the British. Iberville returned to Louisiana in late 1701 with three ships, erected Fort St. Louis at Mobile, and encouraged by missionary activities, those of coureurs de bois and others, the creation of interlocking alliances and associations with the Indian tribes who alone had the power to prevent English encroachments; he was greatly assisted by Henri de Tonty, La Salle's erstwhile lieutenant. Iberville went back to France in 1702, never to return to the American continent although he retained his deep interest in Louisiana, writing a succession of memoirs for French officials concerned with that region. Although in ill health from malaria and other causes, he was given command of a squadron of 12 vessels in 1705 to harass the English in the West Indies; his savage despoliation of Nevis Island and ruthless treatment of its population is beyond the scope of American frontier interest, but it provides a clue to his basic character. While "an undoubtedly remarkable man," whose "outstanding energy and ability and incredible feats of heroism" made him "the first truly Canadian hero," he was afflicted by avarice, apparently lack of scruple and other less worthy characteristics. Yet his "exploits, like those of no other in New France, illustrate the physical and moral strength, the resourcefulness and adaptability that were required in some measure of the whole colonial society to survive and prosper in the exacting wilderness conditions of North America."

Thwaites, JR, LXIII, 305-306n27; DCB, II; CE; DAB; Parkman, *A Half Century of Conflict*, I.

Le Moyne, Simon, Jesuit missionary (Oct. 22, 1604-Nov. 24, 1665). B. at Beauvais, France, he became a Jesuit and reached Canada in 1638, going to the Huron country and working with them until their dispersion by the Iroquois. In 1653 he was sent as an ambassador to the Iroquois and opened a mission among the Onondagas in the present New York State, retaining contact with them or other bands of the confederacy for five years. While there he visited New Amsterdam (New York) and formed a strong friendship with Johannes Megapolensis, the Dutch minister who had abandoned Catholicism for Protestantism but had aided Jogues in an earlier captivity among the Iroquois. Le Moyne made repeated trips to the Iroquois country; his courage was legendary even among the courageous Jesuits. His 1661-62 undertaking, it was written, "is a Mission of blood and fire, of toils and tears, of captives and Barbarians. It is a country where the ground is still stained with the blood of Frenchmen; where scaffolds are still standing, strewn with their ashes; where survivors of the cruel torture bear its direful marks on feet and hands, with nails torn out and fingers and toes cut off; where... Father Simon le Moyne (might) share all the afflictions of his beloved flock." He spent some time with the Cayugas, "least cruel" of the Iroquois, but he also worked repeatedly among the two other western tribes of that people, the Onondagas and Senecas. Scarcely had he returned from one mission before he was sent back on another, willingly braving the most frightful perils to establish peace between those peoples and the French and on at least one occasion to free numerous French captives of the Indians. His efforts were not without result; at his death most of the Iroquois nations were seeking peace with the northern whites. Le Moyne, one of the relatively unsung but greatest of the missionaries, died at Cap de Magdeleine, adjacent to Three Rivers, of fever.

Thwaites, JR, XIV, 288n16; LXVII, 175, 191-219; DCB; J. Franklin Jameson, *Narrative of New Netherland 1609-1664*. N.Y., Barnes & Noble, 1909.

Le Moyne de Bienville, Jean Baptiste, colonial official, explorer (c. Feb. 22, 1680-

Mar. 7, 1767). B. at Montreal he served as a midshipman in King William's War along the New England coast and elsewhere and was wounded in action. In 1698 he sailed with his brother, Iberville to the Gulf of Mexico, entering the Mississippi River March 2, 1699. When Iberville returned to France, Bienville was left as second in command at Biloxi, Mississippi. He explored the Red and Oauchita rivers region west of the Mississippi and was given command of Fort de Mississippi not far above the mouth of the stream and then, upon death of his superior, became commandant at Biloxi. When Iberville returned to France for the last time in 1702, Bienville despite his youth became in effect governor of Louisiana, guiding its destiny by means of his diplomacy, tact, and knowledge of Indian customs and to some extent, their languages, although his rivals and enemies among the French population persistently pressed charges against him alleging various forms of misconduct — charges that never were substantiated. Cadillac was named governor in 1710, reaching Louisiana in 1713 and Bienville was made military commander from the Ohio to the Gulf; in this capacity and in view of Cadillac's ineptness in Indian relations, it was Bienville who maintained what peace there was between the colonials and the natives. When Cadillac was removed, Bienville served as acting head of the colony until the new governor, Jean Michel de Lespinay arrived in 1717. That year the office of royal governor was abolished and Bienville was made commandant general with responsibilities as far north as Illinois. He founded New Orleans in 1718, in 1719 seized Pensacola, Florida when war broke out between France and Spain and took it back again after the Spanish had recaptured it. Bienville was summoned to France in 1725, but with the Natchez uprising in 1729 and a change in the political organization of Louisiana, he once more was named governor in 1732 and returned to New Orleans the following year, guiding the colony through difficult times amid pressures from abroad, slavery issues, troop desertions, Indian difficulties and natural catastrophes. He supported the Choctaws in their conflicts with the English-backed Chickasaws and welcomed the Apalachee refugees from Florida, but his ultimate failure to subdue the Chickasaws and generally ineffectual cam-

paigns against them in 1736 and 1739 led to the termination of his public career in 1742. He left Louisiana in 1743 for Paris where he lived the remainder of his life secure in the knowledge he had "nurtured a sickly outpost into an enduring center of French culture" and in comfortable financial circumstances resulting from his lifetime of service to France and his wise investments. He never married.

Literature abundant: Thwaites, JR, LXVI, 342n27; DAB; DCB; CE.

Le Moyne de Longueuil, Charles, frontiersman (Aug. 2, 1626-Feb. 1685). B. at Dieppe, France, he reached New France in 1641 at 15 and spent four years in the Huron country as an indentured servant of the Jesuits, then was released to become an interpreter and soldier at Three Rivers, Quebec, later moving to Montreal. He survived almost continual skirmishes with the Iroquois whose language, closely related to Huron, he came to speak fluently. His bravery was proverbial; on occasion he barely escaped massacre, and sometimes he took prisoners. In 1657 he instituted an exchange of French and Iroquois prisoners, an uncommon event for the time. In 1665 he was taken prisoner by an Iroquois war party, but was set free by an Onondaga chief, a friend of the French. In January of 1666 Le Moyne commanded an advance party of frontiersmen for Remy de Courcelle's futile expedition to the Mohawk River valley of New York, and that fall he operated with Tracy in a campaign against the Mohawks. Later he escorted a party to Lake Champlain. In 1671 he was sent as interpreter on expeditions to Lake Ontario; in 1682-83 he had a significant role in negotiations between the French and Iroquois. Married in 1654 to a 13-year-old girl, he fathered 14 children, including Iberville, a noted soldier and explorer, and Bienville, founder of New Orleans. In 1668 he was ennobled by Louis XIV of France, became a major land holder, the richest and one of the most prominent citizens of Montreal. He was captain of Montreal militia, interpreter for the city, and was a bulwark of French colonization in a critical period. He died at Montreal and was buried there.

Thwaites, JR, XXVII, 312n10; DCB.

Le Moyne de Longueuil, Charles, army officer (Oct. 18, 1687-Jan. 17, 1755). B. at

Longueuil, Quebec, he became the second baron of Longueuil. He early entered the army in France, returning to Canada in 1712 and in 1726 became commandant of Fort Niagara, where he could supplement his officer's pay by means of the fur trade. In 1733 he became town major of Montreal, and six years later was sent to Louisiana to assist Bienville, his uncle, in an operation against the Chickasaws. He returned to Montreal in 1740, became governor of the community and for a few months was acting governor of New France. He died at Montreal.

Thwaites, JR, LXXI, 396n29; DCB, III.

Le Moyne de Sainte Hélène, Jacques, army officer (Apr. 16, 1659-c. Dec. 3, 1690). The second son of Charles Le Moyne de Longueuil, he took part as a militia officer in La Barre's futile Iroquois operation of 1684 and two years later he accompanied his brother Iberville on an expedition to Hudson Bay to oust the British who had established fur trading posts; the French efforts were successful due largely to the audacity and courage of the Le Moyne brothers. In 1687 he commanded 300 Indians of Denonville's operation against the Senecas. In 1689 he again went to Hudson Bay and returned in time for a winter operation against Schenectady, an incident of the King William War then raging between the French and English colonies. With 210 men, 114 of them French, Le Moyne, sharing command with Nicolas d'Ailleboust left Quebec in February and on the 18th reached their target. The inhabitants, mostly Dutch, were asleep as the French and Indians surrounded the town and launched a night attack, overrunning the place, massacring 60, sparing 50 and taking off 25 prisoners, burning all but five or six of the 80 houses of the town. Le Moyne had "learned the art of fighting in the immense savagery of the North American continent. He derived from the Indian his technique, his courage, and also his cruelty." In October Le Moyne was of the defense forces of Quebec protecting the city from William Phips's attack. On October 20 he was wounded in the leg; the wound, at first thought to be slight, proved mortal and he died at Quebec.

Thwaites, JR, LXIV, 275n7; DCB, I.

Le Moyne de Serigny, Joseph, naval officer (c. July 21, 1668-Sept. 12, 1734). B. at Montreal,

he was a brother of Iberville and Bienville and by 1686 was a midshipman at Rochefort, France. The next year and in 1689 he served as interpreter for Iroquois captives sent from Canada to serve in French galleys following Denonville's Seneca campaign of 1687, and in 1689 as the survivors were returned to Canada. As he rose slowly in the French navy, Serigny served for some years in Hudson Bay operations against the English. In 1701 he reached Louisiana with Iberville's third expedition, remaining a year; he returned to Louisiana in 1706, following Iberville's sack of Nevis Island and was accused in France of fraudulent disposal of booty taken and related matters. Although apparently guilty he weathered that situation. In 1718 he was sent to Louisiana again to serve as joint commandant of the colony with Bienville. In 1719 he captured the Spanish center at Pensacola, Florida. He returned to France in 1720, was promoted to naval captain; Serigny became governor of Rochefort, a post he held at the time of his death.

Thwaites, JR, LXVI, 341n19; DCB, II.

Leon, Alonso de, explorer, military officer (1637-1691). B. at Cadereyta, east of the present Monterrey, Nueva Leon, Mexico, he was believed the first to attempt a permanent white settlement in Texas. He was governor of Nueva Leon and in 1687 became first governor of Coahuila, and captain of the new presidio of Monclova. He led five expeditions into and across the Rio Grande country. In 1686 he went from Monterrey to the river, following it to the Gulf coast and south along the shore to the Rio de las Palmas. In 1687 he crossed the Rio Grande, but was turned back by a river he called the Salado, or Solo. He heard early in 1688 that a French survivor of the La Salle expedition was living among the Rio Grande Indians. In May De Leon crossed the river and captured Jean Henri (Juan Jarri), took him to Monclova, then sent him to Mexico City for examination. This intensified interest in discovering the remains of La Salle's Fort St. Louis (on Matagorda Bay) and perhaps more French survivors. In 1689, accompanied by Father Damian Massanet, De Leon went to Matagorda Bay with Jean Henri as guide and found the remains of Fort St. Louis. He conferred with the chief of the Nabedache, a Caddo tribe. On this expedition, planned as a settlement attempt although the notion proved abortive, De Leon picked up more survivors of the La Salle expedition: Jean l'Archévèque, Pierre Meusnier and Jacques Grollet. They were not sent to Spain as reported, but found their way eventually to New Mexico. In 1690 De Leon made a fifth expedition, assisting Massanet to found a mission, San Francisco de los Tejas near the Neches River, the beginning of Spanish settlement of Texas although the mission was shortly abandoned to be re-established years later. On this final effort De Leon burned the remains of Fort St. Louis lest they prove attractive to the French or others. The next year De Leon died, probably at Monclova.

Herbert Eugene Bolton, *Spanish Exploration in the Southwest, 1542-1706.* N.Y., Charles Scribner's Sons, 1916; *Porrua; HT.*

Leonard, William (Billy the Kid), jeweler, desperado (c. 1850-June 6, 1881). B. in New York, he opened a jewelry store at Las Cruces, New Mexico, in June 1879, and later at Mesilla, New Mexico. He then moved to Las Vegas, where he became friendly with Doc Holliday and perhaps Wyatt Earp, and may have taken part in stage holdups. He fled an assault to murder charge and made for Arizona. Being an expert in reducing gold and silver bullion, he was considered by outlaws "a handy man to have around." As one "division of the Las Vegas gang," he centered his activities around the Shakespeare, New Mexico-Galeyville, Arizona, area with Harry Head, Bill Diehl and others, "wrestling with his conscience..., wanting to be a business-man, yet yearning for the smell of horse leather, cactus blossoms and gunsmoke." He may have taken part in rustling and stage holdups, but the record is most confused by rival charges and claims. Earp apparently wanted Leonard, Head and Jim Crane set up to murder them, yet he is suspected of having a *subrosa* affiliation with them. Leonard and Crane had a ranch near Cloverdale, New Mexico, and somehow enmity arose between them and Head on the one hand, and William and Ike Hazlett of Eureke (Hachita), on the other. The Hazletts at nearby Owl City, New Mexico, killed Leonard and Head, and were themselves later killed by a Crane-mustered crowd of cowboys.

1880 U.S. Census for Ariz.; Ed Bartholomew, *Wyatt Earp: The Man & The Myth.* Toyahvale, Tex., Frontier Book Co., 1964.

Leonard, Zenas, mountain man (Mar. 19, 1809-July 14, 1857). B. in Clearfield County, Pennsylvania, he was raised as a farm boy, received some education, and at 21 hiked to Pittsburgh where he worked some months for a merchant uncle before going on to St. Louis to enter the western fur trade. Hired as clerk by the trapping firm of Gantt and Blackwell, he left St. Louis April 24, 1831, reached the Laramie River after some hardships, and when the partnership was dissolved, became a Rocky Mountain free trapper. Zenas took part in the famous Battle of Pierre's Hole in July 1832, his narrative being one of the standard primary accounts of the affair. He trapped the upper Rockies and Big Horn Basin the following season, and at the 1833 rendezvous met Bonneville and was hired as clerk for Joe Walker's expedition westward. With this party Leonard crossed the present states of Utah and Nevada, surmounted the Sierra Nevada and, according to belief, was among the first Anglos to see the Yosemite Valley and the giant Sequoia trees, reaching the coast in November. The expedition returned by way of Walker's Pass, south of the earlier crossing, and regained the Bonneville Bear River camp in 1834. Still working for Bonneville, Leonard trapped the Crow country in the Yellowstone and Wind River valleys the ensuing winter and returned to Independence, Missouri, with Bonneville August 29, 1835. He went on to his Pennsylvania home. After a few months he established a store and trading operation at the site of Fort Osage (the present Sibley), Missouri, and also operated a boat on the Missouri River as far as St. Louis. He must have completed his manuscript by about 1838, basing it upon diaries and recollections. Leonard's *Narrative* "appears to be the revelation of an honest, average man who resisted any temptation to portray himself as the hero of every exciting adventure." He was a good observer and his work is "of permanent value." His record of the Walker expedition is "the most complete and accurate account" of that important endeavor and for that reason alone the *Narrative* would have unique value. Leonard married and fathered three children, two girls and a son named for him. He was buried in the old Sibley Cemetery.

Zenas Leonard, *Adventures of Zenas Leonard Fur Trader,* ed. by John C. Ewers. Norman, Univ. of Okla. Press, 1959.

Leonis, Miguel, frontiersman (Oct. 20, 1824-Sept. 20, 1889). B. at Camboles-Baines, France, Leonis, of Basque parentage, became a smuggler between Spain and France and reached southern California where he became a sheep rancher in the San Fernando Valley. He married an Indian woman who owned a ranch near present Calabasas and combined his land with hers. Whether deserved or not, Leonis acquired a reputation for keeping squatters from his lands by force, came into a feuding relationship with Andrew Banks, said to have had Civil War experience although not listed in Heitman, and in a shooting incident Banks was wounded mortally. Leonis was in and out of the courts almost constantly; he was either assassinated or died in an accident, leaving his wife reportedly about $500,000 and a home which today is a historical museum at Calabasas, California.

Martin Cole, "The Giant Basque of Calabasas." *Oldtimers Wild West,* Jan. 1975, 12-15.

Leopold, (Rand) Aldo, forester, game manager, conservationist (Jan. 11, 1887-Apr. 21, 1948). B. at Burlington, Iowa, he was graduated from Yale in 1908 and the next year became a Forest Assistant with the U.S. Forest Service in the southwest. He became supervisor of Carson National Forest in 1912 and assistant district forester in charge of operations in 1917. He left the Forest Service in 1924 to become associate director of the Forest Products Laboratory, Madison, Wisconsin, in 1925, but soon entered game management work, being a pioneer in the field, and in 1933 becoming professor of wild life management at the University of Wisconsin. Leopold is best known for his pioneer work in establishment of a wilderness preservation system and for his eloquent writing in its behalf. He was a key figure in creation of the first permanent wilderness reservation, the Gila Primitive Area of New Mexico which he formally proposed in 1922; it was established in 1924. He was influenced in this concept by Arthur Carhart of Colorado and a colleague, Ward Shepard, but the primary moving force was Leopold. A bronze plaque set in a boulder overlooking the Gila Wilderness commemorates Leopold: "Forester and wildlife manager, outdoorsman, ecologist, philosopher and practical idealist, interpreter of nature, pioneer in wilderness preservation, he taught an ethic of the land and by his teaching, his writing and his example gave added depth, breadth and insight to conservation." The tablet was placed by the Wilderness Society, of which he was a founder. His writings include the near-classic, *Sand County Almanac* (1949), and also *Round River* (1953), and the technical works: *Game Survey of the North Central States* (1931) and *Game Management* (1933). He died of a heart seizure while fighting a grass fire on a neighbor's farm in Wisconsin. His survivors incuded sons Aldo Starker Leopold (1913-1983), a noted biologist, and Luna B. Leopold (1915-), geologist and hydrologist.

Works cited; *Los Angeles Times,* June 2, 1974, first edition; *Who's Who;* Boyd Gibbons, "Aldo Leopold: A Durable Scale of Values." *Nat. Geog.,* Vol. 160, No. 5 (Nov. 1981), 682-708; *Wilderness,* Vol. 48, No. 168 (Spring, 1985), 3-30.

Le Petit, Joseph, pioneer child (July 1647-pre 1653). The son of Pierre Le Petit of Beauport, near Quebec, he was captured by Iroquois about 1650 and taken to their villages in the present New York State. Attempts by "a good Scotch Lady" of Fort Orange (Albany) to ransom him were futile, and he died among his captors sometime before 1653, according to the Jesuit Joseph Poncet.

Thwaites, JR XL, 143, 255-56n7.

Le Petit, Mathurin, Jesuit missionary (Feb. 6, 1693-Oct. 13 or 18, 1739). B. at Vannes, France, he became a Jesuit and reached Louisiana in 1726, becoming a missionary to the Choctaws. He remained among them two or three years and then was named superior of the Louisiana mission, residing at New Orleans. He died in Louisiana.

Thwaites, JR, LXVII, 342n44, LXXI, 168.

Lerole: *see* Canchy de Lerole, Louis de

Leroux, Antoine, frontiersman (c. 1801-June 30, 1861). B. Joaquin Antoine Jacques Leroux at St. Louis, he may have been part Indian. He received some education and went up the Missouri River in 1822 with Ashley; he reached Taos in 1824. Leroux trapped the southwest, and in 1833 was married to a Spanish woman of the Vigil family, thereby acquiring a land grant. He guided the Mormon Battalion to California, helping blaze the southern trail to the coast, followed by many California emigrants. Leroux was one of a jury which decreed death for the Taos insurrectionists. He guided military expeditions into the Navaho country and in 1849 against the Utes, engaged in sheep ranching and trading and guided troops retaliating for the White ambush. He was wounded in 1851 while guiding the Sitgreaves expedition exploring another California route, later followed by the Santa Fe railroad. In 1852 he guided the Bartlett Boundary Survey party on its return from San Diego, returning to Taos from El Paso. In 1853 he guided Gunnison over the Colorado Rockies, averting one Ute attack, returned to New Mexico and guided Whipple to Los Angeles, arriving in March 1854. Leroux guided a relief party with New Mexico livestock to Fort Bridger in 1857 for the Johnston expedition against the Mormons, harsh winter weather making the journey a cruelly difficult one. Leroux guided a punitive expedition against Comanches and Kiowas in 1860 out of Fort Union. He died at his ranch (the grant subsequently confirmed by the U.S. Congress), and was buried in the nave of the parish church, later bulldozed away (in 1960) to make room for a new structure. Bones uncovered at the time were thought to be those of parish priests, the memory of Leroux having faded away.

Forbes Parkhill, *The Blazed Trail of Antoine Leroux*. Los Angeles, Westernlore Press, 1965.

LeRoy, Kitty, character (c. 1849-1877). An actress or entertainer of sorts, she had become a "jig dancer" in Dallas in the middle 1870's, then migrated to Deadwood, South Dakota, where she danced in the Gem Theater and presided at the Mint, a gambling house, in addition to getting married to five men by the time she was 27. An expert at extracting from miners their dust, she was shot by Sam Curley, a faro dealer, in the room above the Lone Star Saloon; he had married her bigamously as it turned out, and he was incensed for that reason. Curley thereafter killed himself.

Wayne Gard, *Sam Bass*. Lincoln, Univ. of Nebr. Press, 1969; Gard, "Kitty LeRoy, Queen of Hoofers." *True West*, Vol. 24, No. 1 (Sept.-Oct. 1976), 11, 41-42.

Lescarbot, Marc, writer (c. 1570-1642). B. at Vervins, France, he was well educated in the classics, canonical and civil law, and became an attorney and equally known for his legal prowess and his writings. He visited Acadia, in New France, leaving his homeland May 13, 1606 and reaching Port Royal, Nova Scotia, in July, spending the winter of 1606-1607 there. In the spring he explored the coast from the mouth of the St. John River, New Brunswick to the St. Croix River, between New Brunswick and Maine. Upon his return to France he wrote a great deal on Acadia, his best-known work being the *Histoire de la Nouvelle France* (1609). A strong partisan of Poutrincourt and De Monts and "while a Catholic in name, he was a Huguenot at heart," according to Thwaites, he seems to have been "a man of judgment, tact, and intelligence." He is supposed by many to have been the author of the widely-circulated pamphlet, the *Factum*... (1614), reprinted in 1887, interpreted widely as an attack upon the Jesuits, particularly Biard and Massé; it is this document which alleges Biard served as guide for Argall on his expedition to destroy Port Royal, rather than as an unwilling captive, as the priest indicated he had been. Rene Baudry, in the *Dictionary of Canadian Biography* discounted Lescarbot's authorship of the pamphlet on the rather slender ground that he had been in Switzerland when the work appeared. Lescarbot lived in Europe for the remainder of his life, writing prolifically on a wide range of subjects.

Thwaites, JR, I, pp. 306-307, III, pp. 298-99; DCB; Parkman, *Pioneers of France in the New World*.

Leslie, Frank (Buckskin Frank), gunman (c. 1842- c. 1922). B. probably at Galveston, Texas, his father's name reportedly was Kennedy and Frank used his mother's. He no doubt had a better than average education; when sober he was genial and intelligent, but uncontrollable when drunk. Leslie reported he had been an army scout in the Dakotas, Oklahoma and Texas in the 1870's and certainly so served during the Geronimo campaign in Arizona-Old Mexico. He reached Tombstone in 1877, tended bar in San Francisco and returned to Tombstone in 1880. On June 22, 1880, he and George Perrine shot Mike Killeen, with whose estranged wife Leslie had been keeping company, Killeen expiring five days later. William Claiborne believed Leslie killed John Ringo in July 1882, but this was not generally accepted. On November 14, 1882, Leslie killed Claiborne at Tombstone. He was divorced in 1887. He was suspected of murdering Mike Bradshaw, whose estranged girl friend Mollie

Williams (or Bradshaw) had become Leslie's companion, and was suspected of such crimes as stage robbery. On July 10, 1889, he killed Mollie Williams and wounded Jim Neal, a ranch hand. He was sentenced to life in the Yuma territorial prison, but was pardoned November 7, 1896. Hired as a guard for the Southern Pacific railroad geological expedition to Old Mexico, Leslie reportedly killed three Mexicans allegedly stealing wood. He claimed he had killed 14 people, one the woman for whose murder he was sentenced. He may have taken part in the Alaska gold rush, returning to the San Francisco area where he did odd jobs, being last reported in 1922 as a derelict swamping a saloon in Oakland. In 1926 when William (Billy) Breakenridge, an old friend, tried to locate him, no trace of Leslie could be found. Bailey thought, however, he had committed suicide.

Colin Rickards, *Buckskin Frank Leslie: Gunman of Tombstone*.   El Paso, Tex. Western Press, 1964; Tom Bailey, "I Saw Wyatt Earp's Commission." *True West*, Vol. 8, No. 3 (Jan.-Feb. 1961), 54-55.

Lesperance, Pierre, trapper (Oct. 10, 1791-1879). B. in Quebec, he reached St. Louis about 1811 and New Mexico as a trapper within about three years, under arrest but soon released. By 1822 he had returned to New Mexico, becoming a citizen in 1830, occasionally tried prospecting and ranched near the future San Geronimo, west of Las Vegas, where he was buried.

Janet Lecompte article, MM, Vol. VI.

Le Sueur, Jacques Francois, Jesuit missionary (July 22, 1865-Apr. 28, 1760). B. in Coutances, France, he became a Jesuit and reached Canada about 1716 intending to labor in the Illinois country, but instead studied Abenaki and worked for some time at St. Francis Xavier Mission near Bécancour, across the river from Three Rivers. Later, serving in eastern Canada, he occasionally visited the Abenakis of the mission at Narantsouak, or Norridgewock, Maine; the remainder of his career was spent in Canada. His short paper, "History of the Calumet and of the Dance," was published in 1952 by the Museum of the American Indian, Volume 12, Number 5 of its *Contributions,* the museum holding the original manuscript. He died at Montreal.

Thwaites, JR, LXV, 267n22; DCB, III.

Le Sueur, Pierre Charles, explorer, fur trader (1657-1704). B. at Artois, France, he reached Canada as a Jesuit *donne* and was sent to Sault Ste. Marie where by 1680 he had left the Jesuits and become known as a coureur de bois, being principally involved in the Sioux trade in the upper Mississippi country. He was with Perrot May 8, 1689, when Perrot took possession of the northwest for France, and was commandant at Chequamegon, on the southwestern shore of Lake Superior, by 1693, remaining there several years. In 1693 he was directed to keep open the Bois Brulé and St. Croix trading route (across northwestern Wisconsin to the Mississippi) and for this purpose built forts on Madelaine Island in Lake Superior and on a Mississippi River island near the present Red Wing, Minnesota. He discovered lead mines on the upper Mississippi and went to France for permission to work them; his license was suspended by Frontenac, perhaps to keep him in the more lucrative fur trade or to prevent his fur trading; the record is confused. Le Sueur returned to France and went to Louisiana in December 1699; the next summer Iberville, a relative of his wife, sent him with others to seek copper mines in the Sioux country; he found deposits and sent ore samples to France (Frontenac by then had died). Le Sueur went south to Mobile, then returned to France in 1702 himself to argue the value of the country he had explored. Upon his request the king appointed him a judge at Mobile, with permission to recruit men for exploration work in the north and with payment for his work among the Sioux. He sailed from France early in 1704; the ship paused at Havana where a plague was raging and Le Sueur died at sea between Havana and Louisiana which the vessel reached in July. His wife and four children arrived at Mobile, perhaps unaware until then of his death. Nasatir, in the *Dictionary of Canadian Biography,* believes that his son, Jean Paul Le Sueur, may have been "the Canadian" later active with Bienville against the Natchez.

Thwaites, JR, LXVI, 337-38n7; DCB, II.

Leverson, Montague R., promoter of causes (Mar. 2, 1830-post 1910). B. at London, he "espoused many causes," and according to Angel was "the great American letter, newspaper &c. writer." He became an attorney and solicitor in England, practicing at London from 1852, and came to the United States in 1865. He obtained a doctorate at Gottingen in 1872 and by 1873 was practicing law at Golden, Colorado. He visited New Mexico and was "appalled" at the lawlessness in Lincoln County and elsewhere, engaging in an extensive and probably effective letter writing campaign to Schurz, President Hayes and others to have Governor Axtell removed. According to Angel, Leverson "knows 6 times more than he can prove & 6 times more than any one else," adding, for the benefit of new governor, Lew. Wallace, "he can be of service to you. Use him. Don't commit yourself. Strong McSween man...." In 1879 Leverson moved to San Francisco, took up the Henry George single tax cause, became president of the Anti-Vaccination Society of America, was elected to the California Legislature in 1881 and received a medical degree in 1893 from Baltimore Medical College; he later lived at New York City and in 1910 lived in the Bronx.

Angel; Robert N. Mullin, ed., *Maurice G. Fulton's History of the Lincoln County War*, Tucson, Univ. of Ariz Press, 1968; *Who Was Who*; Information from New York Hist. Soc.

Levis: *see* Strauss, Levi.

Lévis, Gaston François, chevalier (later Duke) de. French officer (Aug. 20, 1719-Nov. 26, 1787). B. at Languedoc, he entered the French army and distinguished himself in numerous European engagements. In 1756 he went to Canada, commanded initially the Lake George sector, was in the attack on Fort William Henry the following year and led an abortive operation into the Mohawk country in 1758. His abilities were everywhere recognized and he became second in command to Montcalm in Canada. After the capture of Quebec, which need not have been lost in Lévis's view, he attempted to retake the city from the English but after a long siege was forced to abandon the attempt on May 16, 1760. Lévis fell back on Montreal. He held that city until an English army forced him to surrender it, with all of New France, on September 8, 1760. Lévis and his army were sent back to France where he was promoted, and continued his distinguished service in the French armed forces. He died at Arras, France.

Thwaites, JR, LXX, 312n29; DCB, IV.

Levy, James H., gunman, gambler (1842-June 3, 1882). B. in Ireland of Jewish extraction, he emigrated to this country and by 1871 was a miner at Pioche, Nevada, where in May he engaged in a quarrel with one, Mike Casey, and killed him, being wounded in the jaw by one of Casey's friends. It was supposed by some that he shot Casey for the $5,000 offered by a mortally wounded Thomas Gossan whom Casey previously had done in. Levy was acquitted. Levy may have had other fights in Nevada; in 1873 was believed to have killed Thomas Ryan and was arrested for it, but not convicted. He moved to Virginia City, Nevada, where he took up gambling, and in 1876 joined the gold rush to the Black Hills. He soon went to Cheyenne where on March 9, 1877, he had his celebrated fight with Charlie Harrison and earned his greatest frontier fame. In a street fight Harrison fired several times at Levy, and Levy mortally wounded him, Harrison dying March 22. Levy was not convicted. Bat Masterson, Wyatt Earp and others held up the fight as an example of calm deliberation giving a gunman an edge over a fast but erratic shooter, but the facts do not warrant that interpretation. Levy was briefly at Leadville, Colorado, reached Tombstone early in 1882 and at Tucson became involved in a feud with John Murphy, a local gambler. They agreed to a duel below the Mexican border, but Levy was killed by Murphy and two colleagues at Tucson while unarmed. The three killers were arrested, but broke jail and were never apprehended.

William B. Secrest, "Jim Levy: Top-notch Gunfighter." *True West*, Vol. 25, No. 6 (July-Aug. 1978), 24-26, 56-58.

Lewis, Aaron B., frontiersman (fl. 1830s). He reached New Mexico in 1831 from Fort Towson, Arkansas, after a most arduous trip, not fully recovering until May of 1832. Lewis trapped beaver in the middle Rockies, then on southern Plains rivers, eventually reaching Fort Smith, Arkansas, late in 1832. He is said to have joined the army, then led a party to California.

Harvey L. Carter article, MM, Vol. V.

Lewis, Alfred Henry, writer (1858-Dec. 24, 1914). B. at Cleveland, Ohio, he became a lawyer in his twenties but in 1881 went to Meade County, Kansas, to work on a cattle ranch. As a cowboy he drifted to Denison, Texas, then to Colfax County, New Mexico, where he became a newspaperman, working for the *Mora County Pioneer* and later editing the *Las Vegas Optic.* He reached Tombstone a few years after the OK Corral fight, and in 1885 returned to Kansas where he resumed the practice of law. In 1890 he wrote his first story on "Wolfville" — i.e., Tombstone, Arizona. Shortly he joined the staff of the *Kansas City Star,* in 1894 becoming chief of the Washington bureau of Hearst's *New York Journal.* He published the novel, *Wolfville,* in 1897 and its success was such that he could leave newspaper work and concentrate on fiction. Lewis published four other Wolfville books: *Wolfville Days* (1902), *Wolfville Nights* (1902), *Wolfville Folks* (1908) and *Faro Nell and Her Friends* (1913). Lewis wrote two other western books, *The Sunset Trail* (1905), a fictionalized biography of Bat Masterson, and *The Throwback* (1906) in addition to nine other books. In 1911 he made his only other trip to the west, visiting El Paso to report on the Mexican Revolution. He died at New York City on Christmas Eve.

R.R. White, "Wolfville, Arizona." *True West,* Vol. 29, No. 2 (Feb. 1982), 32-37.

Lewis, Andrew, frontier soldier (1720-Sept. 26, 1781). B. in Ireland, he settled on the upper Roanoke River near present Salem, Virginia, where he became locally prominent politically. He was present at Washington's surrender at Fort Necessity, and with Braddock's command, but not at the defeat. He participated in border fighting and treaty-making with the Indians. In 1774 during Lord Dunmore's War, Lewis was in command of one wing of the militia forces, Dunmore of the other. Lewis reached Point Pleasant, above the confluence of the Ohio and Kanawha rivers by early October. At daybreak October 10 his force of 800 men was attacked by an equal Indian force, 81 Virginians were killed and 140 wounded; about 200 Indians were killed. By Lewis's skill and courage his forces scored an important victory which had far-reaching effects on the frontier, keeping the Indians quiet for three years, opening the way for the George Rogers Clark expedition and westward expansion. Lewis was commissioned a Brigadier General, but saw no important service during the Revolution. He was upwards of 6 feet tall, agile and strong, and reserved in manner, fathered five sons and a daughter, and left his widow a considerable selfmade fortune.

DAB; *Documentary History of Dunmore's War*

1774, ed. by Reuben Gold Thwaites, Louise Phelps Kellogg. Madison, Wisc. Hist. Soc., 1905.

Lewis, David, Mormon pioneer (Apr. 10, 1814-c. Aug. 1854). B. in Simpson County, Kentucky, he became a convert to Mormonism. He was a survivor of the massacre at Haun's Mill, Missouri, August 30, 1838, when 17 church members were murdered by a mob; he wrote an account of the massacre "in all its horrible detail." Lewis reached Utah in October 1850, and about 1853 was sent south to Parowan. Six feet, 1 inch, tall, weighing 200 pounds, he was blue-eyed; Lewis was a farmer, cooper and a photographer. He died at Parowan, Utah.

Frank Essholm, *Pioneers and Prominent Men of Utah.* Salt Lake City, Western Epics, 1966; Juanita Brooks, *John Doyle Lee.* Glendale, Calif., Arthur H. Clark Co., 1961.

Lewis Elmer (The Mysterious Kid, Foster Holbrook), desperado (Mar. 1876-Feb. 26, 1896). B. near Neosho, Missouri, he was a minor outlaw, who may have worked as a cowboy for a time but by 1894 had fallen into bad company under his alias, Foster Holbrook. He traveled with George (Red Buck) Waightman for a time, joined the Christian gang and April 20, 1895, was part of the ambush that killed Deputy Sheriff William C. Turner of Pottawatomie County, Okla. He was acquitted by a jury. He was persuaded to help authorities run down the Christian gang, later rejoined Waightman, taking part in assorted deviltry. With another minor outlaw, Foster Crawford, he attempted to rob the City National Bank, Wichita Falls, Texas, February 25, 1896, killed one bank employee, and in the attempted getaway Lewis' horse dropped. The two were captured by Texas Rangers under Bill McDonald and lodged in the county jail from which they were taken by a mob and lynched.

Jeff Burton, "The Mysterious Kid." *English Westerners' Tally Sheet,* Vol. 20, No. 4 (Pub. No. 198), (July 1974), 4-10.

Lewis, Frank (Kid), desperado (d. Feb. 1882). This Kid Lewis ran a dance hall in Albuquerque's Old Town in 1881 and no one remembers how long before that. He headed up a gang which headquartered at Cranes, 25 miles east of Gallup, their robberies creating a reign of fear in the environs. A posse under a deputy sheriff named Jones cornered them in their headquarters building and in a resulting battle Lewis, James Lynch, one known only as "Kid," and a civilian, Conrad Knease were killed. Harry French (alias Simpson) surrendered and was jailed at Las Lunas, New Mexico. In March masked men broke into the jail, took out French and two murderers, Charles Shelton and James McDermott, and lynched them all.

Philip J. Rasch, "Three More Named 'Kid' Lewis." *Real West,* Vol. 23, No. 173 (Dec. 1980), 38.

Lewis, James, fur company clerk (d. c. June 15, 1811). Lewis, an Astor clerk aboard the ill-fated *Tonquin,* was reported by Irving as probably responsible for blowing up the ship off Vancouver Island, but this seems a mistake as he was reported killed by Indians there (see entry for Stephen Weeks).

Gabriel Franchere, *Adventure at Astoria 1810-1814.* Norman, Univ. of Okla. Press, 1967; Chittenden.

Lewis, Jim (Kid, James Bartlett), desperado (c. 1863-Sept. 21, 1883). B. in Missouri he reached the Clifton, Arizona, region in June 1883 reputed to have been a member of Billy the Kid's crowd in New Mexico, although probably was not. He was suspected of killing G.W. Gray in a Clifton robbery June 6, but discharged for lack of evidence. He was believed by some to have killed two men across the New Mexico line. September 11 he shot his girlfriend, Jessie Stiles, wounding her mortally, but said the shooting was accidental. September 21 a posse found Lewis and three others fording the Gila River 14 miles below Clifton, wanting some of them for questioning in another shooting. Lewis went for his gun and was killed and another was wounded.

Philip J. Rasch, "Three More Named 'Kid' Lewis." *Real West,* Vol. 23, No. 173 (Dec. 1980), 38.

Lewis, Meriwether, explorer (Aug. 18, 1774-Oct. 11, 1809). B. near Charlottesville, Albemarle County, Virginia, of distinguished lineage, Lewis received a good education from private tutors and became avidly interested in the outdoors while still a boy. At 18 he undertook management of his mother's estate but at 20 volunteered for the militia Washington called to put down the 1794

Whisky Rebellion. From that service on May 1, 1795, he became an ensign in the 2nd Sub-Legion, serving under William Clark in Anthony Wayne's Ohio Indian campaign that culminated with the Battle of Fallen Timbers. Lewis did not forget his favorable impression of Clark although it is doubtful whether the two met again for several years. Lewis transferred to the 1st Infantry November 1, 1796, becoming a lieutenant March 3, 1799, and a captain December 5, 1800. He served at Memphis where he learned something of the Choctaw language; he was then stationed at Detroit until 1801. Jefferson had been interested in sending an expedition to the Pacific coast by way of the Missouri River; Lewis in 1792 had applied to lead such an endeavor, but the idea was not then taken up. When Jefferson was elected President he invited his friend, Lewis to become his private secretary; while serving in that capacity Lewis was encouraged to perfect his scientific studies in the matters of astronomy and navigation and in other directions. Thus in 1803 when Congress was persuaded by a confidential message from Jefferson to finance an expedition to the Pacific, Lewis successfully importuned the President for the opportunity to lead it. His suggestion of William Clark as co-leader suited Jefferson who intended to appoint Clark to the rank of captain, equal to Lewis's rank, although a mixup resulted in a commission only as second lieutenant of artillery reaching Clark; nonetheless, and although Lewis was nominal leader of the expedition, the two were in effect equal co-leaders throughout, with never a trace of tension or rivalry between them. The expedition gathered in Illinois, across from the mouth of the Missouri River and left May 14, 1804, on August 20 suffering the only personnel loss of the entire trip when Sergeant Charles Floyd died of a ruptured appendix. Members saw their first antelope September 5 and the first prairie dogs two days later, both creatures well known through travels of French fur men and explorers, but new to science. October 26 they reached the Mandan villages of present North Dakota, where they wintered. While not necessarily the better observer, Lewis, the more educated of the leaders authored most of the scientific information in the expedition journals, although Clark did his share. April 7, 1805, the westward trek resumed, the Great Falls of the Missouri in present Montana reached June 13, the Bitterroot Mountains crossed and by way of the Clearwater they reached the Snake and then the Columbia rivers, boating down the latter to the Pacific which they saw November 7, 1805. They wintered at Fort Clatsop, which they built, and not discovering shipping upon which they might have embarked for the east by sea, commenced on March 23, 1806, the return overland. While Clark explored down the Yellowstone, Lewis took nine men to the north, crossed the Rockies by what is now Lewis and Clark Pass on July 7 and reached the upper Missouri July 11, finding plenty of buffalo from whose hides they constructed bullboats for crossing the stream. Lewis and three men explored the Marias River, named for Lewis's cousin, Maria Wood. On this trip the only serious clash with Indians occurred: July 27 Blackfeet sought to steal weapons and horses from Lewis's reduced camp. Two of the Indians were killed, one by Lewis himself, and the remainder run off. Lewis brought his party hurriedly down the Marias to the Missouri (lest the Indians muster a greater force and renew the action), where he joined the remainder of his division and continued down the river. August 11 Lewis was shot "through the thighs" by Pierre Cruzatte who mistook him for an elk. The wound healed within a month. The Lewis party rejoined that of Clark August 12 near the mouth of the Yellowstone and the united expedition pushed on down the Missouri, reaching St. Louis September 23, 1806, after an absence of two years, four months and nine days and having been given up for lost by border residents. Influence of the wholly successful expedition "upon subsequent political acts of the United States, affecting the Oregon territory and international boundary lines was... great.... It gave to geographers much new material... and to science many previously unknown... animals and birds." It was the most excellent exploration accomplishment in the history of America, to the lasting credit of both of its leaders. In November 1806 Lewis and Clark went to Washington, D.C., where Lewis resigned from the army March 4, 1807, and immediately was appointed by Jefferson governor of Louisiana Territory, that region comprised in the Louisiana Purchase, though he did not assume the office for a year. He was "unsuited by temperament and experience"

for the position and soon became unpopular with many of his subjects, quarreled with some officials and became estranged from Washington for failure to maintain communications and consultations. He served as governor about 18 months when he left for Washington to straighten out some misunderstandings and hasten publication of the expedition's journals. He traveled overland, by way of Chickasaw Bluffs (Memphis) and reached the Natchez Trace where it crossed the Tennessee River. At an inn on the night of October 11, 1809, he died at the age of 35, either a suicide or by murder; no money was found on his body and his watch was recovered at New Orleans. Lewis had never married. He was serious-minded, moody but congenial with friends, and he was one of the great explorers of history.

Richard Dillon, *Meriwether Lewis: A Biography.* N.Y., Coward-McCann, 1965; *History of the Expedition Under the Command of Lewis and Clark,* ed. by Elliott Coues, 3 vols. N.Y., Dover Pubns., 1965; DAB; REAW.

Lewis, Robert Alpheus, miner, stockman (1858-Feb. 15, 1900). B. in Kentucky, he was the 15th miner to reach Tombstone, Arizona. He had come from San Francisco in November 1878, visited Bisbee, and in April 1879, went to Fort Huachuca, Arizona, and heard about the Tombstone strike. Later he settled at Lewis Springs, Arizona, naming it for his father, Alpheus Lewis, and remained there until 1884. Lewis died following a bobsledding accident in Oregon.

Will C. Barnes' *Arizona Place Names,* rev. and enl. by Byrd H. Granger. Tucson, Univ. of Ariz. Press, 1960.

Lewis, William Henry, army officer (c. 1829-Sept. 28, 1878). B. in Alabama, he was graduated from West Point and joined the 1st Infantry at the frontier post of Fort Brady, Michigan. He transferred to the 5th Infantry in 1850, serving at various posts in Texas until 1855, was on the Utah Expedition from 1857 to 1859, after taking part in Seminole disturbances in 1856-57. He took part in Navaho expeditions in 1860 and 1861. During the Civil War he served in New Mexico, being stationed at Forts Marcy and Union and taking part in the battle of Apache Canyon. As a major of the 36th Infantry he commanded Fort Douglas, Dakota Territory, in

1866. Lewis was at Fort Fred Steele, Wyoming, in 1869-70, then was assigned to the Plains posts of Camp Supply, Idaho Territory, and Fort Dodge, Kansas. As a lieutenant colonel of the 19th Infantry near Fort Wallace, Kansas, on Punished Woman's Fork of the Smoky Hill River, he was mortally wounded September 27, 1878, by the Dull Knife Cheyennes during their attempted movement northward from their Oklahoma exile.

Heitman; Cullum.

Lewis, William P., adventurer (fl. 1841). B. in Pennsylvania, he was a "young man" in 1841. He had lived at Santa Fe and Chihuahua City at least as early as 1835, leaving the latter place with Samuel Howland to join the Texas Revolution; in 1839 a "Lt. Lewis" is mentioned in connection with frontier service, and this might be the same man. He was appointed captain of artillery in the Texan-Santa Fe Expedition of 1841, and was one of the approximately 90-man party headed by William G. Cooke and John S. Sutton to initially cross the Staked Plains. Unaware that the Mexicans at Santa Fe were up in arms over what appeared a Texas invasion of New Mexico from several directions, Lewis, with five others, was sent ahead to San Miguel, southeast of Santa Fe, to prepare the way for the expedition; instead the emissaries were captured. Lewis, fluent in Spanish, appears thereafter to be used as a tool by the Mexicans, and to have become a traitor by Texan thinking; he returned with Armijo's force and persuaded Cooke and the large contingent that an overwhelming force was bearing down upon them, that the Mexicans always relieved travelers into their territory of all arms, that no harm would befall them if they surrendered their weapons, and talked them into laying down their arms. Thereupon the Texans were instantly made prisoners by the Mexicans, except for Lewis, who appears to have been trusted by them. Lewis was denounced by Cooke, Lubbock, Kendall, and others, and defended by no one. He appeared to have profited most from the Texan debacle, and Armijo spoke highly of his services in "assisting me to capture these Texans." According to Kendall and Lubbock, Lewis went from Chihuahua to Guaymas, Sonora, thence to the Hawaiian Islands, and "under an assumed name," according to Kendall, to Valparaiso, Chile, or elsewhere; thereafter he disappears. One report on the other hand suggests that he lived in Mexico "for many years" after the 1841 incident, although this version is not proven.

Noel H. Loomis, *The Texan-Santa Fe Prisoners.* Norman, Univ. of Okla. Press, 1958.

Lewis, William Winslow, Texas Ranger (Sept. 7, 1855-Oct. 20, 1934). B. at Carrollton, Kentucky, he went to Abilene, Kansas, at 16, joined a trail outfit returning to Texas, went to Old Mexico briefly, returned to Texas and worked for W.T. Burnham, going up the trail with a herd in 1873 as far as Nebraska, then returned once more to Texas. In 1874 he enlisted in Captain C.R. (Rufus) Perry's Company D, Texas Rangers. On July 12, with Major Jones, he participated in a very hard fight with Kiowa Indians at Lost Valley, near Jacksboro, in which the Rangers, with 37 men, had 14 killed or wounded. With a brief interlude during which he returned to Kentucky at the death of his father, Lewis served with the Rangers until late 1877 when he retired and entered business at Menard. He held various public offices and died in that community.

Frontier Times, Vol. 4, No. 11 (Aug. 1927), 7; Robert W. Stephens, *Texas Ranger Sketches.* Dallas, p.p., 1972.

Leyba, Marino, desperado (c. 1859-Mar. 29, 1887). B. along the Pecos River, New Mexico, he became a horse thief in youth near San Antonio, Bernalillo County, New Mexico, and in October 1880, probably participated in the murder of Charles Potter of a socially prominent family. Leyba is said to have been associated with Billy the Kid. On December 10, 1880, he was shot and seriously wounded by Pat Garrett at Puerto de Luna, Garrett remarking that Leyba was the "quickest man with a six-shooter" he had ever seen. Arrested following the shooting, Leyba escaped and in a pursuit he was again wounded and surrendered. He was fined $80 for the attempt on Garrett's life and given seven years, one month for theft of stock, but was pardoned July 21, 1886 for saving the life of a warden from a murderous convict. About March 5, 1887, he and two others probably killed three stockmen in San Miguel County, New Mexico, for purposes of robbery. His two companions were taken and after a relentless search Leyba was killed by deputy sheriffs Joaquin Montoya and Carlos Jacomo seven miles west of Golden, New Mexico. Leyba was said to have been a handsome man with dark blue eyes, black hair, reddish-black mustache, was 6 feet tall and weighed about 180 pounds.

Philip J. Rasch, "Los Bravos." English Westerners' Soc., *Brand Book,* Vol. XV, No. 2, Pub. 184 (Jan. 1973), 18-21; Robert R. White, "The Murder of Colonel Charles Potter," *New Mexico Historical Review,* Volume 62, No. 3 (July 1987). 249-62.

Leyva de Bonilla, Francisco, military officer (fl. 1593-1594). A Portuguese, he became a military officer in Spanish Mexico and in 1593 was assigned to punish depredating Indians in Nueva Vizcaya (Chihuahua) on the northern frontier. Joining his expedition was Antonio Gutiérrez de Humaña and some of his followers. The commanders were warned by Governor Diego Fernández de Velasco not to penetrate beyond Nueva Vizcaya on penalty of royal displeasure, but nonetheless took their expedition into New Mexico. They worked up the Rio Grande to San Ildefonso, 25 miles north of today's Santa Fe, spending about a year in the New Mexico pueblos. Then they traveled eastward to the buffalo plains and northeastward into today's Kansas. In the vicinity of either the modern Great Bend or Wichita, Kansas they came upon a large native village with houses of poles and straw (perhaps a Wichita settlement). Near this point a disagreement arose between Leyva and Humaña and the latter murdered Leyva with a butcher knife, shortly afterward being cut down with all his men by Indians of undetermined tribe. Five of their own Indians escaped, three becoming lost on the plains, two reaching New Mexico pueblos where one was slain and the other, Jusepe, surviving to tell the story.

George P. Hammond, Agapito Rey, *The Rediscovery of New Mexico, 1580-1894.* Albuquerque, Univ. of New Mex. Press, 1966; Herbert Eugene Bolton, *Spanish Exploration in the Southwest, 1542-1706.* N.Y., Charles Scribner's Sons, 1916.

Libby, Orin G., historian (June 9, 1864- Mar. 29, 1952). B. near Hammond, Wisconsin, he was graduated from the University of Wisconsin, took graduate work under Frederick Jackson Turner and pioneered studies into American Constitutional history, receiving his doctorate in 1895. In 1902 after seven years instructing at the University of Wisconsin he moved to the University of North Dakota at Grand Forks where he became interested in western history. He reorganized the State Historical Society and became its secretary, helped organize the Mississippi Valley Historical Association and was its fourth president. He also was interested in ornithology, publishing articles on that specialty as well as historical pieces. He studied and wrote papers on a history of the Mandans and Hidatsas, the Verendrye travels and the Custer fight of 1876. In 1912 he interviewed on the Fort Berthold Reservation nine Arikaras who had been scouts with Terry and Custer, publishing the results in North Dakota *Collections,* Volume 6 (1920, repr. 1973). He launched the *North Dakota Historical Quarterly* in 1926 which he edited, as well as the *Collections.* Libby retired at 81 in 1945 and died six years later, regarded as "the father of North Dakota history, the founder of its state historic parks, and a stimulating teacher." Most of his publications were in scholarly journals.

Robert P. Wilkins, "Orin G. Libby: 1864-1952." *Ariz. and the West,* Vol. 16, No. 2 (Summer 1974), 107-110.

Lillie, Gordon William (Pawnee Bill), showman (Feb. 14, 1860-Feb. 3, 1942). B. at Bloomington, Illinois he received a high school education and worked as a bookkeeper briefly when the family moved to Wellington, Kansas. At 16 Lillie went trapping for a season with Tom Evans. Various accounts of his wild Plains experiences about this time seem quite unverifiable. In August 1882 he rode on a roundup for the Zimmerman Ranch on the Skeleton River, then was appointed secretary to Agent Edward Hale Bowman and teacher in an industrial school at the Pawnee Agency, Indian Territory, where he learned the Pawnee language. He later billed himself the "white chief of the Pawnees." He was introduced to Buffalo Bill Cody by Major Frank North, an authentic great of the frontier who had brought Lillie along as interpreter for Pawnees taking part in the show of that year. Pawnee Bill in 1888 organized his own wild west show which toured briefly and then collapsed. In 1889 he led a large party of boomers into Oklahoma, part of which had been opened for settlement. He again organized a wild west show in 1890; it this time prospered. With it Lillie toured for almost 20 years, occasionally in Europe. From 1908-13 he was a partner with Cody in the latter's productions, the two shows having merged; when the partnership was dissolved, Lillie returned to his 2,000-acre ranch near Pawnee, Oklahoma. He was active in work among the Pawnee Indians and for the perpetuation of the buffalo and established an Old Town and Indian Trading Post for the public, near Pawnee. His own place was called Pawnee Bill's Buffalo Ranch. He became vice president of the Fern Oil Company and wrote several books. Lillie was a factor in the establishment of the Wichita Wildlife Refuge. Lillie and his wife were involved in an automobile accident in 1936, his wife being injured fatally and Lillie, because of his injuries, remaining in poor health the rest of his life. He is buried at Pawnee.

Glenn Shirley, *Pawnee Bill: A Biography of Major Gordon W. Lillie.* Lincoln, Univ. of Nebr. Press, n.d.

Lilly, Ben(jamin) Vernon, hunter (Dec. 31, 1856-Dec. 17, 1936). B. in Wilcox County, Alabama, and raised in Kemper County, he became a legendary backwoods hunter and character, who would never lift a hand on Sundays and would quit a good job rather than work for a man who would do so. "It is doubtful if there has ever been a better marksman among hunters of America," judged Dobie, adding however, "but he could not demonstrate that marksmanship in public.... In shooting... he was himself only in solitudes." His reputation spread as did his toll of panthers, bears and anything else that came before his rifle sights. In October 1907 he hunted with Theodore Roosevelt in Tensas Bayou, Louisiana. Although Lilly found plenty of bears, Roosevelt managed to get only a lean old she-bear. Roosevelt described Lilly as "spare, full-bearded, with mild, gentle, blue eyes and a frame of steel and whipcord. I never met any other man so indifferent to fatigue and hardship. He equalled Cooper's Deerslayer in woodcraft, in hardihood, in simplicity — and also in loquacity." By 1904 Ben Lilly, according to Ned Hollister of the Biological

Survey, "is said by everyone to be the best hunter in Mississippi and Louisiana." Lilly was hired by the Survey to send in skins and skeletons for its specimen collection, and over the years he forwarded otter, ivory-billed woodpecker, wolf, deer and bear from Louisiana, Texas, Mexico, Arizona and New Mexico. He never became a conservationist but "it is doubtful if any field naturalist has ever learned as much about bears and panthers as Ben Lilly learned during more than half-century's hunting." Lilly is quoted in many reports of naturalists and scientists who studied game matters in the southwest, his observatiuons, comments and specimens covering species as varied as passenger pigeons and grizzlies. Early in 1906 he left Louisiana for good, entering the Texas Big Thicket, quitting forever home and family ties (he married twice). By 1908 he was in Coahuila, Mexico. After a year he hunted on west into Chihuahua and then the Sierra Madre, market hunting sometimes, hunting for the sport of it more often. By 1911 he was in New Mexico. He commenced bounty hunting for stockmen. In the Animas Mountains he killed 13 lions, several grizzlies and a dozen black bears with a few wolves. In 1912 he moved to Clifton, Arizona and in a week killed six bears and four lions. He went to work in the Apache National Forest as a trapper at $75 a month. For six or eight years he hunted north and south along the Arizona-New Mexico line, averaging about 50 lions and bears a year. In 1916 he commenced working for the Biological Survey at $100 a month, remaining with it four years. Occasionally he raised lions from cubs to grown animals, not as pets but to observe their habits, and detecting a new one delighted him. Literate, he usually took a tablet and pencil with him to make notes; sometimes he kept a diary, and was a voluminous correspondent. He also wrote narratives or started them, of his life and his understandings of wild animals. In 1921 Lilly guided Oklahoma oilman W.H. McFadden on his grand hunt from Mexico to Canada through the Rocky Mountains. Lilly guided and hunted for the lavish party as far as Idaho, but no farther north. Dobie believed Lilly had killed no more than 1,000 lions and bears in his lifetime, adding however that "considering his time(s), this was an enormous toll." Lilly died at a nursing home near Silver City, New Mexico. In 1947 a plaque to his memory was placed in the Gila National Forest of New Mexico, overlooking the Mogollon Mountains — good lion and bear country.

J. Frank Dobie, *The Ben Lilly Legend.* Boston, Little Brown and Co., 1950, and bibliography thereto.

Limoges, Joseph de, Jesuit Missionary (Sept. 19, 1668-Jan. 30, 1704). B. at Vannes, France, he became a Jesuit and arrived at Quebec in 1698. In 1700 he joined Du Rue in Louisiana and labored at a mission among the Houma Indians, east of the mouth of the Red River. Limoges was recalled to France in 1703 and died at Vannes.

Thwaites, JR, LXV, 266n18.

Linderman, Frank B., writer (Sept. 25, 1869-May 12, 1938). B. at Cleveland, he was educated in public schools until at 16 he went to Montana, heading for the Flathead country as "the least civilized area in the United States" and there became a trapper. He remained at that occupation with "no more ambition than... an Indian," from 1885 until 1891. He married in 1893 and more or less settled down, living in a variety of Montana communities, eventually becoming a newspaper publisher, state representative, Montana's assistant secretary of state and a successful insurance agent. He turned to writing in middle life, settling at Goose Bay on Flathead Lake, frequently visited by such friends as Charley Russell, Hermann Hagedorn and others. Linderman came to know well the Flatheads, Kootenais, Crows, Blackfeet, Crees and Chippewas and was adopted into the Blackfeet, Cree and Crow tribes. His books included *Indian Why Stories* (1915); *Indian Lodge-Fire Stories* (1918); *On a Passing Frontier: Sketches from the Northwest* (1920); *Indian Old-Men Stories* (1920); *How It Came About Stories* (1921); *Bunch-Grass and Blue-Joint* (1921); *Kootenai Why Stories* (1926); *American: The Life Story of a Great Indian, Plenty-coups, Chief of the Crows* (1930); *Red Mother* (1932), republished as *Pretty Shield: Medicine Woman of the Crows* (1974); and *Recollections of Charley Russell* (1962), ed. by H.G. Merriam. He died at Santa Barbara, California.

Harold G. Merriam, "Sign Talker with a Straight Tongue," *The Red Man's West,* ed. by Michael S. Kennedy, N.Y., Hastings House, 1965, 245-60; *Montana Adventure: The Recollections of Frank B. Linderman,* ed. by Harold G. Merriam, Lincoln, Univ. of Nebr. Pr., 1968.

Liotot (Lanquetot), surgeon and assassin (d. May 1687). Enlisted as a surgeon of the great La Salle expedition to colonize the Gulf coast, Liotot according to Parkman was a man of property with a large pecuniary interest in the operation. The expedition founded Fort St. Louis at Matagorda Bay on the coast of the present Texas. Simon Le Gros, on Easter Sunday of 1685 was bitten by a rattlesnake; the leg "mortified" and was amputated by Liotot, the first such operation in Texas so far as the record shows, but the patient died. Liotot seems to have been of average competence at his profession, but the wilderness had brought to the surface unattractive qualities, and he swore vengeance on La Salle for as Liotot believed having caused the death of a relative at the hands of Indians. The surgeon was of a party headed by La Salle who desperately sought to reach Illinois from the Texas colony, but while near the Navasota River joined with others following a dispute over buffalo meat and killed La Salle's nephew, Moranget and two others. Then on March 19, 1687, La Salle was assassinated from ambush. Liotot and Duhaut, the other arch-criminal, planned to return to Fort St. Louis where they and their mutineer colleagues would escape somehow from the doomed colony. But the mutineers fell into a dispute over the spoils and Liotot and Duhaut were killed by Hiens and Ruter.

Parkman, *La Salle and the Discovery of the Great West;* HT.

Lippincott, Henry, army surgeon (Sept. 22, 1839-Jan. 24, 1908). B. in Nova Scotia, he enlisted as a surgeon July 15, 1865, in the 6th California Infantry and was mustered out at Benicia Barracks, October 31, by the muster out of the regiment. He became assistant surgeon in the army February 28, 1866, and shortly was on the Plains. He was surgeon with Custer during the Washita campaign and at the commander's order made a detailed description of the nature of the wounds of casualties of the command in the November 27, 1868, battle. Custer praised him as "skillful and kind-hearted... unceasing in his attentions to the wounded." Lippincott also accompanied Custer's subsequent expedition into the Texas Panhandle during which hostile Cheyennes were rounded up and two white captives, Anna Morgan and Sarah White were liberated. Lippincott, in his 40 years of active duty, became the first chief surgeon of the military Department of the Pacific and the 8th Army Corps; he served with Merritt at the taking of Manila, and at the time of his retirement was chief surgeon of the military Department of the East. He died at Brooklyn.

George A. Custer, *My Life on the Plains.* Lincoln, Univ. of Nebr. Press, 1966; Stan Hoig, *The Battle of the Washita.* Garden City, N.Y., Doubleday & Co., 1976; Heitman; *New York Times,* Jan. 26, 1908.

Lisa, Manuel, fur trader (Sept. 8, 1772-Aug. 12, 1820). B. at New Orleans, he became the first great developer of the western fur trade in its finished form. As an itinerant trader he had plied the waters of the Mississippi and Ohio rivers, in 1796 establishing a frontier post at Vincennes. Against strong opposition from entrenched St. Louis interests, Lisa entered the Osage trade in 1802; a shift in the status of the Louisiana Territory assisted him in broadening his enterprises. He was a supplier of Lewis and Clark, projected an idea for trade with Santa Fe and although little developed from it, he retained for a number of years the desire to expand in that direction. His principal attention however was directed to the Missouri River and the fur country about its upper reaches. Upon the return of Lewis and Clark, Lisa formed a partnership with Menard and Morrison to develop trade in that direction. With a keelboat expedition he set off up the river in 1807, the first of his 13 trips up the Missouri. He surmounted opposition from Arickaras, Mandans and Assiniboins and reached the confluence of the Yellowstone and Big Horn rivers, establishing there Fort Raymond, later Fort Manuel. Lisa had been joined by John Colter, of Lewis and Clark experience. Lisa's imagination and experimentation had devised and formulated the directions the fur trade would follow in decades to come. Established St. Louis trading personalities became aware of Lisa's potential and now joined him in creation of the St. Louis Missouri Fur Company. In 1809,

the first year of the new company's operations, necessary upriver posts were established and certain successes scored, but on the whole results were not what had been wished largely because of Blackfoot opposition and similar factors. In 1810, lessened enthusiasm of his partners and feared competition from Wilson Price Hunt of Astor's fledgling operation forced Lisa, with minimum resources, into a frenzied race up the Missouri, vying with his rival, as he imagined, for the upper country trade his men presumably were mastering. The two parties came to an amicable parting of ways. Lisa's agents brought back to St. Louis furs to assure a profitable season, if not so much as had been hoped. Financial difficulties were partially overcome, the company reorganized, and Lisa in 1812 ascended the river once more. War now seemed likely between Britain and the U.S., and Indian hostility mounted, but Lisa persisted, though it was a bad season financially; earnings did not cover expenses and early in 1814 the Missouri Fur Company was dissolved, Lisa promptly forming a new organization. William Clark appointed him sub Indian agent for tribes above the Kansas River as best fitted to keep important bands at peace, and he again went up-stream, wintering with the Omahas where he found a wife. The next season Lisa continued his important political moves which effectively kept the western tribes out of the War of 1812. By 1816 he could return his full attention to trade. In 1817 he brought to St. Louis $35,000 in furs, a very good season. Lisa entered a new company and went north late in 1818. His wife had died and he married Mary Hempstead Keeney; the new company was dissolved after only a year, and in 1819 Lisa organized a fresh Missouri Fur Company. He went upriver one more time, but returned in the spring, suffering from the ailment which proved fatal. He was buried at what is now Bellefontaine Cemetery, St. Louis. Lisa had not only devised the form and method of operations that would guide the fur trade in future years, but his men had conducted important explorations and he had been instrumental in preventing the western frontier from becoming disastrously involved in the War of 1812. His contribution to the development of the west had been monumental.

Literature abundant; Richard Edward Oglesby, *Manuel Lisa and the Opening of the Missouri Fur*

Trade. Norman, Univ. of Okla. Press, 1963; Chittenden; DAB; Oglesby article, MM, Vol. V.

Little, Olga Schaaf, packer (July 26, 1883-Sept. 7, 1970). B. at Hamburg, Germany, she was brought by her parents to America in 1884, eventually settling in Animas City, across the river from Durango, Colorado. She and her brothers became horse breakers and Olga skilled in handling teams. In the early 1900's she was asked by Frank Rivers, a miner, to take a pack-string of burros to his mine in the San Juan Mountains and bring out ore. She had never packed, but undertook the job, launching a career she followed for many years. She generally packed burros but sometimes mules. In 1913 she married Bill Little, a Scot coal miner who also became a packer. Eventually they owned a dairy ranch and other properties. In 1958 Olga was featured on a national television show, and in 1963 the Littles marked their 50th wedding anniversary. She died at Durango and is buried there. In 1983 the federal Board of Geographic Names approved Olga Little Mountain as title for one of the San Juan peaks near Durango.

Kit Stone, "Olga Little, Lady Packer." *True West,* Vol. 24, No. 2 (Nov.-Dec. 1976), 26-29, 36.

Little Beaver, Delaware hunter (d.c. 1848). A member of Jim Swanock's band, he became a hunter and trapper in the Rocky Mountains, was a member of Lucien Maxwell's party attacked by Indians in Manco Burro Pass, New Mexico, June 20, 1848, was wounded and perhaps died therefrom.

Harvey L. Carter article, MM, Vol. VII.

Little Crow (Chetan-wakan-mani; Ta-oya-te-duta), Mdewakanton chief (c. 1803-July 8, 1863). A chief of the Kaposia division of the Mdewakanton Sioux (a branch of the Santees), he was the son of Little Crow and grandson of Little Thunder, and was b. in a village on the west bank of the Mississippi about ten miles below the mouth of the Minnesota River. In 1846 while drunk he was wounded by his brother. This caused him to discourage drinking among his followers and may have induced him to ask of the Fort Snelling agent for a missionary; Thomas S. Williamson, a Presbyterian physician and minister was sent. Under protest Little Crow signed the Mendota Treaty of August 5, 1851.

In the spring of 1855 he and Willis A. Gorman, governor and superintendent of Indian affairs went to Washington to discuss annuities, the payment of which had seriously lagged. In 1858 he went to Washington again on a four month visit with selected chiefs to sign a new treaty, but this time was more hesitant. He told Indian Commissioner Charles E. Mix that "we have been so often cheated that I wished to be cautious, and not sign any more papers without having them explained, so that we may know what we are doing." However he X'd the treaty on June 19, and the next day left for home. Again the pact was a source of dissension. Earlier Little Crow had assisted in the pursuit of Inkpaduta, perpetrator of the Spirit Lake massacres on the Iowa line. Between July 18 and August 4, 1857, Little Crow and his warriors pursued Inkpaduta, killed three or four of his band and captured three. The great Indian war of 1862, led by Little Crow and which involved the slaughter of around 800 whites according to many estimates (although Roddis counts only 360 civilians and 126 military dead) resulted from "the imperfect performance or non-fulfillment of treaty stipulations, failure to pay annuities fairly and promptly, a bad crop year which added hunger to Indian woes, the increasing pressure of whites usurping Indian lands and as a spark, a chance slaying by young Indian men of four whites, all combining to make the summer war in the valley of the Minnesota inevitable. Little Crow became its leader, although reluctantly. Tradition has it that he recognized the futility of the war and argued against it until taunted with cowardice, then agreed to become leader, directing that it start the following morning, which it did. The ravages extended more than 200 miles along the valley. At Redwood Ferry August 18 the military lost 24 killed and half a dozen wounded; other battles occurred at Fort Ridgely, August 22-23 (where Little Crow was wounded slightly); New Ulm, August 19 and 23, with many civilian casualties and much of the town burned; Birch Coulee, September 2 and Wood Lake September 23. Total Indian losses were unreported but Roddis believes no more than 50 Indians were slain in combat, even including those killed in subsequent campaigns in Dakota, although 38 Sioux, including three half-breeds, were hanged for their part in the uprising at Mankato,

Minnesota, December 26, 1862. No whites were hanged. Little Crow fled to the Plains, or to Canada with two hundred or more of his followers; later they returned to Minnesota where further depredations were laid to them. Little Crow was killed near Hutchinson, Minnesota by a settler, Nathan Lampson and his son, Chauncey; the Indian's son, Woinapa was wounded and captured later. Little Crow's body was brought to town, thrown upon a refuse heap at a local slaughterhouse. Later his skeleton, it was said, was placed on public exhibit and ended up at the Minnesota Historical Society. In 1971 it was turned over to his descendants, to be buried at a Santee Sioux cemetery near Flandreau, South Dakota. Little Crow had been married six times and fathered 22 children.

Hodge, HAI; Roy W. Meyer, *History of the Santee Sioux.* Lincoln, Univ. of Nebr. Press, 1967; Louis H. Roddis, *Indian Wars of Minnesota.* Cedar Rapids, Iowa, Torch Press, 1956; Doane Robinson, *A History of the Dakota or Sioux Indians.* Minneapolis, Ross & Haines, 1956; *Minnesota in the Civil War and Indian War,* 2 vols. St. Paul, Pioneer Press Co., 1891, 1899.

Little Dog, Piegan chief (d. May 28, 1866). Believed to have been a first cousin of Natawista Iksana (Mrs. Alexander Culbertson), he was described by W.T. Hamilton as a "fine looking specimen of an Indian chief, over six feet in height, straight as an arrow." He became head chief of the Piegans and was regarded by Alfred Vaughn, Blackfoot agent, as one of the bravest and proudest Indians on the Plains. A determined friend of the white Americans, he almost alone turned to farming as the Indians were advised to do, but gave it up after a short test. Isaac I. Stevens described him as a man of character and probity. Little Dog and his son were murdered near Fort Benton by a drunken party of his own people led by Three Suns, perhaps because he was too friendly with the whites. Little Dog was buried at Fort Benton.

Montana, Contributions, Vol. X, 1940, 255; John C. Ewers, *The Blackfeet: Raiders on the Northwestern Plains.* Norman, Univ. of Okla. Press, 1958.

Little Raven (Hosa), Arapaho chief (c. 1810-1889). B. on the central Plains he was the son of a chief and became head chief of the Southern Arapaho around 1855. He married a Kiowa-Apache and in 1840 acted as intermediary in gathering near Bent's Fort his own people, along with Southern Cheyennes, Kiowas, Comanches and Kiowa-Apaches. They agreed to a peace among themselves permitting hunting on each other's ranges, the peace never thereafter being broken. Little Raven's people usually wintered against the Rockies in the region where Denver and Boulder, Colorado now stand, and the gold rush of 1858-59 brought increasing pressures upon them by a vast influx of whites. A reporter in 1859 said that Little Raven at that time had seven wives and many children and was a handsome, manly looking Indian who spoke no English. He was first to sign the Fort Wise (Fort Lyon), Colorado Treaty of 1861, but shortly became disillusioned with it, claiming its provisions had not been properly translated to him, and that the whites did not live up to its promises. He refused to go with a delegation of chiefs to Washington, D.C., in 1863 because Left Hand, another Arapaho chief who spoke fluent English did not go and he did not trust anyone else to interpret for him. Little Raven took part in hostilities against the whites for a period thereafter. Although Chivington claimed Little Raven was killed at Sand Creek, November 29, 1864, this was not the case; he was not present. While not as determinedly for peace as Left Hand, Little Raven was a reasonable man. He joined in the 1867 Medicine Lodge (Kansas) Treaty, by which his and other tribes accepted reservation status. In 1871 Little Raven joined a group of Indian leaders visiting Washington and other eastern cities and through an interpreter addressed a large audience at Cooper Union in New York City. He held most of the Arapaho at peace during the southern Plains warfare of 1874-75. Little Raven died at Cantonment, Oklahoma, in the winter of 1889 after maintaining for 20 years the leadership of the progressive element of his tribe. He was succeeded by Niwot (Nawat), or Left Hand the younger, no relation to the Left Hand killed at Sand Creek.

Hodge, HAI; Margaret Coel, *Chief Left Hand: Southern Arapaho.* Norman, Univ. of Okla. Press, 1981; Stan Hoig, *The Sand Creek Massacre.* Norman, 1974; Hoig, *The Western Odyssey of John Simpson Smith.* Glendale, Calif., Arthur H. Clark Co., 1974.

Little Reddy: *see* Robert McKimie

Little Robe (Ski-o-mah), Cheyenne chief (fl. 1853-1875). Little Robe was a major Cheyenne chief who late in life became known to the whites as head chief. He, as did Black Kettle, belonged to the faction inclined usually toward peace with the whites. Little Robe first is mentioned in an 1853 expedition against the Pawnees which he helped organize and which had few positive results. In August 1863 he and other Cheyenne chiefs refused to meet with Governor Evans of Colorado for a treaty council, claiming that the previous treaty, at Fort Wise (Lyon), Colorado, had been a "swindle." Although Chivington claimed he killed Little Robe (along with Black Kettle) in the Sand Creek Massacre of November 29, 1864, he was wrong on both counts; if Little Robe was even at Sand Creek he escaped as did Black Kettle. Little Robe signed the important Medicine Lodge Treaty of October 1867. In June 1868 Little Robe, with Tall Bull and Whirlwind led a large revenge expedition against the Kaws in Kansas but although there was plenty of shooting, no one was killed and the raiders withdrew. In mid-November 1868 Little Robe and Black Kettle visited Fort Cobb, Indian Territory to talk about making peace; the agent could offer little advice except to contact Sheridan, already in the field and beyond reach, so they returned to their encampment along the Washita River. Little Robe probably was in the Battle of the Washita November 27, 1868, and survived it as Black Kettle did not, agreeing to surrender at Fort Cobb December 31, 1868, although he said it took time to bring people in, which he did at Fort Sill April 7, 1869. In 1871 Little Robe with Stone Calf and others traveled east, visiting Washington, New York, Philadelphia and Boston; Little Robe also went east in 1873 for a conference at Washington. When the difficulties of 1874 threatened, Little Robe moved closer to the agency with his people, taking no part in hostilities. His later career is unreported.

Donald J. Berthrong, *The Southern Cheyennes.* Norman, Univ. of Okla. Press, 1963; George B. Grinnell, *The Fighting Cheyennes.* Norman, 1956.

Little Thunder (Waki-nyan Chika), Brulé Sioux chief (d. 1879). Said by one account to be the son of Black Moon and by another of Chief Big Thunder who still was living in 1842,

he must have been born in the first quarter of the 19th century. Winter counts tell that in 1840-41 five of his brothers were killed by Pawnees. In 1843 at Fort Laramie Little Thunder was reportedly the most influential chief of the Brulés, and the head of the most important band of the tribe. He was 6 feet or more in height, handsome with a commanding bearing and termed by a Laramie trader the bravest and most honorable of Sioux chiefs and of superior intelligence. June 27, 1843 the Brulés scored a huge victory over the Pawnees on the Loup Fork of the Platte and Little Thunder no doubt was in the fight. According to Salway by 1851 the two big chiefs of the Brulés were Little Thunder and Conquering Bear (Brave Bear), with the latter having a bit the edge, and government officials and traders regarding Conquering Bear head chief. At the Grattan massacre of August 1854, Conquering Bear was killed and Little Thunder henceforth became head chief of the Southern Brulés. He had sought to stop hostilities connected with the Grattan affair and was considered friendly to the whites. In anticipation of army retaliation, Twiss sent runners to the Sioux camps announcing that the Platte was the deadline and friendly camps were to move south of that river, but Little Thunder ignored the advice and maintained his camp on the Blue Water, north of the river near Ash Hollow. Here Harney launched a devastating attack September 3, 1855, reportedly killing 85 and taking off 70 women and children captives. Little Thunder escaped. It is said Harney later conceded he had struck a friendly camp and regretted the action. In February 1856 he called Little Thunder into Fort Pierre and told him he had appointed him head chief of the Brulés. Little Thunder then signed a treaty Harney dictated, but it never was confirmed by the Senate nor put into effect. Little Thunder was interviewed by Richard Burton, an English traveler, at Fort Laramie in 1860, complaining bitterly that the white agent, Twiss, was swindling the Indians on annuities and rations. There is little mention of Little Thunder, or Spotted Tail, his successor as head chief, thereafter, they spending their days far to the south, hunting game and killing Pawnees. As Little Thunder grew older, Spotted Tail came more to the fore, the older chief gradually fading from view. He spent the winter of 1877-78 in a Brulé camp south of Herrick, South Dakota, and

Frank Little Thunder, a grandson or great grandson, believed he died the next year at Rosebud Agency on Hay Creek, where he was buried. Another account said he died in Chief Milk's camp, south of Herrick and was buried there. It is regrettable that today's Sioux have all but forgotten this very important man.

George E. Hyde, *Spotted Tail's Folk.* Norman, Univ. of Okla. Press, 1961; Robert M. Utley, *Frontiersmen in Blue.* N.Y., Macmillan Co., 1967.

Little Turtle (Michikinikwa), Miami war chief (1752-July 14, 1812). B. at a Miami village on the Eel River in Indiana, his father was a Miami chief, his mother a Mahican and so he was considered from birth a Mahican and was not named chief by descent from his father. Through his outstanding talents, however, he became chief while a comparatively young man. He was friendly with the British, and organized a massacre of 80 whites and Indians under Augustine Mottin de La Balme who had intended to conquer Detroit, in Ohio in 1780, during the last phases of the American Revolution. Little Turtle was the principal leader of the Indian forces that defeated and routed Josiah Harmar's force in October 1790 with a white loss of 183 killed and 31 wounded to an estimated Indian loss of 120. Again Little Turtle led Indian forces at the disastrous defeat of Arthur St. Clair's force on November 4, 1791, the worst beating organized American forces ever suffered at the hands of Indians with 647 dead and 217 wounded, while Indian losses were unknown but in Roosevelt's view were probably not "one-twentieth that of the whites." Little Turtle and the Shawnee, Bluejacket were leaders in the fight at Fallen Timbers, August 20, 1794, where they were routed by Anthony Wayne whom Little Turtle knew as the "chief who never sleeps." Little Turtle had entered the engagement reluctantly and after the defeat he accepted the treaty of Greenville, Ohio August 3, 1795, remarking as he stepped forward: "I am the last to sign it, and I will be the last to break it." He was faithful to his promise, and remained at peace until his death. In early 1797, accompanied by his son-in-law William Wells, he visited George Washington at Philadelphia, meeting Constantin Volney, the future count who was "an intelligent and sympathetic observer" of the

American Indian, and General Thaddeus Kosciusko, Revolutionary War hero. The General presented Little Turtle with his own pair of elegantly mounted pistols. Little Turtle in succeeding years signed various treaties by which the Indians sacrificed much of their lands to white importunities and toward the end of his life his people began to mistrust his leadership, or his judgment. But he convinced the majority that it was necessary to acquiesce to demands upon them, rather than go to war again. Tecumseh tried to draw him from his peaceful relations with the whites, but Little Turtle resisted. He married once and fathered a daughter, lived in his late years on a government pension (perhaps given him in return for his tractability in the face of increasing demands upon the Indians) and died at Fort Wayne, Indiana, under care of an army surgeon.

Hodge, HAI; Dockstader; Bert Anson, *The Miami Indians.* Norman, Univ. of Okla. Press, 1970.

Little Whirlwind's Voice, Cheyenne: *see* David Stanley

Little Wolf (Ohkom Kakit), Northern Cheyenne chief (c. 1820-1904). B. near the confluence of the Eel and Blue rivers, Montana he became chief of the Bowstring Soldiers, a tribal military society. By the middle of the 19th century he had won a reputation as a great war leader in actions against other tribes. Charles King said he probably was present at the Fetterman massacre in December 1866, and took part in the Custer fight in June 1876. Whether he was present in Dull Knife's village when Mackenzie attacked it in November 1876 is uncertain, but he surrendered soon after and like Dull Knife, was sent to Indian Territory to live with the Southern Cheyenne. In September 1878 he and Dull Knife led about 300 of their people out to the north, in a long and masterly flight of 1,500 miles on which it is said Little Wolf was the principal tactician. After crossing the North Platte River the bands split, Dull Knife going in to surrender at Fort Robinson, Little Wolf continuing northward into Montana, which his people regarded as their homeland. Here after wintering with Red Cloud's Sioux, Little Wolf was contacted by his white friend, First

Lieutenant William Philo Clark, who persuaded him to surrender without conditions, although Little Wolf was permitted to remain in Montana. He served briefly as a scout for Miles. He killed one of his fellow tribesmen however, and this may have affected his standing with his people, although Dockstader reports that until the end of his life, and even after he had become blind in his advanced age, he remained "a respected figure with an alert mind." He died at about 84.

REAW; Dockstader; Mari Sandoz, *Cheyenne Autumn*. N.Y., Avon Books, 1953; George Bird Grinnell, *The Fighting Cheyennes*. Norman, Univ. of Okla. Press, 1956; Grinnell, *The Cheyenne Indians*, 2 vols. Lincoln, Univ. of Nebr. Press, 1972.

Livermore, William Roscoe, army officer (Jan. 11, 1843-Sept. 26, 1919). B. at Cambridge, Massachusetts, he was graduated from West Point in 1865, appointed a first lieutenant of engineers, and was promoted through grades to colonel by 1904. Most of his professional life was devoted to fortification work, but in 1879 he led a surveying party through the Big Bend country of Texas, charting a route followed shortly by the Southern Pacific Railroad from the vicinity of Fort Davis to Fort Clark (Brackettville). A Congressional appropriation had been made ostensibly to "establish sites for a series of military posts to defend the frontier lands from any possible plundering raids from Mexico or from the Indian reservations, and to protect the scanty population from outlaws," but the survey of course was really intended to benefit the Southern Pacific. Livermore's expedition included an 8th Cavalry detachment and some of Bullis's Seminole Scouts; the places where they camped, 20 or 30 miles apart, became stations along the Southern Pacific when the railroad exploited the route. In the summer of 1880 Livermore's scouts performed duty against Victorio briefly. Mount Livermore in the Davis Mountains, 8,382 feet, next to Guadalupe Peak the highest point in Texas, was named for the officer who used it as a point of observations and placed a base monument atop it. Livermore was for a time chief engineer of the military Department of Texas. In 1868 he and Sir Charles Bright had laid the first American cable from the U.S. to Havana, Cuba. With Colonel A.H. Russell he invented several magazine and automatic rifles, including the method of loading by clip, patented in 1880. Livermore retired in 1907, but was recalled in 1917 on special duty with the Chief of Engineers. His home was at Washington, D.C.

Heitman; *Who Was Who;* Carlysle Graham Raht, *The Romance of Davis Mountains and Big Bend Country* (with a gold-engraved sketch of Mount Livermore upon its cover). El Paso, Rahtbooks Co., 1919.

Livernois, Joseph, frontiersman (c. 1801-1882). B. probably in Canada, he became a trapper for the North West Fur Company. He went to St. Louis and by 1820 had reached Taos, engaging in trading and occasional trapping with Ceran St. Vrain, Sylvestre Pratte and others. In 1828 he joined the American Fur Company at St. Louis, trapped on the upper Missouri, returned to St. Louis in 1831 and wintered that year or the next in what became Idaho. In a skirmish with the Blackfeet Livernois was shot in the eye. He was at Pueblo, Colorado in 1847 and at Taos in 1850. He moved then to Colorado permanently and died at Walsenburg.

Janet Lecompte article, MM, Vol. V.

Llewellyn, William Henry Harrison, lawman, frontier character (Sept. 9, 1851-June 11, 1927). B. at Monroe, Wisconsin, he was graduated from Tabor College, Iowa, and in 1866 at 15 went to Montana where he prospected in Trinity Gulch. In May 1879, he was commissioned a special agent of the Department of Justice, with the goal of catching the notorious Nebraska horse thief and outlaw, David C. (Doc) Middleton, which he did in July 1879. In the spring of 1881 Llewellyn became agent for the Mescalero Apaches of New Mexico. The following year he was named agent for the Jicarilla Apaches and in 1883 removed them to the Mescalero Reservation, a transfer that was short-lived. In 1885 he entered private law practice at Las Cruces, became involved in politics, was elected at various times to the legislative assembly of territory and state. Named captain of Troop G, in the Rough Riders, he served "with great gallantry and distinction" at Las Guasimas and San Juan Hill. A friend of Theodore Roosevelt, he was named U.S. Attorney for New Mexico. He died at El Paso, Texas.

John Carson, *Doc Middleton, the Unwickedest Outlaw.* Santa Fe, Press of the Territorian, 1966; Twitchell, *Leading Facts,* II, 541-42.

Lloyd, Dick, cowboy (d. 1881). B. in Texas, he rode for J.P. Collins of the Graham Mountains, Arizona. He got drunk in Maxey, the town for Fort Thomas, Arizona, stole a Joe Olney (Joe Hill) horse, rode it into the saloon where Olney and others were playing poker, and was shot dead. The game went on, one pot going for Lloyd's inquest and funeral expenses.

Ed Bartholomew, *Wyatt Earp: The Man & the Myth.* Toyahvale, Tex., Frontier Book Co., 1964; Larry Kellner, "William Milton Breakenridge: Deadliest Two-Gun Deputy of Arizona." *Arizoniana,* Vol. II, No. 4 (Winter 1961), 20-22.

Lloyd, Thomas, sourdough (c. 1855-c. 1915). An Alaskan sourdough, he organized the first successful climb of Mt. McKinley, although he did not accompany it to the top. Convinced that Frederick A. Cook had not climbed the peak as he had publicly claimed, Lloyd recruited Pete Anderson, Billy Taylor, Charley McGonogal, E.C. Davidson who later became surveyor general of Alaska, and two others. In December 1909, the party, backed by three Fairbanks businessmen, left that city for McKinley, established a winter camp at Cache Creek and a mountain camp February 27. Lloyd and Davidson came into contention (one report mentions a fist fight), and the latter with two others quitted the expedition. On April 11 Lloyd reached Fairbanks alone, claiming that on April 3, 1910, he, Anderson, Taylor and McGonogal had all climbed both peaks of McKinley. His story was written by W.F. Thompson, editor of the *Fairbanks Daily Times,* and taken by wire around the world. The story was challenged, however, photographs were unsatisfactory, and Lloyd got word to the other three who had remained working on their claims at Kantishna, Alaska, 150 miles from Fairbanks, to make a second climb and take a flagpole up. This was done, the climbers reaching the summit of the more difficult (and slightly lower) North Peak May 17, 1910, planting the pole and raising a flag, the staff seen and verified by Stuck three years later. Their feat was among the most remarkable in

mountaineering annals; Lloyd himself did not get above 11,000 feet, although the group is still largely known as the "Lloyd party." He tried to sell the story of the purported April climb, but was unsuccessful.

Terris Moore, *Mt. McKinley: The Pioneer Climbs,* College, Univ. of Alaska Press, 1967.

Lobillo, Juan Rodriguez, military officer (c. 1522-post 1543). At 16 he joined the De Soto expedition into the southern United States, becoming a captain of infantry; earlier he had come from Peru with De Soto, bringing along a fortune of around $35,000 and a taste for fine clothing and luxury. Once landed at Tampa Bay, Florida, Lobillo was sent on a mission to capture Indians if he could, taking with him 50 infantry including crossbowmen and harquebusiers. He brought back four women and six wounded men, one of whom died. Occasionally afterward Lobillo was reported leading scouts or separate missions which he appears to have done capably. On one occasion he returned without two of his men who had become lost. De Soto roundly berated him, sent him back without food or rest and told him if he didn't return with the lost men he would put him to death. The matter was resolved satisfactorily. Later a black, Juan Bizcayan, who spoke Spanish and was a slave to Lobillo turned up missing near Kusa in southern Alabama. No doubt remembering the previous incident, Lobillo went back to hunt for him, holding up the expedition for a day; when he returned (without the black) De Soto again bawled him out. Apparently Lobillo accompanied the expedition throughout its peregrinations and to Mexico, returning at last to Spain.

Bourne, *De Soto,* I, II.

Lockwood, Francis Cummins, historical writer (May 22, 1864-Jan. 12, 1948). B. at Mt. Erie, Illinois, and raised in Kansas, he was the son of a Methodist minister. Frank Lockwood graduated Phi Beta Kappa from Baker University at Baldwin City, Kansas, in 1892, receiving his doctorate from Northwestern University in 1896. He was ordained to the Methodist ministry and held a parish at Salt Lake City for a year but decided the pulpit was not his profession. He took post-doctoral work at the University of Chicago, received a master's degree in English literature at Wesleyan University, Middletown, Connecticut, taught from 1898 to 1901 at midwestern colleges and settled at Allegheny College, Meadville, Pennsylvania, from 1902 until 1916. Lockwood dabbled in politics without much success and in 1916 joined the faculty of the University of Arizona at Tucson, quickly becoming interested in Arizona and Southwestern history. He wrote *Arizona Characters* (1928); *The Life of Edward Everett Ayer* (1929); *Tucson — The Old Pueblo* (1930); *Pioneer Days in Arizona* (1932); *With Padre Kino on the Trail* (1934); *Story of the Spanish Missions in the Middle Southwest* (1934), and *The Apache Indians* (1938), still a useful reference work nearly half a century after publication. He published *More Arizona Characters* (1943); *Life in Old Tucson, 1854-1864* (1943), and *Thumbnail Sketches of Famous Arizona Desert Riders 1538-1946* (1946). He died at Tucson. Lockwood was married and fathered two daughters.

John Bret Harte, "Frank C. Lockwood: Historian of the Southwest." *Ariz. and the West,* Vol. 9, No. 2 (Summer 1967), 109-30.

Loco, Mimbres Apache chief (c. 1823-Feb. 2, 1905). Loco was probably b. in the Mimbres country of southwestern New Mexico and though he must early have come to prominence in his tribe, was not well known to the whites until after the Civil War. According to family belief, he won his Spanish name from his uncontrollable frenzy as a warrior in his younger days, when he also lost an eye, reportedly during a scuffle with a grizzly. Loco was related to Mangas Coloradas; when Mangas was killed, Delgadito succeeded as chief of the Mimbres, and when he was slain around 1860, Loco and Victorio became joint chiefs, although Loco, somewhat the elder, was senior to a slight degree, at least until Victorio's emergence as leader of the militant faction in the 1870s. Upon reaching his maturity Loco seemed inclined toward peace, a novel attitude for a respected leader of warlike Apaches. The Mimbres and other Apaches had been involved in Civil War turbulence in southern New Mexico although they had long wearied of it and in 1869 Loco reached Fort Craig seeking a sound peace and a good agent for his people. From that time forward he remained quiet and worked closely with agent Charles Drew and subsequent officials. Although speaking "very bad Spanish," Loco was always willing to talk

with white leaders. Initially he seems to have had a marked taste for whiskey, but soon learned to shun it. In the summer of 1871 he was sent to bring in Cochise for talks, but the mission was aborted by Crook. In early 1872 Loco was invited, with Cochise, Victorio and others, to visit Washington, but they all turned the suggestion down. Loco agreed to relocation of the Mimbres from Ojo Caliente to Tularosa, New Mexico as Indian officials desired, but became dissatisfied and after a couple of years his people were brought back to Ojo Caliente. From here they were gathered by Agent John Clum of San Carlos, Arizona, in 1877 and transferred to that crowded reserve. Neither Victorio nor Loco liked the place and within months broke out in an effort to regain their old homeland in New Mexico. In October 1877 they surrendered at Fort Wingate, New Mexico. They were permitted to move once more to Ojo Caliente, their ancient home area, and were happy except that this move too was temporary, the Indian Department being determined to return them once more to hated San Carlos. In the fall of 1878 Loco and a little more than half the Mimbres in New Mexico were removed once more to San Carlos, a trip made miserable by vile weather and their dread of their destination. Victorio took to the mountains and within a year his famous war commenced, although Loco had no part in it. In April 1881 he learned at agent Tiffany's urging that Victorio definitely had been killed in Chihuahua in October 1880, and persuaded the agent to agree to accept the few survivors of Victorio's band to live under Loco at San Carlos and become his responsibility. Loco took no part in the Cibecue affair, in Juh's and Geronimo's bolt into Mexico afterward and remained with his people at San Carlos until 1882. In April of that year Juh brought a band of raiders north and in an amazing feat extracted Loco (at rifle point, it was said) and several hundred of his people from San Carlos, convoying them through several skirmishes and battles with troops to Old Mexico. About 78 of them, all but 11 women and children, were slain by Lieutenant Colonel Lorenzo Garcia in Sonora but the remainder gained the sanctuary of the Sierra Madre. This is known as the Loco campaign, but actually it was Juh's and Loco was an unwilling participant although, being chief his name was attached to it. Crook saw the permanent threat for the entire border region of the resulting pool of hostiles in Old Mexico and in 1883 conducted his great campaign into the heart of the Sierra Madre to persuade the Apaches to return north of the Border. May 25 Loco joined Crook and accompanied him back to San Carlos, arriving in mid-June. When Geronimo and Chihuahua broke out in May 1885 Loco and most of his people refused to go along and sat out the Geronimo war, although many Warm Springs enlisted as scouts for the campaign. When Geronimo and Naiche surrendered in September 1886, Loco and Chatto were sent tu Washington to confer with government leaders; enroute back they were held at Fort Leavenworth, then sent as prisoners of war to Florida where they were joined by the Chiricahuas and Warm Springs the government had exiled east, whether friendly or late-hostiles. From Florida eventually they were sent to Mt. Vernon Barracks, Alabama, and from there at last to Fort Sill, Oklahoma. Here Loco became head of Loco's Village and his son, John was enlisted as a scout. Loco was the last chief of the Ojo Caliente (Warm Springs, Mimbres) Apaches. He was married three times, fathering children by each of his wives. His wives were Chiz-pah-odlee, Chich-odl-netln and Clee-hn. Loco died at 82 and is buried in the main Apache cemetery by Beef Creek on the Fort Sill Military Reservation.

Griswold; Dan L. Thrapp, *Victorio and the Mimbres Apaches.* Norman, Univ. of Okla. Press, 1974; Thrapp, *General Crook and the Sierra Madre Adventure.* Norman, 1972; information from John A. Shapard Jr., principal biographer of Loco.

Logan, Harvey (Kid Curry), desperado (c. 1875-July 9, 1903). B. part Cherokee in Rowan County, Kentucky, he was raised by an aunt at Dobson, Missouri, and with two brothers drifted to Wyoming sometime before 1892, became associated with George Curry, a possible relative, and moved on to Landusky, Montana, where the Logans commenced ranching. On December 27, 1894, Logan shot dead Pike Landusky, the town's founder, in the course of a drunken brawl, fled to Hole in the Wall, Wyoming, contacted George Curry again and commenced a career of outlawry beginning with rustling, stage holdups and similar activities. He apparently participated in the killing of Deputy Sheriff William Deane on April 13, 1897. June 28, 1897, he attempted with five others to rob the Belle Fourche,

South Dakota, bank; one was captured in town and the others taken shortly, but escaped the Deadwood jail November 4, committed two small robberies and regained Hole in the Wall where they successfully fought off a posse and remained secure. Shortly he and his brother, Lonny, joined Butch Cassidy's Wild Bunch, both becoming members of the so-called Train Robbers' Syndicate. Harvey Logan was considered "the most dangerous man who ever associated with Cassidy." He participated with Cassidy in the Wilcox, Wyoming, train robbery of June 2, 1899; with his companions he fled to Alma, New Mexico, where he went to work under the name Tom Capehart on the WS Ranch. Logan may have taken part in the July 11, 1899, Folsom, New Mexico, train robbery with Elza Lay and Sam Ketchum, helping Lay make his getaway, wounded, from a subsequent Turkey Canyon shootout with a posse. On May 27, 1900, it was reported Logan killed Sheriff Jesse M. Tyler of Moab, near Thompson, Utah, in retaliation for Tyler's having killed George Curry; Deputy Sheriff Sam Jenkins, who accompanied Tyler, was killed at the same time. On August 29, 1900, Logan took part with Cassidy and Longabaugh in the Tipton, Wyoming train robbery and on July 3, 1901, the three with Camilla Hanks, pulled off the Wagner, Montana, train robbery, obtaining some $65,000 in unsigned bank notes. Logan is said to have killed W.H. (Jim) Winters July 26, 1901, near Landusky, Winter having previously killed Harvey's brother, Johnny, who had planned to assassinate him. Harvey Logan fled to San Antonio, Texas, then, having passed sufficient money, to Knoxville, Tennessee, where he wounded two officers and was himself badly wounded. He was captured December 15, 1901, and lodged in the Knoxville jail. Logan escaped, perhaps with collusion, June 27, 1903, on July 7 with others robbed a train near Parachute, Colorado, and two days later, being wounded by a posse, shot himself near Glenwood Springs, where he was known as Tap Duncan. The body was fairly well identified. Logan has been accused of a number of killings, including at least three sheriffs, but the evidence is confusing; nevertheless, he was a major outlaw and gunman.

Charles Kelly, *The Outlaw Trail: The Story of Butch Cassidy and the "Wild Bunch."* N.Y., Bonanza Books, 1959; James D. Horan, *The Wild Bunch.* N.Y., Signet Books, 1958.

Logan, John (Tah-gah-jute), chief (c. 1725-1780). A very famous chief, he was b. at Shamokin (Sunbury), Pennsylvania, usually called a Cayuga, sometimes a Mingo (Iroquois living beyond their "proper" boundaries), considered by some to be the second son of Shikellemus, a white man taken prisoner in Canada, raised among the Indians and later made chief of those residing at Shamokin. Or, by a Draper manuscript, the father was a Montreal Frenchman prisonered as a child and adopted by the Oneida, the mother being a Cayuga which therefore became his tribe. The son may have taken his white name from John Logan, onetime acting governor of Pennsylvania and friend of John Logan. Logan lived for many years near Reedsville, Pennsylvania, supporting himself and family by hunting and trapping, and during the French and Indian War maintaining strict neutrality. About 1770 he moved to the Ohio and was living on Beaver Creek when visited by Heckewelder in 1772 while in 1774 he lived at Old Chillicothe, now Westfall, in Pickaway County, Ohio. About April 30, 1774 some 13 of his relatives were murdered on Yellow Creek in a brainless massacre perpetrated by border ruffians in supposed retaliation for depredations by somebody upon white settlers. In furious revenge Logan wrought all the harm he could to whites to initiate the Shawnee War that became the Dunmore War, he purportedly boasting that "I have killed many. I have glutted my vengeance" upon the race whose firm friend he had been, until the atrocity against his family. He was not present at the Battle of Point Pleasant which terminated the Dunmore War. Dunmore sent his interpreter, John Gibson to bring Logan to the peace conference which followed, but Logan refused to attend, stating as his position the famous speech quoted as an example of Indian eloquence by Thomas Jefferson in his *Notes on Virginia,* although there was considerable difference as to its authenticity, particularly its attribution of the murders of Logan's people to Michael Cresap, who probably was innocent of them. It is now generally believed that the substance of the speech was Logan's, but it was presented in polished form by Gibson who may have reconstructed it from notes. Logan's remaining life was generally obscure, although highlighted at odd intervals. He moved to Pluggy's Town on the Scioto, then to Mad River in Logan County

and later to the vicinity of Detroit. In 1778 he saved Simon Kenton from being burned at the stake and the following year purportedly was recognized among the Indian raiding party against southwestern Virginia. He was killed by a nephew, Todkados, near Detroit. Although in many respects a reserved, dignified and accomplished leader, he also had an alcohol problem and became dissolute in his advanced years. His wife was a Shawnee woman; they had no children. A monument to Logan stands in Fair Hill Cemetery, near Auburn, New York.

Hodge, HAI; Reuben Gold Thwaites, Louise Phelps Kellogg, *Documentary History of Dunmore's War.* Madison, Wisc. Hist. Soc., 1905, 305-306.

Logan, Johnny, desperado (c. 1872-Jan. 16, 1896). B. in Rowan County, Kentucky, he was a brother of Harvey Logan and was raised by an aunt at Dobson, Missouri. With Harvey and Lonny, another brother, he reached Wyoming by 1892, the Logans moving on to Montana where they established a ranch near Landusky. Johnny was killed by W.H. (Jim) Winters whom the Logans planned to slay for an alleged abuse, near Landusky. Lonny's murderous brother, Harvey, is said to have killed Winters in retaliation on July 26, 1901.

Charles Kelly, *The Outlaw Trail: The Story of Butch Cassidy and the "Wild Bunch."* N.Y., Bonanza Books, 1959; James D. Horan and Paul Sann, *Pictorial History of the Wild West.* N.Y., Crown Pubrs., 1954.

Logan, Lonny, desperado (c. 1873-Feb. 28, 1900). B. in Rowan County, Kentucky, he was a brother of Harvey Logan and like him was raised at Dobson, Missouri. With two brothers he drifted to Wyoming, then to Montana where they operated a ranch for some time before Harvey killed Pike Landusky and the Logans turned toward outlawry, homing initially at Wyoming's Hole in the Wall, then migrating into Butch Cassidy's Wild Bunch. Lonny may have taken part in the Wilcox, Wyoming, train robbery of June 2, 1899, and no doubt in other deviltry. He visited the home of his Dobson, Missouri, aunt, who had raised him, in early 1900, was trapped there by a posse, and killed.

Charles Kelly, *The Outlaw Trail: The Story of Butch Cassidy and the "Wild Bunch."* N.Y., Bonanza Books, 1959.

Logan, William, army officer (Dec. 9, 1832-Aug. 9, 1877). B. in Ireland, he migrated to the United States and enlisted in 1850 in the army, being promoted to sergeant by 1863. He had married and fathered a son, William R., at Fort Belknap, Texas (1856-1912). As first sergeant, Logan commanded a company in two actions in the Civil War, and was commissioned a second lieutenant, 7th Infantry, in 1864, rising to captain by 1874. Logan commanded Company A of Gibbon's 7th Infantry during the march of the Montana column in 1876, and in command of the same organization he was killed at the Battle of Big Hole, Montana, an event of the Nez Perce campaign. Logan was slain by a woman. In charge of the center column of a three-pronged attack on the Indian village, he was engaged in hand-to-hand action among the willows, killing an Indian whose woman, perhaps his sister, picked up the warrior's weapon and shot Logan through the head. His son, William R. Logan, as a civilian also took part in the engagement.

NCAB, Vol. XVI, 389-90; Heitman; Helen Addison Howard, Dan L. McGrath, *War Chief Joseph.* Lincoln, Univ. of Nebr. Press, 1964; John M. Carroll, Byron Price, *Roll Call on the Little Big Horn, 28 June 1876.* Ft. Collins, Colo., Old Army Press, 1974.

Logan, William R., Indian official, park superintendent (Mar. 27, 1856-Feb. 7, 1912). B. at Fort Belknap, Texas, he was the son of William Logan, an army officer killed at the Battle of Big Hole, Montana, in 1877. Young Logan enlisted in the army and was reported to have been a scout in the Sioux campaign, although details are lacking. It was reported he was recommended for a commission, but declined because it would have meant service in the black 9th Cavalry. Logan was reported to have continued as an enlisted man and scout against Sitting Bull, who shortly crossed into Canada, again declined a commission, and did not re-enlist. He was post trader at Fort Missoula, Montana, for two years, and scouted against the Nez Perce in 1877. In 1879 he began cattle and sheep ranching and tried mining. In 1898 he was named agent for the Blackfeet, then became agent at the Fort Belknap Reservation at Harlem, Montana. On July 2, 1902, he became United States supervisor of industries for Indians. In August 1910, he became superintendent of road construction in the new Glacier National Park, and March 6, 1911, was named first superintendent of the park, a position he held until his death at Chicago. Logan Pass on the Going-to-the-Sun Highway was named for him. He was said to have spoken Sioux fluently and to have had knowledge of several other Indian tongues.

NCAB, Vol XVI, 389-90; Information from the Great Northern Railway.

Lomax, John Avery, folklorist (Sept. 23, 1867-Jan. 26, 1948). B. at Goodman, Mississippi, he was a graduate of the University of Texas and studied at Harvard and the University of Chicago. A lecturer on American folklore and folk songs he was president of the American Folklore Society and in 1934 was appointed honorary curator of folk songs at the Library of Congress. He died at Greenville, Mississippi. His publications relating to the frontier included: *Cowboy Songs and Other Frontier Ballads* (1910); *Book of Texas* (1916); *American Ballads and Folk Songs,* with Alan Lomax, his son (b. Jan. 31, 1915) (1934); *Adventures of a Ballad Hunter* (his memoirs) (1947), and *Folk Songs,* with Alan Lomax (1947).

EA; EB; CE.

Lompre, Joseph, frontiersman (fl. 1842-1868). Said to have been a mountain man who trapped in the Bitterroot Range of western Montana as early as 1842, he became a trader to emigrants on the Oregon Trail, exchanging Flathead horses for worn-out work oxen and cattle. Late in 1856 he began farming near Fort Owen in the Bitterroot Valley where he last was reported in 1868.

George F. Weisel, *Men and Trade on the Northwest Frontier.* Missoula, Mont. State Univ. Press, 1955; *Montana, Contributions,* II (1896).

London, Jack (John Chaney), writer (Jan. 12, 1876-Nov. 22, 1916). B. at San Francisco, he wrote about 40 books, the best of them near-classics. He adopted the name of his stepfather, being of illegitimate birth and was raised at Oakland, Alameda, Livermore and countryside California. At 17 he shipped to Japan and the Bering Sea as an able seaman; he was an oyster pirate, a seal hunter, joined the Alaska gold rush, searched for paradise in the South Seas, and wandered around the world. His *The Son of the Wolf* appeared in 1900, *The Call of the Wild* in 1903, *The Sea-Wolf* in 1904, *White Fang* in 1905 and the

semi-autobiographical *Martin Eden* in 1909.
Success destroyed him, and he committed
suicide.

Literature abundant.

London, Robert, army officer (c. 1850-Dec.
12, 1892). B. in North Carolina, he went to
West Point and was commissioned a second
lieutenant in the 5th Cavalry June 13, 1873,
posted to Arizona. London participated in the
Apache campaign of 1874, engaging in a fight
near Camp Pinal and six skirmishes with
hostile Indians in the Pinal and Santa Teresa
mountains including one in which the
murderer of Lieutenant Almy was killed. He
was twice recommended for a brevet. In
January 1875 he commanded a scouting party
from Camp Apache to Camp Verde and
return on which four parties of Tonto
Apaches were struck with 15 men killed and
22 men and 90 women and children captured.
He was transferred to Fort Gibson, Indian
Territory and in June 1876 was assigned to the
Big Horn and Yellowstone expedition against
the Sioux in the North Plains, taking part in
the actions at Indian Creek, Wyoming (where
Cody killed Yellow Hand) and at Slim Buttes,
Dakota. Subsequently London served at
Forts McKinney and D.A. Russell, Wyoming;
Sheridan and Robinson, Nebraska and Fort
Reno, Indian Territory. He became a first
lieutenant May 1, 1879, and a captain January
14, 1892, eleven months before his death.

Heitman; Cullum; Powell; Price, *Fifth Cavalry.*

Lone Wolf (Guipago; Quirl-Parko), Kiowa
chief (c. 1820-1879). The Cheyennes tell of a
Lone Wolf who lost a celebrated fight to a
great Cheyenne named Mouse's Road in 1837;
it may have been this man or a predecessor of
the same name. Lone Wolf, a Kiowa chief,
was one of nine signers of the Medicine Lodge
Treaty of 1867 by which the Kiowas first
agreed to accept a reservation. In 1872 he
headed a delegation to Washington, where
fine portraits of him were taken by Bureau of
Ethnology photographers. In 1873 his son was
killed on a raid into Texas and during the
following year Lone Wolf became a leader of
the hostile portion of the Kiowas, in part to
revenge the death of his son; he led the Lost
Valley raid in Texas. June 27, 1874 Lone Wolf
led the Kiowas in the second battle of Adobe
Walls in the present Hutchinson County,
Texas, in which four whites and about 15
Indians were killed. Lone Wolf surrendered at

Fort Sill in the spring of 1875 and was sent
into confinement at Fort Marion, Florida,
where he remained for three years. He died of
malaria shortly after his return to the
reservation and was buried secretly on the
north shoulder of Mount Scott. He was
succeeded as head chief by his adopted son,
Mamay-day-te who assumed the name Lone
Wolf.

Hodge, HAI; HT; Dockstader; Wilbur Sturtevant Nye. *Plains Indian Raiders.* Norman, Univ.
of Okla. Press, 1968.

Lonergan, Jerry, soldier (c. 1841-c. 1872). B.
in County Cork, Ireland, he enlisted in
Company M, 7th Cavalry, December 26,
1867, at New York City. On July 17, 1870, he
was wounded in a saloon fight at Hays City,
Kansas, by James Butler (Wild Bill) Hickok,
who also fatally wounded John Kile.
Lonergan was shot through the knee cap, it
was reported, was admitted to the post
hospital at Fort Hays, released August 25, and
was discharged October 17, 1871. According
to report, he was killed "a little later in Kansas
by a man named Kelly belonging to an
infantry regiment."

Joseph G. Rosa, *They Called Him Wild Bill,* 2nd
ed. Norman, Univ. of Okla. Press, 1974.

Long, Aaron, desperado (d. Oct. 29, 1845).
Long, with his brother John Long and
Granville Young were members of a bandit
gang operating along the Mississippi River in
Illinois. On July 4 1845, they tortured to
death a noted frontiersman, George Davenport in a search for loot at his Arsenal Island
home near the present Rock Island, Illinois.
The three were hanged publicly, but Aaron not
without some difficulty. His rope broke on the
first attempt after which he confessed the
crime, was given a drink and hanged again.
Aaron's body was shipped to Dr. P.P. Gregg,
a St. Louis physician, "for scientific study,"
enclosed in a barrel of rum. The boatmen,
"either ignorant or heedless of the special
contents of the keg, drained off and consumed
the rum during the trip and the doctor
received only the body and the dry keg."

Information from Will Leinicke, Hauberg Indian
Museum, Rock Island, Ill.;*Arizona Daily Star,* July
14, 1978; Edward Bonney, *Banditti of the
Prairies.* Norman, Univ. of Okla. Press, 1963.

Long, Ira, Texas Ranger (May 27, 1842-
Mar. 8, 1913). B. in Indiana and raised in

Missouri he fought for the Confederacy in the Civil War, much of the time in Texas. He made his home at Decatur, Texas, where his first wife lived and became a cowboy and stockman, hiring out to Dan Waggoner as foreman and bossing several trail drives to Kansas, sometimes losing stock to Indian raiders. In 1872 he joined the Texas Rangers. From 1874 until 1876 he served as first lieutenant in Captain George W. Stevens Company B of the Frontier Battalion, then commanded Company A, Frontier Battalion. He was a leader in the Lost Valley battle in 1874, losing two men killed; in an engagement near the present town of Breckenridge three Indians were killed. In 1875 Indians raided settlers and ran off horses; Long again performed outstandingly in an ensuing fight, personally accounting for some of the enemy, one in a hand-to-hand fight; he was commended by Major John B. Jones for admirable coolness and courage. He captured desperado Sam Hare alive after the outlaw had sworn he would never be taken "walking." Long's first wife died in 1872 leaving four children; in 1878 he married again, his second wife surviving him. He left the Ranger service in 1880 and retired to his place near Decatur, where he died.

Frontier Times, Vol. VIII, No. 1 (Oct. 1930), 22-31; Robert W. Stephens, *Texas Ranger Indian War Pensions.* Quanah, Tex., Nortex Press, 1975.

Long, James, adventurer (c. 1793-Apr. 8, 1822). B. in Culpeper County, Virginia, he studied medicine and served as a surgeon-physician in the War of 1812, participating in the Battle of New Orleans in 1815. He married Jane Wilkinson, niece of General James Wilkinson, and lived successively at Natchez, Port Gibson, and Vicksburg. Anger rose among expansionists over the so-called Adams-Oñis Treaty on 1819, which rejected any American designs of Texas, and Long was named to head a filibustering expedition to open the country. He led 300 to Nacogdoches where he proclaimed an independent republic, established Galveston as a port of entry, while Jean Lafitte, erstwhile pirate, was assigned to organize "privateers," under its flag. Long formed an alliance with José Trespalacios, a Mexican revolutionist, but after skirmishing with Spanish forces, was captured and sent to Monterrey. He eventually reached Mexico City where he was shot and killed under somewhat mysterious circumstances, perhaps at the instigation of Trespalacios. Long's was one of the first determined attempts to wrest Texas from Hispanic control.

DAB; HT.

Long, John, fur trader (fl. 1768-1791). B. in England, he reached Montreal in 1768 as a clerk and spent seven years learning the Indian trade, becoming fluent in Mohawk and residing for some time at Caughnawaga, a Mohawk settlement south of the St. Lawrence. He joined the British armed service early in the American Revolution, leading Indian parties in guerilla warfare, on one occasion capturing Ethan Allen. In May 1777 he left Montreal for Mackinac from where he was to lead voyageurs on fur trading enterprises in the region north of Lake Superior and south of Hudson Bay. Long was very successful in this endeavor during two hard years. In June 1780 he took a party from Michilimackinac to Prairie du Chien, Wisconsin, successfully retrieving furs that otherwise might have fallen to American or Spanish interests. After a short visit to England he returned to America, in 1785 going to New York where a fur trading expedition among the Iroquois failed and the British commandant at Oswego confiscated his goods. Financial troubles increasingly plagued him and in 1788 he returned to England, three years later publishing his narrative, *Voyages and Travels of an Indian Interpreter and Trader...,* which enjoyed some popularity, was translated into French and German and is reprinted by Thwaites. "The interest of the work, aside from incidental historical references..., lies in the author's intimate knowledge of Indian life and customs...; and in the light he incidentally throws on the history of the fur trade," wrote Thwaites. To his narrative, one of the earliest important fur trade autobiographical accounts, Long appended extended lists of words in Eskimo (Inuit), Chippewa (Ojibway), Mohawk, Mohegan, Shawnee and Algonkin; the lists have considerable value.

Thwaites, EWT, II; DCB.

Long, John, desperado (c. 1800-Oct. 29, 1845). Leader of a bandit gang which operated along the Mississippi River, he was one of three including his brother Aaron and Granville Young who tortured and murdered

George Davenport, noted pioneer and
founder of Davenport, Iowa, at Davenport's
home on Arsenal Island, July 4, 1845. The
three were hanged to the strains of a specially
written dirge before a crowd of about 5,000 at
3:30 p.m., in an area just south of the Rock
Island (Illinois) Courthouse. For decades
Long's skeleton was kept hanging in a wooden
display case with a glass front at the arsenal
which gave the island its name; it then was on
display for about 20 years at the Rock Island
Courthouse, and finally was given to the
Hauberg Museum at the Black Hawk State
Historic Site. The remains were buried in
1978, 133 years after Long's execution, in
Pioneer Cemetery in the Black Hawk State
Park at Rock Island, Illinois.

Information from Will Leinicke of the Hauberg
Indian Museum, July 25, 1978; *Arizona Daily Star,*
July 14, 1978; Edward Bonney, *Banditti of the
Prairies.* Norman, Univ. of Okla. Press, 1963.

Long, John J., teamster (Nov. 7, 1851-c. Aug.
15, 1925). B. in Fayette County, Pennsylvania,
he was hired as teamster at Fort Leavenworth,
Kansas, in 1874, to work with the Miles Red
River expedition. It left Fort Dodge, Kansas,
with 36 six-mule teams, visited Fort Supply,
Oklahoma, crossed the Canadian River near
the confluence with the Oasis, then went up
McClellan Creek. Long took part as a
teamster in the expedition's various movements and occasional Indian skirmishing,
visited Adobe Walls, knew something of that
fight and also the buffalo wallow fight, and his
reports of the Red River undertaking and
related affairs are intelligent and informative.
He continued freighting, scuffling with
rustlers and others, on the South Plains. He
also knew something of early Mobeetie where
he conducted a general merchandise store for
many years. "No man in the Panhandle was
better known nor more universally loved
than he." The article reviewed here resulted
from an interview with Long by J. Evetts
Haley and Olin Hinkle, June 17-18, 1925.

Frontier Times, Vol. 5, No. 1 (Oct. 1927), 14-16.

Long, Oscar Fitzaland, army officer (June 16,
1852-Dec. 23, 1928). B. in New York, Long
went to West Point and was commissioned a
second lieutenant in the 5th Infantry June 15,
1876. He served as aide to Miles in the Bear
Paw expedition of 1877 against the Nez Perce
Indians. On September 30, 1877, he was

directed by Miles to order one of the cavalry
troops to advance. Finding both of its officers
wounded Long voluntarily assumed command and took the troop forward under
heavy fire, placing it in its required position.
For this he was awarded a Medal of Honor.
He became a first lieutenant October 21, 1881,
and captain in 1892. In the Spanish American
War he became a Brigadier General of
Volunteers and a Brigadier General in the
army July 10, 1904, retiring the following day.
Long then became president of the Union Belt
Railway Company of Oakland, California
and had other business connections in that
community. He died at Piedmont, California.

Heitman; *Deeds of Valor,* II, 250-53; Cullum.

Long, Stephen Harriman, military officer
(Dec. 30, 1784-Sept. 4, 1864). B. at Hopkin-
ton, New Hampshire, he was graduated from
Dartmouth in 1809, taught school in New
Hampshire and Pennsylvania and was
commissioned a second lieutenant of Engineers December 12, 1814. He became a brevet
major of the Topographical Engineers April
29, 1816 (and major July 7, 1838). He was
assigned to St. Louis and helped establish and
appraise military posts in Illinois and the
upper Mississippi region the following year.
Long went to Arkansas, selecting a site for
Belle Point (Fort Smith), proceeding southwest toward the Red River, arriving at the site
of the later Fort Towson. Returning to St.
Louis and then to Washington, Long
proposed construction of a steamboat for use
in exploration of the west via rivers; he was
named to command such an expedition,
supervised construction of the *Western
Engineer* at Pittsburgh, assembled scientists
and secured a suitable military escort. Leaving
Pittsburgh May 5, 1819, the *Western Engineer*
descended the Ohio, reached St. Louis and
started up the Missouri June 22, reached St.
Charles the 27th, visited Fort Osage and
continued to Council Bluffs, reached September 17 when winter quarters were established.
Orders in the spring were to quit the expensive
and non-productive steamboat and continue
with the expedition overland, to ascend the
Platte River to its source, locate also the
source of the Red River and return to the
Mississippi by the Arkansas and Red rivers.
The expedition followed the Platte to the
forks, then the South Platte to the mountains
which first were sighted June 30, Long's Peak

being named for Stephen Long. July 5 Long reached the site of Denver and July 12 Colorado Springs, from which Pike's Peak was climbed by three of the party: Edwin James, Lieutenant William Swift and Joe Bissonette, an old mountain man. The expedition reached the Arkansas above today's Pueblo, the Royal Gorge was discovered and deemed impossible to negotiate, and a descent of the Arkansas commenced July 19. Near La Junta, Colorado, the party divided, Long's division to explore the Red River and a party commanded by Captain John R. Bell to descend the Arkansas. Long's party crossed to the Canadian, believing that the Red descended it to the Arkansas before realizing their error and proceeded eastward to Fort Smith where they arrived September 13 to find Bell's group waiting for them. The expedition reached Cape Girardeau, Missouri October 12, Long and Bell proceeding to Washington. Results of the expedition were disappointing, Long himself reporting that the country crossed was "almost wholly unfit for cultivation, and of course uninhabitable for people depending upon agriculture," although it might have some value by limiting the westward expansion of the populace and as a difficult barrier for any invading power from the west. The expedition also failed to attain either of its objectives: determining the sources of the Red and Platte rivers. Yet the effort did add to geographical knowledge in a practical way, and its scientific work greatly enlarged knowledge of the west. In 1823 Long was sent to locate sources of the Minnesota River and northward of it. For his explorations and for ten years in grade Long was breveted to lieutenant colonel April 29, 1826. For many years thereafter he was engaged in railroad surveys and construction and in 1829 published the *Railroad Manual,* the first treatise in this country on railroad building. He became a major with organization of the Topographical Engineers as a separate corps; September 9, 1861, he became chief of the corps with rank of colonel and transferred to the Engineers March 3, 1863, retiring June 1 of that year. He died at Alton, Illinois.

Thwaites, EWT, XIV-XVII; Richard G. Wood, *Stephen Harriman Long: 1784-1864.* Glendale, Calif., Arthur H. Clark Co., 1966.

Long Horse, Crow chief (d. 1874). He had a small following, his fame stemming from his giant size, he being more than 6 feet, 10 inches in height. He was slain by a Blackfoot, Weasel Calf, in the spring of 1874. In the duel each was armed only with a shield and lance. Weasel Calf's lance passed through the shield and body of his opponent who was buried on a tree scaffold, but the skeleton later was removed.

Montana Contributions, Vol. X, 1940, 295.

Long(a)baugh, Harry (Sundance Kid), desperado (c. 1870-1909?-Aug. 28, 1957?). Little is known of his early life, but he served 18 months in a Sundance (Wyoming) jail for horse theft and from that came his nickname. In 1887 when applying for a wrangler job on the Suffolk Ranch, Wyoming, he said he was from Colorado. Charged with robbing an old man of Lusk, Wyoming, of $80, he escaped jail. In December 1892, he, with others, held up a Great Northern train at Malta, Montana, was captured and escaped; he teamed up with Harvey Logan and two others to rob a bank at Belle Fourche, South Dakota, on June 27, 1897; the gang was captured, but he and Logan escaped from the Deadwood jail October 31, 1897. In 1900 he and George Parker (Butch Cassidy) met at the Hole in the Wall or Brown's Hole, and became close friends. Longabaugh became a member of the so-called Train Robbers' Syndicate headed by Cassidy. August 29, 1900, he, Cassidy and Logan robbed a Union Pacific train at Tipton, Wyoming, getting negligible loot; Longabaugh, Cassidy and Bill Carver held up the Winnemucca, Nevada, First National Bank, September 19, 1900, obtaining $32,540; July 3, 1901, Longabaugh helped Cassidy and others hold up a Great Northern train near Wagner, Montana, seizing $65,000 in unsigned bank notes. Somewhere Longabaugh picked up Etta Place and the couple with Cassidy, shipped for South America February 20, 1902, where, after a few years of ranching, the erstwhile desperadoes began their lawless activities again (see George LeRoy Parker entry for details). Whether they were wiped out at San Vicente, Bolivia, in 1909, or at Mercedes, Uruguay, in 1911, or returned to the United States is uncertain; probably they died at San Vicente. According to Robert Longabaugh, who claimed to be the son of Harry and Etta Place, the trio returned to the United States, where Harry died in 1957 and was buried at Casper, Wyoming.

Charles Kelly, *The Outlaw Trail: The Story of*

Butch Cassidy and the "Wild Bunch." N.Y., Bonanza Books, 1959; James D. Horan, *The Wild Bunch.* N.Y., Signet Books, 1958; *English Westerners' Tally Sheet,* Vol. 19, No. 3, Pub. 187, Jan.-Feb. 1973.

Longerell, James J., chief of Indian police (c. 1850-post 1880). B. in New York he was named chief of Indian police at the San Carlos, Arizona Apache agency May 1, 1880. He served until June 30, when he resigned and was succeeded by Frank Bennett.

Record of Employees, San Carlos Agency, Vols. 9, 10, RG 75, Nat. Archives.

Longley, William Preston (Wild Bill), desperado (Oct. 6, 1851-Oct. 11, 1878). B. in Austin County, Texas, his family moved to Old Evergreen, Lee County, Texas, in 1853 and Longley killed a black there in 1867, two more blacks in Lexington, Texas, that year, and perhaps a couple of other men. From then until 1870 he was teamed with bandit chieftain Cullen M. Baker, operating in East Texas and Arkansas. Seized by vigilantes, he was hanged but exuberant pistol work cut the rope and his life was spared. He is said to have hanged a vigilante from the same tree, but with more definitive results. Longley returned to Old Evergreen, and other unexplained deaths accompanied his progress. He became Texas' most wanted desperado. He worked a trail herd to Abilene, killed the trail boss, in Leavenworth killed a soldier and went to Cheyenne, where he worked for the government. He was jailed for murder, sentenced to 30 years, escaped, and took up with the Ute Indians. Eventually he returned to Texas. In 12 years he is estimated to have killed 32 men, or perhaps more. "Sometimes he killed men because he thought they needed killing, but...he mainly killed to keep from being killed." He himself wrote that "I have always acted in self defense," blaming many of his killings on the "murderous mobs" that he said ruled much of Texas, which is true. "The report of my killing negroes for pasttime just to see them kick, is an ungodly falsehood. It was the villanous Ku Klux bunch that did all the killing among the negroes, and laid it on me..." On another occasion, "I have always known that I was doing wrong, but I got started when I was just a fool boy, led off by older heads..." Once when he became associated with Lon Sawyer, a badman in Uvalde County, Sawyer tried to turn Bill in for the reward; Longley had himself deputized under an assumed name in order to take Sawyer. In a prolonged gunbattle, Sawyer shot at Longley 14 times but only killed his horse; Longley shot at Sawyer 18 times, 13 bullets taking effect. "A dirty job it was," one comment had it, but Longley said Sawyer was "the bravest man" he had ever confronted. Finally, after many adventurous escapades he recorded, some probably fictitious as he related them, he returned to the Old Evergreen country and killed Wilson Anderson, whom he suspected of killing his cousin, Cale Longley. He was captured at Camp Wood, Edwards County, Texas, by Sheriff Bill Henry, taken to Austin where Gov. E.J. Davis refused to pay the reward or receive the prisoner, and he was released. He was rearrested in De Soto Parish, Louisiana, May 13, 1877, imprisoned and tried September 3, 1877, at Giddings, Texas, and removed to Galveston while awaiting the result of an appeal from his death sentence. This was denied and he was returned to Giddings and hanged. Many of his letters during his confinement were published, and are revealing. He was described as 6 feet tall, 150 pounds weight, "tolerably spare built," black hair, eyes and whiskers, sometimes neatly trimmed in various styles though sometimes he was full-bearded. He was slightly stooped, his hair occasionally shoulder length. "He can be recognized in a crowd of 100 men by the keeness and blackness of his eyes." He was buried in a cemetery west of Giddings.

Ed Bartholomew, *Texas Outlaw Bill Longley: A Texas Hard-Case.* Houston, Frontier Press of Tex., 1953; HT.

Looking Glass (Allalimya Takanin), Nez Perce chief (c. 1823-Oct. 5, 1877). B. in the Wallowa Valley of northeastern Oregon he became a noted warrior and war chief in battles on the buffalo plains to the east, most importantly in 1874 when he and his people joined the Crows in a memorable victory over the Sioux. Looking Glass came to head the Alpowai band of the non-treaty Nez Perce counting about 40 fighting men, and although originally for peace, because of his reputation and for other reasons he became the de facto leader of much of the notable 1877 Nez Perce exodus from Idaho 1,200 miles nearly to Canadian sanctuary. In 1863 a minority of the Nez Perce had signed a treaty restricting themselves to a modest reservation so that gold-hungry whites could overrun their former country; five bands refused to sign and were called thereafter the non-treaty Nez Perce. It was government insistence that they withdraw to the reservation that led to the 1877 conflict. Looking Glass and his people were camped along the Clearwater River, upon the Lapwai Reservation and took no part in the Battle of Whitebird Canyon, Idaho, June 17, 1877. At Howard's direction troops under Captain Stephen G. Whipple were sent to Looking Glass's village July 1 because it was rumored that the young men of the camp had joined the hostiles. The soldiers brought white "volunteers" or border ruffians with them; these provoked a fight in which there were some Indian casualities, their horses and cattle were driven off and Looking Glass and most of his people were goaded to war and joined the hostiles. Looking Glass became the accepted leader of the hostiles although they had no actual single commander. At a council near the present Weippe, Idaho the Nez Perce pondered whether to lose themselves in the Snake River wilderness or make for the buffalo plains to the east. Looking Glass harangued the council with a fiery appeal, urging that the people make for the Crow country because the Crows, he cried, "are the same as my brothers! If you go there with me you will be safe!" The leading men agreed to do so and "Chief Looking Glass was now in supreme command," the people starting at once, July 16, over the difficult Lolo Trail across the Bitterroots and into Montana. His influence remained strong until the Battle of Big Hole, Montana. He had urged that the people were beyond reach of the white military and might safely rest; the camp was attacked unawares and the Indians suffered severely before rallying. Estimates of Nez Perce losses vary, but probably totaled around 60 or 70 killed, including women and children, while the whites suffered at least 29 killed and 40 wounded, but in the affair some of the bravest and most highly acclaimed Indians were lost and this had a dispiriting effect upon the remainder. Looking Glass was blamed for mistakenly believing the Nez Perce had reached safety, and from this time forward he was rejected as the primary military leader although his advice was carefully listened to, as before. Poker Joe (Lean Elk, Wahwookya Wasaaw), who had joined the Nez Perce in

Bitterroot Valley now took over as war leader and principal strategist, a development not to Looking Glass's liking (McWhorter, 406-407). When approaching the Bear Paw Mountains, not far south of the Canadian Border, Looking Glass again assumed command of the weary column and encouraged them to rest at the northern end of the uplift because he was sure the soldiers were far away. Once more he was wholly wrong, and his leadership proved disastrous. Miles and his forces caught up and the disastrous battle of the Bear Paws resulted. There were numerous casualties on both sides on the first day of the action, September 30, and only one thereafter; Looking Glass was killed on the final day of the siege, October 5 (see Milan Tripp entry), and that marked the end of the Nez Perce hegira, although a considerable number of Indians under White Bird evaded the military and did reach Canada. Looking Glass was described as a "fine looking man," and had a loyal following, but his two mistakes in judgment spelled disaster for his people.

McWhorter, *Hear Me;* Dockstader; John D. McDermott, *Forlorn Hope: The Battle of White Bird Canyon and the Beginning of the Nez Perce War.* Boise, Id. State Hist. Soc., 1978.

Loomis, Willis Anson, lawman (c. 1860-Oct. 17, 1952). B. probably at Lansing, Michigan, he ran away to the west as a boy, reportedly worked on railroad construction and as a cowboy. Reportedly he was at Leadville, Colorado, in 1886, becoming city marshal, then was employed at the Colorado Penitentiary, Canyon City. For 14 years, he said, he was captain of detectives at Denver. Loomis said he helped capture Harry Orchard (Albert Horsley) in Idaho in 1908, the labor agitator purportedly confessing to the killing of 14 persons in union strife. Loomis said he became chief of police at Everett, Washington, in 1915, and of Venice, California, in 1920, then worked for private detective agencies until his retirement in 1945. He died at Santa Monica, California.

Los Angeles Times, Oct. 18, 1952.

López, Diego, military officer (fl. 1540-1542). A onetime councilman at Seville, Spain, he came to Mexico and was appointed a cavalry captain to serve with Coronado on his 1540-42 expedition into the American southwest. Near the mouth of the Rio Chiametla where the army had paused to reprovision itself, Lope de Samaniego, second in command was killed by Indians; Diego López swiftly took command of the foraging party, many Indians were hanged and López was appointed to fill Samaniego's role as field commander and second in command of the expedition. He was with the advance party that moved through Arizona to Háwikuh, the first pueblo of the Cibola group, southwest of Zuñi on the Arizona-New Mexico line. He was prominent in the reduction of Arenal in the Tiguex War of early 1541 on the Rio Grande, and it was his silence after promising quarter to Indians who surrendered in good faith that led Cárdenas (unaware of the pledge) to execute scores of them; this apparent breach of faith caused much trouble for the Spanish later. Cárdenas was second in command during the advance on Quivira in central Kansas, but when he broke an arm, López succeeded him. After some great adventures hunting buffalo and generating a buffalo stampede, López was chosen as second in command of the 30 to accompany Coronado in the final dash to Quivira. After Coronado had fully investigated the villages which the Turk had said were Quivira and had found none of the gold the guide had promised would be there, López was assigned to investigate charges of mendacity and treachery against the Turk, and if they proved valid, to execute him. He presided at the garroting of the hapless Indian. Upon the expedition's return to Mexico, Diego López settled at Culiacán, Sinaloa.

George Parker Winship, *The Coronado Expedition, 1540-1542.* BAE, 14th Ann. Rept., Wash., Govt. Printing Office, 1896; Herbert Eugene Bolton, *Coronado: Knight of Pueblos and Plains.* Albuquerque, Univ. of New Mex. Press, 1964.

López, Francisco, Franciscan missionary (d. c. 1582). B. in Andalusia, he was ordained a priest in the Franciscan order and appointed superior of the three missionaries with the Rodriguez-Chamuscado expedition from Chihuahua into New Mexico in 1581-82. They visited around three-score pueblos in New Mexico, many never before seen by whites, and conducted explorations in various directions although heavy snow prevented their reaching the Hopi pueblos of Arizona. February 13, 1582 the Franciscans determined to remain in New Mexico to perform missionary work despite urgent entreaties of Chamuscado to accompany him back to Chihuahua since otherwise they would surely be killed by the Indians. They remained. López was bludgeoned to death while at prayer at Puaray, near the present Bernalillo, New Mexico. His body was recovered by Rodriguez and given a Christian burial (Rodriguez shortly was slain as well). In 1614 the remains were disinterred and deposited in the church at Sandia Pueblo with great ceremony, a number of priests attending the rites for the martyr-missionary.

George P. Hammond, Agapito Rey, *The Rediscovery of New Mexico, 1580-1594.* Albuquerque, Univ. of New Mex. Press, 1966; Twitchell, *Leading Facts,* I.

Lopez, Francisco, gold discoverer (fl. 1840's). Said by some to have been the initial discoverer of gold in California, he apparently was preceded by Baptiste Ruelle. Lopez was secretary to the alcalde at Santa Barbara in 1841, was given a land grant in 1842, and was said to have been majordomo of Mission San Fernando, in Placerita Canyon, four miles east of the present Newhall, California, in that year. On March 9, 1842, while pulling up wild onions, he found flecks of gold adhering to their roots. This generated a minor rush and gold from the canyon was sent for "many years" to the U.S. mint at Philadelphia for coinage, at least according to report. A plaque was placed at the site in 1930.

Bancroft, *California,* Vols. 4, 5; press release, Los Angeles County Dept. of Parks and Recreation, Apr. 21, 1959.

López, Nicoláa, Franciscan explorer (fl. 1680-1684). López, a Franciscan priest, became custodian of the Franciscan district of New Mexico and for a time Secretary to Procurador General Francisco de Ayeta. As such he took part in Otermín's abortive entrada into New Mexico in 1681 following the great revolt of the Pueblo Indians, and had a role in questioning captured or other Indians who had taken part in the ousting of the Spaniards from New Mexico. He was considered an "entirely trustworthy religious" by Ayeta, and was sent to Mexico City with what information could be gleaned. In 1683-84 he was a leader with Juan Domínguez de Mendoza of an expedition to the Jumanos Indians living at

La Junta, the Spanish name for the region at the confluence of the Conchos and Rio Grande rivers of Texas (see Mendoza entry for details). Two temporary missions were established in Jumano country: La Navidad de las Cruces in today's Presidio County, Texas, and Apostol Santiago on Alamito Creek, southeast of the present community of Presidio. Little further is reported of López, although there is an indication in Bancroft that he became Procurador General for New Mexico late in the decade of the 1680s when the territory still was held by Pueblo Indians.

Herbert Eugene Bolton, *Spanish Exploration in the Southwest, 1542-1706.* N.Y., Charles Scribner's Sons, 1916; Charles Wilson Hackett, Charmion Clair Shelby, *Revolt of the Pueblo Indians of New Mexico,* 2 vols. Albuquerque, Univ. of New Mex. Press, 1970; Bancroft, *Arizona and New Mexico.*

López de Cárdenas, García, military officer, explorer (fl. 1535-1550). The second son of a Spanish nobleman, he married well and went to South America in 1535, spending a year there and in Cuba before going to Mexico City. He was ill for about a year, then took up a number of missions for Viceroy Antonio de Mendoza to whom he was related distantly. Cárdenas became a cavalry captain under Coronado, although he said later he went to Cibola unwillingly; he took along 12 horses, three sets of Castilian armor, two pairs of cuirasses and a coat of mail. When Lope de Samaniego in March 1540 was killed by Indians, Cárdenas succeeded him as *maestre de campo* (field commander) and became Coronado's principal lieutenant. Coronado divided his army at Culiacán and at the head of about 80 horse and some foot and Indian auxiliaries set out for Cibola with Cárdenas commanding the military. In Arizona Cárdenas with 15 men advanced a day ahead of the column to scout the way. At the crossing of the Little Colorado they met their first Cibola natives. The Cibolans later attacked the Spanish camp at night, running off most of the horses and Cárdenas narrowly escaping death. He led the July 7 advance upon Háwikuh, southwest of Zuñi, New Mexico, and was prominent in the attack; it was to Cárdenas that the pueblo surrendered after Coronado was wounded. Dispatched by Coronado to locate the great river reported to the northwest, Cárdenas left August 25, 1540

with 25 horsemen. He reached a native town called Tusayán and 20 days later, sometime in September came out upon the South Rim, the first European to view the Grand Canyon. Bolton supposes that Cárdenas's vantage point was Grand View, but no one knows. A bold trio, Captain Pablos de Melgosa, Juan Galeras and another attempted to descend into the gorge but got only one-third of the way down. Cárdenas traveled west along the rim for a short distance, but gave it up for want of water. He went more than 100 leagues inland, finding no villages other than Hopi towns already located, and returned to Cibola November 14. He established winter quarters for the expedition at Alcanfor among the complex of pueblos near today's Bernalillo. At the pueblo of Arenal a Spanish soldier molested an Indian woman and Cárdenas said he was unable to identify the culprit (Juan de Villegas, brother of a high Mexico City official), who thus went unpunished. This was one of the precipitating reasons for the Tiguex War early in 1541, but there were other causes. The Indians heavily fortified Arenal and Cárdenas led an assault upon it, after fruitless attempts to arrange a peace. In several days it was taken with heavy slaughter of Indians and not inconsiderable Spanish casualties. He ordered prisoners to be burnt after they had been promised quarter unbeknown to Cárdenas; this led to a permanent conviction among the pueblos inhabitants that Spanish pledges were worthless. At the fortified town of Moho on February 20 Cárdenas was trapped and stunned by mallet blows upon the head, was almost carried inside the hostile pueblo to certain death, but was rescued at the last moment. Cárdenas accompanied Coronado toward Quivira in the summer of 1541 but broke an arm on a buffalo hunt and returned to Tiguex. There he heard that his older brother had died and Cárdenas had inherited estates and business interests in Spain. He commenced his return to Mexico City, but at Suya in the Corazones Valley of Sonora he found that an Indian uprising had devastated the region and he returned to Tiguex, then accompanied Coronado to Mexico City in 1542. From there he went to Spain where he was known as García Ramirez de Cárdenas, the change of name unexplained. Because of rivalries, jealousies or political intrigue in Mexico the Council of the Indies at Madrid was given a dossier of alleged crimes committed by Cárdenas on the Coronado expedition, highlighted by the burning of the Indian captives at Arenal. Cárdenas was imprisoned or out on bail for several years before being found guilty. His initially heavy sentence of December 20, 1549, was modified and after its fulfillment he returned to his Madrid home (Bolton discusses the charges and events in some detail, 382-94). The date of his death is not reported.

George Parker Winship, *The Coronado Expedition, 1540-1542.* BAE, 14th Ann. Rept, Wash., Govt. Printing Office, 1896; Herbert Eugene Bolton, *Coronado: Knight of Pueblos and Plains.* Albuquerque, Univ. of New Mex. Press, 1964.

López de Haro, Gonsalez, navigator (fl. 1788-1789). "First pilot," or navigator on expeditions dispatched by the Spaniards in 1788 and 1789 up the northwest coast of North America, he explored Puget Sound to some extent and his name was given to Haro Strait, the present boundary between the United States and Canada northward of Juan de Fuca Strait.

Thwaites, EWT, XXIX, 76n.

Lord, George Edwin, surgeon (Feb. 17, 1846-June 25, 1876). B. at Boston he became a contract surgeon with the army April 27, 1871, serving at Fort Ripley and Leech Lake, Minnesota, and at Whetstone Agency and Fort Randall, Dakota. His contract was cancelled at his request November 3, 1873 when he returned to Limerick, Maine, but the following May 22 he again became a contract surgeon in Dakota. June 1, 1874 he worked with the escort for the Northern Boundary Survey Commission, then was assigned to Fort Ripley. Once more the contract was annulled at his request but January 18, 1875, he signed a new contract and worked in Minnesota and Dakota. He was appointed assistant surgeon with the army rank of first lieutenant June 26, 1875 and the following spring took part in the Sioux expedition into Montana. He was killed in the Battle of the Little Big Horn, buried first on the battlefield and in 1877 reinterred at the National Monument cemetery.

BHB; John M. Carroll, Byron Price, *Roll Call on the Little Big Horn.* Fort Collins, Colo., Old Army Press, 1974.

Lord, Richard S.C., army officer (1832-Oct. 15, 1866). B. in Ohio, he went to West Point and was commissioned a brevet second lieutenant of the 7th Infantry July 1, 1856, a second lieutenant of the 3rd Artillery October 31, 1856, and transferred to the 1st Dragoons June 22, 1857. He was posted to Arizona, stationed at Forts Buchanan and Breckinridge and became somewhat interested in Arizona mining. Lord was involved, although in no position of authority, in the Cochise-Bascom affair in Apache Pass early in 1861 and became a first lieutenant April 23 (the 1st Dragoons became the 1st Cavalry that summer). With transfer of troops from Arizona to New Mexico with the start of the Civil War, Lord, becoming a captain October 26, 1861, operated in the Rio Grande Valley. He participated in the Battle of Valverde February 21, 1862, then went east and won brevets for actions at Gettysburg and Five Forks. He died of tuberculosis at Bellefontaine, Ohio.

Heitman; Cullum; Constance Wynn Altshuler, *Chains of Command.* Tucson, Ariz. Hist. Soc., 1981.

Loring, Frederick Wadsworth, writer (Dec. 12, 1848-Nov. 5, 1871). B. at Boston of middle-class parents he was something of a prodigy, being "well versed" in Shakespeare at 7. He attended Harvard where he pursued his interest in literature and was befriended by James Russell Lowell. He wrote a play, *Wild Rose,* produced "with success" at Boston. Upon graduation in 1870 he became associated with several periodicals, contributing to others, the *Atlantic Monthly* and *Appleton's Journal* among them. A serial, "Two College Friends," was pubished in book form in 1871. That year he joined First Lieutenant George M. Wheeler's survey expedition to the lower Great Basin as correspondent for *Appleton's,* nominally as "barometric observer and recorder." The expedition assembled at Elko, Nevada, by May 3. Loring proved "a most unimaginative young man. The best he could do was pep up his reports by writing in a flippant style," according to one student. He was harshly critical of the Mormons. The expedition studied southern Nevada, southwestern Utah, crossed Death Valley, and with several flat-bottomed boats worked up the Colorado River from Camp Mohave through fearsome canyons to Diamond Creek in the

Grand Canyon. Loring, with William Salmon and P.W. Hamel of the Wheeler expedition, four other men and a woman, Mollie Sheppard, "of disreputable character," set out with the stage from Wickenburg, Arizona, toward La Paz on the Colorado River. Eight miles west of Wickenburg the stage was attacked by Yavapai Indians, Loring and five others killed outright including Salmon and Hamel, another dying of wounds. Loring, while supercilious, was a man of intelligence, and with maturity might have developed into a worthy writer.

DAB; Dan L. Thrapp, *Al Sieber, Chief of Scouts.* Norman, Univ. of Okla. Press, 1964; Richard A. Bartlett, *Great Surveys of the American West.* Norman, 1962.

Loring, Leonard Young, army surgeon (Feb. 1, 1844-Apr. 1, 1903). B. at St. Louis, he was commissioned a first lieutenant and assistant surgeon in the army May 14, 1867, and served in the field against hostile Indians in Kansas and Indian Territory until June 1872, becoming a captain May 14, 1870. Part of the time he was in the field with the 6th Cavalry. After a brief service at eastern posts he was assigned to Camp (later Fort) Apache, Arizona, from July 1874. While there he wrote and submitted January 11, 1875, an extended "Report on (the) Coyotero Apaches," a copy of which is at the Bancroft Library in manuscript form. It included biographical treatments of many prominent Apaches and much ethnological information. Loring was assigned to Fort Yuma until October 1877. He was at Forts Hays, Dodge and Camp Supply in Kansas and Indian Territory until October 1882 and later in the decade was stationed at Fort Mojave, Arizona. Loring frequently was on sick leave, became a major October 9, 1888, and retired February 27, 1891. He died at 59.

Heitman; Powell; information from the Bancroft Library.

Loring, William Wing (Old Blizzards), army officer (Dec. 4, 1818-Dec. 30, 1886). B. at Wilmington, North Carolina, he went as a youth to Florida where he became a second lieutenant in the Florida Volunteers and fought against the Seminoles in 1837. He studied law, then was commissioned a captain in the Mounted Rifles in 1846 for the Mexican War, losing an arm at Chapultepec, Mexico.

He was the youngest line colonel in the old army, his commission dating from December 30, 1856. In 1857 he was with Bonneville for an extended sweep of Apache country, the command having a skirmish with Indians across the Arizona line from New Mexico, and another on the way back. Loring, as commander in New Mexico, turned over his charge to Canby in 1861, and although suspected of treason in attempting to get United States stores to the Confederacy, made his way to Texas. He became a Confederate Brigadier General May 20, 1861, and a Major General February 15, 1862. He was one of the last ranking officers to surrender, capitulating in April 1865, and went abroad. He served under the Khedive of Egypt from 1869, rose to General of Division and twice was decorated. He returned to the United States in 1879. Loring died at New York City and was buried at St. Augustine, Florida.

Heitman; Ezra J. Warner, *Generals in Gray: Lives of the Confederate Commanders.* Baton Rouge, La. State Univ. Press, 1959.

Lott, John S., frontiersman (Nov. 25, 1830-May 24, 1910). B. at Lottsville, Warren County, Pennsylvania, he and his brother, Mortimer H., ranched in Kansas for three years. John then went to Fort Kearny, Nebraska, where he worked as a carpenter. At length he left for Idaho in a Mormon wagon train, his team including an ox and a trained buffalo he had purchased at the fort. His attentions to a Mormon girl caused her suitor to shoot the buffalo, claiming it was a "wild" animal and he had a right to kill it. Enroute to the Montana gold fields John and Mortimer met again, going to Bannack and eventually Nevada City, near Virginia City, Montana, where they opened a store. John was the sixth man to join the committee heading up the Vigilance organization; he became its treasurer and captain of a company. John wrote the original oath which every vigilante was required to swear and uphold. He also was in the forefront of vigilante activities and it was he who led the band of four to Bannack where, with assistance from like-minded men there, they caught and hanged Henry Plummer and his deputies, Ned Ray and Buck Stinson; it was Lott who arrested Plummer. He also was active in other scouts and executions. In 1867 Mortimer and John Lott moved to the present site of Twin Bridges,

Montana, where they operated a store, hotel and livery stable large enough to accomodate 34 teams of horses. They also built three toll bridges, two across the Beaverhead and one across the Big Hole River. Each was 100 feet long and ten feet wide. Eventually they turned to ranching, raising blooded shorthorn cattle and Morgan horses. At one time they were raising from 1,000 to 1,200 horses, John being particularly interested in that activity. He died at Twin Bridges.

Register; Great Falls (Mont.) *Tribune*, Dec. 6, 1959; Hoffman Birney, *Vigilantes*. Phila., Penn Pub. Co., 1929.

Lott, Mortimer Hewett, frontiersman (Dec. 25, 1827-Oct. 4, 1920). B. at Lottsville, Warren County, Pennsylvania, he was a brother of John S. Lott; together they ranched for three years in Kansas and when John went to Fort Kearny Mortimer tried gold mining in Colorado and New Mexico. He was at California Gulch on the upper Arkansas River, Colorado, when he heard of the gold discoveries in Montana and headed for there by way of South Pass, Fort Bridger and Salt Lake City. He met John enroute and they arrived at the Big Hole Basin July 16, 1862. With his brother he operated a lumber production operation for about a year when they opened a general store at Nevada City, near Virginia City, Montana. Mortimer, like John was reported to have been a leader among the vigilantes, although he does not figure as prominently as his brother in those activities. In 1867 the brothers moved to the present Twin Bridges, Montana, where they engaged in a variety of pioneering activities and ranching. Here Mortimer died at the age of 92, his descendants continuing to work the ranch the brothers founded.

Register, 189; *Great Falls* (Mont.) *Tribune*, Dec. 6, 1959.

Louderback, David Henry, soldier (fl. 1861-1865). Louderback testified before the 1865 military commission investigating the Sand Creek massacre of eastern Colorado, November 29, 1864. Major Anthony, commander at Fort Lyon, Colorado, had asked John Smith to discover for him the intentions of the Black Kettle band of Cheyennes camped on Sand Creek; Smith requested permission to trade with them as a measure of cover-up and that Louderback and a teamster be assigned to go

with him. Anthony agreed. Louderback testified it was the only time he had been in an Indian camp, and the only occasion he engaged in Indian trading, except, "a little with the squaws here at the post," Fort Lyon. The Indians disarmed Louderback and Smith upon their arrival at Sand Creek, he added, because, "they thought I was a spy, sent out there by Major Anthony to see what they were doing and leave marks to show the soldiers the way out." Although Anthony had urged Chivington to be careful to spare the three whites during the assault, little was done to this end and they repeatedly were fired upon by white soldiers until Chivington at last put them under his wing. It was, Louderback testified, "the tightest place I was ever in." Even after he was picked up by the officers, Louderback and the others repeatedly were threatened by other members of the command; he had much to say about Jack Smith's murder and refused to remain quiet when told to hold his tongue. "I considered my tongue my own," Louderback testified. "I did not consider that it belonged to the government," and he continued to speak out. Louderback was assigned to nurse the wounded Captain Pressly Talbot, whom Chivington sought to use as a tool in his unexplained effort to "impeach" Louderback's testimony, an unsuccessful endeavor. Louderback was a private of G Company, 1st Colorado Cavalry during his military career.

Sand Creek Massacre.

Love, Harry, ranger (c. 1810-June 28, 1868). B. in Vermont he was a descendant through his mother's side of Ethan Allen, went to sea at an early age and said he later served as a scout in the Seminole wars of Florida and the 1832 Blackhawk War in the upper Mississippi Valley. He fought with Texas in the war of independence in 1836 and in the 1846-48 Mexican War. Love then went to California where he became deputy sheriff at Santa Barbara and Los Angeles. May 17, 1853, Governor John Bigler signed an act creating the California State Rangers with Love as captain, authorized to recruit about 20 men for three months' service against bandits who were over-running Mariposa and neighboring counties. July 25, 1853, after a long search a bandit camp was struck and the outlaw known as Joaquin, or Joaquin Murrieta and his lieutenant, Three Fingered Jack were killed. Love and his rangers received $6,000 in reward and expense money from the State Legislature. Love operated a sawmill in the Santa Cruz Mountains until 1862 when it was washed out by floods. In 1858 he married a wealthy widow, Mary Bennett, but they wrangled continually and lived apart much of the time. Love developed a problem with alcohol and his suspicions grew that a handyman, Chris Iverson was alienating the "affections" of his 300-pound wife. He ambushed the couple on their return from San Jose, California, and in a resulting shootout both Iverson and Love were wounded, the latter seriously. He died during surgery for amputation of his wounded arm. He was described as 6 feet tall, with a light complexion, blue eyes and brown hair which he wore shoulder length; he also had a walrus mustache.

William B. Secrest, "Hell for Leather Rangers." *True West*, Vol. 15, No. 4 (Mar.-Apr. 1968), 20-23, 58-49; information from William B. Secrest.

Love, Nat (Deadwood Dick), cowboy (fl. 1877-1907). Love, a black cowboy sought to become accepted as the prototype of the dime novel "Deadwood Dick" of the Black Hills, far from Love's usual stamping ground, but the soubriquet did not stick. He published *The Life and Adventures of Nat Love, Better Known in the Cattle Country as 'Deadwood Dick'* (1907), but in a critique of it Ramon Adams said Love, "either has a bad memory or a good imagination." Love said he met Billy the Kid at Anton Chico, New Mexico, in 1877, was in Silver City, New Mexico, and Holbrook, Arizona, in 1880 and had personal experiences with the Kid and Garrett throughout the Lincoln County War.

Wayne Gard, "The Myth of Deadwood Dick." *Frontier Times*, Vol. 43, No. 6 (Oct.-Nov. 1969), 10-11, 48-50; Ramon F. Adams, *Burs Under the Saddle*. Norman, Univ. of Okla. Press, 1964.

Love, Thomas D., lawman, cattleman (Nov. 10, 1862-Oct. 20, 1934). B. at Gatesville, Texas, he became a Panhandle cowboy. December 17, 1881, a "Tom Love" was peripherally involved in the shooting of Michael Meagher (see entry) at Caldwell, Kansas, by a party of cowboys headed by Jim Talbot(t). Love was arrested for firing a revolver in a saloon, but was freed by companions. Later he was arrested as an accessory to the shooting of Meagher, but was

acquitted January 24, 1882, at his preliminary hearing at Wellington, Kansas. From age 18 Love was a cowboy in Scurry and Borden counties, Texas, and manager of the Alabama and Texas Cattle Company from 1883-91. He was elected first sheriff of Borden County when it was organized in 1890, remaining in office eight years (reportedly serving at various times as sheriff in other Texas counties). During his incumbency in Borden County he learned of a large reward for capture of Indian Territory desperadoes headed by Bill Cook (see entry). According to common report he picked up the trail of Cook, followed it into New Mexico and single-handedly arrested the notorious outlaw near Fort Sumner on January 11, 1895. Bartholomew however urges caution in accepting this version at face value, reporting Texas Ranger A. John L. Sullivan as stating Love "beat me out of Cook" with assistance of Roswell, New Mexico officers. As a cattleman Love at one time reputedly was worth $1 million. He also proudly claimed the "mumble-ty-peg championship of the West." He was widowed in 1933 and died the following year at Sierra Blanca, Texas where he had lived since 1891.

Information from Ed Bartholomew, Mar. 23, 1984; *Frontier Times*, Vol. 12, No. 4 (Jan. 1935), 146; Nyle H. Miller, Joseph W. Snell, *Why the West Was Wild*. Topeka, Kan. State Hist. Soc., 1963.

Love, William H., cowboy (d. July 20, 1899). A rider for Francis W. Springer, general counsel for the Maxwell Land Grant & Railway Co., he was informally deputized by U.S. Marshal Creighton M. Foraker for the Wilson (Memphis) Elliott posse which was repulsed by the Sam Ketchum, Will Carver, Elza Lay train robbers in Turkey Canyon, near Cimarron, New Mexico. Love was wounded badly and died four days later.

Jeff Burton, "Suddenly in a Secluded and Rugged Place." English Westerners' Soc., *Brand Book*, Vol. XIII, Nos. 3, 4 (April, July 1972); Ed Bartholomew, *Western Hard-Cases*. Ruidoso, N.M., Frontier Book Co., 1960.

Lovelace, Francis, colonial governor (c. 1621-fall 1675). Probably b. in Kent, England, he was the second governor of New York, being appointed to the position in 1667 and reaching the colony the following March. He was a better-than-average administrator and, of frontier interest, was vexed occasionally by

Indian troubles and was interested in Indian missions. He also purchased Staten Island from the natives. Through no fault of his, the Dutch seized New York anew in 1673, and this brought him to hard times. He was captured by Turks in the Mediterranean in 1674 and imprisoned briefly in 1675 in the Tower of London; he died near Oxford.

DAB; EA.

Loveridge, A., Mormon pioneer (fl. 1857-1892). A man of this name was listed by *Mormonism Unveiled* as at the scene of the Mountain Meadows Massacre of southern Utah, September 11, 1857, either participating in or consenting to the tragedy. The book said in 1892 he was "of Cedar City," Utah.

Mormonism Unveiled, 380.

Loving, Frank, gambler (c. 1854-Apr. 1882). A drifter known as Cock-eyed Frank, at Dodge City, Kansas, he killed Levi Richardson in a Long Branch saloon gunfight April 5, 1879. He was released on a plea of self defense. After a stay at Las Vegas, New Mexico, Loving was killed by John Allen at Trinidad, Colorado, with whom he had fought a bloodless duel the preceding night. Loving, shot in the back, died instantly, leaving a wife and two children.

Ed Bartholomew, *Wyatt Earp: the Untold Story.* Toyahvale, Tex., Frontier Book Co., 1963.

Loving, Oliver, trail driver (c. 1812-July 1867). B. in Hopkins County, Kentucky, he moved to Lamar County, Texas, in 1845 and the next year to Collin County, engaging in ranching, farming and freighting as a sideline. In 1855 he took his cattle to Palo Pinto County and three years later with John Durkee drove a longhorn herd to Chicago, the first such drive of record. Part of his route west of the Mississippi later was known as the Shawnee Trail. In 1859 he sought to tap the Colorado gold rush market, driving cattle to Denver by way of Pueblo. He furnished beef to the Confederacy during the Civil War and afterward became associated with Charles Goodnight. In 1866 they pioneered the Goodnight-Loving Trail from the Red Fork of the Brazos River to Fort Sumner, New Mexico, where there was a market at the Bosque Redondo Navaho Reservation. The next year they tried again. Indians and stampedes caused losses and delays. Loving

and William J. (Billy) Wilson set out in advance of the drive for Fort Sumner to assure purchasers there that the herd was enroute. The two ran into Indians and Loving was shot through the wrist and side. Believing his wound fatal, he directed Wilson to leave him and return to the cow camp which, after great difficulties Wilson succeeded in doing. Loving meanwhile had not perished, but managed to drag himself to the trail and after seven days with no food was picked up by Mexicans whom he hired to take him to Fort Sumner. Amputation of Loving's arm seemed indicated, but the inexperienced doctor hesitated. Goodnight and Wilson learned that Loving was at Fort Sumner and when they arrived found that amputation was urgently required, prevailing upon the doctor to attempt it. But gangrene had set in and Loving succumbed after about three weeks. His last request reportedly was for Goodnight to take him back to Texas for burial since he did not wish to remain on "foreign soil." This was done, the burial being in Greenwood Cemetery, Weatherford, with Masonic rites. The *Handbook of Texas* believed Loving deserved the title of "Dean of the Trail Drivers" for his pioneering of three famous cattle trails from Texas.

Hunter, TDT, II, 908-13; REAW; *Frontier Times,* Vol. 52, No. 5 (Aug.-Sept. 1978), p. 4.

Low, William Hall Jr., army officer (Sept. 3, 1848-July 24, 1886). Heitman gives his middle name as Hale; Low was b. in New York, graduated from West Point in 1872, assigned to the 20th Infantry and served at such frontier posts as Fort Snelling, Minnesota, and Fort Pembina, Dakota, until May 1876, when he was assigned to Fort Abraham Lincoln, Dakota. He was in command of the Gatling Gun battery with the Sioux expedition until September of 1876. Low was on a Yellowstone expedition from April to December 1877, did scouting duty out of Fort Gibson, Indian Territory, from 1883 until 1885, and was stationed at Fort Assiniboine, Montana, until his death.

Heitman; Cullum; Don Russell, *The Lives and Legends of Buffalo Bill.* Norman, Univ. of Okla. Press, 1960.

Low Horn, Piegan chief (fl. 1855). Low Horn was said to be the principal Piegan chief at the Judith River council of Montana where he signed the Blackfoot treaty of October 17,

1855. Stevens called him "the quiet, and even meek spokesman," and the first to extend the hand of friendship to western Indians who also attended the council. He cautioned however that even the chiefs could not control their young men who were ambitious for honors of war and the chase. Low Horn signed the Blackfoot Treaty No. 7, September 22, 1877, on the Bow river of Canada. He is said to have died at extreme old age on the Marias River of Montana.

Montana Contributions, Vol. X, 1940, 274.

Lowdermilk, Walter Clay, conservationist (July 1, 1888-May 6, 1974). B. at Liberty, North Carolina, he was taken west as a child by his parents, they becoming pioneer settlers engaged in lumbering, farming and engineering. Lowdermilk studied chemistry and majored in geology and engineering at the University of Arizona, was a Rhodes scholar, and studied forestry in Germany. He was a member of the 1914 Hoover Commission for Belgian Relief, and served three years in France, part of it with the Lumberjack Division of the 10th Corps of Engineers. Afterward he worked on famine prevention in China where he became interested in the reconstruction of land ravaged by wasteful agriculture and other harmful practices due to man's lack of a positive relationship with the land. He became a world figure in combating erosion and promoting ecological balance, long before "ecology" became a household word. Loudermilk planned a 50-year study of the San Dimas hydrocological watershed in California. He was summoned by President Franklin Roosevelt to help start the Soil Conservation Service and was instrumental in drafting the Soil Conservation Act (1935) and Flood Control Act (1936). He studied the effect of climate on the decline of agriculture in the old Roman Empire. In Jerusalem he drafted and broadcast by radio an "11th Commandment," which he said Moses might have uttered had he foreseen man's destruction of his surroundings, the text of which has been widely quoted and used effectively by conservationists. Lowdermilk, a Christian, was a powerful influence in forming plans for reclaiming the Holy Land where the Lowdermilk School of Agricultural Engineering was launched at Haifa, becoming important in developing sound agricultural practices in that country. He died at his Berkeley, California, home.

New York Times, May 9, 1974; *Who's Who.*

Lowe, Joseph and Kate (Rowdy Joe, Rowdy Kate), characters (Joe: c. 1845-c. 1899; Kate: c. 1851-?). Both were born in Illinois. On July 24, 1869, Joe and a Jim Bush drugged and robbed a man at Ellsworth, Kansas, where Joe and Kate ran a disorderly house. They moved their operation to Newton in 1871. On February 9, 1872, Joe shot and killed a man named A.M. Sweet. The couple moved once more to West Wichita, Kansas, a lawless place where Joe was his own policeman, administering order by pistol-whipping offenders and in other ways at their house of prostitution. The place narrowly escaped destruction June 5, 1873, when irate 6th Cavalry troopers swarmed about to avenge the shooting of two soldiers and a girl earlier at E.T. (Red) Beard's house next door; on October 27, 1873, in a melee, Red was mortally wounded by Joe, who was slightly wounded himself; two others were shot. Lowe was acquitted of killing Beard December 11. He fled the county to avoid another warrant, and Kate, too, disappeared. Joe was arrested with more than $8,000 on him at St. Louis on January 3, 1874, where Kate showed up by train with two pets, a bulldog and a yellow lapdog, obtained the money, and got Joe released despite a request from Kansas for him. In October 1874, the Lowes were in Denison, Texas, and later that month Joe was reported killed by Indians while enroute for the Black Hills gold fields. Other reports however continued to place him in Texas; he was fined for assaulting Kate at San Antonio in May 1875. In 1899 it was reported that Joe finally was killed in a Denver saloon by a former policeman. Kate's date and place of death are uncertain.

Nyle H. Miller and Joseph W. Snell, *Great Gunfighters of the Kansas Cowtowns, 1867-1886.* Lincoln, Univ. of Nebr. Press, 1967.

Lowther, William, frontiersman (Dec. 22, 1743-Oct. 28, 1814). B. in Augusta County, Virginia, he volunteered at 17 under David Scott to help repel Indians from the border, continuing in that service for some time. He received a good education. Lowther reached the Hacker Settlement, Virginia, with his parents in 1767, and moved on to the vicinity of Nutter Fort, Harrison County, by 1772 where, as captain of a small body of frontiersmen, he became prominent in Indian-white hostilities. He married Sudna Hughes, sister of famed scouts Jesse, Elias and Thomas Hughes. Lowther was prominent in efforts to alleviate hunger in "the starving year" of 1773, earning lasting gratitude with the success of his rifle against buffalo, elk, deer, and bear which saved the embryo settlements from disaster. "During the war of 1774 (Lord Dunmore's War) and subsequently, he was the most active and efficient defender of the settlements against the savage foe, and many a successful expedition against them was commanded by him." His adventures with Indians and with wild game were almost countless and continuous, his control over the rough rangers and scouts absolute and never resented. In 1781 George Rogers Clark offered him a commission as major for his projected expedition against Detroit, but after a short time at Fort Pitt he resigned. In 1787 Lowther was named colonel of the north-western part of Virginia, retaining his command until Wayne's treaty of 1795 effectively ended the Indian menace. Lowther was a justice of the peace, the first sheriff of Harrison County, a delegate to the state assembly and a community leader in many directions. He was foremost among the pioneers of the northwestern Virginia region, giving freely of his services, his purse, the successful issue of his many hunts, and the peace he largely had brought. He is buried on his old farm on the West Fork, Monongahela River, West Virginia.

Lucullus V. McWhorter, *The Border Settlers of Northwestern Virginia.* Hamilton, O., Republican Pub. Co., 1915.

Lubbock, Thomas S., frontiersman (1817-Jan. 23, 1863). B. in South Carolina, he reached New Orleans and Texas in 1835 to participate in the siege of Bexar (San Antonio). Lubbock worked for a time on a Brazos River steamer, and in 1841 joined the Texan-Santa Fe Expedition as first lieutenant of Company C. Captured with the others in New Mexico, through the supposed treachery of their companion, William P. Lewis, Lubbock was taken to Mexico City where he escaped from Santiago with a companion, Louis Mazur, a Frenchman, making his way to Vera Cruz and hence home by way of New Orleans. He took part in the Somervell Expedition, an inept Texas attempt at a reprisal invasion of Mexico which ended with the tragic Mier Expedition. Lubbock's valuable narrative of the Santa Fe expedition was printed in the *Colorado Gazette and Advertiser* of Matagorda, Texas, June 4, 1842, although the original is lost. Lubbock went into business at Houston, Texas, while his brother, Francis Richard Lubbock, went on to become governor of the state. Tom Lubbock entered the Confederate service in the Civil War, became a lieutenant colonel, and was given command of Terry's Texas Rangers, but illness caused his death, probably in Kentucky. Lubbock and Lubbock County, Texas, are named for him.

Noel H. Loomis, *The Texan-Santa Fe Pioneers.* Norman, Univ. of Okla. Press, 1958; HT.

Luce, Jason, frontiersman (d. 1863). An express driver for A.J. Oliver out of Bannack, Montana, Luce upbraided Sam Bunton for a brutal shooting and was beaten up by Bunton. Later the two met again at Salt Lake City and in a renewal of their feud Luce slit Bunton's throat. Found guilty of murder he was given his choice of hanging, shooting, or beheading, and elected to be shot.

Langford.

Lucier, Auguste, interpreter (May 4, 1814-Aug. 19, 1854). B. at St. Charles, Missouri, he reached the middle Plains by about 1850, had a Sioux wife named Ena Tiglak and two daughters who married the Clifford brothers, according to Hyde; Gilman says Henry Clifford, the elder, had married a Cheyenne, and Mortimer (Monte) married Julia, a daughter of Lucier (whom she calls Augustine Lutice) and related to Spotted Tail. Lucier was a hunter and guide for William Drummond Stewart in 1843. Lucier was "very quarrelsome, particularly when drunk," and in 1854, hated Indians who had run off his horses. He as taken along as interpreter by Grattan although drinking heavily, shouting insults at the Sioux, and Grattan could not quiet him. When the Grattan fight started, Lucier was first to flee, accompanied by a soldier, but they were overtaken by the aroused Sioux and killed.

George F. Hyde, *Spotted Tail's Folk: A History of the Brulé Sioux.* Norman, Univ. of Okla. Press,

1961; Musetta Gilman, *Pump on the Prairie.* Detroit, Harlo Press, 1975.

Lucier, Etienne, trapper (c. 1793-March 18, 1853). B. at Montreal, he joined the Wilson Price Hunt overland expedition to the mouth of the Columbia where Astoria was founded, arriving in 1812. He was taken over, with Astoria, by the North West Company and made at least one trip to Montreal. As a free trapper, he continued to cooperate with the Hudson's Bay Company when it absorbed the North West Company. He lived the life of a wandering trapper and hunter, working sometimes as far south as California, then became a pioneer settler in Champoeg County, Oregon.

Harriet D. Munnick article, MM, Vol. VI.

Lucier, Jean Baptiste (Gardipe), frontiersman (c. 1810-Aug. 16, 1850). B. probably in western Canada as half Cree, he reached the Oregon country by 1830 and became an engage for the Hudson's Bay Company, working with the Snake River brigade. By 1834 he had settled near French Prairie on the Willamette River of Oregon. In 1841 he served as guide for Wilkes and in 1846 was of a party mapping an emigrant route to Fort Boise, Idaho. He died at his Willamette farm.

Harriet D. Munnick article, MM, Vol. VIII.

Ludlow, William, army officer, engineer (Nov. 27, 1843-Aug. 30, 1901). B. at Islip, Long Island, he was graduated from West Point in 1864, joined Sherman's forces and by war's end had been brevetted up to lieutenant colonel. As captain he became chief engineer, Department of Dakota. Ludlow surveyed the later Yellowstone National Park in 1873 and 1875, and in 1874 accompanied Custer's Black Hills expedition with the responsibility of mapping its course. His official report was published in the *New York Tribune* September 14. He had secured the scientific assistance of Newton H. Winchell and George Bird Grinnell who accompanied the party and made their own reports. Ludlow found the region "admirably adapted to settlement," and while mentioning that gold was found, declined to predict whether it would be present in paying quantities, leaving such speculation to the scientists. Ludlow later pursued engineering work in the east; in the Spanish American War he was named

Brigadier General of Volunteers, commanding a brigade in the attack on El Caney and investment of Santiago, Cuba, and as Major General of Volunteers became governor of Havana briefly in 1900; he died in New Jersey while under orders to go to the Philippines.

DAB; Herbert Krause, Gary D. Olson, *Prelude to Glory.* Sioux Falls, S.D., Brevet Press, 1974.

Luján, Natividad, story teller (c. 1840-1918). B. at San Carlos, Chihuahua, on the Rio San Carlos west of Santa Elena Canyon off the Rio Grande, he was raised in that crossroads for Mexicans, Apaches and Comanches, and was thoroughly imbued with the legends, folklore, history and myths of that wholly frontier situation. As such he comes most clearly to focus in his engaging stories written by Williams as a result of his many months of surveying in the Big Bend country of Texas when it was wild and little known. Luján had much to tell him of Indian raids, natural history and the myths and legends associated by Mexicans with each. In November 1894, Luján, who had come to odds with the Roy Bean-like political leader of San Carlos, was kidnapped by that leader, one Matías Zuñiga, for reasons of spite, and taken to San Carlos where had he been found guilty of *any* infraction whatever, Luján believed he would have been executed, for Zuñiga had that authority as autonomous judge and peacekeeper at San Carlos from the Mexican central government. But Luján had committed no such infraction and had to be turned loose. Next he and others caught Zuñiga on the American side of the Rio Grande, took him to Polvo (Redford), and thence to Alpine, Texas, where Zuñiga was tried on a kidnapping charge March 7, 1895, and served two years in the Texas penitentiary. After his release Zuñiga returned to Mexico, and Luján no longer returned to that country "because, you see, Zuñiga lives over there." Yet eventually he did cross at Mulato, across the river from Polvo, was captured in 1918, taken to Ojinaga, opposite Presidio, Texas, and was hanged.

Williams, Oscar.

Lummis, Charles Fletcher, southwest enthusiast, writer (Mar. 1, 1859-Nov. 25, 1928). B. at Lynn, Massachusetts, he was educated at Harvard, edited a newspaper briefly at Cincinnati, Ohio, and in 1884 walked from

Ohio to Los Angeles, sending articles to the *Los Angeles Times* as he did so, becoming city editor upon his arrival after covering 3,507 miles in 143 days. He worked for *The Times* for two years, was the publisher's correspondent to Fort Bowie, General Crook's headquarters, in the spring of 1886 during the Geronimo tumult. For five years, to recoup his health, he lived in the Indian pueblo of Isleta, New Mexico, learning much of the language and customs of that people. He traveled widely over the southwest by horseback and also visited Mexico and Peru. He founded *Out West* magazine in 1894, editing it until 1909; was Los Angeles librarian 1905-10, introducing many worthy innovations. He founded the Landmarks Club to preserve historic sites, the Sequoyah League ("to make better Indians"), was president of Warner's Ranch Indian Commission, securing improved homes for 300 evicted Indians. He founded the Southwest Museum, 1907; was a member of many archaeological, literary, and historical organizations, and was a driving, innovative influence in most of them; he did much to shape the culture of the southwest, and to better orient it toward respect for its varied past. Lummis was married three times, each ending in divorce. His published works were many, among them: *Birch Bark Poems* (1879); *A New Mexico David and Other Stories and Sketches of the Southwest* (1891); *A Tramp Across the Continent* (1892); *The Land of Poco Tiempo* (1893); *The Spanish Pioneers* (1893); *The King of the Broncos and Other Stories of New Mexico* (1897); *Mesa, Cañon and Pueblo: Our Wonderland of the Southwest* (1925); *A Bronco Pegasus* (1928).

Dudley Gordon, *Charles F. Lummis: Crusader in Corduroy*. Los Angeles, Cultural Assets Press, 1972; *Dateline Fort Bowie: Charles Fletcher Lummis Reports on an Apache War*, ed. by Dan L. Thrapp. Norman, Univ. of Okla. Press, 1979.

Lumpkins, Tom, buffalo hunter (d. Apr. 27, 1877). A West Texas buffalo hunter, Lumpkins refused to join others in an impromptu campaign against the Comanches, made slighting remarks about those who had undertaken it, was reprimanded in a saloon at Rath City, Texas, shot and wounded one man and was shot and killed by Limpy Jim Smith, second in command of the expedition. Lumpkins' was the first grave in Rath City's boot hill cemetery.

John R. Cook, *The Border and the Buffalo*. Chicago, Lakeside Ed., 1938; Wayne Gard, *The Great Buffalo Hunt*. Lincoln, Univ. of Nebr. Press, 1968.

Luna y Arellano, Tristan de, conquistador (1510-Sept. 16, 1573). B. in Spain of noble family, he reached Mexico with Cortez in 1530 and after a brief visit to Spain again returned to Mexico where in 1535 he resided in the home of Viceroy Antonio de Mendoza. He was named a captain of cavalry for the 1540-42 Coronado expedition and remained at Culiacán for a time when Coronado went rapidly ahead with a picked force toward Cibola; later Luna y Arellano followed at a more leisurely pace. Luna y Arellano left part of his men near the present Ures, Sonora, where he founded a town, and continued with the bulk of it northward. He reached Cibola in November and wintered with the army at the Tiguex pueblos on the Rio Grande, arriving there after the Tiguex War had broken out. He accompanied Coronado the following spring toward Quivira, but was detached at Palo Duro Canyon June 15, 1541, and sent back to Tiguex, arriving July 9. Awaiting Coronado's return he undertook minor explorations, assembled supplies for the coming winter, and had a skirmish or two with Indians, returning to Mexico with Coronado. He settled at Oaxaca, Mexico around 1545 and married a twice-widowed and very wealthy woman. He put down an Indian uprising in 1548 and in 1551 became governor of the estates of the Marques del Valle. Viceroy Luis de Velasco in 1559, on orders of Philip II of Spain named Luna y Arellano to head up a fresh attempt to conquer Florida and he shipped out July 11 with the titles of governor and captain-general. The endeavor did not prosper however, and proved very costly; the leader fell ill in 1560, and returned to Mexico. He went to Madrid in 1561 but failed to recoup his fortune and returned to Mexico about 1567, wholly impoverished.

Herbert I. Priestley, *Tristan de Luna, Conquistador of the Old South*. Glendale, Calif., Arthur H. Clark Co., 1936; *Porrua;* George Parker Winship, *The Coronado Expedition, 1540-1542*. BAE, 14th Ann. Rept., Wash., Gov. Printing Office, 1896; Herbert Eugene Bolton, *Coronado: Knight of Pueblos and Plains*. Albuquerque, Univ. of New Mex. Press, 1964; John R. Swanton, *Early History of the Creek Indians and Their Neighbors*. Wash.,

BAE Bull. 73, 1922; Swanton, *The Indians of the Southeastern United States.* Wash., BAE Bull. 137, Smithsonian Inst. Press, 1979.

Lupton, Lancaster P. army officer, fur trader (1807-Aug. 2, 1885). B. in New York State, he was graduated from West Point in 1829, but resigned from the army in 1836. The year before he had accompanied Colonel Henry Dodge up the Platte River to the Rocky Mountains, and after he retired went to Fort Laramie, then to the South Platte where he erected a trading post, withstood heavy competition, married a Cheyenne girl and fathered four children. He then built another post on the North Platte near the mouth of the Laramie Fork; he soon disposed of it. During the winter of 1846-47 he operated a store and farm at Hardscrapple, near the upper Arkansas River. He joined the 1849 gold rush to California, settled finally at Arcata where four additional children were born, and where he died.

Ann W. Hafen article, MM, Vol. II; Heitman; Cullum; Guy L. Peterson, *Four Forts on the South Platte.* Fort Myer, Va., Council on America's Military Past, 1982.

Luxan, Diego Pérez de, soldier, diarist (fl. 1582-1583). Luxan and his brother, Gaspar de Luxan, both "natives of Seville," were members of the Espejo expedition of discovery into New Mexico from Nueva Vizcaya (Chihuahua) in 1582-83. Little is known biographically of either, but Diego Luxan's day-by-day diary is an invaluable record of the course of the expedition, and events connected with it. Luxan, as "alguacil mayor" or chief constable or administrative head under Espejo went with the leader and three others on April 30, 1583 west from the Hopi towns on an important exploration journey into Arizona which extended as far as the present Jerome on Mingus Mountain east of Prescott. It was the first Spanish penetration into that region, a copper deposit being located there May 8, after which the party, disgusted that no silver outcroppings of importance had been found, turned back to the New Mexico pueblos and eventually returned to Nueva Vizcaya. Luxan was an intelligent, careful observor and his meticulous recounting of distances traveled, skirmishes with Indians, reception at the various pueblos and observations upon the

Indians and natural features encountered do much to illuminate Espejo's own narrative. Little further is known of Luxan's life.

George P. Hammond, Agapito Rey, *The Rediscovery of New Mexico, 1580-1594.* Albuquerque, Univ. of New Mex. Press, 1966; Herbert Eugene Bolton, *Spanish Exploration in the Southwest, 1542-1706.* N.Y., Charles Scribner's Sons, 1916.

Lyden, John, scout (fl. 1868). One of 50 frontiersmen serving under George A. Forsyth against Indian hostiles on the middle Plains, Lyden took part in the battle of Beecher Island in mid-September 1868. By 1905 he had died, according to the *Beecher Island Annual* of that year.

Simon E. Matson, ed., *The Battle of Beecher Island.* Wray, Colo., Beecher Island Meml. Assn., 1960.

Lyman, Robert, westerner (Aug. 18, 1847-May 9, 1938). B. at Rushville, Indiana, he served in the heavy artillery during the Civil War, then returned to Rushville, where he married. In 1880 the Lymans moved to Girard, Kansas, and in 1894 to Wray, Colorado. Lyman was greatly interested in the Beecher Island battle which occurred some miles south of Wray on the Arickaree Fork of the Republican River in September 1868. He was president of the Beecher Island Battle Memorial Association for many years and edited the Beecher Island Annual. He also was instrumental in securing a stone memorial for the site. He died at Wray.

Simon E. Matson, *The Battle of Beecher Island,* Wray, Colo., Beecher Island Battle Meml. Assn., 1960.

Lyman, Wyllys, army officer (Apr. 4, 1830-Feb. 1, 1900). B. in Vermont, he became a first lieutenant of the 10th Vermont Infantry August 15, 1862, and emerged from the Civil War a major. He was commissioned a captain in the 40th U.S. Infantry July 28, 1866, transferred to the 25th Infantry April 20, 1869, and to the 5th Infantry December 15, 1870. Lyman took part in Miles's Red River campaign of 1874 and in September with his Company I escorted a 36-wagon train from near McClellan Creek, Texas, toward Camp Supply, Indian Territory. Enroute he met a Mexican train bringing supplies, transferred them to his own wagons and started the return. Kiowa, Comanche and perhaps Cheyenne Indians attacked near the Washita River, Texas, the wagons were corraled and the four-day engagement became celebrated in South Plains legend. Relief arrived at length from Camp Supply, and from Miles's immediate command; an officer was wounded, an enlisted man killed and three others wounded for an undetermined Indian loss; 20 mules were killed and others so weakened by loss of water and forage that the train in effect was immobilized. For his leadership, Lyman was breveted to lieutanant colonel. He became deputy governor of the Soldiers' Home at Washington, D.C., in 1884, and from 1885 served in the War Department records section. He became major July 4, 1892, when he retired.

Heitman; Powell; G. Derek West, "Baldwin's Ride and the Battle of Lyman's Wagon Train." London, *English Westerners' 10th Anniv. Pubn.,* 1964; James L. Haley, *The Buffalo War.* Garden City, N.Y., Doubleday & Co., 1976.

Lynde, Isaac, army officer (c. 1804-Apr. 10, 1886). B. in Vermont, he was graduated in 1827 from West Point, and with the 5th Infantry served at Jefferson Barracks, Missouri; Leavenworth, Kansas, 1829; Mackinac, Michigan, 1829-32; Fort Howard, Wisconsin, 1832-37; Fort Winnebago, Wisconsin, 1837-39; Fort Snelling, Minnesota, 1839-40, and Fort Gratiot, Michigan, 1841-45. Lynde served in the military occupation of Texas in 1845, and in the Mexican War the next year. During the next 12 years he was stationed in Arkansas, Indian Territory, Texas and Dakota. In 1858-60 he took part in the Utah Expedition, and by 1860 was in New Mexico at Fort Webster and later at Fort McLane, the site for which he selected. Here he sought to keep peace between gold miners at nearby Pinos Altos and the Mimbres Apaches, whom they exasperated continually; it was a losing struggle, and Lynde himself suffered from Apache stock raids. In 1861 Lynde was at Fort Fillmore, where his actions are most controversial. He abandoned Fillmore to Texas Confederates and "subsequently surrendered his command to an inferior force of insurgents." He was captured. In 1866 he was promoted to major, 18th Infantry, and retired from active service, being 62 years of age. He died at Picolata, Florida.

Cullum; *Annual Reunion of West Point Graduates,* June 10, 1886; Dan L. Thrapp, *Victorio and the Mimbres Apaches.* Norman, Univ. of Okla. Press, 1974.

Lynn, John, scout (fl. 1782). A "celebrated spy" and scout, Lynn warned Wheeling, (present West Virginia), of the approach of British-led Indians about September 1, 1782, in time for an effective defense to be organized in this "last engagement of the Revolution where the British flag was in evidence," at least in the trans-Allegheny country.

Lucullus V. McWhorter, *The Border Settlers of Northwestern Virginia.* Hamilton, O., Republican Pub. Co., 1915.

Lynn, Wiley, gunman (c. 1900-July 17, 1932). His date of birth is conjecture. Born probably in the Oklahoma panhandle, he was a prohibition agent about Madill, Oklahoma, and reportedly wore two nickel-plated, pearl-handled six shooters and a white Stetson hat in his work, and he drank about as much whiskey as he confiscated. On November 1, 1924, he killed Bill Tilghman, veteran peace officer who was trying to arrest him, at Cromwell, Oklahoma, and got off on a plea of self-defense. Lynn left the prohibition service, lived on a farm near Madill, continued to drink, and nurtured enmity against Crockett Long and others on the local police force. In a drug store he accosted Long, who was hard of hearing, and in a shootout Long was killed and Lynn, shot twice, wounded mortally. A by-stander, Rody Watkins, also was killed and another crippled. Lynn was buried at Madill.

Tulsa, Okla., *Daily World,* July 24, 1932; Carl W. Breihan, *Great Lawmen of the West.* N.Y., Bonanza Books, 1963.

Lyon, Hylan Benton, army officer (Feb. 22, 1836-Apr. 25, 1907). B. at River View in Caldwell (now Logan) County, Kentucky, he was orphaned at 8 and went to West Point in 1852. Lyon became a second lieutenant in the 3rd Artillery in 1856 and a first lieutenant in 1860. He did escort duty in the northwest with the crews building the Mullan Road between Fort Benton, Montana and Fort Walla Walla, Washington. Lyon participated in Wright's campaign against the Coeur d'Alenes and eastern Washington tribes in 1858. He served the Confederacy in the Civil War, becoming a

Brigadier General. He was taken prisoner in 1862 at Fort Donelson but exchanged after seven months. Lyon was at Vicksburg, escaping Grant's siege with his command and served ably under Forrest. For a time he was in command of the District of Western Kentucky. After the Civil War he withdrew to Mexico, but returned to Kentucky in 1866 and farmed near Eddyville until his death.

Heitman; Cullum; Ezra J. Warner, *Generals in Gray: Lives of the Confederate Commanders.* Baton Rouge, La. State Univ. Press, 1959.

Lyons, Hayes (Haze), desperado (d. Jan. 14, 1864). A member of Henry Plummer's band of desperados in southwestern Montana, Lyons' mother, a brother and sister lived at Hook's Station, Nebraska, but where he was born is uncertain, as is his age at death. He took part in an assault on friendly Indians near Bannack in the early spring of 1863, wounding one. He was a "roadster," or holdup man of the gang, being a participant in various stage robberies and, in June 1863, the murder of Don or John Dillingham, an honest deputy sheriff, at Virginia City. For this he and two others were tried by a "miners' court," but the court proved ineffectual, and they were freed. Lyons was picked up with four others by vigilantes and all five hanged from a single rafter in an unfinished building at Virginia City, Lyons being the last to go and seemingly penitent. He directed that the gold watch he wore be returned to his mistress, who was not a witness to the execution.

Langford; Dimsdale; Birney.

Lyons, Jack, gambler (d. Feb. 1881). he was known at Dodge City, Kansas, Fort Griffin, Texas, and Las Vegas, New Mexico, where he was a constable under Hoodoo Brown. Lyons got drunk and shot up Rincon, New Mexico, above Las Cruces, until a "saloonist" shot him.

Ed Bartholomew, *Wyatt Earp: The Man & the Myth.* Toyahvale, Tex., Frontier Book Co., 1964.

Mc

McAdow, Perry W. (Bud), pioneer (July 28, 1838-July 14, 1918). B. at Maysville, Mason County, Kentucky, his parents moved to Platte County, Missouri, while Perry was an infant. He reached Montana with William Graham by way of the Missouri River in 1861 aboard the only steamboat up the river that season, the *Spread Eagle.* At Fort Union he transferred to the *Chippewa,* an American Fur Company mountain boat. She blew up below Fort Benton when a thirsty deckhand trying to tap barrels of Indian trade alcohol inadvertently set her afire. McAdow and others reached Fort Benton afoot on July 4 and eventually arrived at Fort Owen in the Bitterroot Valley. From there he and Abraham Sterne (Sterny) Blake made their way to Gold Creek, northwest of the present Deer Lodge and settled in to prospect with James and Granville Stuart and other prospector-adventurers. They returned to Fort Owen for the winter. With spring McAdow returned to Gold Creek where the Stuarts, John W. Powell, Fred H. Burr, James Minesinger and others were camped. After some time mining he went to Bannack where a major strike had been made, and then to Virginia City, Montana. With Tom Cover, McAdow established a sawmill in 1864 near Virginia City. In the late summer they sold out and in partnership launched the first commercial grist mill in Montana at the present Bozeman; Cover sold out in 1868 and with his brother, William McAdow, Perry continued the partnership until 1879. He then moved to Billings, Montana, "where he amassed a large fortune." In 1889 he was a member of the constitutional convention that established Montana as a state. He spent his years after c. 1892 at Punta Gorda, Florida, where he died. McAdow was popular, possessed a lively sense of humor, was progressive, active and had many interests.

Register; Progressive Men of Montana. Chicago, A.W. Bowen & Co., 1902, 723; P.W. McAdow to W.S. Bell, August 4, 1908, letter in the Mont. Hist. Soc. archives; Granville Stuart, *Forty Years on the Frontier.* Lincoln, Univ. of Nebr. Press, 1977.

McAllister, John, cowboy, butcher (d. May 13, 1881). He plied his trades near Galeyville, Arizona, and was killed with three other cowboys near Fronteras, Sonora, by Mexicans led by José Juan Vasquez. The incident had repercussions.

Ed Bartholomew, *Wyatt Earp: The Man & the Myth.* Toyahvale, Tex. Frontier Book Co., 1964.

McArthur, Neil McLean, frontiersman (fl. 1846-1859). From 1846 to 1849 McArthur was an apprentice clerk with the Hudson's Bay Company at a post on the Flathead River above Thompson Falls, Montana. He later was assigned to Fort Hall but resigned in 1855 to become a trader to emigrants on the Oregon Trail, acquiring stock which he recouped in the Flathead Valley or Bitterroot Valley. McArthur later established a kind of ranch headquarters in Grass Valley, near the present Missoula, Montana. He later took his stock from there to the Fraser River country of British Columbia where he managed to lose all his capital, estimated at $150,000. The last word of him was as a prospector in that region. McArthur was intellectually oriented with a cultivated taste in literature.

George F. Weisel, *Men and Trade on the Northwest Frontier.* Missoula, Mont. State Univ. Press, 1955; Granville Stuart, *Forty Years on the Frontier.* Glendale, Calif., Arthur H. Clark Co., 1925.

McCall, D.T., miner (d. Feb. 21, 1867). A prospector and miner of Mohave County, Arizona, he worked in the Wauba Yuma District in the early 1860's until Indian hostility prevented. In 1865 McCall and some others returned to the mines and on November 11, he was named recorder of the district. He filed a claim March 24, 1866, but a year later was killed by Indians in Union Pass, northeast of Hardyville, Arizona.

Roman Malach, *Hualapai Mountains.* N.Y., Graphicopy, 1975.

McCall, John (Jack; Buffalo Curly; Bill Sutherland), assassin (c. 1852-Mar. 1, 1877). B. in Jefferson County, near Jeffersontown,

Kentucky, he left home about 1869, wandered among buffalo camps on the Plains, under the purported nickname of Buffalo Curly, and in 1875 he was in Wyoming, reportedly employed by a stage line, having adopted the name, Bill Sutherland. He reached Deadwood, South Dakota, sometime in 1876. On August 2, he stepped behind Wild Bill Hickok, playing poker in Saloon No. 10, and shot him in the head. Tried by a miner's jury before Judge W.L. Kuykendall, McCall was found not guilty, the jury allegedly having been bribed. At Laramie, Wyoming, he was rearrested August 29, 1876, sent to Yankton, South Dakota for a new trial, since the first was ruled illegal because Deadwood was not a legally constituted community and local acts of justice were not recognized by law. An attempt to escape jail on November 9 proved abortive, and McCall was tried December 4-6, being found guilty and sentenced by Judge P.C. Shannon January 3, 1877, to hang. It was suggested that McCall had been hired to assassinate Hickok, but the perpetrators, if any, were never punished. The judgment was carried out, McCall dying bravely. He was about 5 feet, 6 inches, in height, had chestnut hair, crossed eyes, a sandy mustache, and was plainly dressed throughout. He was buried in the Catholic cemetery at Yankton.

Joseph G. Rosa, "The United States vs. John McCall: Indictment for Murder." London, *English Westerners' 10th Anniv. Pubn.,* 1964.

McCall, William H.H., army officer, scout (c. 1838-June 13, 1883). B. in Pennsylvania, he enlisted as a sergeant in the 5th Pennsylvania Volunteers June 5, 1861, and rose to brevet Brigadier General by war's end, being breveted for heroism in actions at Fort Steadman, and Fort Sedgwick, Virginia. In the former action he retook the place after it had been captured by Confederate General John B. Gordon. "McCall, like many another good man of either army, had drifted West since the close of the war, been unsuccessful, became a bit dissipated," commented Forsyth, and leaped at the opportunity to become one of the scouts Forsyth led to the battle of Beecher's Island. McCall was enlisted as first sergeant of the informal organization and was wounded slightly. March 28, 1872, McCall and Ranald Mackenzie met at Fort Sill, according to Robert G. Carter who said McCall thereafter led "the adventurous and

checkered career of a border spirit." He became a miner near Prescott, Arizona. He had witnessed the shooting of Sheriff Robert Broddus in Montague County, Texas, by George Wilson (who later went by the name of Vaughn), and ran into Wilson/Vaughn again at Prescott in 1877. McCall was a member of the posse which ran down Vaughn and Robert Tullos October 16 of that year, both gunmen being killed. McCall was married in 1878, fathered two children, lost his wife in 1882 and died of hepatitis at Prescott.

Simon E. Matson, ed., *Battle of Beecher Island,* Wray, Colo., Beecher Island Battle Meml. Assn., 1960; George A. Forsyth, *Thrilling Days in Army Life.* N.Y., Harper & Bros., 1900; Robert G. Carter, *On the Border With Mackenzie.* N.Y., Antiquarian Press, 1961, 299; Robert F. Palmquist, "Virgil Earp in Prescott, 1877." *Real West,* Vol. 23, No. 173 (Dec. 1980), 32-34, 48.

McCanles, David Colbert, frontiersman (Nov. 30, 1828-July 12, 1861). B. in Iredell County, North Carolina, he married in 1849 and became deputy sheriff of Watauga County, North Carolina, in 1852. He left under something of a cloud, taking Sarah Shull, to whom he was not married, westward, settling at Rock Spring, Nebraska, where he bought and operated a stage station. In March 1861, James Butler (Wild Bill) Hickok settled there; differences arose between McCanles and Hickok, some of them purportedly over Shull, but there were contributing factors. McCanles was slain, probably by Hickok, in the celebrated shooting at Rock Springs, in which two other men were killed, James Woods, wounded by Bill and despatched by another; and James Gordon, also wounded, probably by Hickok, and finished off by someone else. Bill was cleared by court action.

Joseph G. Rosa, *They Called Him Wild Bill,* 2nd ed. Norman, Univ. of Okla. Press, 1974.

McCarty, Joseph: *see* Joseph Antrim.

McCarty, William H., or Henry: *see* Billy the Kid.

McCleave, William, army officer (c. 1823-Feb. 3, 1904). B. in Ireland he enlisted October 7, 1850, in the 1st Dragoons and rose to first sergeant by 1860. He was commissioned captain of the 1st California Cavalry August 23, 1861, and a major May 1, 1863. In March

1862 McCleave and nine of his men were captured by Confederate Captain Sherod Hunter at the Pima Villages west of Tucson without a shot being fired. After the surrender, McCleave proposed to Hunter he should be released and with his nine men fight Hunter's whole company, an offer Hunter declined. McCleave was paroled four months later after reaching the Rio Grande; he had served a decade under James Carleton who regarded him highly and a major effort was made to effect his release earlier, but to no avail. Upon receiving his back pay, McCleave returned the $582.50 accrued while he was a prisoner, saying he hadn't earned it and in view of "times like these when the government is engaged in such a desperate struggle I can but render my humble assistance in the noble work." January 30, 1863, McCleave and 20 men at Pinos Altos, New Mexico, attacked Mimbres Apaches supposedly under Mangas Coloradas, killing 11 and wounding the chief's wife. Indians swept off the horse herd of Fort West, New Mexico, March 22, 1863, and McCleave took up the pursuit with a command of more than 80 men. The trail was followed westerly for 70 miles to the Gila, then to the Rio Negro and on the 27th a rancheria was attacked with 25 Indians killed and one soldier mortally wounded. The Indians attacked the command on its return, wounding Lieutenant Albert H. French and suffering three killed. McCleave served under Kit Carson in the first Battle of Adobe Walls, November 25, 1864, against Kiowa and Comanche Indians and was praised by Carson for his work. McCleave, with a brevet to lieutenant colonel was mustered out of the Volunteers service October 19, 1866, already commissioned a second lieutenant in the 8th U.S. Cavalry the preceding July 28; after service in Nevada he became a first lieutenant in Arizona March 6, 1867, and a captain August 10, 1869. In the middle of August 1869 a noted Yavapais war chief, Big Rump, was reported killed by Pimas and Maricopa Indians south of Arizona's Bradshaw Mountains. A month later McCleave and Jack Swilling, a well-known frontiersman were sent to confirm the slaying which was a matter of significance for the army. They found Big Rump's body as reports said it would be, along with numerous papers including blank muster and pay rolls and enough greenbacks to implicate the slain chief in a recent raid on a mail stage. McCleave retired March 20, 1879, and settled at Berkeley, California, where he died. He was married and fathered six children, two of his sons becoming army officers.

Heitman; Orton; Dan L. Thrapp, *The Conquest of Apacheria.* Norman, Univ. of Okla. Press, 1967; Thrapp, *Victorio and the Mimbres Apaches.* Norman, 1974; Constance Wynn Altshuler, *Chains of Command,* Tucson, Ariz. Hist. Soc., 1981.

McCleery, Edward H., wildlife conserver, physician (July 23, 1867-May 23, 1962). B. at Milton, Pennsylvania, McCleery became a physician and eventually practiced at Cheyenne, Wyoming, where he became intensely interested in the buffalo wolf or Great Plains wolf. He returned to Pennsylvania, settling at Kane, in McKean County. He became aware of government intentions to exterminate wolves in the western country and secured permission to obtain 25 live-trapped wolves from Wyoming and the Plains states. These he transported to Kane and bred the animals at his Lobo Wolf Park, a tourist attraction. In 1961, shortly before his death at the age of 94, he sold the park and 32 wolves to Jack and Marjorie Lynch who about 1971 moved the animals to Gardiner, Washington, they shortly numbering more than 100. Around 1980 Lynch moved his wolves from Washington to a small town just north of Yellowstone Park where he had "park officials worried — in that he might try his own reintroduction program," according to one comment. Ronald M. Nowak, taxonomist for the Fish and Wildlife Service wrote a memorandum in 1974 to the Office of Endangered Species, stating in part: "Regardless of taxonomic nomenclature, and the possibility that some inbreeding has occurred, (this) group of wolves... contains the genes, no longer available in the wild, of a kind of wildlife that had a major role in the ecology and history of the western United States. There is no other captive group of wolves that is known to have had its primary genetic origin on the northern Great Plains and Rocky Mountains of the lower 48 states." McCleery died at Bradford, Pennsylvania, and was buried at Kane. He had been married and was divorced.

Dick Randall, "Wolves for Yellowstone." *Defenders Mag.,* Vol. 54, No. 4 (Aug. 1979), 207-208; McCleery death certificate; Randall to author, Nov. 11, 1980.

McClellan, Robert, fur trader (1770-Nov. 22, 1815). B. in Pennsylvania and probably raised in Maryland, he early became a packer and hunter. McClellan served in the army in Ohio against Indians, becoming a lieutenant by 1795 and principally a scout, surviving a number of close encounters by his athletic ability. He undertook a trading venture to New Orleans in 1799, overcame yellow fever and reached St. Louis about 1801, the next year entering the fur trade as "the earliest of the long line of American fur traders to engage in the Missouri River traffic." He soon came into bitter enmity with Manuel Lisa over trading matters. McClellan formed an association with Ramsay Crooks in 1807; the partnership was dissolved in 1809 and in 1810 McClellan joined Wilson Price Hunt of the Astorians, reaching Astoria in January 1812. He resigned March 1, 1812, and after an abortive start eastward and one sharp Indian skirmish, joined Robert Stuart June 29; on October 1, in the vicinity of Pierre's Hole, McClellan decided to go it alone, but soon rejoined the party which negotiated South Pass October 21 and went on to St. Louis where McClellan was imprisoned briefly for debt, opened a store, took part in the Sink Hole Fight May 24, 1815, died after a brief illness and was buried on the farm of his friend, William Clark. McClellan was honest, restless, fearless but afflicted with a "sometimes ungovernable temper."

Harvey L. Carter article, MM, Vol. VIII; Stella M. Drumm, "More about Astorians." *Oreg. Hist. Quar.,* Vol. XXIV, No. 4 (Dec. 1923), 335-36.

McClernand, Edward John, army officer (Dec. 29, 1849-Feb. 9, 1926). B. at Jacksonville, Illinois, the son of Major General of Volunteers John Alexander McClernand, he was graduated from West Point and commissioned a second lieutenant, 2nd Cavalry June 15, 1870. Sent to Montana he served on frontier duty at Fort Ellis and was engaged against hostile Indians at Pryor's Fork, August 14, 1872. He was acting engineer of the Sioux expedition and for the District of Montana from April 1 to September 29, 1876. McClernand was on the Nez Perce expedition commanded by Miles, was engaged in the heavy action at the Bear Paw Mountains and there won a brevet and a Medal of Honor; with but a few men he moved far down the Snake River valley, rounded up more than 600 head of Nez Perce horses and in driving them off beat back vicious attempts of the Indians to recapture them. He was promoted to first lieutenant May 9, 1879, and served at Montana posts until 1884 with exception of a period as instructor in tactics at West Point. He became an aide to Gibbon at Vancouver Barracks in 1885 and became captain March 24, 1890. McClernand served in Arizona and New Mexico from 1890-93 and participated in operations against an Indian village at Orati (Oraibi?), Arizona, in July 1891. In 1894 from Fort Wingate, New Mexico, he commanded an expedition against Navaho horse thieves in June. During the Spanish American War and related operations he served in Cuba, winning a Silver Star for gallantry at Santiago; he later served in the Philippines. He was a military attache with the Japanese armies in the 1904-5 Russo-Japanese War. McClernand became a Brigadier General in 1912 and retired December 29, 1912, but was twice recalled to active duty, the last time during World War I. He died at Washington, D.C.

Cullum; *Deeds of Valor,* II, 250-53; Edward J. McClernand, *With the Indian and the Buffalo in Montana, 1870-78.* Glendale, Calif., Arthur H. Clark Co., 1969.

McClintock, James Harvey, historical writer (Feb. 23, 1864-May 10, 1934). B. at Sacramento, California, he went to Arizona in 1879, taking up various occupations until hired by the adjutant general's office at Fort Whipple late in the Geronimo campaign. That affair concluded he enrolled in the Tempe Normal School for a year, then entered newspaper work; being often paid space rates he learned to pad his stories and that led to development of an interest in historical data and characters. McClintock volunteered in the Spanish American War and as captain commanded Company B of the 1st Volunteer Cavalry, the so-called Rough Riders, was wounded at Las Guasimas June 24, 1898, and thereafter walked with a limp. He returned to Arizona a major. In 1902 he became colonel of the 1st National Guard Infantry serving eight years with occasional calls to active duty. He pursued his historical interests and newspaper work meanwhile. He wrote under commission from the S.J. Clarke Company of Chicago the three volume *Arizona: Prehistoric - Aboriginal - Pioneer - Modern* (1916) which didn't pay him much, but until after World

War II was the best Arizona state history except for Bancroft. In 1919 McClintock became state historian and published *Mormon Settlement in Arizona* (1921). He died at Sawtelle Veterans Hospital, Los Angeles. He had assembled a considerable collection of manuscripts and related materials, but it was deposited in the Phoenix Public Library where much was lost during a flash flood, or otherwise disappeared.

Bert Fireman, "James Harvey McClintock: 1864-1934." *Arizona and the West,* Vol. 4, No. 4 (Winter 1962), 303-308.

McClintock, Walter, ethnologist (Apr. 25, 1870-Mar. 24, 1949). B. at Pittsburgh, Pennsylvania, he was graduated from Yale in 1891 and in 1896 went to Montana on a government forestry expedition, coming into contact with the Blackfeet Indians. He remained with an Indian guide, Siksikaikoan (William Jackson) and lived with the Blackfeet for several years, making detailed studies of their way of life and beliefs. He became a member of the tribe, adopted by Chief Mad Wolf and collected by phonograph recordings their songs, legends and took extensive photograph (still and movie) studies of these Indians. McClintock lectured before scientific and educational institutions in this country, Germany and England from 1907-13, became a fellow in ethnology at the Southwest Museum of Los Angeles and curator of the Yale Library. His writings included *The Old North Trail* (1910); *Old Indian Trails* (1923); *Tragedy of the Blackfoot* (1930); *The Blackfoot Beaver Bundle* (1935); *The Blackfoot Tipi* (1936); *Painted Tipis and Picture-writing of the Blackfoot Indians* (1936); *The Blackfoot Warrior Societies* (1937); *Dances of the Blackfoot Indians* (1937); *Saitsiko, the Blackfoot Doctor* (1941), and *The Blackfoot Medicine-pipe Ceremony* (1948). McClintock was buried at Pittsburgh. McClintock Peak in Glacier National Park was named for him.

NCAB, C-134; *Who Was Who;* Library of Congress Union Catalogue.

McCloskey, William, cowboy (d. c. Mar. 9, 1878). McCloskey's movements in the troubles preceding the Lincoln County War, New Mexico, follow no pattern; he worked for Tunstall for a time, and after Tunstall was murdered McCloskey appears in the group that arrested Baker and Morton, two of those who killed the Englishman; then Morton considered McCloskey a "friend" of his. McCloskey was killed with Baker and Morton while the pair was being taken to Lincoln for presumed jailing; the circumstances of the killing of McCloskey are not clear and are variously reported.

Robert N. Mullin, ed., *Maurice G. Fulton's History of the Lincoln County War.* Tucson, Univ. of Ariz. Press, 1968.

McComas, Hamilton Calhoun, attorney (c. 1830-Mar. 29, 1883). B. in Virginia, McComas practiced law in Illinois until about 1868 when he moved to Fort Scott, Kansas, where he married (wife, b.c. 1849). Here he was counsel for settlers in celebrated Osage and Cherokee land suits, and also became prominent in politics. About 1877 he moved to East St. Louis, Illinois, and two years later to Silver City, New Mexico, where he practiced law and engaged in his mining interests "which were quite extensive." In his law practice he was first in partnership with Andrew Sloan, then with John M. Wright, and was said to have been a judge in a federal court. Judge and Mrs. McComas, accompanied by their 5-year-old son, Charley, left Silver City for Leitendorf Springs, near Lordsburg, New Mexico, March 28, 1883, to visit another son. Their buckboard at Thompson's Canyon at noon next day was intercepted by Chatto and his Chiricahua Apache raiders, the adults shot down and the boy abducted. His fate was never certainly ascertained. McComas was chairman of the board of commissioners of Grant County at the time of his demise. Mrs. McComas was a sister of Eugene F. Ware, writer and later a U.S. Pension Commissioner.

Oscar Williams; *Indian Raids as Reported in the Silver City Enterprise... 1882-1886,* Silver City, N.M., 1968. 2-4.

McConnell, George W., soldier (1848-post 1870). B. in Adams County, Indiana, he was of the military escort accompanying the 1870 Washburn Yellowstone expedition, serving as Doane's orderly. He did not reenlist.

Aubrey L. Haines, *Yellowstone National Park: Its Exploration and Establishment.* Wash., Nat. Park Service, 1974.

McConville, Edward, military officer (June

25, 1846-Feb. 5, 1899). B. on a northern New York farm he enlisted at 15 in an infantry organization, was slightly wounded at Antietam and Bull Run, re-enlisted after the Civil War and fought Apaches in Arizona; he was mustered out at Fort Lapwai, Idaho, in 1871. In 1877 when the Nez Perce war commenced McConville raised Company I, 1st Idaho Volunteers June 16 from the Lewiston region and led it for two months in close cooperation with O.O. Howard's regular army forces, eventually being elected colonel of the regiment. His field operations ended when Howard followed the hostiles from Idaho into Montana; there was occasional skirmishing, but McConville appears not to have taken part in any of the pitched battles of the Idaho campaign. In 1878 he again operated with volunteers in the Bannock War in Idaho. Colonel and Mrs. McConville headed the Kamiah Nez Perce school after the war, becoming friendly with the Indians he had grown to admire; later they worked at Lapwai, Idaho, and Forest Grove, Oregon, and by 1890 were back at Lapwai where McConville became superintendent of the school system. When the Spanish American War broke out McConville as major took the 1st Idaho Volunteers to San Francisco and the Philippines. He was killed at the Battle of Santa Ana.

Eleanor Morrill Allen, "Edward McConville." *Idaho Yesterdays,* vol. 13, No. 1 (Spring 1969), 11-15; McConville's Nez Perce War journal is reprinted in "Idaho Volunteers and the Nez Perce." *True West,* Vol. 28, No. 7 (Aug. 1981), 52-54.

McCoy, Isaac, Indian manager, missionary (June 13, 1784-June 21, 1846). B. near Uniontown, Pennsylvania, he was raised in Kentucky, moved to Indiana in 1804 and was ordained a minister of the Maria Creek Baptist Church. In 1817 he was appointed a missionary to the Miami and Kickapoo Indians along the Wabash River and later to the Potawatomi and Ottawa in Michigan. He became convinced that the Indians must be removed from white contact and early became a champion of and instrumental in resettling the tribes west of the Mississippi, seeking to establish an Indian state. His plans were approved by John C. Calhoun, secretary of war, and in 1828 he was named to a commission to conduct a survey and aid the Indians in settling in a new territory; he spent a decade in the later states of Kansas,

Nebraska and Oklahoma, choosing and charting locations for transplanted tribes. His plans for an Indian state were never fulfilled, but he was responsible for selecting many reservations that endured. In 1842 he became secretary and general agent of the American Indian Mission Association at Louisville, Kentucky, serving in this capacity until his death. He wrote a number of pamphlets and lesser pieces, as well as *Remarks on the Practicability of Indian Reform* (1827), and *A History of Baptist Indian Missions* (1840). His diary and correspondence, totaling 38 volumes, is held by the Kansas Historical Society; his books have lasting value. McCoy's was a positive influence on Indian affairs.

DAB; EA.

McCoy, Joseph Geating, cattleman (Dec. 21, 1837-Oct. 19, 1915). B. in Sangamon County, Illinois, he became a farmer-cattleman in Illinois. In 1867 he purchased for $2,400 the township of Abilene, Kansas, on the newly built Kansas Pacific Railway. He was aware of vast herds of Texas cattle stagnating for lack of a market, and knew of the beef hunger of the eastern states. He laid out stockyards at Abilene, built facilities for pasture and hospitality, and laid out a trail to Corpus Christi, Texas. By advertising and persuasion he encouraged Texas cowmen to attempt this new endeavor; the first herds went north in the summer of 1867 and 35,000 head in all reached Abilene that year, to be followed by millions in succeeding years, reaching Abilene and later market communities. The railroad which first offered him economic encouragement, severed business relations with him and although he recovered something by legal means, this break cost him heavily. McCoy was largely responsible for the definitive report on Texas livestock movements in the 11th U.S. Census. He later helped create the cattle trails to Wichita, assisted in opening the Chisholm Trail and other cattle routes, entered politics unsuccessfully, and for the remainder of his life was a noted resident of the south central Plains country. He wrote *Historic Sketches of the Cattle Trade of the West and Southwest* (1874), the basic work for historical research upon the trail driving industry; it was reprinted in 1951. Married, he left a son and two daughters. He died at Kansas City, Missouri.

Literature abundant; EA; DAB.

McCoy (McKoy), Simon, adventurer (fl. 1800-1821). A native of either Opelousas, Louisiana, or Natchez, Mississippi, he was a carpenter by profession and joined Philip Nolan's 1800-1801 wild horse expedition into Spanish Texas. He was captured along with the others after Nolan was killed in the Trinity River area, and taken to Chihuahua City. All foreigners in Mexico were freed by Royal decree in 1820, and in September, McCoy, with others, headed homeward, reaching Fort Smith on the Arkansas River in January or February 1821. Little more is known of him.

Bennett Lay, *The Lives of Ellis P. Bean.* Austin, Univ. of Tex. Press, 1960; MM, Vol. III, p. 29.

McCoy, Timothy J. (Colonel Tim), showman (Apr. 10, 1891-Jan. 29, 1978). B. at Saginaw, Michigan, he went to Lander, Wyoming, as a youngster, worked as a cowboy, filed a homestead claim on Owl Creek, and learned a smattering of sign language from Arapahoes and Shoshones. With World War I he entered officers' training and was commissioned a captain in the cavalry, rising to lieutenant colonel. After the war he served as adjutant general of Wyoming with rank of Brigadier General. He resigned in 1922 to become technical director for the film, *The Covered Wagon,* the greatest of frontier-oriented motion pictures. He was directed to take Indians out to exploit the film and did it so well that Metro-Goldwyn-Mayer hired him in 1925 to do a series of westerns. He was a top star for a decade, then joined Ringling Brothers Wild West show. Colonel Tim McCoy's Real Wild West and Rough Riders of the World emerged in 1938, opening at Chicago April 14. It lasted less than a month; "it was a bad year for outdoor shows," one writer commented wryly. McCoy served in the Air Force in World War II, attaining the rank of colonel and earning a bronze star and other commendations. After the war he made some motion pictures, did considerable television work, joined a circus briefly, and continued in show business with his western specialties with rope, bullwhip and firearms until well into his eighties. He lived in retirement near Nogales, Arizona, and died at the Fort Huachuca, Arizona, military hospital where he was being treated for a heart ailment. He was survived by two sons.

Don Russell, *The Wild West: A History of the Wild West Shows.* Fort Worth, Amon Carter Mus., 1970; George E. Virgines, "Colonel Tim McCoy — Westerner All-Star." *Westerners Brand Book,* Chicago, Vol. XXIX, No. 11 (Jan. 1973), 81-83; *Arizona Daily Star,* Jan. 30, 1978.

McCreery, George, surgeon (July 22, 1854-Aug. 23, 1898). B. in New York he was graduated from Bellevue Medical College in 1877 and became an army assistant surgeon February 17, 1880, being ordered to the Department of Arizona the following month. He became post surgeon at Fort Apache where he remained until August 1882. He was with Colonel Eugene Asa Carr in the affair at the Cibecue August 30, 1881, and two days later was present in the fight at Fort Apache with hostile Apaches. Later he served as a witness for the prosecution at the trial of allegedly mutinous scouts involved in the Cibecue affair (three of the scouts were hanged). At the trial however, McCreery also testified for Dead Shot, one of those convicted and executed. McCreery reported he had "frequent and extended field service" during his period in Arizona. He was stationed at Fort Whipple, Arizona, from late 1882 until May 1883 when he was assigned to a field station near San Bernardino, in southeastern Arizona during Crook's Sierra Madre expedition. McCreery was stationed at Fort Meade, South Dakota, from 1884 until 1888, then was assigned to Fort Warren, Massachusetts. He became a major in 1898 and served at Santiago de Cuba where he was stricken with yellow fever. Enroute from Santiago to Camp Wikoff, New York, aboard the transport *Catania,* he contracted dysentery, died and was buried at sea.

Heitman; Powell; Sidney B. Brinckerhoff, "Aftermath of Cibecue: Court Martial of the Apache Scouts, 1881." *Smoke Signal* 36, Tucson Corral of Westerners, 1978; information from Peter D. Olch, History of Medicine Division, National Library of Medicine.

McCue, John, soldier (c. 1848-July 25, 1871). B. at Albany, New York, he enlisted September 20, 1870 at New York City in Company F, 12th Infantry, being stationed at Beale's Springs, Arizona. He deserted July 21, going to Union Pass, not far to the west, where he was joined several days later by other deserters. The band was come upon by Captain Thomas Byrne of Company F and Hualapais Indian trailers; five of the deserters surrendered, but McCue would not and was shot to death by Byrne, his body left for the vultures (although later buried by citizens); there was no investigation.

Dennis G. Casebier, *Camp Beale's Springs and the Hualpais Indians.* Norco, Calif., Tales of Mojave Road Pub. Co., 1980.

McCulloch, Ben(jamin), frontiersman (Nov. 11, 1811-Mar. 7, 1862). B. in Rutherford County, Tennessee, he became friendly with David Crockett and intended to accompany him to Texas, but missed the Crockett party and reached Texas only in time to take part in the battle of San Jacinto, as an artillerist. While working as a surveyor, McCulloch also participated in several Indian scouts and fights, including the noted Plum Creek action (near present Lockhart) August 11, 1840, another on the Llano River in 1841, and scouted for Jack Hays in 1842; sometimes he headed a detachment of the Texas Rangers, or militia-type frontier fighters. He served from Gonzales County in the Texas Legislature, and raised a company of Texas Rangers to serve as scouts for Zachary Taylor in the Mexican War. He went to California in 1849, was sheriff of Sacramento County for a term, then returned to Texas where he became U.S. marshal. In 1857 he was a U.S. commissioner sent to Utah to try to solve the Mormon difficulty. He was active in the Confederate cause from the outset of the Civil War, being commissioned a Brigadier General; he fought in the battle of Wilson Creek, August 10, 1861, and was killed in the battle of Pea Ridge, Arkansas. He was buried at Austin. McCulloch was generally considered one of the handful of strong men who set the tone and were the greatest of Texas Rangers, as he was among 'he first of them.

CE; HT; Walter Prescott Webb, *The Texas Rangers.* N.Y., Houghton Mifflin Co., 1935; *Frontier Times,* Vol. 5, No. 9 (June 1928), 353-54.

McCurdy, Elmer J. (Frank Curtis, Frank Davidson), desperado (d. Oct. 7, 1911). McCurdy, who according to a United Press International writer "came to one bad end after another," first appears as a leader of Oklahoma outlaws who robbed an Iron Mountain-Missouri Pacific train near Coffeyville, Kansas, in March 1911, may have taken part in bank holdups and other depredations, and on October 4, 1911, held up a Missouri, Kansas and Texas passenger train No. 29, south of Okesa, Osage County, Oklahoma.

McCurdy was trapped in a barn on the Charley Reward place near Pawhuska, Oklahoma, and in a shootout was killed. His remains were embalmed and sold by "someone in the... sheriff's office" to a carnival operator and became a sideshow attraction. Louis Sonney, founder of a firm called Entertainment Ventures, loaned the old "carney" $500 and received McCurdy's mummy as security; the loan never was repaid. Sonney himself used the mummy as a freak show attraction but after World War II when the appeal of such gifts tapered off, stored the item in his firm's warehouse at Los Angeles. In 1968, by now coated with wax, it was sold to the owner of the Hollywood wax museum, that organization later selling the cadaver to a Long Beach, California, Fun House amusement park with an assortment of wax dummies, supposing that the mummy also was of wax. Here Elmer was "hanged" for public view until it was decided to use him with several dummies in making a motion picture, when McCurdy's arm fell off, revealing it to be a corpse, rather than a wax mannequin. Research by Jerry Cohen of the *Los Angeles Times* uncovered the mummy's past.

Los Angeles Times, Dec. 11, 1976; *Pawhuska* (Okla.) *Capital,* Oct. 5, 12, 19, 1911; *Pawhuska-Osage Journal,* Oct. 12, 1911; Okla. City *Daily Oklahoman,* Oct. 8, 1911.

McCusker, Philip, scout, interpreter (d. c. Dec. 22, 1884). McCusker may have been b. in Kentucky and was said to have been of "middle age" in 1867. He reached the south Plains and later centered his activities around Fort Sill, becoming one of the best known interpreters, guides and scouts in the region. He early identified with the Comanches, married a Comanche woman and raised a family, "was a very intelligent man, and was the official interpreter for the Comanche tribe." He also was said to be fluent in Kiowa and Kiowa-Apache. McCusker was at Camp Radziminski in the later Oklahoma during the winter of 1858-59 when Van Dorn was there. In 1859 he assisted in moving Penateka Comanches from their reservation in Texas to one near Fort Cobb, Indian Territory, where it was hoped they would be safely removed from white hostility. October 23, 1862, McCusker with Leeper and a few other whites escaped the Fort Cobb massacre when many Tonkawas were killed by a party of Indians from Kansas Agency, including Osages, Shawnees and Delawares. In 1865 McCusker was working for the government with Agent Jesse H. Leavenworth of the Kiowas and Kiowa-Apaches; he may have been responsible for recovery of some white prisoners of the tribes. Occasionally he engaged in the Indian trade. Since Comanche was the *lingua franca* of the seven major tribes at the Medicine Lodge Treaty Council of 1867, McCusker was principal interpreter, and he was trusted by all concerned. In this role the value of his services could "hardly be exaggerated. The Peace Commission agreed, paying him more than they paid any other interpreter — $583.65." For some time thereafter "he seems to have been employed as special scout and interpreter to keep the Commissioner of Indian Affairs informed on matters pertaining to the South Plains frontier. His reports are informative and manifest a thorough understanding of the Indians." He was not present at the Battle of the Washita, November 27, 1868, but secured the Indian views of the action and forwarded them to Washington. He was always popular with the Indians and they sometimes asked that he be considered a member of their tribes. In 1871 he accompanied a delegation of chiefs to Washington, D.C., among them Little Raven of the Arapahoes, the Cheyennes Bird Chief and Little Robe and the Wichita, Buffalo Goad. After he left the Indian service, McCusker raised stock. During the disturbances of 1875 he accompanied expeditions as volunteer interpreter and guide. It was reported on December 29, 1884 that he had drowned in the Red River with Thomas Russell and George Thomas, but the report was corrected later with the assertion that McCusker alone had perished. His death occurred while enroute from Texas to the Wichita Agency, Indian Territory; he had swum a creek but it was bitterly cold and he could reach no ranch, had unsaddled his horse and tied it nearby intending no doubt to light a fire, but the cold intervened and he froze to death sitting against a tree. He left a brother, James H. McCusker of 202 Manjer Street, Brooklyn.

Rupert Norval Richardson, *The Comanche Barrier to South Plains Settlement*. Glendale, Calif., Arthur H. Clark Co., 1933; Douglas C. Jones, *The Treaty of Medicine Lodge*. Norman, Univ. of Okla. Press, 1966; George E. Hyde, *Life of George*

Bent. Norman, 1968; Wilbur Sturtevant Nye, *Carbine & Lance: The Story of Old Fort Sill,* Norman, 1951; Alfred A. Taylor, "Medicine Lodge Peace Council." *Chronicles of Okla.,* Vol. 2, No. 1 (Mar. 1924), 106-107; Stan Hoig, *Peace Chiefs of the Cheyennes.* Norman, 1980; Darlington, Indian Terr., *Cheyenne Transporter,* Dec. 29, 1884, Jan. 29, 1885; information from the Okla. Hist. Soc.

McCutchen, William, pioneer (c. 1816-April 17, 1895). B. at Nashville, Tennessee, he and his wife Amanda, 24, and their daughter Harriet, 1, joined the Donner party for California from Jackson County, Missouri, in the spring of 1846 (see George Donner entry). He and Charles Stanton volunteered to go ahead of the train to California and return with supplies to hasten the Sierra transit of the company as winter loomed. They left about September 18 and made their way to Sutter's Fort where McCutchen became ill and was unable to accompany Stanton on the return. He joined James Frazier Reed in a relief party to cross the Sierra in midwinter, however. This initial attempt failed but McCutchen joined the Second Relief Party, again with Reed, this time reaching Donner Lake and bringing out the Breens and others, performing heroically enroute. His daughter had died February 2, 1847, but his wife had come out with the "Forlorn Hope" party, seven of whom reached safety January 17, 1847. The McCutchens settled at San Jose, California. Amanda died in 1857. William married Ruth Randall, a widow, in 1860 and died at San Jose.

C.F. McGlashan, *History of the Donner Party.* Stanford Univ. Press, 1947; Bancroft, *Pioneer Register.*

McDaniel, John, desperado (d. Aug. 16, 1844). A Missouri borderer, said to be "lately from Texas," McDaniel reported he was recruited in 1842 by "Texas Colonel" Charles A. Warfield to raise a company and plunder Mexican wagon trains in 1843 on the Santa Fe Trail. Sixty men of the 1st Dragoons were sent in their wake to arrest them after McDaniel's people left for the Plains, but could not overtake them. About April 7, 1843, McDaniel intercepted the Mexican merchant, Antonio José Chavez, eastbound with five men, one wagon (another had been abandoned earlier), and five mules, all left of his herd after severe weather decimated it.

Accosting the trader near the Rice-McPher-
son counties line, Kansas, McDaniel seized
and robbed the Mexican, forced him to march
westward with the banditti for two days,
divided among the robbers the spoils
including some $10,000 in gold and specie and
a small quantity of furs. Seven of the banditti,
not wishing to participate in murder, departed
then for Missouri: Dr. Joseph R. De
Prefontaine, Samuel O. Berry, William and
B.F. Harris, Nathaniel Morton, John
McCormick and B.F. Talbert. Their horses
stampeded and they were forced to bury most
of the loot enroute. The other eight were John
and his brother, David McDaniel, Joseph
Brown, William Mason, Gallatin and Christopher Searcy, Schuyler Oldham and Thomas
Towson. They took Chavez south of the Trail
four or five miles, murdered him and threw his
body and equipage into a ravine tributary to
Cow (Jarvis) Creek, Rice County. Five of the
desperadoes, including three of the murder
party, never were caught. The others were
arrested, Mason turned state's evidence, John
McDaniel and Brown were hanged publicly
before a large crowd at St. Louis. Some served
prison terms, clemency was urged in some
cases.

Barry, *Beginning of West;* Josiah Gregg,
Commerce of the Prairies. Norman, Univ. of
Okla. Press, 1954; Twitchell, *Leading Facts,* II.

McDaniels, James (Jimmy), cowboy, desperado (d. Mar. 2, 1881). His place and date of
birth are undetermined. He was a foreman for
John Chisum and went to New Mexico with a
Chisum herd in 1872, took part in a shootout
near Fort Sumner, was jailed and escaped. He
may have taken part later in a battle with a
Mexican posse; he killed a black that fall. In
1874 he and others were raiding Mescalero
Apache horse herds; he is said to have pursued
rustlers into Old Mexico, captured and
returned them, only to have them lynched. On
January 1, 1876, he, Kinney, Evans and Diehl
through the windows shot up a dance hall
near Fort Selden, New Mexico, killing three
men among the crowded 8th Cavalry
troopers. In June 1877, McDaniels engaged in
a bloody Bowie knife fight with Ben
Reinhardt. February 23, 1878, he wounded a
rustler at Mesilla. He participated in the
Lincoln County War's Five Days Battle, New
Mexico, in July 1879. McDaniels himself was
arrested for alleged rustling and again for

larceny in 1880, but died before trial at Las
Cruces, New Mexico, of undetermined
causes.

Philip J. Rasch, "They Fought for the House,"
Portraits in Gunsmoke, ed. by Jeff Burton.
London, English Westerners' Soc., 1971.

McDonald, Angus, trader (1816-1889). B. in
Scotland he entered the Hudson's Bay
Company service in 1838 and reached Fort
Colville, Washington, the following year.
Eventually he became a chief trader for the
HBC. In the 1840s he married a Nez Perce-
Iroquois woman with whom he raised ten
children. McDonald was stationed at Fort
Hall, Idaho, in 1846, described by the visiting
John R. McBride as courteous and extremely
helpful to his party of travelers. In 1847
McDonald was sent to complete Fort
Connah, Montana, remaining there among
the Flatheads until he was placed in charge of
the Colville district in 1852. When the HBC
abandoned Colville in 1872 McDonald
returned to Fort Connah, Montana, where he
established a ranch, acquired considerable
wealth and where he died.

George F. Weisel, *Men and Trade on the
Northwest Frontier.* Missoula, Mont. State Univ.
Press, 1955, 170n.; MM, IX, 178 (Note: Most other
references to "Angus McDonald" in this series are
to another individual).

McDonald, David Newton, army officer (Jan.
16, 1857-Jan. 8, 1902). B. in Tennessee, he was
the son of Colonel H.B. McDonald of the
Tennessee militia in the War of 1812. David
McDonald was a West Point graduate
appointed in 1877 an additional lieutenant of
the 4th Cavalry and a second lieutenant the
following May; he did frontier duty at San
Antonio, Texas, and Forts Sill and Reno,
Indian Territory, until July 1878, was
promoted to first lieutenant in October 1881
and resigned in 1888. In January 1882
commanding Indian scouts McDonald
crossed the Mexican border from New
Mexico toward Lake Guzman, Chihuahua,
then bore westerly and at Asunción was
arrested by Mexican authorities. He was
jailed four days for improper penetration of
Mexican soil; the "hot pursuit" provision for
crossing the Line was unclear and McDonald
may have been innocent of intentional
wrongdoing. In April 1882, he led a small
command of six scouts and two enlisted men

hunting hostiles in the Stein's Peak range on the New Mexico-Arizona border; he was ambushed by Juh's hostiles escorting the Loco people from San Carlos to Old Mexico; four of his scouts were killed and McDonald and the others narrowly escaped. His first-person account of this adventure is in Forsyth's *Thrilling Days in Army Life.* After retirement McDonald kept a hotel at Carthage, Tennessee, and farmed near there. He died at 45 at Nashville, Tennessee, it was reported although the State Archives have no record of his death. Lummis described him as "herculean and intelligent."

Cullum; Heitman; Dan L. Thrapp, *Conquest of Apacheria, General Crook and the Sierra Madre Adventure.* Norman, Univ. of Okla. Press, 1967, 1972; George A. Forsyth, *Thrilling Days in Army Life.* N.Y., Harper & Bros., 1900; his obituary is in the *Annual Reunion of the Association of Graduates* of West Point, 1919.

MacDonald, Finnan, frontiersman (1782-Dec. 3, 1851). B. at Inverness, Scotland, he joined the North West Company about 1804 and worked at several posts, arriving at Pend d'Oreille Lake in 1809 where he took up with an Indian woman whom he formally married 20 years later. He erected Kalispell House and led his Pend d'Oreille Indians in 1810 to challenge the Piegans on the buffalo plains, defeating them and opening the way to the great herds for his adopted people. MacDonald fulfilled important roles in development of the northwestern fur trade at Kalispell, Spokane House and elsewhere, particularly after the amalgamation of the North West and Astor enterprises. He continued his services after the Hudson's Bay Company took over the North West Company. MacDonald extensively explored and trapped the Pacific northwest. On his way to Ontario retirement, in 1826, he had a famous hand-to-horn fight with a buffalo in which he was mauled severely, but survived. He died at his Ontario farm.

Merle Wells article, MM, Vol. V.

MacDonald, Philip, frontiersman, writer (fl. 1779-1786). B. in Edinburgh, Scotland, and a resident of Virginia with his friend Alexander MacLeod he enlisted in the Army for operations against Indians in May 1779. While on a scout they were captured June 17 by Chickamauga Indians, as they later reported, and in a largely

fictitious broadside, *A Surprising Account...,* alleged that they had been held for some time, escaped, made their way across the continent (26 years before Lewis and Clark), were picked up by a Russian frigate and returned after a circumnavigation of the globe. Their pamphlet went through at least seven early editions.

A Surprising Account of the Captivity & Escape of Philip M'Donald & Alexander M'Leod. Fairfield, Wash., Ye Galleon Press, 1973.

McDougall, Duncan, fur trader (d. c. 1817). His date and place of birth are not ascertained, but when McDougall conferred with Astor and others in 1810 at Montreal, he had been employed by the North West Company "for some years." He became a partner in Astor's northwest coast fur trading enterprise. He reached the mouth of the Columbia River aboard the *Tonquin* in 1811 and was a principal founder of Astoria. He befriended the North West Company's great explorer, David Thompson, out of Astor's stores, Thompson returning east possibly with the understanding that the British firm should acquire the Astor interests. This was done in 1813. McDougall's part in the affair, "equivocal enough," is not clear in all aspects, but his connivance seems obvious; McDougall remained in charge at Astoria, renamed Fort George, under the new management. His relationships with Alexander Henry, who succeeded him, were not entirely amicable. When Henry perished in 1814, Donald MacKenzie and George Keith took over, McDougall apparently was discredited, and returned to Fort William on Lake Superior in 1817. He came to a "miserable death" at Bas de la Riviere, the date not established.

Chittenden; Alexander Ross, *Adventures on the Oregon,* ed. by Milo Quaife. Chicago, Lakeside Press, 1923; Carl P. Russell article, MM, Vol. V.

McDougall, George, adventurer (d. 1872). B. in Ohio, he was an overland immigrant from Indiana and at Fort Hall in 1845 was instrumental in forming what became known as the (William F.) Swasey-(William L.) Todd party of about a dozen young horsemen who with pack animals pressed on to California in advance of the following teams. They reached New Helvetia (Sutter's Mill) safely. McDougall lived at Santa Cruz and Gilroy, served "as kind of an unattached volunteer in the California Battalion" in 1846-47 and in 1847-48 was a gambler at San Francisco where he amassed much real estate in city lots; the next year he was a trader at Sacramento. McDougall made several trips east where he had a family, and about 1853 commenced a wandering life, "rarely making his whereabouts known" and spending a great deal of time among the Indians of Arizona and Mexico, the details of this existence not being reported. In 1867 he was found by a naval commander in Patagonia, in far southern South America. He returned to Indiana and in 1869 settled at Washington, D.C., where he died. Bancroft notes that McDougall was "an eccentric but brave and popular man," the details of whose life, if known, would be of great interest.

Bancroft, *Pioneer Register, California,* IV; Thwaites, EWT, XXX, 89n.

McDougall, Thomas Mower, army officer (May 21, 1845-July 3, 1909). B. at Fort Crawford, Prairie du Chien, Wisconsin, the son of brevet Brigadier General Charles McDougall of the Medical Corps, he served as second lieutenant and volunteer aide-de-camp when only 17 in Louisiana. From Kansas he was commissioned second lieutenant of the 48th U.S. Colored Infantry February 18, 1864, being severely wounded at Lakeville, Louisiana. He was mustered out June 1, 1865, and the next day became a captain in the 5th U.S. Volunteer Infantry, was in an Indian skirmish near Ellsworth, Kansas, and was mustered out again August 10. He was commissioned a second lieutenant of the 14th U.S. Infantry May 10, 1866, at Fort Laramie, transferred to the 32nd Infantry September 21 and became a first lieutenant November 5. After brief service at Fort Vancouver and Fort Walla Walla, Washington, McDougall went to Arizona in 1867, engaged in scouting and had fights with Indians in Aravaipa Canyon, Tonto Basin, Point of Mountain and Rock Springs. McDougall joined the 7th Cavalry December 31, 1870, and was engaged with Sioux at the mouth of the Big Horn River, Montana August 11, 1873 when accompanying the David Stanley Yellowstone expedition. He also was on Custer's 1874 Black Hills Expedition, commanding Company E. McDougall became a captain December 15, 1875. He accompanied Custer's 1876 expedition against the Sioux with Company B and

commanded the guard for Mathey's pack train which was detached on a fruitless detour before the engagement at the Little Big Horn. But with the train and Mathey he joined the Reno forces for their hilltop fight June 25-26. On the night of June 26 McDougall with two enlisted men recovered the body of Lieutenant Hodgson who had fallen in the valley fight, and buried it on Reno Hill, the Indians having withdrawn by that time. McDougall was engaged in scouting in Montana during the Nez Perce troubles in 1877, and commanded part of the escort for the surrendered Chief Joseph and his people from Bear Paw Mountain, Montana, to Fort Abraham Lincoln, Dakota. He remained in Montana and Dakota Territory until 1880 and returned to Dakota in 1882, remaining until 1888. He was retired for disability in line of duty August 22, 1890, promoted to major on the retired list May 24, 1904, and died July 3, 1909, at Brandon, Vermont.

Heitman; Powell; BHB; Edgar I. Stewart, *Custer's Luck.* Norman, Univ. of Okla. Press, 1955.

McDowell, Irvin, army officer (Oct. 15, 1818-May 4, 1885). B. at Columbus, Ohio, he was educated in France and went to West Point, was commissioned a brevet second lieutenant of the 1st Artillery July 1, 1838, a second lieutenant a week later and first lieutenant October 7, 1842. McDowell served on the Canadian border, taught at West Point, was aide to Brigadier General John Wool in the Mexican War and served in army headquarters staff positions until the Civil War by which time he was a Brigadier General. His reputation was tarnished, unfairly, by the disasters of First and Second Manassas (Bull Run) and he never afterward held a field command, although a court of inquiry cleared him following the second affair. July 1, 1864, he assumed command of the Department of the Pacific of which the Department of California (California, Nevada, Arizona) was a part. In 1867 McDowell and Colonel John Gregg engaged in a curious official dispute over which Indians to fight in Arizona without, at the same time, enlarging the theatre of operations beyond the capacity of the army to handle. McDowell was succeeded by Ord in 1868, returning then to eastern posts. July 1, 1876, McDowell again headed the Division of the Pacific, the overall command on the west coast comprising the departments of California, the Columbia and Alaska. He was relieved October 15, 1882, by Schofield, McDowell retiring to live on in San Francisco until his death. Utley (366-67 n26) provides an insight on McDowell's ambitions and the methods he sometimes used to bring them to fruition. McDowell was something of an intellectual, enjoyed music and painting, architecture and landscape gardening and was famed in the army for his hospitality, while being considered by some blunt to the point of tactlessness and though honest, insensitive to others.

Cullum; Heitman; Robert M. Utley, *Frontier Regulars: The United States Army and the Indian, 1866-1890.* N.Y., Macmillan Co., 1973; Dan L. Thrapp, *The Conquest of Apacheria.* Norman, Univ. of Okla. Press, 1967; Bancroft, *California,* VII.

McElderry, Henry, surgeon (Aug. 12, 1842-Apr. 17, 1898). B. in Maryland he enlisted in the 10th Maryland Infantry June 19, 1863, and became a hospital steward, being discharged January 29, 1864, to become a medical cadet for a year, then commissioned an assistant surgeon February 28, 1866. He won a brevet to major for services in an action May 7, 1869, under Captain George William Smith near the Double Mountain Fork of the Brazos River, Texas, along with his work January 17, 1873, against Modoc Indians in the Lava Beds of northern California. He accompanied the Jackson command at the Lost River battle of November 29, 1872, which opened the Modoc War of 1872-73 in northeastern California. McElderry performed his duties in the arduous Modoc War satisfactorily and was prominent in assisting the wounded of the Wright-Thomas disaster. He testified at the court-martial of Captain Jack and other Modoc ringleaders. After the execution of four of them, McElderry retrieved their heads, skinned away the soft parts and shipped them to the Surgeon General's office at Washington, D.C., ultimately to be transferred to the Smithsonian Institution, where they remain. McElderry became post surgeon at Fort Klamath, Oregon, in 1874. He was promoted to major in late 1884 and died at 56.

Heitman; Powell; Richard Dillon, *Burnt-Out Fires.* Englewood Cliffs, N.J., Prentice-Hall, 1973.

McFadden, Joseph, frontiersman (c. 1835-c. 1866). B. in Pennsylvania, McFadden had been on the Harney 1855 Sioux expedition, but whether as an enlisted man or officer is not stated. He was married to an Indian woman, perhaps Pawnee, and in 1864 was a clerk in the trader's store on the Pawnee Agency, near the present Fullerton, Nebraska. He was named "captain" with Frank North as "lieutenant" and directed by Major General Samuel R. Curtis August 25, 1864, to raise a company of Pawnees for scouts and irregulars. Eventually the McFadden company went with Brigadier General Robert Mitchell, while North continued with Curtis. McFadden died at Columbus, Nebraska.

Man of the Plains: Recollections of Luther North, 1856-1882, ed. by Donald F. Danker. Lincoln, Univ. of Nebr. Press, 1961.

McFadden, William C. (Pecos), cattleman (Feb. 11, 1885-Mar. 5, 1972). B. at Throckmorton, Texas, he was brought by his father, William T. McFadden, with the family and a herd of cattle to Holbrook, Arizona, in 1887, the father establishing a ranch in Pleasant Valley a few months before the Graham-Tewksbury feud broke out. After a year of dodging too many bullets, McFadden senior re-established his ranch in the Sierra Ancha Mountains where Pecos was raised. He became a friend of Al Sieber and other frontier luminaries, retaining for the rest of his life clear recollections of them. Pecos McFadden eventually owned cattle ranches in central Arizona: Pleasant Valley, near Livingston and elsewhere. He retired in 1943 to Phoenix where he lived until his death. He was married.

Interview with McFadden, Dec. 10, 1958; Roscoe G. Willson, *Pioneer and Well Known Cattlemen of Arizona,* Vol. II. Phoenix, McGrew Commercial Printery for Valley Nat. Bank, 1956; *Tucson Citizen,* Mar. 8, 1972.

McFarland, Amanda R., Alaskan missionary (1832-1912). B. in Brooke County, West Virginia, she married the Reverend David F. McFarland in 1857, assisting her husband in parish work and at a Female Seminary at Mattoon, Illinois, until her husband, in 1867, was assigned to start Presbyterian missions in New Mexico. Amanda crossed the Plains several times by stagecoach between 1867 and 1873, on one occasion her vehicle being pursued by hostile Indians. To benefit McFarland's health, the couple removed to San Diego, California, in 1873, but two years later became missionaries to the Nez Perce in the Northwest. Here McFarland died. Amanda moved to Portland, then again met Sheldon Jackson, Presbyterian mission superintendent whom she had known in New Mexico and who now was interested in Alaska. She accompanied him there, taking charge of a school August 10, 1877, at Fort Wrangell. Jackson left her in charge, the only Christian white woman there, for seven months the only Protestant missionary in Alaska, and for 12 months the only one at Fort Wrangell. During that time she served as clergyman, physician and legal consultant for the Indians, settling their political, religious, physical and moral problems, presided over a native constitutional convention, interfered in cases of witchcraft, and acted as spiritual adviser for a white man whom vigilantes had determined to hang. Amanda McFarland became of immense influence in southern Alaska.

Alfred Nevin, *Encyclopaedia of the Presbyterian Church in the United States of America.* Phila., Presby. Encyclopaedia Pub. Co., 1884.

McFarland, John, Mormon pioneer (fl. 1857-1892). A man of this name was placed by *Mormonism Unveiled* at the scene of the Mountain Meadows massacre of Utah September 11, 1857, either participating in or consenting to the tragedy. The book, published in 1892, said McFarland was "attorney at law, St. George, Utah." A John McFarlane was one of the defense attorneys in Lee's first trial for the murders in July 1875.

Mormonism Unveiled, 380; Bancroft, *Utah.*

McGaa, William W. (Jack Jones), pioneer (1822-Dec. 15, 1867). B. in Great Britain, he became a seaman and reached the Rockies from the Pacific coast. By 1858 he became associated with Indian interpreter John S. Smith in Colorado. In November 1858, McGaa with others founded Auraria and then Denver nearby, becoming one of the notable pioneer settlers. He married a half-Sioux woman and fathered a son. McGaa's death was hastened by alcoholism.

Ann W. Hafen article, MM, Vol. VIII.

McGarry, Edward, army officer (c. 1823-Dec.

31, 1867). B. in New York State he was commissioned a second lieutenant of infantry April 1, 1847, joining the 10th Infantry on the 9th and becoming a first lieutenant September 13 of that year. He received his discharge August 21, 1848 and settled as a merchant in Napa Valley, California. McGarry was commissioned major of the 2nd California Cavalry October 17, 1861, its regimental headquarters at Camp Douglas near Salt Lake City, Utah. In October 1862 McGarry in an operation along the Humboldt River killed three captive Indians and, continuing a search for hostiles who had slain some whites of an emigrant train, he secured more prisoners. When the enemy refused to come in he executed his four prisoners. In various related affairs a number of Indians were slain "trying to escape" custody of the troops. McGarry's sweep was hailed by a newspaper as "very successful... save and except in his inability to find trees on which to hang the murderous savages," but he managed occasional executions in any event. November 30, 1862, McGarry was sent to retrieve a white boy held by Bear Hunter's band of Shoshones north of Salt Lake City. He found the Indian camp deserted but took some prisoners and after a fight with hostiles Bear Hunter and other leading men surrendered. They were held hostage until the boy was returned, when they were released. In January 1863 McGarry accompanied Patrick Edward Conner's Bear River expedition on which the commander "could promise no prisoners — it was not his intention to have any." Bitterly cold weather incapacitated a third of the command. McGarry commanded four companies or 200 cavalry of the 2nd California as the expedition approached the Indian camp near today's Preston, Idaho, on the 27th. A several hours' engagement was costly for both sides: the Indian loss was reported at 224, including Bear Hunter killed, 160 women and children captured, the camp burned and 175 Indian horses taken for a soldier loss of 21 killed or wounded mortally, three officers and 43 men wounded, some seriously, and 75 men incapacitated by frostbite resulting in some cases in amputations. The feat won War Department praise and no doubt contributed to McGarry's promotion to lieutenant colonel October 18, 1864, and colonel November 29 when he took command of the 2nd California Cavalry. He ended the Civil War a brevet

Brigadier General of Volunteers, was mustered out March 31, 1866, and commissioned a lieutenant colonel of the 32nd U.S. Infantry July 28 of that year. McGarry had developed a drinking problem however and it interfered with his duties. He was named to command the new Subdistrict of the Santa Cruz, in southern Arizona, created for him March 12, 1867, and he brought from Nevada his harsh ideas of Indian control. Apache depredations caused him to send out punitive expeditions with the instructions: "The officer in command... is authorized to hang all (Indians) he may capture. No prisoners will be brought back." This generated consternation in higher headquarters and McDowell directed that McGarry be informed that "no killing in cold blood will be authorized. If the Indians are captured they will *not* be put to death. This is due to the character of civilized warriors." Thus no prisoners were executed, or if they were, it was not made a matter of record. In July 1867 McGarry was directed to scout the Chiricahua mountains for Cochise, but the effort was without important result. Shortly McGarry was relieved from his command because of persistent inebriation or illness, and he left Arizona for San Francisco where he cut his throat in a hotel room.

Heitman; Orton; Constance Wynn Altshuler, *Chains of Command.* Tucson, Ariz. Hist. Soc., 1981.

McGillivray, Alexander (Hoboi-hili-miko), Creek Chief (1759-Feb. 17, 1793). B. of a Scot father (Lachlan McGillivray), his mother was Sehoy Marchand, daughter of a French commander of Fort Toulouse and a Creek mother; through the mother she was member of the strong Hutali, or Wind, clan from which it was customary to elect the nation's chief. Thus though only one-quarter Creek, McGillivray would become head chief. From 14 Alexander was given a classical education at Charleston under care of a relative, Farquhar McGillivray and at 17 was placed in a counting house. He left shortly to return to his home at Little Tallassee near Fort Toulouse at the confluence of the Coosa and Tallapoosa rivers. McGillivray at once became a minor chief and shortly head chief through his own brilliance. His authority extended over the Seminole and Chickamauga tribes and one report, no doubt exaggerated, said he could muster 10,000 warriors. McGillivray however was not notable as warrior or war chief although his men depredated for years against American settlers to the north. His health was ever bad; he was perennially troubled with gout, rheumatism, sharp headaches, confinement to bed and a venereal disease which hampered him throughout life. "He was often so weakened that he could not mount a horse, so stiffened by rheumatism that he could not grasp a quill, so racked by pain that he could not enter into conversation or exercise his full powers in the administration of tribal business," yet his intelligence was ever evident as were his education, deportment and courtesy. It was said he possessed "the polished urbanity of the Frenchman, the duplicity of the Spaniard, the cool sagacity of the Scotchman, the subtlety and inveterate hate of the Indian," while James Robertson, who knew him, contemptuously referred to him as "half Spaniard, half Frenchman, half Scotchman, and altogether Creek scoundrel," an assessment common among Americans who detested McGillivray's pro-Loyalist bias and his pro-Creek and hence anti-American opportunist positions. McGillivray was reported in 1783 presiding over a grand national council of his people at Coweta, on the Chattahoochie River. During the Revolution he received the rank and pay of colonel and position of Indian agent from the British but the treaty of 1783 left him "without cause or party," although the ensuing decade "constituted his real career (as) the most remarkable son of Alabama and an Indian statesman unsurpassed." Swanton wrote that "in the last decades of the eighteenth century, the internal organization of the (Creek) Confederacy was almost revolutionized by Alexander McGillivray... who set up a virtual dictatorship and raised the Confederacy to a high position of influence by his skill in playing off one European nation against another." The Creeks found themselves faced with the Spanish in Louisiana and Florida, aggressive American traders pressing upon them from Carolina and Georgia, and Britain rapidly fading as a viable power. Spanish proposals arrived through McGillivray's Florida business partner, William Panton and in 1784 at Pensacola he entered into an agreement with Spain on behalf of Creeks and Seminoles. McGillivray also was constantly confronted with internal problems of the Confederacy, proposals for common action with Indians of the Ohio basin in addition to relationships with the white powers. "Furthermore these factors were dynamic, changing from year to year," according to Caughey. "The attitude that was indicated toward some particular locality or official in 1785 might have to be modified in 1787, reversed in 1789, reverted to in 1790. Inconsistency with regard to the particulars was often the only means of working consistently toward the ultimate goal." McGillivray was not convinced America could endure as a nation, and so turned for permanency to Spain as well as because its ports seemed necessary for his trade and Creek purposes. Yet he did not shun altogether relations with the fledgling America. In 1790 he made a triumphal pilgrimage to New York where he met George Washington, was appointed a Brigadier General of the American army and August 7 signed a treaty providing for increases in Creek-American trade, use of American ports, the education of a limited number of Creek youths, the payment to McGillivray of $100 a month as agent of the United States and to selected chiefs of the Confederacy $100 a year to cement them to the American cause. McGillivray also had been named Spanish agent for the Creeks and Seminoles; it was reported that in 1792 he virtually repudiated the American treaty by a fresh agreement with Spain in return for an annual $3,500 payment for his services and influence (while continuing to receive his American pension). But through it all he was loyal principally to his Creeks and committed to their national integrity. He had become wealthy: he had received $100,000 compensation for Georgia property confiscated from him for his Loyalist position early in the Revolution; the trade of McGillivray and Panton was worth 40,000 pounds sterling a year; he owned two or three plantations, 60 black slaves, 300 head of cattle and many horses. He had at least two wives, one of them the daughter of Joseph Curnell (Cornells) and another, the mother of his son, Alexander and two daughters. McGillivray died at 34 at the home of Panton in Pensacola, and was buried with Masonic honors in the Panton garden. The son, Alexander was sent to Scotland to be educated by his grandfather, Lachlan McGillivray.

John Walton Caughey, *McGillivray of the*

Creeks. Norman, Univ. of Okla. Press, 1959; Hodge, HAI; CE; REAW; NCAB; XVIII, 371.

McGillivray, Lachlan, frontiersman (c. 1719-post Apr. 10, 1809). B. at Dunmaglass, a dozen miles south of Inverness, Scotland, he reached Charleston, South Carolina, by ship around 1735. He soon became interested in trading, rudimentarily at first since he had few resources, and went with a pack train to Chattahoochie where he commenced his new occupation by swapping a penknife for several deerskins which he later sold at Charleston, the beginnings of a large fortune. McGillivray became "one of the boldest and most enterprising traders in the whole country," and his fortunes were not harmed by his marriage to the beauteous Sehoy Marchand, 16, the half-Creek daughter of a French officer commanding Fort Toulouse where he was killed in 1722 by his own mutinous men. The marriage could have taken place no later than 1738 or 1739. Through his wife and her influential relatives McGillivray received favored treatment as a trader among the Creeks. He established his principal trading house at Little Tallasse, four miles above Wetumpka on the east bank of the Coosa River in present Alabama. He became very wealthy, owned two plantations, with stores at Savannah and Augusta, Georgia; he remained a firm Royalist. When the Revolutionary War broke out, he and his wife and some of their relations were at Savannah which was captured by the British December 29, 1778, and besieged unsuccessfully by the Americans in 1779. When the British evacuated the city in July 1782 McGillivray abandoned his plantations, Negroes, wife, son and two daughters and sailed back to Britain which he had left half a century before. He was still living in April 1809 at Inverness, his name appearing on certain land transactions of that date. He died perhaps there or at his birthplace, Dunmaglass, a short distance east of Loch Ness. Lachlan McGillivray was the father of the famous Alexander McGillivray, most noted of Creek chiefs and was related through the marriages of his daughters to many of the leaders of the Creek nation and of the war of 1813-14, including William Weatherford.

Albert James Pickett, *History of Alabama.* Birmingham Book and Mag. Co., 1962; H.S. Halbert, T.H. Ball, *The Creek War of 1813 and*

1814. Univ. of Ala. Press, 1969; John Walton Caughey, *McGillivray of the Creeks.* Norman, Univ. of Okla. Press, 1959; information from the Department of Scottish History, Univ. of Edinburgh, and from the Scots Ancestry Research Soc., Edinburgh.

McGillycuddy, Valentine T., surgeon, topographer, Indian agent (Feb. 14, 1849-June 7, 1939). B. in Michigan, he completed a brief medical course and practiced for a short time before his health dictated a temporary change of occupation. He joined the U.S. Lake Survey under brevet Brigadier-General Cyrus Ballou Comstock; as an accomplished topographer he joined the U.S. Boundary Survey in 1874, fixing the northern border with Canada; he served as topographer-physician with the 1875 Walter P. Jenney expedition to ascertain the extent of gold occurrence in the Black Hills. On July 26, 1875, he became the first white man known to have ascended Harney Peak, highest point in the Black Hills, where his ashes now rest. He also became the first mayor of Rapid City, South Dakota, founded in 1876, and a pioneer president of the South Dakota School of Mines. He was with Crook at the Rosebud action, and accompanied him on his arduous march to the Black Hills thereafter, some of it following maps McGillycuddy had drafted. When he practiced as a physician in the Black Hills, it is said Calamity Jane sometimes served him as nurse. As post surgeon at Camp Robinson, Nebraska, he became a friend of Crazy Horse and gently nursed that Indian after a mortal stabbing by a bayonet-wielding soldier. In 1879 McGillycuddy was named agent for the Oglala Sioux, succeeding James Irwin. He reached Pine Ridge March 10. He quickly came to a confrontation with the influential chief Red Cloud, and the two became bitter enemies, although McGillycuddy, according to Bourke, was an admirable agent, who "managed to do the work of 20 men," and carried the weight "equal to one-third the United States Army." Nevertheless the dispute between agent and chief grew in intensity until, combined with political partisanship and other matters, McGillycuddy was relieved in May 1886. He was an official observor for the South Dakota governor at the 1890 Wounded Knee affair which he might have prevented had Miles given him the opportunity; he did profession-

ally what he could for the wounded survivors. McGillycuddy died at Berkeley, California. Tall, broadshouldered, vigorous, he was hot-tempered, impulsive, opinionated, but brave and of generous impulses. He was a fine writer, of striking turn of phrase and lively humor, qualities that appeared even in his official reports. He needs competent biographical treatment.

Julia B. McGillycuddy, *McGillycuddy, Agent.* Palo Alto, Calif., Stanford Univ. Press, 1941.

McGinty, William M., bronc rider (1870-May 22, 1961). B. in Mercer County, Missouri, he was raised in western Kansas, became a cowboy at 14 and shortly turned to breaking horses although he was but 5 feet, 4 inches in height and weighed only 135 pounds. During his career at various ranches on the south Plains he became acquainted with such outlaws as Bill Doolin, Bitter Creek George Newcomb and Roy Daugherty (Arkansas Tom) during their cowboy phases, and retained their friendship as long as they lived. McGinty took part in one cattle drive in 1889, from the south Plains to Montana, but most of his career was spent breaking horses, sometimes more than 400 a season. He joined the Rough Riders and fought in Cuba, became acquainted with Theodore Roosevelt, toured with Buffalo Bill's Wild West Show for three years and after a spell of ranching for another two years during which he was "the only man to ride a bucking bronc on the stage," at the Vanderbilt Theatre on New York City in 1907. In 1954 he was elected president of the Rough Riders Association for life.

Wayne T. Walker, "Billy McGinty, World's Best Darn Bronc Buster." *Real West Special,* Spring 1882, 26-29, 68.

McGivern, Ed(ward), handgun expert (Oct. 20, 1874-Dec. 12, 1957). B. at Omaha, Nebraska, of immigrant Irish parents, he became a foremost handgun shooter, possibly the best who ever lived. His records are enduring. He worked his way through Creighton University, Omaha, but became fascinated with handguns on a trip to Wyoming; he moved to Montana in 1904. McGivern reportedly studied neurology, anatomy, psychology, physiology and became proficient at ballistics, mechanics and practical electricity in pursuit of his hobby;

professionally he was in the outdoor advertising business. He developed his own timing device with stop watches refined down to 1/20ths of seconds and verified by the U.S. Bureau of Standards. He experimented with semi-automatic pistols but found double-action revolvers to be faster in his hands, the favorite barrel length 4 to 6 inches. With these he was astonishingly accurate over sizable distances, calculating that at 200 yards an experienced hand-gunner would stand a 50/50 chance against a rifleman. His feats were many. At the Lead, South Dakota, Club Range August 20, 1932, he fired twice from 15 feet five shots in 45/100's of a second, which could be covered by a silver half dollar. September 13, 1932, at Lewistown, he fired a five shot group into the outline of a hand in 2/5ths second. That December 8 he fired 20 five-round strings, four of them in 2/5ths second. His favorite weapons were factory-run .38 caliber revolvers, sometimes with special grips and front sights, but no other modifications. He could hit a tin can tossed in the air six times before it struck the ground, drop a match box from waist high, draw with the same hand and perforate it before it struck the ground. He could toss with a single motion five wooden blocks, about 1½ inch square into the air with his right hand, and using the same hand draw and puncture each block before it reach the earth. Most of his expertise was available to guide law enforcement officers. Of his array of 140 experimental, training, exhibition and aerial shooting feats, at least 15 were designed specifically for police work. McGivern was a stumpy, barrel-shaped 5 feet, 5 inches tall, man though never fat or pudgy and always in good physical condition; he had sharp blue eyes. Although he received some help from manufacturers, the financial backer enabling him to shoot up countless cases of cartridges and wear out revolver bores was Walter Groff, wealthy Philadelphian, the principal disciple and devotee of the McGivern system. McGivern defined this in his *Fast and Fancy Revolver Shooting and Police Training,* Chicago, Wilcox Publishing Co., 1938, repr. 1957. He died at Butte, Montana.

"Fast and Fancy," and Russell S. Stewart, "Memories of McGivern, The Master from Montana." *Amer. Rifleman,* Vol. 122, No. 10 (Oct. 1974). 23-27.

McGlashan, C.F., newsman, attorney (1847-Jan. 6, 1931). B. at Janesville, Wisconsin, at 2 he was taken to California by his family. He taught school at Hangtown (Placerville) and worked in the gold fields during the 1860s, in 1871 settling at Truckee. He became an attorney and newsman, in 1874 writing an important series of articles from Utah on the Mountain Meadows massacre which formed the basis for the government's case against John D. Lee. As publisher of the *Santa Barbara Press* he entered state politics, served in the California Assembly, joined the gold rush to Coeur d'Alene, Idaho, in 1885 and followed often eccentric hobbies all his life, which despite interludes elsewhere always centered upon Truckee. In his career McGlashan applied for a score of patents on such things as a railroad telegraph, an improvement on the Roman catapult and a device for controlled breeding of moths and butterflies. He had taken over the *Truckee Republican* when in 1876 he got the notion of writing a history of the ill-fated Donner party, nearly half of whose members had perished while snowbound in the Sierra Nevada. He announced he would run the serialized account in his newspaper before he had even attempted the research, and response was so overwhelming that he found himself trapped by his own concept. Nevertheless he plowed ahead and as he published segments of the story the response grew and he came into ever more detailed information. He found 26 survivors still living in 1879 and obtained information from 24 of them. He received 2,000 letters and communications, including diaries and firsthand recollections. Members of the Graves, Murphy and Reed families could give intelligent cooperation in fixing the sites of episodes important to the story, few having been disturbed until that time. In addition McGlashan made use of all published narratives dealing with the disaster until then. He completed his work within 18 months, a remarkable achievement. He may have omitted much that he learned, but this is conjecture. He is frank about the mistakes and shortcomings of the Donner party. Shortly before he died McGlashan systematically burned all papers and correspondence relating to his book rather than risk damaging a friendship or violating a confidence. The volume appeared in a revised edition in 1880 and ran through 12 printings. It has been a primary and indispensable source for every serious attempt to relate and discuss that tragic episode in frontier history.

C.F. McGlashan, *History of the Donner Party: A Tragedy of the Sierra,* with foreword, notes and bibliography by George H. Hinkle and Bliss McGlashan Hinkle. Stanford Univ. Press, 1947.

McGonogal, Charles, sourdough, mountain climber (1867-post 1937). An oldtime Alaska sourdough, prospector and roamer, he operated dog teams on the trail to Valdez (since, the Richardson Highway), and was a pioneeer mail driver. In 1909 he, Billy Taylor, Pete Anderson and others were recruited by Tom Lloyd to climb Mt. McKinley on a bet. The first attempt, undertaken by McGonogal, Taylor and Anderson, was turned back in early April 1910, four hours below the summit by an approaching storm; in May the trio attempted the climb again on the urging of Lloyd. This time Taylor and Anderson reached the top of the more difficult but slightly lower North Peak and McGonogal attained 18,000 or 19,000 feet but did not reach the summit. His partners planted a flagpole atop the peak. McGonagall Pass and McGonagall Mountain (the name misspelled) were named for him. The pass is at 5,600 feet north of Muldrow Glacier in Mt. McKinley National Park; the mountain is a 6,560-foot peak nearby.

Terris Morre, *Mt. McKinley: The Pioneer Climbs.* College, Univ. of Alaska Press, 1967; *Dictionary of Alaska Place Names.*

MacGowan, Alexander Bartholomew, military officer (Dec. 16, 1830-post Dec. 16, 1894). B. at Edinburgh, Scotland, he was commissioned from civil life a first lieutenant, Company H, 1st California Infantry August 16, 1861, and served with the California Column in Arizona and New Mexico. He became captain of D Company, 6th California Infantry, February 14, 1863, and was transferred to A Company July 11 of that year, being mustered out at San Francisco October 31, 1865, following the Civil War. MacGowan was commissioned a second lieutenant, 12th U.S. Infantry February 23, 1866, and a first lieutenant the same day; he became a captain August 30, 1871. He was reported to have "conferred with Cochise" on the San Pedro River during Arizona service,

but whether it was while the Apache was nominally hostile is not clear. Of an intellectual bent, MacGowan was reported unconfirmedly to have been an attorney and member of a bar, said that he served "several times" as a physician on military operations, was for a time an Indian agent while commanding Fort Yuma around 1872, and served variously as quartermaster, ordnance or signal officer. He was stationed in the East after the Civil War, then returned to California, was in Idaho for the 1877 Nez Perce and 1878 Bannock wars, and was posted again to Arizona. In 1879 he directed construction of an 80-mile wagon road from Fort Thomas to Fort Apache, and at the latter post served heroically when it was attacked by Apaches August 31 and September 1, 1881, winning a brevet to major. Colonel Eugene Carr cited MacGowan for "distinguished gallantry and worthy of special commendation and reward for exposing himself freely in defense of the Post, and for retaking the sawmill from which guard had been driven." As commander at Fort Apache later MacGowan was an important figure in attempts to quell turmoil in eastern Arizona. He was among those affirming that Juh had led the Loco emeute from San Carlos in April 1882. Later MacGowan served in South Dakota. Upon reaching the mandatory retirement age of 64 he left the army; his subsequent activities are unreported, the National Archives stating it holds no pension file for MacGowan.

Heitman; Powell; Orton; Dan L. Thrapp, *General Crook and the Sierra Madre Adventure.* Norman, Univ. of Okla. Press, 1972; William T, Corbusier, *Verde to San Carlos.* Tucson, Dale Stuart King, Pubr., 1968; Hayden File, Ariz. Hist. Soc.

McGrath, Dan(iel) Lincoln, researcher (Nov. 20, 1906-July 13, 1945). B. at Missoula, Montana, McGrath supplied the research for the book, *War Chief Joseph* (1941, 1964), a superior narrative of that Nez Perce leader; he is listed as co-author with Helen Addison Howard, although Howard did the final writing. McGrath's mother spoke Nez Perce fluently, and her parents were frequent hosts to the Nez Perces when they were enroute to or from the buffalo country on their periodic hunts. McGrath was graduated from the University of Idaho, then joined his widowed mother at Hollywood where an injury rendered him temporarily incapable of normal employment; he and Howard decided to research and write of Chief Joseph, the book resulting. He enlisted in the army in World War II, became a staff sergeant, and died at Paris, France, following a heart attack. His older brother, George McGrath, supplied the sketches for *War Chief Joseph.*

Information from Helen Addison Howard; Univ. of Idaho.

MacGregor, Gregor, adventurer (1786-1845). B. in Scotland, MacGregor served in the British army and went to Caracas, Venezuela in 1811 where he became commandant of cavalry and Brigadier General in the Venezuelan army under Miranda and Bolívar during the wars of independence. He then conceived the idea of liberating Florida from Spanish rule and in June 1817 with a company of adventurers from the fringes of American society, captured Amelia Island, northeast Florida, but abandoned the place as unsuitable to his purposes after several months. MacGregor then went to Nassau in the Bahamas where he completed plans to organize the Indians and with British veterans of the War of 1812 establish a settlement at Tampa Bay, then march overland to capture St. Augustine. He sent Ambrister to further his plans, but with Ambrister's capture and execution by Jackson, gave up this scheme. MacGregor apparently had planned to establish a free government and then annex Florida to the United States when he would lead his victorious army to South America to complete winning the independence of those colonies. After failure of his Tampa Bay project MacGregor was active in the Caribbean region and in Central America until he finally withdrew to Caracas and asked for his old commission back, which was granted. He died at Caracas.

T. Frederick Davis, "Pioneer Florida: The Beginning of Tampa. *Fla. Hist. Quar.,* Vol. XXIII, No. 1 (July 1944), 39-40; Davis, "MacGregor's Invasion of Florida, 1817." *Fla. Hist. Quar.,* Vol. VII, No. 1 (July 1928), 3-71.

McGregor, John, adventurer (c. 1802-Mar. 6, 1836). B. in Scotland, he was a second sergeant at the Alamo, San Antonio, Texas, and surely the only one of its defenders versed in playing the bagpipe. Mrs. Almaron

Dickerson, a survivor of the holocaust, recalled that when the fighting would lull, "John McGregor and David Crockett would give a sort of musical concert, or rather a musical competition, to see which one could make the best music, or the most noise — David with his fiddle, and John with his bagpipes." McGregor always won, with the instrument making "strange, dreadful sounds," foreign to a frontiersman's ears.

Amelia Williams, XXXVII, 271.

McGrew, William, military officer (d. Oct. 4, 1813). William and John McGrew, British Royalists, were forced to leave their Atlantic seaboard homes at the time of the Revolutionary War and settled north of St. Stephens near the Tombigbee River of Alabama. They were reputed to be exemplary men and became "good Americans," it was said. William took part in the battle of Burnt Corn, July 27, 1813, which opened the Creek War of 1813-14. As a militia lieutenant colonel at the head of 25 mounted men he left the St. Stephens region of Alabama and reached a small stream called Bashi which joins the Tombigbee River just north of Wood's Bluff where the party was ambushed by Creeks. McGrew was shot off his horse, Edmund Miles also was killed and Jesse Griffin wounded severely, with three men missing. The incident became known as the skirmish of Bashi Creek, in Creek War annals.

H.S. Halbert, T.H. Ball, *The Creek War of 1813 and 1814.* Univ. of Ala. Press, 1969; Albert James Pickett, *History of Alabama.* Birmingham Book and Mag. Co., 1962.

McIntosh, Archie, scout, interpreter (Sept. 14, 1834-May 6, 1902). The son of John McIntosh, a Scotsman and Charlotte Robertson McIntosh, a full-blood Chippewa, Archie was b. at Fort William, Ontario, and was the older brother of Donald McIntosh (see entry). The father was employed by the Hudson's Bay Company, necessitating frequent moves by the family; John McIntosh was killed in an ambush on the Fraser River, British Columbia, but Archie, his mother, three sisters and three brothers escaped to Fort Vancouver, Washington, being received and cared for there by Dr. John McLoughlin. Archie was well educated, including two years of study at Edinburgh, Scotland. Upon his maturity he became a scout, interpreter and associate on many army expeditions beginning in 1855.

That year he was interpreter for Major Granville O. Haller on his Snake River expedition, an endeavor one historian referred to as an "Indian hanging expedition" in retaliation for previous native depredations. At Kamloops, British Columbia, Archie was married to Susan Grant, and by her fathered a daughter. McIntosh served in Captain Nathan Olney's Independent Regiment of Oregon Cavalry in 1864 and two years later came to the attention of Crook who made good use of him in his 1866-67 expedition against the Pit River Indians. He participated in actions at Steen's Mountain, Oregon on June 19, 1867, in which Archie led Indian scouts and was named as commander of the attackers; August 22 at Surprise Valley, California, where he again led his scouts, and in the very hard fight September 26-28 at Infernal Caverns in the Pit River where Crook was in command. Crook thought so highly of McIntosh that when he became commander of the Arizona Department in 1871 he brought Archie with him to serve as scout. For many years McIntosh was active in operations against the Apaches, frequently being mentioned in significant skirmishes, scouts or activities. He was a guide for troops at the famous Salt River Cave battle in late December 1872. At length McIntosh established a ranch at Black Mesquite Springs, Pinto Creek, and married a half-breed Apache, Dominga (no mention of what became of his first wife). He fathered at least one son, Donald, named for his brother, who had fallen with Custer. In December 1879 and January 1880 McIntosh was instrumental in securing the surrender of the dread Apache chief Juh and Geronimo and their 100 followers who were escorted to San Carlos Reservation. In the spring of 1883 McIntosh was a member of Crook's great Sierra Madre expedition, although not as head scout, that position going to Al Sieber with whom McIntosh never was overly friendly. Both however performed valuable service on this dangerous operation. McIntosh thereafter was assigned to San Carlos where Captain Emmet Crawford was in charge; in 1884 Crawford was informed via a letter to Sieber from a civilian that McIntosh was involved in diverting rations from the Indians to his own ranch for resale and his profit. McIntosh admitted the truth of the charge and was dismissed from government service. He was described by an acquaintance as "tall, slender ... a good drinking man and a hell of a talker. He always had an audience." In 1895 McIntosh wrote John G. Bourke who had been no particular friend, seeking Bourke's recommendation of McIntosh "to some officer of the 7th Cavalry," the regiment in which his brother had served and then in Arizona. McIntosh sought a commander for himself and five Indians of his choice in tracking down the Apache Kid, which he insisted he and no one else could bring about. Archie was after only the reward money, "the officer can have the name & honours" for the feat. Nothing came of the suggestion. He died apparently of cancer and was buried at old San Carlos, but the grave site is not known today.

Juana Fraser Lyon, "Archie McIntosh, the Scottish Indian Scout." *Jour. of Ariz. Hist.,* Vol. III, No. 3 (Autumn 1966), 103-22; Dan L. Thrapp, *The Conquest of Apacheria.* Norman, Univ. of Okla. Press, 1967; Thrapp, *General Crook and the Sierra Madre Adventure.* Norman, 1972; *General George Cook: His Autobiography,* ed. by Martin F. Schmitt. Norman, 1960; McIntosh to Bourke, July 31, 1895, Bourke Collection, Box 2, folio 22, Nebr. Hist. Soc.

McIntosh, Donald, army officer (Sept. 4, 1838-June 25, 1876). B. at Jasper House, near Montreal, he was a younger brother of Archie McIntosh, George Crook's noted scout. He resided at several Hudson's Bay Company posts in Canada until his father was slain on the Fraser River. Donald and other members of his family fled to Fort Vancouver, Washington, in 1846. He lived at various posts in Oregon and Washington until 1860, when he removed to Washington, D.C., arriving June 1, 1861. He married Mollie Garrett October 13, 1866 (becoming a brother-in-law of First Lieutenant Francis M. Gibson of the 7th Cavalry). McIntosh entered the Army as a second lieutenant August 17, 1867, was appointed to the 7th Cavalry August 22, named first lieutenant March 22, 1870, and was acting captain of G Troop for some months prior to the Little Big Horn fight. With Major Marcus Reno's command McIntosh directed troops in line along the river, protecting the led horses at the outset of the engagement. He had one horse shot from under him, but was given another by a trooper who remarked that since everyone was going to be killed anyway he, the soldier, might as well die afoot. McIntosh was pulled from this horse and, according to one account, tomahawked, his scalp torn and cut off from the forehead to the neck and his body savagely mutilated, presumably because he had Indian blood, as has been asserted. He wore a buckskin shirt with his name on it, which helped identification. He was buried on the field and his grave "nicely marked." McIntosh was well educated, with a clear, cogent mind and was described by an acquaintance as a "faithful and brave officer." He was reburied at Arlington National Cemetery.

Service and pension file, NARS; W.A. Graham, *Custer the Myth.* Harrisburg, Pa., Stackpole Co., 1953; Juana Fraser Lyon, "Donald McIntosh: First Lieutenant, 7th U.S. Cavalry." *Clann Chatain,* Vol. V, No. 2 (1965), 118-24.

McIntosh, Donald, Apache leader (Jan. 19, 1880-Sept. 17, 1967). The son of Archie McIntosh, Donald was b. at San Carlos, Arizona, although his parents were not married until June 1, 1880. He attended the Carlisle Indian School in Pennsylvania and served as tribal councilman and judge on the San Carlos Apache Reservation of Arizona. He died at Phoenix. Donald McIntosh fathered several children.

Interviews by author, and correspondence.

McIntosh, Lachlan, army officer (Mar. 17, 1725-Feb. 20, 1806). B. in Scotland, he removed to Georgia in 1736. He raised and was appointed colonel of a battalion of troops in 1776, then was promoted to Brigadier General. In a duel he mortally wounded Button Gwinnett, and was transferred to Washington's headquarters whence in 1778 he was sent to command the West, out of Fort Pitt. Nothing came of his plans against Detroit and the northern Indians. Within a year he had been. sharply criticized by subordinates Daniel Brodhead and George Morgan and was withdrawn from the frontier. He was breveted Major General following the Revolution. He was one of four commissioners treating with the Southern Indians in 1785-86. McIntosh died at Savannah.

DAB; BDAC.

MacIntosh, William, Creek leader, traitor (1775-May 1, 1825). B. at Coweta, an Indian village in the present Carroll County,

Georgia, he was son of William MacIntosh, a Scots trader and captain in the British army, and a Creek woman. Intelligent, he was well educated and came to prominence in the Creek nation through ability. In 1802 the United States persuaded Georgia to relinquish claims to Mississippi territories in exchange for Creek lands (which the federal government had no honest right to tamper with) as quickly as it could be peaceably arranged. By a treaty of November 4, 1805, at Washington which MacIntosh signed, millions of Creek acres were transferred illegally to Georgia. Alarmed by the continuing Georgian clamor for Indian land title the Creeks in 1811 on the motion of MacIntosh adopted a law forbidding sale of their remaining land under penalty of death, although this restriction in time lapsed. MacIntosh by the War of 1812 had become chief of the Lower Creeks, was given the rank of major and led Creek allies on the side of the Americans; he and his men had a principal role in the massacre of 200 hostile Creeks at Atasi, November 29, 1813. MacIntosh also was prominent in defeat of the Creeks March 27, 1814, at Horseshoe Bend, Alabama, when nearly 1,000 hostile warriors were killed with no prisoners taken. MacIntosh signed the treaty of Fort Jackson, Alabama, August 9, 1814, when a large part of the lands of the conquered tribe was confiscated and opened to white settlement. He signed the treaty of Creek Agency, Georgia, January 22, 1818, when more lands were transferred. MacIntosh, by now and perhaps far earlier in the pay of the United States signed the treaty of January 8, 1821, at Indian Springs, Georgia, for still another land cession; a dozen other chiefs controlled by him also signed, while 36 chiefs present refused to sign, making clear the irregularity of a cession with a party representing only 10 percent of the Creek nation. The law providing death for those disposing of Creek lands was re-enacted in 1824. Finally, February 12, 1825, MacIntosh and his clique signed away what was left of the Creek lands. Although Secretary of war John C. Calhoun declared he would not recognize a treaty which he considered illegally obtained, the Senate had no such scruples and promptly ratified it. A formal sentence of death was passed on MacIntosh and he was executed by a party of warriors who surrounded his house and shot him and a companion as they tried to escape. MacIntosh was married three times and a widow and son survived him. He was buried near the present Whitesburg, Georgia.

Hodge, HAI; Dockstader.

McIntyre, Lawson, pioneer (d. Sept. 11, 1857). A member of the Fancher emigrant wagon train which left Fort Smith, Arkansas, late in March 1857 for California, McIntyre was killed with the others at Mountain Meadows, Utah, by Mormons and Mormon-led Indians.

William Wise, *Massacre at Mountain Meadows.* N.Y., Thomas Y, Crowell Co., 1976.

McKay, Charles, fur trader (c. 1798-post Sept. 20, 1826). B. in Scotland, he joined the Hudson's Bay Company in 1816 and learned the Blackfoot language, then was assigned to the Columbia district and reached Fort Vancouver in 1824. He joined Ogden's first Snake River expedition in December 1824, skirmished with the Blackfeet, and on May 12, 1825, sighted Great Salt Lake. McKay wintered in 1825-26 at the Flathead post, made his way to York Factory on Hudson Bay and sailed away from the fur trade forever.

John C. Jackson article, MM, Vol. IX.

McKay, Donald, frontiersman (1836-Apr. 19, 1899 or Apr. 18, 1902). B. in eastern Oregon he was son of Thomas McKay and grandson of Alexander McKay, both of whom reached Oregon in 1811 with Astor's Pacific Fur Company (Alexander was killed by Indians at Vancouver). Donald's mother was a Cayuse woman, Thomas's second wife (the first was a Chinook). Donald was a government scout for many years, rendering valuable service. In 1864 he commanded a company of Warm Springs Indians against the Bannocks, Shoshones and other tribes, and he frequently was interpreter between Klamaths, the Warm Springs and the whites. McKay saw his most extensive service in the Modoc campaign, again leading Warm Springs scouts and himself served as a scout, guide and interpreter, being one of the principals in the capture of Captain Jack in 1873. He learned during his career to speak fluent English, French and several Indian languages. Because of the renown which came to him through his Modoc War service he took Warm Springs scouts east in 1874 and gave exhibitions for two years before the company disbanded.

Donald then joined Texas Jack Omohundro's 1876 show and went to Europe. In all he remained in show business for eight years, being an expert rifle shot, roper and rider. On his return he married a Warm Springs woman who died shortly after the birth of a daughter. About 1888 he promoted medicine show productions, a hallowed American tradition by then, specializing in "Donald McKay's Great Indian Worm Eradicator" for $5 a bottle. He died at his home at the Umatilla Agency near Pendleton, after breaking a hip which failed to mend. He was buried in the Catholic Cemetery.

Information from the Oreg. Hist. Soc.; Keith A. Murray, *The Modocs and Their War.* Norman, Univ. of Okla. Press, 1959; Bancroft, *Oregon* II; Richard Dillon, *Burnt-Out Fires.* Englewood Cliffs, N.Y., Prentice-Hall, 1973; Jeff C. Riddle, *The Indian History of the Modoc War.* Medford, Oreg., Pine Cone Pubrs., 1973.

McKay, Thomas, fur trader (c. 1796-1850). His place of birth is not recorded, but he was a quarter Cree; his father, Alexander McKay, resigned from the North West Company to join Astor, bringing Thomas along as a clerk. Thomas reached the Oregon coast aboard the *Tonquin* in 1811, his father perishing in the Indian attack on the ship later off Vancouver Island. Tom survived an Indian attack in January 1814, near The Dalles. When the Astoria company was sold to the North West Company, McKay transferred his allegiance. He became involved in the Red River dispute between North West and Hudson's Bay Company men, taking part in the Massacre of Seven Oaks in 1816, returning to the Columbia River probably with Ogden. McKay trapped western Oregon for several seasons, his services being retained when the HBC absorbed the North West Company in 1821. Initially favored by George Simpson, HBC governor, McKay fell into disfavor for unexplained reasons, and never rose much in the company, but he became a principal lieutenant of Ogden's. He tried farming in 1833 near Champoeg, Oregon, became an independent trader in 1834. He worked occasionally for HBC thereafter, had a role in the aftermath of the Whitman massacre, went to California briefly during the Gold Rush, and returned to die in Oregon.

David Lavender article, MM, Vol. VI.

McKee, Joel, frontiersman (c. 1824-c. 1905). B. in Indiana, he went to Oregon in 1847, returned to Illinois and then joined the California Gold Rush, profiting somewhat in the mines. About 1855 he went to Texas, settling near Palo Pinto where he owned a horse ranch and from time to time skirmished with Indian raiders. During the Civil War he became a Confederate captain, serving in New Mexico where he was captured, taken to Denver, escaped and rejoined the Sibley forces in New Mexico and fought at Glorieta Pass, eventually returning to Texas, by his own report (he does not appear, however, in Martin Hardwick Hall's exhaustive *The Confederate Army of New Mexico,* 1978). McKee moved to Oklahoma in 1900, where he died.

W.N. Bate, "Frontier Legend."   *Old West,* Vol. 8, No. 3 (Spring 1972), 33.

McKee, John, Indian agent (1771-Aug 12, 1832). B. in Augusta (now Rockbridge) County, Virginia, he attended the predecessor academy of Washington and Lee University and was named agent for the Choctaw Indians of Alabama/Mississippi in 1802, remaining such until 1816. McKee was at Nashville, Tennessee, when news arrived of the Fort Mims massacre of August 30, 1813. Andrew Jackson directed McKee to return to his post and recruit as many Choctaw and Chickasaw Indians as he could and march them against the Creek town at the Falls of Tuscaloosa, Alabama. McKee did as requested, but arrived at the Falls to find that the Creeks had evacuated their town and nothing remained but burn it, which he did. With George Strother Gaines, McKee was principally responsible for bringing the important Choctaws into the Creek War on the side of the Americans and preventing their joining the hostiles. McKee was one of the first settlers of Tuscaloosa County, Alabama. He was a member of the commission to settle the boundary between Kentucky and Tennessee, three times was elected to the U.S. Congress and helped negotiate the Treaty of Dancing Rabbit Creek, September 27, 1830, although he did not sign it; by this pact a large area west of the Tombigbee River was obtained from the Choctaws. McKee died at his home near Boligee, Green County, Alabama.

BDAC; H.S. Halbert, T.H. Ball, *The Creek War of 1813 and 1814.*   Univ. of Ala. Press, 1969.

McKelvey, George A., lawman (c. 1852-post 1881). B. in Pennsylvania, he became a constable at Charleston, Arizona, about 1880 and on January 14, 1881, arrested Michael O'Rourke (Johnny-Behind-the-Deuce) for the killing of Henry Schneider; contrary to legend he had no trouble with any mob enroute to Tombstone, Arizona, with his prisoner. When Till Barnes and Club-foot Jack Lambright tried to hold up a Charleston stagecoach, McKelvey engaged them in a gunbattle as a result of which Lambright was killed, Barnes seriously wounded. McKelvey spent July 1881, in the Tombstone hospital for an undisclosed ailment, but at county expense, suggesting it was incurred in line of duty.

1880 U.S. Census; Ed Bartholomew, *Wyatt Earp: The Man & The Myth.*   Toyahvale, Tex., Frontier Book Co., 1964.

McKenney, Thomas Loraine, Indian office official (Mar. 21, 1785-Feb. 20, 1859). One of the originators of the Indian Removal program, he was b. at Hopewell, Maryland, of Quaker parentage, was in business for a time, joined the armed forces in the War of 1812, participated in the battle of Bladensburg and witnessed the burning of Washington. In 1816 he was appointed a superintendent of Indian trade which, at the time, was based upon the so-called factory system already in disfavor as financially unviable. McKenney saw the factory program as a means to bring civilization to the Indians; he also urged a long series of reforms in the practices of private traders dealing with the Indians, but the factory system was abolished in 1822, and McKenney's position with it. A Congressional investigation completely cleared him of corruption, fraud or any intentional wrongdoing in his management of the system which had consistently lost money while private fur trading organizations, using less scrupulous methods, as consistently made huge profits. In 1824 McKenney was placed in charge of the Office of Indian Affairs under the Secretary of War. He served until 1830. McKenney made the new office into a cohesive, effective instrument to serve its purpose, and was "a major architect of two government progams that had tremendous impact on the native Americans at this period: reform and removal." Largely at his prompting, Congress passed the Indian Civilization Act, providing

$10,000 annually for Indian education, principally by church or missionary agencies, and in 1830 the Indian Removal Act, providing for resettlement of eastern tribes west of the Mississippi. McKenney journeyed in 1826 and later to the upper Great Lakes country with Michigan Governor Lewis Cass and negotiated treaties with northern tribes, then visited the civilized tribes of the south, seeking to persuade them to accept removal. Accused of irregularities in the matter of contracts for feeding Indians during and after removal, McKenney was ousted from office, bitterly insisting that his reluctance to participate in corruption was the cause of his dismissal, and this appears to be true. He left office "a bitter and impoverished man," devoting his time to politics and writing, publishing between 1836 and 1844 his *History of the Indian Tribes of North America,* a 3-vol. work selling by subscription for $120. His 2-volume *Memoirs* appeared in 1846, the first volume being reissued in 1973 with a valuable introduction and assessment by Herman J. Viola. McKenney died in Brooklyn obscurity, his monument the sturdy Office of Indian Affairs, a tightly knit, durable government organization, in the course of the management of which McKenney had proved a pioneer of American ethnology in addition to his other contributions.

DAB; *Thomas L. McKenney: Memoirs, Official and Personal,* intr. by Herman J. Viola. Lincoln, Univ. of Nebr. Press, 1973.

MacKenzie, Donald, fur trader (June 15, 1783-Jan. 20, 1851). B. in Scotland, at 17 he entered service in the North West Company in Canada but March 10, 1810, he enrolled in Astor's Pacific coast enterprise and left St. Louis with Wilson Price Hunt October 21, wintering near the present St. Joseph and proceeding up the river in the spring. Hunt had been named to overall command of the enterprise, a fact MacKenzie resented. After a difficult journey MacKenzie reached Astoria January 18, 1812. He participated in the deliberations through which Astoria was sold to the North West Company, presumably fearing it would be taken over by the British in any event and by this means its owner would receive some compensation. Initially Astor had no suspicion of MacKenzie, who reached New York overland with a report of the transaction in November 1814, but later

believed that the Scotsman had intrigued against him. MacKenzie re-entered the North West Company and was assigned to the northwest again. He constructed Fort Boise in 1819, and was instrumental in opening up the rich Snake River country to the fur trade; he explored widely. In 1823 he became chief factor of the important Red River district of the Hudson's Bay Company which had acquired the North West Company. In 1825 MacKenzie was made governor of the Red River colony, retiring in 1833. It is reported that he first interested William H. Seward in the Russian territory of Alaska, Seward later negotiating its purchase. MacKenzie died at Mayville, New York. He "was eminently fitted, both physically and mentally, for life in the wilderness. His knowledge of the Indians was remarkably keen and accurate." He weighed more than 300 pounds, but was so energetic he once earned the nickname of "Perpetual Motion." He married in 1825 and fathered 13 children.

DAB; Edgar I. Stewart article, MM, Vol. V.

McKenzie, Kenneth, fur trader (Apr. 15, 1797, Apr. 26, 1861). B. at Bradlack, Scotland, he arrived in America in 1816, becoming a clerk for the North West Company, but quit and removed to St. Louis in 1822. McKenzie joined the Columbia Fur Company, eventually becoming president. With establishment of Fort Union near the junction of the Missouri and Yellowstone rivers, McKenzie guided operations of his organization, which had been merged into the American Fur Company, to blanket the upper country, opening trade even with the hitherto implacable Blackfeet. By 1833 control of the entire Missouri River by the American Fur Company was assured and McKenzie widely considered the "King of the Missouri" and the "Emperor of the West." Competition however caused him to begin distilling whiskey for the trade and this with other events brought troubles that led McKenzie to retire in 1834. He eventually became a St. Louis businessman, operating a wholesale liquor business. He accumulated considerable wealth.

Ray H. Mattison article, MM, Vol. II.

McKenzie, Owen, frontiersman (1826-summer 1863). B. near Fort Pierre, Dakota, he was the son of Kenneth McKenzie and an Indian mother. About 1838 he and other children of Kenneth were sent to the Red River settlement of Canada for schooling, Owen alone returning to the upper Missouri River. Audubon, in 1843 at Fort Union, found Owen McKenzie a post hunter, commenting often on his skill and horsemanship. Palliser said of him in 1847 that McKenzie was "a splendid rider, first rate shot, and... on foot and horseback the best hunter I ever saw." Owen then was in charge of a fur trade post on the White River. McKenzie's record of loading and shooting 14 times in one mile of a buffalo chase was well known. In the winter of 1862-63 he was in charge of a small post for Harkness and La Barge on the Missouri above Union; in the summer of 1863 he was sent to take charge of Fort Galpin at the mouth of the Milk River for the firm. (Egbert) Malcolm Clarke (1817-1869) and his son, Horace, engaged in a brawl with McKenzie over money matters. Clarke shot and killed McKenzie, then fled to escape the wrath of McKenzie's many friends. Clarke later was killed by Piegans, his death precipitating the Baker operation and Marias River massacre.

Montana, Contributions, Vol. X, 1940, 293; Robert J. Ege, Strike Them Hard! Bellevue, Nebr., Old Army Press, 1970.

McKenzie, Peter, frontiersman (fl. 1837). McKenzie was one of 18 whites who treacherously attacked the Mimbres Apache leader, Juan José Compá, on April 22, 1837, in the Animas Mountains of present New Mexico, slaying 20 and igniting extended Apache-white hostilities.

Rex W. Strickland, "The Birth and Death of a Legend: The Johnson 'Massacre' of 1837." Ariz. and the West, Vol. 18, No. 3 (Autumn 1976), 257-86.

McKimie, Robert (Little Reddy), desperado (c. 1855-post 1879). The illegitimate son of Rose McKimie and Charles Richards, he was b. at Rainsboro, Ohio, and enlisted in the Army at 14, but deserted or was dismissed in Kansas, made his way to Utah. He joined a group depredating on stage lines "murdering and robbing whenever opportunity offered." He reportedly killed a man in southern Utah, was sentenced to 15 years in a Utah penitentiary, but escaped with Jack Williamson after serving a year and reached the Black Hills of South Dakota, continuing in outlawry. He reportedly participated in a

stage holdup in February 1877, and on March 25, 1877, he was with the Sam Bass-Joel Collins band that held up a stage near Deadwood, McKimie with a shotgun killing the popular driver, Johnny Slaughter, for his error being run out of the band by its leaders. McKimie admitted firing the fatal shot, saying it was an accident. He continued in outlawry until it seemed advisable to leave South Dakota when he went to St. Louis, then briefly to Texas, thence to Philadelphia and returned to Ohio where he purchased a business. He was arrested by Seth Bullock, a Black Hills lawman who had been informed of McKimie's whereabouts by M.F. Leech who had uncovered the Bass-Collins gang after their robbery of the Union Pacific train in Nebraska. McKimie, with plenty of money for lawyers, fought extradition; on February 11, 1878, he escaped jail, became involved in further robberies in Kentucky and Ohio, was recaptured and returned to Hillsboro, Ohio, for trial. His ultimate fate in unknown. Ohio prison records and historical archives do not reveal any trace of him; perhaps county newspapers would provide information, but they have not been microfilmed. He may have been returned to the Black Hills or even to Utah to face charges.

J.W. Bridwell, Life and Adventures of Robert McKimie... Hillsboro, O., Gazette Office, 1878, repr. in Ed Bartholomew, Some Western Gun Fighters. Toyahvale, Tex., Frontier Book Co., 1954; Agnes Wright Spring, The Cheyenne and Black Hills Stage and Express Routes. Lincoln, Univ. of Nebr. Press, 1965.

McKinn, Santiago (James), captive (c. 1874-c. 1950). B. as James, the second son of William McKinn, an Irish-born dairyman and his wife, Luceria, Santiago (as he came to be called) and his older brother, Martin on September 11, 1885, were herding cattle on Gallina Creek, a tributary of the Mimbres River near the present Sherman, north of Deming, New Mexico. Apaches burst upon them. Martin, aged 15 was killed and Santiago, 11 was captured "after putting up quite a battle with sticks and rocks." The Indians took him to Mexico where he spent the following several months in the camp of Chihuahua, and became attached to that chief. When most of the hostile Apaches surrendered to Crook in March/April 1886, Santiago McKinn was brought in and turned over, although he was very reluctant to part with his new friends, the Apaches with whom he seems to have had a generally good time. He was sent back April 6 to his parents, reaching Deming "clad only in a 'gee-string,'" but was outfitted with new clothes by a sympathetic mercantile firm. McKinn married a woman named Victoria and fathered four children. He was working for blacksmith W.A. Tenney of Silver City, New Mexico, in 1908 when he wore a beard and spoke good English; eventually he moved to Phoenix, Arizona, where according to Aranda he died in the 1950s, although there was no death certificate filed for him during that period.

Daniel Aranda, "Santiago McKinn — Indian Captive." *Real West,* Vol. 24, No. 177 (June 1981), 41-43; G.B. Hudson, "Chief Geronimo's Captive." *Frontier Times,* Vol. 5, No. 9 (June 1928), 354-55; Dan L. Thrapp, ed., *Dateline Fort Bowie: Charles Fletcher Lummis Reports on an Apache War.* Norman, Univ. of Okla. Press, 1979.

McKinney, Charles, pioneer (c. 1836-May 28, 1871). B. in Ireland, in 1870 he was farming on the San Pedro River near Camp Grant, Arizona. The Aravaipa Apache, Eskiminzin who was his friend was invited to eat supper with him although then considered hostile. After the meal and a smoke the Apache killed McKinney, explaining later that "any coward can kill his enemy, but it takes a brave man to kill his friend." Eskiminzin was the only surviving witness and the full facts of the incident will never be known.

Don Schellie, *Vast Domain of Blood: The Story of the Camp Grant Massacre.* Los Angeles, Westernlore Press, 1968; U.S. Census of Ariz., 1870.

McKinney, John Augustine, military officer (c. 1846-Nov. 25, 1876). B. at Memphis, Tennessee, he went to West Point and was commissioned June 12, 1871, a second lieutenant of the 4th Cavalry, joining his regiment at Fort Richardson, near Jacksboro, Texas. Carter wrote that he was "a fine looking officer with dark chestnut hair and brown eyes, about six feet in height, slim and straight (and) gave promise of being a valuable addition to the regiment." Ranald Mackenzie also was taken with the man, although McKinney occasionally found himself deeply in debt and with an affinity for

the bottle, faults Mackenzie quietly corrected. McKinney earned high praise from the colonel for his work as adjutant on an extended 1872 scout onto the Staked Plains, and also performed creditably on an 1874 Mackenzie expedition through Blanco Canyon, West Texas. He became a first lieutenant May 17, 1876. In Mackenzie's fight with the Cheyennes on the North Fork of the Powder River, Wyoming, November 25, 1876, McKinney charged into an ambush and was killed instantly, Mackenzie "weeping like a child" at the news. McKinney was the only officer killed in the engagement.

Cullum; Robert G. Carter, *On the Border with Mackenzie.* N.Y., Antiquarian Press, 1961; John G. Bourke, *Mackenzie's Last Fight with the Cheyennes.* Bellevue, Nebr., Old Army Press, 1970; Ernest S. Wallace, ed., *Ranald S. Mackenzie's Official Correspondence Relating to Texas, 1871-73 and 1873-1879.* Lubbock, West Tex. Mus. Assn., 1967, 1968.

McKnight, John, frontiersman (pre 1790-c. 1823). An older brother of Robert McKnight, he was b, in Augusta County, Virginia, became a merchant at Nashville, Tennessee, reached St Louis in 1809 where with his brothers he engaged in commerce. In 1821, learning that Robert, who had been imprisoned at Santa Fe 10 years before, was held or living in Mexico, John journeyed there, found Robert and the two returned to Missouri in 1822. They then engaged with Thomas James in trade with the Comanches, John being killed by that people whom he had visited to invite in for commerce.

Rex W. Strickland article, MM, Vol. IX.

McKnight, Robert, frontiersman (1790-1846). B. in Augusta County, Virginia, he reached Missouri about 1809 and in 1812 entered a partnership with James Baird and others for the Santa Fe trade. Arrested at Taos they were sent to Chihuahua, McKnight later settling in Sonora. He returned to Santa Fe in 1822 with his brother, John, who had gone into Mexico to find him. Robert McKnight left Santa Fe June 1 with the Glenns to return to St. Louis. Robert and John McKnight and Thomas James formed a partnership that autumn to trade with the Comanches; John was killed by Indians, Robert returning to St. Louis late in 1832. He went to New Mexico again in 1824, married a

Mexican woman and shortly engaged in operation of the Santa Rita copper mines near present Silver City, New Mexico, giving the project up in 1834 because of Apache hostility, transferring his mining operations to near Corralitos, Chihuahua, about 1838. McKnight died at Corralitos.

Rex W. Strickland article, MM, Vol. IX.

McLain, E(a)rnest, cattleman, (fl. 1889). With five others McLain was charged with the lynching of Ella Watson and James Averell July 20, 1889, in the Sweetwater country of Wyoming; he was placed at the scene by eyewitnesses who alleged he had been instrumental in accosting the Watson woman and taking her off to her death. One of the witnesses reported a "loud" argument among the lynchers as they were taking their prisoner to the place of execution, and it may be that McLain, as he later claimed, was "an unwilling" participant in the murders. McLain "left the country a few years after the unfortunate affair and has not since been heard from and it is supposed that he is dead," wrote Mokler in 1922.

Alfred James Mokler, *History of Natrona County, Wyoming, 1888-1922.* N.Y., Argonaut Press, 1966 (first published in 1923).

McLanahan, Josiah, adventurer (d. post 1830). He was appointed sheriff of St. Louis in 1805, and may have become interested in the Wilkinson-Burr project. He joined Reuben Smith for a controversial expedition in 1809 to New Mexico, was arrested, held in Chihuahua under harsh conditions, released and returned to Missouri by 1812. On June 18 McLanahan wrote Gov. Benjamin Howard of Missouri, his explanation of the journey and its results, the letter now in the Missouri Historical Society's Dalton collection.

W.A. Goff article on Reuben Smith, MM, Vol. VII.

McLaughlin, James, Indian official (Feb. 12, 1842-July 28, 1923). B. at Avonmere, Ontario, he reached Minnesota in 1863 and the next year married a woman of white and Sioux origin who, familiar with the Indian language, was to be of immense help to him in his work with the Sioux. McLaughlin entered the U.S. Indian service in 1871 as assistant agent at the Devil's Lake Agency near Fort Totten, North Dakota, within five years becoming agent. In 1881 he was transferred to the Standing Rock Agency; meanwhile he had been learning Sioux himself, and could converse readily, if imperfectly, with his charges by voice and sign. McLaughlin was sympathetic with the Indians, but felt he had a mission to civilize them and worked to abolish such customs as the sun dance and other alleged backward notions of the people. Although he was instrumental in persuading the Indians to accept the cession of much land to the whites on several occasions, he also won them some concessions. During the ghost dance unrest of 1890, McLaughlin came to cross-purposes with Miles who favored a strong military control, McLaughlin arguing that the fever would soon pass and that he could control his Indians without the use of force. The dispute centered originally over the usefulness of arresting Sitting Bull and shipping him out of the Sioux country for a period. The question of timing was all-important; McLaughlin aborted one attempt by Cody, at Miles's instigation, to arrest the medicine man, but later ordered his own Indian police under a military directive to undertake it. A clash resulted on December 15, 1890, in which Sitting Bull and a number of others died. This was a contributing factor to the Wounded Knee fight which occurred on the Pine Ridge Agency in South Dakota, not part of McLaughlin's charge. However, as a result of it, Miles, commander of the Division of the Missouri, used his authority to place a military officer in charge at Standing Rock and others at various agencies of the Sioux. McLaughlin lodged massive protests against what he considered a usurpation of his authority and a move calculated to confuse and make inefficient the operation of the agencies. Before Washington could act to nullify Miles's high-handed directive however an army shakeup solved the situation: the Division of the Missouri was abolished, a Department of the Missouri created and Miles lost his control over the departments of Dakota and the Platte — and over the Sioux. The agencies reverted to civilian status. McLaughlin continued to be held in high regard in the Indian office at Washington and in 1895 was offered the post of assistant commissioner of Indian affairs, a position he declined; he became instead inspector under the personal direction of the Secretary of the Interior, and in fulfilling this function became familiar with Indian matters all over the country. He died at Washington, D.C., and was buried at McLaughlin, South Dakota. He wrote *My Friend the Indian* (1910), "a contribution of high rank to the study of the Indian question, to Sioux history, and especially to the Indian side of the battle of the Little Bighorn."

Report of the Secretary of the Interior. 1st Sess., 52nd Cong., Vol. II, Wash., Govt. Printing Office, 1902; Robert M. Utley, *The Last Days of the Sioux Nation.* New Haven, Yale Univ. Press, 1963; DAB.

McLaury, Robert (Frank), cattleman (Mar. 3, 1848-Oct. 26, 1881). B. at Kortwright, New York, and raised at Hazelton, Iowa, he reached Texas as a young man, eventually settling near Fort Worth, but left there by 1877 for southern Arizona. He and his brother, Tom, started a ranch east of Tombstone, Frank being considered the "young, independent" brother (see Tom McLaury entry for added details of their Arizona experience). Tom was unarmed at the OK Corral fight and Billy Clanton, a particular friend of Frank's, was armed and was killed. Frank, though mortally shot, managed to wound Morgan and Virgil Earp and slightly wound Doc Holliday before his death. There is no surviving evidence that either of the McLaurys ever committed any crime; they probably were shot for what they knew, or were supposed to know, about Holliday and stage robberies. Their funeral was largely attended.

See Tom McLaury references.

McLaury, Tom, cattleman (June 30, 1853-Oct. 26, 1881). B. at Kortwright, New York, and raised near Hazelton, Iowa, he reached Fort Worth, Texas in young manhood and by 1877 had left there for southern Arizona. He and his brother, Frank, started a Sulphur Springs Valley ranch, east of Tombstone, and Tom was said to have been the "more sober and industrious" of the two. The ranch, established first at the later Hereford Springs, was removed to Antelope Springs and finally to Mustang Springs, closer to Tombstone. The McLaurys became associated with the so-called "cowboy element," including Brocius, Ringo, the Clantons and others, a loose-knit faction that came to odds with the Earp people of Tombstone; the origin of the feud is obscure, but may have had to do with stage robberies in which Doc Holliday and others perhaps participated, and information about the crimes held by the McLaurys or supposedly held by them. There is no surviving proof that they were rustlers or in any way lawless, although their lives on a rough frontier no doubt brought them from time to time into contact with desperado elements, as it did everyone else. They quitted their ranch in the fall of 1881 for Tombstone because of unrest caused by the Apache Juh's bolt from San Carlos for Old Mexico. The McLaurys sold out and were planning to return to Iowa at the time of the OK Corral fight. On the morning of October 26 Wyatt Earp brutally beat Tom McLaury about the head with a pistol (McLaury was unarmed); later that day Frank McLaury and Billy Clanton reached town from Charleston. Tom was unarmed at the time of the OK Corral shooting, and was murdered by Holliday's shotgun. The funeral was attended by some 2,000, according to report.

Correspondence, Steve McLaury with author, Oct. 7, 1979; Ed Bartholomew, *Wyatt Earp: The Untold Story, Wyatt Earp: The Man & the Myth.* Toyahvale, Tex., Frontier Book Co., 1963, 1964.

McLaury, William Roland, attorney (Dec. 6, 1844-Feb. 16, 1913). B. at Kortwright, east of Oneonta, New York, but raised near Hazelton, Iowa, he was a full brother of Frank and Tom McLaury who were killed in the OK Corral affair at Tombstone, Arizona, October 26, 1881. A McLaury ancestor was Matthew McClaughry who left Scotland for Ireland in 1690 to help King William III put down a rebellion; descendants had reached this continent early enough to have served in the Revolutionary War, one of them a Minuteman. The son of Robert H. McLaury, an attorney, Will served to brevet captain in the 47th Iowa Infantry during the Civil War. He then apprenticed in an uncle's law office in the Dakotas, prospected for gold in Colorado, and arrived by stagecoach in 1876 at Fort Worth, Texas, where he opened a law office. He had married, his wife Leona coming from Ohio; McLaury fathered John G., born in 1874; Birdie, born in 1876; both in Dakota Territory; Maggie born in 1878 in Texas; and other children, some by a second wife. McLaury complained that at Fort Worth "for two years I could get hardly any business, because I was a radical," a problem he resolved and practiced his profession there for 30 years. When word reached Will that his brothers had been killed, he hastened to Tombstone, arriving November 4, 1881, and planning to leave after court adjourned December 20. It is suggested that he made financial and perhaps other contributions toward retaliation against the Earps and their people. In a letter to his father April 13, 1884, he wrote "...My experience out there (at Tombstone, presumably) has been very unfortunate — as to my health and badly injured me as to money matters — and none of the results have been satisfactory — The only result is the death of Morgan and crippling of Virgil Earp and death of (Sherman W.) McMasters — Wyatt Earp was in this town (Fort Worth) about a month ago and stayed about six hours ..." After Morgan's death, McLaury apparently gave up any further attempts at retaliation. He became a judge of the superior court of Texas, "went to the land opening of western Oklahoma," practiced as an attorney in a tent at Lawton, Oklahoma, bought some farms at Snyder, Oklahoma, and retired to them. He died at Snyder and is buried there. A son, Finley, was a lieutenant in the U.S. Air Corps during World War I, and a grandson served in the field artillery as a major in World War II.

Ariz. Hist. Soc. archives; information from Ross McLaury Taylor and Steve McLaury; letter, Ed Bartholomew to author, Sept. 16, 1976.

McLean, Thomas F.M. (Bison, Bise), renegade (c. Dec. 1824-Sept. 29, 1872). B. at Smithland, Randolph County, Missouri, he studied at the University of Missouri for several sessions and his application for an appointment to West Point was endorsed by W.W. Hudson, professor of mathematics who considered McLean "gentlemanly, studious, and intellectual ...," President John Hiram Lathrop of the university who highly recommended him, and others. McLean was admitted to West Point July 1, 1844. He was dismissed August 7, 1848, "after being declared deficient in Conduct in June 1848." McLean protested his dismissal, pointing to his high standing in his class, but was not reinstated. Shortly afterward he reached California "as a sharp and exceedingly dangerous type of desperado." According to Carter he was run out of California by

vigilante activity and reached New Mexico or some neighboring territory where "he joined a band of Comanche Indians and became in time a sort of sub-chief or leader among them." He remained with the Indians some years apparently. Carter quotes Lieutenant Colonel (brevet Major General) John P. Hatch who had been associated with McLean briefly at West Point: "While serving in Texas, shortly after the Civil War, about 1867-68, I happened to be in or near the town of Fredericksburg just after a raid (by) Comanches, ... and upon walking up the street I met a man who seemed to be a stranger in the place and we gave each other a quick and steady glance ... In an instant the coarse shock of red hair, the large features and awkward gait of 'Bise' McLean flashed across my mind. There was no mistake: it was he!" But he could not relocate the man and never saw him again. September 29, 1872, Colonel Ranald S. Mackenzie with five troops of the 4th Cavalry attacked Mo-way's (Mo-wi's) 200 lodge Comanche village on McClellan's Creek, a tributary to the North Fork of the Red River, Texas. Some 23 warriors were killed, 120 prisoners (mostly women and children) captured with few cavalry losses. Among the hostile dead were several Mexicans and half-breeds, no doubt prisoners of the Comanches, and one Anglo. Carter wrote that "That man had a thick shock of red hair and the unmistakable features as described by General Hatch," and no doubt was Bise McLean. At any rate he was never heard of from that date forward. He had won his nickname of Bison, or Bise, because of his shaggy red hair and what Carter described as "uncouth ways," which is not the characterization given him by his university professors and other acquaintances upon his application for a Military Academy appointment.

NARS RG 94, Records of Adjutant General's Office, 1880s, 1917, File No. 201, 1843 pertaining to U.S. Military Academy Application, Papers of Thomas F.M. McLean; information from Kenneth W. Rapp, acting chief, USMA Archives; R.G. Carter, *On the Border with Mackenzie.* N.Y., Antiquarian Press, 1961; Rupert Norval Richardson, *The Comanche Barrier to South Plains Settlement.* Glendale, Calif., Arthur H. Clark Co., 1933.

McLellan, Curwen Boyd, army officer (Apr. 7, 1829-Aug. 24, 1898). B. in Scotland he enlisted in Company B, 3rd Infantry November 17, 1849, and served to first sergeant in that and in Company A, 1st Dragoons by November 17, 1854. He enlisted in Company H, 2nd Calvary and quickly rose to sergeant. McLellan was severely wounded October 1, 1858, in Van Dorn's hard fight at the Wichita Village on Horse Creek in the later Oklahoma. He was commissioned second lieutenant of the 3rd Cavalry May 14, 1861, joined the 6th Cavalry August 3 and emerged from the Civil War a first lieutenant with brevets to major for gallantry in actions with the Army of the Potomac. He became a captain July 28, 1866, and was posted to the southwest. Commanding at Camp Bowie, Arizona, in 1876 he had a role in the removal of the Chiricahua Apaches from their reservation to San Carlos, away from the Mexican border. In 1880, commanding Arizona troops in an offensive against Victorio in southern New Mexico, McLellan rescued Henry Carroll in a stiff fight in the San Andres Mountains, winning another brevet for this action. He also was active in events following the Cibecue affair in Arizona in 1881, although not engaged in the Cibecue operation itself. McLellan became major in the 10th Cavalry December 30, 1881, lieutenant colonel of the 3rd Cavalry May 6, 1892, transferred to the 1st Cavalry May 26 of that year and retired April 7, 1893. He had married but was widowed by 1880.

Heitman; Powell; Harold B. Simpson, *Cry Comanche: The 2nd U.S. Cavalry in Texas.* Hillsboro, Tex., Hill Junior College Press, 1979; Dan L. Thrapp, *General Crook and the Sierra Madre Adventure.* Norman, Univ. of Okla. Press, 1972; Thrapp, *Victorio and the Mimbres Apaches.* Norman, 1974.

McLendon, Benjamin (Nigger Ben, Ben Huggins), prospector (d. 1864). B. in Merriwether County, Georgia, he was said to have admitted being an escaped slave and arrived on the Hassayampa River, with the Weaver party from Yuma in about 1863, the first black miner in Arizona. The group included Pauline Weaver, Abraham H. Peeples, Charles B. Genung and others, 10 in all. The party located several gold sites, the most promising being Rich Hill. In 1864 Ben purportedly made his own strike, but kept its location secret, appearing in the new community of Wickenburg from time to time with dust. He was found murdered, purportedly by Indians, next to his dead burro, four miles from Wickenburg. Apparently he left a son. His "find," whether factual or not, generated one of the enduring lost mine sagas of the southwest.

Carol Ann Muller, "Nigger Ben McLendon and His Lost Gold Mine." *Jour. of Ariz. Hist.,* Vol. XIV, No. 4 (Winter 1973), 379-84.

MacLeod, Alexander, frontiersman (fl. 1779-1786). B. at Williamsburg, Virginia, and with a fair education, he and Philip MacDonald enlisted in May 1779 in an army unit to fight Indians beyond the settlements. They were captured by Chickamaugas June 17 while on a scout, as they later reported. In a largely fictitious broadside, *A Surprising Account of the Captivity & Escape...*, they reported that they had been held for some time, then escaped and crossed the continent (26 years before Lewis and Clark), were picked up by a Russian frigate and returned after a circumnavigation of the globe. Their pamphlet went through at least seven early editions.

A Surprising Account of the Captivity & Escape of Philip M'Donald & Alexander M'Leod. Fairfield, Wash., Ye Galleon Press, 1973.

McLeod, Alexander Roderick, frontiersman (c. 1782-June 11, 1840). McLeod joined the North West Company in 1802, soon becoming a clerk on Peace River in the northwest. In 1821 he became a chief trader when the Hudson's Bay Company absorbed the North West Company, serving in the Athabasca and Mackenzie River countries; in 1825 he was transferred to the Columbia district. He trapped in south Oregon, led brigades in that region on subsequent years, then was transferred, in 1827, to the Fraser River briefly. He soon was back at Fort Vancouver. He led a punitive campaign against Puget Sound Indians, because of his "harshness" being turned down for promotion. McLeod led the party which buried Jedediah Smith's massacred men in southern Oregon, being criticized for "dilatory" leadership of that expedition. McLeod led the first HBC brigade to trap central California in 1829-30. His trip was a failure and McLoughlin sharply criticized him. McLeod was transferred to the Mackenzie River area, where he ended his service.

Doyce B. Nunis Jr., article, MM, Vol. VI.

McLeod, Hugh, military officer (Aug. 1, 1814-Jan. 3, 1862). B. at New York City he went to West Point and was commissioned a brevet second lieutenant of the 3rd Infantry

September 18, 1835, but resigned June 30, 1836, and went to Texas, serving in the Texas army from July to December 21, 1837. He was aide to Thomas J, Rusk in the October 16-18, 1838, battle at Kickapoo Town, Anderson County, Texas. The following year McLeod read law and soon went into the practice of it. He became adjutant general of the Texas army in 1839, and was wounded July 16, 1839, while again serving with Rusk, this time against the Cherokees. March 19, 1840, he took part in the Council House treachery at San Antonio in which Comanches who had come in for a council were trapped and a fight erupted with seven whites and 35 Indians killed, "the greatest blunder in the history of Texas Indian relations." McLeod and William G. Cooke headed the Texas delegation meeting with the Indians. McLeod was breveted Brigadier General in 1841, and commanded the Texan Santa Fe expedition; he was captured by New Mexicans with others of his force, sent as prisoner to Mexico City and released in 1842. McLeod served in various public and military positions until the Civil War when he joined the Confederacy, directed the movement against United States forces on the Rio Grande. He died of pneumonia as colonel of the 1st Texas Infantry.

Thwaites, EWT, XX; HT; Arrell M. Gibson, *The Kickapoos.* Norman, Univ. of Okla. Press, 1963; George M. Kendall, *Narrative of an Expedition... From Texas to Santa Fe.* London, David Bogue, 1845.

McLoughlin, John, Hudson's Bay Company factor (Oct. 19, 1784-Sept. 3, 1857). B. in the parish of Riviere du Loup, Quebec, the son of an Irishman and a mother of Scot-French Canadian origin, he was educated as a physician, serving as such at various North West Fur Company posts. When the company merged with the Hudson's Bay Company in 1821, McLoughlin was in charge of the post of Fort William on Lake Superior. He became chief factor for the Hudson's Bay Company in 1824 and supervisor of the Columbia District, remaining at Fort George (Astoria) and later at Fort Vancouver on the Washington side of the mouth of the great river until 1846. He ever was interested in natural science, making contributions from observational anthropology to botany. The trading area over which he reigned as a kind of baron was immense, he once describing it as "from St. Francisco ... to Latitude 54 North and the Interior as bounded by the Rocky Mountains." His trade touch contacted the Russians in the north, the Spaniards in the south, and the Hawaiians in the Pacific. McLoughlin often was called upon to deal with American trappers, missionaries, adventurers of one sort or another, or the distressed, and he did so competently, charitably, intelligently, and strongly. His domain represented a virtual plantation, northwest style, and from it he shipped out furs valued at up to $150,000 a year, bringing in immense stores for maintenance, barter and to dispense to the needy, which most emigrants were; although the company policy forbade assistance to Americans, McLoughlin freely granted it to all comers, on easy terms, and often was not repaid except in gratitude. He was an extraordinary personality and commanding presence, possibly 6 feet, 6 inches, in height, well-proportioned, dignified, with the gift of command, and he controlled Indians as he controlled whites, by force of personality and fair dealing. His wrath was dreaded, as his largesse was welcomed. He married a half-breed Indian woman, the widow of Alexander McKay, by whom he had four children. McLoughlin retired from the company to become an American citizen at Oregon City at the falls of the Willamette, building a fine home, today a National Historic site. Here he reigned as "the father of Oregon," which he in fact was.

Literature abundant: DAB; MM, Vol. I.

McLoughlin, Joseph, fur trader (c. 1808-c. Dec. 14, 1848). A son of John McLoughlin, his mother is unknown as are the circumstances of his birth and education, although he may have been born at Sault Ste. Marie on the Great Lakes of mixed blood. He reached Oregon about 1825, working in the coastal trade for a year, then trapped with McLeod's southern brigade for two seasons, returning to Fort Vancouver where he remained several years. He rejoined the southern brigade about 1839, contracted tuberculosis, settled in the Willamette Valley, Oregon, where he died.

Ruth Stoller article, MM, Vol. IX.

McLoughlin, Louis A., scout (d. Jan. 19, 1915). McLoughlin was one of Forsyth's scouts at the famous Beecher Island battle in eastern Colorado in September 1868, his account being published in *The Battle of Beecher Island,* 56-59. In February 1908 he was living at Beagle, Kansas, and the place of his death may have been Kansas although its Vital Statistics Department has no record of that event.

Simon E. Matson, *The Battle of Beecher Island.* Wray, Colo., Beecher Island Battle Meml. Assn., 1960.

McMahon, John Mott, soldier (Aug. 25, 1842-Aug. 30, 1917). B. in Fifeshire, Scotland, he emigrated to the United States and at Baltimore on March 7, 1866, enlisted under the name of John Mott in the 3rd U.S. Cavalry, being assigned to F Company. With his company, commanded by Lieutenant Howard B. Cushing, he moved to New Mexico. While drilling in October 1868 as sergeant of F Troop, Mott's pistol was discharged while his horse was leaping down an embankment, the weapon struck by chain sidelines, or hobbles and Mott was wounded seriously in the leg; he was in the hospital at Fort Bascom, New Mexico, for some time, and was sent to Monument Creek, Texas, to rejoin his troop before the injury was fully healed. He re-enlisted March 10, 1869, at Fort Stanton, New Mexico, and shortly accompanied the troop to Arizona, being stationed at Camps Goodwin and Grant. He took part in many scouts after Apaches, including much fighting, and was characterized by Bourke as an "excellent man." He was with the detachment that went to rescue survivors of the ambushed Kennedy-Israel train near Grant in May of 1870. He came down with malaria and typhoid fever, but recovered in time to take part in Cushing's long scout against Chiricahua Apaches. In an action in the Whetstone Mountains, May 5, 1871, Cushing and two others were killed and Mott assumed command, rescuing the remainder of the party in a hard fight against Juh's Apaches, although he lost several horses and had a man wounded. He and four others received Medals of Honor for the action. Mott became regimental quartermaster sergeant and was discharged March 10, 1874 at Fort McPherson, Nebraska, upon expiration of his term of service. He then resumed his full name of John Mott McMahon; McMahon worked at the Quartermaster Department, Chicago, as a civilian clerk in 1874-75; was with Crook and

other officers in the field as a Quartermaster employee until 1885, and thereafter resided at Omaha, where he died. He never married. As a young man McMahon was 5 feet, 3 inches, in height, and had grey eyes, fair complexion and light hair.

Dan L. Thrapp, *The Conquest of Apacheria.* Norman, Univ. of Okla. Press, 1967; Mott's service and pension record, Nat. Archives; John G. Bourke, *On the Border with Crook.* Glorieta, New Mex., Rio Grande Press, 1969.

McMasters, Sherman W. (Little Bill), desperado (d. c. 1882). McMasters was one of the Dodge City, Kansas "gang" of fringe elements in the middle 1870s. He was at Las Vegas, New Mexico, in the days of Hoodoo Brown, 1879, and drifted then to Tombstone, Arizona, where he associated with the Earps and their followers. He was suspected of taking part in three stage holdups, and appeared to be friendly also with the Curly Bill-Diehl-Leonard party, generally in opposition to the Earp faction. On one occasion Virgil Earp, lawman at Tombstone, "attempted" to arrest McMasters, firing five shots at him and, by inference, intentionally missing while McMasters stole a horse or two at Contention and fled to the Huachuca Mountains of Arizona. Although charged with horse theft, robbery and perhaps murder in Arizona, he was at least verbally appointed in 1882 a U.S. deputy marshal by Dake. McMasters was in the Tombstone saloon when Morgan Earp was assassinated March 17, 1882, took part in the murder of Stilwell at Tucson, Arizona, and of Florentino Cruz, sometimes called Indian Charley, two days later. McMasters was one of those who fled Earp's purported confrontation with Brocius the next day. He was killed, in either New Mexico or the Texas Panhandle, by November 13, 1882, in Bartholomew's belief, when a charge against him for larceny was stricken from the court docket at Tombstone. Will McLaury suggested in a letter to his father April 13, 1884, that he had been a factor in the death of Morgan Earp, wounding of Virgil Earp, and killing of McMasters (see McLaury biography).

Ed Bartholomew, *Wyatt Earp: The Man and the Myth.* Toyahvale, Tex., Frontier Book Co., 1964; Bartholomew to author, Sept. 16, 1976.

MacMillan, Donald Baxter, arctic explorer

(Nov. 10, 1874-Sept. 7, 1970). B. at Province-town, Massachusetts, he also died there. MacMillan was graduated from Bowdoin College, Brunswick, Maine, in 1898 and later studied at Harvard. He joined the Peary Arctic Expedition of 1908 by which Peary reportedly reached the North Pole in 1909, and the next year MacMillan joined the Cabot expedition to Labrador. In 1911 and 1912 he made ethnological studies of the Labrador Eskimo. He organized the first independent expedition in 1913, attempting to confirm or disprove the existence of Crocker Land, which Peary reported sighting but had not visited. MacMillan, in the Arctic until 1917, by a noteworthy trip over the pack ice, proved that the sighting had been an illusion and Crocker Land did not exist; he also explored much of Grant Land on Ellesmere Island and completed other useful work. He was appointed professor of anthropology at Bowdoin College in 1918. In 1920 he visited the Hudson Bay region and in 1921 explored Baffin Land; in 1923 and 1924 he conducted researches on glaciers in the Kane Basin. In 1925 MacMillan accompanied the first expedition of Richard E. Byrd seeking to fly to the North Pole; it ended unsuccessfully. In 1926 and 1927-28 MacMillan visited Labra-dor, Baffin Land and Greenland. In 1938 he returned with more than 40,000 arctic plants; in 1944 he commanded an expedition which made aerial surveys of those regions, and followed it with expeditions in 1946 and 1947 as well. He also conducted studies in Ellesmere Land and Baffin Land in 1948 and also in 1949 when he made his 28th voyage of exploration. He wrote *Four Years in the White North* (1918); *Etah and Beyond* (1927), and *How Peary Reached the Pole* (1934).

CE; EA.

McMurdy, Samuel, Mormon official (fl. 1857-1876). Reportedly a lieutenant of John M. Higbee and taking part in the Mountain Meadows massacre of September 11, 1857, McMurdy was also a counselor of Bishop Philip Klingonsmith, a leader in that sordid affair. McMurdy drove a wagon into which the Fancher emigrants piled their arms, then stowed the youngest children before quitting their besieged fortress-corral. When Lee approached the wagon to kill some of the prisoners, his pistol went off prematurely creasing McMurdy across the thigh, McMurdy

protesting, "Brother Lee, keep cool, you are excited... there is no reason for being excited," or so Lee reported later. Lee added that he had told Brigham Young that McMurdy, Samuel Knight and he had "killed the wounded men in the wagons..." and Bancroft details this. After the slaughter McMurdy drove the youngest children to Hamblin's ranch nearby where they would be distributed among Mormon families. McMurdy testified at both of John D. Lee's trials, at neither testifying against himself; at the first he recalled nothing derogatory against Lee, either, but at the second, after the church officials apparently had decided to sacrifice Lee, McMurdy's memory improved. After the massacre, he moved to the Utah village of Paradise, south of Logan.

Juanita Brooks, *The Mountain Meadows Massacre.* Norman, Univ. of Okla. Press, 1966; William Wise, *Massacre at Mountain Meadows.* N.Y., Thomas Y. Crowell Co., 1976; Bancroft, *Utah;* Juanita Brooks, *John Doyle Lee.* Glendale, Calif., Arthur H. Clark Co., 1961.

McNac, Sam: *see* Sam Moniac

McNamara, Eugene, Catholic priest, expan-sionist (fl. 1845-46). B. in Ireland, he reached California aboard the British ship *Juno* in June 1846, after asking the president of Mexico the previous year for sizable land grants in California to be settled by Irish colonists, to advance Catholicism and "put an obstacle in the way of further usurpations on the part of an irreligious and anti-catholic nation," i.e., the United States, and in opposition to "the methodist wolves." He suggested initially 1,000 families, each to have a square league on San Francisco Bay, a second colony near Monterey and a third at Santa Barbara. At Monterey he appealed to Pico for specified grants of land, the governor approving the idea. About this time the U.S. occupation of California was underway, documentary confusion clouds the issue, and McNamara left California aboard the British ship *Collingwood* enroute for Honolulu and Mexico. Bancroft supposed that a group of London speculators, suspecting that Cali-fornia soon would become American and that land prices would skyrocket, employed a Catholic priest to approach a Catholic country (Mexico), for the grants hoping they would be honored — to the adventurers' immense profit — by the incoming government, but the legitimacy of the grant made by Pico was never tested, and McNamara disappears from view.

Bancroft, *California*, V.

McNeal, Hugh, soldier (fl. 1803-1811). B. in Pennsylvania he lived in Kentucky when he enlisted in the Lewis and Clark Expedition. He was an excellent hunter. Clarke said he was on the army muster rolls as late as September 1811, but Clark lists him as dead by 1825.

History of the Expedition Under the Command of Lewis and Clark, ed. by Elliott Coues. N.Y., Dover Pubns., 1965; Clarke, *Lewis and Clark.*

McNelly, Leander H., Texas Ranger (1844-Sept. 4, 1877). B. in Virginia, he reached Texas with his family in 1860, and was raised on a ranch in Washington County, becoming a sheep-herder. He enlisted in the 5th Regiment, Texas Mounted Volunteers, Sibley's Brigade, in 1861 and fought at Valverde, New Mexico, later at Galveston, Texas, and accompanied the brigade to Louisiana. As captain he later raised his own company and fought creditably during the remainder of the Civil War, being wounded April 8, 1864. He remained in service, searching out deserters, following the war, then farmed west of Brenham, Texas, and served with the state police from 1870-73. When the Texas Rangers were recreated in 1874, McNelly was commissioned to head a special force to deal with the Sutton-Taylor feud in Dewitt County, Texas, when the outfit went to the Rio Grande for police work. His company was recommissioned a special state force on July 26, 1876, and with it McNelly was effective in quieting border turmoil, but had contracted tuberculosis and died on his farm in Washington County. He was buried at Burton. McNelly was one of the great Texas Rangers, although he was of slight frame and quiet manner. Webb described him as "a tallish man of quiet manner, and with the soft voice of a timid Methodist preacher."

HT; Walter Prescott Webb, *The Texas Rangers: A Century of Frontier Defense.* Boston, Houghton Mifflin Co., 1935.

McNelly, William T., pioneer (Apr. 3, 1849-Feb. 2, 1938). B. at Avalon, Maryland, he moved to Chicago and enlisted about 1870 in the 8th Cavalry, serving in New Mexico against Mimbres Apaches for several years. As a corporal of A Company he accompanied a scout from Fort Bayard, New Mexico, to Mount Graham, Arizona, and on July 27, 1872, killed the only Apache the operation accounted for; it was commanded by First Lieutenant William A. Stephenson. McNelly was mustered out in 1875, a sergeant and shortly reached Globe, Arizona, where he spent the remainder of his life. He operated a popular saloon and was a particular friend of Al Sieber, onetime sheriff and historian Dan Williamson, Bushrod Crawford and other characters of the mining camp. He was described as "very handsome, tall, straight, with black, wavy hair and a reddish mustache and blue eyes. Much too generous and always willing to help people." McNelly fathered a son, Benjamin A. (1886-1957). Bill McNelly engaged occasionally in mining and other frontier activities as sidelines.

"Frederick E. Phelps: A Soldier's Memoirs," ed. by Frank D. Reeve. *New Mex. Hist. Rev.,* Vol. XXV, No. 2 (Apr. 1950), 114; information from Margaret E. (Mrs. Benjamin A.) McNelly, Jan. 18, 1959; Dan L. Thrapp, *Al Sieber, Chief of Scouts.* Norman, Univ. of Okla. Press, 1964.

McNew, William Henry, frontiersman (d. June 30, 1937). B. in Texas, he was tried with Oliver Lee and Gililland in connection with the Fountain murders in New Mexico and "reportedly he was the meanest and most vicious of the three." Tall, slender, with hard blue eyes, he was a tough gunman who, according to Rickards "was one of the pioneer ranchers of the Tularosa region and had a ranch on the edge of the White Sands at a place known as 'Point of Sands.'" Then he went to work for Lee, wrote Metz, first proving his usefulness in 1892 during election strife in southern New Mexico. He was charged with cattle rustling along with Lee, but was not convicted. McNew and the others were strongly suspected of doing in the Fountains, but proof was hard to get. McNew was arrested first and held in the Las Cruces, New Mexico, jail for about a year, but he, Lee and Gililland ultimately were acquitted. A source Hutchinson identifies only as "Cowman," believed that if any of Lee's partisans had anything to do with the Fountain killings "it was Wm. McNew. He was inclined to be mean and a bit locoed at best. The job was done by... and Bill McNew. Curry told me that Oliver Lee never spoke to McNew after the killings. This would seem to bear this out." In the spring of 1937 McNew suffered a small stroke and almost died; a later stroke finished him off.

Leon Claire Metz, *Pat Garrett: The Story of a Western Lawman.* Norman, Univ. of Okla. Press, 1974; Colin Rickards, *How Pat Garrett Died.* Santa Fe, Palomino Press, 1970; C.L. Sonnichsen, *Tularosa: Last of the Frontier West.* Old Greenwich, Conn., Devin-Adair Co., 1972; W.H. Hutchinson, *Another Verdict for Oliver Lee.* Clarendon, Tex., Clarendon Press, 1965.

McNitt, Frank, historian (Dec. 5, 1912-Dec. 10, 1972). B. at Cleveland, he studied art at Yale and in New York and spent two years as a professional cartoonist. He became a newspaperman at Los Angeles, interested himself in frontier history, particularly that of the Four Corners area. He became advertising manager for the Farmington, New Mexico, *Daily Times,* then sales manager for the University of New Mexico Press, meanwhile exploring the Navaho country. He published *Richard Wetherill, Anasazi* (1957); *The Indian Traders* (1962); edited *Navaho Expedition: Journal of a Military Reconnaissance from Santa Fe... to the Navaho Country,.... 1849 by Lieutenant... Simpson* (1964) and, his major work, *Navajo Wars: Military Campaigns Slave Raids and Reprisals* (1972), which appeared two weeks after his death from a heart attack. It covers Navaho contacts with the whites from Coronado until the Fort Fauntleroy massacre of 1861; he had planned to follow it with a volume completing the tribe's military history. McNitt had moved to Massachusetts in 1957. He bequeathed his "priceless, orderly collection of historical data" to the New Mexico State Records Center.

New Mex. Hist. Rev., Vol. XLVIII, No. 2 (Apr. 1973), 169-71.

McPherson, John, lawman (d. c. Aug. 10, 1879). McPherson, former police chief at Las Vegas, New Mexico, and Charles (Slick) Karl engaged in a shooting match August 6, 1879, purportedly at the instigation of Hoodoo Brown, who wanted McPherson out of the way. Both men were wounded, McPherson mortally. His funeral was largely attended.

Ed Bartholomew, *Wyatt Earp: The Man & the Myth.* Toyahvale, Tex., Frontier Book Co., 1964.

McQueen, James, adventurer (1683-1811). McQueen said he was b. in Scotland, joined the British Navy and served with it in Queen Anne's War. In 1716 his ship was cruising the Florida coast when at St. Augustine, McQueen struck one of the officers and fled to the Creek nation, being one of the first whites to live among that people. He married a Tallassee woman and settled on Tallassee Creek in Alabama, remaining there until 1750 when he moved with his people down the Tallapoosa River where he spent the rest of his life. "He controlled and in a manner shaped the future course of the Tallassee Tribe whilst he lived, and it is said that there are very few of the Tallassee Indians who have not some of the McQueen blood in their veins." He died in 1811 in that nation "at the remarkable age of 125 years," according to Dreisback. McQueen, originally partial to the French, became disillusioned after their destruction of the Natchez Indians around 1730. Thereafter McQueen used his influence to have the French settlements upon the Coosa and Tallapoosa rivers broken up.

James D. Dreisback, "Weatherford — 'The Red Eagle'." *Ala. Historical Reporter,* Vol. 2, No. 4 (Mar. 1884), n.p.

McQueen, Peter Creek chief (c. 1780-c. 1819). Probably a son of James McQueen, Peter was b. near Line Creek in today's Montgomery County, Alabama, and as a Tallassee chief became one of the most important leaders in the Creek War of 1813-14 against the United States, and in the 1818 First Seminole War in Florida. He was half Creek and listened earnestly to Tecumseh on the great Shawnee's mission to the Creek towns in 1811 or 1812. McQueen headed the delegation which went to Pensacola, Florida, in July 1813 to acquire arms for the restless Creeks, and this led to the opening engagement of the Creek War when whites attacked the returning Indians at Burnt Corn Creek, July 27. McQueen took a leading role with Weatherford in the Fort Mims massacre of August 30, 1813. Described by Pickett as "the brutal McQueen," he no doubt was active in later phases of the Creek War, but details are lacking. McQueen probably was not present at the Battle of Horseshoe

Bend, March 27, 1814, but joined the migration into Florida of about 1,000 Creeks. In the Seminole War of 1817-18 in which he again was with the hostiles, he was defeated at the Battle of Econfinnah, then moved to southeastern Florida where shortly he died.

H.S. Halbert, T.H. Ball, *The Creek War of 1813 and 1814*. Univ. of Ala. Press, 1969; Henry S., Marsha Kass Marks, *Alabama Past Leaders*, Huntsville, Ala., Strode Pubrs., 1982; information from the Ala. Dept. of Archives and Hist.

McSween, Alexander A(braham?), attorney (c. 1843-July 19, 1878). B. perhaps at Charlotte-town, Prince Edward Island, Canada, he seems to have been adopted in infancy by Murdock McSween, an emigrant from Scotland, and remained with the elder McSween until a grown man when he migrated to the United States. His original name and place and circumstances of birth are unknown. On August 23, 1873, he was married at Atchison, Kansas, to Sue E. Hummer of Eureka, Kansas (1845-1931), the McSweens arriving in New Mexico March 3, 1875. The attorney settled at Lincoln, Lincoln County, where he practiced law. He handled many matters for John Chisum, principal cattleman of the area and, "aggressive and frankly ambitious," became known as a high-priced lawyer "who usually gave value received by winning his cases... He had high professional ideals and did not hesitate to decline cases he felt were not just. And a sincere interest in bringing law and order... made him observant of the corruption overspreading the area...." An ardent Presbyterian, he urged the church to send home missionaries to Lincoln, and contributed liberally toward their work. He became involved in politics as a Republican. McSween was opinionated and sometimes contentious. When John H. Tunstall reached Lincoln in 1876 with money to invest and plans for commercial ventures, McSween became his attorney; when Tunstall ran afoul of L.G. Murphy & Co., McSween also was involved, and when Dolan took over the Murphy enterprise and desire for monopoly, he exacerbated the feud. When Tunstall was murdered February 18, 1878, McSween remained the principal target for the Dolan faction, but the Dolanites were determined in any case to wipe out opposition by one means or another. This they did as the climax of the noted Five Days' Battle at Lincoln in July 1878, centering on the McSween home. The engagement "was inevitable.... Leadership ...had been thrust upon Lawyer McSween. Hounded and harrassed by citations and writs issued out of Judge (Warren H.) Bristol's court, the result in part of District Attorney (William L.) Rynerson's maneuvering, poor Mr. McSween gave every evidence... of being in a state of resigned confusion (but was) convinced that he had no alternative but to stand his ground and fight." McSween's home was set ablaze during the battle and McSween was killed by shots from the Peppin posse that had besieged the place, the killer never certainly identified. Three of his supporters also were killed as was Bob Beckwith of Peppin's posse.

Literature abundant: *Maurice G. Fulton's History of the Lincoln County War,* ed. by Robert N. Mullin. Tucson, Univ. of Ariz. Press, 1968; William A. Keleher, *Violence in Lincoln County 1869-1881.* Albuquerque, Univ. of New Mex. Press, 1957.

McSween, Sue (Susan) Hummer, frontierswoman (Dec. 30, 1845-Jan. 3, 1931). B. at Gettysburg, Pennsylvania, she moved to Eureka, Kansas, and married Alexander A. McSween of Atchison, Kansas, August 23, 1873, moving with her husband within two years to Lincoln, New Mexico, where McSween, an attorney, became a central figure in the Lincoln County war of the late 1870s. Sue, of an aggressive disposition and "vivid personality," was a staunch and fearless supporter of her husband through all vicissitudes including the Five Days' Battle where he met his death despite her parading through a ring of besiegers to plead with Dudley for safe conduct for him. Her courage, tenacity and abilities continued to support her after his demise, Angel pointing out that: "Sharp woman now that her husband is dead. A tiger. Use her however ('Molasses catches more flies than vinegar.')" Mrs. McSween hired Huston I. Chapman as her attorney after McSween was killed; Chapman soon was murdered also. Threats against her life did not dismay her. Widenmann neglected his duties as administrator of the estate and soon left the Territory, so Sue herself was confirmed as administratrix. She acquired Dick Brewer's ranch in lieu of payment for a note McSween had held against him, sold it and with funds from McSween's estate launched a ranching operation away from Lincoln in the Three Rivers area west of the Sierra Blanca Mountains, possibly being assisted by a gift of a small cattle herd from John Chisum. "This courageous woman was presently a successful rancher in her own right." In 1884 she married George Barber, a Virginian; they were divorced in 1891. Her ranch operation prospered, her herds grew to 8,000 head; she located a silver mine and retained a half-interest in it. She was hospitable as a hostess who could sing competently and play the piano, and occasionally presided at light dances for her guests. In 1917 she finally sold her Tres Rios Ranch to Albert Bacon Fall and retired to White Oaks where she died.

See Alexander McSween references; "Frank Warner Angel's Notes on New Mexico Territory 1878," ed. by Lee Scot Theisen. *Arizona and the West,* Vol. 18, No. 4 (Winter 1976).

McWhorter, Lucullus Virgil, historical writer (Jan. 22, 1860-Oct. 10, 1944). B. in a log cabin in mountainous Harrison County, (West) Virginia, he was the son of a minister and physician whose people had lived in the region since pre-Revolutionary times. Young McWhorter disliked school but was fascinated with local history and accumulated material in that field. He was offered a West Point appointment, but declined. His interest in Indian artifacts and lore led him to assemble a collection now at the Department of State Archives and History of West Virginia. In 1893 he and two others founded *The American Archaeologist,* the organ of the American Archaeologist Association. In 1897 he moved with his wife and family to a farm near Fort Jefferson, Darke County, Ohio, where he specialized in raising blooded Devon cattle. In 1903 he again moved, to North Yakima, Washington, taking the pick of his cattle with him and establishing another farm. He became friendly with Yakima Indians and soon was deeply involved in a bitter dispute on their behalf for irrigation rights. In 1913 he successfully sought aid from the Indian Rights Association; eventually the Yakimas won their fight, in a sense a personal victory for McWhorter. He published a 56-page pamphlet, *The Crime Against the Yakimas* (1913) in the course of the long campaign. In 1915 he published *The Border Settlers of Northwestern Virginia from 1768 to 1795 Embracing the*

Life of Jesse Hughes and Other Noted Scouts of the Great Woods of the Trans-Allegheny, a very creditable work. Another writing concerned the Yakima uprising of 1855: *The Tragedy of the Wahk-Shum: Prelude to the Yakima Indian War, 1855-1856* (1917). He became interested in Indian "nationalism" then sweeping the tribes and with an Indian founded the short-lived *The American Indian Tepee,* which first appeared in 1920. McWhorter also was attracted to the Nez Perce Indians who traveled past his farm, delving deeply into their history and ethnology and becoming a confidante of some of the leading men, one of whom was Yellow Wolf, a veteran of the hegira of Chief Joseph from Idaho toward Canada. Out of this friendship came *Yellow Wolf: His Own Story* (1940), the only account to that time from the Indian side of the 1877 saga. But Mc Whorter had numerous other Indian informants and accumulated a great deal of material on that event. He gradually compiled a massive work, although the final chapters were not written and some revision remained when he died. The task was completed and edited by Mrs. Ruth Bordin and was published as *Hear Me, My Chiefs!* (1952). McWhorter's two books on the Nez Perce were solid, authoritative, honest and substantial enough to become cornerstones for every subsequent work of any importance on the Nez Perce history of the period. McWhorter was interested in a wide variety of topics and lent his strengths to many causes, not least for the humane treatment of animals, a concern in which he felt strongly. His extensive collection of papers and related material was deposited by his son, Virgil O. McWhorter with the State College of Washington Library at Pullman, Washington; it has been catalogued (the listing published) and remains a monument to a remarkable man. "When one considers McWhorter's lack of formal training, his lack of funds or leisure to pursue his study and research on any large scale, his accomplishments seem surprising . . . the record of a hard-working rancher who found the time and energy to pursue the myriad facets of his interests and to help preserve some of the story of the American past."

Nelson A. Ault, "The Papers of Lucullus V. McWhorter." *Research Studies of Wash. State Coll.,* Vol. XXVI, Nos. 2, 3, 4 (June, Sept., Dec. 1958), 85-118, 158-90, 216-44; Vol. XXVII, Nos. 1, 2, (Mar., June 1959), 39-62, 85-108.

M

Macfarlane, Daniel S., Mormon pioneer (fl. 1857-1896). Macfarlane was described by Wise as a son-in-law of Isaac Haight and acting adjutant to Higbee at the time of the Mountain Meadows massacre, September 11, 1857, in southern Utah. While the emigrants were piling arms in the wagons and preparing to evacuate their fortress under the supposed protection of armed Mormons who had promised to shield them from hostile Indians, Macfarlane "rode up, with orders from Major Higbee to hasten their departure, as the Indians threatened to renew the attack." On June 29, 1896, Macfarlane had notarized a statement on the affair "for the sake of the living as well as the dead." He said he was one of a company of volunters who went out to bury the dead but "when we reached 'the meadows' the Indians were still fighting the Imigrants." he said that Mormon help for the Indians was given reluctantly; he told how the slaughtering was engineered, placing the blame principally upon John D. Lee, the selected scapegoat, and Klingonsmith, an apostate who by then had been murdered. "No one knew of the treachery before hand unless Lee and (Klingon)Smith," wrote Macfarlane. At the time of the tragedy he resided in Cedar City, Utah, and continued to live there at least until the paper was drafted.

Juanita Brooks, *The Mountain Meadows Massacre.* Norman, Univ. of Okla. Press, 1966; William Wise, *Massacre at Mountain Meadows.* N.Y., Thomas Y. Crowell Co., 1976; Bancroft, *Utah.*

Mackay, James, fur trader (c. 1759-Mar. 16, 1822). B. at Arrichliney, Scotland, he emigrated to Canada about 1776, entering the fur trade, exploring the wilderness and in 1787 reaching the Mandans. About 1792 he changed his alliance from British to Spanish interests, dropping down to the Illinois country and in 1795 became manager of the Missouri Fur Company's operations on the upper Missouri River. He ascended the stream in 1795, wintering among the Omahas and erecting Fort Charles; John Evans was among his party. Until 1797 he explored the country as far as the Mandan Villages, although Mackay himself may not have gone as far, Evans conducting trade among them. Mackay returned to St. Louis by 1797. He visited New Orleans in 1798, and was appointed captain in the Spanish army and commander of San André, a Missouri post about seven leagues from St. Louis. He differed with Spanish officials on American immigration (which he favored because, though non-Catholic it would strengthen the frontier against Indians). He became an important frontier official. When the transfer of Louisiana took place (1804), he was commandant of San André and perhaps of St. Charles; he held minor positions under the Americans. Although married late in life, he fathered nine children. Mackay died at St. Louis.

Abraham P. Nasatir article, MM, Vol. IV.

Mackay, James Ormond, army officer (Dec. 22, 1857-Jan. 17, 1911). B. in Nova Scotia, Mackay was graduated from West Point (having been appointed from Nevada) in 1879, and joined the 3rd Cavalry. He took part in Crook's great Sierra Madre Expedition of 1883. Mackay served at Texas posts including Nevills Spring, San Antonio and Fort Brown, and helped control Texas and Mexican border disturbances in 1893. He retired July 10, 1900 for disability in line of duty and settled at San Antonio, where he died.

Heitman; Cullum; U.S. Milit. Acad. at West Point, *Annual Reunion of the Association of Graduates,* 1911.

Mackenzie, Ranald Slidell, army officer (July 27, 1840-Jan. 19, 1889). B. in New York City, he was graduated No. 1 in the West Point class of 1862, and assigned to the Corps of Engineers, taking part in many major engagements of the eastern theatre of the Civil War, being wounded twice and winning four brevets for gallantry, up to Major General of Volunteers. After brief service as colonel with the 41st and 24th Infantry regiments he became colonel of the 4th Cavalry late in 1870, retaining its command until he retired as Brigadier General, March 24, 1884. He had become insane and died of paresis. His frontier service was distinguished. He assumed command of the 4th February 25, 1871, at Ft. Concho, Texas, and with it cleared the state of hostile Indians and to some extent Mexican guerillas. He received a bad arrow wound in 1871 in a Comanche fight. On one occasion (in 1873) he raided deep into Mexico to punish Kickapoo Indians he considered hostile to border interests. The regiment was transferred to Ft. Sill, Oklahoma, in 1875. In an accident that autumn he struck his head severely, leaving him "increasingly sensitive and irritable." He helped corral the northern hostiles, Sioux and Cheyennes, in 1876 out of Ft. Robinson, Nebraska, striking the Dull Knife band of Cheyennes sharply on the Red Fork of the Powder River, on November 25, 1876. Mackenzie returned to Ft. Sill. Late in 1877 he was stationed again at Ft. Clark, Texas, and restored peace along the Rio Grande. He harshly removed the Utes from western Colorado to a reserve in Utah in the early summer of 1881, and later that year was sent with several companies into southeastern Arizona in the wake of Apache flareups, but saw no action. October 30, 1881, he assumed command of the District of New Mexico. His health began to fail, however, and he was granted an extended leave. He returned to Santa Fe in February 1883, was reassigned October 27 to command the Department of Texas, bought a ranch at Boerne, north of San Antonio, planning apparently to wed and for his retirement. He was treated for his growing mental instability at New York City early in 1884, and was retired over his protests, removed to his boyhood home at Morristown, New Jersey, and in 1886 to Staten Island where he died. He was buried at West Point. Mackenzie, who had been considered by Grant "the most promising young officer in the army," was a brevet Major General at 24. He was demanding, often irascible, an officer of great courage, intelligence and dedication, and extraordinarily solicitous of his men, winning outstanding loyalty from them. He endeavored to be eminently fair and just to them and even to enemies. He was 5 feet, 9 inches, in height, weighed 145 pounds in his

youth, was smooth-shaven, although later he grew a mustache, had sensitive, ascetic features, gray eyes, brown hair. He worked long hours, slept little, ate moderately, did not drink and had great endurance. He was a great officer.

DAB; Ernest Wallace, *Ranald S. Mackenzie on the Texas Frontier.* Lubbock, West Tex., Mus. Assn., 1964; John G. Bourke, *Mackenzie's Last Fight with the Cheyennes.* Bellevue, Neb., Old Army Press, 1970; R.G. Carter, *On the Border with Mackenzie, or, Winning West Texas from the Comanches.* N.Y., Antiquarian Press, 1961; Dan L. Thrapp, *General Crook and the Sierra Madre Adventure.* Norman, Univ. of Okla. Press, 1972.

Mackey, Elkanah D., Presbyterian missionary (Sept. 16, 1826- Sept. 6, 1858). B. at Colerain, Pennsylvania, he was graduated from Princeton Theological Seminary in 1856 and ordained a missionary to the Indians. He and his wife reached Fort Benton, Montana, to work among the Blackfeet, Mrs. Mackey being "the first white woman in the country," but the Mackeys did not remain long, leaving September 15 for the states, Mackey dying in Maryland.

Montana, Contributions, Vol. X, 1940, 279-80.

Maddox, Thomas John Claggett, surgeon (c. 1852-Dec. 19, 1885). B. in Maryland the son of Dr. Thomas Maddox of Washington County, he was commissioned an assistant surgeon in the army October 22, 1881 and assigned to the Department of Texas. He was sent to Arizona when Crook requested surgeons following the May 1885 Geronimo breakout. Maddox was killed by Josanie's Apache raiders near the WS Ranch of Alma, New Mexico, along with four enlisted men while operating under the command of Lieutenant Samuel Warren Fountain. He was buried on the WS Ranch, the body later removed for shipment east, but the site of the original burial marked by a government headstone about 1950. The hillside site is two miles north of Alma, within view of the present highway.

Heitman; Dan L. Thrapp, *Conquest of Apacheria.* Norman, Univ. of Okla. Press, 1967; *Los Angeles Times,* Dec. 22, 1885.

Madigan, John, army officer (c. 1840- Sept. 27, 1867). B. in Ireland he was taken as a child to Jersey City, New Jersey. He enlisted October 12, 1861, in the 88th New York Infantry in which he was commissioned a second lieutenant December 13, 1862, and mustered out in 1863 when he became a first lieutenant of the 2nd New Jersey Cavalry, being mustered out November 1, 1865. He was commissioned a second lieutenant in the 1st U.S. Cavalry in February 1866, becoming a first lieutenant April 25, 1867. Madigan took part in a campaign under Crook against the Pit River Indians of California in September 1867. In a very hard fight at Infernal Caverns, Madigan and seven enlisted men were killed and a dozen others wounded while the Indians suffered about fifteen or twenty killed. Madigan, of whom Crook wrote, "a braver officer never lived," won a posthumous brevet to captain for his work at the caverns.

Heitman; Bancroft, *Oregon,* II, 538-44; *General George Crook: His Autobiography,* ed. by Martin F. Schmitt. Norman, Univ. of Okla. Press, 1960; 153-54; NARS, Madigan military record.

Madsen, Chris, soldier, lawman (Feb. 25, 1851-Jan. 9, 1944). B. at Copenhagen, Madsen served in the Danish-Prussian and Franco-Prussian wars, and in the French Foreign Legion in Algeria. He was wounded in the Sedan battle. He reached New York January 21, 1876, and enlisted in the Seventh Cavalry, was transferred to the Fifth Cavalry, stationed at Fort Reno, Oklahoma, then Fort Russell, Wyoming. On July 17, 1876, he witnessed Bill Cody's famous fight with Yellow Hand, and left an account of it. He was said to have taken part in the burial of some of Custer's men, and sketched a map of the Little Big Horn battlefield for correspondent John Finerty. Madsen served in various Indian campaigns from 1876 to 1880, and remained in the army for another decade. He had married in the meantime and January 21, 1891, became a deputy U.S. marshal out of El Reno, becoming with Bill Tilghman and Heck Thomas, the "Three Guardsmen" of Oklahoma history. Madsen took part in countless pursuits and arrests and in the occasional shootout was always cool and deliberate, avoiding gunplay and killing if possible. He led the posse that killed Red Buck Waightman about March 4, 1896, near Arapaho, headed the pair that cornered and killed Oliver Yountis, a bank robber near Orlando, Oklahoma, and eliminated other trouble makers. Madsen was reportedly quartermaster for the Rough Riders during the Spanish-American War. He tried to enlist in World War I, but was too old. He served as chief of police at Oklahoma City and in other law enforcement capacities. He died at Guthrie, and was buried at Yukon, Oklahoma. He was a brave, worthy officer of integrity and fine judgment.

Glenn Shirley, *West of Hell's Fringe.* Norman, Univ. of Okla. Press, 1978; Paul I. Wellman, *A Dynasty of Western Outlaws.* Garden City, N.Y., Doubleday and Co., 1961.

Magee, Augustus William, soldier of fortune (1789-Mar. 10, 1813). B. at Boston, he entered West Point June 15, 1808, was graduated third in his class January 24, 1809, and became a second lieutenant in the Regiment of Artillerists. He served under James Wilkinson at Baton Rouge, Louisiana, and Natchitoches, "did good work in keeping down the freebooters of the Neutral Ground," and with Samuel Davenport and Bernardo Gutiérrez de Lara laid plans for an invasion of Texas. Refused a promotion, he resigned from the U.S. Army June 22, 1812, and became a colonel of a Mexican Patriot army. He became involved in what one source called the "Gachupin War" and another termed the "Gutiérrez-Magee Expedition". He left Natchitoches August 2, 1812, crossed the Sabine River six days later, and entered Nacogdoches August 12. He captured Fort Bahía (since 1829 known as Goliad) on November 14, where were found the guns of Louis XIV, brought to San Barnardo (Matagorda Bay) by La Salle in 1685. Magee became seriously ill of tuberculosis or malaria, and died at Fort Bahía (or Nuestra Señora de Loreto Presidio).

Cullum; HT.

Magnus, (Quaiapen, Old Queen, Saunk Squaw), woman chief of the Narragansetts (d. July 2, 1676). One of six sachems of the Narragansetts, she was a sister of Ninigret and remained aloof from hostilities early in King Philip's War which broke out in 1675. As the Narragansetts became more involved, however Magnus edged to the fore as among the strongest leaders in the uprising and by autumn she was fully committed. She escaped the Great Swamp Fight of December 19, 1675, when 1,000 Indian men, women and children were killed near Kingston, Rhode Island. An expedition under Major John Talcott attacked a Narragansett village near Nipsachuck, Rhode Island, July 2, 1676, killing or capturing 171 Indians; among the fallen was Magnus, "a gruesome picture of Indian majesty laid low."

Hodge, HAI; Leach, *Flintlock.*

Magoffin, James Wiley, frontiersman (1799-Sept. 27, 1868). B. at Harrodsburg, Kentucky, Magoffin was trading into Old Mexico by 1825, being one of the first to engage in that occupation. On March 3, 1825, he was named consul at Saltillo in southern Coahuila; served there and as consul at Chihuahua City for 15 years. The dangerous overland trade was "very lucrative" and Magoffin, "who evidently had the brave frontier spirit combined with inherited Irish buoyancy and joviality" became not only well-to-do, but was liked by Mexicans and Anglos equally. During the aftermath of the ill-fated Texan Santa Fe Expedition of 1841, he and his wife extended courtesies and what help was possible to the unfortunate prisoners who reached Chihuahua. He had married in Chihuahua, Maria Valdez (d. Jan. 1845), and fathered six children. After his first wife died, he married her sister. Magoffin's friend, Senator Benton of Missouri, was instrumental in Magoffin's being assigned to precede Kearny to Santa Fe in 1846, preparing the way for the American invasion. Magoffin persuaded Governor Manuel Armijo to retire, enabling the occupation of New Mexico without bloodshed. He attempted to duplicate this success in Chihuahua, but was arrested as a spy, being saved from execution only through his genuine popularity; Magoffin ultimately was paid $30,000 by the Washington government for his Mexican services. After release by Mexican authorities following the war, Magoffin settled in the present El Paso, Texas, founding Magoffinsville, centering largely around his baronial estate. John Russell Bartlett's surveying party made it a headquarters for a time. In December 1853, Magoffin came into dispute with Mexican salt gatherers over deposits on the east slopes of the San Andres Mountains of New Mexico, Magoffin having a claim of sorts over the springs; the trader persuaded Sheriff Jerry Snyder to protect his interests. The lawman raised a posse armed with a howitzer and other weapons and in a resulting clash one man was wounded, according to some reports, or three killed according to others. Magoffin was showered with legal troubles over the incident, but ultimately returned confiscated property to the salt gatherers, paid damages, and the matter was forgotten. Magoffin supported the Confederacy in the Civil War, contributing to the initial successes of Baylor and Sibley, was said to have served briefly in the Confederate army in Virginia, but spent most of the war in Texas and though his El Paso property was confiscated, he ultimately recovered most of it. His two sons served in the Confederate Army, one being killed, and a brother was governor of Kentucky (elected 1859). Magoffin died at San Antonio and was buried at San Fernando Cathedral.

Literature abundant; HT; DAB; Leon Claire Metz, *The Shooters.* El Paso, Mangan Books, 1976; "Dust from the Archives: The Claim of James W. Magoffin." Potomac Corral of Westerners *Corral Dust,* Vol. III, No. 3 (Sept. 1958), 20-21.

Maigneret, Pierre, Jesuit brother (1642-Oct. 1722). B. in France, he arrived in Canada September 25, 1667 and at times was assigned to the Iroquois missions in present New York State. In 1683 the Jesuit Thierry Beschefer wrote of Maigneret's intrepid work among that volatile people. He died at Quebec.

Thwaites, JR, L, 215, LXII, 243, LXXI, 151.

Maillet, Louis R., frontiersman (Feb. 1, 1834-Aug. 1906). B. near Montreal, Maillet became interested in the West and in 1849 went to St. Louis, working there and at St. Joseph, Missouri, until 1851 when he joined a trading expedition to Fort Laramie and beyond. About 40 miles west of Fort Laramie they were surrounded by Crows, but the incident passed without bloodshed. Maillet remained at Salt Lake City for two months when he met Neil McArthur, in charge of the Hudson's Bay Company post at Fort Hall, Idaho, and accompanied him to the post; McArthur, wishing to improve his French, made Maillet his clerk, part of his duties being language lessons. In 1852 Maillet and McArthur journeyed to Fort Vancouver, Washington, taking furs and exchanging them for supplies. Maillet remained in Oregon for several months, then became manager of a trading post at The Dalles. In 1853 he agreed to accompany McArthur back to Fort Hall and engage in trading with emigrants for their worn down stock, which would be recouped on rich Montana grasslands, then resold hopefully at a profit. Their initial ventures were not successful, but in time they did accumulate valuable herds of horses and cattle, and Maillet obtained a wife, the half-Blackfoot daughter of Louis Matt. Maillet and McArthur established a headquarters, or ranch, near the present Missoula, Montana. Maillet traded on the Beaverhead River with Bannocks and Snakes for a good profit in 1857. In 1858 he returned to Canada for a visit with his family by way of Fort Benton and St. Louis. On his return about 1860 he accompanied as interpreter, "Colonel" Frederick W. Lander, bringing annuities for the Snakes. Near the head of the Green River Maillet quit Lander to drive 400 head of John Grant's cattle to California; one member of the party was lost to Indians but the cattle were delivered, whereafter Maillet took a boat to The Dalles once again. When he arrived back at his ranch in Montana he found McArthur had lost all their accumulated possessions, worth about $150,000 and had gone prospecting on the Fraser River. Maillet became manager of a small store for John Grant on the Little Blackfoot River in Montana. In 1861 he went back to the States again, but found the Civil War in progress and hastened back, in the Big Hole Valley of Montana having a narow escape from assassination at the hands of Little Wolf, a Nez Perce, and although captured by those Indians, made his escape. His goods which he had shipped from St. Louis aboard the ill-fated *Chippewa,* were lost when she blew up, but he opened a store on the Little Blackfoot anyway, collected cattle and drove them to Elk City, Idaho, for sale. He took advantage of the mining boom which then struck Montana, trading, mining and freighting. For a time he operated a grist mill in the Bitterroot Valley, went to Canada for his second wife who accompanied him back to Montana, entered the cattle business in earnest about 1880, and at various times owned stores and other mercantile interests. He died at St. Hyacinthe, Quebec.

Montana, Contributions, IV (1903); George F. Weisel, *Men and Trade on the Northwest Frontier.* Missoula, Mont. State Univ. Press, 1955.

Malaspina, Alejandro, navigator, explorer

(Nov. 5, 1754-Apr. 9, 1810). B. of noble parentage at Mulazzo, in the Duchy of Parma, Italy, he commenced a naval career at 20 at Cadiz and served as an ensign in the Mediterranean, the Atlantic and the Philippines. During the American Revolution he fought against and was taken prisoner by the English. By 34 he had circumnavigated the world and achieved a position of some rank and prestige. He and a colleague, Commander José Bustamente y Guerra, five years his senior, then suggested an ambitious plan to survey Spain's empire and assembled a competent coterie of scientists and artists and two corvettes, each of 306 tons, with experienced crews; the expedition left Cadiz July 30, 1789, on its five-year voyage, spent two years in South America and on the west coast of Mexico, and reached the northwest coast of North America in mid-1791. By June it had arrived at Yakutat Bay, Alaska, and through trade commenced a notable collection of Pacific Northwest artifacts, calculated rather accurately the altitude of Mount Elias, discovered today's Malaspina Glacier, then progressed 900 miles southeast to Nootka Sound where Spain already had a small settlement. The expedition continued south to Monterey, California; a scientist of the party, Tadeo Haenke, became the "scientific discoverer" of the coast redwoods while more than 250 other botanical species were described. Malaspina reached Acapulco in the early autumn and proceeded across the Pacific as far as Australia, then returned to South America and to Cadiz where the expedition arrived five years and two months after its departure. Initially well received and the vast work of the expedition intended for publication, Malaspina came afoul of court intrigue, was imprisoned for eight years and banished to Italy where he died in obscurity at Pontremoli. In publications of some of the results of the great expedition, his name was even deleted. A Malaspina exhibit in America in the late 1970's did something to re-establish him to the position he deserved.

Warren L. Cook, *Flood Tide of Empire: Spain and the Pacific Northwest, 1543-1819.* New Haven, Yale Univ. Press, 1973; Donald C. Cutter, "The Return of Malaspina," *American West,* Vol. XV, No. 1 (Jan.-Feb. 1978), 4-19.

Maldonado, Alonso del Castillo, explorer (fl. 1527-1537). From Salamanca, he was a member of the Pánfilo de Narváez expedition of 1527-28 to Florida, and with Cabeza de Vaca, Andrés Dorantes de Carranza and the black, Estevánico, he was a survivor reaching the Texas coast in 1528. With the former three, Maldonado made the remarkable journey across the continent, living from time to time with Indians, and reached Culiacán, Sinaloa, on the west coast of Mexico in 1536. From there the four castaways ultimately arrived at Mexico City. Maldonado may have returned to Spain to claim reward for his sufferings, but if so shortly returned to Mexico. Terrell asserts he married a wealthy widow, settled in Mexico and fathered 11 daughters, no sons.

George Parker Winship, *The Coronado Expedition, 1540-1542.* BAE, 14th Ann. Rept., Wash., Govt. Printing Office, 1896; John Upton Terrell, *Estevánico the Black,* Los Angeles, Westernlore Press, 1968; *Southwestern Hist. Quar.,* Vol. XXVIII, No. 1 (July 1924), 122-34 (appendix to Oviedo).

Maldonado, Francisco, explorer (fl. 1538-1540). From Salamanca, Spain, he joined the De Soto expedition into southern United States, reaching Florida in 1539, and "a good knight and one of the most valiant in that army," was made captain of infantry. He accompanied De Soto to Apalachee (the present Tallahassee) on one occasion having his horse badly wounded and almost losing his lance to a bold Indian; it might have gone ill for him had De Soto himself not dispatched the native. December 28 Maldonado was directed to take 50 men and a boat and run the coast to the west, looking for a usable bay or harbor. Maldonado was overdue three or four days, but returned with the report he had found a sheltered port with water of sufficient depth about 160 miles to the westward of Apalachee. De Soto, pleased, directed he go to Havana for provisions, bringing them back to the new port where De Soto intended to meet him. Should De Soto not be there, however, Maldonado was to return once more to Havana and come back the following season. Maldonado left for Havana February 26, 1540, Juan de Guzman named captain of infantry to succeed him. After the disastrous battle of Mauvila, October 18, 1540, in southern Alabama, De Soto learned that Maldonado awaited at the port of Ochuse (probably Pensacola Bay, of which Maldonado was the effective discoverer), six days'

distant. He learned this through the interpreter, Juan Ortiz, who probably had discovered the fact from friendly Indians. De Soto told Ortiz to keep the matter secret. He had lost the 200 pounds of pearls which he had intended sending to Cuba by Maldonado and upon which he counted to stimulate Cuban interest in his enterprise. He feared if he sent nothing back it would be impossible to raise more men for a continuation of his endeavor, should they be needed. "So he determined to send no news of himself until he should have discovered a rich country." Nothing further is heard of Maldonado who doubtless returned to Havana.

Bourne, *De Soto,* I, II.

Maldonado, Rodrigo, military officer (fl. 1540-1560). From Guadalajara, Spain, he was an aristocrat, brother-in-law of the Duque de Infantado and signed on as a captain of cavalry for the Coronado expedition of 1540-42 into the American southwest. He was a close friend of Coronado. From northern Sonora he was sent to the Gulf of California to look for the ships of Alarcón bringing supplies for the overland expedition. He failed to contact Alarcón but returned with a Seri Indian so huge he was the marvel of the Spanish soldiery. From Háwikuh, a pueblo on the Arizona line southwest of Zuñi, New Mexico, Maldonado joined Coronado in pushing eastward to Tiguex, on the Rio Grande River near the present Bernalillo, where they established winter quarters. Maldonado took a vigorous part in quelling the Tiguex uprising in the early spring of 1541, fighting particularly at the pueblo of Moho in the Tiguex complex of towns. In a spring reconnaissance of the buffalo plains to the east, Maldonado first came across Teyas Indians hunting bison, and using some of them as guides discovered Tule Canyon cutting through the eastern face of the Staked Plains uplift. Maldonado was taken as one of the select 30 by Coronado to discover Quivira, in central Kansas which was done in the summer of 1541. December 27, 1541, Maldonado and Coronado were riding together when the latter fell from his mount, his head being struck by the hooves of Maldonado's horse and Coronado injured nearly fatally although the accident was no one's fault. The friendship of the two continued without interruption, Maldonado testifying for Coronado in early 1547 at a Mexico City inquiry into management of the expedition. Coronado was cleared.

George Parker Winship, *The Coronado Expedition, 1540-1542.* BAE, 14th Ann. Rept., Wash., Govt. Printing Office, 1896; Herbert Eugene Bolton, *Coronado: Knight of Pueblos and Plains.* Albuquerque, Univ. of New Mex. Press, 1964; George P. Hammond, Agapito Rey, *Narratives of the Coronado Expedition.* Albuquerque, 1940.

Maley, Thomas Edward, army officer (d. July 1, 1896). B. in Ireland, he emigrated to this country and enlisted in the 5th (then the 2nd) Cavalry at St. Louis in May 1855, and was assigned to Texas where he was commended for his part in a fight with hostile Indians on the Guadalupe River March 8, 1856. After his enlistment, he was commissioned a first lieutenant of the 6th Pennsylvania Cavalry in 1861, the next year rejoining the 5th Cavalry as a second lieutenant. He saw continual service with the army of the Potomac and was made a captain in 1866, in 1869 being sent to Kansas where he had a significant role in the decisive victory over the Cheyennes at Summit Springs July 11, 1869, and took part in other actions. Disability from a Civil War wound led to his retirement in the rank of lieutenant colonel. He became a farmer in Cook County, Illinois, and died at Englewood, Illinois.

Price, *Fifth Cavalry;* Heitman.

Mallery, Garrick, military officer, ethnologist (Apr. 23, 1831-Oct. 24, 1894). B. at Wilkes-Barre, Pennsylvania, he was graduated from Yale in 1850, studied law at the University of Pennsylvania and was admitted to the Philadelphia Bar in 1853. Commissioned a captain in the 71st Pennsylvania Infantry June 4, 1861, he served creditably in the east during the Civil War, and was twice severely wounded, captured and held at Libby Prison until exchanged. He ended the war a lieutenant colonel of Volunteer cavalry and brevet colonel and was mustered out November 5, 1866, already (July 28, 1866) commissioned a captain of the 28th U.S. Infantry. He joined the 1st Infantry December 15, 1870. In the interim, while unassigned and stationed in Virginia, he served occasionally as acting Governor of the state by reason of offices held in the military occupation. He was

assistant to the Chief Signal Officer, U.S.A., at Washington, D.C., from 1870 until August 1876 when he was assigned to Fort Rice, Dakota Territory. Here he became deeply interested in the Indian sign language, pictographs and the mythology of the Plains Indians and June 13, 1877, joined Major John Wesley Powell, then engaged in a geological and geographical survey of the Rocky Mountain region. Mallery undertook field work until July 1, 1879, when he retired from the Army because of the lingering effects of his Civil War wounds. Then as an ethnologist he joined the Bureau of American Ethnology, which Powell headed. With the BAE he wrote several papers of merit, published by it or other scientific organizations, the first being *A Calendar of the Dakota Indians* (1877). It was followed by *The Former and Present Number of Our Indians* (1878); *Introduction to the Study of Sign Language Among the North American Indians as Illustrating the Gesture Speech of Mankind* (1881); *Pictographs of the North American Indians* (1886); *Israelite and Indian: A Parallel in Planes of Culture* (1889), and *Picture Writing of the North American Indians* (1893) among the most notable of his works. Mallery was a founder and president of the Anthropological Society of Washington, D.C., president of the Philosophical Society, vice president of the American Association for the Advancement of Science and was a member of other scientific and cultural organizations. He was married.

Powell; Heitman; DAB.

Mallet, Pierre-Antone, explorer, trader (June 20, 1700-post June 1751). B. at Montreal as was his brother, Paul, the family moved to Detroit around 1706, the brothers reached the Illinois country in 1734 and five years later set out with seven companions for Santa Fe, New Mexico, of which they had heard, their purpose to open a trade relationship. They ascended the Missouri River, then the Platte River and its south fork and guided by an Indian, reached the Picurís pueblo and mission and July 22 arrived at Santa Fe without their trade goods which they had lost crossing a river. Word of their arrival was sent to the viceroy at Mexico City along with a request for instructions on dealing with them. The decision came within nine months: the French were to quit Spanish territory and not return without permission. May 1, 1740, seven of their party (two had married Spanish women and settled at Santa Fe) left for the Pecos River, New Mexico; there the party split, three men heading northeast for the Illinois country while four, including the Mallets, continued east to Arkansas Post near the confluence of the Arkansas and Mississippi rivers, and thence downstream to New Orleans, reporting to Governor Bienville. The Mallets were requested to guide a fresh expedition to Santa Fe under Andre Fabry de La Bruyère. This group, financed by Bienville, left New Orleans late in August 1741 but the expedition failed to reach Santa Fe. In 1750 Pierre, a resident of New Orleans, decided to make a third expedition to Santa Fe (his brother had settled near Arkansas Post on a farm). Although French Governor Vaudreuil could provide no official funds for the effort he gave permission and letters to his counterpart in New Mexico. Mallet and three companions stayed at Natchitoches, Louisiana, for a time, went on to the present Texarkana and thence overland to the Pecos River, losing most of their merchandise enroute to Comanches. They were arrested in November 1750 at Pecos, sent to Santa Fe, then to El Paso, to Chihuahua and Mexico City, where they arrived in February 1751. From there they were sent to Spain where Nasatir believed Pierre probably was imprisoned and died. Paul in 1749 was listed as a farmer in the present Arkansas; his date of death is uncertain.

A.P. Nasatir, *Before Lewis and Clark,* 2 vols.   St. Louis, Hist. Docs. Found., 1952; Nasatir article in DCB, III; Noel M. Loomis, Abraham P. Nasatir, *Pedro Vial and the Roads to Santa Fe.*   Norman, Univ. of Okla. Press, 1967; Henri Folmer, "The Mallet Expedition of 1739... to Santa Fe." *Colo. Mag.,* Vol. XVI, No. 5 (Sept. 1939), 163-73.

Mallory, Samuel, hatter, pioneer (1823-June 13, 1883). B. probably at Danbury, Connecticut, he was of the family that founded and operated the famed Mallory Hat Company and occasionally a part owner of it. He served in three state legislatures: Colorado, 1864, Connecticut, 1866-67, and Montana, 1873-74. In 1860 he transported one of the first quartz mills to Colorado, moving it from St. Joseph, Missouri to near Gregory's Gulch, Gilpin County, Colorado. After several years there,

Mallory left Denver for the new mines at Bannack, Montana, March 28, 1864, reaching Virginia City, Montana, by July 11. From there Mallory and his wife went overland to Fort Benton at the head of navigation on the Missouri River, thence by water to St. Louis and back to Danbury where Mallory again became associated with the family hat business. In 1867 he returned to Madison County near the town of Sheridan, Montana, where he became a ranchman. He sold out in 1881 and returned to his former home in Connecticut, where he died.

Agnes Wright Spring, "Samuel Mallory." *Mont. Mag.,* Vol. XV, Nos. 2, 3 (Spring, Summer 1965), 24-37, 69-79.

Malone, William T., adventurer (1817-Mar. 6, 1836). B. near Athens, Georgia, he was one of the younger men to fall at the Alamo. He ran away from home at 17, reaching Texas by way of New Orleans, and enlisted as an artilleryman in the Texas defense forces. Mrs. Almaron Dickerson said she saw him die, "fighting bravely."

Amelia Williams, XXXVII, 270; HT.

Maney, James Allison, army officer (Dec. 10, 1855-July 4, 1920). B. in Tennessee, he was the son of George Maney and of the fifth generation descended from French Huguenot immigrants to North Carolina. George Maney had served in the Mexican War, been admitted to the bar, became a Brigadier General in the Confederate service and thereafter held legislative and diplomatic posts for his state and the United States. James Maney was graduated from West Point in 1877, becoming a second lieutenant in the 15th Infantry and reaching Fort Bayard, New Mexico, late in December. He had a significant role in the Victorio War, commanding Indian scouts effectively and even operating at times in Old Mexico. He took part in the hard fight in Hembrillo Canyon in April 1880. Maney was at Fort Buford, North Dakota, in 1890. October 30, 1893, he killed Captain Alfred Hedberg of the 15th Infantry, was indicted for murder but not convicted and the incident seems to have done little damage to his career. Maney became captain in 1897, and major of the 17th Infantry in 1902. He was on the China Relief Expedition of 1900, and in the Far East intermittently from 1900 to 1905. He retired as colonel in 1911 for disability in line of duty, and died in Monrovia, California.

Cullum; Heitman; Dan L. Thrapp, *Victorio and the Mimbres Apaches.* Norman, Univ. of Okla. Press, 1974.

Mangas Coloradas, Apache chief (c. 1795-Jan. 18, 1863). Perhaps the greatest of Apache leaders of record, Mangas was born probably in the southwestern portion of present-day New Mexico, and through extraordinary ability and personal qualities became the dominant chief of the Eastern Chiricahuas, which included several bands eventually consolidated into the groupings known to whites as the Mogollon and Mimbres Apaches. There is no report that Mangas had any part in the Juan José Compás massacre of about 1837, but he apparently succeeded Juan José in overall leadership, or at least influence, among the Eastern Chiricahuas. Mangas earned his fearsome reputation by incessant, widespread and devastating raids upon Mexican ranches and perhaps communities in Chihuahua and Sonora, and by 1846 he was already widely known and greatly feared though a universally respected leader. October 20, 1846, he met Brigadier General Stephen Kearny on Mangas Creek, a tributary to the Gila, when his people sought to enlist American help in their unceasing war on the Mexicans. Emory's description of Mangas' people at the time is memorable. In February 1852, Mangas and some of his followers came into contact with John Russell Bartlett and his Boundary Survey, Bartlett reporting that the name of Mangas and his subchiefs "have struck terror among the people of Sonora, Chihuahua and those portions of New Mexico and Texas which border on the Rio Grande." Mangas' association with Bartlett during the days the latter spent at Santa Rita, southern New Mexico, was amicable. Later that year Mangas signed a treaty at Acomas providing for cessation of his raids on Mexico, but neither he nor the whites had any illusions about its bringing more than a temporary lull in hostilities. Yet it was the first treaty seeking to normalize relations between the United States and the Eastern Chiricahuas. Mangas declined to sign a provisional compact of 1853, however, and he stubbornly refused to be a party to the treaty of 1855 which further

increased the domination of the U.S. over his Apaches. During this period his ascendancy over the various bands of the Eastern Chiricahua became more complete. Discovery of gold at Pinos Altos (nine miles above the present Silver City, New Mexico) in the heart of the Eastern Chiricahua homeland, brought complications, and he soon came to cross-purposes with the belligerent, combative miners whose hostility he had never sought. They were suspicious of his obvious dominance over his people; thefts of stock, from whites by Indians and from Indians by whites, exacerbated the situation. Abuse of Mangas, whom Cremony said was publicly whipped and humiliated by brainless miners, worsened the situation, and with the coming of the Civil War, hostilities erupted. Mangas was prominent, perhaps with Cochise, in Cooke's Canyon and Doubtful Canyon skirmishes with isolated parties of whites, and July 14, 1862, together took part in the battle of Apache Pass with the California Column commanded by James Carleton. Mangas was reported wounded in a related skirmish (with a solitary soldier, John Teal), and was taken to Janos where, according to Cremony (who can not always be believed) he was treated by a Mexican physician under threat of revenge if the patient did not recover. Carleton, then commanding the Department of New Mexico, ordered on October 12 that all Apache men were to be killed when encountered, and directed Brigadier General Joseph R. West, at Fort West, near Mangas Springs on Mangas Creek, "to chastise... Mangus Colorada's Band," with the "punishment of that band of murderers... thorough and sharp." West got the message. Several versions of the end of Mangas Coloradas are extant. The most reliable account reports that the Indian was captured by a mixed party of mountain men under Joseph Walker and soldiers, was taken to Fort McLane, New Mexico, goaded by his soldier guard during the night to rouse himself when he was shot "trying to escape," an event that seems sheer murder. West's various reports of the circumstances are fabrics of lies from beginning to end. Mangas was a huge man for an Apache, some accounts asserting he was well over 6 feet in height, and built proportionately; a man of great intelligence (his skull, with a brain capacity said to equal Daniel Webster's, was recovered and sent to Orson Squire Fowler, an eastern phrenologist), notable leadership and generalship capacities, and was highly regarded by all who knew him, red or white. His influence extended far beyond the geographical range of his people, although Cremony's famous summation of his influence and range of operations is patently exaggerated. Mangas possessed a high degree of statesmanship, as well. His sons included Seth-mooda, killed at Pinos Altos, and Mangus, who died at Fort Sill in 1901. His daughters were Dos-teh-seh, who married Cochise; Nah-ke-de-sah, who married a Bedonkohe Apache leader; and Ilth-tooda, who married a Chiricahua Apache. Through these marriages and subsequent liaisons, Mangas' descendants today are also related to Cochise, Victorio and Loco. There may have been other daughters and sons by other wives, but these are not recalled today by his people. Mangas Coloradas' murder by whites was long remembered and still is resented by the descendants of his people.

Literature abundant, but scattered: Griswold; Daniel Ellis Conner, *Joseph Reddeford Walker and the Arizona Adventure.* Norman, Univ. of Okla. Press, 1956; John C. Cremony, *Life Among the Apaches 1850-1868.* Glorieta, N.M., Rio Grande Press, 1969; Ray Brandes, "Mangas Coloradas: King Philip of the Apache Nation." *Troopers West,* Frontier Heritage Press, San Diego, 1970; Dan L. Thrapp, *Victorio and the Mimbres Apaches.* Norman, 1974; Lee Myers, "Mangus Colorado," manuscript.

Mangum, John, Mormon pioneer (1814-May 1881). A convert to Mormonism, Mangum reached Utah in October 1852, with the Jacob Bigler company, and eventually settled in St. George, Utah. One of his three wives was a daughter of Jacob Hamblin, Indian specialist. Mangum took part in the Mountain Meadows Massacre of September 11, 1857. He was a marshal at Nephi, Utah, a high church official, farmer and stockraiser. He died in Arizona.

Juanita Brooks, *John D. Lee.* Glendale, Calif., Arthur H. Clark Co., 1962; Frank Esshom, *Pioneers and Prominent Men of Utah.* Salt Lake City, Western Epics, 1966.

Mangus, Mimbres Apache leader (1846-Feb. 9, 1901). The son of Mangas Coloradas, Mangus was born in southwestern New Mexico with Seth-mooda a full brother, and

his full sister the wife of Cochise and the mother of chiefs Taza and Nachez (Naiche) of the Central Chiricahuas. After the death of his father in 1863, Mangus followed Victorio and Loco for a time but with the remnants of the Mimbres Apaches gradually melded into the Central and Southern Chiricahuas. Here Mangus became associated more or less closely with Geronimo. He came in to San Carlos after Crook's 1883 expedition into the Sierra Madre, and was a leader with Geronimo in the bolt of some of the Chiricahuas in May 1885, although the extent to which he is to blame for the outbreak is uncertain. In any event, he shortly separated from the Geronimo faction and remained in the deep Sierra Madre, committing few if any depredations; he had but one or two warriors with him, and their families. Geronimo surrendered in early September 1886, and Mangus and his party were enroute north in October to surrender at Fort Apache when they were intercepted by Captain Charles L. Cooper, 10th Cavalry, and shipped to Florida with the Chiricahuas. From Florida the Apaches were sent to Alabama, and eventually to Fort Sill, Oklahoma. Mangus married Dilth-cley-ih, a daughter of Victorio, and had one son and four daughters. At Mt. Vernon Barracks, Alabama, he enlisted in Company I, 12th Infantry. At Fort Sill Mangus and his son, Frank, served in Troop L, 7th Cavalry; in 1897 Hugh Scott enlisted him as a scout, and he held that position until his death.

Griswold; Dan L. Thrapp, *Conquest of Apacheria.* Norman, Univ. of Okla. Press, 1967.

Manly, William Lewis, emigrant, pioneer (Apr. 6, 1820-Feb. 5, 1903). B. at St. Albans, Vermont, he is best known for his book, *Death Valley in '49,* which is regarded as a pioneering classic, although he may not have written it entirely. Enroute for California with John Rogers, the two attempted to float down the Green River, were wrecked, rescued by the Ute, Walkara, and dispatched to Salt Lake City where they met the Asabel Bennett family, also emigrants, and decided to accompany them westward. Captain Jefferson Hunt was guide. Hunt and some followers split off, but the Bennett party went southwest, finding themselves in Death Valley just before Christmas, trapped by the soaring Panamint Range. Camped at Tule Spring or the Eagle Borax Works site, Manly and Rogers left the Bennetts and went for help, reaching present Castaic Junction. They secured animals and in an arduous journey regained the camp whose people were in desperate straits, and brought out the emigrants. Manly's acount appeared in preliminary form in the *San Jose Pioneer* and in magazines, his book was published in 1894 in San Jose, and has appeared in various editions. A prospector at times, Manly died at San Jose, California, and was buried at Woodbridge. It was learned by ranger-naturalist Bernarr Bates of Death Valley that a man named Munn had helped Manly with his manuscript, but Munn's identity has not been established.

L. Burr Belden, "Manly of Death Valley." *Westways,* Vol. 56, No. 11 (Nov. 1964), 27-28; Lawrence Clark Powell, "William Lewis Manly's Death Valley in '49." *Westways,* Vol. 61, No. 11 (Nov. 1969), 30-33, 52.

Mann, James Defrees, army officer (May 15, 1854-Jan. 15, 1891). B. at Syracuse, Indiana, he was graduated from West Point in 1877, assigned to the 7th Cavalry and promoted to first lieutenant in July 1890. Assigned to K Troop under Captain George D. Wallace, he took part in the action against the Sioux at Wounded Knee Creek, South Dakota, December 29, 1890. Wallace was killed. Mann was wounded mortally December 30 in an action at the Drexel Mission, four miles from Pine Ridge Agency. He was taken to Fort Riley, Kansas, where he died.

U.S. Milit. Acad. at West Point, *Annual Reunion of the Association of Graduates, June 12, 1891;* Robert M. Utley, *Last Days of the Sioux Nation.* New Haven, Yale Univ. Press, 1963.

Manning, Frank, frontiersman (c. 1846-Nov. 14, 1925). B. probably at Mobile, Alabama, he with his brothers George (Doc) and James reached Belton, Texas, after the Civil War, and then moved on to El Paso, Texas. As the Southern Pacific railroad built toward the city from the west, Frank ran a floating saloon at the railhead keeping pace with it, and after it reached El Paso he opened the Manning Saloon. February 14, 1882, his brother James killed Doc Cummings; Frank's role in the incident is obscure. Stoudenmire believed the Mannings responsible for several assassination attempts against him; he was killed by

Doc and James Manning. Frank Manning on April 18, 1883, succeeded James B. Gillett as El Paso city marshal, but was dismissed and shortly left El Paso. He prospected in Arizona for some years. As he aged he became increasingly erratic, was committed to the Arizona State Hospital in 1922, and died there. He never married.

Leon Claire Metz, *The Shooters.* El Paso, Mangan Books, 1976.

Manning, George F. (Doc), physician (Oct. 27, 1837-Mar. 9, 1925). B. probably at Mobile, Alabama, he was graduated from the medical department of the University of Alabama and served the Confederacy as an artillery officer. After the Civil War he went with a brother to Old Mexico, returned to Alabama then he and his brothers, James and Frank, settled near Belton, Texas, where George married. By about 1880 he was at El Paso where his brothers entered the saloon and related businesses. The Mannings came into a feuding relationship with city marshal Dallas Stoudenmire who suspected them of instigating several assassination attempts against him. A peace was sought by the principals and others, Stoudenmire by now a deputy U.S. marshal. On September 18, 1882, Doc and Stoudenmire became involved in a gunfight, Doc's shot smashing the other's left arm, Stoudenmire shooting Doc in the gun arm in turn. The little doctor grappled with the big marshal to keep from being killed, and his brother James fatally shot Stoudenmire. Both Mannings were acquitted of murder. George Manning moved to Flagstaff, Arizona, where he served for many years as a respected physician, although his injured arm remained virtually useless to him. He died at Flagstaff. Manning played the violin, was a small man "possessing a temper a sharp as his scalpel," and was generally well thought of, according to Metz.

Leon Claire Metz, *The Shooters.* El Paso, Mangan Books, 1976.

Manning, James, frontiersman (c. 1839-May 27, 1915). James, with his brothers George (Doc) and Frank, was probably b. at Mobile, Alabama. The Mannings reached Belton, Texas, after the Civil War, moving on to El Paso, Texas, where Frank operated a saloon and the three became prominent in the boisterous town. James married the attractive

Leonor Isabelle Arzate of Juarez, helped finance the El Paso *Times,* opened the Coliseum Saloon and Variety Theatre, and once ran for mayor, but lost. The Mannings early came into a feuding relationship with Dallas Stoudenmire, town marshal and later U.S. deputy marshal. On February 14, 1882, after considerable goading, Jim killed Doc Cummings, a Stoudenmire crony. Stoudenmire accused the Mannings of trying to engineer his assassination, finally on September 18, 1882, fought Doc Manning, a small, slight man, each being wounded. Jim Manning then finished Stoudenmire off. He was acquitted of murder. James shortly left El Paso with his wife, remaining for a time in Arizona, then moved on to Washington State. He died at Los Angeles, California, of the effects of an old bullet wound and of cancer and is buried in Forest Lawn Memorial-Park. Before his death Stuart Lake suggested writing his biography; Manning demurred, and suggested Lake see Wyatt Earp. Earp became famous as a result, Manning remaining obscure.

Leon Claire Metz, *The Shooters.* El Paso, Mangan Books, 1976.

Manning, William Cheney, army officer (Sept. 19, 1842-May 5, 1901). B. in New York he enlisted from Maine in the 1st Massachusetts Infantry May 22, 1861, and rose to sergeant major by 1863 when he was commissioned a first lieutenant in the 35th U.S. Infantry, emerging from the Civil War a major in the 103rd Infantry. He joined the 23rd Infantry September 21, 1866, as a second lieutenant, becoming a first lieutenant February 7, 1867. Manning served in the Department of California in 1866-67, the Department of Columbia 1867-72 and the Department of Arizona in 1872-73, taking part in Crook's offensive and winning a brevet for his part in an action against Apaches December 13, 1872, in the Mazatzal Mountains of Arizona; 11 Indians were killed. The rest of Manning's professional career had little frontier interest. He retired with rank of major March 2, 1899.

Heitman; Powell.

Mansker (Mansco), Kaspar, long hunter (1749-1822). B. on shipboard of German immigrants, he was raised near the south fork of the Potomac River and by 20 joined a large party of long hunters bound for the trans-Allegheny where, in Roosevelt's words he became "a wonderful marksman and woodsman (and a) famous Indian fighter." The group spent more than a year in the Cumberland country of today's Tennessee. There is a possibility that Mansker, with Isaac Bledsoe and a few others had penetrated Tennessee in 1768 and one report placed him on the middle Cumberland in 1762, but since he then was 13 this is unlikely. The great hunting party of 1769 split once in the wilderness. With Bledsoe, Uriah Stone, Joseph Drake and Henry Scaggs, Mansker penetrated southern Kentucky, and he and Bledsoe later reached Bledsoe's Creek in present Sumner County, Tennessee, eventually gaining the mouth of the Cumberland. Mansker went west alone to Mansker's Creek, then retraced his steps, killing 19 deer before rejoining Bledsoe. Late in 1769 most of the larger party went home, but Mansker and others stayed on, killed bear and buffalo for hides and meat, made five bull boats and floated down the Cumberland until they met French traders with whom they dealt their peltries for salt, tobacco, flour and taffia, or rum. Eventually they reached Natchez on the lower Mississippi. Kaspar met a trader with a drove of horses, helped him drive them to Georgia and returned to his home on New River. Mansker knew Daniel Boone and most of the other famous long hunters. For 25 years he was a wilderness rover, in countless Indian fights, was wounded several times but through superb woodsmanship survived all, his fame ever expanding. He spoke with a heavy German accent, and was sometimes called "the Dutchman"; eventually he became a colonel of frontier militia. He settled at length at Mansker's station, a dozen miles north of present Nashville, and died at 73.

Harriette Simpson Arnow, *Seedtime on the Cumberland.* N.Y., Macmillan Co., 1960; Theodore Roosevelt, *The Winning of the West.* N.Y., G.P. Putnam's Sons, 1900, I, 188-95.

Manson, Donald, fur trader (1798-Mar. 1880). B. at Thurso, Scotland, he reached Canada by 1817, learning the fur trade at Canadian posts and in 1825 becoming clerk to the Hudson's Bay Company's John McLoughlin at Fort Vancouver. In 1834 he opened a fort on Milbank Sound among the Bella Bella Indians, remaining five years, then being promoted to chief trader he held positions of responsibility. He retired in 1857 to French Prairie, Oregon, on the Willamette River. He is buried at the Champoeg Cemetery.

Harriet D. Munnick article, MM, Vol. VII; Thwaites, EWT, XXIX, 284n.

Manuelito, Navaho chief (c. 1819-1893). B. near Bear's Ears, southeastern Utah, he was said to be a son of Cayetano and in his maturity about 6 feet, 6 inches, in height, of powerful frame and became one of the great war leaders of his nation. Later he became a son-in-law of Miguelito, another important man. A member of the Bit'ahnii (Folded arms People) clan, in 1835 he took part in the defeat of Mexican and Pueblo forces under Captain Blas de Hinojos at Washington Pass, northwestern New Mexico. Manuelito signed a November 1846 treaty with Doniphan, a pact which failed of its purpose. Manuelito took a prominent part in the July 1855 conference with Governor David Meriwether at Laguna Negra, asserting he was now chief spokesman for the Navahos. For the first time the July 17 pact mentioned restricting the Navaho to reservation-like boundaries. At an 1856 council with Henry Dodge and Major Henry Lane Kendrick, Manuelito seemed more adamant, said the Navahos had always raided Mexicans and would continue and complained bitterly about land cessions to Meriwether. Manuelito's rancheria was 20 miles from Fort Defiance and in 1858 he came into dispute with the post commander, brevet Major William T.H. Brooks over haying prairies, both Indians and whites claiming the same acreage. Manuelito sought to return symbols of his office given to him by Meriwether on the ground they no longer were respected by New Mexicans, Pueblos or even Navahos, but Brooks curtly refused to accept them. A confrontation in May 1858 between Manuelito and Brooks led to several years of Navaho-white hostility ended only with removal of much of the tribe to Bosque Redondo on the Pecos River. A slight skirmish between troops and Manuelito's people led to the slaughter of some Navaho livestock and recognition by Brooks of Zarcillos Largos as new head chief of the Navahos. Late in 1858 troops attacked rancherias they believed Manuelito's, but with scant results. In 1860 Manuelito was reported

to have taken part in several actions near Fort Defiance and in the direct attack on the post by about 1,000 Navahos on April 30; they were driven off with three white casualties, one mortal, and about 12 Navahos killed. The action was a rare occasion when Indians attacked a western military post. February 16, 1861, Manuelito was among 24 headmen signing a peace treaty with Canby, but it was never ratified. In 1863 many Navahos were removed to Bosque Redondo, but Manuelito refused to go, continuing to roam his accustomed country and proving an irritant to Carleton who feared this would lure young Navahos from the hated new reservation back to the old free life. However in the fall of 1866 Manuelito and around 50 of his followers surrendered at Fort Wingate and were shipped to the Bosque. Manuelito proved cooperative with his captors for the limited time the Bosque experiment continued. It was dissolved late in 1868, and the Navahos returned to their own country. Thereafter they applied themselves to peaceful pursuits. Manuelito was head chief from 1870 to 1884 and in 1872 he was given command of the native police force. In 1876 he visited President Grant at Washington, D.C. He died on the reservation.

Hodge, HAI; Frank McNitt, *Navajo Wars.* Albuquerque, Univ. of New Mex. Press, 1972; Gerald Thompson, *The Army and the Navajo.* Tucson, Univ. of Ariz. Press, 1976; Dockstader.

Marcelo, Mimbres Apache chief (d. Apr..22, 1837). Marcelo was one of the Mimbres Apaches killed in the John Johnson massacre of Juan José Compá and a score of his people near the southern end of the Animas Mountains in present New Mexico.

Rex W. Strickland, "The Birth and Death of a Legend: The Johnson 'Massacre' of 1837." *Ariz. and the West,* Vol. 18, No. 3 (Autumn 1976), 257-86.

Marcos de Niza, Franciscan missionary (c. 1495-Mar. 25, 1558). Probably b. at Nice, Savoy, of French parentage, he became a Franciscan friar about 1531 and went to New Spain, possibly Santo Domingo. In January 1534 he went to Peru with Pedro de Alvarado. Atahualpa had been executed August 29, 1533, so Marco's later assertion that he had witnessed the slaying was not true unless he had made an earlier trip to Peru, which is not impossible. Whether Marcos returned with

Alvarado late in 1534 is uncertain, but September 25, 1536, he appeared as witness at Santiago, Guatemala, regarding Alvarado's Peru expedition. Shortly afterward he went to Mexico where he was by April 1537, at least. In September 1538 he was commissioned by Viceroy Antonio de Mendoza to attempt to seek out and report the facts on the rumored great cities of Cibola, word of which had come to Mendoza from Cabeza de Vaca and his companions who, however, had never seen the sites themselves. He left Culiacán, Sinaloa March 7, 1539, with Estevánico, the black slave as guide, who had made the transcontinental peregrination with Cabeza de Vaca and two other whites. Estevánico went ahead some leagues, and Marcos followed after. The black approached the first of the Cibola cities, the pueblo of Háwikuh on the Arizona line southwest of Zuñi, New Mexico, and was killed. Word of his assassination reached Marcos who to pacify his Indian companions divided the trade goods with them, saved only the religious articles, and hastened back to Mexico never having seen Cibola nor any of the "fabulous" cities to the north, nor having come within 200 miles of them. His reports, exaggerated in part perhaps by himself but more by editorial additions and interpretations of others, encouraged the Coronado expedition which greatly added to geographical knowledge beyond Spain's northern frontiers. The date of his return to Culiacán is not known but probably it occurred by June 15, in which case he reached Compostela around July 1. Marcos apparently was elected Provincial of the Franciscan order in Mexico, an event which Wagner found "extraordinary" unless it was through pressure from Mendoza. In any event, the friar went north again and left Culiacán April 22, 1540, with Coronado and the advance company of horsemen bound for Cibola. Coronado captured Háwikuh July 7 (although Marcos was not present) and August 3 Marcos, with Melchior Diaz and Juan Gallego left Cibola for Mexico once more, the friar somewhat discredited although his own report had differentiated between what he himself had seen and what he had been told by others, and the passionate interest in Cibola as a land of abundant gold stemmed less from what he had actually said than the fervid imaginations of those who had embroidered his report. Marcos took part in the 1541 Mixton War against rebellious natives of Nueva Galicia, west of Mexico City, counseling severest measures against the insurgents. Partially paralyzed he retired to Jalapa where was living in 1554 in the direst poverty, having to beg of his old friend, Archbishop Juan de Zamarraga a monthly dole of wine for his "lack of blood and natural heat." Thinking that his hour of death was near, Marcos retired to a monastery at Xochimilco, near Mexico City, where he died.

Henry R. Wagner, "Fr. Marcos de Niza." *New Mex. Hist. Rev.,* Vol. IX, No. 2 (Apr. 1934), 184-227; George Parker Winship, *The Coronado Expedition, 1540-1542.* BAE, 14th Ann. Rept., Wash., Govt. Printing Office, 1896; A. Grove Day, *Coronado's Quest.* Berkeley, Univ. of Calif. Press, 1964; Herbert Eugene Bolton, *Coronado: Knight of Pueblos and Plains.* Albuquerque, Univ. of New Mex. Press, 1964.

Marcy, Randolph Barnes, army officer (Apr. 9, 1812-Nov. 22, 1887). B. at Greenwich, Massachusetts, he was graduated from West Point and commissioned a brevet second lieutenant of the 5th Infantry July 1, 1832, becoming a second lieutenant November 25, 1835. He missed the 1832 Black Hawk War in the Middle West because of illness but married and was stationed four years at Fort Howard, Wisconsin. He became a first lieutenant June 22, 1837, and was stationed at Fort Winnebago, also in Wisconsin, remaining there until 1840 when he was assigned to recruiting duty in the east. Later he was stationed at Fort Gratiot, near Detroit until 1845. Marcy was posted to Texas at the start of the Mexican War and took part in the battles of Resaca de la Palma and Palo Alto, but ill health again caused his transfer east; he had become captain May 18, 1846. In late 1848 he took command of Fort Towson, Oklahoma, leaving early in 1849 for Fort Smith, assigned to escort some 2,000 emigrants to Santa Fe, they bound for California and the gold fields. It was the first of five major expeditions he would lead through the West on one of which in 1852 he traced the course of the Red River to its source, the first to do so. Marcy drafted "the first reasonably accurate" maps of the southwest and was instrumental in initiating a chain of forts from eastern Oklahoma to western Texas including Fort Sill, the site for which he selected in 1852 although the post was not established until 1869. The other posts for which he chose the sites were Fort Arbuckle, Oklahoma, and Forts Belknap and Chadbourne and Camp Cooper, Texas. Marcy participated in the 1857 Seminole War in Florida, then went to Utah Territory during the so-called Mormon War. He led a dramatic mid-winter march of 634 miles from Fort Bridger, Wyoming, southward to New Mexico in 1857-58 to secure relief supplies, although he could not return until the following June. Marcy became a major August 22, 1859, a colonel inspector general August 9, 1861, served as chief of staff to his son-in-law, George B. McClellan early in the Civil War, and ended the conflict a brevet Major General of Volunteers. He became Brigadier General and inspector general December 12, 1878, and retired January 2, 1881. Marcy was best known to the general public for his interesting and valuable books on plains travel: *Prairie Traveller* (1859), a handbook for the emigrant; *Thirty Years of Army Life on the Border* (1866), and *Border Reminiscences* (1872). The journals of two of his expeditions, both edited by Grant Foreman also have been published: *Marcy and the Gold Seekers,* dealing with the 1849 expedition, appeared in 1939, and *Adventures on Red River,* his 1854 expedition, was published in 1937. He also wrote articles on various subjects for popular magazines.

Heitman; Cullum; W. Eugene Hollon, *Beyond the Cross Timbers: The Travels of Randolph B. Marcy.* Norman, Univ. of Okla. Press, 1955.

Mares, José, soldier, explorer (fl. 1787-1788). A retired army corporal, Mares was sent by Governor Fernando de la Concha of New Mexico to straighten out the route between Santa Fe and San Antonio, Texas, which earlier had been traced by Pedro Vial. Mares took Vial's companion, Cristóbal de los Santos and Alejandro Martín, a Comanche interpreter, left Santa Fe July 31, 1787, and went east to the Taovaya villages, then southwest again before heading south to reach San Antonio October 8. He cut Vial's mileage between the two termini by more than 200 miles; on his return January 18 to April 17, 1788, by a still more direct route, he cut away another 200 miles, tracing the best course between the communities. On his return he had gone northwest to Palo Duro Canyon, then almost due west to Santa Fe, being guided by Comanches on this journey. His explor-

ations added considerably to geographical knowledge of the area.

Noel M. Loomis, Abraham P. Nasatir, *Pedro Vial and the Roads to Santa Fe.* Norman, Univ. of Okla. Press, 1967; Herbert Eugene Bolton, *Texas in the Middle Eighteenth Century.* Austin, Univ. of Tex. Press, 1916, 1970.

Marest, Joseph Jacques, Jesuit missionary (Mar. 19, 1653-Oct. 1725). B. at Laval, France, he became a Jesuit, reached Canada in 1688 and was sent at once to Michilimackinac. The next year he accompanied Nicolas Perrot to the country of the Nadouesioux, or Sioux Indians. After this expedition, on which Perrot claimed the upper Mississippi region for France, Marest returned to Michilimackinac where Cadillac was post commandant from 1694-97 and with whom Marest came into difficulties because of Cadillac's "brandy diplomacy" among the Indians, whom the priest thought debauched by the lavish use of liquor for trading purposes. Marest, who became superior of the Ottawa mission, the principal upper lakes mission, initially favored Cadillac's desire to build Detroit as the center for the fur trade and move the Indians to it, but after the post was established, about 1700, Marest came to oppose the idea when many Indians objected to removal. He and Cadillac engaged in a verbal feud that lasted until Cadillac was named governor of Louisiana in 1710. Marest had made a second expedition to the Sioux in 1702. He died at Montreal.

Thwaites, JR, LXV, 338n7, LXXI, 156; DCB, II.

Marest, Pierre Gabriel, Jesuit missionary (Oct. 14, 1662-Sept. 15, 1714). B. at Laval, France, he became a Jesuit and reached Canada in 1694 with an Iberville expedition to Hudson Bay of which he was chaplain. He wintered with the party at Hudson Bay, suffering somewhat from scurvy, remained in the arctic when the Iberville group returned to France in the summer and when Hudson's Bay Company ships recaptured the French positions was taken prisoner to England. He returned to Canada in 1697 and the next year was assigned to the Illinois mission, working with a confederacy of tribes that included the Kaskaskias, Peorias and others. He quickly learned the native tongues and in 1700 moved south with the Kaskaskias to the region of the Cahokia mission where they came into rivalry with the Seminary of Foreign Missions priests; forced to leave that station, the Kaskaskias and Marest moved to the site of the present community of Kaskaskia. In 1711 he set out for Michilimackinac where his brother, Joseph Jacques Marest was superior of the Ottawa mission, but met him at the mission on St. Joseph River in the present Michigan. They went on together to Michilimackinac where they remained two months, Gabriel Marest then returning to Kaskaskia. He died during an epidemic of unspecified nature. In 1727 his remains were reinterred in a new Kaskaskia church.

Thwaites, JR, LXV, 264n12, LXXI, 158; DCB, II.

Marguerie, Francois, interpreter (c. Oct. 10, 1612-May 23, 1648). B. at Rouen, Normandy, he reached Canada about 1627 and in time became interpreter for the Algonquins, remaining among the Indians during the 1629-33 occupation of Canada by the English. In February 1641, he and Thomas Godefroy de Normanville were captured by the Iroquois and carried off to their village, presumably in what became New York State; the two occupied their time in perfecting their knowledge of the Iroquois tongue. When the Iroquois organized an attack on Three Rivers in the following summer, the pair were taken along as a lure. Marguerie volunteered to negotiate for the town while Godefroy remained with the hostiles; however he dissuaded the governor from accepting the treacherous Iroquois proposals, then returned to the enemy as he had pledged. Subsequent negotiations resulted in the release of the two. Marguerie was drowned with Jean Amiot when his canoe overturned during a storm near Three Rivers; Godefroy was tortured to death by Iroquois within four years. Marguerie was famed for a fine physique, for courage and for having led a "blameless" life.

Thwaites, JR, X, 320-21n7; XXI, 21-45; DCB.

Marion, Joe, cowboy, buffalo handler (d. c. 1950). A top hand for Michel Pablo, Flathead Reservation rancher in Montana and a savior of the buffalo, Marion was instrumental in moving the 300 or more animals of the herd from Montana to Canada in 1907-12. Marion died at Missoula "in the winter of 1949-50 and many memories of this unique event died with him." His photograph accompanies the Kidder article.

John Kidder, "Montana Miracle: It Saved the Buffalo." *Mont. Mag.,* Vol. XV, No. 2 (Spring 1965), 63.

Marion, John Huguenot, editor (c. 1836-July 27, 1891). B. probably at New Orleans, he went to California in 1853 or 1854, and returned to St. Louis in 1856-57. He went back to California, leaving there October 6, 1863, for Prescott, Arizona, prospecting and exploring for several years. He purchased the *Miner,* in 1867, made it the voice of central Arizona, and became Prescott's best-known and most able newspaperman. He left the *Miner* in 1877, briefly published the *Arizonian* and the *Enterprise* and in 1882 established the *Morning Courier.* "He wielded his pen sometimes like a rapier, sometimes like a bludgeon. Right or wrong, he was never dull, and he was widely beloved and admired." He was anti-Indian, but recognized they had a right to exist, if they would only become civilized. Marion was a ranchman, in a minor way, and an incidental politician. He married Flora E. Banghart by whom he had three children, one named for George Crook. When she ran away with another man he divorced her and married Ida Jones, by whom another son was born. Marion died and was buried at Prescott. His death, wrote John Bourke, "comes like a crushing blow... He was one of God's noblemen." Marion was a man of humor, integrity, strong political passions and was a master of the vivid phrase. "His newspapers formed an inseparable part of the pioneer days of Arizona."

Estelle Lutrell, *Newspapers and Periodicals of Arizona 1859-1911.* Tucson, Univ. of Ariz. Press, 1949; J.H. Marion, *Notes of Travel Through the Territory of Arizona,* ed. by D.M. Powell. Tucson, 1965.

Marlow, Boone, desperado (1865-Jan. 24, 1889). Marlow and his four brothers, Charlie, George, Alf and Llewellen (Lep) were sons of a stockman and physician. The family lived variously in California, Missouri, Oklahoma, New Mexico, Old Mexico and Colorado, settling at length in the Navajo Mountains of Wilbarger County, Texas. In 1886 Boone, the youngest of the brothers, killed James Halstein (or Holdson); he was indicted by the county grand jury for murder. Boone was not present when his brothers were arrested on a warrant charging all five with rustling ponies from Indian Territory tribesmen, Boone being picked up later; all five were released on bond. When word of the murder indictment was received however, an attempt was made to rearrest Boone for that more serious crime; Boone Marlow shot and mortally wounded Sheriff Marion Wallace of Wilbarger County and escaped. His brothers were rearrested, two (Alf and Llewellyn) were killed January 19, 1889, by mob action in which the other two were wounded along with three other people killed and three more wounded (see Edwin W. Johnson biography). On January 28, 1889, Boone Marlow was brought dead from Indian Territory to Graham, Texas, by three white men, Martin Beavers, J.E. Direkson and G.E. Harboldt who claimed he was killed January 24 on Hell Creek, 20 miles east of Fort Sill, showing bullet holes in the body in evidence. It developed later however that they first had poisoned Boone while supplying him with food during his hiding out, then put bullets into his dead body. Instead of the $1,500 reward they each received a penitentiary term, according to Johnson. George and Charlie Marlow "lived to be old men," O'Neal reports.

Edward W. "Ted" Johnson, "Deputy Marshal Johnson Breaks a Long Silence." *True West*, Vol. 27, No. 3 (Jan.-Feb. 1980), 6-11, 48-54; O'Neal, *Gunfighters.*

Marquette, Jacques, Jesuit missionary-explorer (June 1, 1637-May 18, 1675). B. at Laon, France, he attended the Jesuit university at Reims, entered the Jesuit novitiate at Nancy in 1654 and was ordained in 1666 by Bishop Andre de Saussay at Toul. He had volunteered for the missions, was sent to Canada, and began study of Montagnais near Quebec, shortly removing to Three Rivers where he remained two years. He became proficient in six Indian languages. In 1668 he was settled among the Chippewa on Lake Superior, shortly undertaking work among refugee Hurons as well, and in 1672 was at St. Ignatius, which he founded on the straits of Mackinac. In 1673 he was directed to undertake a journey "toward the Pacific or Chinese Sea with French and Algonquin companions," and to spend the summer in explorations toward the west. He and Jolliet, with five men, left in mid-May, 1673, crossed the Lakes, went up Green Bay to its head and the Fox River, to the present site of Portage, Wisconsin, crossed to the Wisconsin River,

and descended it to the Mississippi at Prairie du Chien, arriving June 15. They descended the great river for 990 miles, past the Illinois, the muddy Missouri, the Ohio, probably to about the mouth of the Arkansas River. The explorers began their return in mid-July by way of the Chicago River to Lake Michigan (Jolliet later suggesting a canal to connect the two waterways). Marquette, ill with dysentery, remained at a mission near present De Pere, Wisconsin. The next summer he resumed his missionary work, but illness caused him to winter near the present Chicago. With the spring he went down the Illinois River, preaching on Holy Thursday to Indian listeners, but once more illness forced him to withdraw northward to near the present Ludington, Michigan, on the river since named for him. Here he landed, said Mass, requested the two voyageurs who accompanied him to leave him to his private devotions, and here he died. His remains two years later were removed to St. Ignace.

Literature abundant: Thwaites, EWT, XXVII, 41; Thwaites, JR, Vol. LIV, 85-235; Raphael N. Hamilton, *Marquette's Explorations: the Narratives Reexamined.* Madison, Univ. of Wisc. Press, 1970; the best brief article about Marquette and the controversy over his record as priest and explorer is in DCB, Vol. I, 490-93.

Marquis, Thomas Bailey, physician, historian (Dec. 19, 1869-Mar. 22, 1935). B. at Osceola, Missouri, he was graduated from the University Medical College at Kansas City and practiced medicine briefly at Anaconda, Ennis and Bozeman, Montana, where he and his wife established their home. In 1914 he passed the Montana State Bar examination, but never practiced law. During World War I he served overseas as a captain in the Medical Corps; upon his return he practiced medicine at Livingston, Whitehall and Alberton, Montana. About 1922 he served a few months as agency physician for the Northern Cheyennes; he learned sign language well so that he but rarely had to rely upon interpreters and spent the next decade interviewing and gathering material from Cheyennes, Crows and other Indians, as well as white survivors of the Custer fight of 1876. He wrote numerous magazine articles on this affair as well as six pamphlets: *Sketch Story of the Custer Battle; Rain-in-the-Face, Curley, the Crow; She Watched Custer's Last Battle;*

Which Indian Killed Custer? Custer Soldiers not Buried; Two Days After the Custer Battle; and *Sitting Bull, Gall, the Warrior.* He also wrote three books: *Wooden Leg: A Warrior Who Fought Custer* (1931); *Memoirs of a White Crow Indian* (Thomas H. Leforge), *as told to Thomas B. Marquis* (1928, 1974), and *Keep the Last Bullet for Yourself: The True Story of Custer's Last Stand* (1976), published posthumously. Marquis gave up his medical practice in 1931 settling at Hardin, Montana, where he opened a small museum filled with Custer memorabilia, much of it contributed by his Indian friends. He died of a heart attack, and is buried at the Custer Battlefield National Cemetery.

Biographical notes printed in most of the pamphlets cited; additional information in *Keep the Last Bullet for Yourself.* N.Y., Two Continents Pub. Group, 1976.

Marsh, Grant, steamboat captain (1834-Jan. 2, 1916). B. at Rochester, Pennsylvania, he became a cabin boy on a riverboat at 12. He reached St. Louis as a deckhand in 1852, and for a time worked on boats on the St. Louis-Omaha run; by 1858 he was a first mate on the *A.B. Chambers No. 2,* with Samuel Clemens (Mark Twain) as second mate. During the Civil War Marsh worked with craft in the Union fleet on the lower Mississippi until 1864 when he served one of the boats in Sully's fleet on the upper Missouri. With the war ended he worked as pilot and captain on the St. Louis-Fort Benton run. He moved to Yankton, South Dakota, in 1873 as a captain of a boat of the Sanford Coulson line, at intervals was an independent operator, and by the time of the Custer disaster was "the most popular steamboat captain on the upper Missouri" and was "always ready to take any chances when the services of his government demanded them." Marsh's *Far West* was leased to the army at $360 a day for the duration of the 1876 Sioux campaign; the 190-foot vessel with a passenger capacity of 30 drew only 20 inches of water when laden. Marsh took her to the mouth of the Big Horn River to ferry Gibbon's command across to the right bank; she then moved up the Big Horn as a support vessel and in "an amazing piece of maneuvering, Captain Grant Marsh took his steamer some miles upstream above the mouth of the Little Big Horn." The 7th Cavalry wounded

from the Custer fight reached the boat June 30, by July 3 Marsh had ferried them to the north bank of the Yellowstone, then sped downstream with the wounded and 54 hours and 710 miles later, with the ship draped in black and showing her flag at half-mast, he reached Bismarck at 11 p.m., July 5, with the stunning news of the Custer debacle. Marsh continued to work for the army on occasion; in 1881 with the *Eclipse,* he headed a flotilla of five boats ferrying about 1,500 newly-surrendered Sioux from Montana to the agencies in Dakota. He died at Bismarck, North Dakota.

Edgar I. Stewart, *Custer's Luck.* Norman, Univ. of Okla. Press, 1955; *Peter Thompson's Narrative of the Little Bighorn Campaign 1876,* ed. by Daniel O. Magnussen. Glendale, Calif., Arthur H. Clark Co., 1974; William E. Lass, *A History of Steamboating on the Upper Missouri.* Lincoln, Univ. of Nebr. Press, 1962; Joseph Mills Hanson, *Conquest of the Missouri.* Chicago, A.C. McClurg & Co., 1909; archives of the Mo. Hist. Soc., and State Hist. Soc. of No. Dak.

Marsh, John S., army officer (c. 1838-Aug. 18, 1862). B. in Canada, he and the family settled in Fillmore County, Minnesota, from which Marsh was commissioned a first lieutenant in the 1st Minnesota Infantry of 1861; his company was dismissed because the quota for volunteers was filled, and Marsh enlisted as a private in the 2nd Wisconsin Infantry, serving at Bull Run and in other engagements in Virginia. In 1862 his brother, Josiah F. Marsh, seven years John's senior, raised a company and John Marsh was commissioned a first lieutenant in it, shortly being promoted to captain of the 5th Minnesota. He became commander at Fort Ridgely on the Minnesota River in April 1862. That summer he was involved with Agent Thomas J. Galbraith in difficulties with the Sioux over annuities the Indians had expected but not received. August 18 Marsh heard that the Sioux had commenced hostilities near Redwood Ferry at the Redwood (or Lower) Sioux Agency about a dozen miles northwest of Ridgely. With 44 men of his garrison and interpreter Peter Quinn, Marsh hurried to the ferry where his force was ambushed, 24 being killed (among them Quinn), and five wounded. Marsh himself drowned in the river when attempting to swim across; one Indian was killed in the engagement. Marsh's body was recovered four weeks later and buried with others of his command at Fort Ridgely.

Minnesota in the Civil and Indian Wars, I. St. Paul, Minn., Pioneer Press Co., 1891; Louis H. Roddis, *The Indian Wars of Minnesota.* Cedar Rapids, Iowa, Torch Press, 1956; Isaac V.D. Heard, *History of the Sioux War.* Millwood, N.J., Kraus Reprint Co., 1975.

Marsh, Othniel Charles, paleontologist (Oct. 29, 1831-Mar. 18, 1899). B. at Lockport, New York, he was graduated from Yale in 1860, studied three years in Germany and in 1866 was given the chair of paleontology at Yale, which he held for the balance of his life. Soon after his appointment he went west in pursuance of his intense interest in vertebrate fossil remains, searching out deposits on the Plains while much of the region still was coursed by hostile Indians. His first formal expedition in 1870 explored the Pliocene deposits of Nebraska, the Miocene of northern Colorado, studied the Bridger Basin of Wyoming, the Uinta Basin of Utah and proceeded to California. On this trip and others he became acquainted with Cody, Omohundro and other Plains personalities. Until 1880 he financed his several expeditions himself but in 1882 he was appointed vertebrate paleontologist to the U.S. Geological Survey, remaining associated with it until his death, and this relieved him of the burden of financing his own explorations, although his inherited means provided for his needs and tastes throughout his life. He published widely, his most comprehensive single paper being *Introduction and Succession of Vertebrate Life in America* (1877). Marsh was "the first to describe the remains of fossil serpents and flying reptiles" in western America, and to him goes credit for systematizing the vertebrate record of ancient American life. He was a sizable man of robust health who never married, his tastes were wide, and he received many honors. He died of pneumonia.

Literature abundant; DAB; Don Russell, *The Lives and Legends of Buffalo Bill.* Norman, Univ. of Okla. Press, 1960.

Marshall, James Wilson, prospector (Oct. 8, 1810-Aug. 10, 1885). B. at Hunterdon County, New Jersey, he was a carriage maker, wheelwright and carpenter by trade. He moved west, took up land near Fort Leavenworth and farmed it for a season or two and left May 1, 1844, for Oregon with a wagon train, wintering at Fort Hall. He reached the Willamette Valley. In 1845, guided by James Clyman, a party of which he was a member worked south, reaching Sutter's Fort (Sacramento) in July. Marshall quickly obtained a small ranch nearby but when the Bear Flag Revolt broke out in 1846 he joined it, ultimately becoming associated with Fremont's "battalion," mustered out at San Diego and making his way afoot back to Sutter's place. He was forced to sell his ranch to survive, then contracted with Sutter to construct a sawmill, in the course of which on January 24, 1848, he made the first important discovery of gold in California (see Ruelle and Gutierrez for earlier gold discoveries). By late spring the stampede was on. Sutter's place, the sawmill with it, was overrun by lawless rushers, and neither Marshall nor Sutter profited from the discovery, Marshall becoming bitter and "misanthropic, bringing to himself other misfortunes." For six years California paid him a pension, but this was discontinued in 1878 and he ended his life as a gardener near Coloma, his cabin being preserved in a state park.

DAB; Bancroft, *Pioneer Register.*

Marshall, Robert (Bob), wilderness proponent (Jan. 2, 1901-Nov. 11, 1939). B. at New York City he early was attracted to mountains and the outdoors. With his brother George, he climbed all 46 Adirondack peaks over 4,000 feet; one day in July 1932 he climbed 14 separate mountains for a total of about 13,600 feet. He was graduated from Syracuse University College of Forestry in 1924, earned a master's degree in 1925 from Harvard and a doctorate from Johns Hopkins University's Laboratory of Plant Physiology. Marshall joined the U.S. Forest Service in 1924 and from 1925-28 worked on silvicultural research at the Northern Rocky Mountain Forest Experiment Station, Missoula, Montana. In 1929 he made the first of four notable journeys to Alaska, exploring the Upper Koyukuk region of the central Brooks Range and its Arctic slope. That year he wrote the initial major article of the 96 he produced, "The Problem of Wilderness," appearing in 1930 in *Scientific Monthly,* and projecting Marshall to the forefront of American wilderness proponents. In 1930-31 he spent 15 months in the Brooks Range, based at Wiseman. He explored unmapped country, became interested in Eskimo culture and developed a conviction that Arctic Alaska should be preserved forever wild for the benefit of Alaskans and all Americans. Upon his return he collaborated with the Forest Service on *A National Plan for American Forestry*, writing important segments of it. In 1933 Marshall published two books: *Arctic Village*, which had a wide circulation, and *The People's Forests*, stressing the urgency for conservation of America's resources, as well as the need for wilderness preservation. He was appointed in 1934 director of forestry for the Office of Indian Affairs at Washington, D. C., and in 1937 became chief of the new Forest Service Division of Recreation and Lands, a position he held until his death. His legacy included the Wilderness Society, organized January 21, 1935, in large part through his inspiration and dominant voice. Besides Marshall, founders included Benton MacKaye, Bernard Frank, Harvey Broome, Harold C. Anderson, Aldo Leopold (see entry), Ernest Oberholtzer and Robert Sterling Yard, with Marshall providing funds to help it through its formative years. He died at 38 of a heart attack on a train between Washington and New York. Marshall was considered the "most effective militant conservationist of his generation," and was described as "an unwearied, unsentimental, common-sense radical who never supported any movement without participating in it wholeheartedly and responsibly." He also was interested and active in civil rights causes, which brought him at times under scrutiny from right wing groups. His *Arctic Wilderness*, edited by George Marshall from his papers and notes, appeared in 1956; a new edition in 1970 carried a Foreword by A. Starker Leopold, a son of Aldo Leopold. The huge Bob Marshall Wilderness Area of Montana was named for Robert Marshall.

George Marshall, "On Bob Marshall's Landmark Article: The Problem of Wilderness," *Living Wilderness,* Vol. 40, No. 135 (Oct.-Dec., 1976), 28-35; Robert Marshal, "Exploring the Brooks Range," *Living Wilderness,* Vol. 43, No. 145 (June 1979), 4-41; Paul Brooks, "The Wilderness Ideal: How Aldo Leopold and Robert Marshall Articulated the Need for Preservation," *Living Wilderness,* Vol. 44, No. 150 (Sept. 1980), 4-12; Stephen Fox, "We Want No Straddlers," *Wilderness,* Vol. 48, No. 167 (Winter 1984), 5-19; *New York Times,* Nov. 12, 1939.

Marshall, William, adventurer (d.c. Dec. 15, 1851). B. probably in New Hampshire, he reached California from Providence, Rhode Island, in 1845 aboard the whaler *Hopewell,* deserted at San Diego and made his way into the interior, becoming a foreman at Warner's Ranch and storekeeper there and marrying an Indian woman. In December 1846 he entertained Stephen Watts Kearny's dragoons, showing them "every attention." Marshall reportedly assisted Pegleg Smith in 1850 when the latter tried to relocate the gold deposit he had reported discovering in 1829 on the desert east of Warner Springs; the expedition was unsuccessful. Marshall was suspected of instigating the Pauma Indian uprising under Antonio Garra; nine whites were killed in the event. Marshall and Juan Verdugo were court-martialed and hanged. Several Indians including Garra subsequently were executed.

Bancroft, *California,* IV, 731; V, 567-68; Joseph J. Hill, *History of Warner's Ranch and Its Environs.* Los Angeles, p.p., 1927, 116, 121, 126, 140-41; Philip A. Bailey, *Golden Mirages.* N.Y., Macmillan Co., 1940.

Marshall, William Louis, army officer, engineer (June 11, 1846-July 2, 1920). B. at Washington, Kentucky, he enlisted in the 10th Kentucky Cavalry in 1862, dropping out for health reasons in 1863 but being sent to West Point in 1864. He was commissioned a brevet second lieutenant in the Corps of Engineers in 1868, became a second lieutenant the following year and a first lieutenant in 1871. From 1872 until 1876 Marshall served with the George M. Wheeler surveys in the central Rockies. He commanded one element of the Survey in Colorado and in late November 1873 because of a severe toothache while at the raw mining camp of Silverton, southwestern Colorado, determined to go to Denver, 300 miles distant for treatment despite the rugged nature of the intervening country, deep snows and wintry weather. With Packer Dave Mears he set out and enroute discovered what today is famed as Marshall Pass over the main Rockies, use of which cut off 125 miles from the trip between Denver and the San Juan area. It now is traversed by the Denver and Rio Grande Railroad. In 1875 Marshall discovered gold placers in the Marshall Basin along the San Miguel River. He later served on river surveys, inland waterways and harbor improvement projects, useful enough but with

little frontier interest. In 1908 he was named
Chief of Engineers as a Brigadier General and
retired two years later. He was married,
fathered a daughter and died at Washington,
D.C.

Heitman; Cullum; *Who Was Who;* DAB;
Richard A. Bartlett, *Great Surveys of the American
West.* Norman, Univ. of Okla. Press, 1962.

Marshall, William Rainey, army officer (Oct.
17, 1825-Jan. 8, 1896). B. in Boone County,
Missouri, he became a surveyor of government lands in Wisconsin in 1847 and the next
year was elected to the Wisconsin Legislature.
In 1849 he moved to Minneapolis, Minnesota,
where he established a store and that year
became a member of the first Minnesota
Legislature. Marshall founded the St. Paul
Daily Press (now the *Pioneer Press)* in 1861.
When the Sioux under Little Crow launched
their devastating assault down the Minnesota
River valley in 1862 Marshall was commissioned lieutenant colonel of the 7th Minnesota
Infantry, organized at Fort Snelling. He took
command of five companies moving to report
to Sibley. Marshall was very active in the
campaign. He marched to the relief of Captain
Hiram P. Grant at Birch Coulee, lifting the
siege against Grant's battered command, then
routed the savages at Wood Lake, another
famous engagement of that war. In 1863 he
commanded the regiment in an expedition to
Devil's Lake and thence to the upper
Missouri River and in the battle of Big
Mound he "took the most prominent part in
driving and pursuing the enemy." Marshall
became colonel in 1863. He served largely in
the Mississippi Valley during the Civil War,
taking part in the battles of Tupelo and
Nashville and in the siege of Spanish Fort,
Alabama. He was breveted Brigadier General.
Marshall was elected governor of Minnesota
in 1865 and re-elected two years later; his later
life in finance and business was creditable but
with little frontier interest. He was married to
Abbey Langford, sister of Nathaniel Pitt
Langford March 22, 1854. They had one son.
Marshall died at Pasadena, California.

Who Was Who; NCAB, Vol. X, 64; William H.C.
Folsom, *Fifty Years in the Northwest.* St. Paul,
Minn., Pioneer Press Co., 1888; *Minnesota in the
Civil War and Indian War, 1861-65,* 2 vols. St.
Paul, Pioneer Press, Co., 1891, 1899.

Marshland, Stephen, desperado (d. Jan. 16,
1864). A college graduate from the East, he
was probably 22 or 23 at his execution by
vigilantes whom he begged to spare him
"because of his youth." But he was a member
of the notorious Henry Plummer band of
desperados in southwestern Montana although he is not known to have killed anyone
and seemed averse to murder. He was
described by Red Yager as a "roadster," or
holdup man. In the fall of 1863 he was
wounded through the chest in an attempt to
rob a Milton S. Moody/Melanchthon Forbes
train of wagons and pack animals bound from
Bannack to Salt Lake City. Marshland got
away but badly froze both feet while wandering in the mountains and when accosted by
vigilantes at an isolated ranchhouse suffered
from chills and probably gangrene. The
evidence against him was confirmed by his
still-visible wound, and he was hanged at
Clarke's Ranch in the Big Hole Valley of
Montana. His body had to be guarded all
night for the scent from his rotting feet
attracted wolves; it was buried in the early
light.

Langford; Dimsdale; Birney.

Martin, Agustin (Augustus?), frontiersman
(fl. 1837). Martin was one of 18 whites who
treacherously attacked the Mimbres Apache
leader, Juan José Compá, in the Animas
Mountains of present day New Mexico on
April 22, 1837, slaying 20 and igniting
extended Apache-white hostility. Bancroft
lists an Augustus Martin who in 1847 he cites
as "a witness at Los Angeles," California.

Rex W. Strickland, "The Birth and Death of a
Legend: The Johnson 'Massacre' of 1837." *Arizona and the West,* Vol. 18, No. 3 (Autumn 1976),
257-86; Bancroft, *Pioneer Register.*

Martin, Albert, adventurer (c. 1806-Mar. 6,
1836). B. in Tennessee, he resided at Gonzales,
Texas, and was at the Alamo at San Antonio
early in the Mexican siege. He was sent to get
reinforcements, returning March 1 as captain
of 32 men from Gonzales; all perished at the
Alamo.

Amelia Williams, XXXVII, 270.

Martin, Charles, desperado, (d. Mar. 20,
1868). B. probably at Lexington, Missouri, he
appears to have grown up with desperado
inclinations, filled before he reached Cheyenne, Wyoming, in the summer of 1867,

formed a partnership with Andy Harris in a dancehall operation, killed Harris, was acquitted by a trial jury and was hanged by vigilantes forthwith.

James Chisholm, *South Pass, 1868; James Chisholm's Journal of the Wyoming Gold Rush,* and cited literature. Lincoln, Univ. of Nebr. Press, 1960.

Martin, Douglas D., newsman, writer (Sept. 9, 1885-Sept. 26, 1963). B. at Benton Harbor, Michigan. He was a newsman, working for the *State Journal,* Lansing; *Detroit News; Detroit Free Press,* where he became managing editor; and briefly, the *Tombstone Epitaph* in Arizona. In addition to his two volume, *An Arizona Chronology,* he wrote *Tombstone's Epitaph, Yuma Crossing, The Earps of Tombstone, Silver, Sin and Sixguns,* and *The Lamp in the Desert,* a history of the University of Arizona where he headed the journalism department until his retirement in 1956.

Arizona Daily Star, Tucson, Sept. 27, 1963.

Martin, Emanuel (Old Manuel, the Spaniard), guide (d.c.1873). A Mexican trapper he had trapped the Rockies from his own country to Montana. In the early 1850s he guided the first wagons to the Bitterroot Valley of western Montana, where he first was reported in 1851. He worked for John Owen of Fort Owen there for many years and died near that place.

George F. Weisel, *Men and Trade on the Northwest Frontier.* Missoula, Mont. State Univ. Press, 1955; *Montana, Contributions,* II (1896).

Martín, Hernán, explorer (fl. 1650). With Diego del Castillo, Captain Martín was sent in 1650 on an exploration journey eastward from Santa Fe. He reached the Nueces River of Texas in the waters of which pearls were found. The expedition continued 50 leagues down the Nueces to the country of the Tejas Indians then returned to New Mexico. The pearls were sent to the viceroy at Mexico City, who immediately ordered further exploration of north central Texas although no important wealth of pearls ever was found.

Bancroft, *North Mexican States and Texas,* I, 384; HT; Herbert Eugene Bolton, *Spanish Exploration in the Southwest, 1542-1706.* N.Y., Charles Scribner's Sons, 1916.

Martin, John William, army officer (Sept. 24,

1850-post 1891). B. in New York, he went to West Point in 1869, but left in 1871 without graduating, although he was appointed a second lieutenant in the 4th Cavalry in the summer of 1872 and made captain by 1884. He took part with Mackenzie in 1873 in the attack on Kickapoo and Lipan Indians in Old Mexico. He may have taken part in Mackenzie's raid on the Cheyennes in 1876. Martin was wounded in April 1882, in Forsyth's attack on Apaches in Horseshoe Canyon, New Mexico, during the Loco exodus from San Carlos to Mexico. Martin retired February 24, 1891.

Heitman; "Ranald S. Mackenzie's Official Correspondence Relating to Texas, 1871-1873," ed. by Ernest Wallace. *Museum Journal,* Vol. IX (1965), Lubbock, West Tex. Tech. Coll., 1967; Dan L. Thrapp, *Conquest of Apacheria.* Norman, Univ. of Okla. Press, 1967; Powell.

Martin, Pete (Pedro Martinez), hunter (fl. 1853-1864). A Mexican, he was hired as hunter by I.I. Stevens at Fort Union in September 1853. In 1859 he moved with his family from Fort Union to a settlement on the Little Blackfoot River, Montana, and resided in Deer Lodge County. His son, Dan Martin, 80 in 1940, was an interpreter at Fort Buford for many years.

Montana, Contributions, Vol. X, 1940, 296.

Martin, William A. (Hurricane Bill), desperado (fl. 1874-1881). B. probably in Texas, he turned up in Wichita, Kansas, in 1874 a gunman, dangerous but with wild humor and ready wit, born to be a character, which he was. He was jailed at Wichita for undefined offenses a time or two, and earned a reputation as a "happy-go-lucky frontier rollicker." Four years earlier he confessed he had shot a policeman somewhere, being wounded himself. He was charged by the army with stealing Indian horses. Bill may have visited the Black Hills about 1876. Later he showed up in Dodge City, Kansas, was released on $1,000 bail put up by Dog Kelley and John Selman, and disappeared, bound for Texas where he surfaced in Shackelford County, centering on Fort Griffin. He was arrested by rangers at Castroville, near San Antonio, returned to Griffin, tried on an assault to kill charge and released. He claimed he was forced to marry a prostitute, Hurricane Minnie, then was charged with living with one. By March 19 1879, he was a deputy sheriff at Otero, New Mexico, roping his prisoners like a cowboy, tying them to telegraph poles because the town lacked a jail. He was dismissed after three months "due to incompetency and drunkeness." He apparently settled in the San Simon cattle-raising region of eastern Arizona and western New Mexico. He disappears from western history about the time of the June 6, 1881, killing of Leonard and Head by the Hazlett brothers of Eureka (Hachita), New Mexico. Bartholomew suspected Bill might have been killed with Leonard instead of Head. Bill was 6 feet tall, 200 pounds, well proportioned, with a "fine address," light hair, blue eyes, well dressed, a rather "outgoing sharp face."

Ed Bartholomew, *Wyatt Earp: The Untold Story, Wyatt Earp: The Man & the Myth.* Toyahvale, Tex., Frontier Book Co., 1963, 1964.

Martinez, Estéban José, navigator (c. 1742-Oct. 28, 1798). Navigator or mate under Juan Perez (see entry) in the 1774 expedition to the Northwest Coast from San Blas, Mexico, Martinez became most famous for activities which largely launched the celebrated Nootka Sound controversy, beyond the scope of this work. He was a combative, fractious man whose activities nearly brought on war between Spain and Britain, with other countries perilously concerned. He died at Loreto on the western shore of the Gulf of California, at 56.

Bancroft, *Northwest Coast,* I; Warren L. Cook, *Flood Tide of Empire.* New Haven, Yale Univ. Press, 1973.

Mason, Edwin Cooley, army officer (May 31, 1831-Apr. 30, 1898). B. in Ohio he was commissioned a captain in the 2nd Ohio Infantry in 1861 and emerged from the Civil War after service with various organizations a brevet colonel and brevet Brigadier General of Volunteers. He was a captain of the 17th U.S. Infantry dating from 1861, transferred in 1866 to the 35th Infantry, to the 20th Infantry in 1869 and became major of the 21st Infantry September 5, 1871. In 1872 he was ordered from Fort Vancouver with two companies to Fort Klamath, Oregon, to counter Modoc hostility in northeastern California, left Washington December 3 and camped at Tule Lake, California by Christmas. His battalion was in the first Battle of the Stronghold

against the Modocs January 17, 1873, in which the troops suffered about 40 casualties. Mason apparently had been ear-marked for assassination in April when Canby was killed by Modocs, but was uninjured in his camp some miles east of the General's. Mason and his men also were engaged in the second stronghold battle of April 26 when troop casualties were greater than in the first action. Mason was in on the sweepup of the Modoc country after disintegration of the Indian fighting force (all had been captured by June 1, 1873), then returned to Fort Vancouver. Under Howard's overall command Mason was active in the Nez Perce campaign of 1877. On July 17 he was sent with cavalry, scouts and volunteers from Weippe, Idaho, up the Lolo Trail in pursuit of Chief Joseph's emigrating Indians, but after a light skirmish, hastily withdrew. For his actions in the Modoc lava fields and in Idaho Mason won a brevet to Brigadier General. He became lieutenant colonel of the 4th Infantry May 19, 1881, colonel of the 3rd Infantry April 24, 1888, and retired May 31, 1895.

Heitman; Keith A. Murray, *The Modocs and Their Wars.* Norman, Univ. of Okla. Press, 1965; McWhorter, *Hear Me.*

Mason, George Fawlkes, army officer (c. 1845-Mar. 1, 1870). B. in Washington, D.C., he was commissioned a second lieutenant in the 5th Cavalry from Michigan on August 19, 1867 and became a first lieutenant two years later. In August 1868 he was assigned to frontier duty in Kansas, participating in a number of engagements with hostile Indians, commanded a company during the Canadian River expedition, participated in the Republican River expedition and was distinguished for gallantry at the decisive battle against the Cheyennes at Summit Springs, July 11, 1869. He was shot by a clerk in the Quartermaster's Department at Fort D.A. Russell, Wyoming. Mason, grandson of Major General Alexander Macomb, "was a man of marked energy but very erratic, brave to a fault, and sacrificed his life in seeking redress for an affront which was beneath his notice."

Price, *Fifth Cavalry.*

Mason, John, Indian fighter (c. 1600-Jan. 30, 1672). B. in England, he early became a soldier and served under Thomas Fairfax in the Netherlands, where his ability and courage brought him to attention. He was very tall, of large physique, energetic, but not impulsive, stern, "moral, yet not religious." Before mid-1633 he had reached Massachusetts where he became militia captain of Dorchester and a founder of Windsor on the Connecticut River. It was "Puritan John Mason (who exemplified) the Puritan creed of extinction for the heathen," by means of the Pequod War. On May 20, 1637, Mason with 90 Englishmen and 70 Indian allies set out for Saybrook on the lower Connecticut, skirmishing with the hostiles enroute and after reaching the fort. May 29 the expedition went by sea to Narragansett, Rhode Island, secured permission to pass through the country of the Narragansett Indians on their punitive raid. With their Indian allies swollen to about 500, Mason's expedition set out overland, fording the Paucatuck River and on June 5, attacking the principal Pequod fort, or palisaded town, although most of his native allies had withdrawn in fear. The place was stormed, Mason personally slaying several Indians with his sword and finally firing the fort himself, his efforts assisted by his men, while the enemy, surrounded by flames, were mowed down by musket fire. Mason lost two killed, 20 wounded, took seven prisoners with perhaps as many escaping the holocaust, while between 600 and 700 of the natives perished to flame or arms. He withdrew to his ships, then marched back overland to Saybrook, skirmishing frequently with roving bands of hostiles who had missed the great massacre of their fellows. Although Mason was criticized severely for the barbarity of his fight, he "was a soldier, with a soldier's conscience, and once he had put his hand to the plow, with him there was no turning back.... Mason was rough, but of good mettle; a man of stern policies and unyielding in his determination." Besides, said Sylvester, while Mason's was "an act of great cruelty,... the Pequods had no right to ask for quarter," and of course they had no opportunity to do so; their cruelty perhaps matched that of the Puritans. At Fairfield Swamp the eradication of the Pequod people was virtually completed with Mason killing or capturing another 700 individuals, the remnants of the people fleeing to the Mohawks, being hunted down by the Mohegans or Narragansetts, a few finding refuge with the Niantics and some perhaps wandering as far south as Virginia and the

Carolinas. Mason wrote a history of the Pequod War, printed first as *A Relation of the Troubles that Have Hapned in New England* (1677) without attribution, and reprinted as *A Brief History of the Pequot War* (1736), with a sketch of Mason's life. He continued for 30 years after the conflict to devote himself to public affairs in Connecticut, being a deputy governor from 1660 to 1669, chief military officer and handling Indian relations for Connecticut and the New England Confederation. He was a founder of Norwich, Connecticut, in 1660. Mason married twice and fathered eight children.

Literature abundant: Sylvester; DAB; CE.

Mason, John Sanford, army officer (Aug. 21, 1824-Nov. 29, 1897). B. at Steubenville, Ohio, he went to West Point and was commissioned a second lieutenant in the 3rd Artillery July 1, 1847, becoming a first lieutenant September 7, 1850. He spent some months at Fort Yuma in 1854 and additional time in California that decade. Mason became a captain of the 11th Infantry May 14, 1861 and ended the Civil War a Brigadier General of Volunteers and brevet Brigadier General in the army. With a regular commission as a major, he transferred to the 35th Infantry September 21, 1866. Arizona was shifted from the Department of New Mexico to that of California February 4, 1865, and Mason was assigned on the 20th to command in Arizona. He reached Yuma May 14, 1865, with about 2,800 men at his direction in addition to four companies of Arizona volunteers of dubious value. Mason was active, intelligent, dedicated and in most respects able, but he had enormous difficulties to counter including a chronic lack of supplies, poor communications, the need to depend upon unreliable or volatile native auxiliaries, and subordinates undistinguished in performance of the exacting duties required of them. In June 1865 Mason visited Fort Bowie and shifted its location slightly. From Prescott on October 31, 1865, he issued his General Order 11 which stated that "All Apache Indians in this Territory are hostile, and all men large enough to bear arms who may be encountered will be slain wherever met, unless they give themselves up as prisoners," though no harm was to befall women and children. An offensive against hostile Indians set for November 25 accomplished very little. Mason was adjudged "even less successful than General Carleton has been," and he received much of the abuse Arizonans customarily meted out to military commanders whose effectiveness they did not appreciate. Yet acording to Farish, Mason's "plan was not much different from General Crook's who finally achieved success, but he lacked the means to carry it out." Bancroft concluded that while Mason "was not a very brilliant Indian fighter... it does not clearly appear how any officer could have done much better in his place." Mason was relieved from his command May 26, 1866. He transferred to the 15th Infantry March 15, 1869, became lieutenant colonel of the 14th Infantry December 11, 1873, transferred to the 20th Infantry February 25, 1881, and became colonel of the 9th Infantry April 2, 1883, retiring August 21, 1888. He died at Washington, D.C.

Heitman; Cullum; Farish, IV; Bancroft, *Arizona and New Mexico.*

Mason, Julius Wilmot, army officer (c. 1837-Dec. 19, 1882). B. in Pennsylvania he was graduated from Kentucky Military Institute, was an engineer until the Civil War when he was appointed a second lieutenant in the future 5th Cavalry. He fought at Bull Run, in the Peninsular campaign, at Antietam, Gettysburg, the engagements about Richmond and was in at Lee's surrender. He was sent to Fort D.A. Russell, Wyoming, in 1870, and reached Camp Hualpai, Arizona, in 1872, commanding at the important engagement against the hostiles at Muchos Cañones, September 25, 1872, for which he was commended by Crook. Mason participated in the Sioux campaign of 1876, the Big Horn and Yellowstone expeditions, and in the affair at Slim Buttes. He had transferred to the 3rd Cavalry but continued to serve with the 5th through the Sioux campaign, when he joined his proper organization, commanding at Forts Robinson, Fetterman and Washakie in Wyoming. He was transferred to Arizona in 1882, commanding troops in the field until the fall when he was named commandant of Fort Huachuca where he died of apoplexy. He was an able officer, frequently bringing his engineering training into use for army construction. He was plagued with illness during most of his later career.

Price, *Fifth Cavalry.*

Mason, Richard Barnes, army officer (Jan. 16, 1797-July 25, 1850). B. in Fairfax County, Virginia, he was the great grandson of George Mason (1725-1792), famed constitutional theorist. Richard Mason was commissioned September 2, 1817, a second lieutenant in the 8th Infantry, becoming a first lieutenant the 25th of that month and a captain July 31, 1819. He transferred to the 3rd and then the 1st Infantry in 1821. In 1824 Mason commanded a keel-boat on a Kearny-led Yellowstone expedition that by August 26, 1825, had reached 120 miles above the mouth of the Yellowstone River on the Missouri, returning to St. Louis that same season. He was stationed at Fort Crawford near Prairie du Chien, Wisconsin, and August 2, 1832, took part in the Battle of Bad Axe which terminated the Black Hawk War. Mason became major of the newly created 1st Dragoons March 4, 1833, at Fort Gibson, Indian Territory. In 1835 he held a memorable council with Comanche and Wichita Indians at Fort Mason, named for him, near the present Lexington, Oklahoma. In 1836 Mason succeeded Kearny in command of Fort Des Moines, Iowa, becoming a lieutenant colonel July 4; he was made colonel June 30, 1846. Mason did not accompany Kearny to California but took ship at New York for Panama, crossed the isthmus and boarded the *Erie* for San Francisco, arriving safely if quite ill. He succeeded Kearny as military governor of California May 31, 1847, and later became acting governor. It was a transition period and his term was troubled; during it occurred the discovery of gold at Sutter's Mill, his report of August 17, 1848, constituting the most authoritative account of that event, copied all over the world, published in many newspapers and appearing in thousands of pamphlets, doing much to generate the Gold Rush of 1849. Mason was breveted Brigadier General May 30, 1848. After relief from his California offices he returned to Jefferson Barracks, Missouri where he died. He was married and fathered two daughters.

Heitman; Dwight L. Clarke, *Stephen Watts Kearny: Soldier of the West.* Norman, Univ. of Okla. Press, 1961; Clarke, *Original Journals of Henry Smith Turner.* Norman, 1966; Thwaites, EWT, XX.

Massai, Mimbres Apache (c. 1847-1911). Massai, who became one of the most famed

Apaches by reason of a great exploit and his subsequent career, was b. in southeastern Arizona or southwestern New Mexico. He fathered several children at San Carlos, Arizona, where he and his people were taken from Warm Springs, New Mexico, in 1877. Whether he was married at the time of removal is not known, but his wife at San Carlos was Nah-go-tsi-eh, born it is said in 1850; she subsequently married Stephen Kyzha, and then Chino, and died on Christmas Day 1908. Massai did not join Victorio in the break-out from San Carlos in the fall of 1877, but remained with Loco and the balance of the Mimbres. Betzinez said he enlisted as a scout in 1880 during the Victorio hostilities and, if so, he may have served under Lieutenant James Maney and Chief of Scouts Henry K. Parker, among the most successful leaders of Apache scouts of the period. Betzinez, who knew Massai well, said that two years later, in 1882, Massai while being transported by train with other scouts learned that the Loco band of Mimbres had been herded out of San Carlos and were being convoyed to Old Mexico by the noted Juh and others. "Massai jumped from the train and, eluding capture in a country infested with troops who were following the runaways, headed south for the Sierra Madres." This incident is almost an exact parallel with his greatest exploit more than four years later. Betzinez added that Massai was always restless and became bored with life in the great mountains of Old Mexico, stole Betzinez's horse and made his way secretly back to San Carlos; perhaps his wife had remained there. He could not have been too enamored of life on the reservation either, for when Geronimo broke out for the last time in 1885 Massai went with him although his family remained. After several months he deserted the war party and returned to the reservation by himself. "Seeing him coming our Indians were thrown into fear and confusion, thinking that the hostiles were coming to drive us off the reservation as they had done in 1882," Betzinez recalled. "He calmed us by calling out that he was alone. Once more he was reunited with his family." He was enlisted as a scout in Company A, 2nd Battalion by Marion Maus at Fort Apache on November 7, 1885, his age listed as 38 and his occupation as a farmer. He was discharged May 6, 1886, a corporal because of expiration of his term of service. By late 1886 when the Chiricahua-Warm Springs or Mimbres were all rounded up, taken to Holbrook, Arizona, and placed on a train for Florida, Massai was with them. While awaiting transportation to Holbrook, Betzinez added, Massai "tried to stir us up to revolt," but finding no one to follow him, he subsided. On the train trip east, Massai managed to borrow a butcher knife, and as the train slowed in moving up a long grade short of St. Louis, he eased out a car window and escaped. His odyssey then commenced. Knowing very little English (although he could speak Spanish reasonably well), unable to read directional signs or to ask his way, with no money to buy food or other supplies, and traversing a country he had never seen before, like a wolf remaining unseen in thickly settled regions, he yet worked his way toward the southwest, eventually, perhaps as long as three months later, regaining his original homeland, the still remote and thinly settled Black Range in southern New Mexico. After he had lurked for some time in the mountains he made his way to the Mescalero Reservation, just east of the Rio Grande, and stole a young woman, Zan-a-go-li-che, taking her back to the Black Range where she became his wife, bearing him four children in all. For 25 years they lived thus. One day in 1911, about sunset, Massai and his eldest son chased a horse north of the former agency at Warm Springs; Massai went ahead and approached the horse when a shot was fired by some unseen assailant and he was struck. The boy told his mother that he didn't know whether his father had been killed or only wounded, but subsequently it is said his mother found some of his burned bones and a belt buckle identifiable as his by a dent caused by a bullet in years past and, realizing that he was dead the woman gathered her children and returned to the Mescalero Reservation; historical writer Eve Ball came into possession of the buckle, given to her by Massai's daughter, Alberta Begay. During his years of exile the existence of Massai somewhere in the mountains was known to the whites, and legends about him and his deeds multiplied although quite naturally proof was more often lacking than not. It was said he ran with the Apache Kid at times, and he may have done so. Massai was accused of assorted deviltry as far west as the San Carlos-Fort Apache reservations, where his distinctive track was reported seen on occasion by scouts and others. He was credited with scattered killings and thefts of food or stock, the waylaying of lone travelers on occasion, but it was a wild country and no one could be sure who was responsible for various deeds; the fact is that he survived. His enlistment record shows that in 1885 he was 5 feet, 8 inches in height, had black hair and eyes and was of "copper" complexion. It is interesting to note that Massai perished almost to the day that Ishi, the noted primitive Indian of California, was captured, but Ishi was a stone-age native in culture, while Massai was not. Yet each had perpetuated his wild free existence for many years within a region settled and supposedly thoroughly dominated by white populations. Massai too came to wide public attention by the publication of Paul Wellman's novel, *Broncho Apache* and the motion picture made from it, as well as by earlier writings of Frederic Remington, Nelson A. Miles and Betzinez. Although he appeared to many whites the paradigm of the Apache warrior, Betzinez made clear that his fellows "never considered him to be outstanding as a fighter. He was just an average Apache." Average or not, his record and his career were quite unique to most whites.

Griswold; Frederic Remington, "Massai's Crooked Trail." *Crooked Trails,* N.Y., Harper & Bros., 1899; Jason Betzinez, *I Fought With Geronimo.* Harrisburg, Pa., Stackpole Co., 1959; Alberta Begay, Eve Ball, "Massai — Broncho Apache." *True West,* Vol. 6, No. 6 (July-Aug. 1959), 6-9, 44-48; information from Allan Radbourne.

Massanet, Damian, missionary (fl. 1683-1694). Probably a Franciscan, he was one of 19 missionaries from Majorca, Spain, who founded the college of Santa Cruz de Querétaro, Mexico, in 1683. He conducted several missionary journeys into the north. Stationed at the mission of La Caldera in Coahuila, he questioned Jean Henrí, a survivor of La Salle's Fort St. Louis on Matagorda Bay, Texas. Massanet accompanied Alonso de León on a 1689 expedition to search for the ruins of the fort. They found two more survivors, Jean L'Archévèque and Jacques Grollet living with the Tejas Indians; Massenet promised to return to teach the Indians and when León made another expedition north, accompanied him and was

granted the right to work at the mission of San Francisco de los Tejas, May 25, 1690. He recommended to Mexican authorities that seven missions be established in the present Texas. Once more Massanet went into Texas, this time in 1691 with an expedition under Domingo Terán de los Ríos, but Terán and Massanet could not get along and Massanet remained at the mission of San Francisco when Terán withdrew. Hard times came upon it from natural disasters and disinclination of the Indians to settle nearby. Massanet urged that a presidio be established there and when that request was denied, he burned the mission October 25, 1693, and returned to Coahuila, his party lost for 40 days on the return. Massanet appears to have been disenchanted with missionary life and retired to the college at Querétaro. He was a man of undoubted courage and vision, but contentious and found difficulty in working amicably with his lay superiors. The date of his death is not reported. His writings, judged Bolton, "are among our most important sources of information regarding the beginnings of Texas."

Herbert Eugene Bolton, ed., *Spanish Exploration in the Southwest 1542-1706.* N.Y., Charles Scribner's Sons, 1916; John Francis Bannon, *The Spanish Borderlands Frontier 1513-1821.* N.Y., Holt, Rinehart and Winston, 1970.

Massasoit, Wampanoag chief (d. 1661). B. presumably near the later Bristol, Rhode Island, he had become a grand sachem, or intertribal chief of the Wampanoags when the Pilgrims established Plymouth Colony, and doubtless it was due to his cooperation, and the skills he imparted to the whites, which enabled the fledgling community to survive. He visited the colony in March 1621, with Samoset, his colleague who already had made friendly overtures to the whites. The benefits of peaceful trade and relations between the races were apparent to both factions, one Pilgrim writing that "There is now great peace among the Indians themselves, and we, for our part, walk as peaceably in the woods as in the highways of England." From Massasoit's Indians the colonists learned to make corn pone, planked shad, baked beans, and roasted clams. In 1623 when Massasoit was dangerously ill, he was nursed to health by the Pilgrims who valued his friendship, with Governor Edward Winslow himself taking part. Massasoit was powerful enough to enforce peace while he lived, but under increasing threats of land-hungry whites the Wampanoags grew more restless. Massasoit left two sons, one of whom became "King Philip," who led his people into a violent war with the whites.

Famous Indians: A Collection of Short Biographies. Wash., Govt. Printing Office, 1974; Hodge, HAI.

Massé, Enemond, Jesuit missionary (Aug. 3, 1575-May 12, 1646). B. at Lyon, France, he was ordained about 1602 and after an interval as associate of the confessor to King Henry IV, he was selected to accompany Pierre Biard as an initial Jesuit missionary to Canada, leaving Dieppe January 26, 1611, and reaching Port Royal, Nova Scotia, May 22. A man of considerable common sense, he earned the soubriquet of Father Useful; Massé backed Biard in the latter's endless bickering with Poutrincourt and Biencourt, and accompanied his colleague with the La Saussaye expedition from Port Royal to found a colony at Mt. Desert Island (site of the later Bar Harbor, Maine); when the endeavor was wiped out by Argall, Massé, with La Saussaye and a few others were permitted to take a longboat back to France, arriving in October 1613. Massé earnestly desired to return to Canada and was with the first group of Jesuits that reached Quebec in 1625; he was again expelled by the English under David Kirke in 1629. Massé returned to Quebec in 1633; in 1643 he was at Sillery, near Quebec City, where he taught the Montagnais language to Druillettes. He died at Sillery, leaving his good works but very little written material upon his worthy life.

Thwaites, JR, I, 314-15; Parkman, *Pioneers of France in the New World,* II, *The Jesuits in North America,* I, II; DCB.

Massure, Baptiste, frontiersman (fl. 1837). Massure was one of 18 whites who treacherously attacked the Mimbres Apache leader, Juan José Compá, in the Animas Mountains of present New Mexico April 22, 1837, slaying 20 and touching off extended Apache-white hostilities.

Rex W. Strickland, "The Birth and Death of a Legend: The Johnson 'Massacre' of 1837." *Arizona and the West,* Vol. 18, No. 3 (Autumn 1976), 257-86.

Massure, Laurent, frontiersman (fl. 1837). Massure, perhaps related to Baptiste Massure, was one of 18 whites who treacherously attacked the Mimbres Apache leader, Juan José Compá, in the Animas Mountains of present New Mexico April 22, 1837, slaying 20 and igniting extended Apache-white hostilities.

Rex W. Strickland, "The Birth and Death of a Legend: The Johnson 'Massacre' of 1837." *Arizona and the West,* Vol. 18, No. 3 (Autumn 1976), 257-86.

Masterson, Edward J., lawman (Sept. 22, 1852-Apr. 9, 1878). B. at Henryville, Ontario, he moved with his parents and their six younger children to Wichita, Kansas in 1869, and with his brothers, Bat (William Barclay) and James P., engaged in buffalo hunting west of Dodge City in 1872-73. Ed worked briefly in a restaurant for Mayor James H. (Dog) Kelley, then rejoined Bat for another hunt. He was appointed a policeman at Dodge June 5, 1877, assistant marshal in July of that year, and marshal December 4. In a shooting affair at the Lone Star Dance Hall in November 1877, Masterson was one of four people wounded, being shot in the chest, but quickly recovered. In an affray that followed his attempt to disarm a drunken cowboy, Masterson was wounded fatally, the cowboy, Jack Wagner, died the next day, a third man badly wounded, Alf M. Walker, ultimately recovered. Ed was buried not at Boot Hill, but in a military cemetery at Fort Dodge; his body later was removed with others to another cemetery, then moved again, and the identification of the remains was lost.

Fred Huston, "Ed Masterson — He was More than just Bat's Brother!" *Golden West,* Vol. X, No. 2 (Jan. 1974), 34-37, 43-45; Nyle H. Miller, Joseph W. Snell, *Great Gunfighters of the Kansas Cowtowns, 1867-1886.* Lincoln, Univ. of Nebr. Press, 1967.

Masterson, James P., lawman (1855-Mar. 31, 1895). B. in eastern Canada, he moved with the family to a farm near Wichita, Kansas, in 1871 and the next year, with his brothers, Edward J. and William Barclay (Bat) Masterson, he engaged in buffalo hunting in southwestern Kansas, continuing in that pursuit off and on until 1878. He became a policeman at Dodge City June 1, 1878. Either he or Wyatt Earp on July 26, fatally wounded a spreeing cowboy, George Hoy or Hoyt. While a policeman, Jim became a deputy sheriff of Ford County under the sheriff, his brother Bat, from 1878-1880. Jim Masterson became marshal of Dodge City November 4, 1879, discharged with a change of city government April 6, 1881. He became involved in a minor shooting affray, his brother, Bat, was summoned from Tombstone, Arizona, to help out and a Front Street incident April 16, 1881, resulted in the wounding of Al Updegraff, bartender, seriously, though not fatally. Jim Masterson, ordered out of Dodge City, returned in January 1889, to become involved in a county seat dispute, then went to Oklahoma, becoming a first settler of Guthrie, deputy sheriff of Logan County, Oklahoma, and in 1893 was named a deputy U.S. marshal by E.D. Nix. He took part in the celebrated gun battle with the Doolin crowd and other outlaws at Ingalls, Oklahoma, September 1, 1893, and in various significant incidents. He remained a deputy marshal until his death, of "quick consumption," and was buried at Wichita.

Nyle H. Miller, Joseph W. Snell, *Great Gunfighters of the Kansas Cowtowns, 1867-1886.* Lincoln, Univ. of Nebr. Press, 1967.

Masterson, William Barclay (Bat), lawman, frontier figure (Nov. 26, 1853-Oct. 25, 1921). B. in the parish of St. George, Henryville, Iberville County, Quebec, he was christened with the name Bartholomiew but in early manhood adopted instead the name of William Barclay Masterson although retaining the nickname Bat which, with the variant Bart, derived from his baptismal name. He moved through Illinois to near Wichita, Kansas, in 1871. The next year with brothers Edward and James, he removed to Dodge City, tried railroad construction, and went buffalo hunting in the autumn of 1872. He took part, June 27, 1874, in the Battle of Adobe Walls in the Texas Panhandle between buffalo hunters and Comanches and other Indians, in which four whites and about 13 Indians died. On August 5, 1874, Bat signed on as civilian scout with Miles for the Canadian-Panhandle expedition. He was discharged October 12, and returned to Dodge City, reaching there by March 1, 1875. January 24, 1876, he probably shot and killed Sergeant Melvin A. King at Sweetwater (later

Mobeetie), Texas in a dispute over a woman, Molly Brennan, who also was reported killed. By the spring of 1877 Bat operated a Dodge City saloon, serving as under sheriff to Charles E. Bassett that summer. On September 17 Bat was appointed a city policeman briefly, while still serving as under sheriff. On September 27 he accompanied Bassett in a futile search for train robber Sam Bass. He was elected sheriff succeeding Bassett, taking office in January 1878, serving until January 1880. During his first month he captured Dave Rudabaugh, a noted desperado, and Edgar West, following their attempt at train robbery near Kinsley, Kansas. In his posse were Kinch Riley, who had fought with Bat at Adobe Walls, Prairie Dog Dave Morrow, and John Joshua Webb, noted western characters. Bat may or may not have taken part in the shooting affair in which his brother, Edward, was killed. On October 5, 1878, Masterson headed a posse including Wyatt Earp, Bill Tilghman, Charley Bassett and William Duffey that wounded and captured James W. Kenedy (Kennedy), charged with the killing of Dora Hand, for which he later was acquitted. In January 1879 Bat returned the notorious horse thief-outlaw Dutch Henry Born(e) from Trinidad, Colorado, to Dodge City; Henry was acquitted of rustling. Later that month Masterson was appointed a deputy U.S. marshal. In February he brought back from Leavenworth seven Cheyennes of Dull Knife's band charged with five murders in Ford County, Kansas. They were given a change of venue to Lawrence, Kansas, and the cases ultimately dismissed for want of evidence. Masterson, still as sheriff of Ford County, was asked in March 1879, for help when the Santa Fe railroad contested right of way through the Royal Gorge of the Arkansas River, with the Denver and Rio Grande Western but although he recruited about 30 heavily armed men and they spent some time in Colorado, there was no bloodshed. Bat was beaten for sheriff November 4, 1879, by George T. Hinkle. Masterson had been a busy and probably honest lawman for the times but the politics of Dodge City were acrimonious, involved and confusing and he was caught in the web. He went to the Colorado mines February 25, 1880, but returned, disillusioned in them, by late spring. He made a quick trip to Ogallala, Nebraska to bring back Bill Thompson, wounded in a gunfight, lived in

Kansas City for a time and went to Tombstone February 8, 1881, where he remained without coming to much notice until called to Dodge to help his brother, James, in a dispute with Al Updegraff and A.J. Peacock. In one of Dodge City's better known gunfights, Updegraff was wounded seriously, but not fatally, by Bat. Masterson spent some months in Colorado, returning to Dodge City in May 1883, for the "war" between Luke Short and city officials, but the affair was brief and without shooting. He roamed the west, Kansas, Texas, Colorado, for a period, returning to Dodge City for a time, writing his first sports article (on horse racing) July 4, 1884. He arrived quickly on the scene when Dave Mather killed Tom Nixon July 21, 1884, but had no role in it. He was named deputy sheriff briefly, protected a temperance figure from a mob, refereed a prize fight, moved to Denver when Dodge City saloons were closed in 1886, and was married November 21, 1891, to Emma Walters. In 1892 he was said to be city marshal at Creede, Colorado. He removed to New York City in May or June 1902, becoming sports writer on the *Morning Telegraph,* eventually sports editor and secretary of the company. He died at his desk. Masterson was something of a dandy, dressed well when he could, made numerous friends and some enemies, was blue-eyed and of moderate build.

Nyle H. Miller, Joseph W. Snell, *Great Gunfighters of the Kansas Cowtowns, 1867-1886.* Lincoln, Univ. of Nebr. Press, 1967; Richard O'Connor, *Bat Masterson.* N.Y., Bantam Books, 1958; Robert K. DeArment, *Bat Masterson: The Man and the Legend.* Norman, Univ. of Okla. Press, 1979.

Mastin, Thomas J., frontiersman (Sept. 13, 1839-Oct. 7, 1861). B. at Aberdeen, Mississippi, he reached Quincy, Plumas County, California, in 1857. The next year he settled at Gila City, near Yuma, Arizona, becoming an attorney. By August 15, 1860, he had become a merchant at the gold camp of Pinos Altos, New Mexico, continuing to practice law, and having success as a miner and stock raiser. As a delegate to a Mesilla conference, he voted for secession. On July 18, 1861, he enrolled and commanded the "Arizona Guards" at Pinos Altos and the following month the organization was mustered into Confederate

service at Fort Fillmore. The guards engaged in numerous scouts and forays against the Apache. September 27, 1861, Mastin and a detachment of 15 men repulsed an attack on Pinos Altos of an estimated 250 to 300 warriors (an exaggeration, unquestionably), the captain being wounded in the arm, from which injury he died.

Martin Hardwick Hall, "Captain Thomas J. Mastin's Arizona Guards, C.S.A." *New Mex. Hist. Rev.,* Vol. XLIX, No. 2 (Apr. 1974), 143-51.

Mastin, Virgil, frontiersman (d. May 14, 1868). If Virgil was a younger brother of Thomas J. Mastin, as is possible, he probably was b. at Aberdeen, Mississippi, sometime after 1839. He reached southern New Mexico at least by 1860, although, as a friend of the Ourys, he also was familiar with southern Arizona. On May 17, 1861, he was wounded at Mesilla by John Portell, one of the ill-fated Freeman Thomas party and a Unionist. Virgil Mastin was killed by Apaches on the road between Fort Bayard and Pinos Altos, three miles from the latter town. At that time he owned a ranch near Hot Springs, New Mexico, the ranch having been attacked by Mimbres Apaches on occasion.

Letter May 20, 1868, from John A. Ketcham to C.P. Clever, New Mex. delegate to Congress, microfilm roll 555, Letters Rec'd., Off. of Ind. Aff., 1824-1881, New Mex. Superintendency.

Matheney, Daniel, pioneer (Dec. 11, 1793-Feb. 1, 1872). B. in Virginia he moved successively to Kentucky, Indiana and Illinois. He served in the War of 1812 receiving his discharge following the Battle of New Orleans. Matheney was married in 1819. He served as first lieutenant in Captain John Stinnett's Company of the Odd Battalion of Mounted Rangers under Atkinson in the Black Hawk War of 1832 in the upper midwest. He also served as a captain during Mormon difficulties in the early 1840s. Matheney joined the immigration to Oregon in 1843 and was very active, exploring and opening the road from Fort Hall to The Dalles. Having met George Gay in 1844 Matheney settled near him and operated a ferry across the Willamette near Wheatland, Oregon where he died.

Thwaites, EWT, XXX, 174n.; Bancroft, *Oregon,* I.

Mather, Dave (Mysterious Dave), gunman (b. 1845). A lineal descendant of Cotton Mather, clergyman of early New England, Mather was born in Connecticut. In 1873 he was reported a member of a rustler band in Sharp County, Arkansas, perhaps with Dave Rudabaugh and Milton Yarberry, among others. The next year Mather was a buffalo hunter on the Staked Plains, eventually reaching Dodge City, Kansas, where he was almost killed by a knife-wielding gambler, being saved by the "first major surgery" in the town's history. In gratitude Mather thereafter sometimes rounded up strays requiring a "physical examination" at $5 each, to benefit the physician, Dr. T.L. McCarty. Mather may have led the lynching party which executed John Callahan mistakenly for rustling in April 1876, but he was never formally accused of it. Part-time gambler, part-time lawman, Mather was reported at Mobeetie, Texas, with Wyatt Earp trying to sell phony gold bricks to unsuspecting buyers, and in July 1879, reached Las Vegas, New Mexico. August 14 he was aquitted of a train robbery charge, then became a constable with indifferent success. In a saloon gunfight, January 22, 1880, Marshal Joe Carson was killed and Mather killed William Dandall, mortally wounded James West (James Lowe), and seriously wounded Tom Henry. January 25 he shot and mortally wounded Joe Castello. February 7, 1880, he may have been part of a mob that lynched three men near Las Vegas. In March Mather resigned and returned to Dodge City, moving then to Colorado and later to Texas where he was jailed at San Antonio for handling counterfeit money. After an eventful wandering around Texas, Mather returned to Dodge City in 1883, and became assistant marshal about June 1, serving simultaneously as deputy sheriff under Pat Sughrue. Thomas C. Nixon succeeded Mather as assistant marshal April 10, 1884, and bad blood between the two developed. On July 18 Nixon shot at Mather, but missed; on July 21 Mather shot down Nixon, mumbling, "I ought to have killed him six months ago." He secured a change of venue to Edwards County where he was acquitted early in 1885. On May 10, 1885, following a gambling dispute in a Dodge City saloon, Dave or his brother, Josiah W. (Cy) Mather, killed Dave Barnes; Dave Mather and two other men were wounded, none

seriously. The Mathers jumped bail and left Dodge City, Dave becoming marshal of New Kiowa, Barber County, Kansas. He reportedly reached Long Pine, Nebraska, in mid-1887, remaining there a year. One report said he had died in Alberta in 1916; another that he had served in the Royal Mounted Police, and was living in Canada in 1922. The place and date of his death are uncertain.

Colin Rickards, *Mysterious Dave Mather.* Santa Fe, N.M., Press of Territorian, 1968; Nyle H. Miller, Joseph W. Snell, *Gunfighters of the Kansas Cowtowns, 1867-1886.* Lincoln, Univ. of Nebr. Press, 1967.

Mathews, Jacob Basil (Billy), pioneer (1847-June 3, 1903). B. in Tennessee, he served in the 5th Tennessee Cavalry with the Confederacy during the Civil War, and in 1867 moved to Gilpin County, Colorado, engaging in mining. He removed to Elizabethtown, New Mexico, and mined for five years, then ranched northeast of Roswell, New Mexico, with Frank Freeman until he moved to Lincoln, becoming involved in the Lincoln County War. He clerked for Dolan and became a silent partner in Dolan & Company's store at Lincoln. Mathews was in charge of the posse that killed Tunstall. He was a member of Peppin's posse that besieged the McSween house in the famous Five Days' Battle in July 1878. He was deputized to guard Billy the Kid when the gunman was transferred from the Mesilla to the Lincoln jail in April 1881. Later he ranched on the Penasco River, then moved to Roswell, where he became postmaster. Mathews died at Roswell.

Robert N. Mullin notes: *Maurice G. Fulton's History of the Lincoln County War,* ed. by Robert N. Mullin. Tucson, Univ. of Ariz, Press, 1968; "Frank Warner Angel's Notes on New Mexico Territory 1878," ed. by Lee Scott Theisen. *Arizona and the West,* Vol. 18, No. 4 (Winter 1976).

Mat(t)hews, James, Mormon pioneer (July 4, 1823-June 21, 1871). A man of this name was placed by *Mormonism Unveiled* at the scene of the Mountain Meadows Massacre of southern Utah September 11, 1857, either participating in or consenting to the tragedy. Esshom lists a James Nichols Mathews who reached Utah by mule team in 1849, and who was sent as a missionary to southern Utah to work with the Indians and assist in development of the region. A teacher and farmer, he married once and lived at Pine Valley, Utah. He fathered five children.

Mormonism Unveiled, 380; Frank Esshom, *Pioneers and Prominent Men of Utah.* Salt Lake City, Western Epics, 1966.

Mathewson, William (Buffalo Bill), frontiersman (Jan. 1, 1830- Mar. 22, 1916). B. in Broome County, New York, he wandered the northeast, trapped in Wisconsin and Minnesota, and joined the American Fur Company in 1849, reaching the Rocky Mountains. He freighted and pursued other occupations on the Plains, opened a trading post at the future Great Bend, Kansas, and the first store where Lyons, Kansas, later was built. He also was an influence at Wichita, Kansas, and was said to have accumulated considerable wealth. Because of his prowess at buffalo killing in pre-Civil War days, he was billed on his tombstone at Wichita as "the original Buffalo Bill." Gard reported that Mathewson started down Jesse Chisholm's trace in July 1867, taking two boys he had rescued from the Comanches. At Fort Arbuckle he turned them over to the commandant. There he met "a Texas drover" enroute north with a longhorn herd, Mathewson directing him over the new trail and guiding him as far as the North Canadian River where he could begin to follow Chisholm's wagon tracks, thus having a role in development of the famed Chisholm Trail. Later he brought the first women to travel over the Trail, his wife, Lizzie and Miss Fannie Cox of St. Joseph, Missouri. Mathewson died at Wichita.

Sam Henderson, "Those Other Buffalo Bills." *Real West,* Vol. XVIII, No. 139 (June 1975), 14-20, 58-60; Wayne Gard, *The Chisholm Trail.* Norman, Univ. of Okla. Press, 1954.

Mathey, Edward Gustave, army officer (Oct. 27, 1837-July 17, 1915). B. in France, he was described by Stewart as "so addicted to blasphemy that he had been nicknamed 'Bible-Thumper'." He enlisted in the 17th Indiana Infantry May 31, 1861, was commissioned a second lieutenant May 1, 1862, resigned in August and became a second lieutenant in the 81st Indiana Infantry September 1, 1862, emerging from the Civil War a major. He became a second lieutenant in the 7th U.S. Cavalry September 24, 1867. Mathey served on the Plains and was on Custer's Washita Expedition, but changed

places because of alleged snow-blindness with Louis Hamilton (who was killed in the Battle of the Washita) and remained as train guard while the bulk of the command went into action; this was at Hamilton's urgent request since he desperately wanted to get into the affair. Mathey became a first lieutenant May 10, 1870. On Custer's Sioux expedition of 1876 Mathey commanded the pack train and was detached on a wide detour by Custer before the action but managed to bring up the packs and join the beleaguered forces on Reno Hill where he acted with competence and coolness during the affair. In 1877 he was in the operation against the Nez Perce and was promoted to captain to rank from September 30, at the height of the Bear Paw Mountain action which terminated Chief Joseph's movement toward Canada. Mathey retired because of disability in line of duty December 11, 1896, with the rank of major, being promoted to lieutenant colonel on the retired list April 22, 1904. He died at Denver.

Heitman; BHB; Edgar I. Stewart, *Custer's Luck.* Norman, Univ. of Okla. Press, 1955; Stan Hoig, *Battle of the Washita.* Garden City, N.Y., Doubleday & Co., 1976.

Mato-tope (Four Bears) Mandan chiefs (c. 1800-1861). the first of these two individuals was the second chief of his people when Catlin painted his portrait in 1832 as Bodmer did in 1834. Mato-tope is reported to have led his people in battles against their enemies and in 1837 became chief, the year of the frightful smallpox epidemic that all but annihilated the Mandans. Catlin described his death as he learned it from a trader who was present: "This fine fellow (Mato-tope) sat in his wigwam and watched every one of his family die about him, his wives and his little children, after he had recovered from the disease himself; when he walked out, around the village, and wept over the final destruction of his tribe...then he came back to his lodge, where he covered his whole family in a pile, with a number of robes, and wrapping another around himself, went out upon a hill...where he laid several days...resolved to *starve* himself to death. He remained there till the sixth day, when he had just strength enough to creep back to the village, when he entered the horrid gloom of his own wigwam, and laying his body along-side the group of his family, drew his robe over him and died on the ninth day of his fatal abstinence," on July 30, 1837. De Voto found Four Bears "a remarkable Indian... The tribe's ancient splendor survived in him; he was mighty in council and mightier in war, by far the greatest warrior of them all. He had led his people against all their enemies... he had many coups," and was a persistent friend of the whites, appreciative recipient of white trade. His son succeeded him as chief over what remnants of the Mandan remained. He succeeded in uniting the Arikara and Hidatsa in forming a settlement on the Missouri where Fort Berthold, North Dakota, later an army post, was placed. Four Bears the younger died in 1861.

George Catlin, *North American Indians*. N.Y., Dover Pubns., 1973, II 258; William H. Goetzmann, Joseph C. Porter, *The West as Romantic Horizon*. Omaha, Center for Western Studies, 1981, 28, 58; Bernard DeVoto, *Across the Wide Missouri*. Boston, Houghton Mifflin Co., 1947.

Matt, Louis, blacksmith (d. 1877). Of French-Irish blood he was born either in Quebec or Maine, reached Idaho around 1849, worked for John Owen in the Bitterroot Valley of Montana about 1850-51 and for the Hudson's Bay Company in 1853-54. He married a Blackfoot woman and fathered a daughter, the first wife of Louis Maillet. He died near the Flathead Indian Agency, Montana, his descendants still living on the reservation.

George F. Weisel, *Men and Trade on the Northwest Frontier*. Missoula, Mont. State Univ. Press, 1955.

Matthews, Washington, army surgeon, ethnologist (July 17, 1843- Apr. 29, 1905). B. at Killiney, County Dublin, Ireland, he was brought to America as a child, raised in Wisconsin and Iowa and earned a medical degree at the University of Iowa in 1864. Matthews served as acting assistant Army surgeon at Rock Island Barracks, Illinois, until May 1865. He became post surgeon at Fort Union, Montana, later in 1865 and served at Fort Berthold, Dakota Territory, until he joined Terry's Dakota expedition of 1867, thereafter being stationed at Forts Stevenson, Rice and Buford, Dakota Territory, until October of 1872 when he was transferred east. During his time on the northern Plains Matthews became interested in Indian languages and mythology, leading to publication of a grammar and dictionary of the Hidatsa (Gros Ventres), and a paper on the ethnography and philology of those Indians of Siouan linguistic stock most closely related to the Crows. After service at a number of eastern posts, Matthews was ordered to California in 1875, served in the field during the Nez Perce campaign in 1877 and the Bannock War of 1878 and was post surgeon at Fort Wingate, New Mexico, from October 1880 until April 1884. This service resulted in several papers on the Navaho, on their silver-smithing and weaving, their rituals and legends. In 1885 Matthews became interested in physical anthropology. He wrote 58 papers in all, most of them of enduring value in the study of the American Indian. He retired September 26, 1895, and died at Washington, D.C. He was married.

Powell; Heitman; DAB.

Mattison, Ray H., historian (Sept. 15, 1903-Oct. 8, 1980). B. at Belgrave, Nebraska, he served as a historian for the National Park Service from 1941 to 1965, much of the time as Midwest Regional Historian. During that period he headed Missouri River Historical Research work in anticipation of the development of water impoundments and dam construction which would flood many promising archaeological sites. Mattison was also an authority on the fur trade and contributed 11 articles on fur trade luminaries to the multi-volume *Mountain Men and the Fur Trade* series. Included were biographies of Francis A. Chardon, Alexander Culbertson, John Pierre Cabanné Sr., James Kipp, Kenneth McKenzie, David Dawson Mitchell, Henry A. Boller, James A. Hamilton, William Laidlaw, Alexander Harvey and Joshua Pilcher. Mattison was interested in military sites and posts of the Upper Plains and Santa Fe Trail region and wrote of them in periodicals, although he wrote no books. Following his retirement from the National Park Service he was superintendent of the North Dakota State Historical Society from 1965-69, then retired to Tucson where he became associated with Westerners International and like organizations. He was married and left his widow and two daughters.

Headquarters Heliogram 130, Council on Abandoned Military Posts, Dec. 1980; information from Mrs. Ray H. Mattison.

Maurepas, Jean Frederic Phelypeaux, Count de, French politician (1701-1781). He served as secretary of state in France from 1725-49 when he was forced into exile by penning a satirical bit about Madame de Pompadour, a favorite of Louis XV, but with the accession of Louis XVI he came back into power. He bestowed patronage upon scientists and encouraged exploration, sending out important expeditions. Among these was that of La Verendrye (1738), which led to the discovery later by his son of the Rocky Mountains, or their northern extension.

Literature abundant: Thwaites, JR, LXVII, 343n46.

Maus, Marion Perry, army officer (Aug. 25, 1850-Feb. 9, 1930). B. in Burnt Mills, Maryland, he was graduated from West Point in 1874 and joined the 1st Infantry, becoming a first lieutenant in 1879 and a captain in 1890. Maus was engaged in operations against the Sioux in the Black Hills, South Dakota, and was cited for gallantry in the action against the Nez Perce in the Bear Paw Mountains, Montana, in 1877. In 1885-86 he was second in command to Captain Emmet Crawford on an expedition penetrating the Sonora Sierra Madre in pursuit of Geronimo; when Crawford was killed by Mexican irregulars, Maus assumed command, courageously extricated the scout unit, and arranged for the March meeting of Geronimo and Crook; he later received the Medal of Honor. Maus took part in the Sioux operation of Wounded Knee, South Dakota, in 1891. He accompanied Miles as aide to observe the Graeco-Turkish War and various maneuvers in Europe, rose steadily if unspectacularly in rank, and was an inspector general during the Spanish-American War, being present at the surrender of Santiago, Cuba, taking part in the Puerto Rico operation and later serving in the Philippines for three years. He was at San Francisco during the 1906 earthquake, commanded the Department of California briefly and the Department of the Columbia, being named Brigadier General in 1909 and retiring that year. He died at New Windsor, Maryland.

Heitman; *Who Was Who;* George Crook *Annual Report,* 1886; Nelson A. Miles, *Personal Recollections.* Chicago, Riverside Pub. Co., 1897, 450-71.

Maximilian, Prince Alexander Philip, naturalist, traveler (Sept. 23, 1782-Feb. 3, 1867).

B. at Neuwied on the Rhine River in Prussia as the eighth child of the ruling Friedrich Karl of Wied-Neuwied, Maximilian was inclined toward scholarly pursuits, particularly natural history, but entered the Prussian army and attended the Battle of Jena October 14, 1806, was captured and imprisoned but exchanged and returned to his studies when a fresh military crisis called him up; he rose to become a Major General, won the Iron Cross at Chalons and entered Paris with a victorious army March 13, 1813. He then returned to the university, undertook an expedition to Brazil in 1815, spending two years there and other years in publishing the important results, which won scientific acclaim. May 17, 1832, he embarked for the United States, accompanied by a Swiss artist, Karl (Charles) Bodmer whose fine representations of Indian, primitive and Missouri valley life and themes became a lasting memorial to the expedition. Maximilian reached St. Louis in March 1833, interviewing Sauk and Fox Indians at General Clark's home and visited Chief Black Hawk, defeated in his recent war and jailed at Jefferson Barracks, Missouri. Maximilian and his entourage boarded the *Yellowstone* April 9, 1833, and went up the river to Fort Pierre, South Dakota, trans-shipping June 5 to the *Assiniboine,* a shallow-draft vessel, reached Fort Clark, North Dakota, June 16 where Maximilian's ethnological tastes were captivated by the Crows; the expedition reached the mouth of the Yellowstone and Fort Union June 24, 75 days out of St. Louis. July 6 Maximilian boarded the *Flora,* a keelboat, to work farther upstream to Fort McKenzie among the Piegans and Bloods, 34 days beyond Fort Union. August 28 came a battle about the fort between Piegans on one side and Assiniboins and Crees on the other, a scene which Bodmer immortalized in a graphic painting. Maximilian believed he killed an Assiniboin when he fired at him with a rifle doubly-loaded, himself being stunned by the recoil. Maximilian and his party left September 14 and made their way downstream to Fort Clark, arriving November 8. Maximilian wintered there studying the Mandans (of whom Bodmer painted numerous pictures), organizing his notebooks and recovering from scurvy with the aid of wild-onion stew. The prince's summaries of his findings included the view that American Indians "were not savages. They were as civilized as Caucasians, in terms of their environment, as intelligent as whites, as moral, and at least as peaceful." In addition they were as honest, generous, hospitable, and cleaner and with a subtle sense of humor. Their artistic sense of color and composition was good and they had numerous other enlightened qualities and customs — views very novel for his day. His natural history notes were many, interesting, exact and original in his interpretations. In the spring the party headed downstream and reached St. Louis May 28, 1834; enroute to New York he visited Niagara Falls and left New York City July 16 for Le Havre. Maximilian spent the next few years writing of his travels and findings, producing "one of the greatest works of the West," although he was distressed when the *Assiniboine,* bringing downstream his collection of flora and fauna specimens in 1835 was destroyed by fire and her cargo lost. To his great work on Brazil he had now added his work on the American West, inadvertently heightened in value by the fearsome smallpox epidemic of 1837-38 which killed upwards of 15,000 Indians, all but wiped out the Mandans and devastated other once-powerful tribes. Virtually the entire results of his American tour, including diaries, paintings he did himself, notes and other manuscript material was obtained in 1962 by the Northern Natural Gas Company of Omaha and is on permanent loan to the Joslyn Art Museum of that city where some of it is on exhibit.

Thwaites, EWT, Vols. XXII-XXV; Marshall Sprague, *A Gallery of Dudes.* Lincoln, Univ. of Nebr. Press, 1979; information from Joseph C. Porter, Joslyn Art Museum.

Maxwell, Joseph Edward, army officer (c. 1827-June 30, 1854). B. in Georgia, he went to West Point and was commissioned a brevet second lieutenant of infantry July 1, 1850, being posted to Fort Bliss, Texas. Maxwell became a second lieutenant of the 3rd Infantry March 5, 1851, and served at Santa Fe and Forts Union and Conrad, New Mexico, until 1854 when he was assigned to scouting duty. June 30 he and a small detachment followed Jicarilla Apache Indians up the Mora River into an ambush near Fort Union when a volley of arrows killed Maxwell. He was 27.

Cullum; Heitman; Veronica E. Velarde Tiller, *The Jicarilla Apache Tribe: A History, 1846-1970.* Lincoln, Univ. of Nebr. Press, 1983.

Maxwell, Lucien B., frontiersman (Sept. 14, 1818-June 25, 1875). B. at Kaskaskia, Illinois, he reached New Mexico about 1835, and using Taos as a base traded widely with Plains tribes and the Utes. He may have worked at Fort St. Vrain on the South Platte for a time. Back at St. Louis he was hired by Fremont as a hunter on his first expedition, after which Maxwell returned to trading. He was with Fremont briefly on his second expedition, but did not serve through it all, though he did join the third, on one occasion in the San Joaquin Valley, California, killing an Indian in a hand-to-hand fight. He accompanied Kit Carson with dispatches eastward, but when Carson joined Kearny, Maxwell returned to Taos and became an Indian trader again. On June 20, 1848, he was wounded in an Indian ambush in Manco Burro Pass, Colorado. He acquired a huge New Mexico ranch through his father-in-law, Judge Carlos Beaubien, and by purchase and otherwise became sole owner of a 1.7 million acre place, centered on Rayado, New Mexico. It became known as the Maxwell Land Grant. In 1853, with Carson and others, he drove sheep to California most profitably. Headquarters for his ranch was moved to Cimarron in 1854; Maxwell lived in baronial style, at one time owning 1,000 horses, 10,000 cattle and 40,000 sheep. In 1870 he sold out to English capitalists for $1,350,000, tried banking, then railroad building, finally returning to ranching near Fort Sumner, New Mexico. He died there. His wife, his one son, Peter Menard Maxwell (Pete), and most of his eight daughters survived him.

Twitchell, *Leading Facts,* II; W.A. Keleher, *The Maxwell Land Grant, a New Mexico Item.* Santa Fe, Rydal Press, 1943, 1964; Lawrence R. Murphy, "Lucien B. Maxwell: The Making of a Western Legend." *Arizona and the West,* Vol. 22, No. 2 (Summer 1980), 119-24.

Maxwell, Martha Dartt, taxidermist (July 21, 1831-May 30, 1881). B. at Dartt's Settlement (Charleston), Pennsylvania, she early came to a love of nature in exploring the woods about her childhood home; her mother, an early widow, moved with her second husband to Wisconsin where at 10, it is said, Martha saved her 4-year-old sister from a rattlesnake by shooting the reptile. She later attended Oberlin College, Ohio, and Lawrence College and married a widower, James Maxwell, moving in 1860 to Colorado where her husband operated sawmills. Here she became interested in taxidermy; in 1868 the Maxwells moved to Boulder, Colorado, and Martha commenced collecting and stuffing wild creatures. Her collections grew through many trips into the remote Rocky Mountains with her husband. She pioneered techniques of fitting skins of wild creatures over plaster casts she had made, preserving their lifelike shapes. In 1870 she sold a good collection to Shaw's Botanical Gardens of St. Louis, and began to rebuild her own collection. She accumulated exotic specimens from other collectors as far distant as California. She opened the Rocky Mountain Museum at Boulder, moving it in 1875 to Denver; in 1876 she exhibited her collection at the Sesquicentennial Exposition at Philadelphia and later at Washington, D.C. At one time she had 47 species of mammals and 224 birds in her exhibit. She died at Rockaway Beach, New York, and was buried at Woodmere Cemetery, Far Rockaway, Long Island.

Floyd and Marion Rinhart, "Martha Maxwell's Peaceable Kingdom." *Amer. West*, Vol. XIII, No. 5 (Sept./Oct. 1976), 34-35, 62-63; Lawrence T. Paddock to author, Jan. 31, 1977.

May, William Francis Perry, frontiersman (c. 1797-Feb. 28, 1855). B. at Nashville, Tennessee, he served with the Tennessee Militia against the Creeks for eighteen months, beginning October 1, 1813. By 1822 he was in charge of a trading post for the Missouri Fur Company among the Mandans, returning to St. Louis in 1823, shortly entering the Santa Fe trade. He was robbed of livestock by the Kiowas in 1826. From 1830 until 1843 he traded in the upper Missouri country, but ruthless competition caused him to transfer his operations to the Fort Laramie area. In 1854 he engaged as guide to the Colonel Steptoe expedition. May died at Salt Lake City.

Adrienne T. Christopher, LeRoy R. Hafen article, MM, Vol. IV.

Maynard, David Swinton, pioneer (1808-Mar. 13, 1876). B. in Vermont, he studied medicine, was married in 1828, moved to Cleveland and fathered two children. He started a successful medical school, but was ruined in a financial crash. In 1850 he left his wife and children and went by wagon train to the West Coast, enroute combating a cholera epidemic and becoming aquainted with a woman widowed by that plague. The two reached Olympia, Washington, in September, Maynard working at frontier occupations and his medical practice, traveling to California but soon returning to Washington Territory. He became a friend of Chief Seattle and April 3, 1852, settled on the site of the later city of Seattle, for which he suggested the name. He became active in public and pioneer affairs, obtained a divorce and married the widow, Catherine Broshears. He served as agent during the Indian war of 1855-56 and "played a principal role in keeping (Puget Sound) tribes out of the fighting." Maynard opened the first hospital at Seattle, studied for the bar and passed the examination but never practiced law much, concentrating instead on his medicine. He was popular and convivial, enjoyed a drink and it was said was a better physician "full than when sober." He died at 65 at Seattle; his first wife died two years later and his second at more than 90 in 1906.

James R. Warren, "Doc Was Colorful Pioneer." *Seattle Post-Intelligencer*, Aug. 16, 1981.

Maynard, Ken, actor (July 21, 1895-Mar. 23, 1973). B. at Mission, Texas, he ran away from home at 14 to join a medicine show, studied engineering at the Virginia Military Institute, and served as an army engineer in World War I. He was a rodeo rider, worked with Ringling Bros. Circus, and became a motion picture actor, starring in about 125 films, his last made in 1946. Maynard was said to have been the prototype for "Nevada," in Harold Robbins' novel *The Carpetbaggers*.

Los Angeles *Herald Examiner*, Feb. 1, 1974.

Mays, Ruben E., Confederate officer (c. 1835-Aug. 11, 1861). Mays enlisted in Lavaca County, Texas, April 15, 1861, as a second lieutenant of the 2nd Texas Mounted Volunteers and was sent to West Texas, being stationed at Fort Davis. Late in July or early in August Mescalero Apaches under Nicholas attacked the Manuel Músquiz ranch about five miles from Davis, killing three persons and running off stock. Mays took up the pursuit with 12 soldiers and four civilians on August 5, on the 10th recovering about 100 head of animals; according to one story Mays wished to return with the stock, but his militant Lavaca County riders insisted he go on, and the next day he led a pursuit of a small body of warriors into an ambush; the only survivor was a Mexican herder who hid in a cave while the lieutenant and his command were annihilated. Since there was only the one white witness, whose full name is unknown, and the exact site of the engagement is uncertain (the bodies were never recovered), details of the operation must remain unestablished. Scobee believes the action took place in the vicinity of Corozona Peak, southwest of Persimmon Gap in the extreme northern extension of the present Big Bend National Park.

Tex. Archives, Mays file; Barry Scobee, *Old Fort Davis.* San Antonio, Naylor Co., 1947; Scobee, *Fort Davis Texas 1583-1960.* El Paso, pub. by Barry Scobee, 1960; Carlysle Graham Raht, *The Romance of Davis Mountains and Big Bend Country.* El Paso, Rahtbooks Co., 1919, 146-47; *Frontier Times,* Vol. 7, No. 9 (June 1930), 390; Martin H. Hall, *The Confederate Army of New Mexico.* Austin, Tex., Presidial Press, 1978.

Meacham, Alfred B., Indian superintendent (Apr. 29, 1826-Feb. 16, 1882). B. in Orange County, Indiana, his father lost everything in the financial crash of 1837 and moved the family to Iowa, settling in Iowa City. At 15 Alfred signed a temperance pledge which he broke only once in his life and then involuntarily. In 1845 he assisted in removing the Sauk and Fox Indians to a reservation they had been assigned following the Black Hawk War. From then until 1850 he contracted to "break prairie" with ox teams preparatory to farming. He then with a brother set out by ox team for California, prospered in the mines, returned to Iowa to marry and took his bride to Oregon. In 1869 he became superintendent of Indian Affairs for Oregon; he persuaded Captain Jack, then encamped on Lost River in southern Oregon to settle on the detested Klamath Reservation, thus averting hostilities for a short time. Meacham was rather a weak Indian superintendent, but he did know the Modoc leaders and they trusted him. He was removed in favor of T.B. Odeneal in 1872 and went to Washington, D.C., where he was when the Modoc War (1872-73) erupted. President Grant appointed him nominal chairman of a Peace Commission to settle hostilities, and Meacham returned to Oregon. Canby gradually assumed leadership of the Commission in the absence of strong guidance from Meacham, though he continued as official chairman. Initial contact was made with the Modoc hostiles who remained adamant in their insistence upon a reservation in their own country and in fair dealing; this the commissioners were not prepared to grant. April 11, 1873, at a council session, Canby and Thomas were assassinated, and Meacham shot several times and severely though not mortally wounded. An attempt to scalp him by Boston Charley was less than successful, but gave Meacham an interesting scar he later made use of in lecture tours. His life probably was saved by Tobey Riddle, the woman interpreter who had warned the commissioners that the Modocs would assassinate them though her advice was ignored. Meacham also was forced to violate his temperance pledge when the doctor forced some brandy down his throat in the course of field treatment. Meacham testified at the court martial that doomed Captain Jack and three others to the gallows and almost accepted Jack's plea that he speak for him, the Indian having no other defender, but at the last moment decided against doing so. After the conflict he organized a lecture tour that lasted several seasons, taking along some of the former hostile Modocs from their Quapaw Agency, Oklahoma, and Frank and Tobey Riddle for color. He became known as the foremost exponent of Indian rights, labeled by Interior Secretary Carl Schurz the most faithful and generous friend the Indians had, although castigated by anti-Indian westerners. Meacham wrote *Wig-wam and Warpath* (1876) and *Wi-ne-ma* (1877) and in 1878 started a journal, *The Council Fire,* "probably his greatest contribution toward the reform of Indian policy." In 1880 he was placed on the Ute Commission seeking a resolution of problems confronting the Colorado Uncompaghre Utes, largest division of the tribe. This was a difficult mission, not helped when A.D. Jackson, a drunken freighter, killed a popular young Ute leader, Shavano's son, and was lynched in retaliation. Meacham was indicted as an accomplice in the murder (which he was not), but the indictment died without trial. He finally persuaded the Utes to give up their ancestral lands and move to the Uinta Reservation, Utah. In failing health Meacham returned to Washington where he died of apoplexy and was buried in the Congregational Cemetery.

Jeff C. Riddle, *The Indian History of the Modoc War*. Medford, Oreg., Pine Cone Pubrs., 1973; Richard Dillon, *Burnt-Out-Fires*. Engelwood Cliffs, N.J., Prentice-Hall, 1973; Marshall Sprague, *Massacre: The Tragedy at White River*. Boston, Little, Brown and Co., 1957.

Meade, William Kidder, lawman (Sept. 21, 1851-Mar. 14, 1918). B. in Virginia, he arrived in Arizona as a mining man and settled in the Florence area, becoming prominent in Democratic politics. He desired the Arizona governorship, but President Cleveland instead appointed him U.S. marshal, in which post he served from 1885-90, and from 1893-97. He had been active in Tombstone mining ventures, and while there sided with Sheriff Behan in the feud with the Earps; Fred Dodge, an undercover man for Wells Fargo, sided with the Earps, and being Republican politically, did not get on well with Meade, although they worked together on various cases. A train robbery band, Larry Sheehan, Tom (Dick) Johnson, Dick Hart and Jack Bount, had pulled two jobs on the Southern Pacific near Pantano Wash, southeast of Tucson, and now held up a third train February 22, 1888, near Stein's Pass, New Mexico, on the Arizona border, getting substantial loot, according to report, and rifling the mails, which brought them under Meade's concern. With a posse of four whites and four Papago trailers, Meade took up the trail, following it to Janos, Chihuahua. Here their horses were taken from them, the posse arrested and held 14 days. The incident had international repercussions; Robert H. Paul, noted lawman and longtime detective for the Southern Pacific, quietly secured Mexican permission and assistance, and shot down three members of the outlaw band; the other was killed later in Sonora. Meade's deputies arrested seven suspects in the Wham payroll robbery case in Graham County, but although apparently guilty, they were cleared by a court. Meade later saw several of them sentenced to the penitentiary for train robbery. He was in Alaska during the gold rush, again engaged in mining, then returned to Arizona, and died at Tombstone.

Larry D. Ball, "'This High-Handed Outrage': Marshall William Kidder Meade in a Mexican Jail." *Jour. of Ariz. Hist.*, Vol. 17, No. 2 (Summer 1976), 219-32; Fred Dodge, *Under Cover for Wells Fargo*, ed. by Carolyn Lake. Boston, Houghton Mifflin Co., 1969.

Meadows, Charlie (Arizona Charlie), frontiersman, showman (Mar. 10, 1859-Dec. 9, 1932). B. in a covered wagon under an oak tree during a snowstorm at Visalia, California, as Abram Henson Meadows, his name was changed before he was 10 to Charlie Meadows, and as Arizona Charlie he became widely known. He was one of twelve children of John Meadows, a preacher and rancher, and grew up as a cowboy, adept at ranch work. When he was 18 his father moved the brood to Arizona where the Meadows family settled beneath the Mogollon Rim in the Tonto Basin. In July 1882 hostile Apaches swept through the area (just before the Battle of Big Dry Wash) and Charlie hired out as an army packer. He had only been with the troopers a few hours when word came that Apaches had struck the Meadows ranch (July 15), killed John Meadows Sr., wounded Charlie's brothers John V. and Henry, and had driven off most of the stock, and Charlie at 23 had become head of the family. Henry died of his wound and John V., although he lived, was crippled for life. Charlie worked as a cowboy throughout central Arizona; he took no part in the Pleasant Valley War although personally he favored the Tewksbury faction. Among his skills was with a lasso, and he became a top steer roper: "always a gambler, he would bet his purse and skill against all comers, and he was usually the winner." July 4, 1886, he won a silver buckle at Prescott for throwing and tieing a steer in 59 1/2 seconds, excellent time for the feat and the day. Charlie developed a liking for publicity and kept scrapbooks of news items about himself. November 25, 1888, the *Tucson Star* reported that Meadows had bested Tom Horn in a steer roping contest at Payson; the next year Horn beat Meadows by establishing a world's record of 49 1/2 seconds. This well-attended contest was witnessed by William F. Cody (Buffalo Bill) who invited both ropers to join his Wild West Show. Horn flatly dismissed the idea, but Charlie Meadows accepted, made a date with the showman to meet at his Cody, Wyoming, ranch to discuss details, kept the appointment but Cody had forgotten it and gone east. Meadows returned to Arizona still afire with enthusiasm for a showman's life, let his hair grow long, and wrote letters to all the wild west organizations he could learn about, signing them "Arizona Charlie." Early in August 1890, Charlie's sister, Maggie was married to Thomas Beach, and Julia Hall married to Charles Cole, both couples on horseback in cowboy regalia as was the Justice of the Peace who performed the ceremony near Payson. Charlie handed a lariat to each of the grooms and promised them as a wedding present all of his semi-wild cattle they could rope before sunset, losing 32 head that way. On August 30, 1890, Charlie sailed from San Francisco for the trans-Pacific with Harmston's Wild West Show. After two years in the Far East he caught up with Cody at London and for several weeks traveled with that show. Back in the United States he formed his own exhibition and toured this country and Mexico. Gold was discovered in the Klondike and Charlie took off to establish the first theater and dance hall in the Yukon, becoming a legend in the north country over a period of several years. He bought and wrecked two paddle-wheel steamers for materials for his Palace Grand Theater at Dawson City, which could seat 501 persons; it has been reconstructed and may still be in use. From Alaska and the Yukon, Meadows drifted down the Pacific coast promoting carnivals, street fairs, fiestas and wild west shows. He moved into Colorado and was arrested for staging a bull fight. Having been born in a snowstorm, Charlie fervently believed he would die in one, and thought Yuma, Arizona, was a good place to postpone that event as long as possible so he moved to a ranch at the mouth of the Gila on the Colorado River, near Yuma. He became involved in politics. He started a newspaper, and was sued for libel. He organized a filibustering expedition to take over Tiburon Island in the Gulf of California, but the Mexican government put a stop to that. Finally, for one of the few times in the recorded history of the region it snowed in Yuma, and on that day Arizona Charlie Meadows died at 73. He was a very tall man, about 6 feet, 6 inches in height, was slender and of picturesque appearance.

Don Meadows (second cousin of Charlie), "Arizona Charlie Was Hero." Prescott *Courier,* Centennial Edn., May 15, 1964, C 7-8; correspondence with Don Meadows, Jean King; *New York Times,* July 4, 1962; author's file on Meadows.

Meagher, Michael, lawman (c. 1843-Dec. 17, 1881). B. in Ireland, Meagher was named marshal of Wichita, Kansas, April 13, 1871,

and his brother, John (b. in Ireland c. 1845), assistant. John resigned August 16 and was elected sheriff November 14. Mike served until April 15, 1874, when he resigned; he served as deputy U.S. marshal that summer, but on April 5, 1875, was elected Wichita city marshal again. On January 1, 1877, he shot and killed Sylvester Powell who had attempted to murder him. Meagher moved to Caldwell, Kansas, in the spring, being elected mayor April 5, 1880. When George Flatt was killed June 19, 1880, Meagher was soon on the scene; he and his police force were arrested by county authorities, charged with complicity, but were acquitted. Meagher did not run for re-election, but was named city marshal of Caldwell briefly in July. He and George Speers were killed by five cowboys, Jim Talbot, Bob Bigtree, Bob Munson, Jim Martin and Doug Hill, who escaped after a spirited chase. Hill in 1887 did six months after pleading guilty to manslaughter. Talbot (James D. Sherman), was acquitted in 1895; in 1896 he was killed at Ukiah, California (see Thomas D. Love entry).

Nyle H. Miller, Joseph W. Snell, *Great Gunfighters of the Kansas Cowtowns, 1867-1886.* Lincoln, Univ. of Nebr. Press, 1967.

Meagher, Thomas Francis, nationalist, soldier (Aug. 23, 1823-July 1, 1867). B. at Waterford, Ireland, he was educated at the Jesuit College, Kildare, and at Stonyhurst College, Preston, England. In 1845 he joined the strongly nationalist Young Ireland party, was sent on a mission to France in 1848, and on his return was arrested, charged with treason. He was sentenced to death, the sentence commuted to lifelong banishment, and he was sent to Tasmania, arriving in July 1849. He married there in 1851, but in 1852 escaped to the United States. His wife died in Ireland; he married again in 1855. He became naturalized, studied law and practiced in New York City until 1861. When the Civil War broke out he organized a company of Zouaves, took part in first Bull Run, then organized the "Irish Brigade," and was commissioned Brigadier General of Volunteers May 3, 1862, serving until May 15, 1865. He was appointed secretary of Montana Territory, and served from September 1866 until his death as acting governor, directing suppression of Indian hostilities among other things. He boarded a steamboat at Fort Benton for an inspection trip down the Missouri and disappeared at night, presumably having fallen overboard and drowned.

Literature abundant; DAB; EA; NCAB, Vol. V, 364-65.

Meany, Edmond S., historian (Dec. 28, 1862-Apr. 22, 1935). B. at East Saginaw, Michigan, his father was a tugboat captain who took his family to Washington Territory in 1877 and drowned while his son was at the University of Washington. Edmond was graduated in 1885 and became a newspaper reporter, served a term in the state legislature, became secretary to the Board of Regents and registrar of the University of Washington and in 1895 was appointed instructor in history and forestry. He studied summers under Frederick Jackson Turner at the University of Wisconsin and came into contact with Thwaites and other ranking historians. Meany founded the *Washington Historical Quarterly* in 1906 (the present *Pacific Northwest Quarterly*) and published and edited many books and papers. Among them are *Vancouver's Discovery of Puget Sound* (1907); *History of the State of Washington* (1910, 1924); *Governors of Washington* (1915); *Origin of Washington Geographic Names* (1923), and edited, among other items, *A New Vancouver Journal on the Discovery of Puget Sound* (1915); *Mount Rainier, A Record of Exploration* (1916), and *Diary of Wilkes in the Northwest* (1926). He died following a stroke at Seattle.

Kent D. Richards, "Edmond S. Meany: 1862-1935." *Arizona and the West,* Vol. 17, No. 3 (Autumn 1975), 201-204.

Meares, John, sea captain (c. 1756-1809). B. in England, he served to lieutenant in the British Navy. After the Peace of Paris of 1783 settling the American Revolutionary War, he entered the merchant service and founded a commercial house at Calcutta to trade with the northwest coast of North America. He was first to establish a camp (in 1788) at Friendly Cove, Nootka Sound, on the west coast of Vancouver Island, a move which foreshadowed the celebrated Nootka Sound incident, highlighting the struggle for control of the north coast between Spain and Britain, which was only resolved by a 1790 convention opening the coast northward to British commerce. The controversial Meares first came to the north Pacific in 1786, commanding the ship *Nootka;* he made a landfall on the

Alaskan coast late in the season and wintered at Prince William Sound where scurvy killed 23 of his crew before spring, when he returned to Canton. In 1788 to avoid his lack of proper British commercial licensing, Meares flew the Portuguese flag, using Portuguese nationals as a front for his activities. He made his landfall at Friendly Cove, said he "purchased" for a brace of pistols land from a native chief, a claim later denied by the Indian. While his fort and a schooner were being constructed, Meares cruised southward, visiting the Strait of San Juan de Fuca and continuing as far as Tillamook Bay on the north Oregon coast, but he failed to detect the mouth of the Columbia River, leaving its effective discovery to Robert Gray in 1792; Meares again returned to Canton. In 1789 his establishment at Nootka was destroyed by the Spanish and Meares returned to England from China. His book, *Voyages Made in the Years 1788 and 1789 From China to the Northwest Coast of America* appeared in 1790. Meares did not again serve in the navy, but became a commander February 26, 1795. He had no further significant role in American Pacific affairs.

Warren L. Cook, *Flood Tide of Empire: Spain and the Pacific Northwest, 1543-1819.* New Haven, Yale Univ. Press, 1973; Thwaites, EWT, VII, 112n.; DNB.

Mears, Otto, pioneer (May 3, 1840-June 24, 1931). B. at Courland, Russia, of English and Hebrew stock, he reached San Francisco at 12 to live with an uncle who he learned had departed meanwhile for Australia. Mears sold papers, worked at various jobs in the city and mining camps, and enlisted as a private in Company H, 1st California Infantry, August 17, 1861, accompanying his unit to the Rio Grande. He took part in an Apache campaign in West Texas, then Carson's Navaho expedition, and an Apache campaign into southeastern Arizona in 1864. Mears was discharged, still a private, at Las Cruces, New Mexico, August 31, 1864. He entered commerce at Santa Fe, but within a year went to southern Colorado where he operated a general store at Saguache; prospering, he increased his influence throughout the region, and became politically potent among the Mexican-Americans of the area. He built hundreds of miles of toll roads "which opened the San Juan area to mining and development." His first road was over Poncha Pass and its success led him into other similar ventures. Mears became influential among the Utes largely through his friendship with Chief Ouray; he learned their language, served as an interpreter for 1873 treaty negotiations, and accompanied a Ute delegation on a trip to the East. In 1880 he again accompanied a Ute delegation on a trip to Washington following the so-called Meeker massacre, and in June was chosen by President Hayes one of five commissioners to implement a treaty negotiated the previous March providing for the relocation of the Uncompaghre band of Utes. It is possible that Mears used bribery to get the Utes to ratify the treaty; he helped them select land near the confluence of the White and Green rivers of Utah for their new home. When the Utes showed reluctance to move, they were forced to do so by Colonel Ranald S. Mackenzie, some reports asserting that Mears was instrumental in this use of strength to clear the Uncompaghre Valley. Some of Mears' toll roads were later used, as he had envisioned, for railroad rights of way and he became an important figure in railroad expansion and construction. Mears suffered heavily in the panic of 1893, many of his enterprises being jeopardized or wiped out. He visited New Mexico, North Carolina and British Columbia to examine mines thereafter, and in 1897 became interested in eastern railroad building. He returned to Silverton, Colorado, in 1907, remaining there until his retirement to Pasadena, California, in 1917. A small man physically (he was only 5 feet, 5 1/2 inches tall), he was large in every other way, and was highly regarded by officials and public alike. A man of many interests, he was generous with his money when he had it, donated to a variety of charities, was good newspaper copy all his life, and was something of an empire-builder. He was married and fathered a family.

James G. Schneider, "Otto Mears — Pathfinder of the San Juan." Chicago, *Westerners Brand Book,* Vol. XXXI, No. 11-12 (Jan.-Feb. 1975), 81-83, 87-88; DAB.

Medina, Mariano, mountain man (c. 1810-June 25, 1878). B. at Taos he became a trapper and mountain men, living for a time with the Flatheads. After slaying an Indian in a quarrel, he moved to the Fort Bridger area, trading with emigrants, scouting for the army,

and about 1858, established a trading post near the later Loveland, Colorado, it becoming a famous frontier site. He died there.

Harvey L. Carter article, MM, Vol. VIII.

Meek, Joseph Lafayette, mountain man, pioneer (Feb. 7, 1810-June 20, 1875). B. in Virginia, he went to Lexington, Missouri, and left for the Rocky Mountains with William Sublette March 17, 1829. He spent 11 years in the mountains, becoming an outstanding trapper and rover, taking part in countless adventures with a rollicking good humor that built a lasting reputation. He took part in the celebrated battle of Pierre's Hole in July 1832, and the next year became a free trapper. Meek accompanied Joe Walker on his California expedition of 1833-34, in the summer of 1834 returning to take part in the final Green River's Ham Fork rendezvous of the Rocky Mountain Fur Company. After countless adventures during the waning days of the trapping industry, Meek and his third Indian wife reached the Willamette Valley, Oregon, on December 15, 1840. Despite the astonishing originality of his spelling, Meek was not an unintelligent man and was widely read among the classics of the day; his sense of humor and braggadocio made him outstanding and, being empty of vanity, endeared him to many, missionaries as well as less-refined characters. He had a strong sense of loyalty and justice. He worked for various farms in the Oregon country, then became sheriff, a popular choice. By 1845 he was a prosperous farmer himself, won a seat in the Legislature and, having been converted at a Methodist meeting in 1847 emerged as a strong temperance man. When he learned of the massacre of his friends, the Whitmans, he and others took news of the disaster to the states, reaching St. Joseph May 11, 1848, and Washington May 28 where Meek greeted his cousin, Mrs. James Polk and the President. Oregon was quickly made a Territory, and Meek its marshal; he picked up the new governor, Joseph Lane, in Indiana, and accompanied him back to Oregon City which they reached March 2, 1849. Meek became deeply involved in political affairs in the Territory, complicated by anti-Indian hysteria and complex cross-currents which he had neither the training nor the sophistication to handle, and with a change of administration was swept from

office. He served in the Yakima Indian war in
the Oregon Volunteers, emerging as major. A
Democrat from Virginia by tradition, he still
was strongly pro-Union and helped found the
Oregon Republican Party. Meek's children,
of mixed ancestry, came afoul of the
unreasonable anti-Indian emotionalism of the
time and place, but Joe weathered it all,
remaining himself to the end, a man of great
potential and unusual accomplishment, and
withal one of integrity, judgment, courage and
great magnetism, a born leader.

Literature abundant: Francis Fuller Victor, *River
of the West*. Hartford, Conn., Columbian Book
Co., 1870 (rep. Long's College Book Co.,
Columbus, O., 1950); Stanley Vestal, *Joe Meek:
The Merry Mountain Man*. Caldwell, Ida.,
Caxton Printers, 1952; Harvey E. Tobie article,
MM, Vol. I.

Meek, Stephen Hall, mountain man (July 4,
1805-Jan. 11, 1889). An older brother of Joe
Meek, Stephen was born near Abingdon,
Virginia. He joined fur trader William
Sublette at St. Louis in 1828 and left for the
Rocky Mountains in 1830. He accompanied
Joe Walker to California in 1833-34 and in
1835 joined the Hudson's Bay Company,
trapping in California and elsewhere. He
returned to St. Louis in the winter of 1836-37,
but then went back to the mountains. In 1840
he was wagonmaster for the Magoffin
brothers to Chihuahua where he remained
two years, joining scalp hunter James Kirker
for a time. Meek guided a wagon party from
Independence to the Columbia in 1842, and
another from Oregon to California in 1843.
He took ship in 1844 as far south as
Valparaiso, Chile, then returned to Panama
and made his way to New York, thence to his
Virginia home after an absence of 17 years. In
1845 he guided a train of 500 wagons to Fort
Hall, settled with his bride near Oregon City
on the Willamette River until 1848, then took
his family to California in time for the gold
rush, dividing his attentions between California and Oregon for several years. He took
wagons and mining machinery from California to Boise, Idaho, in 1867, and participated in a Shoshone Indian campaign. He
died near Etna, California.

Harvey E. Tobie article, MM, Vol. II.

Meeker, Ezra, pioneer (Dec. 19, 1830-Dec. 3,
1928). B. near Huntsville, Ohio, he moved to

Indiana as a boy and in 1851 to Iowa. The next
year he joined an emigrant train from Council
Bluffs to Portland, Oregon, arriving October
1, then moving to McNeil's Island, Puget
Sound, and later to Puyallup, Washington. He
made several prospecting trips to the Yukon.
In 1906 with an ox-team he retraced the
Oregon Trail, thereafter devoting his life to
publicizing and preserving traces of the trail
and its points of interest. He traversed it
several times, finally by automobile and then
by airplane. In 1926 he founded the Oregon
Trail Memorial Association, at New York
City. He died at Seattle. Meeker wrote widely,
many of his works devoted to Oregon Trail
subjects.

Literature abundant; DAB.

Meeker, Nathan Cook, Indian agent (July 12,
1817-Sept. 29, 1879). B. at Euclid, near
Cleveland, Ohio, the grandson of a man who
contributed 18 sons to the American Revolution, he roved widely and took up many
occupations, as a newspaperman, teacher,
businessman. He was a devotee of Fourierism
and even wrote a novel. In 1865 he became
agricultural writer for Horace Greeley's *New
York Herald* and increased his interest in
cooperative farming and living. In 1869 he
was sent west to study Mormon work in this
direction. He did not reach Utah, but
envisioned an agricultural colony in Colorado
and in 1870 located at the future Greeley,
where he remained eight years. In March
1878, he was named agent at the White River
Ute Reservation in northwest Colorado,
applying for any agency in order to pay off a
$1,000 debt. He was given the Ute Agency
because it was believed he had the experience
to improve the lot of the Indians agricultur-
ally. As an agent he was creative, but his
influence was tempered by his tactlessness.
The White River Utes at this time were falsely
accused of destroying timber by fire, charges
manufactured no doubt so whites could steal
the rest of their lands. A dispute arose. Meeker
called for troops to quiet his Indians, they
regarding the advance of soldiers as an act of
war, being unsettled in any event by fears they
were to be shunted aside by greedy whites. The
troops were ambushed some distance from the
agency, while Meeker and seven agency
personnel were killed, apparently by Chief
Douglas, a Yampa Ute, and his men, and all
but one of the agency buildings were burned.

The outbreak was settled largely through peaceful efforts of Chief Ouray.

HAI; DAB; Marshall Sprague, *Massacre: The Tragedy at White River.* Boston, Little, Brown and Co., 1957.

Megapolensis, Johannes, Dutch clergyman (c. 1603-late 1669). B. probably near Coedyck, North Holland, in his young manhood he "relinquished Popery and was thrust out at once from my inherited estate." He became a minister and preached at three parishes before sailing in 1642 for New Netherlands with his wife and four children, reaching Fort Orange (Albany, New York) August 13. "A man of scholarship, piety, energy and good sense, he was trusted by the patroon, perhaps more than any one else in the colony, in important matters." In 1643 he commenced preaching to the Mohawks, three years before John Eliot began his work among Massachusetts Indians, and quickly absorbed enough of their language to be understood by them. Jameson prints his "A Short Account of the Mohawk Indians," written in 1644, in which he describes the people, tells of his work and close association with them, and a great deal about Dutch relationships with the Iroquois at this important period. Megapolensis reported that as many as eight Indians would sometimes be lying and sleeping on the floor around his bed, and that occasionally ten or 12 would attend his lengthy services, smoking long tobacco pipes and wondering what he found to talk about so long to his white congregation. Although Megapolensis desired authorities to stop the immigration to New Netherlands of Jews, he took up a collection to aid 23 Jews who had arrived destitute from Brazil. He opposed creation of a Lutheran church and work of the Quakers and was strongly anti-Catholic, yet he saved the life and became very friendly with the Jesuit Isaac Jogues who had been captured by the Iroquois, and was hospitable to Simon Le Moyne, curtly rejecting, however, Le Moyne's plea that he return to the Roman church. Megapolensis urged Stuyvesant to submit to the English and afterward accepted British rule, continuing to minister to his congregation the rest of his life.

J. Franklin Jameson, ed., *Narratives of New Netherland, 1609-1664.* N.Y., Barnes & Noble, 1909; DAB.

Meiaskwat, Charles, Montagnais leader (fl. 1640s). A member of the Montagnais people of eastern Canada, Meiaskwat was an early convert of the Jesuits, became a catechist, assisted Jean du Quen, erecting his first chapel, and made extended tours through neighboring regions visiting tribes or bands of his own nation. Charles was directed to guide to the Abenakis a onetime prisoner upon whom the Algonquins had inflicted intense torture and whom the French had brought back to health. Meiaskwat eagerly accepted the assignment and once among the Abenakis attempted to evangelize them. He went with them to visit the English settlements in Maine; he showed the Protestant English his Catholic beads and was verbally rebuked for having "the Devil's inventions," but stoutly affirmed his faith. He proudly became a "captain of prayers" in his Canadian homeland and remained a paradigm of Jesuit work in New France.

Thwaites, JR, XX, 185-205; XXI, 104-105; XXIV, 57-63; XXV, 175-81.

Meinhold, Charles, army officer (c. 1826-Dec. 14, 1877). B. in Prussia, he emigrated to the U.S. and enlisted in 1851 in what later became the 3rd Cavalry. He was appointed 1st lieutenant of the 5th New Mexico Infantry early in 1862. He transferred to the 1st New Mexico Cavalry, then resigned and in 1862 was commissioned in the 3rd U.S. Cavalry, becoming captain in 1866. Meinhold had taken a "notable" part in the Battle of Valverde, New Mexico, and Indian skirmishing. He fought in the southern theatre against the Confederacy, being twice brevetted for gallantry. Bourke found him in New Mexico in 1870 "an elderly man, of fine physique and great personal attractiveness," and Finerty, on the northern Plains, later described him as a "very fine looking German officer with a romantic history." Meinhold was assigned in 1871 to investigate the somewhat controversial "Wickenburg massacre" of a coach full of people by Apache Mohaves, his report laying to rest some of the suspicions concerning that action. As commander of Company B, 3rd Cavalry, he played a conspicuous role in the June 16, 1876, Battle of the Rosebud, Montana, under Crook, and took part in the subsequent summer campaigns against the Sioux, suffering however from exposure. He died, aged 51, at Clifton Springs, New York, from ailments contracted in the field.

Heitman; J.W. Vaughn, *With Crook at the Rosebud.* Harrisburg, Pa., Stackpole Co., 1956; Dan L. Thrapp, *Al Sieber, Chief of Scouts.* Norman, Univ. of Okla. Press, 1964; F. Stanley, *Fort Craig.* Pampa (Tex.) Print Shop, 1963.

Meldrum, Robert, fur trader (1806-July 10, 1865). B. in Shelby County, Kentucky, the son of Scotch-Irish immigrants who reached the county in 1804, he learned blacksmithing and went west at 16. He may have been with Bonneville in the Rocky Mountains. He was at any rate on the upper Missouri in 1835, for Larpenteur wrote that he had been sent to the Crows that summer and had killed a Blackfoot. Culbertson wrote that he had lived with the Crows before he joined the American Fur Company and knew the tribe and their language better than any white man. Denig explained to Kurz that although Meldrum had distinguished himself among the Crows by his warrior ability, he was esteemed by them rather for his liberality "on account of which he has fallen into debt instead of accumulating money." Meldrum was in charge of Fort Alexander, Montana, the winter of 1848-49, "the most dangerous post in the country." He helped complete construction of Fort Sarpy and from 1850 to 1859 was chief trader at this Crow post. Raynolds in 1859 described him as the "best living authority (on) the Crows... having spent 30 years in their country... spending only 19 days in St. Louis" in that time. "He had lived long among these Indians, assuming their dress and habits, and by his skill and success in leading their war parties has acquired distinction.... He of course speaks their language perfectly and says it has become more natural to him than his mother tongue." He was known to the Crows as Round Iron, because of his blacksmithing skill. Meldrum, after discontinuance of the Crow post went to Fort Union and married a Blackfoot woman. He died at Fort Union, and was buried there the next day. Culbertson said Meldrum was a "man of gentle but courageous character who used excellent language and held the attention of his listeners by his lively and intelligent description of his adventures. When he went to live at Fort Union he resumed the dress and customs of the white man."

Montana, Contributions, Vol. X, 1940, 284-85.

Melgosa, Pablos de, military officer (c. 1516-post 1546). Of Burgos, Spain, he reached Mexico and was appointed a captain of infantry with Coronado's 1540-42 expedition into the American southwest. Melgosa commanded the foot soldiers accompanying Coronado's advance upon Háwikuh, southwest of Zuñi, New Mexico, which was taken in 1540 and though badly bruised was not "wounded" in its capture. Melgosa was with García López de Cárdenas in discovery of the Grand Canyon and with Juan Galeras and another attempted to descend into the chasm but they could get only one-third of the way down "because of the great obstacles they encountered," and were forced to return. Melgosa was prominent in the Tiguex War in early 1541 at the complex of pueblos on the Rio Grande near today's Bernalillo. It was he and Diego López who granted beleaguered Indians quarter at the recapture of Arenal; when the captives subsequently were sentenced to death by Cárdenas, who was unaware of the pledge given them, Melgosa and López stood silently by and did not correct him. The reputation the Spanish won for treachery by this incident did them lasting harm. After the expedition Melgosa returned to Europe, served as a soldier in Flanders for a time and then went home to Burgos. Here in 1546 he testified for Cárdenas at the latter's trial for misdeeds on the great expedition, although Cárdenas was convicted, in part for the offense against the Indians at Tiguex which was more the fault of Melgosa than Cárdenas.

George Parker Winship, *The Coronado Expedition, 1540-1542.* BAE, 14th Ann. Rept., Wash., Govt. Printing Office, 1896; Herbert Eugene Bolton, *Coronado: Knight of Pueblos and Plains.* Albuquerque, Univ. of New Mex. Press, 1964.

Méloche, Pierre, pioneer (1701-1760). B. at Montreal, he reached Detroit soon after his marriage and settled there. He ran a sawmill on the south side of the strait, though his home was on the north side. Méloche was an intimate friend of Pontiac; after Méloche's death Pontiac made his house his headquarters in 1763.

Thwaites, JR, LXIX, 308n73; Parkman, *The Conspiracy of Pontiac,* I, II; *Journal of Pontiac's Conspiracy 1763,* trans. by Robert Navarre. Detroit, Mich. Soc. of Colonial Wars, 1910.

Men, Rodriguez, explorer (d. Oct. 18, 1540). A Portuguese from Elvas, his name was carried as Men, Rodriguez (his last name was not Men). He enlisted with others of his townsmen in De Soto's expedition to the southern United States and was killed in the great battle at Mauvila, Alabama; he was termed by Ranjel "a fine Portuguese gentleman."

Bourne, *De Soto,* I, II.

Menard, Pierre, pioneer (1766-June 13, 1844). B. in Quebec, he reached Vincennes, Indiana, about 1780, then moved to Kaskaskia, Illinois, becoming a major Indian and fur trader in partnership with Francois Vallé. By a second marriage he became brother-in-law to Pierre Chouteau Jr., and soon formed a business arrangement with Manuel Lisa. He was one of the many partners in the St. Louis Missouri Fur Company, making his first wilderness trip up the Missouri in the spring of 1809 and wintering at Fort Raymond, at the mouth of the Big Horn, trapping in the spring with Andrew Henry on the Three Forks of the Missouri. Blackfeet hostility hampered them, and Menard returned to St. Louis. He never went up the river again. Menard became first lieutenant governor of Illinois, was sub Indian agent in 1813, and maintained an interest in Indian welfare all of his life. He named Keokuk, Iowa, after a Sauk chief, and occasionally was called upon to mediate Indian matters. He was a prominent and worthy pioneer.

Richard E. Oglesby article, MM, Vol. VI.

Menard, Rene, Jesuit missionary (Sept. 7, 1605-Aug. 1661). B. in Paris (the *Dictionary of Canadian Biography* gives his date of birth as March 2, 1605), he became a Jesuit and reached Canada in 1640, accompanying Ragueneau to the Huron country. Menard and Raymbault started for the Nipissing villages, were driven back by storms, but in 1642 Menard and Pijart reached the goal and spent a year among that people. Menard thereafter was connected with the Huron mission until the destruction of the Hurons by the Iroquois in 1649. He joined the Iroquois mission in 1656 and worked there two years, when he and other missionaries were forced to flee for their lives to Quebec. In 1660 Menard was sent with Ottawas to their home on Lake Superior, wintering with them probably near the present L'Anse, Michigan, "suffering great hardships and privations, — harshly treated by most of the Indians, though converting a few of them and baptizing some at the point of death." In the spring he heard of some Huron refugees from the Iroquois encamped near the Black River, Wisconsin, and set out for that place. When almost there he became lost and was not seen again; whether he perished from hunger or some other cause is not known. Several years later his breviary and cassock were discovered in possession of the Sioux, who said they had found them.

Thwaites, JR, XVIII, 256-57n5; DCB.

Menchaca, José, revolutionist (d. Aug. 18, 1813). B. probably at San Antonio (Bexar), Texas, Menchaca was described by Bancroft as "a man of vigor, bold and resolute, but rude and uneducated," adding that his "influence with the Mexicans was unbounded." As a Mexican, he headed his people and Indians of the Magee-Gutiérez liberating expedition into Spanish Texas, and was in opposition to Toledo, a Spaniard, the nominal commander-in-chief. Menchaca fell leading his men at the battle of Medina.

Bancroft, *North Mexican States and Texas,* II; HT.

Mendenhall, John, army officer (July 29, 1829-July 1, 1892). B. in Indiana he went to West Point and became a brevet second lieutenant in the 1st Dragoons July 1, 1851, transferring to the 4th Artillery February 20, 1852. He was in an engagement with Indians in 1855 in Kansas and hostilities with the Florida Seminoles in 1857, then spent two years on frontier duty. By the outbreak of the Civil War he was a captain. He served in California from 1873 to 1876, taking part in the Modoc War of 1872-73 in southern Oregon and northeastern California. He sat on the military court which tried Captain Jack and other leaders of the Modoc outbreak and sentenced six of them to hang (four eventually were executed, two reprieved). Mendenhall served at Fort Sitka, Alaska, from 1876-77 and in California again in 1882-83. At his death he was colonel of the 2nd Artillery.

Heitman; Powell; Keith A. Murray, *The Modocs and Their War.* Norman, Univ. of Okla. Press, 1965.

Mendenhall, John S., pioneer (Oct. 18, 1835-Feb. 1, 1896). B. at Vevay, Switzerland County, Indiana, he went to Leavenworth, Kansas, in 1855 and joined a freight outfit to Salt Lake City, where he remained two years before going on to California. He took a ship to New York City, but returned overland to Salt Lake City once more, working there until 1862. In May of that year he and Robert P. Menefee took a party of about 25 men equipped with ox wagons northward intending to go to the Florence, Idaho, gold fields, about 40 miles southeast of Grangeville. They reached Fort Lemhi where they learned the intervening country was impassable for wagons. They then turned east via Lemhi Pass, reaching Gold Creek, Montana, July 15. On August 26, 1862, Mendenhall stood only 15 feet away while C.W. Spillman was hanged for horse stealing, the first vigilante victim in Montana. Mendenhall returned to Salt Lake City and brought a cargo of merchandise to the new mining camp of Bannack where he made considerable profit on the goods. He prospected in the Virginia City, Montana, region in 1863 and in the Kootenai region of British Columbia in 1864, then moved to the Gallatin Valley of Montana, settling in the new community of Bozeman. He farmed with Menefee until 1868 when he entered the grocery business at Bozeman, remaining with that pursuit the rest of his life. He held various public positions. Mendenhall was married and fathered a son who survived him, as did his widow.

M.A. Leeson, *History of Montana, 1739-1885.* Chicago, Warner, Beers and Co., 1885; *Bozeman Courier,* Feb. 8, 1896; Virginia City, Mont., *Madisonian,* Sept. 1, 1899; Bozeman, *Gallatin County Tribune,* June 24, 1971.

Mendoza, Juan Domínguez de: *see* Domínguez de Mendoza, Juan

Menefee, Robert Philip, pioneer (Apr. 13, 1833-July 18, 1906). B. in Marion County, Missouri, he went to Kansas at 22 and took part in the border struggles from 1855-58 when he drove an ox team to Salt Lake City where he became clerk for a government contracting firm. On May 7 or 8, 1862, he and John S. Mendenhall left Salt Lake City with a party of 25 bound for the gold diggings at Florence, Idaho, about 40 miles by road southeast of Grangeville. They crossed the Snake River at present Blackfoot, Idaho, arrived June 9 at Fort Lemhi and, giving up their attempt to reach Florence because of the difficult country intervening, turned east over Lemhi Pass, reaching Horse Creek Prairie, Montana. June 20 and after some aimless wandering, Gold Creek, Montana, June 15. Menefee became assistant postmaster at Virginia City, Montana, in 1863, shortly moved to Bozeman where he became a pioneer resident. He was a partner of Mendenhall in a ranching undertaking until the latter went into the grocery business. During Cleveland's first administration Menefee was postmaster at Bozeman. He never married. He died at Bozeman and was buried there.

Bancroft, *History of Washington, Idaho & Montana;* Virginia City, Mont., *Madisonian,* Sept, 1, 1899; *Register;* Helena, *Montana Daily Record,* July 18, 1906.

Menéndez de Aviles, Pedro, Spanish captain-general (Feb. 15, 1519-Sept. 17, 1574). B. at Aviles, Asturias, Spain, he early went to sea. By 30 he was fighting French pirates and at 35 became under Charles V captain-general of the Indies fleet, making several voyages across the Atlantic besides serving Philip II in Europe. In the Indies "he found means to amass vast riches." He returned to Spain in some disgrace, however, the Council of the Indies had him arrested and he was heavily fined on charges which have not survived; Philip reduced his fine by half, "a strong presumption of his guilt," according to Parkman. Menéndez secured royal permission to conquer and settle Florida at his own expense and within three years. Before he could leave Spain word had been received of the rival attempt by France to colonize the peninsula. Menéndez with the title of adelantado of Florida and orders to oust by any means colonists deemed by Spain to be illegally within its realm, sailed from Cadiz in June 1565; he founded St. Augustine, Florida, and confronted without much result Ribaut's fleet at the St. John's River to the north, withdrawing then to St. Augustine. Ribaut had brought reinforcements for the Huguenot colony of Laudonniere and this place Menéndez resolved to destroy, although France and Spain were nominally at peace and their kings brothers, according to Parkman. Menéndez pledged to treat well those French colonists who might be Catholic, while destroying those he called "Lutherans," or Protestants; he kept his word. When Ribaut's fleet moved south to attack St. Augustine, Menéndez marched overland to capture the French post at Fort Caroline, massacring with singular savagery 142, almost all of the surrendered adult male inhabitants, while piously sparing about 50 women and infants; only a few escaped but these included the wounded and ill leader Laudonniere, who succeeded in regaining France. Menéndez withdrew his forces to St. Augustine from before which the French fleet had been scattered by a violent storm, perhaps a hurricane. Some of the ships were beached in the vicinity of Matanzas Inlet, south of St. Augustine. Here Menéndez accepted the surrender of two groups of Frenchmen to talling more than 200 individuals including Ribaut, bound them and had them murdered; the event shocked even atrocity-hardened Europe, though not the pious King Philip II of Spain, who directed that Menéndez be informed "that, as to those he has killed, he has done well..." Menéndez proceeded with plans to colonize the coasts of Florida, to explore the peninsula and to manage the Indians with whom, Parkman wrote, he "dealt honorably" while attempting to save them from exploitation. He returned to Spain in 1567 seeking support for his program, but this was small, and in 1568 he made his fifth voyage to the west. He returned to St. Augustine in 1571 where he found conditions "deplorable." He went back to Spain in 1572, the next year asked permission to conduct a war against the Florida Indians who had finally exhausted his patience, but died at Santander, his body removed 17 years later for final burial at Aviles. "Menéndez," judged Parkman, "was a man of honor and of strong religious feeling, an expert seaman and a bold and resourceful leader... (who) did succeed in establishing Spanish power in Florida," but is best remembered in this day for the unprovoked slaughter of the French colonists which "can be explained but never excused."

Parkman, *Pioneers of France in the New World;* Parkman also wrote the biographical sketch of Menéndez which appears in DAB.

Menewa (Monahwee), Creek chief (c. 1765-c. 1865). A half-breed, he became second chief of the Lower Creek towns on the Tallapoosa River in Alabama. In his early life, as Hothlepoya (Crazy War Hunter) he was noted for daring and ability, frequently making forays against white settlers on the Cumberland for their horses. Because of one depredation, Georgians raided and burned one of the Lower towns, and Menewa suspected his rival, William McIntosh of instigating the attack. When Tecumseh visited the south to persuade Creeks to join his plan to fight with the British against the Americans, Menewa readily joined the movement. He began the Creek War and became the war chief of the hostile faction, the head chief being a medicine man, Monahee. Relying upon a prophecy of the latter Menewa made a wrong disposition of his men at Horseshoe Bend, Alabama, where in an action March 27, 1814, the Creeks were all but destroyed by Jackson's overwhelming force. Menewa himself killed Monahee for his error. Of his 900 warriors, it was estimated 850 were killed; Menewa, with several wounds, was left for dead upon the field. With nightfall he recovered sufficiently to leave the scene by canoe and reach the hidden Creek camp in the swamps, but even here his village was destroyed, his wealth in stock and trade goods taken. After his wounds had healed however he resumed authority over the remnants of his bands and in later years became a leader in the Creek faction which opposed further cession of land and resisted white encroachments. His rival McIntosh, on the other hand readily acquiesced to giving up tribal lands and in the proposal to remove the Creeks west of the Mississippi. For this he was condemned as a traitor and Menewa, however reluctantly, carried out the sentence of execution. In 1826 Menewa with a delegation visited Washington (where his portrait was painted, now owned by the Smithsonian Institution). He protested the treaty McIntosh had signed for the minority of the Creeks January 8, 1821, ceding to the United States Creek lands. Menewa proposed reserving some of the land to be allotted in severalty to those Creeks electing to remain in Alabama rather than emigrate. That land granted Menewa proved unsuitable however, and he purchased other acreage for his own use. In 1836 when some Creeks became involved in the Seminole War he led his men against the hostiles. In consideration for his services he was tentatively granted permission to remain in Alabama, but this agreement, like so many others, proved false and he was transported with his people to Indian Territory during the 1836-40 removal. He died there, never reconciled to the move.

Hodge, HAI; Dockstader; James W. Holland, *Andrew Jackson and the Creek War: Victory at Horseshoe Bend.* Univ. of Ala. Press, 1968.

Mengarini, Gregory, Jesuit missionary (July 21, 1811-Sept. 23, 1886). B. at Rome he entered the Society of Jesus in 1828 and reached the United States in 1840, eager to become a missionary in the Rocky Mountains. In 1841 he left St. Louis with the De Smet party of six Jesuits and helped found St. Mary's Mission in the Bitterroot Valley of western Montana, among the Flathead Indians. He remained at St. Mary's from 1841 to 1850, spent two years in Oregon and in 1852 helped found Santa Clara (California) University, where he remained until his death. In addition to his mastery of several European languages, he became so well versed in Kalispel that even some Indians conceded he knew the language better than they; he also was noted for his skill in medicine and the use of herbs in the treatment of human ailments and contributed articles to ethnological and anthropological journals. He published a Salishan grammar in 1861 and prepared a Salishan-English dictionary.

Thwaites, EWT, XXVII, 193n.; *Guide to the Microfilm Edition of the Oregon Province Archives of the Society of Jesus Indian Language Collection: The Pacific Northwest Tribes.* Spokane, Gonzaga Univ., 1976; Fr. Gregory Mengarini, *Recollections of the Flathead Mission...,* tr. and ed. by Gloria Ricci Lothrop. Glendale, Calif., Arthur H. Clark Co., 1977.

Mennich, Peter, soldier (d. June 8, 1885). A sergeant of G Troop, 4th Cavalry, he was on detached service guarding a supply train that was traveling through Guadalupe Canyon between Arizona and New Mexico. It was jumped by Chihuahua's Apache raiders and three men including Mennich were killed. The sergeant was shot through the hips and immobilized and fell easy prey; the Apaches found the train to be carrying 10,000 rounds of ammunition, 40 days' rations and other useful supplies.

"The Reluctant Corporal: The Autobiography of William Bladen Jett," ed. by Henry P. Walker. *Jour. of Ariz. Hist.,* Vol. XII, No. 1 (Spring 1971), 34, 48, n48.

Mercer, Asa Shinn, newspaperman, writer (1839-Aug. 1917). B. at Princeton, Illinois, he was graduated from Franklin (Indiana) College, then removed to Washington Territory where he became active in its development. He evolved a scheme to supply marriageable women to lonely bachelors in the Northwest. Twice he traveled east for this purpose and in 1865 brought back 46 single women who "hardly dented the woman shortage (while) Mercer's carelessness with money dismayed his backers. But the publicity he achieved glossed over these shortcomings." It is said he founded the University of Washington before moving to Oregon for eight years and in 1876 to Texas where he developed his journalism bent, in seven years owning and operating four newspapers. In 1883 he moved to Cheyenne, Wyoming, started the *Northwestern Live Stock Journal,* which depended heavily upon advertising and support from the Wyoming Stock Growers Association and in return became its mouthpiece to a large extent. Mercer approved of the lynching of James Averell and Ella Watson for alleged rustling (although later in his famous book he reversed himself). Despite the support from the association Mercer's publication did not prosper, nor did he, particularly. After the so-called "invasion" of Johnson County by hired gunmen in the spring of 1892, Mercer's support for the cattlemen commenced to waver. He charged that they had withdrawn advertising and other support when he offered to go bail for a fellow-newsman, E.H. Kimball who had been arrested on a charge of libeling the stockmen, but records show that Mercer's offer of bond was not accepted; he used that incident as an excuse for shifting sides from the large cattle raisers to the settler element, but politics probably were at the root of the shift, since Mercer had decided to abandon the Republican for Democratic interests. He became as vitriolic against the Republicans as he formerly had been against Democratic causes; harassment of the editor followed and grew in intensity. Mercer refused to surrender to it. October 14, 1892, he printed George Dunning's lengthy and detailed "confessions," which named big names and cited chapter and verse on the cattlemen-inspired operations against Johnson County settlers. Mercer left Wyoming to attend the World's Fair opening at Chicago and while he was gone his printing shop was attached for allegedly unpaid bills. Mercer was sued twice for libel by cattleman John Clay, although the suits ultimately were dropped. Mercer wrote his renowned book, *The Banditti of the Plains, or The Cattlemen's Invasion of Wyoming in 1892 (The Crowning Infamy of the Ages)* in a run of 1,000 copies in 1893 or 1894. It was printed at Denver and sold for $1 a copy. He and his sons promoted the book in a tour of Wyoming in the fall of 1894, their visit and the volume being mentioned in various contemporary newspapers. Accounts of book burning, injunctions and personal threats against Mercer are unsupported by surviving evidence, but nonetheless the book was suppressed, even if details are sparse. Suppression made it rare and with it, famous. It brought lasting publicity to the Johnson County War and the participants. Mercer thereafter slipped into obscurity, took up a homestead at Hyattville, in Big Horn County on the west slope of the Big Horn Mountains, doing a bit of writing though producing little of later importance. He died "not knowing that he would come out the winner.... His book has stood the test of time and the perspective of history remarkably well. Many of his most angrily disputed charges have been justified. The book stands as a strange mixture of diatribe and distortion with solid historical fact. But it stands."

A.S Mercer, *The Banditti of the Plains,* foreword by William H. Kittrell. Norman, Univ. of Okla. Press, 1954; Helena Huntington Smith, *The War on Powder River.* N.Y., McGraw-Hill Book Co., 1966; Lewis L. Gould, "A.S. Mercer and the Johnson County War: A Reappraisal." *Arizona and the West,* Vol. 7, No. 1 (Spring 1965), 5-20.

Merchant, Claiborne W. (Clabe), cattleman (Aug. 31, 1836-Mar. 9, 1926). B. in Nacogdoches County, Texas, he became a cattleman in 1869 after Civil War service, in 1874 moving to Callahan County, Texas, acquiring ranch interests, and joining a group of Texas cattlemen in establishing an operation in the San Simon valley of eastern Arizona. Although he suffered financial reverses in 1885, he reestablished cattle interests in Arizona in 1888 and had ranches as well in New Mexico and Texas. He was a civic and business leader in the Abilene and Amarillo areas.

Ed Bartholomew, *Wyatt Earp: The Man & the Myth,* Toyahvale, Tex., Frontier Book Co., 1964; HT.

Mercier, Charles (Moultier, Rondin), frontiersman (1803-Dec. 1891). B. at The Portage, 40 miles above St. Louis, he was of French Canadian descent and had limited education. He learned boat building at Carondelette, below St. Louis and was engaged from 1827 as a boat builder by the American Fur Company at various upper Missouri River posts; generally he built their mackinaw boats for transporting furs to St. Louis. His second winter in the upper country was spent at the mouth of the Marias River and in the spring of 1829 one man was killed in an Assiniboin attack; the party then moved eight miles and built Fort McKenzie, trading with the Blackfeet for 14 years with only minor skirmishes with natives. Following the Harvey massacre of Blackfeet, the post was burned and the company moved to Fort Chardon, at the mouth of the Judith River; it too the traders destroyed and eventually the company established Fort Benton. Mercier remained at Benton until the American Fur Company sold out to the North West Company in 1866, moving then to Fort Union where he remained more than five years, until its abandonment. Mercier resettled at Benton. In 1831 he had married a 13-year-old Indian woman, remaining with her until she died in 1878 and fathering 11 children by her. One daughter married Henry Bostwick, killed in 1877 at the Nez Perce Battle of the Big Hole, Montana.

Montana, Contributions, Vol. X, 1940, 299-301.

Meriwether, David, statesman (Oct. 30, 1800-Apr. 4, 1893). B. in Louisa County, Virginia, he was taken at 4 to a Kentucky farm near Louisville, making that his home thereafter. He entered the Missouri River trade about 1819, and in 1820 freighted trade goods to the Pawnee villages. He reconnoitred the Santa Fe route that year, was captured by Mexicans and taken to Santa Fe, but released and returned to Council Bluffs by March 1821, shortly going back to Kentucky. In 1823 he married there, eventually fathering 13 children. Meriwether traded occasionally to New Orleans and once to Cuba, and in 1852 by appointment succeeded Henry Clay as U.S. Senator. In 1853 he was named governor of New Mexico Territory where, in general, he proved an intelligent and progressive force. He was active in attempting to bring peace and some kind of stability among numerous

Indian peoples during his four years. He often succeeded, sometimes failed, but on the whole his influence was positive. He returned to Kentucky in 1857, re-entered politics and was an influence in the state for the rest of his life.

David Meriwether, *My Life in the Mountains and on the Plains*, ed. by Robert A. Griffen. Norman, Univ. of Okla. Press, 1965; BDAC.

Mermet, Jean, Jesuit missionary (Sept. 23, 1664-Sept. 15, 1716). B. at Grenoble, France, he became a Jesuit and reached Canada in 1698, being assigned to the Miami mission on the St. Joseph River in present Michigan and another on the site of Chicago until 1702, when he was transferred to Kaskaskia on the Mississippi River. He was assigned in 1702 as chaplain to the Charles Juchereau de St. Denys operation for founding a tannery near the junction of the Ohio and Mississippi rivers and worked with Mascouten Indians who were drawn there; the tannery endeavor collapsed, in part because an epidemic swept off the leader and many of the Indian workers, and Mermet quitted the post in 1704. He arrived back at Kaskaskia about 1705 and remained there until his death. In spite of continued ill health, Mermet's zeal never faltered and his ministry at Kaskaskia was a success.

Thwaites, JR, LXVI, 339n10, DCB, II.

Merritt, Charles W., army officer (Jan. 7, 1849-Dec. 12, 1879). B. at Belleville, St. Clair County, Illinois, he was the youngest brother of Lieutenant Colonel Wesley Merritt, brevet Major General and before retirement to become army Major General. Wesley Merritt made every effort to have Charles commissioned, although his examination probing his fitness found him barely admissable. Charles Merritt on October 1, 1873, was commissioned a second lieutenant in the 9th Cavalry, a black regiment his brother commanded. The 9th was in Texas when Merritt joined it late in 1873. His brother took a leave the following May and never returned to the 9th which in 1875 was posted to New Mexico under its new colonel, Edward Hatch. Charles Merritt seems shortly to have encountered personal problems. In 1877 his corporal John Rogers reported that Merritt repeatedly tried to enter Rogers' quarters at night "after his wife had retired" and while Rogers presumably was on duty elsewhere. The corporal requested an

investigation. The matter came to the attention of General William T. Sherman, army commander-in-chief who, noting that "the humblest soldier of the Army, must be protected in his family," directed that the case be fully investigated "even to arrest and trial." Apparently insufficient evidence was found against Merritt, for neither trial or punishment is recorded. In August 1878 Merritt was on a Ute expedition, camping on the Platte River in Colorado. By 1879 he was in command of Ojo Caliente in the heart of the turbulent Mimbres Apache country of New Mexico. February 7 the dread Victorio and 22 of his followers, then on the warpath, hallooed the post. Merritt instructed his company to hold themselves in readiness, sent for Andy Kelley, a noted interpreter and daringly "went to where Victorio was, and he said he wanted to have a talk with me... On the following day I went out... and sent up my interpreter to tell him I was ready for a talk, to come down. He said he would not come down, for me to come up to where he was." Victorio insisted the officer and interpreter approach without arms and without escort. It was talk, or no surrender. In one of the most intrepid acts recorded in white-Apache history, Merritt fulfilled his duty: he and Kelley, without weapons, climbed the mountain and met the feared chief, face to face. Victorio agreed to surrender, providing he obtained passes for two representatives to visit the Fort Stanton Reservation east of the Rio Grande and bring back Nana and other late-hostile leading men and their families. Merritt saw no other way to end hostilities and agreed to give the passes. This provoked a sharp reprimand from higher authority until the officer explained the circumstances and the end he had in view, when he was cleared of wrong-doing and his recourse adjudged warranted. Victorio shortly would bolt the Ojo Caliente post in the belief he was to be transferred with his people to the hated San Carlos Reservation in Arizona from which they previously had fled, but this fiasco was not Merritt's fault. By this time the officer had developed an alcohol problem. He was court-martialed August 18, 1879, on three charges and seven specifications, most charging that he was drunk on duty or had been a public nuisance and one alleging he had been negligent in action against hostile Indians, remaining in his quarters asleep while his company was engaged against the enemy. He was found guilty on virtually all counts and dismissed from the army November 26, 1879. He died at 30, according to Heitman, 14 days later, the circumstances neither reported nor any explanation given.

Heitman; Dan L. Thrapp, *Victorio and the Mimbres Apaches.* Norman, Univ. of Okla. Press, 1974; Merritt's personnel file, NARS.

Merritt, Ezekiel, frontiersman (d. post 1848). Merritt may have been the "Captain Merritt" reported to have gone to California with Joe Walker in 1833; he was at New Helvetia (Sutter's Fort, later Sacramento) in 1841. In 1844 he was implicated in an attempt to rescue the English surgeon, Edward Bale, who had been imprisoned for shooting Salvador Vallejo in a private dispute. He served with Captain John Gantt in the Micheltorena campaign of 1844-45 during one of California's political upheavals. Merritt stole Francisco Arce's horses in 1846 at the start of the Bear Flag Revolt and nominally commanded the Bears at the outset, subsequently went south with Fremont at one time going as far as San Diego. Later he became a partner of William C. Moon on a Tehama County ranch. He is said to have died in the winter of 1847-48, but Bancroft believes it was somewhat later. He described Merritt as "a coarse-grained, loud-mouthed, unprincipled, whiskey-drinking, quarrelsome fellow, well adapted to the use that was made of him in promoting the filibusters' schemes."

Bancroft, *Pioneer Register.*

Merritt, Wesley, army officer (June 16, 1834-Dec. 3, 1910). B. at New York City, he was appointed to West Point from Illinois and upon graduation in 1860 named to the 2nd Dragoons (2nd Cavalry), serving briefly in Utah, then returning with his regiment to Washington, D.C. He became a well-known cavalry leader in the East, ending the Civil War a Major General of Volunteers on Sheridan's recommendation. He became a lieutenant colonel of the newly formed 9th Cavalry in 1866, assuming command near San Antonio, Texas, where a brief "mutiny" of the untrained recruits enlivened his initial takeover. With six companies he reoccupied Fort Davis, West Texas, spending the next

eight years in that state, with time out for trips abroad, on one of which he was married. In 1875 he became special cavalry inspector for the Division of the Missouri. A year later he was made agent for the Sioux at the Red Cloud Agency. He was promoted to colonel July 1, 1876, taking command of the 5th Cavalry in Wyoming. Merritt was appointed chief of cavalry for the Big Horn and Yellowstone Expedition when his regiment joined Crook on August 3, enroute having his first Indian skirmish with the Sioux on War Bonnet Creek, an encounter which also featured Buffalo Bill Cody's famous duel with Yellow Hand. The most important frontier operation of Merritt's career was the Crook expedition from August until October 1876. In its course Merritt took part in the action at Slim Buttes, September 9-10. Following the expedition he commanded Fort D.A. Russell (Cheyenne, Wyoming) until 1880, conducting scouting operations during the Nez Perce campaign of 1877, but without contacting the hostiles. He scouted with a like result during the Bannock War of 1878 and in early 1879 sat on the Reno Court of Inquiry at Chicago. In the autumn he marched 170 miles in 70 hours to relieve Thornburgh's command besieged by Utes on Milk River, Colorado. He continued to serve generally in the West until 1882 when he began a five-year stint as superintendent of West Point. In April 1887, upon the retirement of Willcox, he was promoted to Brigadier General, given command of the Department of the Missouri and later of the Department of Dakota. He took no part in the ghost dance or Wounded Knee affairs. In 1895 Merritt was promoted to Major General. In 1898 he commanded the expedition to the Philippines and August 13 captured Manila, briefly governed the Islands, and returned home by way of France in December. He retired in 1900 to Natural Bridge, Virginia, where he died. He was buried at West Point. In April 1890, he published in *Harper's New Monthly Magazine,* "Three Indian Campaigns," an article describing operations only one of which, that to Milk River, he participated in personally; the other two descriptions, however, are not without value. Merritt was married twice, his first wife having died in 1893.

Barry C. Johnson, *Merritt and the Indian Wars.* London, Johnson-Taunton Military Press, 1972.

Mesplex, French hero (d. Jan. 25, 1730). Mesplex and five other Frenchmen volunteered to carry to the hostile Natchez Indians of Mississippi who had recently risen in revolt and massacred many whites, terms of peace from the Chevalier de Loubois, commander of French troops. They did this "that they might be able under this pretext to gain information with regard to their force, and their present situation." Three of them were killed outright and three captured, one of the prisoners was returned with Indian demands for a great deal of goods in return for their peace, and "on the very same day, with every refinement in cruelty they burned sieur Mesplex and his (remaining) companion" at the stake.

Thwaites, JR, LXVIII, 191.

Metacom (Metacomet, King Philip), Wampanoag chief (c. 1638-Aug. 12, 1676). B. in Massachusetts, he succeeded his older brother, Wamsutta (Alexander) who had followed their father, Massasoit, as grand sachem of an Algonkin confederacy of Wampanoags. Differences between the colonists and the Wampanoags and other Indians arose principally over land, the Indians having little concept of personal ownership, the whites knowing no other means of managing it, and ofttimes unscrupulous "developers" making steady encroachments by "purchases," or acquisitions of land the tribal leaders considered communally theirs. It is believed by some that Metacom spent his first nine years as chief in preparation for war to push back the colonists; more likely his frustration continued to mount during that period, and his hostility kept pace. By 1674, realizing that the Wampanoags alone could not handle the situation, he sent messengers to other tribes seeking support. In January 1675, the conflict known as "King Philip's War" was generated when an Indian named John Sassamon was found dead under the ice of a Plymouth pond. A convert to Christianity, Sassamon spoke English well; he had returned to the forest as Philip's secretary, although he became a traitor to his people. Three Wampanoags caught by the English as Sassamon's killers, were executed the following June and the war commenced, the Wampanoags being joined by several neighboring tribes, or at least they

catching fire, launched their own hostilities against the whites concurrently. The initial successes were with the Indians. Of 90 colonial towns, 52 were attacked, 12 destroyed. Bands of Nipmucks attacked settlers in western Massachusetts; Philip's men, allied with Sakonnets, Pocassets and others, ravaged the Connecticut valley. Had there been more cohesion and stronger leadership, the Indians might have wiped out the colonists. Even so, "only treachery among the natives in all probability saved the colonists from extinction." Slowly, however, the tide began to turn against the insurgents, and by 1676 the resolution of the struggle became clear, even as the savagry of the whites became more pronounced. Metacom at length returned, or was driven back, to his ancestral home at Mt. Hope, Rhode Island, where he was betrayed by an informer and killed by an Indian in a night ambush-battle that wiped out or dispersed the last knot of his warriors. Philip was quartered and beheaded, the head born triumphantly to Plymouth where it was displayed on a pole for a quarter century as evidence not only of the terror he had brought to the colonial whites, but the barbarism with which they retaliated once they had secured the upper hand. His wife and little son were sold into slavery in the West Indies. Most authorities believe that Metacom, or Philip, "can not but be considered a man of marked abilities," but Douglas Edward Leach, the foremost modern student of the man and his war, believes that "Philip was not the great leader he was once assumed to be." Leach thinks Philip "early lost his control over the situation," and subsided into one leader among many and, in sum, he was "more futile than heroic, more misguided than villainous," and a man who became "more victim than leader" of the events he had set into motion. The truth probably is somewhere between the two views. The war fought in his name wrought "awful destruction." Leach wrote that "In proportion to population, King Philip's War inflicted greater casualties upon the people than any other war in our history. Several thousand persons lost their lives... The line of English settlement had been pushed more than twenty miles southward in the Connecticut Valley, and an even greater distance eastward from Brookfield toward the coast." Deerfield, Brookfield, Lancaster and other towns were totally destroyed and others at least partially burned, in addition to which the cost of the war was staggering and trade had been seriously disrupted in many areas, though loss of the war by Metacom foreshadowed the virtual extinction of the New England Indian peoples. The war, in short, had a profound effect on the maturing of the New England colonies, and upon their future course, even as its effect upon the social, economic, military and cultural fabric of white settlement was very great.

Literature abundant; HAI; reference works; Leach, *Flintlock.*

Metcalf, Archibald Charles, frontiersman (1815-c. 1850). B. in New York, he became an Indian trader about 1840 on the upper Platte, the Arkansas and other streams and at Taos. He sold out to Lancaster P. Lupton on the South Platte, transferring his operations to Pueblo about 1844. Metcalf was sheriff at Taos in 1847, hanging the Taos insurrectionists with some satisfaction. He continued to engage in pioneer activities, being a man of few apparent scruples, and disappeared because of cholera, Indians, or for other cause.

Janet Lecompte article, MM, Vol. IV.

Meurin, Sébastien Louis, Jesuit missionary (Dec. 26, 1707-Aug. 13, 1777). B. at Charleville, France, he became a Jesuit and reached Canada in November 1741. The following year he was assigned to Illinois where he worked principally at Kaskaskia until the Jesuit expulsion of 1763. He virtually alone received permission to remain in the country, and became curé of the French parish at Cahokia. He was appointed vicar general of the West but for long was unable to attend to those duties. He died at Prairie du Rocher, Illinois.

Thwaites, JR, LXX, 310-11n24, LXXI, 174.

Meusnier, Pierre (Pedro), adventurer (c. 1669-post 1699). A Parisian, Meusnier was a member of the 1684 La Salle expedition to the New World and accompanied that leader on his exploratory wanderings in east Texas. Whether he was one of the conspirators who did away with La Salle March 19, 1687, on the Trinity River of Texas is not reported, but at any rate he survived, living among the Indians for two years until, along with L'Archévèque and Grollet, he was picked up by a Spanish

expedition out of Mexico under Alonzo de Leon. In 1699 all three of the Frenchmen were in New Mexico, Meusnier and L'Archévèque soldiers at the presidio of Santa Fe and Grollet at Bernalillo. Nothing further is reported of Meusnier.

Adolphe F.A. Bandelier, "The Betrayer of La Salle." *Nation,* Vol. XLVII, (47), No. 1209 (Aug. 30, 1888), 166-67.

Meyer, Lipman, freighter (c. 1831-post 1865). A freighter out of Leavenworth, Meyer testified via deposition against the character of Captain Silas Soule on the basis of an alleged scout the two made with a small troop escort. The deposition was designed to show Soule "was afraid, got drunk, and stole blankets," and was thrown out by the military commission investigating the Sand Creek Massacre of November 29, 1864, at the instigation of Lieutenant Colonel Samuel F. Tappan, commission president, largely because it was not relative to the study, and was presented after Soule had been assassinated and could not rebut the testimony.

Sand Creek Massacre.

Miantonomo, Narragansett chief (c. 1600-Sept. 1643). A nephew of Canonicus, he became a noted chief of the Narragansett Indians of Rhode Island and in 1632 visited Boston where he was received by the governor. Occasionally suspected of hostility toward the English he cleared himself when once more called to Boston in 1636. During the Pequot War of 1637 he actively sided with the English and warred against the Mohegan, and Miantonomo in 1638 signed the tripartite agreement between the English of Connecticut, the Narragansett and the Mohegan. During 1640-42 he was again suspected by the English of "treachery," by which they meant hostility, but once more satisfactorily explained his position. Miantonomo appeared to have been impressed by the preaching of Roger Williams, although to what extent was unknown. In 1643 he became embroiled in a conflict with Uncas, a Mohegan sachem and was captured in a battle in which his people were defeated. Miantonomo was delivered into the hands of the English who had become disenchanted with him for his disposal of some of his lands to rival English colonists. "Performing a feat of semantic prestidigitation, they made Miantonomo into a treaty violator," although in fact he had scrupulously complied with all treaty provisions. But the English found they could not manage him as they chose and, distrusting his intelligence and ability they determined to murder him; yet they would not do this themselves, so handed him back to Uncas with instructions that he should assassinate the chief which was done "barbarously" by Uncas's brother, Wawequa in Uncas' presence. Miantonomo was said to have been "respected and loved by everyone who was not fearful of his power," which no doubt bothered the English. His son, Nanuntenoo, was a leader in King Philip's War of 1875-76.

Hodge, HAI; Francis Jennings, *The Invasion of America.* Chapel Hill, Univ. of No. Car. Press, 1978.

•

Micanopy, Seminole chief (c. 1780-1849). The descendant of King Payne and thus a hereditary chief since 1814 of the Seminoles, he was sometimes known as Halputta Hadjo, or "Crazy Alligator," but he was a wise and industrious man while giving the impression of slothful indolence. He possessed large herds of cattle and horses and 100 black slaves, and he stood by Osceola and most of the tribe in determination to remain in Florida and not assent to United States demands that the Seminoles remove to Indian Territory. Neither he nor Osceola signed the April 23, 1835, agreement to emigrate and on December 1 when the agent informed them they must hand over their horses and cattle and assemble for the long journey, they sent their women and dependents deep into the interior while the warriors armed themselves. The whites, seeing that the Seminoles intended to resist, abandoned their farms along the border, which the Indians immediately sacked. Troops were ordered in and the seven year conflict known as the Second Seminole War began. Its first startling event was the slaughter of Major Francis Dade and more than 100 of his men, December 28, 1836, Micanopy by report shooting the commander with his own hand, although he is not known to have taken any further part in the hostilities. In 1837 he agreed finally to emigrate, was kidnapped by young warriors for his defection, later that year came in under a white flag to arrange a treaty with Thomas S. Jesup, but Jesup had him taken prisoner regardless of the truce symbol. Micanopy was sent to Charleston, South Carolina, and from there with about 200 of his fellows to Indian Territory. Micanopy never again was absolute head chief and he died at his home there. He was twice married and later in life developed an alcohol problem.

Hodge, HAI; Dockstader; Frank Laumer, *Massacre!* Gainesville, Univ. of Fla. Press, 1968.

Michaux, André, explorer, botanist (Mar. 7, 1746-Nov. 1802). B. at Satory, Versailles, France, he early became interested in botany and traveled to England and in 1782-85 to Persia pursuing that interest. In 1785 the French government requested he study forest trees of North America with a view to the importation of valuable species. He spent months in New York, and in 1787 bought a plantation near Charleston, South Carolina, from where he explored the mountains of the Carolinas and the swamps of Florida, sending back to France many thousands of specimens. In 1794 he undertook a difficult expedition to arctic regions around Hudson Bay. Upon his return he suggested an exploration of the far west by way of the Missouri River, but this expedition never was undertaken, for Michaux was drafted by the French minister to communicate with Kentuckians about a scheme for a filibuster-like assault on Spanish Louisiana; this project collapsed however, although Michaux did go to Kentucky to see about furthering it; he quickly returned to his botanical interests. His financial situation had deteriorated and in 1796 he sailed for France, being shipwrecked on the coast of Holland though his life, some of his manuscripts and part of his collection were saved. He wished to return to America but received no encouragement from the government of France and instead accepted a position with an expedition to New Holland (Australia), but died of fever on Madagascar.

Thwaites, EWT, III; DAB

Michaux, Francois André, botanist, traveler (Aug. 16, 1770-Oct. 23, 1855). The son of the botanist André Michaux, he was b. in France and after his mother died went with his father to New York. He accompanied his parent on several arduous exploratory journeys in the interior although principally entrusted with management of the nursery at the Charleston plantation his father had purchased. He returned to France in 1790 to study medicine, but soon turned his attention anew to botany and in 1801 was commissioned by the republican government of France to revisit North America. He traveled west of the Alleghenies and east of the Mississippi, writing journals that were published and circulated widely in several languages. In 1806 he started once more from France for Charleston, but was captured by the British and held on Bermuda which resulted in his scientific study of that island. In the United States again he spent three years, traveling widely in the east, gathering material for his three-volume *North American Sylva, or a Description of the Forest Trees of the United States, Canada, and Nova Scotia...*, which appeared in French in 1810-13 and was translated and published in English in 1818-19. He died at Vauréal, near Pontoise, France.

Thwaites, EWT, III; DAB.

Michler, Francis (Frank), army officer (c. Nov. 1848-May 29, 1901). B. in New York he entered West Point from Pennsylvania and in 1870 was commissioned a second lieutenant in the 5th Cavalry, joining in October at Fort D.A. Russell, Wyoming and shortly moving to Arizona with the regiment. Here he was stationed at Camp Hualpai and took part in many actions, including an important affair at Muchos Cañones for which, and another, he was breveted, and fights at Red Rock, Clear Creek, Tonto Creek and in the Mazatzal Mountains, among others, all in Arizona. Michler prepared the map of the Muchos Cañones fight which was filed with the action report. In January 1874 he became aide to Major General Schofield, serving at San Francisco and at West Point. He became adjutant of the Military Academy in 1878, remaining there until 1881. He rejoined his organization at Fort Niobrara, Nebraska, and in the late spring of 1882 made a survey of part of southwest Dakota for a wagon road requested by the Sioux. Michler later served at Fort D.A. Russell, and at Fort Sidney, Nebraska. He was stationed at Fort Elliott, Texas, in 1890 and at Fort Reno, Indian Territory, from 1890 to 1892. He had become a first lieutenant in 1876, captain in 1888 and a major in 1901, being military secretary to Miles from 1900 to 1901. He died at Washington, D.C.

Heitman; Cullum; Price, *Fifth Cavalry; Annual Reunion of West Point Graduates,* 1902.

Middleton, David Charles (Doc) (Texas Jack Lyons, and many other aliases), horse thief, outlaw (Feb. 9, 1851-Dec. 27, 1913). B. in Mississippi, he became a Texas cowboy and trailed a longhorn herd to Ogallala, Nebraska, in 1876, rumor having it he left Llano County, Texas, because of a shooting. January 13, 1877, he killed James Keefe, a 5th Cavalryman, in a Sidney, Nebraska, saloon. He fled via Fort Robinson to the Dakotas, organized a band of horse rustlers called Pony boys, and stole hundreds, perhaps thousands of head from Indians and others, marketing them as far south as Texas. On the side he became friends with such frontier notables as Bill Cody, Jim Cook, Print Olive, the Norths and others. The tales about Doc are legion, some of them no doubt true. His nemesis was William Henry Harrison Llewellyn, special agent for the Department of Justice, who by a ruse in July 1879, took him but the outlaw, seriously wounded, escaped in a shootout in which two men were killed and another wounded. Middleton was recaptured. His wife, Pood Richardson, abandoned him while he was doing time (three years, five months) and after his release, on June 18, 1883, he married her younger sister, Irene. He returned to Gordon, Nebraska, opened a saloon, became a deputy sheriff. He entered the famed Chadron, Nebraska, to Chicago horse race in 1893, the year of the Columbian Exposition in the latter city, and finished, although he didn't win. He opened a saloon at Ardmore, Nebraska, fathered four children, did a little bootlegging to the Sioux on Pine Ridge agency, incurred the enmity of Fort Robinson soldiers who wrecked his saloon, ruining him. He opened a bootleg place near Douglas, Wyoming, was arrested, fined $150 and costs, but died before payment. He was a courageous, honest, able crook, a dangerous man but with the glint of real humor in his eyes, something of a Robin Hood and believed in by more men than he robbed.

John Carson, *Doc Middleton, the Unwickedest Outlaw.* Santa Fe, Press of Territorian, 1966.

Middleton, Eugene, stagecoach driver, pioneer (Feb. 7, 1861-Apr. 24, 1929). B. in California his parents, William and Miriam Middleton took their family to Arizona, settling first at Tucson and about 1876 at Globe, a mining camp in Gila County; they then established a ranch eight miles from

Pleasant Valley. In September 1881 the ranch was attacked by Apaches following the Cibecue incident, and Gene, who was at Globe, quickly brought assistance. Later Gene was with a party of "Globe Rangers" oraganized to fight the Apaches who, however outguessed them and stole their mounts. In November 1889 Gene who, with his father was proprietor of a small stage line, agreed to haul eight Apache prisoners along with Sheriff Glenn Reynolds and William Holmes as guards, to the railroad, two days distant. Among the prisoners was one known as the Apache Kid. On the second day, near present Kelvin, Arizona, the Indians turned on their guards, killed one, the other dying of a heart attack, and Pas-lau-tau shot Gene Middleton, dropping him from the driver's box, the bullet entering the right cheek and emerging from his back. It is reported that one of the prisoners wanted to finish Middleton with either a rock or a shot, but was dissuaded by the Apache Kid, though the record is obscured by the several versions Middleton apparently told; it would seem however that the Indian desired to spare his life since the Apache Kid to that time had neither attacked nor killed any white. Middleton lived at Globe the remainder of his life, being described on his death certificate as an "apartment house owner" at the time he succumbed to "natural causes which are unknown."

Jess G. Hayes, *Apache Vengeance.* Albuquerque, Univ. of New Mex. Press, 1954; Dan L. Thrapp, *Al Sieber, Chief of Scouts.* Norman, Univ. of Okla. Press, 1964; author interview with Leroy Middleton, July 13, 1958.

Middleton, Henry, pioneer (c. 1863-c. 1949). B. probably in California he reached Arizona with his parents about 1873; the Middletons established a cattle ranch in the Sierra Ancha Mountains north of Globe about 1879. In September 1881 the ranch house was attacked by Apaches as a spinoff of the Cibecue affair, two men were killed and Henry Middleton was shot above the heart; he had no medical attention for four days until he could be gotten to Globe, but survived to recover completely. Middleton had a close brush with hostile Apaches just before the battle of Big Dry Wash in the summer of 1882 but escaped unscathed although his horse was shot. He was a brother of Eugene (Gene) Middleton who was wounded seriously in an Apache Kid

outbreak in 1889. Lee Middleton said that Henry "lived to die at 86 at Seattle," but there does not seem to be an official record of his death there at the date cited.

Interview with Leroy (Lee) Middleton July 13, 1958; Clara T, Woody, Milton L. Schwartz, *Globe, Arizona.* Tucson, Ariz. Hist. Soc., 1977.

Middleton, Leroy (Lee), stagecoach driver (Jan. 24, 1874-May 31, 1967). B. at Tucson, Arizona, he was taken by his family to Globe in 1876 and later to their ranch in the Sierra Ancha Mountains near Pleasant Valley, also in Arizona. When Apaches attacked the place in September 1881, Lee with two other children and their mother were in the milkhouse; the mother dragged the three through a hail of bullets safely into the log home. Lee was a stage driver between Globe and Florence, Arizona, on the line run by his father and older brother, Gene, who was seriously wounded in 1889 during an Apache Kid outbreak. On one occasion Lee was held up by Henry Blevins who took from the strongbox some bars of silver (later lost in a flash flood). Middleton at that time did not know who the robber had been, but Blevins and his partner were arrested and did time for the affair. In December 1921 Lee ran into Blevins in a speak-easy and they got drunk together. Middleton worked copper claims on Pinto Creek, Arizona, in 1902-1904 during which time he became friendly with Al Sieber; later in life Lee lived in Phoenix, where he died.

Interview, July 13, 1958.

Middleton, William, pioneer (c. 1827-Feb. 19, 1891). B. in Kentucky, he went to California in 1849 where his son, Eugene (Gene) Middleton, later wounded in an Apache outbreak, was born. Middleton, a blacksmith by trade, brought his growing family (which eventually included nine children) to Tucson, Arizona about 1873 and after a few months moved to Hayden's Ferry (the present Tempe, Arizona). He refused an invitation to accompany John Sullivan, an ex-soldier, in his search for a silver lode he had discovered while in the service and thus missed out on possible wealth in the vicinity of the present Globe, which Middleton reached in 1876. About 1880 the Middletons located a cattle ranch in the Sierra Ancha Mountains near Pleasant Valley; the place was attacked twice by hostile Apaches, in 1881 and 1882. One son, Henry, was seriously wounded in the first affray and a daughter, Hattie narrowly escaped death while two young men at the ranch were slain. The Middletons took no part in the Pleasant Valley War, but as a result of the tense atmosphere in the surrounding area they removed to Globe, the sons operating stage lines and the father running a blacksmith shop in town and later becoming head blacksmith for the Old Dominion Copper Smelter at Globe. In early 1891 heavy rains caused the flooding of Pinal Creek at Globe and Middleton was killed either in a 75-foot fall to the water or by drowning.

Globe, *Arizona Silver Belt,* Feb. 21, 1891; Clara T. Woody, Milton L. Schwartz, *Globe, Arizona.* Tucson, Ariz. Hist. Soc., 1977; interview with Leroy (Lee) Middleton, July 13, 1958.

Midnight, bucking horse (c. 1918-1954). B. in Canada he was said to have been part Morgan, part Percheron; he never had good conformation, but his bucking qualities were superb, all who saw or attempted to ride him agreeing that he ranked at the pinnacle of his specialty. He came to international attention in 1926 when Pete Knight drew him at the Calgary Stampede; the horse quickly became a sensation, was used at countless U.S. and Canadian rodeos and "bucked off the best men of his time." Prize money was offered anyone who would ride him, but there were never any amateur takers. Owned by Verne Elliott of Platteville, Colorado, from 1923 to 1930, he was ridden by only four riders; of these only Frank Studnick at Pendleton, Oregon, in 1929, was not subsequently thrown, Studnick not trying a second time. Midnight died at the age of 36 and is buried at the National Cowboy Hall of Fame, Oklahoma City, Oklahoma.

Anthony Amaral, "They Don't Make 'Em Like They Used To!" *Ariz. Highways,* Vol. LVI, No. 5 (May 1970), 2-9, 36-39.

Miera y Pacheco, Bernardo, pioneer (fl. 1743-1778). B. at Valle de Carriedo, Burgos, Spain, he reached Mexico in 1743, came to El Paso from Chihuahua, and to Santa Fe in 1754. He was a talented man, an army engineer, Indian fighter, trader, cartographer and artist, government agent and rancher. Miera y Pacheco accompanied the Escalante Expedition of 1776 as far north as Utah Lake, then down to Arizona and across the Colorado River at the Crossing of the Fathers, returning to Santa Fe early in 1777. In 1778 he completed a useful map of the expedition's travels. As a painter and sculptor his works decorated many New Mexico churches and a large painting of St. Michael still exists on the altar screen at the Chapel of San Miguel, Santa Fe. Miera y Pacheco also wrote a report on the Dominguez/Escalante Expedition which was published by Bolton.

The Dominguez-Escalante Journal: Their Expedition in 1776, trans. by Angelico Chavez, ed. by Ted J. Warner, Provo, Brigham Young Univ. Press, 1976; Herbert E. Bolton, *Pageant in the Wilderness.* Salt Lake City, Utah State Hist. Soc., 1951.

Miguel, (Esh-ke-iba), Cibecue Apache chief (d. 1874). Miguel, known as "One-Eyed Miguel," because he had lost the use of an eye early in life, was an older brother of Diablo, another famous Western Apache chief. John Marion wrote that despite his handicap Miguel managed to "see clearer with (one eye) than do any of his brother chiefs with their two eyes. In a word, he is by far the shrewdest, ablest Indian of the tribe." Miguel was the most prominent chief of the Carrizo Creek Apaches in the 1860s. In 1850 he had driven Pedro to the east in a clan feud, the latter settling near the later Fort Apache with his band. In 1869 Miguel and Diablo had brought to the future site of Fort Apache three white men, Corydon E. Cooley, and two others, from Fort Defiance, virtually initiating relations between the whites and White Mountain Apaches. The three were there when the army arrived to establish Camp, later Fort, Apache. Miguel welcomed the soldiers. In 1871 he and Petone, a son of Pedro, killed an Indian wanted for the slaying of a white clerk at the post trader's store. Miguel supplied recruits for the first unit of Apache scouts enlisted by Crook later in 1871. General Howard took Miguel, Pedro and Esh-kel-dah-silah, an influential though now aged chief to Washington, D.C. in 1872, pausing at New York to purchase Miguel a glass eye which he ever afterward wore with pride. When Crook because of intra-tribal frictions caused the Cibecue (and Carrizo Creek) Apaches to move in closer to Fort Apache where the army could keep an eye on them, this increased tensions among them and led to a mounting series of small clashes. In

the course of one of them, Miguel and eight
other Cibecue men were killed along with two
White Mountain Apaches. Diablo avenged
Miguel's death.

Lori Davisson, manuscript on White Mountain
Apaches, 1978; J.H. Marion, *Notes of Travel
Through the Territory of Arizona,* ed. by Donald
M. Powell. Tucson, Univ. of Ariz Press, 1965, 24;
O.O. Howard, *Famous Indian Chiefs I Have
Known.* N.Y., Century Co., 1908, 93-111.

Mike, Jim, guide (May 3, 1872-Sept. 30,
1977). B. probably in southern Utah, Mike
was a Paiute Indian who guided the white
"discoverers" of Rainbow Bridge in northern
Arizona in 1909, although another Paiute,
Nasja Begay (d. 1918) is generally credited
with leading the explorers to the site. In 1908
William Boone Douglass of the General Land
Office (now the Bureau of Land Management)
while surveying the future Natural Bridges
National Monument learned from one of his
axemen, Mike's Boy (who later took the name
of Jim Mike), of a rainbow-shaped bridge
near Navaho Mountain. From Washington
he received instructions to seek it out. Jim
attempted to guide him to it in December
1908, but snow blocked them. On August 9.
1909, again with Jim as guide, Douglass
headed an expedition out of Bluff, Utah. At
the same time another party under Dr. Byron
Cummings of the University of Utah, was
setting out with the identical objective. The
two groups joined forces; which first sighted
the bridge August 14, 1909, is a matter of
dispute, but Jim Mike seems to have
credentials equally good with Nasja Begay or
his father, Nasja, generally credited with
leading to the discovery. Mike said he had first
sighted the "bent rock with the hole in it" as a
boy, and that he had told Nasja of it, both
being members of a band living in Paiute
Canyon; no Navahos then lived in the area or
knew of the bridge, Mike believed. Mike lived
his latter years at White Mesa, a Paiute
community 10 miles south of Blanding, Utah.
In June 1974, the National Park Service gave
him $50 for his discovery of the bridge.

Information and enclosures from James D.
Harpster, chief, Office of Communications and
Public Affairs, Nat. Park Service Regional Office,
Denver; Zeke Scher, "The Man Who Discovered
Rainbow Bridge." *Empire Magazine of the
Denver Post,* Vol. XXIV, No. 49 (Dec. 9, 1973); *The
Discovery of Rainbow Bridge,* Tucson, Cummings
Pubn. Council, Inc., 1959.

Milam, Benjamin Rush, frontiersman (Oct.
20, 1788-Dec. 7, 1835). B. at Frankfort,
Kentucky, he served in the War of 1812. He
went to New Orleans in 1815, with others
chartered a schooner to trade in South
America but yellow fever defeated them. He
traded with Comanche Indians on the
Colorado River of Texas in 1818 and the
following year joined Trespalacios and Long
in a filibustering expedition into Texas, from
that time forward being involved in the
turbulent events surrounding the Mexican bid
for independence and the later moves by Texas
for its own freedom from Mexican rule. He
was killed in the successful Texan attempt to
seize San Antonio from the forces of Mexican
leader Martín Perfecto de Cós. Milam was one
of the major heroes of the Texas War of
Independence.

Lois Garver, "Benjamin Rush Milam,"
Southwestern Hist. Quar., Vol. XXXVIII, Nos. 2, 3
(Oct. 1934-Jan. 1935), 79-121, 177-202; HT.

Miles, Dixon Stansbury, army officer (1804-
Sept. 16, 1862). B. in Maryland, he was a West
Point graduate commissioned in 1824 in the
4th Infantry, performed frontier duty at Fort
Gibson, Indian Territory, in 1825-28 and was
a quartermaster in a Seminole War from
1839-42 in Florida. Miles was engaged in the
military occupation of Texas in 1845-46. He
was breveted for Mexican War actions at Fort
Brown, Texas, and before Monterrey,
Mexico. He was on frontier duty in Indian
Territory from 1848-51. In New Mexico as
major of the 5th Infantry he made a sweep
against the Mescaleros bringing them to a
peace, and temporarily was in command of
the department, directing expeditions into the
Navaho country more as a demonstration of
force than for hostile purposes. Miles was
characterized by New Mexico governor
William Carr Lane as "a walking sponge,
martinet & a -----," the governor leaving his
last judgment blank. Miles led one wing of
Bonneville's Gila River expedition against the
Apaches in 1857 and the next year again was
in the Navaho country, leading an expedition
at direction of Brigadier General John
Garland. Miles was considered unenthusiastic
in his hunt for hostile Indians, although he
penetrated the Canyon de Chelly and there
was some slight skirmishing with the enemy.
The campaign and related operations required
some four months, when Miles concluded an

agreement with certain Navaho leaders ending the "war." He was at Fort Kearny, Nebraska, in 1860-61 and at the outbreak of the Civil War was at Fort Leavenworth. He was killed by an exploding shell at Harper's Ferry after capitulating to the Confederates because he had been insufficiently supported. The shell burst was accidental.

Appleton; Heitman; Cullum; Frank McNitt, *Navajo Wars.* Albuquerque, Univ. of New Mex. Press, 1972.

Miles, Nelson Appleton, army officer (Aug. 8, 1839-May 25, 1925). B. near Westminster, Massachusetts, he was commissioned a first lieutenant of the 22nd Massachusetts Infantry September 9, 1861, and became lieutenant colonel of the 61st New York Infantry May 31, 1862, and colonel September 20. His Civil War record was exceptional, Miles fighting in all but one of the important engagements of the Army of the Potomac, being wounded four times and earning the Medal of Honor. At war's end he commanded the II Army Corps and became Major General of Volunteers October 21, 1865. Miles became colonel of the 40th Infantry July 28, 1866, and transferred to the 5th Infantry March 15, 1869. For 15 years he was engaged against an assortment of Indian tribes on the Plains and Far West. From July 25, 1874, until June 2, 1875, Miles was a field commander in the so-called Red River War against Comanches, Kiowas and Southern Cheyennes; there was much campaigning, no very important engagements but the activity brought peace after more than a century of warfare to the South Plains. In a winter campaign in 1876-77 Miles swept up the fragments of Sioux resistance on the North Plains, pursued Sitting Bull to the Canadian border and brought peace to the upper country as he had to the southern reaches; again there were no massive engagements but Miles lost no opportunity to ably vanquish what resistance remained, and his service once more was distinctly creditable. In the major operation of his Indian fighting career he led a forced march of his 5th Infantry, Mounted and elements of the 2nd and 7th Cavalry to attack the Nez Perce in the Bear Paw Mountains of Montana at the conclusion of their epic peregrination from Idaho toward Canada. The principal engagement occurred September 30, 1877, Miles losing 24 men, including two officers killed, 50 wounded for an Indian loss of 17 killed and 418 shortly made prisoner; about a third of the Nez Perce did manage to slip away and reached their Canadian sanctuary. Miles became a Brigadier General December 15, 1880, and commanded the Department of the Platte until early 1886 when he succeeded George Crook as commander of the Department of Arizona; Crook had virtually ended the long, episodic Apache wars when Geronimo and a handful of others slipped away from him to resume raiding. Crook was sharply criticized for what was not his fault, and asked to be relieved, Miles named to take over. A difference between Miles and Crook soon became bitter and a lasting enmity developed that endured as long as Crook lived. Miles was directed to make the utmost use of white troops to wind up the Apache campaign, but this proved futile and he resorted at last to the disparaged practices of Crook, sending Gatewood and Apache scouts to bring Geronimo in. The intrepid lieutenant succeeded in entering the camp of the hostiles and persuading Geronimo to submit; Miles accepted the surrender in September 1886 and the Apache wars were over. In November 1887 Miles was awarded a rather unearned sword from the people of Arizona for ridding the territory of hostile Apaches, a feat more properly accomplished by his predecessor although Miles accepted the honor unblushingly. Miles commanded the Division of the Pacific from 1888-90 when he returned to the Northern Plains to direct the military operation which culminated in the Wounded Knee debacle, during which time Miles commanded the Division of the Missouri with Chicago his headquarters when not in the field, as he was in Dakota. In 1890 with the death of Crook there was a vacancy in the ranks of Major Generals and Miles was named April 5, 1890, to fill it, an appointment that would surely have irritated Crook had he known of it. In 1895 Miles became commander in chief of the army and a Lieutenant General June 6, 1900. During the Spanish American War however he did not lead forces in Cuba because he was involved in a bitter public quarrel with the Secretary of War, a controversy with the navy, and had been censured by future President Theodore Roosevelt, who referred to him as a "brave Peacock," in reference to Miles's taste for lavish dress uniforms with every embellishment possible for himself and officers under his command. Miles did lead the operation against Puerto Rico, an undertaking without much glory and that went virtually unnoticed by the public. The General retired August 8, 1903. A very able officer, Miles was rather unimaginative; he was vain, pompous and markedly insensitive to the feelings and rights of others, whites or Indians, unless he felt they could further his inordinate ambition. He generated a wide circle of influential enemies in the army and out of it, and this failing no doubt prevented him from rising to the extreme heights he coveted. While one of few successful Indian-fighting generals, he was acutely defensive over his lack of West Point credentials and formal military training, and this was revealed throughout his outstanding career. Miles died at Washington D.C., and suitably his end came during the National Anthem at the Ringling Brothers Circus. Miles had told his own story in *Personal Recollections and Observations* (1896), and *Serving the Republic* (1911).

Literature abundant: Virginia W. Johnson, *The Unregimented General: A Biography of Nelson A. Miles.* Boston, Houghton Mifflin Co., 1962; James L. Haley, *The Buffalo War.* Garden City, N.Y., Doubleday & Co., 1976; Robert M. Utley, *Frontier Regulars.* N.Y., Macmillan Co., 1973; Odie B. Faulk, *The Geronimo Campaign.* N.Y., Oxford Univ. Press, 1969; Utley, *The Last Days of the Sioux Nation.* New Haven, Yale Univ. Press, 1972.

Milfort, LeClerc, partisan leader (c. 1750-1817). B. at Tiriles-Motiers, near Mezieres, France, he fled his homeland after killing a King's servant in a duel. In May 1776 he arrived at Coweta, Georgia, on the Chattahoochie River, where he settled. Milfort became an acquaintance, then a friend of Alexander McGillivray, whose sister he married. Milfort was created a Tustenuggee, or grand war chief, of the Creeks, leading expeditions against the Whigs, or American rebels during the American Revolution. After nearly 25 years he returned to France in 1799, and Napoleon Bonaparte commissioned him a Brigadier General. Milfort wrote a history of the Creeks which was published at Paris in 1802: *Memoire... sur mes differens voyages et mon sojour dans la Nation Creek.* In 1814 he narrowly escaped with his life during an attack on his home by a party of Russians. Shortly after he died.

Thomas McAdory Owen, *History of Alabama and Dictionary of Alabama Biography,* 4 vols. (1921), IV. Spartanburg, So. Car., Reprint Co., 1978; information from the Ala. Dept. of Archives and Hist.; Albert James Pickett, *History of Alabama.* Birmingham Book and Mag. Co., 1962.

Millar, James Franklin, army officer (d. Mar. 23, 1866). B. in New York he entered the army from Oregon as a private in the 2nd Ohio Infantry April 17, 1861, and was commissioned a first lieutenant in the 14th Infantry May 14. He emerged from the Civil War a captain and brevet major and joined Dr. Benjamin Tappan in traveling from the Pima villages to old Fort Grant at the junction of the San Pedro and Aravaipa rivers in Arizona. Thirty-five miles west of Grant they were attacked by Indians. Millar was killed instantly, four of the six soldiers of the escort also died while the other two soldiers, a teamster and a Mexican "attendant" escaped. Dr. Tappan was wounded and perished of thirst wandering about in the desert.

Prescott, Ariz., *Miner,* Apr. 11, 1866; Heitman.

Miller, Alfred Jacob, artist (Jan. 2, 1810-June 26, 1874). B. at Baltimore, Maryland, he studied art with Thomas Sully and went abroad, continuing his education in 1833-34 at the College of Fine Arts, Paris, visited Rome and Florence, Italy, and returned to the United States to establish a studio at Baltimore in late 1834. By 1837 he was settled at New Orleans, attempting to make a living through portraiture. Miller met the British traveler William Drummond Stewart at New Orleans, the Scottish sportsmen retaining Miller as artist to accompany his party that summer across the Plains to a Mountain Man rendezvous on the Green River in the present Wyoming and to "sketch the remarkable scenery & incidents" to be encountered. The Stewart party joined an American Fur Company brigade, leaving Independence, Missouri, in late spring, reaching Fort William (Laramie) within five weeks and continuing on to the rendezvous, Miller becoming so far as is known the only artist to attend such a singular fur business fair. He made hundreds of sketches and extensive notes to enable him to produce finished pictures upon his return to his studio. Miller may have accompanied a briefer trip to the mountains with Stewart in 1838, these two journeys being his only personal visitations to the Rockies though from them emerged his life's work. He foresook New Orleans to return to Baltimore where he opened a studio once again. Here Miller produced many pictures, oils and water colors, based upon his western experiences; in 1840 he went to Scotland, visited Stewart's Murthly Castle and painted a number of works for his patron. Miller returned to Baltimore after two years and continued to produce finished works from his western sketches and memories. The artist was virtually ignored by contemporary critics, but interest in his work revived as historians came to appreciate its unique quality and value as a testimony, virtually the only one, to an interesting and important phase of American history. Collections of Miller's work are held by the Stark Museum of Art, Orange, Texas; the Walters Art Gallery, Baltimore; the Joslyn Art Museum, Omaha; and the Thomas Gilcrease Institute of American History and Art, at Tulsa, Oklahoma. A manuscript annotating 166 of his western studies is believed to have been compiled by Miller himself and is held by the library of the Gilcrease Institute. Miller died at Baltimore.

Marvin C. Ross, *The West of Alfred Jacob Miller.* Norman, Univ. of Okla. Press, 1951; Bernard DeVoto, *Across the Wide Missouri.* Boston, Houghton Mifflin Co., 1947; REAW.

Miller, Clell(and D.), desperado (Dec. 16, 1849-Sept. 7, 1876). B. in Lincoln County, Kentucky, he was one of eight children, a brother, Edward (b. c. 1856) being killed, perhaps by Jesse James. The family settled near Kearney, Missouri. Miller served as a guerilla with Bloody Bill Anderson during the Civil War and was wounded in a fight with Union forces near Albany, Missouri, captured two days later, held at St. Louis and released in April, 1865. He may have become acquainted with the James brothers in his guerilla days; they lived not far from his family home. He joined the James gang in time to take part in the Corydon, Iowa, bank robbery of June 3, 1871. Miller was arrested by a ruse, tried and acquitted on the testimony that he was "elsewhere" at the time of the robbery. He was said to have taken part in the Otterville, Missouri, train robbery of July 7,

1876, with the James/Younger people. He was killed in the James gang's Northfield, Minnesota, bank robbery. Clell Miller's body was taken to the University of Michigan medical school where it was claimed by his relatives, returned to Missouri for burial.

William A. Settle, *Jesse James Was His Name.* Columbia, Univ. of Mo. Press, 1966; Settle to author, Jan. 19, 1979; Colin Rickards, "Bones of the Northfield Robbers." *Real West,* Vol. 22, No. 161 (Jan. 1979), 28-31, 60; M.C. Eden, "Clell Miller and the Corydon Bank Robbery." *Brand Book,* Vol. 20, Nos. 3, 4 (Apr.-July 1978), London, English Westerners' Soc., 1978.

Miller, George, desperado (1890s-1920s). With Redbuck, "a Plains Indian," Miller depredated in western Oklahoma until by 1898 the pair had good express company prices on their heads. Redbuck was killed and Miller, wounded in the right wrist, surrendered in an 1898 shootout, probably in Washita County. Miller went to the penitentiary for about 20 years. In the 1920s he was deputy sheriff for the oilfield town of Three Sands; a drunken Indian he was trying to arrest killed him.

Tom Dale, "Oklahoma Outlaw Incident." Potomac Corral of Westerners *Corral Dust* Vol. III, No. 4 (Dec. 1958), 29.

Miller, George Lee, rancher, showman (Sept. 9, 1881-Feb. 1, 1929). B. at Baxter Springs, Kansas, he was a son of George W. Miller, who founded the 101 Ranch near Ponca City, Oklahoma, in 1892, making of it a diversified commercial empire and from which emerged the famous wild west show which toured for many years. George Lee Miller during his lifetime was part owner of it all. He died in an auto accident on an icy road.

Who Was Who; Don Russell, *The Wild West: A History of the Wild West Shows.* Ft. Worth, Tex., Amon Carter Mus., 1970.

Miller, Henry, stockman (July 21, 1827-Oct. 14, 1916). B. Heinrich Kreiser at Brackenheim, Wurttemberg, Germany, he came to this country in 1847, was a New York butcher until 1850 when he changed his name to Miller and went to San Francisco, again operating a meat market until 1857, then forming a partnership with Charles Lux, an Alsatian butcher. They entered the cattle business in 1857 and in 1863 the firm of Miller & Lux bought a ranch in the

San Joaquin Valley of California with funds supplied by wealthy San Francisco friends of Lux. More than 15 ranches came under their control, the largest ranching enterprise on the Pacific slope and one of the most extensive on record, covering 800,000 acres in California and other ranges in Oregon and Nevada; at one time they counted 80,000 cattle and 100,000 sheep. Lux died in 1887; Miller engaged in a 20-year court battle with Lux's heirs, then incorporated as the Pacific Livestock Company. It was said that at one time a million head of cattle grazed on Miller lands or those in which he had an interest. He early saw the agricultural possibilities of the San Joaquin valley, built storage dams and irrigation systems and commenced to farm around 500,000 acres, ruthlessly acquiring water rights and engaging in endless litigation with the state and settlers, usually winning his cases although there is no surviving evidence of bribery or other illegal influences with the courts. He was an unscrupulous man however and obtained much of his land and influence by fraud or connivance. One of the positive actions of Miller's long career was his determination to preserve the last remnants of the distinctive tule elk of the San Joaquin Valley; that the species still exists is due to his efforts. Miller was not a particularly pleasant man, penurious to the point of miserliness, humorless, interested only in his holdings and their extension and one whose critics said that "what he couldn't steal for himself, he paid the courts to steal for him." He died at his mansion at San Francisco.

Who Was Who; REAW; James P. Degnan, "Portrait for a Western Album." *Amer. West,* Vol. XV, No. 6 (Nov./Dec. 1978), 30-31; Edward Francis Treadwell, *The Cattle King, a Dramatized Biography.* N.Y., Macmillan Co., 1931.

Miller, Joseph, army officer, fur trader (fl. 1799-1813). B. at Baltimore of a good family, he was well educated but of short temper. He became a cadet in the 2nd Infantry in June 1799, a second lieutenant February 16, 1801, transferred to the 1st Infantry April 1, 1802, and resigned June 21, 1805, because he was denied a furlough. He went to St. Louis and became experienced as a fur trader, hunter and trapper. In 1809 he was a member of the Crooks-McClellan party and with them joined the Astorians. In the autumn of 1809 he became disgusted with the lack of success of

the enterprise and abandoned it and his share in the company at Fort Henry on the Snake River. He met Stuart on his overland journey in 1813 and acted for him as guide, returning with that party to St. Louis. Nothing further is known of his career.

Thwaites, EWT, V, 106n.; Heitman; Gabriel Franchere, *Adventure at Astoria, 1810-1814.* Norman, Univ. of Okla. Press, 1967.

Miller, Josiah, pioneer (d. Sept. 11, 1857). Miller and his wife, Mathilda Cameron Miller, daughter of William and Martha Cameron, all from Johnson County, Arkansas, with their four children: William, 8 or 9 years old; Alfred, 7; Eliza, 4 or 5, and Joseph Jr., 1 or 2, joined the Fancher emigrant wagon train at Fort Smith, Arkansas. The company left, late in March 1857, for California, but was massacred except for the infants at Mountain Meadows, Utah, by Mormons and Mormon-led Indians.

William Wise, *Massacre at Mountain Meadows,* N.Y., Thomas Y. Crowell Co., 1976.

Miller, Marcus Peter, army officer (Mar. 27, 1835-Dec. 29, 1906). B. in Massachusetts, he was graduated from West Point in 1858 and became a brevet second lieutenant in the artillery, becoming second lieutenant of the 4th Artillery in 1859. He did frontier duty at Fort Crittenden, Utah, in 1860-61, served in the east during the Civil War, emerging a captain and brevet lieutenant colonel. Miller served in the Lava Beds against the Modocs, winning another brevet in part for his service there April 17, 1873 and for his role in the Clearwater, Idaho, battle with the Nez Perce when he was of Howard's command July 11-12, 1877. He had performed frontier duty at Fort Stevens, Oregon most of the time from 1872 until June of 1877, served on the Nez Perce campaign from June until October in the latter year, and the Bannock campaign from June to September 1878. The remainder of his duty was largely in the east and not connected directly to the frontier; he became a major of the 5th Artillery in 1883, lieutenant colonel of the 1st Artillery in 1894, colonel of the 3rd Artillery in 1897, a Brigadier General of Volunteers in 1898 and appointed to the same rank in the army in 1899, retiring March 27 of that year. He died at Fort Barrancas, Florida, but had lived in retirement at Stockbridge, Massachusetts. Howard, p. 133, described him as of "middling height, well knit for toughness, with light beard and lightish hair, handsome forehead, blue eye, and a pleasant face," adding that he managed "to take a sincere pleasure in every loyal duty."

Heitman; Cullum; Powell; O.O. Howard, *Chief Joseph: His Pursuit and Capture.* Boston, Lee and Shepard Pubrs., 1881; Keith A. Murray, *The Modocs and Their War.* Norman, Univ. of Okla. Press, 1965.

Miller, Thomas, R., frontiersman (c. 1795-Mar. 6, 1836). B. in Tennessee, Miller reached Texas in 1830, settling in the DeWitt Colony at Gonzales, east of San Antonio. He was one of 18 men who held off a Mexican attempt to seize the cannon at Gonzales and enabled the Texans to win a battle there September 29, 1835. March 1, 1836, he and 31 other Gonzales men reached the Alamo, dying with its defenders.

Amelia Williams, XXXVII, 272; HT.

Millet, Pierre, Jesuit missionary (Nov. 19, 1635-Dec. 31, 1708). B. at Gourges, France, he became a Jesuit and reached Canada August 5, 1667. He worked with Julien Garnier at the Onondaga mission in present New York State until 1672 when, already a master of the language, he moved to the surly Oneidas; he became popular among them and worked in their villages for several years. In 1684 he and other missionaries were forced to return to Canada by Iroquois hostility. He was chaplain at Fort Frontenac where he served also as interpreter for nearly four years, including one spent at the Niagara fort. In 1689 he was captured by the Oneidas; a convert woman on one occasion saved his life. Millet remained in captivity until late 1694, when the Oneidas sent him back to Montreal, and he worked for the rest of his life in Canada. In February of 1697 when Christianized Oneidas moved to Montreal, they asked that Millet be assigned to them as missionary. He died at Quebec. In addition to being an expert interpreter, he was often made use of for his skills as a negotiator, and he maintained at times contacts with English officials of New York.

Thwaites, JR, LXIV, 67-107, 275n8.

Mills, Albert Leopold, army officer (May 7, 1854-Sept. 8, 1916). B. in New York he was graduated from West Point and commis-

sioned a second lieutenant in the 1st Cavalry June 13, 1879. He served at Forts Walla Walla and Colville, Washington, in 1882 and at Fort Coeur d'Alene and in the field in Idaho in 1883 and 1884. Mills was at Forts Keogh and Custer, Montana, in 1884. After eastern service he went to Montana again in 1887, participating in the Crow Indian campaign of that year and the action at the Crow Agency, Montana, November 5, 1887 when an enlisted man was killed and two wounded for seven Indians killed, ten wounded and nine captured. He won a Medal of Honor July 28, 1902 near Santiago, Cuba, for encouraging men by his bravery and coolness after being shot through the head and entirely without sight temporarily. Mills became a Brigadier General in 1904 and served on the General Staff in 1912.

Heitman; *Who Was Who;* Powell.

Mills, A(lexander) Ham(ilton), lawman (c. 1837-c. Oct. 25, 1882). B. in Arkansas, he was half-brother to Steph(en) Stanley and like him a crack shot. They demonstrated this talent at one point by shootng off the first joints of each other's finger. The family reached New Mexico about 1868, both men taking up farms or ranches in Lincoln County and Mills marrying Maria Hammonds before 1870. Mills was sheriff of the county in 1873 and 1874, during the so-called Horrell War and at one time was shot near the heart, the bullet following a rib around his body and the result a painful but not dangerous wound. Four days after the December 1, 1873, breakout of the War, Mills and a posse surrounded the Horrells at a grist mill and for a day exchanged shots, then withdrew; Mills and his deputies lost control of the situation and after the Horrells had killed a number of people Mills conferred with Governor Marsh Giddings at Santa Fe, admitting he was beyond his depth, but by that time the Horrells had swept up much of Mills' and Stanley's stock and were enroute back to Texas. Mills was indicted on an embezzling charge in April 1875, being sentenced merely to pay costs of the action. In October he was accused of manslaughter in the death of Gregorio Balensuela; he was convicted, sentenced to a year, but never served time. Mills was reported to have been wounded again in the fall of 1876, but details are lacking. Soon after Tunstall's murder,

February 18, 1878, McSween's Regulators commenced an extermination program against members of the posse which shot him and Mills, who had been with the posse, fled to Texas though his family remained in Lincoln County; he reappeared a year later, but only enroute to Arizona, as he said. November 4, 1882, a Silver City, New Mexico, newspaper reported he had been killed by Mexicans the previous week near Georgetown 18 miles northeast of Silver City. Mills was described by the newspaper as "a very dissipated man and was only remarkable as being (when sober) a crack shot."

Philip J. Rasch, "A. Ham Mills — Sheriff of Lincoln County." *English Westerners' Brand Book,* Vol. 4 (Apr. 1962), 11-12.

Mills, Anson, army officer (Aug. 31, 1834-Nov. 5, 1924). B. near Thornton, Indiana, he spent two years at West Point but did not graduate. In 1857 he went to west Texas where he worked as a surveyor, helping to lay out the city of El Paso and in 1860 surveying for Texas on the boundary between that state and New Mexico. Mills also established a ranch north of El Paso and in 1860 took part in the gold rush to Pinos Altos, New Mexico, where again he laid out the camp, using improvised instruments. Mills was an anti-secessionist and left Texas at the outbreak of the Civil War, was commissioned a first lieutenant in the 18th Infantry May 14, 1861, and emerged from the war a captain with brevets to lieutenant colonel. After the war he served on the Kansas frontier, being engaged in skirmishes along the Arkansas River where he rescued a white captive of the Cheyennes, Mary Fletcher, near Fort Dodge. Stationed at Fort Bridger, Wyoming, he became a friend of Jim Bridger, mountain man and guide. Mills transferred to the 3rd Cavalry December 31, 1870. In Arizona he founded Fort Reno in the Tonto Basin and occasionally operated against Apaches. Mills, as battalion commander, had an important role in Reynolds' Powder River campaign and fight at a Cheyenne village in March 1876; unlike some other officers who were criticized for their parts in the disappointing action, Mills performed creditably throughout, even to the point where he leveled a shotgun at a corporal who "refused to obey my order... and threatened to kill him." The soldier then followed instructions. Mills' map of the battle

area was sufficiently accurate to be used in court-martial proceedings subsequently. Mills commanded a battalion of four 3rd Cavalry companies in Crook's Battle of the Rosebud June 17, 1876, again performing without fault. He received a brevet to colonel for his part in the Slim Buttes, Dakota, action of September 8-9, 1876 where he was in effect field commander. Crook's criticism of Mills for attacking hastily without awaiting the arrival of the larger command to assure capture of the hostiles, seemed premature; considering Mills' information of the whereabouts of Crook, he did what any good cavalry officer would have done, and struck the enemy with what force he had. Mills became major of the 10th Cavalry April 4, 1878, and served in the later phases of the Geronimo campaign of 1886. He became lieutenant colonel of the 4th Cavalry March 24, 1890, colonel of the 3rd Cavalry August 16, 1892, a Brigadier General June 16, 1897, and retired one week later. Mills was of an inventive turn of mind. He devised an improved cartridge belt and other equipment for soldiers and sportsmen, established a business and, having accumulated a fortune, sold out in 1905. He died at Washington, D.C.

Heitman; Powell; Anson Mills, *My Story.* Wash., D.C., Press of Byron S. Adams, 1918; J.W. Vaughn, *The Reynolds Campaign on Powder River.* Norman, Univ. of Okla. Press, 1961; Vaughn, *With Crook at the Rosebud.* Harrisburg, Pa., Stackpole Co., 1956; Jerome A. Greene, *Slim Buttes, 1876.* Norman, 1982.

Mills, Emmett, frontiersman (Dec. 15, 1841-c. July 23, 1861). B. near Thorntown, Indiana, he was a brother of Brigadier General Anson Mills. With another brother, William W., he followed Anson to El Paso, Texas, the three establishing a ranch, "Los Tres Hermanos," 18 miles above El Paso about 1859. This became a stop on the Overland Mail line, and Emmett Mills a stageline employe. In 1861 because of Union sympathies and trying to avoid the Confederates moving up the Rio Grande, Mills joined six others in a stage trip for California. The party was under Freeman Thomas but is known often as the Free Thompson group. On July 21, the stage was ambushed a mile west of Cooke's Spring, New Mexico, by Apaches led by Mangas Coloradas and Cochise, and in a three day battle all the whites were killed. Mills, with Roeschler,

Portell and Avaline, died within the breast-work they had erected; the other three died outside, apparently trying to escape. Citizens at Janos later reported hearing from Indian sources that Mangas, having lost about 40 men in killed and wounded, withdrew after two days, leaving Cochise to finish off the whites.

Anson Mills, *My Story*. Wash., D.C., Press of Byron S. Adams, 1918; *W.W. Mills: Forty Years in El Paso*, Rex W. Strickland, ed. El Paso, Carl Hertzog, publr., 1962.

Mills, Enos A., naturalist, writer (Apr. 22, 1870-Sept. 21, 1922). B. near Kansas City, Kansas, he went to Colorado as a youth and by 1886 had a cabin on Long's Peak, a 14,255-foot mountain with which he was to become identified; he climbed it more than 250 times. He was a Colorado "snow observor" in the mountains in 1907 and 1908. His rambles through the Rocky Mountains in several states, were made alone, afoot and without firearms, and he was a strong advocate of conservation and the National Park system, earning the soubriquet of "the father of Rocky Mountain National Park." He did much to awaken America to the wonders of the mountains and the need to preserve its scenic and wildlife heritage. His books included: *The Story of Estes Park* (1905); *Wild Life On the Rockies* (1909); *The Spell of the Rockies* (1911); *In Beaver World* (1913); *The Story of the Thousand Year Pine* (1914); *Rocky Mountain Wonderland* (1915); *The Story of Scotch* (1916); *Your National Parks* (1917); *The Grizzly, Our Greatest Wild Animal* (1918); *The Adventures of a Nature Guide* (1919); *Being Good to Bears and Other Stories* (1919); *Waiting in the Wilderness* (1921); *Watched by Wild Animals* (1922); *Wild Animal Homesteads* (1923); *Rocky Mountain National Park* (1924); *The Ro mance of Geology* (1926); *Bird Memories from the Rockies* (1931).

Who Was Who; Carl Abott, "The Active Force: Enos A. Mills and the National Park Movement." *Colo. Mag.,* Vol 56, Nos. 1, 2 (Winter-Spring 1979), 56-73.

Mills, Henry, frontiersman (1808-post 1870). Mills, b. probably in Kentucky, a black, may have worked for the American Fur Company as early as 1839, and may have been a slave of Kenneth McKenzie. Mills was living in Chouteau County, Montana, in 1870, with an Indian wife and a daughter. His son, Dave, lived on the Blood reserve in Canada, employed as an interpreter, suggesting his mother was a Blackfoot.

Montana, Contributions, Vol. X, 1940, 281.

Mills, Stephen Crosby, army officer (May 8, 1854-Aug. 3, 1914). B. at New Hartford, New York, he was a West Point graduate who, as second lieutenant of the 12th Infantry participated in actions in the southwest, principally as commander of Apache and Pueblo Indian scouts. He took part in the hard fight against Victorio in the San Andres Mountains, New Mexico, April 7, 1880, and the equally difficult action against Loco at Enmedio Mountain, Sonora, April 28, 1882; he won a brevet for both affairs, although he probably should have been awarded one for each. By 1898 as a major he was named inspector general of volunteers, later that year became inspector general of the U.S. Army. He was appointed chief of staff, Division of the Philippines, later of the Department of the East, and died as a colonel before his retirement.

Heitman; *Who Was Who;* Dan L. Thrapp, *Victorio and the Mimbres Apaches.* Norman, Univ. of Okla. Press, 1973; Thrapp, *General Crook and the Sierra Madre Adventure.* Norman, 1972.

Millsaps, Isaac, pioneer (c. 1795-Mar. 6, 1836). B. in Mississippi, he reached Gonzales, Texas, where he was living in early 1836 with a blind wife and seven children. Millsaps was one of 32 men from Gonzales who rode to the rescue of the Alamo at San Antonio, and died with its defenders.

Amelia Williams, XXXVII, 272; HT.

Milner, Moses Embree (California Joe), scout (May 8, 1829-Oct. 29, 1876). B. near Stanford, Kentucky, he journeyed overland to California in 1849, reportedly being captured by Utes, then rescued enroute. He spent some time in the California gold fields, and in 1852 moved to near Corvallis, Oregon, where four sons were born to him and his Tennessee wife. In addition to running his farm he operated pack trains to mining camps near Walla Walla and in the mountains to the east. He followed rushes himself to the Salmon River and Bannack, Montana, where, it was reported, he fought three claim jumpers, killing one and wounding another. At Virginia City, Montana, he acquired his nickname, and about 1862 killed another man "for kicking my dog." The vigilantes apparently ran him out of town, and he returned to Oregon, then wandered through New Mexico, Nevada and Texas where he killed another man, this one in 1867. By 1868 he was named chief of scouts under Custer (who made him famous in his writings), but Joe got drunk and missed the fight on the Washita, having assured Custer previously, according to Jack Corbin, there were no hostiles on that stream. Joe made two trips back to Oregon, in 1873 established a ranch of sorts near Pioche, Nevada, then guided a prospecting party into New Mexico, and in 1874 was a scout-guide on Custer's Black Hills expedition, being the first, according to rumor, to loose the report of gold in that region. He prospected illegally into the Hills himself. In the spring of 1875 he was guide for Professor Walter P. Jenney's Black Hills expedition to verify Custer's report of gold and the next year, when the Black Hills were acquired and thrown open for settlement, Joe staked out a homesite on the site of Rapid City, South Dakota. With Jack Crawford and five other men Joe ambushed a party of Sioux in May 1876, reportedly killing 15 of a party of 23. He guided for Crook in September 1876, and for Mackenzie in October. Tom Newcomb shot him in the back after they had quarreled, Joe dying instantly. He was buried at Fort Robinson. It was reported that two years later Newcomb was shot in the back, presumably by one of Joe's long-memoried friends. More than 6 feet in height he was well-built, hirsute, slouchy of dress, ever smoking a pipe and chewing tobacco at the same time, garrulous except about his past, usually rode a mule, and was "brave, self-reliant, and faithful. His skill as a scout, trailer, and marksman is attested by all under whom he served."

DAB; Rex Bundy, "California Joe." *Best of the West,* no vol., no no., (1973), 10-11, 45-46; Joe E. Milner, Earle R. Forrest, *California Joe: Noted Scout and Indian Fighter.* Caldwell, Ida., Caxton Printers, 1935.

Milton, Jeff Davis, lawman (Nov. 7, 1861-May 7, 1947). B. near Marianna, Florida, he was the son of Civil War governor John Milton. In 1877 he moved to Navasota, Texas, a year later working on a cattle ranch near

Fort Phantom Hill on the Clear Fork of the Brazos. In 1880 he joined the Texas Rangers, serving three years and emerging a corporal. May 16, 1881, he and Ranger L.B. Wells killed cattleman W.P. Patterson at Colorado City, Texas. As a deputy sheriff in 1884 in Socorro County, New Mexico, he and cowboy Jim Hammil killed three Mexican gunmen who had sought to ambush them, Milton being wounded in the leg. While chief of police at El Paso, Texas, Milton and George Scarborough on June 29, 1895, shot Martin Morose in a midnight fight. In July 1898 in a gunfight Milton and Scarborough badly wounded Bronco Bill Walters and mortally wounded Bill Johnson near Solomonville, Arizona. While working for Wells Fargo as an express messenger Milton fought five members of the Burt Alvord outlaw band at Fairbanks, Arizona, February 15, 1900. Three-Fingered Jack Dunlap was wounded mortally and Milton suffered a crippled left arm. On November 3, 1917 at Tombstone, Arizona, in a Model T Ford he ran down bank robber Fred Koch, wounded and captured him. At various times in his life Milton had been a range detective, a mounted inspector along the Mexican Line, a prospector, oil man, worked for the Immigration Service, was a rancher and followed other occupations. At times he had contacts or fights with such notables as John Wesley Hardin, Black Jack Ketchum, John Selman, Billy Stiles as well as Scarborough and Alvord. He retired in 1930, lived at Tombstone for several years and moved eventually to Tucson where he died. His ashes at his request were scattered over the desert. He was married, his widow surviving him.

J. Evetts Haley, *Jeff Milton, a Good Man With a Gun.* Norman, Univ. of Okla. Press, 1948; O'Neal, *Gunfighters.*

Mims, Samuel, frontiersman (d. Aug. 30, 1813). Samuel Mims, married to a white woman, settled near Lake Tensaw, Alabama, in the present Clarke County, in 1797. He had at least three sons, David, Alexander and Joseph. Mims established a place a mile east of the Alabama River and one-fourth mile from the Tensaw boatyard. A square stockade was built around the house, enclosing about an acre (some 200 feet to a side) and entered through an eastern and western gate; within the enclosure were several buildings, the Mims home being near the center. At the time of the Fort Mims massacre of August 30, 1813 there were gathered here according to Pickett 553 persons, including Anglos, some Spaniards, blacks and mixed breeds; 250 were soldiers, volunteers or militiamen commanded by Major Daniel Beasley (see entry), and about 100 of the others were children. Samuel Mims' wife was not at the stockade at the time and his three sons escaped but Samuel Mims was killed in the attack led by William Weatherford, Peter McQueen and involving perhaps 1,000 Creek warriors. Mims was a wealthy, generally respected and solid citizen.

H.S. Halbert, T.H. Ball, *The Creek War of 1813 and 1814.* Univ. of Ala. Press, 1969; Albert James Pickett, *History of Alabama.* Birmingham Book and Mag. Co., 1962; information from the Ala. Dept. of Archives and Hist.

Miner, Charles Wright, army officer (Nov. 2, 1840-Sept. 27, 1928). B. at Cincinnati, Ohio, his date of birth at his death was given as October 21, 1840. He enlisted in the 2nd Ohio Infantry in 1861, was commissioned a captain in the 22nd Ohio Infantry in 1862 and served through the Civil War. He was commissioned a second lieutenant in the 19th U.S. Infantry in 1866, shortly transferring to the 28th Infantry where he was promoted to first lieutenant and in 1868 became captain in the 22nd Infantry. In Montana Miner with four infantry companies escorted a train of 94 wagons from the mouth of Glendive Creek intending to reach a cantonment at the mouth of the Tongue River. The train was attacked the night of October 10, 1876 by several hundred Sioux under Sitting Bull, several animals were wounded, 47 mules captured and the train's progress next day was stopped short of Clear Creek, its immediate objective. Miner returned to Glendive Creek for reinforcements. His civilian teamsters were demoralized and 41 were discharged, soldiers being detailed to drive. The escort was increased to five infantry companies under command of Lieutenant Colonel Elwell S. Otis and started off again. October 15 at Spring Creek the Indians, also reinforced, attacked the train which in compact columns struggled on. Infantry repeatedly charged the Indians, Miner winning a brevet for gallantry. The party reached Clear Creek where the Indians fired the grass, the wagons continuing through the flames, the entire escort being engaged in beating the hostiles back repeatedly. The train reached the Tongue and returned to Glendive Creek October 26. Miner became a major of the 6th Infantry in 1894, lieutenant colonel in 1898 and a colonel the following year. He participated in the battles of San Juan Hill and Santiago, winning a Silver Star in the latter; he became military governor of the island of Negros, Philippines and retired in 1903 a Brigadier General. He then served with the organized militia of Ohio until January 8, 1906. He died at Columbus, Ohio, and was buried there.

EHI; *Chronological List;* Powell; Heitman; Columbus, Ohio, *State Journal,* Sept. 29, 1928; information from the Ohio Hist. Soc.

Miner, Thomas, prospector (1835-Nov. 6, 1919). B. in Kentucky he went to California about 1861 where he probably first heard of a purported gold strike in Arizona known as the Doc (Abraham D.) Thorne Mine, became enamored of it, obtaining or drafting "maps" based on what he had heard or learned. About May 1869, he joined the silver rush to White Pine, Nevada, and reached Prescott, Arizona, in the summer of 1871, where he created the "Mogollon Mining Company." He told how he had made the great strike himself, how rich it was, how he had very narrowly escaped the dangers and hardships thrust upon him, including a sandstorm so severe it buried his mules so that only their ears protruded, and so on. Strangely, pragmatic men bought his tales. He set about recruiting followers. Miner influenced Governor A.P.K. Safford, who helped him gather a total of nearly 275 men for a grand prospecting expedition in 1872 into the Gila River country. It split into six divisions and combed the area well but of course found nothing. Miner soon became hopelessly lost, but the humor of the situation became apparent even to the prospectors and although Miner was discredited, he was not lynched. He drifted back to Tucson and, eventually, to San Francisco. He is probably the Thomas Miner who died at Thompson's Flat, near Oroville, California, of "general debility from old age." Miner was described by Spring as "a sandy-haired, red-faced Irishman." Apparently he never married.

John Spring's Arizona, ed. by A.M. Gustafson. Tucson, Univ. of Ariz. Press, 1966; Dan L. Thrapp, *Al Sieber, Chief of Scouts.* Norman, Univ. of Okla. Press, 1964; Butte County, Calif., death records, Bk. B, p. 189.

Minesinger, Henry, cattleman (Nov. 5, 1860-Aug. 25, 1941). The son of James Minesinger and his Shoshone wife, Quick-to-See, Henry was born at Deer Lodge, Montana. In 1875 he joined a trail drive of 300 cattle and a small remuda of horses to the Red River Valley of Manitoba. Enroute the cattle became so mingled with wild buffalo they were recovered only with great difficulty. Minesinger worked in the Red River country as a cowboy for 10 years, then moved to southern Alberta where he worked as a top hand for the Bar U Ranch. He married a métis, Mary Borsow (Bourassa), who became a noted midwife. Minesinger Lake and Minesinger Creek in Alberta were named for Henry Minesinger. About 1900 his wife died and Henry moved his family to Polson, Montana where in 1904 he married again, this time to Eliza Finley, a white woman; by the two marriages he fathered 17 children "or maybe more." He is buried in the Catholic cemetery at Polson.

James Madison Minesinger — Quick-to-See Family Association Christmas Newsletter, 1978, courtesy Walter K. Miles, historian-genealogist, compiler.

Minesinger, James Madison, frontiersman (c. 1824-May 16, 1894). B. in Tennessee he reached Montana in 1856 as a drover with Fred Burr's herd of cattle from Salt Lake City and with his partner, John W. Powell wintered in the Beaverhead Valley. He worked for three years variously for John Owen of the Bitterroot Valley and for Burr. In the spring of 1859 with Powell he helped save from starvation Boone Helm who had been lost during the winter in the Idaho-Montana wilderness. That year Minesinger settled at Grantsville on the Little Blackfoot River, also in Montana. He moved to Gold Creek and mined for a time. In the winter of 1862-63 he camped in the Big Hole Valley and in 1876 he was living at Missoula. He married a Shoshone woman and fathered children; many of his descendants live today in the Northwest. Minesinger died at Calgary, Alberta.

Montana, Contributions. I, 1876, 343; II, 1896; Granville Stuart, *Forty Years on the Frontier.* Glendale, Calif., Arthur H. Clark Co., 1925; George F. Weisel, *Men and Trade on the Northwest Frontier.* Missoula, Mont. State Univ. Press, 1955; information from Walter K. Miles, Mar. 21, 1980.

Minesinger, Nellie (Quick-to-See), Shoshone (Dec. 25, 1826-June 21, 1932). The daughter of William Monroe of Utah Territory and a Shoshone woman named Mary, of Fort Washakie, Wyoming, Nellie was born at Skolko, Montana, and because she was of the mission at St. Ignatius, Montana, the exact date of her birth may have been bestowed upon her many years after the event. She married James Minesinger of Tennessee probably in the 1860s and outlived her husband by almost 40 years. She died at St. Ignatius, Montana, at the age of 105 years, 5 months and 25 days, leaving numerous descendants in Montana, Alberta and Manitoba.

Nellie Minesinger death certificate; *James Madison Minesinger—Quick-to-See Family Association Christmas Newsletter,* 1978, courtesy of Walter K. Miles, historian-genealogist, compiler.

Ming, Daniel Houston, (Hugston), frontiersman, stockman (Feb. 23, 1845-Nov. 12, 1925). B. near Louisville. In 1863 he became a freighter for Joseph Kenard of Terre Haute, Indiana, moved with him to St. Joseph, Missouri, and freighted to southwestern Montana as assistant wagon master, reaching Virginia City, Montana, without incident. Then Ming bought his own freight outfit and hauled from Salt Lake Valley to the Montana mines, later making his headquarters at Idaho Falls, Idaho. In 1865-67 he worked for the Overland Stage Co., east of Green River and for the government at Camp Sanders, near Laramie, Wyoming. He returned to the States to farm, team and went to the cattle towns of Abilene and Wichita in 1870 or thereabouts. At San Angelo, Texas, he contracted to deliver a herd of 2,000 cattle to the Gila River settlements. He became a packer in late 1873 at Camp Apache, was hired by James E. Roberts, agent at the White Mountain Reservation, then helped Agent John P. Clum move Chiricahuas from their reservation to San Carlos. He worked on and off the reservations under various agents, was deputy sheriff of Pima County briefly and chief of police on the San Carlos Agency at times. He served under Lawton in the Geronimo campaign, ran a livery stable, became a stockman, was a member of the 19th Arizona legislature, and ran freighting enterprises. In 1886 at a cattleman's meeting called to consider a serious drought, Dan Ming was asked to render a prayer, a novel undertaking for him. He considered and uttered: "Oh Lord, I'm about to round you up for a good plain talk. Now, Lord, I ain't like these fellows who come bothering you every day. This is the first time I ever tackled you for any thing and if you will only grant this I'll promise never to bother you again. We want rain, good Lord, and we want it bad, and we ask you to send us some. But if you can't, or don't want to send us any, for Christ's sake don't make it rain up around Hooker's or Leitch's ranges, but treat us all alike. Amen." Ming signed on as an army packer in 1899 and served in the Philippines. He died at San Francisco and reportedly is buried in the Presidio cemetery.

Interview with Thaddeus (Bud) Ming, Dan's son.

Minuit, Peter, colonial administrator (1580-1638). Of French Huguenot descent, he was b. at Wesel in Germany's Ruhr and moved to Holland about 1624. In 1625 he left for New Netherland, largely in present New York State, became a member of the director's council under Willem Verhulst, the Dutch West India Company's provisional director-general, or acting governor. Minuit probably returned to Holland late in 1625, but went back to New Netherland, arriving May 4, 1626, shortly to be appointed by the council as director-general and governor. May 6 Minuit reportedly purchased from the Manhattan Indians (of the Wappinger confederacy, an Algonquin people) the island of Manhattan for trade goods worth 60 guilders, or $24 (although see Weslager, 68-74, for discussion). The Dutch managed to live at peace with surrounding Indians during his governorship, although the tribesmen would be virtually destroyed during the Kieft War of 1643-45. After several years Minuit came into dispute with Dutch Reformed ministers, was recalled to Holland and in 1632 was relieved of his governorship. He then turned to Sweden and in late 1637 sailed from Gothenburg with two ships for the mouth of the Delaware River where the colony of New Sweden was planted in March 1638 (it lasted 17 years). Minuit, as governor, established Fort Christina, named for the reigning Swedish queen, on the present site of Wilmington, Delaware, the first permanent settlement on the Delaware River. Enroute back to Europe, Minuit called at St. Kitts (St. Christopher) in the West Indies. In the late summer, while visiting aboard a Rotterdam merchantman, a hurricane blew in, the ship was lost, Peter Minuit with it. He was married; whether his wife perished with him is not reported.

C.A. Weslager, A.R. Dunlap, *Dutch Explorers, Traders and Settlers in the Delaware Valley 1609-1664,* Phila., Univ. of Pa. Press, 1965; *Narratives of Early Pennsylvania, West New Jersey and Delaware, 1630-1707,* ed. by Albert Cook Myers, N.Y., Charles Scribner's Sons, 1912; David P. Henige, *Colonial Governors from the Fifteenth Century to the Present,* Madison, Univ. of Wisc. Press, 1970.

Mitchell, Charles R., pioneer (d. Sept. 11, 1857). Mitchell, his wife whose name is unknown, a son and two brothers, Joel D. Mitchell and Lawson Mitchell, joined the Fancher emigrant wagon train which left Fort Smith, Arkansas late in March 1857, bound for California. The Mitchells were from Marion County, Arkansas. With most of the rest of the company they were murdered by Mormons and Mormon-led Indians at Mountain Meadows, Utah.

William Wise, *Massacre at Mountain Meadows,* N.Y., Thomas Y. Crowell Co., 1976.

Mitchell, David Dawson, fur trader (July 31, 1806-May 31, 1861). B. in Louisa County, Virginia, he joined the Upper Missouri Outfit in 1830; was placed in charge of a succession of upper Missouri fur trading posts. He was a man of courage, decision and ability, exhibited most clearly in his operations among the Blackfeet. He was host to Prince Maximilian and his artist, Karl Bodmer, in 1833. Mitchell became a partner in the company in 1835. From 1841 to 1852 he occasionally was superintendent of Indian affairs at St. Louis. During the Mexican War he served under Price and Doniphan and led the American Army into Chihuahua City. He promoted the Fort Laramie Peace Council, leading to an important treaty, September 8-17, 1851. In 1855 Mitchell helped organize the Missouri and California Overland Mail and Transportation Company, and for a time was president of it. He died at St. Louis.

Ray H. Mattison article, MM, Vol. II; DAB; *Who Was Who.*

Mitchell, Levin, frontiersman (c. 1809-post 1854). B. probably in Ohio, he reached the Rocky Mountains as a trapper by 1830, perhaps with the William L. Sublette brigade. He trapped with Joe Meek, Mark Head and others, becoming a thorough mountain man; he visited the southwest, either Arizona or California in 1834 and about 1840 he was at Fort Davy Crockett in Brown's Hole, Colorado. With Bill Williams, Pegleg Smith and others he raided for horses in southern California, later appearing at Fort Laramie, Bent's Fort, and returned to St. Louis in 1842, 1843, and 1846. By 1845 he had become a trader at Pueblo, Colorado. He was a deputy sheriff at Taos under Wootton in 1848, served occasionally as army scout, later ranched in eastern New Mexico, then removed to the upper Arkansas River country, and finally into Kansas, where traces of him are lost.

Janet Lecompte article, MM, Vol. V.

Mitchell, Luther, rancher (c. 1812-Dec. 11, 1878). Said to have been "from Merrick County," Nebraska, he was married and was considered by the Print Olive people a rustler. Robert A. Olive, who as deputy sheriff sought to arrest him and Ami (Whit) Ketchum in late November 1878, was shot and fatally wounded purportedly by Mitchell. The two were arrested by Sheriff Barney Gillan, turned over to the Olive crowd, lynched and the bodies burned in one of the celebrated incidents of central Nebraska history. Print Olive and a confederate eventually went free.

Solomon D. Butcher, *Pioneer History of Custer County, Nebraska.* Denver, Sage Books, c. 1965, 43-62.

Mitchell, Robert A., cattleman, partisan (fl. 1877). Mitchell was a Lampasas County, Texas, cattleman and brother-in-law of Pink Higgins, becoming a chief Higgins lieutenant in the sanguinary Horrell-Higgins feud of the 1870s. On June 14, 1877 Mitchell, Bill Wren, Higgins and another were involved in a town square shootout with the Horrells at Lampasas, lasting three hours. Only Wren was wounded among the combatants, but Frank Mitchell, Bob's brother, was killed although he was an innocent by-stander; Alonzo Mitchell, another brother and their father, also a noncombatant were witnesses to the affair, but were uninjured. Mitchell may have been a participant in the siege of the Horrell ranch house by the Higgins faction in July. It ended without major incident, but was the cause of Texas Ranger Captain John B. Jones' intervention. Jones persuaded the factions to accept truce agreements, which Mitchell, Higgins and Wren signed for the one faction, the three Horrell brothers for the other. The truce held.

Walter Prescott Webb, *The Texas Rangers.* Boston, Houghton Mifflin Co., 1935; Bill O'Neal, "The Horrell Brothers of Lampasas." *Frontier Times,* Vol. 54, No. 3 (Apr.-May 1980), 44-45.

Mitchell, Robert Byington, army officer, governor (Apr. 4, 1823-Jan. 26, 1882). B. at Mansfield, Ohio, he became a lawyer but was commissioned a first lieutenant in the 2nd Ohio Infantry September 4, 1847. A man of great personal bravery he was so badly wounded at Chapultepec that he was reported dead. He was mustered out July 26, 1848, and returned to the practice of law, in 1855 serving as mayor of Gilead, Ohio. In 1856 he moved to Kansas as a Free Stater. He became colonel of the 2nd Kansas Infantry (eventually commanding the 2nd Kansas Cavalry) May 23, 1861, and was badly wounded again at Wilson's Creek, Missouri August 10, 1861, cited for bravery and devotion to duty even though his wound was critical. He became Brigadier General of Volunteers April 8, 1862, and served east of the Mississippi. In the Battle of Chickamauga in 1863 he arrested 350 of his own men and threatened to shoot them for mutiny, thus establishing himself as "an arrogant, unyielding leader whose command bordered on the despotic." In 1864-65 during a critical period of Plains Indian hostility, Mitchell commanded the District of Nebraska, then the District of North Kansas and finally the District of Kansas. He was mustered out of the armed forces January 15, 1866, and December 14 was named governor of New Mexico, giving it a three-year period of political turbulence not quickly forgotten; he was succeeded August 16, 1869, by William A. Pile. Hastening Mitchell's departure was his executive proclamation of war August 2, 1869, against the Gila Apaches and Navahos, who had been troublesome. This was his last official act as chief executive, generating clamor and protests from Congress, the State Department, the army and even his own official family. Few believed he had authority to issue it and thought it likely to provoke a costly and prolonged Indian war; he was ordered by Washington to annul the proclamation. Mitchell resigned and returned to Kansas, moving in 1872 to Washington, D.C., where he died a decade later. He was a tall, black-bearded man, intelligent and sometimes able, but self-seeking, intemperate and not of balanced judgment.

Heitman; Ezra J. Warner, *Generals in Blue: Lives of the Union Commanders.* Baton Rouge, La. State Univ. Press, 1964; Calvin Horn, *New Mexico's Troubled Years.* Albuquerque, Horn & Wallace, Pubrs, 1963; Dan L. Thrapp, *Victorio and the Mimbres Apaches.* Norman, Univ. of Okla. Press, 1974; Twitchell, *Leading Facts.*

Mix, Tom, actor (Jan. 6, 1880-Oct. 11, 1940). B. at Mix Run, near Driftwood, Pennsylvania, he was raised at Du Bois, west central Pennsylvania. Enamored of the West he was "employed in the dude ranch department of the (Miller brothers') 101 Ranch (of Oklahoma)... and learned to tell tall tales. Perhaps in this category were his reports of service in the Spanish-American War, the Philippines, Boxer War in China and the Boer War. Will Rogers is said to have taken him to task for his 'yarning'." He is said to have spent a decade with the famous 101 and the show it sponsored, learning the tricks and stunts he later used in motion pictures; there is little evidence to support his or his press agent's claims, which included service in the Texas Rangers and in various law enforcement activities, all of which seem likely candidates for the tall tales bin. Mix entered motion pictures around 1909, remaining so employed for many years and becoming a top cowboy star. He also appeared on occasion with wild west shows. He organized the Tom Mix Circus and Wild West Show in 1935; it lasted three seasons. Mix was killed in an automobile accident near Florence, Arizona.

New York Times, Oct. 12, 1980; Don Russell, *The Wild West: A History of the Wild West Shows.* Fort Worth, Tex., Amon Carter Mus., 1970; Ellsworth Collings, Alma Miller England, *The 101 Ranch.* Norman, Univ. of Okla. Press, 1972.

Moise (Moses), Flathead chief (d. 1868). Moise, second chief of the Flatheads, claimed to have seen Lewis and Clark at Ross's Hole in 1805, so he must have been born shortly before the turn of the century. He headed a delegation which met De Smet in 1841. A distinguished horseman and according to De Smet the "handsomest Indian" he ever met, Moise refused to sign the 1855 Treaty negotiated by Isaac Stevens because, he said,

"my brother is buried (on the land to be given up by the Flatheads). I did not think you would take the only piece of ground I had." Yet his name was added to the published document. He was a fervent Catholic and always a staunch friend of the whites. Moise was chief leader of his people's buffalo hunts on the Plains in 1858 and 1862. He died in the Bitterroot Valley in 1868. The town of Moise, headquarters of the National Bison Range in Montana, is named for his son, Antoine Moise, also a prominent Flathead leader.

George F. Weisel, *Men and Trade on the Northwest Frontier.* Missoula, Mont. State Univ. Press, 1955; John Fahey, *The Flathead Indians.* Norman, Univ. of Okla. Press, 1974; Robert Ignatius Burns, *The Jesuits and the Indian Wars of the Northwest.* New Haven, Yale Univ. Press, 1966.

Monaghan, (James) Jay, IV, historian (Mar. 19, 1891-Oct. 11, 1980). B. at West Chester, Pennsylvania, he was educated in part in Switzerland and earned a doctorate at Monmouth College, Illinois. He became a cowboy in Wyoming and western Colorado during the summers of 1908 and 1909 and worked for wagon freighters in western Colorado where he also owned and operated cattle and sheep ranches from 1913 to 1934, holding office in various wool grower organizations. Monaghan taught school on the Uinta Indian Reservation of Utah in 1914-15. He did field historical research in Colorado, Kansas and Missouri, was with the Illinois State Historical Library and Society from 1939-50 and held positions with other historical organizations. Among his books those of frontier interest included *The Legend of Tom Horn* (1946); *The Overland Trail* (1947); *The Great Rascal* (Ned Buntline) (1952); *Civil War on the Western Border* (1955); *Custer* (1959); *Australians and the Gold Rush* (1966); *Chile, Peru and the California Gold Rush* (1973). He edited the *Book of the American West* (1963), and wrote *A Tenderfoot in Colorado* (1968). He died at Santa Barbara, California. His historical works were of varying reliability; he had a tendency to fictionalize for the sake of readability and he failed to develop a pronounced field of interest that would identify him as a specialist in a given area, but his work is not without merit.

Who's Who; Council on Abandoned Military

Posts *Headquarters Heliogram,* 135 (May-June 1981), 4

Moncachtapé, Yazoo explorer (fl. 1700-1758). A Yazoo Indian, his name meant "Killer of Pain and Fatigue." He is famed for his purported lengthy journeys which he recounted to historian Le Page du Pratz who published them in his *Histoire de la Louisiane,* Volume II, 89-128 (1758). Du Pratz obtained the narratives first hand when Moncachtapé was "a very old man," so the purported journeys, if made, must have been completed early in the 18th century. The Indian said that after losing his wife and children he had turned to traveling. On his first extended journey he said he had passed up the Ohio River, visited the Shawnees and Iroquois, wintered with the Abenaki, then returned via the St. Lawrence and Mississippi rivers. His second journey was to the Northwest Coast a century before Lewis and Clark. He mentioned the Tamaroa, Kansa and Amikwa tribes, alluded to many tribes he reportedly encountered on the Columbia but named none. On the Pacific coast, presumably at the mouth of the Columbia he and companions he had picked up encountered a small boatload of bearded white men who "came from sun-setting, in search of a yellow stinking wood which dyes a fine yellow color." He and other Indians ambushed the party, killing 11, of whom two bore firearms. Hodge said that this story "so far as it relates to the western trip, is very doubtful on its face," although some accept it as credible "and that Moncachtapé understood a number of languages is clearly proven." Moncachtapé said he had spent five years on his western journey, his descriptions of the route of the Missouri and over the Bitterroot Mountains to a tributary of the Columbia, down it to the sea and what he learned about the coast north and south seems to give some evidence of firsthand knowledge. John Dunn Hunter may have been influenced by this story.

Hodge, HAI.

Moncravie, John B., frontiersman (c. 1797-July 18, 1885). B. at Bordeaux, France, as Jean Baptiste Moncravie, he reached the U.S. and enlisted in the army in 1820 at Philadelphia, serving until 1829, largely on the Minnesota frontier. He entered the fur trade, being stationed for some years at Fort Union

where he was noted for his interest in women and the bottle, but he also had some artistic ability and skill as an entertainer. He later served at Fort Pierre, South Dakota, and Fort John, near Scotts Bluff, Nebraska. He died at Brownville, Nebraska.

Charles E. Hanson Jr. article, MM, Vol. IX.

Moniac, David, army officer (c. 1802-Nov. 21, 1836). William Moniac, a Hollander, arrived in the Creek nation of southern Alabama in 1756 from Natchez on the Mississippi where the Natchez tribe had been destroyed by the French. William married a Tuskegee woman and fathered Sam Moniac, who married a sister of William Weatherford, noted Creek war chief. Sam and McGillivray went to New York to confer with George Washington. Sam was the father of David Moniac, who thus was mixed white and Creek. He went to West Point and was commissioned a brevet second lieutenant in the 6th Infantry July 1, 1822, went on leave of absence until December 31, 1822, when he resigned. In the Second Seminole War of Florida, David Moniac was commissioned captain of the Creek Mounted Volunteers August 17, 1836, and became major November 15. He was killed "while crossing a difficult morass" in the face of heavy enemy fire in one phase of the Battle of Wahoo Swamp, a five-day action directed by militia Brigadier General Richard Keith Call and in which 55 of the military were killed and wounded to estimated Indian losses of about 95.

Cullum; J.D. Dreisback, "Weatherford — 'The Red Eagle,'" *Ala. Hist. Reporter,* Vol. 2, No. 6 (May 1884), n.p.

Moniac, Sam (Sam McNac), frontiersman (c. 1758-1837). Sam Moniac, whose name frequently appeared in variations, was a son of William Moniac, a Hollander who had reached the Creek nation in Alabama in 1756 from Natchez on the Mississippi. William became the trusted interpreter of Alexander McGillivray who April 4, 1787, sadly reported William's death from "a dry Belly Ache," adding that he was "a Just & faithfull man... I Shall never have Such another again." Yet Sam Moniac to a point filled his father's role with McGillivray, first as a packhorse man as McGillivray reported in August of 1788, then as interpreter since Sam Moniac was half Creek and married to a sister of William

Weatherford, thus was perfectly fluent in Creek as he was in English. Moniac accompanied McGillivray in his 1790 visit to New York where he conferred with George Washington in August, and no doubt served as interpreter in preparation of the Treaty of New York of August 7 though Joseph Cornell signed the document as sole interpreter; there must have been others since 23 chiefs in addition to McGillivray were involved. In 1799 Moniac and William Weatherford were instrumental in capturing the notorious adventurer, William Bowles who, representing himself as a British officer had sought to enlist Creeks to invade and capture Spanish Florida. Indian Agent Benjamin Hawkins assigned Moniac, Weatherford and two others to seize Bowles, which they did, taking him to Mobile to be turned over to the proper authority. Moniac attended at least one of Tecumseh's councils when the great Shawnee visited the Creeks to urge support for his confederation and war against the Americans. Sam Moniac lived near Catoma Creek, Alabama, for some time maintaining a lodging house for travelers on the Federal road, but in June 1813 was driven off, his blacks and cattle stolen by troublesome Creeks. He protested to Jim Boy (see entry), a hostile leader, that he was sorry he had been friendly with whites, and from Jim Boy extracted information about the hostile intentions shortly to break out and kill pro-white chiefs of the Creeks as "traitors," whereafter there would be an uprising against the Americans. Moniac and Weatherford, returning from Mississippi in 1813 ran upon some Creek chiefs gathered near the Alabama River. The chiefs told Weatherford and Moniac they must join the hostiles or be killed. Weatherford accepted but Moniac leaped onto his horse and when Francis (see entry) grabbed the bridle, Moniac snatched a warclub from the chief's grip, sharply struck the Indian (who was his brother-in-law) and escaped in a hail of bullets. Moniac was in the Battle of the Holy Ground December 23, 1813, and to him as guide was attributed the failure of Major Cassels to occupy his assigned position in time to block escape of many Creeks. In March 1818 Moniac lived near Pinchoma on the Federal Road, and reported that the Creeks again were restless. He died at Pass Christian, Alabama, and buried with him was a medal presented to him by George Washington when in 1790 he had accompanied the Creek chiefs to New York.

James D. Dreisback, "Weatherford — 'The Red Eagle'," *Ala. Hist. Reporter,* Vol. 2, Nos. 4, 5, 6 (Mar., Apr., May 1884), n.p.; John Walton Caughey, *McGillivray of the Creeks.* Norman, Univ. of Okla. Press, 1959; Charles J. Kappler, *Indian Treaties 1778-1883.* N.Y., Interland Pub., 1972; Albert James Pickett, *History of Alabama.* Birmingham Book and Mag. Co., 1962; H.S. Halbert, T.H. Ball, *The Creek War of 1813 and 1814.* Univ. of Ala. Press, 1969.

Monroe, Hugh, frontiersman (May 4, 1784-Dec. 7, 1892). B. near Montreal, he received a good education and at 18 joined the Hudson's Bay Company as apprentice-clerk at Edmonton House on the Saskatchewan River. At 21 he married a Blackfoot woman (d. 1876) and after a dispute with his supervisor, left the company to live with the Indians, making his home mainly with the Kootenais. He learned a variety of languages, became an expert at sign language and familiar with the geography of his region, discovering St. Mary's Lake in 1836, which he named, erecting there a large cross. An occasional visitor to frontier forts, he became known as a man of influence among the restless northwestern tribes. In 1853 he was guide and interpreter for Stevens from Fort Benton to Walla Walla. Monroe fathered 10 children, three surviving to advanced ages. "He participated in many conflicts with hostile tribes, and has had many hair breadth escapes and thrilling adventures ...He carries on his person the scars of several old arrow wounds and is blind in his left eye" from a personal encounter in 1850 with a Sioux. He died aged 109 at Milk River, Montana, and was buried at the Holy Family Mission cemetery.

Montana, Contributions, Vol. X, 1940, 255-56.

Montcalm, Louis Joseph, Marquis de, French officer (Feb. 28, 1712-Sept. 14, 1759). B. at Candiac, France, he was commander of French troops in North America at the climax of the French and Indian War; as such he is of interest principally to the rivalry between England and France and not specifically to the frontier *per se.* He entered the French army at 15, fought in Italy, Bohemia and elsewhere and was a Major General when appointed in January 1756, to command in North America, promoted to Lieutenant

General October 20, 1758. He scored initial successes against the English, capturing Forts Oswego and William Henry, and winning the battle of Fort Ticonderoga, but losing Louisbourg, Fort Frontenac and Fort Duquesne. In the summer of 1759 a strong English force under James Wolfe attacked Quebec, culminating in the battle on the Plains of Abraham September 13 in which Wolfe was killed and Montcalm mortally wounded. The city capitulated September 18 and with it inevitably came the fall of the French empire in North America, although various political developments kept a French presence on the continent for another 40 years. W.J. Eccles, in an article on Montcalm in the *Dictionary of Canadian Biography,* concluded that Montcalm himself was responsible for the French defeat, that he had thrown away an opportunity to destroy Wolfe's army and that, while a brave and experienced soldier, he was an improper commander for the task of preserving French empire in North America.

Literature abundant: Parkman, *Montcalm and Wolfe;* Thwaites, JR, LXX, 311-122n27; DCB, III.

Monteith, John B., Indian agent (Oct. 22, 1836-Aug. 7, 1879). B. in Kentucky he was the son of a Presbyterian minister, the Reverend W.J. Monteith (June 16, 1808-Aug. 29, 1876) who later was assigned to Oregon and eventually settled at Lewiston and Lapwai, Idaho, as a missionary. Under the practice of supplying Indian agents from nominees of the various denominations, Monteith was appointed (perhaps upon the recommendation of his father) to be agent for the Lapwai Nez Perce, and was named to this post in February 1871. Monteith was honest, strong-willed and dedicated to his charges, but he was infected by the assimilationist thinking of his times; he worked closely with Lawyer, the great pro-white Nez Perce chief, his goal to strip the "indian" out of the Indians, bring about their tribal and cultural disintegration, convert them from buffalo hunting to truck gardening and make them templates of the "superior race," for only by such conversion could their future be assured, as he believed. "Under his administration missionaries and teachers deliberately made the Indians ashamed of their own tradition, history, culture, and lore," and Monteith could not see the futility of this: that whites refused to accept the reformed tribesmen as equals and thus left them in a twilight zone between the races, stripped of qualities for re-establishing themselves as persons. Of course this widened the schism between the treaty Nez Perce under Montieth's control, and the non-treaties under their leaders Joseph, Olikut, Looking Glass and White Bird, and was a major factor in producing the disastrous 1877 Nez Perce War after the non-treaties found it impossible to accede to peremptory demands they migrate to the Idaho reservation within a stated and unrealistic time frame. Monteith, who originally had favored leaving Joseph and his people in their native Wallowa Valley of Oregon had long since abandoned that idea, deciding it would be better for all concerned if they were concentrated on his reservation. In April or May of 1879, two years after the war, Monteith resigned because of failing health caused by the consumption he had brought to Idaho from Kentucky. He died of it within months, and was buried at the Lapwai Mission Cemetery, Spalding, Idaho, beside his father who had died three years previously.

Information from the Ida. State Hist. Soc.; Terry Abraham, manuscripts-archives librarian, Wash. State Univ., Pullman; Lewiston, Ida., *Teller,* Aug. 8, 15, 1879; Alvin M. Josephy Jr., *The Nez Perce Indians and the Opening of the Northwest.* New Haven, Yale Univ. Press, 1965; Robert Ignatius Burns, *The Jesuits and the Indain Wars of the Northwest.* New Haven, 1966.

Montero, Antonio, fur trader (fl. 1830s, 1840s). B. at Oporto, Portugal, he appears as an employee of the American Fur Company in 1833, and became a leader of a fur brigade under Bonneville, but his activities are largely obscure. He trapped as far north as the Crow country, and appears as far south as the Arkansas River. Being literate he appears to have been a man of some responsibility, but references to him are contradictory and often mistaken. Montero built the so-called Portuguese Houses on the Powder River in 1834, and from them directed activities of about 50 trappers. He was at Independence, Missouri, in 1838, then returned to the Portuguese Houses. Montero was at Bent's Fort in the spring of 1841, settled for a time in northern New Mexico, and may have removed then to Texas, but disappears about 1845.

Edgeley W. Todd article closely examining the evidence of Montero's activities, MM, Vol. II.

Monteur, (Montour), George, interpreter, trader (d. Oct. 10, 1877). Probably he was a member of the Montour family of French-Indian origin whose members won fame on the frontier from the late 17th century. Weisel believed him possibly the son or grandson of Nicolas Montour, a member of the old North West Company in 1787 or a second Nicolas Montour, a fur company clerk in the early 19th century. George Monteur, considered a half-breed, became an interpreter for the Hudson's Bay Company and a trader and guide. From 1858 he worked for John Owen of Owen's Fort in the Bitterroot Valley of Montana and with Owen was captured by Spokane and Kalispel Indians, but released unharmed through "the influence and ability of Monteur." Monteur was killed in a drunken brawl at an Indian camp in the Blackfoot Valley, Montana, and buried a few miles east of Ovando. An engraved headstone was placed over the grave by J.W. Blair, a banker from Helmsville and paid for by "pioneer friends." Monteur Creek, a tributary of the Big Blackfoot River is named for him.

George F. Weisel, *Men and Trade on the Northwest Frontier.* Missoula, Mont. State Univ. Press, 1955; Dale L. Morgan, *The West of William H. Ashley.* Denver, Old West Pub. Co., 1964.

Montez, Lola (Marie Gilbert), lady of pleasure (1818-Jan. 17, 1861). B. in Limerick, Ireland, daughter of an army officer and his Spanish wife, Lola was vaguely romantic in relating numerous variations of her background and lived with, perhaps loved, such men as a Russian emperor, a Polish prince, an Irish lord, a Bavarian king, novelist Alexander Dumas, composer Franz Lizst and many others, becoming incidentally a stage "actress" of sorts and obviously handling her own publicity. By 1853 she was in California where there was much gold, settling at Grass Valley where her house is today a state historical landmark. She remained two years, entertaining miners with lavish parties, taking Lotta Crabtree, an embryonic dancer, under her guidance, and working at her nominal profession as an actress, at which trade she was less convincing than at others. In 1855 Lola migrated to Australia, where notable gold deposits also were being worked. She

returned to California, and moved eventually to New York where she became a member of an Episcopal Church, died following a stroke, and was buried in Greenwood Cemetery.

New York Times, June 6, 1976; Ronald Dean Miller, *Shady Ladies of the West.* Los Angeles, Westernlore Press, 1964.

Montezuma, Carlos, physician (c. 1866-Jan. 31, 1923). B. in central Arizona, of Yavapai parentage, his mother was Thil-ge-ya, and his father Co-cu-ye-vah, a chief. He was captured at the band's camp in the Superstition Mountains of Arizona about 1871, taken to Florence, Indian Territory, where he was sold by the Pima captors to Carlos Gentile, an Italian photographer-painter, for $30, and was named by him Carlos Montezuma. With Gentile he traveled to Washington, D.C., thence to Chicago where the boy went to public schools. Gentile turned Carlos over to the Rev. G.W. Ingalls of the Indian Department of the American Baptist Home Mission Society, the Italian then committing suicide. Educated further in the Urbana, Illinois, high school, Carlos was graduated *cum laude* from the University of Illinois with a degree in chemistry, then entered Chicago Medical School, a branch of Northwestern University. Montezuma became a society physician, but retained his interest in Indian affairs and carried on a voluminous correspondence on those and related subjects with Indians and others. He became a strong spokesman for Indian rights, and fought determinedly against injustices to his people; he was jailed at Fort McDowell, Arizona, charged with sedition for opposing the draft of Indians during World War I, but was released upon President Wilson's intervention. Stricken with diabetes and tuberculosis, he continued to publish his *Wassaja* journal focused on the struggle for Indian rights, until he decided that only a return to the warm sunlight and outdoor life might enable him to recover his health. He died in a primitive wickiup on the McDowell Reservation, his funeral conducted by the Phoenix Masonic Lodge.

Literature abundant; see Edward H. Peplow Jr., "Wassaja," in *Outdoor Arizona,* Vol. XLVI, No. 4 (Apr. 1974), which mistakenly considers Montezuma to have been an Apache, but includes a good summary of where primary materials relating to his life are located.

Montgomerie, Archibald, army officer (May 18, 1726-Oct. 30, 1796). B. in Scotland he was major in the 36th Foot when Pitt at the start of the Seven Years (French and Indian) War sought to raise regiments of Highlanders. Montgomerie quickly raised a regiment of 13 companies of Highlanders, the 77th Foot, or Montgomerie Regiment. He was appointed lieutenant colonel commandant January 4, 1757, taking it to America where it formed the advance of the second expedition to Fort Duquesne, Pennsylvania, under Brigadier General John Forbes; the fort was discovered deserted and the British flag raised over it. Afterward Montgomerie and his men "went through much adventurous service in the remote wilds" of the western country until in 1760 he was sent by Amherst with 1,300 men against the Cherokees. Montgomerie's forces killed 60 to 80 Indians in a fight at Estatoe in the southern Alleghenies June 1-2, while on the 27th they were forced to fight their way out of an ambush losing 17 officers and men killed and 66 wounded plus unreported losses among provincials and rangers. Failing to achieve his objective of burning out the Cherokee towns, Montgomerie pulled back to the Carolina coast, leaving the Indians under the impression that his withdrawal resulted from weakness, hence improving native morale. Montgomerie's regiment was disbanded in 1764, but in 1769 he became colonel of the 51st Foot. That year he succeeded his brother, Alexander, as tenth Earl of Eglinton. He became a Major General in 1772, Lieutenant General in 1777 and died a full General and colonel of the Scots Greys. He married twice and left two daughters.

DNB; Francis Parkman, *Montcalm and Wolfe,* II; David H. Corkran, *The Cherokee Frontier.* Norman, Univ. of Okla. Press, 1966.

Montgomery, John, pioneer (c. 1830-1924). As owner of a livery stable and Tombstone's OK Corral, Montgomery was inadvertently involved occasionally in that frontier towns's violence. He had no part in the Earp-Clanton confrontation in 1881, although it took place in front of his corral, and he was an eyewitness to the gun-battle. He was "not called to testify" and believed it was because "John Behan wanted it to appear Tom McLaury was not armed," Montgomery said to have been able to "testify he saw a revolver in the hand of Tom McLaury." Montgomery was partial to

the Earps in the Tombstone rivalries. He was somewhat more involved in the William Greene-Jim Burnett shootout of 1897. Montgomery died at Mason City, Illinois, where he was buried.

Robert N. Mullin notes, based on information from Wayne Montgomery, John's grandson; C.L. Sonnichsen, *Colonel Greene and the Copper Skyrocket.* Tucson, Univ. of Ariz. Press, 1974.

Montgomery, Lemuel Purnell, army officer (1786-Mar. 27, 1814). B. in Wythe County, Virginia, he was related to the General of his name who fell at Quebec and was of a family noted in early American history. He was educated at Washington College, Tennessee, read law and practiced at Nashville from where he frequently led mounted posses into the Cumberland Mountains in pursuit of notorious desperadoes. He was commissioned major of the 39th Infantry July 29. 1813, and served under Jackson, whose close friend he was. Montgomery was killed at the Battle of Horseshoe Bend; the first man to mount the hostile breastwork he was shot through the head by a Creek. When the battle was over Jackson wept over his body, lamenting that "I have lost the flower of my army!" Montgomery's eyes were black, his hair auburn and he weighed 175 pounds; he was 6 feet, 2 inches in height and "was altogether, the finest looking man in the army." The county of Montgomery, Alabama, was named for him, but the city of Montgomery was named for his relation who fell at Quebec.

Albert James Pickett, *The History of Alabama.* Birmingham Book and Mag. Co., 1962.

Montgomery, Robert Hugh, army officer (Apr. 6, 1838-Sept. 19, 1905). B. in Pennsylvania, he enlisted in the 5th Cavalry August 6, 1860 (serving initially at Fort Inge, Uvalde County, Texas) and rose to first sergeant by November 29, 1862, when he was commissioned second lieutenant. Montgomery was captured October 29, 1863, while on picket duty at Elk Run, Virginia, his name dropped from army rolls, but when the circumstances became known he was restored to duty. He became a first lieutenant April 25, 1865. He served at Fort Niobrara, Nebraska, and participated in the Republican River expedition and the operation on Prairie Dog Creek, Kansas, and became a captain January 3, 1870. He arrived in Arizona in early 1872. He took part in Mason's fight at Muchas Cañones late in 1872 and in actions on the Santa Maria River, Sycamore Creek, in the Red Rock country and on Pinto Creek, all in Arizona. In 1874 he took part in affairs on Lake and Canyon creeks. Montgomery was breveted major for his Arizona work. In July 1875 he was stationed at Fort Lyon, Colorado and Fort Hays, Kansas, and took part in the Crook summer campaign of 1876, being present at the battle of Slim Buttes, Dakota, September 9-10, 1876; after this campaign he was assigned to Fort D.A. Russell, at Cheyenne, Wyoming. He was on field service in northern Wyoming in 1877 and 1878 and took part in the capture of disaffected Indians at Ross Fork, Idaho, in January 1878. Montgomery was on the Ute expedition in the fall and winter of 1879, participating in raising the siege at Milk Creek, Colorado. He became major of the 10th Cavalry March 8, 1891, retired April 8, 1892, and died at Washington, D.C.

Heitman; Powell; Price, *Fifth Cavalry;* John M. Carroll, Byron Price, *Roll Call on the Little Big Horn.* Fort Collins, Colo., Old Army Press, 1974.

Montigny, Francois (Jolliet) de, missionary (1669-Dec. 19, 1742). B. at Paris, he began studies for the priesethood and reached Canada in 1692 where he continued them, being ordained in March 1693 at Quebec, and becoming vicar general for the colony in 1697. In 1698 he was named by the bishop to head up a Seminary of Foreign Missions project for Mississippi River tribes in regions which had been considered the domain of the Jesuits. He and two other priests, Jean Francois Buisson de St. Cosme and Albert Davion reached Michilimackinac in September, there meeting Henri de Tonty who agreed to take them as far south as the Arkansas River, where they arrived before the end of the year. Montigny settled Davion among the Tunica Indians in the present state of Mississippi and St. Cosme among the Tamaroas in Illinois. Montigny himself went south to work among the Natchez and neighboring Indians, but within a year he became discouraged and went back to France. In 1701 he went to China, working there until 1709 when he returned to Europe. He died at Paris.

Thwaites, JR,LXV, 262n7; DCB, III.

Montour, Andrew (Henry), frontiersman (c. 1705-post 1770). The year of birth is conjecture; he was said by Hodge to have been the firstborn of Madame Montour, who had several children by her first husband (a Seneca chief whom she called Roland Montour), and by 1711 she was married to a second, Carondowanen, or Robert Hunter, for he appeared with her that year at Albany. Raised as an Indian, some sources say Andrew was the son of the second spouse of his mother. He first appears in 1742 when Zinzendorf, head of the Moravian Church, visited Madame Montour and Andrew at the former's place near the later Montoursville, Pennsylvania. In 1744 Andrew was captain of an Iroquois warrior band moving against the Carolina Catawbas; he fell ill enroute to the James River and returned to the important village of Shamokin, near the present Sunbury, Pennsylvania. In May 1745, he accompanied the Indian agent and interpreter, Conrad Weiser, with a message from the Pennsylvania governor urging the Six Nations to attend a peace conference with the Catawbas at Williamsburg, Pennsylvania. In June 1748, Montour, said to live among the Six Nations between the forks of the Ohio and Lake Erie, was introduced to the president and council of Pennsylvania as a "faithful and prudent" interpreter and friend of the English. In July Andrew interpreted at George Croghan's house at Pennsboro, Cumberland County, with Six Nations' and Conestoga chiefs. Lieutenant Governor James Hamilton informed the Pennsylvania Assembly that Montour was of use and "discreet" in keeping the Six Nations inclined toward the British. At one critical period George Croghan wrote that "Montour takes a great deal of pains to promote the English interest among the Indians, and has great sway" among them, the French offering "a large reward" for Montour and Croghan, or for their scalps, they considering him a "French Canadian deserter," although he had been born among the Indians and never was a resident of French-controlled country. Montour during this period seems to have been an official interpreter in the employ of Pennsylvania. He was given permission to settle beyond the Blue Mountains in present Perry County, Pennsylvania, where he had long desired to live, to keep squatters out or report them to the government. Thus he settled at the mouth of Montour's Run, northwest of present Harrisburg. In 1752 he interpreted for the important conference at Logstown, about 14 miles down the Ohio from present Pittsburgh, Pennsylvania. The next year the Six Nations chose him one of their formal counsellors; Montour was back and forth between the tribes and official Pennsylvania, informing the whites of Indian desires and attitudes as much the Indians of those of the whites. He interpreted for the significant Winchester, Virginia, council between the Six Nations and the English when the latter assured the tribes of ammunition and support against the French. The Six Nations insisted that there be no white settlement on the Allegheny, although they were uncertain whether to welcome a "strong house," or fort against the French; Montour interpreted not only their words, but their feelings and attitudes, trusted by Indian and white alike. June 9, 1754, he met with George Washington on the Monongahela River, and was with him at the surrender of Fort Necessity, July 3, commanding a mixed company of whites and Indians. Montour may have taken part in the Braddock operation; at least he was active in scouting the French activities following the English-man's defeat. He was interpreter at a meeting May 10, 1756, between Oneida chiefs and Sir William Johnson. In July at a great meeting of many tribes with Johnson, Montour was appointed captain of a party of Indians and "sang his war song," though little fighting developed. The next year Montour again interpreted for Johnson who met with some Six Nations people and Cherokee delegates. He also interpreted at the great council which finalized the Treaty of Easton, Pennsylvania, and in 1759 and 1760 interpreted for several important meetings at Pittsburgh and elsewhere. Montour accompanied Robert Rogers and his command occupying Detroit after the French in Canada capitulated and on December 8, 1760, left Detroit for Mackinac with Rogers to take possession of that place, but ice and winter conditions forced them back. During the Pontiac War Montour was active along the frontier, scouting as much as interpreting, and in 1764 Johnson sent him with about 200 Six Nations Indians and a few rangers against hostile Delawares on the upper Susquehanna River, the war party capturing Captain Bull and about 40 men and in April destroying two towns and committing depredations against the Delawares. In 1768 Montour was interpreter for a great confer-

ence at Fort Pitt between Croghan and many Ohio River tribes. In compensation for his long and valuable service, Montour was given a tract of 880 acres in the present Lycoming County, Pennsylvania, and another of 600 acres about five miles above Fort Augusta (at Shamokin, or Sunbury, Pennsylvania). In 1742 Zinzendorf described Montour in this way: "His cast of countenance is decidedly European, and had not his face been encircled with a broad band of paint, applied with bear's fat, I would certainly have taken him for one. He wore a brown broadcloth coat, scarlet damasken lapel waist-coat, breeches, over which his shirt hung, a black Cordovan neckerchief decked with silver bugles, shoes and stockings, and a hat. His ears were hung with pendants of brass and other wires plaited together like the handles of a basket." Addressed in French, he replied in English.

William M. Darlington, *Christopher Gist's Journals.* N.Y., Argonaut Press, 1966; HAI; Arthur Pound, *Johnson of the Mohawks.* N.Y., Macmillan Co., 1930; Charles Hamilton, *Braddock's Defeat.* Norman, Univ. of Okla. Press, 1959.

Montour, Catherine, frontierswoman (fl. 1779-1791). A noted Pennsylvania-New York character, she was a sister of Esther Montour, daughter of French Margaret Montour, and granddaughter of Madame Montour. She married Telelemut (Thomas Hudson), a Seneca chief, and mothered a son, Andrew, and two daughters. Catherine's Town, near present Catherine, New York, was named for her and destroyed in 1779 by General John Sullivan's expedition. In 1791 she was living "over the lake" beyond Niagara. Her son, Andrew, became a Moravian and was living at New Salem, or Milan, Bradford County, Pennsylvania, in 1788. Catherine's brothers were John and Roland Montour, both prom-inent in border warfare against the English. Whether Graymont considers Esther and Catherine identical is unclear.

HAI; Barbara Graymont, *The Iroquois in the American Revolution.* Syracuse (N.Y.) Univ. Press, 1972.

Montour, Esther, frontierswoman (fl. 1772-1778). A daughter of French Margaret, and granddaughter of Madame Montour, Esther became known as "the fiend of Wyoming" for her alleged role in the Wyoming Valley

Massacre of Pennsylvania. She was the wife of Eghohowin, a ruling chief of the Munsee, a division of the Delaware, and in 1772 was living in the later Bradford County, Pennsylvania. Later she moved about 6 miles away, founding "Queen Esther's Town," and when that was destroyed in 1778 by Colonel Thomas Hartley of the 11th Pennsylvania, she removed probably to Chemung, New York. Her "bloody work at Wyoming, July 3, 1778, has made her name execrated wherever known." Captured militiamen "without mercy and with the most fearful tortures... were ruthlessly butchered," Esther herself dispatching 16 men held motionless by Indians, it was said, and later nine more. Only one escaped to tell the story. The entire legend was considered fiction by Graymont, however.

HAI, Vol. I, p. 938; Barbara Graymont, *The Iroquois in the American Revolution.* Syracuse (N.Y.) Univ. Press, 1972.

Montour, John, frontiersman (1744-1830). B. in Pennsylvania, he was a son of Andrew (Henry) Montour, and a grandson of Madame Montour on that side of his family, his mother a granddaughter of the Delaware chief Olumpias (Allompis) on the other, and in her right John was considered a Delaware chief. From 12 he was educated by Pennsylvania colony at Andrew's request. John Montour was with Lord Dunmore in 1774, adhered to the colonists' cause during the Revolution, was active on the frontier during that period, received a captain's commission in 1782 and as late as 1789 was reported living on the island later known as Neville Island, near Pittsburgh, although Heckewelder in 1788 reported him killed by Mingos.

William M. Darlington, *Christopher Gist's Journals.* N.Y., Argonaut Press, 1966; Reuben Gold Thwaites, Louise Phelps Kellogg, *The Revolution on the Upper Ohio, 1775-1777.* Madison, Wisc. Hist. Soc., 1908; Paul A.W. Wallace, ed. *Thirty Thousand Miles with John Heckewelder.* Univ. of Pittsburgh Press, 1958.

Montour, Louis Couc, frontiersman (c. 1674-1709). The date of birth is conjecture. He was born in Canada, a brother of the later Madame Montour, son of a Frenchman named Montour, or Couc, and a native woman, probably a Huron. In 1694 he was wounded by Mohawks near Lake Champlain;

later, wandering westward, he settled in with the Miamis or Wyandots, and came to lean toward the British influence already strong among these peoples. Perhaps in British pay or bribery, he assisted Edward Hyde Lord Cornbury, colonial governor of New York, in drawing the outer tribes (12 of them) to visit and trade at Albany and thus became anathema to the French at Montreal. He was killed by French units under Lieutenant le Sieur de Joncaire by orders of Marquis de Vaudreuil, governor of Canada, who said he preferred that Montour had been captured alive so he could have been properly hanged. Montour, whose sister had been captured independently by the Iroquois, may have been in contact with her before his death and for him she apparently retained a strong affection, naming a later son, Louis. Their other sister married into the Miamis, whether under duress is not known, and it may be this woman, who must have been familiar with Detroit, who was named Elizabeth and is sometimes confused with Madame Montour.

William M. Darlington, *Christopher Gist's Journals.* N.Y., Argonaut Press, 1966; DCB, Vol. III, pp. 147-48; HAI.

Montour, Madame (Elizabeth Couc), interpreter, wilderness dame (c. 1684-c. 1754). The facts of this remarkable woman's life are difficult to establish, and reports of her career are wildly contradictory, but she was a matriarch of some magnitude on the Iroquois frontier. Darlington (1893) said her father was a Frenchman named Montour, her mother a Huron woman by whom he had three children: a son and two daughters. Hunter (1974) said she may have been born about 1667 at Three Rivers as Elizabeth, daughter of Pierre Couc, and a native woman. According to the older account, she was captured at 10 by Iroquois; the later version said that, already married to a Frenchman (who is not identified), she was captured, ransomed by a relative, taken to Michilimackinac, and somehow came afoul of Cadillac who asserted disdainfully she had been "kept by more than 100 men," as preposterous as would be the statement that each of the 100 men had kept a series of 100 women. By 1704, according to this account, she was living at Detroit under the name Chenette or Techenet, later accompanying a Frenchman who had deserted Detroit "to live in the woods." She subsequently went with her brother, this account said, to New York colony where she and he lived among the Iroquois. It seems possible this version confuses the later Madame Montour with her sister who eventually married into the Miamis, according to report. The older, and more plausible, version said that her brother, whom Hunter determined was Louis Couc Montour, was wounded by the British-inclined Mohawks on Lake Champlain. After the affray, he went to live among the "Far Indians," the Miamis and Wyandots, deserted the French cause and influenced them at length to trade with the British at Albany. For this he was killed by the French in 1709; this, one may suppose, might have influenced Madame Montour to firm up her own inclinations toward the British. She eventually resided on the Susquehanna and Ohio rivers, evolving into interpreter for the English. According to Hodge, she married first a Seneca, whom she called Roland Montour, and after his death, she wed a noted Oneida chief named Carondowanen, who assumed the name Robert Hunter in honor of a New York governor. He was killed by the Catawba in 1729 in the south. Madame Montour was the mother of several children by her first husband, Hodge reported: Andrew, sometimes known as Henry, French Margaret, and perhaps Robert and Louis, or Lewis. Madame Montour first appeared as interpreter at an Albany conference in 1711, at which Governor Hunter met the sachems of the Five Nations and where Montour's Indian husband probably took the name of the white official. The council sought to allay fears that the Iroquois of the north would join their relatives, the Tuscaroras of the Carolinas, in a war on the frontier. Colonel Peter Schuyler was directed to take Montour as interpreter and her husband the next year to the Onondagas to assure their friendship; in 1714 the Tuscaroras migrated north, allaying fears they would ignite the flame of border war. Montour's influence and fame among the pro-British Iroquois was so great that the French sought to induce her to remove to the northern dominion; to counter this the British offered her "a man's pay" for her services, which she found acceptable, and she remained inclined toward British service. She attended a July 1727 conference at Philadelphia as interpreter between British officials and chiefs of the five (now Six) Nations. At times

Madame Montour appeared to have lived among the Miamis, into which people her sister had married. In 1734 she lived on the Susquehanna where the present Montoursville is situated, being host to Conrad Weiser, who spoke well of her, and Count Zinzendorf, head of the Moravian Church, listening with interest to his preaching. In the summer of 1744 she attended the great treaty council between the Six Nations and officials of Pennsylvania, Maryland and Virginia, held at Lancaster, Pennsylvania. Here she was visited by Witham Marshe, who took down the particulars of her life and who described her as genteel, of polite address, and once handsome. Madame Montour moved by 1745 because of a smallpox epidemic to the present Sunbury, Pennsylvania, where she lived until her death. She was blind in her advanced age. Of the varying accounts of her life, that which relates her capture as a child seems most probable; her thorough acquaintance with the language and customs of the Iroquois and her status among that people would have been unlikely to come about if the Michilimackinac account were true. Through generations which followed her Madame Montour's influence continued.

William M. Darlington, *Christopher Gist's Journals.* N.Y., Argonaut Press, 1966; HAI; DCB, Vol. III, article by William A. Hunter.

Montour, Mary, frontierswoman (fl. 1780's). A sister, or perhaps a daughter, of Catherine Montour, she became the wife of John Cook, a Seneca chief whose Indian name was Kanaghragait. He sometimes was called the "white Mingo," and died at Fort Wayne, Indiana, in 1790. Zeisberger said that when Mary was a child she was baptized a Catholic at Philadelphia, but in 1791 became a convert to Moravianism, accompanying its mission from New Salem (Milan), Pennsylvania, to Canada that year. He said she was "a living polyglot of the tongues of the West, speaking English, French, Mohawk, Wyandot, Ottawa, Chippewa, Shawnee and Delaware languages."

HAI.

Montoya, Estanislao, stockman, pioneer (d. before 1891). With his sons, Desiderio (d. before 1891), and Eutimio (d. post 1891), Estanislao Montoya was a resident "for many years" at San Antonio, New Mexico, doing business under the firm name E. Montoya &

Sons. Described as "one of the oldest citizens and most reliable," Montoya furnished transportation to return the Mimbres Apaches from Ojo Caliente, New Mexico, to San Carlos, Arizona, in 1878, Montoya being "personally known to almost every one of Victorio's band." On March 12, 1880, the Mimbres ran off about $3,000 worth of mules, horses and cattle from his place at Nogal, eight miles west of San Antonio. He and his sons tried to recover their losses under the Depredation Act, but were denied.

Arizona Star, Apr. 6, 1880; Montoya v. United States, 180 U.S. 261, 21 S. Ct., 358, 45 L. Ed. 521, Judgment on appeal from Court of Claims.

Mooar, John Wesley, buffalo hide man (June 12, 1846-May 24, 1918). B. at Pownal, Bennington County, Vermont, Mooar was a brother of J. Wright Mooar. He was comparatively well educated, financially independent and was living at New York City in 1871 when his brother shipped him from Kansas 57 buffalo hides to try and market. John W. Mooar sold them to a Pennsylvania tanner thus launching, or being among the first to launch, the buffalo hide business which resulted in wiping out the Great Plains herds and almost the entire species. John Mooar immediately joined J. Wright Mooar at Dodge City, Kansas, and they commenced hunting buffalo as equal partners; eventually they formed a company, Wright doing most of the hunting, and John the marketing of hides and buffalo products, although he participated in the hunting sufficiently to become famous in his own right at that pursuit. By 1878 the Mooar brothers had branched out into cattle ranching in Fisher, Scurry and Mitchell counties, settling near Colorado City, seat of Mitchell County, Texas. Mooar married Margaret Adams McCollum (Aug. 17, 1862-Feb. 25, 1918), and was a factor in the initial growth of Colorado City. He retired from the Mooar firm in 1905 as "a well-to-do man. He was a good business man" and was "one of the largest property owners in Colorado City." He died at Colorado City, and is buried there.

Southwest Collec., Tex. Tech Univ.; "J. Wright Mooar." Frontier Times, Vol. 5, No. 12 (Sept. 1928), 449-53.

Mooar, J(osiah) Wright, buffalo hunter (Aug. 10, 1851-May 1, 1940). B. at Pownal,

Vermont, of Scot descent, he moved to Michigan at 18 and to Chicago a year later, eventually reaching Kansas where he found a job chopping cordwood for Fort Hays. He soon joined five others on a buffalo hunt, securing meat rather than hides, and marketing it at Quincy, Illinois, and Kansas City. But Mooar sold some hides to W.C. Lobenstein of Leavenworth, Kansas, who had contracted to supply a limited number to English tanners. Mooar had 57 hides left over which he shipped to his brother, John Wesley Mooar, at New York City in May 1871. J.W. Mooar contacted a tannery, but a Pennsylvanian tanner bought the hides before the transfer was completed, paying $3.50 each; this was said to be the first sale of "buffalo flint (dry) hides on record." The Pennsylvania tanners experimented with them and ordered 2,000 more. John Mooar immediately joined his brother at Dodge City and they commenced hunting buffalo in earnest, marketing many hides through the Charles Rath company. The Mooars then formed a company themselves, J. Wright doing the hunting and J.W. the marketing. The Mooar hunters operated as far south as the Texas Panhandle over the next two years, skirmishing with Indians occasionally and wintering in sheltered canyons of the Staked Plains. The Sharp's Rifle Manufacturing Company, Bridgeport, Connecticut, developed its .50 caliber buffalo gun at least in part after correspondence with the Mooar brothers. Wright Mooar had a 12-pound Sharp with which he killed 4,000 buffalo, and a 14-pound Sharp with which he killed 6,000, including a white buffalo; in all Mooar was estimated to have killed 20,000 buffalo. Hides and buffalo products were marketed mainly through Dodge City, but also via Denison, Texas, Leavenworth and even New York City. In 1876 J. Wright Mooar went on horseback to Dallas and by train to New York City, thence to Vermont. Shortly afterward the Mooar brothers began raising cattle in Fisher County, Texas, although they continued buffalo hunting for two more years, until the southern herd was wiped out. In April 1878, Mooar led eight mule teams with dried buffalo meat to Prescott, Arizona, remaining in that Territory until 1880, then with his brother entering a livery business at Colorado, Texas. Their cattle ranching enterprise also expanded. He married in 1897. Mooar died at Snyder, Texas.

"J. Wright Mooar." *Frontier Times,* Vol. 5, No. 12 (Sept. 1928), 449-53; see bibliographical references in Wayne Gard, *The Great Buffalo Hunt.* Lincoln, Univ. of Nebr. Press, 1968.

Moody, Joe: *see* Bill Finn

Mooers, John H., surgeon (d. Sept. 20, 1868). B. in Vermont, he had been a surgeon and a major in a New York Volunteer regiment during the Civil War. He moved west for adventure and established a practice at Hays City, Kansas. Mooers was a practicing physician there when he joined the Forsyth scouts "for excitement" and is generally given the ranking of army assistant surgeon, although Heitman does not list him. On September 18, 1868, in the first day of the Beecher Island fighting, Mooers, while dressing the wounds of the commander, George A. Forsyth, was shot in the head, wounded mortally, dying two days later. He was buried on the island, but when an effort was made in November to remove his and other bodies, Mooers', Beecher's and William Wilson's were gone, apparently having been taken by hostiles. Bodies of Culver and Farley, the other two who died on the island, were removed to the Fort Wallace, Kansas, cemetery.

Simon E. Matson, *The Battle of Beecher Island,* Wray, Colo., Beecher Island Battle Meml. Assn., 1960, 100, 118; George A. Forsyth, *The Story of the Soldier.* N.Y., D. Appleton and Co., 1900.

Moon, William C. frontiersman (c. 1795-1878). B. in Tennessee he probably was a mountain man and trapper who reached California in 1841 with the William Workman party from Santa Fe. He was reported at Los Angeles in 1842 and at Monterey in 1844. The following year he mined for "grindstones" in the Sacramento Valley and in 1848 and 1849 mined for gold. He later settled on a Tehama County ranch, where he died. Bancroft described him as a "famous hunter, and a partner of Ezekiel Merritt."

Bancroft, *Pioneer Register;* Paris Swazy Pfouts, *Four Firsts for a Modest Hero.* Helena, Grand Lodge, Ancient Free & Accepted Masons of Mont., 1968, 58ff.

Mooney, James, ethnologist (Feb. 10, 1861-Dec. 22, 1921). B. at Richmond, Indiana, he taught school and worked briefly for a newspaper before joining the Bureau of American Ethnology with which he made his career. He wrote a number of important monographs that today remain standards in their fields. Mooney was a major assistant to Frederick Webb Hodge in preparation of the *Handbook of American Indians* (1907, 1910) and wrote many articles appearing in it, some being signed with his initials, J.M. His "Sacred Formulas of the Cherokees" appeared in the *Seventh Annual Report* of the BAE; "The Ghost-dance Religion and the Sioux Outbreak of 1890" in the *Fourteenth Annual Report;* "Calendar History of the Kiowa Indians," *Seventeenth Annual Report,* and "Myths of the Cherokees" in the *Nineteenth Annual Report.* He also wrote "The Siouan Tribes of the East," which appeared as Bulletin 22 of the Smithsonian Institution, Bureau of Ethnology. Mooney supplied background information for *Miscellaneous Publications Number 3* of the BAE and wrote *Indian Missions North of Mexico,* reprinted from the *Handbook* as *Miscellaneous Publication Number 9* of the BAE. He was married. In the course of his researches he often visited the frontier; his facility for getting along with Indians was very marked.

Who Was Who; List of Publications of the Bureau of American Ethnology, Bull. 200, Wash., D.C., Smithsonian Inst. Press, 1971; Neil M. Judd, *The Bureau of American Ethnology.* Norman, Univ. of Okla. Press, 1967; DAB.

Moonlight, Thomas, army officer (Nov. 10, 1833-Feb. 7, 1899). B. at Forfarshire, Scotland, he ran away at 13, shipped as a forecastle hand and reached Philadelphia without a penny. He worked in New Jersey until May 17, 1853, when he enlisted in Company D, 4th Artillery, in three years rising to first sergeant. Moonlight served in Texas until 1856 and for a year in Florida against the Seminoles, being mustered out at Fort Leavenworth in 1858. He worked as a civilian at Leavenworth, then farmed in the vicinity until 1861 when he was commissioned a captain of artillery, rising to colonel of the 11th Kansas Cavalry and brevet Brigadier General of Volunteers by 1865. He was active against Plains tribes in that year and commanded the District of the Plains with headquarters at Fort Laramie, succeeding Lieutenant Colonel William A. Collins. In May 1865 two Oglala Sioux chiefs, Black

Foot and Two Face arrived at Laramie with a white woman, Mrs. Lucinda Eubanks and her child, whom they had purchased from their Cheyenne captors and brought in to show good faith. Instead Moonlight and Lieutenant Colonel William Baumer, both while drunk it was reported, ordered the chiefs hanged and left as a "warning" to other Indians. The friendlies camped about Fort Laramie were incensed rather than cowed by the incident. In June Moonlight with a force of 234 Volunteer Cavalry pursued some of the erstwhile friendly Sioux east of Fort Laramie; about 120 miles from the post the Indians stampeded his horses and he and his command had to trudge back to the fort afoot. Shortly afterward he was relieved of command of the District and it was said only his political influence saved him from a court-martial; he was mustered out July 17, 1865. Moonlight became prominent in Kansas politics. In 1868 he was elected secretary of state; having switched affiliation from Republican to Democrat, then a minority party in Kansas. He was defeated for governor, for Congress, and in other races. Grover Cleveland in 1884 appointed him governor of Wyoming and, under Cleveland's second administration, minister to Bolivia. When he returned from South America in 1898 he settled on a ranch near Leavenworth, but died within a year. Married he left three daughters and a son who served in the Spanish American War.

Heitman; *Trans. of Kan. State Hist. Soc. 1903-04*, Vol. VIII, 353-54n.; *Portrait & Biographical Record of Leavenworth, Douglas and Franklin Counties.* Chicago, Chapman Pub. Co., 1899, 142-43; Robert M. Utley, *Frontiersmen in Blue.* N.Y., Macmillan Co., 1967; George E. Hyde, *Life of George Bent.* Norman, Univ. of Okla. Press, 1968; information from the Kan. State Hist. Soc.

Moore, Alexander, army officer (c. 1835-Sept. 30, 1910). B. in Ireland he was commissioned a first lieutenant in the 13th Wisconsin Infantry in October 1861 and ended the Civil War, in which he had served primarily in staff positions, a captain and brevet colonel of Volunteers. He became a captain in the 38th U.S. Infantry January 22, 1867. August 27, 1868, he led an attack upon Apaches in the Hachita Mountains of southern New Mexico, with no losses to himself and three Indians killed. Moore commanded Fort Cummings,

New Mexico, in 1869 when he was troubled not only by Mimbres Apaches, but by mail contractors demanding escorts. He believed that "it is as impossible for the military authorities to keep thieving parties of Indians from attacking the mail, as it is for the civil authorities to keep pickpockets out of New York." He was unassigned from November 11, 1869, until he became captain of the 3rd Cavalry December 15, 1870. Moore was placed in command of Fort Crittenden, Arizona, and was there when Cushing was killed to the eastward by Juh's band of Southern Chiricahuas May 5, 1871; Moore promptly led out scouting parties seeking to intercept and punish the slayers, but without success. In July 1871 Moore was sent by Crook, commanding the Department of Arizona to intercept a party of Apaches in the Sulphur Springs Valley, but Moore muffed his opportunity which led to Crook's intense displeasure and suspicion that Moore lacked courage, and ultimately contributed to his court-martial in 1876. Moore had a key role in the March 17, 1876, attack on the Cheyenne village on the Powder River, Wyoming but subsequently was court-martialed along with Colonel Reynolds and Captain Noyes following the debacle, Moore being charged with failure to cooperate in the assault and misbehavior before the enemy. He pleaded not guilty to the charges and specifications. He was found not guilty of disobeying orders nor of withdrawing his command after an Indian counter-attack, but guilty of conduct to the prejudice of good order and military discipline though not guilty of misconduct before the enemy nor of "cowardly failing" to cooperate with other troop elements. He was sentenced to be suspended from command for six months and confined to the limits of the post for that period, the sentence approved by General Grant but remitted in view of his Civil War record, which had been good. However Moore resigned August 10, 1879, ranched near San Antonio, Texas, became quite wealthy and died at Washington, D.C. He left his widow and a son, Dan T. Moore, of the Field Artillery.

Heitman; *Chronological List; General George Crook: His Autobiography,* ed. by Martin F. Schmitt. Norman, Univ. of Okla. Press, 1960; J.W. Vaughn, *The Reynolds Campaign on Powder River.* Norman, 1961.

Moore, Charles, soldier (1846-Feb. 17, 1921). B. in Canada, he was of the military escort for the 1870 Washburn Expedition to the Yellowstone country, and sketched the first known pictorial representation of Yellowstone features. He had enlisted in 1868 with the 2nd Cavalry; in 1874 he reenlisted in the Engineers, retiring a sergeant in 1891. He was 5 feet, 5 1/2 inches tall, dark-haired and blue-eyed.

Aubrey L. Haines, *Yellowstone National Park: Its Exploration and Establishment.* Wash., Nat. Park Service, 1974.

Moore, Edwin Ward, Texas naval officer (June 1810-Oct. 5, 1865). B. at Alexandria, Virginia, he entered the U.S. Navy as midshipman at 15 in 1825, serving aboard the *Hornet* in the West Indies and the *Fairchild* in the Mediterranean, but resigned in 1839 to take command of the Texas Navy with the courtesy title of commodore and few resources. He succeeded in destroying Mexican shipping in the Gulf of Mexico and, allied with Yucatan rebels, captured Tabasco, Yucatan, later engaged Mexican naval strength triumphantly, but came afoul of President Houston, being charged with "disobedience, contumacy and mutiny" for his continued enthusiasm for the Yucatan cause and paying less attention to the Texas interests. Vindicated by the Texas Legislature, Moore spent most of the remainder of his life trying to further clear his name and win compensation for his service to Texas, in which he was partially successful; he died in Virginia.

HT; DAB.

Moore, Isaiah N., army officer (c. 1827-Jan. 16, 1862). B. in Pennsylvania he went to West Point, became a brevet second lieutenant in the 1st Dragoons July 1, 1851, a second lieutenant February 21, 1853, and a first lieutenant March 3, 1855. He reached Arizona with Steen in 1856 after service in New Mexico. He had taken part in an expedition against the Mimbres Apaches earlier in 1856 and in April participated in an unwarranted attack on a peaceful village of Delgadito's; there were no repercussions. Moore was involved in the celebrated Bascom Incident at Apache Pass in February 1861, launching the Cochise War which lasted a decade. He was sent with a reinforcing party to the Pass where a confrontation already had occurred and voted with Irwin and others to hang Apaches

taken prisoner either in reprisal or as a notification to Cochise that the whites were powerful and determined. When Bascom demurred, Moore agreed to accept responsibility and the captives were executed, an unfortunate miscarriage of justice. Moore was of a group which purchased the Patagonia (or Mowry) Mine in southern Arizona, but apparently profited little from it. He was promoted to captain April 20, 1861, and ordered to abandon Fort Breckenridge which with Fort Buchanan was to be destroyed at the outset of the Civil War to prevent their falling into the Confederate hands. Avoiding Southern forces he led his Dragoons and two Infantry companies safely to Fort Craig, arriving August 8, 1861. Moore died in defense of Fort Craig.

Heitman; Cullum; Dan L. Thrapp, *Victorio and the Mimbres Apaches,* Norman, Univ. of Okla. Press, 1974; Robert M. Utley, "The Bascom Affair: A Reconstruction." *Arizona and the West,* Vol. 3, No. 1 (Spring 1961), 59-68; Benjamin H. Sacks, "New Evidence on the Bascom Affair." *Arizona and the West,* Vol. 4, No.3 (Autumn 1962), 261-78; Constance Wynn Altshuler, *Latest From Arizona!* Tucson, Ariz. Pioneers Hist. Soc., 1969.

Moore, James, adventurer, military officer (d. 1706). B. probably in Ireland, he reached Charlestown (Charleston), South Carolina around 1675, soon became active in protest movements and took part in toppling Governor James Colleton in 1690. He had married the widow of a former governor and managed plantations for her and William Walley, then commenced Indian trading, at which he was extraordinarily successful. Moore made many enemies and as many adherents, came to be a valuable man in the province, and frequently was entrusted with militia commands for one purpose or another. In 1699 he already had explored 600 miles to the westward of Charlestown and requested some 500 pounds sterling to finance an expedition of 50 whites and 100 Indians to march overland and discover the "Meschasipi" (Mississippi) River, locate its mouth and establish the true latitude of it (already ascertained by the French), but the money was not forthcoming and the endeavor languished. Moore served as governor from September 11, 1700, to 1703, had a bill introduced into the Assembly giving him a monopoly over the Indian trade and when the bill was defeated, dissolved the Assembly. He led an expedition in August 1702 of 600 English and as many Indians against the Spanish fortress of St. Augustine, Florida, Moore personally commanding several small ships supporting it. The expedition besieged the post for more than a month, but when two Spanish "men of war" (they later proved to be small frigates of 16 and 22 guns, respectively) appeared, he burned his vessels and returned to Charlestown by land, the expedition having cost two allied lives and doing little more damage to the Spanish who had used St. Augustine as a base for occasional raids against the South Carolina English. In the winter of 1703-1704 after being succeeded as governor by Sir Nathaniel Johnson, Moore invaded Apalachia to the west with 50 South Carolina volunteers and 1,000 Creek auxiliaries; he broke up nearly completely the Apalachee nation. The expedition left Ockamulgee December 9, attacked a place called Ayaville and burned it, killing 25 men and taking prisoner about 170 including women and children at the cost of two whites killed and a number wounded. At St. Lewis Fort, manned by Spanish a heavy fight developed between an enemy force of 400 Indians and 23 whites in which the enemy commander was taken prisoner, five or six of his men killed and about 200 of the enemy Indians slain, for a loss unspecified but including two British officers killed. Moore then marched through a series of hostile fortified places which "submitted and surrendered to me without condition," taking numerous prisoners and leaving Apalachee with but one town and those who had fled before the English; also taken were "Indians now having a mighty value for the whites." Moore added that "we have made Carolina as safe as the conquest of Apalatchie can make it," while depriving the Spanish at St. Augustine of a great deal of their support from satellite tribes of the interior. He brought back more than 1,300 of the formerly hostile, Indians, the expedition returning in mid-March 1704. Spanish and French accounts conceded that the Moore operation was successful, adding tales of English barbarity toward prisoners, white and red. The Apalachee carried away by Moore were settled near New Windsor, South Carolina, where they remained until 1715. When the Yamasee War developed that year, the Apalachee joined the hostiles and disappear

from English colonial history. Moore died from yellow fever at Charlestown.

Narratives of Early Carolina 1650-1708, ed. by Alexander S. Salley Jr., N.Y., Charles Scribner's Sons, 1911; John R. Swanton, *Early History of the Creek Indians and Their Neighbors.* Wash., BAE Bull. 73, 1922, 120-24.

Moore, Michael, army officer (July 4, 1800-Aug. 3, 1897). B. at New York City, he enlisted as a musician in the 13th Infantry and served from 1812 to 1817, being present at the capture of Fort George and pursuit of the enemy northward. In 1819 he enlisted in the 2nd Infantry, also as a musician, and was with the detachment establishing a post at Sault Ste. Marie. In 1826 he went with Cass and an escort to the head of Lake Superior to make a treaty with Indians, the party transported in batteaux of their own construction which they rowed the entire distance, "there being no vessels on the lake at that time." At Fort Mackinac the element with which Moore served largely rebuilt the barracks and rehabilitated them. In 1832 Moore served in the Black Hawk War "or, as General Scott termed it, 'The Cholera Campaign.'" In 1837 he went to Florida for three years against the Seminoles. On January 1, 1869, he was commissioned a second lieutenant, 9th Infantry, and retired December 15, 1870.

Powell; Heitman.

Moore, Thomas, packer (Dec. 10, 1832-May 17, 1896). B. at St Louis, Moore crossed the Plains to California in 1850, wandered into Idaho where he commenced packing to the Salmon River mines, and may have been a stage driver in Colorado in about 1868. In 1871 he joined General Crook as packer in Arizona, and helped that officer revamp and reinvigorate pack transportation for the Army, bringing it to the peak of efficiency for which Crook's mule operations were noted, Moore was with Crook in three Sioux campaigns. In the Rosebud campaign he organized 20 packers into a company of auxiliary sharp-shooters who did fine work during the fight with Crazy Horse, and later at Slim Buttes. Moore was in charge of five pack "trains" and 62 packers on the Reynolds campaign, 300 mules on the Rosebud operation, and 400 mules on Ranald Mackenzie's operation against Dull Knife's village in November of 1876. Moore worked with

General O.O. Howard in the Nez Perce war of 1877, with Miles against the Bannocks, was with Merritt at Milk Creek in 1879, with Crook in Arizona from 1883 to 1886, at Wounded Knee in 1890, and in a Bannock affair in Jackson Hole in 1895. He was highly praised for his efficiency, intelligence and endurance by many army officers. Crook called him "the only man in the country" who could properly make fit his pack transportation. He made his base for the last years of his life at Camp Carlin, Wyoming, the present Francis E. Warren Military Base near Cheyenne. Moore died of a cerebral hemorrhage. He was a brother of Carrie Nation, the famous Kansas saloon-buster. Henry W. Daly, also a noted packer, worked under him. Moore was married twice and a daughter and his second wife survived him.

Agnes Wright Spring, "Prince of Packers." *True West,* Vol. XVIII, No. 1 (Sept.-Oct. 1970), 24-25, 42-46,

Moorhead, Max Leon, historian (Dec. 28, 1914-Jan. 25, 1981). B. at Grand Junction, Colorado, he earned a master's degree at the University of Oklahoma in 1937 and his doctorate at the University of California at Berkeley in 1942. Most of his professional life was spent with the history department of the University of Oklahoma. He edited Josiah Gregg, *Commerce of the Prairies* (1954) and wrote *New Mexico's Royal Road* (1958), *The Apache Frontier* (1968) and *The Presidio* (1975), each in the upper echelon of historical studies. Moorhead died at Norman, Oklahoma.

Contemporary Authors; New Mexico Hist. Rev., Vol. 56, No. 2 (Apr. 1981), 140; Oakah L. Jones, "Max L. Moorhead: 1914-1981." *Arizona and the West,* Vol. 26, No. 1 (Spring 1984), 1-4.

Morain, Jean Jesuit missionary (June 20, 1650-Jan. 3, 1690). B. at Coutances, France, he became a Jesuit and reached Canada in 1674, completing his preparation for the priesthood and being ordained in 1676 or 1678. His work in Canada is not clearly stated, but it is said he was an "evangelist" among the Seneca in present New York State from 1679 to 1684 after several years in eastern Canada. He then went back to the St. Lawrence region where he worked until his death.

Thwaites, JR, LX 322n32.

Morco, John (Happy Jack), lawman-gunman (d. Sept. 4, 1873). B. probably in California, he had come to Ellsworth, Kansas, in 1872 from California via Oregon where he claimed to have killed 12 men in Portland in "self defence." He also said he had been fighting Modoc Indians in California lava beds. His estranged wife, an actress, reported he had shot four men at one time who had come to her help when he, drunk, was abusing her. Someone referred to him as an "illiterate moron." Morco became a member of the Ellsworth police force in 1873 under Brocky Jack Norton. Morco "hated Ben Thompson and all Texans in general," it was said, and was a central figure, with John Sterling, in the confrontation with Ben and Billy Thompson that led to the shooting by the latter of Sheriff Whitney. Morco fled to Salina, Kansas, by freight train, where he was arrested for return to Ellsworth. Salina authorities then declined to turn him over to Ellsworth officers, but Morco came back on his own and was killed on Main St. by city marshal J. Charles Brown after he had strutted about, defying officers and at last drawing on them.

Ed Bartholomew, *Wyatt Earp: the Untold Story.* Toyahvale, Tex., Frontier Book Co., 1963; Nyle H. Miller, Joseph W. Snell, *Great Gunfighters of the Kansas Cowtowns, 1867-1886.* Lincoln, Univ. of Nebr. Press, 1967.

Moreau, Pierre (La Toupine), fur trader (1639-Aug. 1727). B. near Xaintes, France, he reached Canada and became a noted fur trader and *coureur de bois.* In 1671 he was with St. Lusson at a great council with the Indians at Sault Ste. Marie. On October 1, 1672, he joined Louis Jolliet and five others in a commercial endeavor to trade for furs with the Ottawa. In 1673 Moreau probably was one of five Frenchmen who accompanied Jolliet and Marquette on their great expedition which formally "discovered" the Mississippi River, or its upper reaches. The next year he and "a companion who was not only a trader but a surgeon as well" built a cabin and became the first settlers, however temporarily, of the future Chicago, being host over the winter to Marquette, who lay ill during that season. Moreau in 1677 was married at Quebec, fathering in all 13 children. The next year he was arrested for illegal fur trading (a difficulty in which many wilderness fur men found themselves from time to time), but was released at Frontenac's directive. He was considered "one of Frontenac's adherents; it was charged that he, with other coureurs de bois, was shielded in illicit trading by the governor's influence." Moreau made his home when not on the frontier in the upper town of Quebec; he died in that city.

Thwaites, JR, LIX, 314-15n44; DCB, I, 394, II, 532; Joseph Kirkland, *The Story of Chicago*. Chicago, Dibble Pub. Co., 1892, I, 18.

Moredock, John, frontiersman, Indian killer (c. 1770-1830). B. in the Monongahela Valley of southwestern Pennsylvania, his birth date is conjecture. His father, Barney Moredock, perished in 1786 and his mother married Michael Huff. With his family, Moredock embarked by flatboat in 1786 at Red Stone (the present Brownsville) on the Monongahela, reaching the Ohio and floating down that stream to its junction with the Mississippi, then working up the latter to Grand Tower, 15 miles southwest of present Carbondale, where the party was attacked by Indians. Moredock's mother and a brother were killed before his eyes; later Huff was slain between Kaskaskia and Prairie du Rocher, Illinois, about 45 miles upriver (according to report Moredock's own father and another stepfather had been killed by Indians in Pennsylvania); from these incidents Moredock derived the hatred which made him one of the Old Northwest's most famed Indian killers. Though still a youth, he stalked his family's assassins for more than a year. With other whites he attacked them on the Mississippi River island, killed all but three, then tracked down and slew each of the survivors. His overall score of Indians killed was reported high. Left some means by Huff, Moredock settled on American Bottom, downstream from East St. Louis, and became a substantial citizen, though with eccentricities, some of them described by Herman Melville in *The Confidence-Man; His Masquerade* (1857). Educated only rudimentarily, he was inclined to indolence in some matters and was energetic in others. "He possessed a mind of extraordinary ability," acquired French by ear, was an accomplished dancer and something of a fiddler, delighted in horseracing, cards, singing, hunting, woods-roving and Indian stalking, and was of considerable natural dignity. He was "a model of symmetry and masculine beauty, rather above the ordinary size of men, and somewhat corpu-

lent. He was as straight as an arrow and of a dark complexion; his eyes were large and black and displayed an uncomon brilliancy; his head was large and forehead uncommonly capacious." Aside from his hatred of Indians, Moredock was "benevolent and kind and possessed no malignity or malice," and had he "received a competent education, he would have been a great man." In 1802 he was a member of the territorial legislature at Vincennes, Illinois, being then part of Indiana Territory. In the War of 1812 he was a state militia officer, working with ranger forces; he figured in Governor Ninian Edwards' campaign late in 1812 to Lake Peoria, and in an 1813 operation under Brigadier General Benjamin Howard. On November 10, 1813, he was elected from St. Clair County to the Legislative Assembly at Kaskaskia. In December 1814, his antipathy to Indians caused the death of William Hewitt in a needless tragedy, Hewitt being probably the last Illinois man to die in the war. Because of his popularity among rough frontiersmen, Moredock was prominently spoken of for governor when Illinois State was created in 1818, but he declined to run. He died at his home in Monroe County, was buried in Miles cemetery where vandalism has destroyed traces of his grave. Moredock married a Miss Garrison and fathered children.

Information from the Monroe County (Ill.) Hist. Soc.; John Reynolds, *The Pioneer History of Illinois*. Chicago, Fergus Printing, Co., 1887; James Hall, *Sketches of History, Life, and Manners in the West*, 2 vols. Phila., Harrison Hall, 1835; Melville's *Confidence-Man*, ed. by Elizabeth S. Foster. N.Y., Hendricks House, 1954; *Herman Melville, Confidence-Man . . . An Authoritative Text, Backgrounds and Sources, Reviews, Criticism: An Annotated Bibliography*, ed. by Herschel Parker. N.Y., W.W. Norton & Co., 1971.

Morehead, Frank Carter, army officer (fl. 1867-70). B. in Kentucky, he was commissioned a second lieutenant in the 5th U.S. Cavalry in 1867 from Missouri, served in the southeast until April 1869 when he was assigned to the frontier, participating in several actions against hostile Indians, including the decisive victory over the Cheyennes at Summit Springs, July 11, 1869. Upon reduction of the army he resigned at his own request October 1, 1870, and returned to Louisville, Kentucky.

Price, *Fifth Cavalry*.

Morel de la Durantaye, Olivier, army officer (Feb. 17, 1640-Sept. 28, 1716). B. near Nantes, France, he reached Canada in 1665 a captain in the Carignan-Salières regiment, assisted in the construction of Fort Ste. Anne at the head of Lake Champlain and in the fall of 1666 took part in the Tracy expedition against the Mohawks. He returned to France but came back to Canada in 1670, continuing as an army officer and also becoming involved in the fur trade. In 1682 he went to the Great Lakes region at La Barre's request in an attempt to control illegal coureurs de bois fur dealings with the Indians and inquire into the activities of La Salle, whom La Barre cordially hated. Durantaye commanded Fort Michilimackinac on the Strait of Mackinac from 1683 until 1690. In 1684 he had collected about 500 Ottawas and others to assist La Barre in an operation against the Iroquois, but the effort came to nothing. In 1686-87 he was active in military affairs on the lower lakes and in this capacity took part in Denonville's hapless expedition against the Senecas. Durantaye was relieved at Michilimackinac in part because he was partial to the Jesuits, who were in something of disfavor at Quebec. He was in France from 1704 until 1708; he died in Canada.

Thwaites, JR, LXII, 274n12; DCB, II.

Moreno, Andres, frontiersman (July 11, 1840-July 16, 1887). B. in Sonora he came to Tucson as a child and about 1865 enlisted in Co. E, 1st Battalion, Arizona Volunteer Infantry, organized to protect settlements from Indians. He is said to have engaged in several sharp fights, presumably with Yavapais or with Tonto Apaches, the first February 11, 1866, out of Camp Lincoln, (Fort Verde) in central Arizona. In the summer of 1866 he returned to Tucson. After 1880 he worked in mines around Globe, Arizona. He did some freighting until 1887. He was murdered by Knox Lee on the Mogollon Rim west of Baker Butte, where he is buried alongside the high road. Lee received six years for manslaughter.

Maurice Kildare, "Arizona's Tragic Hero." *Real West,* Vol. XIV,No. 90 (Feb. 1971) 13-17, 59-63.

Moreno, Joseph Matías, Franciscan missionary (May 1744-July 17, 1781). B. at Almorza, Spain, he joined the Franciscan order in 1762 and in 1769 was stationed at the college of Santa Cruz de Querétaro, Mexico. He was sent to the Sonoran missions and when the Colorado River missions were begun among the Yuma Indians, Moreno joined Juan Díaz at Mission San Pedro y San Pablo north of Fort Yuma. Here the two missionaries were killed in an uprising, their bodies ultimately buried at Querétaro.

Maynard Geiger, O.F.M., *Franciscan Missionaries in Hispanic California.* San Marino, Huntington Library, 1969; Jack D. Forbes, *Warriors of the Colorado.* Norman, Univ. of Okla. Press, 1965.

Morgan, Anna Brewster, captive (Dec. 10, 1844-June 11, 1902). B. near Trenton, New Jersey, her father and a brother were killed in the Civil War in which another brother, David, also served. After the conflict, he took up a claim in Ottawa County, Kansas, where Anna joined him; their mother had died in an insane asylum in Pennsylvania. September 13, 1868. Anna married James S. Morgan and within a month (one source says two weeks), her husband was seriously wounded and she was carried into captivity by Cheyennes according to Quaife, or by Sioux who later traded her to Cheyennes, other sources report. Her husband ultimately recovered at the Fort Hays, Kansas military hospital. With Sarah White, another captive, Anna was taken to the present Wheeler County, Texas, being rescued in March 1869, by Custer and the 7th Cavalry, and the 19th Kansas Cavalry. Anna Morgan gave birth to a half-Indian child after her release, the infant dying within three years; she resumed life with her husband, but he eventually left her and she lived at Delphas, Kansas, with her brother, David Brewster. Anna became insane and died after two years at the Home for the Feeble Minded at Topeka, Kansas; whether her ailment was hereditary or caused by the great hardships during her captivity can not be determined but they must at least have aggravated her emotional stress. Anna Morgan was described by Sarah White as "a beautiful young woman with blue eyes and thick lustrous hair of yellow hue." David, her brother, had accompanied Custer as a civilian during the rescue operation, the officer judging that he "displayed more genuine courage, perseverance, and physical endurance, and a greater degree of true brotherly love and devotion, than I have ever seen combined in one person."

George A. Custer, *My Life on the Plains,* ed. by

Milo M. Quaife. Lincoln, Univ. of Nebr. Press, 1966; Stan Hoig, *The Battle of the Washita.* Garden City, N.Y., Doubleday & Co., 1976; *Concordia* (Kansas) *Empire,* Sept. 1, 1898; *Kansas Optimist,* Oct. 22, 1953.

Morgan, Dale. L. historian (Dec. 18, 1914-Mar. 30, 1971). B. at Salt Lake City, he was a descendent of Orson Pratt, one of the most prominent of early Mormons. Morgan was afflicted with total deafness at 14 because of meningitis and later suffered some loss of normal speech. In his silent world he was forced to turn to the written word and became a pre-eminent historian of the American fur trade. At the University of Utah he read voraciously in history, biography, literature and philosophy but received a bachelor's degree in 1937 in commercial art. Unable to find employment with advertising agencies because of the Depression and his afflictions, he worked for the local branch of the Historical Records Survey of the Works Progress Administration. He soon became an editor, prepared model guides for county archives and was appointed in 1940 state supervisor of the federal Utah Writers Project. His first major book was *Utah: A Guide to the State* (1941), in the WPA guide series. In 1942 he went to work for the Office of Price Administration at Washington D.C., the location permitting him to visit many eastern libraries and archives. His *Humboldt, High Road of the West* (1943) and *Great Salt Lake* (1947) preceded his loose association with the Utah State Historical Society that lasted from 1948 until 1953 and helped provide him a living; he wrote *Santa Fe and the Far West* (1949). A bachelor, he was gregarious, retained an interest in art, painting and sports throughout his life. He was a Mormon, though not devout, and over 30 years assembled a bibliography on Mormonism, some of it incorporated in a project of the University of Utah Press. In 1954 Morgan became an editor and author at the Bancroft Library of Berkeley, California. He already had published *Jedediah Smith and the Opening of the West* (1953), which brought him nationwide attention as an historian of the fur trade. With Carl I. Wheat he now published *Jedediah Smith and His Maps of the American West* (1954); edited *The Overland Diary of James A. Pritchard* (1959; edited *California As I Saw It...* (1960); with

George P. Hammond compiled *A Guide to the Manuscript Collection of the Bancroft Library* (1964); wrote *The West of William H. Ashley... 1822-1838* (1964, which Morgan justly regarded as his *magnum opus;* with George Hammond wrote *Captain Charles M. Weber* (1966); edited, with Eleanor Towles Harris, *The Rocky Mountain Journals of William Marshall Anderson: the West in 1834* (1967). He was forced in 1970 by failing health to resign from the Bancroft Library and died in Maryland of cancer. Morgan received many awards for his writing. He carried on a voluminous correspondence throughout his life. It has been estimated that he wrote, edited or collaborated in the production of around 40 books, in addition to numerous papers, book reviews and articles.

Everett L. Cooley, "Dale L. Morgan: 1914-1971." *Arizona and the West,* Vol. 19, No. 2 (Summer 1977), 103-06; REAW.

Morgan, Emily, unwitting heroine (fl. 1836). Emily was a comely mulatto slave of the household of James Morgan (1786-1866), owner of much property at the later Morgan's Point at the mouth of the San Jacinto River, Texas, where the town of New Washington subsequently was laid out. When Mexican forces under Santa Anna moved into the area, Morgan's buildings were burned and his property confiscated, Emily becoming a "serving girl" for Santa Anna, "a notorious woman chaser." According to legend he was dallying with Emily during the siesta period when Sam Houston's forces attacked and easily won the decisive 18-minute Battle of San Jacinto which assured Texas independence; had it not been for Emily and her charms, the result might have been different, or at least less pivotal. Early Texas historians chose to ignore the incident and the first person to mention it was an English ethnologist, William Bollaert, who obtained his information directly from Morgan, Emily's master, or former master. Emily is believed to have inspired the famous song, "The Yellow Rose of Texas," a handwritten copy of which, probably made in 1836 soon after the Battle of San Jacinto, is held by the Texas University Archives at Austin, Texas. It is signed only "H.B.C.," the name for which the initials stood being uncertain at this date. Nothing is known of Emily's later life or, for that matter, of her life before the San Jacinto affair.

Martha Anne Turner, *The Yellow Rose of Texas: The Story of a Song* (which includes a photographic reproduction of the earliest manuscript). El Paso, Univ. of Tex. at El Paso, Southwestern Studies Monog. 31, 1971; *The Eagle: The Autobiography of Santa Anna,* ed. by Ann Fears Crawford.   Austin Pemberton Press, 1967, 265.

Morgan, George Horace, military officer (Jan. 1, 1855-Feb. 14, 1948). B. in Canada he went to West Point from Minnesota; he was a classmate of George Converse (see entry) and with him was posted to the 3rd Cavalry as a second lieutenant June 12, 1880. As a commander of Apache scouts with Al Sieber (see entry) as chief of scouts, Morgan took part in the hard fight against Apache hostiles July 17, 1882, in the Battle of Big Dry Wash, Arizona; Morgan was severely wounded (as was Converse) and won a Medal of Honor and a brevet for his role in the fight. He became a first lieutenant November 26, 1884. He served at Fort Clark and elsewhere in Texas until 1891 and was a professor of military science and tactics at the University of Minnesota from 1891-95 during which he completed law studies and was admitted to the Minnesota bar, but remained with the army. He became a captain March 15, 1896. Morgan was recommended for a second brevet for bravery in the Battle of Santiago, Cuba, July 1, 1898. He became a major of volunteers and later served actively in the Philippines at various times. He became a lieutenant colonel, 11th Cavalry March 3, 1911, a colonel of the 15th Cavalry April 26, 1914, and was retired by operation of law January 1, 1919. He died at Washington, D.C., aged 93.

Correspondence: Morgan, Converse and Cruse with Britton Davis, 1927; Cullum; Heitman; Dan L. Thrapp, *Al Sieber, Chief of Scouts.* Norman, Univ. of Okla. Press, 1964.

Morgan, John Day, frontiersman (May 15, 1819-June 30, 1899). B. at London, England, he was brought to America at 8, residing at Philadelphia and then in Indiana. Here he was recruited to go to Texas "to fight Mexicans and Indians," reaching Texas in July 1836, settling in Bastrop County and becoming friends with Wiley Hill, an early pioneer. Bastrop County then was on the frontier, and Morgan quickly learned the arts of survival, weathering experiences with hostile Indians and wild life-ways. Morgan was a member of

the Texan Santa Fe Expedition of 1841, being taken from New Mexico with others to Mexico City a prisoner; he was paroled, reached Vera Cruz and shipped for Texas, arriving in time to take part in the Mier Expedition, was captured at Salado; avoiding execution he was marched a prisoner once more to Mexico City, at one point was sentenced to be shot, but escaped that fate at the last moment. He escaped, made his way to Vera Cruz again, and shipped on an American vessel for Texas. In the Mexican War he drove a commissary wagon for three months for Zachary Taylor's army, then resigned. Morgan returned to Cincinnati where his parents still lived, and was married to Rebecca Rogers, bringing his bride back to Bastrop County again, settling on Oscar Creek, 12 miles west of Bastrop. He died there.

Frontier Times, Vol. 4, No. 5 (Feb. 1927), 4-8; HT.

Morison, Samuel Eliot, historian (July 9, 1887-May 15, 1976). B. at Boston, he became an outstanding narrative historian, best known for his sea-related works. His publications had neither the depth nor the cohesiveness of those of Parkman and Prescott, however, and Morison cannot be compared with those master craftsmen in a historian sense nor in the permanence of his product except perhaps for his works on Columbus. He lived mainly in New England, being genuinely attracted to its coasts and seas, and was a salt water man throughout his writing career. Those of his works having some frontier interest include: *Maritime History of Massachusetts* (1921); *Portuguese Voyages to America in the Fifteenth Century* (1940); *Admiral of the Ocean Sea* (1942), a biography of Columbus; *Journals and Other Documents of Columbus* (1963); *Old Bruin: The Life of Commodore Matthew C. Perry* (1967); *The European Discovery of America, The Northern Voyages* (1971); *The European Discovery of America: the Southern Voyages* (1974); and *Samuel de Champlain, Father of New France* (1972). His research was sometimes spotty, reflecting his major interests. There are curious gaps evident in his work; for example, his *Voyages* contain few of the insights one might expect (from a blue-water specialist) on early voyages or those not related in some way to his principal enthusiasms. Morison's life of John Paul Jones was a re-write of earlier biographies, revealed only slight research and contained no important fresh understandings; his 15-volume *History of U.S. Naval Operations in World War II,* although officially "unofficial," actually could not have been researched and written without official authority and assistance at every turn, no doubt including financial aid; it was undertaken with the warm endorsement of President Franklin Roosevelt, himself a friend of Morison's and a salt water enthusiast. Withal, however, Morison was a major American historian and writer, and some of his work deserves to endure.

New York Times, May 16, 1976; *Terra Incognitae; The Journal for the History of Discoveries,* Vol. XV (1983).

Morlete, Juan, military officer (d. 1596). B. at Arcila, Morocco (probably in the mid-sixteenth century), he was of part-German descent. He reached Mexico about 1575, settling at Mazapíl, northeastern Zacatecas. By 1585 Morlete was a royal scribe at Saltillo, southwest of Monterrey and held the military rank of captain. He was sent to Almaden, Nueva León on behalf of the new viceroy, Luís de Velasco to warn Caspar Castaño de Sosa, lieutenant governor, to cease slave raiding among Indian tribes, and forbidding him to make an entrada into New Mexico, as Castaño intended. When Castaño nevertheless set out on his entrada to the north, Morlete, a rival and said by some to be his bitter enemy, was sent with 40 soldiers and some Guachichil Indians to bring him back in chains. He located Castaño in March, 1591 near the pueblo of Santo Domingo on the Rio Grande and manacled him for return to Mexico City. There Castaño was tried by the audencia, found guilty of various charges and exiled to the Philippines, although the Council of the Indies later overturned the conviction. Morlete was named "protector" of the Guachichil Indians, holding the position until his death and in 1591 also became protector of the Tlaxcalan Indian colony adjacent to Saltillo. In 1593 he was alcalde mayor of Saltillo. He was an efficient, able and intelligent officer whose integrity was absolute and who spent sizable funds of his own to carry out his royal duties, a fact noted appreciatively by higher authority. Morlete died, presumably at Saltillo, late in 1596.

George P. Hammond, Agapito Rey, *The*

Rediscovery of New Mexico, 1580-1594. Albuquerque, Univ. of New Mex. Press, 1966; Thomas H. Naylor, Charles W. Polzer, S.J., *The Presidio and Militia on the Northern Frontier of New Spain: A Documentary History,* Tucson, Univ. of Ariz. Press, 1986.

Morrill, Laban, Mormon official (Dec. 8, 1814-Dec. 8, 1900). B. at Wheelock, Vermont, he joined the Mormon sect and reached Utah in 1852 with the Daniel D. McArthur company. He married once, fathered nine children and became a blacksmith, farmer and stockraiser. He was high priest and member of the city council of Cedar City, Utah. Morrill firmly opposed the killing of members of the Fancher train of emigrants in the Mountain Meadows Massacre and according to a daughter his life was threatened for his stand. Morrill died at Junction, Utah.

Frank Esshom, *Pioneers and Prominent Men of Utah.* Salt Lake City, Western Epics, 1966; Juanita Brooks, *The Mountain Meadows Massacre.* Norman, Univ. of Okla. Press, 1966.

Morris, father and son, victims (d. Dec. 1, 1870). Morris, a Douglass, Kansas, druggist and his son were hanged with two others by vigilantes near their home, the four suspected of being supportive of horse thievery. Four suspected rustlers, including Custer's scout, Jack Corbin, had been lynched three weeks earlier, also near Douglass. None of the vigilantes was ever certainly identified except Dr. J.S. McGinnis of the county who subsequently admitted being one of them.

Butler County Hist. Soc. archives, El Dorado, Kan.

Morris, Robert Murray, military officer (May 12, 1824-Dec. 7, 1896). B. at Washington, D.C., he entered West Point in July 1841, but resigned in January 1842. He was commissioned a second lieutenant in the Mounted Rifles May 27, 1846, and remained with that regiment until it was designated the 3rd Cavalry. In 1863 he became a major in the 6th Cavalry, remaining in that regiment until his retirement in 1873. He then returned to Washington, in 1889 moved to Martha's Vineyard, Massachusetts, and died at Philadelphia. "Morris was a colorful character and his later career was unfortunate. He fought bravely in the Mexican War," receiving two brevets, and two more for Civil

War actions. "He was in New Mexico when the (Civil) War started, and was in command of a cavalry company at Valverde.... After the war he served in Texas on frontier and Reconstruction duty.... He evidently had a serious drinking problem of long standing." His various assignments included one at Fort Vancouver, Washington, in 1850-51, as escort for a topographical survey party in Utah in 1853-54, and various stations in Kansas and Texas after the Civil War.

Information from David Perry Perrine; Heitman.

Morris, Thomas, British officer (d. 1818). B. at Carlisle, England, he was baptized April 22, 1732, and entered Winchester College in 1741. He joined the 17th Infantry in 1748. After 15 months study in France, Morris reached America in 1758, a lieutenant in the 17th Infantry. He saw service in the siege of Havana and at Louisburg and was with Amherst in a campaign near Lake Champlain in 1759. He became a captain in 1761, assigned to Fort Hendrick at Canajoharie in the Mohawk Valley of New York, learning something of the Iroquois Indians. He reached Detroit in 1762. Morris undertook a 1764 mission to Pontiac (then hostile) and the Illinois Indians whom he was to wean from the French to the British cause. He was sent from Detroit by Bradstreet August 26 with Jacques God(e)froy and others; they visited Pontiac and his hostile warriors one of whom nearly stabbed Morris to death, being prevented at the last moment by Godfroy. At Fort Miami farther west Morris was captured by frenzied hostiles who stripped and almost put him to the torture, Godfroy standing staunchly by to lend what assistance to the captain he could; at the last moment the torture was held off and once again Morris had escaped narrowly. He wished to continue his mission to the Illinois but was warned repeatedly that to do so would mean inevitable death at the hands of enemy Indians. At last he desisted, he and Godfroy regaining Detroit September 17, "half dead with famine and fatigue." Bradstreet had withdrawn to Sandusky and Morris sent him his journal, a copy of which is presented by Thwaites from Morris's book, *Miscellanies in Prose and Verse* (1791), printed at London. Morris, wrote Thwaites, "evinced a steadiness of courage, endurance, hardihood, fortitude under disaster, and an unflinching determin-

ation to do his duty, as well as a power of attaching men to his service, that would do credit to any man... He bore no grudge against his savage tormentors... His appreciation of the qualities of the French Canadians, and his remark upon their conduct of Indian affairs show keen observation, astuteness, and a judgment free from prejudice." Morris returned to England in 1767. He retired from the army in 1775 and wrote a miscellany of fiction, songs, biographies and verse, the last appearing in 1802. Like his father and younger brother, Charles, Thomas Morris was a song writer of repute in his day; his literary output also included narratives.

Thwaites, EWT, I; Parkman, *The Conspiracy of Pontiac;* DCB; DNB; *Journal of Captain Thomas Morris,* with portrait. London, 1791, repr. Readers Microprint, 1966.

Morrison, Pitcairn, army officer (Sept. 18, 1795-Oct. 5, 1887). B. in New York, he was commissioned a second lieutenant in the Artillery Corps October 27, 1820, joined the 4th Artillery the following June, the 2nd Artillery in August and the 4th Artillery August 29, 1822. He became a first lieutenant August 26, 1826, and a captain September 13, 1836. Not much is known of his service until the Mexican War in which he won two brevets for his part in the battles of Palo Alto and Resaca de la Palma, Texas. Morrison became major of the 8th Infantry September 26, 1847, and lieutenant colonel of the 7th Infantry June 9, 1853. He reached Arizona in October 1860, his headquarters near the mines in the south of the territory at Fort Buchanan, moving the post about a mile east to the site of the later Fort Crittenden. Apaches raided the nearby John Ward ranch January 17, 1861, stealing stock and abducting Ward's foster son who later became the famous Mickey Free. Morrison sent a detachment under Second Lieutenant George Bascom to trail the depredators and recover the boy and stock, if it could be done. Thus was launched the operation which culminated in the historic confrontation between the whites and Cochise's Chiricahua Apaches at Apache Pass. Morrison went on leave in March to seek an assignment in the theater of the Civil War then developing in the east. He became colonel of the 8th Infantry June 6, 1861, but retired October 20, 1863. He died at Baltimore.

Heitman; Constance Wynn Altshuler, *Chains of Command.* Tucson, Ariz. Hist. Soc., 1981.

Morrison, William, fur trader, businessman (Mar. 14, 1763-Apr. 9, 1837). B. in Bucks County, Pennsylvania, he established a fur trading-mercantile business at Kaskaskia, Illinois, in 1790, his operation ultimately extending to the Rocky Mountains, Sante Fe (in a primordial way), and New Orleans. He also speculated in land by dubious means, was associated with Manuel Lisa, became a partner in the Missouri Fur Company of St. Louis and entered numerous other fields; he was active in supplying the army during the War of 1812. His economic empire dwindled thereafter however, he retired in 1830 and died at Kaskaskia.

Richard E. Oglesby article, MM, Vol. III.

Morrow, Albert Payson, army officer (Mar. 10, 1842-Jan. 20, 1911). B. at Payson, Illinois, he enlisted in the 17th Pennsylvania Infantry February 18, 1861; he was commissioned in the 6th Pennsylvania Cavalry March 27, 1862. Morrow was captured near White House, Virginia, paroled, captured again at Chancellorsville and once more paroled, and was wounded severely at Dinwiddie Court House March 31, 1865; in addition he suffered throughout his army career from rheumatism, arthritis and related ailments which did not, however, affect his energy, resourcefulness or ability. He became captain of the 7th Cavalry July 28, 1866, serving at Fort Hays, Kansas, joined the 9th Cavalry as a major March 6, 1867 in Texas, serving with it at Brownsville and Forts McIntosh, Clark, Quitman and McKavett, with occasional field expeditions or other duty through 1874. Early in 1875 he was with a battalion under Mackenzie into Indian Territory and in 1876 moved over to Fort Bayard, New Mexico, operating occasionally against Apaches. He was at Fort Union, New Mexico, in 1878 and in the fall undertook an expedition against the Ute Indians. Returned to Bayard, he again operated against the Apaches, becoming a key officer in the Victorio War. When that Apache broke out in late 1879, it was Morrow who guided the gruelling, exasperating pursuit around the Black-Mimbres Mountains and eventually deep into Mexico where, after a march accompanied by almost unbelievable hardships, he engaged Victorio,

Juh and others in a very hard fight in the Guzman Mountains; the fight was a draw. For a year he was engaged in the impossible task of corralling the hostiles; he had an occasional fight with them, and in June 1880, succeeded in killing Victorio's able son, Washington, but he could not round up the main body, although he followed many of them south to the Mexico line. "I am heartily sick of this business...," he wrote a friend. "I have had eight engagements with the Victorio Indians ...and in each have driven and beaten them but there is no appreciable advantage..." In the fall of 1880 Morrow was one of several observors of the French Army maneuvers and upon his return from Europe held a staff position until 1883 when he became commander at Fort Huachuca, Arizona. He became lieutenant colonel of the 6th Cavalry December 17, 1882, and colonel of the 3rd Cavalry February 18, 1891. He spent his final year of active duty at Fort McIntosh, Texas, taking part in a series of engagements against Mexican bandits, marauders and would-be revolutionists. He retired, in part for reasons of health, August 16, 1892, and died at Gainesville, Florida.

Heitman; Powell; Dan L. Thrapp, *Victorio and the Mimbres Apaches.* Norman, Univ. of Okla. Press, 1974.

Morrow, David (Prairie Dog Dave), pioneer (Apr. 14, 1837-Oct. 18, 1893). B. in Washington County, New York, he had reached California at the outbreak of the Civil War. He enlisted in Company G, 1st California Cavalry, May 25, 1863, and was mustered out at Santa Fe, New Mexico, May 25, 1866. During his three years of service he is said to have seen action against the Navahos and perhaps Apaches. After leaving service, Morrow moved to Hays City, Kansas, and for a time was a buffalo hunter, meanwhile acquiring his soubriquet. The most believable legend for the origin of his nickname was that he once captured two prairie dogs, tamed them, and sold them for $5 to a train passenger from the east; with an eye for business, he devised means of capturing more of the creatures, but soon glutted the market, the price tumbled all the way to 50 cents a pair, and he gave the enterprise up. A less believable version has Dave's ears trimmed by disgruntled desperadoes until "he looked like a prairie dog." By 1873 Morrow had moved to

Dodge City, Kansas, where his fame spread. During the winter of 1872-73 he shot a white buffalo, the only one known to have been killed in the Arkansas River valley, and sold the skin for $1,000 to hide dealer Robert M. Wright who exhibited it widely. It was acquired by the state legislature which held it until 1904, whereafter it was held by the Hubbell Museum of New York for some time. In the late spring of 1874, Morrow was tried at Dodge City for the shooting of one, Lawrence, who recovered; Dave was acquitted. In 1875 Morrow was arrested, possibly on a charge of illegally hunting in Indian Territory; nothing was done about the matter, so far as the record reveals. Morrow, with a tame buffalo and an occasional prank, became a noted character of Dodge City. In 1875 he was constable for Ford County; two years later he was on Dodge City's police force, and in 1878 he was deputy to Sheriff Bat Masterson. In 1883 Morrow was an active partisan of the Masterson-Short-Earp faction in the so-called Dodge City "war," a wholly bloodless affair. Later he served as deputy under Sheriff Ham Bell. Eventually he took up farming near Ingalls, Kansas. He died at the Kansas State Soldiers Home at Fort Dodge, Kansas.

Gary Leland Roberts, "Prairie Dog Dave." *Frontier Times*, Vol. 37, No. 6 (Oct.-Nov. 1963), 46-47, 70; Kan. State Hist. Soc. archives; Ed Bartholomew, *Wyatt Earp: The Untold Story*. Toyahvale, Tex., Frontier Book Co., 1963, p. 216.

Morrow, John Andrew (Jack), frontiersman (1831-July 7, 1876). B. at Washington, Pennsylvania, he established a famous road ranch about 12 miles west of Cottonwood Springs, Nebraska, near the forks of the Platte River. Morrow was a man of some controversy, being considered "notorious" by John S. Gray, a "whole-souled good fellow," by Percival G. Lowe, and an often-drunken schemer and conniver by Eugene F. Ware. Ware wrote that the Morrow ranch was south of the junction of the Platte rivers, Morrow cutting thousands of cedar logs from a nearby canyon for his own use and sale, and for telegraph poles. "He claimed to have cattle and goods and improvements worth $100,000, but he overstated it." Ware described him as "a tall, raw-boned, dangerous-looking man, wearing a mustache and a goatee on his under lip. He was said to be a killer, to have shot a

man or two, and to have passed his life on the plains. He was said to have daily altercations with pilgrims, and to have gone on drunks that were so stupendous in their waste of money and strange eccentricities that he was known from Denver to Fort McKearney and very largely in Omaha. He was said to have an Indian wife..." Yet in the view of Paul D. Riley of the Nebraska State Historical Society, Ware "certainly over-reacted to Morrow, considering the conditions of the times and the way business was done." He added that "it is interesting that few contemporary accounts (aside from Ware's) say anything negative about Morrow."

Eugene Ware, *The Indian War of 1864*. N.Y., St Martin's Press, 1960; *Man of the Plains: Recollections of Luther North, 1856-1882*, ed. by Donald F. Danker. Lincoln, Univ. of Nebr. Press, 1961; Musetta Gilman, *Pump on the Prairie*. Detroit, Harlo Press, 1975; Riley, research associate, Nebr. Hist. Soc., to author, Dec. 13, 1976.

Morrow, Stanley J., photographer (c. 1843-Dec. 10, 1921). B. in Ohio and raised in Wisconsin, he enlisted about 1861 in the 7th Wisconsin Infantry and served throughout the Civil War, taking part in the battles of Antietam, Fredericksburg and Gettysburg. In early 1864 he became acquainted with photographer Matthew Brady, learning the profession from him. After the war he returned to Wisconsin and in 1869 took his wife and daughter to Yankton, then capital of Dakota Territory. There he opened a photographic gallery. That year he journeyed up the Missouri River, photographing Indians and military posts, the first of many such trips, In 1876 he visited Deadwood during its gold rush and when Crook's "Starvation March" column neared the place Morrow hurried out to photograph it, his forming the best pictorial record of the concluding days of that operation. Morrow later established galleries at Forts Custer and Keogh and in 1879 accompanied Captain George K. Sanderson, 11th Infantry to the Custer Battlefield where graves were refurbished and the area cleaned up, Morrow's being the earliest known photographs of the site. In 1883 Morrow removed from Yankton to Florida and about 1888 to Atlanta; he died at Dallas, Texas. His photograph collection was widely dispersed; he sold many of his North Plains negatives to L.A. Huffman (who distributed them under his own imprint). Others were destroyed by fire at Jacksonville, Florida, where they had come into possession of another photographer, and some of his Crook stereographs bear the imprint of E.P. Batchelder of Stockton, California.

Paul L. Hedren, *With Crook in the Black Hills: Stanley J. Morrow's 1876 Photographic Legacy.* Boulder, Colo., Pruett Pub. Co., 1985.

Morse, Jedidiah, minister, geographer (Aug. 23, 1761-June 9, 1826). B: at Woodstock, Connecticut he was graduated from Yale and became a Congregational minister stationed briefly at Midway, Georgia, then at Charlestown, Massachusetts. His ministry was distinguished and important, but the frontier interest in Morse lies in his secretaryship of the Society for Propagating the Gospel among the Indians and his work as the "father" of American geography. In 1819 he was commissioned by the government to investigate Indian matters and to render a final study which was published as *Report to the Secretary of War on Indian Affairs* (1822). It resulted from his tour among Indian tribes over the whole frontier, although he did not visit all parts of it in person. But it was a balanced, judicious assessment in which he included population estimates, locations of tribes as remote as those in Old Oregon and Florida, and pertinent observations. He advocated termination of the factory policy, confinement of Florida Indians on reservations remote from the coast and contact with smugglers, removal of the Oneida Indians from New York to a new reserve in Wisconsin, and many other suggestions of value. He presented a tribe-by-tribe listing, incomplete of course, of populations, arriving at a total of approximately 471,136 Indians within the then territorial boundaries of the United States. Morse was even better known in his times for his several geography studies and texts, most of which went into numerous editions and in sum represented the available published knowledge about the geography of the United States. He was an important — and controversial — figure in American Congregationalism, the father of Samuel F.B. Morse, and devoted to Indian affairs and American history until his death at New Haven, Connecticut. He was married and fathered many children, three surviving infancy.

Literature abundant: Thwaites, EWT, many references (see Index); CE; DAB.

Morton, pioneers (d. Sept. 11, 1857). A family of this name, its composition unknown, perished with others of the Fancher emigrant wagon train at Mountain Meadows, southwestern Utah, at the hands of Mormons and Mormon-led Indians.

William Wise, *Massacre at Mountain Meadows.* N.Y., Thomas Y. Crowell Co., 1976.

Morton, Charles, army officer (Mar. 18, 1846-Dec. 20, 1914). B. at Chagrin Falls, Ohio, he participated with the 25th Missouri Infantry in the Civil War battle of Shiloh and various other actions. He went to West Point immediately following the Civil War and was commissioned a second lieutenant of the 3rd Cavalry June 15, 1869, posted in Arizona. He joined his company, A of the 3rd at Fort Union, New Mexico, and by 1870 was in Arizona, being stationed first at Camp Rawlins and then at Camp Verde where he "practically built" the post. In June 1871 he was ordered to pursue a band of Tonto and Pinal Apaches who had attacked the Agua Frio Ranch, killed herders and run off 160 head of stock. Morton followed the hostiles into the Tonto Basin, having "four successful and successive" actions with them in a celebrated operation in Arizona annals. He accompanied his regiment to Fort D.A. Russell, Wyoming, then scouted regularly from Sidney Barracks, Nebraska. He chased Cheyennes in 1875 and that summer was engineer officer on a Black Hills expedition designed to corroborate Custer's report a year earlier of gold in that region. Morton was on Reynolds' Powder River expedition of March 1876, performing creditably in the actions it undertook, and was with Crook during the summer campaigns against the Sioux. He participated in the Battle of the Rosebud, June 17, the "starvation march" to the Black Hills and the engagement at Slim Buttes, Dakota, September 8-9. Morton took part in various expeditions, scouts and operations on the North Plains until late 1878 and was ordered back to Arizona in May 1882 following the Loco emeute from San Carlos and resulting renewal of Apache hostilities. There he "participated in hard field work" and at least one expedition after Indians. He was at Fort Apache, Arizona when promoted to captain, November 17, 1883, and in 1885 moved with his regiment to Texas where he remained during the Geronimo campaign except that in April

1886 he was detached to return to Arizona and accompany the remains of Captain Emmet Crawford, 3rd Cavalry, who had been killed by Mexican irregulars in Sonora, to their final resting place at Kearney, Nebraska. In Texas Morton served at Forts Concho, Clark and Duncan. He became major of the 4th Cavalry September 23, 1898, lieutenant colonel of the 8th Cavalry March 24, 1901, colonel of the 11th Cavalry February 25, 1903, transferring to the 7th Cavalry two months later. He became a Brigadier General in 1907 and retired in 1910.

Heitman; Powell, which should be consulted for Morton's very interesting Civil War service; Dan L. Thrapp, *Al Sieber, Chief of Scouts.* Norman, Univ. of Okla. Press, 1964; John F. Finerty, *War-Path and Bivouac.* Lincoln, Univ. of Nebr. Press,n.d.; Cullum; *Who Was Who.*

Morton, Howard, scout (1840-Feb. 7, 1925). B. in Massachusetts, he was the son of a shipbuilder and early imbued with a love of the sea. While a boy he followed that bent, circumnavigated the globe and served on several ships. December 10, 1861, he enlisted in the 39th Massachusetts Infantry, and was discharged in 1865 a captain. He then moved to Kansas. Morton was one of Forsyth's scouts at the engagement at Beecher Island in September 1868, where he lost an eye but continued fighting throughout the affair. He was then hospitalized at Fort Wallace, from where he wrote a brother in the East about the engagement. Morton resided at Beverly, Kansas (Howard Township was named for him) until well after the turn of the century when he removed to Palo Alto, California, where he died. Morton had expressed the wish to be buried at sea. His widow had him cremated, Commander R.S. Culp of the USS *Argonne,* under orders from his superior, took the ashes to Lat. 27 degrees 52' N., Long. 115 degrees 49' W., and in the presence of all hands, and with military honors due an army captain, Morton's ashes were committed to the waters. In addition to his widow Morton was survived by seven daughters and two sons.

Simon E. Matson, *The Battle of Beecher Island.* Wray, Colo., Beecher Island Battle Mem. Assn., 1960.

Morton, Thomas, fur trader (d. c. 1647). B. in England, of the Anglican faith and of aristocratic birth, educated at Oxford and a lawyer who had practiced at Clifford's Inn, he was accomplished in Latin, Greek and the classics, wrote poetry, was a drinking companion of Ben Johnson and in 1620 courted a client, an elderly and wealthy widow, and married her for her money, which quickly disappeared. He reached New England in 1622 with trader Thomas Weston's company, but stayed less than a year. He returned in 1625 with a Captain Wollaston who established a colony at what was called Mount Wollaston at today's Quincy, Massachusetts. Wollaston left for Virginia within two years, and Morton, perhaps a former partner of Wollaston, took over the settlement, renamed it Ma-re Mount, which soon came to be called Merry Mount. Because Morton was a convivial soul, little given to Puritan austerity, he and his rambunctious settlement promptly came to cross-purposes with the Separatists, their mores and their legal organizations. "Shrieks of laughter and snatches of song soon rang through the forest and echoed as far away as Plymouth — to the mounting concern of the Saints." More serious was Morton's invasion of the fur trade, and his success in collecting beaver pelts from the woods Indians, thus cutting into the Massachusetts colonies' economic base. Morton extended his commercial operations to Maine, and according to Pilgrim charges, trafficked as well in guns and ammunition with the Indians, a forbidden practice. "Arms were being sold to the Indians also by English fishermen and the French," as well as the Dutch of New Netherlands, but these sources were beyond reach of the Pilgrims, while Morton was not. A nine-man force under Miles Standish seized Morton and in 1628 he was packed off to England on charges of selling arms to the natives and harboring runaway servants. He returned in 1629 and resumed Indian trading, again was brought to court and in 1630 sent to England once more. He came under the wing of Sir Ferdinando Gorges, a powerful and not over-scrupulous protector, and returned once more to the Massachusetts Bay colony, where he was imprisoned anew, held at Boston for a year. Released, he moved to Maine, Gorges' realm, and there he died. His book, *New England Canaan* (1637), was reprinted in 1883 with notes by Charles Francis Adams.

CE; DAB; George F. Willison, *Saints and Strangers.* N.Y., Reynal & Hitchcock, 1945.

Morton, William Scott, gunman (Sept. 1856-c. Mar. 9, 1878). B. near Richmond, Virginia, he was orphaned and lived at Springfield, Missouri, for a time, then went to Denver and finally to New Mexico where he was employed by James J. Dolan and thus sided with the Murphy-Dolan faction in Lincoln County troubles. On March 9, 1877, he became foreman of the Dolan-Riley cow camp on the Pecos. Robert A. Widenmann, an employee of John Tunstall claimed Morton killed a man on the Pecos, two men in Lincoln County and killed his partner in an Arizona mining endeavor. February 18, 1878, he was a member of the group that killed Tunstall, thus starting the Lincoln County War, Morton believed to have fired the fatal shot with a rifle. In early March a group of Tunstall supporters arrested Morton with Frank Baker and executed them enroute to Lincoln. On the way Morton had time to write a letter to Richmond, Virginia, to an acquaintance, H.H. Marshall in which he revealed his belief he was to be killed.

Robert N. Mullin notes; Philip J. Rasch, "They Fought for 'The House'," *Portraits in Gunsmoke,* ed. by Jeff Burton. London, English Westerners' Soc., 1971; William A. Keleher, *Violence in Lincoln County.* Albuquerque, Univ. of New Mex. Press, 1957.

Moscoso de Alvarado, Luis de, explorer (fl. 1530-1543). B. at Zafra, Spain, he may have been related to Pedro de Alvarado, prominent in the conquest of Mexico and served under him in Guatemala and Ecuador. Moscoso and two of his brothers, Cristóbal de Mosquera and Juan de Alvarado joined the De Soto expedition into southern United States, Luis as *maestre de campo,* or field commander. Landed at Tampa Bay the expedition explored and marched overland to Apalachee (today's Tallahassee, Florida) for winter quarters, Moscoso frequently sent on scouts or reconnaissances with separate commands, and as often commanding the army as a whole. He figured prominently in the most important battle with Florida Indians September 15, 1539, at Napetaca on a tributary of the Suwannee River. Moscoso had a creditable role in the disastrous battle of Mauvila, Alabama, October 18, 1540, but was less efficient at the Chickasaw battle of March 8, 1541, disregarding De Soto's instructions that a careful night guard be mounted, with the result that the Indians attacked by surprise

at 4 a.m., set fire to the town and waited outside for the flames to flush the Spaniards out. "Having had no opportunity to put on their arms (the Spaniards) ran in all directions, bewildered by the noise, blinded by the smoke and the brightness of the flame, knowing not whither they were going... they saw not the Indians who shot arrows at them." Many of the invaluable horses burned to death before they could be untied and liberated. The Indians did not realize the extent of Spanish confusion or they might have wiped out the expedition; as it was 11 or 12 Spaniards died, along with 50 horses and 400 swine which the Spanish had driven along for food. Clothing, saddles and arms had been destroyed and the Spaniards must contrive replacements as they could. The affair was a disaster (although it might have been worse) and De Soto replaced Moscoso with Baltasar de Gallegos as field commander, although the leader's anger soon cooled and he ever considered Moscoso one of his most valuable officers. When De Soto lay dying of fever on the western bank of the Mississippi in Arkansas, May 20, 1542, he called in his officers and leading personages and bid farewell to them. Baltasar de Gallegos, as field commander or second in command, asked De Soto to name his successor and De Soto, forgiving past lapses chose Luis de Moscoso, whom all the expedition willingly accepted as their leader. Moscoso surreptitiously submerged De Soto's body in the depths of the river, auctioned off the leader's property to members of the command, assured the Indians that De Soto had not died but gone to heaven from where he would return at his pleasure (in order that the natives hopefully might continue to think him immortal — which they never in fact did). The Gentleman of Elvas conceded that some Spaniards were glad De Soto had died, expecting that Moscoso, "who was given to leading a gay life" would soon take them out of this frightful and unending wilderness so they could return to Europe. Moscoso polled the expedition members, most asserting they ought to make for Mexico overland since "the voyage by sea (was) held more hazardous and of doubtful accomplishment," an adequate boat could probably not be built and even if it could there was no pilot, chart, compass or knowledge of distances to be covered. Moscoso, desiring "to get out of the land of Florida in the shortest time" agreed to lead them overland and June 5, 1542, they set out toward the southwest. By October they were on the river Daycao, identified as the Trinity River or perhaps the Brazos of Texas, in a desert land, as they considered it and they dare not forge ahead on that course, so it was decided to return to the Mississippi where perhaps after all they could construct boats. Moscoso "who longed to be again where he could get his full measure of sleep, rather (than go on) conquering a country so beset... with hardships," led them back to the great river again. Here were constructed seven brigantines (not the "brigantines" of recent past but durable craft that could be rowed or sailed with a single sail raised on a single mast), the Spaniards showing much ingenuity in contriving them. Planks were cut from logs by means of saws they had carried with them throughout the four year hegira; nails were made of melted iron chains they had used to retain Indian captives and slaves. The nails were too short to permit the use of planks of desireable thickness, and thinner planks had to do. They had no tar or pitch to properly caulk the vessels, so it must be done with dry and shredded tree bark, and there was nothing with which to pay the hull bottoms. But the boats were completed and they would have to do. The Spanish set out July 2, 1543, after the spring floods, heading down the Mississippi. Several sharp clashes with Indians occurred, some involving hand-to-hand fighting with Spanish as well as Indian losses. The trip downriver required 17 days and 52 more were necessary to round the Gulf of Mexico to Pánuco, on the Mexican coast. The expedition's 311 survivors were well received in Mexico and most of them returned to Spain or Portugal, including Luis de Moscoso.

Bourne, *De Soto*, I, II; *De Soto Expedition Commission.*

Moseley, Samuel, frontiersman (June 14, 1641-Jan. 1680). B. at Braintree, Massachusetts, he was married by 1665 to Ann Addington and professionally was a cooper. It was reported that he had been a "privateer" out of Jamaica and perhaps had been schooled by Morgan, "the result of which was to bring home to Boston two prizes taken from some unmentioned enemy." He had been in command of a ketch and a small flotilla defending the New England coasts against unspecified enemies, perhaps Dutch. In a confusing operation he was named commander of a reprisal expedition against the Dutch February 15, 1674/75 and fought them under three flags at once: English, French and (renegade) Dutch, bringing the prizes or results back to Boston by April 2. As the hero of the enterprise, Moseley became the most notable man in the colony, although he held no actual military office. When the Indian conflict known as King Philip's War broke out he enlisted 110 men to form an independent company of volunteers, many of them old privateers or pirates and other reckless elements. Captain Daniel Gookin accused him of "high-handed cruelty" toward Indians; he engaged in many skirmishes with hostiles and with his company scouted the Narragansett country. When the Indians fell upon Lancaster, Massachusetts, August 22 and killed nine settlers, Moseley picked up eleven praying Indians (Christian converts) at nearby Marlborough and sent them bound to Boston, where they were acquitted and his ruthless proceeding sorely criticized. From September 14 Moseley was scouting out of Deerfield, Massachusetts, and on the 18th, hearing the guns that signalled the attack on Captain Thomas Lathrop at Bloody Brook, rushed up 70 men. He was too late to prevent the disaster which cost the life of Lathrop and many of his men, but Moseley chased the Indians seven miles from the scene. On October 16, 1675, Moseley's men captured an Indian woman and after extracting information from her he reported "the aforesaid Indian was ordered to be torn to peeces by doggs and she was so dealt with," an indication of his ruthlessness. In November Moseley and his company joined others in a great expedition under Josiah Winslow against Philip. He was in the Great Swamp Fight December 19, 1675, near the present South Kingston, Rhode Island, in which 80 English were killed or wounded mortally, 150 wounded "that recovered," and 1,000 Indian men, women and children slain. At this action Moseley, a contentious man with superiors or other officers, overrode the half-hearted decision of Winslow to save the fort (at Church's suggestion) for use by the English, in the face of Moseley's determination to burn it and, in fact "the exploits of Church in this campaign seem not to have been known to any... except (Church) himself," the inference being that Moseley was the man of iron who brought about its bloody and savage results. Moseley's "popularity with the army, and the violent party of Indian-haters, together with his eminent success in the field... supported him in many notorious acts of insubordination and insolence toward his superiors..." In 1676 Moseley was engaged in the campaign "in the west," or Connecticut Valley. In June 1676 he was sent with Captain Thomas Brattle and his troops on a campaign in Plymouth Colony, they capturing about 150 Indians. His later military activities, if any, are obscure. He apparently died away from home, but the place is unascertained; he left many descendants in the New England colonies.

George Madison Bodge, *Soldiers in King Philip's War*, 3rd ed.   Boston, p.p., 1906; Leach, *Flintlock*.

Moses, Chief, Sinkiuse-Columbia tribal leader (1829-Mar. 25, 1899). Moses was b. among his people who dwelt on the east side of the Columbia River from Fort Okanogan to Point Eaton. The tribe was believed originally quite numerous (one estimate gives the aboriginal population of these people and the related Wenatchee as 10,000, before smallpox decimated them), but by the time of Lewis and Clark they numbered fewer than 1,000. Moses was known in childhood as Loo-low-kin (Head Band); as a warrior as Que-tal-li-kin (Blue Head Horn) and in later life as Sulk-stalk-scosum (Half Sun, or Sun Chief), the name of his father, but in his dealings with the whites used the name Moses, said to have been given him by I.I. Stevens. He was chief of his people during the last 40 years of his life; he was never a Spokane chief, although sometimes described as such. In the spring of 1858 he was one of several eastern Washington tribes who conferred with Colonel George Wright. By 1858 abrasive incidents had occurred between the Moses people and white immigrants, prospectors and wanderers, and at some point during this period Moses and the "Dreamer," Smohalla are supposed to have had their celebrated combat. In 1858, driven to hostility by Major Robert Garnett, Moses and others may have taken part in the action at Four Lakes and surely he was in that on the Spokane Plains after which he came in to confer again with Wright about peace. Moses had come into the chieftainship of his people in 1858 when his brother, Quil-te-ne-nok was killed by a white, Quil-te-ne-nok having

become chief upon the death of their father, Sulk-stalk-scosum, killed by Blackfeet in Montana about 1846. During the 1860s gold finds throughout the northwest encouraged a generous influx of whites, increasing pressure upon the native inhabitants. July 2, 1872 Grant established the Colville Reservation, and here eventually Moses and his people would be settled; an adjacent reservation known as the Columbia, or Chief Moses Reservation was soon eliminated. The Nez Perces always bitterly denied that Chief Joseph had ever sought Moses' help in the Nez Perce War of 1877 as Howard believed thay had and insisted there was no contact between them. Moses had no part in the "originating causes" of either the Bannock or Paiute wars of 1878, although in the general unrest that accompanied these events, all Indians, including Moses and his people came under white suspicion. In late 1878 Moses and several of his men who had been hunting the murderers of a white couple were themselves accosted by a volunteers organization, ironed and thrown into jail at Yakima, Washington. Moses and his followers subsequently were released. With others Moses was taken to Washington, D.C., in 1883 for a meeting which led ultimately to the Chief Moses Agreement (of July 7, 1884), eliminating the Chief Moses (Columbia) Reservation and restriction of his people to the neighboring Colville Reservation. In 1885 Moses and most of his people moved permanently onto the Colville Reservation, the chief building a house near Nespelem where was located the reserve headquarters. This was his home until he died of pneumonia at 70.

William Compton Brown, *The Indian Side of the Story*.   Spokane, Wash., C.W. Hill Printing Co., 1961; O.O. Howard, *Famous Indian Chiefs I Have Known*.   N.Y., Century Co., 1908; McWhorter, *Hear Me*.

Moses, George Nelson, frontier lawman (Apr. 15, 1844-Sept. 10, 1911). B. at Olean, New York, his family located near Sedalia, Missouri, and he was trained as a mason. After Civil War service in an Illinois infantry regiment, he saw action in the Missouri border war with the Jim Turley "gang" against bushwhackers, participating in the killing of Archie B. Clements at Lexington in 1866. Later he hunted buffalo in Kansas, visited Colorado, was a deputy U.S. marshal in

Arizona and New Mexico, and guided the party that located Great Bend, near the former Fort Zarah, Kansas. Moses marked the Texas cattle trail there after that to Abilene was abandoned. He was the first sheriff of Barton County, 1871-75, killing at least one horse thief near Hays City whence he had pursued him from Great Bend, and resolutely handled other hard cases. He was five times mayor of Great Bend and had extensive business interests there and at Gunnison, Colorado.

Biographical History of Barton County, Kansas, Great Bend, *Tribune,* 1912, 27-30; *Kansas, a Cyclopedia of State History.* Vol. III, Pt. 1, Chicago, Standard Pub. Co., c. 1912.

Mosquera (Moscoso), Cristobal, explorer (fl. 1538-1543). A brother of Luis de Moscoso, last commander of the De Soto expedition into the southern United States, Mosquera was known as "the best thrower" of the expedition but even he could not toss a rock across an unidentified but wide south Georgia river the party reached March 5, 1540; the Chronicler called it the Capachequi. Mosquera was joint commander of a brigantine during the 1543 descent of the Mississippi and from there to Mexico. He returned to Spain.

Bourne, *De Soto,* II; *De Soto Expedition Commission.*

Moss, John Thomas, frontiersman (Mar. 4, 1839-Apr. 11, 1880). B. in Utica, New York, he removed with his family to Mitchell County, Iowa. He went west in 1857 and reached Arizona two years later, having lived successively with the Paiutes of Utah, Hopis, Yavapai, Mohaves and Pimas of Arizona. He scouted for the army out of Fort Mojave briefly. In the spring of 1861, Moss claimed, he had floated on a raft alone from Lee's Ferry, southern Utah, to Camp Mojave through the Grand Canyon, a frightening trip for which no authentication exists. In April 1862, or thereabouts, with the Mohave chief, Iretaba as guide, Moss, Frank Skinner and Bill Francis made a strike in El Dorado Canyon, along the Colorado River in Arizona, opening up the San Francisco Mining District. Moss sold a mine for about $30,000 and took Iretaba and the Pima chief, Antonio Azul, to Washington, D.C., late in 1863 by way of San Francisco and Panama. They reached New York February 6, 1864,

and eventually Washington, where Iretaba reportedly met President Lincoln. The trio returned to California, reaching Fort Mojave again June 30. Moss went back to Washington the following year, unsuccessfully seeking an Indian agency. He prospected for a time in the Sierra Nevada. A report shows J.T. Moss as married in 1866 at Keysville, California, but nothing further is known of this union. Moss made a grueling crossing of the Mojave Desert afoot, visited Iowa in 1871, then resumed prospecting in the San Bernardino County area of California. He was peripherally — and innocently — involved in the famed diamond hoax of 1872, and in 1873 opened the San Juan mining region in Colorado. He founded what he called Parrott City, La Plata County, southwestern Colorado, named for his San Francisco backers, and was elected recorder. In September 1874, he guided photographer William H. Jackson to Mesa Verde. On October 20, 1875, Moss married Alida Olson, the first wedding recorded in the county. He was elected to the state legislature, but soon returned to San Francisco, which he had visited at intervals. He died at San Francisco of complications from a gunshot wound, reportedly inflicted by an Indian in southern California. Moss, though lean and wiry, was a hard user of alcohol, and some of his tales are of dubious veracity, but he was, on the whole, a worthy pioneer.

William B. Secrest, "Iretaba's Outrageous Lie." *Frontier Times,* Vol. 48, No. 6 (Oct.-Nov 1974), 22-23, 43-44; Secrest, "The Saga of John Moss." *True West,* Vol. 22, No. 6 (July-Aug. 1975), 8-12, 53-54.

Mossman, Burton, lawman (Apr. 30, 1867-Sept. 5, 1956). B. near Aurora, Illinois, he was raised in Minnesota but reached New Mexico by the age of 16. He worked as a surveyor in the Sacramento Mountains, as a cowboy near Monticello, the former Cañada Alamosa, and elsewhere. An assassination attempt against him failed, his assailant later being killed by Bill Hardin, cousin of John Wesley Hardin, Bill himself being shot by Juan Boca. Mossman visited Dodge City and Pueblo, Colorado, briefly and after various jobs managed a Bloody Basin cattle layout in Arizona, then became manager of the huge Hash Knife outfit out of Holbrook, Arizona, in December 1897. Here he received valuable experience combatting outlaws and rustlers.

Mossman became first captain of the Arizona Rangers, mounted lawmen organized in 1901 to curb rampant lawlessness in the southeastern part of the Territory. The rangers "captured or drove out of the territory many notorious outlaws and made definite progress" toward ending banditry, placing 125 major criminals behind bars during their first year. Before resigning in 1902 Mossman pursued the Mexican murderer, Augustino Chacón, who later confessed to having killed 52 men, including 37 Mexicans, in his lifetime. Mossman employed the services of two former outlaws in chasing Chacón whom he captured in Sonora, spirited back across the border and turned over to law officers to be hanged at Solomonville November 21, 1902. After a brief visit to New York City, Mossman re-entered the cattle business at Roswell, New Mexico. His son, Burton Jr. (Billy), an Air Force major, was shot down in 1943 and killed. Mossman married twice, owned the expansive Diamond A ranch for many years, and died at Roswell.

Jay J. Wagoner, *Arizona Territory 1863-1912: A Political History.* Tucson, Univ. of Ariz. Press, 1970; Carl W. Breihan, *Great Lawmen of the West.* N.Y., Bonanza Books, 1963; Frazier Hunt, *Cap Mossman, Last of the Great Cowmen.* N.Y., Hastings House, 1951.

Mott, John: *see* John Mott McMahon

Mott, Seward, army officer (Aug. 21, 1861- Mar. 11, 1887). B. at Mechanicville, New York, he reportedly had earned a degree at Syracuse University before going to West Point from which he was graduated in 1886, becoming a second lieutenant in the 10th Cavalry July 1, and being sent to Arizona where he was assigned to the San Carlos Apache Reservation, among other duties as an instructor in farming and irrigation methods. A dispute arose with a young Apache, Nah-deiz-az, over land the Indian thought belonged to his family. Mott was wounded mortally on March 10 and died the next day. He was buried first at Fort Thomas, Arizona, with the remains later transferred to Hamilton, New York. Nah-deiz-az was convicted of murder and hanged at Globe, Arizona, December 27, 1889.

Jess G. Hayes, *Apache Vengeance.* Albuquerque, Univ. of New Mex. Press, 1954; Hayes, "... *And Then There Were None* ..." Globe, Ariz., Tyree Printing Service, 1965.

Moulton, Elijah, pioneer (c. 1820-Jan. 28, 1902). B. in Canada, he left home in his teens and became a trapper and mountain man, reaching California by 1844 when he settled in the vicinity of Los Angeles, "becoming one of the very first Anglo-Saxon men to make this his home." Moulton welcomed Fremont to Los Angeles and quickly joined the American side in the war with Mexico. He became a sheepman and dairyman, settling east of the community, and eventually retiring to live in Los Angeles. He apparently was a part-time clairvoyant, and was associated with the Helm boys, cousins of the notorious Boone Helm, to an unclear extent. Moulton died at Los Angeles.

Los Angeles Times, Jan. 29, 1902.

Mountain Chief, Piegan chief (d. Mar. 1872). A leader of the Piegan band of the Blackfeet, he was a different Indian from the Blackfoot, Mountain Chief (1848-1942) who transferred the land that is now Glacier National Park to the nation. The Mountain Chief here discussed by 1858 was second in rank among Piegan chiefs and upon the murder of Little Dog in 1866 (reportedly either by Mountain Chief himself or a close relative) he became head chief after a brief exile. During the latter he, his two sons and two nephews lived among the Crows of Bear Tooth's band; during this period the five Blackfeet shot and killed John M. Bozeman and wounded Tom Cover on the Yellowstone River April 20, 1867. In 1868 he signed a treaty as head chief of the Piegans, but it was not ratified by the Senate. Shortly afterward Mountain Chief asked the Indian Commissioner to oust troublesome white men from the Indian country; for that he was abused by certain white men at Fort Benton, Montana and became openly hostile. Colonel E.M. Baker was directed to lead an expedition against the band and "strike them hard." He struck hard, but unfortunately against a friendly chief and band rather than Mountain Chief whom he had planned to attack. Yet the affair convinced Mountain Chief that successful hostility against the whites was impossible and within two months he met with the Rev. John Imoda, S.J., expressing his desire for peace, which once made was never broken. Mountain Chief was shot and killed by another Blackfoot, perhaps by mistake.

John C. Ewers, *The Blackfeet: Raiders on the*

Northwestern Plains. Norman, Univ. of Okla. Press, 1967; *Montana Post,* July 20, 1867.

Mountain Chief, Blackfoot leader (1848-Feb. 2, 1942). The last hereditary chief of the Blackfeet, he succeeded the Piegan Mountain Chief who was killed in 1872. The later Mountain Chief became known as a war leader, after engagements with the Crows, Atsinas and Kootenais, but he was not prominent in hostilities against the whites. He signed a treaty of 1886 ceding some of his people's lands and in 1895 signed a treaty transferring the present Glacier National Park land to the nation. He made several trips east, met four Presidents, and instructed Hugh L. Scott in the Indian sign language at which he was particularly adept. Mountain Chief went blind in his advanced age. He died at 94 and was buried at Browning, Montana, leaving a son and daughter.

Dockstader; John C. Ewers, *The Blackfeet: Raiders on the Northwestern Plains.* Norman, Univ. of Okla. Press, 1967.

Mourelle de la Rúa, Francisco Antonio, Spanish naval officer (1755-May 24, 1820). B. at San Adrian de Corme, near La Coruña, Galicia, Spain, he had seen service in the Guianas, Trinidad and the Antilles before reaching San Blas on the west coast of Mexico in 1774. There he joined the Hezeta-Bodega expedition of 1775 to the Northwest Coast of America aboard the schooner *Sonora,* commanded by Juan Bodega y Quadra (see Bodega entry for details) and like Bodega, he was a superior officer, possessed of intelligence, dedication, energy and a delightful sense of humor. On July 29 at around Latitude 49 degrees Bodega and Mourelle became convinced Hezeta intended to come about with the *Santiago* and return southward, his assigned mission of reaching 65 degrees north latitude unfulfilled. So the two officers during the night gave the *Santiago* the slip with the little *Sonora,* and continued northward, eventually reaching 58 degrees 30' north. On the entire voyage, north and south, the two young officers, Mourelle and Bodega had a continuing series of exhilarating adventures that sometimes bordered on disaster, but they came through. The vessel reached Monterey Bay October 7 and San Blas November 20. Somehow Mourelle's journal reached London clandestinely, and

was translated and published, being of assistance to Captain Cook on his own Northwest explorations. Mourelle was second in command under Bodega aboard the *Favorita* in the 1779 expedition commanded by Arteaga. This endeavor reached 61 degrees north latitude, or Hinchinbrook Island at the head of the Gulf of Alaska, determining that Alaska, which Arteaga deemed an archipelago rather than extension of the continent, curved in a great bight and from 61 degrees bore southwestward in the course of which they coasted the Kenai peninsula. The expedition, out of San Blas, extended from February 11 until November 21 when it returned to port. Mourelle was directed to command still another expedition northward in 1792, but circumstances prevented. Mourelle was transferred to Spain in 1793, promoted to frigate captain in 1799, to ship's captain in 1806 and to commodore in 1811. His career was distinguished on every side. In 1818 he was to command a squadron to put down a rebellion in the Rio de la Plata, but the endeavor never got underway and Mourelle died shortly afterward at 64.

Warren L. Cook, *Flood Tide of Empire.* New Haven, Yale Univ. Press, 1973; Bancroft, *Northwest Coast,* I; *Alaska.*

Mouse's Road, Cheyenne warrior (d. 1837). Mouse's Road and three companions were attacked by a war party of Kiowas and Comanches near a tributary of the Red River of Texas and the three other Cheyennes were killed. Mouse's Road's bow was broken by a rifle ball, and he threw it away. A Comanche chief, seeing him unarmed, rode up with a lance to kill him, but Mouse's Road avoided the weapon, pulled the Comanche from his horse and killed him with his knife. Lone Wolf, a Kiowa chief and a Mexican captive charged down upon Mouse's Road but the Cheyenne instead of fleeing, ran toward the Mexican, pulled him from his horse and knifed him to death. Lone Wolf dismounted and sped up to help the Mexican, but Mouse's Road dropped the dead man and turned upon Lone Wolf, dodged the Kiowa's lance and knifed Lone Wolf in the hip; as the Kiowa turned to run Mouse's Road caught him by his hair ornament and with all his force stabbed the Kiowa's back, but the knife struck one of the silver hair plates and broke off, leaving only four inches of blade on the handle. The

Cheyenne dodged the weapon and with the lance he had taken from Lone Wolf pierced the Comanche and dropped him from his saddle, dead. To the Kiowas and Comanches it seemed they had seen a man swifter than a horse, more agile than a panther, strong as a bear and one against whom weapons were useless. Though there were more than 100 of them they commenced to move off but a few, braver than the others, called to Mouse's Road to pick up the slain Comanche's horse and ride away to his village to boast of his prowess. Mouse's Road replied that if he did so he would only spend his time mourning his three slain companions, so his enemies must kill him. He mounted then and started to chase the Kiowas; two, armed with guns, sat on the ground awaiting him and when he was almost upon them fired, one shot breaking his thigh. He fell from his horse. Another Kiowa crept up from behind the Cheyenne and shot him in the back, and he fell over. Then all the Kiowas and Comanches rushed back to him; someone cut off his head but in a reflex action Mouse's Road's torso sat up, which frightened his enemies away. They sped to their camp with the news they had killed a medicine man who had come to life again and would kill them all, and the camp was moved so swiftly that some of the lodges were left standing. This was a story told by the Kiowas; since no Cheyennes survived, they had no account of it save what came from their enemies. The Kiowas and Comanches agreed that Mouse's Road was the bravest man they ever saw or heard of.

George Bird Grinnell, *The Fighting Cheyennes.* Norman, Univ. of Okla. Press, 1956, 14-17.

Mowry, Sylvester, army officer, promoter (1833-Oct. 13, 1871). B. at Providence, Rhode Island, he was graduated from West Point and became a brevet second lieutenant in the 3rd Artillery July 1, 1852, a second lieutenant the following year and a first lieutenant March 3, 1855, three years before resignation of his commission. He had been attached briefly to a railroad exploration party near the Columbia River, then served under Steptoe in Utah, reaching California in 1855 with that command and arriving at Fort Yuma October 1, soon becoming interested as were many other army officers in mineral resources. By nature a promoter and visionary, Mowry's fingers strayed into many pies, particularly

after he had resigned from the army to devote himself to entrepreneurial and mining activities. Three times he was elected a delegate to Congress from "Arizona," still unincorporated as a territory for which reason he was not seated. In a dispute that turned personal and bitter, Mowry fought a bloodless duel July 8, 1859, with Edward E. Cross, editor of the Tubac *Weekly Arizonian,* the first newspaper in Arizona, then bought the press, moved it to Tucson and saw that it resumed publication under a different editor; Mowry never edited it himself. He inspired and may personally have developed "Mowry City," on the Mimbres River in southern New Mexico, advertising the place in 1859 with a letterhead showing steamboats on the frequently dry "river," which rarely boasted enough water to float anything. That year he also was named special agent for the Gila River Indian Reservation, serving briefly. In April 1860 he purchased for $22,500 the Patagonia Mine (renamed later the Mowry Mine) in southern Arizona with his older brother, ship's captain Charles Mowry as operator. Sylvester Mowry is reported to have grumbled that it took a gold mine to successfully operate a silver mine in Arizona, but the Patagonia seems to have been profitable for him; he struggled hard enough to keep it. He also was appointed a commissioner in 1860 to fix the Nevada-California boundary, and spent some time in Guaymas, Sonora, which he hoped would develop into a port for Arizona. When Confederate forces invaded New Mexico and sent armed reconnoitering parties into Arizona in the summer of 1861, Mowry's situation became ambiguous: from his vantage it looked as though the Southerners would control Arizona for some time and in any case, his military training persuaded him that any operations in the far Southwest would be irrelevant to the outcome of the developing Civil War. He was of Northern birth with a brother who died in Northern service during the war, but in Arizona he was amidst predominantly Southern partisans and sentiment; he was much more interested in Mowry and his promotions than in political embroilments back east, and being a thorough-going opportunist he cottoned up to the Confederates as he would have to any other conquering element. This earned him a reputation as a Southern sympathiser, although the only thing he was truly in sympathy with was himself and his ambitions. It proved his undoing. When Carleton reached Tucson with his California column in mid-1862, part of his mission was to sweep up or neutralize what Secessionist influences existed and in so doing he caused to be arrested Mowry and a good many others, although to hear Mowry tell it he alone was being persecuted. The underlying reason, he complained was a vendetta against him by Carleton, although in fact that officer appeared to be fairly objective while personally convinced Mowry was a "traitor and a spy." Mowry and others were placed under a lenient form of house arrest at Yuma while his case was investigated. Against him were letters he had written to prominent Confederates, including President Jefferson Davis. In a letter to Sibley he passed along what gossip he picked up about movements of Union troops which added nothing to what Sibley already knew. Rather than "treason," as some writers label it, the letter was pure opportunism and militarily innocuous. Mowry was released from his nominal confinement without a trial and with no definitive resolution of his case, once all danger to Arizona from Confederate forces had been eliminated. He went east, published a book, *Arizona and Sonora: The Geography, History and Resources of the Silver Region of North America* (1864) which drew attention to the Southwest, although he was not permitted to come again to Arizona during the Civil War; his last visit was in 1870. He engaged in a lengthy lawsuit to regain control of his mine, but without positive result; control eventually reverted to him, but it did not again become profitable. A libertine notable even in that day, Mowry was married once and divorced, the charges against him being drunkeness and desertion; custody of his children was awarded to the mother. He died at London where he had gone for medical attention.

Constance Wynn Altshuler, *Latest From Arizona!* Tucson, Ariz. Pioneers Hist. Soc., 1969; Altshuler, "The Case of Sylvester Mowry; The Charge of Treason." *Arizona and the West*, Vol. 15, No. 1 (Spring 1973), 63-82; Benjamin H. Sacks, "Sylvester Mowry: Artilleryman, Libertine, Entrepreneur." *Amer. West*, Vol. I, No. 3 (Summer 1964), 14-24, 79; Estelle Lutrell, *Newspapers and Periodicals of Arizona 1859-1911.* Tucson, Univ. of Ariz., 1949.

Moyano, Spanish soldier-explorer: *see* Boyano.

Moylan, Myles, army officer (Dec. 17, 1838-Dec. 11, 1909). B. in Massachusetts, he enlisted in the 2nd Dragoons June 8, 1857, serving in Kansas and with the 1857-58 Utah Expedition. Moylan was in Nebraska from 1859-60 and July 11, 1860 was engaged in a fight with Kiowas at Blackwater Springs, Kansas. In the Civil War he participated in Lyon's campaign in southwestern Missouri and was in the Battle of Wilson's Creek before being transferred east where he was in on the capture of Forts Henry and Donelson, the battles of Shiloh, Corinth and becoming first sergeant by 1863. He was commissioned a second lieutenant in the 5th Cavalry February 19, 1863. Moylan was in a number of important eastern engagements, including the action at Gettysburg, being a company commander despite his low rank. He was dismissed October 20, 1863 for being in Washington, D.C., without permission. Moylan then re-enlisted under the name of Charles Thomas in the 4th Massachusetts Infantry on January 25, becoming a captain by December 1, 1864. He enlisted under his own name in the mounted service January 25, 1866, and was sergeant-major of the 7th U.S. Cavalry by December 16 when he was commissioned a first lieutenant, becoming a captain March 1, 1872. He served in Kansas, Kentucky, Dakota and Montana. Moylan was engaged in the Battle of Washita November 27, 1868, was on the 1873 Yellowstone expedition and commanded a squadron in an engagement with the Sioux on Tongue River, Montana August 4, 1873; he was in an action on the Big Horn River August 11, 1873. He was on Custer's Black Hills Expedition of 1874, and in the great Custer fight against Sioux and Cheyennes on the Little Big Horn River, June 25, 1876. Moylan was severely wounded and won a brevet and a Medal of Honor September 30, 1877, in a fight with Nez Perce Indians in the Bear Paw Mountains, Montana. In 1881 he was a company commander at Fort Meade, Dakota. November 5, 1887 he was in action with the Crow Indians in Montana. December 29, 1890, he was in the Battle of Wounded Knee in South Dakota. Moylan became a major in the 10th Cavalry in 1892 and retired

April 15, 1893. He died at San Diego, California.

Heitman; Price, *Fifth Cavalry;* BHB; *Chronological List.*

Muir, John, naturalist, conservationist, writer (Apr. 21, 1838-Dec. 24, 1914). B. at Dunbar, Scotland, he came to America at 11 and was raised on a Wisconsin farm. He studied four years at the University of Wisconsin, but took no degree. He walked to the Gulf of Mexico, thence to California where he arrived in 1868, spending about six years in and about Yosemite Valley, with which he was entranced, always keeping a journal for his jottings and sketches. In the Sierra he discovered 65 residual glaciers during his ramblings. On April 14, 1880, he married Louie Wanda Strentzel, horticulturist, devoting a decade to management of a fruit orchard, from which he became financially independent. He had explored Nevada, Utah, the Pacific Northwest and Alaska, where he discovered Glacier Bay and Muir Glacier, and in 1880 he accompanied the search for the G.W. De Long expedition in the Arctic; in 1903-4 he traveled in the Caucasus, Siberia, Manchuria, Japan, India, Egypt, Australia and New Zealand. His books and articles contributed greatly to strengthening the National Park system and creation of such parks as Yosemite and Sequoia. Around him conservationists rallied in such organizations as the Sierra Club, a now-national body he founded in 1892 and served as president until 1914. Muir's publications include *The Mountains of California* (1894); *Our National Parks* (1901); *My First Summer in the Sierra* (1911); *The Yosemite* (1912); among those published posthumously was *Travels in Alaska* (1915). Muir died at Los Angeles and was buried at Martinez, California.

Literature abundant.

Muir, John Theodore, cattleman, pioneer (Oct. 15, 1861-Jan. 7, 1945). B. in Montgomery County, Tennessee, he reached Santa Fe at 19 and in 1885 moved on to Grant County, southwestern New Mexico where he decided to remain. On December 19, 1885, carrying dispatches for First Lieutenant Samuel Warren Fountain to Fort Bayard, he rode in advance of the command a quarter of a mile, passing unsuspectingly through an Apache ambush laid by Josanie (Ulzana) which closed

upon the column in his rear. Five soldiers, including a surgeon were killed and two, including an officer, were wounded. Muir engaged in freighting and in 1888 established a ranch near Lordsburg where he raised cattle largely, although experimenting from time to time with goats. Muir was a state representative for ten years, and became interested in banking. His wife, Mrs. Emma Marble Muir (Sept. 20, 1873-c. 1950), born at Virginia City, Nevada, became a locally-noted historian, writing prolifically on southwestern frontier subjects. She arranged to have permanent headstones placed on graves of frontier notables at the nearby Shakespeare, New Mexico, cemetery. John and Emma Muir were buried at El Paso, Texas.

Dan L. Thrapp, *Conquest of Apacheria.* Norman, Univ. of Okla. Press, 1967; *Service Record, World War I and II, Hildago County.* VFW Post 3099, Lordsburg, (c. 1950), 85-87; recollections of the author.

Mulford, Ami Frank, soldier (c. Apr. 24, 1854-Aug. 4, 1890). B. probably at Corning, New York, he enlisted at Fort Leavenworth, Kansas, September 5, 1876, in Company M, 7th Cavalry, on December 1 becoming trumpeter. He served and probably kept a diary until July 12, 1877, when on Sandy (or Sunday) Creek, Montana, he was thrown by his horse, injuring his right side so severely that his bladder, liver and kidneys were damaged as well as the nerves of his right leg which resulted in progressive atrophy of the limb. He was treated at Tongue River Cantonment until November 1877 when he was transferred to Fort Rice, Dakota Territory, was discharged December 17 and pensioned for disability in line of duty. He lived subsequently at Corning and later at Horsehead, New York. It was at Corning that he published his well-known book, *Fighting Indians in the 7th United States Cavalry,* a volume which according to Rickey "contains more material on rank and file life in the West than does any other," and has often been cited. The work is somewhat misleading however, in that Mulford never took part in any actions against hostiles, may never have seen any and "it is more than likely that Mulford received the story of the (Nez Perce) campaign from his wounded comrades (in his hospital ward) with background material from Howard's report." It is probable he inserted this information to make his book more dramatic and thus more acceptable to the public.

Ami Frank Mulford, *Fighting Indians in the 7th United States Cavalry.* Bellevue, Nebr, Old Army Press, 1970; Rod McNeil, "Trumpeter Mulford and the Seventh Cavalry in the Nez Perce War of 1877." *English Westerners' Tally Sheet,* Vol. 27, No. 2 (Jan. 1981), 28-34.

Mullan, John, explorer, road builder (July 31, 1830-Dec. 28, 1909). B. at Norfolk, Virginia, he was graduated from West Point in 1852, being assigned first to the topographical engineers, then to the artillery. He was a member of the I.I. Stevens party directed to Washington Territory, to explore on the way the country and a route for a northern railway to Puget Sound. In the winter of 1853-54, Stevens left Mullan and Doty in western Montana to mark a wagon and railroad route from Fort Benton, on the Missouri River by way of Coeur d'Alene Lake to navigable waters on the Columbia. This was to become known as the Mullan Road, a route of supreme importance in development of the Northwest. During the winter of 1853-54 Mullan traveled about 1,000 miles, crossing the Continental Divide six times from October to January. The survey expedition "determined the existence of an atmospheric river of heat, varying in breadth from one to a hundred miles, giving mild winters in the lofty regions of the Rocky Mountains," and making the proposed road particularly attractive. Indian troubles interrupted construction of Mullan's Road, however. He was promoted to first lieutenant in February 1855, and transferred to Florida for two years of fighting the Seminole Indians. He returned to Washington Territory and from 1858 until 1862 was engaged as chief of construction in building the wagon road across the Rockies, with time out for Indian fighting. In 1858 he commanded 30 Nez Perce Indian volunteers, garbed in U.S. Cavalry uniforms and assigned as scouts and guides. They took part in an action called the Battle of the Four Lakes, August 31-September 1, 1858, in which considerable forces were engaged but losses negligible for the whites and light for the hostiles. Mullan's *Report on the Construction of a Military Road from Fort Walla Walla to Fort Benton* (1863), described the task, which was entirely successful. Mullan also wrote:

Miners' and Travellers' Guide to Oregon, Washington, Idaho, Montana, Wyoming, and Colorado, via the Missouri and Columbia Rivers (1865). Mullan was married in 1863; he had been promoted captain in 1862 and now resigned to begin ranching near Walla Walla, an endeavor that failed. He secured a contract to deliver mail from Chico, California, to Ruby City, Idaho, but was forced to relinquish his contract within a year. He opened a successful law practice at San Francisco, moved to Washington, D.C., in 1878, and died in that city.

Bancroft, *Washington, Idaho and Montana;* DAB; CE; Robert Ignatius Burns, *The Jesuits and the Indian Wars of the Northwest.* New Haven, Yale University Press, 1966.

Mullin, Henry K., soldier (c. 1779-Dec. 13, 1825). B. in Virginia and a Washington, D.C., printer, Mullin enlisted in 1803 in Amos Stoddard's company of Artillery at Pittsburgh and in 1807 was named sergeant major of the 1st Infantry. He was copyist for much of the journal of Zebulon Pike on his upper Mississippi River expedition of 1805-1806, and on his western expedition; Mullin previously had been copyist for Stoddard and for Brigadier General James Wilkinson before serving Pike. Pike may have helped him secure a commission; Mullin was named ensign July 2, 1812, was promoted to second lieutenant a year later and was regimental adjutant of the 15th Infantry from 1813 to 1815 when he received his discharge. He died at New York City.

Donald Jackson, ed., *The Journals of Zebulon Montgomery Pike,* 2 vols. Norman, Univ. of Okla. Press, 1966; Heitman.

Mullin, Robert N., historical researcher (Aug. 10, 1893-June 27, 1982). B. at Lincoln, Nebraska, he was taken by his parents to El Paso, Texas in 1901 and remained there until 1927. As a boy he was acquainted with' Pat Garrett, Mannie Clements and other famous or notorious figures of the region. From 1912 he operated a bookstore for a few years, weathering several exciting adventures during the Mexican Revolution across the Rio Grande, the action occasionally spilling over into the El Paso environs. Around 1914 Mullin visited Tombstone, Arizona, and employed his time there drafting a sketch-map of the community as it had been in the wild

1880s, revealing who owned what real estate, and so on. It later was professionally redrawn and had a wide distribution. During those years Mullin became fascinated with the history of the Southwest, particularly Lincoln County, New Mexico, became acquainted with Maurice Garland Fulton, Eve Ball and many other students of the wild old days, and commenced assembling a huge collection of biographical and historical notes on key figures and events of the Lincoln County War and other significant events of the area. Eventually these filled nine filing cabinets added to by an excellent library of the region. Mullin's business career was spent with various oil companies; he remained with Gulf Oil Corporation for 25 years, retiring in 1956 as Division General Manager with territory from Ohio to Yuma, Arizona under his direction. He then settled at South Laguna, California. Mullin is best known for having edited and brought to publication *Maurice G. Fulton's History of the Lincoln County War* (1968). He also compiled *A Chronology of the Lincoln County War* (1966), *The Boyhood of Billy the Kid* (1967), *The Strange Story of Wayne Brazel* (1969), and *Stagecoach Pioneers of the Southwest* (1983) published posthumously. He also wrote numerous articles of unvarying merit for historical journals. He died at South Laguna and was buried at El Paso, survived by his widow and two daughters. His library and collections went to the Nita Stewart Haley Memorial Library at Midland, Texas, the founder of which was J. Evetts Haley, a long time friend of Mullin.

Taped interview with Mullin by author, May 27, 1975; correspondence with Mullin over several years.

Mulvey, (Mulrey?), Bill, victim (c. 1844-Aug. 23, 1869). If the man "Mulvey," or some variant, is the "John Murphy" listed by assistant marshal M.E. Joyce as one of three persons shot during the year at Hays City, Kansas, he was a soldier, born in New York. He was killed by James Butler (Wild Bill) Hickok in an attempt by Hickok to keep the peace.

Joseph G. Rosa, *They Called Him Wild Bill*, 2nd ed. Norman, Univ. of Okla. Press, 1974; Nyle H. Miller, Joseph W. Snell, *Great Gunfighters of Kansas Cowtowns, 1867-1886.* Lincoln, Univ. of Nebr. Press, 1963.

Murie, Adolph, wildlife biologist (Sept. 6, 1899-Aug. 15, 1974). B. at Moorhead, Minnesota, he joined the National Park Service in 1934 and retired from it in January 1965. During that period he was biologist for the NPS except 1946-47 when he was with the U.S. Fish and Wildlife Service. Dr. Murie was married in 1932 and fathered a daughter, Gail, and a son, Jan O. Murie. His important publications included: *The Moose of Isle Royale* (1934); *Following Fox Trails* (1936); *Ecology of the Coyote in the Yellowstone* (1941); *The Wolves of Mount McKinley* (1944), and *Naturalist in Alaska* (1961). He died at his home at Moose, Wyoming. His *The Grizzlies of Mount McKinley* (1981), completed by zoologist Jan Murie, was published posthumously.

Information from Mrs Louise G. Murie, his widow, in correspondence with auther, July 13, 1975.

Murie, James, scouts officer (c. 1843-Dec. 26, 1910). B. in Scotland, he emigrated to Nebraska and married a Pawnee woman. When Frank North enlisted his battalion of Pawnee scouts, Murie, who spoke their language, was named on October 24, 1864, a lieutenant, later as captain and company commander, serving, he stated, until October 1, 1866. He accompanied North with the Pawnees on the Connor expedition of 1865, doing effective work. In January 1866, he led a scout along the Republican River, giving young Luther North his first taste of action. Despite the discharge date he gave, Murie participated in August 1867, in a fight with Turkey Leg, a Cheyenne who had taken part in a railroad derailment at Plum Creek, Nebraska, and in 1869 he commanded a company of Pawnees under Frank North, probably participating in the decisive battle of Summit Springs, July 11, 1869, against the Cheyennes. In the 1870 U.S. Census, James Murie was listed as a farmer, with an estate of real and personal property totaling $2,500, but described as "insane," which may have been a temporary condition. He later listed a cause for his disablement as "a Sun Stroke received while in the line of duty (with the result that) he is Mentally and Physically unfit to perform any kind of labor." The 1870 Census showed that he had a white wife, who had been born in Illinois; she was perhaps in addition to his Pawnee mate. He had two children by his white wife. On June 25, 1888, he applied for admission to the Nebraska Soldiers' and Sailors' Home (today the Nebraska Veterans Home) of Grand Island, where he died and is buried. He was 5 feet, 9 inches, in height, of fair complexion with blue eyes and, at 45, had grey hair.

Records of the Nebraska Veterans Home; George Bird Grinnell, *Two Great Scouts and Their Pawnee Battalion.* Lincoln, Univ. of Nebr. Press, 1973; *Man of the Plains: Recollections of Luther North 1856-1882,* ed. by Donald F. Danker. Lincoln, Univ. of Nebr. Press, 1961; information from Paul D. Riley, Nebr. State Hist. Soc.

Murie, Olaus, J., naturalist, wilderness exponent (Mar. 1, 1889-Oct. 21, 1963). B. at Moorhead, Minnesota, he was graduated from the University of the Pacific, Stockton, California, and studied at the University of Michigan. He served with the Army balloon service in World War I. A mammalogist of international stature, he conducted field investigations from Labrador, Hudson Bay and Arctic Alaska to the temperate regions of the U.S. For 25 years he worked for the U.S. Fish and Wildlife Service and its predecessor, the U.S. Biological Survey. In 1949 he led the scientific party of the New Zealand-American Fjordland Expedition. He was president of the Wilderness Society from 1950 to 1957, and held other offices for it, becoming chairman of its governing board. His important writings include: *Alaska-Yukon Caribou* (1935); *The Elk of North America* (1951); *A Field Guide to Animal Tracks* (1954); *Jackson Hole with a Naturalist* (1963), and many professional articles. His pen-and-ink illustrations were widely reproduced. In 1924 he married Margaret E. Thomas; they had four children. He was a brother of Adolph Murie, of the National Park Service. Olaus died at Jackson, Wyoming.

New York Times, Oct. 24, 1963; James, Regina Glover, "The Natural Magic of Olaus Murie," *Sierra,* Vol. 72, No. 5 (Sept./Oct. 1987), 69-73.

Murphy, James, spy (c. 1853-June 7, 1879). B. probably in Denton County, Texas, he was the second son of Henderson Murphy (b. c. 1820 in Virginia), a well-to-do hotel keeper at Denton (his estate in 1860 was valued at $4,650). At 17 Jim became acquainted with Sam Bass, then 19, who had reached Denton

County from Indiana; the friendship continued when Bass went on the outlaw trail. Murphy was even friendlier with Frank Jackson, who became Bass's closest colleague, Jackson at one time working as a cowboy for Murphy. Murphy permitted the Bass gang to camp on his place, served at times as go-between for them, and in May 1878, he, Henderson Murphy, and Jim's brother, Robert (b. c. 1848), were arrested by Sheriff William C, Everheart of Grayson County, charged with harboring the Bass crowd, and jailed at Sherman, Texas. From there they were taken to Tyler, Texas. The Murphys soon were out; Jim Murphy had arranged for this by agreeing to betray the Bass gang. On June 15, 1878, Bass contacted Murphy and suggested he join the gang, and Murphy did so, determined to prove their undoing in order to win permanent freedom for his father and himself. At one point he came under strong suspicion, with Bass and Barnes determined to kill Murphy, whose life was saved by Jackson's strong defense of him. Yet Murphy managed to communicate to Rangers Bass's determination to strike a bank at Round Rock, Texas; he remained apart from the resulting action in which Bass was mortally wounded, Barnes and a deputy sheriff, A.W. Grimes killed on July 19, 1878. Murphy returned to Denton, found himself less a hero than anathema to his fellow townsmen. Late in August 1878, Murphy wrote to Ranger Major John B. Jones and said he had been contacted by Jackson who had escaped the Round Rock debacle, who desired to give himself up and help hunt down Henry Underwood, another gang member, in return for a reprieve, but Jackson never came in and was lost to history. Suffering from eye trouble, Murphy procured medicine from a drugstore and accidentally — as is supposed —swallowed some of it, which caused his death.

1860 U.S. Census, Denton County; Wayne Gard, *Sam Bass.* Lincoln, Univ. of Nebr. Press, 1969; Walter Prescott Webb, *The Texas Rangers.* Boston, Houghton Mifflin Co., 1935; *Frontier Times,* Vol. 3, Nos. 5-7 (Feb., Mar., Apr., 1926).

Murphy, Lavinia, pioneer (c. 1796-Mar. 19, 1847). A widow, Mrs. Murphy with four sons and three daughters left Tennessee by way of Missouri and joined the Donner party for California, departing in early May from

Independence (see George Donner entry). With the others she was snowbound east of the Sierra Nevada and because of her age there was little likelihood that she could walk out, although she exhibited truly herioc reactions to the community suffering. She also was a woman of spirit and frankly accused Keseberg of killing little George Foster, but the details upon which she based her suspicion are not known. When most of the others left with the Third Relief Party Mrs. Murphy remained and died at her cabin at Donner Lake. Her sons Lemuel Murphy, 12 died in the Sierrra December 28, 1846, and John L. Murphy, 15 died January 3, 1847, at Donner Lake. A daughter, Mary M. Murphy (b. c. 1833) married William Johnson in 1847 and he apparently died shortly for in 1848 she married Charles Covilland; in 1850 the city of Marysville, California, was laid out and named for her. She gave birth to five children and died before 1880.

C.F. McGlashan, *History of the Donner Party.* Stanford Univ. Press, 1947; Bancroft, *Pioneer Register.*

Murphy, Lawrence Gustave, merchant (c. 1831-Oct. 20, 1878). B. at Wedford, Ireland, he may have studied for the Roman Catholic priesthood; he emigrated to the United States as a young man. He enlisted in the 5th Infantry and served with it 10 years; he was in Utah in 1859. Murphy reached New Mexico where he enlisted in the 1st New Mexico Volunteers July 27, 1861, was commissioned a captain and ended the Civil War a major, being mustered out in 1866. He then became sutler at Fort Stanton, New Mexico, resigning after three years following a dispute with Major David Ramsay Clendenin, the commanding officer. In 1869 Murphy moved to Bonito (the later Lincoln), nine miles distant, establishing a firm known as L.G. Murphy & Co., taking in eventually as partner Emil Fritz and, after Fritz's death in 1874, J.J. Dolan. Murphy severed his relation with the firm on April 20, 1877, before the so-called Lincoln County War actually broke out, but with the factionalism which led to it well established. In addition to the store, Murphy had substantial ranching interests in the county, centering about 12 miles south of White Oaks, the ranch after his death being acquired by Thomas B. Catron. Murphy died at Santa Fe, apparently of cancer. Angel had characterized him in 1878 as "now a drunkard; no reliability.

He believes himself a martyr and McSween the devil — Handle him with gloves." Murphy was strongly supportive of Governor Axtell, a controversial figure.

William A. Keleher, *Violence in Lincoln County, 1869-1881.* Albuquerque, Univ. of New Mex. Press, 1957; "Frank Warner Angel's Notes on New Mexico Territory 1878," ed. by Lee Scott Theisen. *Arixzona and the West,* Vol. 18, No. 4 (Winter 1976).

Murphy, Thomas B., scout (May 1, 1844-Dec. 4, 1929). b. probably in Missouri he was a Civil War veteran and in 1867 was in charge of the ambulance train that brought the Washington, D.C., negotiators from Fort Larned to Medicine Lodge, Kansas, for the noted Plains treaty. He also was wagonmaster for freight outfits at various western forts, including even Fort Sill. Murphy was one of about 50 plainsmen enlisted by George A. Forsyth to fight hostiles and with the group engaged in the famous September 1868, Battle of Beecher Island in eastern Colorado. Murphy always claimed that the band retired to the "island" in the nearly dry streambed because he and Stilwell suggested it, and that this position was all that enabled most of the party to survive. He gave his version of the engagement in *The Battle of Beecher Island,* 37-39, and in a lengthy interview printed in the *Caldwell* (Kansas) *Messenger.* Murphy was not wounded in the fight. Subsequently he worked for Custer for some time and eventually settled near Corbin, eight miles north of Caldwell. He married Nancy Jane Thompson of Missouri May 28, 1872, and fathered 12 children. Murphy raised purebred shorthorn cattle, some of them winning state fair prizes for several years. He was next to the last known survivor of the Beecher Island fight, being outlived only by Charles H. Cormack (see entry) so far as the record shows, although the dates of death of some of the scouts are not known.

Simon E. Matson, ed., *The Battle of Beecher Island.* Wray, Colo., Beecher Island Battle Mem. Assn., 1960; *Caldwell Messenger,* Dec. 5, 1929; Caldwell *Daily News,* Apr. 15, 1961; information from Mrs. Ed Fein, Wellington, Kan.

Murrieta, Joaquin: *see* Joaquins

Musgrave, George, desperado (c. 1874-Aug. 15, 1947). B. in Texas, raised in New Mexico, he became associated with the Black Jack

Christian band of outlaws after fleeing a rustling charge which followed a betrayal by George T. Parker. Musgrave used many aliases: Jeff Davis, Jesse Miller, Jesse Johnson, Jesse Williams. He was working on ranches in southeastern Arizona when he became a member of the High Fives outlaw band, including the Christians and others (see William Christian biography for details of their depredations). October 19, 1896, he killed Parker at a Diamond A roundup wagon on the Rio Feliz, southwest of Roswell. After the death of Black Jack Christian, Musgrave continued to ride with Bob Christian through 1897, was arrested with him at Fronteras, released from jail December 9, 1897, and disappeared for a dozen years when he was recognized in Colorado, arrested at North Platte, Nebraska, December 25, 1909. He was acquitted June 3, 1910, at Roswell, New Mexico, of the Parker shooting and became "a legend in the range country of several South American republics" before his death.

Jeff Burton, *Black Jack Christian: Outlaw*. Sante Fe, Press of Territorian, 1967.

Musgrove, Mary: *see* Mary Bosomworth

Musselman, Robert, adventurer (c. 1805-Mar. 6, 1836). B. in Shelby County, Ohio, Musselman volunteered for the Seminole War in Florida, and while he was away his father died; soon upon conclusion of his Florida service, he went to New Orleans and enlisted in the Texas armed forces in the war of independence; he was a sergeant at the Alamo where he died with its defenders.

Amelia Williams, XXXVII, 273.

Muybridge, Eadweard, photographer (Apr. 9, 1830-May 8, 1904). B. at Kingston-on-Thames, England, he became a specialist in motion photography, a predecessor of motion pictures, but the frontier interest is largely as a photographer of the Modoc War of 1872-73 in northeastern California. He was born Edward James Muggeridge, but changed his name to Eadweard Muybridge. He migrated to this country, settled at Palo Alto, California, where he became a friend of Leland Stanford and went on to an interesting and innovative career. In early 1873 he journeyed north to record some phases of the Modoc War on glass negatives; some of his work (not always credited) appears in Riddle. The army used Muybridge's and Louis Heller's photography to show the American public what a fearsome task it was to clear the Lava Beds of hostile Indians. Muybridge died in England.

Jeff C. Riddle, *The Indian History of the Modoc War*. Medford, Oreg., Pine Cone Pubrs., 1973; Keith A. Murray, *The Modocs and Their War*. Norman, Univ. of Okla. Press, 1965.

Myers, Lewis B. (La Bonte?), mountain man (Oct. 26, 1812-1893). B. at McConnellsville, Bedford County, Pennsylvania, he went to St. Louis at 18 and shortly afterward to the Rocky Mountains as a trapper until about 1847, when he met the English adventurer-writer George Frederick Ruxton who may have immortalized him as "La Bonte" in *Life in the Far West*. He joined a Mormon party at Pueblo, Colorado, in 1847, continuing with it to Salt Lake where he helped the Saints explore the region and settle, then in 1849 he moved to California. He reached Sacramento in July, having married Maria Lane the previous month, fathering the first white child born at Greenwood, California, and several later children. He died at his ranch near Greenwood.

Ruxton, *Life in the Far West*. Norman, Univ. of Okla. Press, 1951; Ann Woodbury Hafen article, MM, Vol VII.

Mysterious Kid: *see* Elmer Lewis

N

Nah-deiz-az, Apache (1865-Dec. 27, 1889). B. along the Verde River, Arizona, he and his parents were taken to San Carlos Reservation in 1875. Nah-deiz-az was sent to Carlisle Indian School in Pennsylvania and won the Arizona soubriquet of the Carlisle Kid, hence is sometimes confused with the Apache Kid, although the latter never received any formal education and never went east to school. Nah-deiz-az adapted himself to farming, a pursuit encouraged by the whites managing the reservation, but in early 1887 he came into dispute with Second Lieutenant Seward Mott who oversaw the farming operations, and on March 10, 1887, mortally wounded the officer whom he believed was trying to push him off of his land. He surrendered voluntarily and received a life sentence, imprisoned first at Yuma, Arizona and then transferred to a federal penitentiary at Menard, Illinois. Because of jurisdictional problems, however he was returned to Arizona, then tried a second time in October 1889 and in the same term of court which convicted the Apache Kid and his band of attempted murder. In the second trial, Nah-deiz-az again was convicted, but this time sentenced to hang. The execution was a badly bungled affair; Nah-deiz-az was buried in the Globe cemetery beside two white desperadoes who had been lynched some years previously.

Jess G. Hayes, *Apache Vengeance.* Albuquerque, Univ. of New Mex. Press, 1954; Hayes, "...*And Then There Were None*..." Globe, Tyree Printing Service, 1965.

Nahl, Charles Christian, artist (Oct. 18, 1818-Mar 1, 1878). B. at Kassel, Germany, he was baptized Karl Heinrich Christian Nahl, the seventh generation of artists and art collectors. His home life was not particularly happy. Nahl began sketching at 10 and at 17 had completed a painting purchased by the king of Wurttemberg. In 1846 his mother moved the family to Paris, and in 1849 they came to America, the passage given in exchange for a Nahl protrait of the ship-owner. The Nahls lived and the artist worked in Brooklyn for 20

months. In March 1851, they left by ship and the Isthmus of Panama for California, Charles sketching and painting all the way, picturing the stirring scenes all about him; San Francisco was reached May 23, 1851. The Nahls, including Charles and his artist half-brother, Arthur (1833-1889), headed for the mines at Rough and Ready. "He drew constantly. The miner types became models for his facile pen and ink that would some day be used in the great paintings he planned." Unsuccessful in mining, the Nahls settled at Sacramento, where Charles became a sign painter by profession and portrait painter by avocation. Many of his sketches were reproduced in the *California Farmer,* the *Pioneer,* and the *Wide West Weekly.* A flood in March 1852, and a fire in November that year, wiped the Nahls out; they moved to San Francisco where a loan of $400 established them once again. Charles and Arthur quickly placed their work anew. Charles was the more successful, and "there remains a rich store of his art work, much of it related to California history.... None could match him in versatility or productivity. As an illustrator, designer of important certificates, a successful portraitist and genre painter, animal life, birds and flowers, landscape and seascape, he had no equal in quantity, variety or technical excellence." He died at San Francisco of typhoid fever.

Ada Kruse Gibeau, "Charles Christian Nahl: Artist of the Gold Rush," San Diego Corral, Westerners, *Wrangler,* Vol. 9, No. 3 (Sept. 1976), 1-8; Ada Gibeau to author, Jan. 18, 1977.

Naiche (Natchez, Nachite), Apache chief (c. 1856-Mar. 16, 1919). The younger of two sons of Cochise, Chiricahua chieftain, Naiche's mother was Dos-teh-seh, daughter of Mangas Coloradas, Mimbres chief. As a child in 1861 Naiche was captured with his mother during the portentous Cochise-Bascom confrontation at Apache Pass, taken to Fort Buchanan and shortly released. He was with his father during the meeting with Brigadier General O.O. Howard in 1872 when the Chiricahua

Reservation was arranged. Naiche became tall for an Apache, was considered handsome and was attracted and attractive to women. When Cochise died, Taza, his older son, became chief and in 1876 after Taza died at Washington, D.C. Naiche became the last chief the Chiricahuas would ever have. He was less able than Cochise or Taza, but was a fine warrior and held the respect of his people, closely associating first with Juh and then with Geronimo (see entries); Naiche remained nominal leader during Geronimo's campaigns, deferred to by the other who was a war leader but never himself a chief. In September 1880 Naiche accompanied Juh and probably Geronimo in a bolt from the San Carlos (Arizona) Reservation into the Sierra Madre of Mexico. He accompanied Juh and Geronimo in the great 1882 raid on San Carlos when Loco and several hundred of his followers were forced back to Mexico where all remained until 1883 when Crook penetrated the hostile region and persuaded the Apaches to return to the Arizona reserve. Naiche again bolted with Geronimo in May 1885, returning to the Sierra Madre; he and Geronimo agreed to surrender to Crook in March 1886 but were frightened off by bootlegger lies and struck out once more for Mexico, surrendering finally September 4, 1886, to be sent to eastern exile. At Mt. Vernon Barracks, Alabama, Naiche enlisted in the all-Indian "I" Company, 12th Infantry, and at Fort Sill, Oklahoma transferred to the all-Indian "L" Troop, 7th Cavalry during its short-lived existence. In 1897 he was enlisted as scout by Captain Hugh L. Scott (see entry) along with Geronimo, Chihuahua, Mangus and others. Naiche was a strong proponent for removal of the Apaches from Fort Sill to the Mescalero Reservation of New Mexico, going there in 1913. He was married three times, his first and second wives dying at Fort Sill; in all he fathered eight sons and six daughters of whom six sons and two daughters died at Fort Sill, the others at Mescalero where Naiche died of influenza at the Mescalero Hospital. Dorothy, Naiche's daughter by his second wife, married James Kaywaykla, and there are numerous descendants of that union and those of other surviving children in New Mexico.

Griswold; Angie Debo, *Geronimo: The Man, His Time, His Place.* Norman, Univ. of Okla. Press, 1976; Dan L. Thrapp, *Conquest of Apacheria.*

Norman, 1967; Frank C. Lockwood, *The Apache Indians.* N.Y., Macmillan Co., 1938.

Nails, Henry, frontiersman (c. 1810-Apr. 12, 1846). B. in Alabama, he joined a company of trappers under Robert Bean at Fort Smith, Arkansas, in 1830, and trapped in the Rocky Mountains for three years. He reached California probably with Joe Walker in late 1833. By 1836 he and others, operating a distillery near Monterey, became involved in Mexican political-revolutionary affairs, being a principal in the so-called "Graham affair." He entered lumbering, cattle raising and other enterprises, and was killed at Santa Cruz, California, by James Williams in a property rights dispute; Williams was acquitted.

Doyce B. Nunis Jr. article, MM, Vol. III.

Nana (Kas-tziden), Apache war leader (c. 1800-May 19, 1896). An important Mimbres leader but neither a chief nor a sub-chief, Nana was born in the Mimbres country of present southern New Mexico, a nephew of Delgadito. He came to white prominence during and after the Victorio War (1879-1880). Nana's early wife or wives are unknown, but one may have been a Mescalero, since he spent much time with that people. By a wife unknown he fathered a daughter, Geyahnum; his known wife was Nah-dos-te, a Bedonkohe Apache who was full sister of Geronimo. They had one son who died or was killed in 1878. By some Nana is believed to have been the tactical brains behind Victorio, though this probably is in error. Yet he accompanied Victorio on most of the great maneuvers and moved with him into Old Mexico, escaping Victorio's fate at Tres Castillos because he and his followers evaded the ambush and gained the Sierra Madre. As suggested by his Apache name, Nana was lame in his left foot, suffered from rheumatism and, in his great age, failing eyesight, yet in 1881 he led one of the legendary Apache raids into the southwestern New Mexico, during which his handful of warriors, never more than 40 and often only 15, covered more than 1,000 miles of enemy territory, fought a dozen skirmishes with troops, killed 30 to 50 Americans and wounded others, captured two women and at least 200 horses and mules, and raced safely into Old Mexico. Nana rejoined the Sierra Madre hostiles. It was reported he was present at the Cibecue affair of August 30,

1881, in Arizona, but this is unlikely. He surrendered to Crook May 23, 1883, in the Sierra Madre, returning with that officer but bolted with Geronimo on May 15, 1885. Although from time to time reported killed, he probably, because of his age, took small part in depredations until March 1886, when he again surrendered to Crook who considered him "the brains of the hostile bands," and was sent to Fort Marion, Florida. He reached Fort Sill, Oklahoma, in 1894. Nana is buried in the main Apache Cemetery on a knoll overlooking Beef Creek at Sill; his widow died in 1907.

Griswold; Harold Miller, "Nana's Raid of 1881." *Password,* Vol. XIX, No. 2 (Summer 1974), 51-70; Dan L. Thrapp, *The Conquest of Apacheria,* 1967, and *Victorio and the Mimbres Apaches,* 1974, both by Univ. of Okla. Press, Norman.

Nanuntenoo (Canonchet), Narragansett sachem (c. 1630-1676). The son of Mianto-nomo, he signed a 1675 treaty calling for neutrality in the King Philip's War, but secretly aided the enemy. He escaped from the Great Swamp Fight of December 19, 1675, and on March 26 reportedly took part in the virtual annihilation of the command of Captain Michael Pierce on the Pawtucket River, about five miles north of Providence, Rhode Island. It was one of the notable disasters of the war for the English. In April, however Nanuntenoo was surprised and captured by an English force and taken to Stonington, Connecticut. Here "his old enemies among the Connecticut Indians clamored for his execution," and the English acceded, permitting the Indians themselves to shoot him. His head was sent as a trophy to the Council at Hartford. Nanuntenoo was tall and strongly built, a man of courage and ability and his fame rivaled that of Philip himself. Some of his sayings have been preserved.

Hodge, HAI; Leach, *Flintlock;* Dockstader.

Naranjo, Domingo, insurrectionist (fl. 1680). Domingo was the son of a black African former slave and an Indian woman, both of whom are nameless as such in the records. There is a possibility however that the black was a recently freed mulatto named Mateo, servant to a minor officer, Juan Bautista Ruano who reached New Mexico with the expedition of 1600 and eventually became the peon of Alonso Martín Naranjo, assuming Naranjo's last name. The date of birth of Domingo Naranjo and his date of death are unknown. From the union of the black and the Indian woman emerged a family that endured in New Mexico for generations and produced people of prominence, if rarely in the top echelon. Chavez postulates on research and analysis that sometimes is persuasive, that Domingo Naranjo was the "very tall, black (man with) very large yellow eyes" who claimed to represent the mythical being Pohé yemo and arrived from the north to incite the great Pueblo Revolt of 1680, whose instigator history has most commonly considered the Tewa medicine man, Popé. The rumor that a tall black man with yellow eyes had instigated the uprising was common among all the Indians, Chavez points out, although the Spanish generally considered Popé principally responsible and the rumor of the black giant "a fable." The Indian rumors insist that this black had come from the north, bearing a message from Pohé yemo that all "should rebel," and that any pueblo refusing would be destroyed, its people slain. When Governor Otermín reached the pueblo of Isleta on his 1681 reconnaissance expedition, his men picked up an old sorcerer named Pedro Naranjo, whom Chavez believed was probably Domingo's brother; possibly a half-brother, he was smaller in stature, more Indian in appearance, and perhaps Domingo's agent in the southern pueblos. Thus, Chavez reasoned, Domingo carried out Pohé yemo's "orders" at Taos, and Pedro from San Felipe. Chavez concluded that though Otermín "failed to recognize the chief culprit..., the basic truth did survive, even if in a confused way, in the long memory of the common Hispanic folk... It also had been preserved, although in a more legendary manner, in the tradition of Nuestra Señora de la Macana, in which the Devil himself is said to have appeared in the form of a black giant during the 1680 siege of Santa Fe."

Fray Angelico Chavez, "Pohé-yemo's Represen-tative and the Pueblo Revolt of 1680." *New Mex. Hist. Rev.,* Vol. XLII, No. 2 (Apr. 1967), 85-126; Charles Wilson Hackett, Charmion Clair Shelby, *Revolt of the Pueblo Indians of New Mexico and Otermín's Attempted Reconquest 1680-1682,* I. Albuquerque, Univ. of New Mex. Press, 1970; Bancroft, *Arizona and New Mexico,* 180n.

Naranjo, José, Pueblo Indian/mulatto (c. 1662-Aug. 13, 1720). The grandson of a black onetime slave and an Indian woman, and son of Domingo Naranjo whom Chavez suspects may have instigated the great Pueblo Revolt of 1680 in New Mexico, José was nicknamed *el Mulato* or *el Negro.* Captured by agents of Otermín in 1681, José did not reveal his tribe when he was questioned and Otermín sought to take him back to Guadalupe del Paso but on January 8 he escaped and fled back to the northern pueblos, perhaps rejoining his father at Taos. Here the army of Governor Diego de Vargas found him October 7, 1692. José quickly ingratiated himself with the official and from that moment "cast his lot for good with the Spaniards." José probably accompanied Vargas and his officers on various sorties and either witnessed or took part in battles coincident with the reoccupation of New Mexico by the Spanish. He settled at Santa Cruz. June 13, 1696, he learned that his brother, Lucas Naranjo was a power behind a new insurrection against the Spanish, informed the whites of activities of the rebels and eventually killed his brother and presented his head to Vargas. From then on his rise among the Spaniards was swift. In 1700 he was alcalde of Zuñi and shortly war captain of native auxiliaries of Zuní and Acoma. Ordered to accompany several priests to the fierce Hopis, he defended the missionaries at the risk of his own life and no doubt saved theirs. When the Indians of Santa Clara showed signs of surrender, José, against the advice of the padres, entered their stronghold and brought their leaders to Santa Fe; again he talked the warlike Tano Indians into making peace with the Spanish. At great risk José went to Taos and persuaded the Indians there to again accept a Spanish missionary, even to build a church. For all his services José Naranjo eventually received the title of chief war captain of all pueblo auxiliary troops from the Duke of Linares, Viceroy of Mexico (1711-16), José being the first Indian so honored in New Mexico. He had been in command of Indian scouts at Bernalillo in 1704 during the Apache campaign on which Vargas died. Accomplished in the Apache language through his onetime relationship with an Apache woman, he sometimes acted as go-between or perhaps interpreter between the Spanish and Apaches. In July 1707, Naranjo accompanied the expedition of Juan de Ulibarri northeast of Santa Fe to El Cuartelejo in eastern Colorado, to bring back Picuris Pueblo Indians who had fled during the turmoil of the late 1690s from their New Mexico pueblo and settled at El Cuartelejo. A watering place in Colorado was named for him by Ulibarri. In 1707 he was reported married to a woman named Catalina and father of seven children; the name of his oldest son and heir was José Antonio Naranjo. He several times led his auxiliaries on expeditions against the Navaho and in 1719 urged the governor to send a force against the Utes. The next year he accompanied the ill-fated expedition of Pedro de Villasur, lieutenant governor of New Mexico as chief scout and head of 70 Indian auxiliaries. The party was to seek out Frenchmen reportedly living with Plains tribes; it went to eastern Colorado, then eastward, "farther into the interior than anyone from Spanish America had ever gone before," reaching the Platte River perhaps near its confluence with the Loup (or at the junction of North and South Platte rivers; the location is disputed by excellent authorities). There the expedition was surprised at dawn by Indians, probably Pawnees but perhaps with others. Forty-six of the Spanish party, including Naranjo, Villasur and others were killed, while sixty-three escaped.

Fray Angelico Chavez, "Pohé-yemo's Representative and the Pueblo Revolt of 1680." *New Mex. Hist. Rev.,* Vol. XLII, No. 2 (Apr. 1967), 84-126; Oakah L. Jones, Jr., *Pueblo Warriors & Spanish Conquest.* Norman, Univ. of Okla. Press, 1966; Bernard DeVoto, *The Course of Empire.* Boston, Houghton Mifflin Co., 1952.

Naranjo, Pedro, sorcerer (c. 1601-post 1681). Chavez postulates that this man was a brother of Domingo Naranjo (whom he suspects was the instigator of the great Pueblo Revolt of 1680 in New Mexico), and therefore the son of a black former slave and unnamed Indian woman. He seems to have been not notable for his stature, however, and much more Indian in appearance than Domingo for nowhere is it mentioned that he is mulatto, or sambo, so perhaps he was half-brother of Domingo Naranjo. Pedro Naranjo at the age of 80 was arrested December 8, 1681, at the Pueblo of Isleta by officers of Otermín following the uprising and ousting of the Spaniards. It is largely Pedro Naranjo's information of what transpired following the revolt that our knowledge of that critical period is derived. Otermín described Pedro as "a great sorcerer and idolator" and Hackett interprets that to mean he was accomplished in necromancy. He appears to have been an unusual man, accomplished in Castilian as well as several pueblo languages, perhaps able to read and write a bit, with a viable comprehension of Spanish customs and procedures and some knowledge of the Christian religion. His narration is usually accepted as generally honest and full. Naranjo, who said he was a Queres, or Keres, Indian, came from Taos on behalf of the insurgents intent upon punishing the Isleta pueblo for its failure to fully support the revolt. The young men were to be sent to Taos for cattle the Isletans badly needed; meanwhile the old men of Isleta were to be killed, the women given to the Apaches in an attempt to win friendship or concessions from that wild people, while the young men were to be killed at Taos. Otermín's arrival on his 1681 expedition nipped that plot in the bud however, and Pedro Naranjo concluded his testimony by asking to be retaken into the Church as indication of penitence. His ultimate fate is not recorded.

Fray Angelico Chavez, "Pohé-yemo's Representative and the Pueblo Revolt of 1680." *New Mex. Hist. Rev.*, Vol. XLII, No. 2 (Apr. 1967), 85-126; Charles Wilson Hackett, Charmoin Clair Shelby, *Revolt of the Pueblo Indians of New Mexico*, 2 vols. Albuquerque, Univ. of New Mex. Press, 1970.

Narbona, Navaho head chief (c. 1776-Aug. 31, 1849). One of the "truly important" headmen of the Navaho, he remembered the Spanish advance to the Canyon de Chelly in December 1804. Narbona had risen to be head chief by July 1835 when he appealed for peace to Colonel Antonio Perez, governor of New Mexico. An agreement may have been made for exchange of captives, but no record is extant. In 1841 another agreement was reached with the Mexicans and still another, more formal treaty was agreed to in February 1844. In October 1846 Captain John W. Reid of Doniphan's command led a party to confer with Narbona and the chief signed an agreement with the Americans in November 1846. In May of 1848 still another treaty was agreed to with Colonel Edward W.B. Newby. In 1849 Narbona still disposed toward peace

met with Colonel John Macrea Washington in the Chusca Valley. A dispute over a horse arose, the Indians fled and were fired upon by artillery, and Narbona died from "four or five wounds. He was left where he fell, disturbed only by a trophy hunter of the command who... ripped off the scalp of nearly white shoulder-length hair." Narbona was father-in-law of Manuelito, another famous headman and chief.

Frank McNitt, *Navajo Wars*. Albuquerque, Univ. of New Mex. Press, 1972.

Narbona, Antonio, army officer, governor (1773-1830). B. at Mobile, Alabama, when it was Spanish-held, he began his military career in presidio companies in Campeche and Sonora. In 1795 as ensign of the Company of Tucson and adjutant to Captain José Zuñiga he helped reconnoitre a road from Sonora to New Mexico by way of the Moqui villages of northern Arizona; fighting Apaches was one object of the expedition and Narbona brought back five captives and five pairs of ears, proof of the demise of traditional enemies of Spain. In December 1804 he led an expedition out of Zuñi, New Mexico, against Navahos. The command consisted of 300 troops and a company of Opata Indian auxiliaries from Sonora, along with Zuñi guides and New Mexico militia. The effort commenced inauspiciously in a severe snowstorm, but Narbona reported a great success in Canyon de Chelly or nearby. In this massive engagement on January 17, 1805, some 115 Navahos were killed, 90 of them warriors (including old men) and 25 women and children. Thirty-three were captured including the headman, Segundo, a peace advocate. Narbona had lost on his expedition Lieutenant Francisco Piri, dead of pneumonia (he had commanded the Opatas), and 64 wounded. In the action Narbona's men shot up most of the 10,000 musket loads brought along. In 1813-14 Narbona, by then a captain and stationed in Sonora, led expeditions against Apaches, reporting several successes, although nothing decisive. In 1819 Narbona subdued the Apaches of Tinal, probably in Sonora. On September 6, 1821, he joined the Independence movement as military commander of Arizpe, having become such because the military and political leader of Arizpe remained loyal to Spain and left for Guaymas on the coast. June 23, 1822,

Narbona assumed political control of Sonora
and Sinaloa, separating the two provinces for
the first time. In 1823 he fought Opatas and
Yaquis Indians who had revolted and in April
1825 again fought Indians. Narbona then
went to New Mexico as governor, taking over
in September 1825 from Vizcarra and being
succeeded in May 1827 by Manuel Armijo.
Narbona died at Arizpe, Sonora.
    Porrua; Frank McNitt, *Navajo Wars.* Albu-
querque, Univ. of New Mex. Press, 1972; Bancroft,
History of Arizona and New Mexico.

Narbona, Antonio, military officer (d. Dec.
23, 1847). The son of Antonio Narbona the
elder, he became a prominent Indian fighter as
was his father. The earliest mention of him is
in late 1834 when he led a militia group of 40
men under Governor Manuel L. Arvizú of
Sonora and captured Tutije, probably an
Eastern Chiricahua, or Mimbres Apache, near
the Mogollon Mountains of New Mexico. In
the spring of 1841 he was named line
commander on the northern frontier, although
with only 70 men to protect the area from
Altar to Fronteras, Sonora. April 28, 1844,
Chiricahuas attacked Cuquiárachi, Sonora,
capturing several children and Narbona
parleyed with Mangas Coloradas, Yrigollen
and others, ransoming the youngsters. In
August 1844 Narbona attacked Apaches at
Janos, suspected of hostilities and killed a
score. In March 1847 Narbona operated
against Chiricahuas who had killed, wounded
or captured 20 men between Fronteras and
Cuquiárachi and released an Apache woman
to forestall a Chiricahua attack. Late in 1847
Narbona, by now a colonel, led 120 men into
Chiricahua country of southeastern Arizona,
discovering a rancheria in the vicinity of
Apache Pass. Chiricahuas had threatened to
kill Narbona for alleged treachery on his part,
and did so in the shadow of his house at
Cuquiárachi where seven other defenders
were killed and 12 women and children
captured.
    Francisco R. Almada, *Diccionario de Historía,
Geografía and Biografía Sonorenses.* Chihuahua,
1952; information from Edwin R. Sweeney.

Narváez, Pánfilo de, conquistador (c. 1478-
1528). B. at Valladolid according to some
authorities, but at Valmanzano, Cuéllar,
Segovia, Spain, according to *Porrua,* his year
of birth is also unclear. Bernal Diaz wrote that

in 1520 Narváez was "in appearance about
forty-two years of age, tall, very muscular, of
full face, and he had a red beard. He reasoned
well, and his presence was agreeable; he was
leisurely in discourse, with a voice of great
volume, like that of one speaking in a vault.
He rode well, and was reputed to be
courageous." The Bishop of Chiapa, a
personal friend, added that Narváez was "a
man of commanding person, tall of stature,
complexion fair, inclining to be red, honest, of
good judgment, though not very discreet,
agreeable in conversation, with pleasing
address, brave against Indians, and probably
would have been against other people..., but
over every fault he had, was that of being very
careless." Narváez came to America in 1498
and remained largely in the West Indies
islands (principally Hispaniola, or Santo
Domingo); he collaborated with Diego de
Velázquez in the conquest of Cuba in 1511, his
reputation for cruelty to the Indians being
enhanced during this period. As the chief
captain to Velázquez, he was sent to Mexico
in 1520 to arrest Cortez who was then engaged
in his conquest and operating without proper
authority, Velázquez believed. On the night of
May 23, 1520, Narváez was defeated by
Cortez and several times wounded, losing an
eye to a spear thrust; he was imprisoned at
Zempoala and held until 1521 when he was
released by order of the Council of the Indies,
returning to Spain. He was granted by King
Charles I the right of conquest and colonization of Florida and given the titles of captain
general and governor of the new realm, sailing
from San Lucar, Spain, June 7, 1527, with five
ships, 700 to 800 men and suitable supplies.
The expedition remained 40 days at Santo
Domingo, then went to Santiago, Cuba, where
to a hurricane were "lost many people and
supplies," the men as casualties or through
desertion. From there the fleet grounded on
the shoals of Cannarreo, withstood another
great storm at Guaniguanico "where they
were nearly lost," and still another off Cape
Corrientes at the western tip of Cuba. From
there they sailed for Havana, but a south wind
prevented their making that port and drove
them instead up the west coast of Florida to a
point on the peninsula west of Tampa Bay
where April 16, 1528, Narváez took possession of the land for Spain. Some exploratory
work was done in the vicinity of Tampa Bay
and northward. May 1, 1528, Narváez

addressed a council of his officers stating that he wished to penetrate far inland while the ships cruised along the coast, and asked for comments. Cabeza de Vaca, expedition treasurer, protested vigorously, insisting the ships should not be left unless in a secure and identifiable harbor, that when this was done the land expedition would have a point of reference to which to return. He doubted the wisdom of a land expedition anyway, believing that from all reports it was a poor and miserable country. He said that Narváez was awaiting the arrival of two ships from Havana with more supplies and if he left they would not know where to land them, and put forward still other arguments. Nevertheless, Narváez was detemined to seek out the Apalachee, one of the principal native tribes of Florida whom other natives had reported possessed gold. Taking 40 horsemen and 260 foot he left May 2. They marched inland for 15 days on light rations, swam the Withlacoochee River, and were attacked by about 200 Indians, of whom they captured half a dozen, visiting a deserted town and seizing maize. Narváez sent Cabeza de Vaca back toward the coast to try to locate a good harbor (the effort failed) while he went on toward Apalachee. After 22 days he reached the Suwanee River and seven days later arrived at Apalachee in the present Jefferson and Leon counties, Florida, perhaps on Lake Miscosukee, with the principal town near today's Tallahassee. The Spaniards soon came to blows with the Indians of the place, reporting several battles, but they remained there 26 days probably because they found plentiful maize in the village. Narváez then went eight or nine leagues southerly to Aute, about two leagues, or five miles from a shallow inlet of the sea (probably Ocklockonee Bay) where Narváez would build makeshift boats to replace his ships which never afterward contacted his expedition although they searched the Gulf coast for some trace of them for nearly a year. Meanwhile Indian hostility increased, and Spanish losses from that and illness plus other causes became considerable. Construction of the vessels commenced August 4 with such makeshift tools as they could contrive; they caulked them with palmetto fiber and pine pitch, made sails from their shirts and water bottles from horse hides. The five boats were completed September 20, each 33 feet in length. Narváez divided his men, about 48 to

each boat; he captained one, Cabeza de Vaca another; Andrés Dorantes a third; Alonso del Castillo Maldonado a fourth and a Captain Tellez the fifth. They embarked September 22 and sailed westward, seeking Pánuco on the Mexican coast. After about a week, badly in want of water and rest they went ashore where they were helped by Indians who soon however turned on them with a sudden attack in which Narváez was wounded in the head by a rock. They journeyed on week after week, skirmishing with Indians, suffering greatly from various hardships. Narváez had the swiftest boat and rather than assist the others, keeping them all together, called to them to do the best they could and went ahead, soon passing forever from their view. Cabeza de Vaca and two other Spaniards reported what they could learn of the "wretched fate" of Narváez and his followers. Narváez either drowned off the present Galveston or San Luis Island, Corpus Christi or some similar bay, or died after he reached the shore as did the rest of his men, those who landed surviving until the end by cannibalism in many instances. Their demise can be put in the last two months of 1528 or early in 1529. Of the land party of Pánfilo de Narváez only Cabeza de Vaca, Andrés Dorantes, Alonso del Castillo Maldonado and Dorantes's slave, Estebán years later wandered into Mexico and were saved; all the others perished.

Gonzalo Fernández Oviedo y Váldez, "The Expedition of Pánfilo de Narváez," ed. by Harbert Davenport. *Southwestern Hist. Quar.*, Vol. XXVII, No. 2 (Oct. 1923), 120-29; No. 3 (Jan. 1924), 217-41; No. 4 (Apr. 1924), 276-304; Vol. XXVIII, No. 1 (July 1924), 56-74; No. 2 (Oct. 1924), 122-63; *Porrua.*

Natawista Iksana (Mrs. Alexander Culbertson), trader's wife (c. 1825-c. 1890). Daughter of the Blood chief Men-es-to-kos, her three brothers were head men as was a cousin. About 1840 she married the upper Missouri River fur trader, Alexander Culbertson, a happy marriage and one "of immense value to Culbertson in his business dealings" with her people. Natawista was a very beautiful woman; she greatly assisted Audubon in his 1843 expedition to Fort Union, the German artist Rudolph Kurz, and others. Governor I.I. Stevens credited her with a beneficial influence between whites and Indians, retaining her popularity among the Indians by her wit, intelligence and warm sympathy, and the whites by her charm and friendliness. She was the mother of five children: Jack, Nancy, Julia, Fannie and Joseph. Nancy, born in 1848, drowned in the Missouri about 1851; Fannie was b. about 1850 and Joseph was b. at Peoria, Illinois, January 31, 1859. At Peoria, September 9, 1859, Culbertson and Natawista were formally wed by a Catholic priest so that Natawista might be his legal heir. After Culbertson died, or left the North country, Natawista went to live among her people at the Blood reserve, where she was seen in 1881. She is buried at the mission cemetery. Of her children, Jack died in the 1880's at Williston, North Dakota. Julia married George H. Roberts in 1865, lived in Nebraska until 1883 when they moved to Idaho where Roberts in 1890 was elected the first attorney general of the state. Julia died in 1929 at Boise. Joseph lived in Montana and died in 1923; he had been employed at various Indian agencies. Fannie, educated at the Moravian Seminary at Bethlehem, Pennsylvania, married Louis S. Irvin, a lawyer, about 1880 and died at Great Falls, Montana, in 1939.

Montana, Contributions, Vol. X, 1940, 243-46; a photograph of her faces p. 8; her painted portrait appears on p. 177 of *Wilderness Kingdom: The Journals & Paintings of Father Nicolas Point.* N.Y., Holt, Rinehart & Winston, 1967.

Natchez, Apache chief, *see* Naiche

Nation, Carry (Carry Amelia Moore), saloon buster (Nov. 25, 1846-June 9, 1911). B. in Garrard County, Kentucky, she spent her childhood from age 9 in Cass County, Missouri. She was a sister of Thomas Moore, famous army packmaster in the Indian wars. Carry married Dr. Charlie Gloyd in 1867, discovered he drank and after she "cried most of the time," left her husband because he would give up neither drinking nor his Masonic affiliations, she having developed a fixation against the Masonic Order. He died and she subsequently married David Nation, a newspaperman teetotaler, who did not use tobacco, but had other faults, as it seemed to her. They separated periodically, Mrs. Nation running small hotels, first at Columbia, Texas. Carry had "some sort of a (religious) seizure" in 1884 at a Richmond, Texas, Methodist church, and commenced evangelization meetings at her hotel. Her husband

briefly became a Disciples of Christ minister at Medicine Lodge, Kansas, and Carry rejoined him there; her husband's ministry did not last long and Mrs. Nation became more and more outspoken (some believed, obnoxious) in her extreme views. She soon decided that demon rum was responsible for most of the sin in Kansas (which legally was dry, but with a plethora of bootleg outlets). "I began to harass these dive-keepers," she recalled, and it was pointed out that "harass" was a mild way to describe her actions. Her first truly violent attack on the liquor traffic occurred in a Medicine Lodge drug store where she smashed a keg of "medicinal" whiskey despite opposition from the constable and other males. She broke up her first saloon at Kiowa, Kansas, in June 1889, and was so intoxicated — if that is the word — with her success that she went on to smash two more, gathering quite a crowd to whom she preached, and returned to Medicine Lodge something of a heroine with plenty of publicity to fuel her rising reputation. She was found guilty of slander for some of her remarks, fined $1. At Wichita she assailed a saloon picture of a nude woman, and was kept in jail for about five weeks. Her activities expanded and she became more notorious. At Topeka she first used the implement for which she became famous: a hatchet, thereafter conducting her "hatchetations" more and more freely. Divorced in 1901 she took to the lecture platform and traveled widely, as far as Sacramento and New York City. In the latter place onetime heavyweight boxing champion John L. Sullivan warned he would "push her down the sewer" if she entered his saloon. She took up the challenge and chased him into the men's room where she dared not follow. The press followed her antics enthusiastically, and her publicity was enormous, one New York saloon, for instance, hanging out a sign, "All Nations Welcome Except Carry!" In November 1902, she attended a horse show at Madison Square Garden, and assailed a Vanderbilt woman for her "indecent clothing," for Carry was as opposed to anything she deemed smacking of sexual license as liquor and Free Masonry. She invaded England in 1908, and was fined 35 shillings for destroying a sign, but otherwise confined her activities to loud and raucous declamations. She wrote a rambling autobiography, *The Use and Need of the Life of Carry A. Nation,* published several strident magazines, and lived mainly in retirement during her last years at Alpena Pass and Eureka Springs, Arkansas. She died at Leavenworth, Kansas, and was buried at Cass County, Missouri, where a modest marker denotes the grave.

Anton S. Booker, *Carry Nation of Kansas: Who Fought the Liquor Traffic With a Hatchet,* Little Blue Book No. 1850, ed., by E. Haldeman-Julius. Girard, Kan., Haldeman-Julius Pubns., 1947; Earl F. Nation, "Carry A. Nation." Los Angeles Corral, Westerners *Branding Iron* No. 145 (Dec. 1981), 1, 3-12.

Navarre, Pierre, scout, fur trader (Mar. 28, 1790-Mar. 20, 1874). B. at Detroit, the best account of this obscure man's life is in the *Dictionary of American Biography.* This reference work states that his family moved to the Raisin River area while he was yet young, and about 1807 he and a brother, Robert, built a cabin on the Maumee in present Ohio. Pierre early began trading for furs as far west as Fort Wayne, where he reportedly met and became friendly with Little Turtle. In the War of 1812, Pierre was captured at Detroit, released on parole, and became a scout under Brigadier General James Winchester, escaped the Raisin River Massacre in 1813, then scouted for William Henry Harrison. Navarre took part in the Battle of the Thames, claimed to have witnessed the death of Tecumseh and to have assisted in his burial. After the war he resumed fur trading, working for the American Fur Company in Illinois and Indiana. About 1820 or shortly after he retired to a Toledo, Ohio, farm. Twice married, he fathered children.

DAB.

Neagle, Dave, lawman (c. 1848-Nov. 28, 1925). Neagle may have been the Dave Neagle who ran the Oriental saloon at Panamint City, Death Valley, California, in the 1870s. He went to Arizona after a flood washed him out, reaching Tombstone, becoming one of John Behan's deputy sheriffs in 1881, and succeeding Virgil Earp as town marshal after Earp was wounded in December 1881. Neagle was elected to the office in 1882, later serving as chief of police. He was "credited with being one of the fastest pistol shots in the West,... of indisputable courage." He shot and killed a Mexican "desperado" at Tombstone. He was defeated for sheriff in the fall of 1882. Neagle

supposedly went to Butte, Montana, later served as a deputy U.S. marshal. August 14, 1889, he shot and killed Judge Dave Terry in a hotel dining room at Lathrop, California, believing Terry menaced a judge who was under Neagle's protection. Neagle died at Oakland, California.

Ed Bartholomew, *Wyatt Earp: The Man & the Myth.* Toyahvale, Tex., Frontier Book Co., 1964; California death records; Stacy Osgood, "The Life and Times of David Neagle." Chicago, *Westerners' Brand Book,* Vol. XIX (Apr. 1962).

Neal, William, frontiersman (Mar. 25, 1849-Sept. 30, 1936). B. at Tahlequah, Indian Territory, Neal was Cherokee or part Cherokee and perhaps part black. He reported that he had scouted with Buffalo Bill Cody in Wyoming and Colorado before settling in south central Arizona. He built the Mountain View Hotel at Oracle, north of Tucson, in 1894, and became interested in searching for the mythical Spanish-era Iron Door "mine," which inspired a novel by Harold Bell Wright; Neal decided that the entry must have disappeared under rubble from an earthquake, but he interested Cody in its existence for a time, the showman sometimes staying at Neal's hotel. Neal occasionally freighted Arizona ore, established a cattle ranch and carried the mail between Tucson and Mammoth, Arizona, for 42 years. He died at Oracle, being survived by his widow (Jan. 8, 1870-May 10, 1950).

Ariz. Hist. Soc. archives; Don Russell, *The Lives and Legends of Buffalo Bill.* Norman, Univ. of Okla. Press, 1960.

Neamathla, Seminole chief (fl. 1812-1826). By birth a Creek, Neamathla became an uncommonly able and respected Seminole chief of considerable fame. Florida Governor William Duval considered him "bold, violent, restless, unable to submit to a superior or to endure an equal," while his followers were the most "lawless and vile" in all of Florida. He had come to attention before the War of 1812, but was not mentioned as a chief until 1820 and September 18, 1823, was a signer of the Camp Moultrie Treaty by which about 5 million acres of Florida were ceded to the United States; the treaty was repudiated by most of the bands concerned and Neamathla seems to have been disenchanted with it upon reflection. His town south of the Flint River,

Georgia, was destroyed in the First Seminole War of 1817-18. The chief had warned Gaines that if the Americans sought to cross the Flint River into Spanish Florida they would be annihilated; Gaines responded by sending a force of 250 men to capture Neamathla, while hostiles allied with the chief countered by killing about 50 people of a military expedition on the Apalachicola River. Following the Camp Moultrie agreement Neamathla, although originally accepting the pact, objected to being assigned a badly located reservation and in a two hour speech to his assembled warriors urged them to take up arms to protect their rights. At this point fiery-tempered Governor Duval burst into the assembly alone except for a reluctant interpreter who was muttering "I know we will both be killed," seized Neamathla by the throat and pushed him out of the meeting. He then told the assembled warriors that Neamathla had forfeited his right to be principal chief and that he was appointing John Hicks (see entry) to succeed him. The warriors were too amazed by the proceedings to protest. Duval had no right to take such action, and was criticized by his Washington superiors for having done so, but Neamathla left Florida for the Creek settlements of Georgia "where he belonged," and Hicks took the Florida Indians to their reservation. Neamathla apparently held no grudge against Hicks for the two were in a delegation of Seminoles visiting Washington, D.C., in May 1826 to confer with government leaders, and presented a united front while there. At this time he was living resignedly on the despised Florida reservation, and sometimes even cooperated with the whites in punishing Indian wrong-doers. The date and circumstances of his death are not reported, but it must have occurred before 1832.

Edwin C. McReynolds, *The Seminoles.* Norman, Univ. of Okla. Press, 1967; John K. Mahon, *History of the Second Seminole War.* Gainesville, Univ. of Fla. Press, 1967; Hodge, HAI.

Neapope (Napope, Nahpope: "Broth," or "Soup"), Sauk chief (c. 1802-post 1832). Recognized as the principal chief of the Black Hawk band, he took an active part in the 1832 war, described by Thomas Forsyth as "a smart, active young man (who) has been often to war, and is admitted by his Nation to be descended from some of their ancient and great chiefs, and... a warrior of note," not a bad Indian but very talkative and with a "blustering way." Neapope was the only member of the Sauk chiefs' council to join Black Hawk in his war. Something of a fanatic, he went to the British at Fort Malden, Ontario, in 1831, seeking support for hostilities and believing, apparently, that it had been promised the Sauks. He may have been largely responsible for a mysterious mission to Texas, perhaps seeking alliances, undertaken by three Sauk leaders, two of whom died enroute. Neapope took a prominent part in the Black Hawk War, including the defense of the crossing of the Indians over the Wisconsin River; seeing then the apparent overwhelming force of the whites, he abandoned his family and the others to go among the Winnebagos, by whom he was captured. He was imprisoned with Black Hawk at Jefferson Barracks, Missouri, and while there Catlin painted his portrait. He accompanied Black Hawk east in the summer of 1833. Nothing is known of his later life.

HAI; *Black Hawk War,* I; *Illinois Volunteers,* comp. and ed. by Ellen M. Whitney. Springfield, Ill. State Hist. Library, 1970; *Ma-Ka-tai-me-she-kia-kiak — Black Hawk: An Autobiography,* ed. by Donald Jackson. Urbana, Univ. of Ill. Press, 1955.

Needham, James, explorer (fl. 1670-Sept. 1673). B. in England, Needham in 1670 reached Carolina from Barbados and became a planter on the Ashley River before journeying on to Virginia. He was sent by trader Abraham Wood from Fort Henry with Wood's indentured servant, Gabriel Arthur and eight Indians to explore western Virginia up to and beyond the mountains. Initially they were turned back by Indian reluctance to penetrate and "discover beyond" the mountains, but May 17, 1673, were sent out again. June 25 they met some Tomahitans, the Yuchi of eastern Tennessee. Some of these Indians went on to meet Wood (a well-known trader), while the rest took the two white men and one Appomatoc Indian to their own country, or in that direction. From the Occaneechi, a Siouan people living near the present Clarksville, Virginia they traveled over the mountains to the watershed of the Tennessee River reaching at last a Tomahitan town not clearly identified although some believe to have been Chota at the mouth of the Little Tennessee. No English trader had yet been so far, but the Indians possessed muskets of Spanish manufacture and the whites were told that eight days down the river lived "a white people which have long beardes and whiskers and weares clothing." Needham reported that Arthur would remain with the Tomahitans to learn their language and Needham returned to Fort Henry, Virginia, to report his findings to Wood. September 20 Wood sent Needham back with 12 Tomihitans who had returned with him. Enroute they picked up an Occaneechi, Indian John, or Hasecoll. During a river crossing Indian John had carelessly let his pack fall into the water, was upbraided by Needham and after a long and bitter dispute, killed the white, the exact date uncertain.

John R. Swanton, *Early History of the Creek Indians and Their Neighbors*, BAE Bull. 73. Wash., Govt. Printing Office, 1922; Douglas L. Rights, *The American Indian in North Carolina*. Winston-Salem, John F. Blair, Publisher, 1957; Harriette Simpson Arnow, *Seedtime on the Cumberland*. N.Y., Macmillan Co., 1960.

Neely, Alexander, frontiersman (fl. 1770). Neely accompanied Daniel Boone and others into Kentucky from the Great Kanawha River and by drawing the first blood, killing and scalping two Shawnees, Neely, who soon returned to the settlements, had a role in bringing about lasting Indian-white hostility. Little otherwise is known of him.

Lucullus Virgil McWhorter, *The Border Settlers of Northwestern Virginia...* Hamilton, O., Republican Pub. Co., 1915; Reuben Gold Thwaites, *Daniel Boone*. N.Y., D. Appleton & Co., 1902.

Negabamat (Tekwerimat), Noel, Montagnais chief (c. 1600-Mar. 19, 1666). Negabamat in 1638, who had been attracted by Jesuit Paul Le Jeune's teachings, was the first to settle with his followers at Sillery, near Quebec, and soon was converted. He was baptized December 8, adopting the name of Noel and his wife that of Marie. He became influential in the work of the Jesuits among his own people, the Montagnais, and in 1646 persuaded the French to send Father Gabriel Druillettes to the related Abenakis, accompanying the priest on his mission. On September 1, 1650, he left with Druillettes again for the Abenaki country along the Kennebec River and accompanied the priest on to Boston and other New England communities where they urged English colonials to join the French in a general war against the Mohawks. Although personally received warmly, their appeal was not acted upon and in February they returned to work with the Indians of Maine. In September 1651 Noel, who by this time was often called Tekwerimat or some variant, as Negabamat, reached Quebec from Boston with letters from Druillettes referring to their joint mission. Noel took part in 1653 and 1655 peace negotiations with the Iroquois and was ever a voice for moderation and good sense in the tense relations between the tribes. In 1665 he was prominent, as the outstanding native Christian spokesman of Quebec, in welcoming Prouville de Tracy, but before Tracy had completed subjugation of the Mohawks "this noble-hearted Algonquin died, with the same sentiments of piety that he had cherished during his life," leaving all with a high opinion of his manifest virtues. He was tall, well-built and intelligent.

Thwaites, JR, XIV, 207-13; XVI, 109-11; XXV, 135-53; XXXVI, 83-89; XXXVII, 77-79; XXXVIII, 65-67; XL, 197-99; XLI, 181-83; XLIX, 135-37; L, 119-21; DCB.

Negahnquet, Albert (Bede), Potawatomi priest (1874-Nov. 13, 1944). B. near St. Marys, Kansas, he moved with his parents to the Potawatomi Reservation, now Pottawatomie County, Oklahoma, where he entered a Roman Catholic mission school conducted by the Benedictines at Sacred Heart Mission. He made rapid progress in his studies and later entered the College of the Propaganda Fide at Rome. In 1903 he was ordained a priest, said to have been the first United States full-blood Indian to become a priest. He returned to America in 1903, to assume his work among the Indians. Father Negahnquet died at El Reno, Oklahoma.

Hodge, HAI; information from the Rev. James D. White, Tulsa, Okla.

Neighbors, Robert Simpson, Indian agent (Nov. 3, 1815-Sept. 14, 1859). B. in Virginia he went at 19 to Louisiana and reached Texas early in 1836, although his role in the Texas Revolution is not defined. He served as acting quartermaster afterward for the Texas Army and in 1842 was captured at San Antonio by General Adrian Woll and taken to Mexico, being released in 1844. In 1845 he became agent for the Lipan Apache and Tonkawa tribes and later for the Penateka Comanches, spending much time roaming the frontier with his wards and came to exercise "greater influence over the Indians of Texas than any other white man of his generation." He remained in the Indian service after annexation of Texas and received a federal appointment as special Indian agent in 1847. He was present as an official "witness" to the Treaty of 1846 drafted at Council Springs, Robinson County, with the Comanche, Caddo and other peoples and in 1847 headed off a confrontation and made possible an agreement with the Penatekas permitting German settlement of part of their country. In 1848 he succeeded in establishing relations with the northern and wilder bands of Comanches. In 1849 while at Washington where he had been called to help draft a viable solution to the Texas Indian problem, Neighbors learned he had been supplanted by John H. Rollins for political reasons and "thus did the Texas Indian service lose its most efficient employee through the vagaries of the spoils system." Neighbors remained in public life, helping organize El Paso County in 1850, was a member of the 4th Texas Legislature, sponsored a law opening the way for establishment of Indian reservations in the state, and was a member of the convention which nominated Pierce for President. Thereupon he again was appointed Indian agent and ultimately became supervising agent for Texas Indians. With Captain Randolph B. Marcy he made an extensive reconnaissance of northwest Texas in 1854 to locate suitable lands for reservations. As a result two were established: the Penateka Comanche reserve on the Clear Fork of the Brazos in Throckmorton County, and for other tribes the Brazos Indian Reservation in Young County. While standing firm in the face of the disruptive influence of callous military officers who exacerbated latent friction between the races, and the rising hostility of white Texans, Neighbors realized that his charges would have to be removed to survive, and in August 1859 successfully escorted them to the Washita River country of Indian Territory in the vicinity of the present Fort Cobb where the Wichita Reservation was established. Returning he stopped at Fort Belknap, Texas, where he was murdered by Edward Cornett, a man he did not even know

but who resented some remark Neighbors had made in defense of the Indians. Neighbors, one of Texas's best and most effective Indian men, was buried in the Fort Belknap civilian cemetery. Cornett fled according to Richardson, "was pursued by a band of rangers, captured, 'tried' without benefit of judge or jury, and executed." Neighbors had succeeded in leaving "a record of public service that entitles him to a place in the annals of great American pioneers."

Rupert Norval Richardson, *The Comanche Barrier to South Plains Settlement,* Glendale, Calif., Arthur H. Clark Co., 1933; HT.

Neihardt, John Gneisenau, poet (Jan. 8, 1881-Nov. 3, 1973). B. near Sharpsburg, Illinois, he was graduated from the Wayne, Nebraska, State College and held higher degrees from various universities. He traded and lived among the Omaha Indians from 1901 to 1907 and later associated with the Oglala Sioux. He was editor of a country weekly, the Bancroft, Nebraska, *Blade;* was named poet laureate of Nebraska in 1921; literary editor of the *St. Louis Post-Dispatch,* 1926-38, and was poet in residence and lecturer at the University of Missouri, 1949-65. He was widely honored for his verse and authored about two dozen volumes of poetry, fiction and philosophy, many dealing with American Indian culture, customs and frontier history. His most famous work was *A Cycle of the West,* begun when he was 31 and published as a collected work in 1949, including the "songs" of Hugh Glass (1915), Three Friends (1919), Indian Wars (1925), the Messiah (1935), and Jed Smith (1941). He also wrote *Indian Tales and Others* (1926); *Black Elk Speaks* (1932), and *When the Tree Flowered* (1951). He died at Columbia, Missouri.

Who's Who in America; Los Angeles Times, Nov. 5, 1973.

Nelson, Edward, adventurer (c. 1816-Mar. 6, 1836). B. in South Carolina, he and his brother, George Nelson (b. c. 1805) died at the Alamo.

Amelia Williams, XXXVII, 274.

Nelson, John Young, frontiersman (Aug. 25, 1826-Jan. 1903). B. at Charleston, present West Virginia, he ran away as a youth to New Orleans, then worked as cabin boy in a riverboat back to Missouri where he lived with relatives for a time. He left for a Plains journey with a freighting party, became a hunter, met a band of Oglalas and settled in with Spotted Tail's band of Brulé Sioux, marrying a niece of the chief, the first of a succession of Indian "wives" Nelson claimed but seldom held for long, although from them he absorbed a knowledge of the Sioux language. He said he served as a $40 a month guide in 1847 for Brigham Young across the Plains, reaching Salt Lake. He joined Rocky Mountain trappers, fought the Utes, returned to the Sioux, and asserted he was interpreter at Fort Kearny after the action at Ash Hollow, Nebraska. He established a saloon in the vicinity of Kearny, but left to accompany Johnston to Utah in 1857, the next year accompanying troops to the site of the Mountain Meadows Massacre to bury victims of that affair. Nelson said he shot a man at a hog ranch outside of Fort Floyd, Utah. In 1859 he started for California with a herd of 3,000 cattle, but had a fight with Daniel Spencer, the owner, and returned to Utah, eventually reaching the Plains and taking up freighting as he had in the past. Nelson claimed he was in a "battle" at Denver Hall, Denver, in which he said 17 men were killed and 35 wounded, and later had a dispute with Slade at Julesburg before rejoining the Sioux. He worked for twin brothers, Jerry C. and John K. Gilman in Nebraska, had a part in building Fort McPherson and other construction projects, and often interpreted for the army. Nelson said he had known Cody since 1857 and worked with him on various undertakings, Cody referring to Nelson "as a good fellow though as a liar he has few equals and no superiors." In 1876 Nelson went to Deadwood, South Dakota, and later helped construct the Pine Ridge Agency where he was chief of Indian police for a time. He early joined the Buffalo Bill Wild West Show (c. 1884) with his flowing beard, his current Indian wife and five children, remaining with the enterprise for many years. He died at the Pine Ridge Reservation, and is buried in the Episcopal cemetery there.

Harrington O'Reilly, *Fifty Years on the Trail*. Norman, Univ. of Okla. Press, 1963; Musetta Gilman, *Pump on the Prairie*. Detroit, Harlo Press, 1975; Don Russell, *The Lives and Legends of Buffalo Bill*. Norman, 1960.

Nelson, William, army officer (Aug. 8, 1840-Mar. 17, 1926). B. at Indianapolis, he enlisted September 5, 1861, in the 15th Infantry, rising to first sergeant by mid-1862. He was commissioned a second lieutenant in the 13th Infantry May 31, 1862, ending the Civil War a first lieutenant and brevet major. Nelson joined the 22nd Infantry September 21, 1866, became a captain July 9, 1867, and joined the 21st Infantry December 15, 1870. He commanded old Camp Grant at the confluence of the Aravaipa and San Pedro rivers, Arizona when Vincent Colyer came through on his 1871 peace mission. The Camp Grant Massacre had recently taken place, Apaches still sought to settle under Whitman's umbrella near Camp Grant, and anti-Colyer and anti-Apache sentiment roiled wildly among southern Arizonans. Thus when a reported two hundred "armed citizens from Tucson" approached Grant, Colyer directed that they be diverted from the camp and Nelson issued the necessary orders in accordance with his instructions to fully cooperate with the Colyer mission. For some never-explained reason, Crook at Fort Whipple, near Prescott, took Nelson to task, informing him his action was "unwarrantable," Crook's reaction inexplicable. Naive beliefs that the armed "citizens" were merely a gang of happy miners out scrambling for nuggets do nothing to explain the incident away. After only 13 years in the army, Nelson retired May 29, 1874. He died at Charlottesville, Virginia.

Heitman; Dan L. Thrapp, *The Conquest of Apacheria*. Norman, Univ. of Okla. Press, 1967.

Nero, Iroquois chief (fl. 1662). A famous war leader, he was captured by the French near Montreal in 1662. Known for his "notorious cruelty," he was said to have avenged a brother slain in war by roasting to death 80 men, "all at a slow fire, and to kill sixty more with his own hand. He keeps a tally of these on his thigh, which consequently appears to be covered with black characters." Nero commonly had nine slaves with him, five boys and four girls; he was "a man of dignified appearance and imposing carriage." What happened to him was not stated, but can be imagined.

Thwaites, JR, XLVIII, 169-71.

Nero, black Seminole (fl. 1836). Porter thought it unlikely that this Nero could have been the Nero who commanded several hundred black warriors on the Suwannee River of Florida in 1817, believing that the earlier man had been killed in the defense of a Negro village of Suwannee Oldtown during the First Seminole War of 1817-18. The Nero who figured in the Second Seminole War starting at the close of 1835 served as guide for Richard Keith Call. He had a role as such in the Battle of the Withlacoochee in March and April 1836, but nothing is known of him thereafter.

Kenneth W. Porter, "Negro Guides and Interpreters in the Early Stages of the Seminole War." *Jour. of Negro Hist.,* Vol. XXXV, No. 2 (Apr. 1950), 174-82.

Nessmuk: *see* Sears, George Washington

Netawatwees, Delaware chief (c. 1698-Oct. 31, 1776). He was chief of the Unami or Turtle division of his tribe, and then became head chief of the Delawares. Netawatwees was a signer of the treaty of Conestoga in 1718. "To him were committed all the tokens of contracts, such as wampum belts, obligatory writings, with the sign manual of William Penn and others." In 1758 or early 1759 he founded a village on the Cuyahoga River near the present Cuyahoga Falls, Ohio, following expulsion of the Delawares from Pennsylvania. Netawatwees himself lived at the mouth of Beaver Creek on the Ohio below Fort Duquesne. Later he and his people moved to the Tuscarawas River where they founded another community known as Newcomer's Town (Gekelemukpechink), "Newcomer" being a name under which Netawatwees also was known. The chief failed to attend a council called by Henry Bouquet late in 1764 whereupon the British army officer deposed the chief. Upon conclusion of peace between the English and the French and departure of Bouquet, the Delawares reinstated Netawatwees as head chief. Around 1770 Netawatwees became a Christian under Moravian teachings and urged other Delaware leaders to follow his example. Before he died at Pittsburgh his last message to his nation was in praise of the Moravians and a plea to his people to follow them, the message delivered by his chief councillor, White Eyes who succeeded Netawatwees as chief.

Hodge, HAI; Paul A. Wallace, *Thirty Thousand Miles with John Heckewelder.* Univ. of Pittsburgh Press, 1958; C.A. Weslager, *The Delaware Indians: A History.* New Brunswick, N.J., Rutgers Univ. Press, 1972.

Neva, Southern Arapaho chief (c. 1825-post 1870). A brother of Left Hand, he was approximately of an age since they became close companions in childhood and continued as such until Left Hand was killed in 1864. Like his brother, Neva could speak English though without the fluency of Left Hand. Like him he was generally for peace until the Sand Creek Massacre of November 29, 1864. In 1863 he accompanied a delegation of chiefs of various tribes to Washington, D.C., where they met President Lincoln; Neva listened carefully to assure that John S. Smith, who was not trusted by all Arapaho leaders, interpreted faithfully. In September 1864 Neva attended a conference between peace chiefs of the Arapaho and Southern Cheyenne on the one hand, and Governor John Evans of Colorado and Chivington on the other at Camp Weld, near Denver. Whether Neva was present at Sand Creek during the Chivington attack is unreported, but if so he escaped. Afterward he joined the hostiles and took part in war activities against the whites. On June 16, 1868, he signed a treaty at Fort Laramie calling for the Southern Arapaho to accept reservation in Indian Territory, settled in Oklahoma and after 1870 "simply disappeared" from the record.

Margaret Coel, *Chief Left Hand: Southern Arapaho.* Norman, Univ. of Okla. Press, 1981; Stan Hoig, *The Sand Creek Massacre.* Norman, 1974.

Neve, Felipe de, Spanish administrator, soldier (c. 1750-Aug. 21, 1784). B. in Seville, by 1774 he was a major and governor of Loreto, Baja California. In 1776 he was named governor of Alta California, moving the capital to Monterey the following year. He received orders to found colonies and established San Jose in 1777, and at Mission San Gabriel, September 26, 1781, signed the order by which Los Angeles was founded. In 1782 he headed an expedition against the Colorado River Yumas who had revolted and massacred soldiers, priests and settlers. That year Neve was named commander inspector of the Provincias Internas under Teodoro de

Croix, who became Viceroy of Peru in 1783 whereupon Neve became Commander General of the Provincias Internas. He died at Chihuahua's Rancho Carmen, now called Colonia Ricardo Flores Magon.

Alfred Barnaby Thomas, *Forgotten Frontiers: A Study of the Spanish Indian Policy of Don Juan Bautista de Anza Governor of New Mexico 1777-1787.* Norman, Univ. of Okla. Press, 1932.

Nevill, Charles L., Texas Ranger (Apr. 6, 1855-June 13, 1906). B. at Carthage, Alabama, he was brought by his parents to Fayette County, Texas, where he matured. He joined the Texas Ranger Frontier Battalion at 19 in 1874 and served with it until 1882, ending up as captain. He had many encounters with Indians and frontier desperadoes and became one of the notable Rangers of the period. As a sergeant under Major John B. Jones he took part in the affair at Round Rock in July 1878, when Sam Bass's outlaw career was ended, and it was to Nevill that the mortally wounded Bass surrendered. In early 1881 Nevill with George Baylor and their rangers, destroyed a dozen Apaches said to have survived Victorio's escapades, in the Diablo Mountains of West Texas. On December 19, 1881, Nevill took time out from chasing rustlers and with four of his rangers, plus rancher-surveyor John T. Gano and two others, set out on one of his greatest adventures: making the first trip by boat down the Rio Grande through the three magnificent canyons now incorporated in the Big Bend National Park. They were "the greenest set of boatmen that ever started down any river," and embarked at Presidio del Norte. Other expeditions had been wiped out by fear or obstacles. Nevill's boat was wrecked on a rock. "I was carried down the river like I was shot out of a gun," he recalled. "I had on my big boots, coat, pistol and belts and of course as soon as I struck an eddy I sank. When I came up, I caught on a rock and by standing up my head and shoulders would be out of the water." There he stood, clutching his pipe between his teeth, until he managed to climb out. Yet he persevered. The Nevill-Gano expedition was the first documented trip through Santa Elena Canyon. In November 1882, Nevill married and became sheriff of Presidio County, Texas, serving until 1888. While sheriff he and James B. Gillett formed a cattle ranch partnership "which did not interfere with our duties."

Nevill moved to San Antonio in 1889. For four years he was chief deputy sheriff and held many other offices. He died at San Antonio and is buried there.

Robert W. Stephens, *Texas Ranger Sketches.* Dallas, p.p., 1972; Ronnie C. Tyler, *The Big Bend: A History of the Last Texas Frontier.* Wash., D.C., Nat. Park Service, 1975; James B. Gillett, *Six Years with the Texas Rangers,* New Haven, Yale Univ. Press, 1963.

New, William T., frontiersman (1802-1851). B. in Illinois, he had reached the Rocky Mountains by 1836, becoming a trapper; in 1837 he was placed in charge of Fort St. Vrain on the South Platte as an employee of the Bent and St. Vrain company. By 1838 he was a free trapper, attended a rendezvous or two, and raided southern California with others for horses about 1840. He was reported at a variety of posts in the Great Basin as well as on the western Plains. He worked for Lucien Maxwell for a time and in 1850 was staying at Fort Barclay, New Mexico. He was killed by Jicarilla Apaches.

Harvey L. Carter article, MM, Vol. V.

Newcomb, George (Bitter Creek, Slaughter('s) Kid), desperado (c. 1867-May 1, 1895). B. at Fort Scott, Kansas, he became one of the prominent members of Bill Doolin's outlaw gang of Oklahoma. He ran away from home in the 1880s and became a Texas cowboy. He worked for C.C. Slaughter on the Colorado River of Texas, thereby earning his original nickname. He worked for various Oklahoma ranches until he became associated with the Daltons and Doolin, and was in New Mexico briefly with the former. Newcomb may or may not have been present at the illegal Kansas beer party and shootout that launched Doolin on his outlaw career, but he took part in most of the major crimes attributed to Doolin until Newcomb's death. He assisted in train robberies in Oklahoma at Wharton (Perry), May 8, 1891; Lillietta, September 15, 1891; Red Rock, June 1, 1892; Adair, July 14, 1892. Newcomb took part in the Dalton's disastrous raid on two Coffeyville, Kansas, banks, October 5, 1892, but came on the scene late, joined in the shooting that accompanied the break for freedom, and was the only one of the six-outlaw gang to escape unhit. He participated in the Caney, Kansas, train robbery October 14, 1892, and the Spearville, Kansas, bank job November 1, 1892. He "kind of lived together" with Sadie Conley (McCloskey) of Ingalls, Oklahoma, widow of Deputy U.S. Marshal John Conley, killed in a Cushing, Oklahoma, gunfight, but was believed not to have married her. Newcomb was in on the Cimarron, Kansas, train robbery June 10, 1893. He took part in the start of the historic gunfight at Ingalls, Oklahoma, September 1, 1893, being wounded by a shot from Dick Speed, a city marshal of Perkins, the bullet striking Newcomb's Winchester, smashing the magazine, and part of it entering his body. Newcomb killed Speed, and escaped from Ingalls, was treated for his wound, hidden by gang members, and ultimately recovered. He participated in bank robberies at Pawnee, Oklahoma, January 29, 1894, and Southwest City, Missouri, May 10, 1894, where he was again wounded, not seriously. He was at Dunn's "rock fort" in January 1895, when Bill Tilghman blundered in; there was no shooting. Newcomb took part in the Dover, Oklahoma, train robbery April 3-4, 1895. He and his partner, Charlie Pierce, were assassinated while asleep at the Bee Dunn farm, near Ingalls, by Bee and John Dunn who had been outlaws, but wanted the reward money for the pair, $5,000 each. Newcomb was buried by his parents at Ten Mile Flat, west of Norman, Oklahoma.

Bailey C. Hanes, *Bill Doolin, Outlaw O.T.* Norman, Univ. of Okla. Press, 1968.

Newell, Robert, mountain man, pioneer (Mar. 1807-Nov. 1869). B. in Butler County, Ohio, he went to St. Louis and in 1829 joined a Rocky Mountain trapping party. Somewhat educated and an intelligent man, Newell kept a kind of diary from 1836 until 1840; it has been twice published, describing in detail his part in the trapping and trading operations in the mountains from 1829 until he moved to Oregon. He was very active in the northern Rockies, trapped the Three Forks area, took part in the 1832 battle of Pierre's Hole, and associated with all of the great or notable figures in the mountains during his time there, including Bonneville, briefly. Newell returned to his Ohio home in the winter of 1835-36, then served with Bent and St. Vrain, resumed Rocky Mountain trapping, and traded with the Crows for the American Fur Company for a year. He continued to trap and roam through the Blackfoot country, along the Snake River and the Columbia watershed through 1840. Late that year Newell guided an emigrant-missionary party to Walla Walla and Fort Vancouver, bringing the first wagons through and reaching the Willamette December 15. He settled in with his Nez Perce wife and five sons, first at the later Hillsboro, then near Champoeg, becoming a noted pioneer and holding public office; he was speaker of the Oregon House of Representatives for two sessions. He visited California in 1849-50, then returned to Oregon. He went to Idaho during an 1862 mining rush, becoming Indian Agent at Lapwai. His first wife died and he had 11 children by his second wife, a white woman. After her death in 1867, he married a third time. Newell died at Lewiston, Idaho.

LeRoy R. Hafen article, MM, Vol. VIII; Bancroft, *Oregon,* I, II; Bancroft, *Washington, Idaho & Montana;* Thwaites, EWT, XXX, 179n; Frances Fuller Victor, *The River of the West.* Hartford, Conn., p.p. 1870.

Newman, John, frontiersman (c. 1785-Spring 1838). B. near Newmanstown, Pennsylvania, he joined the army and volunteered for the Lewis and Clark expedition, proving a willing and useful man until the party reached the Mandan villages. Here Newman used "certain mutinous expressions," for which he was court-martialed, convicted and discharged from the permanent party. During the winter, seeking atonement, he performed extremely well, but nonetheless was sent back to St. Louis by Meriwether Lewis in the spring, though so well had he served that he was granted the benefits given other members of the expedition. In 1832 he was married at St. Louis (perhaps a second marriage) and again went up the Missouri, engaged in the fur trade. Chardon's journal reports him killed by the Yankton Sioux while on his spring hunt.

Charles G. Clarke article, MM, Vol. IX.

Newman, Norman: see Billy Reed

Newnan, Daniel, army officer (c. 1780-Jan. 16, 1851). B. at Salisbury, North Carolina, he attended the University of North Carolina and March 3, 1799, was commissioned ensign and second lieutenant, 4th Infantry, becoming a first lieutenant November 1 and resigning January 1, 1802. He then engaged in planting for several years but was commissioned colonel of Georgia Volunteers in the Creek War from 1812 to 1814. Florida Indians, suffering oppression from Georgians for years, received permission from the Spanish governor to make forays across the border, and their successes led to Newnan's invasion of Spanish Florida 100 miles deep to attempt to destroy the centers of Indian power. A drive to take St. Augustine failed in September 1812 and Newnan, who had covered the withdrawal of the attacking force launched an assault on King Payne and his Alachua Seminoles. In a running fight from September 27 to October 11 in which four major actions occurred, Newnan's force barely escaped annihilation, suffering more severely than the Indians, although the Indian leader, King Payne, was either wounded mortally or died from over-exertion following the engagements. "Moreover, the Indian victory hardened the determination of the border dwellers to wipe out the red men, once and for all," and that sentiment was lasting, and grew. Newnan became Major General of Georgia militia in 1817 and served in various public offices including a term as Representative in Congress. He died near Rossville, Georgia.

BDAC; Heitman; Edwin C. McReynolds, *The Seminoles.* Norman, Univ. of Okla. Press, 1967; John K. Mahon, *The History of the Second Seminole War.* Gainesville, Univ. of Fla. Press, 1967.

Newport, Christopher, sea captain (c. 1565-Aug. 1617). Presumably b. in England, Newport became a noted sea captain and privateer. He participated in Drake's engagement with a Spanish fleet at Cádiz in 1587 and led an enormously successful privateering expedition to the West Indies in 1591-92 as captain of the *Golden Dragon.* On August 3, 1592, he and others captured the *Madre de Dios,* which he brought to Dartmouth September 7 with millions of pounds sterling in loot, "the most brilliant feat of privateering ever accomplished by Englishmen." In December 1606 Newport was given command of a colonization expedition to Virginia, on May 13, 1607, selecting the site for Jamestown, the first permanent English settlement in what is now the Untied States. He also explored the James River up to the falls. Newport returned to England in July, coming back to Virginia in October, returning to England once more in May 1608. He made a third voyage to the new

settlement and on a fourth trip westward in 1609 he was shipwrecked in the Bermudas, the episode being immortalized by Shakespeare in *The Tempest.* The castaways built a pinnace and sailed on to Virginia, arriving in May 1610, Newport returning to England in September. In 1611 he visited Virginia a fifth time, bringing out Sir Thomas Dale (see entry) and more colonists. Thereafter Newport served the East Indian Company on several voyages from 1613 until his death at Bantam, in the present Indonesia.

DNB; CE; George F. Willison, *Behold Virginia: The Fifth Crown.* N.Y., Harcourt, Brace and Co., 1952; DAB.

Newport, Thomas: *see* Thomas Savage

Nicholls, Edward, British officer (fl. 1814-15). A British lieutenant colonel of Marines, he was put ashore on the Gulf Coast in August 1814 with three officers, a surgeon, and 100 enlisted men to develop the partisan work commenced by brevet Captain George Woodbine who had begun in May to organize and train Indians in the region of the Apalachicola River. They were to be used in support of the British in the War of 1812. Nicholls' initial action was to formulate an inept broadside to dwellers of Louisiana and the Ohio Valley whom, he said the British would liberate from a "faithless and imbecile Government." It had no marked effect. August 31 he wrote to buccaneer Jean Lafitte, seeking his support, but this endeavor also failed, The British sought to enlist Creeks and Seminoles and about 700 came forward to be trained by Woodbine. Nicholls with a force of 100 marines and about 300 Indians attacked Fort Bowyer, near Mobile but the effort failed with a British loss of a ship and 32 killed, 40 wounded for American losses of four killed and five wounded. Woodbine had constructed an earthen fort on the lower Apalachicola River of Florida. Nicholls stocked it with 700 barrels of gunpowder and great stores of munitions and left it in control of Seminole Indians, who soon were displaced by several hundred Negro former slaves and others, who defiantly garrisoned the establishment, thereafter known as the Negro Fort; it ultimately was destroyed by Edmund Pendleton Gaines (see entry). Nicholls sought to establish a sort of protectorate over the Creeks and Seminoles, and in the summer of

1815 took Francis (see entry) and a Seminole delegation to England. Nicholls did not return to America.

Edwin C. McReynolds, *The Seminoles.* Norman, Univ. of Okla. Press, 1967; John K. Mahon, *The History of the Second Seminole War.* Gainesville, Univ. of Fla. Press, 1967.

Nichols, Crosby B., scout (fl. 1868). Crosby was mustered in at Hays City, Kansas, August 19, 1868, as one of the "First Independent Company of the Kansas State Militia," but soon left to join George A, Forsyth's company of about 50 scouts and plainsmen. With them he was engaged in the battle of Beecher Island on the Arickaree Fork of the Republican River of eastern Colorado from mid-September.

Blaine Burkey, *Custer, Come at Once!* Hays, Kan., Thomas More Prep, 1976; Simon E. Matson, ed., *The Battle of Beecher Island.* Wray, Colo., Beecher Island Battle Mem. Assn., 1960.

Nichols, George Ward, writer (June 21, 1831-Sept. 15, 1885). B. at Tremont, Maine, he was commissioned a captain in the Civil War from New York, rose to lieutenant colonel, and was mustered out October 23, 1865. His one claim to frontier note was his article, published in the February 1867, issue of *Harper's New Monthly Magazine,* immortalizing Wild Bill Hickok through a highly colored and largely fictitious narrative of his life and his fight with the McCanles "gang" (*sic*). Nichols devoted the remainder of his life to Cincinnati, Ohio, music affairs, a field in which he was more at home.

Joseph G. Rosa, *They Called Him Wild Bill,* 2nd ed. Norman, Univ. of Okla. Press, 1974.

Nickerson, Azor Howitt, army officer (Dec. 1837-Feb. 18, 1910). B. at Elmyra, Ohio, he was commissioned a second lieutenant of the 8th Ohio Infantry August 17, 1861, and ended the Civil War a captain with a brevet for gallantry at Antietam and Gettysburg. According to Crook, Nickerson was wounded four times and at Gettysburg "was left for dead & his recovery was regarded as almost a miracle. He has now (1871) a hole in his chest which you can nearly stick your fist in, &...at times suffers terribly from this wound. Notwithstanding all this, his ambition & zeal to do his duty has been so great, that he has been constantly on duty ever since the war."

Nickerson had become a first lieutenant of the 14th Infantry February 23, 1866, and journeyed by steamer to the West Coast with Crook who arranged his transfer to Crook's 23rd Infantry September 21, 1866; he was regimental-adjutant in 1867 and 1868 when he became captain, and was on Crook's staff for ten years. Nickerson wrote an amusing sketch of Crook's surrender conference with the Paiute chief, We-ah-we-ah at Camp Harney, Oregon, in 1868. In Arizona Nickerson did not hesitate to take the field when emergencies arose. May 22, 1872, Indians swept off several thousand sheep from near the department headquarters at Fort Whipple; Nickerson with scouts and soldiers took up the pursuit, continued it after nightfall and recovered most of the sheep. He was active in directing Crook's 1873 offensive in Arizona. Nickerson accompanied Crook to the Department of the Platte in 1875. He had a role in organizing the Reynolds 1876 campaign to Powder River, but apparently did not accompany it. However he was with Crook at the Rosebud battle, June 17, 1876, and took an active part, spending most of the day in the thick of action taking orders to various commands. Possibly because of worsening health, Nickerson, who became a major June 15, 1878, was appointed to the Adjutant General's Department but retired June 28, 1882. His first wife had died and he married again in 1870; after his retirement he sought to divorce his second wife in her absence abroad, and married a third time. The wife returned, contested the divorce with resulting scandal; to avoid court martial, Nickerson resigned from the army's retirement rolls November 15, 1883 and took refuge in Canada. The divorce finally was granted, Nickerson remarried his third wife but was not reinstated on army records. He died at Washington, D. C.

Heitman; Dan L. Thrapp, *The Conquest of Apacheria.* Norman, Univ. of Okla. Press, 1967; *General George Crook: His Autobiography,* ed. by Martin F. Schmitt. Norman, 1960; J.W. Vaughn, *With Crook at the Rosebud.* Harrisburg, Pa., Stackpole Co., 1956; Azor H. Nickerson, *General George Crook and the Indians.* Huntington Library, San Marino, Calif., n.d.; Constance Wynn Altshuler, *Chains of Command.* Tucson, Ariz. Hist. Soc., 1981.

Nicolas, Huron chief: *see* Orontony

Nicolas, Louis, Jesuit missionary, artist (Aug. 24, 1634-post 1678). B. in Aubenas, France, he became a Jesuit and May 25, 1664, arrived in Canada. He quickly learned the Algonquin language and served three years among that people along the St. Lawrence. In August of 1667 he accompanied his Jesuit colleague, Allouez, to Lake Superior, where he wintered. In 1668 he was sent to the Mohawk mission and three years later was directed to work among the Montagnais tribes, He returned to France in 1675 and in 1678 "quitted the Jesuit order," according to Thwaites, or was "defrocked" according to the *Dictionary of Canadian Biography.* But Nicolas left more than his tracks and converts as a result of his work in the New World. In the Bibliotheque Nationale of Paris is an Algonquin grammar, dictionary and other material composed by Nicolas, and there is a suggestion that he wrote an extensive work on New France and the Indians; its whereabouts, if it exists still, is unknown. Sketches, published in 1930 in Paris and entitled *Les Rarétes des Indes,* originally thought to have been executed by Charles Bécart (1675-1703), are now attributed to Nicolas, though whether he did the pictures in Canada or in France is not certain. Also unknown are the date and circumstances of his death.

Thwaites, JR, XLVIII, 297n14; LXXI, 377; DCB, II, 53.

Nicol(l)et, Jean, fur trader, explorer (c. 1598-Oct. 27, 1642). B. at Cherbourg in Normandy, he accompanied Champlain to Canada in 1618 and was directed to live for a winter or two on Allumette Island in the Ottawa River opposite today's Pembroke, to reside with the Algonquins under Tessouat and learn the language and customs of his people and the neighboring Hurons. Nicolet remained two years among the Indians, learned both tongues well, becoming it is said a chief among the Algonquins and even being taken by them to visit the Iroquois. Nicolet returned to Quebec in 1620 and reported on his mission, being then given another: to contact the Nipissings on the lake named for them, further French influence among that people, and assure that furs collected in the area not go to the English at Hudson Bay, but to the French on the St. Lawrence River. Nicolet lived among the Nipissings for nine years, trading with them, learning what he could of the distant lands from which various tribes came to trade and keeping a useful journal, now lost but which was helpful to the Jesuit missionaries, being reflected in their famous *Relations.* During the several years occupancy of Quebec by the English, Nicolet remained among his Indians, thwarting any attempt by the British to win their trade. With the French return in 1633 he secured the right to trade at Three Rivers, but was directed by Champlain first to visit the Winnebagos, create a trade relationship with them, establish peace if possible between them and their neighbors and influence them against the New York Dutch. Although Brulé had preceded Nicolet to perhaps four of the Great Lakes, and others also may have visited some of them, the French ideas of Great Lake geography remained vague; Nicolet while with the Nipissings must have heard intriguing details of lands to the west, but it is unlikely he had visited the Winnebagos before 1634. Probably in July of that year he made his way to the Huron towns near Georgian Bay, secured seven canoemen and taking along a robe of Chinese damask (since the French believed the Winnebagos were people of the "western sea" and had communications with China) launched his expedition which reached Sault Ste. Marie, where Brulé had arrived before him. But Brulé had gone on to discover Lake Superior; Nicolet now returned southeast down the strait, pushed into the Strait of Mackinac and passed through it to discover Lake Michigan or, if he were not the first to see it, he at least was its discoverer of record. He entered Green Bay and reached the Menominee River, meeting Indians of that name and the Winnebagos there, where donned in his startling robe and discharging pistols to stress his importance, he managed to put to flight the wild savages who may never before have seen a white man, although they later gathered to the number of 4,000 or more to meet and confer with him. Nicolet then ascended the Fox River to Winnebago Lake and on to a village of the Mascoutins. From them he heard of the Wisconsin River, which drains into the Mississippi. It appears that he then journeyed southward overland toward the country of the Illinois, although the record is confusing; perhaps he met members of that tribe in what is now the southern counties of Wisconsin. He returned to the Winnebagos, hearing from them of the Sioux, calling upon the Potawatomis, and returning to French Canada, reaching Quebec in the fall of 1635. He is believed to be the first white man to explore any part of what became the Old Northwest of the United States although it is difficult to establish that claim with any assurance. Nicolet settled then at Three Rivers, married, fathered a son and daughter (in 1628 he had fathered an illegitimate daughter while among the Nipissings), and became a leading and universally respected leader of the community. From Quebec in 1642 he was told of an Iroqouis prisoner about to be tortured by the Hurons near Three Rivers; he engaged a shallop to hurry there to save the man, but enroute the boat was overturned near Sillery by a strong wind and Nicolet, unable to swim, drowned.

C.W. Butterfield, *History of the Discovery of the Northwest by John Nicolet in 1634 with a Sketch of His Life.*   Cincinnati, Robert Clarke & Co., 1881; DCB; DAB; Thwaites, JR, VIII, 295n29.

Nicollet, Joseph Nicolas, explorer, cartographer (July 24, 1786-Sept. 11, 1843). B. in Savoy of impoverished parents he was an animal herder in early life (or apprenticed to a watchmaker by other accounts) until a priest became aware of his intellectual acuity and found him a place in the college at Cluses where he revealed himself a mathematical prodigy, interested also from an early age in music. Upon graduation he lived for a time at Paris, becoming an astronomer, a professor at the College Louis-le-Grand, and being awarded the Legion of Honor. In 1832 he migrated to New Orleans following financial reverses, then went up the Mississippi River to St. Louis where he became acquainted with the wealthy and powerful Chouteau family. In 1836 he continued up the Mississippi to Fort Snelling and from there to Leech Lake, seeking the origin of the great river and making careful observations as he progressed; in 1837 and 1838 he explored the upper Missouri and the Red rivers. From his notes he compiled a report and the map accompanying it, covering the area between the longitudes of Madison, Wisconsin, and Fort Pierre, South Dakota, and between St. Louis and Red Lake, Minnesota. It "was a contribution of the first importance to American geography." As an expert astronomer Nicollet himself determined the positions of many important points and checked out

others established by previous explorers, making corrections as indicated. His map "determined all the subsequent cartography of an immense region." Nicollet also studied the Sioux and Chippewa languages. In 1837 he had gone to Baltimore and in the winter of 1837-38 showed his maps and journals to Secretary of War Joel R. Poinsett, who secured him employment by the government for three seasons of work in the Missouri-Mississippi region with second lieutenant John Charles Fremont his assistant. Fremont received training he later would put to good use in his own explorations. Nicollet's health rapidly failed in the 1840s however, and he died at Washington, D.C. His *Report Intended to Illustrate a Map of the Hydrographical Basin of the Upper Mississippi River* was published first by the 26th Congress, 2nd Session (1840-41) as SED 237, Serial 380, and reprinted as HED 52, serial 464, of the 28th Congress, 2nd Session, 1844-45. Nicollet was popular, urbane and ever intellectually-curious; he maintained excellent relations with the Indians, as with the whites, he encountered.

William Watts Howell, *A History of Minnesota,* I. St Paul, Minn. Hist. Soc., 1956; *Joseph N. Nicollet on the Plains and Prairies: The Expeditions of 1838-39 with Journals, Letters, and Notes on the Dakota Indians,* trans. and ed. by Edmund C. Bray, Martha Coleman Bray. St. Paul, Minn. Hist. Soc., 1976.

Nidever, George, mountain man, pioneer (Dec. 20, 1802-Mar. 24, 1883). B. in Tennessee, he joined a hunting and trapping party in 1830 at Fort Smith, Arkansas, after years spent roving and adventuring from Missouri to Texas. Although some turned back, the core of the party reached Taos and in the fall of 1831 set out for the headwaters of the Arkansas River. Nidever took part in the battle of Pierre's Hole, July 1832, accompanied Joe Walker to California in 1833, and remained there, joining George C. Yount in a sea otter hunt which had some success. From Santa Barbara he renewed sea otter hunting, pursuing that profession, along with farming and Pacific piloting for the remainder of his life. He joined Fremont at Santa Barbara in 1846 and accompanied him as interpreter to Cahuenga where a treaty was signed. Nidever tried the gold fields briefly, but with not important success, ranched for a time on San Miguel Island, and rescued Juana Maria, the "lone woman of San Nicolas Island," after she had been many years in involuntary exile there. He died at Santa Barbara.

The Life and Adventures of George Nidever, 1802-1883, ed. by William H. Ellison. Berkeley, Univ. of Calif. Press, 1937; Margaret E. Beckman, William H. Ellison, article, MM, Vol. I.

Niehause, John H., soldier (d. June 8, 1885). Probably b. in Germany, he was the saddler for Troop D, 4th Cavalry and was said to have had about 30 years experience as a soldier, 15 of it continuous when with two other soldiers he was killed by Chihuahua's Apache raiders in Guadalupe Canyon on the border between Arizona and New Mexico. The detail was guarding a supply wagon train which the Apaches captured, including 10,000 rounds of ammunition, abundant rations and other supplies, a windfall for them.

"The Reluctant Corporal: The Autobiography of William Blanden Jett," ed, by Henry P. Walker. *Jour. of Ariz. Hist.,* Vol. XII, No. 1 (Spring 1971), 18, 33, 46n24.

Nigger Ben: *see* Benjamin McLendon

Niles, Franklin J., soldier (Aug. 5, 1844-Oct. 2, 1921). B. in Pennsylvania, he joined the 6th Iowa Cavalry at Davenport January 14, 1863, for two and one-half years of hard campaigning and fighting on the North Plains frontier. What makes his service unusual were the voluminous letters he wrote home, describing his service, battles, illnesses and other features of rugged Indian campaigning under Sully and various officers. Niles served in 1863 at Fort Randall and Fort Pierre, Dakota Territory. A captain was killed by three Sioux who in turn were tracked down, shot and decapitated, their heads on Sully's order stuck on poles around camp. His description of the battle of Whitestone Hill (Sept. 3, 1863), near present Ellendale, North Dakota, in which 22 soldiers were killed, about 50 wounded, as against an estimated 200 or 300 Sioux of Inkpaduta's band being killed, was included in a letter of September 17 and is vivid and personalized. He described another minor action shortly afterward as graphically as the first. Niles helped build Fort Sully about 15 miles from Fort Pierre and wintered there. He was on the Sully Expedition of 1864. Niles was in the battle of Killdeer Mountain, though he gave few original details. After several additional skirmishes and much marching, the command reached the Yellowstone August 12, and Fort Rice September 9, the campaign over. On September 1, 1865, Niles wrote from Fort Randall that he was suffering from typhoid fever. He was mustered out October 17 at Sioux City. Niles eventually married, and lived the rest of his life in the vicinity of Cedar Rapids, Iowa.

Lee E. Echols, "We're A-goin' to Fight the Indians." *Frontier Times,* Vol. 50, No. 3 (Apr.-May 1976), 6-11, 45-51.

Nimham, Daniel, Wappinger chief (c. 1710-Aug. 31, 1778). He is first mentioned in a legal document of October 13, 1730, as "a river Indian of the tribe of the Wappinoes," the Wappingers being a confederation of Algonquian tribes on the east bank of the Hudson from Poughkeepsie to Manhattan, closely related both to Mahicans and Delawares but distinct from either. He became chief sachem in 1740, his residence after 1746 being at Westenhuck. He won attention for his part in the border wars of 1746 and 1754 and also for efforts to recover for his tribe their ancestral lands which had been usurped by the English. In 1755 with most of his fighting men he entered English service under Sir William Johnson. About 1762 with some Mohegan chiefs from Connecticut he went to England to press land claims. They received a favorable hearing, but on return to America the claims were submerged in turmoil leading to the American Revolution, Nimham was killed at the battle of Kingsbridge, New York, while "fighting bravely in the cause of the Americans." He was buried at Pelham's Neck, Westchester County, New York.

Hodge, HAI.

Ninigret, (Nenekunat, Janemo, Ayanemo), Niantic sachem (c. 1600-c. 1680). A sachem of the region around Westerly, Rhode Island, he was cousin of Miantonomo and visited Boston initially around 1637. After the death of Miantonomo in 1643 he began war against the Mohegan in revenge against Uncas who had executed his relative, but the English interfered and a treaty was signed at Boston in 1647. In 1652 he visited the Dutch at Manhattan, arousing English suspicions which proved groundless. The following year he made war on the Long Island Indians and again in 1659 against the Long Island

Montauk. During the King Philip War he remained neutral, although the English gave him trouble for this stance. He secured for himself and heirs the tribal land around Charlestown, Rhode Island. After capture of Canonchet, the last chief of the Narragansett, that tribe was consolidated with the Niantic under Ninigret, He was termed by Cotton Mather an "old crafty sachem" which appears accurate since he retained his pride and his tribal lands without fighting for either. Ninigret in advanced age died before the end of the 17th century. He had always opposed Christianity, retorting to the famous missionary, Experience Mayhew to "go and make the English good first" before trying to sell him their religion.

Hodge, HAI.

Niño Cochise, *see* Cochise, Niño

Nix, Evett Dumas, lawman (Sept. 19, 1861-Feb. 5, 1946). B. probably near Coldwater, Kentucky, he moved to Guthrie, Oklahoma, in 1889 and entered the merchandizing business of Oscar Halsell, rancher-business-man. In March 1893, he was appointed U.S. marshal and named John M. Hale his chief deputy. His field deputies included Bill Tilghman, Chris Madsen, Heck Thomas, Frank Canton, Jim Masterson, John Hixon, Ed Kelly, Frank Lake and about 150 others. One of their jobs was to police the booming Oklahoma area and 60,000 arrests were "made by my force during my administration." Nix himself took part in few confrontations with lawless elements, but he directed the work and "his organization captured or killed more criminals and collected more rewards than ever did that of any other pioneer officer." After his Oklahoma career, Nix went to Joplin, Missouri, where he engaged in the wholesale grocery business, then moved to St. Louis, entering the investment field with land, oil and mining his specialties. He died at St. Louis.

Evett Dumas Nix, *Oklahombres, Particularly the Wilder Ones,* as told to Gordon Hines.   St. Louis, p.p., 1929; Okla. Hist. Soc.

Nixon, George Henry, militia officer (d. 1824). B. in Virginia, he lived some years in South Carolina and moved in 1809 to Mississippi Territory. He was commissioned a lieutenant colonel of militia during the 1813-

14 Creek War and at the head of a considerable force scoured the back country for hostiles, killing and capturing a number. He commanded at several of the rude frontier defense establishments of the area, including Fort Claiborne, Mount Vernon and Fort Pierce, and remained in public service until the end of the War of 1812, considered "an excellent officer." Following the conflict Nixon was a member of the constitutional convention for the State of Mississippi and frequently was elected state senator. He died at Berlington, Mississippi. He was a large, fine-looking man with a fair complexion; he was very popular.

Albert James Pickett, *History of Alabama.*   Birmingham Book and Magazine Co., 1962, 573 & n.

Nixon, Thomas C., buffalo hunter, lawman (c. 1838-July 21, 1884). B. at Atlanta, Georgia, he was a miner in Nevada, a freighter in Kansas, sold shelled corn for horses working in railroad construction near Dodge City, ran a blacksmith and repair shop, and was interested in fast horses and fast women. He became a prominent buffalo hunter in the early 1870s in southwestern Kansas and the Oklahoma and Texas panhandles, hiring additional hunters to work for him. Nixon probably set a record killing 204 buffalo from one stand and once slaying 120 in 40 minutes, using two rifles. Once he killed 2,600 in 24 days. From September 15 until October 20, 1872 (?), Nixon killed 2,173 buffalo in Meade County, Kansas. When the battle of Adobe Walls erupted June 27, 1874, Nixon at Dodge City organized a relief party of about 40 men, many of them buffalo hunters, and hurried toward the site; the Indians had pulled off before they could raise the siege, but the Nixon group escorted some people back to the community. Nixon was a partner in a Dodge City saloon for some time, and ran a "dance hall" or worse, that was reputed to be a very hard place. He was named assistant city marshal of Dodge City (he also had served thus in 1881-82), succeeding Mysterious Dave Mather and a feud between the two developed, among various other things reportedly over a woman; Nixon was said to be living with a prostitute because his wife was an invalid. On the night of July 18 Nixon took a shot at Mather, but missed, and three days later Dave assassinated him, securing a change of venue from Ford to Edwards County, and ultimately being acquitted.

Nyle H. Miller and Joseph W. Snell, *Great Gunfighters of the Kansas Cowtowns 1867-1886.* Lincoln, Univ. of Nebr. Press, 1967; Wayne Gard, *The Great Buffalo Hunt.* Lincoln, 1968; Kan. State Hist. Soc. records.

Niza, Marcos de: *see* Marcos de Niza

No Feet (Seeskoomkee; Attween), Indian slave (fl. c. 1870-1885). No Feet's tribal origin is undetermined. He had been purchased as a slave by Kamaiakin, war chief of the Yakimas, from some tribe farther west or southwest. Because of persistent thievery, he was left shackled by traps one sub-zero night outside the lodge; his feet and one hand froze and had to be amputated, after which No Feet was cured of stealing. Kamaiakin's son, Tomio Kamaiakin gave him his freedom and No Feet settled in with the Lower, or non-treaty Nez Perce where "though crippled, he was a splendid horseman, and made his living breaking wild horses." No Feet was well treated by the Nez Perce. He went through the Chief Joseph hegira of 1877 and escaped from the Bear Paw Mountains battle to reach Canada with White Bird and some other Nez Perce. He settled in among the Sioux of Sitting Bull's village where again he was well-treated, eventually marrying into the tribe. In an altercation with the son of a chief he fatally stabbed the Sioux, but before dying the injured man exonerated No Feet from blame, and successfully persuaded his father not to hold the incident against No Feet.

Lucullus V. McWhorter, *Yellow Wolf: His Own Story.* Caldwell, Id., Caxton Printers, 1940.

No Name, Fox, Reservation, I Don't Know, bucking horse (1901-1927). Foaled in Alberta he began his career as a buggy horse but became a good bucker and was bought by Calgary Stampede officials in 1912. Extraordinarily successful, No Name in 1916 was taken on tour of eastern U.S. cities, later bucked at most of the best rodeos and in his long career threw over 1,000 riders. Only four rode him successfully: Yakima Canutt, 1919 (who also was thrown by him); Hugh Strickland, 1920; Ray Bell, 1922, and Bob Askins, who twice rode him, once to a 1925 championship. No Name was a sorrell gelding, weighed 1,200 pounds, and was 15 hands high.

Anthony Amaral, "They Don't Make 'Em Like They Used To!" *Ariz. Highways,* May 1970, 2-9, 36-39.

Nolan, Gervais, frontiersman (d. Jan. 27, 1857). B. at St. Charles, Canada, he joined the North West Company at Montreal in 1816. He arrived in New Mexico in 1824, settling at Taos as gunsmith, being naturalized in 1829 and engaging at times in beaver trapping. He commenced mining in the 1830s, went to California about 1850, settling near Marysville. He returned to New Mexico, where he died.

David J. Weber article, MM, Vol. IV.

Nolan, Nicholas, army officer (d. Oct. 25, 1883). B. in Ireland, he enlisted in the 4th Artillery December 9, 1852, and in the 2nd Dragoons September 1, 1858, becoming first sergeant of B Company of the 6th Cavalry September 5, 1861. He was commissioned a second lieutenant of the 6th Cavalry July 17, 1862. Nolan served against Indians on the central Plains, endless pursuits of small bodies of hostiles in Kansas, Indian Territory and Texas. In West Texas in 1875 Nolan in a hard scout destroyed a couple of Indian rancherias, but found no hostiles; accused of a dilatory pursuit of the enemy he was ordered to be court-martialed though if any occurred its results were negative. In the summer of 1877 Nolan led an agonizing march onto the Staked Plains where he almost lost his command which went 86 hours in blistering heat without water before finally staggering up to Double Lakes on July 30. Nolan had lost four men to thirst and exhaustion along with 25 horses and four mules, while four other men were court-martialed and dishonorably discharged for desertion under the trying conditions the command had experienced. Nolan was assigned to help patrol the Kansas-Indian Territory border to prevent "boomers" from crossing to seize lands to the south in the late 1870s, but in 1879 was sent to West Texas to operate under Grierson in the Victorio War. July 30, 1880, it was Nolan's arrival with his force which relieved a siege of Grierson by Victorio north of Fort Quitman and perhaps saved the general's life. Again Nolan was involved in the Rattlesnake Springs fight in early August, trailing the withdrawing Apaches until they crossed into Mexico.

Nolan became major of the 3rd Cavalry December 19, 1882, but died ten months later.

Heitman; William H. Leckie, *The Buffalo Soldiers.* Norman, Univ. of Okla. Press, 1967; Dan L. Thrapp, *Victorio and the Mimbres Apaches.* Norman, 1974.

Nolan, Philip, adventurer (1771-Mar. 21, 1801). B. at Belfast, Ireland, by his own statement, or at Frankfort, Kentucky, by another report, he emigrated to the United States and was taken into the Kentucky home of James Wilkinson (see entry) in 1788. He was Wilkinson's bookkeeper and shipping clerk until 1791, he and Wilkinson maintaining a friendship as long as Nolan lived. In 1791 Nolan obtained a passport from Esteban Rodríguez Miró y Sabater, the governor of Louisiana for his first documented trip into Texas. It was purportedly a trading mission but, suspected of handling contraband and a probable spy, his goods were seized. Nolan lived two years among the Comanches and Taovayas (the Tawehash of the Wichita confederacy) before returning to New Orleans. By June 6, 1794, with a fresh passport issued by Francisco Luis Hector de Carondelet, now governor of Louisiana, Nolan returned to Nacogdoches and commenced mustanging, capturing wild horses as far west as the Trinity River, driving them to Louisiana and Kentucky for sale. In Texas he had become friends with Antonio Leal of San Antonio and formed a liaison with Leal's wife, Gertrudes de los Santos, who thenceforth assisted his Texas business matters and at times lived with Nolan. Although Carondelet must have known Nolan was engaged in smuggling, he issued a passport for his third trip to Texas, Nolan going on to Chihuahua and bringing 250 horses back to Natchez, renewing there a relationship with Governor Manuel Luis Gayoso de Lemos, who in 1797 would succeed Carondelet as governor of Louisiana. Nolan met Andrew Elliott (see entry), U.S. surveyor, learning from him the rudiments of surveying and map-making; this all tended to reinforce suspicions in some quarters that Nolan was a part-time spy. In March, 1797, an opportunist at the very least, Nolan suggested to Gayoso a profitable smuggling arrangement into Texas. Gayoso was interested but still attempted to learn more exactly Nolan's political ambitions (Britain and Spain were then at war), without

much success. Carondelet still favored Nolan however, and issued a passport for his fourth trip to Texas. He reached San Antonio in July 1797 and remained in Texas until 1800, collecting about 2,500 horses at Nacogdoches while Spanish unease deepened about his operations. Gayoso, now governor of Louisiana wrote the governor of Texas urging Nolan's arrest as a "consummate hypocrite" who probably had been commissioned by Wilkinson "to make an expert reconnaissance of the country." But Gayoso died in 1799 and Nolan reached New Orleans to make a good impression upon the successor, the Marquis de Casa Calvo. He went on to Natchez where he married Frances Lintot and in May 1800 continued to Washington, D.C., where he met and conferred with Thomas Jefferson. The range of subjects discussed is unreported, but Jefferson did express interest in wild horse hunting on which Nolan had become an expert. At Natchez again he found himself accused of filibustering. Nothing came immediately of that charge but suspicions about him flourished anew and Nolan did not help himself with a damaging letter he wrote to one of his men at Nacogdoches, the missive intercepted by the Spanish. He stated that he had tired of wild horse hunting and hinted at involvement in deeper intrigues. Nolan, without a passport, went to Texas for the fifth time late in 1800 with 27 heavily armed men. They erected rough defense works on Nolan Creek near the present Waco, Texas. Here a Spanish command of 70 regulars and 50 militia under Miguel Francisco Músquiz accosted the invaders. When Nolan resisted he was killed, most of the others, including Ellis P. Bean (see entry) taken prisoner and sent to Mexico. Nolan's ears were cut off and sent to the acting governor of Texas, Juan Bautista Elguezábal. Nolan's son by his wife of brief duration was born after the father's demise but died at 21. Nasatir/Loomis speculate that Nolan's purpose in his final adventure was in line with Wilkinson's adventurism-by-surrogate, part of an ill-defined plot against Spanish Texas. Nolan was astute, personable, literate and resourceful, apparently a man of many intrigues, only some of which have come to light.

Noel M. Loomis, Abraham P. Nasatir, *Pedro Vial and the Roads to Santa Fe.* Norman, Univ. of Okla. Press, 1967; Loomis, "Philip Nolan's Entry into Texas in 1800." *The Spanish in the*

Mississippi Valley 1762-1804, ed. by John Francis McDermott. Urbana, Univ. of Ill. Press, 1974, 120-32; HT.

North, Frank Joshua, Pawnee scout leader (Mar. 10,1840-Mar. 14, 1885). B. at Ludlow-ville, New York, he was raised in Ohio and moved with his father to Omaha, Nebraska, in 1856. Frank moved to the present site of Columbus, Nebraska, with an ox team breaking land for new settlers. In 1858 he went onto the Plains with three wolfers, coming into contact with the Pawnees and learning something of their language. In 1859 he freighted goods to Denver, then freighted between Omaha and Fort Kearny, Nebraska. The next year he worked for agent H.W. DuPuy at the Pawnee reservation near present Fullerton, Nebraska, and with his brother, Luther, hauled sawlogs, Frank meanwhile perfecting his knowledge of Pawnee. The next agent, Benjamin F. Lush-baugh made him interpreter and clerk. In 1864 Frank North was directed by the trader at the Pawnee agency to guide troops to Fort Kearny; Major General Samuel R. Curtis, in command, learned North knew the Pawnees well, and suggested he organize a company of Pawnee scouts for Plains service. Joseph McFadden, who had previous military experience, was named captain of this company and North lieutenant. On the Solomon River in Kansas Curtis sent some of the scouts under McFadden with Mitchell, while he retained the others under North; as a result of North's adept handling of the Pawnees, he was authorized to assume rank of captain and raise a company of 100 Indians with headquarters at Fort Kearny. Because operations were anticipated against the Pawnee enemies, the Sioux, he had no difficulty raising the company. January 13, 1865, his company was mustered into service as Company A, Pawnee scouts, with North captain, Charles G. Small, first lieutenant and James Murie, second lieutenant. The scouts made one winter expedition afoot under adverse conditions, finally were issued horses and ordered to Julesburg, Colorado. Enroute they passed many relics of Sioux hostility. In mid-1865 the Pawnee Scouts accompanied Brigadier General Patrick Connor on the North Plains expedition from Julesburg to the Tongue River. In one skirmish about August 23 the Pawnee killed 34 Sioux and

Cheyennes, giving North and his men great prestige. August 29 the Pawnees guided Connor to an Arapaho village, which was attacked with scores of the enemy killed and 750 horses and mules captured. North and his scouts were instrumental in saving from starvation one wing of the three-pronged Connor operation and uniting the command, whence it safely returned to Fort Laramie, North taking his Indians back to the reservation. By this time he was regarded by the Pawnees as something of a father-figure whose wisdom and courage were not to be questioned. March 1, 1867, North was directed by General Christopher Augur to enlist a battalion of Pawnee scouts, 200 men, divided into four companies, with North as "major" and the Indians to be used to protect from hostiles the Union Pacific railroad, then under construction. The Pawnees working from Plum Creek, Nebraska, to the Laramie Plains, Wyoming, were successful in most of the resulting skirmishing; their fame spread. North and his men engaged Cheyennes who had derailed a train at Plum Creek, and killed some of them. North continued his Pawnee work with successively enlisted scouts in 1868 and in March 1869 made a scout along the North Platte River, then joined Carr and the 5th Cavalry for an extended campaign with three Pawnee companies. The Pawnees and Frank North had a key role in the great victory July 11 at Summit Springs, Colorado, over the Cheyenne leader Tall Bull who was killed, the Norths believed by Frank; Cody was the other claimant. North continued to command Pawnee companies in 1870, incidentally guiding paleontologist O.C. Marsh working the Loup Fork for vertebrate fossils. The winter of 1870-71 North was assigned with his Pawnees to Fort D.A. Russell, Wyoming, operating with the 3rd Cavalry. The Pawnees were moved to Oklahoma in 1874-76, giving up their Nebraska reservation and being reduced to poverty. After the Custer disaster, North was requested to raise 100 of them for field operations. They were outfitted at Sidney, Nebraska, participated in the gathering of the Sioux, worked out of Fort Robinson and Fort Laramie, and had a role in Mackenzie's fight with the Cheyennes November 25-26, 1876, on the north fork of the Powder River. On May 1, 1877, the Pawnee Scouts were finally mustered out as no longer needed; Frank and

Luther North were mustered out June 1. The Norths and Cody entered a ranching partnership on the Dismal River in central Nebraska, and stocked it with Texas cattle. Frank served one term in the Nebraska legislature and toured with Cody's Wild West show in 1883, 1884 and 1885. At Hartford, Connecticut he was thrown from a horse and trampled in 1884, was hospitalized for months, rejoined the show briefly but left it at New Orleans and retired to Columbus, Nebraska, where he died; he suffered increasingly from asthma for years. North was married December 25, 1865, to Mary Louise Smith (1845-1883), and fathered a daughter.

George Bird Grinnell, *Two Great Scouts and Their Pawnee Battalion*. Lincoln, Univ. of Nebr. Press, 1973; *Man of the Plains: Recollections of Luther North 1856-1882*, ed. by Donald F. Danker. Lincoln, 1961; Don Russell, *The Lives and Legends of Buffalo Bill*. Norman, Univ. of Okla. Press, 1960.

North, Luther Heddon, plainsman (Mar. 6, 1846-Apr. 18, 1935). B. in Richland County, Ohio, he was taken to Omaha in 1856 and his father, Thomas Jefferson North (Apr. 5, 1813-winter 1857), froze to death within a year. Luther generally followed his brother, Frank J. North (1840-1885) from one employment to another, reaching the Pawnee Reservation near present Genoa, Nebraska, by 1861, when the Sioux were raiding the Pawnees persistently; on one raid Luther North had a narrow escape from Spotted Tail's Brulé Sioux warriors. Luther enlisted in the 2nd Nebraska Cavalry which joined Alfred Sully's Sioux expedition in 1863, seeing some skirmishing with Indians; the expedition was mustered out at Omaha in December. In 1864 North freighted between Columbus and Fort Kearny, Nebraska, and was nearly killed in one of the first outbreaks of the Sioux war of 1864; he did his first government scouting that year. In 1866 he asked his brother, Frank North, for permission to accompany Lieutenant Murie on a scout along the Republican River; this was Luther's first trip with the Pawnee Scouts, though he had no command. The party had one skirmish with hostiles. When Augur in March 1867, commissioned Frank North, a civilian, a "major" authorized to enlist a battalion of Pawnees, Luther became captain of one of its companies. The battalion's mission was primarily protection

of work crews building the Union Pacific railroad, and although a short-term outfit, it and its successors remained in service for several years. In February 1869, Luther North with a company went to Fort McPherson, Nebraska to join a winter campaign into the Republican River country, and in the summer he was with Carr in the great victory over Tall Bull's Cheyennes at Summit Springs. Luther was in many skirmishes during succeeding years, and had as numerous adventures. In the autumn of 1873 he headed a fossil-collecting party for O.C. Marsh of Yale, working east of Greeley, Colorado. In 1874 he accompanied Grinnell on Custer's Black Hills expedition, remained friendly with Grinnell and a prime informant for him for many years. In 1876 the Norths were commissioned again to raise a company of Pawnees, by now removed from their Nebraska home to Indian Territory. They accompanied the Crook Big Horn and Yellowstone expedition and in November took part in Mackenzie's fight with Dull Knife's Cheyennes. The scouts were mustered out May 1, 1877. Luther joined Frank and Cody in a ranch partnership northwest of North Platte, Nebraska. In 1886 Luther became a deputy collector of internal revenue and until 1890 lived in the Black Hills. He moved to Omaha where he was married. From 1917 the Norths lived at Columbus, Nebraska, where he died; his wife died in 1940, and they had no children. Luther did his best to perpetuate the memory of the Pawnee scouts, and frequently was interviewed about them. As Russell points out, his memory weakened in his later years and while he was always honest, he sometimes was mistaken as to details; yet his was a worthy life and his Pawnee scouts notable guerillas of the Plains.

George Bird Grinnell, *Two Great Scouts and Their Pawnee Battalion*. Lincoln, Univ. of Nebr. Press, 1973; *Man of the Plains: Recollection of Luther North 1856-1882*, ed. by Donald F. Danker. Lincoln, 1961; Don Russell, *The Lives and Legends of Buffalo Bill*. Norman, Univ. of Okla. Press, 1960.

Norton, James M. soldier (c. 1823-c. 1863). Norton enlisted in Harry Love's California Rangers who in the summer of 1853 tracked the bandit group led by Joaquin, sometimes known as Murrieta. In the shootout near the present Coalinga, California, Joaquin and his chief lieutenant, Three Fingered Jack were killed. Norton, who had somehow acquired the nickname "the terrible sailor," volunteered to cut off the head of Joaquin and identifying hand of Jack, which he neatly did, the souvenirs being returned as evidence of the demise of the desperadoes. Norton, or another of his name enlisted September 17, 1861, in Company H, 2nd California Cavalry and was assigned to Utah. He was in Patrick Edward Connor's Bear River fight with Shoshones January 29, 1863, near Franklin, Idaho, and incapacitated by reason of frozen feet, being discharged May 28, 1863, at Camp Douglas, Utah, for "disability." Cossley-Batt says he was "killed at Salt Lake," although giving neither date nor details. He was described as 5 feet, 9 inches in height, of light complexion with light hair and blue eyes.

William B. Secrest, "Hell for Leather Rangers." *True West,* Vol. 15, No. 4 (Mar.-Apr. 1968), 20-23, 48-49; Orton; Jill L. Cossley-Batt, *Last of the California Rangers.* N.Y., Funk-Wagnalls Co., 1928.

Norton, John Wesley, Mormon frontiersman (Nov. 6, 1820-Oct. 20, 1911). B. near Lisbon, Indiana, he became a noted Mormon hunter and frontiersman. Norton went in 1847 to Utah with Porter Rockwell, having been associated with the church since its days at Nauvoo, Illinois. He was on various exploration trips, was a member of the Southern Indian Mission of 1854 which worked with southern Utah Indians while the region was being settled, and later was of a group establishing Panaca, Nevada. He died at Panguitch, Utah.

Juanita Brooks, ed., *Journal of the Southern Indian Mission.* Logan, Utah State Univ. Press, 1972.

Norton, Walter, adventurer (d. Jan. 1633/34). An English sea captain, he linked up with the rogue, John Stone at Plymouth and agreed to accompany him in a pinnace to Jamestown. They detoured up the Connecticut River however, captured two Indians for guides and when anchored at night and asleep were assailed by compatriots of the captives. These killed Stone and his crew and attacked Norton who backed into the galley, defending himself bravely. "Captaine Norton defended him selfe a long time against them all in the cooke-roome, till by accident the gunpowder tooke fire, which (for readynes) he had sett in an open thing before him, which did so burne, and scald him, and blind his eyes, as he could make no longer resistance, but was slaine also by them, though they much commended his vallour."

William Bradford, *History of Plymouth Plantation 1620-1647,* 2 vols. N.Y., Russell & Russell, 1968.

Norwood, Randolph, army officer (Jan. 28, 1834-May 24, 1901). B. in Maryland, he was commissioned a second lieutenant in the 1st Maryland Cavalry October 30, 1861, and was a captain at his muster-out in 1864. February 23, 1866, he was commissioned a second lieutenant in the 2nd U.S. Cavalry, becoming a first lieutenant August 31. His Civil War service was largely on the North Plains and in the Northwest. He was in an affair with hostile Indians near the Sweetwater River in Wyoming in September 1872, became a captain in 1876 and May 7, 1877, under Miles participated in a sharp action on Little Muddy Creek, Montana. On August 20 of that year he was involved in the action at Camas Meadows, Idaho, with the Nez Perce then seeking to escape to Canada. For the Rosebud and Camas Meadows actions he won a brevet to major. He operated with Howard in Montana against the Nez Perce, with Sanford leaving the Howard command in the Judith Basin in September. Norwood died at Blue Ridge, Pennsylvania.

Heitman; *Chronological List;* McWhorter, *Hear Me;* Oliver Otis Howard, *Chief Joseph: His Pursuit and Capture.* Boston, Lee and Shepard Pubrs., 1881.

Nosey, John, Apache scout (c. 1850-c. 1940). A San Carlos or White Mountain Apache, Nosey, according to himself, enlisted with the Indian scouts about 1871, and served for many years. "I engaged in many dangerous battles," he reported late in life. He apparently went into the Sierra Madre with Crook in 1883, and served during the Geronimo campaigns. According to Wharfield, Nosey and Josh, another scout, killed an Apache in 1890 near Fort Apache during a drunken fight, fled to the mountains, but were restored to good graces by bringing in the head of Pash-ten-tah, a companion of the outlawed Apache Kid. Nosey wrote briefly of his career in 1938. Goodwin, in a book published in 1942, said by that time he was dead.

Winners of the West, Mar. 1938; H.B. Wharfield, *Apache Indian Scouts.* El Cajon, Calif., p.p., 1964.

Nouvel, Henri, Jesuit missionary (Mar. 1, 1624-c. 1702). B. at Pézenas, France, he became a Jesuit and arrived in Canada August 4, 1662. He spent seven years among the tribes in the vicinity of Tadoussac, then moved westward. The winter of 1671-72 he worked near Sault Ste. Marie among the Beaver people, beginning his 30 years of labors among the western tribes. He was superior of the Ottawa missions from 1672-81 and from 1688-95. Nouvel died probably at the Jesuit mission on Green Bay, Wisconsin.

Thwaites, JR, XLVII, 317-18n17; LXXI, 148-49.

Novinger, Simon, pioneer (Jan. 14, 1832-Jan. 24, 1904). B. at Halifax, Pennsylvania, he went west in 1863 in a 127-wagon train, twice attacked by Indians, to the Blackfoot country of Montana, by way of Nevada. He prospected in Montana, Idaho, Oregon and British Columbia, removing to Tulare County, California. Novinger reached Arizona in 1871, working at the Rich Hill gold deposits for a time, then bought a tract of land where Phoenix later was established. He was badly wounded in an Indian fight near Four Peaks while prospecting. Novinger became interested in the so-called Lost Dutchman Mine, but of course never found it. He farmed in the Phoenix area until his death.

Farish, VI.

Nowlan, Henry James, army officer (June 17, 1837-Nov. 10, 1898). B. on the island of Corfu he was graduated from Sandhurst in England and served as an officer with the 41st Regiment in the Crimean War, including the siege of Sevastopol. He resigned his commission, came to the United States in 1862, was commissioned a first lieutenant of the 14th New York Cavalry January 17, 1863, and was mustered out of the 18th New York Cavalry a captain in 1866. Nowlan became a second lieutenant of the 7th U.S. Cavalry July 28, 1866, and a first lieutenant December 3. He took part in the Custer Sioux campaign of 1876 but missed the Little Big Horn battle because he was attached to Terry's staff, although he was promoted to captain on the day of the action, June 25, 1876. He was breveted to major for his conduct at the Battle

of Canyon Creek September 13, 1877, in Montana against the Nez Perce. Nowlan commanded Troop I in the Battle of Wounded Knee, South Dakota, December 29, 1890. Nowlan was promoted to major July 17, 1895, and died at Hot Springs, Arkansas, being buried at the national cemetery at Little Rock, Arkansas.

Heitman; Robert M. Utley, *Life in Custer's Cavalry.* New Haven, Yale Univ. Press, 1977.

Noyes, Henry Erastus, army officer (Aug. 23, 1839-July 14, 1919). B. in Maine he was graduated from West Point and commissioned a second lieutenant in the 2nd Dragoons, which became the 2nd Cavalry in 1861. He served through the Civil War in eastern theaters and emerged a captain with two brevets, to major for gallantry in action. He was with the 2nd Cavalry on the frontier until 1879 when he became a major in the 4th Cavalry. Noyes was at Forts Leavenworth and Riley, Kansas, until 1867, in Wyoming at Forts Laramie and D.A. Russell, and in Nebraska until 1876. In 1874 he commanded an escort for engineers making a reconnaissance of northwestern Wyoming. Noyes had a role in the Reynolds Powder River Expedition of March 1876 commanding the Third Battalion which included two companies of the 2nd Cavalry. In the attack on a Cheyenne village on the 16th Noyes was assigned to cut out the enemy pony herd which was done, in part; confusion then attended orders given him and his reaction to them, although his service was creditable in the main though the herd was largely retaken by the Cheyennes. Crook believed the expedition had been a failure, charges were filed and Noyes, along with Reynolds and Captain Alexander Moore was tried by court-martial, the charge against him resting on the fact that he had permitted his men to unsaddle and make coffee at a critical juncture of the action. He was found guilty in a lightly pressed trial and sentenced to be reprimanded. Noyes however was a dependable and able officer. He commanded five 2nd Cavalry companies at Crook's Rosebud action and later on the Big Horn and Yellowstone Expedition from May 23 until October 28, 1876. He served at Forts D.A. Russell and Fred Steele, Wyoming, and Keogh, Montana, until 1878, then at Fort Garland, California, briefly, returning to Kansas with the 4th Cavalry until May of 1880 when he was moved to New Mexico for action against Victorio; he accompanied Buell's expedition into Old Mexico in pursuit of that Apache, then was returned to Kansas. He was at Fort Elliott, Texas, until 1881, Fort Craig, New Mexico, until 1883 and in the field during Crook's Sierra Madre Expedition in the late spring of that year. Noyes commanded Fort McDowell, Arizona, from 1884-86 and was at Fort Lowell, Arizona, later in 1886 during the last phases of the Geronimo campaign. He remained in Arizona until 1890, when the Indian wars were over. Noyes became lieutenant colonel of the 5th Cavalry in 1891, returned to the 2nd the following year and became its commanding colonel in 1898. He served in Cuba during the Spanish American War and retired because of age November 16, 1901, being promoted to Brigadier General on the retired list in 1904. He died at Berkeley. California.

Cullum; J.W. Vaughn, *The Reynolds Campaign on Powder River.* Norman, Univ. of Okla. Press, 1961; Vaughn, *With Crook at the Rosebud.* Harrisburg, Pa., Stackpole Co., 1956.

Nugent, John, newsman, attorney (1829-Mar. 29, 1880). The individual for whom Nugent Pass in southern Arizona was named was b. in Galway, Ireland, and arrived in this country as a boy. He was educated at a New Jersey Catholic college, then joined the New York *Herald.* By 1846 he was its Washington correspondent, and had become close friends with James Buchanan and Stephen A. Douglas. Through Buchanan, then secretary of state, Nugent obtained the text of the secret 1848 treaty ending the Mexican War; the Senate jailed him for refusing to reveal his source, but Buchanan had him freed. In 1849 at San Antonio, Nugent joined Jack Hays's party for California, his narrative being among the liveliest and most complete accounts of that eventful journey. Renegade Jack Gordon (see entry), closely associated with the Apaches, agreed to guide Nugent in advance of the group to the heart of hostile territory at the Santa Rita copper mines which the newsman wished to inspect, Gordon assuming responsibility for his safety among the Apaches. The Hays party generally followed the 32nd Parallel from the Rio Grande to Tucson and in 1854 when Second Lieutenant John G. Parke (see entry) was assigned to survey a practicable railroad route at that

latitude, "I gave him my notes and journal," recalled Nugent. In return Parke named one section of his survey "Nugent's Wagon Road." The writer pointed out however that "I was not entitled to the credit, Hays being the leader of the party and having all the responsibility resting on him." This section, which included Nugent Pass, has been variously located though actually was the route from Willcox Playa, on between the Galiuro and Little Dragoon mountains, descending Tres Alamos Wash to the San Pedro River. The Hays party continued on to Tucson and eventually California by way of the Gila River and Warner's Ranch, Nugent proceeding to Los Angeles and San Francisco. June 1, 1850, Nugent and John E. Foy started the San Francisco *Herald,* Nugent buying out the other for $15,000 the following month, he and Edmund Randolph editing the sheet. William Walker (see entry), later a renowned Central America filibuster, was associated with them by 1851. The *Herald* swiftly became most prominent among the city's 26 newspapers, largely through Nugent's provocative pen. He was, wrote O'Meara, "a master of pure English and keen in invective. His humor was pungent, his satire of the vitriol variety." Another wrote he was "unbending. If he took a position he would hold it against the world," this at length proving his undoing. "Seldom have I met a man toward whom my sympathy went out as toward Mr. Nugent," wrote Bancroft, adding that the newsman was "small, of light complexion and delicate features, soft and slow of speech, modest and sensitive, yet lion-hearted and intellectually great withal." It was Nugent's fiery editorial that sparked the 1851 Vigilante effort to curb lawlssness in the raucous Barbary Coast section of the city, and he strongly supported the endeavor. His fearless writings led him into duels, which he usually lost. In 1852 he fought politically-active William H. Jones wounding him slightly. At Contra Costa July 15, 1852, he and Alderman John Cotter squared off with pistols at ten paces; a Cotter bullet delivered a compound fracture to Nugent's left thigh. June 9, 1853, Nugent and Alderman Thomas Hayes fought a duel at 13 paces with Nugent receiving a compound fracture of an arm. In May 1856 San Francisco was convulsed by the mortal shooting of James King of William by James P. Casey, the incident precipitating the second Vigilante movement. Unlike his attitude in

1851, Nugent now took a stand for law and order and against the popular upheaval. Overnight, public fury brought his newspaper to near extinction by withdrawal of advertising and cancellation of subscriptions. The vigilantes were primarily Republican in orientation; Nugent a Democrat who supported his old friend Buchanan (now seeking the Presidency), while listening ever more indulgently to Southern, hence Democratic, persuasions. The *Herald* became a party newspaper. It gradually recouped its strength but not its patronage, influence or profitability. As the Vigilante movement subsided, Nugent ceased to write regularly for it, studied law and by 1859 was an attorney. He served briefly as U.S. special agent to British Columbia during the Fraser River gold rush of 1858, but soon returned to San Francisco. He ran unsuccessfully for the U.S. Senate in 1860. In 1862 he was reported to have argued a mining case before the Supreme Court; from 1864-67 he was an attorney at Virginia City, Nevada. Nugent tried to revive the failed *Herald* in 1869 but it too died. He was an attorney at Alameda, California, in 1871, again at Virginia City in 1874-75 and in 1877 moved to San Leandro, Alameda County. In 1878 he penned an extensive narrative of his career for *The Argonaut,* the six articles warranting republication today in the view of Doyce B. Nunis Jr., a ranking historian. Nugent died at 57 at San Leandro. He was voted into the California Journalism Hall of Fame October 5, 1959.

See Jack Gordon bibliographical references; Bancroft, *Popular Tribunals,* II; Bancroft, *Inter Pocula;* Edward C. Kemble, *A History of California Newspapers 1846-1858,* Los Gatos, Calif., Talisman Press, 1962; James O'Meara, "Early Editors of California," *Overland Monthly,* 2nd Ser., Vol. 14 (Nov. 1889), 489-99; information from the Society of California Pioneers; information from Robert J. Chandler, Historical Officer, Wells Fargo Bank, San Francisco; information from Wayne R. Austerman, William B. Secrest.

Nuñez Cabeza de Vaca, Alvar: *see* Cabeza de Vaca

Nuño de Tobár, military officer (d.c. Jan. 1543). From Xeres de Badajóz, Spain, he signed on in 1538 as captain-general for the De Soto expedition to the southern United States but ran into trouble during the year the party remained in Cuba. Nuño de Tobár got into difficulties a young woman who was waiting-maid to De Soto's wife and for this the incensed De Soto replaced him as second in command with Vasco Porcallo de Figueroa. Nuño de Tobár married the girl before leaving Cuba for Florida. He was appointed captain of cavalry, and as such operated throughout the four-year trek from Florida and South Carolina to Arkansas and Texas. Nuño de Tobár had some engineering skill and was useful at bridging streams otherwise difficult to cross. He took part in the disastrous battle of Mauvila, Alabama, October 18, 1540 in which his lance shaft was split by an arrow which stuck at right-angles and "made a cross with the lance." Nuño de Tobár in 1542 commanded cavalry at the sack of Nilco, a Quapaw village on the south side of the Arkansas River. Garcilaso reported that Nuño de Tobár died at Aminoya, a Siouian village on the west bank of the Mississippi below the mouth of the Arkansas in the winter of 1542-43.

Bourne, *De Soto,* I, II; *De Soto Exploration Commission.*

Nuttall, Thomas, botanist, traveler (1786-Sept. 10, 1859). B. at Settle, West Riding, Yorkshire, he apprenticed to a printer and at 22 emigrated to Philadelphia where he arrived in 1808, fairly well educated and interested in natural science. Through Dr. Benjamin Smith Barton he became particularly devoted to botany and made several field expeditions down the coast as far as North Carolina. In 1810 he accompanied John Bradbury on an incursion to the Missouri. For eight years he studied plants east of the Mississippi, in 1818 publishing *The Genera of North American Plants and a Catalogue of the Species to 1817,* 2 vols., for which he set most of the type. This brought him to wide scientific attention and membership in various learned societies. In October 1818 he visited the southwest, reaching Arkansas Post January 22, 1819, ascended the Arkansas River to Fort Smith and in May 1819 crossed over to Red River, later investigating plants and native life along the Verdigris and Cimarron rivers. Finally, after much hardship he reached New Orleans February 18, 1820. In 1821 he published his most famous work, *Journal of Travels into the Arkansa Territory during the year 1819, with Occasional Observations on the*

Manners of the Aborigines (reprinted by Thwaites, 1906). In 1822 he became curator of the botanical gardens at Harvard but after several years resigned because he could not obtain a leave of absence, and accompanied Nathaniel Jarvis Wyeth on a journey to Oregon, arriving in 1834, investigating plants in the vicinity of Fort Vancouver until late in the year when he took ship for the Sandwich Islands (Hawaii), arriving January 5, 1835, then back to the California coast for the summer, returning once more to the Sandwich Islands and thence by ship around Cape Horn to Boston and Philadelphia. He published the results of his western travels in the form of essays in the *Transactions* of the American Philosophical Society. His last major work was the 3-volume *North American Sylva: or a Description of the Forest-Trees of the United States, Canada and Nova Scotia...* (1842-49). In 1841 he was left by an uncle the estate of Nutgrove, near Liverpool on condition he reside in England at least nine months of every year for the rest of his life. Reluctantly he went back to his native country, devoting his estate to the cultivation of rare plants. He revisited America once in 1847-48, taking three months at the end of the first year and three at the start of the second to fulfill the terms of his uncle's will. He died in England of a strain caused by moving a case of Asian plants. It was written that "No other explorer of the botany of North America had, personally, made more discoveries," and Thwaites judged his southwestern journal to rank "high as a source of information regarding the native tribes."

Thwaites, EWT, XIII.

Nutter, Christopher, frontiersman (Jan. 21, 1760-Feb. 21, 1845). B. in Sussex County, Delaware, his parents brought him as an infant to Augusta County, Virginia, from where in 1769 they moved to Fayette County, Pennsylvania. In March 1772, they moved to West Augusta, now Harrison County, West Virginia, where Christopher lived the rest of his life. Nutter Fort (Clarksburg) may have been named for his parents. From there in 1780 he volunteered as a militiaman under Lowther and served as scout for six months. In 1781 he served under Jackson in Clark's projected campaign against Detroit, reaching the falls of the Ohio River, August 19, continuing in service until Cornwallis's surrender effectively ended the Revolution,

and being discharged at Louisville, Kentucky. In 1782 he volunteered in Captain Thomas Nutter's company and in 1783 in Captain Christopher Carpenter's company. Thomas Nutter may have been his father, or an older brother. Nutter died probably in Harrison County.

Lucullus Virgil McWhorter, *The Border Settlers of Northwestern Virginia.* Hamilton, O., Republican Pub. Co., 1915.

Nye, John A., vigilante, pioneer (Mar. 24, 1832-June 1, 1906). B. at Unadilla, Otsego County, New York, he reached Colorado probably during the Pike's Peak rush era and from there went to Montana by way of Bridger Pass, Bear Lake and the Snake River crossing at Eagle Rock (which became Idaho Falls). He reached Alder Creek September 12, 1863, becoming a merchant. In December 1863, he was one of five men who met and determined upon organization of a vigilante committee, the other four being Nick Wall, Wilbur F. Sanders, Alvin W. Brookie and Paris S. Pfouts. From this slender beginnings grew the organization which executed most of the Plummer gang with other Montana desperadoes and cleaned the camps of organized crime in a celebrated instance in frontier history. Nye joined the 1876 gold rush to the Black Hills, but did not seem to profit much from it. He resided at Minnesala (now extinct) in Butte County, South Dakota, and eventually moved to Deadwood where he died and was buried. He was described as a "farmer" on his death certificate. He was single.

Register; Paris Swazy Pfouts, *Four Firsts for a Modest Hero.* Portland, Oreg., Dunham Printing Co., 1966; John A. Nye death certificate.

Nye, Wilbur Sturtevant, military officer, writer (Oct. 12, 1898-June 1970). B. at Canton, Ohio, he went to West Point in 1920 and rose to colonel by 1954 when he retired to devote time to historical research and editing. As a junior Field Artillery officer he was assigned in 1933 to write a history of Fort Sill, Oklahoma; an entertaining account of how he embarked upon and developed this research is incorporated in the Introduction to the Third Edition of his published result: *Carbine and Lance,* which had gone through 11 printings by 1983. From 1939-42 Nye was editor of the *Field Artillery Journal* and was chief historian, U.S. Army, Europe from 1950-54. Upon his retirement he became associate editor of the Stackpole Company, publishers, of Harrisburg, Pennsylvania, editing some 40 books for that concern, many of frontier orientation. His own books included besides *Carbine and Lance,* co-authorship with Jason Betzinez of *I Fought With Geronimo* (1960); *Bad Medicine and Good: Tales of the Kiowas* (1962), and *Plains Indian Raiders* (1968), in addition to others of non-frontier interest. Nye also edited *Civil War Times Illustrated* and *American History Illustrated.* Married, he made his home in later life at Wormleysburg, Pennsylvania.

Bernark Klein, Daniel Icolari, *Reference Encyclopedia of the American Indian.* N.Y., B. Klein and Co., 1967; *Contemporary Authors,* Vol. 103, Detroit, Gale Research Co., 1982; Nye, *Carbine and Lance,* 3rd ed.   Norman, Univ. of Okla. Press, 1969.

Nystel, Ole Tergerson, captive (Jan. 4, 1853-Nov. 18, 1930). B. in Henderson County, Texas, of Norwegian immigrant parents, his family moved to Van Zandt County and in 1866 to Bosque County where he lived most of the remainder of his life. On March 20, 1867, he was wounded in the leg by an arrow and captured by Comanche Indians, who continued their raid. After many adventures, Nystel was bought from the Comanches by Eli Bewell, a trader near the Smoky Hill River, Kansas, shortly moving to Council Grove, Kansas. Freed, Nystel made his way back to Texas, thereafter residing at Meridian. His narrative is interesting, and revealing in places. For example he wrote that it was true that the Indians received "at the hands of the government in Kansas and other points their supplies...and still the same miserable creatures going off along the frontier of Texas, committing their acts of atrocity... (but) they knew the difference between the people of Kansas and Texas. They knew those of Kansas looked upon them rather in the light of civilized Indians ... something as they would those of a citizen of the State (while) the Texans would follow and fight them to the bitterest end ..." Thus, he implied, violence begot violence, and good treatment relative order. Nystel died in Bosque County.

Ole T. Nystel, "Three Months among the Indians." *Frontier Times,* Vol. 5, No. 1 (Oct. 1927), 33-42.

O

Oakes, James, army officer (Apr. 4, 1826-
Nov. 27, 1910). B. at Limestoneville,
Pennsylvania, he was graduated from West
Point in 1846 joining the 2nd Dragoons, and
was engaged in the Mexican War from
Chihuahua and the siege of Vera Cruz to
Mexico City, winning two brevets and high
commendations. He was engaged against
Comanches in Texas between the Nueces and
Rio Grande July 11 and August 12, 1850,
being severely wounded twice in the latter
fight. While in the field February 22, 1856, he
overtook a party of Waco Indians and
"severely punished them." He routed a body
of Comanches May 1, 1856, near the
headwaters of the Concho River, and August
30, 1856, had three engagements with hostile
Indians near the confluence of the Pecos and
Rio Grande, killing and wounding some and
forcing the remainder into Old Mexico. He
served as captain in the 2nd Cavalry and was a
major in the 5th Cavalry at the outset of the
Civil War, from which he emerged a brevet
Brigadier General. He became colonel of the
6th Cavalry in 1866, and served with his
regiment in Texas, the Indian Territory and
Arizona. He accompanied Indian agent John
P. Clum to Camp Bowie, Arizona, in June
1876, when the agent sought to transfer
Chiricahuas to San Carlos Reservation, and
rendered efficient service during a turbulent
period. Oakes retired April 29, 1879, his later
military career always hampered by the effects
of wounds received on Indian service in
Texas; he died at Washington, D.C.

Army and Navy Jour., Dec. 3, 1910, p. 379;
George F. Price, *Across the Continent with the
Fifth Cavalry.* N.Y., Antiquarian Press, 1959,
280-84.

Oakley, Annie, sharpshooter (Aug. 13, 1860-
Nov. 3, 1926). B. in Darke County, Ohio, as
Phoebe Anne Oakley Mozee, she early was
attracted to shooting and became locally
famed as a markswoman, hunting game for
the Cincinnati markets. Matched with
sideshow marksman Frank E. Butler, she beat
him; he later married her and incorporated

her into his act, and when she became
universally popular, he took over as her
manager. They joined the Sells Brothers
Circus and, in 1885, the Buffalo Bill Wild
West Show; for 17 years she was a star of the
organization. Some of her shooting feats were
phenomenal; she was an especial success in
Europe, performing before Royalty. She was
badly injured in a 1901 railroad wreck, but
recovered to continue her career. Notably
religious, she supported numerous orphans,
having been fatherless herself from the age of
4. She died at Greenville, Ohio, and was
buried at Brock, Ohio, her husband dying
three weeks later at Detroit and being buried
beside Annie in the Brock Cemetery, Darke
County, Ohio.

Literature abundant; *True West,* Vol. 28, No. 10
(Nov. 1981), 7-8.

Oaks, George Washington, frontiersman (July
30, 1840-Feb. 5, 1917). B. on a Tippecanoe,
Ohio, farm which his father sold in 1853 to go
to California where farming, not gold, lured
him. The Oakses reached Westport early in
1854, joined a wagon train and entered California via Donner's Pass, settling near Marysville. Here Oaks became acquainted with Mary
Murphy, survivor of the Donner debacle, and
often heard her tale of that awful winter. Oaks
enlisted August 17, 1861, in Company I, 1st
California Infantry, was mustered in at the
San Francisco Presidio and shipped to Camp
Drum near the later Wilmington, California;
the command at length was ordered to Fort
Yuma, thence east. "We were the advance
guard of the California Column and our
contingent consisted of Companies B, H and
I... under the command of Colonel Joseph
R. West," Oaks recalled. Oaks claimed that
Jonathan Trumbull Warner (Juan Largo) was
a scout with the command, preceding it to
Tucson. If this was the case, Warner served as
a civilian. Oaks confused Jonathan Trumbull
Warner with Solomon Warner of Tucson who
was a scout with the command preceding it to
Tucson. Warner served as a civilian. Oaks saw
the Oatman multiple grave site on Oatman

Flats along the Gila River, and the skeletons near Maricopa Wells where the Maricopa and Yuma Indians had engaged in a noted battle in 1857. Pauline Weaver guided the column to Maricopa Wells, and Oaks had interesting observations of that ancient Mountain Man, including the fact that Weaver had scouted the Confederate ambush at Picacho Pass, and warned the Union command of it; Oaks knew Barrett who was killed at the Pass. He reported that the arrest of Mowry at his Patagonia mine "wasn't so much what he had done, it was the way he had shot his mouth off" that led to his ruin, and he may be correct. Oaks appears not to have taken part in the battle at Apache Pass between Apaches and the California Column, but to have reached the Pass immediately afterward; he had generous comments on controversial Lieutenant George Bascom whose confrontation with Cochise had precipitated hostilities in the region. Oaks also spoke well of Carleton and of his generosity toward Confederate prisoners. Oaks' service in New Mexico was up and down the Rio Grande from Fort Bliss to Fort Union, where he was mustered out September 30, 1864. He went on into Kansas and in 1868 was a teamster out of Fort Harker, amid much of the Indian hostility of the time. He joined Forsyth's scouts and took part in the Battle of Beecher Island where he was wounded by an Indian arrow; his description of the engagement and incidents surrounding it is graphic and accurate. Rescued by the black 10th Cavalry from that disastrous scrape, Oaks returned to Fort Hays and resumed employment as an army teamster, freighting from Kansas to Camp Supply, Indian Territory. A week before Thanksgiving, 1868, he was directed to drive a wagon in Custer's supply train enroute to the forthcoming Battle of the Washita; one of his friends enroute was California Joe Milner. Although Oaks had no part in the battle itself, he heard the firing and, his wagon loaded with ammunition was brought up just as the fighting ceased and before slaughter of the Indian horse herds had begun. He did not see the Elliott casualties, but heard firsthand accounts from troopers who did. At Fort Hays again Oaks met Buffalo Bill or, as he always called him, "Billy," insisting that Cody was not known as Buffalo Bill until "after Ned Buntline... started him in the show business...." After leaving the army transport service in November 1869, Oaks freighted between the railroad and fron-

tier posts; in 1877 he was at Fort Robinson, Nebraska, where several times he saw Crazy Horse, the great Oglala Sioux, remembering he "had quite a scar on his left cheek which he got at the Big Horn battle." On some of his trips in the middle 1870's he went into Dodge City, Kansas, when it was a booming cattle town, becoming acquainted with the Earps, the Mastersons and other frontier figures. Oaks went on to Tombstone, Arizona, as did many of the others, and had observant things to say about some of them, including the blunt opinion that Captain Harry Wheeler of the Arizona Rangers could have killed all three Earps and Holliday had he been at the OK Corral fight and within reach of Tom McLaury's saddle rifle. In 1883 Oaks worked at Fort Bowie while Crook commanded the Department of Arizona; he was an admirer of both Crook and Indian Agent John P. Clum, and had personal experience of the Miles' operation to corral Geronimo. Oaks admired Johnny Behan and Billy Breakenridge. In 1888 Oaks was named marshal of Tombstone "and had to throw my gun on three or four would-be toughs," but in general his term passed with no undue incident. He was a miner in 1890, a millman in 1892 and in 1898 he moved to Tucson where he lived the remainder of his life, initially serving as chief of police. Here he knew Larcena Pennington Scott, John Dewitt Burgess and Tom Jeffords, who stayed at the same hotel as Oaks at times. Jeffords told him Cochise was "afraid of Crook," and wary of the army after the Apache Pass battle with the California Column, and that Jeffords was wary of Cochise, too. Told by his doctor that he had cancer, Oaks dropped by an undertaker's, picked out a casket and paid for it, and told the undertaker to hold it for him. He died at Tucson, and was buried in the Grand Army plot in Evergreen Cemetery. Oaks never married, but formed a brief liaison with an Arapaho girl while on the Plains; there were no known children. Jaastad described him in his late years as "a slim six-footer, fringe of grey hair, grey mustache and not a tooth in his head... His dark clothes were always neatly brushed and his constant companions were his pipe, cane and a deck of cards."

Ben Jaastad manuscript on his recollections of George Oaks, Ariz. Hist. Soc. Archives, Hayden File; the manuscript, in a somewhat shortened version was published as *Man of the West: Reminiscences of George Washington Oaks, 1840-*

1917, recorded by Ben Jaastad, ed. and annot. by Arthur Woodward. Tucson, Ariz. Pioneers' Hist. Soc., 1956.

Oatman family, pioneers. This family was headed by Royse Oatman, b. in New York State c. 1810, and his wife, Mary Ann (Sperry) Oatman, b.c. 1814 in Illinois. Royse was educated in western New York, grew to 5 feet in height, had a round, happy face and was good humored and popular. He and his wife were parents of seven children by 1851: Lucy, 17; Lorenzo D., 16; Olive Ann, 14; Royse Jr., 10 or 12; Mary Ann, 7; Charity Ann, 4, and Roland, 18 months. Royse Sr.'s parents operated a hotel at La Harpe, Illinois. Royse wed Mary Ann, then 18 and they farmed and operated various businesses profitably until reverses in 1842 wiped out most of their capital. They decided to make for California and in August 1850, left Independence, Missouri, by the southern route in company with other emigrants. By February 1851 the company had reached Tucson, Arizona, where most decided to rest up while the Oatmans and two other families pushed on to the Pima and Maricopa villages 90 miles west on the Gila River. Here all but Oatman and his family decided to remain for awhile. The Oatmans continued on and reached Oatman Flat on the Gila, 80 miles east of Yuma where on March 19 the lone company was attacked by some 19 Indians considered by most to have been Tonto Apaches but probably Yavapais. Royse, his wife and four of their children were slain; Lorenzo was heavily wounded, pitched over an escarpment and left for dead, the raiding party taking Olive and Mary Ann on an arduous trek of some 100 miles to the north; unknown to the girls, their brother recovered sufficiently to regain the emigrant road and start westward. Eventually he was rescued, taken to Yuma where he recovered, and moved on to California, for years retaining a hope that his sisters might yet be alive and that he could recover them. The girls were sold by their captors to the Mohaves and taken to the village of the famed chief, Cairook on the Colorado River. They were not badly treated, given the circumstances, but in the "famine year" of 1852-53 Mary Ann died and Olive was left alone among the Indians who adopted her, tattooed her face and treated her as one of themselves, the chief however repeatedly informing her she was free

to leave if she chose. Of course she had nowhere to go and little idea how to reach white settlements, so she remained. Five years later she was rescued through the efforts of a Yuma eccentric, Henry Grinnell, and a Yuma Indian, Francisco, and brought to Fort Yuma where eventually she was reunited with her brother whom she had thought slain on Oatman Flat. She had almost forgotten English and was considered a mental and physical wreck but within weeks recovered. She went with Lorenzo to California where she was now a celebrity, stories of her ordeal and dramatic rescue receiving nationwide attention. The Reverend Royal B. Stratton escorted Olive and Lorenzo by way of Panama to New York where he published his *Captivity of the Oatman Girls,* a widely circulated book that brought Olive even more fame. The report that she eventually went insane and died in 1877 is false. In 1865 at 28 she married John B. Fairchild at Rochester, New York, lived in Michigan for seven years, and moved with her husband and their two or three children to Sherman, Texas, where she died March 20, 1903. Lorenzo died October 8, 1901 at Red Cloud, Nebraska; he and his sister had remained in close touch throughout their lives.

Literature abundant: Stratton, *Captivity of the Oatman Girls.* N.Y., p.p., 1858; Bancroft, *Arizona and New Mexico;* Farish, I; Alfred H. Schroeder, *A Study of Yavapai History,* I, manuscript, Santa Fe, New Mex., 1959, 77-79; Edward J. Pettid, "Oatman Letters Returned to El Monte." *Landmark,* El Monte, Calif., Hist. Soc., Vol. 4, No. 1 (Jan. 1969), n.p.; Mrs. Marian Oatman Shull, "Review of the Stratton Book," manuscript, Tucson, July 1935, Ariz. Hist. Soc.; Alford E. Turner, "The Oatman Massacre." *Real West,* Vol. 22, No. 187 (Oct. 1982), 25-29.

Oblasser, Bonaventure, missionary (Mar. 7, 1885-Feb. 23, 1967). B. at Portland, Oregon, he became a Franciscan priest, ordained at Santa Barbara, California, June 26, 1908, and served as a missionary among Papago, Pima and Apache Indians of Arizona for more than 50 years. He built mission chapels and schools, became an authority on Indian language and culture, developed the Library of Pima Research, was a member of the committee that formed the Papago Reservation in 1916-17, and worked briefly with

Indians of San Diego County, California. He died at Mission Santa Barbara.

Tidings, Los Angeles, California, Mar. 10, 1967.

O'Brien, Adam, borderer (fl. 1760-93). One of the first settlers of the trans-Allegheny country of Virginia, he had a cabin at the Elk and Holly rivers, and eventually died in Kanawha County. He apparently reached the territory just ahead of assorted sheriffs and law officers, saying that "the sheriffs and constables are worse than Indians, because you could kill Indians, and you dare not kill the sheriffs." He seems to have reached the back country about 1760, where the king's men tried to keep settlers out and everything was peaceful until the law was relaxed, in came "the people... and then came the lawyers and next the preachers and from that time they never had any peace any more." In 1781 Adam secured title to two parcels of 400 acres each though it "cost a good deal of hard swearing," for his claims were very shaky. In one Indian fight he abandoned a wounded companion who thereafter was killed by the warriors.

Lucullus Virgil McWhorter, *The Border Settlers of Northwestern Virginia...* Hamilton, O., Republican Pub. Co., 1915.

Ochoa, Estevan, merchant (1831-Oct. 27, 1888). B. in Chihuahua, Ochoa was of a family a member of whom came to Mexico with Cortez. As a boy he journeyed with his brothers' wagon trains to Independence, Missouri, where he learned English and frontier merchandizing. The Tucson firm, Tully, Ochoa & Co., formed in 1864, became the greatest in Arizona, its "business houses and freighting trains associated with the history of almost every town" in the southern part of the Territory. The coming of the Southern Pacific March 25, 1880, to Tucson, spelled the doom of wagon transport, and the company, although not bankrupt, went out of business. Ochoa died at Las Cruces, New Mexico, his remains later moved to Tucson for burial. A man of the highest character, he was a noteworthy pioneer.

Hayden Files, AHS.

O'Connell, Thomas, scout (fl. 1868). Enlisted as one of about 50 scouts and plainsmen to fight hostile Indians under George A. Forsyth, O'Connell was heavily wounded in the battle of Beecher Island in September 1868. White reports on a basis of information from Ray G. Sparks that O'Connell "later died at Fort Wallace," the sixth man of Forsyth's command to fall as the result of the engagement. If O'Connell did so die, however, that fact was not known to other survivors of the engagement for he was not listed as dead in the second *Annual* published in 1905; he was not listed as known to be living, either.

George A. Forsyth, "A Frontier Fight." *Harper's New Monthly Mag.,* Vol. XCI, No. DXLI (June 1895), p. 56; Lonnie J. White, "The Battle of Beecher Island," *Hostiles and Horse Soldiers.* Boulder, Colo., Pruett Pub. Co.,1972.

O'Connor, Richard, writer (Mar. 10, 1915-Feb. 16, 1975). Born Richard Houseman at La Porte, Indiana, he attended Marquette University, then went on the Broadway stage and was auditioned for a role in the motion picture, "Gone With the Wind," but it went to Leslie Howard. He became a newspaperman, working at various cities, among them Chicago, Washington, Los Angeles and New York. O'Connor wrote about 60 books including, of frontier interest, *Bat Masterson* (1957); *High Jinks on the Klondike* (1954); *Wild Bill Hickok* (1959); *Pat Garrett* (1960); *Black Jack Pershing* (1961). His books were competent, but not researched in any depth. O'Connor died at Ellsworth, Maine, from a heart ailment.

Los Angeles Herald-Examiner, Feb. 22, 1975; *Who's Who.*

O'Conor, Hugo, military officer (Dec. 1734-Mar. 8, 1779). B. at Dublin, his family name was spelled with one "n". He joined the revolutionary cause against England and when the movement failed fled to Spain where he became an officer in an Aragon regiment and in 1763 went to Cuba. There he served under his cousin, Alexander O'Reilly (1735-1794) and was promoted to major. In 1765 with other officers he went to Mexico City to help reorganize the army of New Spain, soon going to Texas to investigate local administrative problems; when the governor was removed O'Conor became interim governor, serving as such from 1766 to 1770, about this time changing his last name to Hugo O'Conór Cunco y Fali. Because of his bright red hair he was nicknamed by Texas Indians, "Captain Red." Requesting a more active command he was made a lieutenant colonel and assigned to the presidio of San Saba, relocated south of the Rio Grande from its original position on the San Saba River of Texas. In 1772 he was instructed by Viceroy Antonio María Bucareli to organize several companies for cavalry service in the north, relocate frontier presidios for greater efficiency, and to take the field against the Apaches. In December O'Conor learned he had been promoted to colonel and named Commandant-Inspector of the Interior Provinces, including in addition to northern Mexico provinces, those of California, New Mexico (and Arizona) and Texas. In the fall of 1773 O'Conor scouted the Davis Mountains of West Texas, routing Apaches he estimated at 600. In September 1775 with about 1,500 presidial troops and militia he launched an offensive against the Gila River Apaches whom he defeated in a series of engagements. His report of January 30, 1776, defined his work on the 19 presidios maintained on the northern frontier and their status, among other things recommending that the Tubac, Arizona, presidio be moved to Tucson, which was done. Early in 1777 O'Conor became governor of Yucatan, where he died.

"The Interior Provinces of New Spain: The Report of Hugo O'Conor...," trans. and ed. by Mary Lu Moore, Delmar L. Beene, *Arizona and the West*, Vol. 13, No. 3 (Autumn 1971), 265-82; Herbert Eugene Bolton, *Texas in the Middle Eighteenth Century.* Austin, Univ. of Tex. Press, 1916, 1970.

Oconostota, Cherokee chief (1710-1783). Oconostota is believed to have been one of six Indian leaders including Attakullaculla, his close associate, who went to England about 1730 and met King George II. In a subsequent war with the French the Cherokees were staunch allies of the British. But the spread of English settlements and unfair and contemptuous treatment altered their sentiments. They commenced to retaliate for acts of barbarity committed by white frontiersmen and refused to surrender the perpetrators. In November 1759 Governor William H. Lyttleton of South Carolina cast into jail a delegation headed by Oconostota that had come to ask peace; Attakullaculla obtained the exchange of Oconostota for one of the murderers demanded. Once freed the young chief laid

siege to Fort Prince George in upper South Carolina, called out commander Lieutenant Richard Coytmore for a talk and shot him. This caused the garrison to butcher Cherokee chiefs they held as hostages. This in turn caused Oconostota to fall upon frontier settlements of Carolina while Cherokees over the mountains captured Fort Loudon, Tennessee, and massacred more than 200 whites. Colonel Archibald Montgomerie with 1,600 men relieved Fort Prince George and destroyed some lower Cherokee towns, marched to the relief of Fort Loudon but was routed in a fierce fight and was replaced by Colonel James Grant the next year. Grant with 2,600 men laid waste the Middle Towns, forced the Indians to sue for peace and accept a 1763 treaty setting the stage for further encroachment by whites. After the war Oconostota, who had been war chief, became civil chief of the nation. The ancient war between the Cherokees and Iroquois was ended by a 1768 treaty Oconostota went to New York to sign. The Cherokees sided with the British against the Americans in the Revolutionary War and in it suffered heavily. At its close Oconostota resigned the chieftainship in favor of his son, Tuksi. He died at Echota, Georgia.

Hodge, HAI.

Odaq (Ootah), Eskimo explorer (c. 1875-May 1955). B. in Greenland, he was the last survivor among four Eskimos who accompanied Robert E. Peary and Matt Henson on their purported trip to the North Pole in 1909. Odaq died near Thule, in Greenland.

Los Angeles Times, May 22, 1955.

Oddie, Tasker Lowndes, miner, legislator (Oct. 24, 1870-Feb. 17, 1950). B. at Brooklyn, New York, and raised in New Jersey, he was admitted to the New York bar in 1895, moved to Nevada in 1898, prospected and engaged in livestock raising in the Tonopah-Goldfield-Austin areas, was an associate of Wyatt Earp for a time, and developed the principal gold and silver mining properties at Tonopah and Goldfield. He held political office, served in the U.S. Senate from Nevada from 1921 to 1933, died at San Francisco and was buried at Carson City.

BDAC; Josephine Earp and Glenn G. Boyer, "The Earps of Tonopah." *True West,* Vol. 22, No. 6 (July-Aug. 1975), 14-15, 38, 44-46.

Odeneal, Thomas B., Indian superintendent (Oct. 21, 1834-June 25, 1886). B. in Kentucky he went to Missouri at an early age and in 1852 to Oregon. A lawyer, he also was a newspaperman, was county judge of Benton County, Oregon, in 1870 and a founder and editor of the *Corvallis Gazette.* In 1872 he was named superintendent of Indian affairs for Oregon, succeeding Meacham, the two men never afterward enjoying friendly relations; Odeneal retained the post until it was abolished in 1874. It was a critical period in white-Modoc affairs and Meacham, who knew the Indians and was trusted by them even if not a strong administrator, was exchanged for political reasons with one who knew none of the Indians, was not familiar with the circumstances prevailing, and compounded the situation by appointing Leroy Dyar, who also knew little of the Modocs as agent over them. Odeneal adopted the unwise policy of using force against the Modocs, with the intent to capture Jack and perhaps other of the leaders and thus force them all to abandon their Lost River homeland for the detested Klamath Reservation in southern Oregon where some of the tribe already lived along with their cousins, the Klamaths with whom they usually were at odds. Odeneal's precipitous decision to use troops against the Indians, and local officers acceding to the request without communicating with higher authority, led to the Battle of Lost River, November, 29, 1872, and the Modoc War of 1872-73. Odeneal was proposed as one of the Peace Commision of which Meacham was to be chairman, but the latter refused to serve if Odeneal or J.H. Wilbur of the Yakima Agency were included, and their names were dropped. Odeneal in 1874 became business manager of the *Portland Daily Bulletin* which merged with the *Portland Oregonian* the next year. He was later clerk of the Oregon Supreme Court. He died at Salem, Oregon.

Jeff C. Riddle, *The Indian History of the Modoc War.* Medford, Oreg., Pine Cone Pubrs., 1973; Keith A. Murray, *The Modocs and Their War.* Norman, Univ. of Okla. Press, 1965; Bancroft, *Oregon, II.*

O'Fallon Benjamin, Indian agent, frontiersman (Sept. 20, 1793-Dec. 17, 1842). B. at Lexington, Kentucky, he was a nephew of William Clark and served as sutler for Clark's Prairie du Chien expedition of 1813. In 1816 he was appointed special Indian agent by Clark and planned to trade with Sioux on the upper Mississippi. He was antagonistic toward the British and most traders, whom he saw as thoroughly unscrupulous. He served at Prairie du Chien until 1818, then became agent for the Missouri River tribes. O'Fallon accompanied Atkinson's 1819 Missouri River expedition which established a permanent post at Council Bluffs; here he proved able enough as an official, if irascible and sometimes contentious. He recommended stronger government regulations over Indian trade and that the Indian agent be empowered to enforce them, and he was an influence in the demise of the factory system for handling trade. He appointed Pilcher and Andrew Henry to Indian management positions further up the river and struggled against military control of the Indian agents, particularly following the Arikara troubles on the upper Missouri. His chronic ill health prevented his taking a more active role personally. He returned to Council Bluffs from St. Louis in 1824, to negotiate a Pawnee-Mexican arrangement and thus facilitate trade with Santa Fe. A firm believer in fixed posts for Indian trade, O'Fallon was alternately buoyed and depressed by the action or inaction of his subordinates and elements with whom they had to deal. In 1825 he accompanied an expedition to the Yellowstone River during which he counseled and conferred with numerous bands of Indians, although with neither the Blackfeet nor Assiniboins as he had desired. For health reasons he resigned in 1826, but maintained his interest in the west and the fur trade in which, since 1823, his sympathies had swung around to the trappers and traders. He died at his Jefferson County, Missouri, home.

John W. Steiger article, MM, Vol. V; DAB; REAW; Thwaites, EWT, Vol. 12, 14-17, 22-24; Dale L. Morgan, *The West of William H. Ashley.* Denver, Old West Pub. Co., 1964.

Off Wheeler: *see* J.J. Harlan

O'Fol(l)iard, Tom (Big Foot), partisan (c. 1858-Dec. 19, 1880). B. probably near Uvalde, Texas, his father, mother and one child died of smallpox, Tom being raised by a Mexican family at Monclave, Coahuila, Mexico, until he was returned to Uvalde by an uncle. He reached New Mexico in the spring of 1878, becoming a trusted lieutenant of Billy the Kid and taking an important part in the Lincoln County War. He was tried and acquitted of horse rustling, was at the McSween house during the celebrated Five Days' Battle in July 1878, at Lincoln, New Mexico, and in April 1879, he pleaded the governor's pardon and was freed from a murder charge, With the Kid, Bowdre, Rudabaugh and others he rode into Fort Sumner when the town was filled with law officers, Pat Garrett among them. O'Foliard was shot and killed on its outskirts, the others escaping briefly. The identity of the slayer is not established, although tradition credits Garrett. O'Foliard was buried at Fort Sumner. He was 5 feet, 8 inches, tall, weighed about 175 pounds, was described by Sue McSween as a "good-natured, rollicking, singing fellow," and was generally popular.

Robert N. Mullin notes; *Maurice G. Fulton's History of the Lincoln County War,* ed. by Robert N. Mullin. Tucson, Univ. of Ariz. Press, 1968; William A. Keleher, *Violence in Lincoln County 1869-1881.* Albuquerque, Univ. of New Mex. Press, 1957.

Ogden, Charles Cornell, army officer (Jan. 4, 1869-July 20, 1893). B. at Indianapolis, Indiana, he was graduated from West Point in 1891 and commissioned in the 13th Infantry at Fort Supply, Indian Territory. He drowned at Hamburgh, Michigan, while on leave following marriage.

Annual Reunion of Graduates (West Point), June 12, 1894.

Ogden, Michael, trader, frontiersman (1824-post 1862). The son of Peter Skene Ogden and Julia Rivet, a Nez Perce, Michael became a head trader for the Hudson's Bay Company in the upper Columbia River country and in 1853 succeeded Angus McDonald as postmaster of Fort Connah, Montana, an HBC post. He became a close friend of John Owen, trader of Fort Owen in the Bitterroot Valley of Western Montana, although they were business rivals. Ogden was a good buffalo hunter, and he was with the Pend d'Oreille chief Alexander when the camp on Milk River was attacked by surprise and some 45 casualties resulted to the action by the Crees and Assiniboins. Ogden turned over his post in 1861 to Lachlan McLaurin and became a rancher in the Flathead Valley. When thrown by a horse however, he fell on his head and his

mind was affected. He was supposed to have hidden a "substantial sum in gold dust" on his place, but after his brain was injured he could not remember where it was.

George F. Weisel, *Men and Trade on the Northwest Frontier.* Missoula, Mont. State Univ. Press, 1955; Gloria Griffen Cline, *Peter Skene Ogden and the Hudson's Bay Company.* Norman, Univ. of Okla. Press, 1974.

Ogden, Peter Skene, fur trader (Feb. 1790-Sept. 27, 1854). B. at Quebec of Tory parents from New York, he was raised at Montreal and became a clerk with the American Fur Company, serving in the Hudson Bay and Athabasca regions and then the lower Columbia River country in the Pacific Northwest. He became a brigade leader in 1820, conducting annual trapping parties. After differences, he joined the Hudson's Bay Company following its merger with the North West Company, in charge of the Spokane House District. Between 1824 and 1830 he made six Snake River expeditions, major trapping operations in the upper Rockies. In 1825 he explored the Ogden River and valley (named for him), the Wasatch Mountains and the Salt Lake valley, but had a serious confrontation with American trappers with the result that his fur take was diminished by defections. His subsequent operations were much more successful and profitable, however, and his explorations extensive. He came more often into contact with American trappers, as the upper Rockies country was ever more heavily trapped. On his fifth expedition he was first to reach the Humboldt River and first to trace its route, and after trapping northern Utah and Nevada, crossed into California, exploring the Pit River. On his sixth expedition Ogden in 1829-30 journeyed from Fort Vancouver to the Gulf of California by the Great Basin route, then back up the length of the San Joaquin and Sacramento valleys; he had discussed this region well with Jedediah Smith, who had covered much of it in 1828. At San Francisco a free trapper party under Ewing Young, which had been following up their course, contacted Ogden, continuing with him to the Pit River, Ogden returning to his post by June 30, 1830. Transferred from his Snake River station to a new one on the Nass River, 10 degrees north of Fort Vancouver in the Fraser River country, Ogden remained three years at what he named Fort Simpson. In 1834 he confronted the Russians on the Stikine River, the result inconclusive though later resolved for the benefit of the British. Ogden was promoted to chief factor January 1, 1835, and assigned to Fort St. James on Lake Stuart, where he remained nine years. In the spring of 1845 he was assigned to head the expedition of Lieutenant Henry J. Warre and Lieutenant M. Vavasour to the Columbia country, to further British interests in the developing Oregon boundary dispute with the U.S. Ogden then was assigned to Fort Vancouver and from 1849 to 1852 was the only chief factor on the Columbia. He was popular with the Americans and following the November 29, 1847, massacre of Marcus Whitman and others at his Waiilatpu (Washington) mission, Ogden by decisive action, great tact and at high personal professional risk, managed to rescue the 47 prisoners of the hostiles, this on the very eve of the so-called Cayuse War. Ogden retired to Oregon City about 1854, where he died and was buried. He had been baptised an Anglican, but stubbornly refused to formally marry his Indian consort of many years, asserting that the fact of their life together and his recognition of the parentage of their children was proof enough of his "marriage." He was wrong, as extensive litigation over his $50,000 estate demonstrated. Ogden was described as short, dark, eccentric, with a good sense of humor, high intelligence, a man of great integrity, "the terror of Indians and the delight" of others. He was an outstanding figure of the northwestern frontier. He wrote *Traits of American Indian Life and Character* (1853).

Gloria Griffen Cline, *Peter Skene Ogden and the Hudson's Bay Company.* Norman, Univ. of Okla. Press, 1974; Archie Binns, *Peter Skene Ogden: Fur Trader.* Portland, Ore., Binfords & Mort, Pubrs., 1967; Ted J. Warner article, MM, Vol. III; DAB; EB.

Ogilby, Frederick Darley, army officer (d. May 30, 1877). B. in New Jersey he was described by Martha Summerhayes as "a great, genial Scotchman." Ogilby was commissioned first lieutenant in the 15th Infantry May 14, 1861, and emerged from the Civil War a captain with two brevets, transferring to the 33rd Infantry September 21, 1866, and to the 8th Infantry May 3, 1869. He went from Fort D.A. Russell, Wyoming, to

Arizona with the regiment. Ogilby was active during the Crook operations in 1872-74 against hostile Indians. In 1875, commanding Fort Apache, Ogilby had an acrimonious dispute with Indian agents over control of Apaches at that post, the fracas having an effect on the Washington decision to remove the Apaches from that reserve to San Carlos; this in turn had a bearing on future troubles in the area, although this was not Ogilby's intention. On February 9, 1876, a tumult arose at the Indian scouts' camp near Fort Apache and Ogilby with other officers hurried to see about it. Ogilby arrested Diablo, believed to be the trouble-maker. Diablo called for assistance and several Indians rushed to his aid, "chasing Major (his brevet rank) Ogilby and Lt. (Samuel) Craig through the camp with loaded rifles." At this critical point a troop of cavalry arrived. The Indians fired on the soldiers, the company charged upon the recalcitrants, dispersing them with two killed and several wounded when they withdrew to nearby mountains. Later the troops beat off a desultory attack upon Fort Apache outskirts. In June 1876 Ogilby commanded Indian scouts assisting in transfer of Apaches from the Chiricahua Reservation in southeastern Arizona to San Carlos. He served under Major Charles Compton, operating in the San Simon Valley northeast of the Chiricahua Mountains; Compton was severely criticized by Kautz for his lack of diligence in the operations to contain the Apaches, but Ogilby was spared, his services apparently satisfactory. Ogilby and his command returned to Fort Apache where he contracted pnuemonia in the subsequent spring, from which he died.

Heitman; Martha Summerhayes, *Vanished Arizona.* Lincoln, Univ. of Nebr. Press, 1979, 23; Dan L. Thrapp, *Conquest of Apacheria.* Norman, Univ. of Okla. Press, 1967; *Army-Navy Journal,* Feb. 19, 1876, 448; Microcopy 666, LR by AGO (Main Series), 1871-1880, Roll 265, 4396AGO1876, June 30, 1876, Kautz, Headquarters, Dept. of Ariz. to AAG, Military Div. of the Pacific; Prescott *Miner,* June 8, 1877.

Ogle, Charles Henry, army officer (c. 1825-Mar. 7, 1863). B. in Pennsylvania, he was graduated from West Point, became a brevet second lieutenant in the 1st Dragoons in 1848 and was assigned to frontier duty at Fort Leavenworth and Fort Kearny, Nebraska where he participated in scouting against Indians, becoming a second lieutenant in

1849. On October 23, 1849, a detachment of Dragoons with Ogle in command struck hostile Pawnees while escorting a mail party on the Blue River in Kansas; three Indians were killed and several wounded, seven dragoons were wounded, two severely, and Ogle was struck in the mouth by an arrow. The next year he was stationed at Fort Kearny and in 1851 at the Cavalry School, Carlisle, Pennsylvania. He was on frontier duty at San Diego, California, in 1852 and other California posts thereafter. In 1853 he scouted against Indians on the upper Illinois River in Oregon and skirmished with them November 24. In 1853-55 he was stationed at Fort Lane, Oregon. Ogle, now a first lieutenant, was on frontier duty from Albuquerque, New Mexico, to California in 1856, stationed at California posts in 1856-57 and engaged in Indian hostilities in California in 1857-58. He was suspended from his army position in 1860-61 and dismissed April 23, 1861, but was commissioned a major in the 1st New York Cavalry in September 1861, and served during the early Civil War in the defense of Washington. He went on sick leave September 26, 1862, was honorably discharged in November; Cullum says he died in December 1862, but Heitman that he died March 7, 1863.

Cullum; Heitman; Barry, *Beginning of West.*

Ogle, Ralph Hedrick, historian (Apr. 10, 1903-Apr. 23, 1958). B. at Eminence, Indiana, he graduated from the University of Indiana, and from Columbia University received a master's degree in 1926 and his doctorate in 1940. Meanwhile he had commenced a teaching career at Colorado Springs. He moved to Arizona in 1929, becoming an instructor at Phoenix Union High School and eventually heading its social science department. Deeply interested in the Western Apaches, he conducted research at Washington, D.C., and elsewhere. his dissertation on the history of that people appeared in segments in the *New Mexico Historical Review.* These were collected and published in 1940 by the New Mexico Historical Society as *Federal Control of the Western Apaches: 1848-1886.* This well-known source book is still widely used. Although somewhat dated and containing minor errors it remains nevertheless generally reliable. It has been reprinted with an informative introduction by Oakah L. Jones Jr. Ogle died at 55. He was married.

Ralph H. Ogle, *Federal Control of the Western Apaches,* intro. by Oakah L. Jones Jr. Albuquerque, Univ. of New Mex. Press, 1970; information from Dee Riegel, *Arizona Republic.*

O'Keeffe, Cornelius C. (The Baron), pioneer (Sept. 12, 1827-Mar.11, 1883). B. at Cork, Ireland, he became in his youth a revolutionary, was captured by the English and sentenced to Van Dieman's Land (Tasmania), but escaped and reached New York in 1853. He then took a ship via Cape Horn to California, moved to Washington Territory and in 1859 joined a John Mullan crew building a wagon road across the northern Rockies. O'Keeffe was attracted to southwestern Montana and settled there. Popular and respected by other frontiersmen, he had an explosive temper and being a man of huge strength on occasion appeared domineering — not without humorous aspects as drolly recounted by Granville Stuart for example in the celebrated case of the Tin Cup Joe suit which O'Keeffe lost after wrecking the court. He became a rancher, imported to Montana the first threshing machine, reaper and mower and farmed intensively on irrigated land. In 1865 he married Anna Lester, an English girl, at Virginia City, Montana. O'Keeffe survived brushes with Indians, and in 1864 when Bob Zachary was sought by vigilantes, extended hospitality to him; when the avengers descended O'Keeffe refused to give Zachary up until he had had a substantial breakfast since, the Baron proclaimed, "ye can't hang a man on an empty stomach!" O'Keeffe had a high sense of honor and personal pride. He became Missoula County commissioner and in 1872 served in the lower house of the Legislature. In 1879 he located on a farm at the mouth of O'Keeffe Canyon, 15 miles west of Missoula. Here he died of Bright's Disease, leaving many descendants in Montana.

Edith Toole Oberley, "The Baron C.C. O'Keeffe: The Legend and the Legacy." *Montana: Mag. of Western Hist.,* Vol. XXIII, No. 3 (July 1973), 18-29; Granville Stuart, *Forty Years on the Frontier.* Glendale, Arthur H. Clark Co., 1925; Deer Lodge (Mont.), *New North-West,* Mar. 18, 1883; Missoula, *The Missoulian,* Mar. 13, 1883.

Old, William A., lawman (c. 1874-May 1, 1914). Old was the posthumous son of William Old, a casualty of the battle of Adobe

Walls June 26, 1874, in the Texas Panhandle. The elder Old and his wife ran a restaurant near the Rath and Leonard store, and Old was killed by the accidental discharge of his rifle. The son, b. not long afterward in Texas, as he reported, or perhaps in Kansas, was said to have been a Texas Ranger for some years, then removed to Arizona where in 1904 he enlisted in the Arizona Rangers, rising to lieutenant by 1907; the force was disbanded February 15, 1909. Old had served throughout the Territory and on occasion had penetrated Mexico in pursuit of his duties. He was a tough, fearless officer, but always brought his captured suspects in alive, and had no known notches on his gun. Old was killed at Pearce, Cochise County, Arizona, by his wife for what was described as "jealousy."

Joseph Miller, ed., *The Arizona Rangers.* N.Y., Hastings House, 1972; *Tombstone Prospector,* May 7, 1914; Lonnie J. White, *Hostiles and Horse Soldiers.* Boulder, Colo., Pruett Pub. Co., 1972.

Old Briton: see La Demoiselle

Old Goose, army mule (c. 1844-c. 1886). B. probably near Leavenworth, Kansas, Old Goose became the most widely-known and "revered" mule of its time. She accompanied the Stephen Watts Kearny overland march to California in the Mexican War, and was bearing Captain Benjamin D. Moore when he was killed at the battle of San Pasqual, California, December 6, 1846. Old Goose "has done good service at most of the military posts on (the Pacific) coast, and is well-known by all the old army officers who served on the Pacific slope." By then a pack mule, she was recognized by Sherman on a visit to the coast about 1883, who directed that "this faithful servant should be pensioned." The mule was formally retired and given "regular rations" at a remount station near Alameda, California.

Los Angeles Times, Feb. 7, 1886.

Old Sun, Blackfoot chief (fl. 1856-77). A chief, perhaps head chief, of the North Blackfeet, his Indian name was Natose-Apiw. He signed the September 1, 1868, treaty at Fort Benton, Montana, and No. 7 of September 22, 1877, on the Bow River of Canada; he may have been a sun priest of the Blackfeet.

Montana, Contributions, Vol. X, 1940, 276.

O'Leary, Dan(iel), scout (c. 1834-Jan. 20, 1900). B. in Ireland, O'Leary reached Arizona by 1864 when he was prospecting with Edmund G. Peck in the Bradshaw Mountains without much luck. He then settled in the Hualapais country of northwestern Arizona. He early became a guide for civilian Indian hunters which led to similar occupations for the army. He took a prominent part in the Hualapais War of 1866-68, guiding Captain S.B.M. Young in January 1868 on an important expedition into the Cerbat Mountains after hostiles and becoming involved in hard fights with Scherum and other Hualapais leaders. O'Leary was a guide for W.J. Palmer's railroad surveying party across northern Arizona and New Mexico in 1868 and it may have been while engaged in this pursuit that O'Leary Peak was named for him northeast of Flagstaff, Arizona; it still bears that name. Dan O'Leary visited the silver boom camp at Treasure City, Nevada, the following year, but did not remain long; he engaged in mining off and on throughout his life, but without much profit. He was a prominent scout and guide for Crook in his 1872-74 operations against central Arizona Indians and was frequently mentioned in the local newspapers for his work or in connection with the countless legends and tall tales that were generated about him, all of them good-humored. On one occasion he saved Crook's life during a melee when the officer sought to arrest Indians responsible for the Wickenburg Massacre of stagecoach passengers. In 1877 O'Leary scouted for Lieutenant Robert Hanna in southeastern Arizona, sending a lengthy description of that country to the Prescott newspaper where it was published and if not heavily edited by the editor it reveals O'Leary to have been a literate and highly intelligent observor. During his southeastern Arizona work O'Leary scouted for Victorio and Pionsenay following the former's breakout from San Carlos Reservation. Following the Cibecue affair of 1881 O'Leary was chief of scouts for a William Redwood Price column trailing the fleeing hostiles as far south as the Mexican Border. During his later years O'Leary scouted for the army occasionally but generally was a minor stockman and a resident of northwestern Arizona, across the river from Needles, California. He was congenial, well-liked by whites and Indians and trusted by both races. So far as is known he never married nor left progeny. He was buried at Needles, but the site of his grave is unknown at present.

Dan L. Thrapp, "Dan O'Leary, Arizona Scout." *Arizona and the West,* Vol. VII, No. 4 (Winter 1965), 287-98; Thrapp, *Al Sieber, Chief of Scouts.* Norman, Univ. of Okla. Press, 1964; Thrapp, *The Conquest of Apacheria.* Norman, 1967.

Olikut (Alikut, Ollocot, Frog), Nez Perce chief (c. 1842-Sept. 30, 1877). B. a "year or two" after the later Chief Joseph, Olikut unlike his more famous sibling was atheletically-inclined, a buffalo hunter and warrior and became like Joseph a Nez Perce chief, much listened to in council. Joseph and other non-treaty Nez Perce by early 1877 had appealed to Howard and Indian authorities to be allowed to move to the Umatilla (Oregon) Reservation (if they must be removed from their beloved Wallowa valley) rather than to the confined Lapwai Reservation in Idaho, and understood that Howard had assented to this. If so, his assent was nullified at Washington without the Nez Perce immediate awareness. At a council early in 1877 Olikut warmly praised the decision that they might live with the culturally more akin Umatillas until sharply rebuffed with the information that their desire had been turned down. In a blaze of anger Olikut castigated the absent Howard and from this incident probably arose the marked antipathy the non-treaty Nez Perce ever afterward displayed for Howard. April 20 Howard had a council at Walla Walla with Olikut and other chiefs at which they reiterated a desire for an enlarged Umatilla reservation that would include the Wallowa Valley; the council ended with no important decision. May 3 at Fort Lapwai a third council was held with Howard, Olikut, Joseph and others when Howard delivered his ultimatum that the non-treaty chiefs must gather with their people on the Lapwai Reservation within 30 days, a deadline considered impossible by the Indians. Young men committed depredations against whites along the Salmon and elsewhere, and the 1877 Nez Perce war was on. Olikut became Joseph's most influential adviser, since Olikut was experienced in war and Joseph was not. Olikut was the principal leader of the young men, the most able warriors of Joseph's people. Until the Battle of Whitebird Canyon, however Olikut with Joseph was for peace and accomodation with the whites. Olikut was a leader in the June 17 Battle of Whitebird Canyon, which was precipitated while Indians

under a white flag and seeking a truce were fired upon by Ad Chapman and his white volunteers. It proved a devastating defeat for the soldiers while the Indians suffered no losses. Olikut was in the skirmish at Cottonwood Ranch July 4-5 and in the Battle of Clearwater, July 11-12, when he led Joseph's warriors. He was largely responsible at the Battle of Big Hole, Montana, August 9-10 for breaking off the engagement and leaving the helpless, wounded white soldiers alone, since he pointed out that they had quit fighting anyway. Olikut however remained with some young warriors to scout and make sure the soldiers were not following the withdrawing Nez Perce. Again he was a leader in the affair at Camas Meadows, Idaho, August 20 when the Nez Perce made off with a few horses and many mules of the troops, leaving them virtually without pack stock. Olikut was killed on the first day of the Battle of Bear Paw Mountains, Montana. He remarkably resembled his brother, Joseph, was a tall, lithe, handsome and active man and very popular among the Nez Perce, particularly the young men.

McWhorter, *Hear Me;* Alvin M. Josephy, *The Nez Perce Indians and the Opening of the Northwest.* New Haven, Yale Univ. Press, 1965.

Olive, Ira Webster, cattleman (Nov. 4, 1847-Sept. 7, 1928). B. in Williamson County, Texas, Ira was a brother of Print Olive and with him became a prominent central Texas cattleman, occasionally making trail trips north. In 1876 when Print decided to leave Texas, Ira accompanied the first of their herds to Nebraska while Print returned to Texas upon an urgent summons from his brother, Jay, involved in feuding with rustler elements. Ira wintered on the Republican River. In the spring another brother, Robert A., a fugitive from Texas, joined him and together they located about where the Dismal and Middle Loup rivers met; Print Olive, effective head of the family business, brought many thousands more Olive cattle north to the new range, Ira returning to Texas to help him bring them up, being described as a "partner" of Print Olive. When Print moved his operations south to Kansas, Ira remained in Nebraska and expanded into other fields. He became a respected banker-cattleman at Plum Creek (Lexington), where he lived to the age of 80.

Harry E. Chrisman, *The Ladder of Rivers: The Story of I.P. (Print) Olive.* Denver, Sage Books, 1962.

Olive, Isom Prentice (Print), cattleman (Feb. 7, 1840-Aug. 16, 1886). B. in Louisiana, he moved with the family at 3 to Williamson County, Texas. Here he grew up a cowboy on a wild frontier, at least once accompanying his father with cattle to New Orleans. He joined the Confederate army although his father, James, had voted against secession, fought at Shiloh, was captured at Vicksburg, paroled, and remained at Galveston, Texas, for the rest of the war. Returned to the Jim Olive ranch, Print headed up the work of branding maverick longhorns out of the brush, and expanded the place in several directions. He shot Rob Murday, or Murray, a cowboy who was driving off some of the Olive-branded stock; then he nursed the wounded man back to health and hired him. February 4, 1866, he married Louisa Reno (b. 1845) who survived him. Several Olive herds were sent north; under Print's direction the "Olive Pens," covering some 20 acres, were constructed for cattle-working on the Taylor Prairie, east of Taylor, Texas; in February 1869, rustlers raided the pens whereafter Olive armed his men and his became known thenceforth as a gun outfit. In the spring of 1869 he accompanied a trail herd north, visiting the Nebraska Ash Creek range for the first time. Back in Texas in 1870 he killed Dave Fream in a horseback duel in which Print was wounded heavily. In 1871 he took a herd to Abilene, Kansas, returning reportedly with $50,000. Another Olive trail herd moved north in 1872, reaching Ellsworth, Kansas, July 3. He was wounded badly in a saloon gunfight with Jim Kennedy who was himself wounded by Olive's loyal employe, Nigger Jim Kelly. Olive returned to Texas by train. In mid-1875 he and his brother Jay ambushed a supposed rustler, W.H. McDonald, badly wounding him; the two were charged with assault, but Print was discharged and Jay paid a $1 fine. It is probable that Olive took part in more gunplay than was made a matter of record, the rustling casualties in Williamson County running high in those years. In March 1876, James H. Crow and Turk Turner, suspected rustlers, were found dead on the Lee County prairie, each wrapped in green hides of beeves they had been butchering, the Olive brand exposed on each "package." The implication was clear. In April 1876, Print determined to move north following the gold discovery in the Black Hills. Print and Jay Olive were wounded in a night fight at the Olive Pens with rustlers on August 1-2, 1876, Jay dying August 20. In September Print reportedly killed a man whom he considered leader of his enemies and responsible for Jay's death. September 7 Print killed one Banks, and wounded another, Donaldson, believing the pair were paid assassins. Olive was found not guilty. Ira Olive, a brother, had gone to Nebraska with the initial Olive herd; Print now followed with three or four other herds and by 1879-80 the clerk of Custer County recorded their cattle holdings as more than 31,000 head. Bob Olive, another brother, was killed while attempting the arrest of purported rustlers, Ami (Whit) Ketchum and Luther Mitchell, for whom Print offered $700 reward. They were arrested; by some means Olive and his men secured custody of them from Sheriff Barney Gillan of Keith County and lynched both, by report Print shooting Mitchell who had shot Bob Olive. The bodies were burned under unclear circumstances but probably after death. Print Olive was indicted for murder, tried at Hastings, Nebraska, and on April 17, 1879, found guilty of second degree murder and sentenced to life. In December 1880, the state supreme court ordered a new trial, and Olive subsequently was freed. Hard winters decimated his herds. Print eventually moved his ranches to the Sawlog and Smoky Hill rivers of Kansas, establishing a home at Dodge City. For one small trail drive in Kansas he hired Joseph J. Sparrow as trail boss, beginning a fatal acquaintanceship. Olive became interested in a new town, Trail City, Colorado, three miles west of Coolidge, Kansas, and established a stable, wagon yard and saloon there. Joe Sparrow opened a saloon and dance hall in competition. Sparrow shot Print following a dispute over a minor sum of money. Olive was buried at Dodge City, Kansas.

Harry E. Chrisman, *The Ladder of Rivers: The Story of I.P. (Print) Olive.* Denver, Sage Books, 1962.

Olive, James, frontiersman (May 21, 1804-July 10, 1882). B. in North Carolina, he reached Mississippi, where in 1836 he married Julia Ann Brashear (May 15, 1820-Dec. 20, 1883), and fathered a notable frontier family. He settled in the later Williamson County, Texas, and occasionally drove a small herd of cattle to New Orleans before the Civil War.

After the conflict, his ranching operations expanded considerably under the guidance of Print, Jim's son; trail herds were sent north to Kansas and occasionally Nebraska. But the Olive operation got caught up in turbulence and strife in Williamson County and the Olives appear to have made many enemies; the facts are most unclear. Conditions worsened, his sons became involved in much gunplay and finally moved to Nebraska, one of them a fugitive. James Olive remained in Williamson County, outliving its days as open cattle country. He was buried between two of his sons who had been killed in range warfare.

Harry E. Chrisman, *The Ladder of Rivers: The Story of I.P. (Print) Olive.* Denver, Sage Books, 1962.

Olive, Robert Allen, cattleman (Nov. 30, 1854-Nov. 30, 1878). B. in Williamson County, Texas, he was a younger brother of Print Olive and became one of the Olive outfit. November 18, 1870, he was acquitted of a charge of horse theft. Bob was increasingly caught up in skirmishing between pro- and anti-Olive forces in Williamson County; on December 14, 1875, he captured a supposed ringleader of the opposition, N.B. Ware; after roughly obtaining information from him, Ware was turned loose. Bob married Lorena Minkler about this time. His new home was shot into by night raiders. Early in January 1876, Bob killed Lawson Kelley, a supposed rustler or, at any rate, of the opposition. In the summer of 1876 Bob murdered a black boy he suspected of having been hired to assassinate him. In early September of 1876 Bob killed Dock Kelley, brother of Lawson. In December at Austin he killed Cal Nutt, whom he supposed to be a leader of the rustler faction that had been harrassing the Olives. In January, 1877, now known as Bob Stevens, he joined his brother Ira in Nebraska, assisting him in a search for a permanent Olive range. He found it, saw the family herds settled, and was shot while serving as a temporary deputy sheriff by two suspected rustlers, Ami Ketchum and Luther Mitchell. He was taken to Texas for burial in the Olive plot; the tombstone gives the date of death as November 28, but Chrisman's narrative as November 30.

Harry E. Chrisman, *The Ladder of Rivers: The Story of I.P. (Print) Olive.* Denver, Sage Books, 1962; Solomon D. Butcher, *Pioneer History of*

Custer County, Nebraska. Denver, Sage Books, c. 1965, 43-62.

Olive, Thomas Jefferson (Jay), cattleman (c. 1842-Aug. 20, 1876). B. in Louisiana, he had reached Williamson County, Texas, as an infant with his father, James and his brother, Print Olive. During the Civil War he remained on the home ranch, learning cattle skills; in September 1865, he married Elmira Gardner, daughter of a neighbor. He performed the usual ranch functions for those Texas times. In 1875 he and his brother, Print, ambushed a rustling trio, badly wounding W.H. McDonald, for which Jay paid a $1 fine. Jay was an integral part of the Olive outfit, but decided to remain in Texas when Print and others, increasingly involved in boiling Williamson County feuds over rustling, decided to go north. He called Print back from Dodge City because of feared trouble. On the night of August 1-2, 1876, the Olive men were engaged in a night battle at the Olive Pens, where cattle were readied for the drives north, and Jay was mortally wounded.

Harry E. Chrisman, *The Ladder of Rivers: The Story of I.P. (Print) Olive.* Denver, Sage Books, 1962.

Olive, William Prentice, cattleman (Oct. 8, 1868-Sept. 8, 1887). The son of Print and Louisa Olive, Bill was b. in Williamson County, Texas, and followed his father to Nebraska, then to Kansas as he moved to new ranch properties. Billy practiced cowboy skills and unfortunately also became interested in the gun, the nemesis of his father and uncles. On April 10, 1886, while drunk at WaKeeney, Kansas, he shot his best friend, Dave Harrison, who died April 20. Olive escaped to the Oklahoma Strip, a no-man's-land, where he roused enmity with his lawless pranks and small-time crimes, until he was shot from ambush by Joe Hodge and a saloonman named Henderson. He was buried at Dodge City, Kansas.

Harry E. Chrisman, *The Ladder of Rivers: The Story of I.P. (Print) Olive.* Denver, Sage Books, 1962.

Olney, Joe, desperado (c. 1850-c. 1883). B. possibly in Burnet County, Texas, he was wanted there for rustling and attempted murder by 1874, and for murder by 1876. Gillett said he was known later in Arizona as

Joe Hill, a friend from Texas days of John Ringo. With two others, one probably Ringo, he engaged in a gunbattle at Cimarron, New Mexico, in which a deputy was killed, one of the trio wounded, and George Hill, another desperado, captured. He settled at the San Simon cienega northeast of the Chiricahua Mountains, Arizona, where he ran stock and where Ringo, Brocius, George Turner and others occasionally gathered. With others, Olney sometimes sold beef to the San Carlos Apache Agency. On one occasion in 1880 Olney, Ringo, Turner and Ike Clanton reportedly shot up Maxey, near Fort Thomas, then Safford, and finally Solomonville, Arizona, but with no fatal results. Again at Maxey he shot and killed a drunken cowboy who had stolen Olney's horse after killing another man, and ridden the animal into the saloon where the boys were playing poker. He died, it was said, "through lack of judgment." Olney apparently went to Texas for Christmas 1881, but returned to Arizona. He generally remained aloof from Tombstone and troubles there, and it was doubtful if he was in town for the October 26, 1881, OK Corral shootout, although he was present for the "trial." Olney died following a fall from his horse. He was described as 5 feet, 6 inches tall, light complected, light, almost white, hair, blue eyes, and at times he wore a beard.

Ed Bartholomew, *Wyatt Earp: The Man & the Myth.* Toyahvale, Tex., Frontier Book Co., 1964.

Olson, Sigurd Ferdinand, writer (Apr. 4, 1899-Jan. 13, 1982). B. at Chicago he studied at Northland College, Minnesota, and the Universities of Wisconsin and Illinois, taking numerous courses in the natural sciences and becoming in time a nationally-known author, conservationist and proponent of wilderness. He was president of the Wilderness Society 1968-71 and helped make conservation a powerful social force in the nation and world. He was head of the biology department at Ely (Minnesota) Junior College from 1922-35, and its dean from 1935-46; he also taught overseas in Army schools after World War II. He served in various public positions. Olson was informal director of the fight to obtain establishment of the Boundary Waters Canoe Area as a federally-protected wilderness area. Among his books were *The Singing Wilderness* (1956); *Listening Point* (1958); *The Lonely Land* (1961); *Runes of the North*

(1963); *The Hidden Forest* (1969); *Wilderness Days* (1972); *Open Horizons* (1977); *Reflections from the North Country* (1976), and *Of Time and Place* (1982), published posthumously. He died of a heart attack while snowshoeing with his wife near his Ely, Minnesota, home.

Living Wilderness, Vol. 45, No. 156 (Spring 1982), 26-27; Angus Cameron, "Sig Olson: A Man of Canoes, Wild Places, Eternal Verities." *Defenders,* Vol. 57, No. 2 (Apr. 1982), 5.

Omohundro, John Burwell Jr. (Texas Jack), scout, showman (July 26, 1846-June 28, 1880). B. near Palmyra, Virginia, he first served the Confederacy as a civilian mounted orderly for Major General John Buchanan Floyd, enlisted February 15, 1864, and was a courier and scout during the Shenandoah campaigns. Joel Chandler Harris made him a master spy in a series of short stories. After the war Jack taught school in Florida, eventually reached Texas where he took part in at least one Indian expedition, rescuing an orphan captive who took the name of Texas Jack Jr., for wild west show work. Omohundro went north with a trail herd, became a scout at Fort McPherson, associating with Cody, Hickok, Milner and others. He guided Dunraven, with Cody, on a Plains hunt in 1870, being described by the Englishman as "tall and lithe, with light brown close-cropped hair, clear laughing honest blue eyes, and a soft and winning smile." Jack accompanied Cody as scout in Reynolds' 1872 expedition in Nebraska; there was only minor skirmishing. Jack was employed by Dunraven for an 1872 hunt and another in 1874. Omohundro joined Cody in late 1872 in a stage endeavor at Chicago, "The Scouts of the Prairie," which was a dreadful play but which launched the frontier figures on their showmen careers, Jack eventually marrying the leading lady, Giuseppina Morlacchi (b. at Milan in 1846) a professional dancer-actress. Omohundro, like Cody, was the principal in one of Ned Buntline's dime novels. Jack played his last season with Cody on the stage in 1875, whereafter he and his wife went it successfully alone, they organizing their own company in 1876. In 1877-78 Jack was well received at New York in the play in which he had first appeared with Cody. He appeared in "The Trapper's Daughter" in Denver in 1880; his wife was billed at Leadville in a musical comedy, and Omohundro died in that community.

Don Russell, *The Lives and Legends of Buffalo Bill.* Norman, Univ. of Okla. Press, 1960.

Oñate y Salazar, Juan de, explorer, colonizer (c. 1549-1624). B. in Mexico he was the son of Cristóbal de Oñate (1504-1567), conquistador of Nueva Galicia who early had served under Nuño de Guzman. Juan was a cousin of Cristóbal de Oñate, named for the elder, and who was executed for insurrection activity. Juan de Oñate was wealthy and prominent by birth (the date of which is as given in *Porrua,* although that compendium follows by apparent error with a brief biography not of Juan but of Cristóbal the elder). Juan's wife was a granddaughter of Cortez and great-granddaughter of Montezuma and he was a prominent citizen of Zacatecas, a founder of which had been his father. In 1595 Juan de Oñate finally was granted a contract for the conquest and settlement of New Mexico, a document for which many other adventurous and influential Spaniards had applied. By the contract Oñate was made governor and captain-general, being granted extensive perquisites with additional ones granted to his colonists. His nephew, Vicente de Zaldívar became recruiting officer. After long delays a start was made from Mexico City early in 1596, but it was not until February 7, 1598 that the expedition at last could be launched from the Conchos River. It included 400 men, 130 with their families, 83 wagons and carts and 7,000 head of stock; among those taking part were four brothers and four nephews of Oñate. The party shortly left the Conchos, moving overland for the Rio Grande below the present El Paso, the site of which was reached May 4. From here Oñate went ahead with 60 men to "pacify the land," and July 7 reached Santo Domingo where he reported receiving the submission of the chiefs of seven provinces. July 11 he arrived at the pueblo of Caypa which he christened San Juan, establishing headquarters nearby (several years later it was moved to Santa Fe); his caravan arrived August 18, 1598. Friars moved out to the various pueblos to commence their work, the establishment of irrigation canals and other works commenced and the province of New Mexico was thus founded. Oñate now sent Vicente de Zaldívar with 160 men guided by Jusepe, the sole

survivor of the earlier Humaña expedition, to the buffalo plains where they failed to capture a live buffalo but brought back plentiful meat and skins. Oñate himself went southeast to the salinas, or salt marshes and Jumano towns, then turned west intending to make his way to the South Sea where he supposed pearls might be in abundance. He visited Acoma, where he narrowly escaped with his life, and Zuñi where he found crosses still in place and several Indians who had come to Cibola with Coronado half a century earlier. He went on to the Moqui towns of northeastern Arizona from where he sent Captain Marcos Farfán de los Godos and Captain Alonso de Quesada to seek out mines to the west reported by Espejo 15 years before. He had ordered Juan de Zaldívar at his San Juan headquarters to turn over command of the place to his brother as soon as Vicente de Zaldívar should return from the plains, and bring 30 men as reinforcements. Zaldivar left San Juan November 18, 1598, to carry out his orders, but December 4 at Acoma was killed with 14 of his men. Vicente de Zaldívar was sent with 70 men to avenge the death of his brother; he razed Acoma in January, 1599, an estimated 800 of its inhabitants were killed and most of the survivors maimed and sold into slavery. This frightful bloodshed produced from the Spanish viewpoint a salutary effect and made their hold on New Mexico secure and for the most part unquestioned by that generation of residents. In June 1601 Oñate with 80 men and several Franciscan friars left New Mexico for Quivira to the northeast, reaching a latitude of 39 or 40 degrees, presumably in central Kansas, and fighting a great battle with the Escanjaques (Kaw or Kansa) Indians, 1,000 of whom were said to be killed. His reconnoitering parties reported some utensils of gold here and there, but these accounts, attractive to Spanish ears as they may have been, were not followed up and Oñate returned to his New Mexico base in the fall, only to discover that most of the colonists and friars had deserted and withdrawn to Santa Bárbara, Nueva Vizcaya. He sent Vicente de Zaldívar to bring them back. Oñate had been charged by the friars with mismanagement to the point where missionary endeavors seemed useless and colonization impossible under his direction, the charges perhaps the outgrowth of the dissension which followed Oñate everywhere, hovering over him like a cloud. Zaldívar, with great cruelty it was charged, forced those settlers he could find to return to New Mexico and the friars at length also came back. The prosperity of the New Mexico colony gradually improved. Having received a troop reinforcement, Oñate in October 1604 with 30 men again explored to the west. He reached Bill Williams Fork, in western Arizona, followed it to the Colorado River and went down its left bank to the Gulf of California, or "South Sea," where he arrived January 25, 1605. He went back to his New Mexico headquarters April 25, 1605, being compelled to eat his horses for sustenance on the return. A year or two later Oñate is said to have explored easterly as far as the Colorado River of Texas. In 1605 he moved his capital from San Juan to Santa Fe, a city founded on a site that never supported an Indian pueblo. Oñate ruled New Mexico until 1608 and is regarded its true founder. He was succeeded as governor by Cristóbal de Oñate y Tolosa Cortez who ruled for two years and was followed in 1610 by Pedro de Peralta who had a four year incumbency. Mexican officials, disappointed that Juan Oñate had discovered no rich mines or transportable wealth tried him in 1614 on charges of misconduct in office and he was convicted. He applied for a pardon which was granted before his death.

Twitchell, *Leading Facts;* I; CE; Herbert Eugene Bolton, *Spanish Exploration in the Southwest, 1542-1706.* N.Y., Charles Scribner's Sons, 1916; *Porrua;* David P. Henige, *Colonial Governors from the Fifteenth Century to the Present.* Madison, Univ. of Wis. Press, 1970.

Ondaaiondiont, Charles, Huron Christian (d. 1646). B. in the Huron country of the present Ontario, he was converted by the Jesuits about 1639 and became influential among the Christians of his tribe. With four other Christians and four pagan members of his people he left Huronia April 13, 1647, on an embassy to the linguistically-related Susquehanna (Conestoga) Indians of the Delaware River basin in southern Pennsylvania, arriving there early in June. The Susquehannas agreed to send a mission to the Iroquois pleading with them to abandon hostilities against the Hurons, but before it returned Charles and most of his companions left August 15 in order to return to Huronia before winter; they arrived October 5. While with the Susquehannas, Charles had visited

the Swedish colonies, three days distant, learning there of the murder by Mohawks of the Jesuit Jogues the previous autumn. He brought back a letter from the Swedes to his Jesuit counsellors in his homeland. Charles had been a Christian for seven years at his death and while in his country had failed to hear Mass only once, it was reported and "even then, it was not his fault." He was slain by Iroquois who overran Huronia in 1649, being shot by an arquebus shortly after kneeling to pray.

Thwaites, JR, XXXIII, 129-37, 183-87; XXXIV, 217.

One Eye, Lone Bear (Nahku-uki-yu-us), Southern Cheyenne subchief (d. Nov. 29, 1864). A prominent leader of the Southern Cheyennes, One Eye's daughter married the white rancher, John Powers whose place was across the river from Fort Lyon, Colorado. One Eye had visited the post before 1864 therefore, and that summer had been given a safe conduct pass by Chivington on one occasion, the officer telling him to exhibit a white flag for his safety, should it seem necessary. In the summer of 1864 he delivered a note written by George Bent from Black Kettle to the commandant of Fort Lyon suggesting peace. Wynkoop, the commander, threw One Eye into jail briefly, then, impressed by the Indian's apparent honesty, took him with a modest-sized expedition to the Smoky Hill River to confer with the assembled Cheyennes; One Eye was an important factor in success of the hazardous mission which resulted in Black Kettle's coming in to Fort Lyon with his people in search of a good peace. One Eye later had been sent by Major Anthony, then commandant at Fort Lyon, as a spy into Black Kettle's camp on Sand Creek to inform the officer of the Indian intentions and movements. Anthony urged Chivington when preparing his assault on the village, to spare the chief if possible, but One Eye was killed with many of his band in that disaster.

Stan Hoig, *The Sand Creek Massacre.* Norman, Univ. of Okla. Press, 1974; George E. Hyde, *The Life of George Bent.* Norman, 1968.

One-Eye Dixie (Artina Choak(u)s), Modoc woman (d. post 1914). The wife of One-eyed Mose, a cousin to Captain Jack, she figured from time to time during the Modoc War of 1872-73 in northeastern California, but never in a hostile way. In February 1873 she and another woman were sent to contact the Modoc warriors in their Stronghold and tell them that white peace commissioners wanted to talk with them; the mission was unsuccessful in itself but it did open the way for negotiations later. In May Dixie and another Modoc were sent to find where the hostiles were; they did not locate the Indians, but did discover the remains of Lieutenant Cranston and five soldiers killed ten days earlier. She and her husband were exiled with others of the Modocs in 1873 to the Quapaw Reservation, Oklahoma and after 1909 were permitted to return home. She and Mose settled at Bly, Oregon, where she outlived him by some years.

Jeff C. Riddle, *The Indian History of the Modoc War.* Medford, Ore., Pine Cone Pubrs, 1973; Richard Dillon, *Burnt-Out Fires.* Englewood Cliffs, N.J., Prentice-Hall, 1973.

One-eyed Mose (Mose Ki-esk), Modoc warrior (d. 1910). A cousin of Captain Jack, he was one of the hostiles involved in the Modoc War of 1872-73 in northeastern California. He was with Hooker Jim conducting raids against settlers north and northeast of Tule Lake November 30, 1872, in the aftermath of the Lost River battle which set off the War. Mose was indicted for his role in February 1873 along with others, but none was tried. After the war he and his wife, One-eyed Dixie were exiled to the Quapaw Reservation, Oklahoma but in 1909 were permitted to return to their homeland. He died near Bly, Oregon.

Jeff C. Riddle, *The Indian History of the Modoc War.* Medford, Ore., Pine Cone Pubrs., 1973; Keith A. Murray, *The Modocs and Their War.* Norman, Univ. of Okla. Press, 1965.

O'Neill, William Owen (Buckey), lawman, soldier (Feb. 2, 1860-July 1, 1898). B. in Ireland, O'Neill won his nickname, it is said, for fondness for "bucking the tiger" at faro. He went to Phoenix, Arizona, in 1879 from St. Louis, as printer and typesetter, edited the *Arizona Gazette* and moved to Prescott, Arizona, two years later, starting and operating *Hoof and Horn,* a livestock newspaper. He was politically oriented, became probate judge in 1886 and in 1888 was elected Yavapai County sheriff. March 20, 1889, four cowboys associated with the Hashknife brand (Aztec Land and Cattle Co.) robbed an Atlantic and Pacific train at Cañon Diablo, Arizona. They were J.J. Smith, Dan Harvick, Bill Stiren and John Halford, getting about $1,300 and some jewelry in the theft, then fading northward into Utah. O'Neill and posse stubbornly pursued them more than 600 miles, taking the four after shootouts and conveying them to Kanab, Utah. Smith escaped on the circuitous route back to Prescott, but was recaptured in August at Vernon, Texas, and with the others, convicted. O'Neill, a Populist, ran twice for Congress, but was defeated. He was elected mayor of Prescott in 1897. With the Spanish American War he was named captain of A Troop, 1st U.S. Volunteer Cavalry (the Rough Riders), served courageously in Cuba, and was killed by a sniper at Santiago, buried first on the island and removed to Arlington National Cemetery May 1, 1899. The famous statue by Solon Borglum commemorating the Arizona Rough Riders, unveiled July 1, 1907, before the courthouse at Prescott, has come to be considered the "Buckey O'Neill statue," but that was not the original intent.

Literature abundant; Ralph Keithley, *Bucky O'Neill: He Stayed With 'em While He Lasted.* Caldwell, Ida., Caxton Printers, 1949; Charles Herner, *The Arizona Rough Riders.* Tucson, Univ. of Ariz. Press, 1970; Jewell Nicholls, "Arizona—in the Spanish American War." *Ariz. Highways,* Vol. XV, No. 5 (May 1939), 4-5, 24.

Ootah, Eskimo explorer with Peary: *see* Odaq.

Opechancanough, Powhatan chief (c. 1545-Apr. 1644). An older brother of Powhatan, head chief of the Powhatan Confederation, Opechancanough succeeded to the effective chieftainship after another brother, Opitchapan had succeeded Powhatan following the latter's death in 1618. Opitchapan apparently continued as nominal head chief for some time, but Opechancanough was the real power. He had captured Captain John Smith about 1608 and took him as prisoner to his brother, Powhatan. Smith soon was released at Powhatan's directive. Subsequently Smith, to alter the attitude of the Indians who refused to sell food to the starving English settlers at Jamestown, Virginia, entered the camp of Opechancanough under the pretext of seeking to purchase corn, seized the chief by the hair and at pistol point took him to the settlement a prisoner. The Indians ransomed him with boatloads of provisions and Opechancanough thereafter "entertained more respect and deeper hatred for the English," although he did not exhibit his ill-temper while Powhatan lived. Upon the death of his brother in 1618, however the vindictive Opechancanough became dominant leader of the nation of some 9,000 souls, 2,400 of them warriors by Smith's estimate. Goaded by white arrogance and persistent exactions, Opechancanough secretly commenced plotting their extinction, correctly viewing their continued presence a threat to Indian survival. Only one Indian, Chanco, a Christian, tried to reveal the plot, but did so too late for the warning to be effective. March 22, 1622, the blow fell, struck by Indians who until that moment had seemed friendly. At least 347 whites were massacred and all the outlying settlements were wiped out, only Jamestown and its immediate environs hanging on, if barely. As soon as the English could recover from the shock a war of extermination against the Indians was begun and massacres occurred; the war went on for 14 years until 1636. Both sides were by this time exhausted and a peace was arrived at, lasting until 1641. Opechancanough, by then an aged man organized another general attack to accomplish his goal of white extermination. The chief was carried into the battle on a litter when the Powhatan on April 18, 1644, fell once more upon the settlements, killing between 300 and 500 whites, But the Indians suddenly desisted as victory seemed within their grasp, "frightened perhaps by some omen," as Hodge suggested. Opechancanough, unable by reason of decrepitude to flee was taken prisoner to Jamestown where a guard treacherously shot him, the wound proving mortal.

Hodge, HAI.

Opitchapan, Powhatan chief (fl. 1608-1620). A brother of Powhatan, chief of the Powhatan Confederation of Virginia, Opitchapan was older than another brother, Opechancanough, who was b. about 1545. Upon Powhatan's death in 1618, Opitchapan succeeded him as chief and while remaining "nominal head-chief" he himself was soon succeeded by Opechancanough who led the Powhatan Confederacy into its destructive wars with the Jamestown English. The year of

death of Opitchapan is not reported, but Opechancanough, who died in 1644, apparently survived him.

Hodge, HAI.

Orapeza, Vincenzo, roper (fl. 1893-1907). One of Buffalo Bill Cody's lariat stars, he was called by Don Russell "a top roper of all time and teacher of Will Rogers," who himself became an expert with a trick rope. Orapeza was a great attraction with Cody's Wild West Shows, with which he appeared in 1893, 1905 and 1907, but biographical material on him is very scant.

Don Russell, *Life and Legends of Buffalo Bill.* Norman, Univ. of Okla. Press, 1960; information from Don Russell.

Ord, Edward Otho Cresap, army officer (Oct. 18, 1818-July 22, 1883). B. at Cumberland, Maryland, he was graduated from West Point, commissioned a second lieutenant in the 3rd Artillery July 1, 1839, and a first lieutenant July 1, 1841. He served in the Second Seminole War (1835-1842) in Florida from 1839-42 and wrote home, "We ought to be brevetted for our sufferings, and have a year's leave of absence when the war is over to polish up and see the ladies." Ord reached California around Cape Horn in January 1847 with Battery F consisting mainly of new recruits, half of them Irish and German. He was sent with two men after three murderers, killed one and brought the others back to be tried by an alcalde court, secured their conviction and when the alcalde refused to act, executed them. He became a captain September 7, 1850, was married at San Francisco in 1854, served on the Yakima expedition of 1855, campaigned against the Rogue River Indians of Oregon in 1856 and against the Spokane Indians of Washington Territory in 1858. In 1859, back east, he took part in the expedition that suppressed John Brown's raid at Harper's Ferry, but was returned to California where he was named a Brigadier General of Volunteers September 14, 1861, then returned east again. His Civil War service was distinguished. Ord became a lieutenant colonel of the 1st Artillery December 11, 1865, a Brigadier General July 26, 1866. He commmanded the Department of the Ohio in 1865-66, and successively commanded the Departments of Arkansas (1866-67), California (1868-71), Platte (1871-

75) and Texas (1875-80), being retired
December 6, 1880; in 1881 he became a Major
General by special act of Congress. Ord was
stricken with yellow fever while enroute by sea
from New York to Vera Cruz and died at
Havana, Cuba, where he had been taken
ashore. He was blunt, honest, impulsive and
according to Sherman, "a rough diamond,
always at work on the most distant frontier."
Utley said that he was "of somewhat disorderly
and imprecise mind," but a "vigorous old
campaigner with a reputation for physical
prowess." Sherman added that as a young
officer Ord "would swim rivers with ice
floating in them when he might have bridged
them, and he would go over the tops of
mountains when he might have gone around."
He ever believed in direct action rather than
diplomacy and saw to it that this thesis was
carried out.

Literature abundant; Cullum; Robert M. Utley,
Frontier Regulars. N.Y., Macmillan Co., 1973;
Bancroft, *Pioneer Register.*

Ordway, John, soldier (c. 1775-c. 1817). B. at
Dumbarton, New Hampshire, he enlisted in
First Lieutenant Daniel or Russell Bissell's
company in the 1st Infantry at Kaskaskia, Illinois and from there volunteered for Lewis and
Clark's expedition January 1, 1804. He was
made a sergeant, being educated kept a
journal and was charged with keeping the
orderly books and other clerical duties. In
addition he often was trusted by the officers
with the command of small detachments
assigned for one purpose or another, and was
high in their esteem. His journal was
rediscovered among the Biddle papers in 1913
and published three years later, being reissued
in 1965 by the Wisconsin Historical Society.
After a brief return to New Hampshire
Ordway settled on the Tywappity Bottom,
near New Madrid, Missouri, where he
acquired land and became a prosperous
planter. He married and he and his wife both
died in Missouri in the same year, leaving no
survivors.

Milo M. Quaife, ed., *The Journals of Captain
Meriwether Lewis and Sergeant John Ordway Kept
on the Expedition of Western Exploration, 1803-
1806.* Madison, Collecs. of State Hist. Soc., 1916,
rep. 1965; Clarke, *Lewis and Clark.*

O'Reilly, Alexander, military officer (1722-
Mar. 23, 1794). B. at Baltrasna, County

Meath, Ireland, he was taken by his parents to
Spain and at 10 became a cadet in the
Hibernia Regiment. He fought for Spain in
Austria and France, eventually becoming a
Major General, going to Havana in 1762. He
saved the life of Charles III during a Madrid
insurrection of 1765. When Ulloa was
expelled by Louisiana insurrectionists in 1768
O'Reilly was sent to restore order. With his
2,000 picked men he descended upon New
Orleans, executed five rebel leaders (thereby
earning the soubriquet of "Bloody O'Reilly"),
and within six months had pacified the region
and demonstrated his magnanimity by
paroling others who had had a hand in the
uprising. O'Reilly was considered generally to
be mild, courteous, soft-spoken and gentle,
but he had a flinty will and was a capable
administrator. Ordered in 1794 to take
command of the army in Catalonia, he died
enroute to his post.

Noel M. Loomis, Abraham P. Nasatir, *Pedro
Vial and the Roads to Santa Fe.* Norman, Univ. of
Okla. Press, 1967.

O'Reilly, Edward Synott (Tex), soldier of
fortune (Aug. 15(?), 1880-Dec. 8, 1946). B. at
Denison, Texas, at 17 he enlisted at Chicago
on the outbreak of the Spanish-American
War, and was assigned to the 4th Infantry.
Sent to Cuba, he had his baptism of fire at the
battle of El Caney. He served also in the
Philippines and China, was wounded in the
Boxer Rebellion. After completing his
enlistment he served in the international
police force at Shanghai, was a bouncer in a
Chinese theatre and an instructor in the
Chinese army, served in the bodyguard of the
Emperor of Korea and ran an English-
language school at Kobe, Japan. Suffering
from "the curse of the meandering foot,"
O'Reilly served in the military forces of
Honduras, Venezuela, Nicaragua and for five
years in Mexico. He was over-age for the
World War I Army, but joined the Texas
National Guard. The war ended before he got
to France, though O'Reilly attained the rank
of major. In 1924 he joined the Spanish
Foreign Legion after negotiating with Abd el
Krim on behalf of a mining company for
which he was under contract. He participated
in the difficult retreat from Seshuan to
Tetuan. He had won a Chinese medal for
heroism at Kiang-su, and for his Moroccan
services was appointed a Knight of the Order

of Isabel la Católica, and won the French Croix de Guerre and Legion of Honor for a daring rescue of a French officer from the Berbers. O'Reilly noted that it is said that soldiers of fortune "go to war for the money there is in it. I never knew one that made a living out of it. They turn to a life of hardship and danger because they are that type of men . . ." He was that type of man — brave, honest, reliable through his service under eight flags during which, he said, he ever had to believe in a cause to fight for it. He died at Sunmount, New York.

Major E.S. O'Reilly, *Roving and Fighting.* N.Y., Century Co., 1918; *Born to Raise Hell: The Life Story of Tex O'Reilly, Soldier of Fortune, as Told to Lowell Thomas.* N.Y., Doubleday, Doran & Co., 1936; *New York Times,* Dec. 9, 1946.

Oréouaché, Cayuga chief (c. 1650-1698). A noted war chief of the Cayugas, he was seized treacherously by the French with others of his people in 1687 and after being tortured by the whites and their Indian allies at Montreal, Oréouaché and more than 40 of his fellows were shipped to France in 1687 where they were sentenced to serve in French galleys during a war in the Mediterranean. The incident provoked, or helped to ignite, an Iroquois war which raged for a decade against the St. Lawrence settlements. Louis XIV in 1689 returned Frontenac to the governorship of New France, and sent Oréouaché and a dozen of his surviving fellows back to Canada with him. Frontenac made special efforts to win the friendship of Oréouaché and succeeded so well that the chief never returned to his people except as ambassador of the governor and to participate in retaliatory attacks on his tribesmen who assailed French posts. He died of pleurisy at Quebec and was buried with full military honors.

Thwaites, JR, LXII, 103-105, 272n8; DCB, I.

Ormsby, William M., frontiersman (Sept. 3, 1814-May 12, 1860). B. in Mercer County, Pennsylvania, he received a good education, reached California in 1849 by way of St. Joseph, Missouri, accompanied by his brother, Dr. J.S. Ormsby and others. The Ormsbys settled at Sacramento. William returned to Pennsylvania in 1852 and escorted a fresh party of emigrants to California, bringing along some thoroughbred horses, "most of which died" enroute. He established

a ranch on the Russian River. Egan quotes a Thomas Scott manuscript from the Bancroft Library to the effect that Ormsby was "one of (William) Walker's filibusters," but does not give the date of such activity nor where he operated with Walker; it may be that from some such enterprise originated his generally-accepted title of "major." Ormsby reached the Carson Valley of Nevada in 1857, perhaps as agent for a California transportation company. He located first at Genoa and later on the site of the future Carson City, becoming prominent in business and public life. By now married to Margaret A. Trumbo (February 4, 1826-July 23, 1866)) and father of a daughter, the major built the famous Ormsby House, a combination mercantile establishment, home and hotel. He got on well with Paiutes and other Indians of the vicinity and took in the noted Sarah Winnemucca (see entry) and her sister who lived for a year in the Ormsby home to perfect their English, this at the request of their father, Chief Winnemucca (see entry). Ormsby was an early proponent and prime mover in the establishment of Nevada as a Territory separate from Utah, and he was the "guiding hand" in formation of the Carson City Rangers as a militia outfit to counter rising Paiute hostility. Depredations occured and white excesses against the Indians exacerbated the situation. Ormsby led 105 of his untrained and undisciplined militia in early May on a sweep against the Paiutes, launching what became known as the Pyramid Lake War. The whites, "apparently more with the idea they would have a lark and a prospecting trip than anything else," were largely supplied with mounts and firearms by Ormsby. They encountered a sizable enemy band led by the war chief, Numaga (d. of tuberculosis in 1871) near the Truckee River south of Pyramid Lake. In the resulting engagement 76 whites were killed and most of the 29 others wounded; among the dead was Ormsby who had been repeatedly wounded, his assailants never individually indentified. He was buried at the site, his remains removed in June to Carson City. Ormsby's widow married Dr. John Hudson Wayman who died in 1867, the couple being buried initially at Carson City. In 1885 Ormsby's daughter had the three bodies removed to Oakland, California, where she was then living with her second husband. Ormsby County (the present Storey County, Nevada) was temporarily named for the major when it was organized in 1861.

Ferol Egan, *Sand in a Whirlwind: The Paiute Indian War of 1860*. Garden City, N.Y., Doubleday & Co., 1972; Bancroft, *Nevada, Colorado & Wyoming*; *Nevada Highways and Parks*, Vol. XX, No. 1 (1960), 14-15, with portrait of Ormsby; information from: Phil Earl, Nevada Hist. Soc.; Jeffrey M. Kintop, Nevada State Library and Archives; Nevada State Musuem.

Orontony (Nicolas), Huron chief (fl 1739-1750). A chief of Hurons settled near Detroit, Orontony became uneasy for his people with enemy tribes about and when his plea to return closer to the center of New France was not acted upon, he took his people to near the present Sandusky, Ohio, where they turned toward the English for trade purposes. At Albany, New York, in the summer of 1743 he won trading privileges for his Hurons. His followers were implicated in hostile operations against the French during King George's War (1745-48) although Orontony professed neutrality and even appeared at Detroit; when the French reinforced that place, Orontony took his people south to settle at Coshocton, Ohio. By 1750 he was greatly strengthening his ties with the English, but by October he was dead, probably the victim of a ravaging epidemic.

Thwaites, JR, LXIX, 300n48; DCB III.

O'Rourke, Michael (Johnny-Behind-the-Deuce), character (Apr. 1862- ?). His birthplace is uncertain, and his name is sometimes spelled O'Roarke, his first name occasionally given as John. He reached Tucson, Arizona, in mid-1878, and became a hotel porter. He went to Tombstone in 1879 and eventually to Charleston, Arizona, where he did odd jobs and gambled for a living. On January 14, 1881, he killed W.P. or Henry Schneider, chief engineer for the Corbin Mill, was arrested by Constable George McKelvey and sent on his own horse to Tombstone for an inquest. Contemporary newspapers confirm that a crowd gathered, perhaps contemplating a lynching, but that Sheriff John Behan, Virgil Earp and city marshal Ben Sippy, held them off and took O'Rourke to Tucson where the next day he was turned over to Sheriff Charles Shibell and jailed. On April 18 he was found to have escaped from jail, was tracked some miles southerly, and disappears.

Lin Searles, "The Short Unhappy Life of Johnny-Behind-the-Deuce." *Frontier Times*, Vol. XL, No. 1 (Dec.-Jan. 1966), 22-23, 44; Ed Bartholomew, *Wyatt Earp: The Man & the Myth*. Toyahvale, Tex., Frontier Book Co., 1964.

Orr, George, prospector (1829-Jan. 12, 1914). By the time he was 30, Orr had become a prospector. In 1861 he was at Orofino, Idaho, and in January 1862 had moved to Florence, Idaho. Later that year he reached Bannack, Montana, where a major strike had been made; Orr secured a claim on Stapleton's Bar, near Bannack, but there is no evidence it paid anything. He joined Bill Fairweather and others in February to prospect along the Yellowstone with the James Stuart party, but dropped out at Deer Lodge, saying he would work there and grubstake the others if they returned broke. Instead they discovered the rich Alder Gulch diggings, and laid out two claims for Orr; whether and to what extent he prospered from them is not known. He died at Hamilton, Montana.

Montana, Contributions, Vol. III (1900), 124-25; VII (1910), 197; VIII (1917), 359.

Ortíz Juan, adventurer (d. c. Feb. 1542). B. at Seville of noble birth, he reached Florida with Pánfilo de Narváez in 1528 and returned to Cuba with Narváez's ships. By command he went back to Florida in a pinnace with 20 or 30 others, no doubt seeking traces of the Narváez expedition which by then was lost from Cuban knowledge. On the upper west coast Ortíz and another were captured by Indians of the town of Ucita, perhaps near Tampa Bay; a chief of the same name resided there. Ortíz's companion, resisting capture, was slain. Ucita ordered Ortíz burned, but the chief's daughter intervened and he was spared. After three eventful years Ortíz was warned by the chief's daughter that his life was in jeopardy and he fled to Mocoso, a neighboring tribe, barely escaping with his life. He was taken in and well treated by the chief, also of the same name as the town. He lived there nine years "having little hope of ever seeing Christians (Spaniards) more," although once he heard of a ship cruising the coast which he failed to contact. When De Soto arrived offshore and landed soldiers Ortíz on June 4, 1539, being mistaken for an Indian, was at the point of being run through by a lance when he blurted out in Castilian who he was and was taken to the leader who, delighted with this discovery, outfitted him with armor, a good horse, and enlisted him in the 600-man expedition. Ortíz, reported Biedman, "knew (the Indian) tongue, and, from the long habit of speaking that only, he was more than four days among us before he could connect an idea without putting to every word of Spanish four or five words of Indian, though he came after a while to recover our speech entirely. His knowledge of the country was so limited that he could tell us nothing twenty leagues (52 miles) off, neither from having seen it nor by hearsay." The primary language he had learned must have been some dialect of the Timucuan linguistic family, but in all probability he had also learned a Muskhogean tongue, for he ably served De Soto as interpreter until his death west of the Mississippi; if he knew Muskhogean he could perhaps (albeit with some difficulty) have made himself understood among tribes of that linguistic grouping including the Apalachee, Creeks, Alabama. Choctaw and Chickasaw among a number of others. Someone served as interpreter among these people, and Juan Ortíz is the likeliest candidate. In his complete knowledge of the Indian character he also proved of value. By September the Spanish were approaching Apalachee when De Soto was saved by Ortíz from a surprise attack although a chief struck the leader in the face so sharply De Soto lost two teeth. The Indian and several of his fellows were executed. Ortíz continued with the expedition during its first three years, sharing its adventures, battles and perils, although on one occasion he purposely mis-translated to avert a De Soto-ordered execution of prominent Spaniards (see Osorio entry). Ortíz went into the third winter camp at Autiamque, probably a Caddoan town on the Arkansas River in present Arkansas. During this season he died, the cause not stated. His death was something of a calamity. It preceded De Soto's passing by a few months. De Soto "greatly regretted" Ortíz's loss "for, without an interpreter, not knowing whither he was travelling, Soto feared to enter the country, lest he might get lost... The death was so great a hindrance to our going, whether (continuing) on discovery or (withdrawing) out of the country, that to learn of the Indians what would have been tendered in four words, it became necessary now to have the whole day: and oftener than otherwise the

very opposite was understood of what was asked; so that many times it happened the road that we travelled one day, or sometimes two or three days, would have to be returned over, wandering up and down, lost in thickets."

Bourne, *De Soto,* I, II; *De Soto Expedition Commission.*

Orton, Richard H., military officer, writer (Aug. 23, 1838-Jan. 8, 1894). B. at Rome, New York, he received a fair education and May 15, 1858, reached California via Panama. He engaged in furniture manufacturing. He joined the state militia soon after his arrival, serving as second lieutenant of Company K, 1st Infantry from October 22, 1861, to June 1862 when he resigned. He joined Company I, 1st Infantry as sergeant from September 1862 until early 1863. Orton was commissioned from Stockton a second lieutenant in F Company, 1st California Cavalry March 7, 1863, and was sent to New Mexico, serving at Camp Mimbres briefly as quartermaster and commissary before assuming command at San Elizario, southeast of El Paso, Texas. Orton was promoted to first lieutenant January 28, 1864. In February 1865 a former Confederate colonel, Bill Leaton, son of the noted Ben Leaton (see entry) was commissioned a colonel by President Benito Juarez of Mexico to operate against French forces under Maximilian. Leaton, authorized to raise a guerilla regiment, established headquarters at Guadalupe, 25 miles downstream from San Elizario, sent recruiting agents across the Rio Grande with such inducements that many Union soldiers deserted and joined his force. To break up this nest Orton, taking 10 to 25 men at a time, made five raids into Mexico, twice surrounding the Leaton rendezvous and surprising his party, capturing numbers of deserters and recovering much government property. In May 1865 Company F was attached to Kit Carson's 300-man expedition to Camp Nichols, on the edge of Comanche country, Orton being adjutant of the operation. His company was stationed for a time at Nichols, near Cold Springs on the Cimarron branch of the Santa Fe Trail, assigned to escort civilian freight wagons passing that point. June 15, 1865, a wagon train was attacked by about 50 Comaches, Company F routing the Indians and causing them casualties. Orton was made captain of

Company M, 1st California Cavalry, October 15, 1865. Stationed at Fort Selden, southern New Mexico, he led an expedition to relieve Janos, Chihuahua, which had been occupied by Apaches who terrorized the inhabitants. The force moved swiftly south, on the tenth day reaching Janos only to learn that the Indians, aware of its approach, had abandoned the town. The month-long operation covered nearly 500 miles. Orton took part in other Indian operations while in New Mexico. He was released at San Francisco January 4, 1867, the last of the California Volunteers mustered out. He re-entered civilian pursuits, meanwhile continuing service with the militia, or California National Guard, as it was called. January 6, 1875, he became captain of Company D, 1st Infantry; major August 14, 1878, of the Cavalry Battalion, including all mounted companies of the state, and retired September 14, 1881, before being elected major of the 1st Infantry April 10, 1885, and lieutenant colonel May 30. He was appointed state adjutant general with rank of Brigadier General November 1, 1887, serving in this capacity for the rest of his life. During this time he compiled the magisterial *Records of California Men in the War of the Rebellion 1861 to 1867* (1890); though he professed the 887-page work somewhat incomplete due to faulty records, it has proven definitive and is the much relied-upon history of California Volunteer units and personnel serving in the Civil War. Orton died at Oakland, leaving his widow, a son and three daughters.

Orton; *San Francisco Call,* Jan. 9, 1894; Win. J. Davis, *An Illustrated History of Sacramento County, California,* Chicago, Lewis Pub. Co., 1890, 561-62; *Illustrated Fraternal Directory,* San Francisco, Fraternal Directory Pub. Co., 1891, 131 (with engraved portrait); information from the California State Library, Sacramento.

Osceola (Asi-yahola), Seminole leader (c. 1803-Jan. 30, 1838). B. probably on the Tallapoosa River in Creek country, his paternal grandfather was a Scot (although Osceola denied this) and his mother a full-blooded Creek. He was not a hereditary chief, nor was he ever elected to that position so far as known, but became a leader and "acknowledged chieftain" because of abilities demonstrated during the Second Seminole War. With most Seminoles he rejected a treaty of Payne's Landing in 1832 and one of Fort

Gibson the following year by which some chiefs agreed to remove from Florida to Indian Territory. He came into sharp opposition with the whites, it is said, when his daughter (technically a slave since his wife had been one) was seized and shipped into slave country against his wishes. Osceola secreted women and children in the depths of the swamps where white troops were unlikely to find them, leaving himself free to organize opposition. He had come to cross purposes with Indian Agent Wiley Thompson, and December 28, 1835, he and his party killed five whites including Thompson, who on a previous occasion had the Seminole arrested and ironed until he would agree to emigrate to Indian Territory; Osceola did so under duress with no intent to comply. The incident launched the Second Seminole War which continued from 1835 to 1842. Osceola led the Seminoles who on the same day, December 28, ambushed brevet Major Francis Dade's column of about 110 men and officers and one civilian enroute from Fort King to Fort Drane, Florida. In the battle near Wahoo Swamp, about 107 of the Dade command were wiped out including the major, the worst reported debacle of the conflict. Beginning with Brigadier General Edmund P. Gaines, a succession of officers was placed in command seeking to eliminate Osceola and his able guerilla fighters but all were unsuccessful until Brigadier General Thomas S. Jesup laid arrangements to seize the Seminole and his attendants October 21, 1837, in "the most notorious treachery" of the war. Osceola was held prisoner at Fort Marion, Florida, then moved to Fort Moultrie, near Charleston, South Carolina, where his health rapidly failed. Catlin talked with him and painted his portrait, the best-known likeness of Osceola; the picture and Catlin's report on the character of the Indian served to enhance his legend, already building because of his martial skill and courage. White doctors sought to save his life, but a medicine man intervened; curtailing their efforts. Osceola, feeling his end drawing near, arrayed himself in his finery, including ostrich plumes and silver medals and died, not so much from a "broken heart" as from malaria and severe quinsy. His fame continued to burgeon and Mahon counted 20 towns, three counties, two townships, one borough, two lakes, two mountains, a state park and a national forest bearing his name. Dr. Frederick Weedon, a physician who treated Osceola in his final illness, cut off the Indian's head, embalmed it and Dr. Valentine Mott finally obtained it for his Surgical and Pathological Museum in New York City. Presumably it burned with the museum in 1866. Osceola was described as tall, slender and straight, with a pleasing though somewhat melancholy countenance.

Hodge, HAI; John K. Mahon, *History of the Second Seminole War.* Gainesville, Univ. of Fla. Press, 1967.

Oshkosh, Menominee chief (1795-Aug. 31, 1850). Oshkosh became a warrior at 17, one of 100 of his tribesmen who joined Robert Dickson of the British army in the capture of Fort Mackinaw, Michigan from the Americans in July 1812. He was with the party in 1813 which unsuccessfully attacked Fort Sandusky, Ohio, and is said to have taken part in other military actions. He did not become a chief until August 11, 1827, when he was named as such by Lewis Cass and Thomas McKenney, United States commissioners who required someone to represent the Menominee tribe. Oshkosh sided with the Americans in the 1832 Black Hawk War and took part against the Sauks and Foxes. He was described as of medium height, possessed of good sense, ability and bravery but addicted to alcohol which led him on at least one occasion to murder an inoffensive Indian. Dockstader said he died August 20, 1858, in a drunken brawl at Keshena, Wisconsin.

Hodge, HAI; Dockstader.

Osorio, Don Antonio, explorer (fl. 1538-1543). A brother of the lord marquis of Astorga, province of Léon, Spain, Don Antonio Osorio with his kinsmen, Francisco and García Osorio joined De Soto on his expedition into the southern United States. In Florida May 30, 1539, Francisco Osorio was in a skirmish with Indians in which two Spanish horses were killed along with two Indians. The three Osorios endured continuing hardships as did other members of the undertaking. Ranjel wrote December 9, 1540, in southern Alabama that he "saw a knight named Don Antonio Osorio...wearing a short garment of the blankets of that country, torn at the sides, his flesh showing, no hat, bare-headed, bare-footed, without hose or shoes, a buckler on his back, a sword without

a shield, amidst heavy frosts and cold. And the stuff of which he was made and his illustrious lineage made him endure his toil without laments...although he...had in Spain two thousand ducats of income through the Church. And the day that (I) saw him (I) did not believe that he had eaten a mouthful, and he had to dig for it with his nails to get something to eat... What was it that a man like him wanted of a land unexplored and unknown?" De Soto went into winter quarters, 1540-41 at Chica(s)a, a chief town of the Chickasaw a mile northwest of Redland in Pontotoc County, Mississippi. From here, probably in January 1541 Francisco Osorio and three other cavalrymen wandered off in search of plunder, seized some skins and "shawls" from Indians they met which raised a great stir among the natives and threatened major trouble. De Soto ordered the four arrested, Osorio and another put to death. This in turn caused consternation among the Spaniards with friars, priests "and other principal personages" begging him to moderate the punishment. He curtly refused. When the two were about to be beheaded, some Indians arrived, sent by the neighboring chief to complain about the depredations. Juan Ortíz, De Soto's interpreter, at the secret urging of Baltasar de Gallegos and others, purposely mis-translated what the Indians said, telling De Soto that the chief understood the culprits had been arrested on his account, that they were not at fault, had not offended him and as a favor asked their release. Ortíz then mis-translated for the Indians De Soto's supposed reply, saying that he had the guilty parties in arrest and they would be punished severely. This mollified the Indians, and De Soto as well, and Osorio and the others were freed. Francisco Osorio was returned to good graces and was joint commander of the sixth vessel in the descent of the Mississippi in 1543, went on to Mexico and returned to Spain. Garcia Osorio, captain of harquebusiers, commanded the seventh vessel on the descent of the river, went to Mexico and also returned to Spain, as probably did Don Antonio.

Bourne, *De Soto,* I, II; *De Soto Expedition Commission.*

Otherday, John, Wahpeton Sioux leader (1801-1871). B. at Swan Lake, Minnesota, he was "passionate and revengeful" as a young man and while drunk slew three or four of his fellows, but he outgrew such weaknesses and became an outstanding Sioux leader. Once in a fight on the St. Croix River with Chippewa he rescued from the field "One-legged Jim" who had been severely wounded and in the same action rescued another disabled Indian. He early became attracted to white ways, adopting white dress, became a devoted Christian and abandoned his intemperate habits. When Inkpaduta perpetrated the Spirit Lake massacre in northern Iowa and carried off two white women, Otherday followed the trail, rescued one of them although the other had been slain before his arrival. In the 1862 Sioux uprising on the Minnesota River Otherday, married to a white woman, learning hostilities were imminent, hurried to the Upper Agency, gathered 62 whites and guided them safely through the wilderness to St. Paul, then returned to the frontier to save others and assist in bringing the killers to justice. To him and other Christian Indians the rescue of 43 more was due. John Otherday served as scout under Sibley and rendered valuable service, taking part in the battles of Birch Coulee and Wood Lake, giving frequent manifestations of intrepidity, while "no person on the field compared with him in the exhibition of reckless bravery." Otherday signed the Sisseton and Wahpeton treaty at Washington February 19, 1867, while Congress granted him $2,500 with which he purchased a farm near Henderson, Sibley County, Minnesota. He was unsuccessful as a farmer however, and in a few years sold out at a sacrifice and moved to the Sisseton and Wahpeton Reservation, South Dakota, where the agent had a house built for him and where he died of tuberculosis. He was buried about 12 miles northwest of Wilmot in Roberts County. His deeds are commemorated by a 52-foot granite monument near Birch Coulee, built in honor of "The Faithful Indians" who served during the Sioux War; John Otherday is one of six names inscribed.

Hodge, HAI, Isaac V.D. Heard, *History of the Sioux War...* Millwood, N.Y., Kraus Reprint Co., 1975; William Watts Folwell, *A History of Minnesota*, II. St. Paul, Minn. Hist. Soc., 1969.

Otis, Elmer, army officer (Feb. 27, 1830-Aug. 18, 1897). B. near Westfield, Massachusetts, he went to West Point from Ohio and was graduated in 1853 becoming a brevet second lieutenant in the 1st Infantry. He transferred

to the 4th Infantry in 1855 as a second lieutenant and within a month joined the 1st Cavalry (which later became the 4th Cavalry). Otis served at Forts Clark, Blake and Duncan in Texas and in 1855 at Fort Leavenworth joined an expedition against the Sioux. His Plains experience continued, he was on the Utah Expedition of 1858 and an operation against the Kiowas in 1860. During the Civil War he held largely non-combat assignments, He was on frontier duty in Oregon and Washington from 1871-76 when he became lieutenant colonel of the 7th Cavalry, and on frontier duty at Fort Rice, North Dakota, and Fort Keogh, Montana, until 1881. Otis became colonel of the 8th Cavalry in 1883 and retired February 7, 1891.

Heitman; Powell.

Otis, Elwell Stephen, army officer (Mar. 25, 1838-Oct. 21, 1909). B. in Maryland he became a lawyer and was commissioned a captain of the 140th New York Infantry in 1862, ending the Civil War a lieutenant colonel, brevet Brigadier General. October 5, 1864, he was wounded by a rifle bullet in the head, an injury which bothered him the rest of his life. He became lieutenant colonel of the 22nd U.S. Infantry in 1866 and served on the frontier for some years, being assistant inspector general of the Department of Dakota in 1874-75. In mid-October 1876 Otis was encamped with six companies of his regiment across the Yellowstone from the mouth of Glendive Creek. Captain Charles W. Miner had been beaten back by hostile Indians when attempting to escort 94 wagons with supplies to a cantonment of Nelson Miles' on the Tongue River. Otis with five companies including 11 officers and 185 men started the wagons out again, many of them now driven by soldiers detailed to replace demoralized civilian teamsters, October 15 on Spring Creek more than 700 Sioux under Sitting Bull and others swarmed about the train which, formed in four compact columns moving abreast, continued on while the infantry escort repeatedly charged the enemy, driving him back but never routing him. At Clear Creek the Indians fired the prairie, the wagons continuing their stubborn advance through the flames, the entire escort being involved in fighting off the enemy though suffering only three or four wounded men, the Indian loss being unknown. October 16 an

Indian runner brought in a note from Sitting Bull ordering the whites off of his hunting grounds. Otis sent a scout (Robert?) Jackson with a reply to Sitting Bull, stating he was taking the train through to the Tongue and would be pleased to accomodate the Indians with a fight at any time. The train proceeded, the hostiles keeping up a long range fire. Two Indians with a truce flag approched saying they were hungry, tired of war, desired peace. Sitting Bull they said wanted to meet Otis outside the escort lines, an invitation the officer declined, inviting Sitting Bull rather to meet him inside the perimeter, a proposal the Sioux rejected. Sitting Bull sent in three chiefs to represent him. Otis presented them with bread and two sides of bacon and suggested the Indians go to the Tongue and treat for surrender with Nelson Miles, an offer they did not accept. On the night of October 18 Miles with his entire 5th Infantry regiment arrived, having been alarmed for the safety of the train. Otis delivered the supplies and returned with his wagons to Glendive Creek October 26. Otis became colonel of the 20th Infantry in 1880. The next year he established the United States Infantry and Cavalry School (which became the Command School) at Fort Leavenworth, conducting its affairs until 1885. He became Brigadier General in 1893, commanded all American forces in the Philippines from 1899, becoming Major General in 1900 and retired in 1902, also holding the brevet rank of Major General "for most distinguished service" in the islands. He died at Rochester, New York. Otis wrote *The Indian Question* (1878).

Heitman; Powell; EHI; DAB.

Ouray, Uncompaghre Ute chief (1820-Aug. 27, 1880). Hodge says Ouray was b. in Colorado, Dockstader that he was b. in Taos, New Mexico of a Ute father and Jicarilla Apache mother; his name was either a corruption of "Willie," given by a white family in his childhood, or a Ute word meaning "The Arrow." He engaged in war with Plains tribes in his youth and his only son was captured by the enemy, never being restored. At his father's death in 1860 Ouray became chief. He was ever friendly with the whites, and always loyal to his people. His relationships with the Anglos began with a treaty between the Tabeguache band of Utes and the United States signed October 7, 1863, by 10 prominent Utes including "U-ray, or Arrow." During the 1860s Ouray was associated closely with Kit Carson and often depended upon him for advice, sometimes operating with him against recalcitrant bands of Utes. Ouray went to Washington, D.C., with others in 1868 and there signed a treaty March 2 (Carson witnessing it for the whites). In 1872 Ouray went once more to Washington, strongly protesting the seizure of Ute treaty lands after they had been pledged to the tribe in perpetuity. He was forced to compromise, but did obtain concessions. In the 1879 Ute uprising Ouray personally directed cessation of hostilities, and for his efforts to maintain peace was granted a $1,000 a year annuity as long as he remained chief of the Utes. Ouray was well educated for his times, could speak both English and Spanish. He was married at least twice and late in life lived in a comfortable house on a farm he owned and cultivated. He died of Brights disease, leaving no children, and was buried south of Ignacio, Colorado, initially, reburied in 1925 at Montrose, Colorado.

Hodge, HAI; Dockstader; Charles J. Kappler, *Indian Treaties 1778-1883.* N.Y., Interland Pub. Inc., 1972.

Oury, Granville Henderson, frontiersmen (Mar. 25, 1825-Jan. 11, 1891). B. at Abingdon, Virginia, he was a brother of William Sanders Oury and with his family migrated to Pike County, Missouri, in 1833, studied law and was admitted to the bar in 1848. The next year he went to California where he practiced until 1856 when he moved from Los Angeles to Tucson, Arizona. He held public positions, including that of chief justice under a provisional government, and was active in efforts to give Arizona formal territorial status. In 1857 when the ill-fated Henry Crabb was trapped in Sonora with his filibuster expedition and faced execution, Gran Oury gathered up Crabb's rear guard of 20 men at Sonoyta, Sonora, and set out to rescue the main force, although he didn't know Crabb personally. The rescue party reached Caborca but could not effect a rescue and fought their way back to Arizona losing four men, according to Bancroft. In 1862 Oury raised a unit for the Southern cause and took it to Mesilla, New Mexico, and seems to have served with the so-called Arizona Mounted Volunteers; later he served with Sibley in the

Louisiana campaign but resigned in 1863, going to San Antonio where he married his cousin, Mina Sanders and when the Civil War ended, fled to Mexico with his wife but after a few months returned and did what he had sworn never to do: took the oath of allegiance to the United States at Fort Mason, Arizona, Ocotober 8, 1865. In 1866 he was elected to the Arizona Legislature and occasionally was speaker of the Assembly; he was twice elected a delegate to the U.S. Congress, then returned to Florence, Arizona, where he practiced law and held various public positions until his death at Tucson.

Cornelius C. Smith Jr., *William Sanders Oury*. Tucson, Univ. of Ariz. Press, 1967; Constance Wynn Altshuler, *Latest From Arizona!* Tucson, Ariz. Pioneers' Hist. Soc., 1969; BDAC.

Oury, William Sanders,,frontiersman (Aug. 13, 1817-Mar. 31, 1887). B. at Abingdon, Virginia, he moved with the family to Louisiana, Missouri, in 1833 and migrated to Texas the following year. He quickly became associated with the independence movement and February 23, 1836 reached the Alamo at San Antonio, but was sent as a courier to Houston one week later, a few days before the climactic battle. He met Houston at Gonzales, retreated with the Texas column to Buffalo Bayou and there fought in the decisive Battle of San Jacinto April 21, 1836. Oury enlisted November 5, 1836, in Company D, 1st Texas Infantry, was made corporal and mustered out January 4, 1838. In the summer of 1839 he joined the Texas Rangers, serving with Jack Hays, Ben McCulloch and other known frontiersmen, taking part in several skirmishes with Comanches including the famous August 11, 1840, action at Plum Creek in which between 60 and 80 hostiles were killed with light Ranger loss. Oury accompanied Hays on expeditions resulting in actions on the Guadalupe River, the Nueces, Sabinal, at Uvalde Canyon and elsewhere over the next two years, and in 1842 at Bandera Pass where five Rangers were killed and six badly wounded. Oury with Hays and others moved to the relief of San Antonio which had been captured by Woll in 1842, harassing Woll on his withdrawal into Mexico. In the fall Oury joined the counter-invasion of Mexico; it rapidly faded down to a hard core, but Oury accompanied this to Mier where with other Texans he was captured late in December. He attempted to escape at Hacienda Salado, south of Saltillo, but was recaptured and in the drawing to determine who would be shot for this escapade, pulled a white bean and was saved. He was imprisoned with the other "lucky" ones at Perote fortress at Mexico City, being released September 16, 1844. On September 28, 1845, he enrolled in the 1st Texas Mounted Rifles and fought in the Mexican War as far as Monterrey, taken in a battle September 22-24, 1846, and served in January and February 1847 with Ben McCulloch's Spy (scout) company. In September 1849 he married Inez Garcia at Durango, Mexico, from Mazatlan took a steamer to San Francisco and remained in California until 1856, with small financial reward. He and his family went by wagon to Yuma, then on to Tucson, Arizona, arriving in February. He settled there for the rest of his life, In 1857 he was named agent for the Butterfield Overland Mail Company, acquired a small ranch on the nearby Santa Cruz River. Early in July 1858 Oury had an altercation with Benjamin H. Miles, a onetime member of the California State Legislature, and in a duel killed him; the subject of the dispute is not remembered. In 1860 he fought a duel with Benito Flournoy, and killed him. Oury and Sylvester Mowry purchased the *Arizonian* of Tubac from Edward Cross for $2,500 and moved it to Tucson. Although part owner, he never edited the paper, although he occasionally wrote articles for other Tucson newspapers late in life; they are of varying value, depending upon whether he was a participant in the action described, or picked it up as local gossip. He visited Apache Pass February 14, a few days after the celebrated "Bascom Incident" which launched the Cochise war, and later told of it in the *Arizona Star* (June 28, July 5, 12, 1877), an account that in places has value. When the California Column occupied Tucson, Oury, although a Confederate sympathiser became land registrar under Major David Fergusson. After Arizona became a Territory in 1863, he was named first mayor of Tucson from 1864 and from 1873-77 was sheriff of Pima County. In 1868 he reportedly introduced Shorthorn cattle to Arizona. In 1871 Oury, always hot-tempered, was a leader in organizing the sordid Camp Grant Massacre in which between 85 and 125 Aravaipa Apaches, almost all women and children, were slaughtered in supposed retaliation for minor depredations which no evidence indicated they were a party to or had participated in — but they were the handiest and the easiest to kill. One historian blandly characterized the atrocity as "not admirable," which is the understatement of the millenium while in fact, just as it was the blackest page in Arizona history, so was it the blackest page in Oury's rather spotty life. One noted participant, upon reflection in later years, even expressed disgust with his own role in the monumental crime. With others involved Oury was acquitted December 13, 1871, in a federally-demanded Tucson trial before a Tucson jury. He held various minor public positions late in life, and died at Tucson.

Cornelius C. Smith Jr., *William Sanders Oury*. Tucson, Univ. of Ariz. Press, 1967; Constance Wynn Altshuler, *Latest From Arizona!* Tucson, Ariz. Pioneers' Hist. Soc., 1969.

Outlaw, Bass, gunman (c. 1865-Apr. 5, 1894). B. in Georgia, supposedly of a good family, Bass Outlaw apparently was his real name. He is said to have killed a man in Georgia and fled to Texas. In 1885 he enlisted in Company E and two years later transferred to Company D of the Texas Rangers. He was highly praised for his good qualities when sober, but "was a maniac" when he became drunk, which was often. Although a sergeant he was forced to resign from the Rangers by Captain Frank Jones for being drunk on duty at Alpine. He became a deputy U.S. Marshal at Alpine. His reputation as a tough, nervy gunman grew. He became well-known and feared as far as El Paso. Here he became involved in a ruckus at Tillie Howard's sporting house, killed Ranger Joe McKidrict, wounded constable John Selman who had been trying to quiet the gunman, and Selman mortally wounded him. He died at Barnum Show Saloon. A small man, with many good qualities, "he was never able to maintain any kind of position" because of his temperament, and proved to be "his own worst enemy."

Leon Claire Metz, *John Selman: Texas Gunfighter*. N.Y., Hastings House Pubrs., 1966.

Outreleau, Étienne d', Jesuit missionary (Oct. 11, 1693-post 1752). B. in the French province of Champagne, he became a Jesuit and arrived in Louisiana July 23, 1727, remaining as a missionary in the Mississippi valley for 20 years. In 1728 he was at "the fort on the

Wabash," or Post Vincennes; later he was a chaplain of the hospital at New Orleans. He returned to France in 1745 and was last reported there in 1752.

Thwaites, JR, LXVII, 342n43, LXXI, 169.

Ovando, Francisco de, military officer (d. Feb. 20, 1541). A member of Coronado's 1540 expedition into the American southwest, he was of the vanguard that first reached the pueblo of Háwikuh, southwest of Zuñi, New Mexico, the initial Cibolan city to be visited. Subsequently he led an exploring expedition down the Rio Grande as far as the Piros towns, south of the Tiguex complex centered on today's Bernalillo. In the Tiguex War Ovando was killed as he crawled through a narrow opening into a room filled with hostile Indians, his body found a month later, still preserved by the winter cold.

George Parker Winship, *The Coronado Expedition, 1540-1542,* BAE, 14th Annual Report. Washington, Govt. Printing Office, 1896; Herbert Eugene Bolton, *Coronado: Knight of Pueblos and Plains.* Albuquerque, Univ. of New Mex. Press, 1964.

Overton, Gilbert Edmond, army officer (Mar. 18, 1845-Sept. 29, 1907). B. at New York City, he gave his year of birth as 1843 when commissioned in 1861 because he was actually only 16, under-age. Overton became a second lieutenant in the 4th New York Cavalry, joined the 12th New York Cavalry in 1862 and emerged from the Civil War a first lieutenant, being appointed a second lieutenant in the 6th Cavalry in 1867, a first lieutenant in 1872, and a captain in 1881. With the 6th Overton saw much frontier duty. November 8, 1874, near McClellan Creek, Texas, Overton, commanding D Troop and serving under Frank D. Baldwin, 5th Infantry, took part in a hard fight against Grey Beard's village of Cheyennes, recapturing Adelaide, 5, and Julia German (or Germaine) 7, who had been taken in a celebrated Indian attack on a wagon train previously. For his part, Overton was breveted captain. In 1877 Overton was in Arizona, chasing hostile Apaches. In October 1881, Overton, out of Fort Thomas, Arizona, was engaged in the pursuit of Juh and Geronimo fleeing south from San Carlos. Overton asked permission to go ahead of the main command because he was concerned about the safety of his family at Fort Grant, in the direction of the pursuit. Taking Troops A and F of the 6th, Overton discovered the bodies of soldiers killed by the Apaches, then collided with the hostiles in the engagement of Cedar Springs, a very hard fight. In 1882 he was peripherally involved in the pursuit of Loco after that Mimbres Apache was extracted from San Carlos by Juh and other Chiricahuas and herded into Mexico. Overton had an undistinguished role in the Geronimo campaigns which began in 1885. He retired in early 1891 because of diabetes and "chronic hepatic (liver) derangement," and worked for an insurance company in civilian life. He died at Milwaukee on a business trip.

Heitman; Lonnie J. White, *Hostiles & Horse Soldiers.* Boulder, Colo., Pruett Pub. Co., 1972; information from David P. Perrine.

Oviedo y Váldez, Gonzalo Fernández, chronicler (Aug. 1478-1557). B. at Madrid, he was the chronicler of the Pánfilo de Narváez ill-fated expedition to Florida of 1528, although Oviedo probably never set foot in America. He died at 79.

Gonzalo Fernández Oviedo y Váldez, "The Expeditions of Pánfilo de Narváez," ed. by Harbert Davenport. *Southwestern Hist. Quar.,* Vols. XXVII, XXVIII, Oct. 1923 through Oct. 1924.

Owen, Francis (Frank) B., trader (fl. 1850-1869). Not much has been uncovered about this brother of John Owen who worked with John at Fort Owen in the Bitterroot Valley of Montana, but he probably was b. in Pennsylvania and reached Montana from Cantonment Loring near Fort Hall, Idaho, in late 1850. He returned to Pennsylvania on a business trip in 1857 by Missouri River steamboat and reached Montana again in 1860; in 1866 he made another journey to the States to bring back supplies. He prospected for a time and lived near Stevensville, Montana, at least until 1869, but nothing is known of his movements after that.

George F. Weisel, *Men and Trade on the Northwest Frontier,* Missoula, Mont. State Univ. Press, 1955

Owen, John, frontiersman (June 27, 1818-July 12, 1889). B. in Pennsylvania, he was an educated, well-read man. Owen was at Fort Leavenworth in 1843, Jefferson Barracks three years later, and in 1849 reached

Cantonment Loring, near Fort Hall, Idaho, as sutler to a rifle regiment. He became acquainted with Jesuit missionaries to the Flatheads in the Bitterroot Valley of present Montana and November 5, 1850, he purchased nine-year-old St. Mary's Mission for $250, the paper accomplishing this becoming the first legal document recorded in what is now Montana. Here, just north of present Stevensville, Montana, he built "Fort Owen," in 1970 named a National Historic Site. Owen palisaded the fort against Blackfeet, adobe shortly replacing the logs, and a trading settlement grew up around it, Owen given the courtesy title of "major." He was a heavy man of medium height with strong features, of a convivial nature although inclined toward laziness. He had a good library, kept a journal of lasting interest, started a school, and operated a number of business enterprises, suggesting his indolence was largely in appearance only. He married a Shoshonean woman named Nancy who died in 1868; there was strong affection between them. Owen temporarily abandoned his fort during Indian troubles in 1853, but returned to it. In 1856 he was named special agent for the Flathead Indians, retaining the position for six years, although often at odds with Washington policy. He resigned in 1862 and left Fort Owen for 14 months, visiting his birthplace in Pennsylvania, and at Washington meeting with President Lincoln. On December 30, 1872, Fort Owen was purchased at a sheriff's sale by W.J. McCormick for $4,100, Owen having become an alcoholic, his mind impaired. He entered a Helena hospital for the deranged in 1873 and late in that decade he was returned to Philadelphia to be cared for by relatives. There he died. Chief Joseph's Nez Perce passed Fort Owen in 1877, but there was no attack, the inhabitants lining vantage points to watch the "hostiles" crossing the river and some of the more enterprising selling supplies to the Indians. Owen was buried at Laurel Hill Cemetery, Philadelphia.

Montana Genesis: A History of the ... Bitterroot Valley, Stevensville Hist. Soc., Mont., 1971.

Owen, Richard Bentley (Captain Honesty), army officer (d. Jan. 1872). B. in North Carolina he was commissioned quartermaster and first lieutenant in Phelps' regiment of Missouri Infantry in 1861 and served through the Civil War. He became a friend of James

Butler (Wild Bill) Hickok from the spring of 1864 when Hickok went to work for him as a scout, and introduced writer George Ward Nichols to him in September 1865. Nichols, with an article in *Harper's New Monthly Magazine,* made Bill nationally famous, quoting "Captain Honesty." as one of his sources; Rosa determined the identity of "Captain Honesty." Owen contributed to Hickok's $2,000 bail after he shot Tutt. Owen became assistant post quartermaster at Fort Riley, Kansas, and there hired Hickok early in 1866. Owen left the army November 3, 1866.

Joseph G. Rosa, *They Called Him Wild Bill,* 2nd ed. Norman, Univ. of Okla. Press, 1974.

Owen, William McKay (McKendree), army officer (1843-July 28, 1891). Owen's middle name is given as McKay on California records and by some who knew him, Banta and others, but by Altshuler as McKendree. He was b. at Monroe, Indiana, enlisted in the 1st California Infantry August 28, 1861, becoming a corporal by September 4, 1863, when he was commissioned a second lieutenant in the 6th California Infantry and a first lieutenant a year later. He was mustered out October 31, 1865. Owen became a second lieutenant in the 14th U.S. Infantry May 4, 1866, transferring to the 32nd Infantry September 21 when he was promoted to first lieutenant. Attached to the 8th Cavalry he had a role in the fight of Captain James Monroe Williams with Apaches near Black Mountain, Arizona, April 16 and 18, 1867, in which 54 Indians were reported killed. Owen himself led a small detachment in a related action causing further hostile casualties. Banta, describing Owen as "a first class game-cock," said he was his warm personal friend, "and by the way, I acted as his 'second' in a duel at one time." Owen transferred to the 21st Infantry April 19, 1869, and was discharged at this own request October 1, 1870. Altshuler reported he later enlisted and served in the 1st and 2nd Infantry regiments as William McKendree.

Heitman; Prescott, Ariz., *Miner* April 20, 1867; *Albert Franklin Banta: Arizona Pioneer,* ed. by Frank D. Reeve. Hist. Soc. of New Mex. Pubns. in Hist., Vol. XIV (Sept. 1953); Constance Wynn Altshuler, *Chains of Command,* Tucson, Ariz. Hist. Soc., 1981.

Owens, Commodore Perry, lawman (July 29, 1852-May 10, 1919). B. on an east Tennessee farm, he left home, reportedly lived in Indiana for a time, reached Texas in the 1870s, became a cowboy, migrated to New Mexico and then to Arizona where he settled at Navajo Springs in 1882. Said to have been an excellent shot, Owens sometimes carried a 45-60 Sharps sighted to shoot a mile accurately, or a Winchester repeating rifle, with one or two hand guns. He managed a stage station south of the Navaho Reservation for a time, and was said to have had skirmishes with Indians. When the station was abandoned Owens moved south to Cottonwood Seep, running cattle on shares and raising horses. He became a deputy sheriff of Apache County and on November 4, 1886, was elected sheriff. September 4, 1887, Owens attempted to arrest Andy Cooper (Blevins) at the Blevins house at Holbrook, Arizona. In the house were Cooper, Sam Houston Blevins, John Blevins, Mose Roberts and Mrs. John (Eva) Blevins, with perhaps other women. In a resulting shootout, Owens with his Winchester killed Cooper, Roberts and Sam Blevins and severely wounded John Blevins, who recovered and later served as a deputy sheriff, but not to Owens. Owens fired but five shots in this celebrated fight. After his term as sheriff of Apache County Owens worked for the Atlantic and Pacific railroad and later for Wells Fargo. His widow told Forrest that Owens also was a United States deputy marshal. He was the first sheriff of Navajo County, Arizona, from March 25, 1895, until December 31, 1896. Around 1900 he went into business at Seligman (ran a saloon, according to one account), died there and was buried at Flagstaff. Gilchriese gives the date of his death as May 28. Owens was 5 feet, 10 inches in height, with grey eyes and blonde hair which at one time he permitted to grow to shoulder length. A sometimes flamboyant dresser, he was a very fearless man.

Glenn G. Boyer, "Commodore Perry Owens Revisited." *Real West,* Vol. 22, No. 187 (Oct. 1982), 12-18; John D. Gilchriese, "The Long-Haired Sheriff." *Arizona Currents,* Mar. 1966; Clara T. Woody, Milton L. Schwartz, *Globe, Arizona.* Tucson, Ariz. Hist. Soc., 1977; Earle R. Forrest, *Arizona's Dark and Bloody Ground.* Caldwell, Id., Caxton Printers, 1964.

Owens, Richard, mountain man (fl. 1834-1849). B. probably in Ohio, he appears in the Rocky Mountains about 1835 as wounded in a fight with the Blackfeet. He joined Kit Carson in 1839 for a trapping expedition in southeastern Wyoming; he may have turned to horse stealing about 1840, first from Shoshones, then from southern California ranchos. Owens settled for a time at the Greenhorn trading post south of Pueblo, Colorado. He joined Fremont with Carson for the officer's third exploration expedition, earning encomiums from Fremont who ranked him with Carson in ability. The Owens River and Lake of California were named for him, though he never saw them. He accompanied Fremont to Oregon, then was appointed a captain of Company A and took part in the conquest of California. He accompanied Fremont to Washington, but was not called to testify for the officer. Owens returned to Taos. He may have guided a party to California in 1849, but there his certain trail is lost.

Harvey L. Carter article, MM, Vol. V.